SOCIOLOGY

Visit the *Sociology, fourth edition* Companion Website at **www.pearsoned.co.uk/marsh** to find extensive chapter-by-chapter **student** learning and study material including:

- **Revise** key themes – summaries to aid you with revision and understanding key concepts
- **Research** links to key articles, websites and books organised around the key themes
- **Investigate** Sociology – chapter-by-chapter exercises, projects and links to interactive media immerse you in the issues
- **Review** – test your learning with interactive questions and opportunities for further thinking

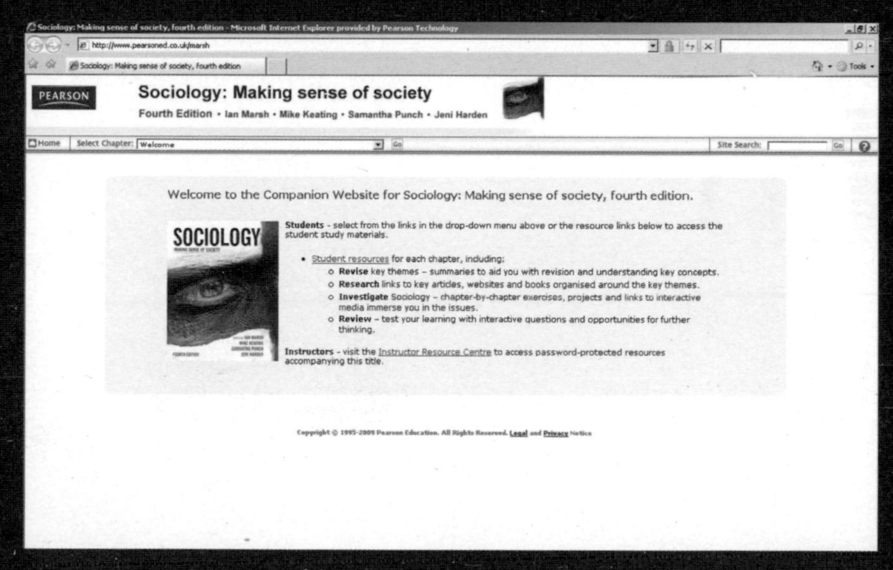

SOCIOLOGY

MAKING SENSE OF SOCIETY

FOURTH EDITION

EDITED BY
IAN MARSH
MIKE KEATING
SAMANTHA PUNCH
JENI HARDEN

PEARSON
Longman

Harlow, England • London • New York • Boston • San Francisco • Toronto • Sydney • Singapore • Hong Kong
Tokyo • Seoul • Taipei • New Delhi • Cape Town • Madrid • Mexico City • Amsterdam • Munich • Paris • Milan

Pearson Education Limited

Edinburgh Gate
Harlow
Essex CM20 2JE
England

and Associated Companies throughout the world

Visit us on the World Wide Web at:
www.pearsoned.co.uk

First published 1996
Second edition published 2000
Third edition published 2006
Fourth edition published 2009

ISBN: 978-1-4058-7357-4

British Library Cataloguing-in-Publication Data
A catalogue record for this book is available from the British Library

Library of Congress Cataloging-in-Publication Data
Sociology : making sense of society / edited by Ian Marsh . . . [et al.]. – 4th ed.
p. cm.
ISBN 978-1-4058-7357-4 (pbk.)
1. Sociology. I. Marsh, Ian, 1952–
HM586.S643 2009
301—dc22

2009002078

10 9 8 7 6 5 4 3 2 1
13 12 11 10 09

Typeset in 9.75/13pt Minion by 35
Printed and bound by Rotolito Lombarda, Italy

The publisher's policy is to use paper manufactured from sustainable forests.

Brief contents

The website facilities for this edition of *Sociology: making sense of society* have been designed to provide opportunities for the student to extend their study of the key issues and concepts from a particular chapter. The material can be utilized either in the classroom, with suggestions for projects, links to media and discussion prompts, or privately, for self-study or revision.

The **Revise** section summarizes key concepts and issues for revision and quick access to the ideas. The **Research** section provides links to key articles, books and websites encouraging and facilitating further study and reading. **Investigate** sociology provides extension activities that can be followed up privately – perhaps for home study or seminar preparation – or used in the lecture hall or seminar room, including suggestions for projects, discussion activities and links to relevant media around which tasks have been built. Feedback to these is also available. Finally, the **Review** section allows you to test what you have learned from each chapter through multiple-choice and further opportunities to reflect.

Supporting resources

Visit **www.pearsoned.co.uk/marsh** to find valuable online resources

Companion Website for students

- **Revise** key themes – summaries to aid you with revision and understanding key concepts
- **Research** links to key articles, websites and books organised around the key themes
- **Investigate** Sociology – chapter-by-chapter exercises, projects and links to interactive media immerse you in the issues
- **Review** – test your learning with interactive questions and opportunities for further thinking

For instructors

- Complete, downloadable Instructor's Manual

Also: The Companion Website provides the following features:

- Search tool to help locate specific items of content
- E-mail results and profile tools to send results of quizzes to instructors
- Online help and support to assist with website usage and troubleshooting

For more information please contact your local Pearson Education sales representative or visit **www.pearsoned.co.uk/marsh**

Contents

Case studies

11. Families and households

12. Work

13. Health, illness and the body

14. Crime and punishment

15. Education

16. Religion

17. The mass media

World in focus

Contributors

Kristin Aune lectures in sociology at the University of Derby. Her research and teaching interests include religion and gender. She is author of *Single Women: Challenge to the Church?* (2002, Paternoster) and coeditor of *Women and Religion in the West* (2008, Ashgate).

Noah Canton received his MSc (with distinction) in Global Movements, Social Justice and Sustainability from the University of Glasgow. He is a research assistant in sociology at the University of Strathclyde doing British Council-funded research on the economic, social and cultural challenges associated with migration from central and Eastern Europe to Scotland.

Colin Clark lectures in sociology in the Department of Geography and Sociology at the University of Strathclyde, Glasgow. His research and teaching interests are in the broad field of ethnic and racial studies. He is co-author of *Here to Stay: the Gypsies and Travellers of Britain* (2006, University of Hertfordshire Press).

Jeni Harden lectures in sociology at the Napier University. Her main teaching and research interests include sociology of health and illness, childhood, the family and qualitative research methodologies.

Mike Keating lectures in sociology and criminology at Liverpool Hope University, where he is course leader for the first-year course in sociology. His main teaching and research interests are in crime, deviance and risk taking at work. He is co-editor of *Classic and Contemporary Readings in Sociology* (1998, Addison Wesley Longman) and a contributor to *Theory and Practice in Sociology* (2002, Pearson Education). He is also interested in Learning and Teaching strategies and is a Registered Practitioner with the Higher Education Academy.

Gayle Letherby is Professor of Sociology at the University of Plymouth. Her teaching, research and writing interests include reproductive and non/parental identity; method, methodology and epistemology; teaching and learning in higher education and travel and transport. Recent publications include *Extending Social Research* (2007, Open University) and *Introduction to Gender: social science perspectives* (2007, Longman).

Jen Marchbank is an Associate Professor in Explorations in Arts and Social Sciences, an interdisciplinary programme at Simon Fraser University in Canada. Her research interests include 'mail order' brides, innovative pedagogies and gendered experiences in education. She is author of *Women, Power and Politics: Comparative Studies of Childcare* (2000, Routledge), co-editor of *States on Conflict: Gender, Violence and Resistance* (2000, Zed Books) and co-author (with Gayle Letherby) of *Introduction to Gender: Social Science Perspectives* (2007, Longman).

Ian Marsh lectures in criminology and sociology at Liverpool Hope University, where he is director of the MA in criminal justice. His main teaching and research interests are in crime, criminal justice and punishment. He has written, co-written and edited a number of texts, including *Crime, Justice and the Media* (2009, Routledge), *Theories of Crime* (2006, Routledge), *Criminal Justice: An Introduction to Philosophies, Theories and Practice* (2004, Routledge), *Theory and Practice in Sociology* (2002, Prentice Hall), *Classic and Contemporary Readings in Sociology* (1998, Addison Wesley Longman) and *Sociology in Focus* (1995, Causeway Press).

Eleanor McDowell is joint partner of McCormick-McDowell Research Partnership specializing in social and environmental policy. From 1995 to 2008 Dr McDowell lectured in the Division of Sociology at Glasgow Caledonian University. Recent co-authored work includes: *Sustainable Working Lives,* (2008, Scottish Council Foundation); *Function and Form: An Independent Review of the Scottish Health Council* (with SCF, 2008), *An Evaluation of the Greenspace Programme* (2008, BTCV, 2008) and she is co-editor of *Sustainable Scotland: Prospects for Sustainability* (1999, Ashgate).

Ian McIntosh lectures in sociology in the Department of Applied Social Science at the University of Stirling. His research and teaching interests include the sociology of work and identities. He is co-author of *English People in Scotland; an Invisible Minority* (2008, Edwin Mellen Press), *Get Set for Sociology* (2005, Edinburgh University Press) and editor of *Classical Sociological Theory* (1997, Edinburgh University Press).

Janet McKenzie is a lecturer in the Faculty of Education of the Open University. Her research and teaching interests include the sociology and politics of education, research methods and child development. She also works as a therapeutic counsellor and trainer, specializing in the support of families bereaved by homicide as well as other types of bereavement. She is author of *Changing Education: A Sociology of Education Since 1944* (2001, Prentice Hall).

Samantha Punch lectures in sociology in the Department of Applied Social Science at the University of Stirling. Her research and teaching interests include the sociology of childhood and the sociology of development. She is co-author of *Get Set for Sociology* (2005, Edinburgh University Press) and co-editor of *Global Perspectives on Rural Childhood and Youth: Young Rural Lives* (2007, Routledge).

Kirstein Rummery is Professor of Social Policy at the University of Stirling. Her research and teaching interests include disability, age, gender, citizenship, and health and social care policy. She is the author of *Disability, Citizenship and Community Care* (2002, Ashgate) and co-editor of *Women and New Labour* (2007, Policy Press).

Preface

This is now the fourth edition of this textbook and in many ways it marks a watershed. We're delighted to have had two new editor-authors – Samantha Punch at Stirling and Jeni Harden at Napier – contributing so much to the new book and helping to bring in new energy, ideas and expertise to what we believe is a more integrated, richer and better textbook this time round. Their editorial contribution to this fourth edition, as well as authored chapters (Age, Global divisions, families and households, Health, illness and the body) plus key contributions to others (Sociological research), has made a significant difference to the book. This has allowed us across the text – along with a new four-part structure – to begin to make more visible and connected some key, current sociological themes, such as identity, inequality, meanings, problems and change.

To this new edition we also welcome brand new chapters on 'Race', ethnicity and nationalism, Disability, Global divisions, Families and households, Health, illness and the body, and Religion, and we are grateful to those authors outside the main editorial team who have made such a telling contribution either by revising or by writing entirely new chapters. To those who have written chapters for previous editions, we'd also like to extend our thanks for helping get the project where it is today.

We're also very pleased that this edition comes in glorious Technicolor, which will no doubt make it a more vibrant and enjoyable read. We hope it communicates the excitement and importance of a sociological understanding, at no time more relevant surely than today.

We would also like to thank Ben Cocking at Roehampton and Jeni Harden particularly for their work in putting together the supporting website for the book.

Ian Marsh
Mike Keating

Guided tour

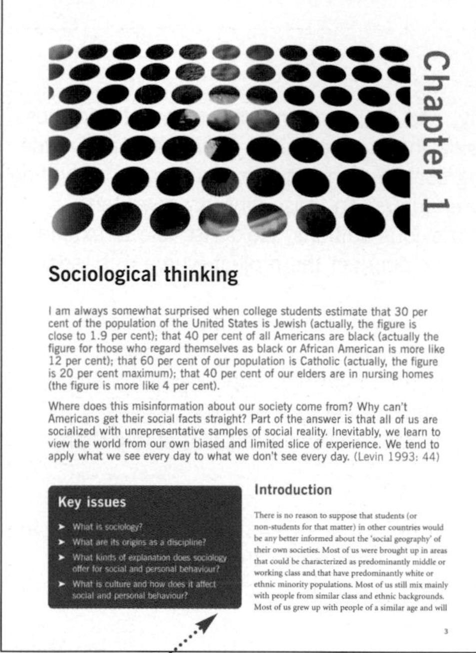

Chapter 1

Sociological thinking

I am always somewhat surprised when college students estimate that 30 per cent of the population of the United States is Jewish (actually, the figure is close to 1.9 per cent); that 40 per cent of all Americans are black (actually the figure for those who regard themselves as black or African American is more like 12 per cent); that 60 per cent of our population is Catholic (actually, the figure is 20 per cent maximum); that 40 per cent of our elders are in nursing homes (the figure is more like 4 per cent).

Where does this misinformation about our society come from? Why can't Americans get their social facts straight? Part of the answer is that all of us are socialized with unrepresentative samples of social reality. Inevitably, we learn to view the world from our own biased and limited slice of experience. We tend to apply what we see every day to what we don't see every day. (Levin 1993: 44)

Key issues

- What is sociology?
- What are its origins as a discipline?
- What kinds of explanation does sociology offer for social and personal behaviour?
- What is culture and how does it affect social and personal behaviour?

Introduction

There is no reason to suppose that students (or non-students for that matter) in other countries would be any better informed about the 'social geography' of their own societies. Most of us were brought up in areas that could be characterized as predominantly middle or working class and that have predominantly white or ethnic minority populations. Most of us still mix mainly with people from similar class and ethnic backgrounds. Most of us grew up with people of a similar age and will

3

Key issues Each chapter begins with a breakdown of the key issues that will be covered, to aid understanding as you read

Stop and think . . . provide the opportunity to reflect on what you have read and think about its applications to the real world

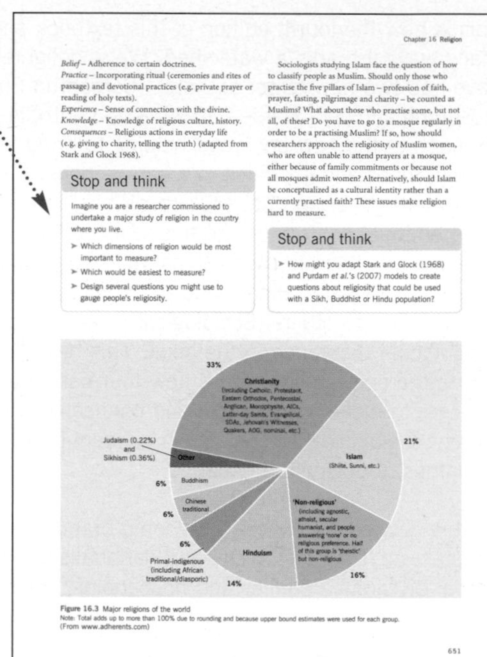

Chapter 16 Religion

Belief – Adherence to certain doctrines.
Practice – Incorporating ritual (ceremonies and rites of passage) and devotional practices (e.g. private prayer or reading of holy texts).
Experience – Sense of connection with the divine.
Knowledge – Knowledge of religious culture, history.
Consequences – Religious actions in everyday life (e.g. giving to charity, telling the truth) (adapted from Stark and Glock 1968).

Stop and think

Imagine you are a researcher commissioned to undertake a major study of religion in the country where you live.

- Which dimensions of religion would be most important to measure?
- Which would be easiest to measure?
- Design several questions you might use to gauge people's religiosity.

Sociologists studying Islam face the question of how to classify people as Muslim. Should only those who practise the five pillars of Islam – profession of faith, prayer, fasting, pilgrimage and charity – be counted as Muslims? What about those who practise some, but not all, of these? Do you have to go to a mosque regularly in order to be a practising Muslim? If so, how should researchers approach the religiosity of Muslim women, who are often unable to attend prayers at a mosque, either because of family commitments or because not all mosques admit women? Alternatively, should Islam be conceptualized as a cultural identity rather than a currently practised faith? These issues make religion hard to measure.

Stop and think

- How might you adapt Stark and Glock (1968) and Purdam *et al*.'s (2007) models to create questions about religiosity that could be used with a Sikh, Buddhist or Hindu population?

Figure 16.3 Major religions of the world
Note: Total adds up to more than 100% due to rounding and because upper bound estimates were used for each group.
(From www.adherents.com)

651

A closer look . . . focuses in on particular issues that arise within the chapter, highlighting the complexities and debates that surround them

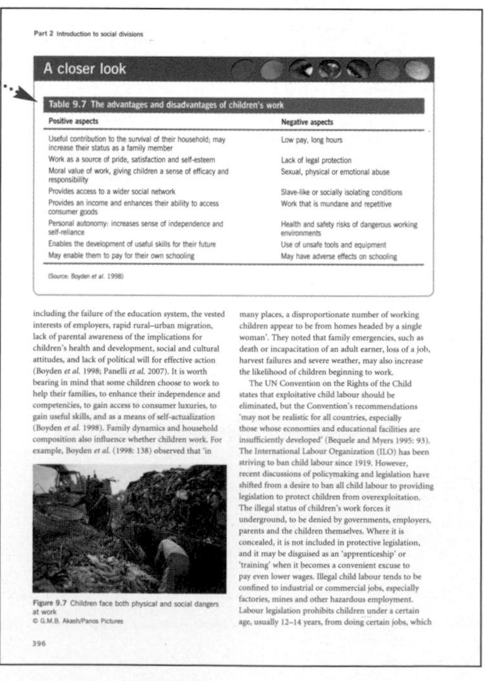

Part 2 Introduction to social divisions

A closer look

Table 9.7 The advantages and disadvantages of children's work

Positive aspects	Negative aspects
Useful contribution to the survival of their household; may increase their status as a family member	Low pay, long hours
Work as a source of pride, satisfaction and self-esteem	Lack of legal protection
Moral value of work, giving children a sense of efficacy and responsibility	Sexual, physical or emotional abuse
Provides access to a wider social network	Slave-like or socially isolating conditions
Provides an income and enhances their ability to access consumer goods	Work that is mundane and repetitive
Personal autonomy: increases sense of independence and self-reliance	Health and safety risks of dangerous working environments
Enables the development of useful skills for their future	Use of unsafe tools and equipment
May enable them to pay for their own schooling	May have adverse effects on schooling

(Source: Boyden *et al*. 1998)

including the failure of the education system, the vested interests of employers, rapid rural–urban migration, lack of parental awareness of the implications for children's health and development, social and cultural attitudes, and lack of political will for effective action (Boyden *et al*. 1998; Panelli *et al*. 2007). It is worth bearing in mind that some children choose to work to help their families, to enhance their independence and competencies, to gain access to consumer luxuries, to gain useful skills, and as a means of self-actualization (Boyden *et al*. 1998). Family dynamics and household composition also influence whether children work. For example, Boyden *et al*. (1998: 138) observed that 'in many places, a disproportionate number of working children appear to be from homes headed by a single woman'. They noted that family emergencies, such as death or incapacitation of an adult earner, loss of a job, harvest failures and severe weather, may also increase the likelihood of children beginning to work.

The UN Convention on the Rights of the Child states that exploitative child labour should be eliminated, but the Convention's recommendations 'may not be realistic for all countries, especially those whose economies and educational facilities are insufficiently developed' (Bequele and Myers 1995: 93). The International Labour Organization (ILO) has been striving to ban child labour since 1919. However, recent discussions of policymaking and legislation have shifted from a desire to ban all child labour to providing legislation to protect children from overexploitation. The illegal status of children's work forces it underground, to be denied by governments, employers, parents and the children themselves. Where it is concealed, it is not included in protective legislation, and it may be disguised as an 'apprenticeship' or 'training' when it becomes a convenient excuse to pay even lower wages. Illegal child labour tends to be confined to industrial or commercial jobs, especially factories, mines and other hazardous employment. Labour legislation prohibits children under a certain age, usually 12–14 years, from doing certain jobs, which

Figure 9.7 Children face both physical and social dangers at work
© G.M.B. Akash/Panos Pictures

396

Part 2 Introduction to social divisions

diseases; many of these diseases could be easily prevented with access to immunization and dehydration sachets, improved access to safe drinking water, better sanitation conditions and increased education.

People who live in economic poverty also suffer from social inequalities, including a lack of access to education and health care, inadequate access to safe water and sanitation, lack of adequate infrastructure

Case study

Inadequate access to basic services in rural Bolivia

This case study illustrates some of the ways in which a lack of resources and basic services can affect people's everyday lives. The two girls pictured in Figure 9.5, Marianela and Luisa, are nine and five years old and live in a relatively isolated rural community in southern Bolivia. They are small for their age as a result of poor diet and lack of adequate nutrition. They have to walk over an hour each way to school every day, but often they are unable to go because they are expected to contribute to the planting and harvesting of crops. They have five siblings so their parents cannot afford to send them all to school. The nearest town is five hours away by bus, but the local bus runs only on Mondays and Thursdays, so if they fall ill on another day of the week, the only means of transport is horseback to get to a doctor in the town.

In Figure 9.5 they are on their way to fetch water from the river, but it is dirty river water that they have to drink. In their community there are no toilets, no showers, no sewage systems, no electricity, no televisions and no telephone lines. It is interesting to compare this with rural Scotland, where even in the most isolated areas people have access to electricity and phone lines, and can even receive their post and have their rubbish collected on a regular basis.

Figure 9.5 Two girls on errands in Bolivia
© Samantha Punch

364

Case study . . . looks at individual events, stories and research findings that bring the topics within each chapter to life

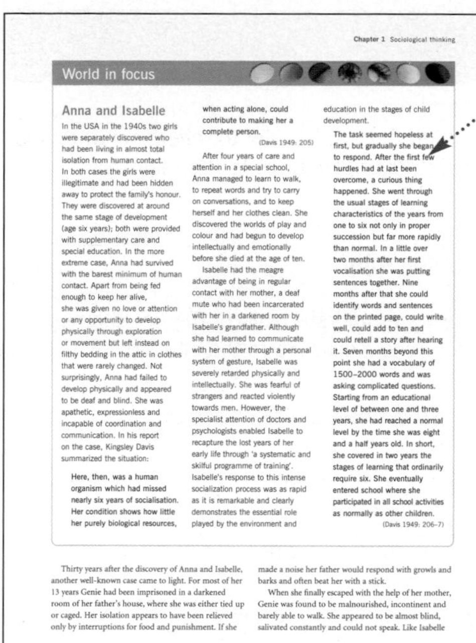

Chapter 1 Sociological thinking

World in focus

Anna and Isabelle

In the USA in the 1940s two girls were separately discovered who had been living in almost total isolation from human contact. In both cases the girls were illegitimate and had been hidden away to protect the family's honour. They were discovered at around the same stage of development (age six years); both were provided with supplementary care and special education. In the more extreme case, Anna had survived with the barest minimum of human contact. Apart from being fed enough to keep her alive, she was given no love or attention or any opportunity to develop physically through exploration or movement but left instead on filthy bedding in the attic in clothes that were rarely changed. Not surprisingly, Anna had failed to develop physically and appeared to be deaf and blind. She was apathetic, expressionless and incapable of coordination and communication. In his report on the case, Kingsley Davis summarized the situation:

> Here, then, was a human organism which had missed nearly six years of socialisation. Her condition shows how little her purely biological resources, when acting alone, could contribute to making her a complete person.
> (Davis 1949: 205)

After four years of care and attention in a special school, Anna managed to learn to walk, to repeat words and try to carry on conversations, and to keep herself and her clothes clean. She discovered the worlds of play and colour and had begun to develop intellectually and emotionally before she died at the age of ten.

Isabelle had the meagre advantage of being in regular contact with her mother, a deaf mute who had been incarcerated with her in a darkened room by Isabelle's grandfather. Although she had learned to communicate with her mother through a personal system of gesture, Isabelle was severely retarded physically and intellectually. She was fearful of strangers and reacted violently towards men. However, the specialist attention of doctors and psychologists enabled Isabelle to recapture the lost years of her early life through 'a systematic and skilful programme of training'. Isabelle's response to this intense socialization process was as rapid as it is remarkable and clearly demonstrates the essential role played by the environment and education in the stages of child development.

> The task seemed hopeless at first, but gradually she began to respond. After the first few hurdles had at last been overcome, a curious thing happened. She went through the usual stages of learning characteristics of the years from one to six not only in proper succession but far more rapidly than normal. In a little over two months after her first vocalisation she was putting sentences together. Nine months after that she could identify words and sentences on the printed page, could write well, could add to ten and could retell a story after hearing it. Seven months beyond this point she had a vocabulary of 1500–2000 words and was asking complicated questions. Starting from an educational level of between one and three years, she had reached a normal level by the time she was eight and a half years old. In short, she covered in two years the stages of learning that ordinarily require six. She eventually entered school where she participated in all school activities as normally as other children.
> (Davis 1949: 206–7)

Thirty years after the discovery of Anna and Isabelle, another well-known case came to light. For most of her 13 years Genie had been imprisoned in a darkened room of her father's house, where she was either tied up or caged. Her isolation appears to have been relieved only by interruptions for food and punishment. If she made a noise her father would respond with growls and barks and often beat her with a stick.

When she finally escaped with the help of her mother, Genie was found to be malnourished, incontinent and barely able to walk. She appeared to be almost blind, salivated constantly and could not speak. Like Isabelle

35

World in focus . . . reports cases of sociological interest from around the globe, helping the reader to question assumptions about the nature of society and to gain a deeper understanding of sociological study throughout the world

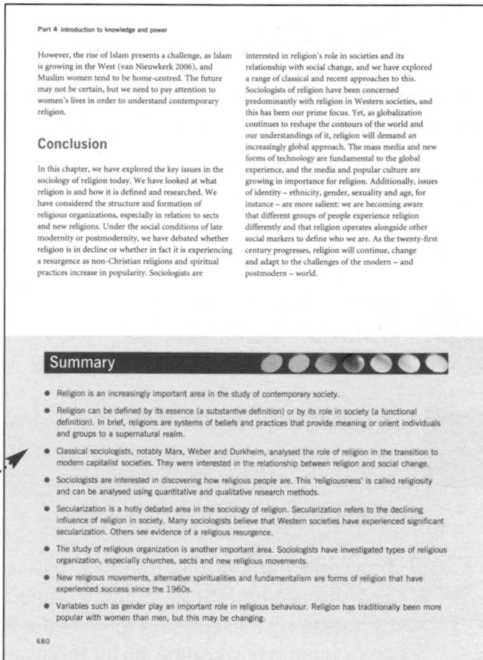

Part 4 Introduction to knowledge and power

However, the rise of Islam presents a challenge, as Islam is growing in the West (van Nieuwkerk 2006), and Muslim women tend to be home-centred. The future may not be certain, but we need to pay attention to women's lives in order to understand contemporary religion.

Conclusion

In this chapter, we have explored the key issues in the sociology of religion today. We have looked at what religion is and how it is defined and researched. We have considered the structure and formation of religious organizations, especially in relation to sects and new religions. Under the social conditions of late modernity or postmodernity, we have debated whether religion is in decline or whether in fact it is experiencing a resurgence as non-Christian religions and spiritual practices increase in popularity. Sociologists are interested in religion's role in societies and its relationship with social change, and we have explored a range of classical and recent approaches to this. Sociologists of religion have been concerned predominantly with religion in Western societies, and this has been our prime focus. Yet, as globalization continues to reshape the contours of the world and our understandings of it, religion will demand an increasingly global approach. The mass media and new forms of technology are fundamental to the global experience, and the media and popular culture are growing in importance for religion. Additionally, issues of identity – ethnicity, gender, sexuality and age, for instance – are more salient: we are becoming aware that different groups of people experience religion differently and that religion operates alongside other social markers to define who we are. As the twenty-first century progresses, religion will continue, change and adapt to the challenges of the modern – and postmodern – world.

Summary

- Religion is an increasingly important area in the study of contemporary society.
- Religion can be defined by its essence (a substantive definition) or by its role in society (a functional definition). In brief, religions are systems of beliefs and practices that provide meaning or orient individuals and groups to a supernatural realm.
- Classical sociologists, notably Marx, Weber and Durkheim, analysed the role of religion in the transition to modern capitalist societies. They were interested in the relationship between religion and social change.
- Sociologists are interested in discovering how religious people are. This 'religiousness' is called religiosity and can be analysed using quantitative and qualitative research methods.
- Secularization is a hotly debated area in the sociology of religion. Secularization refers to the declining influence of religion in society. Many sociologists believe that Western societies have experienced significant secularization. Others see evidence of a religious resurgence.
- The study of religious organization is another important area. Sociologists have investigated types of religious organization, especially churches, sects and new religious movements.
- New religious movements, alternative spiritualities and fundamentalism are forms of religion that have experienced success since the 1960s.
- Variables such as gender play an important role in religious behaviour. Religion has traditionally been more popular with women than men, but this may be changing.

680

Summary . . . at the end of each chapter, key points are highlighted in bullet form as a useful recap and revision tool

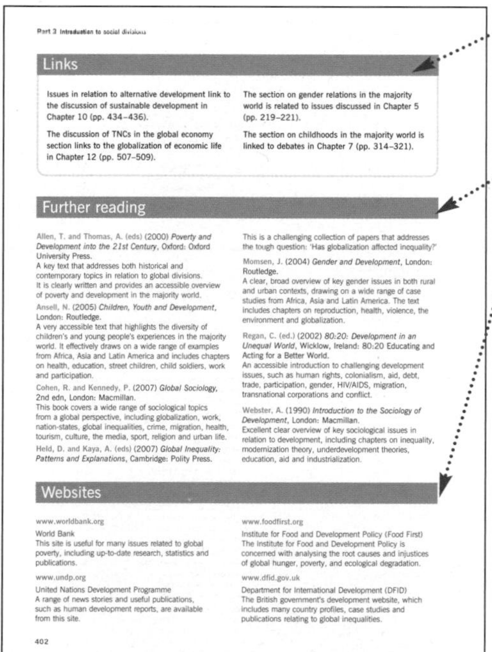

Part 3 Introduction to social divisions

Links

Issues in relation to alternative development link to the discussion of sustainable development in Chapter 10 (pp. 434–436).

The discussion of TNCs in the global economy section links to the globalization of economic life in Chapter 12 (pp. 507–509).

The section on gender relations in the majority world is related to issues discussed in Chapter 5 (pp. 219–221).

The section on childhoods in the majority world is linked to debates in Chapter 7 (pp. 314–321).

Further reading

Allen, T. and Thomas, A. (eds) (2000) *Poverty and Development into the 21st Century*, Oxford: Oxford University Press.
A key text that addresses both historical and contemporary topics in relation to global divisions. It is clearly written and provides an accessible overview of poverty and development in the majority world.

Ansell, N. (2005) *Children, Youth and Development*, London: Routledge.
A very accessible text that highlights the diversity of children's and young people's experiences in the majority world. It effectively draws on a wide range of examples from Africa, Asia and Latin America and includes chapters on health, education, street children, child soldiers, work and participation.

Cohen, R. and Kennedy, P. (2007) *Global Sociology*, 2nd edn, London: Macmillan.
This book covers a wide range of sociological topics from a global perspective, including globalization, work, nation-states, global inequalities, crime, migration, health, tourism, culture, the media, sport, religion and urban life.

Held, D. and Kaya, A. (eds) (2007) *Global Inequality: Patterns and Explanations*, Cambridge: Polity Press.
This is a challenging collection of papers that addresses the tough question: 'Has globalization affected inequality?'

Momsen, J. (2004) *Gender and Development*, London: Routledge.
A clear, broad overview of key gender issues in both rural and urban contexts, drawing on a wide range of case studies from Africa, Asia and Latin America. The text includes chapters on reproduction, health, violence, the environment and globalization.

Regan, C. (ed.) (2002) *80:20: Development in an Unequal World*, Wicklow, Ireland: 80:20 Educating and Acting for a Better World.
An accessible introduction to challenging development issues, such as human rights, colonialism, aid, debt, trade, participation, gender, HIV/AIDS, migration, transnational corporations and conflict.

Webster, A. (1990) *Introduction to the Sociology of Development*, London: Macmillan.
Excellent clear overview of key sociological issues in relation to development, including chapters on inequality, modernization theory, underdevelopment theories, education, aid and industrialization.

Websites

www.worldbank.org
World Bank
This site is useful for many issues related to global poverty, including up-to-date research, statistics and publications.

www.undp.org
United Nations Development Programme
A range of news stories and useful publications, such as human development reports, are available from this site.

www.foodfirst.org
Institute for Food and Development Policy (Food First)
The Institute for Food and Development Policy is concerned with analysing the root causes and injustices of global hunger, poverty, and ecological degradation.

www.dfid.gov.uk
Department for International Development (DFID)
The British government's development website, which includes many country profiles, case studies and publications relating to global inequalities.

402

Links . . . are a useful feature at the end of each chapter, which show the connections between the different chapters – allowing you to learn about specific issues in greater depth

Further reading and Websites . . . are annotated to direct the student of sociology towards other resources for further study, revision and research

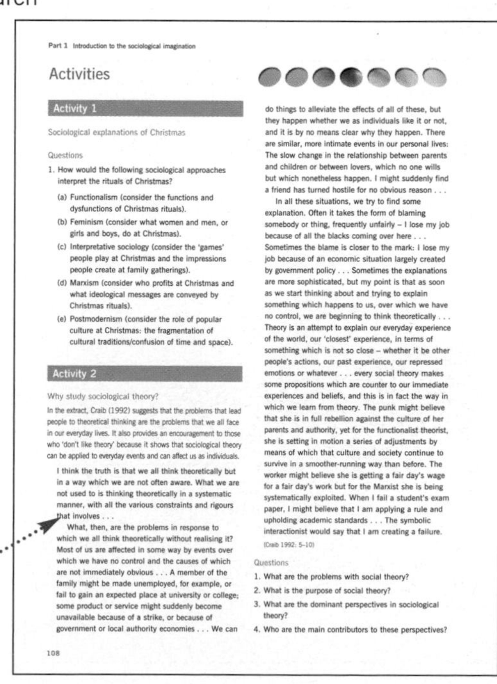

Part 1 Introduction to the sociological imagination

Activities

Activity 1

Sociological explanations of Christmas

Questions

1. How would the following sociological approaches interpret the rituals of Christmas?
   (a) Functionalism (consider the functions and dysfunctions of Christmas rituals).
   (b) Feminism (consider what women and men, or girls and boys, do at Christmas).
   (c) Interpretative sociology (consider the 'games' people play at Christmas and the impressions people create at family gatherings).
   (d) Marxism (consider who profits at Christmas and what ideological messages are conveyed by Christmas rituals).
   (e) Postmodernism (consider the role of popular culture at Christmas: the fragmentation of cultural traditions/confusion of time and space).

Activity 2

Why study sociological theory?

In the extract, Craib (1992) suggests that the problems that lead people to theoretical thinking are the problems that we all face in our everyday lives. It also provides an encouragement to those who 'don't like theory' because it shows that sociological theory can be applied to everyday events and can affect us as individuals.

> I think the truth is that we all think theoretically but in a way which we are not often aware. What we are not used to is thinking theoretically in a systematic manner, with all the various constraints and rigours that involves . . .
>
> What, then, are the problems in response to which we all think theoretically without realising it? Most of us are affected in some way by events over which we have no control and the causes of which are not immediately obvious . . . A member of the family might be made unemployed, for example, or fail to gain an expected place at university or college; some product or service might suddenly become unavailable because of a strike, or because of government or local authority economies . . . We can do things to alleviate the effects of all of these, but they happen whether we as individuals like it or not, and it is by no means clear why they happen. There are similar, more intimate events in our personal lives: The slow change in the relationship between parents and children or between lovers, which no one wills but which nonetheless happen. I might suddenly find a friend has turned hostile for no obvious reason . . .
>
> In all these situations, we try to find some explanation. Often it takes the form of blaming somebody or thing, frequently unfairly – I lose my job because of all the blacks coming over here . . . Sometimes the blame is closer to the mark: I lose my job because of an economic situation largely created by government policy . . . Sometimes the explanations are more sophisticated, but my point is that as soon as we start thinking about and trying to explain something which happens to us, over which we have no control, we are beginning to think theoretically . . . Theory is an attempt to explain our everyday experience of the world, our 'closest' experience, in terms of something which is not so close – whether it be other people's actions, our past experience, our repressed emotions or whatever . . . every social theory makes some propositions which are counter to our immediate experiences and beliefs, and this is in fact the way in which we learn from theory. The punk might believe that she is in full rebellion against the culture of her parents and authority, yet for the functionalist theorist, she is setting in motion a series of adjustments by means of which that culture and society continue to survive in a smoother-running way than before. The worker might believe she is getting a fair day's wage for a fair day's work but for the Marxist she is being systematically exploited. When I fail a student's exam paper, I might believe that I am applying a rule and upholding academic standards . . . The symbolic interactionist would say that I am creating a failure.
> (Craib 1992: 5–10)

Questions

1. What are the problems with social theory?
2. What is the purpose of social theory?
3. What are the dominant perspectives in sociological theory?
4. Who are the main contributors to these perspectives?

108

Activities . . . form a useful starting point for thinking further about what you have learnt in each chapter, individually and in a group environment

How to use this book

Each chapter consists of a number of features outlined below:

Chapter openers – key issues and an opening quote to introduce the reader to the subject.

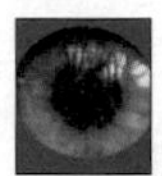

Case studies, which contain specific examples of research, international perspectives and biographies of key writers.

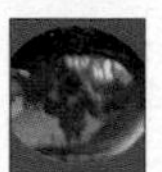

A closer look: boxed sections that highlight definitions and terminology and generally explain in more detail key themes mentioned in the text.

Stop and think points to encourage reflection and discussion. These generally take the form of questions for students to consider either in a group/seminar situation or by themselves. In some cases they ask students to do things and may be developed for class exercises. Some ask for initial and gut reactions to an issue or to what they have read; others require more thought and analysis.

World in focus boxes provide a global view of, or perspective on, a key issue.

Each chapter ends with:

- **A summary** to remind students of the key themes, points and issues discussed in the chapter.
- **Links** to show connections across chapters.
- **Further reading** suggestions.
- **Websites** to encourage further investigation.
- **Activities** that enable a fuller exploration of some of the ideas or material looked at. These could form the basis for group or individual student projects.

At the end of the book there is a glossary that provides brief definitions of key terms and concepts used within the text, and a full list of references.

Acknowledgements

We are grateful to the following for permission to reproduce copyright material:

Figures

Figure 2.5 from Angela Martin; Figure 4.6 from *Income and Wealth: The Latest Evidence*, Joseph Rowntree Foundation (Hills, J. 1997), reproduced by permission of the Joseph Rowntree Foundation; Figure 4.10 from *Poverty, Wealth and Place in Britain, 1968 to 2005*, Policy Press (Dorling, D., Rigby, J., Wheeler, B., Ballas, D., Thomas, B., Fahmy, E., Gordon, D. and Lupton, R. 2007) Figure i; Figure 5.6 after *Bridging the Gender Pay Gap*, reference: MEMO/07/297, copyright European Communities 2007; Figure 7.2 from *Growing Up and Growing Old*, Sage Publications Ltd (Hockey, J. and James, A. 1993) p. 29; Figure 8.1 from *Being and Becoming: Social Exclusion and the Onset of Disability, CASE report 21*, London School of Economics (Burchardt, T. 2003); Figure 8.2 from *Enduring Economic Exclusion: Disabled People, Income and Work*, Joseph Rowntree Foundation (Burchardt, T. 2000), reproduced by permission of the Joseph Rowntree Foundation; Figure 10.4 from *Pollution and Poverty: Breaking the Link*, Friends of the Earth (2001); Figure 12.3 from Flexibility, uncertainty and manpower management, *Report 89* (Atkinson, J. 1984), Institute of Management Studies, Institute for Employment Studies (IES); Figure 15.8 adapted from *Changing Education: A Sociology of Education Since 1944*, Prentice Hall (McKenzie, J. 2001) p. 159; Figure 16.1 from *Who are we? Identities in Britain*, Institute for Public Policy Research (Pew Research Centre 2002); Figure 16.2 from Religion in the UK: an overview of equality statistics and evidence gaps, *Journal of Contemporary Religion*, 22(2), pp. 147–168 (Purdam, K., Afkhami, R., Crockett, A. and Olsen, W. 2007), reprinted by permission of Taylor & Francis Group, http://www.informaworld.com; Figure 16.4 from *God is Dead: Secularization in the West*, Blackwell (Bruce, S. 2002) Figure 1.1; Figure 17.5 from *Mass Communications Theory: An Introduction*, Sage Publications Ltd (McQuail, D. 1994) p. 189; Figure 17.6 from *Mass Communications Theory: An Introduction*, Sage Publications Ltd (McQuail, D. 1994) p. 191; Figure 17.13 from *Sunday Telegraph*, 15 May 2005.

Maps

Map 14.5 adapted from *Guardian*, 8 April 1995, copyright Guardian Media & News Ltd 1995.

Tables

Table 4.1 from How many classes are there in contemporary society?, *Sociology*, 24, pp. 377–96 (Runciman, W.G. 1990) copyright © 1990, reprinted by permission of Sage; Table 4.2 from ESeC User Guide, http://www.iser.essex.ac.uk/esec/guide/table1.php; Tables page 187, 4.3, 4.4 adapted from Sunday Times Rich List 2008, www.timesonline.co.uk/richlist; Table 5.1 from The narrowing education gap between men and women, *Statistics in Focus: Population and Social Conditions*, 130/2007, p. 6 (2007), copyright European Communities 2007; Table 7.1 adapted from *Growing Up and Growing Old*, Sage Publications Ltd (Hockey, J. and James, A. 1993); Table on page 352 from http://www.carersuk.org/Newsandcampaigns/Media/Tenfactsaboutcaring; Table 8.1 from *Understanding Disability: From Theory to Practice*, Macmillan (Oliver, M. 1996) p. 34, reproduced with permission of Palgrave Macmillan; Table 8.2 from *The Politics of Disablement*, Macmillan (Oliver, M. 1990), reproduced with permission of Palgrave Macmillan; Table 9.3 from *80:20: Development in an Unequal World*, 80:20 Educating and Acting for a Better World (Regan, C. (ed.) 2002) p. 127; Table 9.4 adapted from *Introduction to the Sociology of Development*, Macmillan (Webster, A. 1990), reproduced with permission of Palgrave Macmillan; Table 12.1 from *Human Development Report*, Oxford University Press (United Nations Development Programme) http://cfapp2.undp.org/statistics/data/rcrreport.cfm; Table 13.2 after *World Health Statistics 2008*, World Health Organization (2008) p. 82, http://www.who.int/whosis/whostat/2008/en/index.html; Table 13.3 adapted from *World Health Statistics 2008*, World Health Organization (2008) Table 1; Table 14.2 adapted from *Sociology Update*, Olympus Books (Denscombe, M. 2002) p. 24; Table 15.1 from *Education, Culture, Economy, Society*, Oxford University Press (Halsey, A.H., Lauder, H., Brown, P. and Wells, A.S. 1997) Table 17.1, by permission of Oxford University Press, Inc.; Table 16.1 from *Church and State in Contemporary Europe*, Frank Cass (Madeley, J.T.S. and Enyedi, Z. (eds) 2003) Table 3, p. 16; Table 16.2 from Identity, politics and the future(s) of religion in the UK: the case of the religion questions in the 2001 Decennial Census, *Journal of Contemporary Religion*, 19(1), 3–21 (Weller, P. 2004), reprinted by permission of Taylor & Francis Group, http://www.informaworld.com; Table 16.3 from A turning point in religious evolution in Europe, *Journal of*

Contemporary Religion, 19(1), pp. 29–45 (Lambert, Y. 2004), reprinted by permission of Taylor & Francis Group, http://www.informaworld.com; Table 16.6 from Religious toleration and organisational typologies, *Journal of Contemporary Religion*, 22(1), 1–17 (Bruce, S. and Voas, D. 2007), reprinted by permission of Taylor & Francis Group, http://www.informaworld.com; Table 17.1 after Internet World Stats (2008), http://www.internetworldstats.com.

Text

Case Study on page 6 adapted from *Cocky: The Rise and Fall of Curtis Warren, Britain's Biggest Drug Baron*, Milo Books (Barnes, A., Elias, R. and Walsh, P.), with permission from Milo Books; Case Study on page 18 from *Fast Food Nation*, Penguin (Schlosser, E. 2002) p. 152, reproduced by permission of Penguin Books Ltd; Case Study on page 24 after *Sunday Times*, 7 September 1997 (Rayment, T.); Case Study on page 25 after *Sunday Times*, 7 September 1997 (Cassidy, J.); Extract on page 31 from China's strange 'ghost marriages', *The Economist*, 26 July 2007; Case Study on page 36 from Doctor blames parents for 'worst case of malnutrition', *Independent*, 24 November 2004 (Herbert, I.), copyright The Independent; Activity on page 42 from Fly away Peter, *Guardian*, 18 October 1986 (Mair, S.), copyright Guardian News & Media Ltd 1986; Activity on page 44 from *Identity: Cultural Change and the Struggle for Self*, Oxford University Press (Baumeister, R. 1986) pp. 254–5, by permission of Oxford University Press, Inc.; Quote on page 56 from *The Decline of Serfdom in Medieval England*, Macmillan (Hilton, R.H. 1969) 9–30, reproduced with permission of Palgrave Macmillan; Box on page 104 from *Sociology Review*, 8(2), pp. 6–7 (Westergaard, J. 1998), Reprinted by permission of Philip Allan Updates; Activity on page 108 from *Modern Social Theory*, Pearson Education Limited (Craib, I. 1992) pp. 5–10; Box on page 115 from *The Rules of Sociological Method*, The Free Press (Durkheim, E. 1964, translated by Sarah A. Solovay and John H. Mueller, edited by George E.G. Catlin) pp. 1–4, reprinted with the permission of The Free Press, a Division of Simon & Schuster, Inc, copyright © 1938 by George E.G. Catlin, copyright renewed © 1966 by Sarah A. Solovay, John H. Mueller, George E.G. Catlin, all rights reserved; Case Study on page 117 adapted from *For Sociology: Renewal and Critique in Sociology Today*, Penguin (Gouldner, A.W. 1975) pp. 5–6, reproduced by permission of Penguin Books Ltd; Case Study on page 136 from *Hell's Angels*, Penguin (Thompson, H.S. 1967) pp. 52–6, 283, reproduced by permission of Penguin Books Ltd; Case Study on page 195 from Rich – and excluded, *Observer*, 20 September 1998 (Thomas, R.), copyright Guardian News & Media Ltd 1998; Case Study on page 198 from Middle-class professionals are Britain's hidden poor, *Guardian*, 26 July 2004 (Ward, D.), copyright Guardian News & Media Ltd 2004; Extract on page 206 from Wealth gap narrows faster in UK than other developed countries, *Guardian*, 21 October 2008 (Weaver, M.), copyright Guardian News & Media Ltd 2008; Case Study on page 208 from Third of children in the north-west live in poverty, *Guardian*, 12 March 2005 (Carter, H.), copyright Guardian News & Media Ltd 2005; Epigraph on page 216 from *Transliberation: Beyond Pink or Blue*, Beacon Press (Feinberg, L. 1998) pp. 1–4, copyright © 1998 by Leslie Feinberg, reprinted by permission of Beacon Press, Boston; Extract on page 223 from Butch identity development: the formation of an authentic gender, *Feminism and Psychology*, 15(1), pp. 61–85 (Hiestand, K.R. and Levitt, H.M. 2005), c 2005, reprinted by permission of Sage; Box on page 260 from *All ER*, 1st ed., pp. 1066–7 (Lord Fraser 1983), reproduced by permission of Reed Elsevier (UK) Limited, trading as LexisNexis; Case Study on page 263 adapted from *Observer*, 4 January 2004 (Arlidge, J.); Box on page 268 from *The Effectiveness of Employment Equality Policies in Relation to Immigrants and Ethnic Minorities in the UK (Report 38)*, International Labour Office (Wrench, J. and Modood, T. 2000) p. 82, copyright © International Labour Organization 2000; Box on page 279 from Colin Wong, Associate Director of the Undergraduate ITT Programme, Education Deanery, Liverpool Hope University; Box on page 286 from *Intolerant Britain: Hate, Citizenship and Difference*, Open University Press (McGhee, D. 2005) pp. 99–101, copyright 2005, reproduced with the kind permission of Open University Press, all rights reserved; Activity on page 297 from A veil closes France's door to citizenship, *New York Times*, 19 July 2008 (Bennhold, K.), © 2008 The New York Times, all rights reserved, used by permission and protected by the Copyright Laws of the United States. The printing, copying, redistribution or retransmission of the material without express written permission is prohibited; Box on page 312 from *Japanese Society* (Nakane, C. 1973) pp. 27–30, Weidenfeld and Nicolson, an imprint of The Orion Publishing Group, London; Box on page 317 from Research with children: the same or different from research with adults?, *Childhood*, 9(3), pp. 321–41 (Punch, S. 2002); Box on page 320 from *Conceptualising Child-Adult Relations*, Routledge (Alanen, L. and Mayall, B. (eds) 2001) pp. 25–8, copyright © 2001, reproduced by permission of Taylor & Francis Books UK; Case Study on page 323 from *Gender and Later Life: A Sociological Analysis of Resources and Constraints*, Sage Publications Ltd (Arber, S. and Ginn, J. 1991) pp. 41–3; Activity on page 330 from *Towards a Sociology for Childhood*, Open University Press (Mayall, B. 2002) pp. 95–6, copyright 2002, reproduced with the kind permission of Open University Press, all rights reserved; Activity on page 331 from *At Home in the Street: Street Children of Northeast Brazil*, Cambridge University Press (Hecht, T. 1998) pp. 28–9, © 1998, published by Cambridge University Press, reproduced with permission; Case Study on page 338 from Franklin Roosevelt: Ambiguous symbol for Disabled Americans, *The Midwest Quarterly*, Vol. XXIX, No. 1, pp. 113–35 (Duffy, J. 1987); Case Study on page 340 from *Disabled People and Economic Needs in the Developing World: A Political Perspective from Jordan*, Ashgate Publishing (Turmunsani, M. 2003) pp. 51–2, copyright 2003 Ashgate Publishing; Case Study on page 342 from Conductive education: if it wasn't so sad it would be funny, *Disability, Handicap and Society*, Vol. 4, No. 2, pp. 127–200 (Oliver, M. 1989), reprinted by permission of Taylor & Francis Group, http://www.informaworld.com; Activity on page 355 from Deaf activists in Òdesigner babiesÓ storm, *Disability Now*, April 2008 (Emery, S.); Box on page 399 from The impact of primary education on school-to-work transitions for young people in rural Bolivia, *Youth & Society*, Vol. 36, No. 2, pp. 163–82 (Punch, S. 2007), copyright 2004 by Sage Publications Inc. Journals. Reproduced with permission of Sage Publications Inc. Journals in the format Textbook via Copyright Clearance Center; Activity on page 403 from *80:20: Development in an Unequal World*, 80:20 Educating and Acting for a Better World (Regan, C. 2002) p. 190; Lyric on page 414 from *Big Yellow Taxi*, Joni Mitchell, 1969, words and music by Joni Mitchell, © 1970 (Renewed) Crazy Crow Music. All rights administered by Sony/ATV Music Publishing, 8 Music Square West, Nashville, TN 37203, All rights reserved. Used by permission from Alfred Publishing Co., Inc.; Case Study on page 488 from *Work: Twenty Personal Accounts*, Penguin (Fraser, R. (ed.) 1968) pp. 11–12; Box on page 490 from *All Day and Every Day: Factory and Family in the Making of Women's Lives*, Pluto (Westwood, S. 1983) pp. 49–51; Box on page 492 from *Organizations and Identities*, Chapman & Hall (Clarke, H., Chandler, J. and Barry, J. (eds) 1994) p. 364; Box on page 493 from *Myths at Work*, Polity (Bradley, H., Erickson, M., Stephenson, C. and Williams, S. 2000); Box on page 497 from *The McDonaldization of Society*, Sage Publications Ltd (Ritzer, G. 1993) pp. 2–3, copyright 1993 by Sage Publications Inc Books. Reproduced with permission of Sage Publications Inc Books in the format Textbook via Copyright Clearance Center; Activity on page 511 from *The Corrosion of Character*, Norton (Sennett, R. 1998) pp. 9–10, copyright © 1998 by Richard Sennett, used by permission of W.W. Norton & Company, Inc.; Activity on page 512 from Bedroom abuse: the hidden work in a nursing home, *Generations Review*, 4(1), pp. 2–4 (Lee-Treweek, G. 1994); Box on page 514 from *The Body in Society*, Polity (Howson, A. 2004) 1; Box on page 527 from Sky News Forum, http://news.sky.com/skynews/getComments/0,,91251-1306412,.xml; Case Study on page 532 adapted from This UK patient avoided the NHS list and flew to India for a heart bypass. Is health tourism the future?, *Guardian*, 1 February 2005 (Ramesh, R.), copyright Guardian News & Media Ltd 2005; Case Study on page 561 after *The Rules of Sociological Method*, The Free Press (Durkheim, E. 1964, translated by Sarah A. Solovay and John H. Mueller, edited by George E.G. Catlin) pp. 1–4, reprinted with the permission of The Free Press, a Division of Simon & Schuster, Inc, copyright © 1938 by George E.G. Catlin, copyright renewed © 1966 by Sarah A. Solovay, John H. Mueller, George E.G. Catlin, all rights reserved; Case Study on page 578 from *Police and People in London IV: The Police in Action*, Policy Studies Institute (Smith, D.J. and Gray, J. 1983); Case Study on page 579 from *The Politics of the Police*, 2nd ed., Harvester Wheatsheaf (Reiner, R. 1992) pp. 114–22; Case Study on page 594 from *Power, Crime and Mystification*, Tavistock (Box, S. 1983) pp. 44–58; Activity on page 598 from *Sociological Snapshots*, Pine Forge Press (Levin, J. 1993) xvi–xvii, copyright 1993 by Sage Publications Inc Books. Reproduced with permission of Sage Publications Inc Books in the format Textbook via Copyright Clearance Center; Box on page 605 from The dirty little secret of credential inflation, *Chronicle of Higher Education*, 27 September 2002 (Collins, R.), Department of Sociology, University of Pennsylvania; Activity on page 643 adapted from Comparing key dimensions of schooling: towards a typology of European school systems, *Comparative Education*, 44(1), pp. 97–8 (Hofman, R.H., Hofman, W.H.A. and Gray, J.M. 2008), reprinted by permission of Taylor & Francis Group, http://www.informaworld.com; Newspaper Headline on page 645 from Pagan prisoners allowed twigs in their cells to use as magic wands, *Scotland on Sunday*, 11 May 2008, © The Scotsman Publications Ltd; Newspaper Headline on page 645 from Baby with two faces worshipped as reincarnation of Hindu goddess, *The Straits Times*, 8 April 2008, The New Paper © Singapore Press Holdings Ltd, permission required for reproduction; Case Study on page 688 from *The British Press and Broadcasting Since 1945*, Blackwell (Seymour-Ure, C. 1992) pp. 1–5; Case Study on page 714 from http://rts.arfs-test.co.uk/Events_det.asp?art_id=6883&sec_id=3171; Case Study on page 737 from In the hood, *Guardian*, 13 May 2005 (McLean, G.), copyright Guardian News & Media Ltd 2005.

The Financial Times

Table 17.3 from Election 2005: newspaper endorsements, *Financial Times*, 14 April 2005 (Hall, B., Burt, T. and Symon, F.).

Photographs

Figure 1.1 Copyright (c) News Group Newspapers Ltd: Times Newspapers Ltd; Figure 1.2 PA Photos: PA Archive Images; Figure 1.3 PA Photos: PA Wire; Figure 1.4 PA Photos: AP Photo/Police Niederoesterreich; Figure 2.1 Corbis: Bettman; Figure 2.3 Getty Images: Hulton Archive; Figure 2.6 PARIS MATCH/SCOOP: IZIS; Figure 2.7 Getty Images: AFP PHOTO/ADRIAN DENNIS; Figure 3.2 Corbis: PARROT PASCAL/CORBIS SYGMA; Figure 3.3 Getty Images: Chuck Nacke/Timepix/Time Life Pictures; Figure 4.3 PA Photos: AP Photo/Charlie Riedel; Figure 4.11 and 4.12 BBC Motion Gallery; Figure 5.1 Marilyn Humphries: 1998; Figure 5.2 Getty Images: FREDERIC J. BROWN/AFP;

Figure 5.3 iStockphoto: Monika Wisniewska; Figure 6.1 Alamy Images: The Print Collector; Figure 6.5 Kobal Collection Ltd: ICON/LADD CO/PARAMOUNT; Figure 7.1 PA Photos: AP Photo/Charles Dharapak; Figure 7.3 Photofusion Picture Library: Ulrike Preuss; Figure 8.3 Corbis: Image Source.Figure 8.4 Getty Images: MARK RALSTON/AFP; Figure 9.7 Panos Pictures: G.M.B. Akash; Figure 10.2 NASA; Figure 10.2 Bridgeman Art Library Ltd: The Wanderer above the Sea of Fog, 1818 (oil on canvas) by Friedrich, Caspar David (1774–1840, x); Figure 10.3 Panos Pictures: Rod Johnson; Figure 10.5 STILL Pictures The Whole Earth Photo Library: Hartmut Schwarzbach – UNEP; p. 445 Corbis: Pascal Deloche/Godong; Figure 11.1 Corbis: Felipe Trueba/epa; Figure 11.2 BBC Photo Library; Figure 11.3 Corbis: Jose Luis Pelaez, Inc.; Figure 11.4 Alamy Images: Jim West; Figure 11.6 Corbis: Tom & Dee Ann McCarthy; Figure 12.1 iStockphoto: digitalskillet; Figure 12.2 Getty Images: Sean Gallup/Newsmakers; Figure 12.4 Corbis: Sherwin Crasto/Reuters; Figure 13.1 Getty Images: The Bridgeman Art Library; Figure 13.2 Wellcome Trust Medical Photographic Library: Miles Kelly Art Library; Figure 13.5 PA Photos: PA Wire; Figure 13.7 Getty Images: DENIS CHARLET/AFP; Figure 14.1 Getty Images: The Bridgeman Art Library; Figure 14.3 Alamy Images: imagebroker; Figure 14.4 PA Photos: AP Photo/Vincent Yu; Figure 14.6 Corbis: Zaheerudin/Webistan; Figure 15.1 Getty Images: Catherine Ledner; Figure 15.3 Getty Images: ALESSANDRO ABBONIZIO/AFP; Figure 15.9 Corbis: Christine Osbourne; Figure 16.5 Alamy Images: MarioPonta; Figure 16.7 Getty Images: Tim Boyle; Figure 16.8 iStockphoto: naheed choudhry; Figure 17.4 PA Photos: PA Archive; Figure 17.10 Alamy Images: Kevin Foy; Figures 17.11 and 17.12 John Frost Newspapers: NI Syndication.

In some instances we have been unable to trace the owners of copyright material, and we would appreciate any information that would enable us to do so.

Part 1 Introduction to the sociological imagination

We do not need sociology to tell us how important the social environment is in helping us to understand how people live the way that they do – and how this varies from time to time and from place to place. It is fairly self-evident that the social world in which we are brought up will influence the way we live. However, sociological exploration and analysis help to provide us with an understanding of how and why things are the way they are – how the lifestyles of different groups of people in one society vary from those of other groups in that society; and how social life in one society differs from that in another.

Sociology has been criticized for looking at and commenting on everyday issues – for examining the 'common sense'. However, sociological analysis and work have informed social policy and practice in many areas of life, including health care, education, family life, crime and justice.

In Chapter 1, we explore the idea of a 'sociological imagination' and consider how the subject of sociology developed and attained academic rigour and acceptance. In this chapter we spend longer than authors of other introductory books in examining the origins of the subject, but we feel it is important to establish the background and position of the subject you are now studying. After this history, we introduce and discuss a number of key concepts that you will come back to throughout the book and your studies – in particular, we look at culture, socialization and identity. We consider the effects on individuals of cultural deprivation by describing examples of cases where children have been brought up without normal human contact – extreme cases such as children brought up in the wild as well as the recent horrific cases from Austria of girls being imprisoned in their houses for many years.

Chapter 2 provides a detailed introduction to, and examination of, the different theoretical perspectives in sociology. This review follows a basically chronological pattern, starting by looking at the classic theories that helped establish sociology as a serious academic subject. In this section we look at the theoretical works and arguments of Emile Durkheim, Karl Marx and Max Weber and consider their continuing influence in contemporary sociology. The second half of the chapter turns to more recent theoretical work, from, roughly, the second half of the twentieth century. Here we introduce interpretivist sociology and interactionism, feminist theorizing, structuralism and postmodernism. Our emphasis is in looking at how these theories can be applied to everyday contemporary life.

Chapter 3 focuses on sociological research. After raising and considering the debate as to how 'scientific' the study of society can be, we look at the major different methodological approaches to researching the social world and then at the specific methods by which sociologists go about collecting and analysing data and information, including questionnaires, interviews and observation.

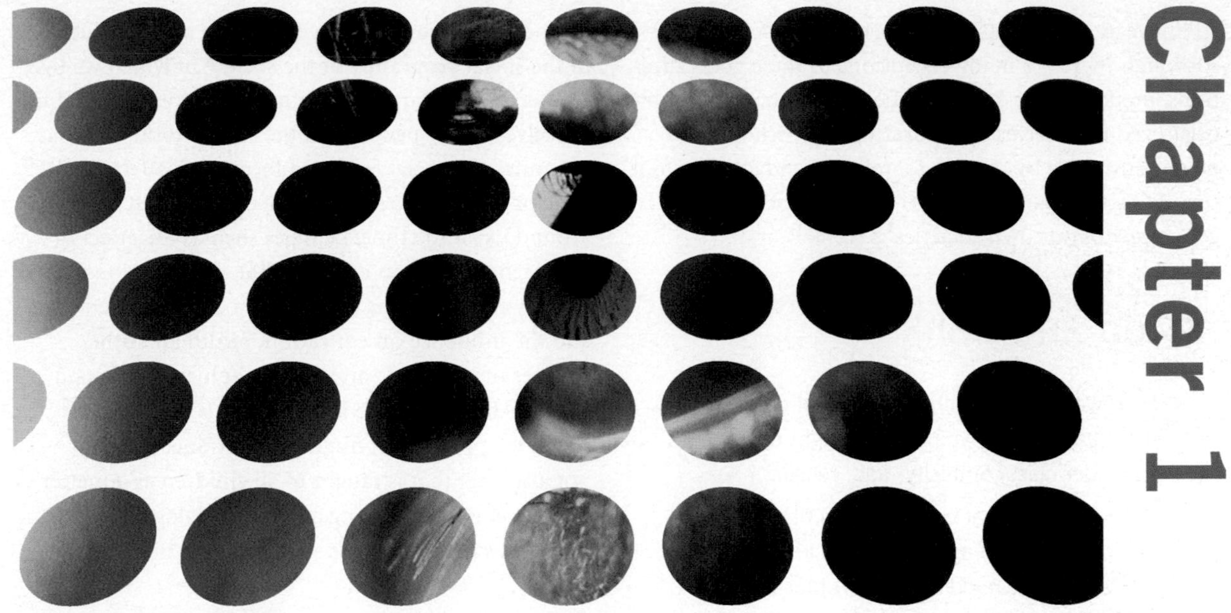

Chapter 1

Sociological thinking

I am always somewhat surprised when college students estimate that 30 per cent of the population of the United States is Jewish (actually, the figure is close to 1.9 per cent); that 40 per cent of all Americans are black (actually the figure for those who regard themselves as black or African American is more like 12 per cent); that 60 per cent of our population is Catholic (actually, the figure is 20 per cent maximum); that 40 per cent of our elders are in nursing homes (the figure is more like 4 per cent).

Where does this misinformation about our society come from? Why can't Americans get their social facts straight? Part of the answer is that all of us are socialized with unrepresentative samples of social reality. Inevitably, we learn to view the world from our own biased and limited slice of experience. We tend to apply what we see every day to what we don't see every day. (Levin 1993: 44)

Key issues

- What is sociology?
- What are its origins as a discipline?
- What kinds of explanation does sociology offer for social and personal behaviour?
- What is culture and how does it affect social and personal behaviour?

Introduction

There is no reason to suppose that students (or non-students for that matter) in other countries would be any better informed about the 'social geography' of their own societies. Most of us were brought up in areas that could be characterized as predominantly middle or working class and that have predominantly white or ethnic minority populations. Most of us still mix mainly with people from similar class and ethnic backgrounds. Most of us grew up with people of a similar age and will still have as our closest friends people of a similar age. Although there are many exceptions to these generalizations, modern, large-scale societies have almost invariably organized themselves by separating their schools and neighbourhoods by race, class, religion and age. It is not surprising that our knowledge of the social facts and geography of our own societies is so inaccurate.

Stop and think

- How would you describe the social geography of the area in which you were brought up (consider class, ethnicity, age, religion)?
- Name an area that could be described as predominantly (a) ageing; (b) black; (c) Catholic; (d) Jewish; (e) middle class; (f) Muslim; (g) Protestant; (h) white; and (i) working class.

Sociology provides us with a more accurate picture of the social geography of the society in which we live. It offers particular and exciting ways of understanding ourselves, other people and the social world. It examines the social facts and forces that affect us all. It helps us to make sense of the changes that occur around us all the time: changes such as the effect of new technologies on everyday life; the variations in employment patterns as factories open or close; and the influence on education, health and other services of economic and political philosophies and policies. In view of the insights into social life that sociology provides, it might seem strange that it is not a subject that is taught to all children as a matter of course. Before looking at what sociology is and how it has developed, we shall consider briefly its 'image'.

Case study

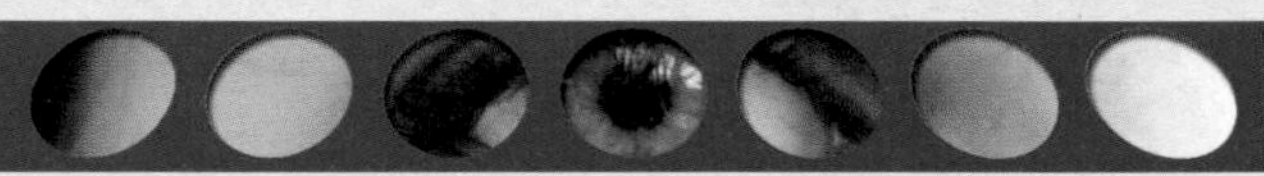

The Kray twins: local heroes?

The Krays were an old-fashioned East End family – tight, self-sufficient and devoted to each other. The name was Austrian, and the twins had Irish, Romany and Jewish blood. The centre of their world was to remain the tiny terrace house at 178 Vallance Road where they grew up and where their Aunt May and their maternal grandparents still lived. The area was badly bombed in the war; before that it was one of the poorest parts of the entire East End and a breeding ground for criminals. It was Bill Sykes' home ground, 'The Rookeries' of Dickens were once just down the road, and Jack the Ripper murdered one of his last victims around the corner in Hanbury Street.

The house, 178 Vallance Road, was tiny, the second in a row of four blank-faced Victorian terraced cottages. There was no bathroom, the lavatory was in the yard at the back, and day and night the house shook as the Liverpool Street trains roared past the bedroom windows. For Violet none of this mattered. Her parents were just around the corner; so was her sister, Rose. Her other sister, May, was next door but one, and her brother, John Lee, kept the café across the street.

And old Grandfather Lee, who still kept his famous left hook in trim, punching a mattress hung up in the yard. He would sit with the twins for hours in his special chair by the fire . . . And sometimes the old man would talk about the other heroes of the old East End, its criminals. Spud Murphy of Hoxton, who killed two men in a spieler in Whitechapel and who shouted to the police that he'd bring a machine-gun and finish everyone off before he was caught; Martin and Baker, two Bethnal Green men who took the nine o'clock walk after shooting three policemen at Carlisle. And for the old man, Jack the Ripper's murders were still a local happening.

(Adapted from Pearson 1972: 12–27)

Ronnie Kray's funeral, 1995

The East End of London accorded one of its most infamous sons the equivalent of a state funeral yesterday. Crowds big enough to gladden the heart of an emperor turned out to shower the last journey of Ronnie Kray with tribute, and to greet his handcuffed twin brother Reggie as though he were a conquering hero . . .

Case study *continued*

Figure 1.1 The funeral of Ronnie Kray, from *The Times* 30.3.95
Photograph by Adrian Brooks, © News Group Newspapers Ltd

Case study *continued*

The Kray twins, who had long ago assumed the status of folk heroes, were each serving 30 years for different murders. Ronnie, the elder of the two by 45 minutes, died of a heart attack in Broadmoor two weeks ago aged 61; Reggie was let out of Maidstone for the day under heavy guard.

(*The Times* 30.3.95: 1)

Crowds gather for Kray's funeral

Large crowds are lining the streets in east London, as mourners prepare to say farewell to gangland killer Reggie Kray.

Six black plumed horses are leading the procession to St Matthews Church for the funeral, which Kray planned in the final days before his death from cancer.

Pavements along Bethnal Green Road have been cordoned off and there is a heavy police presence, as people gather outside the funeral directors where Kray's body was in a chapel of rest.

The last of three notorious brothers, Kray will be buried in the family plot at Chingford, alongside his twin, Ronnie, and older brother Charlie.

The procession is expected to bring the East End to a temporary standstill, with celebrity friends of the Krays among the mourners.

The cortege is scheduled to stop in Vallance Raod, where Kray and his twin brother Ronnie were brought up.

Outside the undertakers, the pavement was bedecked with wreaths – some in the shape of boxing gloves and others in the shape of an 'R'.

One wreath of roses was from the EastEnders actress, and Kray's friend, Barbara Windsor.

(BBC News 11.10.00)

Questions

1. Does social background offer a 'complete explanation' for the Krays' criminal behaviour? What other factors might have played a part?
2. Why do you think the Krays have become 'folk heroes'?

Case study

Cocky: Curtis Warren – Britain's biggest drug baron

Curtis Warren rose from being a street mugger to an international drug baron and one of the richest and most successful British criminals who has ever been caught. He is currently in prison in Holland. The extract below refers to his upbringing in the Toxteth district of Liverpool and is taken from the biography *Cocky: The Rise and Fall of Curtis Warren, Britain's Biggest Drug Baron*.

On July 22, 1960, Curtis, then twenty-five, and Sylvia, twenty-one, were married at St Vincent of Paul's Roman Catholic Church. They took rooms in a Victorian townhouse at 238 Upper Parliament Street, the long, broad Toxteth thoroughfare that dissects the postal district of Liverpool 8 . . . Curtis Francis Warren was born at home on 31 May 1963 . . .

The Granby ward, where the Warrens lived . . . was a close-knit and self-supporting community where everyone knew everyone else. Down at the seaward end of Parliament Street, the dockyards were still busy, the alehouses overflowed and prostitutes lolled under the lamplights, offering cheap sex . . . The streets were a bazaar. Granby Street had its Muslim butchers and its Arab, Pakistani and Bangladeshi food stores displaying strange fruits, vegetables and spices. Old West Indians in Panama hats smoked ganja on their doorsteps . . . At night it came alive. A clampdown on drinking dens in the city centre in 1957 to spruce up the city for an anniversary had pushed many shebeens into Toxteth . . .

Curtis junior followed his brother into the local Catholic primary school before enrolling at a

Case study *continued*

comprehensive with a particularly tough reputation. Apparently he was rarely there beyond his early teens; though his mind was extremely acute, he did not take to the discipline of lessons. He was not alone: some schools regarded twenty per cent truancy as good . . . So Warren and others like him would 'sag' school. They had no money to go anywhere and no gardens to play in, so they spent the days hanging around . . .

Crime also beckoned. As unemployment began to rise from 1974, Toxteth was particularly hard hit. Jobs vanished; even casual work on the docks dried up. If you were black or mixed race, forget it . . . The area drew inwards, became alienated and bitter. By the later part of the decade Granby Street was littered with broken glass, its dwindling number of shops encased in wire grilles to deter burglars . . . In an increasingly tense environment, innocent child pastime paled. Nicking cars and joyriding became a fad . . .

Curtis Warren had just turned twelve when the police stopped him in a stolen car. Though barely big enough to see over the steering wheel, he was charged with the unauthorised taking of a motor vehicle . . . A year later he graduated to the magistrates court, this time for burglary. He was ordered to spend twenty-four hours at an attendance centre. Young Curtis was caught on a spiral of petty offending. It seemed the thing to do. Youth crime was becoming a burning issue in the city. In 1975, a quarter of all people prosecuted in Liverpool were juveniles . . .

Young men of mixed race – like Warren – aroused particular unease in an almost exclusively white police force . . .

On 20 July 1978, the magistrates sent him to a detention centre for the first time, for three months. The centres, known as 'DCs', were schools for crime . . . Warren treated the place as a joke and came out worse than he went in.

(Adapted from Barnes, Elias and Walsh 2000: 14–21)

Questions

The Krays were brought up in the 1940s and 1950s and Curtis Warren in the 1970s and 1980s.

1. Suggest the main similarities and differences between their respective upbringings.
2. What explanations can you offer – both for the similarities and for the differences?

The image of sociology

In the mid-1960s Peter Berger published a very readable introduction to the study of sociology which began by informing us that 'There are very few jokes about sociologists'. He explained that this was probably due to their low profile in 'the popular imagination' (Berger 1967). However, much has changed since then and sociology has a far higher public profile, largely due to its inclusion in the school curriculum, its status as a degree-bearing discipline and the regular appearance of its experts on television and radio documentaries. As a result the sociologist no longer escapes humorous mud-slinging at the professions. Whether it is at the hands of Malcolm Bradbury (*The History Man*), Ben Elton (*The Young Ones*) or simple throw-away comments about the number of sociologists it takes to change a lightbulb, the jokes have not been particularly flattering and have tended to rely on crude and predictable stereotypes.

Dr Christopher Pole made use of the BBC's *Punters* programme (Radio 4, 8 August 1991) to defend the professional and academic status of sociology and to broadcast his objections to the ridicule that sociology often attracts from the media. In the studio debate that followed, Roger Scruton (Professor of Aesthetics at Birkbeck College) castigated the study of sociology as 'an endless quest for knowledge about trivia'. Among other things, he complained that sociology was intellectually sloppy, politically biased and morally corrupting. 'This subject', he said, 'has concentrated on those areas of enquiry which are interesting to someone with a socialist agenda; obsessed with class, with domination, with hierarchy and exploitation . . .

all those old ghastly nineteenth-century ideas. All this amounts to a case to be answered by the sociological establishment.'

Dr Pole was joined in the studio by Professor of Sociology Jennifer Platt, who argued that such misconceptions informed much of the bad press received by sociology and the public ignorance and distrust surrounding it. Dr Pole advocated its continued study on the grounds that it encouraged enquiry, demanded intellectual precision and asked awkward questions:

> **In any kind of sociology it is absolutely essential to question what we are doing and what we are being told . . . what we are studying and from which perspective. That is the very essence of the discipline; that is why I do sociology because I want to investigate, because I want to work at various different perspectives.**

As this was precisely the reason for Professor Scruton's disenchantment, it is hardly surprising that he remained unconvinced. He concluded by warning the audience:

> **There are certain matters which should not be pried into . . . least of all by half-baked lefties from universities . . . Because of this relentless questioning of human institutions and human realities it may be inappropriate for young people to study it.**

Such views are no doubt shared by some politicians, journalists and members of the public, but sociology is also an increasingly popular subject in schools and colleges throughout the Western world. Despite the attacks on its academic credentials, educational status and practical worth, sociology has survived to establish itself not only as a separate discipline but also as an integral part of education in general. As the Higginson Report (DES 1988) pointed out:

> **A free society depends for its strength on the ability of individual members to make sense of their surroundings and to think for themselves.**
>
> (Quoted in McNeill 1990)

Sociology is regarded as an essential part of professional training courses for teachers, social workers and people who work within the National Health Service (NHS) and the criminal justice system. In the United States and in continental Europe trained sociologists are employed as consultants in areas such as industrial relations; it is clear that having a degree in the subject is no barrier to future career prospects. Ministers in both Labour and Conservative Cabinets of recent times have held university degrees in the subject, while Ralph Dahrendorf and Anthony Giddens, formerly Professors of Sociology and Directors of the London School of Economics, have both been elevated to the House of Lords for their contribution to public life.

A review of university vice-chancellors in 1998 showed that the tradition of promoting classical academics from Oxbridge and public school backgrounds has changed and social scientists now account for over 30 per cent of these posts (*Guardian* 14.7.98). In 1999 the *Guardian* could report that ten university chiefs were sociologists, with Anthony Giddens at the London School of Economics (LSE) the best known (19.1.99). This recognition of the value of 'sociological capital' in the labour market has led Sheila Miles (1997) to argue that skills learned on sociology courses can be a definite bonus in 'the process of job hunting'.

A closer look

A view from the girls

In this extract, recent sociology graduates evaluate the usefulness of studying sociology.

Joanne

At university, the individual courses were of varying interest to me. Some in particular stand out as having helped to form my opinions and provide me with a much more tolerant and open view of society. At first, the issues tackled such as race, feminism and poverty gave me an unexpected cynicism about the world, but also made me more aware of different issues and the difficulties facing individuals within society. I feel that I learnt an awful lot about people and the structures within which we live. A focus on the workings of contemporary society has provided me with an insight which I feel has improved my understanding of the world.

A closer look *continued*

Meeta

Learning about culture, race, class and sex has been invaluable during every step of my working life. Although I have worked mostly in administration and computer support, what I have learned from sociology has taught me that there are so many inequalities. Recognizing and understanding how they arise does actually help to confront these challenges in a positive and constructive manner.

Jackie

When I did my teacher training, I realized how much sociology contributed to my understanding of education. It made me realize that people in societies do not behave the way they do by nature only, but they also *learn* behaviour. In my training, it was apparent that education was not just concerned with academic, but also with social learning. When teaching children about acceptable ways to behave, I could see that I was part of the socialization process.

As a social worker, I continue to be part of this process as I act *in loco parentis* to the children with whom I work. Some of these children are estranged from their families. Again, I have found that a sociological outlook has helped me to appreciate the various forces and pressures at work in society and this has helped me to be less judgemental in my work and more understanding of my clients' situations.

This view has also been useful in my general life. I would say that studying sociology has made me more open-minded, more accepting of difference, and more able to question societal norms.

(Adapted from 'Viewpoints from three sociology graduates' in Ballard *et al.* 1997: 372–4)

It was our first term at University. I was concerned that I would regret the decision to go joint and study some Sociology, I thought the ideas might be dull and irrelevant. I was wrong. Sociology just isn't like any other subject. They present their view, their truth, only Sociology says 'this is view, this is what they say is truth'.

Meeting sociological ideas for the first time is a journey, but not an easy one. There are moments, on the street, on the bus, when the familiar world around you seems to shift. Everything you ever thought and believed begins to melt away and that is not without its agony. I bemoaned to my tutor that Sociology was reducing the assumptions of my safe and solid reality to liquid, and that paradoxically I was enjoying it. Yet Sociology itself is unafraid of paradox. It is not so rigid that it insists we only view the world through the perspective in which its interests are invested. With enormous intellectual courage it perceives a multiplicity of worldviews, without fear that that which is uniquely its own will be undone in the process. And a process it is. Even at the personal level, as you encounter for the first time the hideous limitations of your thinking. Face to face you must stand with the massive assumptions of reality and normalcy with which you have walked every day of your life.

Assumptions die hard and I feared that without mine I would be lost in a dark meaningless world forever. Then the very ideas which had damned me to a deconstructed darkness, came to save me. I was lucky enough to attend a primary school for a project. It was there, watching the teachers and pupils interact, that for the first time I saw it. I glimpsed the dance. As if an invisible ball was passing effortlessly from person to person as they wove the construction of their worlds around them. It didn't matter how dimly shone the light of sociological ideas upon my world. It was enough to see the world anew.

(Adapted from Desougi 2005: 28)

Finally, it is worth asking whether the study of any subject should have to be justified in purely vocational terms. Sociology retains its popularity with young and old alike because it asks questions about the very things that directly affect our lives. It has an immediate relevance because it provides insights into the workings of the world we inhabit. Although he was writing in the 1960s, Peter Berger explained that sociology could be viewed as 'an individual pastime' because it transformed the meaning of those familiar things we all take for granted:

> **The fascination of sociology lies in the fact that its perspective makes us see in a new light the very world in which we have lived all our lives.**
>
> (Berger 1967: 32–3)

For a more up-to-date and personal review of the importance of 'discovering sociology' see the recollections of Rex, Heidensohn and Kuvlesky in Ballard *et al.* (1997).

Stop and think

- What did you think sociology was about before you started to study the subject?
- What do other people think sociology is? (Carry out a brief survey of your friends and family.)
- 'Sociology is nothing more than an endless quest for knowledge about trivia.' How would you respond to this attack on sociology from Roger Scruton?
- Why do you think some people – including politicians and journalists – might feel threatened by a subject that encourages the questioning of 'human institutions and human realities'?

The sociological perspective

We have already heard sociology dismissed as 'an endless quest for knowledge about trivia', and it is often criticized as being nothing more than 'common sense'. On the other hand, we find the subject being attacked as 'too theoretical' or obsessed with statistics. If aspects of social life such as poverty, child abuse, crime and educational failure can be regarded as 'trivia', then the first complaint must be true, but it is doubtful whether you would be reading this book if you agreed with it. The apparent contradictions between the view of sociology as common sense and the counter objection (from many students) that it is too complex in its approach to everyday life can be resolved. Although sociology deals with everyday life and common sense, that does not mean that it limits itself to explanations that simply depend on feelings of what makes sense. Such opinions would rely on what Bauman (1990) has called 'a personalised world-view' and should be distinguished from a sociological perspective. Sociology and sociologists have a very strong relationship with common sense in that the object of study is often the common-sense view of social reality held by members of society. It is the way that they study the experience of ordinary people's daily lives, the questions they ask and the concepts they use that distinguish sociologists from other people and disciplines.

The theories and methods used by sociologists are the concern of Chapters 2 and 3, but we should note that in studying people going about their everyday lives, sociologists employ a scientific and theoretical perspective that seeks to establish some kind of factual picture of what is going on. This sociological perspective relies on rigorous procedures and is informed by rational argument, criticism and existing knowledge. In this sense sociology is a combination of common sense, statistical enquiry and social theory and provides a distinct, but partial, view of what is going on:

> **Sociology as an approach to understanding the world, can be differentiated from other approaches in that it attempts to be scientific, that is to produce empirically warranted and verifiable statements about the social world and is basically distinguished by its distinctive assumptions, concepts, questions, methods and answers.**
>
> (Cuff *et al.* 1990: 9)

The idea of 'the sociological perspective' as a way of interpreting and analysing social life should not be taken to indicate that there is a universal agreement as to exactly how sociological investigation should proceed. As we highlight below, the discipline of sociology encourages creative debate, controversy and diversity.

Stop and think

- What common-sense assumptions do you have about (a) yourself; (b) your country and community; and (c) your family?
- What evidence is there for these assumptions?
- Can you test them?
- How widely shared are they?

In the writings of Berger (1967) and C.W. Mills (1970), and more recent contributions from Bauman (1990) and Kingdom (1991), we get a very strong notion of what sociology is, often as a result of stressing what it is not. They make clear that sociology is an antidote to personal and subjective observations and a complete rejection of explanations that are grounded in naturalistic or individualistic assumptions about 'human nature'. The emphasis is quite clearly on the individual as a social animal within the context of a social environment. As this emphasis challenges popular and sometimes deeply held notions of human nature and individual responsibility, it is not surprising that sociology meets a certain amount of resistance. Anticipating what has become known as the 'structure versus agency debate', C.W. Mills pointed out in his introduction to *The Sociological Imagination* that the primary role of the sociologist is to reveal the complex relationship between the individual and society:

> **The sociological imagination enables us to grasp history and biography and the relations between the two within society. That is its task and its promise. To recognise this task and this promise is the mark of the classic social analyst . . . No social study that does not come back to the problem of biography, of history, and of their intersections within a society, has completed its intellectual journey.**
>
> (Mills 1970: 12)

Mills demonstrates that by unifying biography and history we are forced to place our own individual experiences and attitudes in the context of social structure and that societies themselves are not unique but have to be placed within an historical context.

Thus, we have to go beyond personal experience and common sense for answers to our questions. The most vivid example can be seen in Mills's distinction between 'personal troubles' and 'public issues'. Whether we are looking at unemployment, war, divorce or the problems of urban living, there are aspects of our lives over which we have some control – 'personal troubles' for which we bear some responsibility and to which we can offer some private solution. However, there are other conditions that offer no such remedy, because the troubles that we experience (no matter how personally) are beyond our control; they have historical and structural causes and as such represent 'public issues' that can be changed only by large-scale economic developments or social reform.

Writing 20 years later, Zygmunt Bauman reiterates the importance of Mills's early insights into the crucial relationship between history, society and biography:

> **Deeply immersed in our daily routines, though, we hardly ever pause to think about the meaning of what we have gone through: even less often have we the opportunity to compare our private experience with the fate of others, to see the social in the individual, the general in the particular, this is precisely what sociologists can do for us. We would expect them to show us how our individual biographies intertwine with the history we share with fellow human beings.**
>
> (Bauman 1990, quoted in Giddens 1997a: 14)

In Western societies, where the cult of the individual and the notion of voluntary action are crucial aspects of our cultural history, and the coverage of politics is often reduced to the antics of personalities rather than their policies, it is not surprising to hear prime ministers proclaiming that 'There is no such thing as society. There are individual men and women and there are families' (Margaret Thatcher) or referring to 'the classless society' (John Major) as if it were a matter of agreed fact. In such a climate, sociology must struggle to assert the concepts on which its perspective is based; if it does not, it will disappear among the clamour of those whom John Kingdom (1991) has called 'the new individualists'. As Burns reminds us, 'Sociology began as virtually a resistant movement against the trend towards individualism' (1992: 20).

Stop and think

- What do you think Margaret Thatcher meant when she proclaimed 'There is no such thing as society'? What are the broader (a) moral, (b) political and (c) sociological implications of such a statement?

The sociological perspective in practice

Sociology as an empirical enterprise

Sociology has had to fight to establish itself as a social science. Using the principles of the scientific method established by the natural sciences, sociologists have developed methods of data collection that enable them to claim that sociological knowledge is as reliable as that found in any other sphere of the social sciences. This does not mean that sociology can produce infallible laws of the human universe (many natural sciences have failed to do this), but it can endeavour to follow the rules of the scientific method to establish verifiable data and valid correlations that may be used to confirm or deny a hypothesis (or to create a new one). In essence, sociologists demand that theoretical positions be tested against evidence and that this evidence be gathered by the most logical method in an objective manner and interpreted in an impartial way. The application of the scientific method to sociology is examined in Chapter 3. In general terms, the use of the scientific approach enables social researchers to establish two things.

First, through observation and measurement a statistical record of how things are can be compiled, much in the tradition of social accountancy discussed later in this chapter (pp. 19–21). Such statistics are based on and confirm the assumption that social life is largely routine, predictable and unconscious. William James recognized the importance of this when writing about habitual behaviour over 100 years ago:

> **Habit is . . . the enormous fly-wheel of society, its most precious conservative agent . . . It keeps the fisherman and the deck hand at sea through the winter; it holds the miner in the darkness, and nails the countryman to his log cabin and his lonely farm through all the months of snow.**
>
> (James 1890: 143)

We normally take for granted the 'patterned regularity' of social life because we are steeped in the familiarity bred by habit. On a superficial level, these patterns may simply be descriptions of how people normally behave within their culture, perhaps dressing in an 'appropriate' manner for different occasions, such as interviews or funerals. On another level, it may be noticed that some forms of behaviour are exclusive, for example the majority of people do not enter higher education, while patterns may also emerge that change over time, such as the rise in the recorded levels of crime.

Second, the compilation of data allows us to identify possible correlations between the patterns of behaviour so that we begin to notice that certain patterns of behaviour are more commonly discovered among particular groups of people. Some social groups are less likely to pass exams than others, people who live in urban areas may be more prone to burglary than those who inhabit the suburbs or the countryside, and the children most likely to be found anywhere but school in term time come from backgrounds where education is not highly valued. This does not mean that sociology can predict exactly who will fail their exams, get burgled or bunk off from school, but it can make 'tendency statements' about the likelihood of the correlations reproducing themselves.

Sociology as explanation

Social correlations need to be explained, and the emphasis in sociology is on social conditions rather than biological, psychological or genetic factors. This is not to deny that we are, as a species, the product of millions of years of biological evolution or that individual differences call for psychological explanation. However, sociologists resist any generalization that suggests that behaviour can be reduced to biological explanations alone. Not only do such claims have very powerful ideological connotations, but they also fly in the face of the clear evidence linking behaviour to social circumstances and cultural experience. The power of culture and the importance of the learning experience are examined later (pp. 22–27), but the areas we have used so far as examples are clear cases where social circumstances are an essential part of any explanation: educational failure, crime, truancy and mental breakdown are all issues that call for sociological illumination.

In the popular imagination, pure evil may still be the most appropriate explanation for senseless crime, madness may be conveniently dismissed as a disease of the mind, and some individuals are simply ineducatable. Sociology teaches us that educational success is related to gender and class, that recorded crime is committed largely by juveniles, that black people are more likely than whites to be diagnosed as schizophrenic by British and North American psychiatrists, and that the number of British children truanting from school is currently running at about

Cartoon by Mike Keating

30,000 per year – in some parts of inner-city London the rate is as high as 40 per cent. It is not surprising that when things happen to us that we were not expecting, we take it personally or blame it on chance. However, if we are aware of the way in which the odds are stacked, then the element of chance is drastically reduced: your failure to pass your exams is something you share with a lot of other people, your house was the third to be burgled in your street that week, and your children have discovered that their classmates who still attend the local community comprehensive school are now regarded as deviant.

Stop and think

- Think of some of the key events in your own life. To what extent was their outcome affected by (a) social factors (where you live, what school you went to); (b) biological factors (your gender, race); and (c) psychological factors (your intelligence and personality)? How easy is it to distinguish between these different factors?

In this section we have talked of the sociological perspective as if it were a uniform and standardized body of concepts, theories and findings. This would give the impression of a discipline free from criticism and internal division, but it would be wholly incorrect. One of the main difficulties that students of this subject experience is the failure of sociologists to agree with one another and the diversity of opinion that exists within it. Without exaggerating these differences, there are obvious disagreements over methodological procedures and theoretical perspectives, which provide the conceptual backdrop to what sociology is all about and which we explore in Chapters 2 and 3.

Furthermore, there is political disagreement over the value and neutrality of sociology. Apart from the criticisms of philosophers who have argued that sociology cannot logically fit into the scientific frame of reference, there are complaints from within the discipline itself that sociology's claim to be an objective science is undone by its actual behaviour in the real world of research and theoretical activity. Radical and Marxist critics such as Gouldner (1971, 1975) have complained that much sociology has developed into a tame form of social surveillance on behalf of the most powerful groups in society, into 'cow sociology' – a domesticated animal to be watered and fed in return for regular milking. On the other hand, Professor David Marsland has joined forces with Roger Scruton in his attack on the left-wing political bias, which he claims is the overriding characteristic of current sociology.

Whatever its shortcomings, sociology is a rewarding area of study; it offers the opportunity to ask questions, to consider different perspectives, to evaluate evidence and to reflect on those attitudes previously thought of as 'common sense'. As a result, we begin to see ourselves and the social world we inhabit in a different way. As an echo of Berger's claim that the first wisdom of sociology is that 'things are not what they seem', Bauman has summarized the position brilliantly:

> **When repeated often enough, things tend to become familiar, and familiar things are self-explanatory; they present no problems and arouse no curiosity . . . Familiarity is the staunchest enemy of inquisitiveness and criticism – and thus also of innovation and the courage to change. In an encounter with that familiar world ruled by habits and reciprocally reasserting beliefs, sociology acts as a meddlesome and often irritating stranger. It disturbs the comfortingly quiet way of life by**

asking questions no one among the 'locals' remembers being asked, let alone answered. Such questions make evident things into puzzles: they defamiliarize the familiar. Suddenly, the daily way of life must come under scrutiny. It now appears to be just one of the possible ways, not the one and only, not the 'natural' way of life.

(Bauman 1990, quoted in Giddens 1997b: 17)

The origins of sociology

Sociology is generally regarded (by Western sociologists) as a Western academic pursuit. However, as Ritzer has acknowledged, 'scholars were doing sociology long ago and in other parts of the world' (Ritzer 1992: 8). Abdel Rahman ibn-Khaldun, for example, was engaged in what we would now call 'sociological research' and teaching at Cairo University 500 years before its emergence as an academic discipline in Europe. This section, therefore, should be seen as an introduction to the foundations of *Western* sociology.

The intellectual roots of sociology stretch beyond the activists of the nineteenth century to the political and social philosophers of classical Greece, the social contract theories of Hobbes, Locke and Rousseau, and the Enlightenment of eighteenth-century Europe. In their attempts to understand human nature and harness their insights to a vision of social improvement, the early writers discussed issues and employed concepts that were clearly sociological in nature:

In the writings of Aristotle, Plato, Hobbes, Locke and Rousseau there are numerous sociological themes relating to problems of social differentiation, inequality, social conflict and social cohesion, the development of the division of labour and private property – but this does not make these theorists sociologists.

(Swingewood 1991: 9–10)

Swingewood makes an important distinction between the early writers who focus attention on 'human nature as the basis of human society' and the writers of the Enlightenment, who emphasized the importance of social structure and social laws. He suggests that it was not until the Enlightenment of the eighteenth century that 'a peculiarly invigorating mixture of political philosophy, history, political economy and sociology' laid the basis for looking at the world in a new way.

The laws governing these historical and social processes were no longer deferred to as the hidden hand of God working mysteriously behind the scenes. Rather, the dynamics of social order and historical change were seen as open to human inquiry – hidden truths that could be revealed by rational speculation and scientific study.

A closer look

Abdel Rahman ibn-Khaldun (1332–1406)

Ibn-Khaldun was born in Tunis, North Africa, in 1332. He was schooled in the Qur'an, mathematics and history and followed a career in politics, serving in a variety of positions in Tunis, Morocco, Spain and Algeria. After his 'political career', he undertook an intensive five-year period of study and writing and became a lecturer at the centre of Islamic study at the Al-Azhar Mosque University in Cairo. By his death in 1406, ibn-Khaldun had produced a number of studies that shared many ideas and themes with contemporary sociology. He believed in the scientific study of society, empirical research and the importance of locating the causes of social phenomena. He examined social institutions (in the political and economic spheres, for example) and was interested in comparing primitive and modern societies.

(Adapted from Ritzer 1992: 8)

Stop and think

- What differences might there be between a society in which historical and social processes are seen as the 'hand of God' and one in which they are open to rational human enquiry? Can you think of societies in which the two views coexist?

Social theory in Europe and America

European sociology has its recent origins in the intellectual aspirations and social upheavals of the nineteenth century; its foundation as a discipline is usually attributed to Auguste Comte (1798–1857). Comte invented the word 'sociology' and also the term 'positivism'. He established the Positivist Society in 1848 and saw positivism as the search for order and progress in the social world. He felt that a science based on experimentation and open to testing was the only valid form of human knowledge and, in the face of a great deal of academic prejudice, devoted himself to the establishing of sociology as the study of social facts. A year after Comte's death, Emile Durkheim (1858–1917) was born; he continued the fight for sociology to be recognized by the academic community as 'the science of institutions, their genesis and their functioning'.

At the same time, British sociology developed from the theoretical work of political economists such as Adam Smith (1723–90) and the idea of social evolution advocated by Herbert Spencer (1820–1903). However, the major contribution of the early British sociologists was to be found in social research and the belief that social science could solve the social problems of industrial society through statistical analysis and social reform. Some early sociologists had to masquerade as anthropologists or botanists to achieve academic positions, but by 1903 the Sociological Society of London had been founded and in 1907 the London School of Economics and Political Science established the first department of sociology. Liverpool University created a new school of social science in the same year, although the emphasis was on social administration and social work training. Loss of direction, internal divisions and traditional academic resistance within the universities meant that the formal progress of sociology in Britain was very slow. Although the USA could boast 169 institutions teaching sociology as early as 1901, British universities were tardy in recognizing the claim of sociology, and it was not until the 1950s that interest in the subject was revived. By the 1960s there were no more than 40 sociologists in the whole of the UK and only 12 degree courses on offer (Abrams 1968; Kent 1981).

Meanwhile, in Germany the establishment of sociology as a discipline met similar opposition from academics who rejected Marxism as nothing more than a political philosophy but also who refused to take seriously the efforts of Max Weber (1864–1920) and George Simmel (1858–1918), who founded the German Sociological Society in 1910. Both did achieve academic posts, but Weber was dogged by depression and poor health, while Simmel found that academic prejudice against his ideas was compounded by the anti-Semitism that was so deeply rooted in German culture. Both writers probably achieved greater respect in the less prejudiced atmosphere of North American universities.

By contrast, in the USA sociology developed alongside the new universities of the late nineteenth century and as a result was treated with the same respect given to any other academic profession. The first sociology department was founded at the University of Kansas in 1889, and the famous centre of American sociology was established at Chicago in 1892.

Stop and think

- Why do you think sociology was accepted more readily in the USA than in Britain and continental Europe?
- Do you think these reasons are still applicable today?

The emergence of sociology

The emergence of sociology as a new discipline cannot simply be accounted for by identifying its intellectual ancestry. To understand why these ideas flourished in recent history, it is necessary to place them within the context of the economic, social and political upheavals of the eighteenth and nineteenth centuries. In other words, the historical emergence of sociology needs to be treated sociologically. The work of the early sociologists has to be seen as a product of their direct experience, as middle-class intellectuals, of an age characterized by social change. We shall examine this age of transition to try to make sense of the social forces that shaped the interests, priorities and ideas of the major social theorists and researchers of early Western sociology.

Societies that had remained relatively static for centuries now found themselves embroiled in the dramatic transformation from feudalism to capitalism. Just as the religious and political certainties of absolutist monarchies were shaken by the critical attacks of the Enlightenment, so the traditional practices and social relationships of rural life gave way to the new demands of the industrial and political revolutions of the period. The shift from the traditional occupations of cottage industry and agricultural production to the new skills and practices of the factory system saw massive migrations of rural populations to the centres of industrial production and the rise of the 'industrial classes'. While the new middle classes were associated closely with the radical ideas of the Enlightenment and the French Revolution, the working classes were more clearly linked to the social crisis epitomized by urban poverty, crime and poor health and to the new forms of political unrest such as Chartism, trade unionism and socialism.

As Nisbet (1970) has pointed out, many of the terms that we now use in everyday discourse (e.g. industry, ideology, bureaucracy, capitalism, crisis) take their modern meaning from the attempts by nineteenth-century social commentators to make some sense of 'the collapse of the old regime under the blows of industrialism and revolutionary democracy'. The main features of these industrial and political upheavals can be summarized as the Industrial Revolution; the spirit of capitalism; mass society and urban life; political change; and the crisis of the modern mind. We shall look briefly at each of these features.

The Industrial Revolution

Through the Industrial Revolution, technology and the factory system transformed people's relationship to the work process, society and one another. Industrial production as a concept and a practice was not new; Colin Spencer (1986) tells us that the Romans were so keen on fish sauce that liquamen factories were to be found all over the Roman Empire, where catches of sprats and anchovies were salted, fermented and bottled on a grand scale. What was new in the eighteenth and nineteenth centuries was the transformation of working methods to a system of factory production.

This new mode of production, linked to the individualism and enterprise of capitalism, not only uncorked 'productive energies' previously repressed and created wealth on a scale hitherto unimagined but also led to economic and social changes that were regretted by conservative and socialist thinkers alike. In particular, the shift from the family to the factory as the unit of production and the 'degradation of labour' through the destruction of craft skills, the emergence of a specialized division of labour and an emphasis on a 'time-oriented' work discipline were seen at the root of a general decline in status and moral condition for the labourer. Such working practices and conditions not only encouraged feelings of alienation and exploitation but also provided an ideal environment for solidarity and resistance. Not surprisingly, the world of work was a crucial area of social investigation for all the early writers; this tradition was continued by empirical researchers in the field of industrial relations.

The spirit of capitalism

Despite being a contemporary phenomenon that has clear links with the Industrial Revolution, capitalism is not synonymous with it. The principles of enterprise and profit characterize early trading practices and money-lending as well as the agricultural revolution of eighteenth-century Britain. In 'post-industrial' societies the shift from manufacture towards service industries is still underpinned by the ethics of capitalism, while in socialist countries it has been claimed that industrialism is a necessary feature of any post-capitalist revolution and a force for public good.

Nevertheless, capitalism was inextricably bound up with the revolution in production and the industrialization of Western societies. Materialism, commercial enterprise and possessive individualism replaced what Nisbet (1970) calls 'the superior values of Christian-feudal society'. The economics of the free market and laissez-faire attitudes towards the obligations of employers and the rights of the workforce replaced romantic notions of *noblesse oblige* with the 'cash nexus'. The emphasis on money as the basis for relationships between people was mirrored in the relationship with the land. As the importance of landholding declined in the face of share ownership in large-scale industrial enterprises, the allegiance that people had to their roots (in moral communities) was destroyed. While this idea of the link between people and the land might have been romanticized, it formed the backdrop to much of the writings about loss of community; it has been reflected in the feelings of isolation and loneliness that seem to be experienced widely in modern urban society.

Despite the characteristics of individualism and freedom, capitalism also contained contradictory elements that threatened its survival; these included the development of social classes, the intensification of class conflict and the irrational elements of a free-market economy. In the view of Karl Marx, such a system was based on exploitation, alienated labour and political force.

Early sociological theorists differed widely over the nature, development and impact of capitalism (Chapter 2 looks at differing analyses of capitalism offered by the founding writers of sociology, in particular Max Weber's famous study *The Protestant Ethic and the Spirit of Capitalism*). They were, however, clearly aware that anyone trying to make sense of industrial society had to take account of the emergence of capitalism as the dominant Western economic system.

Mass society and urban life

Urbanism is also linked closely with the Industrial Revolution but, like capitalism, it is a separate social phenomenon. The concept of city living has a proud history that predates the Industrial Revolution by centuries. The city states of Greece and Rome, as well as the ancient civilizations of Africa, Asia and South America, all celebrated their cultural and economic achievements in urban centres dedicated to art, politics and learning. Without over-romanticizing ancient and medieval city life, it was the Industrial Revolution that transformed the quality and meaning of urban living.

New cities dedicated to trade and industry emerged across Europe and North America in the nineteenth and twentieth centuries. Sprawling and unplanned, these new centres of economic activity and mass living grew at an alarming rate. They became battery farms for the production of labour for factory work and brought with them the social problems of poverty, overcrowding, poor health and political riot that have been associated with inner-city living ever since. Nisbet highlights the concern with social issues created by modern urban life:

> **It is . . . the city that forms the context of most sociological propositions relating to disorganisation, alienation, and mental isolation – all stigmata of loss of community membership.**
>
> (Nisbet 1970: 28)

The 'mass society' thesis is associated closely with the work of the Frankfurt School and the elitist denunciation of popular culture, mass education and political democracy. This bleak view of modernity is often criticized for encouraging pessimism, exaggerating the homogeneity of the 'masses' and ignoring diversity (see pp. 89–92).

Political change

The new modes of thought, the changes in social relationships and the emphasis on individualism that have already been mentioned went hand in hand with the struggle for democracy. Nisbet (1970) has called this struggle 'the first great ideological revolution in Western history', and it started with the bloody and momentous events in France and North America at the end of the eighteenth century, continued throughout the nineteenth century and fuelled the civil rights movements of the mid-twentieth century. According to the concept of liberal democracy, the values of freedom and liberty were enshrined in the utilitarian principle of 'the greatest happiness of the greatest number', which along with the growth of the secular state became almost synonymous with mass society.

In this new world the rights of the individual and the power of the state challenged the traditional authority of the Christian Church, the monarchy and the guilds. Even the patriarchal family came under attack from those calling for equality in marriage, changes in divorce law and the protection of children. The traditional authority of the family and the Church was further undermined by the transfer of education to state control, where its provision rapidly became a sign of democratic civilization and a matter of legal obligation. The idea of equality (also bequeathed by the French Revolution) led to political aspirations of a different kind. Whereas liberty and freedom were the watchwords of liberal democracy, the egalitarianism of the French Revolution led directly to socialism as an expression of working-class political resistance. The growth of the trade union movement in Britain and syndicalism in France, the flourishing radical press and the writings of Marx and Engels, as well as the activities of the English Chartists and Parisian Communards, all indicate the extent to which revolution, once started, could not be contained by constitutional monarchs and electoral reform.

The crisis of the modern mind

The emergence of science and the decline of religion come together to create what Asa Briggs (1967) has called 'the crisis of the modern mind'. The one does not necessarily exclude the other, but the popularity and prestige of scientific discovery were clearly seen as a threat to religious authority. Science not only offered different types of explanation for the workings of the natural world but also provided the tools for its conquest and exploitation. The discoveries of archaeologists and astronomers had long since struck at the heart of biblical truth, while Darwin's view of the origins of the human race was at the centre of a growing conflict between science and religion. The emergence of this dual phenomenon is clearly reflected in the concern and attitudes of the early sociologists. The decline of religion attracted much attention, and examination of the social significance of religion permeates the theoretical work of Durkheim, Weber and, to a lesser extent, Marx. Meanwhile, the early theoretical models of Spencer and Comte attempt to mimic the mechanical, organic and evolutionary relationships discovered by physics and biology. Even the political manifesto of Marx and Engels was based on the principles of 'scientific socialism'. We have a curious mixture of overlapping themes here; some sociologists were clearly inspired by religion, others thought that sociology was a new religion based on the assumptions of scientific discovery, while a small group felt that sociological enquiry was a useful way of investigating religious belief and established the study of religion as a distinct area of sociology.

All these changes came together to create a dynamic and sometimes chaotic environment into which the early sociologists were born. Many of their ideas were products of the changes to which they were witness, and the major areas of sociological enquiry were more or less established during this period. The themes of religion, urbanism, capitalist development and political stability became essential areas of sociological speculation, while the issues of poverty, crime, industrial relations and family life have retained their place as objects of social enquiry ever since. This connection between the discipline and its historical origins was reflected clearly in both sociological theory and social research.

Confronted with a rapidly changing, fragmented and rootless mass society, the early theorists developed their systematic critiques of the modern world. Whether it is Comte anguishing over the collapse of authority or Durkheim looking for a new moral order, there is a strong conservative element in much sociological theory. This may be contrasted with Marx's celebration of social conflict as an inevitable consequence of class society and Weber's more pessimistic view of the eventual rationalization of society and the replacement of 'magic' with the 'iron cage' of bureaucratic order. Many of these perspectives are dealt with more fully later, but the crucial point is that without the momentous social and political events of the post-Enlightenment there would have been no great social crisis to observe, there would have been no middle-class intellectuals to recount it, and there would have been no social theory.

Case study

The emergence of modern sociology

Many of the factors that led to the emergence of sociological enquiry can be found in Chicago at the beginning of the twentieth century. In a very short space of time 'Chicago had been transformed from a raucous western frontier town to a major city, the railroad and trade centre of the American plains and Midwest' (Lemert 1997: 69). Such intense transformation brought together the achievements and the social problems which accompany rapid economic and urban growth. In Schlosser's account, the application of the production line to meatpacking was Chicago's blessing and its curse.

For more than a century . . . Chicago reigned as the meatpacking capital of the world. The Beef Trust was born there, the major meatpacking firms were headquartered there, and roughly forty thousand people were employed there in a square-mile meat district anchored by the Union Stockyards. Refrigerated sides of beef were shipped from Chicago not only throughout the United States, but also throughout Europe. At the dawn of the twentieth century, Upton Sinclair considered Chicago's Packingtown to be 'the greatest aggregation of labor and capital ever gathered in one place'. It was in his view the supreme achievement of American

Case study *continued*

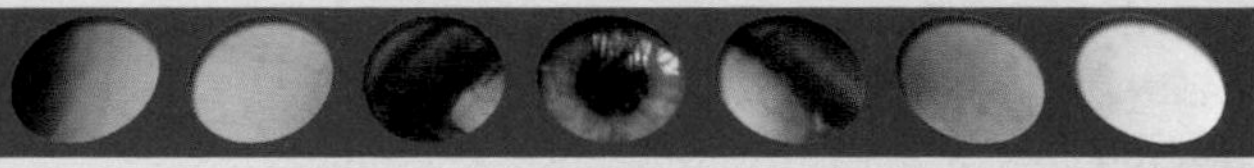

capitalism, as well as its greatest disgrace. The old Chicago slaughterhouses were usually brick buildings, four or five stories high. Cattle were herded up wooden ramps to the top floor, where they were struck on the head with a sledgehammer, slaughtered, then disassembled by skilled workers. The animals eventually left the building on the ground floor, coming out as sides of beef, cans of beef, or boxes of sausage ready to be loaded into railcars. The working conditions in these meatpacking plants were brutal. In *The Jungle* (1906) Upton Sinclair described a litany of horrors: severe back and shoulder injuries, lacerations, amputations, exposure to dangerous chemicals, and memorably, a workplace accident in which a man fell into a vat and got turned into lard. The plant kept running, and the lard was sold to unsuspecting consumers. Human beings, Sinclair argued, had been made 'cogs in the great packing machine', easily replaced and entirely disposable.

(Schlosser 2002: 152)

Questions

1. Why should the working processes and conditions described in Schlosser's account help to explain the emergence of American sociology at Chicago University at the turn of the century? To get a broader picture of the social conditions in Chicago in 1900 you might carry out a quick web search.
2. Conduct a brief enquiry into the origins of the Chicago School and find out:
   (a) Who were its founders?
   (b) What social problems did they investigate?
   (c) What research methods did they use?

In Turner's review of the contribution of sociology's classic writers, he argues that despite their great differences in outlook they were united by an essential belief in the power of 'abstract and analytical thought to understand the social world'. This sense of purpose is as crucial to sociology's future as it was to its emergence in the ninteenth century;

> **Disciplines that have a theoretical canon make a difference in the world. The founders of sociology provided a vision of what was possible; and indeed, gave us many of the critical insights to forge a contemporary canon that can be used to make a real difference in the quality of human life at the close of the twentieth century. What those who begin to practice sociology in the twenty-first century must do is consolidate the canon, make it ever more coherent even in the face of specialization in the academic world, and, if one is still guided by the goals of the Enlightenment, to use sociology to inform public debate, political policy, and social action to reconstruct society.**
>
> (Turner 1997: 77)

Social research

If anything, social research was linked even more clearly to the social changes that were taking place than was social theorizing. The social problems that were related to urban living, particularly those that threatened the established order of society such as crime and political unrest, commanded the attention of early researchers. In the USA, Chicago had become an experimental laboratory in urban survival, while in Britain cities such as London, Manchester and Liverpool attracted empirical social scientists like flies buzzing round a dung heap.

In Raymond Kent's (1981) history of empirical sociology, the British research movement is divided into two camps – the social accountants and the social explorers.

The social accountants

The purpose of collecting statistical data, according to McCulloch (1825), was 'to describe the condition of a particular country at a particular period'. Using survey techniques and official records a statistical history of Britain can be traced back to the *Domesday Book* of 1086. Social surveys of Scotland (John Sinclair 1791–99) and England (Sir Frederick Eden 1797) as well as demographic compilations dating back to John Graunt's account of mortality in 1662 demonstrate that the desire for empirical information was nothing new.

In Bernstein's account, Graunt's study of the official records of births and deaths in London is described as a 'stunning breakthrough . . . [in] statistical and sociological research' (Bernstein 1998: 75). Not only did he develop the concepts of 'statistical inference' and 'market research' but he also created the means by which governments could collect data on health and crime along with the demographic changes taking place. By building up a statistical picture of the rapidly expanding capital, Graunt provided invaluable information for those interested in trade, taxation and recruitment into the army. As Bernstein concluded, Graunt's work challenged contemporary common-sense notions of social reality but also established the methodological basis for empirical social research:

> **The facts Graunt assembled changed people's perceptions of what the country they lived in was really like. In the process, he set forth the agenda for research into the country's social problems and what could be done to make things better . . . [His] pioneering work suggested the key theoretical concepts that are needed for making decisions under conditions of uncertainty. Sampling, averages and notions of what is normal make up the structure that would in time house the science of statistical analysis, putting information into the service of decision – making and influencing the degrees of belief we hold about the probabilities of future events.**
>
> (Bernstein 1998: 83–84)

In the nineteenth century, however, the demand for useful statistics was a consequence not only of the popularity of the social sciences but also of the desire of the political elite to know what was going on in a rapidly changing world. The obsession with statistics developed in the USA and Germany but most obviously in Britain, where the government started its own ten-yearly census in 1801 and maintained an official statistical record of the state of the nation in the 'Blue Books' of the period. Statistical societies were established and attracted social reformers; the Statistical Society of London was, according to Kent (1981), 'almost . . . a branch of government' in its pursuit of politically useful 'state-istics'.

As a result, the emphasis of the social accountants was not simply on the state of society but also on those areas of society that posed a political or moral threat to its survival. Studies of the condition of the working classes in general and social issues in particular dominate a 20-year period after the founding of the first statistical societies in the early 1830s. Then, as now, much attention was paid to the phenomenon of rising crime and much effort was spent on teasing out the patterns of crime and their possible causes. Although the Reverend John Clay (1839) identified moral variables such as 'drunkenness, idleness, bad company, weak intellect and temptation' as the keys to understanding criminal behaviour, Plint's (1851) *Crime in England* has a far more sociological feel to it as he played down the notion of urban decadence and emphasized economic inequality, class position and age as the crucial factors. Similar attention was given to politically sensitive areas such as education, strikes and health, all of which attracted the attention of political economists and social reformers.

Case study

Statistics held to account

Members of the various statistical societies were mostly middle-class men who were professionals, industrialists or members of the establishment, and they espoused policies of free trade and economic laissez-faire. They were suspicious of the factory reformers and preferred to see the towns rather than the factories as the major source of social ills. To them it was urbanization, and the physical environment that it produced, that determined the habits and character of the people; making surveys of their actual condition was the obvious first step to be taken towards its improvement. The goal, however, was not the formation of a welfare state, but the creation of an environment that would foster a thrifty and virtuous working class.

(Kent 1981: 31–2)

Question

1. In what ways are social statistics still used today to justify particular economic and political views and interests? Give some examples.

By the 1850s 'social accountancy' was on the decline, but it had established the importance and usefulness of social statistics for those who felt threatened by movements that they only dimly understood and needed to control. The early use of social statistics can therefore be seen as an attempt by those with economic and political power to chart those areas of the social world that were largely unknown to them, to identify potential trouble spots and to generate ideas for social reform that targeted the habits of the poor rather than the economic system of the day.

The social explorers

The accumulation of statistics was gradually overtaken by social anthropologists, who derived their inspiration and approach from the tradition of the industrial novel and who analysed in depth the condition of the industrial working class. They were more concerned with identifying the structural context of social problems than simply blaming poverty on the fecklessness of the poor.

> **[Social exploration] is the discovery of the unknown and presupposes a rigid class structure in which a representative of a social class consciously sets out to explore, analyse and report upon the life of another class lower on the social scale. It tells the story of one person's journey into alien culture and offers the detailed results of his findings . . . The data that emerge from social exploration are typically qualitative, often emotive, frequently narrative and utilise the imagery of exploration primarily to draw attention to the inequalities in society and to force upon the reader an awareness of his social blindness.**
>
> (Kent 1981: 37)

One of the earliest examples of this approach was Engels' study of Manchester, which marks a reaction against the purely empirical collection of facts found in the work of the statistical societies. Engels' family were wealthy textile manufacturers who owned a factory in Manchester, where he was sent in 1842; while there he wrote his famous account of the *Condition of the Working Class in England* (1845). In it he attempted to describe the conditions of the working population of the day, although his accounts are very much based on personal observation. Mayhew's study (1949) of the London poor in the mid-nineteenth century may be seen as a more structured attempt to create a natural history of the urban underclass, because he was more concerned to record the attitudes and beliefs of the people he was studying in his endeavour 'to collect facts, and to register opinions'. As a result of such studies, the criminal and antisocial behaviour of the urban working class became more understandable as part of a subcultural reaction to harsh economic circumstances.

The journalistic and polemical approach of Engels and Mayhew was followed by the less critical but more thorough efforts of Charles Booth. The wealthy owner of a Liverpool shipping company and member of the London Statistical Society, Booth attempted to weld together the various techniques of social research used by his predecessors to study the problem of poverty. Observation, systematic interviews and official statistics were all employed in his survey of London poverty. Booth's (1889) massive survey was published in 17 volumes and provides a detailed account of social conditions at the end of the nineteenth century. He used sampling techniques and preceded his 20-year project with a 'pilot study' of London's East End. His investigations were based on a subsistence definition of poverty: if income fell below a certain level, then a family could be classified as 'poor' and, if significantly below this level, 'very poor'. Booth found that 35 per cent of people in East London were poor and 12.5 per cent very poor. His work attempted to examine poverty on a formal, impersonal level rather than on an anecdotal basis, which explains its importance as a pioneering piece of empirical sociological research.

Social explorers continued to use statistical analysis to probe 'darkest Britain' in the twentieth century. The Mass Observation studies of Tom Harrison and Charles Madge used another economic depression as an excuse to investigate the important events and hidden 'tribes' of England in the 1930s (Harrison and Madge 1986). The Mass Observation organization aimed to conduct surveys of the population and to report the results as widely as possible. The founders believed that social science should not be purely academic and attempted 'to marry social anthropology to journalism in the interests of revealing Britain to its inhabitants'. The movement involved a network of observers in different parts of the country making observations on how they and other people spent their daily lives. The results provided a very full picture of social change in Britain before and during the Second World War. Initially, Mass Observation tended to be associated with left-wing politics; however, it ended by stimulating the growth of 'market research and public opinion polling . . . rather than social investigation proper' (Mitchell 1968: 210).

Stop and think

- Suggest how (a) social accountants and (b) social explorers would go about studying the following: changing family patterns; the role of religion in society; juvenile crime; and ethnic minority communities in contemporary Britain.

Although the origins of the discipline of sociology are clearly linked with Western industrial societies, and the changes that took place within them, the increasing globalization of the modern world has taken contemporary sociology beyond the traditional 'nation-state' conception of society. No modern societies are self-contained in the way that we might associate with traditional societies. Essentially, globalization refers to the interdependence of societies across the world – there is a constant flow of goods and information around the globe. Perhaps the most obvious changes have been in terms of economic globalization – illustrated by the activities of transnational corporations (TNCs) – and cultural globalization – apparent in the increasingly international flavour of the media and the worldwide interests and activities of particular media companies.

The massive changes associated with globalization (which are introduced and discussed more fully in Chapter 9) have meant that sociological analysis has had to move beyond the study of single societies.

Whether we are concerned about poverty, terrorism, crime or the formation of contemporary identities, we must recognize that whereas early sociological concerns tended to be bound by regional and national boundaries (as in the accounts of American and British sociology mentioned above), it is no longer possible to talk sensibly about social issues without considering the impact of global influences. For example, George Ritzer's concept of the 'McDonaldization of society' began its life as an exploration of the ways in which the principles of the fast-food industry were coming to dominate American everyday life but quickly moved on to examine the 'global existence and implications of McDonaldization'. In his more recent work, Ritzer has introduced the notions of *glocalization* to refer to the opportunities for cultural diversity, which stem from an interaction between local cultures and global systems of communication, and *grobalization*, which reveals the opposite tendency towards cultural imperialism and homogeneity (Ritzer 2004).

Stop and think

- In what ways may the following be understood in terms of 'globalization'?
  (a) Fast food
  (b) Sport
  (c) Pop music
  (d) Nike sports wear
  (e) The deaths of Chinese cockle pickers in Morecambe Bay in 2004
  (f) The bombing of the Madrid express in 2004
  (g) Hollywood movies
  (h) The Bhopal disaster in 1984.

Culture and socialization

In this section, we shall define the key concepts of culture and socialization. The application of these concepts is then explored by assessing the power of culture through cultural diversity and deprivation.

Culture

Stop and think

- What does the term 'culture' mean to you?
- What activities would you describe as 'cultural'?

The activities that we associate with 'culture' tend to include traditional arts such as ballet, literature and painting. Trips to a theatre, art gallery and opera house are seen as examples of cultural involvement (and often recalled by resentful members of school outings). This view of 'culture' is only one definition of the term. It is what Matthew Arnold (1963) called 'the best that has been known and said in the world' and concentrates on the intellectual aspects of a civilization. The subjective and elitist nature of this definition has been questioned in the second half of the twentieth century. This sort of approach has encouraged a division and distinction between what is seen as high culture and mass culture.

In lay terms, a classical symphony or Shakespeare play is seen as high culture; as something of enduring aesthetic merit. In contrast, a TV soap opera or Top Ten single is likely to be seen as an example of mass, or popular, culture; as a commercial product of little aesthetic merit.

However, there is another sense in which the concept of culture can be used. Sociologists prefer a much broader, less subjective and impartial definition that refers to the values, customs and acceptable modes of behaviour that characterize a society or social groups within a society. Indeed, culture and society are closely entwined concepts in that one could not exist in any meaningful way without the other. As Giddens puts it, 'no cultures could exist without societies. But equally, no societies could exist without culture. Without culture no one could be "human" at all' (1997b: 18). Culture, then, refers to the non-biological aspects of human societies – to the values, customs and modes of behaviour that are learned and internalized by people rather than being genetically transmitted from one generation to the next.

This general notion of culture is related directly to social behaviour through the moral goals of a society (its *values*), the status positions of its members (*social roles*) and the specific rules of conduct related to society's values and roles, which are known as *norms*. In other words, those general values that society holds in high esteem are reflected in the norms governing our everyday attitudes and behaviour.

Many sociologists regard the culture of modern societies as differentiated and fragmented. They see such societies as embracing a range of beliefs, values and customs rather than a unified cultural system. Within such diversity, however, some sociologists (among others, those writing from a feminist or Marxist standpoint) would argue that contemporary societies do possess a dominant culture or 'ideology'. In contrast, others would suggest that such societies have a 'core culture' that is more or less shared by everyone.

A closer look

Behavioural etiquette: a Victorian guide

In 1866, Edward Turner Esq. compiled *The Young Man's Companion*, a written record of the sort of advice aspiring young gentlemen might require. It was aimed at 'the very numerous class of young men in this country whose education may have been neglected early in life, and who only require a thorough initiatory elementary knowledge to greatly advance their prospects in the world.' Great value was clearly placed on polite behaviour in the successful performance of the role of gentleman. It is an indication of the extent to which these standards are open to cultural change that the book was reprinted a century later as a joke. Among the hints to be found in the chapter on 'Accomplishments and Graces' we are warned against the social disgrace of enjoying a good laugh:

> Frequent and loud laughter is the characteristic of folly and ill manners. It is the manner in which the mob express their silly joy at silly things.
>
> (Turner 1965: 19)

And later, in his advice on table manners, Turner recommends behaviour that in any other circumstances would be seen as rudeness:

> If you are dining in company with high bred people and there is any article of food on the table, which you know to be very expensive, you should not treat it as such but effect to presume that such a thing is quite common at that table, and help yourself and others with entire freedom . . . Avoid, also, that most vulgar habit which prevails among half-bred country people, of abstaining from taking the last piece on a dish. It amounts almost to an insult to your host, to do anything which shows that you fear that the vacancy cannot be supplied, and that there is likely to be a scarcity.
>
> (Turner 1965: 35)

Case study

Emotion as a cultural phenomenon

Britain's sporting triumphs

In recent years, encouraged by the media, there have been huge outpourings of patriotic, collective public emotion in response to British sporting successes, such as the 2005 Ashes cricket victory over Australia or the array of medals won by Team GB at the 2008 Olympic Games.

Victory parade: jubilant players and fans celebrate England's Ashes triumph

A tired and emotional England cricket team received an ecstatic welcome in Trafalgar Square yesterday where 250,000 people celebrated the long-awaited return of the Ashes.

The team, including Andrew Flintoff, his year-old daughter Holly, Kevin Pietersen and Michael Vaughan, were lionized by crowds up to 10 deep as they passed in an open-top bus . . .

Vaughan, the captain, told the crowd in the square: 'It's been a long night. We've celebrated in true English fashion. Thank you for the support.' He led his team to Downing Street to receive Tony Blair's congratulations and to Lord's for a presentation of the Ashes.

(Daily Telegraph, 15.9.05)

The death of Princess Diana

The death of Princess Diana in August 1997 gave rise to a public expression of grief rarely, if ever, seen before in Britain. There was massive global coverage of Diana's death and her funeral on 6 September. The extracts below illustrate some of the many attempts to 'interpret' the response to Diana's death as a social and cultural phenomenon.

The public cry out for their lost princess

More than 1 million people were in central London to say farewell to Diana. All morning the crowds grew . . . Scotland Yard thought that 30,000 people had

Figure 1.2 Team GB returning from the Beijing Olympics
PA Photos

Case study *continued*

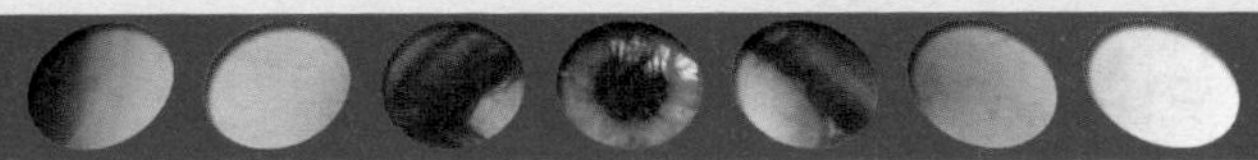

braved the cold overnight. At 6am the mourners were measured in hundreds of thousands; three hours later, when the gun carriage appeared out of Kensington Palace the crowds in Hyde Park were 20 deep. Some wanted to be at the princess's side as long as possible, following the coffin and not letting it out of sight.

They came from all corners of the country, from many other countries and from all walks of life. Those travelling on the Underground noted how the carriages were filled with the sweet smell of flowers, contrasting with the sombre faces of the mourners. . . .

The service was also relayed to the mourners in Whitehall, where skinheads and middle-aged men in suits sat together in sunlit silence. When Elton John sang, some lit candles. The opening bars of the ballad rolled over Hyde Park: the crowd rose and wept as Diana's friend sang of the nation's lost 'golden child'. At the end there was tumultuous applause.

(Tim Rayment, *Sunday Times* 7.9.97)

Back to Blighty, and a vision of a ruling class on the run

On one level, the astonishing reaction to Diana's death can be seen simply as a great national catharsis, an outpouring of affection built up over the years for a troubled, but essentially decent young woman. On another level, however, the unprecedented display of people's power, which overwhelmed the palace, the politicians and the press, has demonstrated something much more profound: Britain is no longer the place it used to be. The empire, the Establishment and the old class system are dead. What will replace them is not yet clear, but it will be a society that is far more fluid, cosmopolitan and informal; in short the country will be more like America.

Many of the traits that we associate with the United States have been on display here during recent days: emotionalism, republicanism, multiculturalism, media overkill and celebrity worship . . .

(John Cassidy, *Sunday Times* 7.9.97)

Questions

1. How might a sociologist explain the reaction to Princess Diana's death?
2. What does this response tell us about British culture?
3. Do you agree with Cassidy's claim that the reaction to Diana's death shows that 'Britain is no longer the place it used to be. The empire, the Establishment and the old class system are dead'? What evidence can you think of to support this claim? What evidence to dispute it?

Stop and think

- The study of 'behavioural etiquette' on p. 23 challenges our views about loud laughter and taking the last piece of food. What other examples can you think of where behaviour appropriate to one cultural context is seen as highly inappropriate in another? (Think of different historical and geographical cultural contexts.)

Socialization

The emphasis on culture, rather than biological instinct, as the key to understanding human behaviour implies that learning plays an essential part in creating social beings. In sociology, the term given to the process by which we learn the norms, values and roles approved by our society is 'socialization'. The survival of children into adulthood and the future of culture itself depend on a society's successful organization of this process.

Unless a society is to rely for its survival on the fear induced by the armed police forces or other agencies of control, socialization is the key to social cohesion and cultural endurance. The rules and customs governing normal social interaction must become internalized by the members of that society in such a way that they become part of the individual's view of the world and of themselves without the individual feeling brainwashed. As Berger makes clear, this balancing act can work only if it is achieved by stealth on the part of the society and through acceptance on behalf of the individual:

> **Society not only controls our movements, but shapes our identity, our thought and our emotions. The structures of society become the structures of our own consciousness. Society does not stop on the surface of our skins. Society penetrates us as much as it envelops us. Our bondage to society is not so much established by conquest as by collusion.**
>
> (Berger 1967: 140)

Gradually, as part of the process of 'growing up', individuals absorb the standards and expectations of a society so unconsciously that they become transformed into social beings almost without noticing it. The requirements, rules and standards of a society have become part of their own identity, motives and desires so imperceptibly that they are experienced as natural and unique although they are clearly social and uniform.

Individuals begin at an early age to become aware of the existence of others and to take this knowledge into account as they form their own identities. A society may not be capable of survival without its members' conformity, but equally individuals cannot develop clear ideas of who they are without some level of social interaction.

Stop and think

- Norms of conduct are often learned from an early age and unconsciously absorbed so that they become part of our 'taken-for-granted' assumptions about appropriate social behaviour. List as many norms of conduct as you can.
- How do these norms differ for different social groups? Consider the differences between (a) young and old; (b) women and men; and (c) poor and rich.

The cases that we mention later in this chapter of children who were deprived of such social interaction in their formative years are clear evidence of the crucial role played by the socialization process in the structuring of identity and the development of the individual.

Charles Cooley, one of the founders of the symbolic interactionist perspective in sociology (see pp. 71–73), examined the development of self-consciousness and maintained that consciousness in general and the self-concept in particular can be understood only in the context of an individual's interaction with society. He called this concept the 'looking-glass self' and argued that it developed on two levels of the socialization process involving primary and secondary groups.

Primary groups are based on intimate relationships and face-to-face interaction; they are crucial in establishing early codes of conduct as well as self-perception, both of which forge the link between an individual and society. The family is the clearest example of a primary group, and it is here that the most basic rules of culturally acceptable behaviour are established. Parents, says Erich Fromm (1960),

in their own personalities . . . represent the social character of their society or class. They transmit to the child what we may call the psychological atmosphere or the spirit of a society just by being as they are – namely representatives of this very spirit. The family thus may be considered to be the psychological agent of society.

(Fromm 1960, quoted in Meighan *et al.* 1979: 129)

Secondary groups are less intimate and more formal organizations that do not provide the personal interaction of primary groups. These groups are often our first contact with society in general; as such, they not only reinforce the lessons learned within primary groups but also introduce us to new standards of behaviour that are universally agreed upon in society at large. These standards are often represented by individuals whose roles symbolize the wider values of society. The school is a good example of a secondary group, as here we begin to learn that we are not unique individuals at the centre of the universe but members of a wider society that will judge us by its rules and standards rather than our own. It has often been pointed out that, after being the big fish in the little pond of family life, children experience school as a microcosm of society within which they pick up the skills, values and tricks that will enable them to get by in the adult worlds of work, leisure and the social security system. In the view of Talcott Parsons (1959), the school classroom can be seen as a miniature social system:

The school is an agency through which individual personalities are trained to be motivationally and technically adequate to the performance of adult roles . . . the socialisation function may be summed up as the development in individuals of the commitments and capacities which are essential prerequisites of their future role performance.

(Parsons 1959, quoted in Miliband 1969: 215)

Culture and identity

The emergence of identity in modern society

According to some writers (e.g. Beck, Giddens, Foucault) the latter part of the twentieth century saw people losing faith with the certainties of religion, social progress, class, community and so on and turning instead to a contemplation of (and obsession with) the self. If the world 'out there' cannot offer security and becomes increasingly shaped by global forces, then it is easy to see why people seek expression (and control) in their lives through local, regional and ethnic identities and become immersed in 'identity politics'. According to Martin Shaw, our response to this sense of powerlessness is to turn away from the big picture (public sphere) to the subjective and personal world of our individual existence (private sphere): 'Most people, most of the time, are concerned overwhelmingly with their private existence' (Shaw 1995: 31).

However, as Baumeister (1986) points out, the concern with identity is a fairly recent development that is related strongly to social change – notably the decline of religion and the perceived importance of the individual in social affairs. These changes have characterized historical change since the sixteenth century. Before (and during) this period of change people had pretty clear and stable ideas about who they were – if they thought about it at all – and saw themselves as almost indistinguishable from family, community and religion.

The notion of identity emerged alongside the ideology of individualism (see above) and the modern obsession with the *self*. However, the word 'identity' comes from the Latin word meaning 'the same'. This occurs because personal identity draws upon two principles that are in a state of tension – if not outright conflict – with each other: on the one hand we experience ourselves as individual personalities open to constant fluctuation and different from everyone else, but on the other hand we remain largely unchanged over time and share many characteristics with other people. This combination of 'similarity' and 'difference' is what enables us to function in society but also to retain some feeling that we are not the same as everyone else.

A sense of identity can therefore be seen to function on three levels:

- *Personal* – Life is given a sense of purpose or direction especially through a clear set of values and priorities.
- *Social* – Successful interaction with others (essential in mass society) relies upon people understanding one another and fulfilling personal and social expectations. The successful accomplishment of such social interaction and the 'people-handling' skills involved not only contributes to social relationships (and social stability) but also reinforces positive feelings of self-worth/social value, which are vital aspects of identity maintenance.
- *Potentiality* – Whereas the two points above refer to those continuous and special aspects of identity that

A closer look

Continuity and differentiation

The whole idea of identity is premised on these contradictory principles:

The principle of continuity

Across time and social situations it is important that we remain recognizable as the same person and behave in more or less predictable ways.

The principle of differentiation

Just as we need some continuity over time to establish an identity of some substance, we also require a feeling that there is something unique or distinctive about this continuous self; something that distinguishes us from 'everyone else'. Some of these elements of differentiation are very broad, for example whether we are male or female, while others, such as our name, are very specific.

Both of these aspects of differentiation are important for establishing who we are to ourselves and to others.

delineate who we *are*, individuals also need to have some idea of who they might become and whether they have the 'right stuff' to achieve it. Achievement is a self-confirming activity that provides personal fulfilment and increases positive feelings about the self. However, failure can undermine self-confidence and cause a crisis of identity.

Theories of identity formation

There are too many theories of identity to consider here, but it is worth distinguishing between two general perspectives on identity before moving on.

- *Essentialism* – An essentialist perspective is one that emphasizes the fixed and usually biological basis of behaviour. According to this view, an individual's identity may be fixed by their genetic makeup, personality traits or basic instincts/drives. It would be wrong to imply that all essentialist arguments are simply a matter of genetics, as there are spiritual explanations that stress essential qualities (good/evil), psychological ones (aggression/sex) and even sociobiological and functionalist perspectives within sociology that stress the similarities between animal behaviour and that of humans. In all of these approaches, identity is determined by some universal characteristics over which people have little control. Consequently essentialists are often criticized as 'reductionist'.
- *Constructionism* – At the other end of the spectrum are explanations that stress the social construction of identity, the cultural variety in identity formations and the opportunities for changing/choosing identities. The emphasis in this perspective is upon learning, culture and socialization; the social roles required by society and the influence upon the individual by the groups to which they belong are crucial. According to this view, the notion of individual identity cannot be separated from the idea of society – without one, the other does not exist.

Baumeister (1986) has argued that the personal and social aspects of identity are not two different points of view but different sides of the same coin (Baumeister's ideas are considered further in Activity 2 on p. 44). Whereas psychologists tend to talk of identity as being 'part of the personality' and sociologists stress identity as 'a set of roles or statutes . . . defined by society', Baumeister has suggested that it is possible to synthesize the 'inner' and 'outer' aspects of identity, particularly in modern societies that provide a loose context for action and a good deal of space within which the individual can 'shape identity by acts of personal choice and commitment' (Baumeister 1986: 252).

The processes involved in identity formation are a combination of the physical, the personal and the social. In this process of 'growing up', the individual does not simply assimilate the influences upon them but reflects, negotiates and incorporates (or rejects) them.

Stop and think

➤ Under the headings of 'physical', 'personal' and 'social', identify the processes that have played the greatest role in the formation of your 'major' identity components.

In conclusion, it is important to understand the distinction between the essentialist position, which tends to suggest that identities are fixed by biology or culture or psychological trauma, and the social constructionist perspective, which emphasizes learning, choice and change. In the next section we consider issues around identity and socialization.

Identity and socialization

One of the growing areas of interest in sociology is the notion of the active subject. The emphasis is not on the deterministic forces of the social structure but on the conscious individual capable of self-awareness and reflection. These ideas stem from Cooley's idea of 'the looking glass self', Mead's work on the 'self-concept' and Goffman's 'presentation of self' (see pp. 71–75). These writers suggest that the identity of an individual is not the outcome of some essential personality but a more fluid creation that develops over time through the interrelationship between the self and those who comprise the outside world. In other words, our identities are a social construction and open to change. This does not mean, however, that we are completely free to choose whatever persona we fancy, and the role of culture in the formation of identities is a crucial one. The process of socialization helps us to become recognizable individuals, but it does so by providing us with options for group membership that shape our identity. The self-concept then is deeply embedded in the process of becoming social, and the resources from which our identity is created are found in key aspects of social life such as family, work and community. For this reason, social identity is not a simple outcome of upbringing but a combination of various and sometimes contradictory commitments that the individual self may have towards a range of identities; a Catholic male homosexual from a working-class background in Ireland who is the head of a suburban girls' comprehensive school in Yorkshire will have to juggle with a range of separate and competing claims on his self-image that raise questions of gender, sexuality, region, nationality, class and ethnicity.

The major agencies of socialization are covered in detail in later chapters, where we look at the contribution of the family, the school, religion and the mass media to the reproduction of culture as it is handed on from one generation to the next. Here we shall look at the way in which the concept of culture has been applied by anthropologists, psychologists and sociologists in their attempts to identify its significance for individuals as well as society.

Stop and think

- Who are the key people involved in the socialization of children and young people at the following ages: (a) 0–4 years; (b) 5–10 years; (c) 11–15 years; and (d) 16–21 years?
- Consider the relative importance of primary and secondary groups at these different ages.

The power of culture

Cultural diversity

How would you feel about being offered dog meat for breakfast? What would be your reaction to a professor giving a lecture wearing nothing but a loin cloth? Would you be surprised to find people of your grandparents' generation using cocaine? Whether we look at fashion, food or leisure activities, anthropology and history reveal a wide range of cultural diversity over all forms of behaviour and belief, which suggests that human activity cannot be reduced to simple biological or social models that have been fixed for eternity. What is regarded as normal and acceptable behaviour by one society or cultural group may be punished as a crime elsewhere. As Matza (1969) reminds us, 'one man's deviation is another's custom', and it is clear that cultural standards are relative to time, place and social position.

Women's work and men's work

The diversity of sex roles is often used as an example of the power of cultural conditioning and is regularly quoted as evidence against conventional explanations for the differences between the sexes. In her analysis of women's work, Ann Oakley (1974a) argues that 'roles in traditional non-industrialised societies are often defined to some extent by sex status' but goes on to emphasize that there is no simple or universal rule for the division of labour by sex. Instead, we find that the rules regarding sex-appropriate tasks vary enormously from one culture to another. To demonstrate this argument she contrasts two African societies – the Mbuti pygmies of the northern Congo and the Lele from the south.

Love and marriage

The importance of culture is also obvious when we consider the relationship between men and women in their pursuit of one another. Courtship, marriage and sexual activity reveal patterns of normal behaviour that are anything but universal, despite the fact that the desires and emotions involved are powerful natural drives genetically transmitted to ensure the survival of the species.

From a Western perspective, the notions of free choice, romantic love and jealousy may lead to the conclusion that monogamy is a natural response to the questions of courtship, marriage and sexual reproduction. However, the briefest review of both Western history and other cultures demonstrates how relative such arrangements are.

Arranged marriages are often associated with the Hindu religion, but this practice is widespread, often touching on cultures where we would least expect to find it. Until the First World War (1914–18) the use of 'dynastic marriage' for political purposes was a crucial aspect of European history. For centuries it was regarded as normal practice for royal marriages to act as a form of international diplomacy to maintain bonds of alliance and peace between states, nations and cultures (Baignent *et al.* 1986). Marriages were also arranged between wealthy families in order to increase their wealth, status or family honour.

Some marriages are still arranged in Japan, where the question of marriage partner is regarded as so important, especially for family honour, that it cannot be left to the romantic preferences of the daughter. A 'go-between' is employed to discover likely partners with good prospects from families of honourable status and background. This is as much an issue of parental concern for the daughter as it is a matter of family honour, because the bride changes family membership on her wedding day and belongs to her husband's family thereafter. To signify this 'death' in her parents'

World in focus

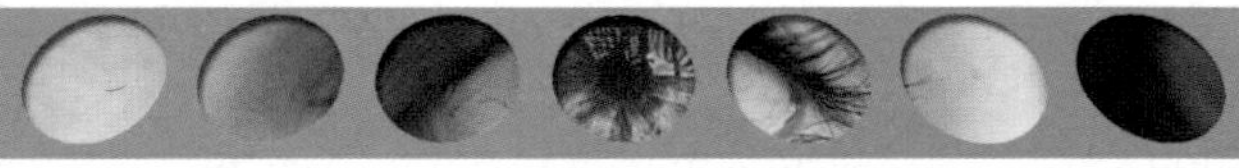

Two African societies: Mbuti and Lele

The Mbuti are a hunter-gatherer people who 'have no rules for the division of labour by sex'. Although there are some very loose practices of 'women's work' and 'men's work', these are related not to general types of activity but to specific tasks (men gather honey, women gather vegetables), while the most important task of hunting is carried out by men and women together. Child care is also shared but is carried out by the middle-aged men and women or by the older boys and girls. There is no division by sex between the worlds of domestic labour and economic production.

The Lele practise a very rigid division of labour by sex, although again they do not distinguish between the worlds of domestic activity and public production; nor do women have an unequal status to men because of the nature of the work they carry out. The division of labour and of life in general is geographical. The men inhabit the forest and cultivate raffia but are excluded from the grasslands, where the women cultivate groundnuts, collect firewood and tend the fishponds. Segregation also affects village life, where men and women keep to different parts of the village and enjoy segregated leisure and mealtimes. As Oakley points out, the main point here is not simply the massive cultural difference in sex-specific behaviour between two geographical neighbours but the general similarity between them when it comes to distinguishing between the domestic world and the economic:

> The situation among the Lele (and among the Mbuti) is the same as that in the majority of traditional African societies: the work done by the women is essential to the economic survival of the society. Despite the ritual allocation of some tasks to men and some to women, men's work and women's work are equal in status and importance . . . the separation between home and work is not a feature of human society as such but of industrialised society specifically.
>
> (Oakley 1974a: 13)

eyes on her wedding day, she wears white, the Japanese symbol of mourning. In Chinese communities, some arranged marriages are known as 'ghost weddings', which makes sense when placed in the context of a culture where a belief in the power of the spirit world still survives. Such practices are growing in contemporary China, as the following extract from *The Economist* illustrates:

> **Parts of rural China are seeing a burgeoning market for female corpses, the result of the reappearance of a strange custom called 'ghost marriages'. Chinese tradition demands that husbands and wives always share a grave. Sometimes, when a man died unmarried, his parents would procure the body of a woman, hold a 'wedding' and bury the couple together. The custom has a long history. In the legends of the classical romance of the 'Three Kingdoms', the warlord Cao Cao finds a corpse bride for his son who died in 208 AD at the tender age of 13. The communists discouraged burials and suppressed ghost marriages as 'feudal superstition'. Yet ancient beliefs die hard. As Marxism wanes, burials are reappearing – and so are corpse brides. The practice is most common in the northern provinces of Shanxi, Hebei and Shandong. This is China's coal-mining heartland. In mountainous Shanxi pit accidents kill many men too young to marry. Compensation to the family is spent giving their son a wife in the afterlife. A black market has sprung up to supply corpse brides. Marriage brokers – usually respectable folk who find brides for village men – account for most of the middlemen. At the bottom of the supply chain come hospital mortuaries, funeral parlours, body snatchers – and now murderers.**
>
> (*The Economist* 26.07.07)

Even if love and marriage do not necessarily go together, we might be tempted to assume that love and sex do. In 'dynastic marriages' it was not expected that the marriage would be fulfilling, but 'courtly love' provided the opportunity for satisfaction outside marriage. The well-publicized indiscretions of the British royal family in the 1990s suggest that such arrangements are still tolerated. However, in west Africa, Nigel Barley's (1986) discussion of adultery with a Dowayo elder reveals that even simple rules regarding sexual attraction are by no means universal:

> **All Dowayos, male and female, were to report on the appointed day and vote. It is the Chief's responsibility to ensure a good turn-out and Mayo humbly accepted this as his lot while Zuuldibo sat in the shade calling out instructions to those doing the work. I sat with him and we had a long discussion on the finer points of adultery. 'Take Mariyo,' he said. 'People always tried to say she was sleeping with my younger brother, but you saw how upset she was when he was ill. That showed there was nothing between them.' For Dowayos sex and affection were so separate that one disproved the other. I nodded wisely in agreement; there was no point in trying to explain that there was another way of looking at it.**
>
> (Barley 1986: 135)

All this discussion has been based on the premise that sexual attraction, courtship and marriage are purely heterosexual activities. However, homosexuality has always been part of social life, even though the cultural and moral response to it varies enormously; while homosexual practice is an offence punishable by death in Iran, it is possible for gay couples to get married in Scandinavia. The issue of homosexual families is raised in Chapter 11.

Monogamy and polygamy

The practice of adultery has meaning only within societies that practise monogamous courtship and marriage. In such cultures, the breaking of these rules can provide the grounds for divorce, justifiable homicide and punishment by the criminal justice system. However, in other cultures, the practice of having more than one partner is not only tolerated but also institutionalized in polygamous marriage.

Among the Nyinba people of north-west Nepal the Western notion of romantic love is thought of as selfish and greedy and the inevitable cause of sorrow. Instead they practise fraternal polyandry, whereby the wife is shared by the brothers of the family she marries into. Such marriages are often arranged, but even when they are based on the sexual attraction of the bride for one particular brother she must still become the wife of the others, spending her wedding night with the eldest brother irrespective of her preference. For the purposes of family stability, it is also important that the wife shows no favouritism to any individual brother and that she demonstrates this impartiality by bearing at least one child for each man. Strict penalties are maintained for anyone caught 'fooling around' outside the marriage.

Case study

Safe passage to the Celestial Kingdom

As Carys Bowen-Jones (1992) has described, girls in the Mormon community are 'turned in' to the priesthood leader once they reach 15 years of age and he 'places' them with an appropriate husband. It does not matter that the husband may already have a wife. Women are expected to share their husband and become 'wife sisters'. This arrangement has been sanctioned by the Mormon belief in 'plural marriage' and fear of social contamination.

> Fundamentalist Mormons see polygamy as a sacred duty. They believe a polygamous lifestyle on earth will ensure their safe passage into a Celestial Kingdom after death, where every worthy male will be given a world of his own to people with his extended family . . . A woman's exaltation after death depends on the number of children she produces, and many women here remain in a state of almost constant pregnancy from their late teens to their late thirties . . . Contact with outsiders – or Gentiles as they're known here – is vigorously discouraged by the church elders, especially among the women . . . The self-imposed social isolation of Colorado City, and of the neighbouring town of Hildale, which houses another 1500 polygamists, is undoubtedly one of the main reasons why such a lifestyle has endured here for 60 years.
>
> (Bowen-Jones 1992: 60)

Question

1. Our discussion of cultural diversity has looked at sex roles and love and marriage. Describe the extent of cultural diversity in the areas of (a) fashion; (b) child-rearing; and (c) recreational drug use. (In responding to this, consider diversity over time and from place to place.)

A more commonly practised version of polygamy is polygamous marriage, which allows a man to have several wives. Despite this being against the teachings of the Bible and the laws of their societies, Mormon fundamentalists still believe that it is a sacred duty for a man to take several brides, even though the Mormon Church rejected the practice in 1890.

Culture and development

Socialization, and in particular the quality of the cultural experiences of children in the early years of the socialization process, is crucial for physical, intellectual, emotional and social development.

This point is demonstrated clearly if we look at what happens when children are deprived of these cultural experiences. The cases that we shall look at illustrate different degrees of exclusion from culture and include examples where children have been partially deprived of what a culture has to offer as well as those extreme cases of children who have grown up beyond the frontiers of human civilization.

Feral children

Children who have been reared in 'the wild', outside human society, are termed 'feral children'. The legends of Romulus and Remus, Mowgli and Tarzan have etched into the minds of many of us distorted and romantic images of children reared in the wild by animals. According to legend these children come to little harm, retain their human characteristics and develop strong identities to become singing and dancing role models of the silver screen. The reality could not be more fantastic or further from the picture portrayed by *Greystoke* and *The Jungle Book*. Since the fourteenth century, more than 53 recorded cases have been found of feral children, including the Irish sheep-child, the Lithuanian bear-child and the Salzburg sow-girl. Other unlikely parents include wolves, baboons, leopards and an Indian panther (Malson and Itard 1972: 80–82). Some of these cases may be 'the stuff of myth rather than experiences' (Maclean 1977), but Armen (1974) recorded the behaviour of a boy reared by gazelles in the Sahara and noted that the boy not only shared the physical characteristics of gazelles (sense of smell, speed, far-sightedness, etc.) but also seemed to participate in their social habits, rituals and games; as Armen made no attempt to capture and return the child to 'civilization' it is difficult to know how long the child managed to survive in the wild by reliance on those skills learned from gazelles.

In 1991 a six-year-old boy, covered with body hair and running wild with a pack of monkeys, was captured in the Ugandan bush and placed with a local orphanage, where he revealed that he had run away from home at the age of three and been reared by the monkeys. John Ssabunnya's story was doubted at the time but subsequent research established that he had learned the ways of monkeys and could communicate with them. He was raised with the other members of the Wasswa family and became a cherished member of the orphan community. In 1998 a similar story caught the attention of the world's press, but this time it did not come from the African bush and it did not involve primate foster care: at the age of four Ivan Mishucov opted for a life on the streets of Moscow in preference to the alcoholic chaos of his family and became the adopted leader of a pack of dogs. In return for food, which Ivan begged from strangers, the dogs offered warmth and security. Eventually the police managed to separate the boy from his guardians and placed him with a foster family, who coped with his canine behaviour and helped Ivan make slow progress with language and social skills.

World in focus

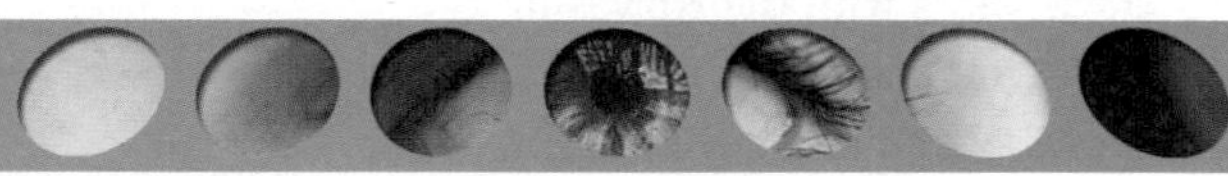

Kamala and Amala: the wolf-girls of Midnapore

In late September 1920, the Reverend Singh responded to appeals for help from local villagers in Bengal. They were being terrorized by ghosts in the form of 'man-beasts', and the Reverend Singh set up a hide from which to observe and destroy the creatures. At first, he tells us in his journal, he saw three wolves followed by two cubs but was then astonished by the apparition that followed:

> **Close after the cubs, came the 'ghost' – a hideous-looking being, hand, foot and body like a human being; but the head was a big ball of something covering the shoulders and the upper portion of the bust leaving only a sharp contour of the face visible. Close at its heels there came another awful creature exactly like the first, but smaller in size. Their eyes were bright and piercing, unlike human eyes . . .**
>
> **The first ghost appeared on the ground up to its bust, and placing its elbows on the edge of the hole, looked this side and that side and jumped out. It looked all round the place from the mouth of the hole before it leaped out to follow the cubs. It was followed by another tiny ghost of the same kind, behaving in the same manner. Both of them ran on all fours.**
>
> (Maclean 1977: 60–61)

The children and wolf cubs were protected by the mother, who was quickly killed by the archers in the hunting party. The offspring were then trapped in sheets and taken into captivity, where the Reverend Singh hoped that he could return the feral children to the fold of God's love and human kindness in the safety of his orphanage.

His account of this struggle to civilize the wolf-children has been diligently researched by Charles Maclean, who reveals how far from recognizable human beings these children had become as a result of their bizarre upbringing. From the start both girls behaved more like wild animals than human children. They appeared frightened by daylight and slept naked on the floor during the middle of the day. They howled at night and shared the eating habits of dogs; they ate carrion as well as raw flesh and gobbled cockroaches, lizards and mice alive. They ran on all-fours and relied heavily on sense of smell, showing a clear preference for the company of dogs over the friendship of other humans. They snarled and growled in fear when approached and even attacked the orphanage children who dared to get too close.

After three months the Reverend Singh had to record in his diary

World in focus *continued*

that the children had made no progress. They did not laugh or smile and continued in their nocturnal and antisocial habits. He was forced to conclude:

> They had cultivated the animal nature and condition of life almost to perfection in the animal world . . . if they were to grow in humanity, they would have to fight with their fixed animal character, formed during those years with the wolves in their care and in the jungle i.e. the whole animal environment. Theirs was not a free growth as is the case of a human child of that age . . . it was hampered growth, consequently very, very slow in all its progress.
>
> (Maclean 1977: 60–61)

Gradually, however, the new environment began to work its changes. Over the next seven months, Mrs Singh's belief that 'love was the key' produced small signs of adaptation to human society. Amala, in particular, showed signs of intelligence and initiative and learned to recognize the names of food and drink. Vegetables were still refused but the children learned to use their hands when eating and drinking and began to play games when food was the reward. A year later they had mastered the skill of sleeping in a bed.

In September 1921, Amala died as the result of illness and the Reverend Singh claims that her 'sister' showed remorse and even cried over the body. Kamala now began to show signs of learning basic skills by copying other children. In June 1923, she stood for the first time and eventually learned to walk upright and moved into the girls' dormitory. By the time of her death in 1929, Kamala had showed the definite effects of her socialization in the orphanage. She had grown afraid of the dark, learned to sit at a table and came to prefer the friendship of other children. She understood language and developed a basic vocabulary of over 30 words, through her combinations of which she demonstrated a basic grasp of a self-concept. She proved to be pretty hopeless at household tasks but did show signs of recognizing the difference between right and wrong to the extent that the Reverend Singh decided that this 'sweet and obedient child' deserved to celebrate New Year's Day by being baptized.

In the case studies we can see not only how important early socialization is but also the extent to which it may be changed by later exposure to human contact.

Extreme deprivation

In the cases above, contact with human beings was replaced by influences from other animals, so that the children learned different survival skills through the processes of imprinting, identification and imitation. We now turn our attention to examples of human beings who have experienced extreme isolation and deprivation, usually as a result of being abandoned, and whose development is retarded rather than different. Again, many of these stories have excited the literary imagination. Alexander Selkirk, abandoned as a castaway on a desert island in 1704, became the inspiration for Defoe's Robinson Crusoe, while Swift based Gulliver's meeting with the Yahoos on his own encounter with Peter of Hanover in 1726. The true story of John Merrick is now famous as the legend of the Elephant Man, and Helen Keller's story has become widely known through her own books and the film of her life.

The most authentic account of such cases, however, remains François Truffaut's brilliant film of Dr Itard's attempts to educate Victor, the Wild Child of Aveyron. Identifying this film as the inspiration for his own research interest into wild children, Michael Newton described his first impressions of *L'Enfant Sauvage*:

> **The film was elegant, beautiful, rationally delicate in its calm delineation of the central relationship between the young physician and the speechless wild child he sought to educate. It captivated me, agitated me: it woke me up.**
>
> (Newton 2002: 9)

World in focus

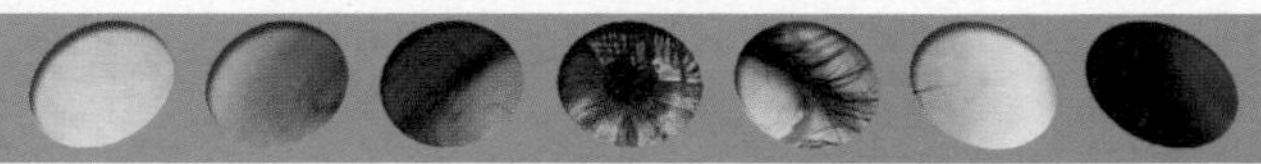

Anna and Isabelle

In the USA in the 1940s two girls were separately discovered who had been living in almost total isolation from human contact. In both cases the girls were illegitimate and had been hidden away to protect the family's honour. They were discovered at around the same stage of development (age six years); both were provided with supplementary care and special education. In the more extreme case, Anna had survived with the barest minimum of human contact. Apart from being fed enough to keep her alive, she was given no love or attention or any opportunity to develop physically through exploration or movement but left instead on filthy bedding in the attic in clothes that were rarely changed. Not surprisingly, Anna had failed to develop physically and appeared to be deaf and blind. She was apathetic, expressionless and incapable of coordination and communication. In his report on the case, Kingsley Davis summarized the situation:

> **Here, then, was a human organism which had missed nearly six years of socialisation. Her condition shows how little her purely biological resources, when acting alone, could contribute to making her a complete person.**
>
> (Davis 1949: 205)

After four years of care and attention in a special school, Anna managed to learn to walk, to repeat words and try to carry on conversations, and to keep herself and her clothes clean. She discovered the worlds of play and colour and had begun to develop intellectually and emotionally before she died at the age of ten.

Isabelle had the meagre advantage of being in regular contact with her mother, a deaf mute who had been incarcerated with her in a darkened room by Isabelle's grandfather. Although she had learned to communicate with her mother through a personal system of gesture, Isabelle was severely retarded physically and intellectually. She was fearful of strangers and reacted violently towards men. However, the specialist attention of doctors and psychologists enabled Isabelle to recapture the lost years of her early life through 'a systematic and skilful programme of training'. Isabelle's response to this intense socialization process was as rapid as it is remarkable and clearly demonstrates the essential role played by the environment and education in the stages of child development.

> **The task seemed hopeless at first, but gradually she began to respond. After the first few hurdles had at last been overcome, a curious thing happened. She went through the usual stages of learning characteristics of the years from one to six not only in proper succession but far more rapidly than normal. In a little over two months after her first vocalisation she was putting sentences together. Nine months after that she could identify words and sentences on the printed page, could write well, could add to ten and could retell a story after hearing it. Seven months beyond this point she had a vocabulary of 1500–2000 words and was asking complicated questions. Starting from an educational level of between one and three years, she had reached a normal level by the time she was eight and a half years old. In short, she covered in two years the stages of learning that ordinarily require six. She eventually entered school where she participated in all school activities as normally as other children.**
>
> (Davis 1949: 206–7)

Thirty years after the discovery of Anna and Isabelle, another well-known case came to light. For most of her 13 years Genie had been imprisoned in a darkened room of her father's house, where she was either tied up or caged. Her isolation appears to have been relieved only by interruptions for food and punishment. If she made a noise her father would respond with growls and barks and often beat her with a stick.

When she finally escaped with the help of her mother, Genie was found to be malnourished, incontinent and barely able to walk. She appeared to be almost blind, salivated constantly and could not speak. Like Isabelle she reacted violently to challenging situations and would urinate and masturbate in public. Under the guidance of a psychologist, Susan Curtiss, Genie learned to dress, eat correctly and use a toilet, but she had probably spent too many years of her bleak early life in isolation to ever catch up on her lost childhood; she never developed her ability with language beyond that of a four-year-old, although her IQ score improved from 38 to 74 in the space of six years.

At the time Genie was seen as an opportunity to test out Chomsky and Lennenberg's new theories on language acquisition; while they both agreed that the origin of language, the ground rules of grammar and the capacity for speech are uniquely human characteristics with which we are biologically programmed, Lennenberg suggested that, for language to develop, it had to be learned during a 'critical period' between 2 and 13 years of age. In Newton's summary of the case, Genie made great progress in her acquisition of vocabulary but did not appear able to develop her natural linguistic potential despite being subjected to intense linguistic experimentation:

> **The results were disappointing in the end, for despite her wide vocabulary Genie failed to use grammatical structures. She had words, but could not make correct English sentences. Her failure appeared to prove Lennenberg's thesis of the critical period for language acquisition. Yet in one sense, Genie really did learn to communicate through words, if communication means simply making oneself understood, though her linguistic attainments were perhaps not sufficient to enable a fully fledged conversation . . . Nonetheless, she mastered the essential facets of language: she could produce novel sentences, play with words, listen, take turns in conversation, speak spontaneously and refer to people or events displaced in time.**
>
> (Newton 2002: 224)

The issue was complicated further by the evidence of damage to the part of Genie's brain that governs language; had Genie's brain not been physically impaired, we cannot say how far she may have progressed. Such speculation and other important questions raised by this case remain unanswered due to Genie's father committing suicide and her mother bringing the support programme to an end with a court case in which she sued the children's hospital for damages (Pines 1981). In a more recent case, a 44-year-old woman called Lola Vina Costello was discovered in a pit in the basement of the family home in northern Spain. She had been there since 1957 and was suffering from severe photophobia (fear of light) and physical atrophy. Consequently, she had lost her powers of sight, hearing and speech and behaved more like an animal than a human being (*The Times* 10.2.97). Such cases are not only historical relics, as the case study below, from Sheffield, reported in the *Independent* in November 2004, illustrates.

Case study

Doctor blames parents for 'worst case of malnutrition'

A doctor who treated twin babies rescued from a house of 'utter squalor' told a court yesterday that it was 'the worse case of malnutrition he had ever seen outside the developing world'.

The emaciated boys, one of them close to death, were among five children rescued from a terraced house in Sheffield, South Yorkshire, last June. The parents, David Askew and Sarah Whittaker, both 24, were each sentenced to seven years at Sheffield Crown Court after admitting five counts of cruelty.

Police officers involved in the rescue said they had difficulty not being physically sick in the filthy bedrooms and kitchen, but were astonished to find a neat living room, filled with state-of-the-art electrical appliances.

The Recorder of Sheffield, Alan Goldsack, told the couple: 'The reality is that behind the closed doors of your home your children were being slowly starved to death. Most members of the public will not begin to understand how in the twenty-first century children can slip through the net in the way yours did.' The court heard how the horror at the three-bedroom house was discovered when, at [her] daughter's

Case study *continued*

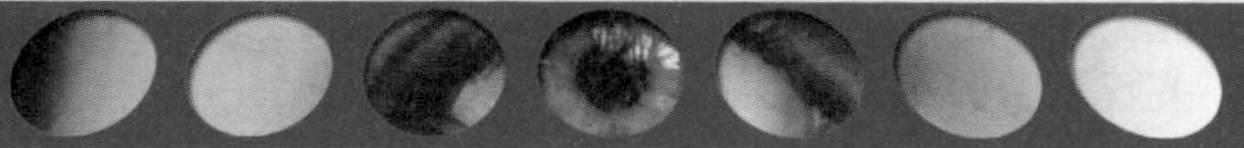

Figure 1.3 The house of 'utter squalor'
PA Photos

behest, Whittaker phoned for an ambulance because one of the twins was 'lifeless'. Paramedics found the boy skeletal and grey, suffering from hypothermia, hypoglycaemia (deficiency of glucose in the bloodstream) and severe malnourishment . . .

Both boys' growth was consistent with a four- to five-month-old baby, according to doctors. The other children in the house – now aged eight, four and three – were also living amid dog and human excrement, with urine-soaked mattresses and soiled clothes . . .

The judge heard that relatives who babysat for the couple had found the children in a terrible state and had told them to sort it out. Social services had never been involved with the family. Askew tried to distance himself from the cruelty, saying it was Whittaker's responsibility to look after the children. He told police that the house 'could do with tidying up'. Whittaker had become pregnant at 15 and had a number of miscarriages and terminations.

The children are now in local authority care. The court heard all five were thriving, although one of the twins may have permanent problems with his sight and hearing.

(Ian Herbert, the *Independent*, 24.11.04)

Question

1. Suggest both social and personal/psychological explanations for the actions of Askew and Whittaker. Which type of explanation do you find more convincing?

As David Skuse has pointed out, the value of these studies is not simply that they demonstrate the importance of nurture over nature or of the environment over inheritance but that we can go too far in the direction of 'super environmentalism' and imagine that behaviour is fixed by experience as opposed to genetic blueprints.

Extreme deprivation in early childhood is a condition of great theoretical and practical

> **importance . . . Most human characteristics, with the possible exception of language . . . are virtually resistant to obliteration by even the most dire early environments. On removal to a favourable situation, the remarkable and rapid progress made by those with good potential seems allied to the total experience of living in a stimulating home and forming emotional bonds to a caring adult.**
>
> (Skuse 1984: 571–2)

However, the best-known recent cases of extreme deprivation have been two examples that came to light in Austria and have attracted massive and worldwide media coverage. Natascha Kampusch escaped from her captor in August 2006 after being held a prisoner for many years. She was kidnapped when aged ten and held for more than eight years. In describing her ordeal to Austrian police, she said her captor kept her in a concealed soundproof chamber in his cellar and made her call him 'master'; she said she dreamed of chopping off his head with an axe. Her captor, Wolfgang Priklopil, killed himself after Natascha escaped. In her interviews Natascha described her kidnapping and how she was shoved into a darkened underground chamber, in which she remained for six months before she was taken upstairs and allowed to bath and read newspapers. Over the next several years, Priklopil became her teacher and mentor as well as her captor and tormentor – giving her toys and presents but also withholding food from her. He never left Natascha out of his sight and told her he would kill her if she tried to contact anyone for help. After her escape (when he turned his back on her while she was vacuuming his car), Natascha was looked after by psychiatrists, therapists and doctors, with some suggesting she may have developed 'Stockholm syndrome', whereby a person who is kidnapped gradually comes to sympathize with their captor. Since then, Natascha seems to have recovered from her ordeal and has become something of a media personality in Austria, even hosting her own talk show on television.

In May 2008 police arrested a 73-year-old man, Josef Frizl, who had kept his daughter locked in a specially built cellar in his house since 1984 (Figure 1.4). Elisabeth Frizl, now aged 42, was imprisoned in the cellar for 24 years and had seven babies by Josef. Of the children, three were kept in the 'upstairs' part of the house and lived a relatively normal life with Josef and his wife (who claimed to know nothing of the cellar and its occupants). The other three – Kerstin, 19, Stefan, 18, and Felix, 5 – were kept in the cellar downstairs and had never seen anyone else apart from each other (the other baby died shortly after birth). It will clearly take many years for Elisabeth and her children to make the transition to 'normal' life – the children kept in the cellar are stooped, anaemic and barely able to communicate apart from through a sort of growling language, while Elisabeth herself is said to be 'destroyed by all means' (Caroline Davies, the *Observer* 4.5.08).

Figure 1.4 Police photo of Josef Fritzl's cellar
PA Photos/Police Niederoesterreich

These two cases have shocked Austria, not to mention the rest of the world, and are clear examples of extreme deprivation. However, both Natascha and Elisabeth were kidnapped and imprisoned after they had been through the early, formative years of acquiring language and culture – Natascha was 10 and Elisabeth 11 when they were kidnapped, so their cases are not the same as children brought up without any meaningful human contact in the early stages of their lives. It is perhaps too soon after the events to assess the impact of the deprivations to which they were subject.

Stop and think

➤ The 'nature/nurture' debate as to how much we are influenced by our environment and how much we are the product of our biological and genetic inheritance has been long and fiercely argued. In what ways might a sociological perspective add to this debate? How could you use the case studies above to illustrate your argument?

Cultural deprivation and social opportunity

In the early studies of crime during the 1920s and 1930s and in the first attempts to understand educational failure, social scientists focused on the role played by cultural deprivation in the creation of deviance and underachievement. The term 'deprivation' was not restricted to intellectual and educational activity but referred to a broader concept that implied a culturally determined notion of desirable standards of material and social existence from which some individuals and families may be excluded. Such circumstances would be synonymous with poverty or poor housing, and 'deprivation' is often used interchangeably with concepts such as 'underprivileged', 'disadvantaged', 'lower class' and, more recently, 'underclass' (Jencks 1993). 'Poor family conditions' have been offered since the end of the nineteenth century as a possible explanation for antisocial and criminal behaviour.

Crime and delinquency

During the early part of the twentieth century, the idea that delinquency could be related to deprivation took root. Juvenile courts began to require reports on the 'home surroundings' of young offenders, and in 1927 a Home Office committee accepted the view of many reformers that delinquent children were themselves victims:

> **There is little or no difference in character and needs between the neglected and the delinquent child. It is often mere accident whether he is brought before the court because he is wandering or beyond control or because he has committed some offence. Neglect leads to delinquency.**
>
> (Home Office 1927: 111, cited in Pachman 1981)

A series of reports between the 1940s and 1960s saw the emphasis shift away from evil and depravity towards the concept of deprivation and 'the lack of satisfactory family life' in the search for an understanding of rising juvenile crime. The social investigations of researchers such as J.B. Mays (1954) and Norman Tutt (1974) confirmed the relationship between delinquency and cultural deprivation.

In his summary of Sprott's (1954) work on lower-class families and 'Delinquent Subculture', Tutt paints a despairing picture of the criminal family type:

> **The . . . families lived in an atmosphere of squalor, possessions were untidy and uncared for, and individual ownership was not prized. The families' leisure was largely taken up with gambling. Irregular sexual unions were frequent and openly discussed . . . Minor acts of physical aggression – mothers clouting children, siblings fighting – were frequent. Parents tended to quarrel openly and violently; the father left the responsibility of bringing up the children entirely to the mother. Children were given pocket money at random to spend as they liked . . . Neither were they encouraged to use their leisure time constructively.**
>
> (Tutt 1974: 25)

Educational failure

Alongside the concern with juvenile crime, and often overlapping with it, was the attempt by social researchers and politicians to understand educational failure in an age when educational opportunity was, in theory, a right for all children. Cyril Burt (1925) was one of the first researchers to confront the issue and, although his emphasis was on the inherited nature of intelligence, his ideas on selective education, which were used to support the development of the notorious '11 plus' examination, were partly justified as a device for rescuing able working-class children from homes blighted by poverty and educational deprivation.

In the 1950s and 1960s, the work of Riessman (1962) in the USA and Douglas (1964) in Britain firmly established the idea that the educational underachievement of children from poor backgrounds was, in part, a result of cultural deprivation. Government investigations such as the Plowden Report in 1967 clearly identified parental attitudes towards education and the lack of educational resources in the home as the key to school performance.

During the 1980s the right of liberal reformers to monopolize the concept of cultural deprivation was challenged from the political right. Beneath the concern to identify the social causes of crime and failure there has always been a hint of moral superiority. It took only a change in the political climate for these feelings to manifest themselves in a way that seeks to 'blame the victims' rather than help them.

Charles Murray, a fellow of the American Enterprise Institute, has argued that welfare dependency and single motherhood have become part of a culture that threatens to destroy family life, social morality and the rule of law:

> **Children learn how to be responsible adults by watching what responsible adults do. The absence of such examples for boys seems especially dangerous. The violence and social chaos in America's inner cities tells us how a generation of males behave when about half of them grow to adolescence without a constraining sense of what it means to be an adult male.**
>
> (quoted in the *Sunday Times* 10.5.92)

According to Murray, unruly males may be the problem, but it is their mothers who are to blame. If the subculture of deprivation is to be broken, then the answer is to stop tinkering with educational reform and eradicate the system of benefit that encourages such attitudes. Murray argued that by refusing benefits to single parents, the values surrounding marriage, family and proper child care will be resurrected. This less obvious aspect of the cultural deprivation argument is increasingly dominating the debates over moral decline, truancy and the rise in juvenile crime (see pp. 203–209 on the 'underclass debate').

Structure and agency

The idea that 'human nature' can be supplanted by the concepts of learning and socialization is often criticized for replacing biological reductionism with a form of cultural reductionism (see Skuse's comment on 'super environmentalism' on pp. 37–38). One of the first sociologists to raise this issue was Dennis Wrong. In his attack on functionalism, Wrong complains that macrosociology tends to exaggerate the power of social structures and processes and loses sight of the conscious and self-determining individual. This he referred to as an 'over-socialized conception of man' in which those individual forces resistant to the power of socialization and the restrictions of role playing are overlooked. If sociologists continued to ignore the unpredictable human element, he warned, 'we will end up imagining that man is the disembodied, conscience-driven, status-seeking phantom of current theory' (cited in Coser and Rosenberg 1969: 131). Wrong's warning anticipated a sociological controversy later known as 'the structure/agency debate'. Since the 1970s different sociologists have tried to accommodate the idea of the individual as an active agent within the powerful social and cultural influences that play upon them.

Summary

- Sociology helps us to make sense of the world in which we live. It asks questions about and seeks answers for the things that directly affect our lives. In studying people and the societies that they live in, sociology relies on rigorous procedures and is informed by rational argument and existing knowledge.
- There is no uniform and all-embracing sociological perspective. Sociologists disagree over research procedures (methodologies) and theoretical perspectives; these different approaches and positions emerged as the subject of sociology developed.
- Modern (Western) sociology is generally seen as originating from the economic, social and political upheavals and revolutions of the nineteenth century, in particular as a result of developments such as the Industrial Revolution and the move to the factory system of production; urbanization; the growth of capitalism; and the wider acceptance of liberal democracy and the support for the rights of individuals.

Summary *continued*

- Culture and socialization are two key concepts used in sociology. Culture is used to refer to the values, customs and styles of behaviour of a society or social group and socialization to the process by which people learn the norms, values and roles approved in their society. Socialization depends on social interaction, and without this individuals could not develop as social beings.
- The importance of these concepts is shown if we look at individuals who have been deprived of socialization and of cultural experiences – children brought up in the wild or shut away and ignored by their families and having no contact with other humans.
- Sociologists have utilized the concept of cultural deprivation to explain patterns of social behaviour such as differences in criminal behaviour and educational attainment between different social groups.

Links

The case study extracts referring to the criminal careers of the Krays and of Cocky Warren link with Chapter 14, particularly the section on theories of crime.

The information on capitalism on pp. 16–17 links with Chapter 2.

The section on socialization on pp. 26–29 links with Chapter 11.

The examination of cultural deprivation and opportunity links with both Chapters 11 and 15.

Further reading

Ballard, C., Gubbay, J. and Middleton, C. (eds) (1997) *The Student's Companion to Sociology*, London: Blackwell.
This is a collection written by an international team (with an American editor, Ballard, and British editors, Gubbay and Middleton) that conveys the excitement of studying sociology. It provides plenty of practical advice for students new to the subject and for those hoping to use their sociological education to enhance their employment opportunities.

Bauman, Z. (1990) *Thinking Sociologically*, Oxford: Blackwell.
An up-to-date and 'theoretical' introduction to sociology that discusses in some depth the relationship between sociology and common sense.

Bennett, T. and Watson, D. (eds) (2002) *Understanding Everyday Life*, Oxford: Blackwell.
This is the first book in a series of four that aims to provide an introduction to the sociological study of modern society. This book looks at how sociology can throw new light on familiar aspects of everyday life. The different chapters consider a range of sites, including the home, the street, the pub and the neighbourhood. The other books in the series are entitled *Social Differences and Divisions, Social Change* and *The Uses of Sociology*.

Berger, P.L. (1967) *Invitation to Sociology: A Humanistic Perspective*, Harmondsworth: Penguin.

Levin, J. (1993) *Sociological Snapshots*, Newbury Park, CA: Pine Forge.
This series of essays tries to relate the familiar, common-sense world of our everyday experiences to the more abstract sociological interpretation and theorizing. The first two sections, on culture and socialization, are particularly relevant to this introductory chapter.

Mills, C.W. (1970) *The Sociological Imagination*, Harmondsworth: Penguin.
Given that this is an introductory chapter, there are no particular substantive studies that provide an overview of the area. However, the introductory books by Peter Berger and C. Wright Mills have had a tremendous impact and been an important influence on many people currently working in sociology. They are still well worth reading; perhaps more than any other introductory studies they capture the excitement and challenge of studying the human world.

Nisbet, R.A. (1970) *The Sociological Tradition*, London: Heinemann Educational.
In this classic introduction to the history of sociology, Nisbet focuses on the period between 1830 and 1900, which saw the emergence of modern sociology. He sets the development of sociology in its political and economic context, in particular highlighting the importance of the 'two revolutions' – the Industrial Revolution of the late eighteenth/early nineteenth century and the political revolution that started in France in 1789 – for nineteenth-century thought.

Websites

www.britsoc.co.uk
The website for the British Sociological Association (BSA) provides information about sociology as a subject, including its history, where to study sociology, and guidelines on good practice in doing sociology (such as appropriate language to use).

www.socresonline.org.uk
The Sociological Research Online website is a mine of useful information that provides details on sociology departments in the UK and other countries.

Activities

Activity 1

Sky burials

Steve Mair describes a burial ceremony in Tibet and demonstrates how the disposal of the dead is dealt with in a radically different manner from the way it is dealt with in contemporary Western society.

Fly away Peter

During a six-week visit to Tibet, Steve Mair set off from Lhasa early one morning to attempt to witness one of the world's most startling spectacles. Photographs were forbidden. And unnecessary.

> It was six-thirty on a cold Tibetan morning and still pitch black when, stumbling and yawning, we set off out of town towards the nearby hills . . .
>
> Previously I'd had no intention of trying to see a sky burial since, although what I'd heard about this custom fascinated me, I thought that to intrude on other people's grief was obscene, to say the least. Joe had felt the same, and besides we had been told that we would not be welcome there and had even heard stories about rocks being thrown at Westerners who did try to go. This turned out to be true, but it was Westerners who had tried, stupidly, to take photographs of the burial after being warned not to do so.
>
> However, two days before, we'd met a New Zealander who said she'd been to see a burial that morning, and that no hostility had been shown to her. Also, and most importantly, she said that there were no family of the deceased present during the ritual. So that was it, that there were no relatives present was the deciding factor (they apparently arrive later, after it's over, just to see that the job has been done and their loved ones properly dispatched). Joe and I both made up our minds to try to witness a burial before leaving Lhasa.
>
> Now here we were, on a hill outside Lhasa, standing in the Tibetan pre-dawn chill with the man by the fire silently stropping his butcher's blade. For a few moments it was quite eerie as we stood gazing at the two covered bodies until finally, in sign language, we asked if we could stay. They asked if we had cameras. We assured them we didn't. They warned us again we should not take photographs, we said we understood, and then after a little discussion they motioned us to sit.

We sat for half an hour in almost total silence, trying to imagine the ceremony, while the Tibetans continued to smoke and drink tea and from time to time produce more large knives to be sharpened . . .

By now it was quite light and we'd been joined by three other Westerners, who had obviously had the same idea, and an old Buddhist monk carrying a large prayer flag, who had come down from the monastery on the opposite side of the hill to preside over the burial. First the monk made himself comfortable in a makeshift altar behind us, and then commenced a soft, rhythmic chanting while setting up a gentle staccato beat on a goatskin drum and blowing down a conch-like trumpet . . .

After he'd been praying for ten minutes or so and with the crisp morning air filled with these strange mystical sounds as well as the sweet smell of burning juniper bushes that one of the workmen had lit all around us, the sun suddenly appeared over the hills to the east instantly bathing the whole tableau in warmth and light. At this point seven of the workmen finished their tea, put out their cigarettes, donned grubby and bloodstained overalls, and set off towards the large rock that was thirty feet in front of us. At last the ceremony began.

Five of the workmen sat down behind the bodies, facing us, while the remaining two drew the large knives from their belts and threw the covers off the bodies. One of the bodies was of a plump female, perhaps in her forties, while the other was that of a skinny, old man. Mercifully they were lying face down so we couldn't see their faces. This was just as well since I think by now most of us had begun to feel a little queasy: I certainly had.

For most of the time we watched the 'butcher' who was working on the woman. He began by making a cut from the nape of the neck down to the buttocks and then on down the back of each leg up to the heel. He pulled off the skin from the back in two pieces and threw them to the ground with a loud slap. At this point the squeamishness left me as the red meat and white fat of the body was revealed: it was just like Smithfields, a side of beef waiting to be cut up. From then on, I watched in total fascination.

As he proceeded to cut up the torso, the knife pierced the gut, and the blood and juices flooded out over the rock and down its side. He chopped off the limbs and removed the bones, which he tossed in turn to the five men sitting down. They were crushers and, using large stone hammers, they began to reduce the bones to a fine powder . . .

Although we all sat and watched this strange spectacle in silence and awe, I came to realise they were just ordinary workmen doing a difficult and messy job. They could have been a gang of tarmac layers in the north of England . . .

After half an hour all that was left of the bodies were the heads. These were first scalped, cutting off all the hair, and then the skin peeled off to leave just the bare skulls. They placed the skulls in one of the shallow grooves that dotted the rock and smashed them open with a large stone. After tipping out the two halves of the brain they tossed the pieces to the crushers to do their job.

After 40 minutes the work was complete and both bodies had been reduced to a small, unrecognisable rubble-heap of flesh and powdered bone mixed with tsampa, the coarse flour made from barley that is the Tibetans' staple diet. By that time a dozen or more vultures had gathered on the slope at the side of the rock and were silently waiting. As the two butchers wiped the blades on their overalls and made their way back to the fire one of the crushers picked up a piece of flesh and tossed it amongst the birds.

It was as if a dinner gong had sounded. A cacophony of screeches erupted from the previously silent birds and suddenly the sky overhead turned black as 60 to 70 of the largest vultures I've ever seen (I'd seen quite a few in India) descended on to the slope by the rock . . .

For a few seconds they milled around on the slope until one of the throng finally flew up on to the rock and began feeding. This seemed to be the signal as all at once the rest of the birds jumped, hopped, and flew on to the rock which became at once a brown, seething unidentifiable mass as, with wings folded and heads down, they began tearing at the food. The noise was terrible as they greedily devoured the remains, squawking and squabbling over the larger pieces, but after 10 minutes or so they had finished . . .

The 'burial' was over. It had taken less than one hour from beginning to end, and there was not a morsel of food left on the rock, just a few dark stains.

By now the men had removed their overalls and were smoking and drinking tea again as they cleaned and packed away their tools. Myself, Joe, and the three other Westerners rose stiffly to our feet (we had sat virtually without moving for over an hour), thanked the Tibetans, who now showed little interest in us, and started back down the hill, still in total silence, each of us trying to assess what we had just seen.

In a land where wood is scarce and at a premium, and the ground is as hard as rock, and where the Buddhist beliefs of the people proclaim the continuity of all life (birth, death, and rebirth) they had developed this unusual method of disposing of their dead. We had experienced no feelings of disgust or horror, merely a sense of wonderment, and also privilege, at having been allowed to witness this unique Tibetan custom.

On the way back to town I finally asked Joe what he had thought of it all. 'Bloody incredible,' he said, 'there's no need for photographs at all, it's something I'll remember for the rest of my life.' I totally agreed.

(the *Guardian* 18.10.86)

Questions

1. What aspects of the sky burials are very different from your own notions of a 'decent burial'?
2. What similarities are there between the Tibetan burial rituals and those practised in contemporary Britain?
3. What possible explanations might there be for the type of burial ceremony described by Mair?
4. How does Mair's account illustrate the relationship of culture to history and economic necessity?

Activity 2

Identity formation

Read the following extract from Baumeister on the role of the family and identity formation and then answer the questions below.

The infant is born into a mini-society, namely, the family. This little society provides the child with identity. The child's relation to that society is at first not problematic for the same reasons that the medieval adult's relationship to society was not problematic. That is, the society is narrow, inflexible and well defined, and the child holds the two basic attitudes that make the individual's relationship to society unproblematic. First, the child is equated with its place in the family. The infant's and small child's role in the family is not open to much redefinition, at least not from the child's perspective. The very young child has no private self or life apart from its role in the family. And if the child has an interesting experience during the parents' absence, the child will probably tell them about it as soon as they return. Second, the child believes fulfilment to be contingent on performing its role in the family. The child trusts the family to love and care for it as long as the child does what it is supposed to do.

As the child grows, these two basic attitudes are undermined and the child's relationship with the family gradually becomes problematic. First, the child slowly ceases to equate itself with its role in the family as its social world expands through school, peer interactions, sports and so forth. The family may remain the most important society for the child, but it is not the only one, and therefore the child can conceptualise itself apart from the family. The second attitude is the belief that one will be fulfilled simply by doing what one's parents tell one to do. This attitude tends to die a complex and multifaceted death. By adolescence, the boy or girl is generally convinced of the necessity of becoming emotionally detached from the parents and seeking fulfilment elsewhere.

(Baumeister 1986: 254–5)

Questions

1. Why does Baumeister regard the family as such an important feature of identity formation?
2. How is this process undermined by 'growing up', and what impact might this have on identity formation?
3. What criticisms can you make of this view of family life and identity formation?

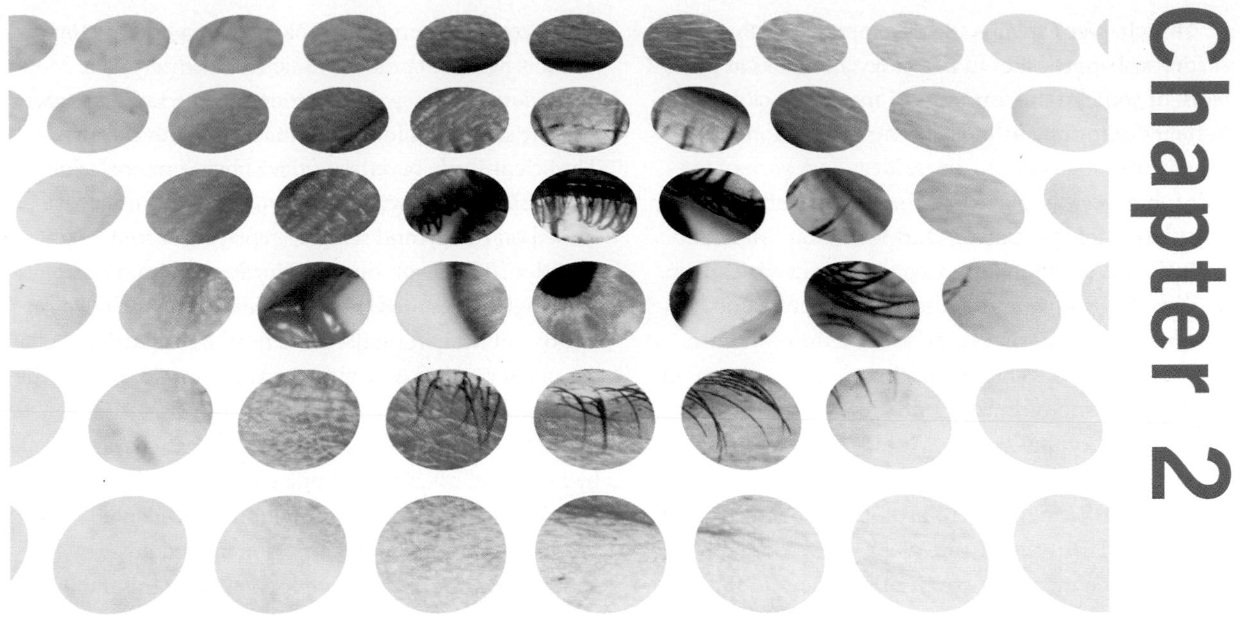

Chapter 2

Sociological theories

To be sure, theory is useful. But without warmth of heart and without love it bruises the very ones it claims to save. (Gide 1952)

Key issues

- What are the major theoretical perspectives in sociology?
- How have the writings of Durkheim, Marx and Weber influenced the development of sociological theories?
- How have the established sociological theories been criticized by feminism and other more recent theorizing?

Introduction

Sociological theory deals with the 'big questions' that we all ask ourselves from time to time. Questions such as: Who are we? Is there a reason for the way we are? How do our lives fit in with the wider society? Who has power and influence over us? Why do some people live in poverty?

Studying theory can and should be an exciting enterprise. However, many people, including students, are suspicious of theory and are keen to extol the virtues of being 'down to earth' and practical. This distinction between practice and theory is not a clearcut one: most of our practical actions and decisions are influenced by the theoretical assumptions we hold. The decision to buy flowers for one's mother on Mother's Day, for instance, might be based on an assumption that males and females have different tastes that reflect their different personalities.

Stop and think

- List the kinds of 'theoretical assumption' that (a) teachers make about their pupils' attitudes to school work; (b) employers make about what motivates their employees; and (c) influenced your decision to study sociology.

This chapter explains the development of the major theoretical approaches in sociology and looks at the work of some of the founders of modern sociology and at their continuing influence. The first section of the chapter will focus on the lives, ideas and work of the three thinkers who have had the greatest influence on modern sociology – Emile Durkheim, Karl Marx and Max Weber. Although not exact contemporaries, all three were born in the nineteenth century and developed theories that responded to the economic, political and social changes of that century – the rapid industrialization of Europe and North America and the effects of capitalism on Western society. It is important to bear in mind that the origins of sociological theorizing were profoundly political. When Marx, Durkheim and Weber tried to understand nineteenth-century industrialization, they did not do it just out of intellectual interest or academic indulgence; rather, they aimed to explore the effects of these changes on the shape and quality of social life – and to consider how the changes might (or might not) improve this quality of life. Indeed, the development of early, 'classical' sociology can be seen as an attempt to answer the question 'What is industrial society?' Durkheim, Marx, Weber and other early theorists tried to explain how industrial society had come about, what held it together and what kept pulling it apart.

However, this is not to imply that there was a general agreement or consensual approach among these early theorists. Marx's theorizing and analysis focused on capitalist society – on the workings of capitalism and the inevitability of its eventual collapse – rather than on industrial society in general. In terms of their own beliefs, Marx was a political revolutionary, while Durkheim rejected the case for revolutionary politics; although attracted to socialism, Durkheim saw it as a protest against the disintegration of traditional social and moral values rather than as a means for promoting the abolition of private property. And although both Marx and Weber emphasized the importance of power and conflict in their social theorizing, Marx held as a general principle that economic relations had primacy over other aspects of the social structure, whereas Weber opposed this general theory of history and stressed the importance of culture and politics, as well as economics.

While sociological explanations and theories might be relatively recent, the questions that interest sociology have been considered by thinkers throughout history. What is new is the modern science of society. The roots of modern sociology can be found in the Enlightenment and the social revolutions of the eighteenth century. The scientific discoveries of the Enlightenment helped to transform the social order, with secular knowledge (based on reason and science) replacing sacred tradition. The revolutions in North America, France and England resulted from social movements based on notions of human rights; these revolutions advocated democracy rather than autocracy. As our account of the origins of sociology demonstrated (pp. 14–19), the world from which sociology emerged was characterized by rapid and often frightening change. The Industrial Revolution, for instance, brought unprecedented productivity at the same time as increased poverty, congested cities, high unemployment and miserable living conditions.

Sociological perspectives

Although there are other, and earlier, writers whose work is important to sociology, Durkheim, Marx and Weber are generally reckoned to be the key figures in the development of sociological theory. Their work and ideas have been developed by later writers into particular schools of thought or perspectives with their own analytical styles and interpretations. You may be puzzled by the diversity of theoretical approaches and perspectives, but it is important to realize that there is no agreed theoretical standpoint in sociology. Giddens (1993) suggests that this lack of agreement is due to the nature of the subject itself: sociology is about people and their behaviour and it is a highly complex task to study such subjects. The lack of one overall theoretical approach should be taken not as a sign of weakness but rather as an indication of the vitality of sociology. Human behaviour is complicated, and it is unrealistic to expect a single unified theoretical perspective to cover all aspects of it. Although there is a diversity of theoretical approaches, there is also a good deal of overlap between them. All sociological theories have in common an emphasis on the ways in which human behaviour and belief are the products of social influences; indeed, this distinguishes sociology from other approaches to human behaviour.

Stop and think

- It is not just sociology that is characterized by theoretical disagreement. Consider the different subjects you have studied or are studying. What different and contradictory approaches or explanations have you come across in these subjects?
- Which subjects appear to have a unified theoretical stance? Why do you think this might be?

In introducing the sociological perspective in Chapter 1, alternative explanations of human behaviour were considered. Until relatively recently (the nineteenth century), interest in social aspects of behaviour had been very limited; non-social approaches to human behaviour were predominant. In reflecting on this lack of interest in the social aspects of human existence, Jones (2003) highlights two important non-sociological explanations of human behaviour – *naturalistic* explanations and *individualistic* explanations.

The naturalistic explanation suggests that human behaviour is the product of inherited disposition; humans, like animals, are programmed by nature. This style of explanation is common enough. For instance, it is sometimes argued that it is 'natural' for women and men to fall in love, marry and live in a small family unit (and, therefore, it is 'unnatural' not to want to do this). However, there are many variations to the supposedly 'natural' family practice in both Western, industrial societies and non-industrial societies.

The individualistic explanation sees human behaviour as a result of the psychological makeup of individuals. Criminals, for instance, are people with certain kinds of personality and may be lacking a sense of right or wrong. Again, wider study casts doubt on these explanations. The bulk of people who are convicted of crime are male, young and from working-class backgrounds: is it feasible to believe that criminal personalities are concentrated in such groupings? And if class is important, why are working-class women underrepresented among the criminal population?

These examples help to illustrate the importance of social influences on human behaviour. Where the particular sociological theories and approaches differ is in their emphasis on what these social influences are and how they can be explained.

Classical sociological theories

Durkheim and consensus

Although there is no definitive version of the history of Western sociology, there is a general agreement that it was developed in nineteenth-century France as a consequence of changes in French society brought about by the democratic revolution of 1789 (see p. 17). The two French writers who did most to 'create' the subject were Auguste Comte, who helped to establish the idea of the study of society as a project and who gave the subject its name, and Emile Durkheim, who gave sociology its academic credibility and influence. Durkheim devoted his life to establishing sociology as a distinctive and accepted field of study by building a profession of sociology in France. He established university departments to train students in the theories and methods of this new science and edited and directed the publication of a journal that was the leading light of the new sociological movement – *L'Année Sociologique*. As well as this organizing role, Durkheim is best known as an author. His four major studies have given him a key position in sociology:

- *The Division of Labour in Society*, 1893.
- *The Rules of Sociological Method*, 1895.
- *Suicide: A Study in Sociology*, 1897.
- *The Elementary Forms of the Religious Life*, 1912.

Durkheim's work

In attempting to answer the question 'What is industrial society?', Durkheim focused on the moral basis of social order and stability – the moral basis of what he termed 'social solidarity'. He believed that social order was based on a core of shared values. This belief is a key aspect of the functionalist approach in sociology, which he helped to establish.

Durkheim argued that, without the regulation of society, individuals would attempt to satisfy their own desires and wishes without regard to their fellows. This societal regulation or constraint had to be based on a shared set of values. Thus, a working society necessitated the individuals within it accepting these common values. Durkheim called this common set of values the 'collective conscience'. This term is a little ambiguous in that the French word 'conscience' means both 'consciousness' and 'conscience'. However, Durkheim defined the collective conscience as 'the totality of beliefs and sentiments common to average citizens of the same society'.

Stop and think

- What common, generally held values make up the 'collective conscience' of modern society?
- Which of these values do you use to guide your everyday life?
- Which of these values are used by (a) your family; (b) your friends; and (c) your teachers?

Durkheim suggested that while we as individuals may think we choose to behave in certain ways, in reality the choices are made for us. The kinds of possibility of thought and experience available to us are not invented by us individually; they are learned. Durkheim uses religion to illustrate this point. Our religious beliefs and practices are learned; they were in existence before us and if we had been born in another society or age it is likely we would hold quite different beliefs and follow different religious practices. Although self-evident, this point is fundamental to the consensus approach in sociology and is illustrated by Durkheim's comment:

> **When I fulfil my obligations as brother, husband or citizen I perform duties which are defined externally to myself and my acts, in law and custom. Even if they conform to my own sentiments and I feel their reality subjectively . . . I merely inherited them through my education . . . The church member finds**

A closer look

Emile Durkheim (1858–1917)

Durkheim's life spanned a period of great change in French and European history. He grew up in the aftermath of the French defeat by Prussia in the war of 1870–71, while the final years of his life were overshadowed by the outbreak of the First World War in 1914. Durkheim was the son of a rabbi and was brought up in an orthodox Jewish family. He was expected to follow in his father's footsteps and become a rabbi, but 'conversion' to Catholicism and then to agnosticism in his youth led him into an academic life. Durkheim was a brilliant student; he studied at the Ecole Normale Supérieure, Paris, where his interests in social and political philosophy developed. His political views matured while he was studying in Paris; he seems to have been pro-democracy and social reform in the face of the reactionary views of the monarchists and Catholic right. However, Durkheim tended to remain aloof from day-to-day political life, preferring to study and debate politics in terms of general theoretical principles. After graduating, Durkheim taught philosophy in several schools between 1882 and 1885. He then spent a year in Germany, where he was deeply impressed by German advances in social science and psychology. The articles he wrote on these developments helped him to get a post as lecturer in social science and education at the University of Bordeaux in 1887 – the first social science post at a French university. It was while at Bordeaux that Durkheim produced his major works; the first three books listed on p. 47 were written during this period of his life. By 1902, Durkheim's academic reputation was established and he moved to Paris as professor of education and social science at the Sorbonne, where he remained until his death.

Figure 2.1 Emile Durkheim

> **the beliefs and practices of his religious life made at birth, their existence prior to him implies their existence outside himself.**
>
> (Durkheim 1964: 1–2)

For Durkheim, then, the achievement of social life among people, and the existence of social order and social solidarity, is ensured by collective standards of behaviour and values. However, while social solidarity is crucial for the existence of society, the specific type or form it takes is not fixed and changes with the changing forms of society. In his first major work, *The Division of Labour in Society*, Durkheim examines the changes in the form of social solidarity from early, premodern societies to complex, modern ones.

The Division of Labour and forms of social solidarity

One of the major academic issues that Durkheim focused on was the significance of the rise of individualism in modern industrial society. *The Division of Labour in Society* attempts to demonstrate how the rise of individualism exemplifies the emergence of a new type of social order – an order that will increasingly transcend traditional forms of society.

Durkheim argues that the function of the division of labour in modern society is the social integration of individuals, which is achieved through their fulfilling a range of complementary roles and tasks. The theme of the study is the relationship between individuals and the collectivity. The question or problem that Durkheim tackles is 'How can a multiplicity of individuals make up a society?' or 'How can a consensus – the basic condition of social existence – be achieved?'

Durkheim addresses this question by distinguishing between two forms of social solidarity. He argues that the basis of social solidarity in pre-industrial, small-scale societies is different from that in modern industrial society; the former he termed *mechanical solidarity*, the latter *organic solidarity*.

In defining and describing the different forms of solidarity, Durkheim is talking in general and abstract terms. He was not suggesting that there is a simplistic and rigid divide between mechanical and organic solidarity: societies do not necessarily exhibit either mechanical or organic solidarity. Societies with a highly developed organic solidarity will still need to have common beliefs; all societies have to have some common set of assumptions about the world. So the collective conscience is vital in all societies; without it

A closer look

Mechanical solidarity

A solidarity of resemblance. Individuals are essentially alike: they feel the same emotions and hold the same things sacred. Individuals are not differentiated, in the sense that there is little job specialization. This type of solidarity has existed throughout most of human history; archaic, preliterate societies were characterized by it. In such situations, collective feelings predominate, property tends to be communally owned and the discipline of the small community and of tradition is dominant.

As societies became more complex, with increased division of labour, so mechanical solidarity becomes less evident and is superseded by organic solidarity.

Organic solidarity

Consensus comes, essentially, from differentiation between individuals. With the increasing range of functions and tasks in complex modern societies comes an increasing differentiation between individuals. Individuals are more interdependent: because people engage in different activities and ways of life, they are very dependent on others, and this dependence leads to the development of networks of solidarity. In these situations, social order does not rest on uniformity but rather on individuals pursuing different but complementary functions. This differentiation releases and encourages individualism and individual talent. In the face of this, society needs a strong moral force and consensus to hold it together and to ensure interdependence. In spite of individuals being unlike one another (in terms of their occupations, for instance) they need to get on together in order for social life to work.

there would just be disintegration into a collection of mutually antagonistic individuals. However, the collective conscience varies in extent and force from one society to another. Where mechanical solidarity is predominant it embraces virtually all of the individual conscience; in modern, differentiated societies characterized by organic solidarity, the scope for individuality is greater – people have greater freedom to follow their own preferences.

Functionalism: Durkheim's approach developed

Emile Durkheim is generally regarded as the principal figure in the establishment of the sociological perspective of functionalism. In explaining social solidarity and the division of labour, Durkheim adapted the arguments of the Victorian sociologist Herbert Spencer that societies evolve according to the basic laws of natural selection, survival and adaptation. Thus, they can be most easily understood and analysed if they are compared to biological organisms. Durkheim suggested that societies or social systems work like organic systems: they are made up of structures of cultural rules (established practices and beliefs, for instance) and people are expected to conform to them. The organic analogy is used by Durkheim and others as a way of getting to grips with the very abstract nature of sociological theory. The comparison of society to a living organism, such as a human being or a plant, provides a model for interpreting human behaviour.

A closer look

Anomie and suicide

Durkheim also referred to 'abnormal' forms of the division of labour. In the context of modern societies, characterized by organic solidarity, the lack of a general and strong consensus that encouraged interdependence between people would lead to a situation of anomie. Durkheim felt that this was likely to be a particular problem in modern, developed societies that were experiencing rapid social upheaval, such as becoming industrialized. In small-scale societies, characterized by mechanical solidarity, it is easier for a general consensus to be upheld.

The term 'anomie' was initially used by Durkheim to refer to situations where there was substantial disagreement over the *appropriate* norms and values for governing social behaviour. It occurred when aspects of a society were regulated inadequately. However, anomie can be applied in an individual as well as a social context. Durkheim's analysis of suicide is the most famous illustration of this application of anomie. One of the four categories of suicide that Durkheim highlighted was 'anomic suicide': without the regulation of norms to define appropriate behaviour, life becomes aimless and the individual is more prone to commit suicide; as a society becomes more anomic in times of economic upheaval, such as periods of depression or boom, the suicide rate tends to increase.

Durkheim also found a link between divorce and suicide in that divorced men are particularly prone to suicide. He suggested that 'conjugal anomie' and the consequent greater likelihood of suicide occurred when the regulation of marriage was undermined. Here too anomie is a weakening of the established normative framework.

Cartoon by Mike Keating

Websites linked to suicides

17 Youth Suicides in a Year

The South Wales community around the town of Bridgend, nearly 20 miles west of Cardiff, have been shocked by the spate of suicides by young people living in or around the town – and all within

A closer look *continued*

2007 and the first two months of 2008. Although no evidence has been found of a suicide pact or even a suicide cult there have been concerns that the suicides are connected with internet social networking sites. A friend of one of the victims, Anne-Marie Eagle, aged 17, said the suicides had become a fixation for local youths and that she had even considered it herself.

(Further details of this phenomenon can be found on www.mnsbc.com)

Questions

1. How relevant do you think the concept of anomie is today?
2. Do you think it helps to explain the growing number of teenage suicides?

Although by no means original, this analogy is central to Durkheim's work and to the functionalist perspective. From this perspective, the institutions of society – the kinds of educational arrangement and family forms it has, for instance – are analogous to the parts of an organism, such as the parts of a body. It is quite commonplace for the history of societies to be explained in terms of the human lifecycle. Like individuals, societies tend to start as small units and get bigger and, sometimes, to wither away; the history of the Roman Empire, for instance, could be described by such a model. Thus, the analogy can be used in describing the development of societies: studies of the USA regularly refer to the 'birth of a nation'. In the development of sociological theory, this approach has been associated with the work of Herbert Spencer, who looked at the evolution of societies and compared them with individual organisms.

Another way in which the model of the organic analogy has been used is in comparing the structure of organisms with societies. As parts of the body, the heart or the liver, for instance, are understood in terms of the function they perform, so social institutions, such as families and schools, have to be understood in terms of their functions for maintaining society. In order to understand how the body works, the various parts have

A closer look

The organic analogy and the functioning of society

The classic exponents of this application of the organic analogy have been anthropologists who have studied other societies 'in the field'. As the British anthropologist Radcliffe-Brown puts it:

> The life of an organism is conceived as the functioning of its structure.If we consider any recurrent part of the life process such as digestion, respiration, etc., its function is the part it plays in the contribution to the life of the organism as a whole.

Applying this analogy he goes on:

> The social life of a community is here defined as the functioning of the social structure. The function of any recurrent activity, such as the punishment of crime or a funeral ceremony, is the part it plays in the social life as a whole and therefore the contribution it makes to structural continuity.
>
> (Radcliffe-Brown 1952: 179–80)

to be examined in relation to one another. If one part was examined in isolation, it would not tell us how life was maintained: scrutiny of the heart or liver by itself would not tell us how the human body 'worked'. Similarly, any part of social life, any social institution, has to be understood in terms of the way it functions to maintain the whole social structure.

The term 'function', then, is used to refer to the contribution an institution makes to the maintenance and survival of the wider social system. In determining the functions of the various institutions or parts of society, the functionalist approach assumes that there are certain basic requirements that must be met for the society to exist and survive; these requirements or needs are called *functional prerequisites*. Examples of these might include reproduction, systems of communication and agreed standards of behaviour.

Given that the parts of society are interconnected and interrelated, each part will affect all the other parts, and for the system to survive there will have to be compatibility between the parts. Functionalists generally argue that this integration is based on value-consensus – essentially an agreement by members of society over values and standards. In Western society, for instance, materialism is valued widely. Hence, the economic system is geared to producing a wide range of consumer goods; the economic system is backed up by the value placed on materialism by the family, the mass media, the education system and so on. The rest of this section will look at how Durkheim's functionalist approach has been applied in the study of specific areas of society. In particular, we shall examine the functionalist approaches to the study of religion and crime.

Stop and think

- The functionalist analysis of any area or institution of society starts by asking what function does it perform for the maintenance of that society. What do you think are the functions of the following institutions: (a) the family; (b) the mass media; and (c) the education system?

Functionalism and religion

The functionalist analysis of religion stresses how and to what extent religious beliefs and practices contribute to meeting the needs (or prerequisites) of society.

Durkheim's study *The Elementary Forms of the Religious Life* (1912) describes how religion provides the basis of the collective conscience – the shared values and ideas – of a society. Religion, therefore, expresses and fulfils a social need and promotes social solidarity and cohesion; in other words, it binds people together.

Durkheim's ideas on the role of religion were based on anthropological material on the religion of the Australian aborigines, which he called 'totemism'. This term referred to the fact that each group of aborigines, each clan, had a sacred symbol or totem that they worshipped. The totem functioned as a symbol of both god and the society and in worshipping it the aborigines were, in effect, worshipping society.

Perhaps the most influential part of Durkheim's theory is the definition of religion by its functions, and the emphasis on religious rites, the collective acts of worship, rather than on what is actually believed. As Durkheim put it:

> **The most barbarous and the most fantastic rites and the strangest myths translate some human need, some aspect of life . . . The reasons with which the faithful justify them may be, and generally are, erroneous . . . [but] In reality there are no religions which are false. All are true in their own fashion; all answer, though in different ways, to the given conditions of human existence.**
>
> (Durkheim 1976: 14–15)

Stop and think

- To what extent do you think we can talk about religions being true or false?
- What functions can religious practices, such as acts of worship, provide for (a) individuals and (b) society as a whole?

The religious rites of the aborigines were seen as a sort of ritual mechanism for reinforcing social integration. Although the aborigines who came together to perform a rain dance have, as far as they are concerned, come together with the purpose of producing rain, Durkheim suggests that this is largely irrelevant. The important point is that they have come together to perform a collective activity that binds them together and that reaffirms commitment to the group's values and norms.

Thus, Durkheim is interested in how religion binds people to society; religion is seen as giving 'sacred authority to society's rules and values'. Functionalists writing since Durkheim have extended his analysis of primitive religions to all religion and have argued that religion of some form is a necessary integrating force in all societies. From this point of view the focus is not on the content of different religions – whether Protestantism, Catholicism or Hinduism, for instance – but on the fact that they all form similar integrative functions.

The importance attached to religion as an integrating force raises the question of what happens when religion declines in importance in society. A response to this has been to emphasize that the functions of religion are still fulfilled by present-day equivalents of religion, such as nationalism or socialism, for example, where political figures become deified and 'worshipped'.

The functionalist approach suggests that religion, in one form or another, is a necessary feature of society. A major problem with this approach is that in modern societies several religions coexist, regulating and integrating their followers differently; thus religious pluralism will tend to work against social cohesion. This criticism implies that Durkheim's analysis of religion is perhaps more appropriate to small-scale, simpler societies. A second important problem is that functionalism focuses on the integrative functions of religion – the provision of shared values and so on – and tends to ignore the effect of religion as a force for division and disharmony in society. There are many societies divided over religious dogma and belief, and such divisions can be so deep-rooted as to lead to bitter and violent conflict, as a glance at both British and world news will soon reveal.

Functionalism and crime

> **Crime is present . . . in all societies of all types. There is no society that is not confronted with the**

Case study

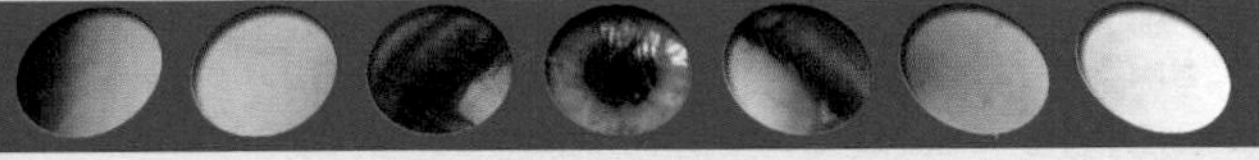

The role of religion

The role of religion in binding people together is regularly stressed by contemporary religious leaders and by political leaders. For example, the Archbishop of Canterbury, in response to criticisms about the Christian Church's lack of moral guidance to young people made after the trial of two ten-year-old boys found guilty of the murder of two-year-old toddler James Bulger in 1993, commented that:

> Somehow we need to recover a sense of belonging to one society. Let us move away from the Do It Yourself morality that has been going on, with everyone doing what is right or wrong in their own eyes. It is not too late to return to a sense of purpose, to a sense of shared values based on the Christian tradition.
>
> (quoted in the *Guardian* 29.11.93)

More recently US presidential candidate Mitt Romney gave a speech entitled 'Faith in America' in Texas in December 2007 in which he emphasized the role of religion in the contemporary world. The following extract is taken from a transcript of the speech broadcast on the American news radio programme, npr:

> There are some who may feel that religion is not a matter to be seriously considered in the context of the weighty threats that face us. If so, they are at odds with the nation's founders, for they, when our nation faced its greatest peril, sought the blessings of the Creator . . . In John Adams' words: 'We have no government armed with power capable of contending with human passions unbridled by morality and religion . . . Our constitution was made for a moral and religious people.'
>
> ('Faith In America', www.npr.org, 6.12.07)

Questions

1. Can you think of any other examples of how religion or religious leaders in the contemporary world have attempted to promote a sense of belonging to society?
2. Can you think of other examples of political leaders using religion to promote their campaigns?

> **problem of criminality . . . To classify crime among the phenomena of normal sociology is not to say merely that it is an inevitable, although regrettable phenomenon . . . it is to affirm that it is a factor in public health, an integral part of all healthy societies.**
>
> (Durkheim 1964: 65–7)

As with other areas of functionalist analysis, the importance of shared values and norms is central to the explanation of crime. Crime consists of behaviour that breaks or departs from the shared values and norms of society. The functionalist approach, as developed by Durkheim, focuses on the functions performed by the various institutions and parts of society – in particular, the function they perform in the promotion and maintenance of social unity and cohesion. This classic functionalist approach can be applied to crime as to other areas of society. Given that crime is behaviour that breaks rules, it might seem odd to talk about its functions. However, functionalists argue that crime is necessary and indeed useful for society; certainly it has to be controlled but it still has positive functions.

Put simply, the functionalist argument is that crime is universal, in that it exists, to some extent at least, in all known societies. Furthermore, as it is normal it must also be functional. And it is functional in that it helps to sustain conformity and stability. The fact that some individuals commit acts that break rules is accompanied by a sense of outrage that reinforces, for the majority, the support of those rules. When someone commits a particularly horrible crime, such as child murder, people often feel closer together through sharing their collective outrage. Through bringing people closer together, crime can have the effect of contributing to social cohesion. Thus, the presence of the criminal allows the rest of society to draw together and reaffirm their values: it strengthens the society or social group. The definition of behaviour as 'criminal' helps social cohesion by distinguishing between those who follow the laws and those who do not and by establishing a boundary between what is seen as acceptable and unacceptable behaviour.

Of course, it is not the criminal actions themselves that draw people together; rather, it is the publicizing and punishing of crime that does this. The reaction to and punishment of crime is of central importance. The public trial of law-breakers and the media obsession with publicizing crime and criminal trials help to clarify the boundaries of acceptable behaviour. The reaction to and the punishment of crime do not always correspond with the extent of social harm done by the particular criminal action. It does, though, according to Durkheim, express the strength of common values and standards. The extent of harm done by an act of violence against a child, for instance, may be slight compared with the number of people harmed by a company ignoring pollution or industrial safety laws. However, the reaction against the child murderer will be far stronger than against the offending company. The reaction to crime is essentially emotional rather than rational, and the demand for punishment seems to demonstrate a desire to see the offender suffer pain – evidenced by the angry crowds outside courtrooms at particularly horrific murder trials. These kinds of response can be best understood if crime is seen as an action that offends widely against strongly held norms and values. Durkheim argued that, for there to be social cohesion and agreement, people need to be able to react against those who depart from the shared rules and values and that crime creates this opportunity. (See pp. 589–591 for a fuller discussion of Durkheim's analysis of the punishment of crime.)

Marx and conflict

Karl Marx, like Durkheim, was concerned with broad questions about the dynamics of societies and how societies change over time. And, as with functionalism, Marxism is a structural theoretical perspective: it concentrates on the structure of society and explains individual actions in terms of the social structure in which they are located. Both functionalism and Marxism stress the crucial and pervasive influence of society. However, in contrast to functionalism, Marx's writings emphasized conflict in society.

Marx's work

For Marx, the way that people live is, in many ways, a consequence of the arrangements they make for survival, and the methods of producing and distributing food will to some extent determine lifestyle, religious belief, custom and so on. Marx starts his analysis of society and history at this point, that the most obvious and vital fact of life is the need to survive by finding food and shelter. The one constant universal factor in human existence is the system that people devise for maintaining existence, and this system will influence all else they do. Thus, subsistence is basic to all societies, and how it is achieved affects their whole structure and organization.

Marx's analysis of society

For Marx, there are two essential components of a society: first, the *economic base* or *infrastructure* (also called the *substructure* in some texts), which provides the material needs of life; and second, the *superstructure*, basically the rest of society, including the family, the education system, ideas and beliefs, the legal system and the political system. This division distinguishes between the material and the non-material world. The material world (the economic base) comes first and determines the non-material, because without it the non-material (the superstructure) would not be possible. The economic base is itself composed of the *forces* of production and the *relations* of production. The forces (or means) of production include factories, machinery, raw materials and technology. The relations of production refer to how people relate to one another at work, in particular to the relations that owners and employers have with those who work for them.

The superstructure is the non-material, but essentially it reflects the economic base. For example, the education system and the legal system protect and support the basic values of the economic structure of society. In contemporary Western society, they support the capitalist economic system or base.

A closer look

Karl Marx (1818–83)

Marx was born in Trier, Rhineland, where his father was a lawyer. He grew up in an atmosphere of sympathy for the ideas of the Enlightenment and the French Revolution. In 1835 he became a student at Berlin University, where his political ideas became more radical. As a student, Marx was influenced by the philosophy of Hegel and his followers, who were critical of the religion and politics of the Prussian state, of which Berlin was the capital. After university, Marx became a journalist (rather than his professed ambition of becoming a university lecturer), writing articles on social and political problems for the radical Cologne paper *Rheinische Zeitung*, which earned him some notoriety.

In 1843 Marx moved to Paris, where he was introduced to the ideas of socialism and communism and where he met Friedrich Engels, who became his lifelong friend and co-writer. During this period, Marx studied economics and came across the theories of classical economists such as Adam Smith and David Ricardo. This interest in economics shaped Marx's belief that political power is linked closely to economic power; his political views cannot be separated from his historical analysis of the development of capitalist society.

After a brief spell in Germany, during the revolution of 1848, Marx moved to London and exile there in 1849. For the rest of his life Marx devoted his time to two major tasks: first, building a revolutionary workers' party; and second, producing a detailed analysis of the capitalist socioeconomic system. These two tasks were connected in that Marx believed that an understanding of capitalism and its problems was a necessary prerequisite to its political overthrow. The quote on Marx's grave in Highgate Cemetery, London, illustrates his commitment to political action: 'The philosophers have only interpreted the world in various ways; the point is to change it.' Marx never finished his analysis of capitalist society. *Das Kapital* (1867–95), perhaps his most famous work, was intended as only a part of this wider project.

Figure 2.2 Dr Karl Marx, the German socialist writer, died 14 March 1883, aged 65

The development of capitalism: historical materialism

Marx was a prolific writer and in his work there are different emphases, hence the difficulty of interpreting Marx and the existence of various different interpretations. However, it is probably fair to say that the essence of Marx's work was to explain the nature and form of modern society, in particular to explain the evolution of capitalism and how it would lead eventually to a communist system.

Conflicts around the system of production, and especially in the relations of production, between workers and owners, were seen by Marx as the essential factors of modern society. These conflicts reveal the nature of capitalist societies and demonstrate how there will have to be a new system of social organization. Marx asserts that capitalism is a necessary stage before the establishment of communism in all modern societies (just as feudalism was a necessary forerunner to capitalism). This emphasis on conflict highlights the vital role of social classes in Marx's theory of social change. In all societies that have existed so far (apart from those characterized by early forms of communism – what Marx termed 'primitive' communism), there has been a broad division into two classes, one of which exploits the other. The struggle between these two class groupings (loosely, the ruling and ruled classes) leads to societies moving from one form of economic system to another. Thus the role of social class and class struggle is a key element of Marx's analysis of society.

Marx's theory of social change, his theory of historical development, is called *historical materialism*. For Marx, social structures are not created randomly: there is a clear pattern to the way societies in different parts of the world and at different periods of history have organized the production of material goods. According to Marx, throughout history societies have exhibited one of five modes of production, which, in chronological order, are primitive communist, ancient, feudal, capitalist and communist. Each of these forms of society leads inevitably to the next. The importance of conflicts of production to Marx's historical analysis is demonstrated in his account of the ways in which societies move from one mode of production to another.

The emergence of capitalism from feudalism

Marx described the feudal relations of production as hierarchical and reciprocal. Hierarchical refers to the allegiance that peasants owed to their feudal lords, to whom they had to give their surplus produce; peasants farmed their own land, provided for themselves and gave the surplus they produced to their feudal masters. Reciprocal refers to the obligations of the lords to look after the peasants' interests by ensuring, for example, their physical security in 'exchange' for their allegiance.

A key development in the decline of feudalism was the enclosure of common land. This encouraged the development of commercial types of agriculture and the establishment of conditions where agriculture could produce a surplus. So early capitalists emerged from within the feudal system; commercial rather than subsistence agriculture led to people owning money rather than just land.

Marx argued that there were very clear differences between feudal and capitalist societies. In feudal societies, for instance, people were supposed to be paid on a fair, just basis rather than on economic calculations, and they were bound to one another by mutual obligations. The feudal lifestyle was in sharp contrast to the emerging capitalist mode of production. The concern that Marx and Engels felt at the destruction of these feudal relationships and ties is illustrated by their comments in the first section of the *Communist Manifesto* (1848):

> **The bourgeoisie, wherever it has got the upper hand, has put an end to all feudal, patriarchal, idyllic relations. It has pitilessly torn asunder the motley feudal ties that bound man to his 'natural superiors', and has left remaining no other nexus between man and man than naked self-interest, than callous 'cash payment'. It has drowned the most heavenly ecstasies of religious fervour, of chivalrous enthusiasm, of philistine sentimentalism, in the icy waters of egotistical calculation. It has resolved personal worth into exchange value . . . In one word, for exploitation, veiled by religious and political illusions, it has substituted naked, shameless, direct, brutal exploitation.**
>
> (Marx and Engels 1952: 44–5)

Marx emphasized the conflicts and contradictions in all societies, including feudal ones; in contrasting feudal and capitalist economic systems, his portrayal of feudal relations as 'idyllic' is clearly somewhat idealized and exaggerated. The extract below is taken from an historical account of serfdom in medieval England.

> **Hereditary servile status in medieval Europe was the lot, by and large, of the bulk of the peasantry . . . The term normally employed by modern historians**

for unfree peasants is 'serfs' . . . The end of the thirteenth century and beginning of the fourteenth was the time when the situation of the customary tenant was most affected by the servile legal status which had been elaborated in the courts to his disadvantage for over a century . . . The villein (serf attached to a farm) could be made to pay for a licence fee before being allowed to sell any livestock; he would certainly have to pay for permission to marry off a daughter or even a son; his daughter would have to pay a fine if she became pregnant out of wedlock; his heir would have to hand over his best beast or chattel as *heriot* (as well as the second best beast as *mortuary* to the parson); he was not allowed to buy or sell land without permission; he was not allowed to leave the manor. These were the basic restrictions implicit in villeinage, and there might be more or less depending on the local custom . . .

In a peasant society the fundamental freedom, obviously enough, was the right of the peasant, if not to the full product of his labour, at any rate to enough to sustain a traditional standard of living. But any medieval peasant knew, of course, that his surplus product was going to be taken away bit by bit by landowner, by lord, by Church and by State.

(Hilton 1969: 9–30)

The capitalist mode of production: pursuit of profit

Marx stressed the importance of the system of production – of the economic base or substructure. In a capitalist society this system is based on the pursuit of profit. In this pursuit the capitalist, the owner of the means of production, must necessarily exploit the worker. For Marx, the essential element in the relationship between capitalist and worker is surplus value – basically the source of profit. Under capitalism the worker is paid a wage designed to enable him or her to survive, yet through the worker's labour power a product that has value over and above the cost of these wages is produced. As well as covering other costs that the capitalist might have – such as the buying of raw materials and renting premises – the surplus value also constitutes the capitalist's profit. For example, a person who works a 40-hour week may, in the first 20 hours of the week, produce all the value that will be received in wages; of the value produced in the remaining 20 hours, that person will receive nothing – it is stolen by the employers. Thus, the value produced by workers far exceeds the value of their wages.

Once a wage is fixed it is in the interests of the capitalist to get as much productivity as possible from the worker. Marx looked at the major ways of increasing exploitation used by capitalists; in *Das Kapital* he looked at how different forms of exploitation appeared and were used in different periods of history. Absolute exploitation would involve squeezing more output from the worker, by increasing the length of the working week perhaps. However, this is a very crude method and would be less likely to be used now. Nowadays the more usual way of raising productivity and therefore profit is to improve the efficiency of work without a commensurate rise in the labourer's wages rather than to increase the time worked by the labourer. Marx saw this method of increasing profit as the dominant form of exploitation in the modern capitalist system.

Stop and think

- To what extent does this account (a) support Marx's idealized picture of the feudal society; and (b) refute it?

The surplus value generated in modern capitalist societies has not only benefited the capitalists. The position of wage earners has improved in certain ways. However, the fact that the working population may get more – in terms of better living standards, ownership of consumer goods and so on – is seen by Marxist writers as necessary for the survival of the capitalist system. To explain this point briefly: as capitalism is a system based on profit, it depends on continual growth and, therefore, it makes sense to give the mass of the population surplus wealth in order to enable them to buy goods; the more goods they buy, the more the system can produce. Of course, the wealthy capitalists will also have plenty of money to spend on luxuries. However, one person can spend only so much, and it is more efficient to distribute surplus value around 20 million families rather than 20,000; then they can all buy televisions, washing machines, cars and cosmetics and thereby generate more production and profit. Personal wealth and savings are still concentrated heavily in a few hands, but most wages are now above subsistence levels and enable the mass of the population to buy a range of consumer goods.

The contradictions in capitalism

In their account of Marx's analysis of capitalism, Cuff *et al.* (1990) suggest that he saw capitalism as a system characterized by:

- the exploitation of many people by a few;
- tensions, strains and contradictions between different social groups;
- the certainty of drastic change via some form of social revolution.

Adopting this categorization, we shall examine each of these statements in turn.

First, Marx argued that there are basic contradictions within capitalist societies due to the conflict of interests between the various groups involved in the economic process: in particular, the conflict of interests between an exploiting and exploited group, between the owners of the means of production and the non-owners. Under capitalism the main link between people is an impersonal cash relationship. Most people have only one marketable asset – their labour. A small number of industrial capitalists own the means of production, such as factories, land and raw materials, and provide the main means of employment for the majority. It is unlikely that individual capitalists regard themselves as exploiters; they are in business to make profits. To do this they have to beat competitors by reducing prices, and a major way of reducing prices is to cut costs. The biggest recurring cost for most employers is likely to be labour, so capitalists, in trying to be competitive, have little option but to keep labour costs down. Essentially, the capitalist wants as much work as possible from as few workers for as little pay as possible: this exploitation is not due to the 'evil' nature of individual capitalists but is a necessary requirement of the whole capitalist system according to Marx.

Second, the capitalist system produces the very conflicts and tension that will eventually tear it apart: in particular, conflicts and tension over pay and conditions between capitalists and employees, but also conflicts and tension between different groups of wage-earners and between capitalists themselves. Marx believed that the tensions inherent in capitalism would intensify, due to certain developments or trends that were inevitable in a capitalist system. These developments included polarization, homogenization and pauperization.

A closer look

Polarization

In modern industrial societies traditional skills were becoming redundant and there was a tendency for the working population to polarize into two distinct and hostile groups – the capitalists and the labourers.

Homogenization

Within these two groups, individuals were becoming increasing alike (or homogeneous). Among the capitalists, for example, competition was eliminating the smaller businesses and the successful ones were expanding, with the typical capitalist enterprise becoming a large and complex concern. Furthermore, workers would become increasingly homogeneous as a result of their dependence on work in these large factories and the decline of traditional skills.

Pauperization

In pursuing profit, capitalists need to keep their wage bills down. They need to ensure that the workers' wages do not rise in relation to those of capitalists, so that, in relation to capitalists, wage-workers are turned into paupers – they are 'pauperized'.

Question

1. **What contemporary evidence is there to support the argument that there is (a) a polarization of the working population; (b) homogenization among major groups of workers; and (c) pauperization of workers in relation to capitalists?**

Third, Marx argued that the capitalist system was doomed: the contradictions would grow and a social revolution was inevitable. Capitalism would disintegrate as developments such as polarization, homogenization and pauperization intensified. This would open the way for the establishment of a new, alternative type of social system. However, for a new system to be created, a new consciousness would have to develop among the exploited workers – a consciousness that would reflect the interests of the workers. Marx felt that this new consciousness could develop only if the exploited group actively opposed the capitalist system; only through struggle would the old, false consciousness be eradicated. The old consciousness is false because it reflects the interests of the privileged ruling groups, not the interests of the bulk of the people. True consciousness for the mass of the population would come about only when they developed an ideology (a set of ideas and values) that supported their interests.

When this new consciousness develops and matures, the proletariat, according to Marx, would overturn the capitalist system. They would take over the means of production and the state – as the capitalists had done before them. This would lead to a fundamental shift in the relations of production and a new abundant society would emerge where everyone could work and live freely and enjoy equality of status:

> **It will be possible for me to do one thing today and another tomorrow, to hunt in the morning, fish in the afternoon, rear cattle in the evening, criticise after dinner, just as I have a mind to, without ever becoming a hunter, fisherman, shepherd or critic.**
>
> (Marx and Engels 1976: vol. 5, 47)

Only in this sort of liberated, communist society could humans fulfil their potential for creativity; in societies where one class group dominates the rest, it is not possible.

This section has focused on the contradictions in the capitalist system: contradictions based on the exploitative relationship between owners and non-owners, between capitalists and workers. It is important to emphasize that we have looked at capitalism in a very general, simplistic manner. Contemporary capitalism differs considerably from early capitalism and from the model of capitalism that Marx wrote about. In the twenty-first century, instead of people actually owning factories and industrial production, ownership usually takes the form of capital investment – stocks and shares. Marxists argue, however, that this does not alter the essentially exploitative features of capitalist society; the bourgeoisie may not make the goods but they still gain the benefit from the surplus value produced by workers. Although exploitation may not be as obvious as feudal masters extracting 'tithes' from their peasants (or as the exploitation of slaves), the relationship between capitalist and wage earner is essentially the same.

Alienation

> **Work is external to the worker, that is it is not part of his nature . . . consequently he does not fulfil himself in this work but denies himself, has a feeling of misery, not of well-being, does not develop freely a physical and mental energy, but is physically exhausted and mentally debased . . . [Work] is not the satisfaction of a need but only a means for satisfying other needs. Its alien character is clearly shown by the fact that as soon as there is no physical or other compulsion it is avoided like the plague.**
>
> (Marx, *Economic and Philosophical Manuscripts*, 1844, in Bottomore 1963: 124–5)

The antagonistic and unequal class structure characteristic of capitalist societies leads to what Marx termed 'alienation'. Alienation refers to the separation, or estrangement, of individuals from themselves and from others. It is a complicated concept as it involves individuals' feelings. Alienation describes the sense of frustration, pointlessness and lack of involvement felt by many working people. Marx saw alienation as a central feature of capitalism and one that could take different forms. As the quote above illustrates, workers became alienated from their work because what they produced was controlled by others. As well as work itself being an alienating activity, workers are alienated from each other. Relationships in a capitalist society are those of competition (the 'dog eat dog' philosophy) rather than cooperation, even among the workers.

Stop and think

- Give examples of 'alienating work' in modern society.
- Describe the extent and sort of alienation that might be found in the following occupations: (a) nurse; (b) shop assistant; (c) car mechanic; (d) taxi driver; (e) food packager; and (f) teacher.
- In what areas of life other than work might alienation occur?

A closer look

Alienation: Marxist interpretations

The notion of alienation has been given different emphases by the different versions of Marxism that have developed from Marx's work. These differing emphases can be seen in the two major divergent strands of Marxist theorizing – humanistic Marxism and structural Marxism.

The more orthodox, structural Marxism is concerned mainly with the economic laws of capitalism and the nature of the capitalist state; this approach formed the basis for the discussion of historical materialism and the contradictions in capitalism provided above.

In contrast, humanistic Marxism has tended to play down the importance of the economic base/superstructure division. The focus has been on Marx's analysis of the dehumanizing effects of the rise of capitalism and, in particular, Marx's writings on alienation. This approach developed from the early 1920s in the work of, among others, George Lukács, Antonio Gramsci and the Frankfurt School (see pp. 89–92). Humanist Marxism suggests that people are essentially cooperative but that the development of capitalism leads to their alienation. This alienation occurs not only in the economic context but also in other contexts due to the general influence of large bureaucracies, the mass media and oppressive forms of government. Alienation can be overcome only by abolishing capitalism.

Rather than stressing alienation, structural Marxism, exemplified in the work of the French Marxist philosopher Louis Althusser (1918–93), focuses on exploitation. The processes and structures of capitalism are seen as exploiting workers. This exploitation can be measured objectively; it is not based on speculative ideas about the 'human spirit'. Thus, structural Marxism focuses on the economic base, where the exploitative mechanisms are located: 'the base/superstructure distinction is of paramount importance – it renders Marxism a scientifically valid method of analysis' (Lee and Newby 1983: 118).

The role of ideology

> **The ideas of the ruling class are, in every age, the ruling ideas.**
>
> (Marx and Engels 1976: vol. 5, 59)

The emphasis given to class exploitation and conflict raises the issue of why disadvantaged and exploited people accept their situation. Now, even in the modern, 'civilized' world a great deal of exploitation is exerted by pure force, particularly in states run by military and authoritarian regimes. However, that does not provide a complete explanation for the apparent acceptance of exploitation. In Marxist theory, ideas, values and beliefs perform a central function in maintaining inequalities and oppression. They act as ideologies supporting the (capitalist) system.

Although, strictly speaking, ideology means the science of ideas, it is generally taken to refer to a system of ideas that belong to a particular social group and is usually used in a negative and pejorative sense as implying false or mistaken ideas, values and beliefs. For Marx, an ideology was a system of ideas that misrepresent reality by serving the interests of the dominant social groups in society, particularly the ruling classes. The notion of ideology as a misrepresentation of reality is very close to Marx's description of false consciousness, and the two terms are, to a certain extent, almost interchangeable. In their discussion of the nature and functions of ideology in Marx's work, Cuff *et al.* suggest that ideologies:

> **Misrepresent reality in various ways: they conceal unacceptable aspects of it; they glorify things which are of themselves less than glorious; they make out things which are neither natural nor necessary as though they were both.**
>
> (Cuff *et al.* 1998: 27)

Stop and think

For a basically exploitative system such as modern capitalism to exist, either the inequalities (the fact that some people own Rolls-Royces and yachts while others can barely afford household bills, for example) and exploitation must fail to be recognized by disadvantaged people or they must be persuaded that such a situation is acceptable and justified.

- Why do you think disadvantaged groups put up with their situation?
- What 'ideas, values and beliefs' might persuade people to accept their disadvantaged and exploited condition?

The importance of ideology highlights the crucial role of the superstructure – of society's cultural aspects and institutions – in ensuring that the economic system is considered legitimate. It also illustrates the importance of the notions of class consciousness and false consciousness to Marxist theory. Marx's theory of historical materialism is a good deal more complex than presented here. For instance, the relationship between the economic base and superstructure is not as rigid as we have perhaps implied. Marx was well aware that there was not a complete 'economic determinism' and that the superstructure had some influence on the economic system and could, indeed, influence the way in which the economic system developed. The variations in the capitalist system from one society to another demonstrate this: the different histories and cultures of Japan, the UK and the USA, for example, have affected the kind of capitalist economic system that prevails in those countries.

Marx and social class

According to Marx, there is a built-in antagonism and conflict between class groups in all societies; as his

Case study

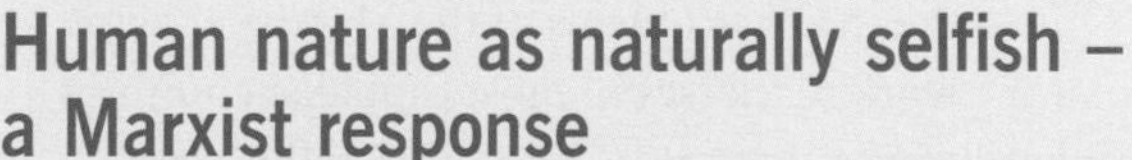

Human nature as naturally selfish – a Marxist response

Cuff and colleagues examine the widely held idea that human beings are naturally selfish and competitive – that selfishness is in the nature of all living things – as an example of an ideological concept:

> Such a view has two features which are common among ideologies: the suggestion that it is simply in our nature to be selfish and self-interested; and the implication that there is nothing we can do to change it because it is built into our natures. From the Marxist point of view, we are not innately competitive in this way. To talk about the natural, immutable competitiveness of the human species offers a false picture of our human natures. Such theories serve to justify a socio-economic system – competitive capitalism – which is based on unrelenting individual competition. These ideas justify that system by suggesting that, first, it gives full rein to our fundamental human natures and is therefore best suited to us and, second, there is little point in disapproving of or attempting to moderate the competitiveness of the system since it is our nature to be competitive . . . In one way or another, systems of ideas play this ideological role of convincing people that they cannot change their society, or that it is not worth their effort to try changing it.
>
> (Cuff *et al.* 2006: 26–27)

Question

1. Suggest how the idea of natural human selfishness can be found in the following areas of popular cultural production:
   (a) TV soap operas (consider the characters from your favourite soaps);
   (b) literature;
   (c) film;
   (d) sport (consider the behaviour/demands of sports personalities).
2. How might a Marxist approach 'interpret' these examples?

famous comment at the start of the *Communist Manifesto* puts it:

> **The history of all hitherto existing society is the history of class struggles.**
>
> (Marx and Engels 1952: 40)

Perhaps Marx's major intellectual aim was to discover the principle of change in society. However, he did not want just to describe divisions in society but to explain which groups had strong interests in maintaining the existing system and which in trying to change it. These groups, with differing interests, Marx saw as social classes.

Classes exist in all non-communist societies. In the ancient mode of production the two main classes were the slaves and the slave-owners. In feudal society they were the servile peasantry and the landed nobility. Under capitalism, there are, similarly, two main classes – the *bourgeoisie*, who own the means of production, and the *proletariat*, who have only their labour to sell. In any class system, then, there are two main classes and, because one exploits the other, they are antagonistic to one another. This antagonism provides the driving force for social change (as we highlighted in discussing the contradiction in capitalism, pp. 58–59).

For Marx, class consciousness was of central importance in defining social class. Members of social classes could be distinguished by two criteria, both of which are necessary for a fully developed social class to exist:

- *Objective criteria* – The sharing of a particular attribute, for example a similar type of occupation or the same relationship to the means of production (being an owner or non-owner).
- *Subjective criteria* – Grouping people in terms of a shared attribute does no more than create a category (all red-headed people could be lumped together in this way, for example); a category is only a possible or potential class and can be transformed into an active social class only when people become conscious of their position.

Marx summed up this distinction by stating that it was not enough for a class to be a class *in* itself; it had also to be a class *for* itself (with a full class consciousness and feelings of solidarity with others of that class). This distinction is central to Marx's theory of class and social change, and the notion of class consciousness is central to his theory of working-class revolution. Awareness and consciousness are necessary for the existence of an active social class; only when a class becomes a class for itself does it exist as a political force.

Marx believed that the working class was bound to develop this class consciousness once the appropriate conditions were present. These conditions would include the growing relative poverty of the proletariat and the increasing 'class polarization' between the proletariat and the bourgeoisie. Members of the proletariat would become increasingly angered by bourgeois exploitation and would organize themselves – locally at first and then nationally – to improve their economic situation. As a consequence of this, they would eventually take control from the bourgeoisie and set up a new society. As this happened the proletariat, according to Marx, would transform themselves from a mere category of people who share the same conditions to a group of people who organize to change these conditions: they would move to become a class for themselves. Ultimately, Marx believed, then, that the proletariat would see through the bourgeois ideology and become revolutionary. He believed the bourgeoisie were incapable of developing a strong overall consciousness of their collective interests, due to the inevitable competition between individual capitalists chasing profit.

One of the major problems of the Marxist analysis is that the working classes in most capitalist countries have hardly ever come close to acquiring this class consciousness and becoming a class for itself. Most Western working-class groups have been content to squeeze the occasional reforms out of the ruling class rather than to challenge the whole basis of class inequality. Linked with this failure to mobilize has been the growth of the middle classes. For Marx, all non-owners of the means of production are, objectively, members of the proletariat. However, what distinguishes the middle class is that they help to administer and perpetuate the capitalist system for the ruling class. They are not part of the ruling class but they are its functionaries; lawyers, teachers, civil servants and so on are seen by Marxists as 'lackeys of the ruling class'. They enjoy more privileges than the exploited working classes but their power is no greater; without property to rely on for income the real interests of the middle classes are bound up with the working classes and in so far as they do not realize this they are victims of 'false consciousness'.

Stop and think

- How might groups of workers develop a sense of collective identity and class consciousness?
- What factors work against this in modern society?
- Where do you think the interests of 'professional' workers and manual workers coincide? Where do they diverge?

With the apparent demise of communism in the late 1980s, perhaps most symbolically represented with the dismantling of the Berlin Wall, it seemed that the work of Marx had little relevance to contemporary society. This judgement may prove to be somewhat premature in view of the economic crises in a number of societies (in South East Asia and Russia, for example) in the late 1990s. Such developments have demonstrated how badly capitalism can go wrong and have led writers such as Eric Hobsbawn (1998) to say of Marx, 'What this man wrote 150 years ago about the nature and tendencies of global capitalism rings amazingly true today.' Echoing Marx's sentiments, Hobsbawm suggests that such crises make a compelling economic, social and moral case for reducing inequality and for promoting a more even distribution of incomes. He highlights the polarization between a concentration of high-income jobs in high-profit-making firms and low-wage, casual occupations, 'between the City dealers and the office cleaners and security staff'. Such polarization is economically and socially unhealthy; in contrast, social and economic equality improves 'a region's health, mortality, crime rates and "civic community". Hence, for those who need such arguments, the lower the financial cost to society'.

Weber and meaning

Max Weber is considered to be one of the 'trinity of founding thinkers' of sociology, along with Durkheim and Marx. Weber and Durkheim adopted quite distinct methods and theories in their sociological work. While Durkheim devoted himself to trying to establish sociology as an academic subject (founding journals and teaching departments), Weber was more a pure scholar, grappling with ideas. Like Marx, Weber was not 'just' a sociologist: his work extended into philosophy, economics, religion and history, for example. This work, however, has not led to the establishment of a coherent doctrine; there is not a 'Weberism' in the same way that there is a 'Marxism'. The focus of this introduction to Weber's work and its influence will be to examine some of the ideas and themes that he developed. His four major studies are:

- *The Protestant Ethic and the Spirit of Capitalism*, 1904–05.
- *The Sociology of Religion*, 1920.
- *The Theory of Social and Economic Organization*, 1922.
- *The Methodology of the Social Sciences*, 1949.

Weber's work

Weber wrote about the nature of sociology and how to go about studying society. He argued that people cannot be studied using the same procedures as those involved in investigating the physical world: people are thinking, reasoning beings who attach meanings to what they do, and sociology has to acknowledge this. Weber felt that sociology should adopt a sort of midway position between the 'hard' natural sciences and the cultural studies such as literature, history and art.

For Weber, the basis of sociological analysis was the meaning that individuals give to the social world and their situation in it. This necessitated sociology following a different kind of method from that of the natural sciences. Sociology could not proceed in the same manner as the natural sciences, because individuals had a degree of free will that led to some unpredictability in their actions. Sociology had to aim to understand human action, and to do this it had to acknowledge the particular and unique rather than always expect to be able to generalize.

In contrast to the other founding writers, Weber was interested in explaining individual social action and what motivates it. The basic unit of investigation should, therefore, be the individual, whereas Durkheim emphasized collectivity and Marx the social class groupings.

In particular, sociology had to adopt what Weber called *verstehen* – a German word meaning, roughly, empathetic or interpretative understanding – in order to show how people's beliefs and motives led to particular types of behaviour and action. Understanding and empathizing with the belief of others does not necessarily mean being sympathetic to or supportive of those beliefs. However, in order to gain a real appreciation of

A closer look

Max Weber (1864–1920)

Weber was born in Germany and spent his academic career there. His first teaching job was in law at Berlin University. As his intellectual interests widened he was appointed to professorships in political economy and then economics at the universities of Freiburg and Heidelberg, respectively. However, mental illness and depression meant that he was unable to hold down full-time teaching positions throughout his whole life. In 1897 at Heidelberg, shortly after the death of his father, he suffered a nervous breakdown that cut short his career as it was beginning to develop. After that his academic life was spent writing and researching, with sociology becoming his main academic field.

Weber's lifetime spanned a period of massive change in German history. The unification of Germany led to the emergence of the modern German state and was accompanied by a phenomenal growth of industry; indeed, it was around this time that Germany challenged and overtook Britain as Europe's leading industrial power. The attempts to create a German empire culminated in the First World War and defeat towards the end of Weber's life.

Weber's work has been described as a debate with the 'ghost of Marx'. Weber was clearly influenced by Marx but was critical of some of his views. He criticized Marx's overemphasis on materialist explanations of historical development and argued that social divisions reflected more than solely economic or class conflict.

Figure 2.3 Max Weber
Hulton Archive/Getty Images

how others feel, we should try to think of ourselves as being in their situation and see things through their eyes.

Although it might seem difficult to empathize with people from different cultures and periods of history, Weber saw *verstehen* as a method that could be applied to the understanding of events from different contexts: 'One need not have been Caesar in order to understand Caesar' (sense can be made of Caesar's actions by seeing them as an understandable sequence).

Stop and think

- How might *verstehen* help in the study of (a) religion; (b) poverty; and (c) crime?
- What difficulties might face someone adopting such an approach?

Thus, sociology, according to Weber, is the study of social action, and it is by placing meaning on and interpreting the behaviour of others that we are able to understand that behaviour. Of course, the meaning of an action requires an interpretation and the problem for sociology, as Weber sees it, is how to discover the meanings that other individuals and groups place on their behaviour. In interpreting behaviour, sociologists will inevitably be left with nagging doubts about their observations and analyses: 'How can I be sure that I have understood the subjective feelings of others? How would I know if I had totally misunderstood and misinterpreted them?'

These kinds of doubts and problems raise the issue of whether there is some standard of social action against which different types of behaviour can be related to and measured. Weber suggested there were four basic categories of action that could provide such a standard:

A closer look

Ideal types

The categories of social action suggested by Weber are 'ideal types', a notion that is an important element of his work. Essentially, an ideal type is a way of classifying things; it is an abstraction that Weber employed in trying to get to grips with the complexities of the social world. Social phenomena cannot always be understood in their entirety, and it is often easier to emphasize certain key features. Thus, our ideal type of capitalism, democracy or whatever will not necessarily represent the 'real thing'; it will be a rather exaggerated and idealized version (a little like a cartoon characterization). Weber saw the ideal type as a sort of yardstick for comparing and evaluating other cases. It is quite possible for different ideal types to be constructed for the same phenomenon; there might be different ideal types of capitalism, for example.

- *Traditional action* – The individual is driven by custom and habit, with behaviour often an automatic reaction. A great deal of everyday activity comes under this heading – eating, washing and so on.
- *Affective action* – The individual is guided by emotions. Such behaviour contains some distinctive and unconscious elements: it may involve seeking revenge or providing immediate sensual gratification, for instance.
- *Value-rational action* – The individual follows strongly held values and morals. Overall objectives or ends are seen as important, and behaviour is guided by ideals – doing the 'decent thing'.
- *Technical-rational action* – The individual chooses the objectives and means rationally, with a full account taken of the consequences. It is this sort of behaviour that is most open to sociological understanding and analysis.

Weber argued that technical-rational action was becoming more and more dominant in Western society and was driving out the other forms of action. This notion of rationality and the spread of it is a key principle of Weber's work.

Weber's work was wide-ranging and encompassed many topics. Here we shall focus on just two of his main concerns: the relationship between religion and the development of capitalism and the spread of bureaucratic administration in the modern world. As well as being extremely interesting and influential in their own right, both of these areas of Weber's work give a good insight into the analytical methods he employed.

The Protestant Ethic and the Spirit of Capitalism

Weber's most famous study, *The Protestant Ethic and the Spirit of Capitalism* (1904–05), attempted to explain how a particular type of religious belief came to influence economic behaviour, thereby making it more rational; this is an application of his argument that technical-rational action was becoming the predominant form of social action in the modern Western world.

Weber studied a range of cultures and religions of the non-Western world in order to show that they had not developed a similar sort of rational capitalism to the West due to religious and cultural factors. This approach can be contrasted with Marx's emphasis on the importance of economic, class factors in the rise of Western capitalism. Weber's work was critical of the Marxist view that religious ideas were always and inevitably shaped by economic factors. Weber did not deny that in certain situations religion may be shaped by economic factors, but he argued that this was not always the case. However, his main interest was in the ways in which religious ideas might affect and determine social change.

So, the 'Protestant ethic thesis' aimed to explain the development of capitalism in terms of the emergence of a particular form of Protestant religion. Weber tried to explain why capitalism had developed fully only in the Western world and had flourished in northern Europe. He argued that religion provided a clue. He suggested that the ideas and practices of Protestantism were particularly appropriate to capitalist development in a way that was not true of other religions, such as Islam, or of other forms of Christianity, such as Catholicism.

The capitalist spirit

Weber argued that there was a capitalist spirit that was based on a desire to be productive and accumulate. In Western society, hard work, investment and steady accumulation were seen as the 'proper' and correct attitudes, with idleness and overconsumption seen as wrong; elsewhere, production was geared more towards the production of goods for immediate use. The sort of Western attitudes that Weber identified with capitalist societies were, he felt, by no means natural. Why not, for instance, just produce enough for our needs and then stop working? Why not spend when we can, rather than save?

In looking at Weber's definition of capitalism, it is important to bear in mind that he was writing at the beginning of the twentieth century, and the attitudes and style of capitalism have changed since then. Also, his description is an 'ideal type': each capitalist society has its own peculiarities. Nonetheless, the essence of capitalism is seen as an 'enterprise whose aim is to make the maximum profit and whose means is the rational organisation of work and production'. This desire for profit in tandem with rational discipline constitutes the historically unique feature of Western capitalism. In all societies there have been merchants eager to make money, but what is unique is that this desire for profit should satisfy itself not by conquest and plunder but by discipline and science. Perhaps the term 'profit' does not fully describe Weber's emphasis on the idea of unlimited accumulation. The capitalist, according to Weber, does not limit his appetite for gain in accordance with tradition or custom but is driven by a desire to keep accumulating.

With regard to the relationship between Western capitalism and religion, Weber suggested that a certain form of Protestantism provided conditions that were particularly favourable for the growth of the capitalist economic system. The key elements of his findings and argument can be summarized as follows:

- In areas of mixed religions (such as his own society, Germany) particular groups of Protestants possessed a disproportionate amount of wealth and important positions.
- This indicated a spiritual affinity – a link – between the Protestant religion and the spirit of capitalism.
- The different styles of religion in different societies help to explain why Western capitalism did not develop elsewhere. Weber studied the religions of a number of areas of the world, including China, India and the Middle East. He argued that a particular attitude to work, determined by religious belief, was the crucial factor present in the West and absent elsewhere that helped to establish Western economic dominance.

The Protestant ethic

What was the particular feature of this 'form of Protestantism' that Weber felt was so influential? The Protestant ethic was a sort of Puritanism that was based on Calvinism (John Calvin was one of the great religious reformers of the sixteenth century and the founder of the Presbyterian religion). The principal features of the Protestant ethic were:

- The existence of an absolute, transcendent God who created the world and ruled over it.

A closer look

Capitalism according to Weber

Weber's definition of capitalism as an enterprise working towards unlimited acquisition of goods and functioning in a rational and disciplined way resembles Marx's definition but also presents various differences.

Similarities with Marx: the essence of capitalism is the pursuit of profit through the market; capitalism has utilized increasingly powerful technical means to achieve its ends – of extra profit.

Differences from Marx: the major characteristic of capitalism is rationalization, which would continue no matter who owned the means of production. The need for rational organization would persist beyond any revolution that might result in the state ownership of production; it would still exist in socialist or communist societies.

- This all-powerful God has predestined each person to salvation or damnation; this predestination cannot be altered.
- God created the world for his glory, and everyone is obliged to work for the glory of God – whether they are to be saved or not.
- Worldly things belong to the order of sin: salvation occurs only through divine grace.

Although each of these features exists separately in other religions, their combination in Calvinist Protestantism was, Weber argued, unique.

Weber saw a coincidence between certain requirements of this Protestantism and capitalist logic. The Protestant ethic asks the believer to beware of the things of this world and emphasizes the importance of self-denial. To work rationally in pursuit of profit that is not consumed but is reinvested is the sort of conduct that was necessary to the development of capitalism. This demonstrates an aspect of what Weber called the spiritual affinity between the Protestant and capitalist attitudes. The Protestant ethic, according to Weber, provided an economic motivation for the 'strange' capitalist behaviour of accumulation for the sake of it – a behaviour that has no obvious parallel in non-Western societies.

Predestination

A central aspect of the Protestant ethic was the idea of predestination, which is a religious conviction based on the belief that God's decrees are ultimate, impenetrable and irrevocable. Grace is either bestowed on an individual or it is not, and there is little the individual can do to alter this. This belief helps to explain the rejection of the sacraments by Protestant religions. In some religions, people can find 'grace' through, for instance, confession and absolution from sins or from last rites. For Puritan Protestants these practices would make no difference to whether an individual was saved or not.

The belief in predestination leads to the elimination of many of the mystical elements of belief and, for Weber, highlighted the increasing rationalization of religion.

Believers in predestination are faced by crucial questions such as 'How does one know that one belongs to the elect?' and 'What is the sign that one is saved?' The early Protestants believed that the sign of election could be found in a personal life that followed religious teachings and in the social achievements of an individual. Social achievement would include success in the individual's professional activity – in their 'calling'. Effective and good work demonstrates the glory of God, so that a successful work career demonstrated a blessing on those activities and could, therefore, be interpreted as 'proof of election'. Individuals acquire the certainty of salvation through the strength of their faith, which would be reflected in success at work.

This notion of successful worldly achievement demonstrating spiritual salvation poses a dilemma. Growing business success will lead to greater affluence, which does not fit in with the rigour of a true Christian life, where worldly possessions would be seen as unimportant. However, Puritan Protestants believed that it was not the acquiring of wealth that was wrong but the enjoyment of the things that money can buy and the temptations it can bring. It was felt that individuals should take from their assets only what was needed for a life of personal sobriety and obedience to God's law and must follow an ascetic lifestyle.

The emphasis on hard work and productivity coupled with the rejection of luxuries led to a lifestyle that encouraged and influenced the spirit of capitalism.

The Protestant ethic thesis: discussion points

The Protestant ethic thesis is essentially a reaction to the Marxist assumption that all social events are reducible to a single factor – the economic context or substructure. Weber's argument is not the opposite of historical materialism; as he put it, 'It is not my aim to substitute for a one-sided materialistic an equally one-sided spiritualistic causal interpretation of history and culture' (Weber 1974: 183). What he demonstrated is that economic activity may be governed by systems of belief, just as at certain times systems of belief may be determined by the economic system. Thus, Protestantism was not seen by Weber as the cause of capitalism but rather as one of the factors that led to its emergence and development. Weber's work has encouraged the recognition that there is no necessary determination of beliefs by economic and social reality, or rather that it is not justifiable to assume a determination of this kind to be the only and ultimate one.

Given its scope, it is not surprising that many doubts have been raised about the validity of Weber's thesis. First, although the early Protestant capitalists advocated an ascetic lifestyle and did not spend a great deal on luxuries, they did have power and status in their communities as well as financial security – and perhaps these things are enjoyments in themselves. Second, many of the early rich capitalists were not Protestants:

A closer look

The Protestant ethic and asceticism

A lifestyle of asceticism was one based on self-denial and abstinence. In the context of the early Protestants, with their emphasis on the virtues of hard work, it was felt that wasting time was a sin: God's time should not be wasted by idle talk, by too much sleep or by sociability, for example. In addition, people should accept the position that God had assigned to them; whatever work one has to do, it should be done to God's greater glory. A person without a vocation was felt to lack the character demanded by asceticism; although irregular work might be unavoidable at times, it was not a good thing. If individuals did not try to be as productive as possible in their work, then they were refusing to be a good steward of God's gifts and were not following a calling. Asceticism was hostile to leisure and cultural pursuits. The theatre was obnoxious to Puritans, as was ostentatious dress: thus the plain clothing worn by Puritans.

The link between this religious asceticism and capitalism was that industry was provided with sober and conscientious workers. Furthermore, it gave an assurance that inequality was part of God's plan and was not to be questioned. Asceticism, and particularly the notion that hard work was highly pleasing to God, was not a new phenomenon; nor was it unique to early Protestantism. However, the emphasis on work as a calling, and a sign of personal salvation, added an extra dimension to the ascetic idea. From a different perspective, it could be argued that the emphasis on work as a calling also provided a justification for employers' exploitation of their workforce, in that employers' business activities were also seen as callings, with profit-making viewed positively.

Questions

1. Which particular stories or parables from the Bible could be used to 'support' the Protestant ethic's emphasis on asceticism?
2. How has the Protestant ethic influenced the way that people think about contemporary issues such as (a) unemployment and poverty; and (b) divorce and changes in family structure?

there were also rich Catholic and Jewish business people. Third, while there probably was a link between capitalism and Protestantism, rather than Protestantism leading to capitalism the reverse occurred and Protestantism developed as a rationalization for capitalism. It justified the wealth of certain people by suggesting that this wealth would be viewed favourably by God. Fourth, some Calvinist communities did not develop along capitalist lines immediately. Scotland, for instance, although strongly Calvinist, had a slower capitalist development than other less obviously Protestant countries. Finally, the accumulation of investment capital in Britain, the Netherlands, New England in the USA and other early capitalist societies was arguably due as much to profiteering through trade with less developed countries as to careful saving by God-fearing Protestant business people.

Of course, Weber realized that capitalism was not solely the result of Protestantism: he was aware of the developments in trade and technology. He felt, however, that the age in which capitalism developed, which was also the age of the Reformation, was one where religion was a major force in society and social scientists should examine and explain the extent to which religious conduct could influence other activities. Weber did not believe he had exhausted the subject, as his comment in the last paragraph of *The Protestant Ethic and the Spirit of Capitalism* illustrates:

> **Modern man is in general unable to give religious ideas a significance for cultural and national character which they deserve.**
>
> (Weber 1974: 183)

Weber and bureaucracy

In the sociological study of organizations, Weber's work is generally taken as the starting point. Weber examined, in particular, bureaucracy, the form of organization that he saw as becoming predominant in modern industrial society. In Britain, the word 'bureaucracy' tends to have negative connotations and to be seen as something of a 'problem'; indeed, the term 'bureaucrat' often doubles as a form of mild abuse. Nevertheless, the bureaucratic type of organizational structure would seem to be a fixed, permanent and perhaps even necessary feature of modern society.

Weber saw that as industrial societies developed they were characterized by the growth and spread of large-scale organizations – the civil service, the armed forces, churches, educational institutions, manufacturing companies and so on. Large-scale organizations were clearly having an increasing influence on all areas of social life.

Weber was particularly concerned with the problem of efficiency in organizations. The 'ideal type' blueprint for bureaucracy that he defined (see p. 70) was, he felt, the best way of ensuring efficiency in the administering of organizations. This 'ideal type' of Weber's was based on his analysis of alternative forms of power and authority. This analysis provides the context for an understanding of Weber's theorizing on bureaucracy.

Power was seen by Weber as the ability to get things done or to compel others to comply with one's commands. *Authority* also involves the ability to get things done but in situations where the particular order is seen as legitimate by those following it. Authority is, in essence, legitimized power, where legitimacy involves the acceptance of the rights of others to make decisions. So, power and authority are closely related concepts for Weber, but the notion of legitimacy is an important distinguishing feature. Weber then defined and distinguished three types of authority based on different 'types' of legitimacy. The three types were traditional, charismatic and rational-legal, and these were found, he argued, in one degree or another, in all forms of society.

In broad historical terms, Weber believed that the traditional and charismatic forms of authority existed in earlier, pre-industrial societies. In modern society, the rationalization process (by this, Weber means the application of scientific thought and the influence of science in behaviour) has meant that authority has become increasingly rational-legal, based on formal

A closer look

Weber's three types of authority

Traditional authority

This is based on the unquestioning acceptance of the distribution of power. Legitimacy is believed because it has 'always been so'; the leader has authority by virtue of the traditional status that the office of leader has.

Charismatic authority

This is based on the commitment and loyalty to a leader who is generally felt to possess very exceptional qualities. Charisma is a unique force that overrides tradition and law. In a system based on charismatic authority the word of the leader is seen as all-important; by its nature, this type of authority is very unstable. First, the particular leader has to keep the loyalty of the masses and, assuming this can be achieved, it is difficult to pass on charismatic authority after the leader's death. Second, the authority of charismatic leaders tends to become routinized over time; they will need to get a staff of assistants as the job of leader evolves. Weber argued that charismatic authority will eventually change its form and become routinized or bureaucratized; it will merge with the third and final type of authority he defined – the rational-legal.

Rational-legal authority

This is based on a legal framework that supports and maintains the distribution of power among individuals and groups in society. This form of authority is characterized by bureaucracy; the emphasis is on the rules rather than either the leader (charismatic authority) or the customs (traditional authority). The organization is supreme, with no one being 'above the law' (remember that Weber was talking in ideal terms!).

Questions

1. Give an example of
   (a) traditional authority;
   (b) charismatic authority;
   and (c) rational-legal authority.

2. Give examples of people who illustrate or have illustrated each of these forms of authority.

rules. And, as suggested above, bureaucracy is the most typical form of rational-legal authority.

Weber's 'ideal type' bureaucracy

Bureaucracy was, for Weber, the characteristic form of administration in modern society. It was not only confined to the political arena but was common to all other forms of administration, including education, religion, the business world and so on. Essentially, Weber's explanation for the spread of bureaucracy was because of its efficiency in relation to other forms of organization.

It is important to note that Weber's belief in the efficiency of bureaucracy did not mean he saw bureaucracy as necessarily a 'good thing'. An overriding fear at the end of his life was that modern society would be subject to a deadening, dictatorial bureaucracy. This fear was tied in with Weber's work on rationalization; bureaucratic development was a logical consequence of increasing rationalization, which was undermining and removing spiritual influences from the world. Rationalization was, for Weber, a key feature of modern society and occurred in the fields of both religious belief and economic activity.

Weber's 'ideal type' model of bureaucracy contained six basic principles:

- *Specialization* – Official tasks and positions are clearly divided; each covers a distinct and separate area of competence.
- *Hierarchy* – There is an ordered system of superordination and subordination; every position or office is accountable to and supervised by a higher office.
- *Rules* – There are clearly established, general rules that govern the management of the office.
- *Impersonality* – Everyone within the organization is subject to formal equality of treatment.
- *Officials* – They are (a) selected and appointed on the basis of technical qualifications (or some clearly recognized criteria); (b) full-time appointments, in that the particular post is the sole or major occupation of the individual; and (c) subject to a formal career structure with a system of promotion according to either seniority or merit (in other words, there are objective criteria for promotions).
- *Public–private division* – There is a clear separation between official activity and private life (the resources of the organization, for instance, are quite distinct from those of the officials as private individuals).

Essentially, then, Weber's 'ideal type' bureaucracy meant ordered administration by officials. Weber laid particular emphasis on the central importance of rules. Rules reduce tension between people; they allow people to feel that they are following a rule rather than a particular individual. Furthermore, rules apply to everyone (in the ideal situation, of course) and they legitimize punishments in that the rule and sanction for breaking it are known in advance. Weber felt that the impersonal quality of bureaucracy was also particularly important: it ensured that everyone received the same treatment and that they could calculate in advance what would happen in particular situations and circumstances.

The major reason for the development and spread of this form of administration has been its technical superiority over other forms of organization. Precision, discretion, continuity and speed are all achieved to a greater degree in a bureaucratic structure. For Weber, bureaucratization was simply the most efficient way of administering; there is a regular chain of command, always a higher authority to refer to.

Stop and think

- What organizations are you a part of or do you have regular contact with? Take each of the six elements of Weber's model of bureaucracy and describe briefly the extent to which they apply to these organizations.
- Following on from these descriptions, evaluate whether Weber's classification is a good basis for assessing the extent to which a particular organization is bureaucratized.

Weber and bureaucracy: criticisms

Weber's argument that bureaucracy is the most efficient form of organization has been criticized by a number of writers. Robert Merton, an American sociologist and a leading figure in functionalist sociology between the 1940s and 1970s, wrote a famous paper, 'Bureaucratic structure and personality' (1952), which focused on the harmful consequences of bureaucracy. He highlighted a number of *dysfunctions* (things that hinder the workings of an institution or activity) of bureaucracy. He suggested that the 'virtues' of discipline and efficiency could become exaggerated in practice, to the extent that officials become obsessed with organizational rules. At the extreme, officials may become so enmeshed in the rules and 'doing things by the book' that they are unable to help their clients speedily or efficiently. Merton's argument is that bureaucracies create a bureaucratic personality – a personality that stresses conformity and, consequently, initiative and innovative behaviour are stifled and replaced with inflexibility and timidity. Merton also pointed out that strict conformity to rules can work against the achievement of organizational goals, particularly in circumstances of rapid change, when new ideas might be necessary. Thus, the dysfunctions or problems of bureaucracy are seen by Merton as due to the stress on rules that become too rigid and cannot be altered to fit special circumstances.

Weber's description of the ideal type bureaucracy does not include concepts such as trust, cooperation and flexibility. Alvin Gouldner (1954), in a study of a gypsum plant in the USA, argued that while a bureaucratic structure might work well in stable, predictable situations, it was too rigid to cope with situations of rapid change, where trust, cooperation and flexibility are essential. In the context of industrial bureaucracies, a rule might be rational for achieving the ends of one group – management, for instance – but might work against the interests of another group – the employees, perhaps.

The importance that Weber attached to following rules was seen by Peter Blau (1963) as, on occasion, working against the efficiency of the organization. Some organizations function more effectively when workers gather into informal groups and disregard or break official rules. To illustrate his argument, Blau studied a federal law-enforcement agency in the USA. He found that officers who infringed rules regularly achieved a higher success rate in enforcing the law. Blau argues that bureaucratic structures can be too inflexible. No set of rules can anticipate all the potential problems, and it is important to study the informal workings of organizations as well as the formal structure.

Bureaucracy in practice is often quite distinct from the ideal type on paper. It must be emphasized that although Weber believed bureaucracies to be efficient, he was not an uncritical supporter of them. Indeed, Weber saw the growth of bureaucratic administration, which he felt was inevitable, as a grave threat to individual freedom (along with other aspects of the general process of rationalization in modern societies). He argued that bureaucracies have an in-built tendency to accumulate power and that, once established, they tend to take on a life of their own and become extremely hard to dismantle.

Weber's relevance in the twenty-first century

In 1989 Kaessler argued that, if there were such a thing as the Sociological Hall of Fame, Max Weber would be honoured among its ranks. What he actually said was that, according to a range of academic criteria, Weber should be accepted as a 'classic' sociologist because his work and insights had stood the test of time.

More recently, George Ritzer (1993) developed the concept of the 'McDonaldization of society', in which many of Weber's ideas on rationality were applied to the economic and social changes taking place in the USA 70 years after Weber's death. These ideas were later applied to other scenarios as Ritzer argued that the processes he was describing were not restricted to the American fast-food industry but could be found in all walks of life on a global scale. In the twenty-first-century edition of his book, and the reader that accompanies it, he demonstrates that, far from being a 'dead white male' and a 'founding father' in sociology, Weber's ideas are probably more relevant today than when he was alive.

Contemporary sociological theories

This section discusses some important developments in sociological theory since the 1920s. Social theory did not come to an end with the deaths of the founding writers; rather, their work has acted as a stimulus for a wide range of theoretical argument in sociology. This general introduction can provide only a flavour of the various complex developments in modern social theory; to capture the excitement and intricacies of these theoretical debates you will need to look at the original sources summarized here or, failing that, texts that focus on modern social theory (see Further reading).

Interpretative sociology

The title 'interpretative sociology' includes a number of more specific sociological theories, the best known of which are probably *symbolic interactionism* and *ethnomethodology*. As with other sociological theories, these approaches attempt to explain human behaviour and do this by examining the social influences on behaviour. However, rather than emphasizing the influence of the social structure and how it constrains people, interpretative theories argue that the most important influence on individuals' behaviour is the behaviour of others towards them.

Interpretative sociology concentrates on the microlevel of social life. Societies are the end result of human interaction rather than the starting point, and by looking at how this interaction occurs it is possible to understand how social order is created and maintained. In focusing on everyday life, this theoretical approach offers a clear contrast with those theories that examine 'grand' questions and issues, such as 'What is industrial society?', and provide a general explanation of society as a whole. Thus, interpretative sociology offers a different approach and style of investigating society to the functionalist and conflict macrotheories and the work of the founding theorists looked at earlier in this chapter.

Meanings

These theories focus on the individual and the process of social interaction. They examine how people are able to understand one another; how they interpret what is going on around them and then choose to behave in particular ways. They emphasize the meanings that people give to actions and to things.

Human behaviour is seen as the product of conscious decisions and, in most cases, individuals have some choice as to how they act. Furthermore, actions are usually purposive: they are directed towards some goal. The particular goal or purpose that is followed is dependent on the way in which individuals interpret the world around them. People choose what to do in the light of their 'definition of the situation'. For instance, you might wake up on a wet morning and decide to work on an assignment or essay; if the weather brightens up, you may decide to make the most of it and abandon the college work and go into town; in town you may meet a friend and decide to forget about any shopping plans and go to a café.

Theories that emphasize the meanings that individuals give to action clearly owe a great debt to Max Weber. The importance Weber attached to explaining individual social action and to the notion of *verstehen* (empathetic or interpretative understanding, see pp. 63–64) demonstrate his role as the founder of the interpretative approach in sociology. However, Weber applied the idea of *verstehen* to the analysis of large-scale social change and did not examine in detail the day-to-day interactions of individuals in specific situations. Interpretativist sociologists have adopted Weber's approach and applied it to small-scale and specific contexts.

Stop and think

➤ How can a greater understanding of social interaction on a microlevel aid our understanding of macrosociological questions?

Symbolic interactionism

There are a number of related theoretical perspectives that fit under the broad heading of interpretative sociology. Symbolic interactionism is perhaps the most well established and will be the focus for this introductory discussion. It suggests that human behaviour is different from that of (other) animals because it uses symbols and attaches meanings to them. When people interact with one another they use symbols, especially in the form of language – hence the name 'symbolic interactionism'.

This theoretical perspective emerged from the writings of US sociologists and social psychologists in the 1920s and 1930s, in particular Charles Cooley, William Thomas and George Herbert Mead. Mead, who began his career as a philosopher, published little while he was alive, and his lectures form the basis for his key role as the founder of symbolic interactionism.

Mead's work emphasized the relationship between the individual and society. He called his approach 'social behaviourism' because it was linked closely with social psychology – the study of social groups. The basic idea behind Mead's approach was that the perceptions and the behaviour of individuals are influenced by the social groups of which they are members. The existence of social groups is essential for the development of what Mead termed the 'self'.

The self is perhaps the key concept of the symbolic interactionist perspective. It refers to how individuals see themselves. We all have a self-image, an identity and some conception of who we 'really' are – which we refer to as the self. This concept of the 'self' is meaningful only in relation to other 'selves'. We carry on a whole series of different interactions with different people; we are one thing to one person and another thing to another.

It is the ability to become self-conscious, to be able to stand outside our own situation and look at our behaviour retrospectively that provides the key to Mead's analysis. Questions such as 'What made me do that?' Mead saw as examples of reflexive questioning – of the individual 'taking the role of others'. So Mead's theory of self and socialization rests on the individual's ability to take the role of others and so of the wider community. This requires the organization of the individual's whole self in relation to the social groups and the community to which that individual belongs. The organized community or group that provides this unity of self for individuals was given the term the 'generalized other' by Mead. The attitude of the generalized other is the attitude of the whole community to which the individual belongs. It is through taking the attitude of the generalized other that individuals are able to see themselves as others do and to understand the attitudes of others towards the various aspects of social life.

The development of the self

The self develops or evolves through understanding the attitude and role of others. This development occurs through stages. Initially a young child adopts the role of particular individuals, for example through playing at being mummy, teacher, doctor and so on, and then gradually adopts the attitude of the whole community or society. The move from adopting individual to adopting general attitudes involves a change from copying behaviour to understanding behaviour. This development is exemplified in the change in a young child's reaction from 'Mummy says no' to 'One does not do this', where the child is relating to the generalized other.

Mead's theory of the development of self lays great stress on the individual's ability to interpret the behaviour of others. During social interaction the individual learns which behaviour is appropriate to particular situations. With experience the individual is able to generalize from specific instances and decide which types of behaviour are appropriate. Part of the process of socialization involves becoming aware of which particular role is applicable to a particular situation. So Mead regards the self as being made up of a series of roles, each of which relates to the social group of which the individual is a part. For a fully developed self, self-consciousness is necessary and is the core of the process of self-development.

Stop and think

- List the different roles you play during the course of one day.
- Do any of these roles conflict with one another?
- If so, how is this conflict resolved?

All the world's a stage: the dramaturgical approach of Erving Goffman

Our discussion of the development of self looked at the ways in which individuals understand and adopt the role of others. The notion that in everyday life

A closer look

Erving Goffman (1922–82)

The view of the 'world as a stage', with individuals performing and acting for their audiences in everyday life, has been particularly associated with the work of Goffman. Goffman wrote a number of widely read and influential books between 1956, the publication of *The Presentation of Self in Everyday Life*, and 1981, when *Forms of Talk*, his last book, was published. In this discussion we shall use Goffman's work, and particularly *The Presentation of Self in Everyday Life* and *Relations in Public* (1971), as a specific illustration of this interactionist approach. Goffman was primarily an observer of social interaction who 'possessed an extraordinary ability to appreciate the subtle importance of apparently insignificant aspects of everyday conduct' (Manning 1992). He argued that individual behaviour follows intricate patterns; in our everyday lives we follow a set of implicit instructions that influence and determine this behaviour.

individuals play roles, negotiate situations and to a certain extent are forced to be 'actors' is the basis of the dramaturgical approach developed by Erving Goffman.

Goffman's work

Goffman saw social encounters and interaction in theatrical terms, with his earlier work concentrating on how people present themselves and their activities to others. Using the theatre analogy, he talked about individuals' behaviour being 'performances' put on for audiences, with different parts or roles played on different occasions. As we mentioned earlier, all of us have many different roles, with different expectations attached to them. Each of you may have a role as a student, where you are expected to sit in classes, reasonably quietly, look interested and do the work set; but you will also have many different roles that will involve you acting in quite different ways – as brother or sister, friend or worker, for instance. Goffman's work provides many examples of how we play different roles and try to create different impressions for others. Bearing in mind that Goffman's research was undertaken in the late 1950s, the following example illustrates female students acting dumb to avoid creating the 'wrong' impression:

> **American college girls did, and no doubt do, play down their intelligence, skill, and determinativeness when in the presence of datable boys . . . These performers are reported to allow their boyfriends to explain things to them tediously that they already know; they conceal proficiency in mathematics from their less able consorts; they lose ping-pong games just before the ending:**
>
> > **'One of the nicest techniques is to spell long words incorrectly once in a while. My boyfriend seems to get a great kick out of it and writes back, "Honey you certainly don't know how to spell." '**
>
> **Through all of this the natural superiority of the male is demonstrated and the weaker role of the female affirmed.**
>
> (Goffman 1969: 48)

As well as playing roles and creating impressions, Goffman highlighted other ways in which everyday behaviour can be compared to a theatrical performance. There is often a division into a back region, where a performance is prepared, and a front region, where it is presented. As the audience in a theatre does not see backstage, so access to certain aspects of everyday behaviour is controlled, to prevent outsiders seeing a performance that is not intended for them. Backstage is private, and it can be embarrassing if outsiders gain access to it; in hotels and cafés, for example, the differences between the front regions and back regions can be dramatic, and customers might be disappointed, or horrified, if they saw backstage. Also, the communication that occurs front and backstage can be quite different: customers who may be treated very respectfully to their faces may be caricatured, ridiculed or cursed as soon as they have gone.

When interacting with others, most people want those others to reach a particular interpretation of their actions. It is possible to use dress, language, gestures and so on to organize and influence how others interpret behaviour and to ensure that they arrive at the desired interpretation. Although the police officer, business person or skinhead might make no apparent attempt to communicate with people who pass them on the street, they are creating an impression that will influence how others think about them (Figure 2.4).

Figure 2.4 A businessman and a skinhead: impression management at work and the outside world
Photodisc; AP Photo/Markus Schreiber

As a rule individuals will try to control or guide the impressions that others form of them, and there are common techniques that can be used to create and sustain these impressions. A fundamental point that underlies all social interaction is that when one individual interacts with others the person will want to discover as much about the situation as possible. To do that it is necessary to know as much as possible about others. Of course, such information is not usually available (we do not know the likes, dislikes, background and so on of everyone we interact with). So in the absence of this knowledge we have to make guesses or predictions about others.

The importance of giving a convincing impression to others, and the obligation to live up to that impression, often forces people to act a role. What people think of one another is dependent on the impression given (as a certain type of person), and this impression can be disrupted if others acquire information that they are not meant to have – as the regular revelations of scandals in the private lives of public figures demonstrate.

Stop and think

- What factors influence the first impressions you have of others?
- How can these first impressions be either supported or altered as you acquire more information?
- It is quite easy to think of examples from our own lives of instances where the 'wrong' person has seen or heard something that we would rather have kept hidden from them. Give examples of aspects of your own behaviour that you try to keep 'backstage' from others. What might happen if such behaviour were to exposed 'frontstage'?

Goffman was aware of the limitations of the theatrical analogy. In his later work he acknowledged the differences between face-to-face interaction in social life and on the stage. When watching a play, the audience generally likes to see a complete performance and to hear all the lines of the actors, whereas in daily life this is often not the case, with interruptions a normal part of social interaction. However, while not offering a complete account of everyday life, the dramaturgical analogy does contribute to our understanding and analysis of aspects of everyday life. It is clear in our interaction with others that we play roles and display great skill in creating and managing impressions.

Normal appearances

Goffman applied the dramaturgical perspective on social interaction to how individuals behave in public, looking in particular at the expectations people hold of what is normal and acceptable behaviour. We have particular ideas about what is right and wrong. Goffman cites a story from the *New York Times* to illustrate this point.

> **A hit-and-run driver fooled several witnesses who saw him hit another automobile. The driver got out of his car after an accident, went to the damaged car and left this note: 'I have just hit your car. People are watching me. They think I'm leaving my name. But I'm not.'**
>
> **The note was signed, 'the wrecker'.**
>
> (Goffman 1971: 312)

This example illustrates the point that when people sense things are normal they will act in a normal manner. Acting normally or naturally is seen by Goffman as a key element in successful impression management. Indeed, it is relatively easy to 'con' people because of the expectations that are held as to what is normal behaviour. This is not to say that it is morally a good or decent thing to do, but that it is often much easier than we initially think to fabricate lies and to make them seem natural.

Perhaps the best examples of the use, or maybe misuse, of normal appearances and expectations occur in the context of criminal behaviour. Criminals have regularly used normal appearances to deceive.

> **Tokyo – The bandit, about 22 years old, wearing the white helmet and black leather jacket of a traffic officer, rode a stolen motorbike up to a bank car carrying bonus money for employees of the Toshiba Electric Co., 20 miles west of Tokyo. He told the unarmed bank men, from the Nippon Trust and Banking Co., that he had information that dynamite had been planted in the car. When the four got out, the bandit got in and drove away with the car and three metal boxes full of unrecorded yen banknotes worth $816,667.**

> **'He looked just like a policeman,' said Eiji Nakad, the driver of the auto. 'He said he had instructions from Koganei Police Station.'**
>
> (Goffman 1971: 360)

Ethnomethodology and the rules of everyday life

The term 'ethnomethodology' means 'people's methods' and was used by Harold Garfinkel (1967) to describe a theoretical branch of sociology that he developed. Garfinkel felt that conventional sociology took social order for granted and assumed that the everyday social world we inhabit was a structured one. Ethnomethodology focuses on how people construct their social world; it investigates the background knowledge and assumptions that people hold and how they help to create and re-create social order. As with other interpretative approaches, there is an emphasis on how people give meanings to and interpret behaviour. However, ethnomethodology is concerned particularly with the processes by which this occurs, and specifically with the methods used by people to communicate with one another.

The importance of the meanings that we give to our actions can be illustrated clearly if we suspend the 'rules' of everyday life. Most of the time we, as individuals, live in a world that is taken for granted; we do not question what goes on. We do not think about the rules underlying everyday actions until something happens to interrupt the routine. During a college or school day it is a reasonably safe bet that nothing will happen to astound us. There is the possibility of a surprise – the building may catch fire, or we might develop a passionate hatred or love for someone we meet. However, we all accept that what is going on is a routine, called college or school education. If this routine were not the case, we would not get much done as we would constantly be being surprised by astounding happenings. Furthermore, even if a definite attempt were made to try something different, this might soon become routine too. If a teacher went into the classroom and stood on a desk to teach, this would soon become routine if done regularly: there would be a change from 'Look what she's doing' to 'There she goes again'.

In focusing on how people go about constructing their social world, one of the key questions that

Case study

Rule-governed behaviour: Garfinkel's experiments

Various experiments have been carried out by interpretativist sociologists to demonstrate how rule-governed our everyday behaviour is. Garfinkel (1967) organized a number of experiments that involved the disruption of everyday life. In one case he asked a group of his students to take part in a new type of counselling. They were to put questions to an 'expert counsellor', who was to help them and give advice, but on the understanding that he would answer their questions only with a 'yes' or 'no' and no more. The 'counsellor' was, in fact, told to answer the questions by reading from a random list of 'yes's' and 'no's' that he had in front of him, paying no attention to the particular questions asked. Although the questions the students asked were meaningful, the answers given by the 'counsellor' were arbitrary and unrelated to the questions. However, because the students believed the answers came from an expert, they imposed meanings and relevance on them. Indeed, when asked by Garfinkel, the majority of the students said they felt the advice had been helpful. Garfinkel argued that this demonstrated how individuals construct meaning from chaos because of a need to fit things into underlying and understood patterns.

Questions

1. What rules and routines do you follow in everyday activities such as (a) getting up; (b) eating; and (c) travelling?
2. How do you feel when you are forced to change your regular routines?

Garfinkel considered was that of how people decide whether something is real or not, how they decide 'what really happened'. In some of his early research, Garfinkel studied how jurors made decisions about a defendant's guilt or innocence. This decision-making necessitated jurors having to decide and act in a legal manner while not being trained lawyers, having to understand psychological motivations of people while not being psychologists, and so on. Similarly, in everyday life, decisions have to be made on a regular basis: we have to decide between fact and fiction, between the real and imagined, between right and wrong answers. Garfinkel's ethnomethodological approach involves examining the ways in which people go about responding to such questions or dilemmas and how these responses act as a basis for deciding what to do next. This detailed examination of how people go about defining and deciding on social reality in everyday situations offers a way of studying how daily life is organized.

The ethnomethodological focus on interpersonal communication and relationships has been criticized for ignoring the importance and complexity of social systems and the ways in which social factors constrain behaviour. Indeed, it could be accused of denying the importance of real phenomena that clearly affect the face-to-face interactions studied by ethnomethodologists. As an illustration of this criticism, Cuff *et al.* (1998) comment that although ethnomethodology might be able to study communication among a group of software engineers meeting to discuss a software project, it would not be able to explain why software engineering had grown so phenomenally in the contemporary world. In other words, its analysis would not be informed by the broader picture. In defence, ethnomethodologists would see the criticism that they reject the wider social context as merely an attack on ethnomethodology for not being like other, conventional, sociology. However, as Cuff and colleagues say, 'the charge of rejecting the wider context refuses to go away' (1998: 177).

Feminist theories

Feminist theory and feminist sociological research have developed significantly since the 1960s in what has been described as a 'second wave' of feminism; the first wave is generally taken to refer to feminist struggles for the vote in the late nineteenth and early twentieth centuries. Feminism has a rich history: the breadth of ideas and theory can be only touched on in this introductory section.

Feminist sociologists have produced an extensive critique of conventional sociological theory. They have argued that sociological theories have been written from a male perspective, which has meant that women's experiences have been marginalized. Not only have feminist theorists criticized male-centred theory but they have also written new theories of society that place women's experiences centrally and attempt to explain divisions between men and women in society.

It is important to outline briefly feminist criticisms of the founders of sociology. A key problem with their work is that the founders either paid little or no attention to the issues of women's subordination or treated this as normal. Durkheim and Weber assumed that it was natural for women to be located in the private sphere of the home and men to be active in the public sphere of paid work. Both associated women with nature, biology and emotion and men with reason, culture and rationality. They treated the sexual division of labour and women's subordinate position within it as natural and inevitable (Sydie 1987). Weber's and Durkheim's analyses of social relations between men and women were shaped by assumptions that there were fundamental biological differences between women and men that suited the two sexes to distinctively different social roles. Sydie argues that, for Durkheim and Weber:

> **This belief in the significance of biological difference means that the hierarchies of power in society, which relegate women collectively to a subordinate status to men, are taken as givens that do not require sociological analysis.**
>
> (Sydie 1987)

This sort of biological approach to gender relations has been identified as problematic by many feminists.

Although Marx acknowledged inequalities between men and women, he failed to treat gender as a crucial factor that shapes social experiences. His work focused on economic class relations and the exploitation of the working class, very much marginalizing gender relations and questions concerning the oppression of women. His theories were gender-blind: the working class were treated as an undifferentiated mass, yet much of his work was concerned with male members of the

Figure 2.5 Feminist cartoon
Cartoon by Angela Martin

proletariat. This failure to treat gender as a crucial determining factor of our social experiences has been a fundamental weakness of much sociological theory, according to feminist theorists (Maynard 1990). Many feminists have formulated theories that place the question of women's subordination and gender relations much more centrally.

Stop and think

- Durkheim, Marx and Weber are sometimes referred to as the 'founding fathers' of sociology. What does this suggest about the origins and development of the subject?
- Why are there no 'founding mothers' of sociology?

When we examine feminism it becomes clear that there are many different tendencies within feminism and that there is no one all-encompassing definition of feminism. Indeed, it is more appropriate to talk about feminisms than feminism (Humm 1992). Contrary to many common-sense interpretations of feminism, feminists do not always agree on ways in which we can explain gender differences and women's subordination.

Stop and think

- What characteristics do you associate with feminists and feminism?
- Do you consider them positive or negative characteristics?
- Consider where you have got these views about feminism from.
- (After reading this section come back to these questions and consider whether any of your assumptions have changed.)

We shall outline here five of the different strands of feminism: liberal feminism, radical feminism, Marxist/socialist feminism, black feminism and postmodern feminism. Although any attempt at classification is likely to be incomplete and somewhat arbitrary, this approach provides a useful way of introducing feminist theorizing. However, it is important to note that some feminists cannot be assigned conveniently to a particular category, not all feminism is encompassed, and nor do these strands represent entirely distinct feminisms. The five types of feminism introduced here represent key tendencies, but there are many other feminist perspectives – ecofeminism and psychoanalytical feminism are just two examples. Feminism is a diverse, constantly evolving body of thought.

Liberal feminism

Liberal feminism has its roots in the liberal tradition of the Enlightenment, which stressed the principles of justice, rationality, citizenship, human rights, equality and democracy. The treatment of women in society violates many of these values. From the days of Mary Wollstonecraft and the publication in 1792 of her seminal book *A Vindication of the Rights of Woman*, liberal feminists have stressed that, as rational beings, women should be entitled to full personhood and hence have the same legal, political, social and economic rights and opportunities as men. They recognize that women are on occasion unfairly discriminated against on the basis of their sex. Much of this discrimination is informal and based on custom, the product of sexist assumptions and prejudices that still endure in our culture and are the product of gender role conditioning. Liberal feminists advocate political action and reform, favouring educational strategies and formal and legislative changes in order to provide women with opportunities and challenge stereotypes and prejudices. Yet many have recognized that formal equality is not enough and have supported legislation that outlaws sex discrimination against women and men.

Some contemporary liberal feminists believe that if the state is to enforce equal rights and ensure equal opportunities, then it must make it economically possible for women to exercise these rights. Hence, the state should fund such things as child-care facilities and refuges for women who have experienced violence from their partners. Liberal feminists have historically put an emphasis on incorporating women into the mainstream, giving women the right to equal opportunities in the public sphere of education and employment. Some have suggested that having women in positions of power and influence will in itself have a knock-on effect, with such women in high-status positions acting as role models for others and taking account of women's interests in the formulation of policy.

Betty Friedan's influential liberal feminist text *The Feminine Mystique* was published in 1963. Friedan argued that North American women had been offered fulfilment through motherhood and wifehood, only to find dissatisfaction: this was the feminine mystique. She criticized this notion that women should only be home-based carers and encouraged women to engage in paid work outside the home to provide more economic power and personal fulfilment. However, she has been criticized for not addressing how difficult it would be for women to combine motherhood and a career without challenging the notion of women as primary carers and considering the need for men to change. Black feminists pointed out that her theory was ethnocentric, i.e. based on the experiences of a particular ethnic group, in this case white middle-class women. Black women have historically had to work in the labour market and this has not brought them liberation.

Liberal feminists have been criticized for a range of reasons, many linked to what other feminists see as strategies that merely operate within the existing system rather than fundamentally changing social relations. While liberal feminism may bring opportunities and rewards for a few token women, it brings little fundamental change in the lives of the large majority of women; despite some reform, men still hold the majority of positions of power (Bryson 1992). Others argue that liberal feminism brings opportunities for women on men's terms, that women working within the status quo merely endorse the hierarchical and competitive structures of capitalism and patriarchy and indeed theoretically does not acknowledge these social relations.

Some feminists argue that liberal feminism encourages women to be male clones, i.e. successful women adopt 'male' strategies and values. It has been suggested, for example, that Margaret Thatcher became very successful because she conducted her politics in the traditional masculine style and that she did little to improve the position of women in British society during her years as prime minister. These concerns reflect a debate within feminism concerning whether women should be struggling for equality with men, which suggests they are the same as men, or recognize the differences between women and men (whether innate or socially constructed) and attempt to shape societies based on 'feminine' values and strategies, which some feminists argue would create a more egalitarian, less competitive and less destructive world order.

Stop and think

- How easy is it to think of women who have been successful in traditionally male-dominated areas such as business or politics?
- Would you describe the successful women you can think of as having adopted 'male' strategies and values?

Radical feminism

Contemporary radical feminism is associated with the women's liberation movement of the 1960s, and yet although many of the ideas expressed by radical feminists were not new, in this period they began to be 'developed systematically as a self-conscious theory' (Bryson 1992). Some women within the movement argued that women's oppression was deeply rooted and that inequality between men and women was a primary source of oppression. This they felt was not being acknowledged in many existing social and political analyses and organizations, which they identified as androcentric (male-centred). As a result, the struggle for women's liberation was being marginalized and a new approach that prioritized women's oppression was needed. Radical feminists argued that gender inequalities

A closer look

Patriarchy

Patriarchy is basically used to describe a structural system of male domination. It encapsulates the mechanisms, ideologies and social structures that have enabled men historically to gain and maintain their dominance and control over women. Stacey (1993) points out that radical feminists have found patriarchy to be useful theoretically as 'it has given some conceptual form to the nature of male domination in society' and has enabled radical feminists to describe 'how and why women are oppressed'.

Mies (1986) notes that it has provided a concept that captures the totality of women's oppression. Men dominate women in every sphere of life, and all relationships between men and women are institutionalized relationships of power; this includes 'private', personal relationships, hence the feminists' slogan 'the personal is political'. Patriarchy is trans-historical, cross-cultural and universal; no area of society is free from male domination. Thus, radical feminists are concerned to reveal how male power is exercised in all spheres of life and how patriarchy emerged historically.

are a central and primary form of social inequality and constructed theories that acknowledged this. Radical feminists explain gender inequalities and women's subordination as the outcome of an autonomous system of *patriarchy*.

Kate Millett's *Sexual Politics* (1970) has been identified as an important radical feminist text because it introduced the concept of patriarchy and contains many typical radical feminist concerns. Millett described all societies as patriarchal; men dominate and women are subordinate, hence all relations between men and women are political relations of power. Patriarchy is maintained via a process of sex role socialization, which takes place in the male-headed family. The family is a patriarchal unit that reflects the rule of men in other areas of society. Millett documents how education, religion and literature reinforce the notion of female subordination and male superiority. She also argued that a whole range of strategies were utilized to control women if they did not conform; these included physical and sexual violence. Similar concerns are evident in the work of other radical feminists.

Radical feminism now constitutes a large and diverse body of thought, with radical feminists taking different positions on a range of issues. Abbott and Wallace (1990) identify three key issues of disagreement within radical feminism: the extent to which gender differences are the product of actual biological differences or are socially constructed; the relationship between feminist politics and personal sexual conduct; and the sort of political strategies that should be adopted to bring about change. An examination of the ideas of specific radical feminist theorists highlights these differences.

Unlike Millett, who stated that the differences between men and women are the product of socialization, the work of some radical feminists has been identified as proposing a biological basis for some differences between women and men. Rich (1977) argues that women's mothering capacity is at the core of men's oppression of women. Men are fearful of women's power to create life, and men sense that women's reproductive powers are somehow mysterious and uncontrollable. Rich and others have contended that, as a result, men have attempted to control women and even to control reproduction and birth itself. Feminists taking such a position are wary of developments in reproductive technology, which are seen as a means of enabling further male control of reproduction (O'Brien 1981). Rich (1977) stresses that motherhood itself is not inherently oppressive for women but has become oppressive under patriarchy. She celebrates female biology and the potential for motherhood and argues this is an important source of power that women should reclaim. She goes on to suggest that woman-centred cultures and societies in which children are raised in line with feminist values of care and nurture can provide the basis for an alternative non-patriarchal society. For other radical feminists, this biological approach to gender differences is unacceptable and reinforces traditional divisions and roles.

Stop and think

> ➤ Some people who have fought for sexual equality or whose beliefs overlap with feminism have refused to be labelled as feminists. What might be their reasons for doing so?

Many feminists accept that women have had less power in sexual relationships than men, but some radical feminists such as Catherine MacKinnon identify sexuality as central to patriarchy. Sexual relations are seen not simply as a reflection of broader inequalities but as a source of power which men can exert over women. As MacKinnon (1982) puts it, 'Sexuality is the primary source of male power.'

For MacKinnon, sexuality is male-defined: in sexual relationships with men, women are powerless and are merely objects to be used for male sexual pleasure. Heterosexual sex is based on relations of dominance and submission. Some radical lesbian feminists such as Jeffreys also place sexuality at the heart of women's oppression, specifically heterosexuality. According to Jeffreys, the construction of heterosexuality as normal and natural and all other sexualities as deviant is the organizing principle of social relations of male supremacy; women are pressured into heterosexuality and this serves the interests of patriarchy:

> **Without heterosexuality it would be difficult for individual men to extract unpaid sexual, reproductive, economic, domestic and emotional servicing from women.**
>
> (Jeffreys 1994: 23)

A whole range of radical feminists have identified violence, both physical and sexual, as a key source of male control over women (Radford *et al.* 1995). The identification of violence against women as a political issue and social problem has been seen as an important achievement of feminism and has been associated particularly with radical feminism; Brownmiller (1976) argued that the act of rape lies at the origins of men's oppression of women. Although not all radical feminists would identify violence as the original source of women's subordination, many have seen it as an important mechanism for maintaining the subordination of women (Kelly 1988). This violence is an expression of power and hatred that controls, humiliates, objectifies and disempowers women.

This brief discussion shows that radical feminists' ideas have generated much debate and criticism from feminists and non-feminists alike. Some non-feminists have identified radical feminism as a misguided political ideology, which, by identifying men as oppressors and women as exploited, has actually fuelled conflict between the sexes (Lyndon 1992). The concept of patriarchy has been identified as a static and rigid category that does not allow for changing and varied gender relations across cultures and across history (Rowbotham 1982). A key criticism of radical feminism is that it has tended to lump women together as a universal group; this is problematic because it masks women's 'varied and complex social reality' (hooks 1984). It ignores and denies the different experiences between women, differences based on factors such as class, race, nationality, age and sexual identity. The emphasis on women as a group with shared experiences and common interests has been identified as particularly problematic by black feminists, who have pointed out that this ignores the way in which racism has impacted on the lives of black women, creating different experiences for black and white women. They also stress that women exploit and oppress other women and that white women have often been in positions of dominance in relation to black women.

Black feminists have stressed that radical feminists have tended to treat all men as equally powerful, yet in systems such as slavery and imperialism black men have been denied positions in the white male hierarchy; patriarchy is racially demarcated (Murphy and Livingstone 1985). Hence, it is difficult to claim that black male dominance over women always exists in the same forms as white male dominance. Black feminists have pointed out that black women have many common interests with black men: the strategies of separatism and the need to organize separately from men, proposed by some radical feminists, have been unacceptable because of the common struggle against racism that they share with black men. The identification within radical feminism of gender as the key source of inequality in society has been rejected by many. Marxist feminists, for instance, argue that gender inequalities are related to economic class relations.

Marxist/socialist feminism

Marxist feminists have attempted to develop Marxist concepts to understand the subordination of women in capitalist societies. They have argued that it is essential to recognize that the oppression of women is inextricably linked to the capitalist order and that, although Marxist analyses of society may have marginalized women, they provide insights into the structure of capitalist society and the position of women within it.

Marxist feminism has been criticized by feminists within and outside the socialist tradition. In historical terms, Marxist feminism has been faulted for failing to account for the oppression of women before capitalism. It has also been pointed out that in revolutionary class struggles and supposedly socialist societies women have often found themselves occupying a secondary position, with relations between men and women fundamentally unchanged. Many individual socialist women have found a contradiction between socialist values of equality, solidarity and anti-exploitation and the treatment they receive from socialist men (Phillips 1987). Some socialist women have therefore questioned the adequacy of Marxism for explaining women's subordination, as it fails to acknowledge men's role in women's subordination and emphasizes economic class relations at the expense of gender relations. Yet these feminists have also rejected radical feminism as it does not place centrally economic relations of capitalism.

Some feminists working in the socialist tradition began to place greater emphasis on patriarchal gender relations in their theoretical analysis. These have been referred to as 'socialist feminists' to indicate a shift away from orthodox Marxism. Michelle Barrett's *Women's Oppression Today* (1980) paid attention not only to the economic but also to the ideological conditions of women's oppression. She argued that women's oppression is the product of not only the economic needs of capitalism but also patriarchal gender ideology, which existed before capitalism. The family–household system is crucial to women's oppression. This system controls women's access to paid labour by handicapping them as the reproducers of children and sexual objects for male pleasure. First, the family–household structure consists of a *social* structure, the household, which consists of a number of usually biologically related people who depend on the wages of adult members, primarily a husband or father, and also the unpaid labour of a wife and mother. Second, it consists of the *ideology* of the family, which defines family life as naturally organized in the above way with a male breadwinner and financially dependent wife and children. So it defines the nuclear family and sexual

A closer look

Marxist feminism

Many Marxist feminists have focused on how the economic class relations of capitalism produce women's continued subordination. They have argued that under capitalism a key cause of women's oppression is the sexual division of labour, which shapes gender relations in a way that reinforces the capitalist relations of production. In this sexual division of labour men are defined as breadwinners and women have been defined as primarily domestic labourers and excluded from wage labour. They have been allocated an exploitative and restrictive role in the household reproducing the relations of production. The traditional nuclear family and the role of women's domestic labour has been a central focus of the Marxist feminist position. Women's domestic and reproductive labour has been identified as a very cheap way of reproducing and maintaining the working class and reproducing the next generation of workers. The value of this labour to capitalism was the subject of the domestic labour debate in the late 1970s. The family was seen as a useful means of social control, disciplining male workers, who must support their dependants, initiating children into restrictive gender roles and also acting as a useful unit of consumption. In terms of gaining liberation, Marxist feminists stressed the need to struggle for a communist society in which the social relations of the labour market and the family would be revolutionized, and child care and domestic labour would be socialized and the responsibility of the state. They also emphasized the need for women to enter productive labour and struggle alongside male workers. Marxist feminists have been very active in examining the exploitation of women in paid work.

division of labour as natural. Within this ideology are notions about 'natural' masculinity and femininity, while sexuality is defined as naturally heterosexual. With Mary McIntosh in *The Anti-Social Family* (1982), Barrett again emphasized the ideological significance of the family rather than the economic role. Barrett and McIntosh stressed that the ideological construct of the family as a haven not only masked the exploitation of women but also attracted attention away from social problems. They argued that the ideology of the family embodied principles that shore up the economic system – such as selfishness, looking after one's own or pursuing private property as opposed to altruism and community.

Some feminists went further, arguing that women's subordination is the outcome of two systems, patriarchy and capitalism. In *Patriarchy at Work* (1986), Walby outlined a range of struggles between male workers and capitalists to illustrate these patterns of conflict and compromise. In contemporary society women are excluded from certain areas of the labour market, which ensures men maintain economic and social privileges in the labour market and the household. Yet at the same time capitalism can utilize female labour in certain sectors of the labour market and pay lower wages by utilizing ideological notions of the male breadwinner, the secondary role of the female worker and women's suitability for certain types of work. Walby developed these ideas in *Theorizing Patriarchy* (1990), where she attempts to develop a theory of patriarchy that not only acknowledges how it interacts with capitalism but also acknowledges that gender and patriarchal relations can change. She also argues that in Western history in the nineteenth and twentieth centuries there have been two major forms of patriarchy. *Private patriarchy* is based on household production, in which a patriarch controls women individually in the household; this control is maintained through the exclusion of women from many aspects of the 'public' world. This reached its peak in the mid-nineteenth century, when violence against women was formally condoned, divorce was difficult to obtain and women were formally excluded from many areas of education and paid work. *Public patriarchy* involves less emphasis on control in the household; patriarchy is maintained through other structures, women can enter public arenas but are subordinated within them. The exploitation of women is performed more collectively: 'Women are no longer restricted to the domestic hearth, but have the whole society in which to roam and be exploited' (Walby 1990).

Most women enter paid work but have lower-paid, lower-status jobs; women have citizenship rights but form only a small percentage of elected representatives; divorce can be obtained, but women remain responsible for children; cultural institutions such as the arts and media allow women's participation but usually in an inferior way. In contemporary British society the public form of patriarchy predominates.

Black feminism

Black feminists have produced criticisms of each of the varying strands of feminism, and indeed have now developed an influential critique of what has been identified as white feminism. The key concerns about much of the theory and research produced by white feminists are that it has been ethnocentric and that it has failed to acknowledge differences between women and specifically the effects of race and racism on women's experiences.

Black feminists have not only criticized white feminists but also proposed new directions for feminist theory. Some black feminists have pointed out that placing black women's experiences centrally, looking at the world from a black woman's standpoint, brings new insights into social relations (Hill-Collins 1990). bell hooks (1984) has noted that the experiences of black women shows that oppression can be resisted, as black women have in very adverse circumstances struggled to survive and resist oppression. Feminists need to focus these strategies and resistances to counter the tendency to talk about women as victims and to develop alternative forms of empowerment. Another thing that is learned about oppression from the experience of black women is that it is complex. Many black feminists have stressed that race cannot be simply added on to existing feminist approaches: this would be mere tokenism (Bhavnani 1993). They have rejected what have been called additive approaches, which simply describe black women as being exposed to a triple oppression of race, class and gender. This approach suggests that you can add together these three factors to end up with the sum of black women's oppression: i.e. race + class + gender = black women's oppression. Yet black feminists argue that these factors interact to produce not necessarily a worse experience for black women but a qualitatively different experience. We can take women's experiences of contraception and abortion to illustrate this argument. In the 1970s and 1980s a key concern of white feminists around these issues was that white women's access to contraception and abortion had been restricted; struggles were focused on retaining legal access to abortion and increasing access to contraception and abortion. Yet black feminists pointed out that black women in Britain did not find it harder to get contraception and abortion but that they did experience concerted attempts to get their fertility restricted. They were more likely than white women to be encouraged to have abortions and also more likely to be offered forms of contraception with possible damaging side effects, such as the injectable contraceptive Depo-Provera™. This black feminist critique has led to the development of a broader reproductive rights movement that emphasizes the rights of women to have or not have children, which has relevance to all women.

Black feminists have stressed that any theoretical model that deals adequately with the experience of all women must recognize and explore the *interlocking* nature of class, race and gender:

> **the realities of our daily lives make it imperative for us to consider the simultaneous nature of our oppression and exploitation. Only a synthesis of class, race, gender and sexuality can lead us forward, as these form the matrix of black women's oppression.**
>
> (Amos and Parmar 1984)

In the same vein, some black feminists have pointed out that it is impossible to list a universal hierarchy of oppressions or to list which set of social relations is the most important and most oppressive. bell hooks (1984) makes reference to her own experience to make this point:

> **I am often asked whether being black is more important than being a woman . . . all such questions are rooted in competitive either/or thinking, the belief that the self is formed in opposition to an other. Most people are socialized to think in terms of opposition rather than compatibility.**
>
> (hooks 1984: 29)

So she warns against theories that prioritize one form of oppression. Black feminists have proposed theories that begin to explore the *interconnectedness* of all forms of oppression, i.e. examine multiple systems of oppression.

Similarly, Hill-Collins (1990) proposes a theoretical model that she refers to as a matrix of oppression, which incorporates all relations of domination and subordination. Within this matrix race, class and gender must be viewed as axes that form part of a complex matrix that has other dimensions such as age, religion and sexual orientation. Feminism needs to explore the connections and interactions between women's oppression and other forms of oppression. In this model women's oppression is part of a more general system of domination; the liberation of women can be achieved only as part of a broader strategy that challenges all relations of domination and subordination. Similar issues have been raised by non-Western feminists, who have pointed out that the dominant voices of feminism have been white Western women, hence the experiences and voices of women in the developing world have been marginalized within feminism. They have stressed that Western feminism needs to incorporate the international relations of inequality if it is to be relevant to the lives of women in non-Western countries and again stressed the need to explore the interaction of gender relations with other social relations such as relations of colonialism (Mohanty *et al.* 1991).

Postmodern feminism

In recent years, post-structuralism and postmodernism have had a significant impact on sociological theory, including feminist theory. Within feminism their influence has led to a questioning of what have been seen as some of the fundamental concepts of second-wave feminist theory and also to the creation of new feminist approaches and ideas. A more general introduction to post-structuralism and postmodernism is provided later in this chapter (pp. 96–105).

If you are new to postmodernism, do not worry if you find it difficult: like many theoretical tendencies it has its own language. You will not be alone in struggling with postmodernism, as the following comment from Caroline Ramazanoglu, a renowned feminist theorist, indicates:

> **I arrived late at a women's studies meeting towards the end of the annual conference of the British Sociological Association a few years ago, to find some women expressing indignation at finding session after session of the conference dominated by men talking in terms of postmodernism. These women felt silenced, intimidated, excluded, put down and angry. They did not know whether 'postmodernism' was something they should take seriously, because they could not engage with a debate which made issues inaccessible to them.**
>
> (Ramazanoglu 1993: 1)

It is not unusual to hear people saying that they do not understand postmodernism or that they find it elitist and exclusionary. For these reasons, some feminists have been wary of postmodernism, concerned that it has entrenched academic elitism and hence that it replicates the worst elements of masculinist social theory.

However, although some feminists have rejected postmodernism (Klein and Bell 1996), others have embraced it positively (Nicholson 1990) and some argue for the need to engage with it selectively and critically (Ramazanoglu 1993; McLaughlin 1997). Some commentators have noted that feminism and postmodernism share certain concerns (Assiter 1996; McLaughlin 1997). For instance, both have developed new forms of social criticism and have challenged 'universal' knowledge claims. In the 1970s and early 1980s, a number of feminists argued that many of the assertions that were put forward as universally true in social theory were only true for men; they were seen as examples of androcentric knowledge.

Postmodernism is a body of thought that has argued that it is misleading to make universal claims about the world. Yet postmodern feminists have argued that much feminist theory has in its own work replicated the universalizing assumptions that it criticized male-centred theory for producing. Hence, postmodern feminism has produced a criticism of what have been called 'universalizing' feminisms (Flax 1990; Nicholson and Fraser 1990). It is argued that much of feminism has been part of grand theorizing, attempting to identify overarching structures that create gender inequality and women's subordination. A key proposition of postmodernism is that it is misguided to search for grand theories, to find one truth or explanation about complex social relations. Such totalizing theories or 'meta-narratives' are rejected within postmodern thought.

Problems with the category 'woman'

A number of feminists influenced by postmodernism have expressed scepticism about the category 'woman' and the concept of gender as it has been used by many feminists. In her book *Gender Trouble*, Judith Butler (1990) outlined the problems she identified with the category 'woman'. As other postmodern feminists have stressed, she proposed that there is no fixed identity of woman, a notion that has often been assumed in feminist theory and activism. She points out that the main subject of feminist theory, and this is the case for many of the strands of feminism outlined in this chapter, has been that of the category 'woman'. The goals of feminism have been concerned with making changes for the social group 'women'; feminist theory and activism have been about representing women and speaking on their behalf.

The problem with this, for Butler and others who share her theoretical analysis, is that a fixed identity of women does not actually exist. This has been a key proposition of postmodern feminism:

> **Feminism has played an important role in showing that there are not now and never have been any generic 'men' at all – only gendered men and women. Once essential and universal man dissolves, so does his hidden companion, woman. We have instead myriads of women living in elaborate historical complexes of class, race and culture.**
>
> (Harding 1987)

Some writers argue that this means that the notion of gender, which has been so important in feminist theory, is meaningless: '[It] is so thoroughly fragmented by race, class, historical particularity and individual difference, as to self-destruct as an analytical category' (Nicholson and Fraser 1990).

Butler argues that feminism has itself had a role in constructing the category of woman and has implicitly set women up as 'different' from men. In doing so it has constructed gender difference rather than challenged it. To talk about women as a category assumes that women share something, that they are 'all the same' and also that they are separate from men. For Butler, this is not far from the conceptualization of gender relations that feminism set out to challenge. She sets out to understand how the division between the sexes has come about and to deconstruct the idea that gender is an essential or indispensable category. The postmodern concerns that are visible in her work include the refusal to accept fixed categories or identities.

Butler's work demonstrates another central postmodern claim: that the individual self is a fiction. Within postmodernism and postmodern feminism the self or subjective identity is understood as an historically conditional construct. Butler explores how gender and gender identity are constructed and describes gender as 'performative, a masquerade, a complex role performance' (Butler 1993). Gender is not simply acted out in a robot-like manner but can involve resistance and mimicry. Like many postmodern feminists she demonstrates a preoccupation with exploring the varied ways in which many possible subjectivities are gendered.

Stop and think

- What sort of analysis might each of the five strands of feminism provide for (a) government policy on single parents; and (b) prostitution?
- Would the different strands of feminism see an increase in the number of women in senior positions and top jobs as a positive step for women?
- In 2008, women in the British army (unlike in the US military, for example) do not actually fight in war situations, although they may be present in other roles on the front line. Do you think women should be entitled to a combatant role? What arguments can you propose for and against women entering combatant positions?

The pornography debate

Theoretical and strategic differences between feminists have manifested themselves in the ongoing debate about pornography. There are two general positions within feminism: the 'anti-pornography' approach and what has been called 'anti-censorship' feminism. A key anti-pornography feminist is North American radical feminist Andrea Dworkin, who has identified pornography as central to patriarchy, describing it as the 'nerve centre of patriarchy' and hence one of the main institutions of male supremacy.

> **At the heart of the female condition is pornography: it is the ideology that is the source of all the rest.**
>
> (Dworkin 1983: 34)

Many anti-pornography feminists share Dworkin's concerns about the effects of pornography. They feel that pornography objectifies women; it constructs an ideology of women as sexual objects to be used by men, hence women are dehumanized within pornography. Some anti-pornography feminists argue that pornography is actual male sexual violence against women. They argue that women used in the making of pornography often suffer actual physical harm and draw on the testimonies of women coerced, harmed or abused in making pornography and women whose lives have been damaged by their partners' use of pornography. They have argued that pornography encourages sexual violence against women. They have drawn on various social and psychological research that indicates the use by sexual offenders of pornography before their assaults and that pornography desensitizes men to rape and makes them more sexually violent. Pornography plays a role in shaping male sexuality and beliefs about female sexuality.

Itzin (1994) contends that it is always difficult to prove causation using scientific evidence but that it is possible to show correlation between two things. She argues that research on pornography shows that it contributes to a sexually violent culture that legitimizes violence against women. So pornography is a violation of women's civil rights that incites sexual hatred. It censors women by presenting them as one-dimensional sexual objects existing only to meet the sexual needs of men. Such representation plays an important role in reproducing sex discrimination and oppression. Anti-pornography feminists have campaigned for legislation that bans or censors pornography or enables women to seek compensation for pornography-related harm. This anti-pornography stance instigated by radical feminists was the dominant position within feminism and still has strong support, but another position has begun to gain ascendancy.

Anti-censorship feminists Elizabeth Wilson and Gillian Rodgerson (1991) contend that pornography merely reflects sexism in wider society; it did not create it. Rubin (1993) suggests that pornography is a modern phenomenon that women's subordination long predates; there are a whole range of social relations that are oppressive to women, and focusing on pornography as Dworkin does marginalizes these. Wilson and Rodgerson argue that feminism needs a broader cultural politics rather than a simple campaign against pornography. They say that pornography is not actual sexual violence; it is merely representational, and a distinction must be made. Rubin (1993) claims that anti-pornography feminists exaggerate the extent of violence depicted in pornography and argues there is a considerable amount of pornography in which women are portrayed as active participants who have their sexual needs met.

Anti-censorship feminists assert that, despite the coercion of some women in the production of pornography, many women who work in the sex industry are not victims but choose to work in the sex industry. Feminists would be better struggling to improve working conditions for sex workers. Furthermore, they contend that the links between pornography and sexual violence are not proven. Many of the studies of the effects of pornography on men are inconclusive; some even show that many men do not express more hostile attitudes to women after viewing pornography (King 1993). They point out that in countries where pornography is widely available sex crimes are no higher than in countries where it is less readily available.

Anti-censorship feminists argue that censorship in any form curtails choice and freedom and is anti-democratic. Campaigning for censorship will only support the moral Right, which opposes sexual freedom and women's liberation. They point out that censorship would be and has been applied first and most strongly against lesbian and gay material rather than the material that feminist campaigners against pornography themselves identify to be most harmful.

This debate to a certain extent is linked to two different analyses of female sexuality. Radical feminists tend to see sexuality as male-centred and male-defined; pornography is a reflection of this male-centred model of sexuality, which shores up patriarchy and controls and disempowers women. Lynne Segal (1994) argues that some feminists have not moved beyond understanding female sexuality in terms of something that is male-defined and connected to sexual violation. In this analysis all women are defined as victims, and this has been reflected in the anti-pornography position. Anti-censorship feminists argue that radical feminism and the radical feminist analysis of pornography focus on women only as sexual victims: women have gained some control over their sexuality and should have the right to the freedom of expression of their sexuality. Segal and Wilson, both socialist feminists, believe that women can be active agents of desire and can actively and willingly participate in a wide range of sexual practices and that some may enjoy the consumption of pornography. Anti-censorship feminists accept that much mainstream pornography is sexist and misrepresents female sexuality, yet they do not see censorship as the strategy to adopt: 'We believe feminism is about choice, about taking control of our lives and our bodies and this must include our sexual choices' (Wilson and Rodgerson 1991: 71).

A proliferation of voices

Clearly feminism is a diverse body of thought. In recent years, because of the arguments of many feminists, particularly black, non-Western and lesbian feminists, there has been an acknowledgement of the diverse experiences that women face. Also the influence of post-structuralism and postmodernism has led some feminists to suggest that, although the concept and experience of being a 'woman' is important in feminist theory and politics, it is misguided to assume one identity and experience and to search for one theory, one truth about women. Indeed, the diversity within feminism can be interpreted as a strength:

> **No one method, form of writing, speaking position, mode of argument can act as a representative model or ideal for feminist theory. Instead of attempting to establish a new theoretical norm, feminist theory seeks a new discursive space, a space where women can write, read and think as women. This space will encourage a proliferation of voices, instead of a hierarchical structuring of them, a plurality of perspectives and interests instead of the monopoly of the one . . . No one form would be privileged as the truth . . . rather knowledges, methods, interpretations can be judged and used according to their appropriateness to a given context, a specific strategy and particular effects.**
>
> (Gross 1992: 368)

A closer look

Waves of feminism

Feminism may be deemed by the British Sociological Association (BSA) (www.britsoc.co.uk) to be the greatest social force of the twentieth century, but it can be traced back to earlier times: in 1792 Mary Wollstonecraft published her treatise *A Vindication of the Rights of Woman*; the first women's rights convention was held at Seneca Falls, USA, in 1848 and by the 1860s British philosopher John Stuart Mill was both publishing and campaigning for women's rights, including presenting a bill to Parliament.

However, it has become common for feminism to be divided into three waves. These are seen as encompassing different periods of time (see below), seeking different agendas and utilizing different

A closer look *continued*

strategies. As each 'wave' built upon previous achievements and theorizing, it is perhaps more appropriate to think of them as three waves within one high tide. In fact, Imelda Whelehan (1995), among others, has suggested that the Second Wave was actually a continuation of the First Wave, while Drude Dahlerup (1986) refers to the years between the first two waves as a period of boom and bloom, alternating with quiet, but continuing struggle. Further, Third Wave feminism developed as a response to the political backlash towards Second Wave feminism and its limitations.

So what are these three waves? A short review is provided below, but first a 'health warning'. Any summary can only include an essence and some main examples; however, each wave has included thinkers, political activists, women of all social classes and backgrounds, those concerned with health and those concerned with expanding opportunities for women and definitions of femininity.

First Wave

Usually refers to feminist activity beginning in the nineteenth century and continuing into the first few decades of the twentieth century. The term was not in use contemporaneously, but was coined retrospectively after the term 'Second Wave' was in common usage. This First Wave feminism existed across Europe, North America, Australia, New Zealand, India, China, Iran and many more places. In Western societies it focused on issues such as suffrage and women's rights to own property and have control of their children. In addition, specific campaigns such as against the British Contagious Diseases Acts (led by Josephine Butler) with its provisions to intimately inspect any woman suspected of prostitution existed. In the USA, leaders such as Susan B Anthony and Elizabeth Cady Stanton emerged from the anti-slavery movement to work on suffrage. It is commonly understood that this wave ended with the winning of women's suffrage, though as shown some scholars argue that it never really ended but rather formed the base for the next wave.

First Wave organizations in Europe

Germany – 1865 – General German Women's Association.

France – 1866 – Society for the Demand for Women's Rights.

Britain and Sweden – 1867 – establishment of movements for women's suffrage.

Russia – 1860s; Italy – from 1890s – establishment of women's rights movements.

Second Wave

This refers to the feminist thought and activism beginning in the 1960s and lasting into the 1980s. The focus for this wave was on economic equality and ensuring the rights of women to equality of treatment in the workplace and society. This feminism also worked to end discrimination. One slogan, 'the personal is political', represents the Second Wave's focus on not only political but also cultural discrimination. Some major campaign foci for this wave were legal abortion; equal pay; equal opportunities in work and education; and later against male violence.

One critique of the Second Wave is that it holds essentialist notions of femininity that overemphasize white, middle-class Western women's experience. However, by the 1980s many black feminists, such as Audre Lorde, Patricia Hill Collins and bell hooks had shown how racism, class oppression and sexism are all linked, with Alice Walker (1983) developing womanism, which argues that black women experience oppression differently and more intensely than white women. Likewise, developing world feminist thought, developed by theorists from countries in the developing world such as Chandra Talpade Mohanty (1988), criticizes Western feminism for being ethnocentric and not taking cognizance of the experiences of women and the activities of feminisms indigenous to the developing world.

Third Wave

Beginning in the 1990s, this wave embraces post-structuralist ideas and, rather than having a focus on rights and equal opportunities, examines the concepts of sex and gender. In attempts to avoid the 'essentializing' aspects of the previous wave, the Third Wave employs queer theory, transgender politics, post-colonial theory, anti-racism and womanist ideas to

A closer look *continued*

explore gender terms and categories. It has strong roots in the Second Wave's debates and negotiations around the intersections of race and gender, debates that sought to add a new subjectivity to feminist thought. According to the Third Wave Foundation (2006) its definition of feminism 'explicitly connect[s] women's issues to issues of race, heterosexism, class, and other forms of oppression'.

The term was first used (in print) by Rebecca Walker[1] (1992) in an article written for the US magazine *Ms* as a response to a famous sexual harassment case in which a Supreme Court nominee, Clarence Thomas, was exonerated of charges. In this article Walker declared herself as 'not a post-feminism feminist. I am the third-wave'.

Third Wave feminism celebrates women's abilities, allows women to seek to be feminine if they choose, to express themselves politically, culturally, sexually, diversely. However, they also seek to build upon the successes of the Second Wave on issues such as maternity leave, sexual harassment, child care and the media representation of women. It has been criticized for an absence of a single cause, but it must be remembered that, although the First Wave won the vote for women and the Second Wave won equal opportunities, neither of these previous waves was unicausal either.

> It is feminism for those who have grown up with feminism, who may not realize the benefits they enjoy from the struggles of earlier waves but who still wish to build and expand upon them, to deconstruct and reinvent, launched from a culture of consumerism, the Internet, 'zines and punk rock rather than from the Civil Rights and anti-war campaigns of the 1960s.
>
> (Baumgardner and Richards, 2000)

[1] Rebecca Walker is the daughter of Alice Walker and the co-founder (with Catherine Gund, Dawn Martin and Amy Richards) of the Third Wave Foundation.

The Frankfurt School and critical theory

In the 1920s, Georg Lukács and Antonio Gramsci criticized the mechanistic Marxist model of society that had become the dominant interpretation of Marxism after the Soviet Revolution of 1917. The mechanistic model, sometimes referred to as structural Marxism (see p. 60), stressed the determining effect of the economic infrastructure: human action was fashioned by the inevitable laws of economic history. In contrast, this new interpretation, sometimes known as humanist Marxism, emphasized the concepts of alienation and ideology and highlighted the value of human struggle against impersonal systems. Lukács and Gramsci attempted to place the individual back at the centre of the stage and stressed the importance of winning the hearts and minds of people in the political struggle for socialism.

These ideas are linked closely to those of the Frankfurt School, which was established in 1923 to 'criticise and subvert domination in all its forms' (Bottomore 1983: 182) and which developed a critical approach to both capitalism and Soviet communism. Faced with the failure of working-class revolution after the First World War and the rise of fascism in Europe at the end of the 1920s, the Frankfurt School developed a very pessimistic view of society and culture that held out little hope of revolutionary change in a world increasingly dominated by bureaucracy, mass culture and authoritarianism. The leading members of the school, including Max Horkheimer, Theodor Adorno and Herbert Marcuse, were forced into exile in the USA by the triumph of Hitler in the 1930s.

In an attempt to explain the failure of the working-class revolution in the West, the critical theorists emphasized the power of culture and the declining importance of the individual. Instead of destroying capitalism the working class had become integrated into it by absorbing its culture and accepting its values and goals. In a pessimistic view of the postwar world, the Frankfurt School argues that, as the working class finds its economic circumstances improved through wage increases and welfare reforms, it becomes increasingly impoverished in psychological, cultural and spiritual terms. The three most important features of this process of domination are instrumental reason, mass culture and the establishment of the authoritarian personality.

Instrumental reason

Instrumental reason refers to the way in which rational thought had ceased to be a critical faculty and had become instead yet another instrument through which the powerful could exercise control and domination. During the Enlightenment and the French Revolution of the eighteenth century, reason had been celebrated as the source of liberation from tradition, superstition and religious bigotry. Under capitalism it had become 'domesticated' (Cuff *et al.* 1998: 194); according to Horkheimer, reason and science had become the tools of capitalism and bureaucracy. Instrumental reason is essentially the means by which we achieve the ends laid down by the system; it is the use of 'technocratic thinking' to achieve limited and practical ends or to solve immediate problems. This use of rational thought may produce short-term results and personal success, but it ignores long-term effects and moral questions about the ends themselves. Instrumental reason may tell us that certain qualifications will lead to more lucrative careers than others, but it does not consider 'ends' such as personal fulfilment. Similarly, cost–benefit analysis demonstrates the efficiency gained by introducing new technology into the workplace, but it takes no account of the resulting levels of unemployment. The laws of supply and demand reveal the economic necessity of committing more and more natural resources to the enterprise of industrial production, even though this may lead to global destruction and pollution.

Science, for so long the optimistic badge of reason, had become tarnished as a form of domination. Instead of fulfilling its promise of freedom and enlightenment, it had become an extension of capitalism and bureaucratic thinking. As society becomes more mechanized and social life more routinized, science and instrumental reason come to symbolize a modern world characterized by conformity and control; we become increasingly adept at servicing the bureaucratic machine but do not have the foggiest idea where it is going.

In *One Dimensional Man*, Herbert Marcuse (1964) argued that the subversive power of critical reason was being displaced by an all-embracing faith in the promise of 'positive science' and progress. Everyday life was becoming colonized by technological and pragmatic rationality as all forms of social and cultural life became dominated by 'mechanisms of conformity', and true individualism declined in the face of a 'totally administered society'. In the ultimate act of repression, our real needs had become transformed into false ones, which were then 'satisfied' by the pleasure industries in an orgy of contentment.

In his exploration of the impact of technological rationality and the illusion of freedom, Marcuse argued that the passive consumption of superficial products leads to short-term contentment but in the long run creates an uncritical and one-dimensional society in which the working classes are incapable of revolt and only a handful of intellectuals present any challenge to the dominant culture. In this vision, the emergence of the authoritarian personality and the role of the culture industry are crucial.

The authoritarian personality

The authoritarian personality is associated largely with the work of Adorno. Using the psychoanalysis of Freud along with his own research, Adorno argued that the forces of instrumental reason and mass culture required the members of technocratic societies to possess conformist personalities suited to the hierarchical structure of society and the routines of modern living:

> **Domination is not simply built into the culture industry, it requires a particular character structure, one that is not only receptive to domination but actually seeks it.**
>
> (Craib 1992: 219)

Whereas early capitalism relied on the repression of individualism and sexuality through strict upbringing and the development of strong personality, the modern age of mass culture and consumerism encouraged the abandonment of self-discipline and the expression of individualism through consumption. With a decline in parental control and the increasing influence of the culture industry, society was becoming inhabited by 'standardized' individuals who looked to the social system for approval. Instead of developing an independent personality based on a strong father figure, the child turns away from the family towards the role models and icons provided by the worlds of politics and popular culture. The weak and anxiety-ridden modern personality is seen as uncritical and incapable of independent judgement. It craves domination and strong leadership to allay the doubts and fears that beset it in an increasingly complex and ambiguous world.

The authoritarian personality relies on stereotypical and rigid thinking: racial prejudice and intolerance are characteristic symptoms, nationalism and fascism the potential outcomes.

> **Rootless, lonely, directionless, 'mass man' thus constituted ready made fodder for totalitarian parties . . . [they] offered him a means by which he might overcome his puniness and isolation, the psychic pain of responsibility, by merging his will with that of a mass movement.**
>
> (Hannah Arendt, in Bennett 1982: 36)

Mass culture

Mass culture attracted the critical attention of the Frankfurt School because of the emphasis it gave to the power of ideas in explaining human action. In its view, genuine art was seen as rising above the mundane and routine world of instrumental reason; indeed, the Frankfurt School would seem to share Picasso's belief in the critical power of art as 'the lie which tells the truth'. This subversive element of 'true' culture has been undermined and superseded by a new popular culture which is not spontaneous, genuine or critical. Popular culture is a false culture devised and packaged by capitalism to keep the masses content.

> **The culture industry concerns itself with the predominance of the effect. It aims primarily at the creation of diversion and distractions, providing a temporary escape from the responsibilities and drudgery of everyday life. However the culture industry offers no genuine escape. For the relaxation it provides – free of demands and efforts – only serves to distract people from the basic pressures of their lives and to reproduce their will to work.**
>
> (Bottomore 1983: 186)

In a fragmented 'mass society' populated by isolated and estranged individuals of weak personality and little substance, the role of the culture industry and its promotion of empty products to satisfy false needs holds a special interest for the Frankfurt School. Instead of being the expression of human potential and an affirmation of all we can achieve, culture is simply another commodity; robbed of its uplifting and inspirational qualities, artistic activity has no meaning other than the value placed on it by the marketplace. Works of art are mass-produced to satisfy general tastes, artists become famous and business people rich from the general 'dumbing down' of culture that results from giving people what they think they want in their pursuit of contentment and conformity. In a savage attack on the commodification of culture, which some would criticize as elitist, Horkheimer and Adorno (1973) defend the achievements of serious art against the bland and predictable clichés of mass culture, which 'is uniform as a whole and in every part' and invades all aspects of life in a deliberate strategy of 'mass deception'.

The ideas of the Frankfurt School attracted a good deal of academic consideration and interest after the Second World War. It championed the cause of the individual in a world increasingly dominated by bureaucracy, strong state government and international capitalism. The critical approach to ideological control and mass culture seemed to focus on the concerns of the postwar period, and the student movement of the 1960s expressed many of its ideas. However, the Frankfurt School became the victim of its own pessimism. It had rejected traditional Marxism and its optimistic faith in the working class and had nowhere to go. As these critical theories lost their influence, Marxist thought turned again to a consideration of its basic themes:

> **the analysis of modes of production, structural contradictions and historical transformations, class structure and conflict, political power and the role of the state.**
>
> (Bottomore 1983: 76)

Attempts have been made to rehabilitate the ideas of the Frankfurt School. Jürgen Habermas (1971a), one-time research assistant to Adorno, developed a more optimistic approach that attempted to bring together the critical insights of Marx, Weber, Parsons and Mead. Utilizing Parsons' notion of 'system' and distinguishing it from the 'lifeworld' of everyday experience, Habermas highlighted the difference between the objective and constraining features of external society and our subjective and personal experience of it in an attempt to reconcile the age-old tensions between notions of 'structure' and 'agency'. While the world of work and the social system are dominated by the forces of instrumental reason, the lifeworld relies on our human ability to communicate with one another. This is at the root of understanding and interpretation (the 'hermaneutic sciences') and provides the basis for his optimistic belief in discussion and debate as a form of 'communicative action' that can resist 'instrumental reason' and encourage free and equal relationships between people. According to this view, the Enlightenment belief in the power of reason to unearth 'universal truths' is resurrected as an achievable ideal.

Case study

Mass culture as mass deception?

Movies and radio need no longer pretend to be art. The truth that they are just business is made into an ideology in order to justify the rubbish they deliberately produce . . . Not only are the hit songs, stars, and soap operas cyclically recurrent and rigidly invariable types, but the specific content of the entertainment itself is derived from them and only appears to change. The details are interchangeable. The short interval sequence which was effective in a hit song, the hero's momentary fall from grace (which he accepts as good sport), the rough treatment which the beloved gets from the male star, the latter's rugged defiance of the spoilt heiress, are, like all the other details, ready-made clichés to be slotted in anywhere; they never do anything more than fulfill the purpose allotted them in the overall plan. Their whole raison d'être is to confirm it by being constituent parts. As soon as the film begins, it is quite clear how it will end, and who will be rewarded, punished, or forgotten. In light music, once the trained ear has heard the first notes of the hit song, it can guess what is coming and feel flattered when it does come. The average length of the short story has to be rigidly adhered to. Even gags, effects, and jokes are calculated like the setting in which they are placed . . .

Real life is becoming indistinguishable from the movies. The sound film, far surpassing the theater of illusion, leaves no room for imagination or reflection on the part of the audience, who is unable to respond within the structure of the film, yet deviate from its precise detail without losing the thread of the story; hence the film forces its victims to equate it directly with reality. The stunting of the mass-media consumer's powers of imagination and spontaneity does not have to be traced back to any psychological mechanisms; he must ascribe the loss of those attributes to the objective nature of the products themselves, especially to the most characteristic of them, the sound film. They are so designed that quickness, powers of observation, and experience are undeniably needed to apprehend them at all; yet sustained thought is out of the question if the spectator is not to miss the relentless rush of facts. Even though the effort required for his response is semi-automatic, no scope is left for the imagination. Those who are so absorbed by the world of the movie – by its images, gestures, and words – that they are unable to supply what really makes it a world, do not have to dwell on particular points of its mechanics during a screening. All the other films and products of the entertainment industry which they have seen have taught them what to expect; they react automatically . . .

It is quite correct that the power of the culture industry resides in its identification with a manufactured need, and not in simple contrast to it, even if this contrast were one of complete power and complete powerlessness. Amusement under late capitalism is the prolongation of work. It is sought after as an escape from the mechanized work process, and to recruit strength in order to be able to cope with it again. But at the same time mechanization has such power over a man's leisure and happiness, and so profoundly determines the manufacture of amusement goods, that his experiences are inevitably afterimages of the work process itself. The ostensible content is merely a faded foreground; what sinks in is the automatic succession of standardized operations. What happens at work, in the factory, or in the office can only be escaped from by approximation to it in one's leisure time. All amusement suffers from this incurable malady. Pleasure hardens into boredom because, if it is to remain pleasure, it must not demand any effort and therefore moves rigorously in the worn grooves of association. No independent thinking must be expected from the audience: the product prescribes every reaction: not by its natural structure (which collapses under reflection), but by signals.

(Horkheimer and Adorno 1973 (original 1944): 121–37)

Questions

1. Do you feel Horkheimer and Adorno's comments apply to contemporary film and music?
2. To what extent do you agree with them?

Structuralism

Structuralist theories originated in the work of Durkheim and Marx and have since taken many forms both within and beyond sociology. Structuralism represents an attack on the importance of the individual 'subject' and advocates explanations of human consciousness and behaviour that refer to fixed and objective forces beyond our awareness and control. It implies that explanations for our thoughts, our actions and our culture are to be found not at the level of direct experience and personal awareness (surface structure) but rather in the hidden forces that construct our world and give it meaning (deep structure). In other words, 'being human involves living in a world which has already been determined' (Trigg 1985, cited in Jones 2003: 143). These ideas re-emerged in France at the end of the Second World War and represent a break from French humanism and, in particular, an alternative to the existentialism of Sartre, which laid so much stress on the role of the individual in history and the reponsibility of individuals for the consequences of their actions. In the view of this new breed of radical thinkers, individualism and subjectivism were a 'bourgeois' trait in philosophical thought that needed to be eradicated by the annihilation of the subject altogether.

These ideas have had a particular influence in three areas of the human sciences: linguistics, anthropology and sociology.

Linguistics

As with advocates of theories such as Marxism and functionalism, structuralists and post-structuralists believe that to explain social life it is necessary to look at structural influences beyond the individual. However, rather than focusing on institutional structures, they emphasize how systems of language provide us with our knowledge of the world: language defines our social reality. Linguistics is, then, clearly associated with the ideas of structuralism. In this context, the work of Ferdinand de Saussure (1857–1913) has particular importance. He made a crucial distinction between the everyday use of speech by individuals in their conscious communication with one another (*parole*) and the underlying system of collective language, which is governed by rules of conduct and meaning (*langue*). Words take their meaning from this language system and it is the system we unconsciously learn and use to impose sense and order on the world. We do this by learning to apply correct words to relevant concepts.

The importance of the rules governing grammar, sentence structure and sounds can be seen when we attempt to learn a new language. Nigel Barley reveals the importance of tone in changing the meaning of a word in the Dowayo language (from Cameroon, West Africa):

> **My rather wobbly control of the language was also a grave danger. Obscenity is never very far away in Dowayo. One day I was summoned to the Chief's hut to be introduced to a rainmaker. This was a most valuable contact that I had nagged the Chief about for weeks. We chatted politely, very much sounding each other out . . . [and] agreed I would visit him. I rose and shook hands politely, 'Excuse me,' I said, 'I am cooking some meat.' At least that was what I had intended to say; owing to a tonal error I declared to an astonished audience, 'Excuse me, I am copulating with the blacksmith.'**
>
> (Barley 1986: 57)

As this body of rules already exists and has to be learned, it is correct to say that language is not a reflection of reality but the definition and creation of it; it can be seen as the underlying structure that gives meaning to our experiences and enables us to share them with others. When a two-year-old child announces that she wishes to go to McDonald's even though she has never set foot in a fast-food restaurant, she indicates the power of language to create conceptual categories that are independent of and prior to direct experience. The price we pay for this gift of communication is our enslavement by language through its power to constrain the way we think. As Doyal and Harris (1986) point out:

> **You must learn from others the language you employ to describe even your most intimate and private feelings; thus even the way you describe yourself to yourself can only happen by using words publicly available, and learnt, by you.**
>
> (cited in Jones 2003: 142)

The idea that words are only one form of communication has been applied by the science of signs known as semiotics. The work of Roland Barthes, for instance, has attempted to unearth the hidden messages of popular culture. Barthes (1972) has tried to illustrate how all forms of cultural phenomenon can be analysed as systems of signs that help us to understand our society. According to this approach a sign is made up of two elements – the actual object ('signifier') and that which it represents ('signified').

Case study

Signifiers and signifieds

Many of us have followed the adventure of a detective who was (like all the classical detectives) a first class semiologist. I am talking about Sherlock Holmes. Inevitably there is some situation that arises that puzzles everyone, which Holmes then 'solves'. He does this by reading signs which others ignore as trivial and inconsequential. In one story, 'The Blue Carbuncle', Watson finds Holmes examining a hat that had been brought to him by a policeman. Watson describes the hat: it was old, its lining was discoloured, it was cracked, very dusty and spotted in places. Holmes asks Watson what he can deduce from the hat about its wearer. Watson examines the hat and says he can deduce nothing. Holmes then proceeds to describe, in remarkable detail, what the man who owned the hat is like. He is, Holmes says: highly intellectual, has had a decline in fortune, his wife no longer loves him, he is sedentary, and probably doesn't have gas in his house. Watson exclaims, 'You are certainly joking, Holmes.' Holmes then shows Watson how he reached his conclusions. He examined the hat, noticed certain things about it (signifiers) and proceeded from there (described the implied signifieds).

Signifiers	Signifieds
Cubic capacity of hat (large brain)	Man is intellectual
Good quality of hat but three years old	Man hasn't a new hat, suggesting a decline in fortune
Hat hasn't been brushed in weeks	Man's wife no longer loves him
Dust on hat is brown housedust	Man seldom goes out
Wax stains from candles on hat	No gas in house

Holmes explains Watson's mistake. 'You fail . . . to reason from what you see. You are too timid in drawing your inferences.' Watson had failed to recognize the signifiers he examined for what they were . . . The meaning in signs, and texts (collections of signs) is not always (or even often) evident; it has to be elicited. And too many people are like Watson, I would suggest – not bold enough in drawing their inferences.

(Adapted from Berger 1991: 9–10)

Question

1. Take three current adverts and describe the messages that they are conveying. (Choose adverts for different types of product – perhaps American jeans, a cleaning product, a car, a soft drink.)

In other words, we inhabit a world of signs, which exist on two levels. On the surface or 'connotive' level, things have a purely empirical status as objects; but they also function at a deeper or 'denotive' level, where they act as symbols for something else – they convey meaning. The task of semiotics is to decode the signs of everyday life (body language, adverts, fashion and so on) in order to establish what they denote. A simple example of this, borrowed from Sherlock Holmes by Asa Berger, is shown above.

Anthropology

Regarded by many as the founder of French structuralism, Claude Lévi-Strauss applied structuralist ideas to the study of anthropology. He focused on the form rather than the content of particular cultures and attempted to explain all social phenomena as communication systems. He argued that myths and stories that might seem unintelligible to us made sense and could be shown to have a clear structure and order when studied as systems of signs and symbols. Lévi-Strauss adopted a similar approach in his examination of other aspects of human societies. His study of kinship structures, for example, revealed universal taboos of incest, which he argued were simply a means of ensuring that marriage took place outside the family. As a result, women became gifts between groups of men; gifts that expressed the value and respect that men had for one another. As with other forms of structuralism, what individuals themselves think or say they are doing is subjective and irrelevant. Ritzer points out that 'to engage in a science, the focus must shift from people to some sort of objective structure' (1992: 502). For Lévi-Strauss, social phenomena are the products of the mind and should be interpreted as reflections of 'the permanent and logical structures of the mind'. Whereas anthropology usually highlights examples of cross-cultural diversity in human behaviour, the structuralist model clearly suggests unconscious and universal similarities that unite human behaviour at a deeper level.

In a rejection of both ethnocentrism and cultural relativism, Lévi-Strauss argues that the distinction between so-called 'primitive' cultures and more rational ones is misleading as all cultures are based on logical thought, which is a universal human characteristic. This quality can be found underlying the construction of a totem pole, the invention of the traffic light and the development of computers.

In l968, Vladimir Propp published his attempt to apply the ideas of structuralism to the fairy tale. Despite the range and variety of fairy tales around the world, he argued that all such stories are simply myths created to communicate deeper meanings about ourselves. They display universal similarities in form irrespective of the differences in content. These shared characteristics can be reduced to a basic menu of 31 functions from which all myths and stories are created. Asa Berger (1991) applied Propp's ideas to various texts to show that the underlying themes can be applied as easily to Frankenstein and Sam Spade as they can to Little Red Riding Hood. He demonstrates that the basic elements in fairy tales recur in various genres:

Genre	Elements from fairy tales
Science fiction	Magical agents, magical powers, etc.; hero leaves home
Detective	Finding kidnapped heroines
Soap operas	Relationships between members of families
Spy stories	Finding false heroes; hero (unrecognized) arrives in a foreign country
Situation comedies	Reversal of problem stories about royal families; stories about tricksters
Western	Hero and villain fight; a chase (reversed, with villain pursued)

In Roland Barthes' work these ideas were applied to popular culture, where he dispensed with the distinction between 'high' and 'low' culture, regarding all cultural artefacts as worthy of study. By analysing the taken-for-granted aspects of everyday life, Barthes revealed the hidden ideological messages behind those things that we see as natural. Clearly influenced by Marxist notions of false consciousness, Barthes argued that all artefacts refer to meanings that are implicitly cultural but appear to be natural because the assumptions on which their meanings are based are so much part of our common-sense view of the world that we recognize them without having to make their cultural origins explicit. In the preface to *Mythologies* (1972), Barthes explains his project as an attempt to remind people of the historical (or cultural) origins of those things which they take for granted:

> **The starting point of these reflections was usually a feeling of impatience at the sight of the 'naturalness' with which newspapers, art and common sense constantly dress up a reality which, even though it is the one we live in, is undoubtedly determined by history. In short, in the account given of our contemporary circumstances, I resented seeing Nature and History confused at every turn, and I wanted to track down, in the decorative display of what-goes-without-saying, the ideological abuse which, in my view, is hidden there.**
>
> (Barthes 1972)

Food and drink, fashion, adverts and sport all contain messages that derive their meanings from underlying ideas of national identity, gender, status and so on, which may appear to be natural but which have a cultural and political history that is disguised by the very naturalness of their appearance. For this reason, Barthes uses the notion of 'myth' to describe how everyday cultural artefacts operate to distort and disguise the social world by representing it as natural and fixed. A magazine photograph of a black soldier saluting the tricolour emphasizes the inclusive nature of French citizenship but negates the colonial history of France in Africa. The drinking of coffee or wine calls up notions of 'Frenchness' and social status but disguises the conditions under which coffee beans or grapes are picked, while an advert for Italian groceries operates in a similar way to appeal to our sense of Italian culinary tradition without thinking too closely about who prepares the meals. The more natural a social practice appears, the stronger its ideological power.

Semiotics – then and now

In the 1950s France was still a colonial power using its military power to resist struggles for independence in North Africa and South East Asia. In this extract from *Mythologies*, Barthes explains how he was struck by the connotive and denotive aspects of the front cover of *Paris Match* (Figure 2.6).

Figure 2.6 The *Paris Match* cover referred to by Barthes
PARIS MATCH/SCOOP

A closer look *continued*

I am at the barber's, and a copy of Paris-Match is offered to me. On the cover, a young Negro in a French uniform is saluting, with his eyes uplifted, probably fixed on a fold of the tricolour. All this is the meaning of the picture. But, whether naively or not, I see very well what it signifies to me: that France is a great Empire, that all her sons, without any colour discrimination, faithfully serve under her flag, and that there is no better answer to the detractors of an alleged colonialism than the zeal shown by this Negro in serving his so-called oppressors. I am therefore again faced with a greater semiological system: there is a signifier, itself already formed with a previous system (a black soldier is giving the French salute); there is a signified (it is here a purposeful mixture of Frenchness and militariness); finally, there is a presence of the signified through the signifier . . . In myth (and this is the chief peculiarity of the latter), the signifier is already formed by the signs of the language . . . Myth has in fact a double function: it points out and it notifies, it makes us understand something and it imposes it on us . . .

Figure 2.7 Christine Ohuruogo celebrates her victory
AFP Photo/ADRIAN DENNIS/Getty Images

Questions

1. Paraphrase (summarize in your own words) this extract to show that you understand what Barthes is saying.
2. After winning gold in the 400 metres at the Beijing Olympics, Christine Ohoruogu was pictured (Figure 2.7) celebrating her victory – but what else does the image tell us?
3. Using Barthes's ideas on signification and myth, what sense can be made of such an image in a national newspaper on the day after her victory?

More recent attempts to apply these ideas to popular culture can be found in Williamson's (1978) work on advertising and Masterman's (1986) analysis of television programmes. Intended as a homage to Barthes, Masterman's edited series of essays concentrates on television partly because it was overlooked by Barthes in the 1950s but largely because of its power in contemporary society:

> **Television, constantly denying its own mode of production, continually manufacturing for its audiences a seamless, plausible and authentic flow of 'natural' images, easily outdoes all other media in its effortless production of cultural myths, 'realities' which go-without-saying.**
>
> (Masterman 1986: 5)

Whether we are looking at the BBC's news coverage of 'the Battle of Orgreave' during the miners' strike, the trivialization of black history by *Blue Peter* or the hidden messages about national identity, gender and sexuality in the coverage of Torvill and Dean (Britain's Olympic ice-skating champions), these essays 'attempt to unearth some of the myths perpetuated by British television' in the early 1980s (Masterman 1986). *Tomorrow's World*, for example, is a popular programme that claims to glimpse the future through the inventions of today, but in Robins and Webster's 1986 account it is guilty of trivializing science, patronizing the audience and avoiding moral issues in a format that naturalizes technological progress and the superior authority of scientists:

> **Far more important, however, than all the image and hype of the *Tomorrow's World* rhetoric, is the way in which the programme mystifies our understanding of science and technology. Like a great deal of television output, *Tomorrow's World* connives in the myth of expertise and knowledge. It asks us to stand in awe at what scientists pull out of their top hats. It invites us to defer to a figure whose status and power (founded upon knowledge) is inverse to that of the viewer (founded upon ignorance). Significantly, however, the figure of the scientist is physically absent from the programme. Perhaps it is felt that his or her mandarin language will alienate the average peak-time viewer. Or perhaps it is assumed that he or she will be lacking in charisma. The consequence, though, is that the authority of the scientist (and of Science) is enhanced. Scientists become remote and revered deities above and beyond the daily run of things. Their expertise is safely protected from scrutiny and possible demystification.**
>
> (Robins and Webster 1986: 111)

Stop and think

- How might the following examples of popular culture be 'read' from a structuralist perspective: (a) *EastEnders*; (b) *University Challenge*; and (c) a meal at McDonald's? (Try to use ideas of 'naturalness' and 'disguise'.)

Post-structuralism

Following the failure of the student revolt in Paris in May 1968, structuralist writers such as Roland Barthes, Jacques Derrida and Michel Foucault began to cast doubt on the promise of structuralist thought and the idea that there was a structural reality to be discovered behind the world of appearances through a scientific analysis of language and signs. To them the very language that the structuralists were forced to use made them as prone to ideological thought as anyone else; instead of revealing the true structures of the mind and the outside world, structuralism was simply another perspective and as such represented a dead end in the search for universal and unifying principles. Language was still seen as a powerful instrument for control, but it no longer offered the key to scientific analysis or social improvement, which were underlying elements of the Enlightenment, structuralism and the later work of Habermas (see p. 91).

In Foucault's (1977) work, the term 'discourse' is used to refer to the ways of talking and thinking that we use to make sense of the world and to communicate with one another. As we refine these tools of language, however, we become ensnared by them; it becomes almost impossible to separate our ideas from the language we use to express them. This implies that all attempts by intellectuals to speak on behalf of humanity in universal terms are corrupted by language and as such simply represent different discourses. This is as true for Marxism as it is for any other set of ideas; instead of providing a scientific analysis of social reality beyond false consciousness, Marxism represents one more ideology in the language of power. The failure of the student revolt in 1968 stands as a symbol of the 'decline [of Marxism] as a dogmatic framework' and led Foucault to consider its 'powerlessness . . . to confront a whole series of questions that were not traditionally a part of its statutory domain (questions about women, about relations between sexes, about medicine, about mental illness, about the environment, about minorities, about delinquency)' (quoted in Kritzman 1988: x).

In breaking away from structuralism in general and Marxism in particular, Foucault suggests a far more relativist and accidental view of history and the development of knowledge/power. According to this perspective, familiar practices such as the treatment of disease in clinics, the care of insane people in asylums and the control of criminals in prisons are the product of particular discourses that can be accounted for by unearthing the unconscious forces that shaped these ways of thinking and talking about the world at that time. This form of historicism is dramatically different from the Marxist notion of 'historical materialism' (see pp. 56–58) because it rejects the notion of a grand design, historical laws and the ultimate role of class conflict in the historical process. It also challenges the idea of a sovereign power centralized in the hands of a ruling class or elite group; rather, power is dispersed throughout the network of institutions, professions and bureaucracies that go to make up the 'carceral' society. These groups all use knowledge as a means of exercising their control over others, with the overall effect of producing a society characterized by surveillance and 'disciplinary control' in all places and at all levels.

Foucault's ideas have been influential not only as a critique of meta-narratives such as Christianity, Marxism and Freudian psychoanalysis but also in their application to substantive areas of sociological enquiry such as crime, health and sexuality. In all these areas, the way in which knowledge is used in conjunction with power is crucial as Foucault strives to demonstrate that knowledge can be used as a form of domination. Instead of being progressive or civilizing influences, the discourses around medicine, prison reform and sexual difference become part of the processes of normalization and self-discipline. In serving the everyday interests of doctors, psychoanalysts and social reformers, the language of benevolence and improvement conceals the new barbarism of social control and disguises the overall social interest that is being served.

By studying the historical context within which these new discourses arose, Foucault attempted to take us beyond what the actors themselves thought they were doing to explain the specific historical circumstances that created the discourses in the first place. Indeed Foucault's historical accounts of madness, sexuality and punishment aimed to show how and why different discourses were established and accepted as defining such phenomena. With regard to madness, he argued that the origins of mental hospitals (initially called 'madhouses') could not be separated from the emergence of the power of reason (the opposite of madness), the medicalization of insanity and the vested interest of psychiatrists. The major explanation for this was institutional and almost accidental: the eradication of leprosy in post-Renaissance Europe had emptied the 'lazar houses' (which segregated lepers until the decline of leprosy in Europe) and provided the opportunity to segregate and incarcerate the 'mad'.

Foucault rejected the idea that the provision of asylums for insane people was inspired by a genuine desire to provide the 'sick' with medical care; rather, this represented a new age of incarceration in an increasingly rational world that sought to persecute the irrational and reinforce social control. In the new medical discourse, reason was the source of a healthy civilization, while madness was a sickness to be healed. Our resulting fear of madness ensures conformity and guarantees social control. Whether he was talking about medicine, punishment or sex, Foucault's unconventional ideas represent an attack on rational forms of knowledge as extensions of institutional control. They are not superior, they are simply dominant. This relativist approach to knowledge is shared by many postmodernist thinkers, who also reject the notion that history is determined by the civilizing forces of science and reason.

Stop and think

- Foucault and others have suggested that certain discourses represent a form of social control. How might this be applied to the way in which certain types of behaviour are defined as rational or insane?
- Give examples of behaviour that is generally seen as rational or insane. Why might society want to encourage the rational and control the insane behaviour?

A closer look

Foucault, post-structuralism and feminism

The French theorist Michel Foucault is one of the key thinkers associated with post-structuralism. Although his work has been of enormous influence in sociology, it has been seen as problematic for feminists, in particular because of his lack of explicit interest in gender. However, some feminist theorists have argued that his ideas can be utilized to help to understand gender relations. Ramazanoglu (1993) argues that Foucault has 'much to offer in enhancing feminist understandings', particularly as regards how power is exercised and how women's bodies are controlled. One of the reasons why feminism should attend to Foucault is that his understanding of power relations can offer feminists new insights into women's relationships with men.

Central to Foucault's work was the concept of disciplinary regimes that exert power over people. He argued that during the nineteenth century there was a rise of a new and unprecedented style of discipline directed at the body. This discipline sought to invade and regulate the body and could be seen in the disciplinary practices in various social institutions, including schools, hospitals and prisons. Through these disciplinary practices, docile bodies were produced through control exerted at the microlevel – control over the movement and space available to the body.

Bartky (1990) draws on Foucault's notion of disciplinary power to understand how women's behaviour and bodies are controlled. She argues that there are significant gender differences in posture, movement, gesture and general bodily comportment. Discursive practices surrounding the body are gendered, and women's bodies are subject to particular control. As Bartky puts it: 'Women are far more restricted than men in their manner of movement and in their lived spatiality, women's space is an enclosure in which she feels confined.'

These discursive practices produce concerns over notions of beauty, for instance, which impact on women: 'A woman's face must be made up, made over and so must her body . . . her lips must be made more kissable.'

She argues that these new forms of control of women are so powerful because women discipline themselves, thus they play a part in imposing such control. These disciplinary practices construct sexual difference and are part of the process through which the ideal body of femininity – and hence the feminine body subject – is constructed. The feminine body is, according to Bartky, inscribed with particular meaning and status which is seen as inferior to the masculine body.

Postmodernism

Since the Enlightenment the search for the truth has dominated philosophy, social theory and scientific research. This search for 'the truth' has resulted in all-encompassing theories of society and history known as *meta-narratives*. Meta-narratives claim to provide ever-improving and logical accounts of historical progress and destiny (and are an essential part of what Crook *et al.* (1992) have called the 'continuous qualitative progression of modernity'). Such accounts have dominated sociological thinking since its infancy, in the optimistic predictions of Marx and the pessimistic warnings of Weber. In the twentieth century, 'meta-narratives' surface in the theories of development put forward by Parsons (1966) and Rostow (1960) and in the post-capitalist theories of Dahrendorf (1959) and Bell (1973). A more recent exponent of the 'project of modernity' is Francis Fukuyama, who has argued that history has been the evolution and final triumph of liberal democracy and global capitalism:

> **What we may be witnessing is not just the end of the Cold War or the passing of a particular period of post-war history but the end of history as such; that is the end point of mankind's ideological evolution and the universalisation of western liberal democracy as the final form of human government.**
>
> **(Fukuyama 1989: 4)**

This triumph of Western values may, however, produce 'soulless consumerism' and a world in which cultural and political differences disappear. This more critical view of modernity was summed up by Malcolm Muggeridge in *Things Past*:

> **What they all want . . . is what the Americans have got – six lanes of large motor cars streaming powerfully into and out of gleaming cities; neon lights flashing, and juke boxes sounding and skyscrapers rising, storey upon storey into the sky. Driving at night into the town of Athens, Ohio (pop. 3,450), four bright coloured signs stood out in the darkness – 'Gas', 'Drugs', 'Beauty', 'Food'. These signs could have shone forth as clearly in Athens, Greece as in Athens, Ohio. They belonged as aptly to Turkestan, or Sind or Kamchatka . . . There are, properly speaking, no Communists, no capitalists, no Catholics, no Protestants, no black men. No Asians, no Europeans, no Right, no Left and no Center . . . There is only a vast and omnipresent longing for Gas, for Beauty, for Drugs and for Food.**
>
> (Muggeridge 1978: 125, quoted in Dizard 1982: 18)

One of the most damning critiques of modernism is Bauman's (1989) analysis of the Holocaust in Nazi Germany. In this work, he dismisses conventional explanations that suggest that the persecution of the Jews, Gypsies and other enemies of the Aryan ideal is an aberration in the 'march of progress' brought about by natural or unique aspects of the German character. Instead he argues that it is a predictable outcome of modernist thinking and behaviour, where man has replaced God and science has supplanted morality; the growth of the modern bureaucratic state may not make such things inevitable, but modernity was a 'necessary condition' of the Holocaust. By applying the principles of technology, bureaucracy and the production line to 'the Jewish problem' we ended up with a 'final solution' symbolized by factories of death:

> **The civil service infused the other hierarchies with its sure-footed planning and bureaucratic thoroughness. From the army the machinery of destruction acquired its military precision, discipline, and callousness. Industry's influence was felt in the great emphasis upon accounting, penny-saving, and salvage, as well as in factory-like efficiency of the killing centres. Finally, the party contributed to the entire apparatus an 'idealism', a sense of 'mission', and a notion of history-making . . . It was indeed the organized society in one of its special roles. Though engaged in mass murder on a gigantic scale, this vast bureaucratic apparatus showed concern for correct bureaucratic procedure, for the niceties of precise definition, for the minutiae of bureaucratic regulation, and the compliance with the law.**
>
> (Bauman 1989: 13–14)

Such doubts about the modernist project have encouraged some writers to challenge the triumph of progress and the validity of scientific knowledge. Instead, it is argued we have entered a new age (the postmodern condition) that has generated a much more relativist view of the world (postmodernism). In general terms, ancient certainties and tried and tested ideologies and methods have come under immense pressure as postmodern ideas and concepts have gained a greater currency within social theory. It is important to understand that it is possible to accept postmodern changes in social life without becoming a 'postmodernist', and as we shall see some sociologists manage to square the two while others reject both the idea of significant change and the postmodernist ideas associated with it.

In the work of writers such as Lyotard (1985) and Baudrillard (1990) the end of modernism is celebrated and a postmodern world of disintegration, confusion and cultural choice opens up. The 'rational and rigid' guidelines of the meta-narratives of modernism have been swept away and replaced by the 'irrational and flexible' elements of a far more relativist position, which says that 'anything goes'. This can be seen most clearly using examples from architecture, where the terms 'modernism' and 'postmodernism' are used widely. For example, housing officials in London decided to 'postmodernize' their high-rise flats with architectural features from earlier epochs and styles such as classical roof shapes, decorative façades and ornate balconies (Strinati 1992).

In sociological theory the shape and impact of postmodernism are less easy to describe, in part because it is not a unified theory but a collection of different positions and ideas. However, there are several identifying features of postmodernist thought that provide some kind of identity, if only because they tell us what postmodernism is not.

The confusion of time and space and the fragmentation of cultural traditions are characteristics of the postmodern consumer society in which we experience the erosion of 'collective and personal

A closer look

Postmodernism and sociology: no special claim to the truth

First, the idea that social history is the rational and evolutionary progress of society towards some kind of end is rejected by postmodernists. The meta-narratives of Marx and Durkheim with their exclusive claims to truth have been replaced with a relativist perspective that treats their work as 'texts' rather than gospels. Postmodernism sees all points of view as valid, with none able to claim superiority; they are simply different ways of looking at things. From this relativist position, all sociological accounts have equal validity. In a postmodern world, grand theoretical accounts such as Marxism and functionalism are obsolete. And sociology itself has no special claim to truth.

Second, postmodernists disdain the artificial classification of knowledge into separate disciplines; they emphasize the pluralistic character of knowledge. The boundaries between sociology, psychology, history, philosophy and so on are merely attempts to preserve one set of grand theories in opposition to all others. By dissolving such distinctions it is possible to become more eclectic in our approach – to 'pick and mix' from a range of disciplines and perspectives in order to create a more exciting blend of ideas. This can be seen in modern politics, where the old organizing principles of class and party are being replaced by issues such as famine, civil rights and the protection of the environment.

Third, in postmodernist writing the importance of popular culture is often stressed, especially in relation to the power of the media to create 'realities' – through advertising, popular music and television soap operas for instance. These new versions of historical reality have no respect for matters of fact or taste; they simply take what they need from the variety of characters, narratives and styles available and create new cultural forms – video games, adverts, comics. In Las Vegas there is a billion-dollar casino based on the Egyptian pyramids but it mixes together historical themes as diverse as Camelot and Henry VIII and characters from Charles Dickens. In this new pluralist culture, art is not the preserve of the elite but is available to all; there is no good or bad, there is simply choice.

identities'. On the one hand, Strinati (1992) argues, we have lost the traditional sources of social identity once found in factors such as social class, religion, community and family life. On the other hand, popular culture has failed to create anything worthwhile enough to provide an alternative source of security. Television is the supreme example of this 'candy floss' culture, which 'speaks to everyone and no one in particular':

> **TV is a constant flow which switches back and forth between different surface messages; it is not a genuine source of identity and belief. But . . . since there is nothing else, nowhere else, but the TV screen, people have no alternative (except perhaps to go to the shops) but to succumb to the TV image, to lose themselves in the blankness of the screen and the hollowness of its icons.**
>
> (Strinati 1992: 7)

Stop and think

➤ *Shooting Stars* is a popular and irreverent TV show in Britain. The presenters have developed the ultimate postmodernist formula in which nothing is taken seriously. If you were the programme controller, would you interrupt the show to announce any of the following news items? If so, how would you 'present' them?

(a) the outbreak of war in Central Europe;

(b) the election result;

(c) the break-up of a royal marriage;

(d) a TV personality involved in a sex scandal;

(e) the birth of kittens to your pet cat;

(f) a dramatic twist in a popular soap.

Many of these ideas emanate from French philosophy and in particular poststructuralism. However, while writers like Barthes and Foucault retained the notion that it was possible to go beyond the 'text' (and the discourses that produced the people who 'created' the texts) to uncover the structural elements responsible for the discourses that characterized specific periods in history, it seems as if the postmodernists have taken the next step to argue that there is no discernible reality beyond the text – there is only discourse. While positivism dismissed early forms of knowledge as myth and narrative (simple stories for simple people) that had been superseded by scientific accounts of the world, postmodernism suggests that *all* accounts of 'reality' are nothing more than stories; science is simply another narrative and sociology is a branch of this tradition of storytelling that refers to social life.

In this argument the work of Baudrillard is most significant, because he is not a philosopher but a Marxist sociologist who demonstrates his roots to argue for the 'death of the social' and the triumph of popular culture. In postmodernism, cultural images take on a life of their own that is indistinguishable from what sociologists like to call 'real life'; they become one and the same thing as the life of signs ('simulacrums') creates a 'hyperreality' engulfing us all. People's lives are so enmeshed with the daily diet of television that it becomes almost impossible to discuss social reality as an experience separated from our media apprehension of it. Consequently, 'postmodernism (totally accepts) the ephemerality, fragmentation, discontinuity and the chaotic . . . half of . . . modernity. But . . . it does not try to transcend it . . . Postmodernism swims, even wallows in the fragmentary and the chaotic currents of change as if that is all there is' (Harvey 1990: 44). In this new set of arrangements, social reality and political struggle are replaced by cultural candy floss and consumerism; the promises of sociology and Marxism are dead.

Sociology has responded to this challenge in various ways, with some writers 'rounding out' the discipline to accommodate aspects of the postmodern critique and others, particularly Marxists, rejecting it out of hand. As Crook *et al.* (1992) point out, it is only those forms of thinking that stress the scientific and structuralist assumptions of positivist sociology that have much to fear from the insights of postmodernism:

> **Sociology is under threat from the 'end of the social' . . . no agenda for sociology is likely to succeed which is based on realist claims for the autonomy of and causal powers of the social. On the contrary, sociology needs to shift its attention to the boundaries between the once-autonomous spheres of modernity in order to gain some purchase on postmodernity. For this reason, if classical models for contemporary society are required, Simmel and Weber have more to offer a postmodernising sociology than do Marx and Durkheim.**
>
> (Crook *et al.* 1992: 238)

By stressing the 'social action' approach, it is argued that a postmodern sociology can develop that lays emphasis on the major areas of 'uncertainty' that characterize postmodernism and the ways in which people respond to these uncertainties in their interpretation and negotiation of everyday life. They also argue that sociology has a role to play in raising public awareness of the ironic and playful aspects of postmodernism and in encouraging policymakers to take these understandings seriously when they make decisions or direct publicity campaigns.

On the other hand, critics of postmodernism dismiss it as an academic parlour game that plays about with words and creates confusion. As such, it is a dangerous distraction that has little or no bearing on the life of most people and the enduring social constraints that confront them; times may have changed, but the issues of inequality, power, unemployment, alienation and so on still shape the lives of people in a society that is 'late modern' rather than postmodern. This has led Marxist writers such as Callinicos to reject completely the notion of a postmodern condition and the postmodernist theorizing that goes with it:

> **Now I reject all this. I do not believe that we live in 'New Times', in a 'post-industrial and postmodern age' fundamentally different from the capitalist mode of production globally dominant for the last two centuries.**
>
> (Callinicos 1990: 4)

In contrast to the modernist and postmodernist perspectives, there is also the argument that the world does have a clear destiny but it is one that is doomed to failure and collapse. In his pessimistic view of the future, Paul Kennedy (1993) argues the case for a world divided by crisis, domination and ecological decline. In the nineteenth century the predictions of Thomas Malthus that British society would be destroyed by the ravages of overpopulation and poverty were avoided through the opportunities offered by colonialism and emigration. In the twenty-first century the world will

A closer look

Sociologists' views on postmodernism

In pursuing their research, sociologists often canvas the opinions of the general public. In an interesting reversal of roles, A-level sociology student Daniel Morgan interviewed prominent sociologists over their views of postmodernism. These interviews were part of Daniel's coursework project in which he was examining 'How leading sociologists evaluate the contribution of postmodernism'. Some of Daniel's findings were included in an article on coursework in the journal *Sociology Review* and are included below. In the first extract, Professor Ken Thompson expresses an essentially positive view of postmodernism; in the second, John Westergaard is more critical. The two extracts demonstrate the divergence of opinion on the relevance of postmodernism among well-known and respected sociologists.

Ken Thompson

The concept of postmodernism has served a useful function for sociological theory in a number of ways. It has been useful in indicating a number of developments that do not seem to fit in with the ruling paradigm which sociology inherited from the Enlightenment meta-narratives of progress, rationalisation and secularisation. The underlying assumption in sociological theories of modernity and modernisation was that all societies were evolving in the same direction, characterised by increasing rationalisation and secularisation. Postmodernism, as related first of all to aesthetics, referred to an increased tendency towards pastiches of incongruent cultural codes, without any single articulating principle or theoretical foundation. This has been extremely useful in various fields of sociological interest for focusing attention on tendencies that are the reverse of those predicted in the paradigm of modernity and modernisation. To take just one example, the sociology of religion has had to take cognisance of religious revivals in various forms of 'fundamentalism', especially those linked with ethnicity, nationalism and cultural identity.

John Westergaard

In my view, postmodernist approaches constitute neither a theoretical advance – on the contrary – nor even a backward step, but rather a declaration of intellectual bankruptcy. There is such bankruptcy involved when reasoned scepticism towards simplistic 'grand narrative' is extended into unreasoned rejection of all analysis of dominant socio-historical trends and shifts of societal configuration; when such rejection is itself at strident odds with postmodernist assumptions of a present transition from 'modernism' to a new era of postulated flux; when ever-observable complexities of social structure are misidentified, in their current forms, as signs of an absence of structure; when, correspondingly, ever-observable intricacies of social causation are taken to rule out significant scope for causal analysis at large; when speculative inferences about allegedly new and structure-freed modes of personal 'identity' are made from impressions unchecked by reference either to relevantly direct evidence or to demonstrable structural constraints on 'identity' formation; when, above all, the implications of such assertions and assumptions is to endorse a relativistic conception of knowledge impossible to square with that pursuit of knowledge in which, after all, even postmodernist enquiry itself purports to be engaged. I may add that the criticisms that I have so very summarily set out apply in my view not only to postmodernist theory – whose openly professed and fully-fledged adherents are few – but to those strands of postmodernist-inclined thinking which, under 'late modernist' or similar labels, tend in the directions I have outlined, albeit within broader and more flexible frameworks of interpretation.

(extracts from an article on coursework in *Sociology Review*, 1998, 8(2): 6–7) have no chance for escape. According to this view, the world is destined to face a crisis between the developed world, based on a wealth explosion, and the developing world, which cannot avoid a massive explosion in population. In this unequal equation, the values of the free market and liberal democracy will evaporate in the face of world domination by multinational companies and global oligarchies.

The end result will be disaster because the long-term problems of ecological decline cannot be grasped by short-term Western political culture, which is incapable of confronting the crises of wealth creation. This view of the future is an indictment of modernist writers and their naive belief in the inevitable progress of science and reason. It is also a reminder of the limitations of postmodernist thinking and its obsession with Western culture. Instead of engineering a new period of history, we may simply be witnessing the disintegration of the old one.

As Kennedy puts it:

> **What is clear is that as the Cold War fades away, we face not a 'new world order' but a troubled and fractured planet, whose problems deserve the serious attention of politicians and public alike . . . The pace and complexity of the forces for change are enormous and daunting; yet it may still be possible for intelligent men and women to lead their societies through the complex task of preparing for the century ahead. If these challenges are not met, however, humankind will have only itself to blame for the troubles, and the disasters, that could be lying ahead.**
>
> (Kennedy 1993: 349)

Case study

Giddens, Beck and the 'risk society'

Recent developments in social theorizing can be found in the arguments of Ulrich Beck and Anthony Giddens, who suggest that at both the structural, macro, level and at the action, micro, level, contemporary life is becoming more uncertain and risky. This risk is felt in terms of the uncertainty at a global level of what the future holds and the supposed greater and more pervasive risks faced by individuals in their personal everyday lives. Giddens distinguished between different forms of risk that reflect different areas of contemporary life. External risk might involve concerns over what nature can do to us while manufactured risk relates to the impact humans have had on the world and nature (for instance, threats to the environment through global warming).

Beck is linked most closely with the idea of the risk society (which was the title of his seminal 1992 text). He felt that the increased dangers of risk in modern society did not signal the end of modernity but rather the beginning of a new form of modernity – a phase of what he called 'reflexive modernization'. Awareness of the greater range of risks has led to doubts over the knowledge of 'experts' and to a questioning of science and scientists. It has also highlighted the importance of risk management – at both the individual and the wider level.

So both Beck and Giddens see contemporary life as much more uncertain and risky than the past and their work in this area considers how a culture of risk and uncertainty affects individual and social life.

In looking at risk in the area of criminal justice, Kemshall cites an article in the *Daily Telegraph* that refers to 'a plethora of risks for the twenty-first century . . . from risks to newborn babies from their mothers' kisses, to vaccines, cot death, food risks and paedophile abductions en route to school' and suggests that 'being a mother in the twenty-first century is a fraught business' (Kemshall 2003: 3).

Questions

1. What risks do we face nowadays that were not present in the past?

2. What risks did people face in the past that are no longer felt to be dangerous? (Consider life in the nineteenth century and in pre-industrial times.)

3. Do you agree that life is more risky today than in the past?

Summary

- In reviewing different theoretical approaches it is important to stress that sociology is more than the sum of different theories. The sociological perspective is not tied to one theoretical point of view, and sociologists should be able to use a range of different theories.
- Durkheim helped to establish sociology as a distinct academic subject. He outlined the scientific basis and methods that sociology should adopt. Durkheim's work emphasized the moral basis of social cohesion or solidarity, an approach that has developed in the functionalist perspective.
- Marx's analysis of society saw the economic base of society as affecting and determining all other aspects of social life. Marx argued that in all societies there are basic contradictions within this economic base, due to the conflict of interests between different social groups involved in the economic process – in particular conflict between dominant and subordinate classes. Since Marx's death a number of strands of Marxism have emerged. In sociological theory, two major forms of Marxism can be identified: (a) structural Marxism, focusing on the importance of the economic base and class exploitation; and (b) humanist Marxism, stressing the alienation of the human spirit as a result of the rise of capitalism.
- Weber moved away from the structural theories of Durkheim and Marx and based his social analysis on the meanings that individuals give to the social world. He focused on social action and the motivations behind it. Weber developed this approach to suggest that structural Marxism, in particular, underplayed the role that non-economic factors might have in determining the development of society.
- There have been a number of important developments in sociological theory since the work of Durkheim, Marx and Weber.
- Interpretative sociology developed from the work of Weber and the importance attached to social action and includes a number of related theoretical perspectives. Symbolic interactionism focuses on the individual and the processes of social interaction. Ethnomethodology examines how people construct their social world. While emphasizing the importance of individuals' behaviour and of human interaction, interpretativists are aware that this cannot be divorced from the social situation in which behaviour and interaction occur.
- Feminist sociologists argued that sociological theory has been written from a male perspective. They have attempted to redress this state of affairs by placing women's experiences as central to the development of social theory and by trying to explain the divisions between women and men in society. There are various strands of feminist theory, including liberal feminism, radical feminism, Marxist feminism, black feminism and postmodern feminism.
- Critical theory, building on the work of Marx and Weber in particular, has emphasized the power of culture and the declining importance of the individual.
- Structuralism argues that the explanation for human behaviour cannot be found in the experience of the individual and that objective forces beyond our control have to be uncovered and examined. These forces can be found in systems of language and in the ideological and political structures of society. Poststructuralists look at how systems of language and ideological structures act as forms of power and control over people.
- Postmodernism suggests that the search for an ultimate explanation of and for human society is an enterprise doomed to failure. This perspective argues that all theoretical approaches are valid: none can claim to tell us the 'truth'.

Links

Sociological theories are applied throughout this book to the different areas of sociology being examined in specific chapters, so theories are applied to education, religion, family and so on. However, particular sections of this chapter are expanded in later chapters:

Functionalism and religion on pp. 52–53 links with Chapter 16, pp. 655–657.

Functionalism and crime on pp. 53–54 links with Chapter 14, pp. 560–563.

Marx and class on pp. 61–63 links with Chapter 4, pp. 166–168.

Mass culture on pp. 91–92 links with Chapter 17, pp. 721–723.

Further reading

This chapter has introduced and reviewed a wide range of sociological theories and theoretical writing, and it really goes without saying that to gain a fuller appreciation of this work you would need to read the original sources referred to. Indeed, it is often rewarding to read the 'real thing' and many of these sources are far more accessible and interesting than might be thought initially. Here, though, we highlight some more general texts that focus on sociological theorizing.

Craib, I. (1992) *Modern Social Theory*, London: Harvester Wheatsheaf.

Layder, D. (1994) *Understanding Social Theory*, London: Sage.

Ritzer, G. (2003) *Sociological Theory*, 6th edn, New York: McGraw-Hill.
These three studies provide thorough discussions of contemporary theories.

Cuff, E.C., Sharrock, W.W. and Francis, D.W. (2006) *Perspectives in Sociology*, 5th edn, London: Routledge.

Jones, P. (2003) *Introducing Social Theory*, London: Polity.

Marsh, I. (ed.) (2002) *Theory and Practice in Sociology*, London: Prentice Hall.

Scott, J. (2006) *Fifty Key Sociologists: The Formative Theorists*, London: Routledge.
These texts offer clear general introductions to the different theoretical positions in sociology.

Andermahr, S., Lovell, T. and Wolkowitz, C. (1997) *A Concise Dictionary of Feminist Theory*, London: Arnold.

Eagleton, M. (ed.) (2003) *A Concise Companion to Feminist Theory*, London: Blackwell.

Nicholson, L. (ed.) (1997) *The Second Wave*, London: Routledge.

Whelehan, I. (1995) *Modern Feminist Thought: From Second Wave to Post-Feminism*, Edinburgh: Edinburgh University Press.
These four texts focus on feminist theory. The first provides an accessible and comprehensive dictionary of feminist thought; Whelehan is a detailed exposition of the various strands of feminist theory; and the two edited collections contain a range of extracts from key feminist theorists across the different strands of feminism.

Lemert, C. (ed.) (1993) *Social Theory: The Multicultural and Classic Readings*, Oxford: Westview.

Marsh, I., Campbell, R. and Keating, M. (eds) (1998) *Classic and Contemporary Readings in Sociology*, Harlow: Addison Wesley Longman.
There are many readers on sociological theory and edited collections of theoretical writing. We particularly recommend these collections, which cover a range of 'classic' and contemporary writing.

Websites

www.sociosite.net
This is a sociology website run by the University of Amsterdam that provides details on important sociologists, including Weber, Marx and Foucault, plus information on courses, journals and university departments.
Details of websites devoted to individual social theorists can be found in *Sociology on the Web: A Student Guide* by Stuart Stein (Harlow: Prentice Hall, 2002).

Activities

Activity 1

Sociological explanations of Christmas

Questions

1. How would the following sociological approaches interpret the rituals of Christmas?
   (a) Functionalism (consider the functions and dysfunctions of Christmas rituals).
   (b) Feminism (consider what women and men, or girls and boys, do at Christmas).
   (c) Interpretative sociology (consider the 'games' people play at Christmas and the impressions people create at family gatherings).
   (d) Marxism (consider who profits at Christmas and what ideological messages are conveyed by Christmas rituals).
   (e) Postmodernism (consider the role of popular culture at Christmas: the fragmentation of cultural traditions/confusion of time and space).

Activity 2

Why study sociological theory?

In the extract, Craib (1992) suggests that the problems that lead people to theoretical thinking are the problems that we all face in our everyday lives. It also provides an encouragement to those who 'don't like theory' because it shows that sociological theory can be applied to everyday events and can affect us as individuals.

> I think the truth is that we all think theoretically but in a way which we are not often aware. What we are not used to is thinking theoretically in a systematic manner, with all the various constraints and rigours that involves . . .
>
> What, then, are the problems in response to which we all think theoretically without realising it? Most of us are affected in some way by events over which we have no control and the causes of which are not immediately obvious . . . A member of the family might be made unemployed, for example, or fail to gain an expected place at university or college; some product or service might suddenly become unavailable because of a strike, or because of government or local authority economies . . . We can do things to alleviate the effects of all of these, but they happen whether we as individuals like it or not, and it is by no means clear why they happen. There are similar, more intimate events in our personal lives: The slow change in the relationship between parents and children or between lovers, which no one wills but which nonetheless happen. I might suddenly find a friend has turned hostile for no obvious reason . . .
>
> In all these situations, we try to find some explanation. Often it takes the form of blaming somebody or thing, frequently unfairly – I lose my job because of all the blacks coming over here . . . Sometimes the blame is closer to the mark: I lose my job because of an economic situation largely created by government policy . . . Sometimes the explanations are more sophisticated, but my point is that as soon as we start thinking about and trying to explain something which happens to us, over which we have no control, we are beginning to think theoretically . . . Theory is an attempt to explain our everyday experience of the world, our 'closest' experience, in terms of something which is not so close – whether it be other people's actions, our past experience, our repressed emotions or whatever . . . every social theory makes some propositions which are counter to our immediate experiences and beliefs, and this is in fact the way in which we learn from theory. The punk might believe that she is in full rebellion against the culture of her parents and authority, yet for the functionalist theorist, she is setting in motion a series of adjustments by means of which that culture and society continue to survive in a smoother-running way than before. The worker might believe she is getting a fair day's wage for a fair day's work but for the Marxist she is being systematically exploited. When I fail a student's exam paper, I might believe that I am applying a rule and upholding academic standards . . . The symbolic interactionist would say that I am creating a failure.
>
> (Craib 1992: 5–10)

Questions

1. What are the problems with social theory?
2. What is the purpose of social theory?
3. What are the dominant perspectives in sociological theory?
4. Who are the main contributors to these perspectives?

Sociological research

Methods are not simply neutral tools: they are linked with the ways in which social scientists envision the connection between different viewpoints about the nature of social reality and how it should be examined. (Bryman 2008: 4)

Key issues

- What is sociological research?
- What different research methods are available to sociologists?
- What are the philosophies that underlie the collection and analysis of data?
- Why and in what ways have feminists criticized conventional sociological research?

Introduction

We all engage in some form of research in our everyday lives by collecting and processing information and coming to conclusions about a product, service or decision. You may have been stopped in the street and asked to take part in market research, testing the latest brand of a particular product. You may have heard research findings discussed in the news. Indeed, research is part of our everyday lives.

In this chapter we look at sociological research and explore why and how sociologists do research. Sociological research can provide explanations for issues that affect us both as individuals and as members of larger groups. It can help us to make the links between personal troubles and public issues, understanding, for example, how your social background can affect your educational attainment and why people in some countries die from diseases that have long since been eradicated in other parts of the world. People hold a vast range of views on social issues, such as why certain people become criminals, why women are massively underrepresented in positions of power in the political and business world, and why fewer people attend religious services now than in the past. The findings of sociological research should lessen the misconceptions and prejudices that often form the basis of common-sense views of many important issues such as these.

Why do sociologists do research?

To help us to answer this question, we can ask another – what does sociological research produce? Some typical answers may be 'facts', 'knowledge' and 'ideas'. Each of these has a particular meaning but can be seen as dimensions of a larger concept – 'evidence'.

Stop and think

Jim and Sarah are ordering food in a restaurant. Sarah wants to order the soup but is unsure whether it is vegetarian. Think about the way evidence is used in their conversation:

Sarah (to waiter) – Is the soup vegetarian?
Waiter – I'll check for you . . . [comes back from the kitchen and tells her it is made with vegetable stock. She orders the soup. It arrives]
Sarah – It is definitely vegetarian – I can taste it.
Jim (to Sarah) – But how do you know it really is and they aren't just saying that? [What proof is there?]
Sarah – I've had it here before anyway.

This is a very ordinary everyday example of how evidence is part of our lives and how we constantly use evidence to make judgements and to give support to what we are saying. In this example we can view evidence as understood and used in a number of ways:

- *Facts* – The soup was made with vegetable stock.
- *Confirmation* – Checking this fact when the soup is served.
- *Proof* – At what point, and why, do you believe the evidence? Sarah wanted the soup so wanted to believe the waiter and the chef. Jim, on the other hand, wanted to tease Sarah so implied that he did not believe it.

Now think of a situation in which you have used evidence and reflect on why you accepted or rejected the evidence.

We can see evidence as information that supports a statement, but we can also see it as a form of knowledge that stems from a range of sources. In every society there are many ways that we know what we know – many of which we take for granted. Scott (2002) identifies six basic categories of knowledge:

- *Common-sense knowledge* – Refers to something everyone knows to be true, for example fire burns.
- *Authority-based knowledge* – We tend to give a lot of credence to expert sources, such as doctors.
- *Experiential knowledge* – We develop knowledge based on our own experiences, which can at times differ from knowledge from experts. For example, some parents believe, from their own experience, that autism is linked to the MMR (measles, mumps and rubella) immunization, but most medical experts deny such a link.
- *Traditional knowledge* – Knowledge can also be based on practices passed down through generations to explain and justify many aspects of their lives, for example the Countryside Alliance, a UK organization supporting working and living in the countryside, often refers to 'tradition' in support of its beliefs.
- *Non-rational knowledge* – Based on faith, for example a belief in God.
- *Scientific knowledge* – Based on systematic, rigorous testing.

We can identify a range of different forms of knowledge that we use in different ways. What we can also begin to see is that they are not all given equal weight: there is a hierarchy, with some forms of knowledge being privileged over others. In some societies, knowledge based on tradition is valued most highly, while in others, non-rational, faith-based knowledge is the dominant form. The nature of what is considered to be privileged knowledge will vary from time to time and from place to place. If we look at Western Europe and trace back the forms of knowledge considered most accurate, and around which people lived their lives, we can see that religious belief (non-rational knowledge) was dominant for centuries. In the sixteenth century it was argued that the earth did not move and that people were the centre of the universe. Copernicus devised a theory that challenged this, claiming that the earth in fact revolved around the sun. He would not allow his theory to be published until he was dying because he was aware that the Roman Catholic Church would treat such a claim as heresy.

Indeed, when Galileo developed the ideas of Copernicus, he was imprisoned by the church (McIntyre 2005).

In contrast to earlier eras, in modern Western societies scientific knowledge is privileged. Science is generally accepted as the most valid form of knowledge, the most accurate way of knowing.

Stop and think

- Why do you think scientific knowledge is the dominant form of knowledge in Western societies?
- What alternative ways of knowing exist in these societies?

We could consider that scientific knowledge is privileged because it works; there are indeed many examples of the triumphs of science, space flight to name but one. Nevertheless, the effectiveness of a particular form of knowledge does not always relate to its general acceptance in society. In the chapter on health, we can see that the successes of many forms of complementary and alternative medicines have not resulted in their widespread inclusion in medical practice within Western societies. Forms of knowledge tend to be regarded as valid only if they fit with the ways in which people already make sense of the world.

Defining sociological research

So where does sociology fit in this discussion: what form does evidence take in sociology? Would it be sufficient for sociologists to base their claims on common sense, personal experience, faith in God, the word of an authority or tradition? Sociologists try to ensure that sociological knowledge goes beyond these forms. Instead, sociology derives its knowledge, its evidence, from research. Sarantakos defines research as

> **the purposive and rigorous investigation that aims to generate new knowledge . . . Social research is about discovery, expanding all horizons of the known, confidence, new ideas and new conclusions about all aspects of life.**
>
> (Sarantakos 2004: 4)

If we pick out some key phrases in this, we can further define sociological research and note the differences with knowledge based on common sense, faith or personal experience. Sociological research:

- *Generates new knowledge* – Sociological research creates new knowledge about a vast range of topics, some of which you can read about in the chapters of this book. Sociological research produces data (for example, statistics, interview recordings and observations) and from these data new understandings of the world around us are built.
- *Expands horizons of the known* – Research does not happen in a vacuum. Sociologists build on and develop the research of others. The critical evaluation of previous research is fundamental to sociology. Research should not produce findings because we want a particular result, or because we have a feeling that it should be that way. Rather, it has to be able to stand up to challenges from others who may disagree.
- *Involves purposive and rigorous investigation* – Sociological research is carried out in a systematic way. There is a clear plan concerning what the research involves and how it will be carried out, and this is documented to enable those reading the

A closer look

Primary and secondary data

There are two forms of data that sociologists work with – primary and secondary.

- Primary data are data collected first hand through a range of methods, including interviews, observations, experiments and questionnaires.
- Secondary data are collected by someone other than the researcher, for example official documents, statistics and media reports.

findings to evaluate the research. All sociological research is planned around a particular methodological approach – a way of producing knowledge. In this chapter we will explore the key methodologies used in sociology and the implications of this for research practice.

The foundations of sociological research

Some of you may be familiar with certain ways of doing research, for example using questionnaires, and you may have learnt the advantages and disadvantages of such tools. However, the choice of research tool is really the end point in planning research. To understand why researchers choose particular methods, and indeed for you to begin thinking about how you could design your own research, we need to consider the foundations of sociological research. In doing so, we will be using four key terms – methods, methodology, theory and epistemology. Crotty outlines their meaning:

- ***Methods*: the techniques or procedures used to gather and analyse data related to some research question or hypothesis**
- ***Methodology*: the strategy, plan of action, process or design lying behind the choice and use of particular methods and linking the choice and use of methods to the desired outcomes.**
- ***Theoretical perspective*: the philosophical stance informing the methodology and thus providing a context for the process and grounding its logic and criteria**
- ***Epistemology*: the theory of knowledge embedded in the theoretical perspective and thereby in the methodology.**

(Crotty 2003: 3)

These definitions indicate how the four aspects relate, but this can be seen more clearly through a diagram. Figure 3.1 shows the movement from epistemology to methods.

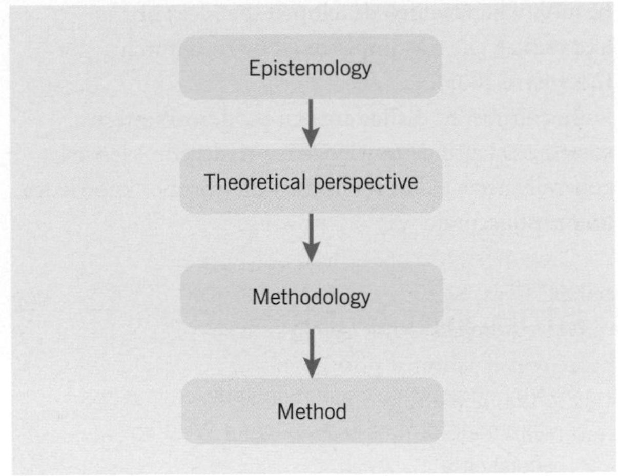

Figure 3.1 The movement from epistemology to methods

Starting from the bottom and working up, we can see that, in order to explain the reason for choosing a particular method, for example interviews, the researcher must have a strategy or plan of action – a methodology. The methodology is influenced by the researcher's theoretical perspective, which in turn is shaped by their wider beliefs about the status of the knowledge that we, as researchers, can access. For example, if, as a researcher, I believe that the meanings and interpretations people give to the world are the fundamental aspects of life that sociologists should study (epistemology), then I am likely to engage with sociological theories such as symbolic interactionism, which reflect those ideas (theoretical perspective). When carrying out research, I need to develop a strategy that fits with my interest in meaning (methodology) and finally I will need to choose tools to enable me to explore meanings (methods).

One of the most important things you learn from studying sociology is that people see and understand the world around them in many different ways. This is reflected in the different theoretical approaches you may have read about in Chapter 2. These different viewpoints have an impact on research because they shape the researcher's views on the type of knowledge that research can produce, and so on the best way to study social life. Here we will focus on the most fundamental difference raised by Bryman's question:

> **Whether social entities can and should be considered objective entities that have a reality external to social actors, or whether they can and should be considered social constructions built up from the perceptions and actions of social actors.**
>
> (Bryman 2004: 18)

Two positions are reflected within that question – objectivism and constructionism – and can be illustrated through an example. Social class can be defined and measured in many different ways. From an objectivist position, social class can be defined through a particular measure, which is likely to involve occupation, skill level and so on. This measure and indeed the class positions themselves exist independently of the perceptions of the people located within them. From a constructionist position, social class is regarded as having no independent, external reality. Rather, it is defined by perceptions, experiences and actions.

These positions are reflected in theoretical perspectives. Marxism and functionalism tend to reflect objectivist beliefs, while symbolic interactionism takes a more constructionist position. In relation to research, this fundamental difference also leads on to a key question – should sociology adopt the same principles for studying the social world as those used by scientists in their study of the natural world? The basic issue is how far the study of human behaviour and social life is fundamentally different from the study of the natural world.

Stop and think

- Think back to lessons you have had in chemistry, physics or other sciences. How were you taught to find out about things?
- How might the methods you were taught in those subjects be used to find out about social issues, such as (a) why some groups get better educational qualifications than others; and (b) why men commit more crime than women do?

There are two very broad theoretical approaches in sociological research: positivism and interpretivism. A positivist approach advocates the application of scientific methods to sociological research, while an interpretivist approach stresses the difference in studying human beings and the need to develop more applicable research strategies. We will look at each in more detail.

Positivism and sociology

Science is usually taken to refer to the natural sciences and (in the educational context) to subjects such as chemistry, physics and biology, which aim to explain the natural world in a logical manner by using specific techniques – the 'scientific method'. Science aims to produce knowledge that can be trusted because it is known to be true in all circumstances and at all times. It produces knowledge that has been empirically discovered and tested, rather than knowledge based on belief or faith.

Whether the scientific method can be applied to sociological research is a question that has excited considerable debate and divided opinion in sociology. Positivism takes an objectivist stance and this is reflected in its support of the scientific method of research. Positivist research in sociology tried to discover 'scientific laws', which could explain the causes, functions and consequences of social phenomena, such as rates of crime and suicide. The term 'laws' reflects a fairly hard-line position; many

A closer look

Positivism and interpretivism

Positivism and positivist research are based on the logic and method of science and scientific enquiry. Positivism sees empirical science (science based on experiments that are testable) as the only valid form of human knowledge. Auguste Comte coined the term when arguing that the application of the methods of the natural sciences to sociology would produce a 'positive science of society'. In contrast, the interpretivist perspective maintains that there is a fundamental difference between the subject matter of the natural and the social sciences.

Interpretivism can be defined as the study of the ways in which people understand and interpret the world in which they live. This perspective derives from the work of Max Weber. Although adopting a 'grand theoretical' approach, he argued that people cannot be studied in the same manner as the physical world. People attach meanings to what they do, and sociology has to acknowledge this and attempt to interpret those meanings.

positivists would aim to discover 'tendencies' rather than laws.

> **The sociologist [must] put himself in the same state of mind as the physicist, chemist or physiologist when he probes into a still unexplored region of the scientific domain. When he penetrates the social world, he must be aware that he is penetrating the unknown; he must feel himself in the presence of facts whose laws are as unsuspected as were those of life before the era of biology; he must be prepared for discoveries which will surprise and disturb him.**
>
> (Durkheim 1964: xlv)

Karl Popper (1902–94) was one of the foremost supporters of the scientific approach to research. In his view, scientific knowledge is the only valid form of knowledge. The development of knowledge is dependent on mutual criticism in that we learn about the world only by testing ideas against reality. Science proceeds by the disproving of generalizations, by refutation, according to Popper. Science should make generalizations or hypotheses that are open to testing. Scientists should be detached observers, suspicious of common-sense ideas and intuitions and able to reject theories that they may hold when there is evidence against them.

Popper's view has been widely accepted as an accurate account of what scientists do and has been instrumental in establishing the 'hypothetico-deductive' method: scientific knowledge and theory develop from the deducing and testing of hypotheses. The procedure is essentially a set of steps that describe how a particular piece of research is carried out. These steps are illustrated using the example of football hooliganism (Figure 3.2):

1. *Identification of a specific social issue or phenomenon that is to be investigated*: football hooliganism.
2. *Formulation of a hypothesis*: football hooliganism is caused by young people in 'dead-end' jobs that have little future and allow no scope for creativity and self-expression.
3. *Selection or design of a particular research method by which the hypothesis might be tested*: checking of

Figure 3.2 Should football hooligans be subjects for 'scientific' research?

police records of people arrested at football matches, followed up by asking those arrested what they feel about their employment situation.

4. *Collection of information*: examine police records and interview or give questionnaires to known football hooligans.
5. *Interpretation and analysis of the information gained*: relating the data gathered to the hypothesis being investigated, how many football hooligans were in 'dead-end' jobs?
6. *Formulation of a theory based on the tested hypothesis and the interpretation of the data collected*: there is (or is not) a causal link between employment situation and football hooliganism.
7. *Reporting the findings and conclusions, which must be open to discussion and retesting by others who may be interested*: in some cases, the findings might be used in the formulation of policy, perhaps in deciding whether to introduce identity cards as a requirement for entry to football grounds or whether to segregate and fence groups of football supporters into self-contained areas of the grounds.

The steps need not be followed in the exact order indicated above. For instance, a scientist may observe something happening and examine it without having any clear hypothesis in mind as to why it occurred; the hypothesis may emerge later in the investigation, perhaps after some information has been collected. In reality, research is rarely as clearcut as a textbook suggests.

Stop and think

- Select another issue or phenomenon that sociologists might investigate and consider how steps 2–7 of the scientific method detailed above could be applied to it. Consider how this scientific method could be applied to an examination of (a) the extent to which the television portrayal of women influences children's attitudes towards the role of women; and (b) the decline in attendance at religious services since the nineteenth century.
- Can you identify any weaknesses with this approach?

Consideration of the scientific method and its applicability to sociology highlights the relationship between sociological theory and method and the difficulty of looking at research methods in isolation. The formulation of a hypothesis and the type and style of questions asked will depend on the theoretical perspective favoured by the researcher. This theoretical perspective is also likely to guide the researcher towards certain 'facts'. Hypotheses do not appear from nowhere: they might derive from beliefs and theories that are already held. In our example of football hooliganism, the hypothesis emphasizing the employment situation could derive from a criticism of government economic

A closer look

Durkheim and 'social facts'

> In reality there is in every society a certain group of phenomena which may be differentiated from those studied by the other natural sciences. When I fulfill my obligations as brother, husband, or citizen, when I execute my contracts, I perform duties which are defined, externally to myself and my acts, in law and in custom. Even if they conform to my own sentiments and I feel their reality subjectively, such reality is still objective, for I did not create them; I merely inherited them through my education . . . Here, then, are ways of acting, thinking, and feeling that present the noteworthy property of existing outside the individual consciousness.
>
> These types of conduct or thought are not only external to the individual but are, moreover, endowed with coercive power, by virtue of which they impose themselves upon him, independent of his individual will . . . If I do not submit to the conventions of society, if in my dress I do not conform to the customs observed in my country and in my class, the ridicule I

A closer look *continued*

provoke, the social isolation in which I am kept, produce, although in an attenuated form, the same effects as a punishment in the strict sense of the word. The constraint is nonetheless efficacious for being indirect . . . Here, then, is a category of facts with very distinctive characteristics: it consists of ways of acting, thinking, and feeling, external to the individual, and endowed with a power of coercion, by reason of which they control him. These ways of thinking could not be confused with biological phenomena, since they consist of representations and of actions; nor with psychological phenomena, which exist only in the individual consciousness and through it. They constitute, thus, a new variety of phenomena; and it is to them exclusively that the term 'social' ought to be applied. And this term fits them quite well, for it is clear that, since their source is not in the individual, their substratum can be no other than society . . . It is true that, when we define them with this word 'constraint,' we risk shocking the zealous partisans of absolute individualism. For those who profess the complete autonomy of the individual, man's dignity is diminished whenever he is made to feel that he is not completely self-determinant. It is generally accepted today, however, that most of our ideas and our tendencies are not developed by ourselves but come to us from without. How can they become a part of us except by imposing themselves upon us? This is the whole meaning of our definition. And it is generally accepted, moreover, that social constraint is not necessarily incompatible with the individual personality.

(Durkheim 1964: 1–4)

Questions

1. Using Durkheim's broad definition, what 'social facts' have had an impact on your actions?
2. What do you think Durkheim means when he says that 'social constraint is not necessarily incompatible with the individual personality'?
3. Compare Durkheim's ideas on 'social facts' with Mills' concept of the 'sociological imagination' (see p. 11)

policy as having caused an increase in the sense of frustration felt by certain groups of people or from a wider theory about the alienating nature of work under capitalism.

As we noted above, positivist views about the applicability of scientific methods to the study of the social world have been disputed. We can now go on to explore a very different set of ideas about sociological research.

Interpretivism and sociology

Interpretivism, influenced by the work of German social scientist Max Weber, is sometimes presented as a reaction to positivist conceptions of science. However, we should not jump to the conclusion that this leads to an abandonment of science. Rather, it is a way of redefining science to enable the development of the best methods of studying the social world. The social world is considered to be very different from the natural world and so, it is argued, cannot be studied in the same way. Human beings live and act in the world in a conscious manner: a crucial difference from rocks, for example. Interpretivism takes a constructionist position, recognizing that people act consciously in order to create and re-create their worlds. We experience the world around us subjectively, and 'society' is not an objective entity; it is nothing more than the perceptions and actions of the people who exist within it. It is these perceptions and actions that are central to understanding human behaviour from an interpretivist stance. Rather than seeking causal relationships or laws that were said to determine people's behaviour, sociology should seek to understand how and why people interpret the social world in various ways. This is a very different form of science from that advanced by positivists, and we can highlight this difference by looking at the issue of value freedom in sociological research.

Can sociological research be value-free?

The positivist argument that sociology should attempt to be as scientific as possible is based on the belief that only science can provide the 'truth'. Scientists discover this truth by being completely objective, by dealing with facts. In their research, sociologists must be objective and neutral, must not take sides and should adopt an approach based on a position of value-freedom. This idea of value-freedom in sociological research – or indeed in scientific research in general – has not been universally accepted by sociologists. The facts collected in research depend on the questions asked, and it has been argued that sociological research is inevitably directed by values – which are cultural products. From this perspective, knowledge is a cultural product. What a society defines as knowledge reflects the values of that society; another society and culture will accord other things the status of 'knowledge'.

Case study

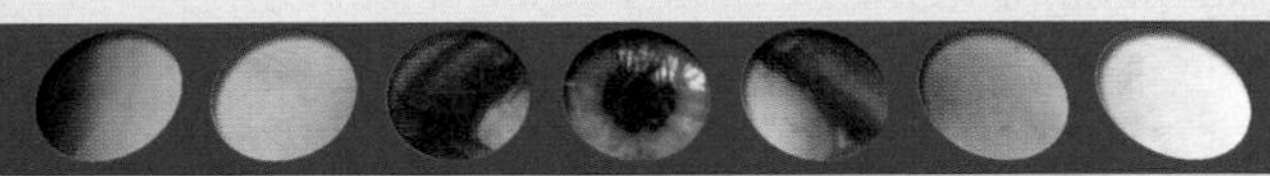

Value-freedom in sociology?

This extract is taken from Alvin Gouldner's attack on the model of objectivity promoted by positivist sociology.

> Does the belief in a value-free sociology mean that sociology is a discipline actually free of values and that it successfully excludes all non-scientific assumptions in selecting, studying and reporting on a problem? Or does it mean that sociology should do so? Clearly, the first is untrue and I know of no one who even holds it possible for sociologists to exclude completely their non-scientific beliefs from their scientific work; and if this is so, on what grounds can this impossible task be held to be morally incumbent on sociologists?
>
> Does the belief in a value-free sociology mean that sociologists are or should be indifferent to the moral implications of their work? Does it mean that sociologists can and should make value judgements so long as they are careful to point out that these are different from 'merely' factual statements? Does it mean that sociologists do not or should not have or express feelings for or against some of the things they study? Does it mean that sociologists should never take the initiative in asserting that some beliefs which laymen hold, such as the belief in the inherent inferiority of certain races, are false even when known to be contradicted by the facts of their discipline? Does it mean that sociologists should never speak out, or speak out only when invited, about the probable outcomes of a public course of action concerning which they are professionally knowledgeable? Does it mean that social scientists should never express values in their roles as teachers or in their roles as researchers, or in both? Does the belief in a value-free sociology mean that sociologists, either as teachers or researchers, have a right to covertly and unwittingly express their values but have no right to do so overtly and deliberately?
>
> I fear that there are many sociologists today who, in conceiving social science to be value-free, mean widely different things, that many hold these beliefs dogmatically without having examined seriously the grounds upon which they are credible. Weber's own views on the relation between values and social science, and some current today are scarcely identical. If Weber insisted on the need to maintain scientific objectivity, he also warned that this was altogether different from moral indifference.

(Adapted from Gouldner 1973: 5–6)

Question

1. In what ways might the values of a researcher influence the following stages of research:

   (a) the choice of research issue;

   (b) the formulation of a hypothesis;

   (c) the choice of research method;

   (d) the choice of questions asked (if any);

   (e) the interpretation of results;

   (f) the presentation of findings?

Howard Becker is an advocate of the view that sociological research need not, and often cannot, be value-free. In his classic study of deviance, *Outsiders* (1963), he argues that it is difficult to study both 'sides' involved in deviance objectively – the rule-breakers and rule-enforcers – and that, whichever group is chosen to study, there will inevitably be some bias. Becker suggests that there is a strong case for sociologists representing the views and attitudes of the deviants as it is their views that will be least known about and therefore most open to misrepresentation. C. Wright Mills, in his renowned introduction to sociology, *The Sociological Imagination* (1970), also makes the point that social scientists cannot avoid choices of values influencing their work. Political and moral concerns are central to sociology and value-freedom is, therefore, impossible. In a similar vein to Becker and Wright Mills, Erving Goffman, in reflecting on his study of mental patients, *Asylums*, argued that it was unrealistic to aim to be value-neutral:

> **To describe the patient's situation faithfully is necessarily to present a partisan view. For this bias I partly excuse myself by arguing that the imbalance is at least on the right side of the scale, since almost all professional literature on mental patients is written from the point of view of the psychiatrist.**
>
> (Goffman 1968: 8)

These arguments contrast with the positivist view that scientists must aim to produce value-neutral knowledge and that sociology should aim to be value-free. As we have seen, the debates raised by this question relate to the particular epistemological and theoretical position of the researcher. If a researcher begins with a view that the social world is objective and external, this will lead them towards a theoretical perspective that reflects this belief – that is, towards a positivist position. If, on the other hand, a researcher begins with a view that the social world is constructed by the perceptions and actions of those within it, then they will favour an approach that sees perceptions and actions as central to understanding behaviour. In the discussion in this section, we have laid the foundations for understanding how research strategies (methodologies) are developed.

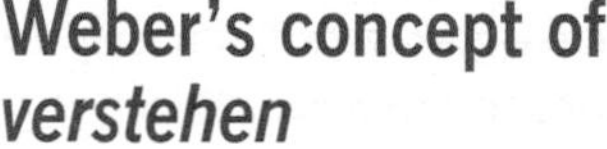

A closer look

Weber's concept of *verstehen*

> Social scientists cannot hope to formulate general laws on the basis of observing [patterns of behaviour] . . . It is clearly impossible to find out about a person's motivations and intentions simply by watching their outward behaviour – the ideas people have about the society they live in and the machinations of their inner world cannot be directly observed. What people do has to be interpreted in the light of the meanings, motives and intentions behind their action . . . Instead, [social scientists] have to ask questions about the beliefs people hold and the meanings they attach to action. They have to concern themselves with the inner world of their subjects in order to understand why they act as they do . . . *Verstehen* essentially involves the attempt to understand social action through a kind of empathetic identification with the social actor. The researcher must try to see the world through the eyes of the research subject in order to grasp the meanings, motives and intentions behind their action . . . through rigorous study, the researcher can build up a picture of how the world appears to others and of the choices and constraints that they perceive . . . When interpretative understanding is achieved, the meaning of a given form of social action becomes clear.
>
> (O'Connell Davidson and Layder 1994: 31)

Questions

1. Contrast this statement with Durkheim's ideas on 'social facts' on pp. 115–116.
2. What methods do you think are appropriate to Weber's ideas on social action and *verstehen*?

Methodologies: how to produce sociological knowledge

Methodology refers to the strategy or plan for carrying out the research that allows the researcher to answer their research questions. It should be clear that the methodological approach of a researcher is not plucked from the air; it is very much shaped by their epistemological and theoretical stance. Positivists argue that it is possible to measure human behaviour in an objective sense and to identify cause and effect relationships. A suitable methodology is one that is deemed to be as objective as possible. Therefore knowledge is best produced by developing hypotheses that can be tested against empirical observations (Popper's hypothetico-deductive method). In contrast, an interpretivist approach would stress the need to understand how people see and interpret the world in which they live. A suitable methodology must facilitate this understanding – that is, it must enable the researcher to get the 'insider's view'. The most significant distinction between methodological strategies is between quantitative and qualitative research.

Quantitative and qualitative research

Although it is not possible to establish hard and fast connections between methodologies and particular theoretical positions, a quantitative methodology is likely to be used by those who favour a 'macrosociological' perspective and a qualitative methodology by those favouring 'microsociology'. Many of the early, 'grand' social theorists adopted a macro-, or large-scale, approach in their writings. Karl Marx, for instance, set out to describe and explain the origins and development of modern industrial capitalist society. He examined different types of society – tribal, feudal, capitalist and communist – and explored how one type of system evolved from another. Consequently, he had little interest in the personal beliefs of individuals or their motives for action and spent little time engaged in trying to discover what individuals actually thought. Marx and other classical sociologists who are regarded as the founders of the discipline, including Durkheim and Weber, based their analyses of society on evidence from second-hand, general and historical sources rather than on original, first-hand research. At a similar period to the writing of these early sociologists, around the turn of the nineteenth century, social reformers such as Charles Booth and Seebohm Rowntree were doing quantitative research in the form of large-scale surveys.

The concern of qualitative research tends to be with the small scale; a close-up view of society is taken. Such sociological research might focus on one aspect of social behaviour, perhaps a religious group or a juvenile gang. Although this form of research might consider broad issues, the emphasis is different; there is less concern with generalizing about whole societies from particular instances and more focus on interpreting the behaviour of individuals and groups.

McNeill (1990) emphasizes the cyclical nature of trends in sociological research. After the Second World War, the importance of objective data and statistical proof was stressed, particularly in the sociological work pursued in the USA and the UK. During the 1960s a reaction against this kind of sociological research developed, and the qualitative approach became the vogue. While various methodological approaches tend to be popular at different times, the extent of the division into an 'either one or the other' approach should not be overstated. Pawson (1989) suggests that the supposed conflict between positivists and interpretivists has led to certain methodological myths being propagated, in particular that the two traditions or approaches are mutually incompatible and in a state of permanent dispute. As he puts it,

> **no good sociologist should get his or her hands dirty with the paradigm wars . . . both qualitative and quantitative approaches face identical problems and need to adopt common solutions.**
>
> (Pawson 1989: 31–2)

Pawson argues that quantitative sociology can be based on non-positivist lines. Sociologists should not be afraid to admit that research is influenced by theory: the fact that sociologists pick and choose the evidence that they will examine according to their theoretical interests should not be seen as a failure of positivism. For example, in the sociological study of religion, one researcher might focus on the high proportions of people who believe in God and the growing numbers who express an interest in superstition and new forms of religious expression as evidence to demonstrate the continuing importance of religion in modern society. Another might emphasize declining attendance at mainstream churches as the key evidence on the importance of religion in society. Pawson also points out that, even in 'respected' sciences such as physics,

A closer look

Quantitative and qualitative research

Quantitative research involves the collection and presentation of numerical data, which can be codified and subjected to detailed statistical testing. It follows the scientific method in so far as it attempts to discover and measure facts about society and social behaviour. Information is collected and analysed in order to test a specific hypothesis (see pp. 114–115). Methods of research include gathering social data through questionnaires and structured interviews. These techniques usually involve studying large numbers of subjects so that the findings can be used as a basis for presenting general conclusions about social behaviour.

Qualitative research focuses on smaller units of society and on the understanding of social situations and the meanings that individuals attach to behaviour. It is a more subjective approach, whereby the researcher aims to understand and interpret the experiences of the individuals involved by viewing the world through the eyes of the individuals being studied. Methods of research include various forms of interviews and observation.

the data collected are influenced by theory; even the instruments used by physicists, such as thermometers, have been developed and constructed on the basis of complex theories. Similarly, Pawson argues that it is mythical to see qualitative research as a coherent and superior alternative that can get to grips with the special character of human meaning.

Therefore, it is important to highlight the limitations of dividing all research into either quantitative or qualitative. There are various subdivisions within the two broad approaches, overlaps between quantitative and qualitative research, and many examples of sociological research that have adopted aspects of both approaches. Nonetheless, this broad division provides a structure for examining the various research methods used by sociologists. Before going on to discuss these methods in more detail, we need to consider the general methodological issues that all researchers need to address – sampling, gaining access and ethics.

Sampling

Researchers, including sociologists, cannot collect data from everyone they wish to survey. A 100 per cent response would be the ideal, but for practical reasons researchers have to *sample* – that is, select people or information – from the population they are researching. All researchers are systematic in their approach to sampling, but the particular approach taken will depend on the methodological strategy and research questions. For example, you may want to find out how many people in Scotland use complementary therapies, what kind of therapies, how often and for what conditions. Your aim is to be able to say that *x*% of the population uses complementary therapies, so it is very important to be able to achieve a sample that is representative of the whole population. However, if your research is a qualitative in-depth exploration of people's experiences using complementary therapies, then your sample will be much smaller and so it is less likely that you would try to achieve a representative sample. Instead, the focus would be on the depth of understanding provided by the study of a particular group.

Sampling methods

- *Random or probability sampling* is where all the members of a population have a chance of selection – for instance, all schoolchildren of a particular age in a particular area – and perhaps one in every 100 is selected.
- *Quota or stratified sampling* is the major form of non-probability sampling. Here, the technique is to make the sample non-random deliberately by splitting it up beforehand, usually into categories such as sex, age or class, and then selecting a certain number for investigation from each category. Random sampling and quota sampling are the most commonly used methods of sampling.
- *Snowball or opportunity sampling* is where one person selected and questioned recommends another person, and so on.

A closer look

Growing Up in Scotland survey

Growing Up in Scotland is a large-scale longitudinal social survey designed to examine the characteristics, circumstances and behaviours of children from birth to late adolescence. It is being carried out by the Scottish Centre for Social Research in collaboration with the Centre for Families and Relationships at Edinburgh University. The sample of children was drawn from child benefit records (CBR) held by the Department for Work and Pensions. In order to accommodate a representative random sample of children that could be accessed efficiently by the interviewers from the study, a process known as primary sampling units (PSUs) was selected. These units enable the fieldwork to be managed efficiently by the study's interviewers, since the selected families are clustered in particular geographic areas. The PSUs are based on aggregations of data zones, which are newly geographic units being increasingly used as the basis of neighbourhood statistics in Scotland. These data zones were randomly selected within a stratification scheme based on region and deprivation. Within these sample PSUs, all eligible children are then sampled for the 0–1 years cohort, and three-fifths of all eligible children are selected for the 2–3 years cohort. Where a 0 to 1-year-old child has a sibling aged 2–3 years, one child is selected at random. A total of 8000 children were enrolled into the study in 2005–06.

Source: Growing Up in Scotland (www.crfr.ac.uk/gus/index.html).

Gaining access

When we decide to do research on a particular topic and with a particular group of people, we need to consider how to access this group. How will we make contact with the group, inform them and ensure there are enough people willing to take part in the research? This involves knowing what sample you want to end up with and identifying places where it is most likely that you will find the kind of people you are aiming to recruit into the research. For example, if you are carrying out research with parents, you could start with plans to contact them through schools, parent and toddler groups and parenting organizations. Often a wide range of recruitment measures are needed; these may include strategies such as advertising in local newspapers and handing out flyers in shopping centres.

Each research project will have its own recruitment challenges. If a topic is very sensitive or not considered important, people may be less willing to participate. The method of research may also have an impact on recruitment. If we want to do face-to-face interviews, then there may be more issues than if we want to do questionnaires. If we want people to be involved repeatedly in experiments or in repeat interviews, that might raise issues about commitment over a period of time. Finally, access to certain groups considered to be 'vulnerable' will require negotiation with 'gatekeepers'. For example, in the UK, if you are carrying out research with children and want to access them through schools, you need first to contact the local council to seek permission to approach the school, then the head teacher must be willing to allow you to contact the children in her school, then parents must give permission for their children to participate, and finally you must ask the child whether they want to participate in the research.

Ethical issues

> **Sociologists have a responsibility to ensure that the physical, social and psychological well-being of research participants is not adversely affected by the research. They should strive to protect the rights of those they study, their interests, sensitivities and privacy, while recognising the difficulty of balancing potentially conflicting interests.**
>
> (British Sociological Association 2002)

Ethical standards require that researchers do not put participants in a situation where they might be at risk of

Case study

Participant observation

Participant observation involves the researcher becoming a part of a group or community in order to study it; initially, then, there is a need to gain access. Roy Wallis's (1976) research into the Church of Scientology illustrates the problems associated with this.

Scientology was founded by L. Ron Hubbard, a science-fiction writer, who developed a religious doctrine based on the idea that humans can regain the spiritual powers they have lost through a process of training that unlocks the doors to these powers. The movement has attracted considerable controversy since the 1960s. Wallis's interest in studying Scientology was hampered by its reluctance to be investigated. As a result he joined and followed an introductory course put on by Scientologists and became a participant observer. As a secret or covert participant observer, Wallis had difficulty in showing his support for and commitment to the beliefs of Scientology and felt uncomfortable deceiving members of the sect, saying 'Disguised or covert participant observation is easy when no participation beyond mere presence is required. When the interaction moves on to a more personal basis and participation of a more active kind is necessitated, role-playing dilemmas present themselves.' He did not complete the course, but the participant observation gave Wallis an insight into Scientology from the perspective of a potential recruit and provided the basis for another approach – this time he adopted an *overt* strategy and applied directly to the leaders for permission to interview members of the Church. He was given permission but, probably due to his earlier deception, his research was hampered by a series of 'mysterious and unpleasant happenings' and his first attempts to publish his findings met with threats of legal action. He was forced to concede some editorial control to the Church and over 100 amendments were made before final publication.

At the end of his study Wallis reminds us that research takes place within the context of power:

> The sociologist's interaction with his subjects forms a part of, and takes place in the context of, the overall interaction between those subjects and the wider society. He may be seen as a potential legitimator or defender of their public image or a threat to it. Those groups which are, or have been, in conflict with agencies of the wider society are likely to view a potential threat to their public image with hostility . . . The sociologist who undertakes to study the social structure and dynamics of powerful groups . . . must expect his revelations to be met with hostility and the mobilisation of strategies to censor or even prohibit his work . . . While in the past sociologists have . . . displayed concern over the dangers of harming the interests of the powerless groups they have chosen to study, they should not altogether forget the problems of the relatively powerless sociologist faced with the threat of censorship.
>
> (Wallis 1976)

Questions

1. What problems of access would be faced by research into (a) inmate culture in prisons; (b) the division of household tasks between partners; (c) sexism and/or racism in the school playground; and (d) the decision-making processes of business and companies?
2. Following the Macpherson Report in 1999 (see Chapter 6), BBC reporter Mark Daly joined the Manchester police force to examine the extent to which 'institutional racism' still existed and kept an undercover record of his experiences at the Police Training Centre in Warrington using hidden cameras. Despite pressure from the government and Mark Daly's subsequent arrest, the documentary *The Secret Policeman* was broadcast in 2003.
   (a) Why do you think Mark Daly chose this method of investigation?
   (b) Do you think he was justified in using this technique?
   (c) What problems do you think this posed for him?

harm as a result of their participation. Although arising in relation to concerns about medical research, the need to protect human subjects from being used as 'guinea pigs' in scientific research is also applied to social science research. Harm can be defined as both physical and psychological, for example causing undue stress, anxiety or emotional distress. The now infamous experiments by Milgram (1974), which explored our capacity for cruelty, illustrate the potential that social science has for causing psychological harm to participants. The volunteers in Milgram's experiments were asked to play the role of either 'teacher' or 'learner'; the teachers were then told to deliver electric shocks to the learners as punishments when they made errors. Although the 'teacher' volunteers did not know the experiment was set up so that no electric shock was transmitted, the majority of them were prepared to deliver what they felt to be severe shocks. If you were one of these volunteers, how would you feel about yourself after you had taken part? For many people, participation in such an experiment may lead to self-doubt and a questioning of identity and so can be seen as causing harm.

Milgram's experiment also raises the issue of what it means to be a research 'volunteer'. The principle of voluntary participation requires that people not be coerced into participating in research. Fundamental to voluntary participation is the requirement for informed consent. Essentially, this means that prospective research participants must be informed fully about the procedures and risks involved in research and must give their consent to participate. However, any group of people who are used to others speaking for them and making decisions for them, such as children, pose a more difficult challenge when it comes to consent (see Chapter 7 for more discussion of this issue). In addition, giving consent should be seen as an ongoing process, and consent can be withdrawn at any time.

In addition to gaining informed consent, researchers must ensure the particpants' rights to privacy. There are two standards that are applied in order to help protect the privacy of research participants. Research guarantees participants' confidentiality and anonymity: the participants are assured that their responses, their interviews and notes about them will not be shown to others until the information has been anonymized – that is, until all identifying features, most obviously names, are removed. Researchers need to anticipate any issues that may arise in order to ensure that confidentiality and anonymity are maintained. In many studies, not only is the identity of individual respondents kept secret, but also the names of schools, organizations and towns are changed in order to avoid identification.

When discussing research ethics, there is an even more fundamental question that we can raise about academic research – research for whom? Who benefits from the research that sociologists do, and what responsibility do we have to those who participate in research with us? The British Sociological Association (2002) ethical code states that

> **Sociologists, when they carry out research, enter into personal and moral relationships with those they study, be they individuals, households, social groups or corporate entities.**

It is the very nature of the relationship we have with the people who participate in research that is the focus here. However, we can really consider the nature of this relationship only by looking in more detail at the issues raised in relation to specific research methods.

Methods of research

We mentioned at the start of the chapter that the choice of method is often the last point in planning research and is shaped by the methodology and in turn by the epistemological and theoretical position of the researcher. When investigating a particular issue or phenomenon, the sociologist is not limited to any one method. What is important is that the method fits – that is, it reflects the research strategy and it helps the researcher to answer their research questions.

Quantitative research

Surveys

The survey is usually a large-scale method of research that involves collecting information from large numbers of people. Although this information is typically gathered from questionnaires or interviews, a survey is not limited to any one technique of collecting information. In contrast to qualitative research, which provides a more in-depth study of social life, surveys tend to produce information that is less detailed but that can form the basis for making statistical generalizations over broad areas.

There are many well-known examples of large-scale surveys that have been used in sociological research, including the studies of poverty in the early years of the

A closer look

Reliability and validity

Examination of the different methods of sociological research should consider the concepts of reliability and validity. The degree of reliability and validity acts as a sort of quality control indicator in the assessment of any particular research method.

Reliability refers to consistency in research; however, the way that consistency is interpreted depends on the researcher's epistemological and theoretical stance. From a positivist approach, reliability refers to when repeated applications of the same technique of collecting or analysing information produce the same results. To ensure this is possible, data collection methods should be highly structured so that any researcher would collect the same types of data from the same respondent. Unreliability would be a human error that could be eliminated. In contrast, an interpretivist approach focuses on the fluid nature of reality based on our perceptions and actions and so would reject the notion that it is possible to repeatedly 'capture' that reality and expect it to be the same. Again, this difference of opinion relates to fundamental differences of understanding about the nature of the social world and how it can be studied. Rather, interpretivists would seek to ensure reliability through consistency, though not necessarily standardization, in research procedures.

Validity refers to the degree to which the findings of research can be relied on, and it involves an evaluation of all the methodological objections that can be made about the particular research. This is an obvious requirement for good research; however, as with reliability, the notion of validity applies differently to different approaches to research. Positivist quantitative research tends to refer to the extent to which a technique measures what the researcher intends it to measure. Qualitative research does not 'measure' social phenomenon, so for some issues we are better asking 'are we accurately reflecting the phenomena under study as perceived by the study population?' (Lewis and Ritchie 2003: 274).

Others argue that reliability and validity are inherently positivist concepts, and not applicable to interpretivist qualitative research, and suggest that new evaluative concepts should be developed. Guba and Lincoln (1994) developed **alternative criteria** to evaluate the trustworthiness of research: credibility, transferability, dependability and confirmability.

twentieth century undertaken by Charles Booth and Seebohm Rowntree, the Oxford Mobility Studies of the 1970s, and the British Crime Surveys of the past 20 plus years. The British Crime Survey was set up in 1982 to investigate crime through a sample survey of 11,000 households that asked people about their experiences of crime. It was established to address the limitations of official crime statistics, particularly the fact that those statistics include only crimes that are known to the police. The British Crime Survey asked this large sample of people whether they had been victims of crime and whether they had themselves committed any crimes over the previous year. The British Crime Survey has shown that there is a great deal of crime, including serious crime, that does not appear in the official statistics. The British Crime Survey also provides information on public fear of crime, perceptions of antisocial behaviour and attitudes to the criminal justice system.

Stop and think

- What kinds of questions could be asked to find out whether people have been victims of crime?
- What do you think might be the problems with and limitations of surveys that ask about people's experiences of crime?

Surveys can be distinguished from other research methods by the forms of data collection and data analysis. Surveys produce structured or systematic sets of data, providing information on a number of variables or characteristics, such as age, sex and political affiliation. As questionnaires are the easiest way of getting such structured data, they are the most common

A closer look

Can surveys measure social change?

Surveys involving the collection of information at one point of time are referred to as **cross-sectional surveys**; they provide a snapshot picture. The data gathered provide information such as who would vote for a particular political party or who belongs to a particular occupational grouping. Cross-sectional surveys that are repeated at different times, such as the British Crime Survey and the General Household Survey, allow some analysis of change over time.

Longitudinal surveys provide data that enable the analysis of change at the individual or microlevel. One of the best-known longitudinal surveys in the UK is the cohort studies of the National Child Development Study, in which a sample of children born in April 1958 have been followed from birth and interviewed at various stages of their lives. More recently, the British Household Panel Survey has been established at the University of Essex. This is made up of 10,000 people who were interviewed annually throughout the 1990s. Such longitudinal surveys are concerned with the behaviour of people over time and are therefore well suited to the analysis of change.

(Adapted from Rose and Gershuny 1995: 11–12)

technique used in survey research. The analysis of data produced from a survey will provide standardized information on all the subjects being studied, for example how much television people watch a week or how people intend to vote. Surveys can also provide detail on the causes of phenomena such as variations in age, and suggest the extent to which this influences television-watching or voting behaviour.

Surveys are one method of collecting and analysing data that usually involve large numbers of subjects. They are seen as highly reliable in that the data collected can be easily coded and analysed and should not vary according to the person or people collecting it. In conducting a large-scale survey, it is clearly impossible to investigate every single case or person, which raises the issue of sampling, and whether a smaller number can be used to represent a larger population (see p. 120). However, the fact that the data gained from surveys are necessarily restricted can be seen as a strength, in that it enables the analysis of these data to focus on standardized questions.

Criticisms of surveys

According to de Vaus (1986), the major criticisms of surveys can be classified as philosophical, technique-based and political. Philosophical criticisms suggest that surveys cannot uncover the meanings of social action: they neglect the role of human consciousness, goals and values as important sources of action. To some extent these kinds of criticism are linked with more general criticisms of quantitative sociology as being too rigidly scientific, being too focused on hypothesis testing and the collection of facts and statistics, and neglecting imaginative and creative thinking. Some surveys do, however, try to discover what people (say they) think; for example, the British Crime Surveys ask respondents about their attitudes to crime.

Technique-based criticisms emphasize the restrictiveness of surveys due to their reliance on highly structured ways of collecting data. The statistical emphasis is seen as reducing interesting issues to sterile and incomprehensible numbers. Political criticisms of surveys see them as being manipulative: the aura of science surrounding them gives power to those who commission and use the data. Survey data can be used to justify and further particular political interests. However, it is important to remember that surveys can provide unreliable information and are sometimes wrong. The surveys carried out before the 1992 general election in Britain predicted a very close-run election; however, the Conservatives were elected for a fourth term of office with an overall majority. The pre-election opinion poll surveys overestimated the Labour vote by 4 per cent and underestimated the Conservative vote by 4.5 per cent. Much of this difference was attributed by the Market Research Society to 'fundamental problems' in the way opinion polls are conducted. With regard to voting intentions, there would seem to be a persistent and growing exaggeration of the Labour vote, which suggests that the sampling procedures used are missing a significant proportion of Conservative voters, or that some Conservatives lie about their voting intentions. Concern about the accuracy of survey polls has led to them being outlawed during election campaigns in some countries: in France, for example, they are banned for a period just before elections.

In defence of surveys

Despite the criticisms, O'Connell Davidson and Layder defend the use of surveys as being part of the armoury of techniques available to sociologists. Surveys may have limitations, but they are a useful means of producing certain types of data:

> **Surveys are not *the* or best method for acquiring objective knowledge. But we should also recognise that survey methods are a valuable adjunct to other techniques. Surveys can play a vital role in confirming more qualitative research, in highlighting gaps in knowledge or issues that require further investigation, and in revealing broad patterns that might be missed if researchers relied solely upon qualitative methods.**
>
> (O'Connell Davidson and Layder 1994: 114–115)

Collecting quantitative data: questionnaires and structured interviews

Although a number of techniques for collecting information are available to sociologists who conduct surveys, information is usually gathered from questionnaires and/or structured interviews. While there are clearly differences between questionnaires and structured interviews – in terms of the way they are administered and the issues and problems they raise – we shall focus here on some of the common elements.

Respondents (the subjects from whom information is sought) can be asked questions, which are either written down in a questionnaire or presented verbally in an interview. The questions used in survey research are always structured – that is, organized into a particular order and wording. However, the range and form of possible responses can vary from providing only a limited number of possible responses such as 'yes', 'no' and 'don't know' or ticking one of a list of statements, or they can be more open-ended. The range of responses affects the extent to which data can be coded and analysed. Using the example of the question on voting given opposite, it would be straightforward to

Case study

Asking questions about sex

We may think that members of the public would keep their sexual behaviour to themselves, but a series of surveys have gained a range of data. Structured closed-ended questions through interview or by questionnaire are the conventional techniques:

- *Kinsey Reports* (1940s–1950s) – Almost 20,000 interviews of volunteers (approximately 90 minutes per interview). Described as a 'scientific voyage to explore the unknown world (of) the sex life of human beings', these revealed some surprising sexual antics in conservative America.
- 1949 mass observation survey of 2000 men and women in UK (also known as 'Little Kinsey') – Regarded as 'too explosive to publish'.
- *Hite Report* (1974) – Thousands of questionnaires to gain data on sexual experiences of women challenged many myths about female sexuality.
- Scully (1990) *Understanding Sexual Violence* – Highly structured (and very long) interviews with 114 rapists.
- *British National Survey of Sexual Attitudes* (1992) – Almost 19,000 men and women in a random-sample survey. Published in spite of government withdrawal of funding.
- *The Global Sex Survey* (2005) – More than 317,000 people from 41 countries took part in the world's largest sex survey.

Visit the website www.durex.com/cm/gss2005results.asp to discover some interesting cross-cultural differences; for example, Greeks come top of the global sex chart, with an average 138 bonks per year, while the Japanese can manage only a weedy 45.

A closer look

Question styles

In a questionnaire or structured interview that aims to provide information on voting, a closed-ended question might be:

How did you vote in the 2005 general election? (please tick)

Conservative

Labour

Liberal Democrat

Other

An open-ended question might ask:

Why did you vote the way you did in the 2005 election?

with space left for a lengthy response.

code 'Conservative', 'Labour', 'Liberal Democrat' and 'other' as 1, 2, 3 and 4: such coding would make the statistical analysis of the data easier.

As questionnaires and structured interviews are considered to provide data that are both reliable and quantitative, their use is generally advocated by positivist research in an attempt to provide a scientific basis for sociology. However, these methods do raise some awkward questions concerning the reliability and validity of sociological research.

How can we be sure that the people we want to question will agree? If they do, can we be sure that they are giving honest answers? Not only will the researcher have little control over these problems – it is not feasible to force people to be involved in research – but there is also the difficulty of ensuring that the way in which the question is asked does not influence the way that it is answered. It is important to be aware of the danger of leading questions and loaded words in the design of questionnaires and interviews.

Order effect

Another factor that can influence people's responses to questionnaires and structured interviews is the way in which questions are ordered. In research into *order effect* in survey questionnaires, Schuman *et al.* (1985) noted a marked difference in the responses to the same question. They asked first: 'Do you think the United States should let Communist newspaper reporters from other countries in here and send back to their papers the news as they see it?' They followed this with 'Do you think a Communist country should let American newspaper reporters come in and send back to their papers the news as they see it?' In that order, 44 per cent of Americans asked said 'yes' to the first question. Using a split sample technique, where half the sample was asked the second question first, the numbers agreeing that communist reporters should be allowed to visit the USA rose markedly, to 70 per cent. It would seem that an initial antagonism to foreign, communist reporters was significantly modified once people considered how they would feel about limitations on access to other countries for their 'own' reporters.

Bias

Survey research, with the use of structured methods of collecting data, is seen as the most effective way to provide an objective science of society. As well as the doubts raised concerning the influence of the wording and ordering of questions on the objectivity of such research, the extent to which bias is eliminated from these methods has been challenged. The way in which people respond to questions may be influenced by *prestige bias*, in that answers that might be felt to undermine or threaten prestige may be avoided. People tend to claim that they read more than they do, for instance, or that they engage in more 'cultural' activities than they do. Answers to certain questions can reflect unfavourably on an individual's lifestyle: negative answers to questions such as 'Are you satisfied with your job?' could be seen as being too self-critical, admitting one's life to be a bit of a failure. Research into deviant behaviour is often confronted with this problem, as respondents may exaggerate or play down levels of alcohol consumption, drug abuse or criminal behaviour.

A classic, widely reported example of respondents reacting to a word concerns the different responses to the terms 'working class' and 'lower class'. A Gallup poll survey in the USA in 1933 found that 88 per cent of a sample of the population described themselves as middle class, while only 1 per cent said they were lower class. Members of the sample had been offered a choice of three alternatives – upper, middle and lower class.

A closer look

Leading questions and loaded words

Leading questions are worded so that they are not neutral: they either suggest an answer or indicate the questioner's point of view. They are called leading questions because they lead the respondent towards one answer over another or to one response only. Kinsey has been accused of this in his sex surveys, when he assumed that all respondents were sexually active and phrased his questions accordingly, for example 'How often do you masturbate?'

Loaded words excite emotions in the respondent that will be likely to suggest automatic feelings of approval or disapproval: the respondent reacts to the particular word or phrase rather than to the question itself.

A similar survey was repeated shortly afterwards, with the term 'lower class' replaced by 'working class'; this time, 51 per cent of the sample described themselves as working class.

Finally, there is also the danger of *interviewer bias*. Even with tightly structured questionnaires and interviews, the respondent might still react to the interviewer – to their age, gender or race, for example – and provide answers that it is felt the interviewer is looking for. In his research into the failure of black children in the US educational system, Labov (1969) found that black children responded differently to white and black interviewers; with the white interviewer, there seemed to be a sense of hostility that limited the responses from the children. Of course, race is not the only factor that influences interview responses. As Lawson (1986) puts it, 'the interviewee may be antagonistic towards interviewers for no other reason than a dislike of the clothes they are wearing'.

Stop and think

- You want to find out about attitudes to (a) unemployment and (b) juvenile delinquency. Give examples of 'loaded words' that you should avoid in framing your questions.
- Write down an example of a leading question for both areas of investigation.
- Write down a 'neutral' version of those questions.
- How might prestige bias and interviewer bias affect the findings from surveys?

This discussion of survey research has not covered the range of research methods that could be put under the heading of 'quantitative', and we shall look at some of the other methods used by sociologists later in the chapter. In essence, quantitative research attempts to follow the scientific method of positivism. The research should be reliable and replicable: the data should be collected systematically and be standardized so that, regardless of who collects the data, the same findings will always emerge. These findings should be generalizable, to a wider population, allowing laws to be established on their basis.

In the next section, qualitative research is examined. Here, the interest is in the smaller-scale research; the focus is on 'meanings' and 'experiences'. An attempt is made to understand the lives of those being studied; as well as the use of less structured, informal interviews, qualitative research has emphasized the importance of observation. At the risk of being overly repetitive, it should be stressed again that sociological research is not simply an either/or choice and that the trend in recent research has been to use a number of different methods, both quantitative and qualitative.

Qualitative research

There is considerable variety in what we term 'qualitative research', but we can outline some basic features. In doing so, it is useful to consider Mason's question: 'What is qualitative about qualitative research?' (2002: 3–4). Qualitative research is:

- *Based on an interpretivist position* – Qualitative researchers are interested in exploring the ways in which participants interpret and experience the world around them.

- *Based on flexible methods of data collection* – Flexibility is central to qualitative research because there is a recognized need be able to respond to context within which research is taking place. This means that highly structured, standardized methods are not considered suitable.
- *Focused on developing explanations that take into account the complexity of the social world and the lives of the participants in the research* – Detail and context are not seen as problems that may lead to unreliability – they are the very essence of the social world to be studied and of the qualitative methodology.

These features of qualitative research enable researchers to

> **explore a wide array of dimensions of the social world, including the texture and weave of everyday life, the understandings, experiences and imaginings of our research participants, the ways that social processes, institutions, discourses or relationships work, and the significance of the meanings that they generate. We can do all this qualitatively by using methodologies that celebrate richness, depth, nuance, context, multi-dimensionality and complexity, rather than being embarrassed or inconvenienced by them.**
>
> (Mason 2002: 1).

Qualitative interviews

Interviews are one of the most common methods used within qualitative research, though they are very different from the structured interview method we discussed earlier. Qualitative interviews can be loosely structured around a set of questions; be based on very little preconsidered structure other than some relevant topics; or be centred on the participant's life history. A fundamental difference between these types of interview is the extent to which the interview is led by the researcher or the participant. All qualitative interviews intend to allow the participant to 'tell their story', but in some the researcher will gently lead the participant towards a discussion of certain topics that they consider to be relevant to their research questions, while in others the participant leads the direction of the interview. Despite this difference, there are features common to all qualitative interviews:

- *In depth* – Qualitative interviews are intended to look at the in-depth opinions and responses of interviewees, rather than yes/no responses.
- *Interactive* – Kvale (1996: 2) noted that 'an interview is literally an *inter view*, an interchange of views between two persons conversing about a theme of mutual interest'.
- *Generative* – Create new knowledge rather than simply excavate existing knowledge. As Gubrium and Holstein (1997: 114) argue, both the interviewee and the interviewer are participants in the social process that is the interview: 'Respondents are not so much repositories of knowledge, treasuries of information awaiting excavation, so to speak, as they are constructors of knowledge in collaboration with the interviewers'.

A closer look

Types of qualitative interview

- *Semi-structured interviews* – Topics or questions are developed for use in the interview (interview guide). The interview guide is intended to initiate discussion from the participants, which will then lead to many further unplanned questions arising from their particular initial responses. This flexibility also means that the questions will not necessarily be asked in a preset order.
- *Unstructured interviews* – At times a very loose set of topics is used, or perhaps a single question is used to start the interview and thereafter the interviewee leads the direction of the topics covered.
- *Life history/biographical method* – The focus of the interview is on the person's life story. While all qualitative interviewing stresses the need for context, it is more explicit in this approach.
- *Focus groups* – Small groups are asked to discuss social issues or services. The direction the discussion takes may be structured by the researcher, or the group may raise its own questions.

- *Informal style* – The aim of good qualitative interviewing is to make the interview seem like a conversation rather than an interview. Despite having the appearance of being a conversation, considerable planning is required beforehand.

Planning an interview

It was indicated above that the interview may appear like a conversation while in fact it requires a lot of planning. Researchers will have developed research questions so will have some topics that they are interested in, and many will develop an interview guide as a starting point to explore these topics. The interview guide helps to clarify the researcher's thinking about the research; it helps them to remember, especially in the first few interviews, what the key topics are. Some interview guides are many pages long and quite detailed; others are very short, with brief headings. However, it should be remembered that the interview guide is not a preset list of questions to be read out, as in the case of a structured interview. The interview guide may be worded as questions, but these will not be all the questions the researcher will ask – far from it – and the interviewer may well not ask the questions in that particular order. In qualitative interviewing, the emphasis is on responding to what the participant is saying: thinking on your feet. This is a challenge and, when doing so, you should try to avoid:

- using terminology;
- using leading questions; for example, asking 'Were you furious when he said that?' rather than 'How did you react when he said that?';
- using emotionally charged words or concepts;
- asking questions that would make people defensive; for example, when asking about child-care arrangements, you might want to ask about the amount of time parents spend with their child. Asking 'Do you spend enough time with your child?' may elicit a defensive response; instead, you could ask 'Do you have any difficulties in managing your time between work and home?'

Beyond questions

Interviews do not have to be simply about asking questions. There are other techniques we can use in an interview situation in order to communicate with interviewees and to generate data. One of the most commonly used is vignettes. Finch (1987) describes them as 'short stories about hypothetical characters in specified circumstances, to whose situation the interviewee is invited to respond'. Vignettes can be used as an icebreaker to start interviews but are often used to facilitate discussion (Barter and Renold 1999). They are often used in research with children in order to reduce any pressure of a one-to-one interview that a child may feel. Vignettes are also useful when tackling sensitive

A closer look

Vignettes

This vignette was used in a project exploring children's and parents' perceptions of risk. Based on a letter to the problem page of a magazine aimed at 10- to 14-year-old girls, it was hoped that it would allow them to speak about whatever they felt were risks to children; about risks and specific locations, such as parks, about parental controls and about age-appropriate behaviour. More specifically, it encouraged them to think about urban and rural differences. After reading the vignette, participants were asked to comment and the discussion then developed in line with their responses.

> My mum and dad are really strict and won't let me go out anywhere. It's like they don't trust me. We lived in a house in the countryside for a few years and it was fine there, but since we've moved to the city it's changed. I'm not allowed to go down to the local park with friends even though I beg them. They say I'm only 13 and they want to keep an eye on me.

topics. Commenting on a story is less personal than asking about direct experience. Vignettes provide the opportunity for participants to have greater control over the interaction by enabling them to determine at what stage they introduce their own experiences.

When writing vignettes, the researcher must ensure that the stories are plausible to the participants. They should seem real and be suitable to the topic and the group with whom you are researching. The vignettes should also contain sufficient context for respondents to have an understanding about the situation being described but be vague enough to encourage them to discuss and speculate.

Interview challenges

Carrying out interviews can be very challenging and requires a range of intellectual, social and practical skills. As the interviewer, you need to be knowledgeable about your subject area; you should be able to interact well with others, actively listening and responding with appropriate questions; and you need to be organized in arranging and recording the interview. While many people will be open to discussing the particular issues that you want to explore, others will seem very reluctant. As a researcher, you need to try and understand the basis of this reluctance and find ways to encourage discussions. At the other extreme, some interviewees may have no problem talking but may talk about anything and everything except the topics on which you want to focus. To a certain extent, you can plan ahead for circumstances such as these, but little can replace direct practical experience in building the skills required.

Power relations in interviewing

The relationship between interviewer and interviewee is necessarily one based on power – you are the researcher and have created the relationship with the interviewee and to some extent may want to shape its outcomes, for example through the range of topics covered. Feminist research has been highly influential in debates around this issue. A wider discussion of the feminist influence on sociological research is found towards the end of this chapter. Here, we will highlight the contribution to debates on the relationship between researcher and interviewee.

While researching certain experiences of women, feminist researchers found existing techniques, or the conventional ways of using these techniques, inappropriate. In her research on the transition to motherhood, Oakley (1981) exposed the limitations of conventional sociological criteria for interviewing. After six months as an observer on a maternity ward in London, Oakley interviewed 66 women on four occasions during their pregnancy. In this context she found that, as a feminist, she had to reassess how she had been trained as a sociologist to carry out interviewing. She argues that in many textbooks the interview is presented as distanced from normal social interaction – as a clinical research tool. In order to maximize data collection, the subject must be put at ease, and yet at the same time the interviewer must remain detached in order to avoid 'interviewer bias'. In order to gain cooperation, interviewers must strike up 'rapport' but avoid involvement. Interviewing is presented as a one-way process in which the interviewer gathers information and does not emit any information. The relationship between interviewer and interviewee is hierarchical, and it is the body of knowledge possessed by the interviewer that allows the interview to proceed successfully. Oakley is critical of this model, which, she argues, is a product of the desire for scientific status often associated with 'malestream' sociology (see the case study 'Critique of positivism: male reason versus female emotion' on p. 142).

Feminist researchers argue that bias is introduced when an interview is taken out of ordinary everyday relations and becomes a constructed and artificial relationship. The orthodox model is highly problematic for feminists whose aim is to validate the subjective experiences of women. Oakley (1981) points out that so-called correct interviewing is associated with a set of values that, in our patriarchal culture, are more readily associated with the masculine, such as objectivity, detachment, science and hierarchy. Oakley argues that interviewing, which relies on subjectivity and equality, is devalued as it does not meet the 'masculine' standards of social science, rationality and scientific objectivity and that it has been seen as potentially undermining the status of sociology as a science. In the social science model of interviewing, feeling, emotion and involvement are conventionally denigrated.

The hierarchical model of interviewing is not congruent with feminist principles, which challenge all relations of dominance and submission. Oakley suggests that when a feminist interviews women, it would be morally and ethically wrong to use prescribed interviewing practice. In her research, Oakley (1981) discussed personal and intimate issues with women in repeated interviews, which inevitably meant that a personal relationship evolved. Oakley built up relationships and became close friends with some of these women; she answered all personal questions and questions about the research. As Oakley herself was a mother, the women would ask about her opinion and experience of young babies and she would share her experience with them. Oakley argues that she could have taken no other direction than to treat the whole research relationship as a two-way process: the relationship cannot be left in the interview room but exists beyond the interview.

Stop and think

- Oakley emphasizes the importance of developing close personal relationships with the women she was researching. What difficulties might she have in doing this?
- How might this influence the information they gathered?
- Do you think this matters?

The relationship between the researcher and the research participants is clearly a contentious issue. Many qualitative researchers point to the need to be reflexive about their role within the research process. Moving away from an emphasis on objectivity leads the qualitative researcher to a more reflexive research position. Qualitative research is an active process, the practice of which involves the researcher continually questioning themselves and their actions. Reflexivity involves critical thinking and awareness about what you are doing and why you are doing it; questioning what assumptions you have about the research; and documenting how your own views and experiences shape the research you do, how you interact with people and how you interpret what they say. As human beings engaging in interactions with others, despite the fact that we consider it to be research, we need to consider the impact that we have on the research. Our gender, ethnicity or social class may shape how participants react towards us or indeed how we react to participants. Equally, our life experiences and values may influence the way we relate to a particular topic or a particular interviewee. For example, Scott (1999) carried out interviews with Caribbean and white women. She noted the significance of her own ethnic identity in doing the interviews. She felt that she was able to gain more trust in the interviews with Caribbean women because of their common background. However, this does not mean that she considered the data from those interviews to be 'better' than the data from interviews with white women. Both sets of data are equally valid, though the context in which they are produced may be different; what must be recognized and included in any analysis of data is the perceived impact that factors such as ethnicity and gender have on the interview process. These issues are also very apparent when analysing qualitative interview data.

Analysing qualitative interview data

There are many different approaches used to analyse qualitative interview data, arising from the theoretical position of the researcher. However, Coffey and Atkinson note that

> **what links all the approaches is a central concern with transforming and interpreting qualitative data – in a rigorous and scholarly way – in order to capture the complexities of the social worlds we seek to explain.**
>
> (Coffey and Atkinson 1996: 3)

Most qualitative researchers try to give meaning to the data, often by developing themes or concepts that help to pull the data together and make sense of them. One such approach is outlined by Ritchie, Spencer and O'Connor (2003). They outline their thematic approach as involving moving through stages from the systematic sorting and ordering of the data through to more in-depth interpretation by developing descriptive accounts, looking for patterns, and ultimately developing explanations derived from the data. They, like most qualitative researchers, argue that, although it is systematic, the analytical process should be flexible and researchers should move forwards and backwards between the stages rather then seeing them as steps moving only in one direction.

Having looked in some detail at qualitative interviewing, we can now go on to consider the observational method. While some of the issues raised are similar, there are also specific challenges and concerns relating to observation.

Observation

Observation can be either participant or not; however, in sociological research, *participant observation* or *fieldwork* (the terms can be used interchangeably in introducing these methods) has been a widely and successfully used approach. Participant observation has its roots in anthropology and the studies of non-Western societies by anthropologists such as Bronislaw Malinowski, Edward Evans-Pritchard and Margaret Mead in the first half of the twentieth century. These researchers lived with the peoples they studied, learned their languages and cultures, and provided fascinating accounts of such societies. More recently, this approach to sociological research has been used to study groups and cultures within Western societies. The work of sociologists at the University of Chicago in the 1930s (led by Robert Park) applied anthropological techniques to the lifestyles they found in the city of Chicago (Park *et al.* 1923). They promoted participant observation, with researchers observing the life of social groups while actually participating in them. Our introduction to participant observation will look at examples of sociological work that have used this method and will discuss some of the issues raised by it.

Cartoon by Mike Keating

A closer look

Ethnography

Hammersley (1992) highlights a basic disagreement over the definition of ethnography: some see it as a specific method of research and others as a more general approach to research. Here, we adopt the latter usage advocated by Hammersley, ethnography being the in-depth study of a specific group or culture over a lengthy period. The emphasis of such study is usually on forms of social interaction (in, for example, a school, factory or juvenile gang) and the meanings that lie behind them. An ethnographic study would typically involve observing the behaviour of a social group and interpreting and describing that behaviour. Hammersley summarized the key assumptions that ethnography makes about the social world and how it should be studied:

- An understanding of human behaviour has to be achieved by first-hand contact with it; thus, ethnographers adopt a naturalistic focus and do their research in 'real life' settings.
- Human actions do not consist of fixed or learned responses; to explain such actions, it is necessary to understand the cultural perspectives on which they are based.
- Research should aim to explore the nature of social phenomena rather than be limited to the testing of hypotheses; the emphasis should be on getting at the meanings and motivations that underlie behaviour.

These assumptions indicate why ethnography is linked with qualitative research and explain why ethnography uses methods of research that are less structured and do not follow the traditional scientific model discussed earlier.

Stop and think

- Participant observation has been used particularly in the study of unusual and deviant behaviour. One reason for this is the fact that such behaviour is, by its very nature, liable to be secretive and/or illegal and thus often difficult to study by more conventional means. Why might participant observation be particularly useful for the study of crime and deviance?
- Participant observation has also tended to be used when researching the less powerful groups in society. Why might this be?

Participant observation enables the researcher to gain insight into behaviour through direct experience. This does not mean that it is an easy method to use; the observer has to remain neutral while at the same time being closely involved with those being studied. Howard Becker (1963), in his studies of the sociology of deviance, attempted to understand such behaviour through observation and close contact with the people he was studying. He described the role of the participant observer as someone who

> **watches the people he is studying to see what situations they ordinarily meet and how they behave in them. He enters into conversations with some or all of the participants in these situations and discovers their interpretations of the events he has observed.**
>
> (Becker 1982: 247)

The influence of the participant observer

The extent to which the participant observer might influence the group or activity being studied has to be considered. People are likely to behave differently when they are being observed, though this will depend to some extent on whether the subjects are aware of the fact that they are being observed. This raises the important distinction between open (overt) and secret (covert) observation. If the observation is going to be done overtly, then the researcher will need to inform the subjects of the research of his or her identity. If it is to be done covertly, then the researcher will need to observe under some sort of guise. Even if the researcher does not tell the subjects and they do not know that they are being investigated, the presence of another person may still, unwittingly, affect their behaviour. Covert participation observation, in particular, highlights ethical issues about observing people without informing them (although, incidentally, this is habitually done by journalists reporting on celebrities).

The points raised above about the influence of the participant observer and the ethics of such observation can be illustrated by looking at examples of sociological research. Eileen Barker's (1984) study of the Reverend Moon's Unification Church adopted several research methods, including participant observation. Barker considered the argument that, in researching religion, more information would be gained if the researcher pretends to believe in the religion being studied – that is, if observation is done covertly. This raised for her the ethical question as to whether it was morally permissible to get information through false pretences. In rejecting the covert style of observation, Barker pointed to the psychological difficulties of pretending to hold beliefs and performing actions that go against one's conscience.

Although this sort of dilemma is not confined to the sociology of religion, it does arise particularly in the examination of secretive religious movements unwilling to be studied. Barker argues that it is possible to carry out overt research even into fairly closed groups such as the 'Moonies'. Although suspicious of outsiders and of publicity, the Unification Church gave her access to a great deal of information and supported her research. Their media image was so bad that the 'Moonies' could not believe that someone who really tried to understand them and listen to them would come up with a worse account than that provided by the media. Barker also pointed out that covert observation can hamper the research by making it impossible to ask certain questions or to appear too curious. In contrast, the recognized, overt observer is expected to ask questions and exhibit curiosity; indeed, they might find themselves being sought out and told things that the believers want to share with a 'stranger' who is not part of the particular organization. Both overt and covert observers have to be careful of the extent to which they influence the behaviour they are meant to be observing.

Two well-known studies of deviant groups that used the method of participant observation and that illustrate the issues and problems attendant on this style of research are described in the following 'World in focus' and case study.

World in focus

When Prophecy Fails

When Prophecy Fails (Festinger *et al.* 1956) is a classic covert participant observation study of a small deviant religious movement that predicted the imminent end of the world. In Christian-based movements this has usually referred to the second coming of Jesus Christ and the establishment of a new Heaven and Earth, accompanied by the destruction of all sinners. Movements such as the Millerites in the 1840s and the Jehovah's Witnesses have prophesied that the world would end at a certain time (although the Jehovah's Witnesses have now abandoned these specific date-centred predictions).

Festinger and colleagues were fortunate to find a small group who appeared to believe in a prediction of catastrophe due to occur in the near future. The group was located as a result of a story in an American provincial paper, the *Lake City Herald*. This story detailed the prophecy of a Mrs Marian Keetch that Lake City would be destroyed by a flood before dawn on 21 December; Mrs Keetch had received messages sent to her by superior beings from the planet 'Clarion' who had visited the earth and observed fault lines in its crust. The authors called on Mrs Keetch to discover whether there was a group of believers based around her. Their initial contact with her made it clear that any research could not be conducted openly. Given this, they described their basic research problem as 'obtaining entry for a sufficient number of observers to provide the needed coverage of members' activities, and keeping at a minimum any influence which these observers might have on the beliefs and actions of the members of the group' (Festinger *et al.* 1956: 234).

The bulk of the study describes how the group prepared for the end of the world and then how the followers came to terms with dis-confirmation of their beliefs. Fascinating though the whole study is, our interest is in the methodology of the research. On the whole, the authors and the additional hired observers they used were welcomed into the group as new converts. It was clear, however, that the involvement of a number of new observers-cum-believers was having a definite influence on the group itself, as the following extract illustrates:

> One of the most obvious kinds of pressure on observers was to get them to take various kinds of responsibilities for recommending or taking action in the group. Most blatant was the situation that one of the authors encountered on November 23 when Marian Keetch asked him, in fact commanded him, to lead the meeting that night. His solution was to suggest that the group meditate silently and wait for inspiration. The agonising silence that followed was broken by Bertha's first plunge into medianship . . . an act that was undoubtedly made possible by the silence and by the author's failure to act himself.
>
> (Festinger *et al.* 1956: 241)

As well as issues concerning access, influence and ethics, participant observation raises practical problems. Because of the difficulties involved in gaining access and trust, it is a time-consuming and therefore expensive method. Furthermore, it may well have significant effects on the lives of the researchers as well as the observed, as the case study below demonstrates.

This case study and the 'World in focus' box above illustrate that research by observation is by no means straightforward. Observers, particularly when working in a covert context, have to be detectives – listening, probing and ensuring that their 'cover' is not blown. Some of the practical and ethical considerations that need to be taken into account when pursuing sociological research are examined further in Activity 1 at the end of this chapter.

Analysing data from participant observation

In concluding this review of research by participant observation, we shall refer to Howard Becker's (1982) reflections on the theoretical problems faced by those who adopt this method. Observational research

Case study

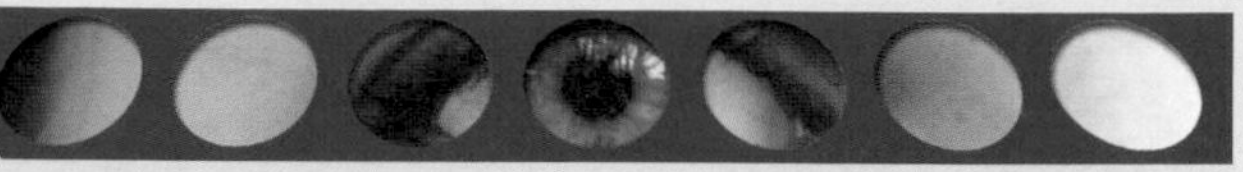

Hell's Angels

Hunter Thompson's (1967) study of the notorious San Francisco Hell's Angels motorcycle gangs highlights the potential dangers of covert participant observation.

> My dealings with the Angels lasted about a year, and never really ended. I came to know some of them well and most of them well enough to relax with . . .
>
> By the middle of summer [1965] I became so involved in the outlaw scene that I was no longer sure whether I was doing research on the Hell's Angels or being slowly absorbed by them. I found myself spending two or three days each week in Angel bars, in their homes, and on runs and parties. In the beginning I kept them out of my own world, but after several months my friends grew accustomed to finding Hell's Angels in my apartment at any hour of the day or night. Their arrivals and departures caused periodic alarm in the neighbourhood and sometimes drew crowds . . . One morning I had Terry the Tramp answer the doorbell to fend off a rent collection, but this act was cut short by the arrival of a patrol car summoned by the woman next door. She was very polite while the Angels moved their bikes off her driveway, but the next day she asked me whether 'those boys' were my friends. I said yes and four days later received an eviction notice.
>
> (Thompson 1967: 52–6)

As well as losing his accommodation, Thompson's research proved physically painful.

> On Labour Day 1966 I pushed my luck a bit too far and got badly stomped by four or five Angels who seemed to feel I was taking advantage of them. A minor disagreement suddenly became very serious . . . The first blow was launched without warning and I thought for a moment it was just one of those accidents that a man has to live with in this league. But within seconds I was clubbed from behind by the Angel I'd been talking to just a moment earlier. Then I was swamped in a general flail. As I went down I caught a glimpse of Tiny, standing on the rim of the action. His was the only familiar face I could see . . . and if there is any one person a non-Angel does not want to see among his attackers it is Tiny. I yelled to him for help but more out of desperation than hope.
>
> (Thompson 1967: 283)

Questions

1. Did being a participant observer influence Thompson's attitude towards the Hell's Angels and his relationships with people outside the group?
2. What other research methods could provide insights into the Hell's Angels? Give reasons for your answer.

Figure 3.3 Hell's Angels
Chuck Nacke/Timepix/Time Life Pictures/Getty Images

typically produces vast quantities of descriptive material, which the researcher has to analyse. This analysis, Becker suggests, needs to be carried out sequentially, while additional data are still being collected – and these additional data will take their direction from the provisional analysis. Becker distinguishes four stages involved in the analysis of data gathered from observational research:

1. *The selection and definition stage* – The observer looks for problems and issues that will help to provide an understanding of the topic or organization being studied. The researcher will be using available data and material to speculate about possibilities. The credibility of the informants will also have to be considered: do they have reason to lie about or conceal information? In assessing the reliability of evidence, the observer's role in the situation has to be examined: was observation overt or covert?
2. *The frequency and distribution of the data have to be checked* – Are the events typical? Does every member of the group respond in the same way?
3. *The data have to be incorporated into a model that will help to explain it.*
4. *The presentation of the evidence and 'proof' of the results* – Quantitative, statistical data are relatively easy to present in tables and charts. However, the qualitative data gained from observation are much more difficult to present adequately. Such data are less easy to count and categorize; the data are also generally too detailed to present in full, which raises the issue of selectivity of presentation.

Other methods of research

Our discussion of different methods of research has focused on those adopted most often in sociological investigations: questionnaires, interviews and observation. Other methods of research are also used, and this section will outline the most prominent.

Secondary data

The research methods we have discussed – questionnaires, interviews and observation – involve the researcher collecting new (primary) data. However, sociologists also use data collected by others, including other researchers and organizations. One of the most common forms of secondary data used by sociologists is statistics from surveys conducted by or for the government. These include the census (a survey of the whole population of the UK every ten years) and smaller surveys based on samples of the population, such as the General Household Survey. Official statistics are available to the public through a range of HMSO (Her Majesty's Stationery Office) publications, including the *Annual Abstract of Statistics* and *Social Trends*, which provide summaries of statistical information under specific headings, such as 'Education', 'Employment' and 'Crime'. See, for example, www.statistics.gov.uk.

Official statistics are a useful source of material for sociologists: they are already available and provide very full information that can be compared from one year to another. However, official statistics are collected by people other than sociologists for purposes other than social scientific research. Official crime statistics, for example, are collected and published by the Home Office and are based on police records of crime; these statistics, then, omit many activities that break the criminal law but remain unknown to the police. There is a 'dark figure of unrecorded crime'. It is impossible to say what this figure may be, but common sense would suggest that, for each crime the police know about, there are likely to be many more that they are not aware of and so unable to record (problems with crime statistics are discussed in more detail in Chapter 14).

In addition to the amount of crime not recorded, the official statistics are also influenced by the way that the police enforce the law. Whether the police decide to arrest and recommend the prosecution of individuals or to 'warn' them will affect crime figures, as will the amount of police resources, including police officers. All the way through the process of dealing with crime, decisions are made about whether individuals are cautioned, arrested, charged and convicted, all of which affect the official crime statistics.

Stop and think

➤ What kinds of problems might the sociologist face in using official statistics on (a) unemployment; (b) religious beliefs; (c) child abuse; and (d) homelessness?

Content analysis and discourse analysis

Content analysis concerns how people communicate and the messages conveyed when people talk or write. It is, essentially, the analysis of the content of communication and involves the classification of this content in order to understand the basic structure of communication. In practice it involves researchers creating categories that relate to the particular issues being studied and then classifying the content of the communication into these categories. Content analysis produces quantitative data that can be measured and analysed objectively, although the extent of this objectivity can be questioned in that subjective judgements have to be made in creating the categories that form the basis of the analysis.

Content analysis has been used widely to investigate how the media transmit ideas and images. If examining the position of women in society, for example, a content analysis of school textbooks would probably find that the majority of characters are males and that women are portrayed in a more limited number of roles than men. A content analysis of television programmes would determine the percentage of leading characters that are male and female. Thus, the content of books, television programmes and films can reveal aspects of the society and culture in which they are situated and so can be an important source of information for sociologists. One of the advantages of content analysis is that it is cheap and easy to conduct, but it is limited in its application and at the end of the day merely records the amount of times a sign or message occurs – it cannot tell us what they are taken to mean or whether they have any effect. As Sumner (1979: 69) has pointed out, 'It is not the significance of repetition that is important but the repetition of significance' – in other words, it does not matter how often a message is repeated if the audience makes no sense of it in the first place.

Discourse analysis is also a text-based research method that looks at and analyses forms of communication, or 'discourses' – in particular, speech and writing. Discourse analysis has been utilized in a number of subject areas, including sociology, and these different subject disciplines (such as psychology, philosophy, history and literature) emphasize different aspects of discourse analysis. However, all approaches highlight the social nature of discourse: the fact that the meanings of words, for instance, depend on who uses them, with whom they are used and where they are used. So, words and their meanings, and hence analyses of them, vary according to the social and institutional situations within which they are used. Thus, a number of different discourses exist at any one time, and these discourses can be, and often are, in competition and conflict with one another.

Discourse analysis does not aim to produce quantifiable data in the way that content analysis does, but rather it adopts a thematic approach, looking at areas and issues that are not (or are not so readily) quantifiable. For instance, Foucault, a key figure in the development of discourse analysis, described and examined discourses of madness (ways of communicating and thinking about the concept of madness) in one of his early studies (Foucault 1967).

Jupp and Norris (1993) identify two broad theoretical strands of discourse analysis, each of which focuses on the relationship between power and discourse. First, the analysis of discourse and power at a macrosocietal level: an approach emphasizing the role of the state in the production of ideologies and associated with structural Marxist analyses and the work of Althusser (see p. 60). Second, the work of Foucault and his concern with why different forms of discourse and knowledge emerge at different points of time. In *Discipline and Punish*, for example, Foucault (1977) discusses how different forms of punishment became dominant during different periods of history. Foucault sees discourses as mechanisms of power and control, but rather than highlighting the role of the state he argues that the state is only one of several points of control: power and control are pervasive throughout society.

Case studies and life histories

Other qualitative approaches to sociological research include case studies and life histories. A case study investigates one or a few particular cases in some depth. Although case studies are only illustrative ('one-offs'), they can be used as guides for further research. McNeill (1990) makes the point that, to a certain extent, any piece of qualitative research could be described as a case study, given that all such research focuses on a relatively small group or on one particular institution. Case studies provide a different sort of data that can supplement other methods of research. As Walters puts it:

> **the use of case studies aids the capturing of a process of events; they provide a sequence and structure that is often omitted in surveys or interviews . . . [they are] a useful means by which to chart ideas and develop themes for analysis.**
>
> (Walters 2003: 179)

Classic examples of case studies include Goffman's *Asylums* (1968), Beynon's *Working for Ford* (1975) and Hunter Thompson's study of the Hell's Angels (1967).

A life history consists of biographical material that has usually been gathered from a particular individual, perhaps from an interview or conversation. As well as relying on people's memories, other sources of information are used to build as detailed a picture as possible of the experiences, beliefs and attitudes of that individual; these sources might include letters and newspaper articles. As with qualitative research in general, the emphasis is on the individual's interpretation of behaviour and events. Like case studies, life histories are unreliable as a basis for generalizing about social behaviour, but they can be valuable sources of insight for the sociologist.

In particular, life histories can provide more detailed information than other methods of research about the development of beliefs and attitudes over time. And, in general terms, it could be argued that an historical outlook and analysis is important in many, if not all, areas of sociological research. In such cases, the life-history method can complement the examination of documents and written historical records. Thomas and Znanieki's (1918) study of the Polish community in Chicago is a classic example of this technique.

Stop and think

➤ Reflect on your own life history. Consider the extent to which your personal development has been influenced by cultural factors.

A multi-method approach

In this chapter, we have introduced and discussed a range of methods by which sociologists gather new evidence and apply already existing information in order to address social issues and problems. We have tried to present these methods as complementary rather than mutually exclusive ways of pursuing research. The complementary nature of different research methods is shown when two or more methods are combined in one research project; this process is given many names but is most often called triangulation. For example, Walters' (2003) use of different styles of interview in his research into the politics of criminology was supplemented by a number of other research techniques. He used case studies so as to 'bring to life' research questions and themes identified through his interviews; he examined academic literature; and he conducted an extensive documentary analysis of official information, including records of parliamentary debates, the League of Nations, the United Nations and reports to the US Congress.

Triangulation can be understood in many ways, often depending on the theoretical position of the researcher (Moran-Ellis *et al.* 2006). From a positivist stance, triangulation involves the idea that each method can corroborate the evidence produced by other methods, thereby producing a more valid account. However, this approach has been criticized by interpretivist researchers because it assumes that 'there is one, objective, and knowable social reality, and all that social researchers have to do, is to work out which are the most appropriate triangulation points to measure it by' (Mason 2002: 190). As we have discussed, this assumption is not something with which many interpretivist, qualitative researchers would agree. Instead, triangulation is understood to be the combining of methods to enable researchers to explore different aspects of the same phenomenon. This illustrates the point made throughout this chapter: decisions around methods are explicitly connected to the researcher's beliefs about what we can and should study in sociology and about what knowledge sociological research can produce. We end this chapter by looking in some detail at feminist research, not only because it illustrates these connections, but also because feminists have made significant contributions to key debates within sociological research as a whole.

Feminist research

Feminists have been concerned with the techniques used in carrying out research, the way research is practised and, more fundamentally, the processes via which sociological knowledge is formulated. They have been concerned with methods, methodology and epistemology. Feminists have produced a scathing critique of orthodox sociological research methodology (Abbott and Wallace 1990).

As research generates the raw material of sociological theory and knowledge, feminists have in turn challenged how sociological knowledge is produced (Spender 1981). They have recognized that knowledge is socially constructed, the product of social and cultural relations. All human beings may generate explanations of the world; not all of them become legitimized and

Case study

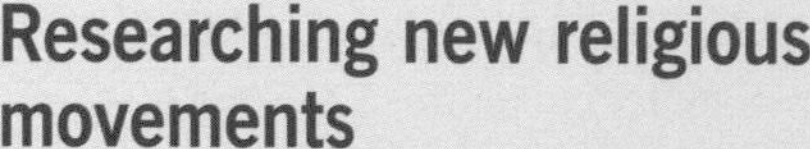

Researching new religious movements

Following a bad press in which the Unification Church was accused of corruption, kidnapping and the brainwashing of its members, Eileen Barker set out to discover whether there was any truth to these allegations.

The research question

> Why should – *how could* – anyone become a Moonie? What possible explanation is there for the fact that men and women will sacrifice their family, their friends, their careers in order to sell tracts, flowers or candy on the streets for 16, 18 or even 20 hours a day? How can well-educated adults be persuaded to abrogate the right to decide whom they will marry, whether they can live with their spouse and whether they can bring up their own children? . . . When asking the question 'Why do Moonies do what they do?' part of the answer is to be found through an understanding of how they came to be Moonies in the first place.
>
> (Barker 1984: 8)

Methodology

In order to find some answers, Barker decided to analyse the question on three levels:

- Personal
- Interpersonal
- Impersonal (social).

She then chose to use triangulation and adopt a different technique to investigate each level:

- *Personal* – In-depth interviews (36 at the start of the research) between 2 and 12 hours.
- *Interpersonal* – Overt participant observation. Over six years Barker lived with Moonies at various centres. She made no attempt to deceive them.
- *Impersonal (social factors)* – Questionnaires. A pilot study (sample of 20), followed by a full study of all Moonies in the UK (about 500). High response rate.
- She also kept a diary and met with parents and anti-cult groups.

Barker's findings

- Moonies attend residential courses and were therefore subject to 'a carefully controlled situation which can exert a considerable influence on some of the guests'.
- Moonies may target individuals in different ways to influence them – to manipulate what 'resonates' with each one.
- Distorted versions of Moonie history and activity may be given to enhance its image.
- She found no evidence of coercion.
- Converts were 'normal' (no special characteristics).
- Individuals eventually decide – 'conversion to the movement is the result of a (limited) number of individual experiences; it is not the result of mass-induced hypnosis'.

Consequently, she concluded:

> I have not been persuaded that they are brainwashed zombies.
>
> (Barker 1984: 233)

Questions

1. Contrast Barker's approach with Wallis' initial attempt to infiltrate the Church of Scientology.
2. Do you think the behaviour of the Moonies would be affected by Barker's presence?
3. Do you think Barker's findings may have been affected by her participation in the group?

accepted explanations. Women have been excluded as producers of knowledge and as subjects of sociological knowledge.

Stop and think

- Name as many sociology books or studies as you can that have been written by (a) women; (b) men; and (c) both.
- What topics were covered by the books and studies in lists (a), (b) and (c)?
- Is there a pattern in the topics researched and written about by female and male sociologists?

Feminists examined the sociological research community itself. This includes academic institutions, departments, funding bodies and publishing houses. Collectively these constitute what Liz Stanley (1990) has called the academic mode of production. She argues that the structure of this has contributed to the production of partial or limited knowledge. Certain individuals and groups have greater control over who can carry out research. Those individuals and groups with greater control include heads of departments, professors, referees and editors; women are underrepresented in these senior positions (Abbott 1991). Abbott and Wallace (1990) have described orthodox sociological research as 'malestream'; they have described several levels on which sociological research has been male-centred.

Research has also been androcentric because it has been based on male experiences. Women have often been absent from research samples. For many years sociological research was carried out by male researchers and on male samples (Abbott and Wallace 1990). The majority of studies during the 1960s and 1970s in the sociology of work were of male paid labour. Findings and theories from these samples were often generalized to the whole population, including women. Goldthorpe and Lockwood's famous affluent worker study suggested that manual workers were becoming increasingly affluent and were increasingly adopting the values and lifestyles of the middle class (Goldthorpe *et al.* 1968). Yet they were describing only the experiences of male workers; women have a different relationship to the labour market.

Men set the research agenda in sociology for many years and, as a result, areas and issues relevant to women were neglected or marginalized. Topics such as sexual violence, domestic labour, childbirth and contraception received very little attention until the feminist impact on sociology. Feminists believe that there must be feminist research that addresses issues and social problems that affect women. A key aim of feminist research is to make women visible, to observe, listen and record the experiences of women, and to write women back into sociological research.

> **[Our central argument] has been that sociology has ignored, distorted or marginalized women. We have also suggested that this is a result of the systematic biases and inadequacies in malestream theories, not just an omission of women from samples. Malestream theories do not ask questions or do research in areas of concern to women, and frequently women are excluded from the samples; when they are included they are viewed from a position that sees males as the norm . . . Feminist sociologists have argued that it is necessary to develop feminist theories: theories that explain the world from the position of women, theories that enable us to rethink the sexual division of labour and to conceptualise reality in a way that reflects women's interests and values, drawing on women's own interpretations of their of their own experiences.**
>
> (Abbott and Wallace 1997: 283)

Feminism has had an impact more broadly on sociology. Mary Maynard (1990) argues that feminism has begun to reshape sociology as many non-feminist sociologists are beginning to consider women and gender in their research and analysis. Feminists have stressed that men are influenced by gender relations, hence gender should be examined not only in research on women but also in all research. They have moved beyond criticism and suggested principles that should underlie feminist research. Just as feminist theory is not a unified body of thought, similarly there is no one feminist methodology (Reinharz 1993).

Feminist principles

Stanley and Wise (among others) have argued that no one research method or set of methods should be seen as distinctively feminist: 'Feminists should use any and every means available for investigating the condition of women in sexist society' (Stanley and Wise 1983).

Feminists have considered how the logistics of particular methods engage with feminist aims, yet it is the principles that underlie selected methods that distinguish a range of emerging feminist praxes (Stanley 1990). Feminist research involves a commitment to a particular way of practising research, and this may shape how the specific techniques are utilized. Liz Kelly (1988) has suggested that 'feminist practice' would be a more appropriate term than 'feminist methodology', in order to avoid the assumption that particular methods are feminist.

Not all feminists share a common view of research methodology: there is debate about what is and what should constitute a feminist methodology (Harding 1987). However, a set of recurring themes and principles does emerge, four of which have been selected here. They are of particular importance to feminist 'practice' (Kelly 1988):

- The centrality of women's experience
- Research for women
- The rejection of hierarchy and empowerment
- Critical reflexivity.

Centrality of women's experience

Feminists in their research draw on new empirical resources, the most significant being women's experiences. Feminism moves away from the androcentric position, which sees male experiences as central, and places women's experiences as the foundation of social knowledge. The task of feminist research is to explore how women see themselves and the social world.

Case study

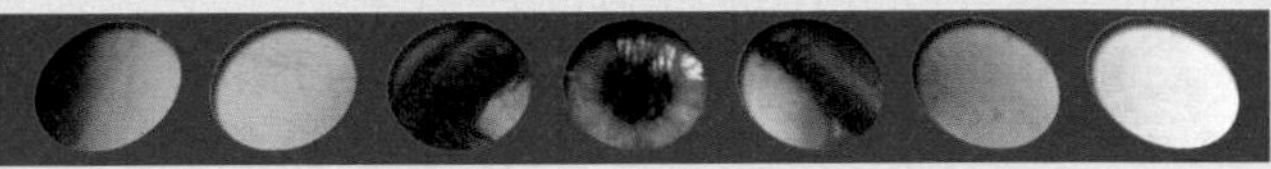

Critique of positivism: male reason versus female emotion

Stanley and Wise (1983, 1993) have argued that positivism is problematic for feminists for several reasons. First, it is based on a series of dichotomies: science versus nature, objectivity versus subjectivity, reason versus emotion and male versus female. The problem is that positivism elevates science, objectivity, rationality and the masculine, hence denigrating nature, subjectivity, emotion and the feminine. Feminists have argued that in Western scientific thought and culture the masculine is associated with reason, science and objectivity, and the feminine with nature, emotion and subjectivity.

Second, Stanley and Wise argue that the positivist emphasis on objectivity divorces sociological knowledge from the social conditions in which that knowledge is produced. Feminists do not see research as orderly; they are suspicious of 'hygienic' research:

> hygienic research in which no problems occur, no emotions are involved, is 'research as it is described' and not 'research as it is experienced'.
>
> (Stanley and Wise 1983)

Feminists argue that researchers are always part of the social relations that produce particular findings. Their beliefs and values will shape the research. The private and public spheres, the emotional and the rational, subjectivity and objectivity cannot be separated. Feminists have argued that personal subjective experience is political and important and should be recognized as such in research.

Third, feminists argue that the scientific approach produces a division and an imbalance of power between social science researchers and those people whose lives they research. Social scientists are seen to have special knowledge and skills, they control the research process, and they come along and do their research on people. Feminists have been keen to involve women in the research process itself in an attempt to reduce the imbalance of power and hierarchical relations.

In challenging the concept of objectivity, feminists have challenged the view that research should be value-free and apolitical. Indeed, they stress that feminist research not only must be of intellectual interest but also should further the political interests of women. Feminists argue that research should raise consciousness, empower women and bring about change.

(adapted from Harding 1987)

Questions

1. What is 'hygienic research' and why are some feminists critical of it?
2. How might a researcher's values influence the way they study (a) crime and (b) poverty?

McRobbie (1991) argues that the most important achievement of feminist research is the revealing of women's hidden experiences, both past and present. Underlying all feminist research is the goal of correcting both the invisibility and the distortion of women's experiences by providing a vehicle for women to speak through. Women's experience must provide the raw material for theory construction. They stress the need to ground theory in research and stress the two-way relationship between experience and theory. Indeed, many feminists reject any divide between theory and research.

Research for women

Ramazanoglu (1991a) notes that there has been a distinct shift in feminist methodology from an earlier position that defined feminist research as research of and by women to research that has a political commitment to be for women. Duelli-Klein (1983) differentiates between research *on* women, which merely records aspects of women's lives, and research *for* women, which 'tries to take women's needs, interests and experiences into account and aims at being instrumental in improving women's lives in one way or another'.

Feminist research is committed to improving women's position in society. Several feminists have stressed consciousness raising as a key role for feminist research in the emancipation process. Pollert (1981), in her participation observation of women factory workers, did not take a neutral stance but challenged both male managers and female workers about the sexist assumptions they made. She treated the situation as a consciousness-raising process for herself and the women in the factory.

Rejection of hierarchy and empowerment

A basic principle of feminist methodology has been not only to challenge relationships typical of traditional research based on hierarchy and power but also to aim to democratize the research process. Stanley (1990) argues that feminists should be committed to a belief that research and theorizing are not the result of the thinking of a group of experts different from those of 'mere people'. Stanley and Wise (1983) warn of the danger of the emergence of an academic elite of feminist researchers who distance their activities from the mass of women. Feminists have attempted to restore their subjects as active participants in the research process and to ensure that knowledge and skill are shared equally between researcher and subject. There has been a range of feminist research aimed at empowering and actively involving the women involved (Lather 1988). The aim to change as well as to understand the world means that some feminists build conscious empowerment into the research design.

Lather (1988) coordinated a group called the Women's Economic Development Project in South Carolina. Low-income women were trained to research their own economic circumstances, in order to understand and change them. This participatory research design involved 11 low-income women working as community researchers on a one-year study of the economic circumstances of 3000 low-income women. Information was gathered in order to bring action as a catalyst for change, to raise the consciousness of women regarding the sources of their economic circumstances, to promote community-based leadership, and to set up an active network of low-income rural women in the state to support new legislation concerning women's work and educational opportunities.

Abbott and Wallace (1990) note that the logic of the feminist position on research seems to demand non-individual cooperative research, where the researcher helps the women involved to undertake their own research. The researcher acts as an enabler. Subject and researcher decide together how the findings are to be used, although in practice this is difficult to achieve.

Stop and think

- Suggest how Abbott and Wallace's notion of cooperative research could be applied in the following areas:
  - (a) male and female roles in the catering industry;
  - (b) the sexual harassment of girls at school;
  - (c) homelessness;
  - (d) the role of women in the police force.
- What are the arguments for and against personal involvement in research?

Critical reflexivity

In the section on qualitative interviewing we looked at the importance of reflexivity in qualitative research, highlighting the work of feminists. As Mauthner notes,

> **Reflexivity is a central tenet of a feminist methodology whereby the researcher documents the production of knowledge and locates herself in this process.**
>
> (Mauthner 2000: 299)

She described how, in her study of sister relationships; her own experiences shaped the research:

> **Clearly, my own sistering experiences coloured my interpretation of the data: they influenced the way that I listened to the narratives, the patterns that I noticed in the data, and the themes that I pursued.**
>
> (Mauthner 2000: 300)

For Oakley (1981) it is essential that the relationship between researcher and participant is reciprocal – that is, it involves the mutual exchange of information, ideas and personal experiences. In doing so, the need to be reflexive becomes a central part of the research process. However, there are also difficulties for feminist researchers in establishing a fully reciprocal relationship. Mauthner describes how she engaged with the participants and shared her own sistering experiences during interviews but noted that, when analysing and writing up the data, she stepped back from this reciprocity. In part this was to preserve her privacy; researchers are not afforded the confidentiality and anonymity of research participants. The notion of a mutual exchange was also limited at the analysis stage by the use of sociological theory in making sense of the data. While theory is an essential part of qualitative data analysis it also 'distances the participants from the research product' because they do not have access to that body of knowledge (Mauthner 2000: 301).

Similarly, McRobbie (1991) argues that feminists must recognize that there is an unequal distribution of privilege. Feminist researchers often represent powerful educational establishments. They must acknowledge that this may be one reason why women are willing to participate in research. For example, she criticizes Oakley (whose work we considered earlier), who she claims fails to consider the imbalance of power between herself as a researcher and the young mothers:

> **She does not concern herself with the fact that pregnant, in hospital . . . the women were delighted to find a friendly articulate knowledgeable woman to talk to [*sic*] their experiences about . . . their extreme involvement in the research could also be interpreted as yet another index of their powerlessness.**
>
> (McRobbie 1991: 79)

There is always the danger that some women will use the experiences of women's oppression to further their careers, with women's suffering becoming a commodity. Angela McRobbie speaks honestly about the fact that doing research sometimes feels like 'holidaying on other people's misery'. She describes an interview with a 19-year-old woman who had been brought up in care:

> **I was almost enjoying the interview, pleased it was going well and that Carol was relaxed and talkative. Yet there was Carol with her eyes filling up with tears as she recounted her life and how her mother had died.**
>
> (McRobbie 1991: 77)

McRobbie also challenges the assumption that the feminist researcher will necessarily understand the women because of their 'shared' oppression. Women have a multiplicity of experiences. Feminists may have valuable personal experience, but they cannot assume that this will be the same as those they are researching. While feminism attempts to foster sisterhood, it cannot naively assume that women are bound together purely on the grounds of gender.

Therefore, although reflexivity is a key strand in feminist 'practice', it raises many challenging questions concerning the relationship between feminist researchers and the women involved in research. Although the principles enshrined in feminist research cannot eliminate the possibility of exploitation, they can serve as a check against it. As part of the conscious reflexivity, feminists attempt to be explicit and open about power relations as they operate in the research process.

Quantitative or qualitative methods?

It is often assumed that feminist research involves only qualitative methods. Some feminist sociologists have been critical of quantitative methods. They have argued that questionnaires and structured interviews precode experience, producing a false body of data that distorts the actors' meanings. Graham (1984b) claimed that survey methods and structured interviews 'fracture women's experiences'. Barbara Smith (1987) argues that there are aspects of women's lives that cannot be preknown or predefined in such a way. Some feminists have stressed that the female subject gets lost in social science survey research. Oppression is such that it cannot be 'neatly encapsulated in the categories of

Case study

Women's Leisure, What Leisure?

Green *et al.* (1990) used a social survey in combination with unstructured interviews and discussion groups in a comprehensive study of women's leisure in Britain, summarized in their book *Women's Leisure, What Leisure?* They wanted to collect both general information about the types and levels of women's leisure participation and more detailed knowledge about women's perceptions and attitudes to leisure. They argued that, as feminists are concerned both with understanding patriarchal structures that oppress women and with seeking to change them, they must utilize the strengths of quantitative evidence. They argued that using a survey enabled them to generalize from their results to the larger female population and to exert greater political influence. They wanted to provide a statistical body of research that could actually form the basis for more informed policy decisions. They pointed out that policymaking bodies were more impressed with statistical data, and it was crucial that such bodies examine and take note of their findings. They were fully aware of the limitations of the survey method in the context of women's lives and hence used qualitative research to complement the quantitative data. Hence the shift towards triangulation (see p. 139) is also reflected in feminist research. Feminists will use any appropriate method to expose and oppose women's oppression.

Question

1. **What 'limitations of the survey method' might there be in pursuing research into women's leisure activities?**

survey research' (Graham 1984b). On many of these points feminist arguments overlap with ethnographic researchers.

Stop and think

- On the whole, feminists have favoured qualitative methods, claiming that they fit more comfortably with feminist principles as well as being more appropriate and sensitive to women's experiences of oppression. Why do you think feminist research has favoured qualitative methods?

Although feminist research has tended to be defined in terms of qualitative research, a growing body of feminists have attempted to break down the distinction between quantitative and qualitative research. They have stressed that there is nothing inherently sexist with quantitative research methods and techniques such as surveys (Jayaratne 1993; Kelly *et al.* 1992; Pugh 1990). If used sensitively, they can complement broader feminist research aims.

Many feminists have also proposed that the use of qualitative methods does not necessarily overcome some of the problems identified with quantitative methods. Stacey (1988) has pointed out that, although ethnographic methods seem ideally suited to research in that they involve empathy and allow for an egalitarian, reciprocal relationship, they may expose the research subjects 'to greater risk of exploitation, betrayal and abandonment by the researcher than does much positivistic research' (Stacey 1988: 21).

There is a great deal of debate about what a feminist methodology should contain. It is important to remember that there is not one easily identifiable feminist research methodology (Reinharz 1993). Yet there is some consensus about principles that feminists should consider when carrying out research. Kelly notes this ambivalent position:

> **There is not, as yet, a distinctive 'feminist methodology'. Many of the methods used by feminist researchers are not original. What is new are the questions we have asked, the way we locate ourselves within our questions and the purposes of our work.**
>
> (Kelly 1988: 5–6)

Summary

- Sociological research involves the gathering of relevant material and data and interpreting and analysing them.
- In undertaking research, the sociologist can use a variety of techniques. The method chosen will be influenced by the researcher's views about the social world and by the theoretical approach favoured by the researcher.
- One issue that has been central to the style of research adopted has been the extent to which sociological research should follow the methodological approach of the natural sciences. A by-product of this issue has been the debate over whether sociology can and should be value-free and the extent to which the data gathered by sociologists are reliable and valid.
- Quantitative research is associated most closely with the conventional scientific methodology. Surveys involve collecting data from large numbers of people, usually from questionnaires or interviews that ask people about their behaviour and attitudes. Surveys are typically based on a sample of respondents drawn from a specific population. The use of official statistics and content analysis are other examples of quantitative research.
- Qualitative research gathers more detailed information from a smaller number of respondents. The focus is on the experiences of people and the meaning given to such experiences. Observation, in-depth interviews and case studies are qualitative methods.
- Feminist research has criticized orthodox sociological research methodology for being 'malestream', i.e. centred on men. Although feminist research is not a unified body of research, a major focus has been on women's experiences and how an understanding of them can help to explain and improve women's position in society.

Links

As with sociological theory, sociological research also underpins all of the topics and areas of sociology covered in the rest of this book. Rather than indicate all of the links, we would urge you to think about the research processes involved in the various studies and examples of sociology you come across in the remaining chapters and to consider the sort of research issues that those studies would raise.

Further reading

Becker, H.S. (1963) *Outsiders: Studies in the Sociology of Deviance*, New York: Free Press.
As well as 'methodology' texts, it is good practice to look at the methodological sections of specific sociological studies. Such sections may be found in the introductions to studies or as appendices. Chapter 9 in Becker's classic study of deviants, *Outsiders*, for instance, discusses some of the key issues attendant on studying deviant behaviour.

Bryman, A. (2008) *Social Research Methods*, 2nd edn, Oxford: Oxford University Press.
Although focusing on social research rather than sociology, this general text provides a very accessible but detailed introduction to all the topics covered in this chapter.

Durkheim, E. (1964) *The Rules of Sociological Method*, New York: Free Press.
With so many secondary sources available, there is a tendency not to consider reading the originals. However, Durkheim's key work on the studying of social phenomena is no more difficult to read than some of the commentaries on it. It is a short study that sets out the requirements that rigorous sociological research needs to follow.

Gilbert, N. (ed.) (2001) *Researching Social Life*, 2nd edn, London: Sage.
This is a collection of papers that outlines the main ways in which sociologists gather data and describes a range of ways of analysing such data. The connections between quantitative and qualitative research methods and their theoretical bases are emphasized throughout. The papers are written by experienced social researchers who reflect on their own research experiences.

Hammersley, M. (ed.) (1993) *Social Research: Philosophy, Politics and Practice*, London: Sage.
This collection contains some particularly useful material on the politics of the research process with articles on, for instance, issues of race, gender and power in social research.

Ritchie, J. and Lewis, J. (2003) *Qualitative Research Practice*, London: Sage.
A very practical book giving advice on 'doing' qualitative research and framed within an interesting discussion of the main debates. There are plenty of examples to illustrate the processes they describe.

Salkind, N.J. (2000) *Statistics for People Who (Think They) Hate Statistics*, London: Sage.
The title says it all – a book for those who want to learn the basics of statistics for social research but who are worried about their abilities in this area.

Silverman, D. (2001) *Interpreting Qualitative Data*, 2nd edn, London: Sage.
The second edition of this popular introductory text takes account of the expansion in qualitative research since the 1990s.

Stanley, L. and Wise, S. (1993) *Breaking Out Again: Feminist Ontology and Epistemology*, London: Routledge.
This updates and reviews the main arguments in feminist thinking and research since the original *Breaking Out* – an important feminist text, first published in 1983, that challenged conventional positivist practices in sociological research.

Websites

www.statistics.gov.uk
The UK National Statistics Gateway
Provides access to a range of links to government statistics.

www.soc.surrey.ac.uk/sru
University of Surrey, Sociology Department
Here you can find articles on research published by the Sociology Department at the University of Surrey.

www.asanet.org/student/archive/data.html
American Sociological Association

www.cessda.org
Council of European Social Science Data Archives

Activities

Activity 1

Problems in researching a deviant religious movement

This extract illustrates some of the difficulties of research into deviant religious movements. It is taken from the methodological appendix to *When Prophecy Fails* (Festinger *et al.* 1956), the classic study of a small group that believed that the world was about to be destroyed and which we referred to earlier in the chapter (p. 135).

In our investigation of the group which gathered about Dr Armstrong and Marian Keetch, our observers posed as ordinary members who believed as the others did. In short, our investigation was conducted without either the knowledge or the consent of the group members. This situation presented a number of problems that merit detailed discussion . . .

Both of our 'local' observers were under pressure at various times in mid-December to quit their jobs and spend all their time with the group . . . Their evasion of these requests and their failure to quit

their jobs at once were not only embarrassing to them and threatening to their rapport with the group, but also may have had the effect of making the members who had quit their jobs less sure that they had done the right thing. In short, as members, the observers could not be neutral – any action had consequence . . .

Observing, in this study, was exhausting work. In addition to the strain created by having to play an accepting, passive role vis-à-vis an ideology that aroused constant incredulity, which had to be concealed, observers frequently had to stay in the group for long hours without having an opportunity to record what they had learned . . .

The circumstances of observation made it impossible to make notes openly except on a single occasion, the meeting of November 23, when the Creator ordered that notes be taken. Apart from this, it was difficult to make notes privately or secretly, for the observers were rarely left alone inside the house and it was necessary to be ingenious enough to find excuses for leaving the group temporarily. One device used occasionally was to make notes in the bathroom. This was not entirely satisfactory, however, since too frequent trips there would probably arouse curiosity if not suspicion . . .

Our observers had their daily lives to care for as well as the job, and were subject to occasional bouts of illness or fatigue from lack of sleep. The job was frequently irritating because of the irrelevancies (from the point of view of our main interest) that occupied vast quantities of time during the all-night meetings.

(Festinger *et al.* 1956: 234–46)

Questions

1. You are a sociologist just starting a research project seeking information on ritualistic abuse. A friend tells you they know of a Satanic cult meeting regularly in the area. Most of their activities are harmless but there is a rumour that an animal is to be sacrificed at Hallowe'en. Your friend tells you they know of a member looking for new recruits. You feel this is a rare opportunity of getting access to the group that may not come up again. How would you continue with your research? (Consider the advantages and disadvantages of alternative methods of research that might be used.)
2. Suggest the practical and ethical consequences of the methods of research that you propose to follow.

Problems in researching female factory workers

This extract is taken from a study of female workers in an electronics factory in Malaysia. It focuses on the problems faced by these workers, who were termed 'Minah Karan' (meaning, roughly, 'loose women'). Daud's research was carried out in a number of stages and involved several research methods: participant observation, in-depth interviews, official documents and surveys (based on questionnaires and including a follow-up survey five years after the initial research).

I started my fieldwork as a participant observer, by becoming a factory worker. It began in October 1976 and continued until June 1977. During the first five months I worked in the Variable Resistance Section (V.R.) and the Electrolytic Capacitor Section, working two-and-a-half months in each section. Then I carried out my in-depth interviews with 100 workers over a period of one month. At the end of the last two months of fieldwork I conducted a survey of 111 respondents to see the changes that had occurred between 1977 and 1982 . . .

Although work in the factory numbed the mind and tired the body, my research was strengthened by real knowledge of the long hours and tough working conditions. I discovered many advantages in becoming a worker in order to understand the real problems and situations of factory life. I could feel for myself the tiredness, depression, tension and other physical hazards; I discovered a lot of truth about the nature of a worker's life. For instance, cohabitation and illegitimate pregnancies were usually subjects for gossip. However, the workers talked about this only within their own groups. I believe that if I had not undertaken participant observation by becoming a factory worker, such private and personal matters would be very difficult to uncover . . .

During the first few days of my work I had asked them whether it was true, as people claimed, that factory workers cohabit. They replied that it was nonsense. But when they had accepted me as one of them, they told the truth . . .

There were drawbacks in becoming a worker and doing this 'undercover' work. Some of them are discussed below. The chief methodological problem was to keep my notes up to date while working normally with others. Each worker sat near another in the 'line' and I found there was a general interest in what I did and how I behaved since I was a newcomer. Only when there was a break could

I write my notes in any detail. By becoming a worker I had to follow work regulations. Workers were not allowed to talk during work . . .

A few seniors especially the 'line leaders' became suspicious and were unhappy with me. They feared that I might be appointed to the supervision post after my 'training'. They viewed this as unfair since they were senior to me. They resented me and refused to be friendly. It is undeniable that becoming a factory worker was a very good method of carrying out my fieldwork. In not disclosing my real identity, I always had to be careful and be on the alert for rumours and suspicion among the workers . . .

The major advantage of using structured questionnaires is that it produces systematic data on information obtained during observation and in-depth interviews. But, there are also a few disadvantages in using this method, namely: I noticed great differences in the quality of information obtained through the methods of participation and descriptive survey . . .

For example, when I asked about their attitudes towards the management, during my period of anonymity, almost all the workers condemned the management and said they hated it. But when questioned during the descriptive survey, half the sample said the management was 'good'. I think this is because they were trying to be careful when answering the questionnaires administered by someone who was no longer their fellow-worker.

(Adapted from Daud 1985: 134–41)

Questions

1. What sort of information on factory work would each of the methods adopted by Daud be likely to provide?
2. To what extent can these different methods be seen as (a) valid sources of information; and (b) reliable sources of information?

Activity 2

How sociological is your imagination?

Take out your notebook, sharpen your pencil, discard your most cherished cultural assumptions and suspend good old common sense. You are an outsider and your job is to observe and describe what you see around you.

Choose one type of activity (preferably one that you are not familiar with) and simply record your observations. This may be as simple as observing people in a café or pub (Who are they? Where do they sit? What do they do?) or it may involve you in an anthropological pursuit of the exotic and the bizarre: a night at the wrestling, an evening at the opera or an afternoon spent watching football or playing bingo (Who are the punters? What do they wear? How do they behave?).

Using your newly found sociological imagination, how do you interpret your observations? Do any patterns emerge? Do any hypotheses suggest themselves? What problems have you encountered in your search for new sociological truths?

Notes for students

This activity is intended to help you to understand the process all observers go through in making sense of the world around them. We all use information previously learned to make sense of situations, and we pick up clues from those we are watching or interacting with. No two people will therefore make sense in exactly the same way. The point of this exercise is to make you aware of what sociologists do when they 'explain behaviour', to raise the issues of subjectivity, value and interpretation. Whether or not you have studied sociology previously, it is hoped that you will be stimulated into thinking differently about the world around you, questioning behaviour that might have been taken for granted.

1. First you must select your observation. Think through some possible choices. Religious and cultural events lend themselves well to this activity, and you may find that local newspapers contain some helpful ideas.
2. You need to decide how you are going to record your observation. Will you keep notes in a book (obviously or unobtrusively)? Will you trust to your memory and write up your impression as soon as possible? Will you use a tape recorder/still camera/video camera? There is no right way in this activity: think about the pros and cons of each recording method.
3. After the observation, note the following. How long did the observation last? Did you know whether the participants were typical? (How would you decide this?) Did anyone explain what they were doing? Were there written instructions (e.g. church prayer book – how much sense did that make?)? Did you make your own sense of what you saw?
4. Let your imagination generate explanations: you are allowed to present competing explanations for what you think you saw and should select the most likely account from your standpoint, explaining in terms of further logical arguments or theories.

Outline

A suggested outline for the written part of the assignment is as follows:

1. *Introduction* – Observation chosen: Where? When? Why?
2. *Method* – How the observation was recorded – pros and cons. Did you remain 'non-participant' or did you participate? What were the effects of this? In retrospect, would you change the way you did the activity?
3. *Explanations* – This section should describe your observation – clues picked up both orally and visually from the participants should be highlighted. You should go beyond pure description and attempt imaginative explanations in order to generate hypotheses about the social behaviour you observed. Factors that may help you in considering explanations and gaining a sociological understanding of what you are observing might include the following: Does there appear to be a shared set of values and rules among the group? Is there a certain social etiquette that must be maintained? What social characteristics strike you about the group? Are they all male? All female? Predominantly older people? Why? What do the participants appear to get out of the interaction? Escape, pleasure, social contact, sense of identity, etc.?
4. *Reflexive account* – In this section you reflect on your own role in the observation: if you had been a different type of person, would you have made another interpretation? It is in this section that you raise issues of objectivity/subjectivity, value and interpretation. You need to account for your own role in the process of understanding – that is, the interpretation you made of the situation. Are you male/female, white/black, disabled/able-bodied, young/mature, middle class/working class? Do you hold certain religious, moral or political beliefs? How did these factors shape your interpretation and shape the behaviour of the people involved in the interaction?
5. *Conclusion* – How useful did you find this exercise?

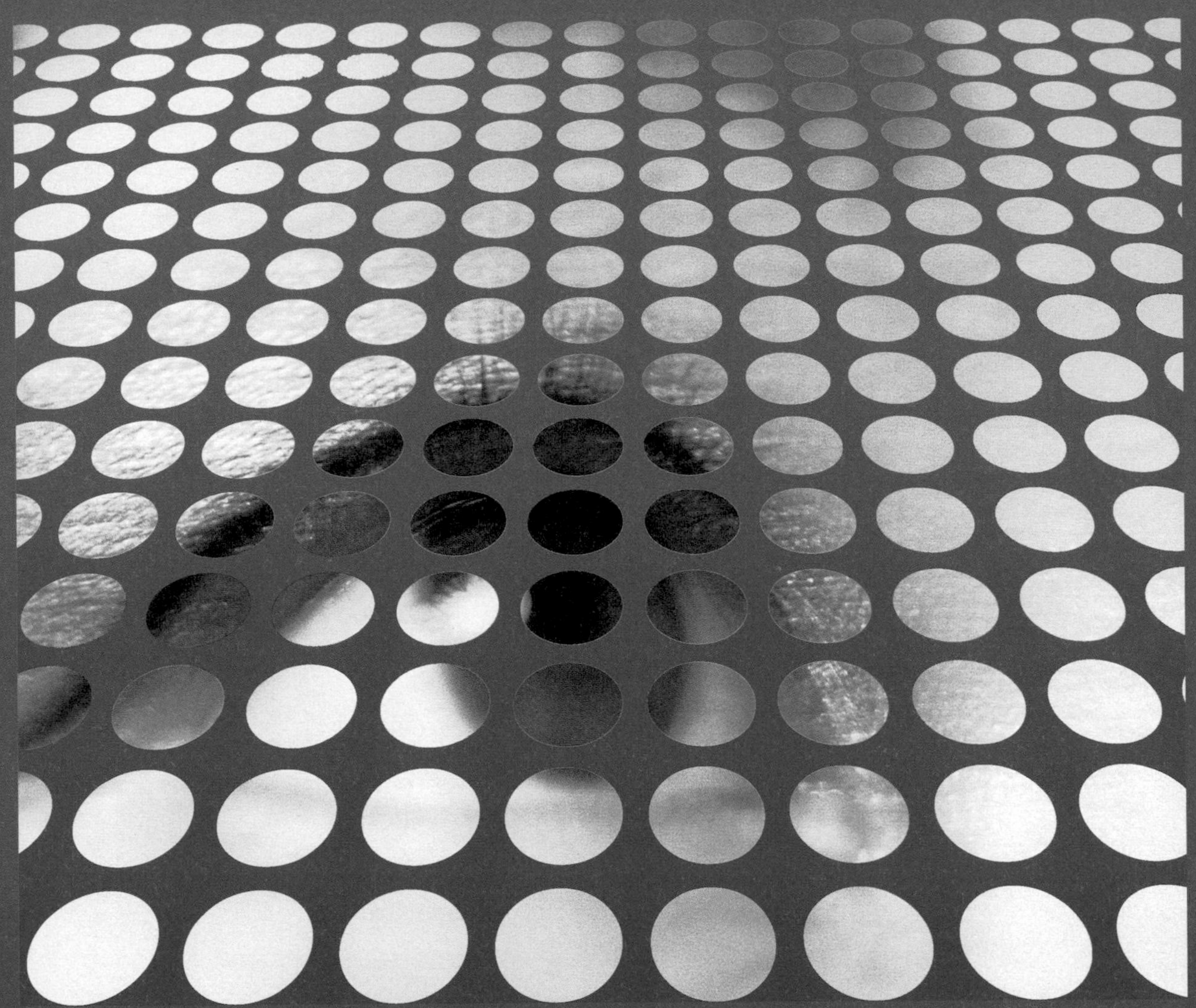

Part 2 Introduction to Social Divisions

If we are to make coherent sense of our own lives, let alone understand what is going on in our society and why society as a whole operates as it does, the idea of 'social divisions' is one of the most useful and powerful tools available. (Payne 2006: 4)

Sociologists have a keen interest in the way society is divided into distinctive social groups: 'each uniting people through their particular and shared experiences and interests that mark them as different from, and possibly in conflict with, other groups' (Braham and Janes 2002: ix). One of sociology's key concerns is the way in which social divisions lead to social stratification, inequality and identity. Each of the following chapters – on social stratification and class; gender; race, ethnicity and nationalism; age; disability and the body; and global divisions – focuses on a specific social division, but they also share some common themes:

- *Social construction of social divisions* – Our understanding of class, gender, ethnicity, age and disability changes both historically and culturally. As sociologists, we need to question how we define social divisions: what do we mean by 'class' or 'gender'? How and why have these social divisions emerged, and what are their key characteristics? The categories of age, gender, class, ethnicity and so on are sociological 'labels' (Payne 2006) that are not static or fixed. Thus, the ways in which we interpret these labels may change over time and place.

- *Identities* – Social divisions are an important part of our identity. Sociology enables us to raise questions about how we view ourselves and others. Our perceptions of ourselves may change according to how others react to us because of how they perceive us at any given point in time. We hope that sociology will encourage you to reflect on your own social identity and the ways in which you categorize yourself and other people as young or old, rich or poor, male or female, able-bodied or disabled. Sociologists are keen to challenge stereotypical assumptions that surround these social groupings.

- *Inequalities* – Social divisions can also result in social inequalities. Key concepts that are explored in the chapters in this part are power, marginalization, social exclusion and discrimination. One of the main roles of sociologists is to understand social differences and try to explain social inequalities.

  Social divisions based around gender, age, ethnicity, nationality, religion, sexuality and disability affect our individual life chances because rewards and privileges are unevenly distributed often according to which of these 'divisions' we may find ourselves in. Consequently, our lifestyle may be constrained or enhanced in relation to our social location (McIntosh and Punch 2005: 88).

  Thus, it is worth remembering that, although inequality can often be conceptualized in highly individualistic terms, it is also collective and shared. Our social positioning shapes the opportunities and constraints that we experience throughout our lives, but as individuals we are not often conscious of this process. As sociologists we should seek answers to questions such as: To what extent does difference result in inequality? Is it possible to retain differences while eliminating inequalities? Does inequality always have negative consequences for society? Do social divisions always imply social disadvantage?

- *Continuity and change* – Social divisions persist and are reproduced over time, yet they also are subject to gradual change. What it means to be rich or poor, male or female, young or old, black or white, and other potential sources of social division, changes at different historical moments. However, we should be careful not to exaggerate such changes as many social divisions remain relatively constant and resistant to rapid change. For example, although more women are in paid employment nowadays, they may still experience inequality at work such as receiving less pay or finding it hard to achieve promotion compared with many men. Social divisions are subject to both continuity and change. The chapters in this section consider the extent to which aspects of each social division have remained constant or gradually transformed over recent decades.

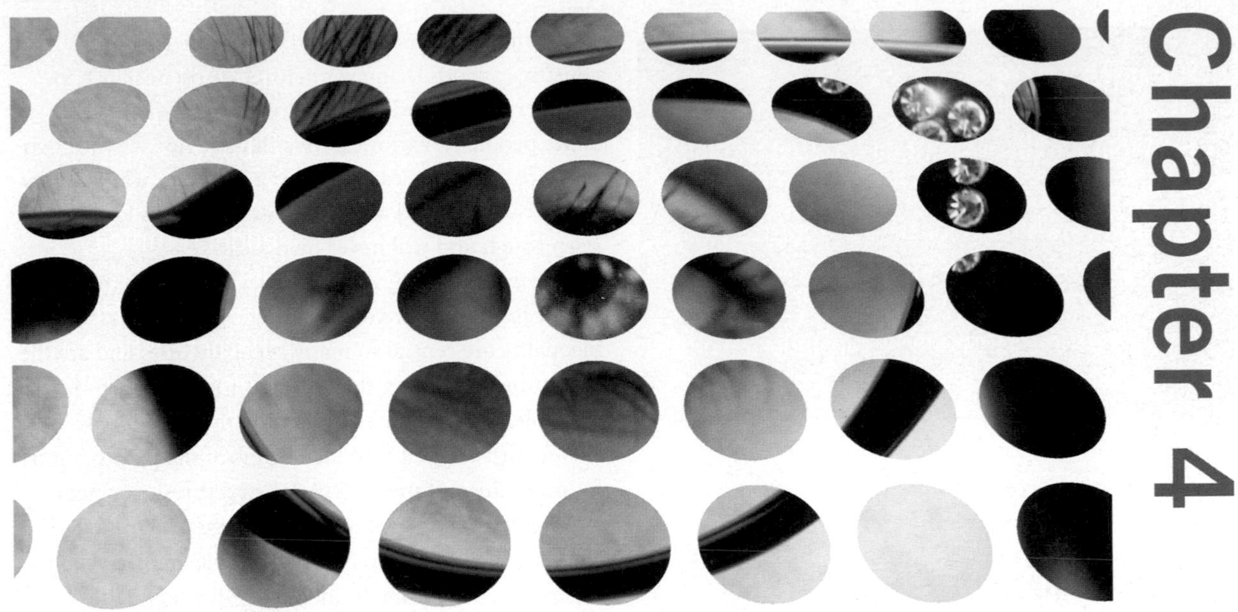

Chapter 4

Social stratification and class

I conceive that there are two kinds of inequality among the human species: one, which I call *natural* or *physical*, because it is established by nature, and consists in a difference of age, health, bodily strength and the qualities of the mind and the soul; and another, which may be called moral or *political inequality*, because it depends on a kind of convention and is established, or at least authorised, by the consent of men. This latter consists of the different privileges, which some men enjoy to the prejudice of others; such as that of being more rich, more honoured, more powerful, or even in a position of exact obedience. (J.-J. Rousseau, quoted in Bottomore 1965: 15)

In a class society everyone lives as a member of a particular class, and every kind of thinking, without exception, is stamped with the brand of a class. (Mao Zedong 1966: 2)

Key issues

- What are the major forms of stratification?
- What explanations have social scientists offered for the advantages and disadvantages that follow from membership of particular social classes?
- Is class analysis still useful in understanding social structure and social opportunities?

Introduction

Stop and think

- What kinds of inequality can you identify that are natural or physical?
- Which ones would you regard as moral or political?
- Do you feel that you are a member of a particular social class?
- If so, which class and what influence does it exert on your life?
- If not, do you feel that you are a member of any other sort of social grouping that affects your everyday life?

While more and more people own more and more consumer goods than ever before, we do not have to look very far to find evidence of gross inequalities. Some people can afford to live in large houses with two or more expensive cars to drive around in, while others live in overcrowded and run-down accommodation or sleep rough and will never own a car.

The examination of inequalities has been a major (if not *the* major) area of sociological enquiry; issues of inequality are central to many social theories and are the key to understanding the different social opportunities available to different social groups and individuals. Sociologists suggest that the origins of inequality can be found in the cultures and social structures of societies themselves. This is not to deny that there are innate and natural differences between people and that such differences contribute to inequality; however, the sociological approach emphasizes how cultures and social structures can create and maintain individual inequalities.

In this chapter we focus on how inequality in societies leads to systems of social stratification, particularly stratification by social class.

Systems of stratification

Although our focus here is on stratification in contemporary society, the origins of social inequality

A closer look

Inequality and stratification

Although not synonymous, these terms are often used interchangeably. *Inequality* refers to differences between people in terms of their abilities and rewards. We notice these differences from an early age. Why am I stronger than my brother? Why is my sister smarter than me? We become aware of their social implications as we grow up. Why do some people get better jobs? Why are some jobs paid more highly than others?

Inequality leads to *social stratification* when people are ranked hierarchically according to their possession of attributes such as income, wealth, power, age, gender and status. This sort of ranking leads to groups of people being classified into layers or strata – like geological rock formations – hence the term 'stratification'. Stratification can be thought of as referring to structured inequalities that persist over time.

Inequality and stratification profoundly affect the quality of people's lives and can make the difference between, say, working in a well-paid job or being unemployed, eating well or going hungry, owning your own home or living on the street, living to an old age or dying young.

can be traced back to ancient times. Historically, four systems of social stratification can be identified: slavery, caste, estates and social class.

Slavery

The oldest and most extreme form of stratification involved the enslavement or ownership of others as a result of conquest, trade, kidnapping, hereditary status or the repayment of a debt. The early civilizations of Babylon, Egypt and Persia relied heavily on slave labour, as did the Greek and Roman empires. Between the fifteenth and nineteenth centuries the industrial and financial might of modern European powers was related directly to the trade in African slaves. This slave labour was crucial to the economic development of the New World and the establishment of black populations in the Americas and the Caribbean.

Although in earlier civilizations slavery was sometimes only temporary, with individual slaves occasionally enjoying high status and the opportunity to earn their freedom, usually it was a permanent state whereby an individual was the property of someone else for whom he or she worked with no prospect of reward, freedom or legal protection. Despite being abolished in the British Empire in 1833, slavery has by no means disappeared. In 1984 the United Nations investigated claims that the West African former colony of Mauritania still allowed 100,000 people to be kept in slavery. Anti-Slavery International has continued to monitor the use of forced labour as well as child prostitution on a global scale.

Caste

The caste system is associated mainly with Indian society and the Hindu religion. It involves a complex and strictly defined division of labour in which occupations are assigned to one of four closed status groups (*varna*). Rank order is not necessarily related to power or money but rather to traditional values that place the Brahmin priests at the top and those responsible for 'unclean' tasks, known as 'untouchables', as outcasts below the four main castes. There is no possibility of social mobility, as these positions are determined by birth. Indeed, a person's position is believed to be based on what was achieved in a previous incarnation. As a result of these beliefs, it is held that the structure of society is divinely ordained and individuals are obliged to accept it and to carry out their duties within it 'without ambition to change' (*dharma*).

Case study

27 million slaves in the world today

Since 1839 Anti-Slavery International has campaigned for an end to slavery around the globe. A fundamental abuse of human rights and the most extreme form of exploitation, slavery still exists on every continent, with rich and poor countries involved in the trade. Since 2001, Anti-Slavery International has worked closely with Free the Slaves, its sister organization in the USA.

According to these organizations, millions of men, women and children are bought and sold, bartered for and exchanged, and even given away as gifts. Although the shackles and chains we associate with the African slave trade are gone, slavery, bondage and serfdom still exist in the twenty-first century and its victims end up as domestic slaves, forced labourers and prostitutes. In West Africa children are kidnapped and sold for as little as $20 to be sold on for $350 or more to traders from richer neighbouring countries. The modern slave trade in women (known as odalisques), which exists between the poorer parts of the Indian subcontinent and the richer states of the Middle East, sees women changing hands for between $3000 and $10,000. At the beginning of the twenty-first century, Dr Charles Jacobs who is president of the American Anti-Slavery Group claimed that there were over 27 million slaves worldwide and quoted a report from the CIA, which estimated that 50,000 slaves were being smuggled into the USA every year.

According to Anti-Slavery International's *Annual Review 2004*, the most common forms of slavery today are:

- *Bonded labour* – This affects millions of people. The person is forced by poverty or tricked into taking a ▶

Case study *continued*

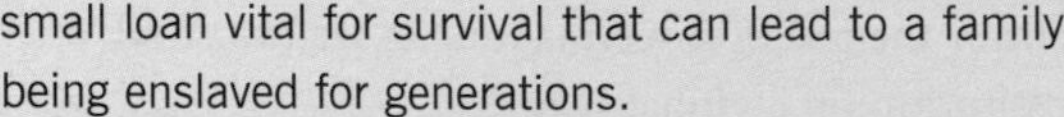

small loan vital for survival that can lead to a family being enslaved for generations.

- *Forced labour* – The person is forced to work under the threat or use of violence or other punishment.
- *Forced marriage* – Girls and women, married without choice, are forced into a life of servitude that is often dominated by violence.
- *Worst forms of child labour* – This affects an estimated 179 million children around the world in work that is harmful to their health and welfare.
- *Human trafficking* – This is the fastest growing form of slavery today. A person – woman, child or man – is taken from one area to another in order to be forced into slavery.
- *Slavery by descent* – The person is either born into a slave class or is from a group that society views as suited to being used as slave labour.

See the following websites for more information about slavery, human trafficking and child labour:

www.antislavery.org

www.iabolish.org

www.anti-slaverysociety.addr.com

www.unicef.org

Questions

1. **Using the websites mentioned above, examine one form of contemporary slavery in depth.**
2. **How would you account for the persistence of slavery?**

These beliefs are further reinforced by taboos governing social interaction, pollution and marriage. Despite being officially abolished in 1947, this system still survives, especially in rural areas, as do the religious beliefs that have underpinned it for the past 3000 years. The term 'caste' has also been used to describe societies based on racial segregation such as South Africa under apartheid and the southern states of the USA before the civil rights movement.

Estates

In the feudal system of medieval Europe a ranking of status groups known as estates became the dominant system. The three major estates were the aristocracy (headed by the divine monarch), the priesthood and the commoners (peasants, servants, artisans, etc.). This system was related closely to property and political power, with land ownership as the key. In a relationship of rights and obligations known as *noblesse oblige* (Figure 4.1), the commoners were allowed use of land in return for providing service and rents to their landlord, who in turn promised protection and support. Just as the tenant was a vassal (dependant) of the lord, so the lord was in debt to the monarch. This interlocking system of rights and obligations was seen as divinely ordained. However, the estate system was not as strictly tied to religious belief as the caste system is, and some historians have argued that feudalism allowed for a degree of social mobility, especially in towns.

Social class

In the previous systems of stratification the social position of an individual was fixed by law, custom or inherited status. These positions were reinforced by a set of norms that clearly governed the relationship between members of the different groups; group membership was often ascribed at birth. Such systems are characterized by very little social mobility and are sometimes referred to as 'closed' societies because the life prospects of individuals are predetermined. Under the process of industrialization the traditional aspects of these stratification systems gave way to a more open system, which was characterized by competition and a higher degree of social mobility. Customary divisions and traditional distinctions were replaced by 'class' distinctions based on property and authority. Class position is therefore determined largely by an individual's place within the economic system and is to some extent achieved. Ideally such a society should become a *meritocracy* (a hierarchy based on achievement and ability) in which class origins are irrelevant to where an individual is 'placed' in the economic system. However,

Figure 4.1 Noblesse oblige
Cartoon by Ian Hering

despite this conception of society as a hierarchy of positions based solely on merit, most sociologists still regard modern industrial societies as being stratified on the basis of social class. Indeed, the idea that contemporary societies can be and are divided into classes is one that is not only popular with sociologists but also shared by members of society at large. A large part of this chapter will be taken up with a fuller discussion of the meaning of class and of its continuing importance in modern society, while the chapters on education, politics and health also make extensive use of the connection between social class, social processes and the quality of life.

Explanations of stratification

Inequalities between people and the stratifi[...] entire societies have always require[...] explanation. Such explana[...] either justificatior[...] regarded as ideolo[...] times these explana[...] natural or social inte[...] (post-Enlightenment) [...] are all born equal (in a[...] has only increased the sp[...]

Divine explanations

Peter Berger has claimed that religion has a special authority when it acts as an ideology of justification, 'because it relates the precarious reality constructions of empirical societies with ultimate reality' (quoted in Daly 1991: 132). This notion of 'ultimate reality' can be applied to various forms of inequality. The Indian caste system is supported by the Hindu belief in reincarnation and the identification of social rank as a sign of spiritual purity. The twin concepts of *karma* and *dharma* are central to this moral justification of a closed social system:

> **Karma teaches a Hindu that he or she is born into a particular caste or sub-caste because he or she deserves to be there as a consequence of actions in a previous life. Dharma, which means 'existing according to that which is moral' teaches that living one's present life according to the rules (dharma) will result in rebirth into a higher caste and thus ultimate progression through the caste system. Both existing inequalities of caste, therefore, as well as any possibility of change in the future, are related to universal religious truths and are thus beyond the reaches of systematic sociological examination.**
>
> (Crompton 1993: 2)

Similar justifications were provided for the estates system by the Roman Catholic Church, which sanctified the feudal hierarchy with the argument that it reflected the celestial order of things and blessed the king with a divine right to rule.

> **One of the greatest achievements of the Middle Ages was the development of this idea of a universal human society as an integral part of a divinely ordered universe in time and in eternity, in nature and supernature, in practical politics and in the world of spiritual essences.**
>
> (Southern 1988: 22)

This universal human society laid great stress on duty and order and allowed for little social mobility. 'Everyman had his station in society, and few men were llowed to sink very much lower or to rise very much her than the station into which they were born' hern 1988: 43). To seek for personal improvement the pursuit of wealth was condemned as a sin), while poverty was cherished as a humble ideas may have originated in the Middle persisted into the Industrial Revolution rise of capitalism.

> **In 'primitive' societies religious explanations were used to come to terms with phenomena which were beyond understanding, but gradually these beliefs and explanations became justifications and legitimations for keeping society as it was. Thus, for example, in the sixteenth and seventeenth centuries, the idea of a 'great chain of being' existed in which the social hierarchy of Gods, kings and bishops, lords, freemen and serfs was argued to be natural and God given. Similarly, in the eighteenth and nineteenth centuries many people thought it was largely senseless to try to do anything about poverty since it was God who had created the rich and the poor, and it was therefore immoral and ungodly to try to change things.**
>
> (Thompson 1986: 36)

Religious explanations have been used to justify both racial and sexual inequality. The relationship between religion and race has always been troublesome. In those societies that depended on African slaves for their economic power, theological debates raged over the 'humanity' of black Africans. The Dutch Reformed Church (DRC) in South Africa (regarded as the 'official religion' of the National Party) introduced segregated worship and persistently sanctioned apartheid from the pulpit. In its 'Statement on Race Relations, no. 1' (November 1960) the DRC stated that it 'could not associate itself unreservedly with the general cry for equality and unity in the world today'. In 1982 apartheid was declared a 'heresy' by the World Alliance of Reformed Churches and the DRC was expelled for its continued defence of racial segregation in South Africa.

The universal subordination of women throughout history has also been explained and approved of by almost all religions. Whether it is through creation myth, spiritual teachings or ritualized practice, the subjugation of women by men has often been given the status of holy law. O'Faolain and Martinez (1979) have shown that holy teachings and practices have provided powerful ideological support for the oppression of women. In many representations of The Great Chain of Being, Man is always closer to God while Woman separates Man from the Beasts. In the 1579 version shown in Figure 4.2, women are absent altogether.

Naturalistic explanations

From ancient times to the present day the explanations of differences between individuals and groups in terms of natural differences have been popular. It appeals to

Figure 4.2 The Great Chain of Being. From Didacus Valades, *Rhetorica Christiana* (1579). In such representations of a divine order, all forms of natural and social species are ordained their place in the hierarchy
Source: reproduced from Fletcher (1999)

our common sense to suppose that the differences and similarities that appear at an early age between members of the same family are caused by nature. Whether a child is regarded as 'a chip off the old block' or 'the black sheep of the family', the cause can be accommodated easily within a model that explains physical, psychological and intellectual characteristics in terms of genetic inheritance. It is a short step to assume that all inequalities within society are part of the same natural condition; 'boys will be boys' is used to explain why brothers are treated differently from their sisters; the idea that the aristocracy have 'blue blood' in their veins is taken to mean that they were 'born to rule'. There are important differences between different types of natural explanation; biological and psychological explanations, for instance, are not interchangeable.

As with divine explanations, appeals to the laws of nature can operate as very powerful conservative ideologies. While Aristotle was insistent that the domination of both slaves and women by freemen was a condition ordained 'by nature', so Plato argued that the clear differences between the three basic classes of human stock in an ideal society should be maintained by a form of state-regulated eugenics.

The importance of selective breeding for the maintenance of a stable class structure (especially in the face of a population explosion among poor people) was stressed in the work of Francis Galton and his admirer Cyril Burt. Both believed that individual talent (and its absence) was essentially inherited and that the unequal

World in focus

Beyond God the Father

Mary Daly (1991), in her book *Beyond God the Father*, has argued that world religions (and Christianity in particular) are part of a conspiracy to retain the status of women as a 'sexual caste' through their own consent via the process of 'sex role socialization', which hides the truth of their caste status. Daly suggests that 'the entire conceptual systems of theology and ethics . . . have been the products of males and tend to serve the interests of sexist society' (Daly 1991: 4).

The biblical and popular image of God as a great patriarch in heaven, rewarding and punishing according to his mysterious and seemingly arbitrary will, has dominated the imagination of millions over thousands of years. The symbol of God the Father, spawned in the human imagination and sustained as plausible by patriarchy, has in turn rendered service to this type of society by making its mechanisms for the oppression of women appear right and fitting. If God in 'His' heaven is a father ruling 'His' people, then it is in the 'nature' of things and according to divine plan and the order of the universe that society be male-dominated.

Within this context a mystification of roles takes place:

World in focus *continued*

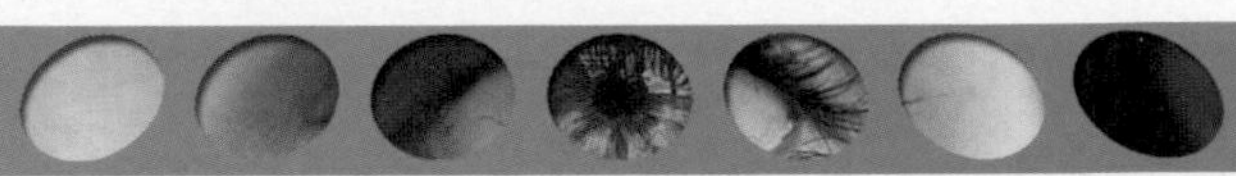

the husband dominating his wife represents God 'Himself'. The images and values of a given society have been projected into the realm of dogmas and 'Articles of Faith', which in turn justify the social structures that have given rise to them and that sustain their plausibility; however, change can occur in society, and ideologies can die, though they die hard.

As the women's movement begins to have its effect upon the fabric of society, transforming it from patriarchy into something that never existed before – into a diarchal situation that is radically new – it can become the greatest single challenge to the major religions of the world, Western and Eastern. Beliefs and values that have held sway for thousands of years will be questioned as never before.

(Adapted from Daly 1991: 14)

Questions

1. In what ways is traditional religion patriarchal?
2. Can you think of any religious beliefs or practices that illustrate this?
3. What does the controversy over women priests in the Church of England tell us about the extent to which the women's movement has successfully challenged patriarchal religious beliefs?
4. How would you feel about being married by a woman priest?

rewards found in society were no more than a reflection of this natural distribution of ability throughout the population. If social classes existed, that was merely a reflection of groupings in nature. The Eugenics movement was also concerned with the issue of racial purity and campaigned for the sterilization and incarceration of disabled and mentally ill people as well as the introduction of strong immigration controls. In the nineteenth and early twentieth centuries the threat to the Anglo-Saxon stock (in Britain) was identified as Celtic and Jewish. Later this fear was extended to African and Asian people. Early on in Britain's imperial history scientists were ready to explain the differential treatment of other racial groups in terms of natural differences between the races. This led to the development of what Peter Fryer (1984) has called 'pseudo-scientific racism', which is clearly linked to attempts to demonstrate that differences in intelligence, aggression and personality have a racial origin. During the twentieth century the work of some psychologists was used to suggest that the social failure of some racial groups is the result of inferior IQ.

In 1916 Lewis Terman introduced the Stanford–Binet Test by highlighting its capacity to distinguish between the abilities of different racial groups in the USA and expose the 'feeble-mindedness' of some groups in particular:

> **Their dullness seems to be racial, or at least inherent in the family stocks from which they come. The fact that one meets this type with extraordinary frequency among Indians, Mexicans and negroes suggests quite forcibly that the whole question of racial difference in mental traits will have to be taken up anew . . . Children of this group should be segregated into special classes . . . They cannot master abstractions, but they can often be made efficient workers . . . There is no possibility at present of convincing society that they should not be allowed to reproduce . . . they constitute a grave problem because of their unusually prolific breeding.**
>
> **(quoted by Kamin 1977: 374–7)**

This debate grabbed the headlines again in the early 1970s when psychologists such as A.R. Jensen (1973) began to repeat the claim that black Americans were intellectually inferior to whites. In the early 1990s Charles Murray and Richard Herrnstein initiated a return to the arguments with their claim that black people in the USA scored on average 15 points below whites in IQ tests. In their book *The Bell Curve: Intelligence and the Class Structure* (Herrnstein and Murray 1994), they argue that a three-part class structure has emerged based on inherited intelligence.

Case study

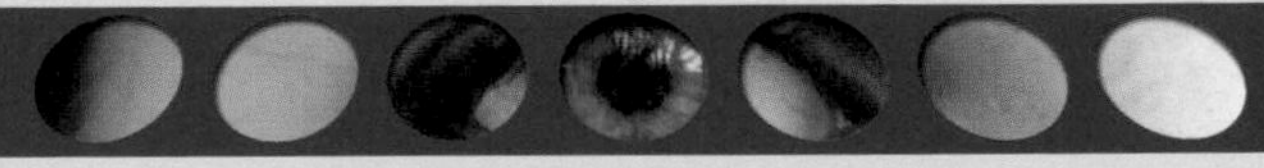

Plato's Republic – the world's first dating agency?

In Plato's ideal world the social structure depended upon the reproduction of the three key classes (guardians, auxiliaries and labourers) for which he used the metaphor of precious and base metals (gold, silver and bronze). In order for these 'natural classes' to be reproduced without mishap, Plato argued for the abolition of marriage and the family and sexual selection to be organized by the state through the regular celebration of 'mating festivals' at which the classes would be kept apart in order to maintain their genetic purity:

> For guardians, sexual intercourse will only take place during certain fixed times of year, designated as festivals. Males and females will be made husband and wife at these festivals for roughly the duration of sexual intercourse. The pairings will be determined by lot. Some of these people, those who are most admirable and thus whom we most wish to reproduce, might have up to four or five spouses in a single one of these festivals. All the children produced by these mating festivals will be taken from their parents and reared together, so that no one knows which children descend from which adults. At no other time in the year is sex permitted. If guardians have sex at an undesignated time and a child results, the understanding is that this child must be killed.

(From: www.sparknotes.com)

A closer look

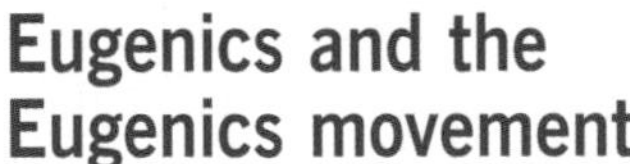

Eugenics and the Eugenics movement

Eugenics refers to the improvement of the human race through genetic policies that would discourage certain people and social groups who were felt to be 'inferior' from breeding and encourage others, who were thought to be more intelligent or superior in some way, to breed.

By the late nineteenth century, scientific interest in the new fields of genetics and evolution led to a Eugenics movement that had a powerful influence on many areas of social investigation and policy, particularly in the USA and Europe.

Society is dominated by a 'cognitive elite' (IQ 125+) and serviced by a middle class of average IQ, beneath whom a largely black underclass with IQs of 75 or less survive and multiply (*The Observer* 23.10.94).

The historical subordination of women and the domination by men of all positions of economic and political power have been given similar treatment by some biologists and psychologists who sought to show that gender differences can be traced back to the natural differences between men and women. According to this view, women achieve very little outside their caring role within the family because they are physically weaker, emotionally unstable and intellectually inferior.

Nineteenth-century 'phrenologists' argued that in terms of head shape the areas responsible for love, approbation and secretiveness were larger in the female but less well developed than those for aggression, self-sufficiency, firmness and ingenuity. Later attempts to locate the source of the differences targeted the brain, hormonal balance and genetically transmitted differences in intellect and personality.

By 1914 the German psychologist Hugo Munsterberg concluded that the female mind is 'capricious, oversuggestible, often inclined to exaggeration, is disinclined to abstract thought, unfit for mathematical reasoning, impulsive [and] over-emotional' (Fairbrother 1983). As Hugh Fairbrother has pointed out, such

A closer look

Social class and race: the underclass

Characterized by poor IQ and educational failure, the 'underclass' (see also pp. 203–209) becomes a breeding ground for 'welfare queens' and criminals. Although Herrnstein and Murray (1994) assert that they are concerned more with social class than race, the racial implications of their work are clear, especially in a society where terms such as 'underclass' and 'crime' are codes for white Americans, meaning 'black'. As Haymes (1996) has argued, this research is an attempt to pathologize and criminalize black Americans as one step towards a 'final solution' of social problems, which scapegoats black urban youth in particular.

> By using intelligence as a 'neutral' medium, Herrnstein and Murray are able to claim surreptitiously that Blacks are biologically predisposed to violent criminal behavior, linking criminality with race. Making this connection allows the authors of *The Bell Curve* to use crime to talk covertly about the black body as being menacing. In other words, Herrnstein and Murray link their explanation of crime with Western racial discourse.
>
> (Haymes 1996: 244)

In *The Race Gallery*, Marek Kohn (1996) has shown that this racial discourse about the biological elements of social class is not restricted to American society. Since the collapse of the Soviet Union and its satellite states, there has been a rebirth of nationalism, which draws on Romantic notions of *Volkgeist* and an emerging 'race science system', both reminiscent of the earlier pronouncements of European Fascism. In countries such as Hungary, Romania and Slovakia, this ideology is directed largely at Romany Gypsies. Once again, pseudoscience is being used to identify an ethnic group as a genetically inferior class, to blame them for society's ills and to make them the focus of social intervention. In 1992 Istvan Csurca, leader of the Hungarian Road movement, conflated the concepts of class and race to express this idea of a biologically created underclass in extreme and fatalistic terms.

> We can no longer ignore the fact that the deterioration of the Hungarian nation has genetic causes as well. It has to be acknowledged that under-privileged, even cumulatively underprivileged, strata and groups have been living among us for far too long. Society now has to support the strong fit-for-life families who are prepared for work and achievement.
>
> (Quoted in Kohn 1996: 187)

conclusions have a strong whiff of male prejudice about them and very little to do with scientific rigour:

> **What we need to do is remind ourselves constantly that our behaviour is not only, or even mostly, at the whim of our physique and physiology. As social beings we share responsibility for each other's behaviour. We create the sexist society which in turn spawns sexist science . . . The crude stereotypes of 'male' and 'female' that the scientists set out to validate have changed and continue to change.**
>
> (Fairbrother 1983: 8–9)

In the modern age the advances in technology have meant that the 'harmless' speculations on genetic engineering of Aristotle and Plato have become distinct and disturbing possibilities, not only in the prophetic pages of Aldous Huxley's *Brave New World* (1932) but also in the real world of genetic engineering and social policy. Hitler's *lebensborn* policy of eugenic breeding to create a 'super-race' was the flipside of the 'final solution' coin.

> **All the good blood in the world, all the Germanic blood that is not on the German side, may one day be our ruin. Hence every male of the best Germanic blood whom we bring to Germany and turn into a Teutonic-minded man means one more combatant on our side and one less on the other. I really intend to take German blood from wherever it is to be found in the world, to rob and steal it wherever I can.**
>
> (Heinrich Himmler, speech to officers of the Deutschland Division, 8 November 1938, quoted in Henry and Hiltel 1977: 143)

The Swedish nation was shocked to learn in 1997 that their Social Democratic governments had been practising a programme of enforced sterilization for 40 years between 1935 and 1975. The campaign targeted ethnic groups, criminals, mentally retarded people and alcoholics, and over the period approximately 63,000 men and women were either paid to take part or offered the operation as a means of achieving a quick release from prison, qualifying for state benefits or retaining custody over their existing children.

In California scientists have engineered 'super-kids' using sperm banks and artificial insemination, and the prospect of cloning identical families is well within the scope of current genetic technology. 'Problem populations' may be dealt with through birth control and immigration legislation. Rather than being old-fashioned philosophies or creations of science fiction, these ideas are now more powerful and potentially dangerous than they have ever been.

Social explanations

Within sociology various explanations have been offered for the persistence of social inequalities. Much emphasis is placed on the role of personal experience, culture and deprivation in explaining why some individuals succeed and others fail, while the openness of the opportunity structure is also a crucial part of the debate. For the moment, however, we concentrate on the purposes and consequences of inequality for society from three perspectives: the functionalist model, the libertarian model and the egalitarian model.

The functionalist model

Derived primarily from Durkheim's analysis of the division of labour, the functionalist model argues that social inequality is an essential part of modern society so long as recruitment is based on merit and rewards are distributed fairly. If this can be achieved, then social cohesion (rather than resentment) will result because it is seen (by the majority) as providing just reward for those who perform jobs of high social value. To some extent this view echoes the belief that market forces can be relied on to produce a 'spontaneous order' (see 'The libertarian model' below), but it clearly possesses a moral dimension with references to social consensus, fairness and merit. For this reason, Durkheim, who is popularly typecast as a conservative thinker, argued against the inheritance of property on the basis that it gave unfair advantage to the offspring of wealthy families.

Developing Durkheim's concern with the moral aspects of inequality, Talcott Parsons maintained that the 'spontaneous order' is not simply a product of market forces but also the result of social consensus ('normative order') over the most important skills (such skills might be bravery, hunting or intelligence) and the extent to which they should be differentially rewarded. Davis and Moore argued that stratification is both inevitable and functional in any society that requires its most important tasks to be carried out efficiently:

> **Social inequality is an unconsciously evolved device by which societies insure that the most important positions are conscientiously filled by the most qualified persons.**
>
> (Davis and Moore 1967: 48)

By compensating those who train to become qualified for the most important positions, this system ensures that the most able individuals are allocated to the key roles in society and motivated to work hard while they are employed in them. As a result, social efficiency is maintained while the high value placed on certain skills is reinforced. At the centre of this model is the assumption that competition for the key places is open to all and that roles are allocated according to individual merit. This is clearly summarized in Turner's model of 'contest mobility'.

> **Applied to mobility the contest norm means that victory by a person of moderate intelligence accomplished through the use of common sense, craft, enterprise, daring and successful risk taking is more appreciated than victory of the most intelligent or the best educated . . . The contest is judged to be fair only if all the players compete on an equal footing. Victory must be won solely by one's own efforts.**
>
> (Turner 1961: 183)

Saunders (1987) has argued for a return to this model, maintaining that, as long as people are guaranteed political and legal equality, the best system must be one in which everyone has an equal opportunity to be unequal. In his discussion of the relationship between meritocracy, inequality and fairness, Saunders draws on evidence from a survey of public attitudes, which suggested 90 per cent support for the ideal that 'people's incomes should depend on hard work and ability' and concludes that social inequality is not only an effective means of running the economy but also a force for social stability:

> **This strong support for meritocracy . . . reflects the fact that most of us understand that inequality is not necessarily 'unfair' – it depends on whether it is justifiable with reference to individual talent and individual effort. If we are convinced that, by and large, those who have the ability and who make an effort can usually find success, and that those who do not will not generally prosper, then the basis is laid for a society which should be able to function reasonably harmoniously. Meritocracy does have a problem in dealing with the social consequences of failure, but this need not be catastrophic as regards social cohesion provided the competition is known to have been fair. Ninety per cent agreement is not a bad basis on which to build and sustain a moral social order.**
>
> (Saunders 1996: 90)

In his discussion of meritocracy, Saunders points out that the functionalist approach has been criticized from the political right (libertarian) and left (egalitarian).

The libertarian model

The libertarian model, which is associated closely with individualistic and naturalistic explanations, emphasizes the importance of an open and free market for talents and abilities so that those with the most marketable skills are rewarded for their ability and motivated to work hard and compete with others for the highest rewards. Neo-liberal economists (sometimes known as 'the New Right') have argued that unequal reward encourages self-interest and competition, which in turn sponsor personal initiative and technological innovation. Capitalism is seen as a dynamic system that gets the best out of individuals by rewarding talent and hard work and penalizing feckless and idle people. As a result we all benefit from the inspiration of creative individuals and harnessing the power of their ideas and effort. Whether we approve of them or not, we inhabit a world that has been greatly influenced by individuals such as Henry Ford, Richard Branson and Rupert Murdoch. Without an unequal reward structure, we would never have heard of any of them or enjoyed the benefits of mass-produced motor cars, the Virgin airline or satellite TV. According to writers such as Friedrich Hayek (1976), Milton Friedman (1962) and Robert Nozick (1974), any attempt to tamper with the 'spontaneous order' generated by the capitalist reward structure serves only to reduce the 'social energy' produced by inequality.

On the surface there seems to be a strong similarity between the idea that the market should be left to determine who gets what and the functionalist conviction that merit should be rewarded. However, the logic of the marketplace has no time for notions of fairness or just reward, particularly where these may impede the freedom of people to do what they will with their talents or their money. For Nozick, people may reap whatever rewards come their way so long as they are entitled to them as earnings or as gifts. Whether people deserve their luck or not does not enter into the argument: millionaire lottery winners, professional footballers on £120,000 per week and windfall profiteers cashing in on the vagaries of the stock market should not be denied their entitlement simply because it is not fair. As Hayek points out, this is an argument about freedom, not fairness; in general the market will reward highly those people who have rare skills and talents, but there is no guarantee that this will happen and sometimes the highest rewards go to those whom we feel least deserve them; as with the lottery winner our response should be 'good luck to them' because, as the advert for the lottery used to say, one day 'It could be you'. In a free society people should be left to make the most of their talents and reap whatever rewards they can get so long as they do not exploit others or break the law:

> **However able a man may be in a particular field, the value of his services is necessarily low in a free society unless he also possesses the capacity of making his ability known to those who can derive the greatest benefit from it. Though it may offend our sense of justice to find that of two men who by equal effort have acquired the same specialized skill and knowledge, one may be a success and the other a failure, we must recognize that in a free society it is the use of particular opportunities that determines usefulness . . . In a free society we are remunerated not for our skill but for using it rightly.**
>
> (Hayek 1960: 82)

The egalitarian model

While the libertarians and the functionalists accept that there are natural differences in talent among the general population but disagree over the extent to which rewards should be unequally distributed and the role of fair play in the allocation of these rewards, the egalitarian argument rejects the principle of unequal reward and the notion of natural differences on which it is founded. The so-called natural differences between people are

A closer look

Tiger Woods

Tiger Woods (Figure 4.3) was ranked number 2 in the Forbes Celebrity 100 for 2007 and is the highest paid sports personality in the world, earning $100 million in that year alone.

According to Forbes:

> Woods is the first athlete in history to bank $100 million in a year, thanks in part to a raise he finagled out of long-time endorser Nike. (The sneaker giant's Tiger-oriented golf division is now a $600 million-a-year business.) He also signed a new deal with Gillette and upped his usual lucrative overseas playing gigs, where he can command, on average, $3 million a pop. Wife Elin gave birth to the couple's first child, daughter Sam Alexis, in June.

www.forbes.com/lists/2007/53/07celebrities_Tiger-Woods_WR6D.html

Figure 4.3 Tiger Woods
AP Photo/Charlie Riedel

created by the social privileges and disadvantages inherent in an unequal society, and reinforced by differential educational opportunities in particular. Consequently the wide differences in reward in society are not a fair reflection of natural differences in ability or effort but a manipulation by those in positions of power to reward themselves at the expense of others. Instead of encouraging fairness, social cohesion and harmony, this model suggests that inequality of reward promotes a dysfunctional world in which the middle and upper classes revel in their superiority and the poor resent their failure. These views are clearly close to those expressed by thinkers on the political left, who believe that all people should be treated equally, but they are also to be found among 'progressive' sociologists, who have condemned the functionalist model as an ideological justification for the status quo.

Melvin Tumin's (1967) attack on the 'principles of stratification' outlined by Davis and Moore (1967) is well documented elsewhere; essentially his argument challenges the assumption that some positions are inherently more important than others, and that stratification provides an efficient mechanism for attracting the most talented individuals in society to these positions. Instead of promoting functional efficiency and fairness, such systems can be socially divisive and dysfunctional, promoting resentment, demotivation and conflict, while the skills and talents that are encouraged by unequal rewards have little to do with intelligence or social worth:

> **Wealth and power tend to accrue to those who are ruthless, cunning, avaricious, self-seeking, lacking in sympathy and compassion, subservient to authority [and] willing to abandon principle for material gain.**
>
> (Chomsky 1972, quoted in Anderson 1974: 82)

As a result, systems of stratification encourage self-perpetuating elites, who pass on their privileges through inherited wealth, private education and intermarriage. As Bottomore (1965) pointed out, social stratification operates to resist the dynamics of openness and social change:

> **Indeed, it would be a more accurate description of the social class system to say that it operates, largely through the inheritance of property, to ensure that each individual maintains a certain social position, determined by his birth and irrespective of his particular abilities.**
>
> (Bottomore 1965: 16)

The arguments of Tumin (1967), Bottomore (1965) and Chomsky (1972) clearly indicate a lack of agreement with the fundamental idea of modern, stratified societies as meritocracies. Instead they would see Turner's model of 'sponsored mobility' in which status is ascribed rather than achieved as being more appropriate:

> **Sponsored mobility . . . rejects the pattern of the contest and substitutes a controlled selection process. In this process the elite or their agents who are best qualified to judge merit, call those individuals who have the appropriate qualities to elite status. Individuals do not win or seize elite status, but mobility is rather a process of sponsored induction into the elite following selection.**
>
> (Turner 1961: 183–4)

Even when the egalitarians concede that there are natural differences in ability and aptitude, they see no reason to accept that this is a fair basis for rewarding people differently. In response to Saunders' argument in favour of a meritocracy, Marshall and Swift put forward the view that ending up with the right genes is no more fair than winning the National Lottery and should not be rewarded as such:

> **It [is] particularly apt to ask whether an inherited characteristic – genetically determined intelligence – is an appropriate basis for reward at all. A crucial issue here would seem to be the distinction between those attributes for which the individual can claim responsibility and those which are his or hers merely by chance. If someone possesses particular talents or skills merely as a result of the natural lottery then it is not clear how justice is served by rewarding such possession.**
>
> (Marshall and Swift 1993: 206)

Stop and think

- Using the three social perspectives (functionalist, libertarian and egalitarian) assess the following cases from each one:
  - (a) Ingvar Kamprad, the head of Ikea, overtook Bill Gates as the richest man in the world when the drop in the value of the dollar against the Swedish krona boosted his wealth to $53 billion.
  - (b) The world's biggest lottery winner ($315 million).
  - (c) A 16-year-old playworker earning £4.10 per hour.
  - (d) A disabled 18-year-old receiving incapacity benefits of £56 per week.

Theoretical concepts of class

> **The discourse of class has become one of the key concepts through which we can begin to understand [the modern world]. Class, therefore, is a major organising concept in the exploration of contemporary stratification systems.**
>
> (Crompton 1993: 4)

> **Slowly but surely the old establishment is being replaced by a new, larger, more meritocratic middle class . . . A middle class that will include millions of people who traditionally see themselves as working class, but whose ambitions are far broader than those of their parents and grandparents . . . I believe we will have an expanded middle class, with ladders of opportunity for those of all backgrounds. No more ceilings that prevent people from achieving the success they merit.**
>
> (Tony Blair, quoted in the *Guardian* 15.1.99)

These two quotes highlight quite contradictory stances on the importance of class in contemporary societies. In the first quote, class is seen as an essential aspect of such societies, whereas Tony Blair's comment suggests that class is becoming less important, with an individual's position increasingly based on that person's own ability. As we mentioned when looking at systems of stratification (pp. 154–157), sociologists would tend to support Crompton's comment and emphasize the continuing importance of social class in modern societies. The 'discourse of class' continues to have a wide and general usage. In thousands of different ways we generate and interpret clues about ourselves and others that indicate class position. How we dress, speak and eat are all indicators of social class. The concept of social class is part of our culture; embedded in this culture are judgements about how we earn our money and what we purchase with it, how we educate our children and where we spend our leisure time.

Marx and social class

Marx died with his aim of providing a precise definition of social class an unfinished project. Nevertheless, the concept remains at the centre of his work. Unlike Durkheim, who rarely used the term 'class', or Weber, who gave it specific and limited meaning, Marx saw class not only as a descriptive device but also as a way of understanding how society and history interact, the maintenance of social order and the dynamics of social

Case study

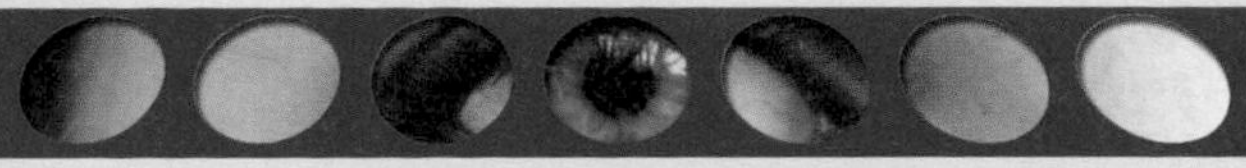

The Duke of Westminster's housing estate

In 1937 the Duke of Westminster made a present of the Page Street housing estate to the Westminster Council on the condition that it should be used exclusively as 'dwellings for the working class . . . and for no other purpose'. Almost fifty years later the 1985 Housing Act gave sitting tenants the 'right to buy' council rented property. Westminster Council attempted to implement this policy, but ended up in the High Court when they insisted that the phrase 'working class' no longer had any meaning. The current Duke of Westminster successfully defended his ancestor's wishes when Mr Justice Harman ruled that parliament 'does not determine the meaning of those words in ordinary English speech'. He concluded that the term was 'as valid today as when it was made'.

(The *Guardian* 27.11.90)

Questions

1. What do you think the Duke of Westminster meant by 'working class'?
2. What does the term 'working class' mean to you?
3. What evidence is there that the public still think in terms of social class?

change. Sometimes Marx talks of 'Society . . . splitting up into *two* great hostile camps'; on other occasions he says that 'wage labourers, capitalists and landlords, form the *three* great classes of modern society'. In more empirical mood Marx allows for six different groups (in Germany) and seven (in Britain), where the working class can be subdivided into productive (factory workers) and non-productive (servants). In his mention of 'intermediate' classes Marx seems to anticipate some of the arguments developed later in Wright's discussion of 'contradictory class positions' (see p. 171). To understand the different ways in which Marx used the term we can distinguish between *objective* and *subjective* class positions.

In Marx's work, then, social class is not simply a category to describe the measurement of social inequality; it is a dynamic force used to explain social change. As the processes of deskilling and proletarianization shape a homogeneous class of workers sharing similar experiences of work and lifestyle, Marx expected that they would also come to a common understanding of their political interests. The radicalization of working-class politics was seen to go hand in hand with proletarianization and, it was argued, would lead to the revolutionary transformation of society through class-based action.

In the more deterministic strands of Marxist thought, especially in the later 1990s, this

A closer look

Objective class position

For Marx, a person's class can exist independently of their awareness of it and affect them in ways they are not conscious of. In this sense class operates as a social force that influences opportunities, governs relationships (between groups) and transforms conflict into change.

As Lee and Newby (1983) have pointed out, Marx used this notion of objective class position both theoretically and empirically. First, it was used to explain the inevitable antagonism that would develop between the bourgeoisie and the proletariat as a result of their diametrically opposed interests and the gradual proletarianization of society, work and politics. The eventual outcome of this class conflict would be a revolutionary transformation of society and the victory of socialism.

►

A closer look *continued*

Second, objective class position was used in a more static and descriptive way to provide a snapshot of the various social classes actually in existence at any particular time without making much comment on the relational aspects of these groupings. This explains why Marx can describe the existence of several classes alongside his more theoretical attempts to explain the importance of the two dominant ones.

Subjective class position

Although Marxism is often accused of being structuralist and deterministic in its emphasis upon the objective nature of social class, Marx himself clearly realized that antagonistic interests did not automatically guarantee social conflict and revolutionary change. People had to be conscious of their interests and committed to achieving them; only when this *class consciousness* developed could a class be transformed from a 'class *in* itself' to a 'class *for* itself'. This development of a class consciousness involved people in an ideological struggle in which 'false consciousness' is replaced by class awareness and a revolutionary consciousness. In the *Manifesto of the Communist Party*, Marx makes it clear that workers will achieve nothing until they share a common consciousness.

revolutionary outcome is assumed to be an automatic result of the forces of history (historical materialism), while in later versions, following Lukács, the roles of class consciousness and ideology are given a more significant part to play in class conflict and revolutionary struggle. The essential question here concerns the extent to which working-class people have a conscious role to play in making their own history or whether they are simply moulded in a deterministic manner by events. This debate within Marxism hints at later sociological interest in the concepts of 'structure' and 'agency', which are given particular attention in Giddens's (1973) work on 'structuration'. For the sociological discourse on the significance of class structure in modern society that concludes this chapter, the objective and subjective elements in Marx's writings are crucial because they set the agenda for the subsequent debate; Marx's ideas on proletarianization, class consciousness and radicalization are challenged by sociologists who feel that the processes of fragmentation, social mobility and embourgeoisment explain the inadequacies of the Marxist concept of class and the failure of communism.

Weber and social class

Like Marx, Weber did not finish his analysis of the concept of class, but he did give a more complete picture of what it meant to him by distinguishing the 'multidimensional' aspects of stratification. According to this view, society cannot be stratified by economic factors alone; status and party coincide and overlap with class as alternative bases for stratification. John Hughes (1984) argued that, rather than reducing inequality to economic factors, Weber regarded *power* as the primary relationship between unequal groups in society with class representing only one form:

> **Power, according to Weber, is the ability of an individual or group to get what they want even against the opposition of others . . . Power can be divided into three spheres of activity: the economic, the social and the political. Within each of these, individuals can be grouped according to the amount of power they are able to command.**
>
> (Hughes 1984: 7)

These three spheres of activity are more commonly referred to as class, status and party, and we need to examine each one in order to understand the extent to which Weber differed from Marx on the issues of class and stratification.

Class

It is not surprising that Weber did not share Marx's beliefs about social class. Weber had a commitment to the possibility of value-free sociology and cautiously welcomed the growth of capitalism and bureaucracy as the inevitable progress of rationality. He was also a Christian with some faith in the possibility of social reform. However, his writings on social class show that he was in close agreement with Marx on the importance of economic classes and the shape that these classes took at the end of the nineteenth century. Weber defined class in clear economic terms and accepted that it often provided the basis for shared social position, life chances and political action. He defined 'class situation' as:

> **The typical chance for a supply of goods, external living conditions, and personal life experiences, in so far as this chance is determined by the amount and kinds of power, or lack of such, to dispose of goods or skills for the sake of income in a given economic order.**
>
> (Weber, quoted in Edgell 1993: 12)

Like Marx, he accepted that 'class situation is by far the predominant factor' in determining social position with ownership (or lack) of property being the 'basic categories of all class situations'. As a result Weber acknowledges the existence of positively and negatively privileged classes, separated by a growing middle class. His description of the prevailing class structure resembles that put forward by Marx:

> **[Weber] identified as 'social classes' (a) the working class as a whole; (b) the petty bourgeoisie; (c) technicians, specialists and lower-level management, and (d) 'the classes privileged through property and education' – that is, those at the top of the hierarchy of occupation and ownership. In short, at the descriptive level, Weber's account of the 'class structure' of capitalist society is not too different from that of Marx.**
>
> (Crompton 1993: 30)

In four other respects, however, Weber's views on social class formation and class action are very different from those espoused by Marx: first, class situation is not determined simply by property relationships but by the shared life chances that people enjoy (or are denied) as a result of the value of their skills and possessions in the marketplace. This means that the possession of particular skills or qualifications may be just as important as the possession of property in determining class situation. It also implies that a person's class position will change with fluctuations in the market.

Second, class position is associated with potential for consumption (income) rather than the relationship to the mode of production.

> **For Marx, class relationships are grounded in exploitation and domination within *production* relations, whereas for Weber, class situations reflect differing 'life chances' in the *market*.**
>
> (Crompton 1993: 30)

This emphasis on consumption and lifestyle is central to Weber's idea of status.

Third, despite his apparent agreement with Marx over the four essential classes of capitalist society, Weber's definition allows for 'multiple classes' because he recognized 'important differences in the market situation of all groups, especially with respect to the various skills and services offered by different occupations' (Hughes 1984: 7). This means that on top of the differences between his four main classes he also emphasizes possible differences *within* these classes. Instead of society becoming polarized into two simple homogeneous classes, Weber's view was that the number of different classes would multiply with the expansion of society. Thus, Weber's conception of the social stratification structure in general, and the class structure in particular, is extremely complex and pluralistic.

Fourth, Weber rejected Marx's *dynamic* view of social class. He did not see class conflict as inevitable, nor did he accept it as the engine of historical change. Weber believed that people are essentially individuals and their class situation is only one of many possible sources of consciousness and political activity. Classes were seen as (merely) representing possible and frequent bases for communal action.

While Marx saw something inevitable in the connection between class position, class consciousness and political revolution, Weber was quite cynical about the political potential of the working classes and very pessimistic about the direction of world history. Working-class people could just as easily be motivated by patriotism and religious fervour as they were by class interest. He believed that rationally organized capitalism was more likely to dominate the future than revolutionary socialism.

Status

For many writers, Weber's greatest contribution to the stratification debate is his view that social differences can be as important as economic ones in the identification of social position even if the two seem very closely related:

> **'Classes' are stratified according to their relations to the production and acquisition of goods; whereas 'status groups' are stratified according to the principles of their consumption of goods as represented by special 'styles of life'!**
>
> (Weber, quoted in Hughes 1984: 8)

Although you may feel that 'lifestyle' is determined by class position, Weber said this is not necessarily the case:

> **Money and an entrepreneurial position are not in themselves status qualifications, although they may lead to them; and the lack of property is not in itself a status disqualification, although this may be a reason for it.**
>
> (Weber, quoted in Ritzer 1992: 128)

Status position is derived from the prestige or 'social honour' that the community attaches to a particular individual or role as well as the expected 'lifestyle' that attaches to it. A community will judge someone's social status according to cultural standards such as education, occupation, speech and dress, as well as the more obvious trappings of a privileged lifestyle.

Weber's concept of 'status group' has allowed modern sociologists to recognize that factors such as age, gender and race are related to 'life chances' in much the same way as class differences are and, for the individuals concerned, may be even more important.

Party

Just as the social order is given autonomy from economic forces, so Weber argues that the political sphere cannot be reduced to economic interests either. In this third arena of Weber's stratification system, people exercise control over others, and inequalities of power become another way in which differentiation manifests itself. Sometimes people organize themselves into political parties that represent their economic interests (e.g. the parliamentary Labour Party), but this is not the only basis for political organization. When political power results from such organization it can be used for the benefit of party members at the expense of other groups in society. In the former Soviet Union, for example, party membership was related closely to social status and economic privileges.

Corruption scandals in Western democracies emphasize this point: political power may be used as a device to increase economic privilege and social differentiation. In developing societies, too, political power may be a source of economic privilege. On the other hand, political policy may be directed towards social reform and the eradication of economic inequality. In both cases, political power is not simply the reflection of economic relations but appears to have a life of its own that sometimes runs in the opposite direction.

Stop and think

Class, status and power – what's the difference?

➤ Awarding a mark for each occupant (with 1 as the lowest and 8 the highest), rate the following for 'class', 'status' and 'power'.

Name	Class	Status	Power
Bill Gates $900,000 per hour			
Justine Whitaker – Nurse of the Year 2007			
George Bush – multimillionaire and ex-president of the USA			
Playworker on £4.60 per hour			
Duke of Westminster – worth £7 billion			
John Palmer (jailed fraudster) worth £300 million			
Mother Teresa of Calcutta – chose a life of poverty to help the poor			
The Beckhams – worth £112 million			

More recent concepts of class

The debate over the concept of class has continued. The main contributors have derived their inspiration from both Marx and Weber, with some clearly representing a neo-Marxist position and others proclaiming a neo-Weberian stance. In the middle there are those who have attempted to use Weber's insights to 'round out' Marx.

Nicos Poulantzas

In the face of changes in modern society, the apparent failure of communism and the emergence of humanistic Marxism, structuralist writers such as Louis Althusser (1969) and Nicos Poulantzas (1979) argued for a return to 'scientific Marxism'. This was largely an attack on individualism and subjectivism within Marxism and sociology, but it was also an attempt to re-emphasize the importance of class position as determined by the mode of production. For Poulantzas, classes were defined not by shared life chances or market situation but by their *role* in the production of *surplus value*. Consequently, those groups who appear to be 'working class' because of similarities in pay and working conditions with other workers cannot be included unless they are directly involved in the production of surplus value. On the political and ideological levels these classes may support one another and pursue the same interests, but they may not be classified together at the economic level. Instead, Poulantzas distinguished between productive and unproductive labour, with only those directly involved in production being allowed the classification 'proletariat'.

Erik Olin Wright

Wright is another neo-Marxist whose ideas developed not only in response to the work of Poulantzas (1979) but also as an attempt to provide an operational concept of class for use in empirical study. He followed the example set by fellow American Marxist Harry Braverman (1974) when he developed a more flexible 'class map' than Poulantzas' (1979) rigid 'production model'. In Wright's view the structure of class relations in modern capitalism is defined not primarily by economic production but also by power relations – that is, control of the workplace and work processes. By including this factor of control in his analysis, Wright allows a much more complex model to develop, which is based on Marxist notions of exploitation and control but also allows for the ambiguous nature of class relationships that develop between different groups in a complex society.

> **According to Wright, the two major classes have unambiguous locations with respect to all three dimensions [of control]. The capitalist controls investment, organises labour power and decides upon the nature of the productive process. The proletariat, on the other hand, is excluded from all forms of control. Other classes, however, have contradictory locations, the new middle class most of all.**
>
> (Hughes 1984: 13)

The concept of 'contradictory class locations' was used to accommodate managers, small employers and self-employed workers into his 'class maps'. In his later works Wright attempts to recognize that, over and above the exploitative power of the owners, the middle classes also found themselves in positions where they could exploit others (Edgell 1993).

In a more recent contribution, Wright (1997) moved much closer to a Weberian notion of class, which he acknowledged 'does not dramatically differ from the class typology used by Goldthorpe'. Goldthorpe's occupational scale is outlined on p. 174.

Frank Parkin

Probably the best-known exponent of the neo-Weberian perspective, Parkin (1972) made clear his opposition to Marxist concepts of class. Embracing Weber's idea of status he argued that ownership of property is only one means of social differentiation and identified occupational status as the most significant criterion for distinguishing between groups in society.

> **The backbone of the class structure, and indeed the entire reward system of modern western society, is the occupational order. Other sources of economic and symbolic advantage do coexist alongside the occupational order, but for the vast majority of the population these tend, at best, to be secondary.**
>
> (Parkin 1972: 18)

In Parkin's model the major distinction appears to be that made between manual and non-manual jobs, with higher professionals at the top of the hierarchy of occupations and unskilled workers at the bottom. Instead of society being driven by class conflict, struggles between status groups are more important. In the battle over resources, those who monopolize economic and cultural assets strive to maintain their privileged position through a process Parkin calls 'social closure'. While the lower-status groups attempt to improve their situation through strategies of 'usurpation', the elite-status groups will resist attempts at equality and social mobility by employing a variety of techniques of social 'exclusion' that effectively deny access to the less desirable social groups. As a result, class boundaries are created not by some objective relationship to the means of production or market situation but out of the strategies and techniques adopted by competing status groups. As Simon Raven boasted in a Radio 4 interview: 'A good club, a good regiment, a good college or a good school; you can only make one by keeping people out.'

Stop and think

- Exactly what strategies do you think status groups adopt on a day-to-day basis to maintain their own prestige and exclude others? See 'The establishment' (p. 193) and the case study 'The overclass' (pp. 195–196).

W.G. Runciman

Following Weber, Runciman (1990) took the three major stratifying elements in society to be 'ownership' (of property), 'control' (of power/authority) and 'marketability' (of skills), but instead of associating each source of privilege with a particular class he argued that these criteria for differentiation cut across simple class boundaries, producing a much more fragmented model of the class structure in which the differences within broad classifications are celebrated rather than disguised. The result was a seven-class model in which a small 'upper class' shares a dominant position with regard to all three criteria (Table 4.1). At the other end, a significant 'underclass' was identified, members of which possess no property, exercise no control over events and have few marketable skills. The two extremes are separated by two broad classes ('middle' and 'working'), internally differentiated by variations in access to property, authority and skill.

Table 4.1 Runciman's seven-class model

Class	Size in 1990
Upper class	<1%
Upper middle class	<10%
Middle middle class	15%
Lower middle class	20%
Skilled working class	20%
Unskilled working class	30%
Underclass	5%

(Source: Runciman 1990: 389)

Anthony Giddens

Giddens (1973) put forward a model of the class system that is very close to Weber's. In this model the power that people enjoy in the bargaining process derives essentially from their 'market capacities' (i.e. the value attached to their possessions and skills). He suggested that modern societies tend towards a three-class model in which class position is determined by market capacity:

Class	Market capacity
Upper class	Capital ownership
Middle class	Educational credentials
Working class	Labour power

Giddens was aware of cultural variations on this model and acknowledged the internal fragmentation that can occur within each group (e.g. the distinction between professional, technical, managerial and clerical workers within the middle class), but he still preferred to simplify the class system into its three major components, based on 'the possession of property, qualifications and physical labour power' (Edgell 1993: 53).

In his ideas on 'class structuration', Giddens was concerned with the ways in which individuals contribute towards a class-based social reality through their actions and beliefs. He was aware that people derive status from their position within a hierarchical division of labour in which some occupations are generally esteemed and others looked down upon. Within these occupations and through the performance of work roles, some people have more control than others and this emphasizes notions of superiority and inferiority, which we also associate with ideas of social class. Finally, the way in which we spend our money can be seen as an expression of class differences in taste and lifestyle. Furthermore we can reinforce the importance of social class division by passing on property, skills and privileges to our children.

Over the following 20 years Giddens changed his emphasis and aligned himself with a less class-based approach to politics and social democracy sometimes referred to as the 'third way' (for a useful discussion of these ideas and how they have influenced political thinking in Europe and the USA, see www.sociologyonline.co.uk/#politics/Giddens_3way.shtml). His new ideas involve a more individualistic approach in which class differences count for little; some individuals may experience more barriers to success than others, and some have more opportunities, but this is no longer determined by a thing called 'class' and is not experienced as such. In the constant and rapid changes brought about by technological change and globalization, life is far more unpredictable and social destinations far less related to their origins (Best 2005: 44–5).

Operationalizing the concept of class

Apart from the theoretical problems posed by the concept of class in sociology, there is also much disagreement over its categorization for the purposes of empirical study. This is an important issue, because if sociologists cannot agree on the best way of operationalizing social class (i.e. turning the concept into a measurable variable), they will use different methods for classification and measurement and end up with data that are not comparable. If this is the case, then apparent changes in social life such as voting behaviour and social mobility patterns may be nothing more than distortions created by changes in our definition and measurement of social class.

Official definitions of 'social class'

The earliest attempts to classify economically active groups in society did not involve class analysis at all. The first UK census in 1801 simply adopted general and vague categories of general employment:

- agriculture;
- manufacture, trade and handicraft;
- others.

Such a scheme may have been useful for assessing proportional shifts in the working population, but it made no attempt to classify people according to their position within the economic and social hierarchy. The revised census of 1851 simply increased the range of categories of employment and only added to the confusion. It was not until 1911 that the classifications were revised again 'to represent as far as possible different social grades'. The five grades that were introduced formed the basis of what we now know as the Registrar-General's scale, which was said to be 'the nearest thing we have to an official definition of "social class" ' (Nichols 1979: 158).

Up until 1981, the occupational scale was based on social status, but after this date it was revised to reflect the level of skill demanded by an occupation (Roberts 2001). By the time of its demise in 1998 this scale had been expanded to six main grades that managed to encompass most occupations and still appeared to reflect the traditional ideas of social status and skill associated with different jobs.

In sociology the occupational scale has become adopted as the most convenient means of converting the problematic concept of social class into a variable that we can easily use. In Goldthorpe's work this neo-Weberian approach is clear to see. He identified 'market situation' and 'work situation' as the important determinants of class consciousness and used an occupational scale for his important empirical studies of class consciousness (Goldthorpe *et al.* 1968, 1969) and social mobility (Goldthorpe *et al.* 1980). His revised version shows how 'social classes' reflect gradations in

A closer look

Registrar-General's scale (pre-1998)

1. Higher-level professionals, managers and administrators.
2. Lower-level professionals, managers and administrators.

3a. Lower-level white-collar workers.

3b. Skilled manual workers.

4. Semiskilled manual workers.
5. Unskilled manual workers.

the workplace and the labour market (Goldthorpe *et al.* 1980).

In the 1990s social scientists in the UK were invited to revise the official scale, and the eventual compromise, based upon the Registrar-General's scale and that proposed by Goldthorpe, was designed by Rose and O'Reilly (1997) and officially adopted by the Office for National Statistics in the following year. The basis for classification of occupations is to place together those that share:

- similar 'market situations', i.e. rewards; and
- similar 'work situations', i.e. levels of control, responsibility and autonomy in the workplace.

An eight-class scale was adapted from Goldthorpe's scheme by David Rose and is now the official class scheme for the UK.

David Rose and his team have developed a new socioeconomic classification for use across Europe, known as the ESeC scale (Table 4.2). This may be

A closer look

Goldthorpe's class scheme (revised version)

1. *Classes I and II* – All professionals, administrators and managers (including large proprietors), higher-grade technicians and supervisors of non-manual workers.
2. *Class III* – Routine non-manual employees in administration and commerce, sales personnel and other rank-and-file service workers.
3. *Class IVab* – Small proprietors, self-employed artisans and other 'own-account' workers with and without employees (other than in primary production).
4. *Class IVc* – Farmers and smallholders and other self-employed workers in primary production.
5. *Classes V and VI* – Lower-grade technicians, supervisors of manual workers and skilled manual workers.
6. *Class VIIa* – Semiskilled and unskilled manual workers (other than in primary production).
7. *Class VIIb* – Agricultural and other workers in primary production.

A closer look

The Office for National Statistics' socioeconomic classification analytic classes (NS-SEC)

1. Higher managerial and professional occupations:
   - 1.1. Large employers and higher managerial occupations.
   - 1.2. Higher professional occupations.
2. Lower managerial and professional occupations.
3. Intermediate occupations (e.g. clerks, secretaries, computer operators).
4. Small employers and own-account workers.
5. Lower supervisory and technical occupations.
6. Semi-routine occupations (e.g. cooks, bus drivers, hairdressers, shop assistants).
7. Routine occupations (e.g. waitresses, cleaners, couriers).
8. Never worked and long-term unemployed.

(Source: www.statistics.gov.uk/methods_quality/ns_sec/)

Table 4.2 European socioeconomic classification

	ESeC class	Common term	Employment regulation
1	Large employers, higher-grade professional, administrative and managerial occupations	Higher salariat	Service relationship
2	Lower-grade professional, administrative and managerial occupations and higher-grade technician and supervisory occupations	Lower salariat	Service relationship (modified)
3	Intermediate occupations	Higher-grade white-collar workers	Mixed
4	Small employer and self-employed occupations (excluding agriculture etc.)	Petit bourgeoisie or independents	–
5	Self-employed occupations (agriculture etc.)	Petit bourgeoisie or independents	–
6	Lower supervisory and lower technician occupations	Higher-grade blue-collar workers	Mixed
7	Lower services, sales and clerical occupations	Lower-grade white-collar workers	Labour contract (modified)
8	Lower technical occupations	Skilled workers	Labour contract (modified)
9	Routine occupations	Semi- and non-skilled workers	Labour contract
10	Never worked and long-term unemployed	Unemployed	–

adopted by Eurostat as the official scale in the European Union (EU). Harmonization of class scales across Europe will make comparative research more valid. When conducting comparative research British sociologists will use the ESeC scale, but they will continue to use the NS-SEC for UK-based study.

Advantages of using occupational scales

The occupational scale incorporates the idea of social status and recognizes the growing importance of the middle classes against the decline of the ruling and working classes.

In modern societies occupation has become the primary status-fixing device. In modern mass societies characterized by large impersonal bureaucracies and a complex division of labour, occupational position becomes a shorthand method for recognizing others. 'What do you do?' is often the first question that we ask someone when we meet for the first time.

In order to measure the possible influence of social class on life chances, it is necessary to have some generally agreed means of categorizing people. Much valuable research has been conducted using occupational scales, and the data produced have been used to inform debate and influence policymaking.

Criticisms of occupational scales

Occupational scales confuse class and status. In this merging of two distinct terms, the emphasis shifts away from property relations and the process of production in favour of prestige as the main measure of social position.

Occupational scale is a *descriptive* device that is good at providing static snapshots of the occupational hierarchy, but it does not explain the relations between classes. This criticism comes from Marxist writers, who believe that class division, class conflict and the dynamics of class struggle are obscured by scales that simply rank the working population by prestige.

Although they appear to offer a neat solution to the difficulty of operationalizing the concept of class, occupational scales are extremely problematic for four reasons. First, people may be classed together by occupational group despite large differences in reward and prestige within each occupation, for example junior hospital doctors and consultants in private practice.

Second, different occupations may be placed in the same social grade despite differences between those occupational groups; for example, Goldthorpe has been criticized for including managers, high-grade technicians and professional workers in classes I and II along with 'large proprietors' (Edgell 1993: 32).

Third, accounts based on occupational scale target the working population and, by definition, overlook those who have retired or do not have a job; for example, how should we class students, housewives and those engaged in voluntary work? It is also difficult, in such schemes, to classify the 'idle rich', who may live by an invested income but do not have a recognized occupation. Nichols (1979: 165) has referred to the absurdity of 'a sort of bald class structure' that has a 'working class' and a 'middle class' but 'nothing on top'.

Fourth, feminists have attacked scales such as Goldthorpe's for classifying women according to the occupation of the male head of household and producing gender-blind accounts of social structure and social change so that women are seen as peripheral to the class system. Writers such as Oakley and Oakley (1981), Stanworth (1984) and Crompton (1989) have argued for a more 'gendered' approach to the class structure by replacing the head-of-household classification with one that recognizes the increasing contribution of women in the workplace.

Stop and think

- What kinds of assumption do you make about people based on their occupation?
- What assumptions would you make about individuals in these occupations:
  (a) professional footballer;
  (b) doctor;
  (c) sociology lecturer;
  (d) secretary?

Consider political views, leisure activities and tastes.

The class structure in modern society

Whether it is still useful to talk of a class structure is a matter of continuing sociological debate; this debate is informed by the theoretical positions outlined in the previous section and by empirical research based on the attempts to operationalize the concept of class.

The demise of class

Since the latter half of the twentieth century, the traditional notions about the significance of social class have been questioned. Such questioning has been inspired not only by Weberian-influenced criticisms of Marxism – by writers such as Parkin (1972), Dahrendorf (1959) and Pahl and Wallace (1988) – but also by writers such as Saunders (1987, 1996) who reject both Weber's and Marx's conceptions of class on the basis that 'they continue to employ essentially nineteenth century ideas to analyze late twentieth century conditions' (Saunders 1987: 319). According to this general viewpoint, it is claimed that changes in the structure of society, the nature of work and the formulation of consciousness have reduced the value of class analysis so that 'class as a concept is ceasing to do any useful work for sociology' (Pahl, quoted in Crompton 1993: 99). In their book *The Death of Class*, Pakulski and Waters (1996) suggested that, in today's world, 'the class paradigm is intellectually and morally bankrupt'.

In general this position is based on the following factors:

- changes in the quality of life;
- social reform and the idea of 'citizenship';
- changes in the organization and nature of work;
- social mobility and the fragmentation of class structure;
- the end of ideology and the embourgeoisment thesis.

Changes in the quality of life

According to Marx, the 'pauperization' of the working class was an essential condition for the survival of capitalism and its eventual downfall. However, since the 1950s, the living standards of many working people have improved due to wage rises and the increasing cheapness of basic goods and mass-produced consumer items. For skilled workers who have retained their jobs, and especially for those 'work-rich' households that have more than one income, material lifestyle has clearly improved. The relative affluence of these groups has promoted an optimistic notion of workers becoming incorporated into a diamond-shaped 'middle mass' society. Pahl (1989) argues that patterns of consumption have replaced productive activity as the means of fixing social identity and position:

> **If the symbol of the nineteenth century city was the factory chimney, the equivalent symbol at the end of the twentieth century in Europe and North America is the shopping mall.**
>
> (Pahl 1989: 718–19)

The fact that many working people can now afford the 'luxuries' previously associated with well-off people and can buy their own houses and shares in public utilities is taken as further evidence of the existence of the 'affluent worker' and the limitations of the 'pauperization' thesis. In this 'property-owning democracy' the assets are no longer concentrated in the hands of a capitalist elite but are shared to such an extent that people who come from working-class backgrounds and occupations 'have a direct or indirect financial stake in capitalist enterprises, and most companies are owned directly or indirectly by millions of workers' (Saunders and Harris 1994: 1).

In the USA, George W. Bush talked up the idea of Americans becoming members of an 'ownership society'. In a speech (16.12.2004) he made clear his belief that economic investment has social benefits:

> **I love the idea of people being able to own something . . . People from all walks of life, all income levels are willing to take risks to start their own company . . . And I like the idea of people being able to say, I'm in charge of my own health care . . . I particularly like the idea of a social security system that recognizes the importance and value of ownership.**
>
> (Quoted by Holland 2005)

Social reform and the idea of 'citizenship'

In 1963 T.H. Marshall published the text of his now famous lectures on citizenship and social democracy. He argued that the social and political reforms of the nineteenth and twentieth centuries, the establishment of a welfare state and the belief in Keynesian economic policies meant that a liberal democratic state had emerged that reflected and guaranteed the interests and rights of all people in society. No matter what class people belonged to, they enjoyed the same rights of citizenship. Within liberal democracies, people had civil and political rights that guaranteed their freedoms before the law as well as the opportunity to participate in the political process, but what was special for the citizens of such democracies was their right to a decent standard of living established through the welfare state. The battle for 'social citizenship' was seen as an essential part of the war against capitalism; its aim was to assist 'the modern drive towards social equality' and reduce class antagonism. According to Marshall, social citizenship would establish

> **a general enrichment of the concrete substance of civilized life, a general reduction of risk and insecurity, an equalisation between the more and less fortunate at all levels – between the healthy and the sick, the employed and the unemployed, the old and the active, the bachelor and the father of a large family. Equalisation is not so much between classes as between individuals within a population which is now treated for this purpose as though it were one class. Equality of status is more important than equality of income.**
>
> (Marshall 1963, quoted in Jordon 1984: 110)

As well as providing a 'universal right to a real income', Marshall's social citizenship had at its centre the right to a decent education, which in turn would widen opportunities and increase rates of social mobility. Under such circumstances it was envisaged that the sharp divisions of capitalism would be reduced and the resulting class antagonisms removed. This idea of citizenship is crucial to the 'third way' developed by Anthony Giddens (1998) in response to the demands of the 'late modern' age and the policies pursued by social democratic parties across Europe, the Americas, Australia and post-communist Russia. Through the extension of 'dialogic democracy' to all parts of society it becomes possible for all people to feel that they have a part to play in creating a 'state without enemies'. The policies of 'social inclusion' pursued by New Labour in Britain since 1997 are a good example: by targeting families, schools and sport it is felt that people from the most deprived communities can feel that they are equal citizens in a democratic world (see pp. 172–173).

Changes in the organization and nature of work

In the traditional model of the class structure, people were clearly stratified according to their position within the system of production. The decisions about planning, investment and development would be made by those who owned and therefore controlled the means of production (factories, mines and railways, for example). This class of manufacturing entrepreneurs employed large groups of workers whose labour power was essential for the production of mass-produced goods. Entire communities emerged that were solely dependent on traditional industries and skills. Within these communities work was often regarded as central to a person's status, and the identity of male workers was inextricably bound up with the work they did.

In the early twenty-first century many traditional industries have declined to the point of extinction. In Britain the steel industry, coal-mining, shipbuilding and deep-sea fishing have all but disappeared. The service industries that have replaced them, in areas such as banking, leisure and retail, require different skills and different attitudes towards work. People are now told not to follow a trade but to pick up as many 'transferable skills' as they can in order to take advantage of the new pick 'n' mix job opportunities thrown up by an ever-changing economic environment. No one can expect a job for life and everyone needs to be able to adapt. There are many consequences of these changes for the modern class structure, but two in particular stand out.

First, the emergence of a new middle class has, at the top end, taken over some of the administrative functions of the entrepreneurial class of owners and at other levels has expanded through the development of the professions and the rapid increase of the non-manual sector. This has given rise to the idea that, apart from a very few rich people at the top and an increasingly marginalized underclass at the bottom, society is now characterized by a large and contented middle class. Despite there being little sociological evidence for this 'middle-class classless' society, the idea has been extremely popular with social commentators and politicians (Edgell 1993: 119); it is certainly true that the majority of working people are now to be found in what may be loosely termed middle-class occupations.

Second, within this growth of non-manual, service-sector jobs, another pattern has emerged – the replacement of men by women. Whereas women in the first half of the twentieth century were largely excluded from the economic structure by their roles as wives and mothers and the 'ideology of domestication' that accompanied these roles, the penetration of women into the labour market and their increased importance as family breadwinners has been remarkable. Various surveys in Britain and Europe show that this trend often involves women in part-time work and concentrated in a narrow band of occupations, particularly within the 'service' sector. For a full discussion of women and paid work see Chapters 5 and 12.

This 'feminization' of service work has several implications for the debate about the class structure. Women workers have been at the forefront of the occupational shift from manufacturing to service industries, so that as men in traditional industries are made redundant they are replaced in the occupational structure by women in a range of non-manual occupations. Despite the evidence that many of these women are being recruited into low-paid and part-time routine jobs, the non-manual nature of the work creates

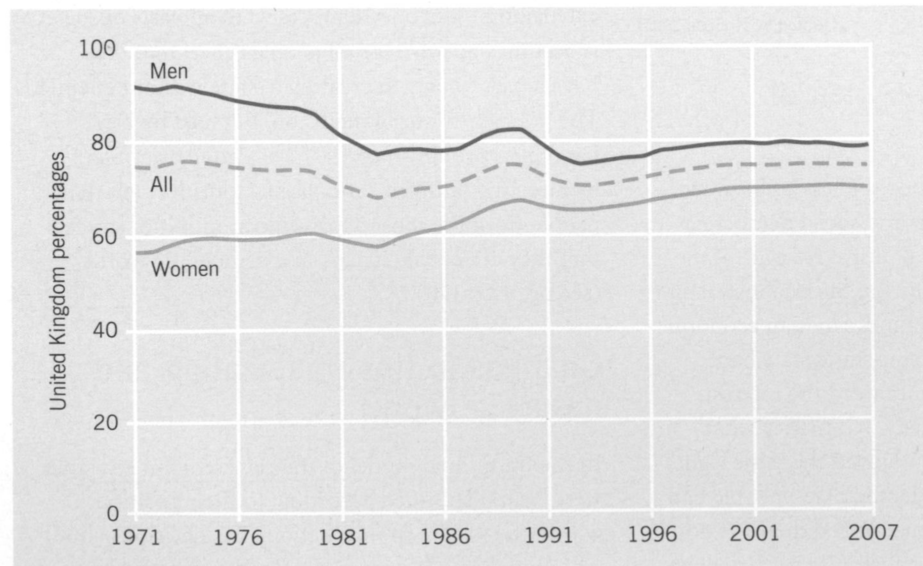

Figure 4.4 Employment rates by sex
Data are at Q2 each year and are seasonally adjusted. Men aged 16 to 64, women aged 16 to 59. See Appendix, Part 4: Labour Force Survey.
Source: Labour Force Survey, Office for National Statistics

the impression that the class structure is becoming more middle class. Although many women may go to work simply to make ends meet, where their income combines with other household incomes, sociologists such as Pahl and Wallace (1988) have argued that 'work-rich', dual-income families, who enjoy relatively high living standards, emerge. Again the impression of a new middle-class family being created by changing patterns of work and income has established itself; this reinforces the impression that modern society is increasingly dominated by middle-class households able to afford a middle-class lifestyle.

Social mobility and the fragmentation of class structure

The growth of a new middle class and the increasing opportunities for social mobility for people from both middle-class and working-class origins has led to the idea that the homogeneous and polarized classes of the traditional model have become so fragmented by differences in skill, pay and consciousness that it no longer makes sense to talk of a class structure. According to writers such as Dahrendorf (1959), the traditional upper class has undergone a process of decomposition largely as a result of increasing share ownership and a managerial revolution that has effectively seen ownership and control of the means of production slip from their grasp (see also Burnham 1945; Galbraith 1967).

At the same time the working class has become fractured by differences in employment opportunities and pay. Not only are there divisions between skilled, semiskilled and unskilled workers, but also an underclass of 'work-poor' families has emerged characterized by unemployment and poverty (Smith 1992). This idea of fragmentation clearly undermines the Marxist notions of class formation and class consciousness and has been used to support the argument for the growth of a new middle class. However, it has been argued that even the middle mass of society is becoming increasingly fragmented by differences in skill and pay and that this has created a hierarchy of differentially rewarded status groups who see the social structure in very different ways (Roberts *et al.* 1977). In his polemic against the 'British obsession' with class, Lord Bauer argues:

> **it remains part of contemporary political folklore that a restrictive and divisive class system is the bane of this country [which acts as] a major barrier to economic progress . . . and also a significant source of justified social discontent.**

In rejecting what he sees as a stereotypical view of modern Britain, Bauer contends that

> **In Britain, class distinctions do exist, but they are not, and rarely have been, significant barriers to social or economic mobility.**
>
> (Bauer 1997: 1)

This view is supported by Saunders (1996), who claims that the research into social mobility by Glass in the 1950s and Goldthorpe *et al.* in the 1970s and 1980s distorts and exaggerates the influence of class background on social destination. From his own research, Saunders concludes that society is 'unequal but fair' and also argues that the meritocratic ideal that 'people's income should depend on hard work and ability' shares widespread support among the British public. In his own analysis of social mobility rates, Saunders (1997, 2002) uses data collected from the National Childhood Development Study (NCDS), which has monitored the achievements of a cohort comprised of all the children born in the same week in Britain in 1958. These children were assessed for ability and aptitude at regular intervals. Saunders analysed these personal data and concluded that, if we use IQ and motivation scores in childhood as our predictors of mobility (rather than social class), we find that the social destination of individuals has more to do with their ability than with their social advantages or shortcomings. Upward and downward mobility reflect individual rather than social differences. These views are supported by psychologist Daniel Nettle (2003), who also analysed the NCDS data.

The German sociologist Ulrich Beck (1992) took these ideas even further in arguing that the predictable patterns of class-related privilege and achievement have been replaced in the modern world by a lack of certainty about the future, which confronts all young people. In the 'risk society' of late modernity the young generation leaving school and college face a world no longer characterized by the class-based certainties of an orderly industrial society revolving around work, family and local community. Instead they perceive social achievement as a matter of individual risk-taking and social position as an outcome of these decisions. In the absence of any real community or class consciousness, people are left to deal with a rapidly changing world alone. In this sense Beck argues not that class is unimportant but that it is no longer perceived as relevant as an explanation or as a basis for action. In a similar vein, Furlong and Cartmel conclude:

> **In the 1990s the traditional links between the family, school and work seem to have weakened and young people embark on journeys into adulthood which involve a wide variety of routes, many of which appear to have uncertain outcomes. Because there are many more pathways to choose from, young people may develop the impression that their own routes are unique and that the risks they face are to be overcome by them as individuals rather than as members of a collectivity.**
>
> (Furlong and Cartmel 1997: 29)

The end of ideology and the embourgeoisment thesis

Despite predictions of a proletarian revolution made by Marx, the failure of the working class to develop a 'class consciousness' that has translated into 'class action' has led many sociologists to challenge the basic assumption that class position, consciousness and political action are automatically linked (Rose 1988). Instead of becoming committed to a radical value system, most working people have rejected rebellion in favour of a more individualistic set of attitudes towards social change. In attempting to explain why workers do not necessarily adopt radical attitudes, Marshall and colleagues (1988) have distinguished between theories of working-class ambivalence and theories of working-class instrumentalism.

Theories of working-class ambivalence

The political passivity of workers is explained in relation to the fragmentation and middle-mass arguments mentioned above. On the one hand, it is suggested that a fragmented working class becomes heterogeneous and divided and as such cannot achieve its role as a revolutionary class. On the other hand, it is argued that sections of the working class become incorporated into the dominant value system and subordinate to it. This view was expressed clearly in the *embourgeoisment* thesis put forward to explain the decline in working-class support for the Labour Party in the 1960s. According to this thesis, the increasing affluence of working-class family life undermined the attraction of radical or social democratic policies for change. Being able to afford the trappings of a middle-class lifestyle had encouraged working-class people to become more conservative. This thesis was partially revived in the 1980s to explain the dramatic success of consecutive Conservative governments in appealing to the 'collective acquisitiveness' of some sections of the working class.

Theories of working-class instrumentalism

In their famous study of affluent workers in Luton, Goldthorpe and colleagues (1968) set out to test the embourgeoisment thesis and effectively demonstrated its limitations as a general economic explanation for the political behaviour of a whole class. Essentially they noted that, despite economic improvements, the workers in their study had not become 'middle class'; nor had they become conservative. They did conclude, however, that a 'new working class' had been created in the post-war environment of full employment, citizenship and consumerism; their goals were increasingly 'privatized' (home-centred) and their political strategies were still collective but clearly instrumental. In other words, affluent workers were prepared to support their trade unions and vote Labour as long as this guaranteed their affluent lifestyle. It was the defection of this group of skilled manual workers to the Conservatives since 1979 after promises of tax cuts, 'right-to-buy' schemes for council tenants and the privatization of public utilities that kept the Labour Party out of power for 18 years.

In their attack on the Marxist model of class and class consciousness, Pahl and Wallace (1988) refuted the deterministic approach as 'simple-minded' and romantic. They argued that the decomposition of the working class along with the dealignment of politics caused by Thatcherism had shown that there are other determinants of political outlook. Drawing on the research of sociologists and political scientists at the University of Essex (Marshall *et al.* 1988), as well as their own study of family life and class in the Isle of Sheppey, Pahl and Wallace argued that the class alignment of working people had been 'fractured' by changes in occupational structure and lifestyle. Four factors in particular provide alternative sources of social identity:

- An increasing number of people are 'non-working' class and depend increasingly on state benefits for their income. It is their experience of unemployment that crucially affects their consciousness.
- The increasing number of women in the workplace means that traditional (male head of household) notions of work, identity and class consciousness have to be re-examined.

- Differential access to private and public services means that differing patterns of consumption appear that may be seen as a more important source of consciousness than occupation. Home ownership, private education, private health care and the ownership of shares may all become points of departure from a traditional class alignment.
- In the world of work itself, further divisions have occurred that are related to the form that work takes rather than the nature of the job. A self-employed maintenance worker may have very different views from one who works for somebody else. Whether that person is employed in the private sector or the public domain may also affect political attitudes.

As a result, it is argued that the 'cultural privatization' of home-centred working-class lifestyle can result in the demise of class identification and class politics. This view was developed further by Pahl and Wallace, who suggested that social identity and consciousness are too complex to be reduced to social class. The social world is experienced through the everyday life of families and it is people's own experiences of their domestic lifecycle that forms their consciousness of the real world: 'Social images, we suggest, may be constructed less in terms of class and more in terms of family and personal biography' (Pahl and Wallace 1988: 136). These findings anticipated Beck's ideas on the decline of class consciousness in the 'risk society' discussed earlier (p. 179).

The Isle of Sheppey study found little evidence of any radical consciousness ('rebels in red'), and nor did it discover the widespread deference often associated with privatized workers ('angels in marble'); but the collective identity it did come across took rather surprising forms. First, steel-plant workers on the island had combined against pickets from other plants to defend their jobs rather than join in a broader struggle. (The defection of the Nottinghamshire miners during the national strike in 1983–84 is perhaps a better-known example of a similar phenomenon.) Second, trade union membership and organization were purely instrumental and were not linked in any traditional way to the Labour Party. Indeed, trade unionists were as likely to be actively involved in the Conservative Party – although the popularity of the Conservative Club seemed to rest on the price of beer as much as anything else! Third, the general collective identity had deep historical roots that went beyond class and touched on the themes of nationalism and patriotism. The victory celebration at the end of the Falklands War in 1982 was seen as an example of 'relatively spontaneous collective action'.

Alongside this rather conservative form of collective identity, Pahl and Wallace (1988) also claim to have discovered 'a strong element of working class individualism', a resentment of 'less respectable' families and a deep-rooted commitment to the values of domesticity. It was within this broader social consciousness that the politics of 'dynamic conservatism' made its mark at the end of the 1970s with the rise of Thatcherism:

> **She presented herself to the working class as the champion of the taxpayer against the Treasury, the worker against the trade union, the council tenant against the landlord and the citizen against the state.**
>
> (Jenkins 1987: 53)

This populist ideology seemed to strike a chord with many working-class people who felt that the Labour Party had let them down and that ownership of property was an important means of 'getting on'. The stereotype was tracked down to its home in Essex where 'Basildon Man' had turned against his working-class roots to vote for the Conservatives throughout their period in office (1979–97). In their two-part study of this phenomenon, Hayes and Hudson explain how Basildon represents a post-war social experiment: attracting its new residents from the working class heartlands of the East End of London, Basildon was from the outset 'an overwhelmingly working-class town' characterized by 'a strong sense of individualism and self improvement' (Hayes and Hudson 2001: 11). At the end of the 1970s Margaret Thatcher swept to power on the promise of extended home ownership, but it was felt by some political pundits that 'Thatcherism had wrought some deeper, more permanent change in the attitudes and outlooks of working class people' (Hayes and Hudson 2001: 38). Between 1981 and 1996 home ownership in Basildon increased from 53 per cent to 71 per cent, and in their first study in 1992 Hayes and Hudson did find some evidence of a more family-centred approach to life that may have been related to a more instrumental attitude to politics and a revolt against Labour:

> **In 1992 Basildon's skilled workers associated the Labour Party with poverty and welfare, hopelessness and failure. They saw it as the party for losers.**

Basildonians said they wanted to help themselves rather than wait around for someone else to sort out their lives. Many saw that Labour was a barrier to taking control of their lives and making something of themselves. For a period, through thick and thin, the pronouncements of the Tories had tapped into their aspirations.

(Hayes and Hudson 2001: 19)

During the final ten years of the Conservative government, Bev Skeggs (1997) conducted an ethnographic study of 83 working-class women from a town in north-west England. Her interviews revealed a high level of insecurity as the women raised concerns about their identities and aspirations. Although they were aware that they did not possess the 'airs and graces' to be considered middle class, they also sought to distance themselves from the 'dirty and dangerous' stereotype of working-class life and its negative associations with loose morality, irresponsibility and poor educational standards. Seeing themselves as 'respectable', they tried to 'disidentify' with the traditional image and aspired to more positive self-images through marriage and vocational (as opposed to academic) education.

Class is experienced by women as exclusion. Whereas working-class men can use class as a positive source of identity, a way of including themselves in positively valorised social category . . . this does not apply for working-class women . . . Overall (this) is a study of how social and cultural positioning generates denial, disidentification and dissimulation rather than adjustment. It is a study of doubt, insecurity and unease: the emotional politics of class.

(Skeggs 1997: 74–5)

Although one of the respondents (June) uses the term to try to make sense of her new and 'respectable' position, she ends up rejecting 'class' as a useful concept:

No, I don't think I'm working class at all now. Not after we bought the house and that . . . I expect I'm now middle class . . . but it's like when we go to Dave's business dos, but I don't really feel like some of them, you know the real bosses' wives with all their talk and that. I sometimes feel really frightened to speak in case I show him up. I expect they're really middle class so I'm not really like them, but I'm not like the rest of our family without two pennies to rub together. You know, I just don't think class is a very useful term. I think I'm probably classless. You know I'm not really one nor the other. I don't really fit.

(Skeggs 1997: 77)

In the 1990s Terry Clark and Seymour Martin Lipset analysed the significance of social class as an international phenomenon by comparing changing trends in the USA, Western Europe and the emerging nations of the old Eastern bloc. In their view the decline of hierarchy in the three major areas of social organization (referred to as 'situses of stratification') had seen a decline in the importance of social class; the democratization and differentiation of the workplace, government and family life had led to the decline of class as a determinant of lifestyle and opportunities, which rendered the idea of class 'an increasingly outmoded concept . . . appropriate to earlier historical periods' (Clark and Lipset 1996).

They concluded that societies are now characterized by 'fragmentation of stratification', which can be summarized as:

the weakening of class stratification, especially as shown in distinct class-differentiated life styles; the decline of economic determinism, and the increased importance of social and cultural factors; politics less organised by class and more by other loyalties; social mobility less family-determined, more ability and educational-determined.

(Clark and Lipset 1996: 48)

Utilizing many of the arguments outlined above, Pakulski and Waters (1996) also claim that class has lost its significance, with people rejecting class as a basis for social grouping and preferring alternative sources of social identity such as ethnicity, gender and age. In a very Weberian analysis, they argue that in contemporary 'first world' societies a series of technological and social changes have ushered in a 'post-industrial' age in which the old class-based communities and identities have disappeared. As the traditional industries of mining, steel production and shipbuilding have declined, the service sector has expanded. In consequence the traditional skills of labour power have been replaced with those of a 'knowledge economy' and people feel less distinguished by the division of labour. On top of this, the wider distribution of wealth and income and the increase in property ownership have created a society organized no longer around class but around 'status conventionalism', in which social esteem and identity are derived from patterns of consumption. Inequalities in income clearly still exist, but the attention has shifted away from how people earn their money to an assessment of how they spend it. As Abbot puts it:

> **For Pakulski and Waters, contemporary societies are stratified, but this stratification is achieved through cultural consumption, not class positioning in the division of labour. It seems that they are claiming that the differences between, say, a skilled worker from Luton, who drives a Ford Escort, lives in a semi-detached house worth between about £80,000 and £100,000 and who goes on package holidays to Spain, and an Oxbridge-educated lawyer living in Hampstead, who drives a Mercedes, has a house worth £200,000 and who holidays in private rented villas in Tuscany, are purely issues of status: it is not that they are members of different classes.**
> **It is all a matter of style, taste and status (prestige), not of location in the division of labour.**
>
> (Abbot 2001: 7)

(These arguments are rejected by Houtt *et al.* (1996), whose position is summarized on pp. 210 and 212.)

Stop and think

➤ Summarize the problems that may arise in trying to 'measure' the following indicators of the importance of social class:

(a) changes in the quality of life;

(b) the importance of social reform;

(c) changes in the nature of work;

(d) the extent of social mobility;

(e) the extent of working-class instrumentalism.

The persistence of class

Many sociologists, particularly those adopting a Marxist perspective, would reject the conclusion that class analysis is no longer useful, although few would argue that the class structure has been unaffected by social and economic change. From this point of view the major divisions in society are ones of class. These divisions still affect life chances and have a major effect on the way that people see themselves and the structure of society.

> **The view that class is dead derives from a very narrow and misleading understanding of class. Properly understood, class points to fundamental social divisions that cross-cut Britain and all other modern societies. Taken along with the closely interlinked themes of gender, race and ethnicity and age, class defines the nature of social stratification, which remains the sociological key to understanding the structure of society.**
>
> (Scott 1994: 19)

Despite the differences already mentioned, sociologists who have been influenced by Marx and Weber still talk of three major classes and emphasize the underlying conflict in the relationship between these classes. In examining the extent to which social class is still important we look at some of the evidence and arguments that suggest that the upper, middle and working classes continue to be important and distinct groups in modern society.

In his review of social class in modern Britain, Ken Roberts (2001) argues that class still matters and that the evidence is 'overwhelming', particularly with regard to the key indicators of opportunity: wealth, health and education. His comments on the five key arguments for the 'demise of class' are worth summarizing.

Changes in the quality of life

Roberts accepts that society has become more affluent and that wealth and income have been redistributed since the war. However, he points out that, despite increases in property ownership among working-class households, this often refers to assets for personal use such as houses and cars as opposed to investments from which an income can be derived, such as shares. Against the view that we have all become mini-capitalists, he points out that only about half the population 'has any significant share in the country's wealth', with less than 20 per cent owning shares, added to which concentrations of wealth and disparities in income still exist. 'The fact that many workers have some assets, and many capitalists also work, does not necessarily prove that there is no longer a glaring class division between them' (Roberts 2001: 179).

Social reform and the idea of citizenship

Democracy and the development of the welfare state may provide the opportunity for everyone to be involved in the political process and to ensure that health, education and social security are properly funded, but that does not mean that rights or benefits are enjoyed in equal measure. As Titmuss pointed out in the early days of the welfare state, equal citizenship rights do not guarantee a more equitable distribution of opportunities or rewards (see Alcock *et al.* 2001). In education, for example, it is still the case that middle-class families tend to get a better share of resources, particularly when it comes to higher education. It is also the case that important services such as medical care, housing and education exist outside state provision for those that can afford them and as such reinforce class differences rather than reduce them.

As Anne Phillips points out, no democratic political system can be separated from the socioeconomic system in which it is rooted and the privileging of certain interests that flow from it:

> **The . . . conditions of corporate capitalism constrain the exercise of popular control, making the supposed freedom and equality of citizens a desperately unbalanced affair . . . The point here is not just that the wealthy find it easier to disseminate their views, to finance newspapers, launch pressure groups, lunch prime ministers. More troubling (because it is more systematic) is the fact that all governments depend upon the process of capital accumulation as the source of incomes, growth, and jobs, and must therefore ensure that the economic policies they pursue do not undermine the prosperity of the private sector. This structural privileging of corporate power means that the democratic playing field is never level.**
>
> (Phillips 1999: 17–18)

Changes in the nature and organization of work

Pakulski and Waters' arguments that there has been a shift from manufacturing industry to a 'knowledge economy' based upon educational qualifications rather than industrial skills are given short shrift by Roberts (2001: 17), who dismisses such ideas as 'plain bunk' because they ignore the relationship between class position and educational achievement in the first instance and the tendency of such differentials to reinforce the class divisions in society in the long term. As Bourdieu has pointed out, educational qualifications are an important source of cultural capital and as such operate as a clear means by which social divisions are maintained. In Fiona Devine's (2004) ethnographic account of the strategies employed by middle-class families in Boston and Manchester to ensure the educational advancement of their own children, it is clear that the perennial dinner-party angst around schooling is treated as a serious aspect of the contest between individual families and social classes for places in the most prestigious schools. In her limited set of interviews with the parents of children from middle-class homes (24 doctors and 24 teachers), she shows the significance attached to education for social advancement and the lengths to which middle-class parents will go to ensure that their kids get the educational advantages they require. In other words we slip behind the rhetoric of 'meritocracy' to appreciate the social reality of self-recruitment and self-advancement from a middle-class point of view. As such, it succeeds in revealing 'the micro foundations of . . . macro reproduction' (Reed 2004).

Social mobility and the fragmentation of the class structure

Despite the arguments of Saunders and others that we live in a meritocratic society in which the inequality of rewards reflect inequalities in ability and motivation, there are many sociologists who argue that achievement is still based upon social factors and that the changes in the class structure have been much exaggerated. (See Chapter 8 in Roberts 2001 for a useful review.)

In the statistical analysis of Glass (1954) and the Nuffield study of Goldthorpe *et al.* (1972), it was suggested that social mobility rates in both absolute terms (the overall movement between occupational groups) and relative terms (the chances of groups from different backgrounds to move up or down when compared with one another) were not great. There has been some movement, especially into the expanding intermediate sector and between adjacent groups, but there was also evidence of high levels of self-recruitment at the top and bottom with very little evidence of a genuine 'rags to riches' meritocracy in operation. The social destiny of young men was seen to be clearly linked to the occupational status of their fathers. Goldthorpe (1996), Breen and Goldthorpe (1999) and Savage and Egerton (1997) dismiss Saunders' conclusion that intelligence and motivation account for patterns of mobility and self-recruitment, arguing instead that 'success' and 'failure' in the job market are still related to cultural and economic advantages rather than individual ones.

In fact, after seven years of Labour government the British prime minister's own strategy unit admitted that the chances of people from lower-class backgrounds improving their chances in the job market had got worse rather than better. As Andrew Rawnsley reported:

> **No one seems to have a comprehensive explanation for why birth, not worth, has again become such a key determinant of life chances, not just in Britain, but across the advanced industrialized countries, not excluding so-called classless America.**
>
> **One reason, I suggest, is that those already enjoying membership of the middle class have got more adept, energetic and aggressive about ensuring they bequeath that privilege to their offspring. Another reason is that, while the number of higher status and earning occupations is increasing, the pool of available jobs is not growing fast enough to let in many incomers from the bottom of the heap. A further factor is the number of people trapped in economic inactivity, like the many on incapacity benefit who say they would actually like to work, or stuck in insecure jobs which offer no skills development and little possibility of escape from low incomes.**
>
> **There are compelling reasons to be concerned about the seizing up of social mobility. It ingrains poverty in crime-ridden sink communities. It hurts the economy when we fail to harness the potential talents of everyone with a contribution to make.**
>
> **And if there aren't the opportunities for people to advance through effort, then they become impoverished, not just financially, but in aspiration. Government has to have a better answer to poverty of ambition in deprived areas than dangling the remote hope of winning the jackpot at a super casino.**
>
> (*Observer* 14.11.2004)

In line with Roberts we may think that people have better opportunities today than they did in the past, but the sociological evidence tells a different story:

> **As far as we can tell, the rate of social fluidity, meaning the social mobility that is not structurally inevitable on account of class differentials in birth rates and changes in the proportions of positions at different levels, is roughly the same at the beginning of the twenty-first century as it was at the beginning of the twentieth. Modern social classes have never been closed groups . . . But most people have ended up, and continue to end up, in either the same class, or in a class close to where they were born. In any case, social mobility transfers people between classes without necessarily weakening the roots of class division.**
>
> (Roberts 2001)

Describing this as 'one of the most startling discoveries in the whole of sociology', Roberts argues that over time and between modern societies it is 'the absence of major variations' that is most apparent.

Despite the different explanations on offer (individual ability versus social advantage) there seems to be general agreement that the chances of social and economic advancement are restricted and the patterns predictable:

> **It is equally startling that this finding, one of sociology's firmer conclusions, has been ignored by virtually all social-policy makers, and by many sociologists who continue to act as if they expect modest interventions in education or labour markets to bring about a significant redistribution of life-chances between the social classes.**
>
> (Roberts 2001: 224)

The end of ideology and the embourgeoisment thesis

The idea that working-class people were becoming more affluent led to the idea that they would adopt more middle-class lifestyles and eventually a middle-class outlook on life, including more conservative political attitudes. Roberts dismisses such simplistic thinking by pointing out that it is flawed on three grounds:

- Income and assets may have improved in absolute terms, but this is true for all groups so that in relative terms the inequalities in income between the classes still persist.
- Consumption patterns may change, but so do people's perceptions of the status attached to goods and property. As items that were once regarded as exclusive become common, they lose their associations with a middle-class lifestyle. Cars, holidays abroad, home ownership and TV sets were all once symbols of high status that most people have now come to expect as part of a normal standard of living.
- Workers who have incomes comparable to those of middle-class professionals still earn their money in a different way, have a different experience of life and continue to see themselves as working class. In

> cultural terms it is unlikely that, by becoming affluent, workers automatically disassociate themselves from their roots and see themselves as middle class.

These ideas are explored in more depth in the next section (pp. 200–209), where we look at the work of Goldthorpe and Lockwood, Fiona Devine, Hayes and Hudson, Simon Charlesworth and Bev Skeggs.

In conclusion, Roberts argues that despite the changes that have occurred class still remains a key factor in shaping lifestyle, opportunities and attitudes and that people still tend to use class as a means of understanding who they are. With regard to the related argument that people now have a range of alternative and competing claims on their identity (see Payne 2000), Roberts acknowledges the higher profile of gender, race, nationality and age as a basis for group membership but points out that these status differences are still striated by class.

In the remainder of this chapter, we look more closely at the composition of the three major classes themselves.

The upper class

Traditionally the upper class is associated with ownership of property and in particular the ownership of land. The landed aristocracy began to be replaced in the nineteenth century by those whose economic power derived from manufacturing industry, retail and banking, although a certain amount of overlap occurred between these interests. More recently it has been argued that a 'managerial revolution' has stripped this class of its power to control events and that a new managerial elite of administrators has taken over.

Occupational scales tend to obscure the existence of the 'super-rich'. Research is thin on the ground, with rich people tending to keep details of their wealth secret, so it is easy to be persuaded by the idea that this group has all but disappeared. However, there is clear evidence that as a class it has adapted in order to survive and even become more powerful through a diversification of interests.

In view of the continued concentration of wealth, many writers, including Miliband (1969), Scott (1991, 1994) and Westergaard (1995) in Britain and Barron and Sweezy (1968) and Zeitlin (1989) in the USA, have argued that the managerial revolution is more imagined than real. The idea that the managerial elite is a group of essentially neutral technocrats operating in the public interest is roundly rejected. The modifications of the class structure in recent times have not altered its essential nature:

> **Property, profit and market – the key institutions of a capitalist society – retain their central place in social arrangements, and remain the prime determinants of inequality.**
>
> (Westergaard and Resler 1976: 17)

At the apex of these key institutions remains a dominant class of between 5 and 10 per cent of the population who derive their position from property ownership and the control that they exercise over resources and other people's lives:

A closer look

Every year *The Sunday Times* publishes the 'Rich List', which documents the changing patterns of wealth around the world and identifies the richest individuals and families who make up the 'super-rich'. According to the 2008 figures (Tables 4.3 and 4.4), British-based Lakshmi Mittal was the richest man in Europe, with a fortune of £27.7 billion, but he trailed behind the Wal-Mart-founding Robson family, who were estimated to be worth £38.4 billion, and the Ambani family, who top the global league with a combined wealth of £43 billion. Under a Labour government, the collective wealth of the richest 1000 people in Britain has jumped from £99 billion to £412 billion. There are still concentrations of considerable wealth in Britain, so that it takes a personal fortune of at least £755 million to gain admittance to the Top 100 club.

A closer look *continued*

Table 4.3 The 10 richest in the world

				2008 wealth	2007 wealth
1	Mukesh and Anil Ambani	India	Petrochemicals	**£43bn**	£19.6bn
2	The Walton family	USA	Retailing (Wal-Mart)	**£38.4bn**	£42.6bn
3	Warren Buffett	USA	Investments	**£31bn**	£26.7bn
4	Carlos Slim Helu	Mexico	Telecoms	**£30bn**	£27.2bn
5	Bill Gates	USA	Software (Microsoft)	**£29bn**	£28.7bn
6	Lakshmi Mittal*	UK	Steel	**£27.7bn**	£19.2bn
7	Karl & Theo Albrecht*	Germany	Supermarkets	**£25bn**	£19.1bn
8	Forrest & John Mars*	USA	Confectionery	**£21bn**	£16.1bn
9	King Abdullah	Saudi Arabia	Oil	**£20bn**	£13.5bn
10	Sultan of Brunei	Brunei	Oil	**£18bn**	£12.4bn

*denotes family wealth

Table 4.4 Rich List, UK, 2008

Rank	Name	Worth	Source of wealth
1	(1)►Lakshmi Mittal and family	£27,700m	Steel
2	(2)►Roman Abramovich	£11,700m	Oil, industry
3	(3)►The Duke of Westminster	£7000m	Property
4	(4)►Sri and Gopi Hinduja	£6200m	Industry, finance
5	★Alisher Usmanov	£5726m	Steel, mining
6	★Ernesto and Kirsty Bertarelli	£5650m	Pharmaceuticals
7	(6)▼Hans Rausing and family	£5400m	Packaging
8	(8)►John Fredriksen	£4650m	Shipping
9	(7)▼Sir Philip and Lady Green	£4330m	Retailing
10	(9)▼David and Simon Reuben	£4300m	Property

★New entry ▲Up ▼Down ►No change in rank (2007 rank in brackets)

The Rich List is made up of:

1019 **men**
96 **women**
762 of the richest 1000 entries are self-made millionaires
238 inherited their wealth

There are:

231 in land and property
167 in banking, insurance, stockbroking, finance
114 in industry, metal bashing, engineering, steel-making
73 in retailing (not food)
60 in computers, software, Internet, telecoms, mobile phones
56 in hotels, leisure, health and fitness, sport
54 in food retailing, food production, drink
50 in construction, housebuilding
49 in media, television, films, publishing, novels
35 in transport
31 in music
29 in car sales, wholesaling and distribution
26 in pharmaceuticals, nursing homes, healthcare
25 in business services, recruitment, office support

To access the Rich List, go to www.timesonline.co.uk/richlist.

Case study

Dwarfs and giants

There is another way of looking at the overall income distribution . . . It involves thinking of a parade of the whole population passing before our eyes in a period of one hour. Each person's height is determined by their income such that the person with the mean income has the mean height (say 5′ 9″). Someone with income half the average would have a height half the average, and a person with income twice the average would be twice as tall as the average. Now suppose they pass before us in order of income (and therefore height) with the poorest (shortest) first until the last second of the sixtieth minute when the richest (tallest) person passes . . .

The first few seconds will actually see a few upside-down people with negative incomes and therefore negative heights. These will be the self-employed who are making losses from their businesses. And then for the first couple of minutes tiny dwarfs of under a foot or so will be passing. The heights of those passing will initially rise quite quickly, reaching 2′ 4″ after six minutes. But then there will be a long parade of dwarfs whose height will increase very slowly, only reaching just over 2′ 10″ (or half average height) by the end of the twelfth minute. Most of those passing at this point will be on social security benefits of some sort.

In the next 18 minutes, taking us up to the half hour, the height of those passing continues to rise gradually, reaching about 4′ 9″ when the half hour is reached. Half-way through and we are still looking down on people nearly a foot shorter than the average. The average height is eventually reached in the thirty-seventh minute, with the height still growing fairly gradually. At this stage, we are seeing mainly working people.

At about the three-quarters-of-an-hour mark, something happens to the parade. The heights of the people passing by start rising much more quickly. It took half an hour for everyone under 4′ 10″ to pass. It then takes another 18 minutes for the height of the parade to reach 7′ 8″. This is the height of people passing with just 12 minutes to go before the hour is up. But over just the next six minutes, the height rises to nearly 10′, and in the last few minutes, the heights start rising very quickly indeed. By the time we get into the last minute, 15′ 6″ giants are passing by. But it is not until the very last few seconds that the real giants are striding past. A merchant banker or chief executive of a large company with a gross income of £1 million per year (say) and net earnings, therefore, of about £12,000 per week would be towering up in the sky at a mighty 265′ or 88 yards tall, over one-and-a-half times as high as Nelson's Column.

Even above the highest-paid executives and employees will be a few entrepreneurs and aristocrats. The very richest in the country are not salaried employees. They either own their own companies (like Richard Branson) or large parts of the country (the Queen, for example). Unfortunately, none of our data contain information on this particular group of the population. When Pen first wrote of the parade, he estimated that John Paul Getty was the richest man in Britain and attributed to him a height of at least ten miles.

(Adapted from Pen 1971 by Goodman *et al.* 1997)

Questions

1. Transfer the above figures on to a graph that represents height (in yards and feet) against time (60 minutes).
2. What does this tell us about income inequality in the UK?

> The core assumptions of our society (property, profit and market) are firmly in line with the interests of one small group. That group comprises top business people and large property owners. It also includes those who derive substantial privilege from their association with this central cluster: the highly prosperous and well established professions, the senior ranks of officials in public service . . . Capital with its associates is still the effective ruling interest. It is not just one elite among several.
>
> (Westergaard and Resler 1976: 252)

This homogeneous view of a capitalist class has been modified more recently by models that suggest a variety of interests constituting a powerful group at the top whose ownership of property confers power. Giddens (1986: 159) has identified three categories of rich people in Britain:

- *Jet set rich* – This includes writers, sports professionals and rock stars who amass large fortunes very quickly as a result of well-marketed publicity. This group represents a very small section of the wealthy and would not normally be regarded as part of the capitalist class. An example is Paul McCartney.
- *Landowners* – These are people whose fortunes have been largely inherited, their estates having been passed down over generations. The concentration of land ownership means that a small group of landed families are still prominent. Because of the responsibilities and costs involved in maintaining such estates, as well as the legal restrictions covering such property, members of this group are not as wealthy as they may appear and do not control the kind of liquid assets that make other rich people very powerful. An example is the Duke of Westminster, an aristocrat who inherited both land and title.
- *Entrepreneurial rich* – These are people who derive their position from the ownership of stocks and shares. The concentration of ownership of these resources puts the control of manufacture, banking, insurance and the retail trades in the hands of a very few people. Although they may not be as wealthy on paper as some aristocrats, these people control assets that give them substantial power. Richard Branson and Roman Abramovich are examples.

John Scott (1991, 1997) has researched the exclusive 'business class' at the centre of the major enterprises that dominate British economic activity. In his view, the landed aristocracy and the highly paid are not necessarily members of the business class simply because of their affluence. The important consideration for Scott is the involvement of wealthy and influential individuals who hold key positions ('economic locations') at the centre of capitalist activity.

> **Capitalist economic locations are positions within a structure of ownership and control over property, and there are two bases for location within the capitalist class: direct participation in control through personal property holdings and administrative participation, as directors and executives, in the impersonal patterns of control through which business enterprises are ruled.**
>
> (Scott 1991: 8)

Behind the rise of joint-stock companies and institutional share ownership there still exists a core of capitalists who represent a business class. Scott suggests that this group may be classified in the following manner:

- *Entrepreneurial capitalists* – Through their personal property holdings, these enjoy direct control over corporate policy in one organization where they have a major or complete stake. The Moores family's domination of the Littlewoods empire is a good example.
- *Rentier capitalists* – These have less day-to-day involvement with company policy, and their personal investment is spread over a range of different companies. Return on investment rather than control is the major consideration – they speculate to accumulate. They have multiple shareholdings and make their money out of share dealing. By their nature, such individuals tend to work behind the scenes and so are not very well known.
- *Executive capitalists* – These have official full-time positions (e.g. chair person) within organizations but do not necessarily hold a large or controlling stake in the business. The senior executives of large concerns such as ICI, British Airways and British Telecom fit this category.
- *Finance capitalists* – These enjoy multiple non-executive directorships across a range of separate companies. These people are not simply passive shareholders but might represent the interests of big financial institutions on the boards of large companies and as a result may be regarded as a sort of 'inner circle' of the British business class.

Although Scott has indicated a more differentiated model of the upper class than that offered by, for instance, Westergaard and Resler (1976), he is clear that they still represent a privileged group in society:

> **Occupants of all these capitalist locations are able to secure advantaged opportunities and life chances for themselves and for their families and they are able to live a life of privilege.**
>
> (Scott 1991: 10)

According to Scott, this group survives as a class, despite the transformation of capitalism from personal to impersonal forms of ownership, because of a series of networks that bind these people together socially, politically and economically to the exclusion of others.

Scott shows that through intermarriage, kinship, private schooling and an exclusive lifestyle, the establishment continues to assert itself as a sort of 'private welfare state' (Crompton 1993: 193). Similarities of social background, club membership and political affiliation (traditionally to the Conservative Party) mean that these people see themselves as a class and act as one. As Crompton concludes:

> **The upper class in capitalist societies *does* manifest all the signs of being both conscious of its material interests and capable of protecting them.**
>
> (Crompton 1993: 198)

Case study

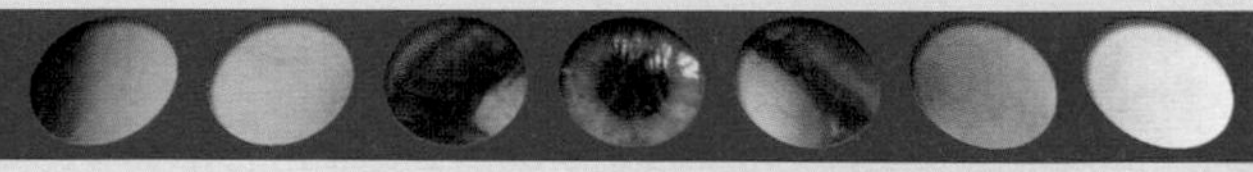

Inequalities of wealth and income

There are two common measures of economic fortune and they are often confused.

Wealth refers to assets such as land, shares, houses, cars and jewellery, and under some circumstances these can be more useful than having money in the bank. It is also important to consider what types of asset we own, as houses and cars are for personal use while stocks and shares are an investment. A car will almost certainly decline in value over time, while houses and shares may well go up in value.

Inequalities in wealth have generally decreased over time. In Britain an official report claimed that 'over the twentieth century as a whole, the distribution of wealth became more equal. In 1911, it is estimated that the wealthiest 1 per cent of the population held around 70 per cent of the UK's wealth. By 1936–38, this proportion had fallen to 56 per cent, and it fell again after world war two to reach 42 per cent in 1960' (Babb *et al.* 2004, quoted in Carvel 2004). By 1991 this trend had fallen to its lowest ebb (17 per cent) before it began to reverse itself. According to figures released since then, the top 1 per cent (the wealthiest 600,000 individuals in Britain) saw their share of the nation's wealth increase from 17 per cent to 23 per cent. At the other end, the share of the poorest 50 per cent shrank from a high of 10 per cent in 1986 to 5 per cent in 2001 (Table 4.3).

In a review of recent research by the American economist Paul Krugman, Chris Hamnett claims that 'wealth inequality has returned to the level of the golden age of American capitalism from the 1870s to 1929'. By comparison the wealth gap in the USA is even greater than that found in Britain or the rest of Europe:

Table 4.3 Distribution of wealth (UK)

Marketable wealth Percentage of wealth owned by:	**1976**	**1986**	**1996**	**1999**	**2000**	**2001**	**2002**	**2003**
Most wealthy 1%	21	18	20	23	23	22	24	21
Most wealthy 5%	38	36	40	43	44	42	45	40
Most wealthy 10%	50	50	52	55	56	54	57	53
Most wealthy 25%	71	73	74	75	75	72	75	72
Most wealthy 50%	92	90	93	94	95	94	94	93
Total marketable wealth (£ billion)	280	955	2092	2861	3131	3477	3588	3783
Marketable wealth less value of dwellings								
Percentage of wealth owned by:								
Most wealthy 1%	29	25	26	34	33	34	37	34
Most wealthy 5%	47	46	49	59	59	58	62	58
Most wealthy 10%	57	58	63	72	73	72	74	71
Most wealthy 25%	73	75	81	87	89	88	87	85
Most wealthy 50%	88	89	94	97	98	98	98	99

(Source: Inland Revenue)

Case study *continued*

Figure 4.5 Shares of total disposable income, 2002–03
Equivalized household disposable income before housing costs has been used to rank individuals.
Source: Babb *et al*. (2004: 43)

The US is even more unequal than Britain in both income and wealth. In the US, the top 1 per cent of wealth owners owned one-third of total wealth in 1983 but this had risen to 38 per cent by 1998, and the top 5 per cent owned 59 per cent. By comparison, the bottom 60 per cent owned less than 5 per cent of total wealth.

What is remarkable about the US is that the group which has increased its share is just the top 1 per cent of wealth owners. The other 99 per cent have seen their share fall. This is very different from Britain, where the top 50 per cent have all gained, and it supports Professor Krugman's claim that America is moving back towards the gilded age of capitalism.

(Hamnett 2004)

Income refers to the non-marketable wealth that a person earns through wages, salaries, dividends, pensions and benefits. It may be regarded as 'the most direct single indicator of material living standards' (Shaw *et al.* 2007: 98). Most forms of income are taxed either at source (direct taxation) or through taxes such as VAT on our purchases (indirect taxation). It is important to distinguish between the disposable income someone earns after tax and gross or pre-tax earnings. It is also important to understand that direct taxation tends to hit those on higher incomes while indirect taxation has more impact on poorer households. In general the gap in incomes in the UK is less well marked than the wealth gap, but it is still very unequal.

Since the start of the new millennium, the issue of 'fat cat' pay has never been far from the headlines, with shareholders and trade union officials quick to criticize the relentless rise in pay for those at the top. In 2002, Income Data Services reported that the average pay increase for the leading executives of those companies listed on the FTSE 100 had been 9.7 per cent for the year. This meant annual earnings of £1.6 million on average for top executives and £600,000 for the directors of these top companies. The Office for National Statistics issued a report in 2004 that showed that 'the pay of the richest 10 per cent of earners rose 4.3 per cent in the year to April to £825 a week – nearly double the average of £422 a week while the pay of the poorest 10 per cent rose only 4.1 per cent to £230 a week' (Seager 2004). The rate of increase appears to be shrinking but 4.3 per cent of £825 is worth a lot more than 4.1 per cent of £230. In their study of the elusive high-earners, Toynbee and Walker (2008) claim 'The top 10% of income earners get 27.3% of the cake, while the bottom 10% get just 2.6%. Twenty years ago the average chief executive of a FTSE 100 company earned 17 times the average employee's pay; now it is more than 75 times.' The *Guardian* newspaper monitors executive pay on a regular basis – updates appear on its website www.guardian.co.uk.

Reporting on a bumper year for bonuses in 2006, the *Independent* claimed that around £7.5 billion was to be added to the salaries of some of the highest earners in the UK:

Case study *continued*

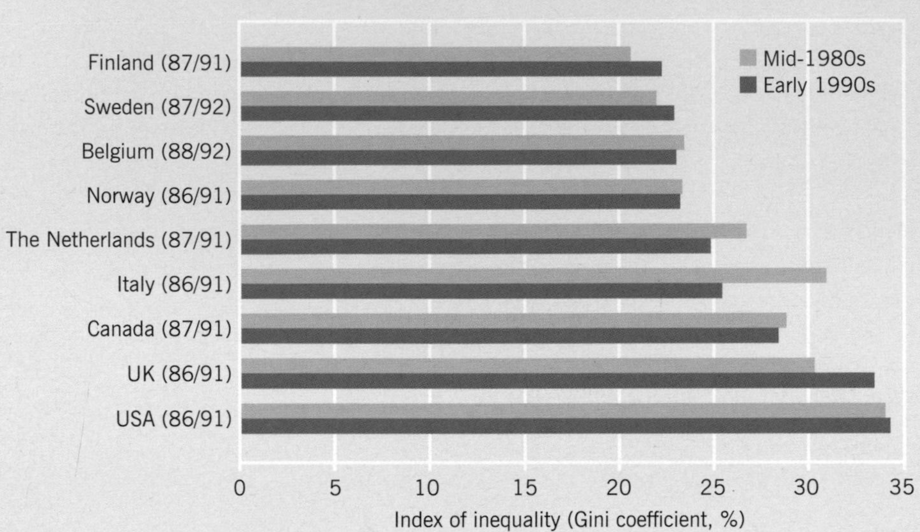

Figure 4.6 Income inequality in the mid-1980s and early 1990s
Source: cited in Hills (1997), and reprinted by permission of the Joseph Rowntree Foundation

> At the top end, about 3000 people, usually at boardroom level at such companies as Goldman Sachs and Morgan Stanley, will get bonuses of more than £1m, with a handful nudging £10m . . . But there are also 330,000 City workers, usually traders, brokers and dealers, who are also getting bonuses ranging from a few hundred pounds up to the magic £1m figure: the average is around £23,000.
>
> (Quoted in Ferguson 2008: 31)

An international comparison

Using the Gini coefficient it is possible to compare inequalities across societies. The closer a society is to 0, the more equal it is in terms of income distribution. As we can see in Figure 4.6, the UK and the USA appear to have the highest levels of income inequality. In countries such as the UK such inequality is increasing, while in Italy it slowed down over the 1990s and in the USA it remains high but unchanged.

Questions

1. How might income differences become translated into social inequalities?
2. What factors might explain the differences in income inequality between societies?

The middle class

The term 'middle class' is one of the most misused in the sociological dictionary. It is used in everyday language to denote a variety of social, economic and cultural phenomena. It can be used to signify a wealthy lifestyle, a managerial occupation or cultural snobbery. In sociology its meaning is not much clearer; it has been used as a catch-all category for anyone found in the intermediate strata of industrial society and to describe and identify a particular set of social values.

In the eighteenth and nineteenth centuries the term tended to refer to those people who made a living from the trade and manufacture of goods and inhabited the middle ground between the landed aristocracy and the poor. As their economic power increased, so did their political aspirations. In some countries (e.g. France) they led successful revolutions against the aristocracy, establishing republican governments and exerting their own economic and political domination. In Britain, integration and reform led to the gradual merger with the aristocracy to form what is loosely referred to as the

A closer look

The establishment

The establishment is not simply a group of people; it is a group of people allied around certain social institutions. These institutions are the Conservative Party, the Church of England, the public schools and ancient universities, the legal profession and the Guards regiments . . . In its informal aspect the establishment is the 'old boy network', the system of social contacts which stem from family and education. Such contacts 'are maintained largely in an informal manner by membership of the London clubs, by the social round of dinners and parties as well as, more formally, in business meetings and at official events'. The contacts which constitute this informal network of social relationships are important in the determination of the life-chances of those who go through the public school and Oxbridge system. Their contacts 'both facilitate their careers and enable them to have more influence in the posts where they eventually land'.

(John Scott 1992, quoted in Giddens 1992b: 88)

'upper class'. In both situations the class that had been in the middle was now at the top, which made the continued use of the term even more confusing. According to Marx, the industrial bourgeoisie had become the new ruling class in opposition to the other major industrial class (the proletariat). In between he also recognized a class of small-traders, self-employed artisans and landlords, whom he referred to as the petit bourgeoisie. However, as economic competition and the growth of monopolies forced them out of business, Marx expected that this group would eventually sink into the proletariat as society divided more clearly into 'two hostile camps'. As we have noted (see pp. 169–170), Weber disagreed fundamentally with Marx here and predicted an increase in the growth of the middle class as an intermediate status group. In the twentieth century the number of people in 'non-manual' occupations undoubtedly grew at the expense of traditional manual occupations. The percentage of the working population in manual occupations is now lower than 50 per cent in many industrialized countries, with the non-manual sector representing anything between 50 and 60 per cent. This shift has been accompanied by a growth in female employment in the service sector and increasing levels of education and social mobility:

> **With the general rise in living standards, the spread of higher education and the transformation of Britain from an industrial to a service economy the middle classes, however defined, have made up an increasingly large proportion of the population.**
>
> (Williams 1986: 112)

Over time, then, the term 'middle class' has ceased to be used to define a class (of manufacturers and traders) and has been applied instead to a status group who are distinguished by the non-manual nature of their work and whose attitudes and values differ from those of the traditional industrial working class. In 1948 Herbert Morrison generalized the middle class as 'that varied section of the community that works with its brain rather than its hands'. They were also seen to be better paid and to have earned a salary (paid into a bank account) rather than a weekly wage (placed in their hand). Along with this they were more likely to have a mortgage and to pay income tax. Some of these distinctions between manual and non-manual workers may have diminished in significance but the middle class is still defined in economic and social terms. Sociologists and advertisers refer to the middle class as those who inhabit grades A, B and C on an A–E scale, where the distinction is still drawn between skilled manual (C2) and skilled non-manual (C1) occupations.

As this non-manual status group is so broad, it is unhelpful to talk about all non-manual employees as if they belong to one homogeneous and conscious middle class, sharing similar economic, social and political interests. As a result, most writers seem to accept that the differences within this group are as important as the similarities that may exist:

> **It is, indeed, much more accurate to talk about the *middle classes* rather than about one single middle class. There is an enormous difference in income, status and lifestyle between the stockbroker at the**

upper end of the upper middles and the shorthand typist hovering uncomfortably between the ranks of the lower middle classes and the skilled manual workers.

(Williams 1986: 112)

Since the 1950s a distinction has been made between the 'old' middle class, whose position derived from property, and the 'new' middle classes, which include a range of 'white-collar' occupations. There is some dispute about the future of the old middle class, but it is clear that some small-scale entrepreneurs have survived. Optimists believe that this class may reassert itself as a result of government support for small businesses and enterprise initiatives. However, the high failure rate of such initiatives and the collapse of small businesses as a consequence of recession and a jittery banking sector may lead us to question the long-term revival of a petit bourgeois class. Early research by Savage *et al.* (1992) suggested that the class position of the self-employed might be an unstable transition from redundancy to unemployment, with over half lasting less than ten years in their trade. However, more recent figures show that after a poor time of it in the 1970s the numbers of self-employed in the labour market rocketed by 45 per cent to over 10 per cent of the workforce by the 1990s. In their review of the 1980s, Fielding (1995) concluded that after ten years approximately 62 per cent remained in self-employment. In comparing this with his own assessment of the period 1971–81, Savage concludes that the petit bourgeoisie are becoming a more secure, distinct and visible group in British society (Savage 1995: 3).

The 'new' middle classes, on the other hand, have been dramatically successful in expanding their size and influence. There is little dispute that the service sector has grown, and that professionals, managers and administrators have become a significant part of the occupational structure. This growth has created a demand for new groups of specialists whose function is to service the emotional and cultural needs of the new middle classes. Media pundits, psychotherapists, fashion designers and health gurus are part of this 'new petite bourgeoisie', which has blossomed in response to an ever-growing appetite for difference in the postmodern age of mass consumption (Crompton 1993: 179–80).

Where this may end up is unclear, but Roberts feels that, despite its cosmopolitan appearance, patterns of inward mobility from lower-class groups may begin to slow down as the middle class consolidates itself and sorts out some notion of group identity:

We have seen that the new middle class has expanded strongly since the mid-twentieth century. During this growth, it has become more diverse in ethnic and gender composition, and is equally mixed in terms of its members' social class origins. During the twenty-first century the middle class is likely to remain just as mixed, if not more mixed, in terms of gender and ethnicity, but it will definitely become increasingly self-recruiting. It is only at this stage that any characteristic forms of consciouness and politics are likely to solidify. Perhaps the most important point to grasp about the new middle class is that it is still in formation.

(Roberts 2001: 168)

The service class

This section of the 'new' middle classes is that which is closest to the capitalist or upper class by virtue of the control and servicing functions that it carries out on behalf of the upper class and because of clear differences in income, education and lifestyle that mark it out from other non-manual groups, but similar to the dominant group in society. As a result, this group clearly has a stake in the status quo, although there is continuing debate about whether it is so privileged that it has become part of the dominant class.

An attempt to make sense of the factors that confuse our analysis of the middle classes at this level can be found in the work of Mike Savage *et al.* (1992). According to their view it is possible to understand the lifestyle and structuring of the upper middle and service classes in terms of the different assets that they possess. These are property, cultural and organizational assets, which are the key to their success and the life chances they and their families enjoy. These assets also correspond to the formation of different groups within the middle class and may explain the differences in cultural outlook at this level.

Property assets

Property is the most important form of asset. It is easy to store and quick to utilize; it represents the most obvious way in which members of this class can establish themselves and get things done. Although property assets are most obviously connected with the formation of the entrepreneurial classes, they can also be important in establishing and maintaining the class position of members of the service class – some of whom enjoy six-figure annual incomes and lucrative share options. In their study *Inequality in the UK*, Goodman *et al.* (1997) conclude that inequalities in income distribution have widened since the 1970s, with the top 10 per cent of the population earning as much as the bottom 50 per cent. This trend was confirmed by the research of the economist John Hills, who studied the growing inequalities in income between 1996 and 2003 in Britain. According to the *Observer*'s Heather Stewart:

> **About 40 per cent of the total increase in income between 1979 and 2003 went into the pockets of the top 10 per cent of Britain's earners. Between them they now take home more than the whole of the poorest half of society.**
>
> (*Observer* 7.11.04)

The overnight fortunes made in the City after the Big Bang in 1986 also provided the basis for the formation of a young and upwardly mobile subclass. The 'yuppie' phenomenon may have been short-lived, but it demonstrates the enduring power of property assets to affect class formation. Because, in Savage's model, this group is almost indistinguishable from what we have already called the upper class, it is safe to assume that they exist within (or on the fringes of) the network that Scott identified as the establishment. Private education, intermarriage, membership of exclusive clubs and the Conservative Party are all badges of 'social exclusion'. Savage and colleagues, however, identified a postmodernist trend among the yuppies of the 1980s whereby cultural taste is less determined by traditional patterns of consumption and is more hedonistic and eclectic in nature. The old divisions between high cultural forms and mass culture disappear in the free market of commodity choice as new patterns of consumption and taste emerge (see pp. 100–105).

Case study

The overclass

The following extract is taken from a feature on an exclusive housing estate in Buckinghamshire, made up of five houses and known as 'The Gate'. The people who live there have used their wealth to ensure that they are 'socially excluded'.

> Meg is interrupted, mid sentence, by an electronic chirruping. 'Oh damn, that's The Gate,' she explains, jumping up. The Gate, along with the winking red eyes in the corner of each room, are symbols of Meg's status: one of the socially excluded . . .
>
> One of the five houses behind The Gate – which is spoken of in reverential terms by residents – can be yours for a million-plus. On the drive of one house are a Mercedes sports car, a Range Rover and a Rolls. One resident has homes on the West Coast of America, Spain and Bermuda.
>
> 'Opulence is the norm here,' says Meg. 'The concentration of wealth is really something.'
>
> The people who live here, then, are not socially excluded through lack of money. On the contrary their wealth allows them to cut themselves off from society's mainstream. All the luxury-house building companies report an increased demand for scaled communities for the gated garrisons of the 'overclass' – a term included in an Oxford University Press dictionary published last month.
>
> Meg's road is private. The children go to private schools. There is a private, 10-acre wood and more cars than people. The infra-red motion sensors in their homes are linked directly to the local police station . . .
>
> The families behind The Gate are the lead characters of the Thatcherite dream, people who worked their way up – self-made, hard-working, risk-taking, entrepreneurial. When Tony Blair says the UK needs more millionaires, these are the people he is talking about. Conchi and husband Peter own a satellite TV firm. Gordon and Pat, a semi-retired Irish couple, built a computer company. Meg's husband, Eddie runs a medical products firm . . .
>
> Celebration of their success means detachment from the less successful. Status plays a part. 'People say "Wow, you've got a gate" when they visit,' says Meg. Security, too – though the scale of the protection seems ill-matched to the threat posed by the communities beyond The Gate. The enclave is in the heart of the most prosperous part of the country . . .

Case study *continued*

According to Professor Tony Giddens, director of the London School of Economics: 'If you allow a situation to develop in which some people cut themselves off, then you pose a threat to the very fabric of society.

'In effect there are two forms of social exclusion – voluntary and involuntary.' In the UK, some gated communities have opted for moats and portcullises to deter the outsider, a powerful echo of a time when society was fractured into baronies, and communities lived in fortresses, safe from marauders.

Giddens says that while the government cannot ban such gated estates, it can work to bring down some of the non-physical barriers.

'We need to foster institutions that enhance the sense of collective identity – which is why I am not in favour of a minimalist welfare state. And we need to do more to lower the hurdles between state and private schools for instance . . .'

'We are in danger of creating a structural breach in society,' says Giddens.

The inhabitants of Gateland deny the charge . . .

Meg says the self-made nature of the inhabitants is a safeguard against rebellion. 'People who have got here because of hard work and risk-taking are less likely to lose sight of the needs of others – of where they came from.'

But Giddens worries that over time, the separation of this group may grow. 'It is one thing to work your way up from humble roots to these places, quite another to grow up in them.'

Currently, the overclass is defined simply by money and a desire to be cut off. If the group begins to have shared political objectives, then a class in the real sense of the term could develop.

(From R. Thomas, 'Rich – And Excluded', *Observer* 20.9.98)

Question

1. What sort of problems or difficulties might such exclusive developments cause for (a) those who live in them; and (b) the rest of society?

Cultural assets

Along with property, and sometimes instead of it, the 'cultural capital' achieved through exclusive and high levels of education can become the key to membership of the professional wing of the service class. This professional middle class clearly takes advantage of the education system to secure the cultural advantages that can lead to social success. These assets may not be as fluid or as effective as property, but a 'good education' is an investment in the future that can withstand inflation and the vagaries of the marketplace.

In the longitudinal '7 Up' study conducted by Michael Apted for British TV, a socially diverse group of seven-year-olds from 1963 are revisited every seven years to see whether there is any truth in the maxim 'Give me a child until he is seven and I will give you the man'. By 1998 most of them were still willing to be interviewed for the '42 Up' episode. One of them, Andrew (who attended Charterhouse – one of the 'top' public schools in England – and Cambridge University, where he studied law) regards education as the most important investment his parents could have made for his future. Echoing the findings of Fiona Devine's study (see p. 184), he says:

> **Education is very important . . . you can never be sure of leaving your children any worldly goods but at least you can be sure that once you've given them a good education that's something that no one can take away.**

However, as opportunities for access into higher education increase, academic qualifications may count for less as employers become more interested in personal qualities such as character, appearance and manners. In a study by Nuffield College Oxford, it is suggested that education as the great hope for a more meritocratic society may be misplaced as individuals are employed for their ability to get on with clients and customers; the skills required are nonetheless social and tend to favour those with a middle-class background where such qualities are the norm. As one of the authors of the Oxford study, John Goldthorpe, puts it:

> **If you are selling high-value things like real estate, you will be interacting with middle-class people and you will do better if you are familiar with their style, manners, etc. . . . It's not much use having some graceless anorak, however impressive his or her degree. The attributes that these people have from their family background have some real commercial use. It's not nepotism. Employers know what they want.**
>
> (cited in *The Economist* 2004)

As a result, cultural assets have enabled a powerful professional middle class to emerge 'alongside but subordinate to [the] propertied class' (Scott 1994: 2). As this group is high on cultural capital but low on economic assets, it is not surprising that in terms of consciousness and lifestyle they can be seen as different from the propertied middle class. This is especially true of those professionals who work in the public sector, who may have different tastes as well as unexpected political allegiances. Their lifestyle has been described as healthy, intellectual and culturally radical; Wynne (1990) called this group 'sporters' because of their ascetic and athletic lifestyle. In political terms they are also less likely to support the Conservative Party. Whereas top professionals have been described as a 'conservative force', this does not apply to all members of the professional middle class. Research has shown that although top professionals in the private sector who are employed within an entrepreneurial model tend to be Conservative, those who work in public service areas such as health and education may support and become actively involved in the Labour Party (Callinicos and Harman 1987; Crompton 1993).

Organizational assets

The least valuable forms of asset are those skills that relate only to the organization being served. Although administrative skills have made managers, as a class, indispensable to large organizations, they provide only a short-term and inflexible basis for membership of the service class. Managers may become redundant as a result of restructuring or new technologies and discover that their skills are no longer required anywhere else. This makes organizational assets alone a very unstable guarantee of middle-class position and lifestyle, especially in Britain, where the managerial middle class has historically been recruited separately from those with cultural assets. This may explain why the children of managers are likely to be well educated and are encouraged to 'trade' their organizational assets for cultural ones. As a result, the children of managers are more likely to become professionals than to follow their parents into management (Savage *et al.* 1992).

The lower middle class

The other element of the 'new' middle classes is a lower or intermediate class, which is comprised of lower-paid non-manual workers engaged in routine white-collar work. Although some writers seem happy to lump this group together with other members of a general middle class characterized by their ownership of educational and technical qualifications (Giddens 1973), there is widespread disagreement among sociologists about the class position of routine non-manual workers. Some would argue that the pay, status and working conditions of these workers make them a distinct 'intermediate' class occupying the social territory between the service class and the working class; others, however, would prefer to see them as part of a broader working class that makes no distinction between mental and physical labour. In essence this debate concerns the process of *proletarianization*, which Marx predicted as the fate of industrial capitalism. Colin Ward provides a clerical worker's view of office routine:

> **One occupational hazard facing a clerk is always the sense of futility he struggles against, and is more often just overwhelmed by. Unlike even the humblest worker on a production line, he doesn't produce *anything*. He battles with phantoms, abstracts; runs a paper chase that goes on year after year and seems utterly pointless. How can there be anything else other than boredom in it for him?**
>
> (Ward 1972: 22)

Westergaard and Resler maintain that the apparent growth of this 'middle class' is really no more than an expansion of opportunities for low-paid drudgery with little prospect of promotion. This is especially true for women who have 'moved from domestic service jobs and skilled manual work into semi-skilled jobs in offices and factories' (Westergaard and Resler 1976: 294). Crompton and Jones (1984) have emphasized the continuation of deskilling in the workplace and the proletarianization of the social and economic position of white-collar workers. Crucial to this process is the 'feminization' of clerical work and the restricted opportunities for women in these organizations relative to men (see p. 184).

A closer look

We argue that, once a person's place in the relations of production is taken as the key to his or her class position, then three groups of white-collar workers must be distinguished: 1. a small minority who are salaried members of the capitalist class, participating in the decisions on which the process of capital accumulation depends; 2. a much larger group, the 'new middle class', of highly-paid white-collar workers, most of whom occupy managerial and supervisory positions intermediate between labour and capital; 3. the majority, routine white-collar workers having as little control over their work as manual workers, and often less well-paid. The crucial conclusion we draw from this analysis is that the growth of this third group represents the expansion, not the decline, of the working class.

(Callinicos and Harman 1987: 9)

Case study

Middle-class professionals are Britain's hidden poor

The plight of Britain's hidden poor – middle-class professionals who have slipped down the social scale – is highlighted in a report published today.

It shows that 3.8 million people, 14 per cent of the country's professional classes, are living on incomes below the poverty line.

For a single person this could mean an income as low as £114 a week.

The report paints a grim picture of the lives of a group that can include teachers, nurses, managers, social workers, solicitors and musicians, as well as others who have social standing but few or no formal qualifications.

The report, published by the Elizabeth Finn Trust, which gives financial support to almost 2000 people a year, including those struggling on low incomes in retirement, was based on a poll of 10,000 adults plus 450 of its clients.

It talks of a 'vicious circle of decline' prompted by factors including money troubles, lack of work, family breakdown, poor health and inadequate pensions.

A major problem for some of the group identified by the charity is their lack of formal educational qualifications 'in an increasingly meritocratic society' where 'who you know' is no longer a guarantee of financial or social status.

Only 6 per cent have a university degree, compared with a national average of almost 12 per cent, and a third have no qualifications at all.

'Among the professional classes, one-quarter leave school without five good GCSEs,' says the report. 'Whereas once this group may have got into the workforce through their connections, this will be increasingly difficult in a world where qualifications are paramount.'

The value of pensions is also a cause of anxiety. 'With the ageing population, we will see an increase in the numbers of retired professionals who are in an ever more precarious position as a result of the increasing uncertainty of personal and company pensions,' continues the report.

'With increasing longevity, their pensions are squeezed at the other end too, since it means that annuities are paying out increasingly smaller amounts, as the money has to stretch further.'

The report concludes that members of the group are less likely to be in work: 40 per cent of them compared with 56 per cent of the total adult population and 70 per cent of their professional peers. They are also more likely to be on benefits.

Case study *continued*

On the whole they tend to be in worse health and are more likely to suffer with problems involving drink or drugs, anxiety, depression, blood pressure, heart problems and strokes . . .

'Overall it seems likely that the professional classes will polarise more in the future, with the educated and the better networked leaving others less fortunate than themselves behind in the workplace and social and leisure life.'

(David Ward, the *Guardian* 26.7.04)

Question

1. Using the ideas covered in this section on the 'new' middle class, which group are most likely to find themselves among the 'hidden poor'?

The proletarianization thesis has been attacked by sociologists influenced by the Weberian perspective. In their view those in white-collar occupations form a distinct 'intermediate class' who can be clearly distinguished from the service class above them and a manual working class below (Goldthorpe *et al.* 1980). In his early study *The Blackcoated Worker*, David Lockwood (1958) argued that, despite a deterioration in relative pay and status, clerical workers enjoyed better job security, pension provision and promotion prospects when compared with manual workers. In his revised edition, Lockwood concluded that changes in the workplace may have benefited white-collar employees:

> **Regardless of the extent to which clerical work may be said to have been proletarianised, there are no grounds for thinking that the majority of clerical workers have experienced proletarianisation. The promotion opportunities of male clerks and the fairly rapid turnover of female clerks more or less guarantee that this is not the case. Secondly, the view that clerical work itself has undergone widespread 'degradation', as a result of rationalisation and mechanisation, is not one that has found much support. Indeed, the most detailed recent surveys and case-studies of the effects of the new technology lead to just the opposite conclusion: namely, that reskilling, even job enrichment appear to be the most general consequences.**
>
> (Lockwood 1989: 250)

Support for this view has been provided by the research of Stewart *et al.* (1980), whose study of male white-collar workers showed that, for over 50 per cent of their sample, clerical work was a route to promotion and social mobility. By the age of 30 years, less than 20 per cent were still in clerical work, which led them to conclude that in the experience of most clerical workers proletarianization did not characterize their work. This view has been endorsed by Marshall *et al.* (1988), whose research shows very little evidence of deskilling and proletarianization among clerical workers but indicates a fragmentation within the lower middle class between this group and personal service workers (e.g. shop assistants), for whom the process of proletarianization is more significant.

There are clearly problems in using a term such as 'middle class' to accommodate all those people who neither own property nor work with their hands. Although the term is used widely in everyday language, its use within class analysis is fraught with difficulties that stem from the fragmentary and contradictory nature of the group who make it up. Abercrombie and Warde provide a clear summary of these difficulties:

> **We conclude that the category of occupations conventionally identified as middle class contains a small number of identifiable, potentially cohesive fractions whose members share many conditions. The service class, still expanding, holds an advantageous position in most respects. Despite its internal differences it stands apart from other fractions, comprises perhaps 30 per cent of the occupied population, and shows no sign of relinquishing its privileges. Its lower ranges overlap with the routine white-collar group beneath, which has neither the control over work nor the rewards of higher managers and professionals. Lower managements, parts of the lower professions and**

technicians nevertheless still have better market and work conditions than clerks or shop assistants. The conditions of routine white-collar workers are also varied, but while the best-rewarded of them have advantages over manual work, the differences are reducing. The petite bourgeoisie is set apart, distinctive in its economic, social and cultural orientations, but despite its recent growth it has limited power and its privileges are precarious. Some independent small proprietors, particularly those selling cultural and professional services, prosper greatly, but others in traditional avenues like shopkeeping and the building trades are unlikely to be much better off financially than skilled manual workers.

(Abercrombie and Warde 2000: 182)

The working class

We have already noted that the idea of a homogeneous manual working class with its roots in traditional forms of manual work, community culture and political allegiance has come under attack as a result of technological and economic change. These criticisms also brought into question the relationship between class position, class consciousness and class action. As a result, the revolutionary role of the working class has been rejected in favour of models that stressed working-class ambivalence and instrumentalism. However, the idea that the decline in the number of people working in some areas of industrial production means saying 'farewell to the working class' (Gorz 1982) has been challenged by many sociologists and Marxist writers, who have argued that the working class has simply been transformed by changes in the structure of the labour market. The nature of work, reward and lifestyle of these workers still distinguishes them from others, while the political consequences of these changes may have been exaggerated. While acknowledging the disagreement over the nature of the working class in modern society, we attempt to categorize the broad groups who may be said to constitute the working class: a traditional working class, an expanded working class and an underclass.

The traditional working class

This group is made up of people (usually men) who work in the traditional areas of industrial production. In the past these industries have included textiles, steel production and coal-mining; more recently, light engineering and the car industry have formed part of this changing area of the economy. Classical sociological studies of family life, work and the community have painted a homogeneous and possibly romantic stereotype of a working-class culture dominated by the male pursuits of sport, drink and trade union politics, but characterized also by a strong matriarchal family and sense of community (Dennis *et al.* 1956; Tunstall 1962; Young and Willmott 1957).

It has been argued that, by the early part of the nineteenth century, in Britain a strong working class with its own distinctive culture had emerged. Working-class people were conscious of their membership of this culture and their separate interests as a class (E.P. Thompson 1968). According to Callinicos and Harman (1987) these interests developed into a fully fledged class consciousness based on collective values and action as a result of 'three waves of industrial struggle' between 1850 and the 1930s. This old manual working class established the basis for collective action through a variety of organizations such as family, community, trade unions and the Labour Party.

Since the 1950s the homogeneity and strength of purpose of the traditional working class has been under attack from the processes of 'embourgeoisment' and 'privatization'. Goldthorpe *et al.*'s (1968, 1969) classic study of 'affluent' workers in Luton repudiated the idea that the working class had adopted middle-class norms and values as a result of a more affluent lifestyle (see p. 180). However, their conclusion that a 'new working class' had emerged who were more interested in a privatized lifestyle and an instrumental attitude to work (and politics) has also been criticized. At the time John Westergaard (1970) disputed the idea that increasing materialism made workers less interested in class action (in fact, he suggested the reverse). In the early 1990s Fiona Devine returned to Luton in order to test the 'new workers' hypothesis in the aftermath of a protracted recession and a decade of Conservative government. Her conclusions suggest that Goldthorpe *et al.* had 'exaggerated the extent of change in working-class lifestyles . . . [and] incorrectly gave primacy to changing working-class norms and values' (Devine 1994: 7). Workers moved to Luton in search of jobs and affordable housing (not to become socially mobile) and, once there, retained ties of kinship and friendship with communities as far afield as Northern Ireland, Scotland and south-east England. These workers identified with the concerns and aspirations of other workers (especially the threats of redundancy and unemployment) and felt that trade unions and the Labour Party were a 'collective means of securing working class interests'.

What had appeared as a 'new' working class in the 1960s had all but vanished in 20 years.

A similar conclusion was drawn by Hayes and Hudson (2001) in their comparative study of Basildon. We have already noted that 'Basildon Man' had been heralded as the new face of working-class politics and that there was some evidence in the 1992 study that workers were becoming more privatized and family-centred and less likely to trust the Labour Party (see p. 181). However, this shift towards the conservatism of the Thatcher government was short-lived and 'skin deep'. In their 1997 follow-up study, Hayes and Hudson discovered 'no rooted ideological shift in the outlook of Basildonians' and suggested that voting for the Conservatives was 'more to do with a rejection of Labour than a positive embrace of Thatcherism' (Hayes and Hudson 2001: 38). Despite the claims that Basildon workers had become more individualistic and middle class, Hayes and Hudson conclude that this was exaggerated by the media and that the idea they represented a new wave of embourgeoisment a myth (see Table 4.4). In any event the 1997 election saw a Labour government returned to power and a victory for their candidate in Basildon with one of the biggest majorities in its electoral history.

Although Basildon workers did not see work as central to their identities or aspirations, and class was not a basis for political action (trade union membership, for example, was in decline), they did see social class as an important part of their heritage and recognized class-based discrimination as a feature of modern life that affected their life chances.

Bev Skeggs (2003) also discovered contradictory trends in her analysis of class attitudes among white working-class women. Despite the fact that the women in her study tried to distance themselves from those aspects of working-class life, culture and self that they did not regard as 'respectable', they were also aware that they lived in a society in which life chances relate to class structure and that their cultural responses enabled social class differences to be reproduced. In much the same way as Willis (1977) has argued that working-class lads contribute to their own reproduction as working-class adults, so these women were aware of the inequalities of social life, their cultural responses to this situation and the impact this had upon their own chances of progress:

> **Class was completely central to the lives of the women. It was not only structural, in the sense that the division of labour organized what economic opportunities were available for them, or institutional, in that the education system was designed on this basis and operated through a multitude of operations of capital transformations and trading. By using Bourdieu's metaphors of capital and space the study mapped how a group of white working-class women were born into structures of inequality which provided differential amounts of capital which circumscribed their movements through social space. These movements were not imposed but put into effect by the women who utilized the forms of capital to which they had access in an attempt to put a floor on their circumstances. They did not have access to . . . those forms of capital which are convertible in an institutional system, such as the cultural capital of the middle classes, which can be converted and traded-up through**

Table 4.4 The truth about Basildon Man

Media image	Reality 1992	Reality 1997
Tasteless: shell suits for men, short skirts and large 'hoop' earrings for women	Some truth in this choice of clothes, but it is based on relatively low earnings	Ordinary or smart dress
Loads of money	64% less than £15,000 p.a.	60% earning less than £15,000; relatively poor
Conservative	Yes; that is, they voted Conservative, but 24% rejected all Conservative policies	No; they voted New Labour and 39% rejected all Conservative policies; they are increasingly disengaged from politics
Classless	75% describe themselves as working class	73% describe themselves as working class

(Hayes and Hudson 2001: 14)

> **education and employment into symbolic capital and economic reward. They made the most of what they had but it rarely offered good trading potential . . . Lack of alternatives was one of the central features of being working-class; they rarely had the potential to re-valorise their classed subjectivities.**
>
> (Skeggs 2003: 161)

Rather than examining aspiring working-class men from Basildon or women from Greater Manchester for evidence of change, Simon Charlesworth (2000) returned to the roots of industrial Britain to see what had become of those people left behind by the technological revolution. He returned to Rotherham (grimly referred to as 'Deadman's Town') where industrial decline and unemployment are the order of the day and an impoverished culture the legacy. Adopting a phenomenological approach he is keen to get 'to the heart of working-class people's experience' and understand their responses to the situation they find themselves in from their point of view. Rather than disappearing, he finds working-class experience and an awareness of it only too prevalent:

> **For the working class, themselves, for whom the economically marginal and socially excluded are family members and neighbours, they have had to deal in the most palpable way with the decline of their own economic role and social position. Since the early 1980s, the gradual decline of the culture of the working class has been one of the most powerful, telling developments in British society. The bleakness of English society, what lies around us in the faces of the urban poor everywhere, emerges from this context, and yet there have been few accounts of the transition and consequences from amongst those who are unable to buy their way out of the conditions and into the protected elite spaces of the English middle and upper classes.**
>
> (Charlesworth 2000: 2)

Despite attempts by middle-class intellectuals (some of whom are sociologists) to render the term meaningless, social class retains a powerful role in the understanding of social life for those the other side of the divide:

> **If one engages with working people one finds a profound sense of the centrality of a common experience of their living conditions and of the society in which they live. This experience is obvious in every constitutive moment in which the society is made and remade and in which the conditions of exclusion and marginality, of hardship and humiliation, are achieved through all the totality of affinities and repulsions that modulate the contours of English social structure.**
>
> (Charlesworth 2000: 154)

These people rely upon their narrowly defined and undemanding culture as a means of survival but are limited by it in turn; a cultural response that deals with frustration and boredom through instant gratification of the physical pleasures available is not one that is likely to enervate or engage. As one person neatly puts it, these pleasures are pretty basic and easily summarized as 'some nice snap t' 'ave a good trough at; plenty'r beer, a shag, some decent kip an' a good shit, the'r in't much mo'ore t' life' (Charlesworth 2000: 279).

In Charlesworth's view the economic decay of the area has infected the culture. Marginalized and redundant, people no longer seem proud of their heritage or positive about the future. He expresses his disquiet in terms that are grim and pessimistic:

> **They may be biologically alive but they do not have access to the resources, symbolic as well as economic, to have a life. They are the zombies that British culture has created by condemning them to a living death of a stigmatized, abject, being.**
>
> (Charlesworth 2000: 281)

Although the number of people employed as manual workers in the traditional industries has clearly fallen, this does not eradicate their significance as a class. Manual workers still play an important role within the economy and continue to account for a large proportion of the workforce. Depending on how we define manual workers, this group still constitutes around 50 per cent. In some parts of the world the proportion is even lower (approximately 40 per cent in the USA), but in areas of recent industrialization the manual working class will continue to constitute the majority class.

The pay and life chances of manual workers have remained a significant part of working-class experience. Despite the fact that some white-collar workers take home less pay than some manual workers, it is still clear that, on average, the comparison favours those in non-manual occupations.

The *New Earnings Survey* 2003(www.statistics.gov.uk/statbase/Product.asp?vlnk=5749) showed that manual workers depended far more than other groups on overtime payments for their total earnings and that they worked longer hours. It is also still the case that manual workers enjoy fewer privileges at work (time off, sick pay, holidays) and have lower levels of job security. They have fewer opportunities for promotion and they are less likely to belong to pension schemes. As a consequence, manual workers are also less likely to enjoy the life chances available to other groups in society. In the areas of health, housing, education, social mobility and leisure, major differences still occur that reveal the significance of being 'working class'. As Ivan Reid's (1989, 1998) work demonstrates, individual life chances are still tied to class background with very little likelihood of improvement for those at the lower end:

> **It is difficult to see that political activity and social change in the 1980s has done much other than to sustain, or even increase, existing class differences. Indeed the large body of unemployed, especially the long-term, may be seen as a new class whose deprivations are many and severe. There is, in short, no evidence to suggest that class differences are anything but alive and well at present and that they will feature prominently . . . into the 1990's and beyond.**
>
> (Reid 1989: 397)

An expanded working class

As noted earlier, the 'proletarianization' debate raised the issue of the class position of the lower middle classes. It has been argued that, as the nature of work has changed to increase the demand for routine clerical and service workers, the conventional distinction between manual and non-manual work has been rendered useless. Instead, the view of neo-Marxist writers such as Callinicos and Harman (1987) is that the routine nature of this work and its relatively low levels of pay and status make this form of employment virtually indistinguishable from manual labour. In the 'hierarchically structured' world of white-collar work, they estimate that a prestigious group of administrators and managers has emerged who represent some 10–15 per cent of the workforce and operate as part of the 'service class' (they use the term 'new middle class'). Below the minority are an 'intermediate grade' of administrative and clerical staff (approximately 15 per cent of the workforce) who aspire to membership of the 'new middle class' but in reality exist just above those on 'routine manual grades' and as a result must be regarded as simply another group of 'exploited workers'. Alongside this group has emerged a strata of lower professionals such as classroom teachers and lower-paid nurses, who also exert little control over their work and have only their labour power to rely upon. In conclusion, they argue that 'the restructuring of industry has produced a restructuring of the working class, not the growth of a new class alongside and comparable in size to the working class' (Callinicos and Harman 1987: 86). If the surviving blue-collar workers and the lower grades of white-collar and routine non-manual workers are combined together, they represent an 'expanded working class' that accounts for 70 per cent of the working population.

The underclass

In the debate over the persistence of the working class, the idea of a growing underclass has emerged that relates to a variety of sociological and political issues. In this discussion we shall have to overlook many of these important issues and focus on the relevance of the underclass to class analysis. In particular we are concerned with the way in which the underclass is defined and with its relationship to the wider class structure.

The idea of an underclass is not new. Marx used the term *lumpenproletariat* in the nineteenth century to refer in disparaging terms to a 'surplus population' living in the most destitute conditions. The writings of Mayhew (1949) and Booth (1889) also painted lurid and frightening portraits of life among the 'dangerous classes' in Victorian London (Chesney 1991). In the twentieth century, the term 'underclass' was coined in order to make sense of the experiences of those living in the black ghettos of the USA and the townships of South Africa. This racial dimension has always made its application to British society problematic, but since the 1960s the term has been used widely to refer not only to inner-city deprivation among ethnic minority groups (Rex and Tomlinson 1979) but also to those suffering from the urban decay found on many of the (predominantly white) post-war housing estates on the fringes of major cities.

Writers such as Giddens (1973) have used the term broadly to describe those people in modern capitalist society who survive in a twilight world between unemployment and the secondary labour market. But Runciman (1990) and Field (1989) prefer to highlight welfare benefits as the key to defining the underclass. As Field puts it:

Poverty: the UK and Europe

The definition of poverty is problematic, but most commentators accept that in an affluent society it makes little sense to use absolute definitions that may be applied to parts of the world where people have to go without food and shelter. Consequently, relative definitions are used that compare living standards against the average income. Depending on our judgement of where the line should be drawn, we end up with different figures for those thought to be living in poverty. In Figure 4.7 from *Social Trends*, we can see what the level of poverty might be using 60 per cent and 50 per cent of the median income as our poverty line.

By using this technique it is also possible to compare poverty levels in Britain with those in other European countries. We can see from Figure 4.8 that Portugal appears to have the highest proportion of its households living below the EU median (set at 60 per cent), while Luxembourg has the lowest.

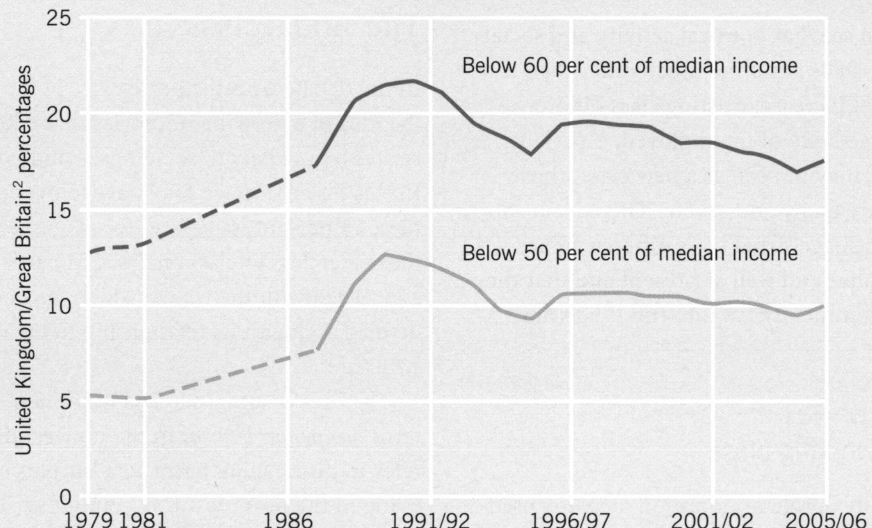

Figure 4.7 Proportion of people whose income is below various percentages of median household disposable income[1,2]

[1] Contemporary household disposable income before deduction of housing costs, using OECD equivalization scale. See Appendix, Part 5: Households Below Average Income (HBAI), and Equivalization scales for variations in source and definition on which the time series is based.

[2] Data for 1994/95 to 2001/02 for Great Britain only.

Source: *Households Below Average Income, Department for Work and Pensions*

This translates as 49 per cent of Portuguese households falling below the EU median and in Luxembourg only 1 per cent below the median. In Britain, Sweden, Finland and France, approximately 15 per cent of households fell below the 'EU poverty line'.

This model can be criticized for comparing all countries against a notional EU standard (60 per cent of the EU median income) and overlooks the massive differences across Europe in earnings and cost of living (many Portuguese people defined as poor against this overall standard would not feel poor unless they left Portugal), so another way of looking at this that gives us a different picture is to compare countries against their own relative levels of income using the 60 per cent of national median income as the poverty line and deriving comparative poverty data from these national snapshots. This allows us to see what proportion may be regarded as living in poverty relative to their own standards. As we can see from Figure 4.9, the UK does less well using this form of comparison.

For a useful discussion of poverty thresholds and other issues related to poverty, see www.poverty.org, which is maintained by the New Policy Institute and supported by the Joseph Rowntree Foundation.

Question

1. **How would you account for the European differences in poverty levels suggested in the chart below?**

Case study *continued*

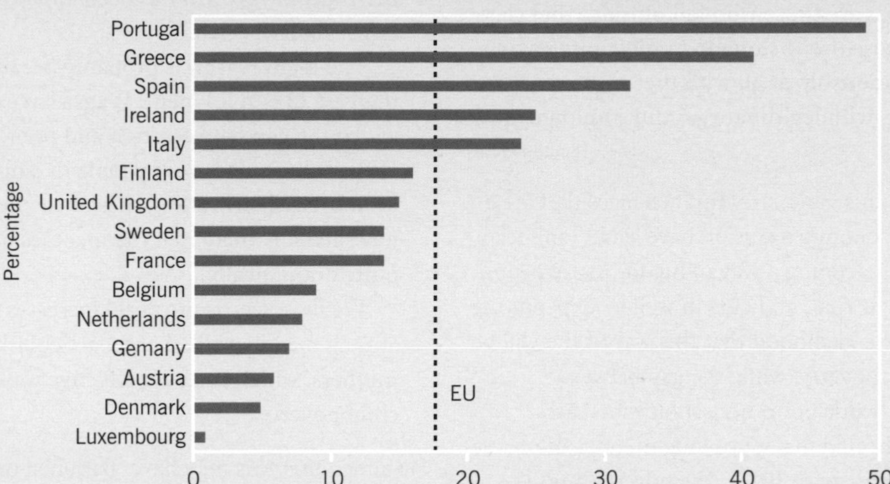

Figure 4.8 Percentage of people with incomes[1] below 60 per cent of the EU median: EU comparison, 2000

[1] Equivalized disposable income in each country.

Source: European Community Household Panel, Eurostat in *Social Trends* 34, 2004: 85

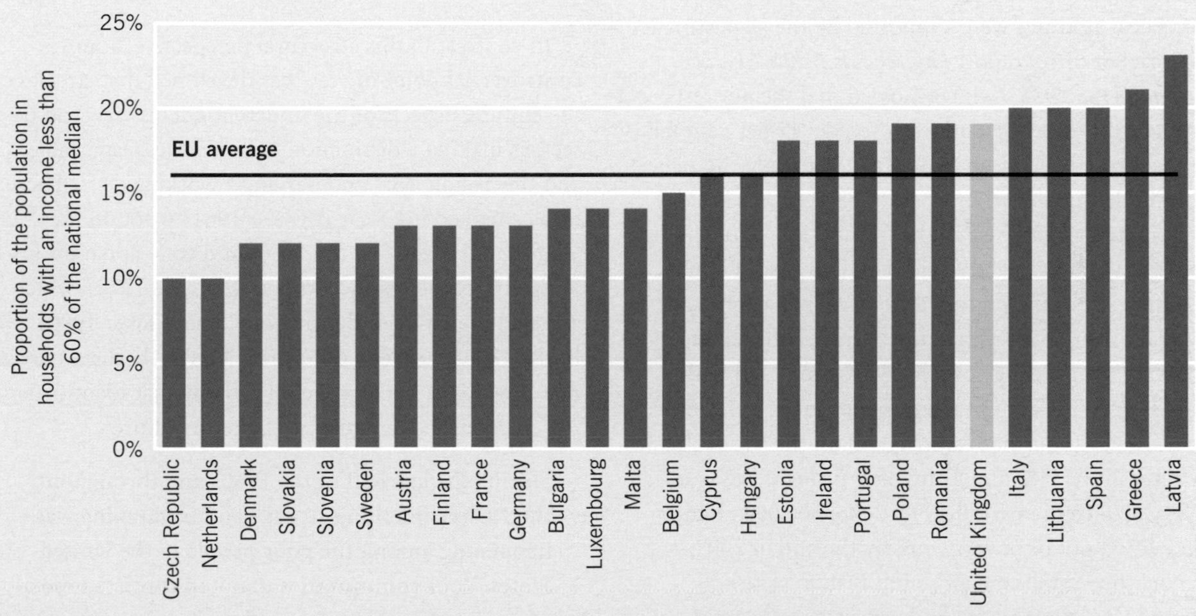

Figure 4.9 The UK has a higher proportion of its population in relatively low income than most other EU countries

Source: Eurostat; the data is for 2006 and is before deducting housing costs; updated January 2008

I accept that Britain does now have a group of poor people who are so distinguished from others on low income that it is appropriate to use the term 'underclass' to describe their position in the social hierarchy.

(Field 1989, quoted in Murray 1990: 37)

He goes on to suggest that the underclass includes three main groups: 'the very frail, elderly pensioner; the single parent with no chance of escaping welfare under the existing rules . . . and the long-term unemployed' (Field 1989, quoted in Murray 1990: 39).

Smith makes a case for defining the underclass in structural terms that are specifically related to legitimate opportunities for regular work:

> **The underclass are those who fall outside [the] class schema, because they belong to family units having no stable relationship at all with the 'mode of production' – with legitimate gainful employment.**
>
> (Smith 1992: 4)

According to this view, structural changes that are a direct result of economic recession have led to long-term unemployment becoming a way of life for many people. Changes in benefit rules and cuts in welfare expenditure have increased the likelihood that this way of life will be characterized by poverty, while the gap between 'work-rich' and 'work-poor' households increases. Studies have indicated that a growing number of people in Britain are living on or below the poverty line. The Joseph Rowntree Foundation report (1995) *Income and Wealth* concluded that inequalities of income and opportunity were widening: the top 10 per cent were becoming better off and the bottom 10 per cent worse off. These findings were supported by the Department of Social Security report *Households Below Average Income* (DSS 1994), which showed that the poorest one-tenth of the population suffered a 17 per cent fall in real income between 1979 and 1992 while the richest one-tenth enjoyed an increase of 62 per cent. It also highlighted an increase in the number of people living in poverty. Overall, 13.9 million children and adults (25 per cent of the population) were living below the official poverty line of half the average income after allowing for housing costs in 1992, compared with 5 million (9 per cent of the population) in 1979. Since 1997 New Labour has campaigned on the issue of child poverty in the UK, and Tony Blair promised to eradicate it by 2020. In the period 1998–2006, 600,000 children were lifted out of poverty but, by the end of 2007, almost three million children in Britain were still living below the poverty line (see www.jrf.org.uk/child-poverty). This suggests that poverty is an endemic feature of capitalist societies (on a global scale, see www.makepovertyhistory.org).

However, a study for the Organization for Economic Co-operation and Development (OECD) by Mark Pearson has suggested that since the start of the twenty-first century the gap between rich and poor in the UK has narrowed dramatically compared with other developed economies, mainly as a result of increasing employment:

> **Both ends of the distribution have been getting richer . . . but the poor have been getting richer more rapidly than the rich. Since the year 2000, their income growth has been about three times larger than the rich.**
>
> **The main reason is probably because of the increase in employment. Wages have continued to widen the gap between rich and poor, but because we have had a lot more people in employment and a lot more redistribution, these two effects combined have actually increased the incomes of the poor quite dramatically.**
>
> **We have seen quite rapid increases in employment among the low-skilled and particularly among mothers, which is a very effective way of reducing child poverty.**

He added that this may have 'flattened out' since 2005 and warned

> **Now we are entering a recession, which may increase inequality and poverty again.**
>
> (*Guardian* 21/10/08)

In contrast to this structural perspective, a more controversial point of view has developed that stresses the cultural aspects of the underclass. This view can be seen as making a distinction between the 'respectable' and the 'rough' (or 'undeserving') working class. These ideas emerged in Oscar Lewis's (1961) work on the 'culture of poverty' in the 1950s and were apparent in Sir Keith Joseph's policy initiatives in the 1970s, which targeted the 'cycle of deprivation' (see Walker 1990). In the 1980s the work of Charles Murray became part of a New Right perspective on poverty that identified the emergence of an antisocial ghetto culture:

> **During the last half of the 1960s and throughout the 1970s something strange and frightening was happening among the poor people in the United States. Poor communities that had consisted mostly of hardworking folks began deteriorating, sometimes falling apart altogether. Drugs, crime, illegitimacy, homelessness, drop out from the job market, drop out from school, casual violence – all the measures that were available to the social scientists showed large increases focused in poor communities. As the 1980s began, the growing population of 'the other kind of poor people' could no longer be ignored, and a label for them came into use. In the US we began to call them the underclass.**
>
> (Murray 1990: 2–3)

A closer look

A study for the Joseph Rowntree Foundation divided the population into five categories:

- *Core poor* – People who are income-poor, materially deprived and subjectively poor.
- *Breadline poor* – People living below a relative poverty line, and as such excluded from participating in the norms of society.
- *Non-poor, non-wealthy* – The remainder of the population classified as neither poor nor wealthy.
- *Asset wealthy* – Estimated using the relationship between housing wealth and the contemporary Inheritance Tax threshold.
- *Exclusive wealthy* – People with sufficient wealth to exclude themselves from the norms of society.

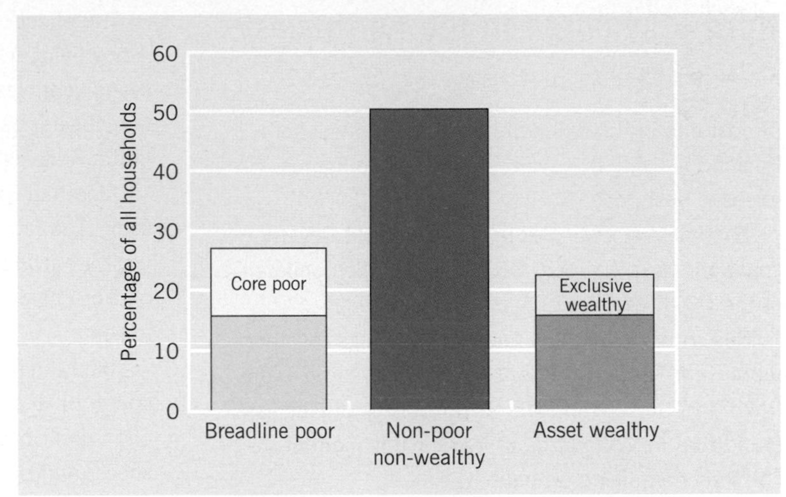

Figure 4.10 Distribution of all UK households, 2000

Within these categories, UK households are distributed as shown in Figure 4.10.

The study concluded:

> Over the past 15 years, more households have become poor, but fewer are very poor. Areas already wealthy have tended to become disproportionately wealthier, and we are seeing some evidence of increasing polarisation. In particular there are now areas in some of our cities where over half of all households are breadline poor.
>
> (Dorling *et al.* 2007: xiv available as a free download from www.jrf.org.uk)

The patterns of poverty may have shifted but the consequences remain stubbornly consistent particularly in relation to social problems:

> People on the edges of the labour market are likely to experience multiple disadvantage – unemployment, poor housing, ill health, disability and poverty. Social workers will tend to work (with these people in) . . . areas characterised by rented accommodation . . . lack of facilities, schools will be low in the league tables (and) students are likely to have low morale, and there will be high rates of absence and truancy . . . These are places of social exclusion where residents are barred from the mainstream of opportunities available to the rest of society.
>
> (Parrott 1999: 51)

When asked to apply his ideas to Britain, Murray found no difficulty in discovering a similar group defined by their 'deplorable behaviour' rather than their structural position. This subculture not only marks them off from the respectable working class but also serves to transmit underclass membership from one generation to the next:

> **I am not talking here about an unemployment problem that can be solved by more jobs, nor about a poverty problem that can be solved by higher benefits. Britain has a growing population of work-aged, healthy people who live in a different world from other Britons, who are raising their children to live in it, and whose**

Case study

A third of children in the north-west live in poverty

Almost one in three children in the north-west of England is living in poverty, according to figures released yesterday.

The latest statistics from the End Child Poverty coalition show that 450,000 of 1.5 million children in the region are living below the breadline.

Research for the coalition, which brings together more than 75 organisations such as Barnardo's, the Children's Society and the Royal College of Nurses, found that in 215 wards at least 30 per cent of children were living on benefits.

Of these poorest wards, 75 were in Greater Manchester, 66 in Merseyside, 46 in Lancashire, 15 in Cumbria and 13 in Cheshire. Among the worst-affected areas were Blackfriars in Salford, where 60.8 per cent of children live on benefits, Hulme in Manchester, where the figure is 68.5 per cent, Princess in Knowsley (69 per cent) and Granby in Liverpool (71.9 per cent).

The coalition says that overall, 3.6 million children (28 per cent of the UK child population) are living in poverty. The proportion of children living below the breadline rose from one in 10 in 1979 to one in three in 1998 . . .

The effect of poverty reduces life expectancy. A boy living in Manchester can expect to live seven years less than a boy in Barnet. A girl from Manchester can expect to live six years less than a girl in Kensington and Chelsea.

Jonathan Stearn, the director of End Child Poverty, said: 'The fact that 450,000 children in the north-west are living in poverty – the highest number in any part of England outside London – is a blight on the region.

'Such high levels of poverty shame a prosperous country like ours. We are talking about children who often don't have warm winter coats, weatherproof shoes, and don't have three square meals a day.'

Figures from the charity in Yorkshire and North Lincolnshire showed that the worst-affected areas were the Manor Estate in Sheffield, where 53 per cent of families live on benefits, and Hull's Myton ward, where the figure was 54 per cent. A third of the 1.1 million children in the region are living in poverty.

(Helen Carter, *Guardian* 12.3.05)

Questions

1. How would you explain such levels of child poverty in the north-west of England?
2. Why should poverty have any impact on life expectancy?

values are now contaminating the life of entire communities.

(Murray, quoted in *The Sunday Times* 26.11.89)

A slightly more sympathetic view, which still adopts a culturalist perspective, is that of Ralph Dahrendorf (1992), who argues that, partly through choice but also due to changes in long-term unemployment and family structure, there is now a distinct category of people who are redundant to the needs of modern capitalism and are in danger of falling out of the social and political system altogether. As such they challenge the idea of 'citizenship' discussed earlier (pp. 183–184) and indeed represent a threat to social order.

In different ways, these writers have used the term 'underclass' to denote a group in society that exists below or beyond the traditional class structure. The term itself indicates that they should be seen as a distinct class; however, few sociologists would agree that people who are poor, marginalized and out of work should be treated as a separate class with its own identity, interests and lifestyle. Although Dahrendorf popularized the term in Britain, he is adamant that 'there is no technical or proper sociological sense in which this particular category can ever be called a class' (Dahrendorf 1992: 55). Marxists such as Stuart Hall (1977) and Weberians such as Ray Pahl (1984) would agree that, despite being largely excluded from the opportunity structure of society, it is misleading to represent the underclass as a permanent and stable class, conscious of its own interests. Rather, it has tended to be seen as constituting a fraction of the

A closer look

Despite difficulties in defining the term, the underclass has entered political discourse and is widely used by journalists and politicians. Labour M.P. Frank Field has been discussing the issue since the 1980s while Labour ministers have talked of intervening in the lives of poor children to deter them from crime. In 2006 the Conservative Party published a report entitled *Breakdown Britain* which identified dysfunctional families in the poorest communities as the source of crime, drug abuse and educational failure. In 2008 Chris Grayling (Shadow Work and Pensions Secretary) fuelled the debate in a speech to the Demos think tank:

'In too many places, in too many communities, we have a Jeremy Kyle generation of young men reaching adult life ill-equipped for it . . . Lacking the right social skills. Lacking a sense of purpose and responsibility. Lacking self-confidence. Lacking the ability to seize on an opportunity and make the most of it and as a result turning against the society in which they live . . . Family break-up often means that there is no father figure in childhood. Teaching recruitment patterns often mean there are few male role models at school.

For those whose skills are not academic, the path into stable employment is much less clear than it was for past generations . . . And so while the craft jobs of today are occupied en masse by young men from eastern Europe, our own young men all too often hang around on the fringes, uncertain about where and how to build their lives.'

There was a danger of this continuing from generation to generation, Mr Grayling added:

'Our young boys are too often drawing lessons about life from footballers and celebrities who behave in monstrously inappropriate ways.'

Accusing Prime Minister Gordon Brown of undermining the role of young men in society, he said: 'The New Deal and the welfare programme have been inadequate, the criminal justice system too soft.

It is morally negligent to abandon so many young men, so, I want this speech to spark a debate about how to end the inequality of hope.

We need to provide leadership in government to create a climate for the social entrepreneurs to flourish and re-engage young men.

Second, we need to promote positive, socially responsible male role models and third, we need practical measures to combat family breakdown, worklessness and poor educational opportunity.'

(adapted from BBC News website 11/2/08)

Questions

1. What do you think Grayling means by 'a Jeremy Kyle generation of young men'?
2. In what ways does he link the underclass with male crime?

working class, despite the fact that it may have a distinct social character in terms of ethnicity, gender, age and cultural attitude.

Although it has excited a good deal of theoretical interest, the underclass has not been subjected to much empirical scrutiny. However, Anthony Heath (1992) used information from the 1987 British Election Survey and the 1989 British Social Attitudes Survey to study the attitudes of members of the underclass, investigating orientation to work and political attitudes of two samples (the long-term and the short-term) of the underclass. He concluded that it was difficult to identify the underclass as a distinct community with negative attitudes towards family values, work and other mainstream institutions.

'Class is dead; long live class'

In this chapter we have examined the concept of social stratification and, in particular, the relevance of social class. Discounted by many writers as an outdated notion more suited to the 'two nations' of nineteenth-century Britain, it retains for many sociologists a significance in the twenty-first century that has hardly been diminished by social, economic or political change. As Scott puts it, 'class remains the sociological key to understanding the structure of society' (Scott 1994: 19).

For Scase (1992), the relevance of class for ordinary people may be somewhat vague, but for sociologists 'it remains a concept that is vital for understanding the structure of present-day capitalist society'. As a Marxist, Scase argues that it is not possible to contemplate society without reference to the role played by social classes in the formation and maintenance of capitalism:

> **The analysis of class is inherent to the study of capitalist society. Western industrial societies are capitalist and, hence, their economic development is determined by the interplay of class forces of one kind or another. The fact that the prime objective of capitalist corporations is to make profits means that they are characterised by relations of exploitation and control and, hence, consist of class relations . . . It is for this reason that social class will continue to remain central to sociological analysis.**
>
> (Scase 1992: 81)

To some extent this view is matched by Edgell (1993), who emphasizes the importance of social class as the major source of structural social inequality. The significance of social class as the basis of social identity and political action may have been diluted over time, but this is due largely to the power of capital and the relative weakness of the 'propertyless classes'. Instead of raising the question of the extent of class consciousness in contemporary society we should be questioning the assumption that society has become a classless meritocracy:

> **The main obstacle to the establishment of a multi-class or non-egalitarian classless democratic society is the persistence of class inequalities . . . Hence, what needs to be explained is not the presumed demise of class, but the tenacity of class-based patterns of inequality and politics, and much else besides. In the meantime, class rules and classlessness remain a dream rather than a reality.**
>
> (Edgell 1993: 122)

Houtt *et al.* (1996) reject the arguments of Clark and Lipset (see p. 182) that the concept of class has been rendered obsolete by the fragmentation of stratification in the workplace, government and family life. They argue that Clark and Lipset have confused social class with social status, which diverts our attention away from the enduring inequalities of wealth and power with vague references to the decline of hierarchy. By returning to the three 'situses' of economics, politics and family life outlined by Clark and Lipset, Houtt *et al.* argue that social class is still related to social opportunities and lifestyle in all three areas of social organization.

Although they acknowledge the changing and complex nature of social class in modern societies, they insist that it still maintains a key role in understanding social relations:

World in focus

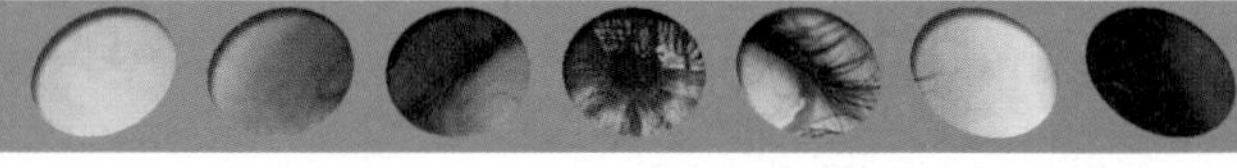

'All comrades are equal but some are more equal than others': inequality in the People's Republic of China

55 years after the foundation of a classless society in China, observers have commented upon the increasing gap between the rural poor and a new elite of wealthy entrepreneurs in its major cities. In a report for the World Bank, David Dollar (2007) reports that the rapid growth of the Chinese economy may have produced a dramatic rise in per capita income and a decline in poverty but it has also created new disparities:

> **'Income inequality has risen, propelled by the rural-urban income gap and by the growing disparity between highly educated urban professionals and the urban working class. There have also been increases in inequality of health and education outcomes'.**

In a Newsnight report, by Paul Mason, a top class restaurant is used as a metaphor for what is happening across the country as a whole.

With 220 tables, 700 staff the Jincaicheng Restaurant (known locally as 'The Aircraft Carrier') is

World in focus *continued*

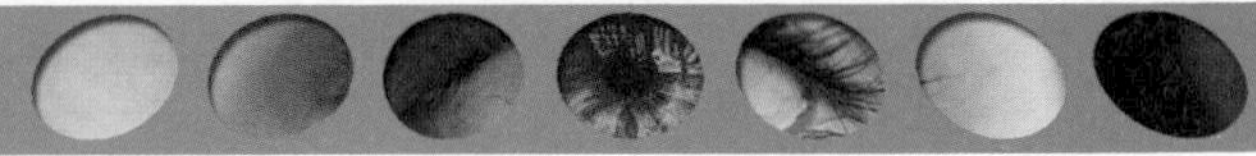

the biggest restaurant in Tianjin, China's third largest city. It caters for guests from a range of backgrounds and employs a variety of skilled staff on very different levels of pay. For this reason Mason chose it as an ideal venue for assessing the impact on the class structure of China's economic boom.

Yang Ming (trainee waitress)

Yang Ming comes from the rural province of Hainan, 2000km to the south of Tianjin where she lived on the eight-roomed family farm and shared the basic agricultural chores. She exchanged this for a bunk bed in a dormitory for 30 girls and a pay packet of £20 per month with one day off per week. Despite concerns for her safety and complaints about the strict discipline she is determined to make a new life for herself:

> **'Living in the village restricts what you see and learn. Some girls stay in the village all their life until they get married. I don't want that kind of life.'**

Figure 4.11 Yang Ming
BBC Motion Gallery

Peasant migrants like Yang Ming are a major component in China's economic revolution – by 2005, 140 million had already made similar journeys from the countryside. At the Jincaicheng Restaurant rural migrants make up 90 per cent of the workforce.

Mu Xing Ha (head chef)

Mu Xing Ha qualified as a chef after leaving school in the 1980s and has noticed changes in his clientele and their tastes:

> **'Before customers came to the restaurant just to eat. Just to fill in their stomachs with food. They didn't want vegetables or seafood much. Nowadays, customers are choosing a variety of food to meet their tastes. They're ordering meat, seafood, vegetables and salad, etc. They're demanding top quality ingredients for every dish, and they're trying different kinds of cuisine.'**

Not only does he enjoy the professional challenges this new affluence brings but his life has improved materially as well. He is in the middle of the management structure at the restaurant and gets paid 20 times what a waitress earns. In the past 20 years his wages have increased ten fold. This may be good news for Ma Xing Ha but it creates a potential headache for China's leadership as such differences in pay make China 'one of the most unequal on earth'.

Ma Ya Cui (CEO)

Ma Ya Cui is the Chief Executive of the Jincaicheng. She would not reveal her pay but Paul Mason suggests that her yuppie life style and posh waterfront apartment indicates a pay scale well above that of her Head Chef.

Despite operating a thriving business, Ma Ya Cui's background is firmly grounded in the state-run business sector from where she was head hunted by TEDA (the state-owned investment organisation which bought out the failing department store that stood on the site of the Jincaicheng). She clearly knows where her loyalties lie and sees no contradiction between being a successful entrepreneur in the free market and faithful servant of the state at the same time:

> **'I've been involved in state-run businesses for the past 20 years,' she says. My philosophy's to be loyal to the Party, because I am a senior manager. I also have to be loyal to the company. In other words, my mottoes are loyalty and obedience.'**

Figure 4.12 Ma Ya Cui
BBC Motion Gallery

▶

World in focus *continued*

As the wealth gap in China grows alongside increasing aspirations for a better life, it could be that the economic dream turns into a political nightmare:

> 'It's created a kind of social escalator' says Mason 'it moves faster at the top than at the bottom, but once you're on it, for now, the only way is up. The problem is, two-thirds of China's population haven't even got a foot on the bottom step. And no one wants to contemplate what might happen if it should ever stop'.

Questions

1. How does the Jincaicheng Restaurant serve as a metaphor for what is happening in China?
2. Why might market reform and wealth creation lead to social unrest?

> **The persistence of class-based inequalities in capitalist societies suggest that in the foreseeable future the concept of class will – and should – play an important role in sociological research . . . As citizens and sociologists we would very much like to live in a world in which class inequalities have disappeared. But . . . class society is not yet dying, and truly classless societies have not yet been born.**
>
> (Houtt *et al.* 1996: 58–9)

The relevance of class analysis, particularly in areas such as health, housing and education, remains clear. However, as indicated in our discussion of Weber, social class is not the only means by which social inequality is transmitted. Since the early 1970s sociologists have become more aware of the relative importance of gender, race and disability as the bases of structured inequality and discrimination. These three areas are examined in Chapters 5, 6 and 8.

Summary

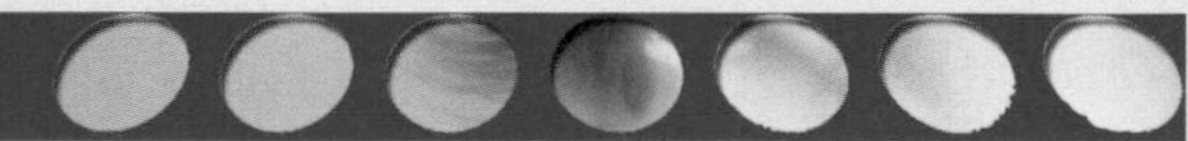

- Historically most societies develop some form of stratification system.
- Most sociologists regard modern industrial societies as being stratified on the basis of social class.
- Sociologists have provided various theoretical 'class maps' and class categories based on Marxist, Weberian and functionalist models.
- The significance of social class in the twenty-first century is a matter of continuing sociological debate.
- On the one hand, it has been argued that changes in the structure of society have reduced the importance of class as a tool for sociological analysis.
- On the other hand, while acknowledging that the class structure has been affected by social and economic changes, there is evidence that social class continues to affect lifestyle, opportunities, consciousness and behaviour; the upper, middle and working classes continue to be important divisions in modern society.

Links

This chapter has strong links to Chapter 2 on sociological theories, particularly the section on Marx and social class (pp. 61–63).

Social class is a factor that strongly influences life chances and opportunities and features in the chapters on work (Chapter 12), health (Chapter 13), crime (Chapter 14) and education (Chapter 15).

Further reading

Crompton, R. (2008) *Class and Stratification*, Cambridge: Polity Press.
A detailed examination of the complexities of class and status, especially recommended for pursuing this area of study beyond foundation undergraduate level. Now in its third edition, it has become something of a classic.

Goodman A., Johnson, P. and Webb, S. (1997) *Inequality in the UK*, Oxford: Oxford University Press.
An empirical study of inequality in the UK.

Lee, D. and Turner, B.S. (1996) *Conflicts about Class: Debating Inequality in Late Industrialism*, London: Longman.
An important assessment of the relevance of class in late-twentieth-century Britain.

Payne, G. (2006) *Social Divisions*, London: Macmillan.
A useful introduction to the debates surrounding social divisions including class, gender, ethnicity, age, disability and so on.

Reid, I. (1998) *Class in Britain*, Cambridge: Polity Press.
An excellent review of the correlations between class position and life chances that covers areas such as wealth, pay, health, education and housing.

Roberts, K. (2001) *Class in Modern Britain*, London: Macmillan.
A useful review of the debates around class structure and mobility in contemporary Britain.

Scott, J. (1991) *Who Rules Britain?*, Cambridge: Polity Press.

Scott, J. (1994) *Poverty and Wealth: Citizenship, Deprivation and Privilege*, London: Longman.

Scott, J. (1997) *Corporate Business and Capitalist Classes*, Oxford: Oxford University Press.
John Scott is one of the few sociologists to undertake a comprehensive analysis of the rich and powerful; these are summaries of the patterns of wealth and poverty distribution in the UK and abroad.

Shaw, M., Galobardes, B., Lawlor, D., *et al.* (2007) *The Handbook of Inequality and Socioeconomic Position*, Bristol: Policy Press.
An essential starting point for anyone wishing to understand the key concepts and criteria used in the measurement of economic and social inequality. Particularly useful for second- and third-year undergraduates specializing in areas such as poverty, social class and social policy.

Smith, D. (1992) *Understanding the Underclass*, London: Policy Studies Institute.
A collection of readings from the key contributors to the underclass debate, such as Dahrendorf, Murray and Field.

Regular sources of updated empirical material are in the journal *Labour Research*, publications of the Child Poverty Action Group and *Social Trends*.

Websites

www.statistics.gov.uk

Provides a wealth of data on class-related trends in the UK.

www.inequality.org

A US-based site that highlights the concentration of wealth, income and power in the USA.

www.trinity.edu/~mkearl

A fascinating sociological trawl through cyberspace – clicking on 'social inequality' provides many sources of information and weblinks (largely American).

www.makepovertyhistory.org

A useful campaign site that highlights a range of issues related to global poverty.

www.cpag.org.uk

Founded in 1965, the Child Poverty Action Group is the leading charity in the fight against child poverty in the UK.

www.jrf.org.uk

With a mission to 'overcome the causes of poverty, disadvantage and social evil', the Joseph Rowntree Foundation has a commitment to achieve this through research and evidence. A great source of information and ideas (essentially UK-focused).

Activities

Activity 1

Value, status and (in)dispensability

Occupational scales

Attempts to reconcile the differences over class and status in evaluation of an individual's position in society have generally involved classifying people according to their job based on the assumption that some jobs are more prestigious/important than others. Rate the following jobs in order of importance from 1 (most important) to 6 (least important): coal-miner; electrician; refuse collector; director of advertising agency; nurse; High Court judge.

Are you a worker?

What is a worker? That's the question . . . provoked by our criticism of the Greenham Common protesters as predominantly middle class.

Ann Roderick, for example, naturally enough feels insulted when she is put – as a school teacher – in the same category as 'vicars' wives'.

The issues raised here are very important. A majority of the workforce in Britain, along with other advanced industrial countries, does white-collar work. Does that mean, as ruling class propagandists (and even some socialists) claim, that the working class is disappearing?

Class

The answer depends, obviously, on what you mean by class. Academic sociologists attach a great deal of importance to status – to how the job is seen by those doing it, and by others. Historically, there has certainly been a difference of status between manual and white-collar jobs. This is reflected in the fact that even today most white-collar workers work shorter hours and enjoy better pension rights than their manual counterparts.

Does this mean that they belong to different classes? Not according to Marx. For him, a person's class position is determined by his or her relation to the means of production. And this relationship is crucial because control over the means of production gives you the power to exploit the labour of others.

Equally, lack of such control makes you liable to be exploited. So, anyone who is compelled by their economic position to sell their labour-power is, according to Marx, a worker. A worker is someone who has the choice between working and starving because they do not control the means of production.

Control

From this standpoint a shorthand typist or word-processor operator is as much a worker as a miner or engineer. Both . . . must sell their labour-power to live.

So what has happened in the past 40 years is that the structure of the working class has changed. There are fewer manual workers in industries such as mining and manufacturing, but more typists and other clerical workers.

The size of the working class has increased overall, not shrunk . . . Most white-collar workers are not middle-class.

But this isn't the end of the story. All white-collar workers aren't middle class, but some of them are. Those that form what is sometimes called the 'new middle class'.

(Alex Callinicos, *Socialist Worker*, undated)

Questions

1. What criteria did you use in 'rating' the six occupations? Which of these criteria were objective and which subjective?
2. Does the order coincide with classifications based on the conventional division between manual and non-manual occupations?
3. The article by Alex Callinicos looks at problems with the division between manual/working-class and non-manual/middle-class occupations. What difficulties do you think there are with this method of categorizing occupations?

Activity 2a

The underclass

The underclass spawns illegitimate children without a care for tomorrow and feeds on a crime rate which rivals the United States in property offences. Its able-bodied youths see no point in working and feel no compulsion either. They reject society while feeding off it: they are becoming a lost generation giving the cycle of deprivation a new spin . . . No amount of income redistribution or social engineering can solve their problem. Their sub-life styles are beyond welfare benefit rises and job creation schemes. They exist as active social outcasts, wedded to an anti-social system.

(Charles Murray, *The Sunday Times* 26.11.89)

Questions

1. What evidence can you find to support Murray's view?
2. What 'solutions' do you feel Murray would offer to deal with the problem of an underclass? What criticisms can be made of this approach?
3. There have been various publicity stunts by Conservative politicians who have claimed that they and their families have managed to live quite adequately for a week on income support. Find out how much you would get on income support and work out how you would spend your weekly payments. What kind of changes would you have to make to your current lifestyle? What are the strengths and weaknesses of approaching a social problem in this way?

Activity 2b

Investigating the rich

Questions

Using *The Sunday Times* Rich List (which can be found at www.timesonline.co.uk), find out the answers to the following questions:

1. Who is the richest man/woman?
2. Who is top of the pops?
3. How many aristocrats are there?
4. Identify oldest/youngest.
5. Which forms of wealth creation tend to dominate the list?
6. How has the creation of wealth changed over time? You will need to track down previous Rich List and Forbes (see below) information to do this.
7. Identify an individual from the Rich List – find out as much as you can about them, how they made their money and what they do with it.

See also the Forbes listing for the richest people in the world at www.forbes.com/billionaires/

How rich are you? Go to the Care International website www.globalrichlist.com/index.php and find out.

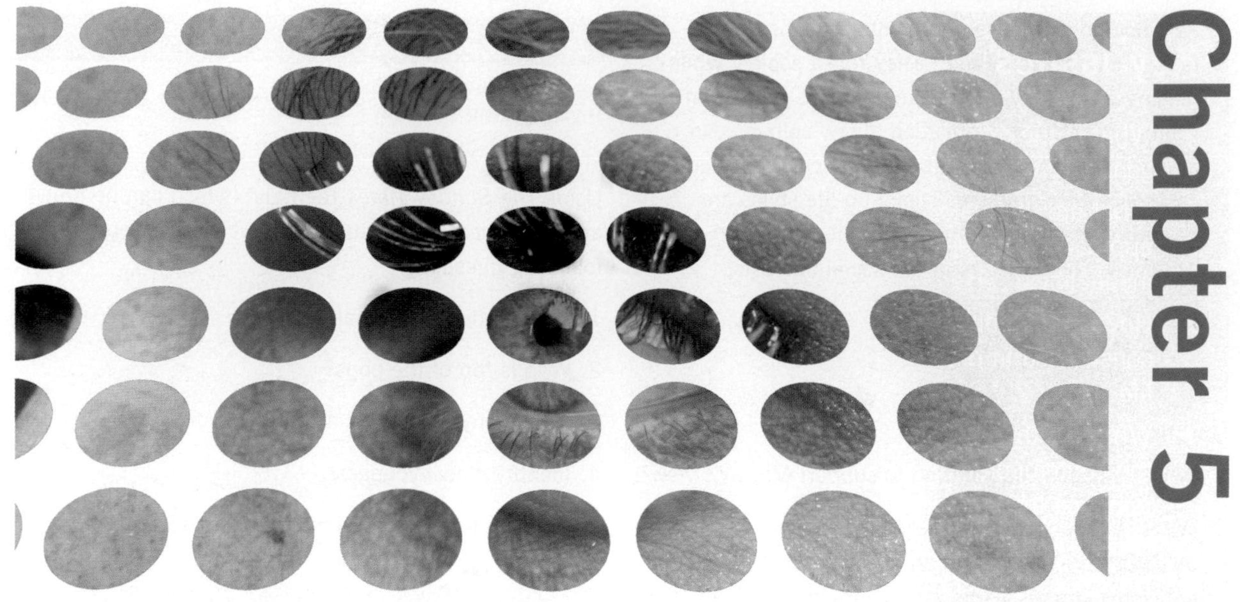

Chapter 5

Gender

Jennifer Marchbank and Gayle Letherby

I am a human being who would rather not be addressed as Ms. or Mr., ma'am or sir. I prefer to use gender-neutral pronouns like sie (pronounced like '*see*') and hir (pronounced like '*here*') to describe myself. I am a person who faces almost insurmountable difficulty when instructed to check off an 'F' or an 'M' box on identification papers.

I'm not at odds with the fact that I was born female-bodied. Nor do I identify as an intermediate sex. I simply do not fit the prevalent Western concepts of what a woman or a man 'should' look like. And that reality has dramatically directed the course of my life . . .

All your life you've heard such dogma about what it means to be a 'real' woman or a 'real' man. And chances are you've choked on some of it. You've balked at the idea that being a woman means having to be thin as a rail, emotionally nurturing, and an airhead when it comes to balancing her checkbook. You know in your guts that being a man has nothing to do with rippling muscles, innate courage, or knowing how to handle a chain saw. These are really caricatures. Yet these images have been drilled into us through popular culture and education over the years . . . These gender messages play on and on in a continuous loop in our brains, like commercials that can't be muted. (Feinberg 1998: 1–4)

Key issues

- What is the difference between sex and gender?
- What are the major theoretical approaches to gender differences and inequalities?
- How are femininities and masculinities constructed in different areas of social life?
- What are the major gender divisions in the contemporary world, and how do they reinforce the subordinate position of women in society?
- How does gender interact with other social factors such as 'race' and ethnicity, sexuality, social class and disability?

Introduction

The author of the extract opposite, Leslie Feinberg (Figure 5.1), is a long-time transgender activist. Sie clearly points out that our concepts of gender are fixed on a binary proposition – in fact, a binary opposition: that of masculinity and femininity being separate and opposite experiences and identities. Gender is understood culturally and theoretically as a dualism. As such, avoiding being treated as a 'man' or a 'woman' is clearly a struggle. Gender is a key factor that shapes social behaviour and social institutions. Yet gender differences are something that we often take so much for granted, that seem so 'normal', that they often remain invisible to us. However, Tam Sangar (2008) argues that the narratives, the stories, of transpeople offer points of resistance that challenge this binary notion and therefore destabilize hegemonic ideas of gender.

A closer look

Sex and gender

From the 1970s social scientists began to make a distinction between sex and gender.

> Gender is usually seen as a socially determined difference based upon the biological differences between the sexes. Sex, the state of being either female or male, is determined by biological characteristics such as anatomical, reproductive and chromosomal attributes. Sex is deemed to be natural whereas gender is seen as the social expression of natural, biological differences primarily based upon the appearance of genitals.
>
> (Marchbank and Letherby 2007: 5)

This distinction between sex and gender implies two concepts that can be separated unambiguously; it also implies that while gender is shaped by social factors, biological sex is not and is based on an assumption that there are two distinct biological sexes. Some sociologists and natural scientists question these rigid distinctions.

Sex = Gender?

Gender is usually described as socially constructed, and sex as biological. The categorizing of all human beings as 'male' or 'female' is left unquestioned. However, this does not always fit with local realities. For example, cultures of eunuchs in India, travestis in Brazil, ladyboys in Thailand and transgender in the USA suggest that there is more to sex than just male and female. Perhaps ideas of sex are socially constructed too.

> You don't need genitals for politics. You need brains.
>
> (Shabna Nehru, the first eunuch politician to run for parliament in India; *New Internationalist*, 2000, 328)

Figure 5.1 Leslie Feinberg
© Marilyn Humphries

Stop and think

- Think about walking down the main street of any Western city or town. What gender distinctions are there between shops and between departments in shops? What gender distinctions are there among the staff in shops? Are most shoppers women or men? Are most car drivers women or men? Are most van and delivery drivers women or men?
- What other gender distinctions between women and men might you see in the street?

R.W. Connell (1987, 2002) describes the street as a 'gender regime'. A gender regime consists of the social relations based on distinctions between women and men. It is a 'theoretical model of gender relations as a regime or system with a limited number of key elements' (Walby 2004a: 9). Connell (1987) points out that all social settings, including formal and more informal organizations, have gender regimes. More recently, the concept has been employed in the investigation of gender equality in the European Union (EU) (Walby 2004b), asylum practices and procedures (Oxford, 2005) and organizational behaviour, such as Joan Acker's (2002) study of change in Swedish banks.

Gender does not exist on its own. It interacts with other social differences; for example, in Western societies, an adult woman wearing makeup is socially acceptable but most people would feel uncomfortable seeing a three-year-old girl in mascara and lipstick. Likewise, the physical strength expected of a man aged 30 is not an integral part of an 80-year-old man's masculinity. Differences also exist across geography and culture; for example, in Australia 'mateship' is a socially acceptable practice of preferring the company of men over women that developed 'in the context of the harsh reality of bush life for men without female companionship' (Pease 2001: 191). Even within single states, in the following case South Africa, cultural practices vary, yet the underlying reason for them may be the same:

> **in a workshop held in a government agency, an Afrikaner man indicated that he was taught, 'ladies first'. An African man who came from the Xhosa community then said in his culture, the rule was 'men first'. The reason, he explained, was to protect the family from an animal or the enemy. In the discussion of these apparently opposite rules, it was noted that both are based on an assumption that women are weaker and need either protection or assistance.**
>
> (Horowitz 2001: 234)

Traditionally, sociology neglected gender as a factor that shapes our social experiences. Feminism, in its struggle to understand women's oppression, has placed gender on the broader sociological agenda. Increasingly it is recognized that gender is a crucial factor in shaping individual experience and identity, as well as social institutions, and must be taken into account by sociologists for a full understanding of all social processes. In 1990 Mary Maynard argued that the study of gender was reshaping sociology. By the fiftieth anniversary of the British Sociological Association in 2001, her view was shared by several past presidents of the association, who, when asked about the highlights and low points in British society over the previous 50 years, cited feminism as a highlight (British Sociological Association 2001). In addition as Stephen Whitehead and Frank Barrett state:

> **we would go so far as to suggest that feminism was the single most powerful political discourse of the twentieth century . . . one of the direct consequences of feminist thinking and action has been to expose and highlight the power, position and practices of men . . . feminism puts men and masculinities in a critical spotlight . . .**
>
> (Whitehead and Barrett 2001: 3)

(See Chapter 4 in Marchbank and Letherby 2007 for further discussion.)

The sociological study of gender shows that gender shapes the experiences of women and men differently in many areas of social life and remains a source of inequality in society.

Explaining gender differences

Although feminism may now be accepted as a main strength of sociological work, this has not always been the case; nor have feminist insights been accepted uncritically. Sociology has attempted to explain gender differences in a number of ways, and here we will look at biological explanations and their critiques, and socialization explorations and their limitations for explaining both female and male experience. We will also consider how the very discourses employed by society assist in the shaping of gender identity and 'norms'.

Born to be a man/woman

Sociologists have concerned themselves with the biological category of sex because sex differences have often been proposed as explanations for the differences in social roles performed by women and men. Essentialist, or biological, arguments attribute the different social roles performed by women and men to underlying biological structures, particularly reproductive differences or hormonal difference. The 'natural' differences between women and men are seen to contribute to an organization of social relations in which women nurture and men go out to work. Biologically deterministic explanations of sexual difference have a long history in scientific and pre-scientific thinking, although the form of the biological arguments has changed over the years as scientific techniques and knowledge develop. Essentialism and biological determinism are umbrella terms for a range of approaches that emphasize biological factors. In the 1950s the functionalist sociologist Talcott Parsons argued that there are natural differences between women and men that mean they are suited for particular roles in society (Parsons and Bales 1955). This sex-role theory, particularly dominant in the years from the Second World War until the re-emergence of feminism in the 1970s (feminist movements had existed in Western and other societies, e.g. in India, from the 1880s to the 1930s), asserted that women have an instinct to nurture that suits them for

A closer look

Difference and inequality

Two key themes recur in sociological theory and research on gender: difference and inequality.

- Difference concerns how distinctions are made between women and men. Various theoretical approaches have been proposed to explain these differences. Sociologists have been concerned with examining how different social relationships, institutions and processes distinguish between women and men and create meanings about femininity and masculinity.
- Inequality concerns how gender distinctions are linked to inequalities, hierarchy and power relations. Sociologists have examined whether social distinctions between women and men create or reinforce inequalities between them, and the unequal distribution of resources and/or access to opportunity.

an 'expressive' role in the nuclear family; male biology, on the other hand, which leads men to be more aggressive and competitive, means that men are suited to an 'instrumental' role in the family, providing economic support and links with the outside world. As such, biological differences were seen to constitute a practical and 'natural' basis for the sexual division of labour. Biological theories also often present heterosexuality as the 'normal' and 'natural' expression of human sexuality, and identify women and men as having different sexual needs and desires.

Biological explanations have been marginalized within sociology for some time, but they still abound in our culture and new biological theories are often proposed. For example, Anne Moir and David Jessel (1989) in their book *Brain Sex* bring together what they argue is evidence to support prenatal hormone theory, based on the influence of testosterone on thought processes and emotions. They suggest that these hormonal differences mean that in effect the wiring of the brain is different in women and men. They are keen to point out that women should be seen as different but not inferior, and they emphasize that women's verbal and people skills should be increasingly valued in the labour market. More recently, psychological studies have entered the ether of the public media.

For many years sociobiologists have provided a whole range of theories for gender differences, connected to Darwin's theory of evolution. A key criticism of these essentialist approaches is that they are

Case study

Male and female brains

Scientists have long debated whether or not there are differences between the brains of males and females. Simon Baron-Cohen (2003) argues that 'the female brain is predominantly hard-wired for empathy, and the male brain is predominantly hard-wired for understanding and building systems'. He goes on to point out that this is not to say all women have a female brain and all men a male one, but that, on average, more males have a systemizing brain and more women an empathizing brain. The results of his experiments show that by a year old, girls will look longer at a face and boys longer at a mechanical mobile. This is determined partly, according to Baron-Cohen, by the presence of testosterone in the uterus during development.

> **We, of course, know that, with time, culture and socialisation do play a role in determining a male brain (stronger interest in systems) or female brain (stronger interest in empathy). But these studies strongly suggest that biology also partly determines this.**
>
> **The theory is saying that, on average, males and females differ in what they are drawn to and what they find easy, but that both sexes have their strengths and their weaknesses. Neither sex is superior overall . . .**
>
> (Baron-Cohen 2003)

In 2005 the US news agency ABC reported on new findings that revealed sex differences in the brain. Amanda Onion wrote:

> **From the way we record information to how we process language to the size of our brains and different regions of the brain, clear differences have emerged through animal studies and the use of technology such as brain scanning. And this is just the beginning.**
>
> (Onion 2005)

Quoting Nancy Forger of the University of Massachusetts, Onion reports that depression is twice as common in women as in men and that 'nearly all neurodevelopmental diseases are either more common in one gender or more severe in one gender'. This variability includes up to 100 sex differences, including how men and women encode memories, how men's and women's brains react to verbal and spatial tasks and why it seems that girls learn to speak before boys do. The answer to why this variability exists is explained in Onion's article as the presence of testosterone in the womb.

(Baron-Cohen 2003)

biologically deterministic and neglect social influences on behaviour (Bem 1993; Oakley 1972). They also neglect how biological features themselves interact with the environment in which they are situated: sociobiology greatly underestimates the contribution of cultures and histories to gender development.

Biological approaches also assume rigid distinctions between women and men and rely on the assumption that the categories 'women' and 'men' are universal groups sharing a universal biology and personality. (See Mead's New Guinea study below for a different view that shows gender roles as malleable.) These theories do not account for diversity: they do not account for biological women who display masculine behaviour and take on masculine roles, or biological men who display feminine traits, except to define them as biological deviants. There is a great deal of autobiographical evidence from individuals who feel that their gender identity does not correspond to their biological sex or who feel restricted by a culture that allows gender identity to be expressed only in terms of the female–male dualism (see Bornstein 1994; Feinberg 1998). Further, sociologists point to the variation across cultures of what it means to be a woman or a man. Much anthropological and sociological research evidence shows cultural variation in gender roles.

Within many contemporary societies, women effectively perform conventional male roles in, for example, the military (Jacobs *et al.* 2000); similarly, men can be found involved in child care and non-traditionally masculine work. Some sociologists have argued that we have become blinkered by gender distinctions. In Western culture we make a rigid distinction between female and male and then judge everyone else in relation to this dichotomy and attempt to place them within one of two categories. We impose social meanings on to our human biology. In the 1970s Ann Oakley (1972, 1974b) argued that it was misleading to think in terms of two distinct sexes and more useful to think in terms of the female and the male being placed at the ends of a continuum, with overlap. Many sociologists now challenge the notion of two distinct sexes and propose that the male–female dichotomy itself is a social construct; the lives of intersex and transgender people indicate that this may very well be the case.

Sociologists have engaged in the nature/nurture debate on whether differences in personality, behaviour and social roles between men and women are the product of biological or sociocultural factors. Are women and men naturally different, or are they made so by the society in which they live? This debate has been of particular importance for feminist writers, who have argued that certain interpretations of women's biology have been used not simply to mark out their difference from men but to justify their subordinate and secondary status and to exclude women from certain areas of society. Gender inequality refers to this inequitable allocation of social status, opportunity and resources (economic, political and social) on the basis of gender. However, even if there are biological differences between women and men, this does not

A closer look

Mead's New Guinea study

Mead's (1935) famous study in New Guinea of three different groups of tribal peoples – the Arapesh, the Mundugumor and the Tchambuli – provides an example of variation. Among the Arapesh, both females and males were gentle, passive and sharing. There was not a rigid definition between the responsibilities and personalities of women and men, and there was a more egalitarian community. Among the Mundugumor, there was more defined sexual division: men were aggressive, hostile and dominant and women were responsible for child care and subordinates. Among the Tchambuli, Mead found what could be interpreted as a reversal of conventional Western gender behaviour: men had a greater responsibility for domestic labour and care of the young and adorned themselves, whereas the women had a greater involvement in leadership and hunting and were more aggressive.

explain why the male gender has higher status; to understand this, we have to look to social and political factors.

Social construction of gender

The predominant view in sociology has been that many of the differences between women and men are the product of social and cultural processes, not biology. Yet the earliest works on social learning were based firmly on biological notions of gender-appropriate learning. Sex-role theory developed out of structural functionalism (see Chapter 2), and it was argued that sex roles were associated with a certain status within society while simultaneously providing a text, a script, for that role. Such texts, providing instruction on appropriate behaviour and attitudes, need to be learned, and this is achieved through the process of socialization. As such, sociologists have focused on gender as a learned set of behaviours and have explored the social processes through which we all learn to be either feminine or masculine. A whole range of social processes have been identified as sites where gendered categories of femininity and masculinity are constructed. Sociologists have explored the diverse meanings attached to femininity and masculinity – so much so that there has been a shift towards talking about femininities and masculinities.

Learning gender

According to social learning theory we learn what is considered gender-appropriate behaviour via socialization, which begins at birth through our interactions with our parents. Girls and boys experience gender socialization in different ways, learning appropriate behaviours, personalities and gender roles and developing their own gender identities (own feelings and consciousness) as parents act differently towards girls and boys (Brannon 2005).

Sociological and psychological research has paid attention to various components and stages of gender development. In the 1970s and early 1980s, there was a mass of research that examined the different learning processes of boys and girls. This included studies of such things as postnatal care, books and magazines, clothing and toys. Many researchers have reported that there are different practices and expectations in relation to girls and boys that encourage or reinforce 'feminine' behaviour in girls and 'masculine' behaviour in boys.

Stop and think

Social learning theory assumes that in our culture there are certain roles, behaviours and characteristics that are stereotyped as either 'feminine' or 'masculine'. Examine the list of characteristics below and decide for each one whether they are considered desirable for a woman or man in British society generally.

Affectionate	Tender	Sensitive to others' needs	Warm
Flatterable	Gentle	Strong personality	Yielding
Analytical	Leadership abilities		Individualistic
Cheerful	Makes decisions easily	Ambitious	Does not use harsh language
Self-reliant	Sympathetic	Child-like	Dominant
Forceful		Athletic	
Softly spoken			
Independent			Loves children

- Was it easy to allocate characteristics to categories?
- If you were asked to allocate the characteristics in line with your own opinions of women's and men's personalities and capabilities, rather than what is considered more desirable and appropriate in British society generally, would there be differences in how you allocated them?
- Did you feel that some of the characteristics could not be allocated to a discrete category?
- Tick those traits that you would use to describe yourself. Have you ticked mainly 'masculine', mainly 'feminine' or a mix of both traits?

The characteristics above are taken from the Bem Sex Role Inventory (BSRI). Sandra Bem (1993) stressed that the traits that were included on her inventory were not selected on the basis of how females and males describe themselves but on the basis of what was culturally defined as gender appropriate in the USA in the early 1970s. She determined this by asking a sample of US citizens whom she saw as her 'cultural informants' to identify for each of the traits whether they were seen as more desirable for a woman or a man 'in American society generally'. Bem went on to develop the BSRI using these traits; the inventory involves individuals assessing their own personality. From the results of her work, Bem has argued that humans are androgynous, expressing a range of 'feminine' and 'masculine' traits.

Some writers have interpreted Bem as arguing that 'the development of typical gender roles and gender stereotyping are not inevitable' (Marchbank and Letherby 2007: 125). In other words, parents can intervene and provide alternatives to the dominant gendered information children receive from a variety of sources, such as peers and the media. Research on a variety of non-traditional family forms confirms that this is possible, although it cannot completely overcome external societal influences (Fivush *et al.* 2000; Fiese and Skillman 2000; Brannon 2005).

Socialization influences surround us everywhere, from messages we receive from our families, in school, from peers and from the media. The exploration of how girls learn to be women was a very important early focus for feminist theorists, who showed how feminine gender roles and dominant ideologies of femininity have been restrictive for women, channelling them into social roles to which lower social status is attached. There has also been a concern that the male sex has been taken as the norm and women have been defined as deviant, lacking, second rate or, as Simone de Beauvoir (1974) argued, 'other'.

Although gender studies began with a concentration on girls and women to balance their absence from, or, when present, often inaccurate, social scientific views, it is not the case that only women 'have' a gender. Masculinity has been studied since the 1950s, though it was only in the 1980s that the pro-feminist New Men's Movement turned the focus on to a critical study of masculinities (see Marchbank and Letherby 2007: 16–19 for an outline of critical studies of masculinity). A commonality in the critique of both femininity and

Girls and boys come out to play

In a study of identity development of butch women (i.e. masculine lesbians), Katherine Hiestand and Heidi Levitt explored childhood experiences of being a tomboy.

Some of the earliest memories of the participants included feelings of perplexity about their gender differences . . . a sense of being 'different' from other girls and privately questioning their status as girls . . . a sense of uneasiness when expected to act feminine. . . . The respondents recalled becoming 'like a boy' or being 'a non-girl' throughout their childhoods. They spent much of their time with boys and adopted these gender norms: 'All my friends were male, and I just pretty much took it upon myself to socialize myself as a male, as far as gestures and behaviours [were concerned]' . . . 'I was very handy with the girls because playing house, playing doctor, anytime there was a male role needed, I filled that role really well . . . No matter what we were playing I was the guy'.

Some of the women remembered wishing to become a boy. 'Because I used to, when I was a child, really really really want to be a guy. I prayed and prayed and prayed to be turned into a boy'. . . . Others did not wish to be a boy, but knew they wanted to express their gender differently. . . . As they compared themselves to the only gender categories they knew, 'boy' and 'girl', they were unable to find their place . . . and struggled to find a way to represent their internal sense of gender:

> I just thought that I was supposed to be a boy. Because I always got, from my parents and my family, 'dress like a girl, act like a girl, be like a girl, do like this, do like that', you know. It was always 'Like a girl', which meant that I wasn't like a girl. I was more like a boy and that was not right. I'm not like a girl; I'm more like a boy. But I am a girl. So what does that mean?

(Hiestand and Levitt, 2005)

World in focus

Hegemony

'Hegemony' is a term originally devised by Gramsci (see Chapter 2) to explain and describe how one social group – in Gramsci's case, an elite social class – through the use of political power and ideology can achieve dominance over other groups. The important aspect for sociology is the use of ideology rather than force to obtain assent. In discussing hegemonic femininity and masculinity, sociologists mean the ideology of the 'ideal' forms. Interestingly, hegemonic influences are used more frequently to describe the forces around masculinity than femininity – although ideal types exist in most cultures. Consider the example below.

> The Catholic hierarchy in Ireland expected strict adherence to the compulsory celibacy rule and the form of hegemonic masculinity was cast around celibacy. At the core of this social order was the private family and heterosexual marriage whose sole purpose was procreation, rather than pleasure . . . sport played a key role in the production of the disciplined, Catholic, self-reliant Irish male body . . . Its [the Gaelic Athletic Association] attempts actively to create a national-minded manhood intensified after the creation of an independent Irish Free State in 1922 . . . A further strand to the configuration of traditional hegemonic masculinity in Ireland was the hard-working man and the 'good provider' role.
>
> (Ferguson 2001: 120–21)

masculinity is the way in which sociologists have examined how socialization has been employed to present and preserve hegemonic views of both.

Dominant notions of femininity have emphasized passivity, dependence, emotion and nurturing characteristics, which have often disempowered women. Many feminists have pointed out that these characteristics are not inherently negative but have been denigrated and unvalued. Socialization into roles that stress romance, marriage and motherhood have been seen as particularly restrictive and as providing an effective way of obtaining female subordination, by consent. Hence it was crucial for feminists to explore how femininity is constructed and to challenge these processes. In the 1970s, Sue Sharpe (1994a) mapped out the process of gender socialization for girls. She found that children's activities performed in the home that distinguished between girls and boys, and parental expectations, rehearse girls and boys for future roles. Girls were encouraged to be girlfriends, wives and mothers, with primary responsibility for domestic labour. Although they expected to engage in paid work this was seen as temporary or secondary, and the jobs they aspired to were conventional low-paid female jobs (see Chapter 12 for more details); girls were being encouraged to have limited aspirations and hence restricted choices.

More recent research shows differences in sex-role expectations and behaviours. In the USA, Fivush *et al.* (2000) discovered that parents will talk more with girls than with boys about feelings and emotions. Other US-based research has explored the way parents with different attitudes towards gender interact with their children, showing that those with more traditional views speak about success in life more to sons than to daughters, while the reverse is the case for parents with less traditional gender views (Fiese and Skillman 2000). Such gender learning occurs early in life. Marion O'Brien *et al.* (2000) found that in the USA by 36 months old children knew about gender roles. However, whereas boys knew more about male stereotypes than about female stereotypes, girls of the same age not only knew much more than boys about female roles but also understood as much as boys did about male roles.

Sociologists also know how such lessons are learned. One main way of learning is through observation; as the old adage goes: children see, children do. Children watch who does what task, and although men's domestic chores have increased it is still predominately women who perform such duties. Children learn not only from their parents but also from each other. A Canadian study of adolescent girls and young women (Matthews 2000) found that popularity among their peers was enhanced by dieting, discussing diets and weight loss, and by being thin or trying to be thin. The earlier message of slimness being important for women, perhaps learned from parents or the media, is reinforced by the very targets of the message themselves. Similarly, British studies of boys' behaviour in school shows that boys who engage in 'laddish' behaviour such as mucking about and displaying an interest in soccer are thought to be more masculine than those who do not (Francis 2000).

As far back as 1981, sociologists such as David Morgan were developing the study of masculinity. Morgan (1981) pointed out that although men may have been the key subjects of sociological research, they had not been approached as gendered beings until more recently. Increasingly, masculinity is receiving more attention from male sociologists. Some men have listened to the tenets of feminism and have responded with new ways of understanding men's behaviour. Masculinity is taken to be socially constructed: men are considered to *become* men rather than 'being a man' being an innate property of the male sex. It has been argued that the hegemony around masculinity operates not to teach what masculinity can be but rather to teach what it is not (Donald 1992).

Feminists pointed out that traditional masculinity often disempowered women and led to their subordination. Masculinity was therefore approached as problematic, and certain aspects of male behaviour particularly so – men's violence and aggression, their sexual activity and their domination of women. Jeff Hearn (1987) identifies men as the gender of oppression and points out that they oppress other men as well as women. The study of men and masculinity has attempted to explore the processes that lead to this domination and to recognize the emotional costs to both men and women of male dominance. Further, modern studies of masculinity developed over the past three decades have examined the different experiences of masculinity in and across societies (Whitehead and Barrett 2001; Pease and Pringle 2001) and explore issues such as men's relationships to their family, interpersonal violence and the interactions of masculinity with culture and ethnicity.

It has been recognized that, although feminism has challenged men's domination, no fundamental changes in gender relations can take place without changes in men. Victor Seidler (1989) has considered the consequences for men of what he identifies as the dominant Western form of masculinity, which is taken to be natural to men. He argued that far from being natural this is a relatively recent historical development. In this model of masculinity, the male mind has come to be seen as separate and superior to the body; masculinity is identified with reason, objectivity and superior mental power. Masculine identity is tied closely to the 'public' realms of work and political life. The consequences of this identity for many men is that they are restricted in developing a more personal sense of self, which makes it hard for men to recognize their own or other people's needs. Dominant masculinity stresses aggression, assertion, competition and reason

A closer look

Social learning theory

There is a school of thought that says that children learn gender just as they learn other things, through observing the world around them and through interacting with other members of society. Social learning is achieved through reinforcing the behaviours that parents (and other significant adults) want in their children, such as saying please and thank you and ignoring a request if such is not forthcoming. When parents present boys with a toy truck and encourage play, hegemonic masculinity is reinforced. When the boy's sister picks up the truck and is then handed a doll, hegemonic femininity is reinforced.

Children also copy. They emulate what they see, especially those they see as the same. This is called modelling. All children model, but some modelling is encouraged and reinforced, and some is not. So, although both little boys and girls may want to help Mummy bake and to try on her high heels, the parental reaction to these behaviours will determine which gender lesson is learned by the child.

rather than emotion. Within this model of masculinity, for men to acknowledge their emotional needs is seen as weakness. Men are then locked into a competitive struggle to prove their masculinity. This has implications for male sexuality. Seidler argues that, as part of this competitive struggle, men approach sex as something connected closely to individual achievement and something that signifies their position in the pecking order of masculinity. Male sexuality is part of the development of a masculine identity in which sexuality is seen in terms of power and conquest. Sex becomes a way of proving manhood.

Stop and think

- Consider the experiences of being a tomboy. Does any of it resonate with your childhood experiences? Make a list of all the obvious messages you've received about gender-appropriate behaviour. Now make a second list of all the subtle messages about the same. You may find it interesting to compare your list with another person, especially if that person differs from you in generation or culture.

Femininities and masculinities: discourses of gender

As we have seen, much of the sociological work on femininity and masculinity has adopted a socialization perspective, in which the main concern has been how people learn gender stereotypes and internalize them. Although many sociologists accept that gender is learned and that socialization plays a key role, an increasing number of writers have pointed to the problems with taking a straightforward learning approach. Social learning theory acknowledges that gender roles and identities are not fixed and may change over history and across cultures. Sylvia Walby (1990) argued that this approach still operates with a static and unitary conception of gender differences: femininity is one set of characteristics that girls and women learn, and masculinity is another set that boys and men learn. Walby argued that this takes insufficient account of the different forms that femininity and masculinity can take and hence it does not account for diversity among women and men. This approach implies that each person is equally conforming to gender ideology and does not explore how masculinity and femininity vary according to a whole range of social factors such as class, age, race and ethnicity. It treats people as relatively passive in their acquisition of gender identity. The emphasis on the passive learning of dominant ideology does not recognize adequately that people such as Leslie Feinberg (see pp. 216–218) may resist, reject or subvert dominant meanings about gender.

This has led to an exploration of the varied content of femininities and masculinities and a shift in emphasis from examining simple sex stereotyping to exploring the processes by which a range of femininities and masculinities are constructed. This shift is the product of a recognition that there are different messages about female and male behaviour, communicated for example via the media and education, and not simply one ideology. Some writers, such as Connell (2000a), contended that by the end of the twentieth century two separate approaches had developed: materialist and post-structuralist.

Post-structuralist approaches to gender argue that the polarity of gender is hegemonic in its dualism, but the difference from social learning lies in the way in which post-structuralism emphasizes the way in which language, discourses, constructs this dualism.

Femininity has been identified in the past very much as a set of characteristics and behaviours that women learn and that then constrain women's lives. Yet some researchers have explored how femininity and feminine identification can be part of social identification from which women can gain positive identity and meaning. Similarly, although masculinity was originally approached as a fixed set of characteristics that disempower women and restrict men, it has been acknowledged that men may feel uncomfortable with some constructs of masculinity and that there are many alternative masculinities. As such, Harry Brod and Michael Kaufman (1994: 4) remind us that we 'cannot study masculinity in the singular, as if the stuff of man were a homogeneous and unchanging thing'.

Stop and think

- What characteristics do Prince Harry, Johnny Depp and Nelson Mandela share?
- In what ways are they different?
- Do you think it is accurate to describe them as sharing similar 'masculine' traits?

Post-structuralist and postmodern thinking have had a key role in shifting debates about gender away from simple social learning theory. Social learning theory identified a clearcut binary division between the category 'male' and the category 'female'. Post-structuralist theorists argue that this does not allow for differences among women, men, resistances or choice. Post-structuralism emphasizes that meanings about gender and gender identity are fluid and historically and socially constituted.

Other post-structuralists, such as Judith Butler (1990), argue that gender is not fixed but variable, and that it changes at different times and in different social contexts. She describes gender as 'performative': we all act out a gender performance – some of us may act out a more traditional one, while others might not. Those that run counter to the traditional or hegemonic are subversive performances/identities, which can lead to what Butler calls 'gender trouble' as they confound and challenge the norm and present alternative identities.

Butler argues that certain culturally hegemonic forms of gender roles exist; these may seem natural and unchangeable, but they are not. She says that through subversive acts, and through creating 'gender trouble', change can be achieved. Given that we all 'do' a gender performance anyway, she argues, why not do it differently? If we choose to 'do' gender differently, for example as a gender-blending androgyne, it may be possible to challenge gender norms and to disrupt the binary thinking regarding femininity and masculinity. This approach sees identity as unconnected to any natural essence, such as biological sex, but rather as free-floating and fluid.

Some post-structuralist theorists have argued that some cultural developments, such as the development of information technology, present another opportunity to challenge rigid gender roles, giving individuals the opportunity to explore different gender identities (Harraway 1991). The Internet has been identified as a cultural site where traditional gender identities can be confounded and transcended as users take on new gender identities in cyberspace; for example, a biological female who identifies as heterosexual may adopt a male bisexual cyber-identity (Di Marco and Di Marco 2003).

A criticism of post-structuralist approaches to gender is that they may have become overly abstract. Hearn (1996) argues that abstract consideration of masculinity can divert attention away from the materiality of men's lives and practices. As such, it weakens our abilities to understand how men relate to women, children and each other. Other work has focused on the practices that men use to protect their interests, such as men's resistance to women in the workplace. Materialist analyses reject not discourse and meaning but rather, as Connell (2000b) notes, work such as 'Hearn's . . . research on men's violence to women is an important example of how material practices – indeed, practices addressed to bodies – can be linked to the construction of meaning, the making of ideology'.

Sex and sexuality

Sex and sexuality are often referred to as the last taboo, but in fact there is a cultural obsession with sex and sexuality that is reflected in the interest that everyone from comedians to politicians has in these topics. As individuals we are encouraged to measure our sexual identity and sexual experiences against a politically and popularly supported ideal, the image of which is predominate in cultural representations.

The attention that different experiences and behaviours receive is varied. For example, homosexuality and homosexual relationships are still not universally sanctioned in law and social policy in the ways that heterosexuality and heterosexual relationships are, and lay opinion still supports the view that heterosexuality is normal and natural. These views are based on statistical (what most people do), religious (what religions permit or prohibit) and cultural (what is encouraged or discouraged) norms. Heterosexuality is also subject to sanction and censure; one example is the sexual subordination of women through the encouragement of the appropriation of women's bodies by men (Jackson and Scott 1996; Abbott *et al.* 2005; Marchbank and Letherby 2007). This cultural obsession is also reflected in the diverse sociological interest in sex and sexuality, and we briefly consider some of the key debates here.

Explanations and theories

Sexuality is often defined as a natural instinct and is often believed to be part of the biological makeup of each individual. This view of sexuality as a natural biological entity is referred to as *essentialism* and is usually linked to heterosexual sex and procreation.

We learn very early on from many sources that 'natural' sex is what takes place with members of

the 'opposite' sex. 'Sex' between people of the same 'sex' is therefore, by definition, 'unnatural'.

(Weeks 1986: 13)

Furthermore, it is widely believed that the sexual needs and desires of men and women are different, with men often thought to have the strongest sex drive and a natural tendency to promiscuity. Any deviation is considered to be pathological. Thus, lesbian, gay and bisexual women and men have been defined as deviant, unnatural and perverse, and women who are perceived as having an active rather than a passive sex drive have been defined as not real women.

Michel Foucault (1979, 1984) and Jeffrey Weeks (1986, 2000) have criticized essentialist views of sex and sexuality. Foucault argues that powerful discourses shape our sexual values and beliefs. So, sex is not a biological entity governed by natural laws; rather, our views of it are culturally and historically specific. Weeks also rejects the idea that there is a true essence of sex, an 'uninformed pattern' that is 'ordained by nature itself' (Weeks 1986: 15), and insists that it is simplistic to reduce a complex pattern of sexual relations and identities to biological factors. His hypothesis is that the sexual categories that we take for granted, that map the horizons of the possible and that seem so 'natural' and secure and inevitable, are actually historical and social labels. He has stressed that it is important to study the history of sexuality in order to understand the range of possible identities, based on class, ethnicity, gender and sexual preference, and argues that it is reductionist to reduce the complexities of reality to an essentialist biological truth. Similarly, Butler (1990, 1993) challenges the assumed causal links between sex, gender and sexual desire and argues that desire is usually constructed as being towards the other gender. Butler adds that heterosexuality is not the only valid form of sexual desire; rather, it is merely one configuration of desire that has come to be seen as natural. Thus, although our sexual desires may seem to be natural, sociologists and others have argued that our sexual responses and identities are actually socially constructed. Sexuality is shaped by the culture in which we live; religious teachings, laws, psychological theory, medical definitions, social policies and the media all inform us of its meaning. This does not mean that biology has no influence: limits are imposed by the body and we experience different things depending on whether we have a vagina or a penis (Plummer 1975, 1995; Hirst 2004; Marchbank and Letherby 2007).

Both heterosexuality and homosexuality are, then, social constructions. Some writers have pointed out that there is no essential homosexual experience, that gay history is complex and the experience of being homosexual varies. Indeed, the use of the term 'homosexual' to describe a certain type of person is a relatively recent phenomenon (Foucault 1977; Weeks 1990, 1991b, 2000); in many historical periods a woman who had sex with another woman would not think of herself or be regarded as lesbian.

A closer look

Sexual citizenship

As Jeffrey Weeks (2000: 239) notes, despite the New Right political concern (in both the UK and America) with social authoritarianism on moral issues that led to real setbacks for a more humane and tolerant order, the 1990s and 2000s have seen 'a recognition of the importance of the freedom of individuals to choose their own ways of being' influenced not least by the lesbian and gay politics of the past 40 years. Yet, despite shifts in attitudes towards gay men, lesbians and bisexuals, 'sexual citizenship' is still not equally experienced by all (Bell and Binnie 2000). As Davina Cooper notes:

> Heterosexual demonstrations are so naturalized they remain unapparent – wearing wedding/engagement rings, talking about marriage/honeymoons/dating, kissing/holding hands in public places. However, analogous signifiers of sexuality by lesbians and gay men, lacking a naturalized status, remain highly visible, and are constructed as flaunting.
>
> (Cooper 1998: 133)

Stop and think

- Why do you think that some sexual identities and behaviours are defined as appropriate and others as inappropriate?
- What are the consequences of a sexually deviant label?

Issues and experiences

Historically and to date, men have been defined as having a stronger sex drive than women and with a natural tendency to promiscuity. Many theorists have argued that men's sexual identity is in some way shaped by masculine ideology, with sexuality being defined as important to male gender identity and to male power. In many cultures women are sexually objectified, as Peter Berger and Linda McDowell note:

> **Men act and women appear. Men look at women. Women watch themselves being looked at. This determines not only most relations between men and women but also the relation of women to themselves. The survey of woman herself is male: the surveyed female. Thus, she turns herself into an object – and most particularly an object of vision: a sight.**
>
> (Berger 1992: 47)

> **Above all, beaches [and other areas where women 'perform'] are arenas for looking . . . men look at women, women look at women, men at men, women at men and adults at children. In all but exceptional locations, however it is the heterosexual male gaze that dominates the displays.**
>
> (McDowell 1999: 167)

An extreme version of objectification is pornography, which Catharine MacKinnon (1987) argues is the foundation of male dominance as it shapes how men see all women. Some theorists also link objectification of this kind to violence against women. Since the mid-1970s feminists have drawn attention to the high levels of violence that women experience at the hands of men. Liz Kelly (1988) found that most women have experienced some form of sexual violence; she identified a continuum of violence, from verbal harassment to rape and murder, which she argues acts to instil fear and control women. A recurring theme in the analysis of male sexuality is that, as part of their socialization, men learn to separate sex from emotion, to be dominant in sexual relations and to see women as sexual objects to please men.

Kelly (1988) and Martin Daly and Mary Wilson's (1988) examination of homicide reveal the use of men's violence to control their female partners across industrial and non-industrial societies. They argue that the killing of women is relatively rare but that the

Case study

Rape and sex crimes in war

Mass rape and other sex crimes have been used systematically throughout history and across geography: over 100,000 women were raped in Berlin in the Second World War (Seifert 1994); over 20,000 Chinese women were brutalised by Japanese soldiers during the 1937–8 'rape of Nanking' (Copelon 1994) and, during the Bangladeshi War of Independence from Pakistan in 1971, it is estimated that 200,000 women were raped (Brownmiller 1975). Research by Karen Parker and Jennifer Chew (1994) estimates that each Japanese Comfort Woman [women captured and imprisoned during the Second World War and used to provide sexual 'comfort' for Japanese soldiers] was raped at least five times a day and that there were at least 100,000 rapes per day by the Japanese authorities and conducted by soldiers . . .

Although rape and other sex crimes during war are predominantly enacted upon women, men and boys are also targeted (Change 1997; Hague 1997; Petman 1996; Trexler 1995) both for rape and sexual humiliation (Goldstein 2001) and to conduct sexual acts upon their own communities (Leibling 2004) to destroy the social fabric of the 'enemy' . . . severe sexual torture predominates, frequently followed by murder.

(Marchbank 2008: 239)

widespread use of violence is not. While men's violence to women is usually characterized as 'losing control' or flying into a 'blind rage', all the evidence suggests that both women who are battered and men who batter tell the same story – that men's behaviour is used as a means of control. On the other hand, although men do experience violent attacks by women, this constitutes the smallest proportion of men's assaults and men are much more likely to be victims of physical and sexual violence from other men (Newburn and Stanko 1994a). Tim Newburn and Elizabeth Stanko argue that men not only victimize women but also victimize each other; thus, it is necessary to consider the experience of men as victims of sexual violence as well as oppressors.

In addition to the risk of violence, there exists an enduring sexual double standard whereby men are judged positively if they engage in sexual encounters and women are judged negatively, such that girls and women risk loss of reputation. Research by Sue Lees (1986, 1993) found evidence of this double standard in the 1980s and 1990s and argued that the name-calling that girls and women are subject to serves as one way of controlling female sexuality. More recently, research by Karin A. Martin (2002) on why adolescents have sex supports this argument: she found that the teenage girls in her study often experienced sexual intercourse as shaming and frightening and many had sex before they wanted to in order to keep their boyfriends. Similarly, Eileen Green and Carrie Singleton (2006: 863), in their study of risk and safety in the leisure lives of young women in England and South Asia, found that 'women "moderated" their behaviour in public to avoid being "gossiped about" and labeled "unrespectable".'

Thus, some theorists stress that the way sexual relations have been institutionalized through heterosexuality has served to control and oppress not only lesbian, gay and bisexual men and women but all women (Rich 1980; Jeffreys 1990; Jackson and Scott 1996). For some individuals, heterosexuality and the social relations that accompany it, such as marriage,

Case study

Teenage pregnancy and double standards

Although teenage pregnancy is not a recent phenomenon in the UK, it is an issue that is receiving increasingly more attention. Young mothers are stereotyped as a burden on the state (e.g. see Phoenix 1991). Despite evidence to the contrary (Phoenix 1991; Ussher 2000; Brown *et al.* 2008), teenage mothers are stereotyped as bad mothers and their children as severely disadvantaged. As Kent (2000) adds, it is the so-called loose morals of these women that are in question, and in each case moral discourses are harnessed to define the 'competent'/'incompetent' and 'fit'/'unfit' mother. Arguably, it is not the age of the woman that is the primary issue but the fact that younger pregnant girls and women are more likely to give birth outside marriage. Hollway (1994) suggests that the male sex drive discourse and the have/hold discourse each affects the dominant views of young unmarried mothers.
The male sex drive discourse implies that men have biological urges and women's sexual needs are subservient to this male sex drive, while the have/hold discourse implies that sex is considered appropriate only within a committed heterosexual relationship sanctioned by marriage. The young pregnant woman or mother has a problematic social identity. Her bump or baby is a stigma and sets her aside as other – as 'inappropriate' – according to dominant sexual and political discourses. Even earlier than this, young women may be sanctioned for their arguably 'sensible' choices in choosing contraception as they are 'actively anticipating intercourse' and 'looking to have sex' (Luker 1975, cited by Petchesky 1985: 218). Thus, young women's experience of pregnancy and motherhood takes place in a 'damned if you do and damned if you don't' context (for further discussion see Wilson *et al.* 2002).

Questions

1. How many negative stereotypes of young mothers can you think of?
2. Are young fathers portrayed in the same negative ways?

have been crucial to the persistence of male dominance. Other theorists have explored the complexities of women's experiences of both the pleasures and dangers of sex (Vance 1992; Jackson and Scott 1996) and the complexity of male sexuality, arguing that sex also has a range of meanings for men, including anxiety and fear (Seidler 1991). Work on the relationship between gender, sexuality and the Internet adds further complications. Nicola Doring (2000) argues that women can achieve qualitatively better sexual experiences via cyberspace because they can afford to be more discerning in their search for partners. As Máirtín Mac an Ghaill and Chris Haywood (2007: 135) point out, 'a key implication of this is that conventional notions of sex (heterosexual and genitally focused penetration) are problematized in cyberspace with a plethora of sexual possibilities emerging that can liberate women's sexual experience and emotional investment.' But the Internet can also be a space of objectification, victimization and abuse where adult and child pornography, harassment, stalking, cyber-rape and so on take place (Doring 2000; Mac an Ghaill and Haywood 2007; Letherby *et al.* 2008).

Representing gender: mass media and popular culture

In contemporary Western society mass media and other forms of cultural influence are all around us and are influential in many ways:

> **We are immersed from cradle to grave in a media and consumer society . . . The media are forms of pedagogy that teach us how to be men and women; how to dress, look and consume; how to react to members of different social groups; how to be popular and successful and avoid failure; and how to conform to the dominant system of norms, values, practices and institutions.**
>
> (Kellner 1995: 5)

Yet some would argue that this approach is overly deterministic and oversimplistic in that:

- it reduces all power relations to gender, which neglects and denies other aspects of power such as class, (dis)ability, 'race' and ethnicity and sexuality;
- it denies the pleasure that women and men derive from the media as active consumers;
- it denies the fact that the media offer us a variety of images and provide us with contradictory images, thus both challenging and supporting patriarchy (Stacey 1994);
- popular culture does not simply serve capitalism and patriarchy, 'peddling false consciousness to the duped masses' (Gamman and Marshment 1988: 1), and the media can be seen as a site of struggle where many meanings are contested and where dominant ideologies can be disturbed.

Stereotypes in the media

Some theorists suggest that, within the mass media, stereotypes about gender, gendered ideologies and gender inequalities are reinforced. Stereotypes are useful because they are simple and easy to recognize; their strength lies in the fact that they are a combination of validity and distortion (Condry and Condry 1976) and reduce individuals and groups of people to a few characteristics by which they can be easily identified (Cranny-Francis *et al.* 2003).

It is argued by some writers that women are represented in a restrictive and stereotypical number of ways, and that the representation of women is determined by the 'male gaze'; that is, women are represented in ways that suit men's interests and pleasures (e.g. Ferguson 1985; Coppock *et al.* 1995). The construction of masculinity in the media has also received attention because, even though men have a greater presence in the media, masculinity is narrowly defined (Jackson 1990; Collier 1992; Beynon 2004).

Early consideration of gendered stereotypes in the media began with analysis of women's magazines. Theorists argued that girls' and women's magazines defined and shaped women's lives and expectations from childhood onwards (McRobbie 1982; Winship 1986; Ferguson 1985). Janice Winship (1986) suggested that women's magazines located and exploited the fragmented position of women in the family and at work, both of which are required for the maintenance of capitalism. She argued that the emphasis of the woman's role in the family helped keep women out of the running for economic and political power. Margorie Ferguson (1985) argued that magazines perpetuated the 'cult of femininity' – what it is to be a good and a real woman – which women must maintain. Ferguson examined women's magazines from the 1940s to the 1980s and claimed that, although the rituals changed slightly, the cult of femininity remains fundamentally unchanged. She suggested that until the late 1970s the dominant themes were 'getting and keeping your man', 'the happy family', 'self-help', 'be more beautiful' and 'the working wife is a bad wife'. In addition to these themes, the image of 'new woman' began to emerge in the 1980s, with the focus on the working wife as a good wife. Thus, not least because of socioeconomic changes such as women's increasing role in the labour market and changing attitudes to sex and marriage, in the late 1970s and 1980s women's magazines contained two conflicting messages: be proud of who you are but at the same time ensure you are a good wife and mother (Ferguson 1985). More recently, Kath Woodward (2003) argues that a new figure of motherhood emerged in the 1990s, in magazines and the media more generally, and that this 'independent' mother was an amalgam of previous figures of caring and working mothers. In addition, 'independent' motherhood adds sexuality to motherhood.

It was only in the late 1980s that a modern group of general interest, glossy 'men's magazines' emerged, containing articles on health, sport, fashion, personal care, relationships with women and children, sex and employment (Collier 1992). John Beynon (2004) argues that this new breed of men's magazines objectifies the male body in the same way that women's magazines objectify the female body. Certainly these publications presented men with contradictory images, sometimes focusing on masculinity characteristics and sometimes offering a more challenging, progressive masculinity as something to aspire to. But whereas the men's magazines of the 1980s did at some level attempt to challenge traditional male (and female) images and expectations, those launched in the 1990s reintroduced a strong heterosexual script that includes soft-porn shots of women and a focus on the 'new lad' rather than the 'new man' through articles on partying, sport and heroes to aspire to. As Beynon (2004: 211) notes, the message of these publications is that 'real men get "loaded", "shag" women and watch football'.

Yet, just as there is confusion and contradiction regarding motherhood, Richard Collier (1992) argues that the media present a similar ambiguous view of fatherhood. The 'ideology of new fatherhood' present in some magazines considers issues of shared parenting and men as active fathers, and yet masculinity is still presented in terms of material and economic success and on the privilege, hierarchy and material benefits that accrue to men. Also concerned with fatherhood, Tabitha Freeman (2003) argues that 'ideal manhood' is now linked with fatherhood.

A closer look

Motherhood, fatherhood and the media

Media reports often focus on mothers as good or bad, with examples of bad mothers including those who abandon their children, leaving them at home while they go on holiday, or selfishly put the interest of their own careers before the care of their children. Fathers are rarely subjected to the same kind of scrutiny or classification as 'bad' parents in similar cases. In addition, women's magazines, alongside other Western media, frequently feature 'celebrity' mothers, and '[s]uccessful motherhood is encoded as "well-off and sexually attractive"' (Woodward 2003: 23–30).

The media has become flooded with representations of high-profile men publicly exhibiting affection for their young children and explicitly promoting their self-image as 'good', involved fathers.

'Why every man should have one' (*Sunday Times* 28 May 2000) pictures the footballers David Beckham and Dennis Wise holding their babies like trophies, alongside a strikingly intimate photograph of the then British prime minister, Tony Blair, lying beside his newborn son. Such open displays of paternal affection are now commonplace, with newspapers and magazines presenting a myriad of visual and textual images of pop stars, actors, sportsmen and politicians proudly parading their offspring and making enthusiastic pronouncements on the virtues of fatherhood (Freeman 2003: 44).

Stop and think

- Compare a woman's weekly magazine, a woman's monthly magazine, a magazine aimed at men and a 'celebrity' magazine. How many different versions of appropriate womanhood and manhood can you find?
- What stereotypically defines a 'good mother' and a 'good father'? How does the mass media perpetuate these stereotypes?

The Internet is a relatively new medium that some authors suggest offers a challenge to gender inequality and stereotypical representations. Mac an Ghaill and Haywood (2007: 137) note that the 'internet provides the possibilities of women being men who are playing women and the alternative position of men being women who play at being men'. Further, Sadie Plant (1996: 265) argues that women are able to use cybernet technologies to subvert patriarchy as the 'Internet promises women a network of lines on which to chatter, natter, work and play; virtuality brings a fluidity to identities which once had to be fixed; and multi-media provides a tactile environment in which women artists can find their space'. However, evidence suggests that men are more likely than women to change their gender identity online (Suler 1999, cited by Mac an Ghaill and Haywood 2007), and women continue to be ascribed traditional gendered characteristics on the Internet (Mac an Ghaill and Haywood 2007). In addition, access to the Internet is unequal and there is still work to be done on the gendered use and control of cyberspace (e.g. Van Zoonen 2002; Gillis 2008).

In an attempt to challenge the 'male gaze' in the 1980s and 1990s, feminists began to consider the concept of a 'female gaze' across the mass media. One response was to attempt to objectify men for women's pleasure but, as Anne Cranny-Francis and colleagues (2003) argue, objectifying men rather than freeing women from objectivity does not solve the problem. There are increasing representations of strong women in the media and challenges not only to gender stereotypes but also to heterosexuality as the norm (Cranny-Francis *et al.* 2003; Marchbank and Letherby 2007). In addition, as well as being vehicles for dominant ideology, media such as women's (and men's) magazines and books, films, the Internet and so on are greatly enjoyed by consumers (e.g. Hermes 1995; Ussher 1997).

Stop and think

- Can you think of some television programmes, films, video games, books or songs that challenge sexism and gender stereotypes?

The media and consumption

A consideration of the media would be incomplete without some reflection on the relationship between media output and consumption. As Ruth Holliday (2008: 187) notes:

> **since capitalism's aim is to generate ever-expanding profits it must sell cheap, mass produced products in a way that fools us into thinking they are designed for us as individuals (Althusser 1971). This also applies to media products that compete for viewing figures in order to secure advertising revenue and which also carry ideological messages about the world to ensure our compliance with the capitalist system as workers and consumers.**

Further, as noted above, the media promote idealized and stereotypical images of women and men, and these images are used to sell products and services. Traditionally, women have been used to sell everything from 'bar snacks' to 'cars' (Holliday 2008) to men, as well as a multitude of products to enable women to fulfil their stereotypical roles and responsibilities in life (see above). Katherine T. Frith and Barbara Mueller (2003) argue that globalization has altered the process of advertising in that advertisements across the world are often created in American and Western styles and the advertisers themselves have usually received their training in American and British universities or been interned in Western advertising agencies. Thus, the forms of representation, particularly of women, often take on globalized or transnational patterns:

> **For thirty years, media have been taken to task for reproducing and reinforcing stereotyped images of women. Yet unfair representations of women in media prevail worldwide. Sex stereotyping has been so deeply ingrained, even glorified, that the women themselves have become desensitized to their own inferior portrayal. The prospects appear even gloomier as the globalization of media progresses.**
>
> (Frith and Mueller 2003, cited in Kyung-Ja-Lee 2000: 86)

Not surprisingly, given the dominant images of 'appropriate womanhood', the fashion, beauty, diet and increasingly healthy eating industries are big business within capitalism and thus within the media. Take the new wave of make-over programmes – for example, *The Swan*, *Extreme Makeover* and *America's Next Top Model* in the USA and *Ten Years Younger* and *What Not to Wear* in the UK – which are aimed at women and focus on how individuals can improve their bodies through consumption (Holliday 2008). Yet, just as feminine stereotypes are reinforced and exploited in advertising, so is masculinity; as Lance Strate (2004) notes, the resulting images are widely available to both children and adults and influential in terms of socialization:

> **Jacks, rock stars, and pickup artists; cowboys, construction workers, and comedians; these are some of the major 'social types' found in contemporary American beer commercials. The characters may vary in occupation, race, and age, but they all exemplify traditional conceptions of the masculine role. Clearly, the beer industry relies on stereotypes of the man's man to appeal to a mainstream predominantly male target audience. This is why alternative social types, such as sensitive men, gay men and househusbands, scholars, poets, and political activists, are noticeably absent from beer advertising . . . in a sense they constitute a guide for becoming a man, a rulebook for appropriate male behaviour, in short a manual on masculinity.**
>
> (Strate 2004: 533)

Of course, in order to continue to sell goods and services, advertisers need to keep up with and respond to cultural change. As feminism could not be ignored by advertisers, it has also been incorporated into advertising and used to sell commodities (Goldman 1992; Holliday 2008). The advent and increasing use of the Internet provides further opportunities for stereotypical and more challenging gendered representations and increased opportunities for advertising and consumption. Yet, here, as elsewhere in the media, we can find challenges to the view of men and women as media dupes.

World in focus

Cyber-chattels: buying brides on the Net

Stereotypes are used to advertise potential brides: prospective buyers are warned of the extra financial outlay attached to women of certain nationalities: 'Whereas a Thai is unprepared for cold German winters – one has to buy her clothes – a Pole brings her own boots and fur coat. And she is as good in bed and as industrious in the kitchen' (Scholes 1999: 168).

However, although popular discourses surrounding men who buy brides are that such men are pathetic, inadequate and unable to attract a woman by the more accepted routes of Western courtship, evidence suggests that many men who seek mail-order brides are economically and professionally successful. So, stereotypically at least, it appears that these men were likely to be 'eligible' to women in their own communities and country.

Similarly, popular discourses surrounding women who offer themselves as brides are frequently judgemental and disapproving, often positioning the women as victims of their husbands and agencies. However, rather than viewing all women on mail-order Internet sites as victimized and exploited, it is possible to argue that, for some, seeking such a match may be an act of agency. Admittedly it may be interpreted as an act of limited agency, for truly free women would not need to seek such a marriage, but it may be the only kind of agency available to women who are entrapped in social and economic structures that limit their life opportunities. Evidence from the USA supports the conclusion that women are seeking improved life chances by offering themselves on 'bride' sites, for they 'for the most part come from places in which jobs and educational opportunities for women are scarce and wages low' (US government report on the mail-order bride industry, www.wtw.org/mob/mobappa.htm).

(Adapted from Letherby and Marchbank 2003: 70–71)

Stop and think

➤ Find some examples of adverts across the media aimed specifically at men and specifically at women. How easy would it be for the advertisers to leave out the specific references to gender in the advertisements?

Gender and the body

A recurring theme in the work on the representation of women and men in the media is that women and men are represented in a particularly limited way. For example, with reference to women in films, television programmes, magazines and other media, women's bodies are presented as 'glamorous', 'beautiful', 'sexy' and often 'thin'. Until recently, social scientists paid little attention to the body, but now some sociologists are exploring how the body is taken up in culture and how culture constructs the body so it is understood as a biological given (Lupton 2003; Fraser and Greco 2005; Woodward 2008).

Jane M. Ussher (1997, 2006) argues that throughout history and across cultures women's bodies have provoked fascination, adoration, revulsion and fear. She states:

> **We see evidence of this dread in representations of the dangers of the menstruating woman, whose 'touch could blast the fruits of the field, sour wine, cloud mirrors, rust iron, and blunt the edges of knives'.**
>
> (Ussher 1997: 643)

Thus, as Foucault (1979: 25) notes:

> **The body is directly involved in a political field; power relations have an immediate hold upon it; they invest it, mark it, train it, torture it, force it to carry out tasks, to perform ceremonies, to emit signs.**

A particularly significant time affecting our current understanding of the relationship between gender and the body in the Western world was the sixteenth and seventeenth centuries. The dominant 'scientific' message that emerged at this time was that women were not only different from men but also physically, psychologically, emotionally and socially inferior to men. In the nineteenth century, middle-class women were thought to be particularly weak and susceptible to illness: menstruation was thought to be an 'indisposition' or illness that sapped women's energy, making it necessary for them to rest; childbirth was termed 'confinement' and a long period of bedrest was thought to be necessary after the birth of a baby; and the menopause was considered a disease that marked the beginning of senility (Marchbank and Letherby 2007). These views of women as inferior, along with the dominance of men in senior medical, legal and other professional positions, have led to continued control over women's bodies.

One response to sexism in health care was the production of books written with the aim of informing individuals about their own body and health. A number of these books hit the bookstores in the 1970s, perhaps the most well known being *Our Bodies, Ourselves*, first published by the Boston Women's Health Book Collective in 1973. These books were written by women and were grounded in women's experiences. However, as Jenny Hockey (1997) notes, these early texts were relevant mostly for white middle-class audiences. It was not until the 1980s that books aimed at black, lesbian, working-class and older women began to appear.

Even today there are fewer books concerned specifically with men's health, although, as Jonathan Watson (2000) notes, during the 1990s men's health was an increasing concern within the media, with reports on increasing stress and incidences of cancer, declining fertility and reluctance to visit the doctor. In turn, all of this has led to further debate on the state of men's health and what to do about it. Because women are often seen as responsible for both their own and others' health, and because of the focus on women's bodies as other than the norm, historically less attention has been given to some aspects of men's health (Watson 2000; Abbott *et al.* 2005). This has led to the need for creative ways to interest men in healthy living. One recent attempt in the UK to encourage men to pay more attention to their health has been the production of a men's health manual modelled on the car manuals produced by Haynes.

Increasingly, bodily ideal is linked not only to a healthy body but also to an aesthetic ideal. Feminists are concerned that the bodily ideal presented to women by the media undermines women's autonomy and works against the development of unity between women, encouraging as it does competition and hierarchy

A closer look

Whose body is it anyway?

. . . written evidence of cases of court-ordered Caesarean Section are rare . . . [although it is claimed that court-enforced caesareans have been performed in the USA since 1973] . . . Most of these early American cases involved women who were poor, or members of ethnic minorities. Many of them did not speak English and had beliefs and attitudes about childbirth which did not coincide with the medical model of their doctors . . . They included cases where the pregnant woman had her wrists and ankles forcibly secured with leather cuffs . . .

In what was probably the most notorious case in the USA, in 1987, a hospital administration went to court to force a pregnant woman who was critically ill with cancer to undergo a caesarean section at 26 weeks 'gestation'. At this point in pregnancy the foetus is barely viable outside of the uterus. Nevertheless, the hospital told the judge that there was a 50 to 60 per cent chance that the baby would survive and a less than 20 per cent chance that it would be handicapped. This move was not only opposed by the woman herself and her family, but also by her obstetricians. The baby died two hours after the surgery, and after being told that her infant had not survived, the woman died two days later . . .

(Weaver 2002: 233–4)

World in focus

Contradictory messages?

In 2005 the magazine *Marie Claire* included an article on 'The Miss Plastic Surgery' contest in China (Figure 5.2), where women and girls as young as 16 compete in the first pageant for 'artificial beauties':

> [A]t the height of the cultural revolution in the Sixties and Seventies, Maoist officials condemned any form of grooming or beautification as 'unrevolutionary' and regularly beat women for owning a hairbrush, wearing blusher or painting their nails.
>
> In the past 30 years, the pursuit of beauty has made a comeback. Good looks are now a vital currency, especially for women in search of well-paid jobs or rich husbands . . . Cosmetic surgery is now a £1.3 billion industry in China, growing at a rate of 20 per cent a year. More than 3.5 million surgical operations were performed between 2002 and 2003 . . .
>
> . . . Dr Fushun Ma, a cosmetic surgeon at a large private clinic in Beijing . . . [is quoted as saying] 'Rounder eyes and a higher nose are basic necessities, like food or water, for beauty-conscious young females . . . They don't deliberately want to copy the West, they just believe these features look prettier . . .'

Marie Claire questioned the celebratory stories of the contestants in the contest, noting the many cases of botched surgery that sometimes result in irreversible damage. They also argued that the increasing demand for 'artificial' beauty adds to the objectification and distress of all women in China. Interesting, then, that at the end of the magazine, there were no fewer than eight pages of adverts offering cosmetic surgery solutions to the readers of the magazine.

(Source: Haworth 2005, cited in Marchbank and Letherby 2007)

Figure 5.2 And the winner of Miss Plastic Surgery is . . .
FREDERIC J. BROWN/AFP/Getty Images

(Chapkis 1986; Wolf 1991; Ussher 1997). Patricia Hill-Collins (1990) argued not only that eternally defined standards of beauty were 'white', which can create anxieties for black women, who cannot live up to the white-skinned, blue-eyed, straight-haired ideal, but also that this white ideal existed only in opposition to the black 'other'. Holliday (2008) suggests that expanding global markets have led to significant increases in the number of black, Asian and East Asian fashion models represented and notes that older models are now being used to appeal to women in their forties and fifties. Despite this, culturally defined bodily ideals are still prevalent. Using breast augmentation as an example, Peter Conrad and Heather T. Jacobson (2003) argue that body enhancements are a reflection of what is socially valued in a given society at a given time and that the history of breast augmentation mirrors society's view of the meanings and values of breasts, with particular reference to the so-called ideal size, shape and function. This shows how social values of bodily ideals are often reflected in medical practice, in that at different times 'small' and 'large' breasts have both been defined as a medical problem. In addition, as Kathy Davis (2003) notes, cosmetic surgery is a gendered practice, as surgeons are almost exclusively male and patients largely female. Davis suggests that men will never seek surgery to the same extent as women, except for hair transplants, because men's bodies are constituted as bodies that 'do' rather than bodies that are 'done to'.

As cosmetic surgery gradually becomes normalized, women who do not seek cosmetic surgery may be at risk of being labelled as abnormal or deviant (Morgan 1991). Increasingly, it is recognized that men, too, are subject to the ideals of the thin, toned youthful body, leading in some cases to obsessive exercising, eating disorders and submissions to surgery.

In leisure activities, the body has moved centre-stage. The idealized desiring body and desired body of late capitalism needs work to produce a sleek and acceptable performance in an era that has seen the triumph of the cult of the fit body. Thinness and fitness, for men and for women, are dominant desires, achieved not only through exercise but also through general improvements in health care and dietary practice (McDowell 1999).

Stop and think

- Describe a healthy person. Is healthy the same as attractive? What gender differences are there between your definitions of healthy men and women and attractive men and women?

Gendered labour

The 'public' world of paid work was often thought of as separate from the 'private' sphere of family. Yet feminist theorists question this notion of separate spheres, pointing out that gender relations in the labour market are related to gender relations in the family and household. One explanation for women's greater domestic labour is that it is necessary to free up men to dedicate their energies to competing in the labour market (Garmarnikov *et al.* 1983). However, more recently there have been moves towards recognizing men's role in the domestic sphere, both from the labour movement and from governments.

Although challenging the notion of separate spheres, feminism argues that this dichotomy has had a very powerful ideological role in constructing gender relations. This public–private split reflected a sexual division of labour within which men were defined as active in the public world, including paid work, and women were primarily defined as residing and working in the domestic world. Both feminism and the field of critical men's studies acknowledge the central role that this dichotomy has had in shaping femininities and masculinities. Both see these as restrictive for women and men: women have been excluded from, and disadvantaged in, paid employment, while the public–private split has created a limited definition of masculinity, one in which the 'breadwinning' role has dominated and created a key source of masculine status and prestige (Morgan 1991).

Unpaid labour

Before we turn our attention to paid employment, it is important to examine unpaid labour. Gender relations in the household interact with and shape paid employment. Throughout the world both women and men perform unpaid labour; a large proportion of this is domestic labour. Feminists have stressed that this labour is real work and can be taxing in ways that paid work is not. One of the first sociologists to theorize unpaid labour was Oakley (1974b). In the 1970s Oakley carried out in-depth interviews with 40 London housewives. She found that women spent an average of 77 hours per week on housework. She applied the criteria used by industrial sociologists to the work performed by housewives and found high levels of dissatisfaction, monotony, loneliness and feelings of low status.

Numerous studies have shown that, despite some shift towards equality, women still perform an unequal share of domestic labour in the home and in relation to child care. Valerie Bryson analysed various studies of domestic labour across both industrialized and non-industrialized countries and concluded that the studies 'unequivocally confirm that women continue to do significantly more unpaid work than men, and that men have not matched their increased time in employment with an equivalent contribution in the home' (Bryson 2007: 154). However, this gap in performing domestic labour is no longer as large as it was, due to the fact that men have increased their contribution to housework since the 1960s, achieved alongside increasing the number of hours they spend in paid employment, and women have decreased their contribution to housework

Figure 5.3 European housewives

and now much of the overall time spent on domestic chores in the past has gone. Put simply, some domestic tasks are just not done these days, and others have been mechanized, such as laundry. One study of the UK found that in almost a third of heterosexual households where both adults are in employment, the man did more housework than the woman (Sullivan 2004). Another study, on lesbian households, found that as most lesbian relationships (in this study) were based on both partners working in the public sphere, the responsibilities for home tasks were much more flexible than in traditional households, being based on principles of egalitarianism. This was especially true when there were children in the household (Dunne 1998).

Paid labour

The experience of work has changed over time (see Chapter 12). One major change has been in the sexual division of labour since the Second World War.

World in focus

Men's and women's time use in Europe

A Eurostat survey conducted by Christel Aliaga found that across Europe patterns of time use are quite similar, although some distinctions can be found.

> On average, women aged 20 to 74 spend much more time than men on domestic work, ranging from less than 50% more in Sweden to over 200% more in Italy and Spain . . . Women spend most time doing domestic work in Italy, Estonia, Slovenia, Hungary and Spain, around 5 hours or more per day. The lowest figures are found in Sweden, Norway, Finland and Latvia – less than 4 hours per day.
>
> Men spend on average more time on gainful work/study than on domestic tasks whereas the opposite is true for women in most of the countries surveyed. The total hours worked per day – i.e. gainful work/study and domestic work – is highest for women in Lithuania, Slovenia, Latvia, Estonia, Hungary, Italy and Spain (around $7^1/_2$ hours or more). It is shorter for men than for women except in Sweden, Norway and the United Kingdom, where it is almost equal or only slightly shorter.
>
> (Aliaga 2006: 1)

References to male breadwinners and housewives are misleading and conceal a diverse and complex range of social relations (Allen and Walkowitz 1987; Pascall 1995; Walby 1990). Gillian Pascall (1995) argues that since the mid-1970s women's position in the UK labour market has changed distinctively. Women have increasingly entered paid employment and in 2001 formed 44 per cent of the workforce, an increase of 1.5 per cent from the previous decade (Twomey 2002). In 2001 in the UK, 69 per cent of women and 79 per cent of men of working age were in paid employment, constituting a decrease in the difference between women's and men's employment rates from 14 per cent to 10 per cent in the decade from 1991 (ONS 2001a). More recent figures are virtually identical, at 69.8 per cent for women and 78.8 per cent for men (ONS 2006).

The changes observed in the last few decades of the twentieth century were due not only to social shifts towards gender equality but also because of economic restructuring: manufacturing jobs declined whereas employment in the service industries increased. Men traditionally dominated many sectors of manufacturing, whereas women have been concentrated in the service industries, hence many of the new jobs created have been taken by women.

These changes have led some commentators to argue that a 'genderquake' is taking place, that women are gaining equality at last and even that an emerging shift in power from men to women is taking place. Yet feminist researchers have argued that, despite significant changes in the patterns of female and male employment, women are still disadvantaged in paid employment

A closer look

Economically active and employed

Statisticians make a distinction between economically active and employed:

Economically active – The whole labour market, those currently in employment and those of working age available for employment but currently unemployed.

Employment rate – The actual number of persons in paid employment.

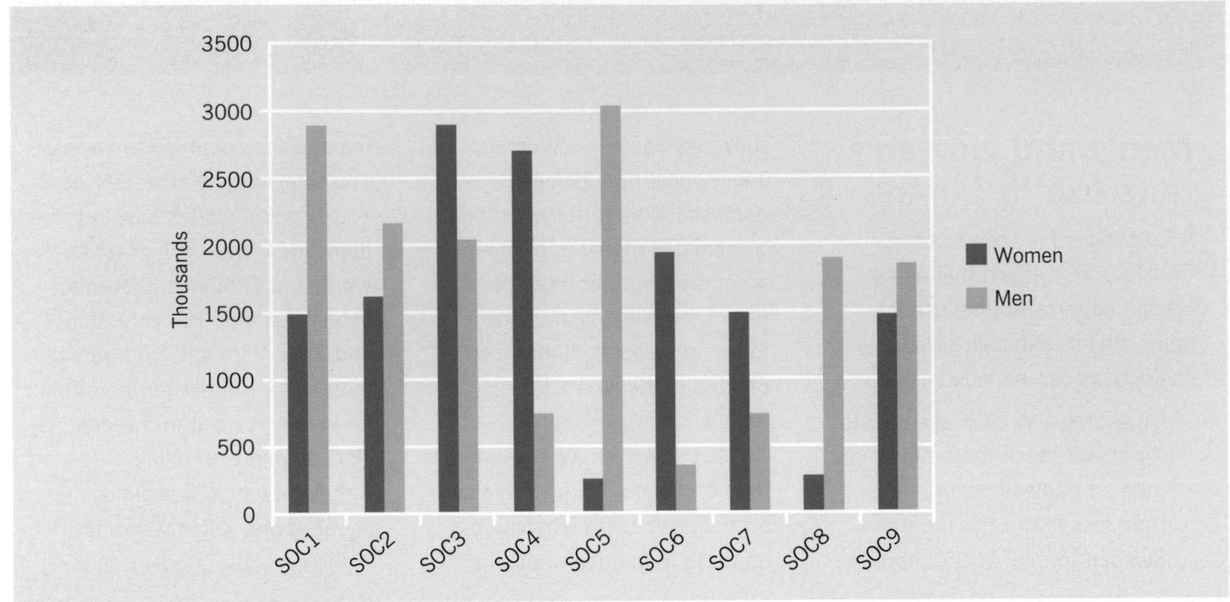

Figure 5.4 Women and men by occupational classification, UK 2007

SOC1: managers and senior officials
SOC2: professional occupations
SOC3: associated professions and technical
SOC4: administrative and secretarial
SOC5: skilled trades
SOC6: personal service occupations
SOC7: sales and customer service
SOC8: process, plant and machine operators
SOC9: elementary occupations

Source: *Labour Force Survey: Employment Status by Occupation and Sex, April–June 2007*, Office of National Statistics

compared with their male counterparts. These persistent inequalities are linked to the different types of work that women and men perform: men and women are still largely segregated into different occupations (Figure 5.4).

In the UK, women remain concentrated in a small range of roles: administrative and secretarial (SOC4: 20.2 per cent of all employed women), personal services (SOC6: 14.5 per cent of all employed women) and sales and customer services (SOC7: 11 per cent of all employed women) account for almost half of all women's employment, yet the same sectors provide only 11.7 per cent of men's occupations (ONS 2007). In addition, women work 'differently' from men: despite restructuring, men's employment remains mostly in full-time posts while a sizeable minority of women work part time: 41.9 per cent of employed women compared with 10.6 per cent of employed men (ONS 2007). However, these figures are less imbalanced than the figures of 43 per cent of women and 8 per cent of men working part time at the beginning of the twenty-first century (Twomey 2002).

The segregated labour market

Horizontal segregation describes the tendency for women and men to be concentrated in different occupations (Hakim 1979). In the UK in the 1980s, Jean Martin and Ceridwen Roberts (1984) found that 63 per cent of women were in jobs done only by women and 81 per cent of men were in jobs performed solely by men. As discussed above, women remain concentrated in a narrower range of occupations and sectors of the economy compared with men and tend to form the majority of part-time workers.

Stop and think

- List six occupations that you would describe as female-dominated and six as male-dominated. Why do you think these jobs are 'gendered'?

A closer look

A note on statistical recording

Beware the limitations of statistical records. Historically, 'estimating the labour participation rates of women is fraught with difficulties given the discrepancies in census data available' (Marchbank 2000: 41), as often the part-time work of married women has not been fully documented (Roberts 1990). Even today not all family businesses record all members as working and, for some women and younger adults, working in the family business can be yet one more strand of unpaid work (Afshar 1994; Delphy 1984).

However, gender is not the only division in the labour market: paid employment is an area that demonstrates the interaction of gender with a whole range of other factors. Black feminists have pointed out that black women have had a different relationship than white women with the labour market; this differential positioning is the product of historical, economic and ideological factors. Whereas white women have found themselves excluded from paid labour and defined as domestic workers, Afro-Caribbean women, since slavery, have been seen as the 'mules of the world', capable of heavy work. Different ideologies of femininity have shaped the experiences of black and white women. Afro-Caribbean women have always worked, which is still reflected in their higher rates of economic activity. Annie Phizacklea (1994) argues that labour markets across Europe are both gendered and racialized, even in traditionally female employment sectors such as home work. In fact, both men and women from ethnic minorities are less likely than white men and women to be in employment; in the UK this is especially so for Pakistani and Bangladeshi women.

Case study

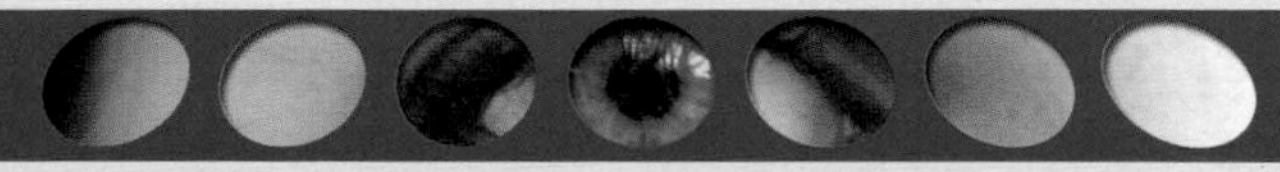

Bangladeshi and Pakistani women in the British labour force

Sameera Ahmed and Angela Dale (2008) have researched the labour market participation of Pakistani and Bangladeshi women in Britain. They used national survey data along with qualitative interviews. They examined participation rates from 2001–05 for women aged 19–60 years (not including full-time students). Their figures show that levels of economic activity vary by ethnicity:

Black Caribbean women – 78 per cent

White women – 77 per cent

Pakistani women – 31 per cent

Bangladeshi women – 21 per cent

They also confirmed that unemployment rates among the economically active are higher for Pakistani and Bangladeshi women:

Bangladeshi women – 16 per cent

Pakistani women – 15 per cent

White women – 3.4 per cent

They conclude that there seem to be particular barriers for Pakistani and Bangladeshi women, including the perceptions of potential employers:

> Attitudes of potential employers are undoubtedly significant influences . . . and are amplified when they are viewed as 'Muslim' women. Respondents in this study were unanimous in their belief that wearing a headscarf or face veil posed major barriers to finding a job.
>
> (Ahmed and Dale 2008: 22)

Comparing Pakistani and Bangladeshi women's rates of employment with those of white women showed that, in 2003, 72 per cent of white women worked while only 22 per cent of Pakistani and Bangladeshi women were similarly recorded (Hibbert and Meager 2003). However, when employed, men and women from ethnic minorities in the UK are no less likely than white men and women to work in managerial or professional activities (Hibbett 2002).

Vertical segregation describes how the division of labour between occupations is paralleled with that within them (Hakim 1979). When women and men work together in the same sector or organization, men are higher up the job hierarchy in better-paid, higher-status conditions. Even in the twenty-first century we still find this vertical segregation: although women have broken into many male-dominated areas of employment, they are still underrepresented and virtually absent from high-status positions. The 'glass ceiling' describes the phenomenon whereby women are progressing into high-status professions but are not making it to the top jobs even though they are as talented and able as the men who hold those positions.

Even where outright prejudice is absent, there remain institutional barriers. The structure of work remains very 'masculinized' – that is, it is based upon notions of male breadwinners who are free to work full time and who have no other commitments. However, there have been some changes to working patterns: in the UK in 2003, 27 per cent of women and 18 per cent of men worked in jobs that allowed for some flexibility (e.g. flexitime, job-sharing, term-time-only contracts) – a total of around six million UK adults (ONS 2003a).

The Employment Act 2002 gave UK parents the right to request flexible work if they are parents of young and/or disabled children; by 2007 this was extended to some employees caring for dependent adults.

> **There have been some signs of a positive impact, that it has been widely implemented and that there have been few major obstacles and many workplace benefits. While the level of requests has not significantly increased . . . the number or refusals by employers has fallen.**
>
> **Although women are the majority of those making requests and having their requests granted, men are also requesting flexibility in significant numbers. Men are more likely to seek options which, unlike part-time work, do not reduce earnings.**
>
> (Hegewisch and Pilinger 2006: 11)

However, even when a greater degree of flexibility is legally provided, patriarchal notions of gender have been hard to challenge. A study of Scandinavian fathers (in Denmark, Finland, Iceland, Norway and Sweden) found that the men had rights to parenting leave but chose not to take that leave for fear of jeopardizing their careers (Kaul 1991). A later study across the European Community by the European Opinion Research Group (2004) found that the rate of non-uptake of parental leave options varied from 33 per cent in Sweden to 95 per cent in Spain and Ireland. One reason for non-uptake was a lack of knowledge: 'over a quarter of men surveyed across the European Union claimed to be unaware of their right' to such leave (Marchbank and Letherby 2007: 83). In addition, in 2004, across 20 EU member states only a quarter of all employees aged 25–49 years (those most likely to be trying to reconcile work and family responsibilities) enjoyed some flexibility in their work schedules; further, 'employees with children seem to be less likely to work in jobs with flexible working arrangements than those without children' (Eurostat 2007c: 4).

It appears that although many men are parents, the majority of parents whose work patterns are determined by parenthood are women (Marchbank 2000). Figure 5.5 shows the amount of time men and women spend exclusively on child care in several European countries. However, note that this is time spent exclusively on child care and, as Bryson (2007: 156) notes, such time-use studies 'cannot capture the "being there" nature of caring'.

Parent status and child care

Across the world, men have a greater rate of economic activity than women. In the UK in recent years there has been a growth in part-time work, a growth that has been greater for men than for women. There is a distinct pattern to men's part-time work: the largest proportion of part-time working men are either under 25 or over 50, due to most of them being students or approaching retirement (Hibbert and Meager 2003). Unlike British men, British women who work part-time come from across all age groups. There is a distinct connection between women's part-time work and their parenting status: those women with young children are more prevalent in the part-time labour market, and this trend decreases with the increasing age of the youngest child. Of working mothers of children under five, 67 per cent work part time, but this falls to 45 per cent

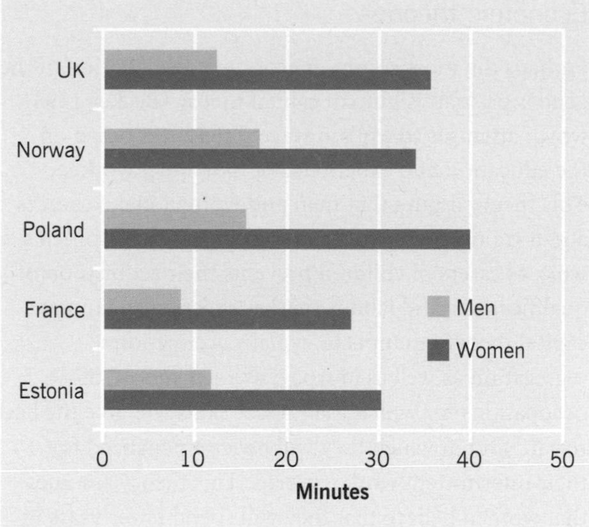

Figure 5.5 Time spent exclusively on child care, selected European countries

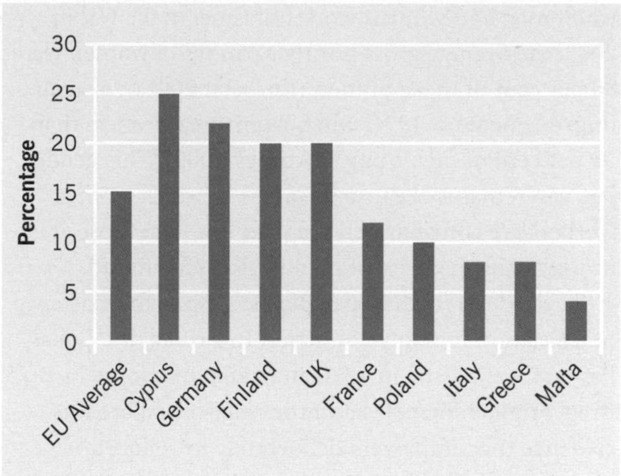

Figure 5.6 Gender pay gap, selected European countries, 2005

for those whose youngest child is over 16 (Twomey 2002). Given that only 32 per cent of childless women work part-time, it is clear that motherhood is a major factor in part-time economic activity; conversely, fatherhood does not seem to be a factor in men's reasons for working part time. White women are more likely than ethnic minority women to work part time, showing that, although ethnic minority women have lower employment rates overall, they are more likely, when in employment, to work full time (Hibbett 2002). One factor affecting the employment of mothers is the availability of affordable child care. Across Europe there is a strong link between the availability of public child care and the number of women who are mothers of under-fives and economically active (Marchbank 2000) (see Figure 5.5).

Pay

In a capitalist society the pay that people receive is a measure of the value of their labour. Compared with their male counterparts, women workers get less for their labour than male workers across the world (see Figure 5.6).

Figure 5.6 shows the gender pay gap in several European countries based on hourly rates of pay. However, if we look at total earnings and focus on the UK, the gender pay gap is overall 40 per cent; that is, women earned 60 per cent of men's wages in 2005. This is due partly to the greater tendency of women than men to work part time. However, a gap remains even

A closer look

Eurostat's definition of gender pay gap

The gender pay gap is given as the difference between average gross hourly earnings of male paid employees and of female paid employees as a percentage of average gross hourly earnings of male paid employees. The gender pay gap is based on several data sources, including the European Community Household Panel (ECHP), the EU Survey on Income and Living Conditions (EU-SILC) and national sources.

The target population consists of all paid employees aged 16–64 that are 'at work 15+ hours per week'.

The data cover EU-Member States, EU-aggregates, Croatia, Norway, and Switzerland.

(Eurostat 2007a)

when men and women work full time: in the UK in 2005, the average gross hourly earnings of women were 80 per cent of those of men (Eurostat 2007a), a small improvement on 1991, when women earned less than 78 per cent of men's pay (Twomey 2002). This gender pay gap remains because the areas in which women workers are concentrated are paid less than those areas in which the majority of men workers are found.

These differences in pay persist despite the existence of legislation in many countries. In Britain, the Equal Pay Act was passed in 1970 and came into force in 1975. In its original form, it had little impact as there was evidence that employers deliberately introduced segregation by sex in jobs where there had been none before in order to avoid giving female workers equal pay. In 1984 the Act was amended to refer to jobs of equal value; it was hoped that comparisons could be made across jobs and that many women performing jobs in which traditionally few men have been employed would come within the scope of the Act. Although some individual cases have been won, problems with the legislation remain. Many women are unaware of the existence of legislation or are reluctant to make claims because of the fear of victimization by colleagues and employees. More fundamentally, differential pay is related to the structure of the labour market, and the Equal Pay Act has had little impact on this structure.

Explanations for gender segregation in the labour market

A range of explanations have been put forward to explain gender segregation in the labour market and specifically why women generally undertake jobs that are relatively low paid and that are perceived as having low levels of skill. We describe some of the most famous theories below.

Economic theories

Perhaps the most common economic explanation of the gender pay gap is human capital theory (Becker 1993), which attempts to explain wage differences based on the education and experience of individual workers. This theory argues that men and women make choices about training and work and recognizes that women's work as carers of children prevents their acquisition of qualifications and labour market experience. Human capital theory attempts to explain occupational segregation as well as low pay: women choose those occupations for which their lesser skills will give the best reward and in which they will be least penalized for their intermittent work patterns. This theory assumes that women believe that they will spend fewer years in the labour market than men and so invest less in their own human capital.

This theory has its weaknesses. First, 'it ignores sex discrimination for it does not explain why women who have equal human capital to men . . . face limitations . . . and do not get promoted posts at the same rate as equivalent men' (Marchbank and Letherby 2007: 242). Second, it assumes that skill is an objective category, that there is consensus about what is skilled work and that all skills are recognized as such. In fact, as the economist Steven Pressman (2002: 31) concluded after studying cross-national data on gender poverty gaps, 'educational levels matter very little' and do not explain gender differences in pay. Across virtually every European Community country, young women have now surpassed young men in attaining formal qualifications and yet gender differences remain in the subjects studied, as women remain predominant in the 'soft' areas of arts, social sciences and welfare (Table 5.1). It appears that it is not the educational level that is achieved that matters but the areas deemed to denote valuable skills.

Table 5.1 Women and men with high educational level, by study field and age, EU25, 2005 (%)

	Women		Men	
Field of study/age group (years)	**25–39**	**40–64**	**25–39**	**40–64**
Arts, humanities, languages	28.0	36.4	12.7	16.2
Social sciences, business, law	36.3	23.7	30.5	24.0
Mathematics, science, engineering	13.6	12.6	43.8	43.6
Health and welfare	17.1	23.3	6.0	9.1
Services, agriculture, other	5.1	3.9	7.9	7.1

(Source: Eurostat 2007b: 6)

Marxist feminist approaches

Economic analyses such as that of Karl Marx examine the ways in which men sell their labour and employers benefit from the surplus value of that labour (see Chapter 12). Despite a virtual absence of women from Marx's analysis, many feminist Marxists have attempted to adapt Marxist theory to include the position of women. Various Marxist theorists acknowledge that women's labour is exploited, and some suggest that this can be understood by considering how the labour market is itself split into two key sectors that provide very different experiences and opportunities. In the 1970s two segments in the labour market were identified:

- *Primary sector* – Skilled secure work, good pay and working conditions, promotion prospects.
- *Secondary sector* – Unskilled, poor working conditions, insecure pay, few prospects (Barron and Norris 1976).

This approach argues that employers segment the labour market as part of a divide-and-rule strategy to control the workforce. They utilize pre-existing social divisions based, for example, on gender or ethnicity. Women are concentrated predominantly in the secondary sector, fitting into this sector easily because they will work for less money as they are not so committed to paid work because of their domestic roles. Women frequently leave work of their own accord and are less likely to join trade unions, making them easier to dispense with; the social distinction between the sexes means that women are demarcated from men, and this becomes a useful way of dividing the labour force (Barron and Norris 1976).

Marxist feminists also explain the experience of women in the labour market as the outcome of the capitalist economic system, and yet they identify the exploitation of women's labour as central to the functioning of capitalism and hence to the subordination of women. In much Marxist feminism, the sexual division of labour in the family and family ideology have been seen as crucial in placing women at a disadvantage when they enter the labour market. A range of explanations are proposed by Marxist feminism.

Marx noted that capital accumulation required a reserve of labour in order to prevent workers from being able to bargain up their wages and conditions in times of increased demand for labour. Veronica Beechey (1978) applied this theory to women, arguing that they constitute a flexible reserve of labour that can be brought into the labour market when boom conditions increase the need for labour and let go to return to the home in times of recession. This type of approach has been applied to Western women's employment during the two world wars, when, due to the shortage of male labour, women were required and encouraged to enter the labour market, particularly in munitions factories, and to engage in trades that had once been a male preserve. Images such as 'Rosie the Riveter' (in the USA) were part of the wartime strategy to encourage women to enter the labour market. Women were 'let go' at the end of the war to make way for the returning men (in some cases, the women were forced out by law), and governments were able to utilize ideologies about domesticity and motherhood, women's suitability as wives and mothers, the need for mothers to rear their children, and men's right to work.

The Marxist feminist approach pays little attention to the role of men in excluding women from work and the role of trade unions in maintaining the segmented labour market (Cockburn 1991). A further weakness of this theoretical position is that

> **it does not take into account the fact that there are women in the primary sector and men in the secondary sector, nor is it able to explain the differential experiences amongst women, for example the fact that ethnicity is related also to pay rates.**
>
> (Marchbank and Letherby 2007: 242)

In fact, one of the most fundamental critiques of this approach is that there is too much focus on the role of capitalism and not enough on gender relations.

Capitalism and patriarchy: the dastardly duo

Some feminists have tried to understand women's position in the labour market as a product of both the economic relations of capitalism and patriarchal gender relations; this reflects a broad change of direction in socialist feminism. A key thinker in this area is Heidi Hartmann (1981), who argued that segregation by sex and women's low pay can be explained only by exploring the way in which patriarchy and capitalism work together to form a system that she referred to as 'patriarchal capitalism'. The basis of male power in this social system is men's control over female labour, in both the family and the labour market. Segregation by sex in the labour market has secured male dominance, and men's demand for a family wage ensures that men have higher wages and economic power in the household. Hartmann argues that men have organized via trade unions to exclude women from certain areas of work. Capitalist employers have benefited from this arrangement chiefly by obtaining women's labour cheaply in many areas of the labour market. Walby (1986) also took a dual-systems approach, but she stressed that patriarchy and capitalism are two separate systems that interact together in a variety of ways, and not always harmoniously as Hartmann proposed. Walby suggested that these two systems have conflicting interests over women's labour. Men dominate in the labour market but this is in tension with capitalist relations, as employers are keen to exploit all forms of labour, particularly women's labour. Women's access to paid work on an equal basis to men would give women greater power and hence undermine patriarchy and male privilege. Walby identifies a pattern of struggles and compromises between employers and male workers and examines a range of historical and contemporary events to illustrate her theory. For example, she considered the Factory Acts passed in the late nineteenth century. Women were entering factory employment in large numbers and capitalists were happy to use their labour, but this threatened the patriarchal family. In excluding women, male workers and trade unions had not only the health and safety of women workers at heart but also the dominance of male workers. Eventually a compromise was reached: women were excluded from certain sectors of the labour market, for example from mining in the UK. Although groups of women opposed this exclusion, their voice was not heeded.

One criticism of this dual-systems approach is that it still does not consider gender enough, in particular the ways in which the sexual division of labour reflects gender-specific roles and functions. This is not just about who does which job but also about the gendered expectations of how that job should be done.

Summary

- The sociology of gender has been developed by feminist women and pro-feminist men concerned with how gender differentiation has meant the subordination of one sex, women, who have been assigned certain gender characteristics and roles. Gender is socially constructed. We are all gendered beings, and more than two possibilities for gender expression exist.
- Sexuality is also socially constructed, which has implications for the relationships between women and men and for the oppression of women and some men. Gendered bodily ideals are also socially constructed, and these ideals alongside expected roles and responsibilities are represented in the mass media.
- Some progress towards equality for women in the household and in the labour market has been achieved, but inequality persists. Gender ideologies still structure labour market choices and opportunities for women and men. The labour market is a site where meanings about femininity and masculinity are constructed and reinforced.
- Gender is a crucial social factor in producing adequate explanations of social behaviour and the organization of social institutions. Gender relations have been researched in all areas of social experience. This is reflected in the fact that many chapters in this book consider gender; perhaps one day there will not be a separate chapter such as this one in sociology textbooks, if gender distinctions and divisions are eroded and gender studies become fully integrated into sociology.

Links

Chapter 9, gender relations in the majority world (pp. 389–393).

Chapter 11 (pp. 449–451).

Chapter 12 (pp. 485–512).

Issues of gender are relevant across most areas of sociology. For instance, Chapter 15 (pp. 627–635) looks at education and gender and Chapter 17 (pp. 722–725) at media and gender.

Further reading

Abbott, P., Wallace, C. and Tyler, M. (2005) *An Introduction to Sociology: Feminist Perspectives*, London: Routledge.
A comprehensive introduction to feminist sociology that considers theory and method and covers a broad range of topics and areas – stratification and inequality; education; the life course; the family and household; crime, violence and criminal justice; politics; and mass media and popular culture.

Jackson, S. and Scott, S. (eds) (2002) *Gender: A Sociological Reader*, London: Routledge.
A book containing 50 short readings that clearly demonstrate the 'gendering' of sociology.

Kimmel, M.S. and Messner, M.A. (2004) *Men's Lives*, 6th edn, Boston and New York: Pearson Education.
A collection of articles focusing on men's lives (particularly in the USA) in both public and private spheres. Topics include boyhood, family life, sexuality, health and the media.

Marchbank, J. and Letherby, G. (2007) *Introduction to Gender: Social Science Perspectives*, Harlow: Pearson Education.
A broad, interdisciplinary introduction to the themes and debates within gender studies. Gender is explored through the disciplines of history, sociology, social policy, anthropology, psychology, politics, pedagogy and geography. The book also integrates the gendered aspects of eight issues, including health and illness, work and leisure, and culture and the media.

Richardson, D. and Robinson, V. (eds) (2008) *Introducing Gender and Women's Studies*, 3rd edn, Houndmills: Palgrave Macmillan.
A comprehensive introductory text with chapters on a wide range of areas of women's experience, including feminist theory; men, masculinities and feminism; feminism and technology; families, domesticity and intimacy; work; media and popular culture; and sexuality and cyberspace. Each chapter outlines and summarizes key research, debates and theories.

Websites

www.gender.org.uk/about/00_prefc.htm
A site discussing what gender is and how it has been studied.

www.newser.com/tag/18210/1/gender-stereotypes.html
An online resource of news stories drawing on gender stereotypes.

Activities

Activity 1

Identifying gender

Go to the following places and observe what people are doing:

- a busy high street or shopping centre;
- a public transport vehicle, e.g. bus or train;
- a children's playground;
- a coffee shop or a public bar.

Questions

1. Can you tell who is male and who is female? How – what clues are there to gender identity?
2. Make a list of the 'different' behaviour of males and females. Are gender differences more evident in some places than in others?
3. Is gender the only signifier of difference? If not, what other aspects of people's identities are significant? How do different aspects of an individual's identity interact?

Activity 2

Personalizing gender

Write your own autobiography focusing on gender relations and how they have affected your life. Among the areas and aspects of your life, you might consider (a) relations with and between family members; and (b) the importance of gender relations at significant stages of, or events in, your life – births, weddings, going to new schools, joining clubs, starting work and so on. How did gender influence your schooling, the jobs you have done or are hoping to do, your leisure pursuits – what you do and what you would like to do?

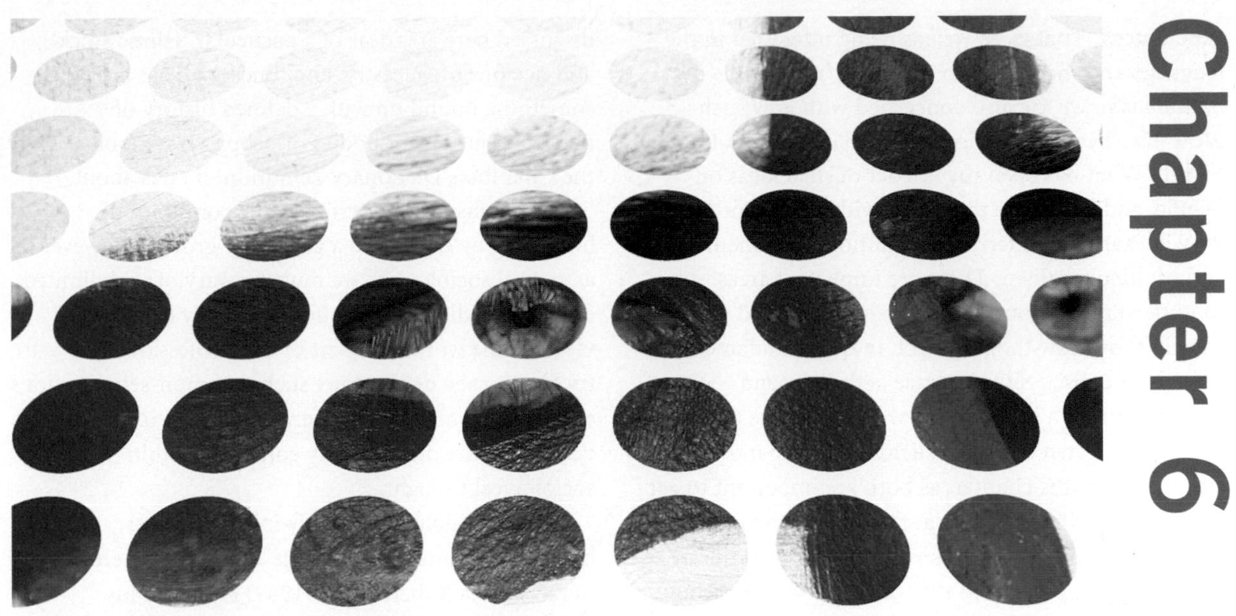

Chapter 6

'Race', ethnicity and nationalism

Colin Clark and Noah Canton

In the latter part of the twentieth century the vast improvements in communications and transport together with the creation of global markets have brought the peoples of the earth more together and, in some respects, have jumbled them up so that the old boundaries between groups are no longer so distinct. As the frameworks have weakened, individuals have become more interested in questions of racial and ethnic identity and the ways in which their subjective experience does not accord with the assumptions of others . . . These trends should increase interest in a bottom up approach to questions of racial and ethnic relations . . . (Banton 1998: 235)

Key issues

- How can we sociologically best explain 'race', ethnicity and nationalism, and what are the connections within and between them?
- In what ways do different groups of people experience racism, and how does it disadvantage them in wider society?
- What connects identity, citizenship and multiculturalism?
- What prompts people to migrate, and what are their experiences of settlement?

Introduction

This chapter explores some questions and answers to the four key issues raised here. We will examine three related and connected areas of sociology: 'race', ethnicity and nationalism. We will unpack some of the historical, conceptual and theoretical aspects of work in these fields and spend some time defining our key terms of reference. However, such work cannot be carried out in isolation from the experience and impact of such ideas, so we will explore the contexts and environments in which 'race', ethnicity and nationalism are experienced. That is, as well as being interested in the language and theory of, for example, 'race' and nationalism, we are also concerned with how such ideas have been *experienced* by people in the 'real world'. What has been the impact of such ideas on people, and how have they dealt with them? Further, we will examine patterns of migration, settlement and multiculturalism. These are important areas to understand in contemporary sociology, and we will show how they connect, in quite fundamental ways, to the discussion on 'race', ethnicity and nationalism. In a similar way, we spend some time looking at related concepts such as identity and citizenship in this chapter, as both are important to get to grips with when looking at the wider dynamics of ethnic and racial studies. As you read through the chapter it is important to try and relate what is being discussed to your own understanding of these ideas. There are various exercises and questions that can help you do this.

Unpacking 'race', ethnicity and nationalism

> **Race is a monster. It is tremendous and terrible and astonishingly resilient. Race changes shape, size and color as the need arises. It is a monster because of the manner in which it has been employed for the justification of a systematic oppression and for the wholesale muder of huge populations. Race is also a monster because of the exacting tenacity with which it survives despite more than a few deliberate and sophisticated attempts to remove the concept from our ideological lexicon.**
>
> (Niro 2001: 1)

Defining key terms

To begin with we need to spend a little time examining the origins and meanings of the term 'race'. Such a term is contested – meaning that there have been lively debates about where the term came from and the way it has been used over the years. For example, an ordinary dictionary (e.g. Cassell's Concise Dictionary) might define 'race' as a major division of human beings descendent from a common stock and distinguished by physical characteristics. What is being discussed here are ideas of a particular 'ethnic stock' and notions of 'ancestry' and 'lineage'. That is, it is something bound up with a defined history of particular groups or bodies of people. If we look at the Chambers Dictionary definition, it talks about 'inherited disposition'; that is, 'the condition of belonging by descent to a particular group'. However, as critical sociologists, we must be wary of such limited definitions: dictionaries offer us socially constructed views of the world and part of our professional job is to try to critically deconstruct such common-sense notions and instead run through the various ways in which definitions are often heavily contested within sociological thought.

In fact, sociology, certainly in recent times, has been less interested in 'race' and more interested in racism. As Robert Miles (1989) argues in his influential text on racism, the two terms are quite different, with racism being sociologically defined as the holding of derogatory social attitudes or cognitive beliefs towards members of a particular group on account of their membership to that group. Indeed, as Augoustinos and Reynolds (2001) suggest, racism includes the belief that racial groups are physically and biologically different, and this can lead, and has led, to the forming of beliefs regarding the superiority of certain groups over others. These beliefs are often translated into actions that seek to maintain these superior and inferior positions and to create artificial boundaries and divisions between the different groups, which are economic, social and political in nature.

Over time, however, 'ethnicity' has arguably replaced 'race' as an everyday term to try to make sense of differences between groups. One of the advantages of using the term 'ethnicity' is that it helps us focus more on the characteristics of *social* groups, which, in turn, can lead us to rely more upon ideas and notions of a common culture and shared identity. What is important here is that such ideas and notions can be real or perceived, and identity can be constructed and based around things such as culture, religion, language and tradition. What is very clear in all this is that there is an uncertain relationship existing between ethnicity and 'race'; and this uncertainty is exactly what the sociology of ethnic and racial studies explores (e.g. in journals such as *Ethnicities*, *Ethnic and Racial Studies*, *Race and Class*, *Journal of Migration and Ethnic Studies*, and *Journal of Refugee Studies*).

Stop and think

1. Be brave (!) and venture into your university library. Track down a few of the above journals and any others that focus on ethnic and racial studies.
2. Flick through a few back copies and get a sense of what the articles are discussing.
3. Try to read, at the very least, the abstracts of five or six different articles from different journals.

➤ From this brief snapshot, what kind of language and terminology are the authors of the articles employing to discuss their fields of study? What are the differences and similarities among the authors and articles?

Explaining prejudice

Another important idea to be aware of in the field of ethnic and racial studies is what might be termed the language of prejudice. Prejudice is an area that has received a lot of attention in the social sciences, especially from disciplines such as sociology and psychology. Prejudice may have both a social and a biological basis to it, although there is much debate on this. What is apparent is that when we talk about prejudice we are really meaning a preconceived and unreasonable judgement or opinion of people or situations (the term literally means to prejudge a person, event or situation). In other words, it happens when we form an impression or opinion that has not been based on evidence or a full examination of the facts – we show *bias*. As we shall see later in this chapter, prejudice (opinions) can often turn quickly to discrimination (actions), and this can leave its mark on people's experience of racism (for example, being refused employment because of skin colour or religious views). Clearly, where prejudice is negative, it often results in harmful or unfavourable consequences for the 'victim'. Psychologists often talk about 'in-groups' and 'out-groups', making reference to the fact that prejudice can be used to render some groups as outsiders or inferior (Nelson 2005).

Stop and think

Sociobiologists and ethologists regard prejudice as something to do with 'animal instincts' of territoriality and feral restraint. Writers such as Robert Ardrey and Richard Dawkins have argued that aggression is an innate characteristic directed against others as a survival mechanism. According to this view, 'it is biologically fixed that humans form exclusive groups, and that these groups succeed internally in so far as they close up against outsiders' (Fernando *et al.* 1998: 17). As this exclusionary behaviour is said to be based upon physical differences it is hard to explain why some of the worst examples of ethnic cleansing involve peoples who are physically alike.

Psychologists have argued that prejudice is more a matter of ignorance and may arise from egotism and inflexible ethnocentrism (if unsure, you should look up this term in your sociological dictionary, although we will examine it below).

Sociologists tend to suggest that prejudice may be bound up with socialization – that the influences we are subjected to at formative stages of our life are crucial to the development of social attitudes (think here of the character Shaun in Shane Meadows' film *This is England* (2006) and how he is 'turned' by Combo).

The literature on prejudice also suggests that there are connections between prejudice and racism that are more structural in nature; that is, prejudice could be a necessary means of creating scapegoats for individuals and/or groups that feel threatened (e.g. asylum seekers and refugees being housed in areas of multiple deprivation where white working-class families feel under pressure and 'swamped').

➤ Based on your own understanding of the concept, what do you think best explains the nature of prejudice?

➤ Why do you think racial differences are such a powerful basis for prejudice?

➤ What is it that makes someone a racist – is it one thing or a combination of several factors?

Ethnocentrism

If someone were to put a proposition before men bidding them choose, after examination, the best customs in the world, each nation would certainly select its own.

(Herodotus)

In looking at prejudice, it is also worth exploring, briefly, the notion of ethnocentrism. This is a key concept in social anthropology and other social sciences, and involves examining any given issue from a viewpoint that has a particular and specific cultural background to it. So, for example, you may judge one culture and set of cultural practices through the restrictive lens of your own culture and cultural practices. To take an ethnocentric view is to look at any given issue in a narrow way. This, in turn, can lead to biased opinions and the formation of stereotypes, which can often be national as well as individual; for example, 'The Scots are mean', 'The English are arrogant', 'The Irish are stupid'. However, this can apply to any person who comes at an issue from a certain ideological tradition and brings with them a certain amount of 'cultural baggage' that involves a range of stereotypes: these are regarded as being relatively fixed and unchangeable sets of oversimplified beliefs about groups of people or events, calling for their simplified representation. For example, loose generalizations and characteristics of people become their essential forms. In a racialized context, stereotypes can be used as a justification for certain social, economic and political actions and policies, and often confer what sociologists call a 'master status' upon the group members concerned. This process of 'stigmatization' has also been examined in our coverage of the social model of disability (see Chapter 8).

Stop and think

But dehumanizing the victim makes things simpler
It's like breathing with a respirator
It eases the conscience of even the most
conscious and calculating violator
Words can reduce a person to an object,
something more easy to hate
An inanimate entity, completely disposable,
no problem to obliterate . . .

Listen to a copy of the song 'Language of Violence' by Disposable Heroes of Hiphoprisy on their 1992 album *Hypocrisy is the Greatest Luxury*. You can also find the video for this song on YouTube. The lyrics explore the tale of a young boy who turns from aggressor into victim through the American criminal justice system.

- Think about the lyrics above. In what ways can 'words . . . reduce a person to an object'? In what ways can such sentiments be related to current media discourses around refugees, asylum seekers and migrants?
- Is this something that *has* to occur, with certain groups being depersonalized and dehumanized?
- What other groups are subject to such processes in the UK? Gypsies and Travellers? Muslims? Who else?
- Why might it be useful to dehumanize a group we seek to victimize?

On origins of 'race' and racism

Like 'nations', 'races' too are imagined, in the dual sense that they have no real biological foundation and that all those included by the signification can never know each other, and are imagined as communities in the sense of a common feeling of fellowship. Moreover, they are also imagined as limited in the sense that a boundary is perceived, beyond which lie other 'races'.

(Miles 1987: 26–7)

When it comes to discussing the origins of 'race' and racism, there are, as you might expect, many conflicting perspectives. For some, particularly Christian religious scholars, it is prudent to look to the Bible where, it is said, 'race' is used to indicate the order in which families or species evolve from one generation to the next. Between the eighteenth and twentieth centuries, certain aspects of the Bible were used by those in power to justify racism and slavery. In particular, the 'Hamitic hypothesis' remained unquestioned throughout this period and was taken seriously by religious scholars, ethologists and anthropologists until the 1930s. It was based upon the story (in Genesis 9: 20–27) that tells of the curse that Ham's father, Noah, placed upon Ham's son Canaan after Ham witnessed his father drunk and naked in his tent. This story has been used to justify both the early Israeli enslavement of the Canaanites (who were said to be descended from Canaan) and the later racist treatment and enslavement of black Africans who were understood to be descended from Ham. Although now thoroughly rejected, these prescientific ideas held sway for a number of years, largely because the 'curse' was said to be a 'darkening of the skin' that affected both Ham and his son Canaan (see also p. 158 in Chapter 4, in which we explore the role of religious ideas as 'divine explanations' of inequality).

From here, it is said, the cultural associations of 'blackness' and 'smitten skin' took on an (ideological) life of their own, and the legacy remains. Such associations are not confined to the vaults of historical and biblical times. Think about the differences between 'whiteness' and 'blackness' in everyday life: why in the UK do we tend to wear black clothes at funerals? Why is blackness associated with sadness, alongside other negative imagery and emotions?

Since early times, blackness has been falsely associated with elements such as dirt, evil and savagery. Think of the terms below and write down what they mean in everyday discourses. You might also want to look up dictionary definitions as well:

Black sheep =

Black comedy =

Black death =

Black market =

Blackwash =

Blackleg =

Blacklist =

Blackmail =

➤ Can you add any others to this list?

Stop and think

In 1556 *A Summarie of the Antiquities, and wonders of the Worlde* was published in England. This popular book included stereotypical images of Africans as 'inherently carefree, lazy and lustful', which drew upon the writings of Pliny some 1500 years earlier:

> Readers were told that Ethiopians had no noses, others no upper lips or tongues, others again no mouths. The Syrbotae were eight feet tall. The Ptoemphani were ruled by a dog. The Arimaspi had a single eye, in the forehead. The Agriophagi lived on the flesh of panthers and lions, the Anthropophagi on human flesh. There were people in Libya who had no names, nor did they ever dream. The Garamantes made no marriages; the men held the women in common. The Gamphasantes went all naked. The Cynamolgi ('dog-milkers') had heads like dogs' heads. The Blemmyes had no heads at all, but eyes and mouths in their breasts.
>
> (Fryer 1984, quoted in Marsh *et al.* 1998: 243)

Aside from biblical reference points, it is important to be aware that representations of the 'other' existed long before European expansionism and colonialism began. Indeed, pre-sixteenth- and seventeenth-century ideas of 'the other' very much influenced the colonial expansionists. Before the fifteenth century Africans and Muslims, in particular, were characterized as being 'other', and in Greco-Roman times notions of 'images of savages' sought to link together physical and animalistic images to associate such 'othering' with hypersexuality, 'monsters' and 'blackness' (Miles 1989). This is worth dwelling on, as it is evident that in defining this mythical 'other' we are, in turn, saying something about ourselves. But what is this? Do we define ourselves in contrast to others?

In the seventeenth and eighteenth centuries, this African and Asian (in the main) 'other' began to be viewed by Western eyes with what could be regarded as an 'environmentalist gaze'. This gaze has a long history to it and sought, in a similar way to the early biblical stories, to explain differences in physical features and skin colour between 'us' and 'other'. With rather fanciful ideas of 'God's curse' on the way out, other ideas were looked to, trying to account for differences between different groups of human beings. Climate was now regarded as a key factor: this was seen as impacting on both the phenotypical (that is, the observable physical or biochemical characteristics of an organism) and cultural characteristics of populations. Indeed, an essay by Samuel Stanhope Smith in 1787 ('Essay on the causes of variety of complexion and figure in the human species') proposed that diversity among the human species was due to environmental influences – or 'climates' and 'states of society'. Smith argued that exposure to 'savage states' had roughened, darkened and coarsened the human condition, which explained physical differences.

It is not surprising, then, to discover scholars of this period making sweeping generalizations about Africans and their culture that are simply racist. David Hume, a distinguished philosopher and empiricist (so he ought to have known better!), condemned black people in the following manner, despite having never set foot in Africa:

> **I am apt to suspect the Negroes, and in general all the other species of men to be naturally inferior to the white. There never was a civilized nation of any complexion than white, nor even any individual eminent in action or speculation. No ingenious manufacturers amongst them, no arts, no science.**
>
> (cited in Fryer 1984: 152)

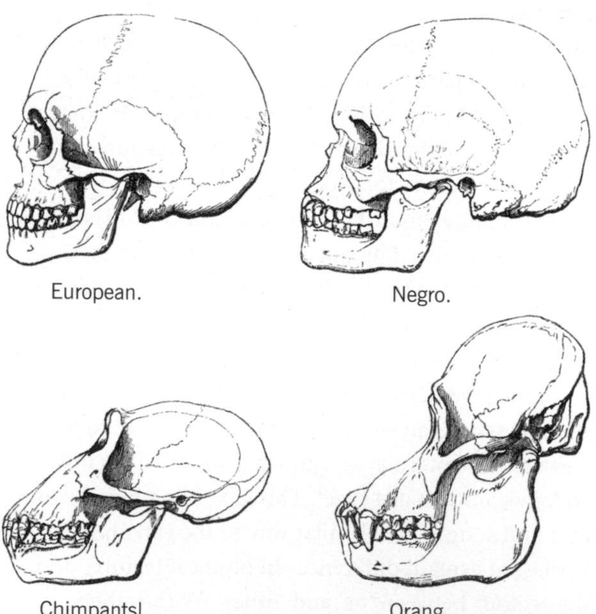

Figure 6.1 An early 'scientific' drawing that attempts to show that the typical Ancient Greek skull shape is more 'advanced' and 'evolved' than that of the 'Negro', which is more akin to that of a young chimpanzee. Such 'science' is now thoroughly discredited as being fundamentally racist and without substance
The Print Collector/Alamy

Monogenism versus polygenism

Such ideas brought into focus questions about 'races' being the same or different species. Here we can trace two different bodies of thought: those advocating a monogenist (genetic sameness) position believed that all people are essentially the same (sometimes referred to as the 'Out of Africa' thesis), while those arguing for a polygenist (genetic differences) position believed that human beings originated in separate parts of the world and had different racial characteristics (see Kohn 1996). This latter view was often used to support enslavement and discriminatory treatment. In the context of the slave trade, for example, polygenists were enslavers while monogenists were liberators. From the sixteenth to the nineteenth century, at least, the polygenists had enormous influence and success in their attempt to establish a dominant ideology of racial differentiation, cultural diversity and hierarchy, which rendered slavery and racial segregation as 'natural' practices. Again, in the context of the slave trade, it made for good business, as whole populations could be subjugated and enslaved for trade with apparent good reason.

This all raises much wider questions about 'race' and genes and the development of polygenist and monogenist ideologies during the slave trade. Although there is not space here to dwell long on this subject, it is important to mention it as it helps us to understand the connections and differences between religious and scientific racism. The polygenists increasingly turned to science to support racism, exploiting the assumed objectivity and reliability of scientific knowledge to advance their cause. However, with the outcome of the US Civil War (1861–65) and other historical moments, the monogenists were winning the moral battle of slavery and racism. Of course, the formal abolition of slavery, which occurred in 1807 in Britain under the direction of William Wilberforce, did not mark the end of racism. Those proposing a polygenist approach turned to science and scientific evidence to try to advance their arguments. It is here that the early social sciences were emerging and offering comment, and it is apparent that some eminent social scientists were advocating positions that would support a scientific racist approach to questions of human division and difference.

The 'science' of 'race'

> **The fact that pre-Darwinian scientific racism flowered in France and the United States more than**

> in England may derive to some extent, paradoxical as it may seem, from the revolutionary legacies of nation-states premised on the equal rights of all citizens. Egalitarian norms required special reasons for exclusion . . . simply being a member of the lower orders would not suffice.
>
> (Fredrickson 2002: 68)

It is worth reminding ourselves of the huge social and intellectual transformation that European societies and America were undergoing in the late eighteenth and early nineteenth centuries. The Enlightenment brought with it, along with new science, ideas and theories, the need for social order and stability in the context of fast-changing societies. For our purposes here, the key point is that 'race', in terms of its ideological usage, was entering debates and discussions about the ways in which humanity can be split into distinct groupings whose members have supposed common or shared physical characteristics. Alongside this usage of 'race', of course, came the development of racism and the historical experiences of slavery and colonialism. But a longer-term view, as we have seen, indicates that there has been a long historical awareness of phenotypical and cultural differences, all the way back to ancient societies such as Egypt, Greece and Rome. However, the point is that divisions during these periods were based not around alleged 'racial' differences but more around what we think of today as class or caste. Before the advent of the Atlantic slave trade and colonialism, it is clear that skin colour had less significance; although Africans in Europe may have faced discrimination (see Fryer (1984) on the treatment of Africans in Britain under the reign of Elizabeth I), it is also the case that they were treated as 'different but equal' (Davidson 1984) and regarded with respect.

Scientific racism

With the Enlightenment and the adoption of more supposed 'scientific' approaches to questions of 'race' (as opposed to religious and environmental explanations), we can trace back the beginnings of racial doctrines and ideologies. Images of 'the other', as we discussed, took on new racialized meanings and people were increasingly being defined by group on a physical basis and categorized within a racial taxonomy that placed Europids at the top, Negrids at the bottom and Mongoloids somewhere between the two (Kohn 1996).

Stop and think

Conduct some independent research and investigate some of the scientists in the UK, Europe and America who worked in the area of 'race'. We have listed five individuals below, but see if you can find five other scientists.

- P. Camper (1722–89) on facial angles.
- G. Cuvier (1769–1832) on Caucasian, Mongolian and Ethiopian types of mankind.
- F.J. Gall (1756–1828) on cranial measurement.
- R. Knox (1791–1862) on English Anglo-Saxon 'race' as superior to all others.
- J.K. Lavater (1741–1801) on appearance as equating to 'intellect'.

We cannot disentangle science from the Enlightenment, and there is a need to look at science in the context of broader philosophical, social, political and economic transformations of the late eighteenth and nineteenth centuries. Certainly, by the early nineteenth century 'race' as a concept contained a number of features and aspects, including the ideas:

- that physical appearance and the behaviour of individuals was an expression of a fixed biological type;
- that cultural variation was due to different biological types;
- that biological variation was the origin of, and resulted in, individual and national conflicts;
- that some 'races' were 'better', 'higher' and 'superior' than others.

An example of where such ideas led can be found in the work of Joseph Arthur Comte de Gobineau (1816–82). Although somewhat ignored when first published, and drawing on areas as diverse as linguistics and anthropology, his paper of 1853–55, entitled 'An essay on the inequality of human races', is now regarded as one of the first examples of scientific racism. Gobineau argues, forcefully, that 'race' is the primary driving force determining world events and issues. Drawing on the work of others, Gobineau maintained that there were three 'races': 'black', 'white' and 'yellow', each with its own distinct culture. He argued that there were 'barriers' between these 'races' and that any form of 'race-mixing' would 'upset' these barriers and lead to a breakdown of society (as, he said, had already occurred in places such as the Indian subcontinent and southern France). In keeping with people such as Robert Knox (1791–1862), Gobineau believed that the 'white' 'race' was superior to all other, coming as it did from the ancient Indo-European culture (Aryan):

> **[History] shows us that all civilisations derive from the white race, that none can exist without its help, and that a society is great and brilliant only so far as it preserves the blood of the noble group that created it, provided that group itself belongs to the most illustrious branch of our species.**
>
> (cited in Banton 1987: 48)

The legacy of Gobineau's thought was heavily edited and used by the Nazi regime to propose that the Aryan 'race' was the creator of the world's civilizations and that the 'mixing' of 'races' was something to be stopped (this is most noticeable in the anti-Semitic Nuremberg 'racial hygiene' laws of the 1930s, but it is also evident in the 'Jim Crow Laws' in the USA after 1877 and the Immorality Act 1949 in South Africa).

As we can see, then, the nineteenth century and the first part of the twentieth century witnessed the emergence and growth of scientific racism and the social sciences played a key role in this, alongside the 'natural' sciences. Gobineau was just one of many. For example, in the UK, a few eminent psychologists, including Galton, McDougall, Cattell and Spearman (Augoustinos and Reynolds 2001) embraced the essentials of scientific racism. Galton and Spencer were arguably the main architects of scientific racism but, for some, it was Charles Darwin who offered a link between Bible-sanctioned slavery and emerging scientific racism. Born at The Mount in Shrewsbury, England, in 1809, Darwin went on to graduate from the University of Edinburgh with a medical degree; he used his training and knowledge to research and write publications such as *On the Origin of Species* (1859), *Descent of Man* (1871) and *The Expression of the Emotions in Man and Animals* (1872). In such work, Darwin offered his theory of evolution – a theory that made historical debates between monogenists and polygenists somewhat redundant. Evolution extended the timescale over which life processes operate and this allowed greater time for the development of diverse types of human being from a common origin. Darwin advocated the dynamic nature of biological change, moving away from formal and static classification. In terms of natural selection, he argued that the origins of variety in the natural world came about via accident or spontaneity, and it was those species that were best able to adapt to new and different environments that allowed for the continuation and growth of species that 'survived'. Darwin did promote a view of the survival of the fittest, but he also suggested that Europeans were related to Africans and that all humans were related to the apes. However, this was more about mechanics and not as some kind of 'league table' of those racial groups that were stronger or lower in terms of civilized development. Of course, Darwin's theories and legacy have been open to much differing interpretation. Neo-Darwinists have suggested that ideas of heredity and variation challenged directly ideas of 'fixed' species types. However, Darwin's work has also been simplified and politicized to support a number of ideas that he would have had issues with, such as the eugenics movement. Having said this, like most people alive during his time, Darwin never considered the 'less civilized races' to be truly human (Bergman 1993), and social Darwinism led directly and indirectly to racism and anti-Semitism. Darwinism was used to justify the concept of 'survival of the fittest', in which only superior nationalities or 'races' survive. Social Darwinism had an enormous impact far beyond the racism championed by the scriptures, such as the Nazi 'project' and the Final Solution.

As we have seen so far, a key moment was arrived at in terms of various attempts to try to explain physical and cultural 'difference' between the human species, differences that appeared, at face value, to challenge monogenist notions. With increasing European travel and exploration came the need to explain human variation, especially physiological, cultural and linguistic differences. It was during the 'enlightened' eighteenth and nineteenth centuries that the belief in science took hold and there was a need for established 'norms' and rules of scientific method. There was to be little place in scientific circles for religious 'stories'. However, when applied to questions of 'race', we have seen that a scientific approach has not always been well intentioned or without prejudice. Biological essentialism and genetic determinism took hold, and in this way a kind of 'you are what you are' ideology became mainstreamed that served to hold good past, present and future. We have touched on social Darwinism already and seen how the 'survival of the fittest' led to war, conquest, subjugation, colonialism and imperialism. However, the eugenics movement of the early twentieth century, alongside the post-1945 Nazi experience, proved to be the death knell for 'race science', and it fell from grace within the natural sciences, at least for a period and in its visible, uncompromising format (Kohn 1996).

Stop and think

Monogenist and polygenist debates continue to this day, although these are often conducted in softened language or high-brow scientific debate. Conduct some Internet and library research to find out more about the following topics and issues, all relevant examples of how the monogenist/polygenist debates continue to play out:

- the 'G' factor (Chris Brand, Arthur Jensen and others);
- the 'underclass' (Charles Murray and others);
- the 'bell curve' (Richard Herrnstein, Charles Murray and others);
- genetic similarity theory (Philippe Rushton);
- the 'selfish gene' theory (Richard Dawkins);
- r-K theory (MacArthur and Wilson, Rushton and others).

Concepts and theories

> **This world is white no longer, and it will never be white again**
>
> (James Baldwin 1955)

Moving on from defining the key terms of reference and examining some of the historical theories on origins, we need to determine the main conceptual issues and theoretical debates in this general field of study. As sociologists, we have to explore some of the dilemmas, contradictions, tensions and areas of controversy, and try to evaluate the relative worth of these ideas and examine the bearing they have on 'the real world' (for example, the way, at times, in which abstract ideas can bear influence on legal systems, policy and politics). With regard to ethnic and racial studies, it is clear that different terms mean different things to different people. This is not an unknown situation within the social sciences across a range of concepts and social divisions, such as gender and class (Payne 2000). From just a brief glance at a website such as www.amazon.co.uk you can see that a multitude of books in the field have advocated a varied range of theories and concepts. Such concepts and theories have been applied within both academic discourses and policy and lay discussions regarding 'race', ethnicity and nationalism. Often, you find that key terms of reference work together, such as 'ethnic minority', or such terms can be used interchangeably, such as 'race'/ethnicity. These terms can raise further, subsequent questions; for example, if we speak of an ethnic minority, then what of the 'ethnic majority'? This is increasingly being problematized as 'the racialisation of Whiteness', whereby authors such as Mac an Ghaill (1999) and Bonnett (2000) wish to take apart the idea of 'whiteness' and subject it to the same critical scrutiny that has been applied to 'blackness' over the years. This is a growing area of interest and one not without its controversies, as can be seen on the BBC website www.bbc.co.uk/white/, which has clips and discussion of a television series on the white working class in twenty-first-century Britain.

The focus on racism instead of 'race'

Despite the post-war public disgrace of scientific racism, notions of 'fixity' in questions of 'race' have refused to disappear fully from public and political discourses. It is not surprising, on one level, as even among critical sociologists who acknowledge that 'races' in this limited genetic/biological sense do not exist there is a tendency to talk and write about the concept, often at some length. However, as we indicated earlier, although the term 'race' itself might still be in use, the vast majority of social scientists are more interested in racism (as an experience) rather than 'race' (as a concept), and in studying the perception of others that 'race' might be real. This shift can arguably be traced back to the 1960s when sociology as a discipline was undergoing something of a radical transformation, not least because of a rebirth of Marxism as an explanatory tool for understanding changes in wider society. Marxist scholars argued that to treat 'race' as a concept was to give it ideological meaning and legitimacy – entirely the wrong approach. Such 'fixed' divisions between supposed different 'races', Marxists argued, were not due to differences in genes (or even belief systems and environmental factors) but rather were concerned with socioeconomic and political exploitation and oppression. This is one reason why we now see a contemporary focus on racism and its many forms, whether individual, group or institutional. This leaves us with a conceptual lacuna (a gap in which something is missing): if 'race' is to be ignored, avoided or sidelined, then what emerges in the sociological and policy forum in its place?

Ethnicity

> **Ethnicity refers generally to the perception of group difference and so to social boundaries between sections of the population. In this sense ethnic difference is the recognition of a contrast between 'us' and 'them'.**
>
> (Wellman 1977: ix)

The concept of ethnicity was first introduced in the 1930s and began to take hold in Europe in the 1950s (Barth 1969; Jenkins 2008). Its growth in importance is attributable to the post-war redundancy of 'race' as an explanatory concept within both the natural sciences and social sciences. As Miles and Brown summarized:

> **In Europe, North America, and Australia, the idea of 'race' is now usually (though not exclusively) used to differentiate collectivities distinguished by skin colour, so that 'races' are either 'black' or 'white' but never 'big-eared' and 'small-eared'. The fact that only certain physical characteristics are signified to define 'races' in specific circumstances indicates that we are investigating not a given, natural division of the world's population, but the application of historically and culturally specific meanings to the totality of human physiological**

Case study

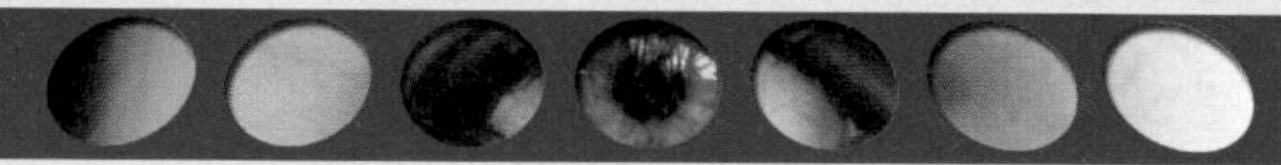

Ethnicity – the new racism?

In 1935 two British academics, Julian Huxley and Alfred Haddon, challenged the increasingly popular racist ideologies of the day in a book entitled *We Europeans*. They argued that the discredited biological concept of 'race' should be replaced with the socially defined notion of 'ethnic group' in the hope that this would undermine ideologies of racial supremacy. However, the idea of racial difference has survived and is often confused with the concept of ethnicity. As Hazel Croall has pointed out, 'Social relationships become racialised when racial differences are assumed to be significant' (Croall 1998: 161). If cultural badges of difference are mistaken for biological ones, we may simply end up with what Martin Barker (1981) has labelled the 'new racism'. In the discussion below, the persecution of groups on the basis of ethnicity is examined through the work of Marek Kohn and Michael Ignatieff.

By the 1930s, the idea of 'race' as a meaningful biological concept had been established through the work of eugenicists in the USA and Europe who, in the name of 'racial science', argued that the innate characteristics of individuals were related to their racial origins. By studying the physiological differences of these groups and identifying their intellectual, psychological and physical traits, it would be possible to identify the strengths and weaknesses of each racial group. These physiological differences usually bring to mind differences in skin colour, body size and shape, but in many parts of the world it is not physical but cultural differences that are seen as significant. In regions such as Central and Eastern Europe where the black/white dichotomy is not in evidence, it is ethnic group membership that is more important as a mark of difference, although racial terminology is still often used and many ethnic groups are talked of as if they are racial groups (for example, the search for the 'Hungarian gene' continued well into the twentieth century).

In his work on 'racial science', Marek Kohn (1996) demonstrates the universal power of racial discourse, whatever we choose to call it. In Europe, for example, attitude surveys have revealed that the Roma (Gypsies) are 'the most unpopular ethnic groups in each country

Case study *continued*

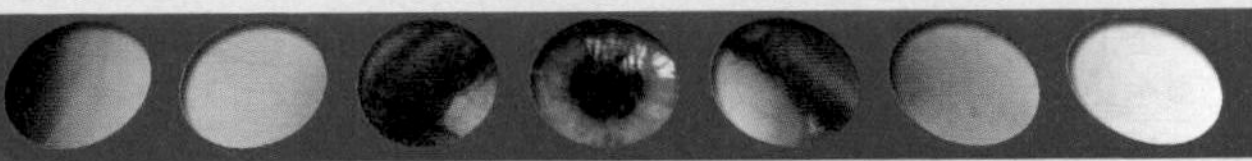

polled'. Using evidence from Slovakia, the Czech Republic, Hungary, Romania and Bulgaria, Kohn concludes that 'hostility to the Roma might therefore be considered one of the principal characteristics of racism in East and Central Europe' (Kohn 1996: 183). Since the Middle Ages, the attitudes and actions of a land-based peasantry towards the nomadic Romani have always been hostile. In the nineteenth century Cesar Lombroso argued that Gypsies were innately criminal because they were 'so low morally and so incapable of cultural and intellectual development', and even under Soviet rule the common perception was that 'Gypsies were untidy, anarchic and archaic, requiring modernization in the same way that horses required replacement by tractors' (Kohn 1996: 192). With the re-emergence of post-Soviet nationalism, it is not surprising to discover that Gypsies continue to be identified as outsiders:

> In the vision that prevails in Central and Eastern Europe . . . nationhood depends on the bond between land and people, hitherto based on the peasant way of life. This implies that the Roma are not an authentic people.
>
> (Kohn 1996: 194)

In 1993 a pogrom in the Romanian village of Hadareni demonstrated how powerful such beliefs can be. Following a fight, villagers with the help of the police revenged themselves on the local Roma by kicking to death two Gypsies being held in custody, burning 13 houses and killing another man. Following the incident, a local resident said:

> We're proud of what we did . . . We did not commit murder. How could you call killing Gypsies murder? Gypsies are not really people, you see. They are always killing each other. They are criminals, sub-human, vermin. And they are certainly not wanted here.
>
> (Kohn 1996: 184)

In *Blood and Belonging*, a work concerned almost exclusively with ethnic division, Michael Ignatieff (1994) examined the impact of nationalism and national identity on societies characterized by ethnic division. His research took him to the former Yugoslavia, the Ukraine, Germany, Quebec, Kurdistan and Northern Ireland. In all cases it was not obvious 'racial' characteristics that inspired conflict and persecution but cultural differences; the closer the physical resemblance between groups, the more violent the response to ethnic division:

> Nationalism is most violent where the group you are defining yourself against most closely resembles you. A rational explanation of conflict would predict the reverse to be the case. To outsiders at least, Ulstermen look and sound like Irishmen, just as Serbs look and sound like Croats – yet the very similarity is what pushes them to define themselves as polar opposites. Since Cain and Abel, we have known that hatred between brothers is more ferocious than hatred between strangers.
>
> (Ignatieff 1994)

As Ignatieff says with regard to the civil war and ethnic cleansing in the former Yugoslavia:

> A Croat, thus, is someone who is not a Serb. A Serb is someone who is not a Croat. Without hatred of the other, there would be no clearly defined national self to worship and adore.
>
> (Cited in Marsh *et al.* 1998)

Questions

1. In your own words, describe the difference between the concepts of 'race' and 'ethnic group'.
2. What evidence is provided in the work of Kohn and Ignatieff to support Barker's idea of a 'new racism' based upon ethnic group membership?
3. Why do you think the Roma are a target for persecution in Central and Eastern Europe?
4. How would you explain Ignatieff's observation that nationalist violence is at its most extreme where the groups in conflict are similar in appearance?

> variation. This is made equally evident by historical evidence that records that certain populations have been categorised as different 'races' at different historical times and in different places. *Thus, the use of the word 'race' to label groups so distinguished by some combination of phenotypical and cultural attributes is one moment in the ongoing social construction of reality: 'races' are socially imagined rather than biological realities.*
>
> (Miles and Brown 2003: 89; our italics)

What makes ethnicity so attractive?

For most critical sociologists, but certainly not all, 'ethnicity' is a much preferred term over 'race'. First, it allows us to avoid the explicit determinism of 'race' with its genetic/biological connotations; second, it allows us to offer some degree of self-ascription – that is, people can have some control over how they are defined and labelled as individuals belonging to wider 'ethnic' groups (Fenton 1999). A constant feature across various theoretical positions advancing the causes and meanings of ethnicity is a reliance on the 'stuff' of culture.

So, although 'race' had been deemed an inappropriate explanatory tool by the international community and the academic community, there was a continued need to make sense of the obvious cultural, social and political differences between groups that had previously been seen as 'racially' distinct. These did not just 'disappear'. These differences could be based on any one of a whole range of characteristics within what we might call 'cultural' – nationality, language, religion, perceived racial background and so on – and usually they were based on a complex combination or fusion of all of them. In particular, there was a need to analyse the tensions and advantages and disadvantages that seemed to be almost inevitably associated with these differences. Thus, with 'race' deemed inappropriate to explain these tensions, 'ethnicity' filled an analytical gap. Some authors suggest that 'ethnicity' is really a 'politically correct' term for what we used to call 'race' and, in reality, little of substance has changed except the language and terms we now use (Miles and Brown 2003: 93). This is an extreme view, but one with some support. What we can say is that, in Britain, 'ethnicity' took on both an academic and a legal importance – although the difference between legalistic and academic definitions is more a question of emphasis than of essence.

Stop and think

Questions of ethnicity and ethnic identity are not just a sociological or abstract theoretical exercise. The British legal system has something to say on this as well; for example, ethnicity has become a key legal category within the Race Relations Act (1976) (amended 2000). In 1983, the issue of ethnicity was given definitive consideration by the House of Lords in the *Mandla* v. *Dowell Lee* case. In his analysis, Lord Fraser argued that there were two 'essential' characteristics and five 'relevant' characteristics:

> For a group to constitute an ethnic group in the sense of the 1976 Act, it must, in my opinion, regard itself, and be regarded by others, as a distinct community by virtue of certain characteristics. Some of these characteristics are essential; others are not essential but one or more of them will commonly be found and will help to distinguish the group from the surrounding community. The conditions which appear to me to be essential are these: (1) a long shared history, of which the group is conscious as distinguishing it from other groups, and the memory of which it keeps alive; (2) a cultural tradition of its own, including family and social customs and manners, often but not necessarily associated with religious observance. In addition to those two essential characteristics the following characteristics are, in my opinion, relevant: (3) either a common geographical origin, or descent from a small number of common ancestors; (4) a common language, not necessarily peculiar to the group; (5) a common literature peculiar to the group; (6) a common religion different from that of neighbouring groups or from the general community surrounding it; (7) being a minority or being an oppressed or a dominant group within a larger community, for example conquered people (say, the inhabitants of England shortly after the Norman conquest) and their conquerors might both be ethnic groups.
>
> (*Mandla* v. *Dowell Lee* [1983] 1 All ER 1066–7)

- Do some Internet research and find out more about the *Mandla* v. *Dowell Lee* case. What was this case about, and what was the outcome of it for those involved?
- In terms of the two 'essential' characteristics that Lord Fraser mentions, can you easily apply these characteristics to your own ethnic group? Try and write some notes addressing the ways in which your ethnic group meets these conditions.
- Look at the five 'relevant' characteristics that Lord Fraser mentions. If you were asked to rank these in terms of their importance, what order would you put them in?
- Given the Mandla criteria, to what extent can people 'choose' or 'wear' their ethnicity, and how does this impact on their relations with others?
- In 2003, David Beckham was named as Britain's 'most famous black man' in a TV documentary entitled 'Black like Beckham'. Is it at all justifiable for David Beckham to be considered a black man? Can we really choose who we want to be in terms of our ethnicity and ethnic identity? The scale or range of this 'choice' can be quite wide, itself illustrating the displays of unity and dedication to the distinct 'cause' of particular cultural identities.

Exploring ethnic identity

> **The question of identity has received extensive attention . . . it is now widely recognised that we do not have one fixed identity but a range of shifting identities and that these are socially constructed. Of critical importance to this process of social construction is representation.**
>
> (Pilkington 2003: 209)

It is evident that there are some 'ethnic' identities that we are 'born into', while others we learn or acquire. In another form, especially for postmodernist scholars, the boundaries of ethnicity are wide open and are little more than a symbolic strength to be relied upon in an instrumentalist fashion. It is useful here to look at the work of Fredrik Barth. Barth edited a collection of essays entitled *Ethnic Groups and Boundaries* (1969), in which he sets the tone in a seminal introductory paper outlining his view that ethnicity involves the negotiation of boundaries between people and groups: the focus has to be on the relations between groups and the ways in which ethnic identities are connected together. Barth goes further and argues that those ethnic labels/categories that are sustained and 'stronger' are those whereby individuals move across boundaries or share identities with individuals in other groups. In other words, for Barth, ethnic identity is created via processes of relationships with others, and the nature of these processes determines, in part, the inclusion and exclusion of certain individuals and groups. The point is this: boundaries establish and help regulate relationships *between* different groups, whether real or perceived. In point of fact, it is primarily much less to do with internal or 'insider' coherence of a distinct ethnic identity. That is, in knowing what we are not, we know what and who we are.

In other words, in the sociology of everyday life, we tend to draw on strengths that we have and play down or relegate our perceived weaknesses. This is true of various identities that we take on. When it comes to ethnicity, its flexibility and management can be impressionistic, and it can be situational as well as relational. In other words, sociology sees ethnic categories and identities as open to change rather than being fixed. In a Western European sense, 'ethnicity' or 'ethnic' is often used as a codeword or synonym of 'difference'; but for some people, 'difference' or 'ethnic' can equate to 'not British', neatly avoiding the question of whether 'Britishness' itself has an uncontested existence. If so, what elements would be included in this cultural mix? This is a useful exercise as it raises wider questions regarding the extent to which we can argue that some aspects of 'culture' are perhaps predetermined (this itself reminds us of debates of nature versus nurture). In such ways, the (stereotyped) behaviours and actions of culture become associated with particular ethnic identities, for example 'the luck of the Irish', 'the Gypsy look' and 'Asian entrepreneurship'. In the cultural worlds of fashion, music, the arts, business and sports, such ideas are widespread, but we must consider what they really tell us.

There are material concerns here about focusing on 'difference' and 'diversity' and trying to make theoretical connections between culture and ethnic identity. For example, in 1997 the Policy Studies Institute (PSI) published its fourth survey report entitled *Ethnic Minorities in Britain: Difference and Diversity* (Modood *et al.* 1997). We will look at the main findings of this study in more depth later on in this chapter. The report was, at the time, the most influential and comprehensive overview of Britain's ethnic minorities in terms of their socioeconomic and political standing. The subheading for this survey report was most telling: for the first time the PSI started to acknowledge the majority/minority problematic alongside the traditional black/white dualism. In other words, the PSI and the authors recognized that diversity between different minority groups is as important as differences from the majority white population. It is also worth noting, as an aside, that not even this comprehensive report was complete in telling the story of Britain's ethnic minorities: nowhere in its pages did it mention the Gypsy and Traveller population of Britain, some 200,000–300,000 citizens. Indeed, there are other tensions as well – we can look at the 'shared experience' of racism across all minority groups, but at the same time it is important to acknowledge the fact that different groups experience racism, and feel its impact, in many different ways as it in turn intersects with complex questions of class, gender, age and sexuality, among other social divisions in society. It should be noted that in much of the ethnic and racial studies literature, especially more recent texts and articles, reference is often made to ethnicity not only in abstract terms of 'culture and identity' (e.g. Hall 1997; Gilroy 2004) but also, arguably, in more concrete, material issues such as citizenship, social exclusion and poverty (e.g. Platt 2007; Woodward 2004). In other words, the construction of identity draws on many resources – physical, positional, cultural and economic – all of which influence what we might regard as 'lifestyle' choices; for example, Tiger Woods will probably have a very different experience of life and view of the world compared with a Puerto Rican single mother living in a trailer park and flipping burgers at McDonald's for a living.

The extent to which social theories present ethnicity as being socially fixed by circumstances has been criticized, and their limits have been tested by alternative points of view and the active resistance to such labels by individual members of the minority groups concerned. Certainly in the UK context between the 1950s and 1980s, there is a sense that minority ethnic identity was often presented as being somewhat static, with individuals and groups being represented as one-dimensional and castigated as perpetual 'victims' in the face of white prejudice, discrimination and violence. This is not to suggest that such prejudice, discrimination and violence did not occur – far from it – but rather to argue that such positions and realities were one of many. It does not help to present a skewed, selective or exaggerated vision – this has a potential danger, in that any sense of minority ethnic agency is seen as removed or is rendered hopeless. There is plenty of evidence of 'ethnic' political mobilization (for example, think of the campaign by the Lawrence family after the racist murder of their son Stephen in 1993) as well as generational differences and changing identities that allow for more public articulation of need.

Stop and think

With regard to changing identities, the golfer Tiger Woods was asked on the *Oprah Winfrey Show* in April 1997 whether it bothered him that people described him as 'African-American'. He replied that it did; he went on to say: 'Growing up, I came up with this name. I'm a "Cablinasian".' This self-ascription of his own ethnicity, a portmanteau, reflects the fact that he is one-quarter Chinese, one-quarter Thai, one-quarter African-American, one-eighth Native American and one-eighth Dutch: 'Ca Bl In Asian' is short for 'Caucasian, black, Indian and Asian'. It is worth noting that the reaction from some sections of America's African-American community to Tiger apparently being 'bothered' when called African-American was not positive, and his assertion of a multiracial identity was regarded as being something of a 'sell-out'.

- To what extent could 'Cablinasian' be considered as a 'real' ethnicity? Could we not all apply such convoluted understandings of our own ethnicities?
- Is an ethnic label such as 'Cablinasian' the ultimate example of a hybrid identity?
- How are popular understandings of 'race' and ethnicity influenced by celebrity and media culture?
- Why do you think Tiger Woods' comments generated such reaction from sections of the African-American community?

The controversy over Woods' comments illustrates the complexity and sensitivity that can arise when choosing to define yourself as *x* or *y* ethnicity, especially if *x* or *y* is infused with other letters to become a plural rather than a singular ethnicity. Yet this is increasingly common as, for example, second and third generations of minority ethnic groups come to grapple with new definitions of self, such as 'Scottish Asian', 'Anglo-Chinese', 'Black British' and so on. What is important is that such new identities are not in and of themselves 'weaker' or 'diluted' in comparison with first-generation groups but rather are different and are constructed from more options than were previously available. Such issues are now a central part of the kind of 'identity politics' that authors such as Stuart Hall (1992) have discussed. This has, in fact, become an increasing part of the language of sociology in relation to what might be thought of as 'pick and mix ethnicity'. It might be argued that, with the impact of post-1960s radical sociology, and, more latterly, globalization, all things identity are, in a sense, 'up for grabs' and as part of a cultural shift we are witnessing more fluid approaches to how we define ourselves in relation to others, vis-à-vis ethnic identity. Within postmodern schools of thought, this is often talked about as multidimensional or provisional identities and ethnicities; there is a discontinuity with the past to embrace a new, less restrictive future. Of course, it is useful to wonder what prompted this shift or, rather, whether this is just 'natural' social change.

Case study

Forget black, forget white. EA is what's hot

It stands for 'ethnically ambiguous', a term embracing a whole new generation, from US mega-stars to Brixton clubbers, who have grown up colour-blind.

In the Plan B bar in Brixton, the DJ plays black R&B music in a part of town once seen as 'Black' but the crowd is mixed. They regard themselves as Generation Ethnically Ambiguous. While many blacks and Asians are casting aside the old ethnic labels as crude and outmoded, many white youngsters are embracing so-called 'black' lifestyle and culture in fashion, grooming, music, sport and language. As Nurj Khan, a nurse from Camberwell, explains: 'Trying to define people by the old race labels just doesn't work any more. Look around you. Can you pigeonhole these people? To me, that doesn't undermine the fact that culture and heritage are an integral part of life, but there is more to it than just colour.'

In the movies and the worlds of fashion and pop music, this fusion of culture and appearance has been well marketed in response to changes in America and the UK . . . Almost one million young Britons identified themselves as members of more than one race or of 'no race' in the most recent census, the first in which respondents could choose their ethnic origin. 'Mixed Race' is now the third largest ethnic minority group in Britain and is set to become the biggest over the next decade.

As blacks and Asians move away from colour-based labels, observers say that white youngsters are moving towards traditional black lifestyles, creating the new 'blended' youth.

'Black urban culture has become the mainstream culture,' says journalist and social commentator Paul McKenzie. 'It represents the triumph of the immigrant black community.'

As with all social trends, the first people to pick up on the rise of Generation EA have been media and entertainment groups. This can clearly be seen in the casting of mixed race movie stars and the 'racially-indeterminate, melting pot aesthetic' characterizing the catwalks of the fashion world. It is also beginning to have an impact on pop music; after years of churning out lily-white, blond-haired, blue-eyed boy and girl bands, the music industry is remixing looks as fast as it remixes singles.

Multiracial bands such as the Sugababes are replacing the likes of Boyzone and Westlife. Even mega-stars are deliberately tweaking their looks, playing with audiences' perceptions of their origin. ▶

Case study *continued*

Among male stars, Eminem and Justin Timberlake, who are white, claim that their music is as 'black' as songs by such US rappers as P. Diddy or 50 Cent.

Ambiguity sells, marketing experts say, not only because it – helpfully – covers all bases but because it suits the times. 'There is a current fascination with the racial hybrid,' says Sean Pillot de Chenecey, a London-based trend analyst and researcher who has worked for Levi's and Coca-Cola. 'For the marketing industry, the focus is on trying to reflect the blending of cultures. It's about art imitating life.'

The transition from segregated cultures to multiracialism is now so marked that some believe the time has come to dismiss race altogether as a useful social indicator. US academic Evelyn Hammond, a professor of the history of science and Afro-American studies at Harvard, recently told the *New York Times* that race was an 'invented concept' used 'to categorize perceived biological, social and cultural differences between human groups'.

In Britain, Michael Eboda, editor of the black newspaper *New Nation*, says, 'The barriers between black and white are really coming down.' At the Commission for Racial Equality, Trevor Phillips agrees: 'The CRE is not just here to go about shouting "racism, racism, racism". I want to bring the word integration back into fashion because I think it is what is going on already. Public bodies need to catch up with real life and work out how to take things even further forward.'

Back on the streets of Brixton, what do those in Plan B bar make of these claims? Is Generation EA a reality? In the multiracial, pluralist culture in which we now live, does race still matter, or has the new climate of crossover, fusion and cultural diversification relegated colour to the margins?

Nick Leader, a 25-year-old research consultant who has travelled from Hampstead, north London, to party with his friends, says: 'People don't make a distinction now because the distinction is dissolving – culturally and even at times physically.

'We are the new mix. We are the remix generation.'

(Adapted from John Arlidge, *Observer* 4.1.2004)

Question

1. Using contemporary Britain as an example, what evidence is there to support or refute Leader's notion of a 'remix generation'?

From theory to the 'real world'

Theory moves on, reflecting changes in the 'real world', and at least two main approaches challenge modernist and structuralist viewpoints. First, feminism has helped us to understand the category of 'women' as problematic and has challenged essentialist positions on both gender and ethnicity, especially the work of authors such as Anthias and Yuval-Davies (1983). Similarly, postmodern and post-structuralist accounts have actively sought to view ethnicity as 'negotiated', whereby one can almost adopt a variety of complex identities to suit the mood, such has been the impact of post-colonial debates that challenge, for example, categories such as 'whiteness' (Rattansi and Westwood 1995). It is evident, however, that, in general terms, the social world is quicker than social theory; social theory *reacts to* rather than *leads* 'real life'. There are many contradictions that theories in ethnic and racial studies struggle with and need to address. One of the more fundamental ones, perhaps, is that on the one hand there is increasing social mobility among minority ethnic groups and reactions against their supposed 'victimology' but on the other hand there is evidence of continued material inequality and differential treatment based on ideas of 'race'. How do social theorists deal with a situation characterized by both continuity (ongoing racial and ethnic discrimination for some) and change (new opportunities and success stories for others)? This dilemma highlights debates between modernists or materialists and the postmodernists. Modernists/materialists are largely concerned with addressing questions of human rights abuses and with social, economic and political actions to confront areas of inequality and discrimination (employment, housing, education etc.). For postmodernists, however, the concern is chiefly one of embracing the 'new world order' and the idea that individuals are too diverse, fluid and fragmented to advocate a 'one size fits all' approach to righting such wrongs. The focus should be one of allowing greater choice, style and diversity, with the celebration of 'difference' as a key goal. However, the ideas of freedom and choice are problematic in a society where resources are not equally distributed; some people have more choices and freedoms than others. There are dimensions here to both public and private spheres – where equality is formally supported, especially in the guise of a multicultural society. The biggest dilemma, perhaps, is how we 'judge' or measure progress – there is a need to look at solid empirical data in order to give the theory and concepts some meaning. This is what we will turn to in the section examining the findings of the fourth PSI survey (Modood *et al.* 1997).

Inequalities and social exclusion

> **The obsession of 'race relations' research with the extent and impact of racial discrimination to the exclusion of most other factors encourages a perspective in which West Indians, Pakistanis, Indians etc, come to be viewed unidimensionally as the objects of other people's beliefs and behaviour.**
>
> (Miles 1982: 65)

Although now over a decade old, the fourth national survey of ethnic minorities conducted by the PSI in London in 1997 is still an important source of data on the ethnic minority experience of inequality and social exclusion in Britain (Figures 6.2–6.4). Entitled *Ethnic*

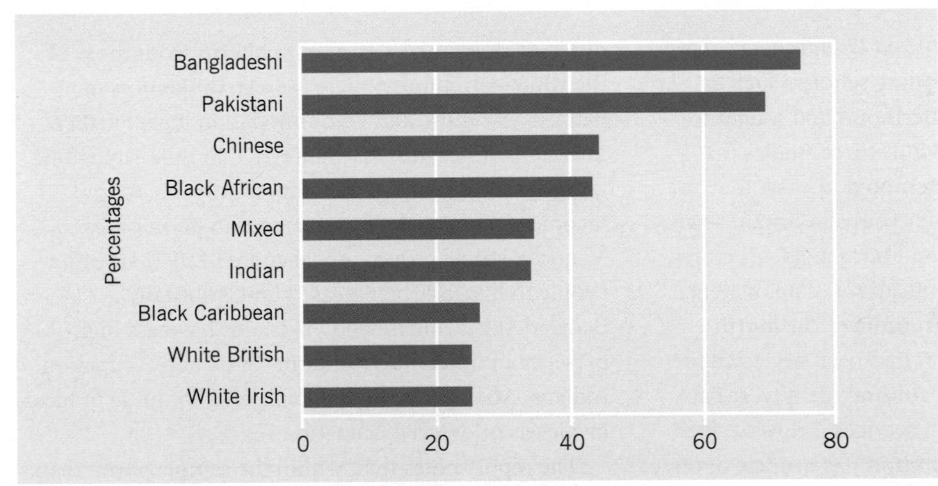

Figure 6.2 Economic inactivity rates of women, by ethnic group, Great Britain, January to December 2004

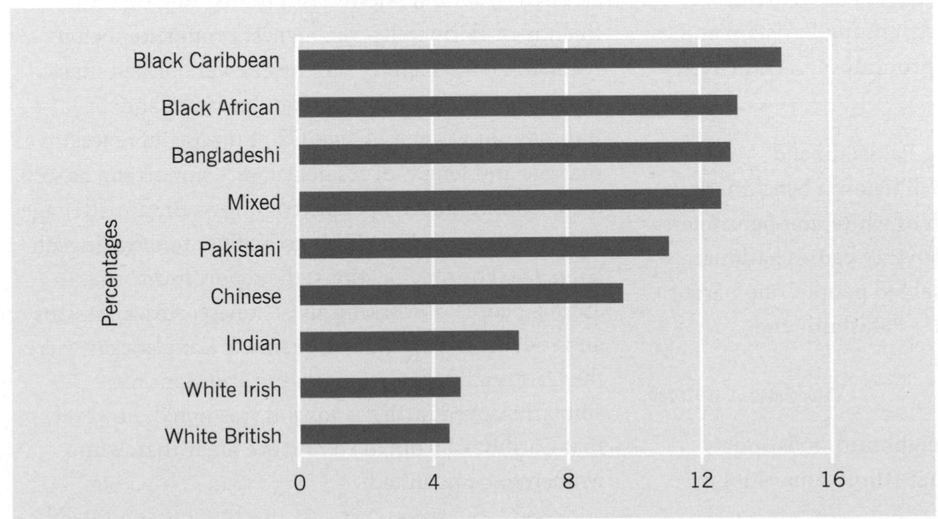

Figure 6.3 Unemployment rates of men, by ethnic group, Great Britain, January to December 2004

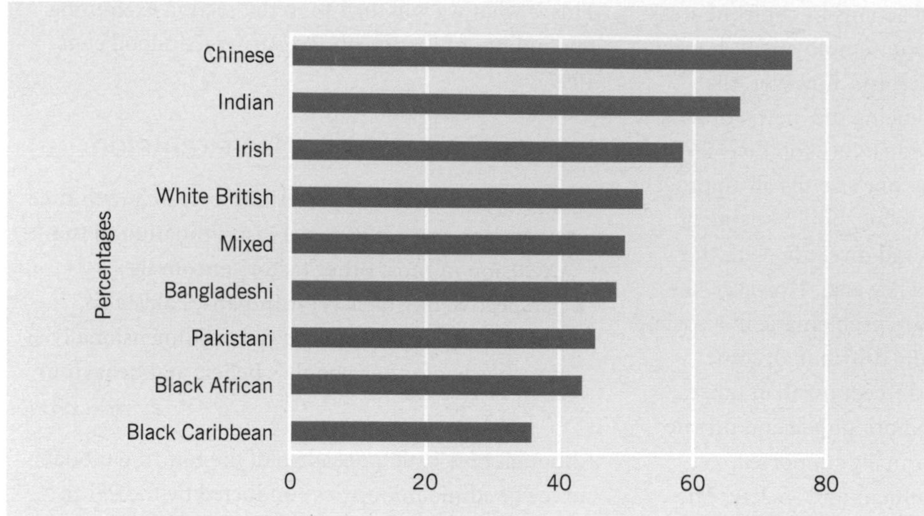

Figure 6.4 Attainment of five or more GCSE grades A* to C or equivalent, by ethnic group, England, 2004

Minorities in Britain: Diversity and Disadvantage, the survey was coordinated by leading scholars such as Tariq Modood and Richard Berthoud and sought to build on the work of the previous three studies that the PSI had conducted; all attempted to chart the experiences of minority ethnic groups in Britain since the 1960s in terms of family and household structures, language, education and qualifications, employment and income, housing and community. The fourth survey took on new issues that had been neglected in the previous surveys, such as cultural identity, racial harassment, health and health services. Below we look at some of the most important findings in a few of these areas.

In relation to income and standards of living, it was noted that rates of poverty among Pakistani and Bangladeshi households are pronounced. As the report states,

> **more than four out of five Pakistani and Bangladeshi households fell below a benchmark which affected only a fifth of white non-pensioners. Name any group whose poverty causes national concern – pensioners, disabled people, one-parent families, the unemployed – Pakistanis and Bangladeshis were poorer.**
>
> (Modood *et al.* 1997: 180)

Similarly, in relation to neighbourhoods and housing, the report argues that ethnic minorities have different residential settlement patterns from those of the white community; there are also differences in patterns of tenure and accommodation type. Further, the report notes the disadvantages that minority ethnic groups face in terms of housing, mostly due to low incomes and histories of settlement in poorer areas. Minority ethnic groups are far more likely than white people to live in urban areas, with Caribbeans, Bangladeshis, Chinese and Pakistanis having a high presence in inner cities. In terms of owner-occupation, Indians, African Asians and Pakistanis continue to have low levels of owner-occupation.

The report notes that, within the sample, more than three-quarters of men in each Asian group were assessed by an interviewer as speaking English either fluently or fairly well – the highest proportion being African Asians. Gender differences were picked up on, especially with regard to Indian, Pakistani and Bangladeshi women. A significant finding here was that age and length of residence were important, as well as age of migration – people coming to Britain after age 25 years were the least likely to be fluent in the English language. For qualifications, the report found that, among people of working age, Chinese, African Asians and Indians were the most qualified. Bangladeshis were the least qualified; Caribbean and Pakistani men similarly lacked qualifications. It was noted, however, that Caribbean women were more likely than white women to be qualified.

Regarding issues of health, the survey reported that levels of ill-health 'vary markedly' (Modood *et al.* 1997: 256) across and between different minority ethnic groups in Britain, with Indians, African Asians and Chinese having similar levels of health to whites, but Caribbeans, Pakistanis and Bangladeshis having worse health than whites. However, the chapter on health warns us of the danger of 'crude stereotyped generalisations' (Modood *et al.* 1997: 257), especially in relation to the South Asian experience of health and wellbeing. Indeed, it is further noted that important differences are 'missed' if several minority ethnic groups are studied together as if they were one homogeneous group.

With regard to racial violence and harassment, the report concluded by noting the 'difference and diversity' of experience across and between ethnic minority groups. For example, similar numbers of white people and South Asian people reported being attacked, whereas significantly higher proportions of Caribbeans and a significantly lower number of Chinese were subjected to physical attacks. For reported property damage, the survey discovered that, apart from Bangladeshis, one in seven of all ethnic groups (including white people) reported having had their property damaged in the past 12 months (Modood *et al.* 1997: 287). Regarding racial harassment, meaning racial abuse and insulting behaviour, 13 per cent of the sample reported suffering from this form of abuse, with Caribbeans, African Asians, Pakistanis and Chinese reporting higher numbers of incidents than, for example, Indians and Bangladeshis. If the sample is extrapolated, this would mean that about one-quarter of a million people were subjected to some form of racial harassment in a 12-month period (Modood *et al.* 1997: 288).

For the purposes of the survey, the research team took a broad view of 'culture and identity' and yet, by their own admission, this section of the report had only 'modest' aims (Modood *et al.* 1997: 291). The discussion, like the rest of the survey, is a quantitative one that examines some aspects and components of culture and ethnic identity, for example self-description and identification, religion, marriage, clothing and sense of 'Britishness'. Although noting the many differences across and between different ethnic minority groups on these issues, the report rather boldly declares that 'a new form' of ethnic identity has emerged in Britain. One of the most significant findings here is that the most common expression of ethnicity is 'not what people do but what people say or believe about themselves' (Modood *et al.* 1997: 332). In other words, minority ethnic communites can have strong associational identities even without direct participation in distinctive cultural practices (for example, practising religion or wearing particular clothing). In terms of 'Britishness', the team asked the sample what they thought about the following statement: 'In many ways, I think of myself as being British' (Modood *et al.* 1997: 328–9). Less than two-thirds of the sample agreed with this statement, with African Asians agreeing the most and Bangladeshis agreeing the least.

Overall, the research team for the fourth PSI survey concluded that during the 1990s all the evidence indicates that Pakistanis and Bangladeshis are 'consistently at a disadvantage' when compared and contrasted with the white experience of life in Britain across many indicators, such as employment, income, health and housing (Modood *et al.* 1997: 342–3). People from Caribbean and Indian origins are more often than not found to experience disadvantage in Britain, although their circumstances are less serious when compared with the situation of Pakistanis and Bangladeshis. Caribbean and Indian people are said by the team to occupy a 'middle position' in terms of the indicators. Finally, the survey found that Chinese and African Asian people are showing signs of 'upward social mobility' and they are in 'broad parity' with the white population; the research team suggests that it is not appropriate to describe such groups as 'disadvantaged'. Importantly, in his concluding thoughts, Tariq Modood argues,

> **equality and social cohesion cannot be built upon emphasizing 'difference' in a one-sided way . . . also required is a recognition of shared experiences.**
>
> (Modood *et al.* 1997: 359)

The emphasis, he suggests, needs to be with common rights and responsibilities (a common notion and something also pushed heavily by New Labour since their election in 1997). New multicultural forms of citizenship are required, forms that are aware of ethnic difference and yet are held together under common ideas of 'Britishness'. This is the challenge that we are still addressing today, and it is hoped that, when a fifth survey is commissioned by the PSI, its findings will reflect increasing levels of social cohesion and social justice across all ethnic groups in Britain.

A closer look

Multicultural Britain – still room for improvement?

Tariq Modood, Director of the Centre for the Study of Ethnicity and Citizenship at Bristol University, has researched patterns of inclusion and discrimination in, for example, education and employment, and discovered a complex set of arrangements in which some ethnic groups do well in education (notably Indians and Chinese) while others (Bangladeshi women and Afro-Caribbean men) do not. These differential trends are reflected in patterns of employment. In a report on employment prospects in 2000, he concluded:

> Overall, there are both positive and negative elements within the British experience . . . Sophisticated quantitative analyses, careful differentiation between groups, linkages between ethnicity, religion, class and gender, new analyses of racism, including 'new' racism, cultural racism and Islamophobia, suggest that while there may be no singular 'black–white' divide, 'race' and ethnicity continue to shape economic as well as wider socio-cultural divisions in Britain. Research shows that by most measures, racial disadvantage is declining and the circumstances of the minority groups are diverging. Some groups are poorly placed in educational and occupational hierarchies, others have overtaken the white population in the acquisition of qualifications, in business ownership and in entry to some prestigious professions, though perhaps all minorities are underrepresented as managers in large establishments. This overall picture reveals employment patterns for some sections of ethnic minority groups which are far better than that painted by surveys in previous decades, which had shown a general confinement of ethnic minorities to low skilled, low paid work.
>
> Whilst the causes of this development are many, it is not unreasonable to suppose that one part of the explanation is the role of equal opportunities policies in breaking down barriers of discrimination and disadvantage . . . The British experience has been that legal and administrative measures, voluntary policies, and the pressure on organisations from the collective actions of workers have all been necessary to bring about progress in the processes of integration of immigrants and ethnic minorities into employment.
>
> (Wrench and Modood 2000)

Nationalism

> **We live in an age of nationalism, but one which spends a lot of time denying that nationalism exists. The orthodoxy is that it is a virus left over from an older more vicious age, which, as if mutating itself against all known antidotes, comes back to wreak its havoc on hapless victims. Centres of power employ the common-sense that they are patriotic while their enemies are nationalistic . . . the most powerful forms of nationalism are those which operate its power while denying its existence.**
>
> (David McCrone 1998: vii–viii)

Imagining nationalism

When we think of terms such as 'race' and 'racism', certain images come to mind. You might think back to history classes and remember seeing pictures of African slaves on plantations or Jews, Slavs and Gypsies in Nazi concentration camps. Or you might pick up a newspaper and see pictures of neo-Nazi skinhead demonstrators in Russia or far-right political leaders addressing crowds in France. This is a useful exercise when it comes to a term such as 'nationalism'. It can evoke strong images in the mind. When you think of this word, what does it say to you? What do you see?

Take a few minutes now to write down what first comes into your head when you think about nationalism.

We imagine that nationalism could be a number of things. You might think of far-off places, certain areas in the world, such as the Balkans or Rwanda, territories that have seen so much destruction and suffering in the name of 'national' or ethnic-based causes. Similarly, you might have thought of recent events in Iraq, the Basque Country, Israel, Palestine, Ukraine, Pakistan or the former Soviet Union – again, countries and areas of the global map that have seen conflict and wars in the name of redrawing maps and pushing the rights of one group of people over another. You might not have thought of a territory at all: you might have thought of a particular ethnic group, such as the Kurds or the Roma, who have fought for years to be accepted as a people. Closer to the UK, you might have thought of 'the Troubles' in Northern Ireland or the racist policies of the British National Party. In Scotland, you might have thought of Alex Salmond and the Scottish National Party, or the Australian actor Mel Gibson playing the part of William Wallace in the Hollywood film *Braveheart*. The point is, nationalism often evokes horrific images of racialized or religious violence, ethnic cleansing, the Holocaust, genocide, political movements, war and terrorism. And this is a key terrain for classic sociology: how do (nationalist) *beliefs* transform into (nationalist) *social actions*?

Like questions about ethnicity and 'race', nationalism has a changing nature. Nationalism is not fixed or static; rather, it is constantly evolving. The one certainty regarding nationalism is that it raises many questions about its key features: for example, is nationalism a progressive and positive force, or a reactionary and negative one, and what are the commonalities and differences in nationalist thinking across different countries? In point of fact, what seems crucial to nationalism is the importance of categories and divisions; there is a need for enemies and comrades, whether real or imagined, so it can be determined who is with you and who is against you in the nationalist order. Nationalism can tell us much about some of the big questions in sociology and politics, such as minority-state relations, democracy, human rights, citizenship and more.

Definitions of nationalism

There have always been two contrasting sides to images of nationalism: one of prejudice and intolerance, where you think of words such as 'reactionary', 'dictatorship', 'ethnic cleansing', 'fascism' and 'Hitler', and one of equality and progressiveness, where you think of words such as 'democracy', 'justice', 'anti-fascism' and 'Mandela'. Clearly, nationalism means different things to different people, and these meanings are relative to time and place. So, how do we define nationalism?

In defining a nation, we need to decide what 'it' (in the plural sense) is that makes a nation. What and whose criteria should be used? Is nation bound up with aspects of identity and culture, in addition to elements of history, myths, memory and language? Or is it more to do with maps, borders and ancient and contemporary struggles over territory?

Untangling these areas is easier said than done, but we can draw out debates on nations, nationalism and the state. For example, how have different authors in the field viewed such matters? For Ernest Gellner, 'Nationalism is primarily a political principle, which holds that the political and the national unit should be congruent', while for Guiseppe Mazzini, 'Every nation a state – only one state for each nation.' The sociologist Max Weber has talked about the state as 'a human community that (successfully) claims the monopoly of the legitimate use of force within a given territory.' Ernest Renan, in 1882, wrote a famous paper entitled 'Qu'est-ce qu'une nation?', in which he argued that there is no objective basis for the nation, as 'A nation is a soul, a spiritual principle'. Renan (1990) talks about the nation as a 'daily plebiscite' and the nation as 'a large-scale solidarity, constituted by the feeling of the sacrifices that one has made in the past and of those that one is prepared to make in the future.' For Ernest Gellner, 'Nationalism is not what it seems, and above all it is not what it seems to itself. The cultures it claims to defend and revive are often its own inventions, or are modified out of all recognition.' In other words, for Gellner, nations are defined by nationalism, not the other way around.

From the quotes above, we can deduce that there are important elements to the nation and the state. It is important to get this distinction and relationship in order. The state offers power and authority over a place and people, having the right to rule and sovereignty. The nation has a collective identity with relations between people who have connections over time and place. However, it is useful to bear in mind that there are such entities as stateless nations (such as the Roma in Europe) and multinational states (such as great empires of years past).

So, what is this thing called nationalism? On one level it is an ideology that imagines community in a national way, foregrounding and preferring this collective identity over other forms. It appears to always seek power in its name – a state for the nation, as Mazzini put it. Nationalism is active, and it sustains and nurtures *national identity*; this identity appears to be open and fluid and can be more cultural than political. National identity also sees you relating to other people as members of that nation; but this is not to deny the attraction of other competing identities (for example, our religious, sexual, gendered or ethnic identities). There is a psychological element here, whereby nationalism becomes a means through which groups and group membership can take form. This national 'membership' can be about searching for a collective identity, and it is one way in which humans can socially organize themselves to help make sense of the world, as social psychologists Reicher and Hopkins (2001) have argued.

The history of nationalism

Nationalism has its beginnings in the nineteenth century, where we can see ideas of nation and nationhood taking academic shape, along with the political and social thought that fostered a way of seeing nationalism that was both positive and critical. More recent writing has drawn on these nineteenth-century traditions and models and is largely accepting of the suggestion that the nation and national identity are inherent to human society. Here we need to look at ongoing academic debates between two crucial positions: primordialists (e.g. Llobera 1994) and modernists (e.g. Anderson 1991). How do these positions see the origins of nationalism? We shall explore these positions, but what we can say with certainty is that, despite all the debates and controversy, each sees a future where nations are inevitable and here to stay, whatever globalization may throw at nation states.

Questioning nationalism

As critical social scientists, we need to look behind the headlines and many of the assumptions within the literature. How, for example, have nations become seen as 'natural' and inevitable when we question so much else in human life and societies? Nationalism is often predatory and instrumentalist: national identity does get used by nationalism in times of conflict and uncertainty. We can see this across the globe in a range of conflicts. Nationalism is called upon, constructed and reproduced from generation to generation. To make any sense of this, we argue that we need to foreground the political and contested nature of identity and culture as it relates to nationalism, so often seen as neutral in certain forms and processes. These two elements are essential to understanding contemporary nationalism. When looking around the globe, it seems evident that national identities are created through what we might call nationalist 'imaginings', and these are not fixed or inherent. These imaginings can be seen as both positive and negative or, indeed, progressive (indigenous movements fighting against colonial rule) and reactionary (the Nazi period in Germany). Nationalism can, of course, be positive, and it might be seen as offering solutions to problems of identity in late capitalism. Although there are connections between nationalism and democracy, we need to question the idea that nationalism is *always* democratic. Indeed, nationalism can be very exclusionary and selective, while democracy is usually more inclusive.

Theorizing nationalism

When it comes to theorizing nationalism, there are a range of positions that need to be examined:

- *Primordialism* – Primordialists argue that nationalism has deep roots with ancient origins and historical depth. Nationalism is seen as 'natural' and 'essential', a key ingredient for human social organization and interaction. Romantic writers such as Herder rejected the Enlightenment ideas of rationality and science and talked of each nation having a soul with its own peculiar *Volkgeist* (Kohn 1996: 31). A revisiting of such an approach can be found in the work of Adrian Hastings (1997), on what he terms *The Construction of Nationhood.* Hastings directly challenges the modernists, such as Eric Hobsbawm, Benedict Anderson and Gellner mentioned below.
- *Modernism* – For the modernists, nations have no natural or spiritual roots but were created in response to political and economic changes, dating from the late eighteenth century. In *Nations and Nationalism*, Ernest Gellner (1983) argues that the shift from agrarian to industrial society required the construction of nations and nationalism. The industrialization process called for fixed borders and nationalist sentiments. Although primordialism and

modernism are the two dominant theories in the field, we should also mention perennialism. As the name implies, this theory suggests a continuous nature for nationalism. which is ever-evolving. Consequently, a socially constructed set of ideas and practices gives the impression of being natural and permanent.

- *Ethno-symbolism* – This is another theory to be aware of. In *The Ethnic Origins of Nations*, Anthony Smith (1986) contends that it is in myths, memories, traditions and symbols of ethnic heritages that nationalism comes alive and brings 'a living past into the present'. Whether the origins of nationhood are primordial or relatively recent creations, they are represented by aspects of culture that carry national sentiments.
- *Feminism* – As with theories on 'race' and ethnicity, nationalist academic work has also felt an impact from the work of feminist positions on nationalism. For example, in *Gender and Nation*, Nira Yuval-Davies (1997) argues that the content of nationalist discourses is often gendered and that questions of nationalist power are bound up with sexuality and oppression. She argues that women often suffer the most in nationalist conflicts, where rape is often used as a method of ethnic conflict, and that the future of the nation is held in women, being childbearers and the primary socializers of youth. In Nazi Germany and the Soviet Union, 'motherhood' was imbued with special status.
- *Postmodernism* – With regard to postmodernist approaches, it is the 'discursive strategies' of the nation that are alluded to – that is, the 'stories' of the nation and relationships with popular culture. Postmodernists are quick to point out the tensions and ambivalence within nationalist projects, focusing on those at the margins and boundaries. In *Nation and Narration*, Homi K. Bhabha (1990a) talks of the 'counter-narratives' of nationalism and 'resistance' to such projects. Such an approach suggests that there is nothing fixed or determined in the emergence of nationalism and that the meta-narratives of primordialism and modernism discussed above have no special claim on the truth. Bhabha asks important

A closer look

How 'natural' are feelings of national identity?

Is anything within national identity 'natural'? Are elements of such identities as English, French, Scottish or Belgian 'naturally' present, or are they being continually constructed and reproduced? In his book *Banal Nationalism*, Michael Billig (1995) argues that we need not only to focus on the 'big' ceremonies and rituals of nationalism but also to examine the day-to-day 'stuff' that produces a 'we' and 'us' view of the world via processes that he calls 'flagging', such as the sport we watch, the papers we read, the flags we wave, the maps we read, the flowers we buy, the food we cook, the buildings we visit and work in and the anthems we sing. All these things and more build up a 'national interest'. However, it is true that the power of socialization can be overstressed at times: 'flagging' can imply rather fixed, static identities that reflect the demands of dominant ideologies. It is true that political elites seek to use nationalism and patriotism for their own ends and that the mass media plays its part in this process (see Chapter 17), but people are not dupes and we use filters to make sense of the world so that we extract different meanings from the information we can process. The point is that national identities can too easily become reified (a thing that cannot be changed or altered); an example of this can be found in the title alone of Carol Craig's (2005) book *The Scots' Crisis of Confidence*.

Questions

1. Do you regard nationality as a 'major component' of your identity?
2. Under what circumstances do you feel national pride/shame?
3. Do you regard these feelings as 'natural'?
4. Using Billig's notion of 'flagging', what 'day-to-day "stuff"' can you think of that maintains your feelings of national identity?

questions about who really speaks in the name of the 'nation' and how 'nationness' is evoked. As a result, his work destabilizes the idea that countries can be regarded as homogeneous entities with shared identities and cultures. All senses of nationhood are 'narrativized', meaning that they are created through the telling and retelling of stories and have no reality other than this. In other words, 'nations, like narratives, lose their origins in the myths of time and only fully realize their horizons in the mind's eye' (Bhabha 1990: 1). Like Benedict Anderson (1991) in *Imagined Communities*, Bhabha and his co-authors suggest that we need to view nationalism not as some natural entity or the outward representation of a political ideology but as part of a large and evolving cultural system.

National identities

Closely related to the subject of nationalism are questions of culture and identity. How do they interact with one another? The past three decades or so have seen lots of work in the area of identity within the national context, shifting from individuals to groups. Postmodernists, for example, have embraced notions of 'hybrid identities' in the global world, whereas other theorists have examined political identities in the context of the state mobilizing people, in times of trouble, as labour and armies; wartime is an obvious example, where workers and soldiers are encouraged to play their part in the defence of the nation.

Regarding nationalism, obvious questions of sameness and difference are thrown up – who is an enemy and who is a comrade? Who exactly constitutes 'us' (insiders) and who constitutes 'them' (outsiders), and why are such categories viewed as being 'national'? In what way is group belonging the same as national identity? Much of this can be tied to questions of citizenship and of rights; as discussed previously, the work of Barth (1969) is useful in reminding us that identities are derived through the construction and operation of boundaries (nation-state borders are one of the most policed and regulated boundaries we know of in the present age). When it comes to the construction of national identities, it is prudent to ask whether these constructions occur from within or whether they are, to some extent, imposed. In his book *Social Identity*, Richard Jenkins (2008) examines the connections between identity and power in relationships and questions whose categories we are part of – do we internalize some imposed identities? A lot of identity is about *categorization*, and including when applied to national identities and nationalism.

The nationalist project

It is apparent that successful national projects need solid foundations; they cannot be situated in shifting sand. Order and structure are required to make nationalist movements achieve their goals, for without such elements fear can take over. In the work of authors such as Erich Fromm (1942), this fear stems from the collapse of the medieval social order in which individuals had a clear idea of who they were and where they stood in relation to one another. The system may have been autocratic and corrupt, but at least people knew their place and had little time to concern themselves with the modernist obsession with the 'self'. The battles for democracy and social equality overturned this system, but in the modern world that replaced it Fromm argues that we confront our new-found freedoms as a curse rather than a blessing. Faced with the loneliness and isolation that freedom brings, people respond to their fears by seeking new certainties in the authority and stability offered by nationalism.

In *The Language of the Self*, Jacques Lacan (1968) applies his ideas to nationalist thinking and argues that much of the project of the nation is bound up with the plural search for common emotion, boundaries and identification. It is the search for a kind of 'exclusive club', where comfort is given to those in need of security. Theodor Adorno (1973) also discusses the appeal of nationalism as being about 'the mobilization of narcissism', as it gives comfort to those disturbed or displaced by modernity and late capitalism. There is a process that occurs whereby in playing up 'our' national identity we fall into a psychoanalytical trap of needing to play down and denigrate other national identities. The national spirit in times of war, for example, focuses on what 'we' are good at and repeats the virtues and values that make 'our' country great. In such times, the primacy of national identity is foregrounded and we support 'our boys' (troops) without question. This is a matter that Benedict Anderson (1991) dwells on a great deal. In *Imagined Communities*, he ponders why it is that so many sacrifice themselves for the nation. Nationhood may be part of some modernist project with benefits for those in power, but it also speaks to the needs of individuals, who may respond with genuine feelings of love and pride that provoke the acts of sacrifice and bravery that become a new chapter in the nation's mythology.

How do questions of culture sit beside nationalism and national identity? For Anthony Smith (1998), in *Nationalism and Modernism*, beliefs and culture are very important in constructing ethnic and then national identity. But what are the 'roots' of these, and can we still talk of 'national cultures' in our increasingly globalized world? For primordialists, cultural continuities are important, with blood and descent, for example, forming the backbone of cultural ties. For perennialists and ethno-symbolists, culture is important too, as it gives a 'rootedness' to older ethnic cultures and groups: it is the place where languages, ideas and stories come from. Here, again, Smith raises interesting notions regarding the subject of *ethnie* and ethnic roots. He argues that it is the cultures of pre-existing ethnies (that is, a community sharing common cultural traits) that is at the heart of modern nationalisms. Is this right? What if ethnic roots are missing, fragmented, forgotten or even reinvented? What about the role of language here and the development of the vernacular (Hastings 1997)? Such questions are at the heart of the national enterprise in relation to questions of culture and illustrate how slippery this connection can be. For modernists such as Ernest Gellner (1983), in *Nations and Nationalism*, nationalism arises from rather more functional requirements of a new mobile industrial society. The state promotes what he calls a common 'high culture' that is inculcated via mass education systems. For Benedict Anderson (1991), in *Imagined Communities*, it is more about the development of mass literacy and the flourishing of print-capitalism: the printed word being read is what really kick-started the 'culture' of nationalism. As early proponents of 'mass education' were aware, literacy was a key means of transmitting social values, including notions of nationality. In other words, there are cultural 'needs' for nationalism to 'work' effectively. For postmodernists such as Bhabha (1990a), it is pretty much all about culture: some postmodernists seem to talk about nothing else! Nationalism is principally about 'narration' and the way in which 'stories' are told to invent, equip and sustain the nation. Importantly, we need to be aware of not reifying a 'common culture' and being critical to exactly how common such a 'common culture' may actually be. Indeed, culture is always contested in terms of content, values and transmission: different people and groups have different memories and acquired knowledges regarding heritage and tradition as well as placing different meanings in symbols and structures. For example, the flag of St George has often been associated with British fascism, signifying racial exclusion, but more recently it has been reclaimed as a simple expression of support for the England football and rugby teams.

There are close connections between 'race' and nationalism. As we have seen, racial categories have been central to the development of nationalisms, and throughout the nineteenth century scientific racism facilitated the spread of nationalist movements (in Hungary, as mentioned on p. 258, the search for the 'Hungarian gene' continued until the outbreak of the Second World War). It is also apparent that certain groups of immigrants have been racialized and that the affinity between racism and nationalism can take the form of setting boundaries and categories, in the sense that racism as well as nationalism can define belonging and exclusion. With the shift to 'ethnicity' in the twentieth century, we have seen that national identity has often been constructed as having an 'ethnic base', as has been well documented in Michael Ignatieff's (1994) brilliant book *Blood and Belonging: Journeys into the New Nationalism*. For example, there is the notion of 'Celtic blood', whereby a range of different ethnic groups and nations are 'connected' via notions of genetic continuity, so this becomes something more about myths, beliefs and culture rather than anything biological.

Stop and think

In October 2007 the editor of the *Sun*, Kelvin MacKenzie, made some comments on the BBC1 programme *Question Time* regarding Scotland and Scots – in particular, he suggested that Scots like spending money but not creating it and that, if it weren't for London, Scotland would be a third-world nation. Below is a quote from the show:

> [Gordon] Brown is a Scot . . . He is a socialist Scot who wants to spend every single penny you earn, never forget that . . . Scotland believes not in entrepreneurialism like London and the south east . . . He couldn't find anyone who would carry his bag better than another Scot so he grabbed [Alistair] Darling from

►

wherever he was . . . The reality is that the Scots enjoy spending it, they don't enjoy creating it which is the opposite of down in the south . . . There's no doubt that if it weren't for London and the South East, Scotland might well be heading towards being a third world nation now.

(Kelvin MacKenzie)

The reaction from various people included the following:

Andrew Neil (media commentator) – *'ugly and contemptible'*

Liz McColgan (athlete) – *'the comments are just retarded'*

Ian Rankin (novelist) – *'ignore him'*

Craig Brown (football manager) – *'shockingly wide of the mark'*

Questions

1. What is being said here by MacKenzie about Scotland and Scottish people?
2. How accurate, would you say, are some of the statements being made in reaction to MacKenzie's comments?
3. Overall, why do you think MacKenzie's comments have generated this kind of reaction – why are people getting so upset about them?
4. Do you think MacKenzie would have made similar remarks about a racial minority?

'Performing' nationalism

It is important to examine the different elements that go into the 'making' of a national identity and how it is 'performed' – that is, how we enact our national identities on a day-to-day basis. What ingredients do we need to include? We can examine the processes of how national identity can be 'performed' by looking at the work of Tim Edensor (2004) along with some further reference to Michael Billig's (1995) influential book *Banal Nationalism*. In terms of locating a 'national culture', we could include at least some of the following aspects: histories, myths, memories, languages, territories and a future. Crucially, the idea of a shared and united past appears important to nationalist rhetoric although, it does beg the question about whose past we are speaking of and how this has been recorded. Here the role of archaeology is important, and archives, libraries and museums are not to be regarded as neutral either.

Hobsbawm and Ranger have written about 'inventing tradition' in relation to the nation and suggest that all history, to some extent, is 'invented' as myths become bound up with fact:

> **Invented tradition is taken to mean a set of practices . . . which seek to inculcate certain values and norms of behaviour by repetition, which automatically implies continuity with the past . . . normally . . . with a suitable heroic past.**
>
> (Hobsbawm and Ranger 1983: 1)

Hugh Trevor Roper's account of *The Highland Tradition of Scotland* examines the ways in which the 'Highland myth' was manufactured to provide a focus for Scottish national pride following subjugation by the English (Roper 1983). However, there are consequences to traditions, myths and an imagined past. Denitch (1994) has written about the 'symbolic revival of genocide', where symbols and emotional content are tied together and past suffering and horrors are used in a strategic and political way to guide an uncertain nationalist future. Finkelstein (2000) has attacked what he calls 'the Holocaust industry' as a cynical attempt by American–Jewish business interests to exploit the memory of the Holocaust for financial and political gain – especially in furtherance of the Zionist project in modern Israel.

The myths of identity and nation are often proposed by elites and more often than not relate to a quest for power. It is crucial to be aware of the fact that remembering and forgetting can be selective and that the past can be reconstructed and deconstructed for the present and future.

Languages and territory also have a central role in many accounts of the 'essence' of national character. The presence of different language communities may, on the face of it, challenge notions of a national identity. The attempts by the English to wipe out Gaelic in Scotland and Ireland and the adoption of Russian as the official language in the old Russian empire and the Soviet Union as part of the process of 'Russification' are but two examples. However, language is not always about exclusion, and it can be inclusive. Language is often seen as a marker of 'difference', and linguistic claims are often political, whereby debates occur over what are to be 'national' and 'standard' languages, in contrast to the position of minority languages and how these are catered for, in terms of translation services. Similarly, territory can evoke heated responses in the search for 'national identity': hills, valleys, streams and mountains can become a lot more than just scenery as they can have a key role in collective memory. For Smith (2001), territory is 'fundamental' to national identity; he talks of 'sacred territory' and the role of the arts and literature (e.g. paintings, novels) in securing territory as part of a national belonging. But this also raises questions about the type of land and its purpose: is it rural or urban? Is it local rather than national? Who owns the land? Crucially, borders change and the drawing of maps and painting of scenery can be political.

The idea of a common future is important in the forming of national identity, and is sometimes tied in closely with religion, whereby notions of a 'common future' and the 'destiny' of a chosen people can be referred to. For example, we can look to Zionism, Afrikaner nationalism or the Third Reich 'of 1000 years' where the search for a lasting 'motherland' or 'fatherland' is desired. It is psychologically comforting to be part of a future and to have a place in it.

In exploring this further and pushing the debates forward, we can look to the interactions between popular culture and national identity by focusing on the work of Tim Edensor (2002). Edensor is interested in the making of nation and national identity; he argues that it is less about the transmission, via cultural elites, of authoritative culture, invented traditions and folk customs but more about the everyday and popular culture. It is suggested that 'high' and 'official' forms of culture are rather passé and that the 'everyday', in terms of cultural icons such as the Millennium Dome, *Braveheart* and Rolls-Royce cars, help reproduce, sustain and transform a sense of national identity in much the same way that the logos of Coca-Cola, McDonald's and Nike can be seen as a celebration of Americanization. He questions how national identity varies across time and space, and how it is contested, and he wonders what the impact of globalization has been upon national identity and culture. In exploring such debates, Edensor argues that national identity is represented, performed, spatialized and materialized. Such processes occur via popular culture and everyday life, in front of our very eyes. National identity is now about landscapes, habits, eating, music, sport, carnivals, tourism and cinema as much as it is about history, memory and myth.

Edensor's framework offers criticisms of previous concepts of national culture, such as 'high' and 'low' culture as argued by the likes of Ernest Gellner (1983). He suggests the use of a metaphor (a 'matrix') to describe how national identity is situated in an ever-shifting conceptual framework. The 'matrix' is used to identify connections between the domestic and the national, the location of places and performances in various settings. It is interesting to consider the extent to which the nation is spatialized within a geographical matrix, for example in national landscapes, symbolic sites and the everyday landscapes of routine and domestic life. The key interest here is the symbolic stages upon which national identities are played out. In terms of 'performance', a key question is how national identities are reproduced. That is, in what ways do sport, dance, carnivals and the tourist industry serve as examples to look at occasions where the use of the body and 'emotional participation' and other activities express national identity? Clearly, there are everyday ways of performing national identity that sustain a common-sense understanding of the nation and who it claims to represent. Importantly, nations also have a material culture. How is this imagined or performed? Edensor argues that there are a number of common objects in households and the shopping we do for goods and commodities that become important 'signifiers' of (material) national identity, as they are embedded with national significance and meaning; such material objects are, crucially, part of the everyday world, and these symbolic images are reincorporated into national identity. In other words, for Edensor, it is things such as the films we watch, the food we eat, the buildings we visit and the cars we drive that make us a 'nation'. Such cultural icons as *Braveheart*, fish and chips, the Millennium Dome and the Rolls-Royce or Mini can transform our many and varied understandings of national identity. Edensor is interested primarily in how our understandings of national identity shift across time and space, the ways in which it is contested and the impact of globalization on 'our' sense of nationhood. This work is important because it addresses gaps in the literature – it assesses the impact of popular culture on nationalist enterprises and asks us to look again at the classic debates between 'high' and 'low' culture' because, in the debate over national identity, at least, a pint of beer can be as significant as a sonnet by Shakespeare.

A closer look

Braveheart and Scots identity

In *The Invention of Tradition* Hobsbawm and Ranger (1983) examine the ways in which history is involved in the creation of national identities. One of the areas they consider is the development of the highland myth in the cultural struggle to establish a Scottish identity.

The film *Braveheart* (Figure 6.5) is used as a more recent example by Edensor to consider some of the debates about the representation of Scotland in film and the manufacturing of a contemporary Scottish identity in an era of globalization. The political and 'general public' responses to the film revealed many complexities of contemporary national identities, and not just a Scottish one. In a similar way, Edensor also examines the construction and use of the Millennium Dome in London and what this says about modern British national identity. He looks at expressions of Britishness through the lens of the Dome and argues that there are multiple and contested ways in which people assert a sense of Britishness. In other words, what sustains the power of national identity is the flexibility of making links within 'the shared cultural matrix'. Edensor's study is useful in that it explores the cultural meanings of national identity on an everyday level and the emphasis is firmly on the cultural, rather than the discursive (that is, practices through which the nation is reproduced). So, according to Edensor, national identity can be viewed within the local and everyday through performances and practices, and also within spatial and discursive frameworks.

Figure 6.5 Australian actor Mel Gibson playing Scottish hero William Wallace, in the film *Braveheart*. What does this image say to you?
Kobal Collection Ltd

A future for nationalism?

Stop and think

Is there a future beyond nationalism?

Another issue that needs to be explored is the idea of a future beyond nationalism. Is there one? What forces are at work here? We must wonder how globalization and the power of transnational corporations impact on nationalism and examine the alleged shift away from old norms and reified notions of nationality and ethnicity. Yet a brief scan of the daily newspapers testifies to the persistence of national differences – such as the struggles between Russia and Georgia and the Ukraine for example. So, are modern nationalisms any better or worse than their nineteenth-century versions? Are they merely old prejudices in new bottles? In a globalized era, should we not be thinking of internationalism rather than nationalism? What about transnational institutions and structures such as the European Union or the World Bank? Do they not render nation states as increasingly redundant? Do such economic and political 'clubs' lead us to a non-national future? The lead question here might be one of democracy – the search for a democratic politics where human rights, citizenship and identities do not require a nation-state or a relationship to a nation to exist. But how do such politics exist or develop?

With the onset and spread of globalization there has been much debate over the future of the nation-state and nationalism, perhaps looking at a future beyond the nation-state. Certainly, globalization has helped to challenge, rather than fixed and reified, national categories and has required us to look at different transnational, international, postnational and cosmopolitan theories. Are we beyond nationalism now? Has the reach of universalism demanded that new types of democracy, rights and citizenship are needed for changing global times? Are there credible alternatives to the 'national'? One obvious way is to begin thinking more internationally than nationally – are there options to world or global citizenship rather than forms of citizenship tied to particular states and borders? Ideas of internationality have existed for a long period of time, but people have always struggled to identify legitimate ways and means of managing the international system based on the existence of self-determining states. Processes of cosmopolitanism have called for the rejection of the nation-state and national identities and the formation of a single political, social and economic community. Cosmopolitanism is strongly pro-humanity and one-world and calls for anti-national attachment and loyalty. This is perhaps why such ideas have never properly taken hold – on both pragmatic grounds and also people's attachment to the 'national', unwilling to let go of flags, symbols and anthems. Other ideas have been positioned such as transnational and postnational ways of moving beyond the national. Here we can look to the work of authors such as David Held (1995) and Rainer Baubock (1994), who have argued for transnational and multiple citizenships based on accepting new global realities. Such theories have raised thorny questions such as whether borders should exist. What about the movement of goods, capital and people? According to Soysal (1994), for politicians, especially nationalist politicians, the thought of open borders would signify the death of the nation-state and the rise of postnational politics. Fundamentally, is the undermining of national-based citizenships in and of itself a bad idea? As we shall see, one concern here is the prospect of nation states 'losing control' of who can and cannot cross certain borders and enter particular territories. In the global age of terrorism, these are fears not easily dismissed. We can also see a clash between national states and international institutions (for example, the European Court of Human Rights with regard to human rights abuses in particular states). Difficult questions are raised, especially with regard to the often made assumption that in the context of globalization the term 'universal' is equated to 'Western European' or 'North American'. Whose values are reflected in this universalism? Indeed, in the European context, we can also look to European networks as perhaps offering a route out of the restrictions of nationalism and nationalist sentiments. The European Union is one such supranational institution that could, potentially, deal with the social, economic and political concerns and issues of a range of currently existing states within its geographical reach and 'badge' them under a new European identity. Would such a federal Europe gather support, though? Would it necessarily lead to a two-speed or two-tier Europe, with some areas lagging behind in terms of development and engagement with the 'project' of Europe? Further, the European Union has been subject to criticisms regarding its supposed undemocratic, unaccountable and bureaucratic nature. Aside from these criticisms, questions have been raised regarding the European Union's approach to matters of immigration and citizenship, whereby the spectre of 'fortress Europe' has been alleged, indicating that the European Union is less than welcoming to certain minorities from other parts of the world.

Various other ideas and solutions have been proposed to try to contain the excesses of nationalism, although two main ones have gained a particular currency in academe: federalism and consociationalism. Both of these ideas rely on changing existing institutional arrangements rather than anything more radical or imaginative, and they are essentially about different groups accommodating each other and learning to live together.

Federalism is a political philosophy and a system of government. As a philosophy it describes a group of people who are bound together with a governing and usually elected head. As a system of government, it refers to a system in which sovereignty is constitutionally divided between a centralized authority and constituent political units (for example, the US federal government and states such as Alaska and Hawaii). Federalism thus involves a federation: a system where the power and right to govern is shared between national and state governments. In the European context, federalists would like the European Union to take on the same kind of role of the federal government of the USA, with countries such as the UK, Germany and France becoming national states that are part of this federal system.

Consociationalism is a social elites endorsed system of 'power-sharing': it refers to a type of government that involves secured and guaranteed group representation in contexts where conflict is rife in divided societies. It has been best discussed by the political scientist Arend Lijphart (1977) as a system of ideas to help regulate ethnic conflict and tension in countries. One of the earliest examples of consociationalism can be traced back to the Netherlands in the early twentieth century, and many of Lijphart's arguments are drawn from this country, where between the 1850s and late 1960s society was divided into four non-territorial pillars – liberal, Catholic, Calvinist and socialist. Like Durkheim, consociationalists are obsessed with social and political stability, avoiding violence, enduring democracy and effective power-sharing agreements. However, apart from a few temporary projects, such as in the Lebanon between 1943 and 1975, it has rarely worked fully in practice as it calls for the accommodation of often impossible pressures and demands, given that, as a system, it lacks accountability and deals in rather fixed identities. As political science theory, it has won prizes (winner of the Ethnic and Cultural Pluralism Award in 1978 given by the American Political Science Association), yet outside the theory it has problems.

Stop and think

After reading the section on nationalism, try to answer the questions below:

- Does the fact that people believe in nations and national identities make them actually exist?
- To what extent are national identities just one identity among many?
- In what ways can national identities be 'performed'?
- What are the political choices taking us beyond the confines of the nation-state?
- Is nationalism a barrier to democracy?

Migration, settlement and multiculturalism

On identity

In the field of sociology there is no single absolute or clear definition of 'identity' (see pp. 27–29 for a further discussion on culture and identity). There are concepts that are used loosely and widely to help us make sense of one's self, feelings and ideas. However, there are also a number of theories that, in different yet interconnected ways, allow us to begin to understand how identities are formed. In terms of definitions, identity can refer to the way in which one is a unique individual on a personal level, being distinct from everyone else, such as the delineation of one's first name or, more broadly, whether one is female or male. In another way, identity can refer to a sense of 'sameness' in the way that one shares common features with, and is associated with, others on a social level such as being a member of an ethnic group or a being a supporter of a particular football team.

It is only in the past 50 years or so that discussions on identity have become popular. One reason for this, according to Baumeister (1986), is the way in which social change over the centuries has increasingly involved people having a more individual sense of who they are and less of a feeling of being tightly attached to, and at times indistinguishable from, religion, community and family. Yet, at the same time, according to research conducted by Canton and colleagues (2008), the individual self, in relation to attachments to, for example, family and community, helps to formulate one's identity.

Personal identity

Personal identity refers to the sense of direction or purpose that one's life is given, particularly through a set of priorities and values. It also includes, as mentioned above, an individual's name, for example. Flicking through a telephone directory will make one aware that names are not completely unique; however, people with common names will regard their own name as being individual personal property. Nicknames differentiate people and help to emphasize individuality. Tattoos are another type of personal identity; however, people with tattoos may be inadvertently identified as belonging to a specific group of people, such as ex-prisoners or bikers, and thus may be perceived as a member of a less than highly esteemed social group.

Social identity

When people feel part of a group, or are thought of by others as seeming to belong to a group, social identity is created. Clusters of personal characteristics share common traits with other groups, which maintain similar characteristics that are linked to social roles, groups and categories, giving rise to the attributing of a person to a social identity. Examples of common social identities attributed to groups include musicians, 'nerds', golfers, heterosexuals, celebrities, migrants and habitual hash smokers. Some of these identities are based on clear identifications with occupational roles, while others correspond to general social roles and some relate to stereotypes. It has been argued that personal and social identities are not mutually exclusive. Baumeister (1986: 252) makes the point that individuals are able to 'shape identity by acts of personal choice and commitment'. In other words, fusing personal and social identities opens up a space for the individual to take a course of action in a direction that she or he chooses to take. Canton and colleagues also suggest that:

> **family, friends and nationality, alongside our work and lifestyle/leisure identities, are routinely drawn upon to construct our overarching social identities. One identity tends to overlap the others and it is in the 'mix' that we know who 'we' and 'others' are.**
>
> (Canton *et al.* 2008: 48)

Multiple identities

Foucault pointed out two dimensions regarding the multiple identities people inhabit. First, 'discourses', or ways in which spoken or written communication is used in particular contexts, can produce varying versions of identity that determine the action one can take. In his book *Discipline and Punish*, for example, Foucault (1977) argued that distinct ways of knowing and thinking about criminals and criminals' minds are produced by penal discourses. However, the way particular discourses, such as the state, religion or sport, can produce divergent versions of someone who is a taxpayer, a cult member, a ballet dancer and a marksman all at the same time can also indicate the way in which identities can overlap. The second dimension for Foucault involves the way in which multiple identities fit into a framework of larger identities, such as sexuality, class, ethnicity and gender.

Hybrid identity

The interweaving of identities leads to a further development of identity by which the concept of a 'hybridity' of cultural identities, regarding ethnic identities emerges. For example, regarding ethnic identities, this can refer to identities as the product of mixing and fusing as a result of the moving, producing a mixture of cultures. This suggests that there are no 'pure' identities. The way in which cultures have moved and continue to move throughout the world – for example, the Jewish Diaspora, the slave trade and even hip-hop music – give testament to hybrid identities. This does not mean that one cultural aspect is assimilated into a different culture, but rather that something new is formed, contributing to the shaping of the modern world.

A closer look

Colin Wong – Chinese, European, English or Scouser?

My parents arrived in England in the early 1960s . . . from Hong Kong with three daughters, one son and their aspirations for a different life. They settled in rented accommodation in Liverpool, with friends and other family members living nearby, working long poorly paid hours in various jobs in local Chinese restaurants and shops.

Growing up in a large family was bliss; even with all the usual sibling dramas it was tremendous fun. Being bilingual was the norm; we spoke Cantonese with our parents and English with others.

[At primary school] I do not recall enduring any of the name-calling that my working family continued to experience in the shop. Ethnic differences were never really highlighted to me at primary school, so I grew up just being me. Labels only started being attached once I reached secondary school.

It was really only at that time that I began to consider my cultural and ethnic identity. As if overnight, the duality of my

A closer look *continued*

life became evident: I attended Anglican schools, yet my home life reflected Buddhism; I celebrated Easter and Christmas, yet my family also celebrated festivals such as Chinese New Year; I believed in God, yet I continued to make offerings to other deities; I spoke English but also Cantonese . . .

During my teenage years it was difficult to decide on my true identity . . . I felt English, but adversaries would remind me of my differences to them . . . I felt Chinese, yet I had never been beyond the UK.

However, on my first visit to Hong Kong for a vacation I felt instantly comfortable with the people, the place, the language and the culture. Within hours, I submerged myself as a 'local' although the real locals spotted my Scouse-accented Cantonese immediately! Strange, but whenever I visit Hong Kong, I never feel like a tourist.

So – who am I?

When I complete Ethnic Monitoring Forms, I tick the Chinese box. When I clear Customs at the airport, I walk through the European channel. When I look in the mirror, I do not see a Chinese face or an English face . . . I just see plain Me.

(Colin Wong is associate director of the undergraduate ITT programme in the Education Deanery at Liverpool Hope University)

World in focus

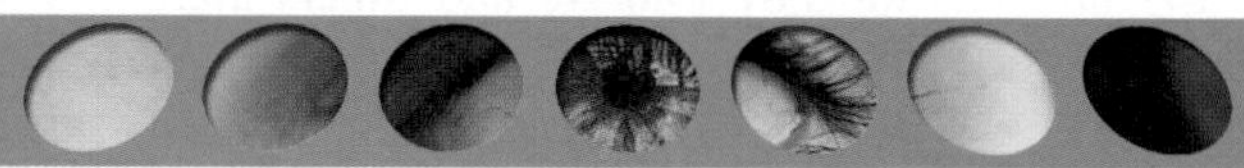

'Old Firm': home away from home in North America

Sociologists Richard Guilianotti and Roland Robertson examined various aspects of Scottish football fans' migration strategies from Scotland to Canada and the USA, including how Scottish migrants transfer, sustain and cultivate their fundamental identities, institutions and practices in North America. The Glasgow-based football clubs Celtic and Rangers are Scotland's two most successful football clubs. Known together as the 'Old Firm', the clubs have fan bases throughout much of the world; in Canada and the USA there are 76 official Celtic supporters' clubs and 42 official Rangers supporters' clubs – jointly referred to as North American Supporters' Clubs (NASCs). Celtic's 76 clubs are administered by the North American Federation of Celtic Supporters' Clubs (NAFCSC), while Rangers' clubs are administered by the North American Rangers Supporters' Association (NARSA). NAFCSC and NARSA both hold annual summer conventions in various North American locations that attract thousands of supporters. The majority of the club members are 45- to 65-year-old Scottish men who left Scotland and migrated to Canada and the USA between 1960 and 1980 and who have made North America their home away from home. On game days NASC members gather at their respective clubs to watch live televised matches that have been beamed in via satellite. Traditional Scottish food is served during matches, and club members dress in their team colours and sing team songs, maintaining and creating a sense of community among Scots and North Americans, while at the same time holding on to national identity. 'Hybridization', or an active synthesis of the local culture and, in this case, Scottish culture, is a form of social integration that migrant communities and local communities create through 'distinctive organizational practices'. For example, club members have come together to lobby television networks to transmit live games from European matches to their North American clubs:

World in focus *continued*

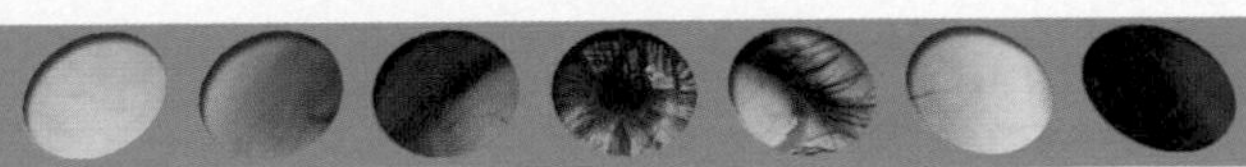

Club names fuse North American location with team affiliation (e.g. Kearny Rangers Supporters' Club, New York Celtic Supporters' Club) . . . Most NASCs produce crested merchandise, notably badges, polo shirts and t-shirts. The crests mix North American and team motifs: for example, the New York Celtic crest combines Scottish, Irish and American flags; and the NARSA crest integrates the Rangers crest and club motto with the Canadian and US flags. The NASCs' hybrid merchandise is not produced for profit, but meets a strong social demand in North America and overseas.

(Guilianotti and Robertson 2007: 143)

Stop and think

- In relation to the examples summarized in the World in focus box above, suggest some similar practices used by other immigrant groups – try to think of examples from both the UK and the USA.
- Can you think of similar practices used by British people living abroad?

Aspects of identity commonly include race/ethnicity, nationality, gender, sexuality, age, abilities and traits, religion, culture, socioeconomic class, and political, philosophical and ethical stances and views – all those factors that make us who we are, both individually and collectively. Identity is neither one nor the other but exists in the relationship between the two. It involves not only our views of ourselves but also considerations of how others view us and what we believe the views of others to be in this regard. Identity concerns both differences and similarities – it is about what makes us

A closer look

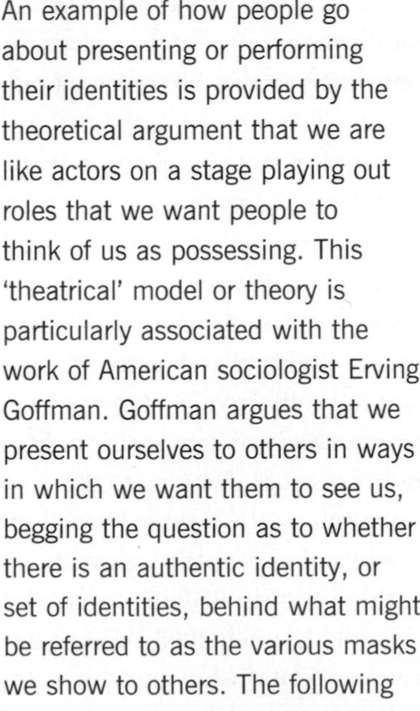

An example of how people go about presenting or performing their identities is provided by the theoretical argument that we are like actors on a stage playing out roles that we want people to think of us as possessing. This 'theatrical' model or theory is particularly associated with the work of American sociologist Erving Goffman. Goffman argues that we present ourselves to others in ways in which we want them to see us, begging the question as to whether there is an authentic identity, or set of identities, behind what might be referred to as the various masks we show to others. The following segment is an excerpt from his well-known and highly regarded book *The Presentation of Self in Everyday Life.* It looks at how people act or perform their 'Englishness' when abroad:

The story of Preedy vacationing on a Spanish beach

> But in any case he took care to avoid catching anyone's eye. First of all, he had to make it clear to those potential companions of his holiday that they were of no concern to him whatsoever. He stared through them, round them, over them – eyes lost in space. The beach might have been empty. If by chance a ball was thrown his way, he looked surprised; then let a smile of amusement lighten his face (Kindly Preedy), looked round dazed to see that there were people on the beach, tossed it back with a smile to himself and not a smile at the people, and then resumed carelessly his nonchalant survey of space.
>
> But it was time to institute a little parade, the parade of the Ideal Preedy. By devious handlings he gave any who wanted to look a chance to see the title of this book – a

A closer look *continued*

Spanish translation of Homer, classic thus, but not daring, cosmopolitan too – and then gathered together his beach-wrap and bag into a neat sand-resistant pile (Methodical and Sensible Preedy), rose slowly to stretch at ease his huge frame (Big-Cat Preedy), and tossed aside his sandals (Carefree Preedy, after all).

The marriage of Preedy and the sea! There were alternative rituals. The first involved the stroll that turns into a run and a dive straight into the water, thereafter smoothing into a strong splashless crawl towards the horizon. But of course not really to the horizon. Quite suddenly he would turn on to his back and thrash great white splashes with his legs, somehow thus showing that he could have swum further had he wanted to, and then would stand up a quarter out of water for all to see who it was.

The alternative course was simpler, it avoided the cold-water shock and it avoided the risk of appearing too high-spirited. The point was to appear to be so used to the sea, the Mediterranean, and this particular beach, that one might as well be in the sea as out of it. It involved a slow stroll down and into the edge of the water – not even noticing his toes were wet, land and water all the same to him! – with his eyes up at the sky gravely surveying portents, invisible to others, of the weather (Local Fisherman Preedy). (Goffman 1969)

Questions

1. Who or what is the *real* Preedy?
2. Do all people role-play all of the time, or do you think there may be occasions when they allow their 'true' identity to come to the fore?
3. What do you think the difference is between cultural 'assimilation' and integration?

distinct and what makes us the same. Together, though, these different aspects of similarity and difference are what make each of us unique and yet also part of a societal whole, which we both influence and are influenced by.

Citizenship

Connecting identity with citizenship

An important connection exists between different forms and types of identity and citizenship. Citizenship is about being accepted as a member of a political community that carries with it both rights and responsibilities. If you have legal rights to political participation in a particular country, then you are deemed to be a citizen of that country. Citizenship covers the same areas as nationality, though it is important to stress that you can have a nationality without being a citizen; that is, you can be legally subject to a nation-state and entitled to its protection, but without the accompanying substantive rights of political participation. Similarly, it is possible to have formal political rights without being a national of the state. In many nation-states, an individual non-citizen or non-national is called a foreigner or an alien. The crucial distinction here is that while national identity usually comes about through things such as place of birth, parents and ethnicity, citizenship comes about through a specific legal relationship with the nation-state. In multicultural nation-states, a question that is often asked is what unites a society when it is populated by people of different cultures, religions and political perspectives. One connection can come through citizenship, although several conditions, according to the political philosopher Bhikhu Parekh, need to be in place in order for this to be effective, including the need for respect for a common body of democratic political and legal conditions; a sense of belonging to the country; a set of public values; the need for equality; the requirement for respecting people's legitimate differences and identities; and (in Britain) a shared sense of a 'British' identity (Parekh 2008). As can be seen, then, there is a clear relationship and connection between identity and citizenship. We will now proceed to look at citizenship in a little more depth.

Historically, a good example of early citizenship can be found in classical Greece, where contributing to the support of the city-state, through military service for example, granted free men citizenship, which enabled them to participate in political debate. Over time and with the expansion of democratization, citizenship has been expanded to include a broader definition of what it means to be a citizen, regardless of gender, ethnicity or age – at least in principle. In France following the Revolution of 1789, the revolutionaries sought to establish the idea of France as a sovereign nation by defining French citizenship as applicable only to native French speakers. This tended to favour Parisians and excluded immigrants and rural minority language speakers (under these rules, Napoleon, as a Corsican, would be excluded). Since then the battle over what actually constitutes 'Frenchness' has attracted racial and cultural definitions, with Jews in the nineteenth century and people of African and Islamic backgrounds more recently experiencing attempts to exclude them. An argument over whether Muslim girls should be permitted to wear traditional dress in French schools was decided only after a national referendum, which supported the ban (see Activity 1, pp. 297–298).

National citizenship

Being a citizen in the UK means that fundamentally you are a full member of society, having rights, entitlements, shared obligations and duties. State policies institutionalize the rights and obligations, while state agencies determine who is and who is not a full member of society. However, even though people live in societies within national borders, this does not always mean that they are treated as full citizens. Children, for example, until they reach an arbitrarily defined age, are not considered citizens. This is equally true of migratory workers from other countries in many cases, though for very different political and economic reasons.

Cosmopolitan and global citizenship

While the traditional perception of citizenship, or national citizenship, involves a direct cultural and legal relationship to a nation-state, Osler and Starkey argue that:

> **citizenship requires more than a legal status. Beyond and in addition to that, however, citizenship involves a feeling of engagement, of belonging in and in feeling part of a community of other individuals who may share some or all of one's ideas or ideals of what it means to be a citizen of a particular nation-state.**
>
> (Osler and Starkey 2005: 13)

Citizenship in this sense is not directly defined in a legal sense or in relation to an area of a specific nation-state. With changing relationships among individuals, as well as the growth in communities and states that has evolved as a result of globalization, there is a growing interest in human rights and the environment that brings with it a degree of universality in relation to the requirements of others and to the practice of citizenship. Ulrich Beck (2006) examined various issues regarding 'cosmopolitan' and 'global citizenship'. Although cosmopolitan and global citizenship are closely related, the latter has closer ties to economic globalization. According to Beck, people have a tendency to sympathize with other people who face difficulties in life, irrespective of whether they know them directly. Therefore, the cosmopolitan citizen is in touch with the moral and universal dimensions in human existence and feels a desire not only to make connections with others and help them but also to do what they can to ensure the preservation and protection of the environment. It can be said that the cosmopolitan citizen is involved in a commitment to addressing inequality, poverty and the attainment of social and ecological justice by:

- advocating fairness among people in the world;
- promoting dignity for all;
- alleviating climate change;
- reducing and eliminating disease, malnutrition and poverty around the world.

Multiculturalism

If we take a look at London today, we see a city rich with cultural diversity. With over 270 nationalities making up its social fabric, over 300 languages spoken on a day-to-day basis, and its countless restaurants serving cuisines from around the world, London is considered to be one of the most multicultural cities in the world. As Levi-Strauss (1994: 424) commented, 'each society is multicultural and over centuries has arrived at its own original synthesis'. He also noted that 'all cultures are the results of a mishmash, borrowings, mixtures that have occurred, though at different rates, ever since the beginning of time'.

Although multicultural societies are not new, the term 'multiculturalism' in a state policy context is relatively new. The concept was first coined by the Canadian government in the mid-1960s as a policy-led attempt to promote a harmonious coexistence between the French-speaking minority and the descendants of the English-speaking settler majority, thus establishing Canada as a bicultural and bilingual society. Beginning around the 1970s, and largely as a result of large-scale global migrations following the Second World War, several other Western nations undertook efforts to recognize the growing ethnic diversification of their societies and adopted official policies of multiculturalism. These policies, in most cases, were developed to meet the needs of new migrants in order to:

- prevent them from being excluded from the education system, welfare services and the labour market;
- encourage positive interaction with those already living in the communities;
- accommodate, recognize and respect diverse religious and cultural priorities.

The following migration timeline provides an example illustrating how, in the past 2000 years, the 'British way of life' has been one of constant migration and settlement, with newcomers bringing with them various identities, cultures, religions, values and reasons for migrating, all the while shaping Britain into what it is today:

ca. 500 BCE	Early Celts (Bronze Age peoples) arrive from central and southern Europe
40s AD	Romans arrive under Emperor Claudius
500s	Angles, Saxons and Jutes (Teutonic peoples) invade and settle
1060s	Normans invade and settle

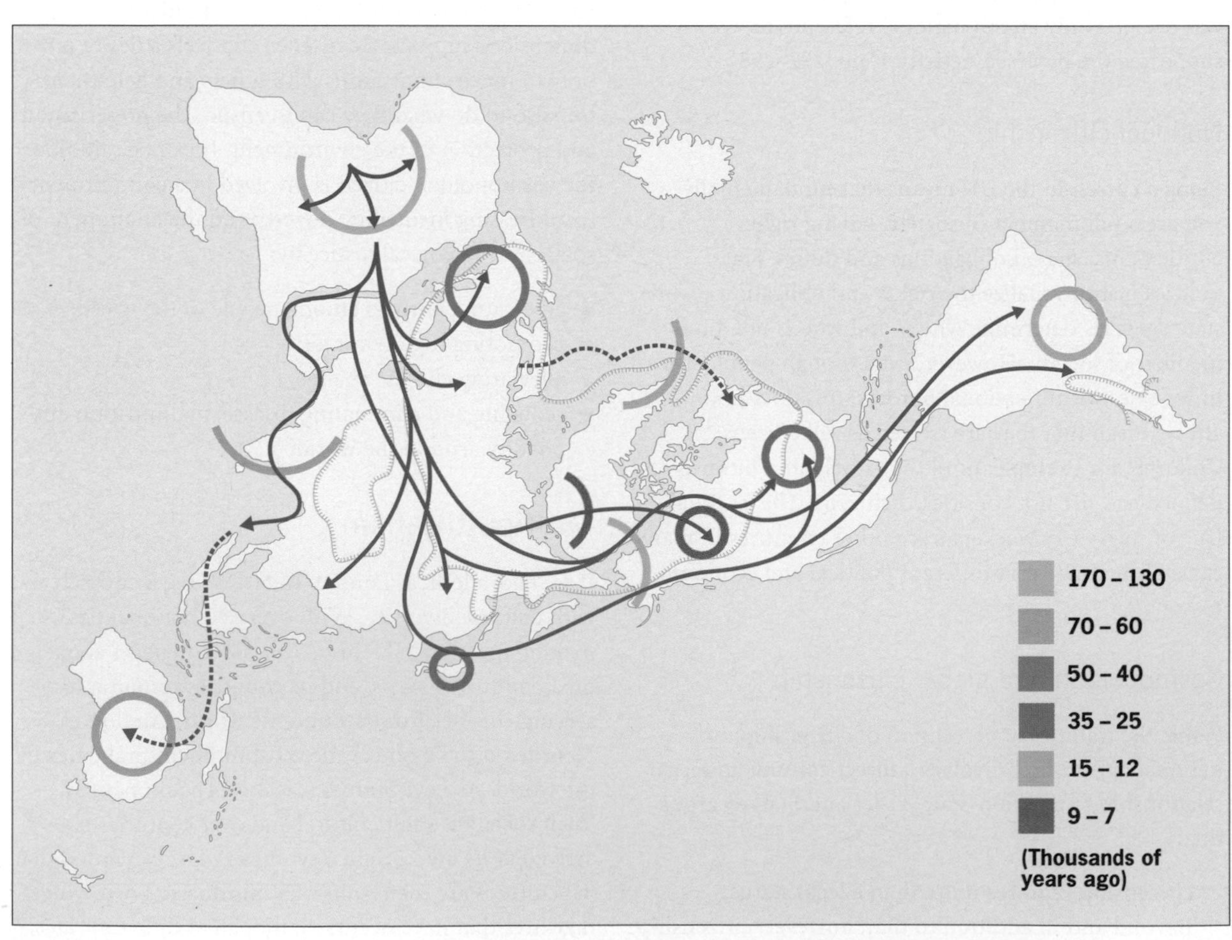

Figure 6.6 World map of human migration as seen with Africa at the top left and South America on the far right

1100s	Dutch and German merchants settle
1500s	French and Dutch Protestants settle
1600s	Asian slaves are taken to England
1700s	French refugees and Chinese sailors arrive
1800s	Jewish refugees from Russia, Poland, the Ukraine and Belarus arrive Irish settle as a result of the potato famine Indian and Chinese traders arrive Italians arrive
1914	Belgian refugees arrive after escaping First World War fighting
1930s	Nazi oppression refugees arrive
1940–1960	Polish homeless from Second World War settle, along with German, Ukrainian and Italian former prisoners of war
1948	Jamaicans and Caribbean islanders arrive to assist in rebuilding post-war Britain
1950s and 1960s	Pakistanis, Bangladeshis and Indians settle Hungarian refugees settle
1970s	Vietnamese, Muslims and East Africans arrive and settle
1980s	Romanian and former Yugoslavian refugees arrive
1990s	Somalians, Bosnians and Sri Lankans arrive
2000s	Cyprus, Czech Republic, Estonia, Hungary, Latvia, Lithuania, Malta, Poland, Slovakia and Slovenia join the EU and over one million migrants have settled for at least some period of time

As the timeline shows, Britain has never been a 'pure' or homogeneous population. On the contrary, the processes of integration and settlement are part of a society's evolutionary processes through which 'newcomers arrive and settle, and, in negotiating aspects of their identity, shape local conditions into which subsequent newcomers settle (Audrey 2000: 9). In this way, 'both parties are an active ingredient and so something new is created' (Modood *et al.* 1997: 24). Yet this is not to say that the newcomers are not met with racist attitudes, unfair treatment and exclusion from certain rights that established 'locals' enjoy. While the existing population often has a tendency to exhibit sympathy and calls for fair treatment for the newcomers (or migrants), there are also feelings of hostility and exclusionary practices are initiated. Migrants, on the other hand, tend to maintain and also modify certain aspects of religious and cultural identities. However, the resulting interaction between the two parties is often complex.

Stop and think

What's in a name?

Using the Internet, try to discover the origins of your family names – remember that women usually drop their family name on their wedding day, so see how much you can find out about the family names on your mother's side of the family tree as well as your own surname. A search should tell you the ethnic origins of your name and what your name means.

The following website is a good place to start if you are 'British': www.searchforancestors.com/surnames/origin/

World in focus

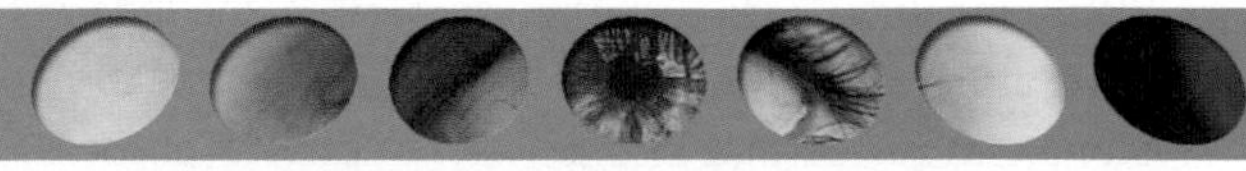

Islamophobia

The infamous attacks on the Twin Towers in New York on 11 September 2001, the London Underground network in July 2005 and Glasgow Airport in June 2007 brought Muslim terrorism and suicide bombers into the world consciousness and have led to an increase in anti-Muslim feeling and actions across the Western world. Indeed, those events are seen as key dates and turning points in recent history and are routinely referred to as 9/11 and 7/7, with phrases such as 'post 9/11' used and understood around the world. 'Islamophobia' has become a widely used term and a major form of racial intolerance. The three

World in focus *continued*

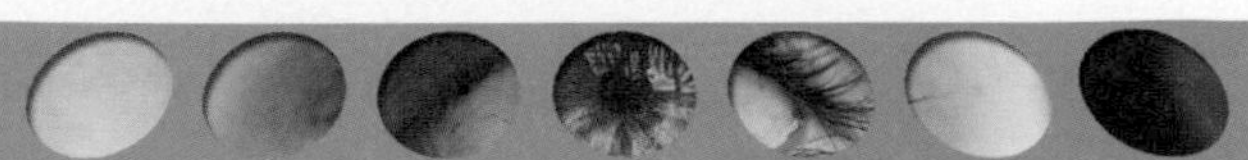

extracts below illustrate the recent growth of this phenomenon. They are from different sources of information – an academic text, a news review and a campaigning website. Read them and consider the questions that follow.

Intolerant Britain

> In the post 9/11 climate . . . Islamophobia in Britain, according to a report published by the Commission on British Muslims and Islamophobia (CBMI) (a think-tank set up by the Runnymede Trust) in May 2004, is becoming increasingly institutionalized . . . Police stop and search practices were singled out as a key indication of institutionalized Islamophobia in the post 9/11 climate because more than 35,000 Muslims were stopped and searched in 2003, with fewer than 50 charged. Three years ago, only around 2000 Muslims were stopped and searched (Doward and Hinsliff 2004). Several sources cite a 300 per cent increase in police stop and search techniques against 'Asians' in Britain between July 2003 and July 2004 . . . The chair of the CBMI, Richard Stone, suggested that in this climate of institutionalized Islamophobia, 'if we don't take positive action to embrace the young Muslim men in this country, we are going to have an urgent problem . . . we are going to have real anger and riots with young Muslims pitched against the police (Doward and Hinsliff 2004) . . .
>
> According to Alexander (2003), the emergent spectres of religious 'fundamentalism' and the threat of terrorism now mean that Muslim young men are becoming increasingly inseparable from the image of violence, which is evidenced in the explosion of the riots in 2001 . . .
>
> The post 9/11 climate is both a culture of fear and a culture of indignation in which established and asylum-seeker migrant communities are viewed with suspicion. In this context, the benevolence of the UK's immigration and asylum policies and championing of multiculturalism (especially in the British tabloids) is being thrown back in the taxpayers' faces. This is clearly fertile ground for Far Right political manipulation . . .
>
> The former Conservative Prime Minister Baroness Thatcher commented in an interview to *The Times* published on 4 October 2001 that she 'had not heard enough condemnation from Muslim priests' of the September 11 attacks. Baroness Thatcher was keen to present the attacks on the USA as an exclusive Muslim problem: 'the people who brought down those towers were Muslims and Muslims must stand up and say that it is not the way of Islam . . . they must say it is disgraceful'.
>
> (McGhee 2005: 99–101)

'Islamophobia' in the UK rises after 11 September

According to research carried out at the University of Leicester following the September 11th terrorist attacks in the United States of America, incidents of discrimination and racism towards Muslims increased, while racist experiences towards Christians and Jews decreased.

The academic study sought to assess the extent of racist and discriminatory incidents against religious and racial minority groups preceding and following the September 11th events. General racist and religious discrimination, as well as 'implicit racism' were measured via a questionnaire. Implicit racism refers to people treating religious and ethnic minorities differently than they would to members of their own similar groups, while denying having obvious prejudices.

The study surveyed close to 500 participants, with the highest religious proportion being Muslim (50%) and the rest being affiliated with other major religions including Sikhism, Hinduism, Judaism and Christianity. The majority of participants lived in Leicester (one of the UK's most ethnically diverse cities), and Stoke-on-Trent (inhabited by an ethnic minority of only 3.1%).

World in focus *continued*

The results of the study indicated that Muslims posed the highest risk of being victims of general discrimination and implicit racism before September 11th and experienced the highest increase of general discrimination and implicit racism after September 11th. Based on the findings, experiences of 'implicit racist discrimination' exist not just on racial grounds, but on religious grounds – indicating 'implicit religious discrimination' towards Muslims and a rise in 'Islamophobia.' Islamophobia refers to a type of racism based on a fear of, and prejudice and intolerance toward, Muslims' physical appearances and cultural and religious beliefs.

Based on the respondents' experiences of discrimination and racism in relation to their religion, it appears that discriminatory behaviour and sentiment may at times be motivated more by religion than by ethnicity or race. Following the major events occurring on September 11th in the United States, religion, more so than race or ethnicity, triggered general discrimination and implicit racism in the UK.

(http://www.le.ac.uk/ua/pr/press/discriminationandracism.html)

Raising awareness

The presence of Muslims in Britain has been one that dates back over a century. Today Islam is the fastest growing religion in the history of the world. Britain's UK 2001 census confirms that, with more than 1.6 million UK Muslims (2.7 per cent of the population), Islam is now this country's second largest faith after Christianity.

British Muslims are a diverse and a vibrant community and they form an essential part of Britain's multi-ethnic, multi-cultural society. Despite their contributions, however, British Muslims suffer significantly from various forms of alienation, discrimination, harassment and violence rooted in misinformed and stereotyped representations of Islam and its adherents – the irrational phenomenon we have come to know as Islamophobia.

Islamophobia has now become a recognized form of racism . . .

In the wake of September 11, in the UK alone, within a space of two weeks, there were more than 600 cases of Islamophobic harassment, violence and criminal damage . . .

The Forum Against Islamophobia and Racism (FAIR) was founded in 2001 as an an independent charitable organization – our aim is to work towards establishing a Safe, Just and Tolerant Britain in which Islamophobia and racism have no place.

(www.fairuk.org)

Questions

1. Why do you think Muslims might be an 'easy' target for racial intolerance and violence?
2. How would you rate the reliability of the three extracts? (Consider the extent to which the comments are based on fact and/or research evidence.)

Multiculturalism as a controversial concept

Issues regarding multiculturalism are connected to national policies on immigration, which essentially not only are determining factors as to who is permitted into the nation but also dictate under what conditions and to what extent newcomers should be expected to 'fit in'. Ien Ang (2005) argued that 'multicultural' is frequently equated with 'multiethnic', which in turn is connected to 'multiracial', implying that multiculturalism debates are generally concerned with issues regarding white, Western societies and the presence of non-white migrant communities living or arriving in those societies.

A closer look

The following quotes exemplify the complexity and controversy involved in issues surrounding multiculturalism, with some seeing multiculturalism as a process of integration, others seeing it as a process of division, and yet others seeing it as neither integration nor division but rather as a constructive coexistence and influence.

> My argument with multiculturalism is not that it respects and tolerates diversity but rather in many ways it emphasizes division.
>
> (Australian prime minister John Howard, 1988)

> Britain is both a community of citizens and a community of communities, both a liberal and a multicultural society, and needs to reconcile their sometimes conflicting requirements.
>
> (Bhikhu Parekh, chair of The Commission's report, *The Future of Multi-Ethnic Britain*, Runnymede Trust Commission on the Future of Multi-Ethnic Britain, 2000)

> If we went on as we are, then by the end of the century there would be four million people of the New Commonwealth or Pakistan here. Now that is an awful lot and I think it means that people are really rather afraid that this country might be swamped by people with a different culture. And, you know, the British character has done so much for democracy, for law, and done so much throughout the world, that if there is a fear that it might be swamped, people are going to react and be rather hostile to those coming in . . . We are a British nation with British characteristics. Every nation can take some minorities, and in many ways they add to the richness and variety of this country. But the moment a minority threatens to become a big one, people get frightened.
>
> (Margaret Thatcher, quoted in the *Guardian*, 31.1.1978)

Much of the current discussion in Britain rests on a false paradigm that counterposes 'multiculturalism' to 'integration', which has replaced the discredited term 'assimilation' but carries similar implications. The choice the paradigm offers is unreal: neither ethnic isolation nor cultural uniformity is possible or desirable. As popularly construed, multiculturalism and integration both misconceive culture as reified and static; both seek to manage diversity through imposed categories.

(Mike Marqusee, in 'Veiled Threats', *Red Pepper* 2.10.06)

Immigrants will have to pass a test of Britishness . . .

Immigrants who want to become citizens of the United Kingdom will have to pass a 'Britishness test' and learn English, David Blunkett said yesterday. The Home Secretary also called on the English to be proud of their heritage and to stop being 'apologetic' about their roots . . .

Mr Blunkett said that an understanding of the UK's history, law, way of life and indigenous languages would help immigrants take part in British society and ensure they are accepted more readily by the existing population. Failing the exam would mean applicants cannot gain a British passport or vote, although their residency status would not be affected . . .

Mr Blunkett said history would be part of the exam only when it was relevant to daily life. 'Knowing the six wives of Henry VIII doesn't constitute being a good citizen,' he said. 'You would need to know about when Britain was last invaded if you were touching on what happened in terms of consequent 20th century wars.'

(the *Independent*, 4.9.2003)

Questions

1. Do you think that 'multiculturalism' is a racial issue?
2. Can laws really impact the way in which people respond to an influx of immigrants?
3. Why do you think people feel threatened by an influx of immigrants?
4. What questions might be used to 'test' someone's Britishness? How effective do you think such a test would be? Try the test yourself at www.timesonline.co.uk/tol/news/uk/article584918.ece

Migration

Approximately 40,000 to 50,000 years ago people began emigrating out of Africa and settling in, and populating, what are now the Middle East, Asia, Australia and Europe. Nearly 30,000 years later people were slowly making their way across to Scandinavia and to the Americas, eventually populating all but a few islands and Antarctica, jumpstarting the movement of humans that would continue through the millennia to the present day. Migration is far from being a new phenomenon and, other than a few exceptions, we are all descendants of migrants.

The push and pull of migration

Reasons for migration are often attributed to factors that 'push and pull' people to leave their homes and resettle in new areas and communities. Reasons people are 'pushed' from their native land typically relate to issues regarding the maximization of security, such as in the case of poverty, famine, persecution and war. 'Pull' factors are usually described as relating to income maximization and risk-taking, such as wealth, adventure and health. However, there is more to migration beyond reasons that push or pull, or represent a combination of both, such as whether migration is voluntary and the extent to which the state shapes opportunities and constraints for migrants.

In the period between 1500 and 1800, an estimated six million Africans were coercively forced out of Africa and into colonies to be used as slaves (Emmer 1993). This type of migration was forced migration, as the slaves, used for their labour, were forced against their will to contribute to what was shaping into the world capitalist economy. After the abolition of slavery, indentured labour was another type of forced migration, which, in the nineteenth century, resulted in more than 30 million workers from India and China being forced to sign contracts that barely gave them subsistence wages and demanded unconditional obedience to their employers (Massey 1994; Jess 1995).

As a result of the capital amassing from the labour of the forced and involuntary migrants, the nineteenth and early twentieth centuries saw 60 million Europeans heading to British colonies in Africa, Australia and the New World seeking wealth (Hirst and Thompson 1996). From 1860 to 1920, an additional 30 million Europeans migrants arrived in the USA (Castles and Miller 1993). According to migration historian Marlou Schrover, this transatlantic mass migration was driven by increasing land fragmentation and growing population pressure in rural Europe (see www.let.leidenuniv.nl/history/migration/chapter52.html#2). A major factor enabling conditions for this migration was the growing presence and accessibility of steam-driven transport (steamships facilitated transatlantic migration and trains provided greater mobility and job opportunities in the rapidly expanding railway industry in the USA). America held out the promise of not just a more affluent life but also the perception of a freer and less oppressive society – a particularly relevant point when many of the migrants were members of oppressed religious minorities or nationalities, including Germans, Jews, southern Europeans and former slaves. This mass migration can be seen as significant in the evolution of historical and contemporary America, introducing, as it did, the influences of a wide range of different ethnicities, cultures and religions.

A closer look

The passport

In 1858, the passport was made available to British nationals as proof of national identity. Before that passports had only been issued to foreign dignitaries as a way to control the migration of subversives. In his book *The Invention of the Passport*, John Torpey writes:

> The creation of the modern passport system signaled the dawn of a new era in human affairs, in which individual states and the international state system as a whole successfully monopolized the legitimate authority to permit movement within and across their jurisdictions.
>
> (Torpey 1999: 9)

Integration and division

As a consequence of international migration, colonial societies of diverse ethnicities occupying different social positions were created, along with a hierarchy based on those 'elites' who possessed power and wealth and those dispossessed and subjugated groups who did not. With this hierarchal power structure came politicized notions of inferiority and superiority that were often tied in directly with ethnic identity (given that the majority of people who occupied low social, economic and political status were not white). For example, Diana Paton's (2004) work on punishment, race and gender in the formation of the Jamaican state during 1780 and 1879 clearly demonstrates the subtle and not so subtle ways in which different groups were subjected to different forms of punishment – often based not on actual or accused crimes but on factors such as gender and ethnicity. Paton's work shows us that British white male migrants in Jamaica constituted the privileged elite, while black Jamaican women were subjected to terrible forms of racist discrimination, not only in the emerging criminal justice systems but also across social life. Stereotypes resulted in crude characterizations of different people and groups, and these were then used to justify inequality. The ethnic stratification of colonial societies such as Jamaica was regarded, incorrectly, as somehow reflecting inborn characteristics rather than resulting from power, wealth and racist positions.

Stop and think

- Does the power hierarchy that existed in the nineteenth century still exist today?
- In what manner has it changed?

Case study

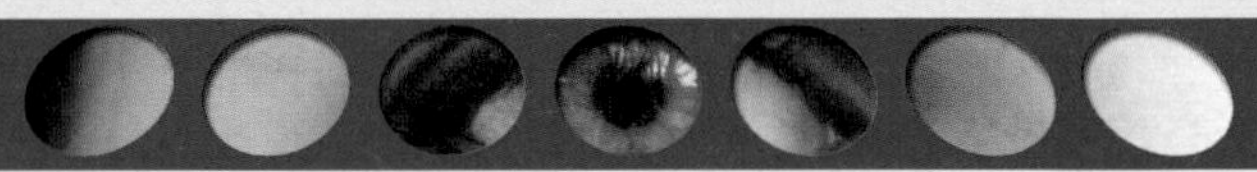

Roma migration across Europe

As explained above, one of the outcomes of international migration in the nineteenth and twentieth centuries was the perpetuation of inequalities and discrimination that those who were thought to be inferior were forced to endure. Among those groups were the Roma, an ethnic group that has suffered social and political discrimination since the Middle Ages and who currently face more social exclusion than any other ethnic group in Europe.

Having emigrated in the eleventh century from northern India, the Roma (referring to the umbrella group under which those who refer to themselves as Gypsies, Travellers, Manouches and Sinti fit), despite having resided in Europe for nearly 600 years, have endured enslavement, ethnic cleansing, Nazi concentration camps, forced sterilization of women and men, the removal of children from families, and absolute poverty.

Over the past century there have been increasing migrations of Roma across Central and Eastern Europe to Western Europe (Figure 6.7). The reasons for this increase are described in Table 6.1.

More recently there has been an effort via government initiatives and projects to bring to light issues regarding

Table 6.1 Push and pull factors of Romani migration (1990–2002)

Push factors	Pull factors
Racially motivated violence, pogroms	Romani Diaspora (relatives and friends from earlier migrations in the receiving country)
Discrimination in employment, housing, education	Possibility for employment
Detrimental economic situation	UK context – social service providers to asylum applications
Lack of prospects for improving socioeconomic situation	Feeling of being accepted in the society
Usury (exorbitant rates of interest on money loaned)	Better education resulting from Romani children being admitted to schools
	Language skills (German, UK context)

(Sobotka 2003: 106)

Case study *continued*

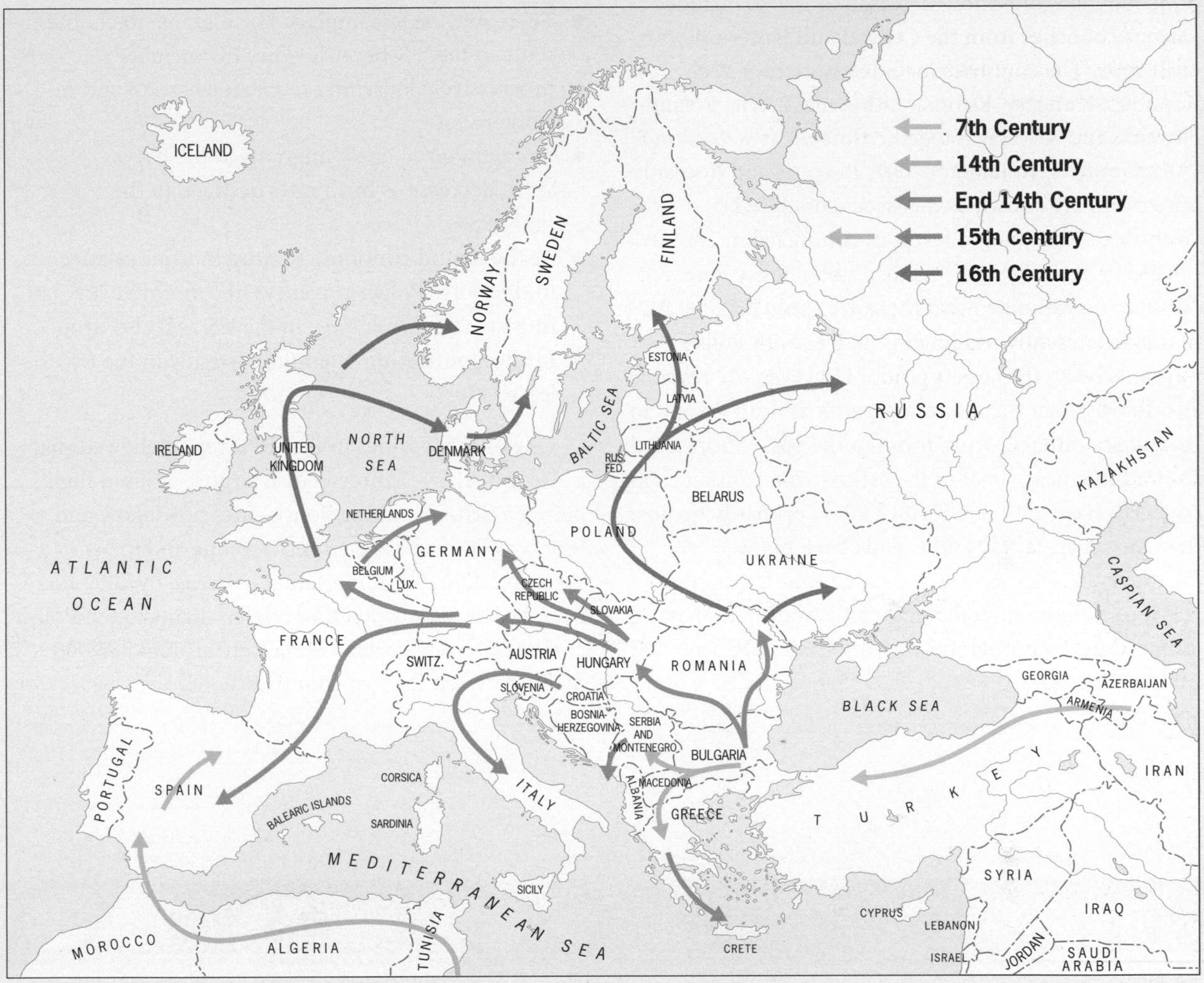

Figure 6.7 Roma migration through the Middle East and North Africa to Europe

the discrimination that Roma face. However, despite new government legislation being implemented to tackle marginalization and poverty, Clark *et al.* point out that

> such efforts are not preventing, or even slowing down, Roma migration from East to West and this, in reality, has little to do with ethnicity or culture and instead everything to do with the wider, global arena in which migration patterns are being played out (in itself this often coming down to class relations). It is the socio-economic and political realities that need to be looked at as a part of a greater transformation in global labour markets and the uninterrupted movement of both labour and capital across Europe and beyond.
>
> (cited in Canton *et al.* 2008: 18)

A new wave of Polish migration

From 1 May 2004, the UK experienced new waves of migration when the European Union, in the tradition of neoliberal economics, increased in size to include various countries from the Central and Eastern parts of Europe. The countries included were the Czech Republic, Hungary, Estonia, Lithuania, Latvia, Poland, Slovenia and Slovakia – together known as 'accession 8' (A8) countries. In January 2007, Bulgaria and Romania joined and are known as the 'accession 2' (A2) countries. According to research conducted in 2008 by Pollard *et al.* at the Institute for Public Policy Research (IPPR), it is estimated that there are about 650,000 A8 nationals presently residing in the UK, with Polish migrants being the largest group. However, the research also showed that the migration patterns from Poland to Britain are different from those in the past. The research showed that nearly half of the estimated one million A8 nationals have left the UK since 2004, primarily because they miss their family and friends back home. Furthermore, the research indicated four factors that will lead to more migrants returning home and may also lead to fewer migrants moving to the UK from new EU member states:

- There is a likelihood that new member states' economic conditions will improve and therefore incentives to move to the UK to find work will weaken.
- There may be less impetus for migrants to choose to settle in the UK because other EU member states are progressively loosening restrictions on A8 and A2 workers.
- The number of likely migrants to the UK is set to decrease as birth rates declined in the mid-1980s.
- As the pound continues to drop in value relative to the zloty (Polish currency), the incentive for migrants to earn money in the UK will also drop, further motivating migrants currently in the UK to leave.

One of the findings in the IPPR report showed that in December 2003 three British airports offered flights between Britain and the Polish cities of Krakow and Warsaw. To maximize airport revenue and to accommodate Polish migration patterns, by 2007 there were 22 British airports that offered flights to ten Polish cities. In December 2007 there were around 385,000 flights between the two countries alone.

Case study

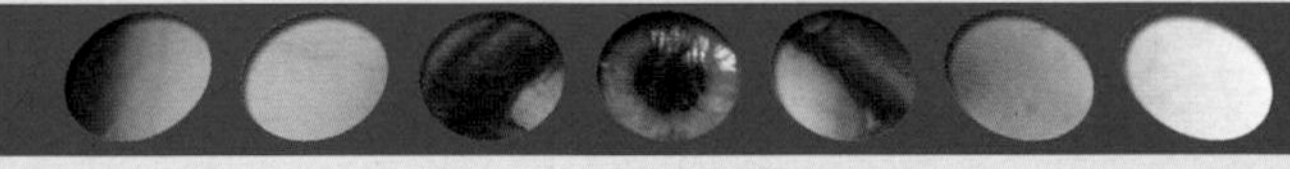

Polish social networks in Glasgow

One of the main reasons for choosing Glasgow as a place of original destination is a pre-existing migrant's social network. Respondents stated that having family or friends who had already resided in Glasgow helped them to reduce their migration costs related to accommodation searching, employment or adjustment to the new type of work and pace of living. Polish migrants have spoken about how important such 'connections' were to them:

> I came here because my friend Emily was here. She offers me some help if I will decide to come to Glasgow. She offers me some help at the beginning like flat and job searching and I could stay with her and her friend, so I just decided on Glasgow.
>
> (Female, 24, Polish recruitment agent)

> My brother was working in Norway with some of his friends. One of his friends went to Glasgow to work for company . . . They find a job there because of the niece of my brother friend. So when the company needed a workers, she called my brother's friend and after a less than a week my brother migrate to Glasgow. And after a while my brother called me and said that the company he is working with is looking for a people. So I made decision and that's how I am here. After a while some of our friends from the place we come from have arrived as well.
>
> (Male, 45, Polish, labourer)

The Sikorksi Polish Club, based near Kelvingrove Park in the affluent west end of Glasgow, is another good example of a social network that has become formalized, to an extent, and acts as a hub for Glasgow's Polish

Case study *continued*

Figure 6.8 Polish parade
© Noah Canton

migrant population. It has over 500 members and self-reports that 70 per cent of its members speak English to at least a basic level. The club acts as a source of information for activities such as language classes, chess tournaments, salsa dancing, legal advice, and mother and toddler groups, as well as offering advice and guidance on seeking employment and accommodation in Glasgow. Membership in the Sikorski Club is open to all nationalities and it has made efforts to incorporate the local Scottish community as well as members of other minority ethnic groups.

The post-EU enlargement migrants have also set up their own newspapers (*Cooltura Goniec Polski*), radio stations and websites. The Sunny Govan Radio in Glasgow was the first in Scotland to broadcast the Polish-language programme *Kraina Deszczowców* (amusingly entitled *The Rainmen's Land*, acknowledging the rather wet and wild Scottish climate and weather). Additionally, members of the Polish population in Glasgow, and throughout Scotland, use dedicated websites in order to exchange information on issues related to employment, housing, health, social benefits and social and cultural events in Glasgow.

The development of readily available communication technology and ever-cheaper transport links has facilitated the A8/A2 migrants to organize and restructure their social networks within these transnational spaces. Interviewed migrants maintain multiple connections, mainly with their family and friends, between and across many national borders. Most of them travel between their new land and homeland or use Web communicators such as Skype to establish and maintain contact with ▶

Case study *continued*

Figure 6.9 A private members' club in Glasgow, for Polish people living and working in the city
© Noah Canton

their relatives and friends. Additionally, some of them send remittances electronically in order to provide financial support for their partners and children in their homeland.

(Source: Canton *et al.* 2008)

Questions:

1. Despite their diligence in maintaining their cultural identity, do you think present-day immigrants share a growing tendency to achieve greater assimilation within their host country?
2. Explain how information technology (IT) and the Internet might contribute to a more stabilized migrant culture.

Conclusion

> **But is there anything more to say that has not been said already?**
>
> (Elkins 1976: 1)

In beginning his famous study on slavery in America, Stanley Elkins wondered whether he could add anything new to the voluminous debates and discussions that had already taken place in this controversial field of study. As it turned out, of course, his investigation, based on his earlier Columbia University PhD study, was hugely influential and innovative. In other words, when it comes to most topics and issues in the social sciences, there is always something new to be said: fresh empirical evidence comes to light and new theoretical arguments can be generated through this acquired evidence. In this chapter, we hope to have made you think about some of the issues we have touched on in new and different ways. We have tried to get around common-sense thinking on 'race', ethnicity and nationalism, and we have attempted to answer four main questions, as outlined in our chapter introduction. To remind you, these questions were:

- How can we sociologically best explain 'race', ethnicity and nationalism, and what are the connections within and between them?
- In what ways do different groups of people experience racism, and how does it disadvantage them in wider society?
- What connects identity, citizenship and multiculturalism?
- What prompts people to migrate, and what are their experiences of settlement?

We started this chapter by exploring some of the most important concepts you need to be familiar with in this field of study. There are many, of course, but we stuck to the main issues and concerns. We took each concept in turn and examined the different ways in which 'race', ethnicity and nationalism have been viewed and discussed over the years. We saw how discussion of 'race', in ancient times, focused on biblical and environmental themes, before the Enlightenment period and science challenged some of these beliefs. Further, we saw how in the early twentieth century the concept of ethnicity came to prominence and cultural factors were deemed to be as important as, or more so than, contested notions of 'biological roots' or similar. Likewise, with the sections on nationalism, we saw how many different theories exist that seek to offer an explanation as to the origins and future of nationalism. We looked at how national identity is constructed and 'performed' on a day-to-day basis to remind us who 'we' are. We also noted, in our discussion of 'race', how most social scientists are now more interested not only in ethnicity but also in racism – that is, the prejudiced social and political actions of individuals who hold racist beliefs. We have looked at the experiences of a range of individuals and groups in this chapter, through the case studies, exercises and questions, and we have documented the work of the Policy Studies Institute (PSI). The PSI study (Modood *et al.* 1997) demonstrates the 'difference and diversity' that exists across and between minority and majority ethnic groups in Britain, and its coverage of issues such as employment, health, housing, cultural identity and racial harassment is comprehensive and insightful. In addition, we examined other concepts such as identity, citizenship and multiculturalism, in the context of debates around migration and settlement. Globalization has seen not only the movement of capital but also the increasing movement of people, leading to new transnational identities and global diasporic cultures. We looked at the experiences of groups such as the Roma and the Poles and their experiences of movement and settlement. Above all else, this chapter has sought to encourage you to find out more about 'race', ethnicity and nationalism and to look at the ways these connect to other chapters in this book. Such matters are a central concern for critical/public sociology and we hope you will want to examine such material in more depth as part of your degree programmes.

Summary

- Sociological interest in the issue of race tends to concentrate on the ways in which 'race' may be socially constructed. These ideas tend to contrast with 'natural' explanations of racial difference that we find in biology and psychology.
- Sociologists also focus on racism (people's experience of racial identification) and the patterns of racial exclusion that occur in areas such as employment, housing and education.
- A distinction is made between race and 'ethnicity', where the emphasis is upon the cultural aspects of group membership and ethnic identity rather than physiological characteristics.
- We also need to consider the importance of nationality and nationalism as a basis for group membership. In some instances ethnicity and race may overlap with ideas of nationhood, but in other situations they are distinct and have little connection with one another.
- In terms of national identity, the notion of citizenship is also important because legal rights and responsibilities define our relationship to the nation-state.
- Race, ethnicity and nation all play an important role in defining who we are, how we see ourselves and how we are treated by others.
- As patterns of migration accelerate, particularly in the era of globalization and international travel, the issues raised above become more important.

Links

Identity and culture (pp. 27–29) in Chapter 1.

Discussion of minority and majority in Chapter 9 (pp. 359–360) raises issues of race and ethnicity.

Further reading

Anderson, B. (1991) *Imagined Communities: Reflections on the Origins and Spread of Nationalism*, London: Verso.
A key work in the debate on the origins of nationalism.

Back, L. and Solomos, J. (eds) (2000) *Theories of Race and Racism: A Reader*, London: Routledge.
A useful collection of articles and a good place to begin some in-depth reading.

Bowling, B. and Phillips, C. (2002) *Racism, Crime and Justice*, Harlow: Longman.
A detailed analysis of racism and the criminal justice process from crime and victimization to policing and punishment.

Cohen, R. (1994) *Frontiers of Identity: The British and the Others*, London: Longman.
An accessible examination of the way the identity of the British people is constantly redefined through various ethnic and national identities, both within and outside the UK.

Eriksen, T.H. (2002) *Ethnicity and Nationalism: Anthropological Perspectives*, 2nd edn, London: Pluto.
Aimed at students of social anthropology, this book looks at the role of culture in the shaping of ethnic identities and examines the relationship between ethnicity, class and gender.

Fryer, P. (1984) *Staying Power: The History of Black People in Britain*, London: Pluto.
Provides a detailed history of black people in Britain.

Kohn, M. (1996) *The Race Gallery*, London: Vintage.
In need of an update and a decent index, but a brilliant review of 'race science'. Simply the best.

Hastings, A. (1997) *The Construction of Nationhood*, Cambridge: Cambridge University Press.
An attack on the work of Hobsbawm, Gellner and Anderson.

Ignatieff, M. (1994) *Blood and Belonging: Journeys into the New Nationalism*, London: Vintage.
Excellent account of various nationalist and ethnic conflicts around the world, such as Yugoslavia and Northern Ireland.

Mason, D. (2000) *Race Ethnicity in Modern Britain*, Oxford: Oxford University Press.

Miles, R. (1993) *Racism after 'Race Relations'*, London: Routledge.
Provides a concise yet comprehensive historical account of the concept of 'racism'. Miles focuses on the multiple definitions of the concept of racism and contests the view that racism is experienced only by black people.

Modood, T., Berthoud, R., Lakey, J., *et al.* (1997) *Ethnic Minorities in Britain: Diversity and Disadvantage*, London: Policy Studies Institute.
This is the fourth report from the Policy Studies Institute into the experiences of ethnic minorities in Britain. It provides a wealth of detailed information on the position of ethnic minorities in Britain in the 1990s; in particular, it highlights the growing differences between the main ethnic minority groups.

Oppenheimer, S. (2007) *The Origins of the British*, London: Robinson.
A readable account of the subject using genetic, archaeological and linguistic evidence to trace the early ancestors of Britain, with some remarkable conclusions.

Bulmer, M. and Solomos, J. (eds) (1999) *Ethnic and Racial Studies Today*, London: Routledge.
A good place to start – especially the opening chapter.

Spencer, P. and Woollman, H. (2002) *Nationalism: A Critical Introduction*, London: Sage.
An excellent book, and a comprehensive introduction to the subject.

Witte, R. (1996) *Racial Violence and the State: A Comparative Analysis of Britain, France and the Netherlands*, London: Longman.
The first comparative study of racist violence in three major European countries covering the history, theory, policy and practice of state responses to racist violence.

Websites

We regularly use the following websites.

www.equalityhumanrights.com
Equality and Human Rights Commission

www.nationalismproject.org
The Nationalism Project

www.carf.org.uk
Campaign Against Racism and Fascism

www.searchlightmagazine.com
Searchlight Magazine

www.refugeecouncil.org.uk
Refugee Council

www.irr.org.uk
Institute of Race Relations

www.lse.ac.uk/collections/gellner/index.htm
Ernest Gellner Resource Site

www.runnymedetrust.org
Runnymede Trust

www.errc.org
European Roma Rights Centre

www.unitedagainstracism.org
UNITED for Intercultural Action

www.srtrc.org
Show Racism The Red Card

www.magenta.nl/crosspoint/uk.html
Crosspoint – Anti-Racism

Activities

Activity 1

A veil closes France's door to citizenship

LA VERRIÈRE, France – When Faiza Silmi applied for French citizenship, she worried that her French was not quite good enough or that her Moroccan upbringing would pose a problem. 'I would never have imagined that they would turn me down because of what I choose to wear,' Ms. Silmi said, her hazel eyes looking out of the narrow slit in her niqab, an Islamic facial veil that is among three flowing layers of turquoise, blue and black that cover her body from head to toe.

But last month, France's highest administrative court upheld a decision to deny citizenship to Ms. Silmi, 32, on the ground that her 'radical' practice of Islam was incompatible with French values like equality of the sexes . . .

So far, citizenship has been denied on religious grounds in France only when applicants were believed to be close to fundamentalist groups. The ruling on Ms. Silmi has received almost unequivocal support across the political spectrum, including among many Muslims. Fadela Amara, the French minister for urban affairs, called Ms. Silmi's niqab 'a prison' and a 'straitjacket.'

'It is not a religious insignia but the insignia of a totalitarian political project that promotes inequality between the sexes and is totally lacking in democracy,' Ms. Amara, herself a practicing Muslim of Algerian descent, told the newspaper *Le Parisien* in an interview published Wednesday.

François Hollande, the leader of the opposition Socialist Party, called the ruling 'a good application of the law,' while Jacques Myard, a conservative lawmaker elected in the district where Ms. Silmi lives, demanded that face-covering veils be outlawed. In an interview at her home in a public housing complex southwest of Paris, the first she has given since her citizenship was denied, Ms. Silmi told of her shock and embarrassment when she found herself unexpectedly in the public eye. Since July 12, when Le Monde first reported the court decision, her story has been endlessly dissected on newspaper front pages and in late-night television talk shows.

'They say I am under my husband's command and that I am a recluse,' Ms. Silmi said during an hourlong conversation in her apartment in La Verrière, a small town 30 minutes by train from Paris. At home, when no men are present, she lifts her facial veil and exposes a smiling, heart-shaped face. 'They say I wear the niqab because my husband told me so,' she said. 'I want to tell them: It is my choice. I take care of my children, and I leave the house when I please. I have my own car. I do the shopping on my own. Yes, I am a practicing Muslim, I am orthodox. But is that not my right?'

Ms. Silmi declined to have her photograph taken, saying that she and her husband were uncomfortable with the idea. Eight years ago, Ms. Silmi married Karim, a French national of Moroccan descent, and moved to France with him. Their four children, three boys and a girl, ages 2 to 7, were born in France. In 2004, Ms. Silmi applied for French citizenship, she said, 'because I wanted to have the same nationality as my husband and my children.' But her request was denied a year later because of 'insufficient assimilation' into France. She appealed, invoking the right to religious freedom. But in late June, the Council of State, the judicial institution with final say on disputes between individuals and the public administration, upheld the ruling.

'She has adopted a radical practice of her religion, incompatible with essential values of the French community, particularly the principle of equality of the sexes,' the ruling said. Ms. Silmi, who resides in France as a legal immigrant, will not lose her right to stay. She has given herself until September to decide whether to make another attempt to acquire citizenship.

Emmanuelle Prada-Bordenave, the government commissioner who reported to the Council of State, said Ms. Silmi's interviews with social services revealed that 'She lives in total submission to her male relatives. She seems to find this normal, and the idea of challenging it has never crossed her mind.' The unease with a very small but growing number of Muslim women wearing face veils is not unique to France. In Denmark, the government barred judges from wearing religious garments and symbols after a rightist political party whose support it needs campaigned for such a ban. Its campaign featured posters showing a judge in a niqab. In Britain last year, a schoolteacher wearing a niqab was told to go home. Several Belgian cities have enacted outright bans on burqas.

M'hammed Henniche, of the Union of Muslim Associations in the Seine-St.-Denis district north of Paris, says he fears that the French ruling may open the door to what he considers ever more arbitrary interpretations of what constitutes 'radical' Islam. 'What is it going to be tomorrow?' he asked. 'The annual pilgrimage to Mecca? The daily prayer? This sets a dangerous precedent,' he said. 'Religion, so far as it is personal, should be kept out of these decisions.'

. . . The Silmis say they live by a literalist interpretation of the Koran. They do not like the term Salafism, although they say literally it means following the way of the Prophet Muhammad and his companions. 'But today "Salafist" has come to mean political Islam; people who don't like the government and who approve of violence call themselves Salafists,' said her husband, a soft-spoken man who bears two physical signs of devotion in Islam: a beard and a light bruising on his forehead caused by bows in prayer. 'We have nothing to do with them.'

His wife said that in 2000 she decided to wear the niqab, which is usually worn on the Arabian Peninsula, because in her eyes her traditional Moroccan djelaba – a long flowing garment with a head scarf – was not modest enough. 'I don't like to draw men's looks,' she said. 'I want to belong to my husband and my husband only.'

France is home to about five million Muslims, three out of five of them French citizens, experts estimate. Criteria for granting French citizenship include 'assimilation,' which focuses on how well the candidate speaks French. Ms. Silmi's French is fluent. Lately, though, President Nicolos Sarkozy has stressed the importance of 'integration' into French life. Part of his tougher immigration policy is new legislation to require foreigners who want to join their families to take an exam on French values as well as the French language before leaving their countries.

Ms. Silmi's husband, a former bus driver who says he is finding it hard to get work because of his beard, dreams of moving his family to Morocco or Saudi Arabia. 'We don't feel welcome here,' he said. 'I am French, but I can't really say that I am proud of it right now.'

(*New York Times* 19.7.2008)

Questions

1. Summarize the two sides of the argument for granting or not granting Faiza Silmi French citizenship.
2. Which do you find most convincing? Give your reasons for your answer.

Activity 2

Is Britain a racist society?

Read the review below of an opinion poll on race commissioned by BBC News Online and consider the questions at the end.

According to the BBC, their News Online team conducted one of the largest online opinion polls on race relations in the UK in 2002. Their findings indicated that while over half of those questioned feel Britain is a racist society, most also believe that society is less racist than it was ten years ago.

The poll was weighted to include the views of Asians, blacks and whites living in Britain. When asked if Britain is a racist society, 52 per cent of whites and 53 per cent of blacks said yes, while only 41 per cent of Asians said yes also.

When asked whether immigration had been a negative force in society over the last 50 years, 47 per cent of whites said it had, while 28 per cent said it had been more of a benefit. Overall, 44 per cent of all those questioned said they believe immigration has been damaging to British society. However, the survey indicated that the majority of respondents support introducing English lessons and citizenship classes for those applying to live in Britain.

Chairman Gurbux Singh, of the Commission for Racial Equality (CRE), had this to say about the immigration issue: 'This is a worrying finding and simply belies the facts. Britain has been collecting different cultures, skills and people for centuries. From Marks and Spencer to the Mini motorcar, some of the most famous symbols of British success have come from people who were refugees and immigrants.'

Positive findings from the survey include 53 per cent of respondents saying they maintain friendships with people from different racial backgrounds. In addition, the majority of those questioned said finding a loving partner is the most important thing in regard to their children marrying outside of their ethnicity.

Singh said, 'Many of us agree that Britain is a modern multi-racial society, and welcome that. Yet, at the same time we think racism is on the increase.' He added, 'Ethnic minority respondents were more likely to feel they were the victims of racial discrimination than whites, showing very clearly the differences in their experiences of living in Britain to the majority of the population.'

Questions

1. **What contradictions can you find in the results of the BBC poll?**
2. **How might they be explained?**
3. **What do you consider to be positive findings with regard to race relations in Britain?**
4. **What do you consider to be negative findings with regard to race relations in Britain?**
5. **Have you witnessed or experienced racism? If so, has it shaped your view of whether Britain is a racist society?**

Activity 3

Inventing tradition

Imagine you are a member of an ethnic majority group in a country made up of several ethnic and religious groups. The 'nation' has been part of a larger empire since the nineteenth century. The empire has begun to collapse and you have broken away to form an independent nation-state that has been recognized by the United Nations (UN).

As a member of the newly formed government, you need to create a strategy for national unity.

Using the following headings (and any others you may think of), how would you set about creating a strong national identity? On your own or in a group, complete the 'Strategic policy' boxes.

Potential areas of intervention	Strategic policy
Territory	
Language	
Culture	
Family life	
School	
Religion	
The media	
Sport	
Youth organizations	
Citizenship	

See also www.nationstates.net, the website for a free nation simulation game that you can play online.

Chapter 7

Age

. . . the development of modern industrial capitalist societies brought increased awareness of age as a basis of social distinctions and greater segregation of age-groups. Whilst most societies have elements of age stratification, capitalism has promoted a distinct form of age inequality which rests upon the socially dependent status of the young and the old. (Bradley 1996: 176)

Key issues

- How do we define and understand age? How does our understanding of age vary over historical time and in different cultures?
- How does age shape our identity? What sociological significance do we attach to the body and biological age?
- How do we separate different stages in the life course? For example, when does childhood stop and youth begin? How do we identify childhood, youth, adulthood and older age – what criteria are we using?
- What are the inequalities between different age groups? For example, why do adults tend to have more power than children, and how do they maintain that power?
- What is the social construction of age-related behaviour? In what ways does our age provide us with opportunities or constraints? What does our age enable us to do, what might it stop us from doing, and why?

Introduction

Imagine a group of 18-year-olds spending an afternoon playing bowls followed by a few hands of bridge at the local bridge club, while a group of 75-year-olds go abseiling before an evening of clubbing at the local night club. Why does this sound strange? It does seem 'inappropriate' for people of those ages to engage in such activities but, we should ask ourselves, why is this the case? We consider these scenarios to be unlikely or somewhat perplexing because of the deeply held notions of age and acceptable age-related behaviour in a society like ours.

Clearly, we live in a world that is structured and ordered by age. Sometimes our age may inhibit us from doing certain things and, at other times, we are able to behave in particular ways because of how old we are. Thus, age can be both enabling and constraining. Our age may influence where we shop, what we buy and even how we pay for goods. For example, older people may prefer to pay by cheque, younger people may be more used to using debit or credit cards, and children may use cash as they are less likely to have access to a bank account. Our age may affect the types of books we read, the music we listen to, the television programmes we watch and the leisure activities we engage in. Thus, our everyday lives are shaped to a certain extent by the way in which our age is understood and expressed in the society we live in.

Stop and think

- In what ways does age shape your identity?
- How do you feel if someone tells you that they think you look younger or older than you actually are? Why might that be?
- Have you ever tried to appear older or younger than you actually are? If so, in what kinds of situation?

For a long time age has divided societies by distinguishing one group of people from another but, apart from some notable exceptions (e.g. Eisenstadt 1956; Mannheim 1952), age has only recently become a topic for sociologists (Bradley 1996). In the past it was assumed that ageing is a biological process that 'naturally' affects everyone. Now it is recognized that age is also socially determined and that our experiences of age can depend on the society we live in. Different cultures attach a range of meanings and values to different age groups, and this affects the way we behave and how we treat others. Thus, age can be seen as a social variable similar to other variables, such as gender, ethnicity and class. Age can differentiate how we are treated in society and how our lives are structured.

However, it is worth bearing in mind that age is only one of several social divisions that shape our lives. For example, our life experiences vary according to whether we are rich or poor, male or female, black or white, young or old. These social divisions overlap and cut across each other, so we need to consider how one variable impacts on another, particularly in relation to power and status. It is not enough to investigate what it is like to be old in society without recognizing, for example, that the life of an older woman from a working-class background can be very different from that of an older middle-class man.

Thus, we live in an age-oriented world, and this chapter begins by highlighting three main reasons why age is an important social category that should be considered alongside other social divisions such as class, ethnicity, disability and gender. Like these social divisions, age can act as a basis for social relationships, social stratification and discrimination. The chapter continues by exploring three different ways of understanding age: chronological, biological and social age. The life course perspective is then considered before we look at the different ways in which age can be used to organize societies. Subsequently, the chapter focuses on a detailed discussion of two stages in the life course – childhood and older age – in order to illustrate the ways in which age is both socially and culturally constructed.

Age and social relationships

Societies are structured and organized by age in a variety of ways; for example, age is used as a basis for group membership for certain institutions. These are known as aged-based institutions as their membership is linked to particular age groups. For example, older people may experience some of their old age living in a residential care home. Children are confined to many age-based institutions, the main one being school, where pupils are segregated into year groups based on age rather than intellectual ability or interests.

Furthermore, there is little mixing between different age groups at school (Ariès 1962) and, even during breaks, children tend to play with those in the same year.

Other age-based institutions for children include playgroups, nurseries and youth clubs. Some of these are also gendered, so boys may go to Cubs and then Scouts when they are older, whereas girls may go to Brownies and then Guides. Children's involvement in age-based institutions can create a peer-group identity for children of similar ages. Consequently, children are separated from much of the adult social world by spending a large part of their lives in age-related contexts with other children. In such ways children develop an understanding of 'appropriate' age relationships and build up knowledge of the ways in which the world is structured through age. They learn about power and authority by seeing the different status given to adults and children. For example, at school children soon discover that they should speak to adults only in certain ways. They may be told 'You don't talk to a teacher like that', but in the playground they can behave more informally with their friends (Devine 2003). Thus, children learn to treat different age groups in distinct ways.

Therefore, involvement in age-based institutions can create a sense of identity with those of a certain age group (or cohort). Karl Mannheim (1952) defined a 'generation' as a particular age group that lives through the same historical and social events. He argued that people of a similar age share a common historical experience and may develop a sense of social solidarity or common consciousness. Thus, history and social change can impact differently upon our age-based experiences according to the generation we are born into.

Furthermore, our generational experiences can be reinforced by consumer goods such as music and clothes, which are targeted to certain generations. Some fashions are perceived to be exclusive to specific age categories and tend to transmit age-related messages (Featherstone and Hepworth 1989). Attitudes can also mark generations as different from one another. Certain attitudes can be perceived as 'old-fashioned' and outdated, particularly when you hear older people talking about things that happened 'in their day'. An example of this is the changing perceptions towards disciplining children. Depending on their age, it is quite likely that, for your grandparents' generation, the beating of children may have been perceived as justified if the children involved had been disobedient. For your parents' generation, beating was perhaps considered too extreme but smacking was regarded as acceptable behaviour. In contrast, a younger generation is more likely to question the suitability of any type of physical

A closer look

Ageism

Johnson and Bytheway (1993: 205) define ageism as 'the offensive exercise of power through reference to age' and suggest that it includes the following:

- *Institutionalized ageism* – For example, legislative discrimination excluding people over 70 from jury service. Age discrimination is also institutionalized in the labour market:

  > It is common both for young job applicants to find themselves passed over for older, supposedly more mature applicants and vice versa, for older people looking for work to find younger, supposedly more lively, people preferred.
  >
  > (Vincent 2000: 148).

- *Internalized ageism* – This occurs during social interactions, such as saying someone is 'childish' or calling someone an 'old bag' or an 'old fogey'. It involves systematic and negative stereotyping on the basis of a person's age. The underlying assumption is that people's experiences are determined only by their chronological age rather than taking into account their social competencies and the environment in which they live.
- *Benevolent patronage* – For example, 'keeping an eye on the old folk' or being overprotective towards children. We tend to assume that all older people and all young children are vulnerable because of their age and thereby need other adults to protect and care for them.

punishment. Nowadays many people are opposed to the smacking of children, which is reflected in the banning of corporal punishment in schools in 1986 in the UK and the banning of smacking in 12 European countries over the past 30 years (although debates are ongoing in the UK regarding this issue). Thus, as Vincent (2003: 115–16) argues, 'Generation is a cultural phenomenon; a set of symbols, values and practices which not only endure but unfold as a cohort ages'.

Age and social stratification

Age stratification involves the unequal distribution of social resources, including wealth, power and status, which are accorded to people on the basis of their age. Victor (1994: 39) suggests that 'Every society divides individuals into age groups or strata and this stratification reflects and creates age-related differences in capacities, roles, rights and privileges'. Key age groupings are childhood, youth, young adulthood, mid-life and old age (Bradley 1996). This chapter focuses mainly on examples from the two ends of the life course, since childhood and old age tend to illustrate the ways in which, at least in British society, we attach less value and status to some age groups compared with others.

Age and discrimination

People can be discriminated against or negatively stereotyped because of their age, and this is known as 'ageism'. As Vincent (2000: 148) points out: 'Ageism, like racism or sexism, refers to both prejudice and discrimination; the first being an attitude, the second a behaviour'. Older people tend to suffer from ageism more than people in other age groups, as the process of ageing is often perceived with fear. We only have to look at the slogans on birthday cards to see the stigma attached to growing older. However, people of all ages can experience negative treatment because of their age: 'ageism places limits, constraints and expectations at *every* stage from birth onwards' (Johnson and Bytheway 1993: 204). Consequently, we need to remember that ageism is not directed only at older people:

> **Thus *all* older people are seen as less suitable for employment on the grounds that they are physically slow, lacking in dynamism, and not very adaptable to change; *all* younger people are suspected of being unreliable, reckless, undisciplined and prone to drug-taking and promiscuity.**
>
> (Bradley 1996: 147)

Bradley (1996) concludes that age is a social division that can create inequality and difference because, on the basis of age, people have different access to social resources, such as wealth, power and status. One of the main roles of sociologists is to understand social differences and to try to explain social inequalities. This in turn can help policymakers to minimize the negative treatment of people on the margins of society. In relation to age, children and older people are those most likely to be socially excluded. Britain is an ageist society and we tend to marginalize certain age groups,

A closer look

Defining the majority and minority worlds

In this chapter we prefer to use the terms 'majority world' and 'minority world' to refer to the developing world and the developed world, respectively. These terms invite us to reflect on the unequal relations between the two world areas. The minority world consists of a smaller proportion of the world's population and land mass despite using the majority of the world's resources. Furthermore, by using the terms we are reminded that what happens in our society, in a minority world context, is not necessarily the way most of the world's population live their lives and that, with greater access to resources, we in the West tend to experience more privileged lifestyles. Case studies from different parts of the majority world are used throughout this chapter to remind us that, like other social divisions, age is a cultural construction.

Majority world (in terms of population and land mass) – Africa, Asia, Latin America

Minority world – UK, Europe, Australia, New Zealand, Japan, USA and Canada especially the very young and the very old. This will be discussed in further detail later in the chapter.

Ways of understanding age

There are three main ways of understanding age: chronologically, biologically and socially.

Chronological age

This is an important concept in the minority world. We are all very aware of how old we are in relation to others. We have birthdays to mark the number of years we have been alive. Our numerical age often determines our access to certain privileges or activities, some of which are linked to laws; for example, eligibility to drink alcohol in pubs and to vote in elections depend on our chronological age. Our age means we are part of a certain 'cohort', which is defined as a set of people who are born at the same time (Vincent 2003). Policymakers need to know how many people are in each age cohort in order to predict the levels of services that will be required. For example, they need to know what percentage of the population will be over 65 in ten years' time in order to estimate the provision of services such as hospitals and sheltered housing.

Stop and think

- What factors account for the rising proportion of older people in society?
- What social and political implications follow from these changes?

Nowadays people live longer because of improved living conditions and health education, better nutrition and advances in medicine. Furthermore, in the minority world, both mortality and fertility rates have dropped (Wilson 2000), leading to what is known as an ageing population. This is when the average age of a population has risen and there is an increase in the proportion of older people compared with the rest of the society (Vincent 2003). In Britain, the number of older people has increased substantially over recent years:

> **For the first time, people 60 and over form a larger part of the population than children under 16 – 21 per cent compared to 20 per cent. There has also been a big increase in the number of people aged 85 and over – now over 1.1 million, or 1.9 per cent of the population.**
>
> (ONS 2003)

Ginn and Arber comment that this

> **has led to fears about rising costs of pensions and of health and welfare services used by older people, together with projections of a rising dependency ratio which has fueled the portrayal of older people as a burden on taxpayers.**
>
> (Ginn and Arber 1993: 6)

However, as they also point out, such attitudes are based on ageism and overlook the diversity of older people and their varied contributions to unpaid domestic and caring labour.

Biological age

Chronological age is linked to biological age, which is based on physical development and the increasing maturity of the body. Biological age is the development over time of how our bodies should function, appear and perform. In terms of physical appearance, biological age is important. In the minority world, there is a strong notion of the youthful body as being central to looking good, and people try to resist the signs of ageing (Vincent 2003). Medical science cashes in on this by providing cosmetic surgery, such as face-lifts, liposuction and chemical peels, in order to try to make people look younger.

One of the reasons why people attempt to reverse the ageing process is because of society's response to biological age. Thus, it is not just about how you look but also about how people respond to the way you look. In British society there is a tendency to assume that notions of success and attractiveness are integrated and often linked to youthfulness. Hence, in a job interview, the young attractive candidate may have an advantage over the older, less attractive candidate, even before either of them says a word. There is a stereotypical assumption that, if you look young and attractive, then you can be thought to be potentially more successful than if you look old and unattractive. Hockey and James (1993: 82) indicate that this is not only experienced by women, as 'Men from their late teens onwards are increasingly aware of the role of a fit, well-groomed body in bolstering the adult individual's social power and status'.

Psychologists are particularly interested in biological age and they explore ideas about the biological and psychological development of individuals. At certain ages, people are expected to be capable of developing specific skills; for example, children are supposed to learn to walk and talk at particular developmental stages that are related to chronological and biological age. In contrast, sociologists are more interested in the significance attached to biological age and the ways in which the body is perceived:

> **The body is lived, experienced, but is done so in ways which are profoundly influenced by social processes and shaped by particular social contexts. We do not simply have bodies that we do things with and to, but we *are* bodies, our sense of who we are is inseparable from our own body.**
>
> (Howson 2004: 12)

Thus, sociologists are keen to explore the ways in which we experience and manage our own and other people's bodies (Shilling 1993). Shilling points out that bodily control is important for ensuring social acceptance, and children are socialized into the regulation of the disciplined body from an early age. It is also recognized that body image impacts upon how we feel about ourselves and how we experience our social relationships. Nettleton and Watson (1998: 2) remind us that our bodily experiences change over time: 'The extent to which we are conscious of our bodies and how we feel about them will vary throughout our lives and within different social contexts'.

Social age

As well as considering different interpretations of the body and biological age, sociologists have a particular interest in social age. Social age refers to the social understandings and significance that are attached to chronological age. Ginn and Arber (1993: 5) define social age as 'the social attitudes and behaviour seen as appropriate for a particular chronological age, which itself is cross-cut by gender'. Social age concerns how you feel in relation to your life experiences and age group rather than fixed ideas based on numerical or biological age. For example, at 70 years of age, a person may be chronologically old, and biologically their physical development may reflect that age as they may have grey hair and wrinkles. However, socially they may feel 'young' and no different from when they were 40. They may engage in the same activities and they might still be fit and healthy. Nevertheless, many people in society may expect their behaviour to reflect their biological age. For example, older people are supposed to 'grow old gracefully' and to avoid looking like 'mutton dressed up as lamb'. Social expectations place pressure on people to look and act their age.

Many ideas about ageing are social and therefore can change. For instance, life expectancy in Britain has increased to 76 years for men and 81 years for women and this has affected our attitudes to chronological age: back in 1901, life expectancy was 45 years for men and 49 years for women (ONS 2003). Thus, when people did not live as long, 60 would have been considered very old, but nowadays, people are not perceived to be very old until they are over 75.

Stop and think

- Think of things that you did as a child or young person that you were not allowed to do. What activities or behaviour were seen as unacceptable for the age you were at the time?
- Consider who decided that you should not engage in such activities and why.

Ideas about age-appropriate behaviour are socially constructed rather than based solely on biology. For example, what children should or should not do tends to reflect their social age rather than their biological age. An eight-year-old can smoke, it is biologically possible, but socially smoking is considered inappropriate for a person of that age. Usually it is adults, parents, policymakers and lawyers who decide what children are allowed to do at different ages, largely because adults perceive children to be immature, vulnerable and in need of protection. Thus, the age at which people can legally drink alcohol, have sex, smoke or drive is often not based on physical or mental abilities but on what society deems to be appropriate. These age-based norms are maintained by ideologies that are resistant to rapid change (Ginn and Arber 1993) but that can change gradually over time. For example, in 1969 the age of majority was lowered from 21 to 18 years (Pilcher 1995), and nowadays you can legally do most things by the time you are 18. Hence your biggest birthday

Figure 7.1 A child soldier: an image that may challenge our assumptions about age
AP Photo/Charles Dharapak

celebration is likely to be your eighteenth, whereas for your parents it was probably their twenty-first. This illustrates that ideas about age and the meanings we attach to different ages can change over time.

Similarly, ideas about age can change according to place: different societies have distinct age norms about what is perceived to be appropriate behaviour. In parts of the USA the legal age for drinking alcohol is 21, but in Britain it is 18. The age of majority also varies in different countries, for example 18 in Austria, 20 in Switzerland and 21 in Malaysia. Therefore, we can conclude that age is a social construction: our understanding of age changes over time and space. The length of time that we live is a biological fact, but the value we place on different age groups is a social construct. Our social experiences of age are affected by the social context in which we live. The way that age is socially constructed can change through history and in different societies, and these issues will be explored in more detail in the sections on childhood and older age.

The life course perspective

Like age, the life course is a social construct. We attach meanings to different age groups, perceiving some age groups as more important than others. The life course perspective is not the same as the life cycle model, which is based on what we perceive to be the 'normal' path of human development. The life cycle sets out what is to be regarded as normal behaviour at different ages; for example, it is not 'normal' to have a baby at 60 or before adulthood. If someone steps outside this pattern, they are labelled as deviant (Becker 1963; see Chapter 14). Thus, the life cycle model is based on biological and chronological age and is used mainly by psychologists and medical scientists. In contrast, the life course model, used by sociologists, takes into account the socially constructed nature of human development and is based on social ageing. It does not suggest that biological and chronological development do not occur, but it believes that we need to understand the social context in which they take place. Elder (1978: 21) suggests that 'The life course refers to pathways through the age-differentiated life span, to social patterns in the timing, duration, spacing and order of events'.

Hence, the life course is a socially defined timetable of events from birth to death, which 'emphasises the interlinkage between phases of the life course, rather than seeing each phase in isolation' (Arber and Evandrou 1993: 9). Thus, the process and experience of becoming old incorporates a notion of past and future. First of all you are born, and then you are socialized from being a child to being an adult. The peak of the life course is adulthood (which is also the physical peak and the time for reproduction), and then you decline into old age and death. Hockey and James (1993) give a metaphorical comparison of this to indicate the values that we place on particular stages of the life course. Childhood is seen as something new and growing; it is metaphorically portrayed as spring or summer, to represent the growth and the dawn of a new life. In contrast, old age is seen as slowing down, metaphorically represented by autumn and winter. Coming to the end of life is compared to evening or twilight.

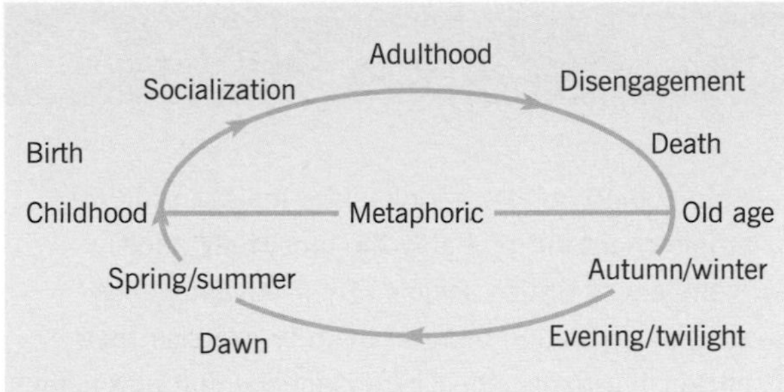

Figure 7.2 Schematic representation of the life course
Source: Hockey and James 1993: 29

As we can see in Figure 7.2, in minority world contexts adulthood is perceived as the central and dominant stage of the life course, representing independence and power (see pp. 308–310). Adulthood is what children are striving for and what older people are trying to hang on to. On either side of adulthood, on the margins, children and older people are more dependent and subordinate to the dominant social category of adults (Hockey and James 1993). Children are growing up and gaining independence. Their move towards adulthood is celebrated and perceived as positive. In the minority world, a frequent question that adults ask children is: 'What do you want to be when you grow up?' This reflects that we focus on adulthood as the important stage of life, indicating that children's social status is marginal. In contrast, while children are growing up, older people are growing down and losing independence: their move out of adulthood is seen as unwelcome and negative (Pilcher 1995). Most people do not look forward to getting older and often try to disguise the ageing process, for example by using anti-wrinkle cream or hair dye.

Thus, children try to look older and are pleased if someone thinks they are older than they actually are, whereas older people try to look younger and are pleased if someone thinks they are younger than they actually are. For example, you know you are getting old when you are pleased that someone tells you that you look young. So, why is this? It is because we place value on the dominant social status of adulthood as a stage in the life course that symbolizes independence, autonomy and power (Hockey and James 1993). Thus, as Pilcher argues, 'The centrality of adulthood has less to do with its position mid-way through the span of human life than with its apparent *desirability*' (Pilcher 1995: 81). Children like to rush towards adulthood and older people like to linger and hold on to it. The old and the young are distant from the centre of social power. This is represented in Table 7.1, which shows the centrality of adulthood compared with the marginality of childhood and old age in our society.

Table 7.1 indicates how age is perceived in our society and the ways in which we socially construct age by placing more value on some age groups than others. The life course perspective indicates that there is an age-based inequality in our society, where children and older people are marginalized in relation to adults. Sociologists are interested in exploring the unequal power relations between adults at the centre of society and children and older people on the margins of society. One of the key roles of the sociologist is to consider power and the way it is played out between different social groups in processes of domination and subordination.

We have seen that, in the minority world, childhood and old age are stigmatized and subordinated in

Table 7.1 Images of ageing in contemporary Britain

Childhood	Adulthood	Old age
Dependent	Independent	Decreasing independence
Lacking autonomy	Autonomous	Losing autonomy
Subordinate	Dominant	Becoming subordinate
Lacking power	Powerful	Losing power
Asexual	Sexual	Increasingly asexual
Vulnerable	Not vulnerable	Increasing vulnerability
Socialization process		*Infantilizing process*
Increasing personhood	Full personhood	Decreasing personhood

(Adapted from Hockey and James 1993)

Case study

Adulthood

We have seen that adulthood is a sought-after status: the peak of the human life course. Yet paradoxically, it is rarely addressed by sociologists as a stage in the life course worthy of study in its own right. While there are sociologies of childhood, of youth and of old age, there is no 'sociology of adulthood' (Pilcher *et al*. 2003). On the one hand, this is because adulthood is taken for granted, and many aspects of sociology indirectly address issues concerning adults without explicitly exploring the life course stage of adulthood. On the other hand, sociologists have an interest in studying marginalized social groups and so are more likely to focus on subordinate social categories when directly exploring the life course. However, it is worth bearing in mind that adulthood is a relatively vague and imprecise social category since it covers a wide range of chronological ages but, like other stages in the life course, it cannot be defined purely in terms of numerical age.

Adulthood has traditionally been associated with productive work roles, parenthood and citizenship rights. Consequently adulthood tends to be linked to notions of responsibility, independence and autonomy. In contemporary Britain, as in many parts of the minority world, adults hold a dominant position in the social world, including 'positions of importance in families and households, in the labour force, in political institutions, and so on' (Pilcher 1995: 87). However, we must remember that not all adults are equally powerful, and an individual's experience of adulthood is shaped by class, gender, ethnicity, sexuality, disability and age. As Pilcher reminds us:

> Able-bodied, white, middle-class males in full-time employment are probably the most fully adult members of British society. Their advantageous structural position enables them to exercise their citizenship rights, their independence and autonomy, to a greater extent than can women, elderly or disabled people, children, the working class, or members of ethnic minority groups . . . Clearly, some grown-ups are more grown-up than others.
>
> (Pilcher 1995: 87–99)

The latter part of adulthood is often referred to as 'middle age', the period before old age, and has become recognized as a distinct phase of adults' lives. It is identified when signs of ageing begin to appear such as grey hair and the 'middle-aged spread', and for women it tends to coincide with the menopause. It is often linked to a change in parenthood such as when children leave home. In popular discourse this period can be referred to as the 'mid-life crisis': a time when people reflect on their family and work status while struggling to postpone the ageing process for as long as possible (Featherstone and Hepworth 1989). Thus, although adulthood is constructed as the dominant powerful stage of the life course, it is important to bear in mind that, like other life course stages, it is not a constant status and it can be experienced in a variety of ways.

Question

1. As a child, can you remember ever being eager to reach adulthood, the peak of the life course? If so, what features of adulthood were you keen to embrace, and why?

relation to the dominance of adulthood. However, it is worth bearing in mind that people are rarely totally independent or dependent; they may be independent in relation to some aspects of their life but not to others. Thus, 'dependence and independence should not be seen as dichotomies, but as part of a spectrum which involves interdependence and reciprocity' (Arber and Evandrou 1993: 19). In addition, we should also remember that children and older people (and other adults, for that matter) are not all the same; they are not homogeneous groups. They are often stereotyped as social groups, and this can mask the wide diversity of social experiences. As already mentioned, their lives will vary according to other important aspects of social differentiation, such as class, gender, disability and ethnicity.

One of the difficulties of studying the 'life cycle' is setting age limits to define the different social groups. Where do childhood, youth, adulthood and old age divide, and how distinct are they as different phases of people's lives? There are many competing definitions for all stages in the life course, and the boundaries between them are often blurred (see the case study below). For example, Abdalla (1988) describes children as people under 12 years old, and young people as being between 12 and 18 years old; Bonnet (1993) defines children as under 15 years of age; and the United Nations Convention on the Rights of the Child (United Nations 1989) states that 18 years of age is the upper limit to childhood. Such wide age ranges to define the boundaries of being a 'child' or a 'young person' reflect that neat age-based categories are not easily set. Thus, understandings of childhood and youth are linked to the social, economic and cultural context rather than to chronological or biological age. This emphasizes why the concept of 'life course', is more appropriate than 'life cycle', as it recognizes that there are overlaps between different stages in the life course and there are no precise chronological markers of when one stage begins and another ends. Therefore, as Pilcher (1995: 82) points out: 'it is important to remember that the life course is best understood as an interconnected and cumulative process'. In contrast to the life cycle, the life course takes into account both cross-cultural and historical variations.

Stop and think

- In Britain at what age can you:
  - (a) vote;
  - (b) watch a PG category film unaccompanied;
  - (c) be convicted of a criminal offence;
  - (d) open a bank account;
  - (e) leave school;
  - (f) marry without parental consent;
  - (g) buy a firearm;
  - (h) become an MP;
  - (i) qualify for a pension;
  - (j) qualify for cheaper fares on public transport?
- How do these ages vary in different countries and at different points in history?

Case study

Youth transitions: from childhood to adulthood

Childhood and youth research widely recognizes that it is inadequate to consider the transition from childhood to youth to adulthood in terms of a linear progression from dependence to independence (Furlong and Cartmel 1997; Wyn and Dwyer 1999). Youth is an age group that is in transition from childhood to adulthood, and consequently young people's status is often ambiguous. In the minority world, due to changes in family structures, education and the labour market (see below), youth transitions have become longer, interrupted and more complex. This has led to more options for young people as they may shift between work and education, but it has also created much uncertainty and increased financial dependency on their parents (Furlong and Cartmel 1997). In the minority world, young people are now more likely to undergo a series of transitions, moving in and out of independence and dependence in different contexts and in relation to different people (EGRIS 2001), and yet still the ultimate goal is to achieve independence (Gillies 2000). Similarly, in the majority world, the notion of 'youth transition' from dependent child to independent adult is problematic, since young people negotiate and renegotiate their interdependence with their parents and siblings throughout the life course. Thus, the notion of interdependence is a useful way of understanding how young people move in and out of relative autonomy and dependence (Punch 2002a).

Case study *continued*

The use of the concept of 'transition' has been questioned in minority world contexts, and Gillies (2000) argues that there are three main drawbacks of using the term. First, it does not allow for greater recognition of the blurred boundaries between dependence and independence. Second, it tends to imply an individualistic transition, while placing less emphasis on family interrelationships and. Third, youth becomes conceptualized merely as a transitional period of change and instability rather than being a special category in its own right. Despite these drawbacks, it is recognized that the concept of 'transition' can still provide a useful framework for exploring the ways in which young people are constrained and their decision-making processes in relation to their chosen school-to-work pathways (Gillies 2000). Apart from the school-to-work trajectories, youth transitions also include leaving home, starting a sexual relationship, having children and acquiring citizenship rights (EGRIS 2001). It is widely recognized that these transitions are interlinked and that it is important to take a holistic perspective in order to understand the interconnections between them (Wyn and Dwyer 1999). Therefore, this case study has shown that, like childhood, 'youth' is 'a *relational* concept, which refers to the social processes whereby age is socially constructed, institutionalized and controlled in historically and culturally specific ways' (Wyn and White 1997: 10–11).

Structural changes since the 1970s leading to extended youth transitions

Labour market changes

- Decline in levels of employment (especially traditional heavy industries and the manufacturing sector)
- Increase in levels of unemployment (young people are often perceived to lack skills and experience)
- Reduction in wages
- Increase in part-time and casual work
- Decrease in entitlement to social security benefits
- Increase in youth training schemes.

Education

- Increasing numbers of young people remaining in full-time education

Family structures

- Increase of average age at first marriage
- Increase of average age at first birth.

(Adapted from Pilcher 1995: 73–8)

Question

1. **In what economic and social contexts do you experience more dependence on family or friends? Do you think that people can ever live their lives totally independently of others?**

The social construction of the life course

We need to bear in mind that the life course, like age, is socially constructed. The process of ageing and the ways in which we perceive very young and very old people are shaped by the attitudes of the society we live in. Our attitudes and understanding of different age categories are shaped by several interrelated factors: the social, political and historical context, ideologies, language and the media. Hockey and James comment that:

> **the precise ways in which childhood is conceived, understood and ascribed with meaning in everyday social practice alters in relation to the economic and political demands of particular societies at particular historical moments.**
>
> (Hockey and James 2003: 15)

Similarly, the meanings we attach to adulthood and older age are also shaped by the politics and policies of a particular society located in time and place. Thus, the specific social context in which people live influences the ways in which different stages in the life course are understood at different points in historical time.

In turn, this leads to the development of ideologies that suggest what childhood or older age should be like for that society. For example, in Britain, partly because children do not engage in full-time work, it is commonly thought that childhood is meant to be the 'happiest time of your life', full of innocence and fun. However, the reality is not always like that: children can be miserable, may hate having to go to school, and may have to care for older or sick parents. Not all children's lives are based on dependence, innocence and carefree playtime. Similarly, in the UK, retirement tends to be thought of as a time to relax and to enjoy leisure activities. Yet some older people find not working a frustrating and boring experience, leaving them with feelings of uselessness. Thus, our stereotypical views of childhood and older age are based on particular ideologies of society and do not necessarily reflect realities.

Our images of age are also shaped by language and popular discourse. For example, older people are often told 'you're too old to act like that', whereas children are asked to 'stop acting like a baby and grow up'. People refer to certain behaviour as 'childish', and we tend to use an ageist vocabulary that reflects our ideas about age. Thus, the way language is used in everyday social interactions shapes our perceptions of age. This is also illustrated in media representations; the next time you watch television or read a magazine, look closely at how children and older people are portrayed, especially in adverts. Children tend to be depicted playing, happy and carefree, in contrast to older people, who are presented as helpless and frail. These particular images of children and older people reflect ideologies and stereotypes. The meanings we attach to different age groups are often part of adult discourses and representations that are expressed through language and imagery (Gittins 1998: 43). Thus, such discourses are often a reflection of adult power in society.

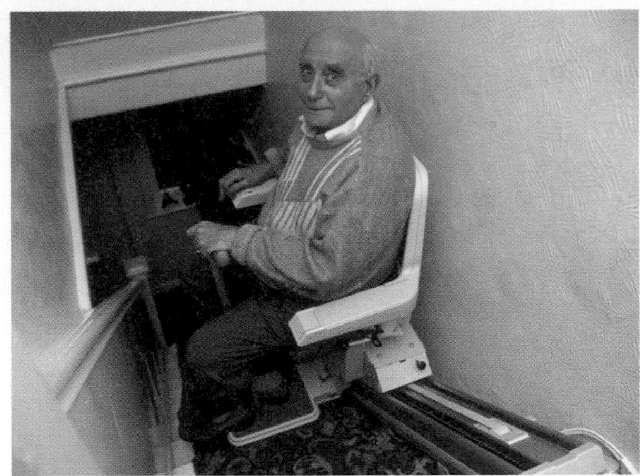

Figure 7.3 New technology can help to give older people independence

The important point to remember is that concepts of ageing are social constructions rather than simple descriptions of biological processes (Hockey and James 1993). The way we understand age and the life course is shaped by the social context, at a specific time in history. Thus, 'the life course is structured around cultural expectations of appropriate behaviour for people of particular ages' (Vincent 2003: 11).

Age as a cultural construction

Cross-cultural and historical comparisons remind us that what happens in our contemporary society is not the only way of doing things. Different cultures use age

World in focus

Horizontal and vertical age relationships

The following two cross-cultural examples indicate that different cultures can use age in distinct ways to organize their society.

Horizontal age relationships: Nyakyusa age-villages

The Nyakyusa are cattle owners and cultivators living in the Great Rift Valley near Lake Nyasa in south central Africa. In this African society age dictates where people live and the power they have in society. Their villages are based on age rather than on kinship ties:

> The age-village starts when a number of herd-boys, about ten or eleven years old, build together at the edge of their fathers' village. They have been

World in focus *continued*

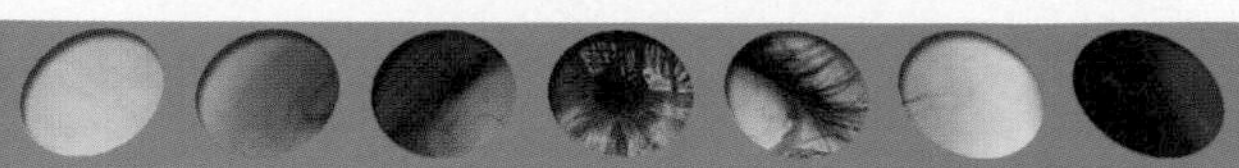

practising building huts for some time, as small boys in other cultures do also, but when they reach the age of ten or eleven they actually go to live in their huts, sleeping and spending their spare time in them, though still going to their mothers' huts for meals. A boy should not and does not eat alone, but a group of friends eat together, visiting the mother of each member of their gang in turn. This system is regarded not only as being congenial to small boys (as with us) but also as moral. For the Nyakyusa eating with age-mates is a corner stone of morality, and a boy who comes home alone often to eat is severely scolded . . .

A boys' village starts quite small, with, perhaps, not more than ten or a dozen members, but it grows as young boys from the fathers' village, or from other men's villages in the neighbourhood, become old enough to join it. When the original members are fifteen or sixteen years old the village is usually closed to any further ten-year-olds, who must then start a new village on their own. Conditions vary with the density of the population in the neighbourhood and other factors, but generally the age-span within a village is not more than about five years, and a village numbers between 20 and 50 members.

The boys who thus establish a village continue to live together through life.

(Wilson 1967: 219–20)

Vertical age relationships: Japanese society

In Japan, the ranking of individuals is more important for determining status and power:

> For the Japanese the established ranking order (based on duration of service within the same group and on age, rather than on individual ability) is overwhelmingly important in fixing the social order and measuring individual social values . . . In this kind of society ranking becomes far more important than any differences in the nature of the work, or of status group. Even among those with the same training, qualifications or status, differences based on rank are always perceptible, and because the individuals concerned are deeply aware of the existence of such distinctions, these tend to overshadow and obscure even differences of occupation, status or class . . .
>
> In Japan once rank is established on the basis of seniority, it is applied to all circumstances, and to a great extent controls social life and individual activity. Seniority and merit are the principal criteria for the establishment of a social order; every society employs these criteria, although the weight given to each may differ according to social circumstances. In the west merit is given considerable importance, while in Japan the balance goes the other way. In other words, in Japan, in contrast to other societies, the provisions for recognition of merit are weak, and institutionalization of the social order has been effected largely by means of seniority; this is the more obvious criterion, assuming an equal ability in individuals entering the same kind of service.
>
> (Nakane 1973: 27–30)

In Japan, the rank of an employee depends on their qualifications and date of entry into the company. Thus, in the workplace, seniority is based on how long someone has been in the company rather than on their chronological age. All those who join a large company at the same time form a club and socialize with each other. In contrast, in Britain, you are more likely to socialize with people your own age rather than those who started work at the same time as you.

Questions

1. In what ways does age structure your life?
2. To what extent does British society enable or constrain you from doing certain things on the basis of your age?

in distinct ways to organize their society. For example, the notion of time passing varies in different cultures. In Britain and in other parts of the minority world, numerical age and the measurement of time are important. The calculation of time passing structures our society and our access to certain activities, such as work and school. Chronological age has not always been as significant as it is today, and it does not have the same relevance in other cultures. During industrialization the notion of structured time became more important when people were working in factories, having to clock on and work a certain length of time (see Chapter 12). Before that, families worked together on the land and time did not need to be so structured. In many pre-industrial societies, time is often marked by events rather than by counting numbers. The passage of time might be remembered by natural events such as an eclipse, a flood or a harvest or by social markers such as puberty or the birth of a first child.

Stop and think

- In British society can you think of any rituals that mark the entry into different stages of the life course? Compare them with rituals in other societies.

In some societies the actual age of the individual can be less important than their stage in the life course. Many traditional societies have 'rites of passage' to mark the movement from one status in the life course to another, such as the onset of puberty. Ritual ceremonies are often used to mark this transition. In modern societies such transitions have become social events rather than formal rites of passage, although there are some exceptions, such as christening and marriage ceremonies. Since these rituals change through history and in different cultures, this reflects the point that age is both a social construction and a cultural construction. In order to reinforce this key point, the remainder of this chapter focuses on two detailed examples of childhood and old age. Each example begins by indicating the ways in which childhood and old age are socially constructed and change over time, followed by a discussion of how they are also culturally constructed and change over place.

Social construction of childhood

Ariès was the first academic to criticize the idea of childhood as a fixed universal state, and his main argument was that childhood changes over time. He was well known for saying that: 'in medieval society the idea of childhood did not exist' (Ariès 1962: 115). He claimed that in the Middle Ages children were like miniature adults, with the same style of dress and engaging in the same work and activities as adults. Ariès argued that, in the minority world, childhood gradually emerged from the fifteenth century onwards, becoming established as different from adulthood only in the nineteenth century once children were banned from working and compulsory schooling was introduced. He was not implying that parents did not love their children, but rather that child-rearing techniques were different. The differentiation between childhood and adulthood was based on the emergence of special clothing and literature for children, and the increase of schooling and new forms of work. Thus, over time, adult perceptions of childhood change and this in turn influences how children are treated and understood in society.

Ariès's ideas have been criticized: he was a social historian whose methods were somewhat controversial, as he relied heavily on the images of children in paintings. His critics (e.g. Pollock 1983) argue that paintings may not depict how things are but how others think they should be, or they may represent ideologies rather than realities. Nevertheless, some of Ariès's ideas were interesting and he was one of the first academics to show that the concept of childhood is a social construction: it is not universal and it changes over time.

In 1973, Hardman made a plea for children to be studied in their own right and not merely as passive objects of society (Hardman 2001). The 1970s witnessed the gradual rise of interest in the social studies of childhood, which developed through the 1980s, mainly in the disciplines of sociology and anthropology. Previous work on childhood had been concentrated mostly in the fields of developmental psychology and education, guided by models of child development and socialization. Thus, until recently, childhood studies focused on children's future worth rather than on their present worth as beings in their own right. Children were perceived only in terms of what they would or could become and were regarded as by-products of

Case study

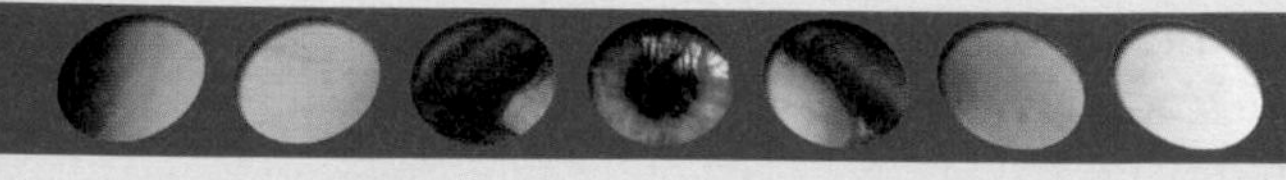

Main influences of changing attitudes to childhood in Britain

Changes in family life

In medieval times family life was open, not private as it is today. Family and community life were mixed and children were integrated into the adult social world. Over time the family became a more self-contained private unit, moving from the public into the private sphere. Thus, children became less integrated into public life and adult contexts.

Changes in work

Before industrialization, children carried out both paid and unpaid labour. Rural families tended to work the land together as a unit, including children. There was minimal separation between home and work (Pilcher 1995: 83). During industrialization, work and domestic life became separated, which meant that some children stopped working, but others began to work in the public sphere, where they tended to be more vulnerable than when working for their families at home. Subsequently, after industrialization, laws were introduced with the aim of banning children from working by the end of the nineteenth century. Hence, the nineteenth century saw the growing dependency of children by denying them a source of income; by the beginning of the twentieth century, children were no longer seen as workers (Hockey and James 1993). Consequently, industrialization led to a change in social relations and the emergence of children's dependency. Childhood became seen as a time when children did not work. It is important to remember that this was because of changing social relations, not because of children's physical abilities. It was connected not to their biological or chronological age but rather to their social age. Thus, as a result of changing social attitudes, children no longer engaged in work and became seen as not participating fully in society.

Changes in education

In medieval times, education was seen as open to all ages, not just children. The medieval school was more like a technical college, with apprenticeships for people of all ages. The school system as we know it developed later, initially with a key role in moral instruction (Heywood 2001). In the seventeenth century there was a focus on the idea that the young were degenerate and in need of control. Gradually schools responded to this social problem by teaching religious values to pupils.

Hoyles (1979) notes that, although educational changes were important, children were affected differently according to their social class. Middle-class boys were the first young people to be constructed as 'children' and use education. This is because their parents had sufficient money to fund them and saw education as a way of providing opportunities for their children's future. The aristocracy did not use education as much because they had alternatives: other traditional jobs were available to them via their aristocratic networks, such as jobs in the army. In contrast, poor children continued to work and were the last to use education. During industrialization poor children worked in mills, factories and agriculture and there was a lot more resistance to viewing working-class children as a separate group from adults. It took some time to remove them completely from the workforce because they were perceived to be too useful. Thus, this example indicates that social class can impact upon children's experience of childhood.

Ariès (1962) argues that, with industrialization, the middle class developed new childhood ideologies. One such ideology was to perceive children as sweet and cute, romanticized as a source of amusement. A later ideology perceived them with concern because of their morally weak nature. These ideas came from religious notions about children being born without sin but being vulnerable to corruption. The outcome of this was that children were seen to be in need of guidance and control. Two notions were developed: that children need discipline and that children should be separated and protected from the adult world.

The school system developed as an appropriate separate place for children: an arena where they could be apart from adults, but also where they could be disciplined and guided. This often resulted in very harsh punishments, sometimes to the point of being cruel. Compulsory education was introduced in 1880 (Heywood 2001), and this contributed to the marginalization of children from the workplace, because it meant that children had to go to school instead of

Case study *continued*

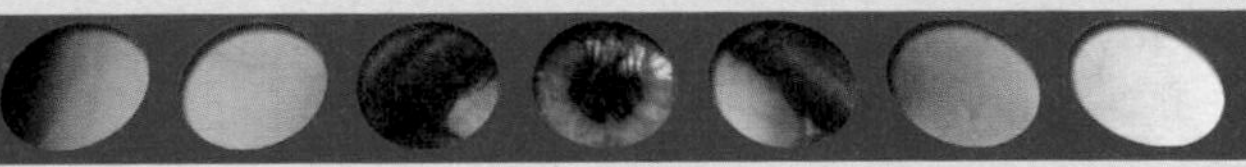

work. Education not only segregated children from world of adults but also led to the economic dependency of children.

Changes in consumer products

As children became separated from the adult world, new markets for children were created. Children became a new group of consumers due to the commercial expansion of markets, such as book and toy industries, that were developed in the eighteenth century. Subsequently, a range of specialist services and products for children were created, including different clothes, toys, books, films and games (Hockey and James 1993). Specialized markets for children reinforced the idea of childhood as a special period in the life course. Children became a separate and distinct consumer group.

Question

1. **In what ways do you think that new technologies, such as email, the Internet and mobile phones, have changed the nature of contemporary childhoods?**

other units such as the family or parents (Saporiti 1994: 193). Traditionally, childhood had been conceptualized as an incompetent, passive and dependent stage in the life course (Hockey and James 2003). The linear developmental model was taken for granted, based on growing competencies increasing with age. Recently, developmental theories of childhood have received widespread criticism: 'this approach both denies the agency of children and ignores the socially constructed character of childhood' (James *et al.* 1998: 173).

The 'new' sociology of childhood was consolidated in the 1990s, focusing on the social construction of children's everyday lives in the present rather than on their future worth as adults. Previous developmental models of childhood did not take into account children's views, and the focus was on the child 'becoming' an adult. In contrast, the sociology of childhood takes children's views seriously and considers children as social actors. Children are perceived as competent active beings who, within certain constraints, are capable of shaping their own lives. Thus, the focus is on 'the experiences of being a child' (James *et al.* 1998: 208), the child as 'being' rather than 'becoming' (Qvortrup 1994). Such a framework facilitates

A closer look

The sociology of childhood

James and Prout offered a new paradigm for the sociology of childhood, highlighting six key features for understanding children and childhoods:

1. Childhood is understood as a social construction. It is not defined in biological terms of chronological age but varies across different cultures and societies. It is not universal but is subject to social and cultural interpretation.
2. Childhood is a variable of social analysis, in the same way as gender, class and ethnicity are considered essential components of social analysis.
3. Children's cultures and social relationships are worthy of study in their own right.
4. Children are not passive subjects but active agents in the construction of their own lives.
5. Ethnography is a useful and appropriate methodology to study childhood, allowing children to have a more direct voice.
6. The emergent paradigm involves a process of the reconstruction of childhood in society.

(James and Prout 1990: 8–9)

sensitivity towards understanding children's issues from their own perspective rather than imposing adult concerns and interpretations on to their lives.

It must also be recognized that the social construction of childhood needs to be understood at three different levels: the structural, the discursive and the situated (Jackson and Scott 2000). At the structural level, childhood is shaped by the institutions of the family, education and the state. The socioeconomic context and the structural constraints of adult–child relations affect the opportunities and restrictions that children face in their lives (Lavalette and Cunningham 2002). At the level of discourse, representations and images of childhood shape common-sense understandings of childhood (Jenks 1996), which vary in different cultures. However, at an everyday, individual level, children are not passive actors in the face of either discourse or structure. Children act to shape and reshape structures and discourses, particularly in their relations with others. They are social actors in the social construction of childhood, which is situated in everyday relations as well as within structures and discourse. Yet it must also be recognized that:

> **children's participation in constructing their own everyday world takes place within the constraints set by their subordinate location in relation to adults.**
>
> (Jackson and Scott 2000: 154)

Perceiving children as social actors means that their own views should be sought when constructing knowledge about their daily lives (Mayall 2002). There is now wide recognition that children should be listened to and their perspectives taken seriously. The 1979 United Nations Year of the Child provided much impetus to child research (Boyden and Ennew 1997: 9). Such interest has continued to increase as a result of the 1989 United Nations Convention on the Rights of the Child, which has been almost universally ratified, except in Somalia and the USA. The Convention has 54 articles covering the following broad areas of rights: survival, protection, development and participation. As well as defining the social, economic, cultural, civil and political rights of children, the Convention outlines the duties and responsibilities of governments and other adults to children and their families. Article 12 focuses on the importance of children being able to express their views freely and having them taken into account in matters that concern them. Children's perspectives should be listened to not only because children have a right to be heard and are capable of expressing themselves, but also because 'only by hearing from children themselves is it possible to learn about their particular childhood experiences' (Boyden *et al.* 1998: 170).

Stop and think

- In what ways and to what extent are children's interests represented in the following social institutions?
  (a) the family;
  (b) different forms of media;
  (c) religion;
  (d) politics;
  (e) education;
  (f) the law.
- In discussing this, you may find it useful to compare and contrast possible responses from adults and children and compare these institutions across time and cultures.

A closer look

Rights of the child

Article 12: State parties shall assure to the child who is capable of forming his or her own views the right to express those views freely in all matters affecting the child, the views of the child being given due weight in accordance with the age and maturity of the child.

(United Nations 1989)

Characteristics of modern childhood in Britain

We have seen that changes in family life, education, work and consumer markets have led to what we understand as modern childhood today. In Britain, as in most societies of the minority world, childhood is perceived as a distinctive and special stage in an individual's life. Children are regarded as 'other': a distinct social group, set apart as a special category with specific needs, different from adulthood (Pilcher 1995). Children tend to be separated from much of the adult world, such as spending much of their everyday lives in aged-based institutions with their peers. Thus, what began as separation from the adult world led on to marginalization, resulting in a construction of childhood as a stage of dependence and subordination to adults. Children experience social, political and economic dependency. Furthermore, their lives are largely controlled by adults (Mayall 2002). They are subject to parental control in the family and to teachers' control in schools. Thus, much of their lives is spent under adult surveillance.

There are two polarized views of children in modern society. On the one hand, children are perceived as vulnerable and innocent, in need of protection from the harsh adult world. On the other hand, they are seen to be vulnerable and corruptible, in need of control. In

A closer look

Research with children

In the past, most childhood research tended to gather second-hand information about children's lives from parents, teachers and other adult carers. Nowadays it is widely accepted that children's own perspectives should also be sought on issues that concern them. However, most societies do not have a culture of listening to children, so how can their views best be heard?

> The challenge is to strike a balance between not patronising children and recognising their competencies, whilst maintaining their enjoyment of being involved with the research and facilitating their ability to communicate their view of the world. A combination of techniques can enable the data-generation process to be fun and interesting for the participants as well as effective in generating useful and relevant data . . . Some children prefer to draw, others to write or talk. As preferences and competencies vary from child to child in the same way as they do from adult to adult, it is impossible to find the ideal methods for research with children.
>
> Using a range of methods, both traditional and innovative, can help strike a balance and address some of the ethical and methodological issues of research with children. Like other child researchers I found that using a variety of techniques was valuable: to prevent boredom and sustain interest; to prevent biases arising from over-reliance on one method; to triangulate and cross-check data; to evaluate the usefulness of different methods and to strike a balance between traditional and innovative methods . . .
>
> It should also be acknowledged that it is misleading to talk about 'child' and 'adult' research methods, since the suitability of particular methods depends as much on the research context as on the research subjects' stage in the life course. The choice of methods not only depends on the age, competence, experience, preference and social status of the research subjects but also on the cultural environment and the physical setting, as well as the research questions and the competencies of the researcher . . . Perceiving children as competent social actors does not necessarily mean that research should be conducted in the same way as with adults. This is because many of the reasons underlying potential differences stem from children's marginalised position in adult society or from our own adult perceptions of children rather than being a reflection of children's competencies.
>
> (Punch 2002b: 337–8)

Britain, as in many other parts of the minority world, childhood is considered as a time dedicated to play and to school, but not to work: a period free from adult responsibilities. As mentioned earlier, this social construction of childhood leads to the view that children are meant to be happy and to lack responsibility. Yet this is the idealized image of childhood in the minority world, which is often presented as universal, and it is important to realize that it is an ideology and not necessarily a reality (Boyden 1990).

However, some writers argue that children are oppressed, that their lives are too controlled, that they are not valued and that they are too dependent on adults (Hood-Williams 1990). Furthermore, the dependence of children on adults is widely recognized, but the idea that adults are, or can be, dependent on children is frequently ignored or underestimated. In the minority world, since most children go to school and do not work full time, they tend to be economically dependent on their parents. However, Leonard (1990: 67) observes that parents in the UK can be emotionally dependent on their children for 'love, loyalty, obedience and moral support'. She suggests that children give meaning to adults' lives and are central to adults' definition of self. Children also create many jobs for adults in terms of child care and schooling. Oldman (1994) argues that adults in the UK may be dependent on children for their employment.

Therefore, adult–child relations are complex and should not be seen merely in terms of independence versus dependence. Elements of exchange in reciprocal relations between adults and children should be considered (Morrow 1994). Adults' and children's lives are interrelated at many different levels, and adults are often not fully independent beings (Hockey and James 1993). It is too simplistic to use the notion of dependency, whether of children on adults, or adults on children, to explain the complexity of adult–child relationships. Adult–child relations should be explained in terms of interdependence that is negotiated and renegotiated over time and space, and needs to be understood in relation to the particular social and cultural context (Punch 2001a).

Many of the characteristics of modern childhood in Britain are found in other minority world societies, but not in all cultures. This definition of childhood is relatively recent, thus illustrating that childhood is a social construction and the way it is understood varies over time. Furthermore, as we shall see in the following section, it is a cultural construction; the way childhood is understood also varies over space.

Cultural construction of childhood

The notion of a universal childhood exists only in so far as it is a generational category present in all societies. That is, childhood is a structural form and a social status in both minority and majority world contexts. However, as Qvortrup argues (1994: 5), we need to bear in mind that 'There is . . . not one, but many childhoods'. The multiplicity of different childhoods requires them to be placed within their particular historical, geographical and cultural context. For example, Blanchet (1996) shows how children in Bangladesh are indulged and protected when they are very young; however, they are treated somewhat severely between the ages of about 10 and 20 in order to prepare them for the harshness of adult life. Similarly, Stafford (1995: 179) comments that children in a fishing village of Angang in Taiwan are often subject to teasing and harsh treatment by adults in order to teach them to be 'clever, resilient or tough'. In the majority world, where many children work, parents may be economically dependent on their children. For example, Boyden (1990) notes that in some countries children can be the main or sole income-earners in the household. Children are often the only source of social and economic support for their parents in old age. Thus, relations between children and adults in the majority world tend to be more interdependent than the generational relationships of families in the minority world.

In the majority world many children work and can be proud about being active contributors to the maintenance of their households. Children tend to be perceived as competent workers and are encouraged to take on adult responsibilities from an early age. Much of their work teaches them useful skills for their future and is perceived to be a central part of their childhood. However, in popular and media discourses, majority world children who work from an early age, 'burdened with adult-like duties and responsibilities' (Kefyalew 1996: 209), tend to be conceptualized as miniature adults (Boyden *et al.* 1998). This is because the notion of the globalization of childhood based on minority world ideals continues to persist, where childhood is perceived as a time for play and school but incompatible with work (Boyden 1990). Childhood is considered as a special time when we need to be protected, often resulting in exclusion from the world of adults, especially from adult responsibilities of work. The popular conceptualization of children who do not live up to such idealism is that they have 'abnormal' childhoods (Edwards 1996). Although not denying that some child work can be extremely exploitative, recent academic studies have shown that work is central to many majority world childhoods and that it is not necessarily detrimental, often having both positive and negative effects (Boyden *et al.* 1998; Woodhead 1999).

Thus, in a global context, it is more common for children to work and go to school than to have a childhood dedicated to play and school. Rather than perceiving majority world children as having 'abnormal' childhoods, it should be remembered that, children in the minority world tend to experience more privileged, protected childhoods compared with most of the world's children. It is also worth remembering that, although most children in the majority world work, this does not mean that they have no time for play; many combine the activities of play with both school and work (Woodhead 1999). For example, rural Bolivian children tend not to have access to manufactured toys because of limited financial resources and the relative isolation of countryside locations but, to compensate, children use their own resourcefulness to make their own toys (Punch 2001a). They use the natural environment and materials that are available to them, such as stones, water, mud and maize (Figures 7.4 and 7.5). They integrate their play activities with work and school, for example by playing on the way to and from school or while taking animals out to pasture (see below).

Nevertheless, this is not to say that all children who work in the majority world have happy childhoods. There are also many street children, child prostitutes and child soldiers who live in particularly difficult circumstances. The important point to bear in mind is that we should not see childhood in poor countries, and

Figure 7.4 A young Bolivian girl cooking
© Samantha Punch

Figure 7.5 A South American child 'being Mum'
© Samantha Punch

children who work, only in a negative light. We should be aware that simplistic stereotypes of childhood hide the complex realities of children's lives. Thus, although the social construction of childhood in Britain means that we perceive work as something negative and potentially harmful for children, we have to remember that these are merely minority world ideas of what childhood should be like. After all, we should not forget that in our society we force children to go to school and do not let them work full time. Who is to say what a 'normal' childhood should consist of?

Thus, there is not one universal childhood but a diversity of childhoods that exist both between and within different cultures. Simplistic distinctions between majority world and minority world childhoods are problematic because children's lives vary according to a range of factors, such as culture, class, gender, age, ethnicity, disability, religion and birth order. For example, in Hecht's (1998) research with street children in Brazil, he differentiates between the protected, nurtured childhoods of the rich and the independent, nurturing childhoods of the poor. As a social category, childhood exists in all societies, but attitudes towards it can be different and so the ways of being a child and the ways in which childhood is understood by adults vary. It is important to consider the particular circumstances in which children live their childhoods. The historical, cultural, economic, social and geographical contexts shape how different childhoods are understood and experienced. Therefore, childhood is both a social and a cultural construction as it varies over time and space.

World in focus

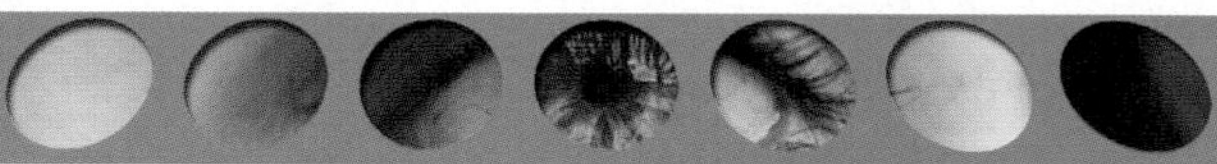

Childhood in rural Bolivia

It is useful to consider examples of childhood in different parts of the world in order to highlight that the minority world construction of childhood is not universal. Research in rural southern Bolivia illustrates that the concept of childhood varies cross-culturally:

> Most of the children in Churquiales face the same broad constraints of relative poverty and geographical isolation. The opportunities for waged employment are limited, and schooling is available only for the first six years of primary education. The community is relatively isolated, having limited access to the mass media, as there is no electricity and no television, and communication networks are not extensive. The main form of transport is foot and there are no cars. There are no push-chairs for young children, so they are tied by a shawl and carried on their mother's back. As soon as they can walk they are encouraged to get used to walking long distances and from as young as three years old they can be expected to walk several miles if necessary. Children cover a lot of ground every day as they walk between their home and school, go to the hillsides in search of animals or firewood, fetch water from the river and carry out regular errands for their parents to other households or to the shops in the community square . . .
>
> In order to provide for the family's subsistence requirements, the households in Churquiales have high labour requirements in three main areas of work: agriculture, animal-related work and domestic work. In the countryside many jobs have to be done every day, such as caring for the animals, food preparation, and water and firewood collection. The household division of labour is divided according to sex, age, birth order and household composition (Punch 2001b). Children are expected to contribute to the maintenance of their household from an early age. Once children are about five years old parental expectations of their household work roles increase, and children are required to take on work responsibilities at home. As they acquire skills and competence their active participation in the maintenance of the household rapidly increases.
>
> Bolivian children in rural areas carry out many jobs without question or hesitation,

World in focus *continued*

often readily accepting a task and taking pride in their contribution to the household. In addition, some household tasks, such as daily water and firewood collection, are such a regular part of their daily routine that they accept responsibility without having to be told to do them. Water collection is a child-specific task, usually carried out by young children as it is a relatively 'easy' job which children as young as three or four years old can start doing. They may begin by only carrying very small quantities of water (in small jugs at first), but by the time they are six or seven years old they can usually manage two 5-litre containers in one trip. Since children are assigned this job from a very early age and it has to be carried out at least once or twice every day, children know there is no point of trying to avoid doing something which is very clearly their responsibility. I observed that children frequently accepted responsibility for such tasks and initiated action to fulfil them rather than merely responding to adults' demands. Their sense of satisfaction for self-initiated task-completion often appeared to be greater than when they were asked to do something.

So, children in rural Bolivia are not only expected to work and are given many responsibilities but they are also aware of the importance of their contribution and often fulfil their duties with pride. Parents encourage them to learn new skills by giving them opportunities to acquire competencies and be responsible. Parents do not expect to have to remind children constantly of their tasks and may threaten them with harsh physical punishment if their obligations are not completed. Children are encouraged to be independent: to get on with their jobs, to combine work and school, and to travel large distances within the community unaccompanied. In addition, children are also expected to maintain interdependent family relations by contributing to the survival of the household. Furthermore, parents teach their children to try to be relatively tough, for instance not to cry if they fall over and hurt themselves, not to sit on adults' laps or be carried on mothers' backs once they are over about three years old, and to be able to look after themselves and younger siblings when parents are away from the household.

(Punch 2001a: 25–28)

Questions

1. What were the opportunities and constraints that shaped your experience of childhood?
2. Consider the responsibilities you had as a child. Did you perceive them as a frustrating burden, or did they enhance your sense of pride and achievement?

Social construction of old age

Stop and think

- Think of terms we use in everyday language to describe older people. What kind of images do they conjure up?
- In what ways are such images positive or negative about the ageing process, and are they gendered (i.e. are different images used to refer to older men compared with older women)?

For many people, growing old can be a time of social withdrawal and loss – loss of job, income, health, independence, role, status, partners, friends and relatives. Old age can be experienced as a time of loneliness and social isolation. It is commonly believed that older people are 'burdens', being dependent on medical and social services. Yet old age can also be associated with having greater life experience and being 'wise', such as when grandchildren look up to the worldly wisdom of their grandparents. However, many of the negative generalizations of older people mask the diversity of their varied experiences. As Victor argues:

> **Although the realities of ageing do not fit the commonly held stereotypes, the myths about ageing continue to find common currency and expression in everyday life.**
>
> (Victor 1994: 78)

This is reflected in the popular terms used to describe older people, such as 'being past it', 'little old ladies' and 'old biddies'.

Most images of older age indicate that in minority world societies older people tend to be marginalized through negative stereotypes that reflect 'the experience of bodily decay or mental deterioration' (Hockey and James 1993: 79). As mentioned previously, young bodies tend to be considered more beautiful in British society, and so physical ageing is often perceived in derogative terms. In particular, images of ageing tend to marginalize older women more than older men (Biggs 1993). This is partly because physical appearance is seen as more important in society for women than for men (Arber and Ginn 1993). Thus, when women lose their physical attractiveness, they are more stigmatized than men. Victor explains why there is a double standard of ageing:

> **Growing older is less problematic for a man because masculinity is associated with qualities such as competence, autonomy and self-control. These valued attributes withstand the ageing process much better than the qualities for which females are desired: beauty, physical attractiveness and childbearing . . . Later life is a time when men become grey-haired, distinguished, wise and experienced whilst women are typified as worn-out, menopausal, neurotic and unproductive.**
>
> (Victor 1994: 82)

It is important to recognize that in relation to gender and ageing, women suffer from both sexism and ageism (see opposite). For example, women are more likely than men to be living in poverty as their pensions tend to be less than those of men. Women are also more likely to live longer than men, since life expectancy for women is higher than for men, which means women are more likely to end up living alone or in residential care in later life (Biggs 1993).

Stop and think

- Do you think that future cohorts of older women will have higher expectations regarding their position in society than previous generations? If so, why?
- In what ways do you think older women in future generations might be able to resist the patriarchal ideal of femininity?

Retirement

The experience of retirement has become one of the defining features of old age in the minority world. In the UK, the age of retirement (65 years) is an arbitrary age that 'bears no relationship to the nature of the individual's personality, vitality, biological condition and mental acuity' (Holmes and Holmes 1995: 53). There is no particular decline in physical or mental abilities at this chronological age, and many older people can still be both mentally and physically capable at 60 or 65. However, the notion of the pensioner, the retired older person who receives a pension, tends to be how many older people become defined, hiding their individual identity. Yet we need to be aware that older people are not a homogeneous group (Arber and Evandrou 1993; Phillipson 1998). For a moment, compare yourself with someone 25 years older than you and imagine how you would feel if you were constantly referred to as being part of their social group. It seems a bit ridiculous to consider that people who are 25 years apart share many similarities, but this is what we tend to do to older people. Society often sees all older people as just part of one big group of pensioners. Yet the group of retired people over 65 can represent a number of different generations. Trying to suggest that the life of a 65-year-old is similar to that of a 90-year-old, simply because they are both in the age of retirement, is not appropriate.

Retirement has become the norm in Britain and is experienced in a variety of ways. Research has shown that, if people are dissatisfied with retirement, it is usually related to their loss of income and reduced social contacts rather than missing the job itself (Victor 1994). Satisfaction with retirement is linked to increased opportunities for leisure activities and greater freedom. However, the experience of retirement is affected by social class (Biggs 1993; Vincent 2000). A middle-class person will be more likely to have a good pension,

Case study

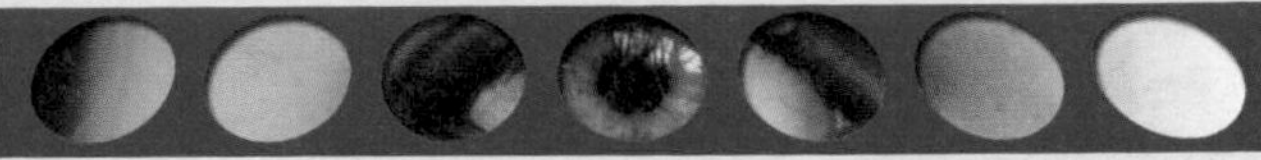

The double standard of ageing

Arber and Ginn (1991) argue that growing older has a different significance for women compared with men:

> Itzin (1990) sees the double standard of ageing as arising from the sets of conventional expectations as to age-appropriate attitudes and roles for each sex which apply in patriarchal society. These are conceptualized by Itzin as a male and a female 'chronology', socially defined and sanctioned so that transgression of the prescribed roles or of their timing is penalized by disapproval and lost opportunities. Male chronology hinges on employment, but a woman's age status is defined in terms of events in the reproductive cycle. She is therefore 'valued according to sexual attractiveness, availability and usefulness to men' (Itzin 1990: 118). The social devaluation of older women occurs regardless of occupation or background, or of the fact that after childrearing they have potentially twenty-five years of productive working life ahead.
>
> Because women's value is sexualised, positively in the first half of life, negatively in the second, it depends on a youthful appearance. Sontag (1972) observes that while men are 'allowed' to age naturally without social penalties, the ageing female body arouses revulsion. The discrepancy between the societal ideal of physical attractiveness in women and their actual appearance widens with age, whereas the signs of ageing in men are not considered so important. This double standard is most evident and acute in the conventions surrounding sexual desirability, as shown in the taboo on asking a woman her age, and in the contrasting attitudes towards marriages where the husband is much older and those (few) where he is much younger. The former practice is socially approved, or at least forgiven, as is the desertion by husbands of their middle-aged wives for younger women. But an older woman who marries a young man is censured as predatory and selfish. Unlike the older man who is admired for this capture of a young bride, the older woman is condemned because she has broken the convention that men remain dominant. Since age seniority generally implies authority, women remain minors in their conjugal relationships (Sontag 1972) . . .
>
> The double standard of ageing is not merely a matter of aesthetics: it is 'the cutting edge of a whole set of oppressive structures (often masked as gallantries) that keep women in their place' (Sontag 1972: 38). Itzin concurs; men's preference for wives younger than themselves at *all* ages shows that the devaluation of women as they age has less to do with appearance than with the sexual division of labour and of power (Itzin 1990).
>
> (Arber and Ginn 1991: 41–3)

Question

1. Think of some examples of well-known women, such as actors and politicians, and consider the extent to which they suffer from the double standard of ageing in comparison with men in similar situations.

A closer look

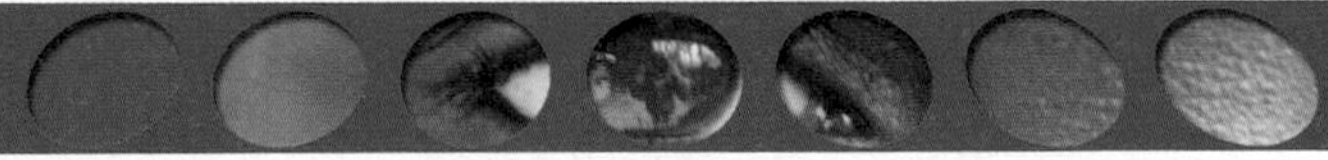

Appropriate terminology

The term 'older people' is a more suitable expression than the more static and homogenized terms of 'pensioner', 'the elderly' and 'old people', since it implies variety and suggests a range of different ages (Wilson 2000).

health insurance, their own home, a car and savings to spend on new activities. In contrast, a working-class person will be more likely to have sparse savings, to receive an inadequate state pension and to be unable to afford a good lifestyle. Thus, the working-class person will be more likely to experience retirement as a time of poverty. The problem of poverty in old age can be acute, and older people feature prominently in the poorer sections of all societies (Vincent 2003). For example, according to the Office for National Statistics, a total of 3000 women and 2000 men aged 75 and over in Britain have neither central heating nor sole use of a bathroom (not including residents of communal establishments). Financial hardship may also be intensified by ill-health and isolation (Bradley 1996). A growing proportion of older people live alone: 14.4 per cent of all households in the UK, of which two-thirds of these (68.2 per cent, or 2,129,000 older people) have no access to a car (ONS 2003b).

Consequently, the experience of retirement, like that of ageing, is extremely diverse and cross-cut by factors such as age, gender, class, marital status, disability and ethnicity (Victor 1994). For example, class can affect the likelihood of an older person suffering from poor health or becoming dependent. However, the persistence of inappropriate negative stereotypes of older people masks the diversity of their experiences and can result in discrimination and prejudice against them (Victor 1994). Phillipson (1998: 139) argues that, in order to understand the complexity of life in old age, we should explore the ways 'in which people "resist" rather than succumb to the pressures associated with growing old'. We should also take account of older people's contributions to society by recognizing that some continue to work or learn (such as by embarking on Open University courses), and many still provide material and emotional support within their families and communities through voluntary and unpaid services. Thus, as Victor (1994) suggests, it is more appropriate to consider notions of interdependence between generations and throughout the life course, rather than a more linear conception of independence and dependence at different life stages. We should not perceive old age to be 'naturally' problematic by focusing only on 'the "burdens" of pensions, caregiving and intergenerational equity' (Wilson 2000: 160). We need to move beyond stereotypical assumptions by also considering the benefits of old age and older people's positive experiences and contributions to society:

> **Older people should be seen as repositories of cultural wisdom and expertise, craft skills and local knowledge – things that are valuable to all. However, it is important to avoid romantic stereotypes of old age, since elders can also be repositories of prejudice and ancient animosities as well as the positive side of tradition.**
>
> (Vincent 2003: 168)

A closer look

The contested nature of sociology

Table 7.2, based on Phillipson's (1998) work, indicates that over time different sociological arguments emerge in relation to specific issues. Initially there was concern that retirement would impact negatively on people's lives. This view then shifted to perceiving retirement as a positive way of coping with mass unemployment. More recently, it has been recognized that there are multiple routes into retirement and that it may be experienced in both negative and positive ways. These different perspectives reflect the complexity and shifting nature of sociological understanding that is often debated and may change over time.

Table 7.2 Different perspectives of retirement

1950s	Concern that withdrawal from work may lead to social and mental health problems
1970s and 1980s	Promoted as a means of coping with mass unemployment
1990s and 2000s	Fragmented and flexible pathways into retirement: redundancy or disability pathways, forced or voluntary early retirement, informal care or unemployment pathways and state retirement

A closer look

Sociological perspectives of ageing

Some writers approach the study of ageing from different theoretical perspectives. Each 'theory', or way of understanding the ageing process, is given a different name.

Disengagement theory

Cumming and Henry (1961: 211) argue that 'Disengagement is an inevitable process in which many of the relationships between a person and other members of society are severed and those remaining are altered in quality'. As the ageing process develops, older people are believed to become increasingly self-preoccupied while society prepares for their final 'disengagement' of death in order to minimize the social disruption it may cause (Phillipson 1998).

The political economy of old age

This theory strives to understand the relationship between the ageing process and the economy. Townsend (1981) refers to the concept of 'structured dependency', which perceives older people to be excluded from work and to have a restricted access to a range of social resources, resulting in their dependent status and increased likelihood of living in poverty. The loss of a productive role in the economy and increased welfare dependence can result in old age being perceived as a social problem (Howson 2004: 149).

Ordinary theorizing

Gubrium and Wallace (1990) suggest that researchers should listen carefully to the questions that older people raise when they are being interviewed. They argue that, in research, older people should not merely be perceived as passive respondents; it should be recognized that 'they develop facts and theories of their own, and the relevance of these deserves wider recognition' (Phillipson 1998: 26).

Stop and think

- Give examples of older people who continue to play leading roles in areas such as the arts, politics and law in contemporary society.
- In what ways do they challenge negative stereotypes about older people?

Cultural construction of old age

We have seen that, in Britain and other societies of the minority world, ageing is devalued and not esteemed (Hockey and James 1993). We need to bear in mind that the disadvantages of old age are not universal or fixed:

> **A decline in strength and a changing physical appearance may be inevitable in old age, but the degree and meaning of change are very variable. The actual impact of physiological changes depends on whether the environment is hostile to disabilities or supportive . . . The cross-cultural approach to the study of ageing shows that most of the attributes of old age are culturally determined. For example, it is not 'natural' for older men or women to live in poverty, or to take care of grandchildren, or to spend time in religious contemplation, but it is easy to believe it is if we are locked into one culture only.**
>
> (Wilson 2000: 3)

Retirement pensions are by no means universal, and globally many people continue working until they are no longer physically capable. There are widespread beliefs that in the majority world old age is revered and, once older people are unable to work, they are cared for by their families. Some cultures have more positive attitudes towards the ageing process, but this does not necessarily mean that all older people in those societies will be treated with respect and importance. Featherstone and Hepworth (1989) note that high status tends to be accorded to those who had power, wealth or status when they were younger.

In some traditional cultures, there can be a tendency to offer older people higher respect and status. For example, some societies worship their ancestors, and it tends to be older men who carry out important ritual ceremonies. Elders can be perceived to achieve almost godlike status; for example, in Ghana older people are a symbol of deity and so, if you offend them, you are thought to offend the gods. The traditional Hindu perception of ageing illustrates the benefits of older age in that culture: 'being old means being more saintly, gaining greater respect and possibly achieving a better position in the next life' (Wilson 2000: 23). Wilson (2000) also points out that in Islamic and Asian countries there can be very strong religious or philosophical beliefs that older parents should be greatly respected. These cultural beliefs, along with a lack of available pensions, often lead to families rather than the state providing support for older people. For example, in Japan there is a strong sense of duty towards older people, and children (usually sons and daughters-in-law) are generally expected to provide economic and social care for older parents. However, because of falling birth rates and greater longevity, Japan has the largest ageing population in the world and is increasingly concerned about whether families will be able to continue to provide support for older people.

Thus, older people can be treated well and may have more power and status in the majority world. However, we need to be careful not to romanticize old age in such cultures, as not all older people in traditional or religious communities are treated well:

> **Even among very small-scale societal types such as hunters and gatherers (or tribal horticultural peoples), a wide variation exists in how older people are evaluated and dealt with. Some such societies regard their older citizens as revered personages to be carried on one's back as communities move over the landscape, while others see them as excess baggage to be left to the elements when they can no longer keep up.**
>
> (Sokolovsky 1990: 2–3)

In addition, widespread poverty can make it difficult for some people to care for the older generation. As Wilson (2000: 26) reminds us, 'not everyone has a family and, further, not all families are dutiful, let alone harmonious'. Hence, even when old age is perceived positively, not all older people will occupy a privileged position. Furthermore, we need to take into account that increasingly the values associated with old age in majority world countries are diminishing in their importance:

> **Wisdom, spirituality and magic powers were seen as attributes of long experience or nearness to death. Now the spread of materialism, industrialization, urbanization and Westernization have led to the breakdown of religious authority and family solidarity and the devaluation of the wisdom of the old.**
>
> (Wilson 2000: 10–11)

World in focus

Older age in Inuit culture

Holmes and Holmes (1995) describe how processes of modernization have impacted upon the role of older people in Inuit culture. Inuits live in a harsh cold environment, mainly surviving on the subsistence activities of hunting sea mammals and fishing. Traditionally, older people have held positions of high status and respect within their communities. Younger family members frequently consulted them about improving their hunting skills, choosing marriage partners and settling family disputes. Older people played an important role in educating children, particularly in economic skills, and were believed to have special knowledge and spiritual power. The Inuit culture developed food-sharing practices in order to ensure that older people would be cared for. For example, some foods were prohibited to be eaten by hunters and were reserved for those who could not hunt for themselves. However, because of contact with Europeans, the traditional Inuit system has begun to experience some effects of modernization. Some of the recent changes are positive, such as access to basic services of running water and electricity, but generally the impact on the role of older people has been negative. For example, the subsistence food-sharing practices are

World in focus *continued*

beginning to be replaced by more commercial hunting. Older people are losing decision-making power and respect, as elected councils with younger people are being formed. Education has become more formal, and children now attend school rather than relying on informal education from their grandparents. This has even led to a language barrier between older people who speak Inuit and children who learn English at school:

> The result is very little intergenerational communication or learning. However, much of the knowledge the old people traditionally have imparted is now largely irrelevant anyway, and both grandparents and grandchildren know it.
>
> The elderly have also lost other traditional functions. Store-bought goods have eliminated the need for old people to make such things as weapons or clothing, and maintaining new mechanical and electrical gadgets requires skills they have never acquired. The elderly at one time performed magical services and taught young people magic songs, formulas, and techniques, but the coming of Christianity has done much to destroy belief in or use of such phenomena. In the larger communities, curing activities and midwife duties have been taken over by trained medical personnel.
>
> (Holmes and Holmes 1995: 157)

Question

1. In what ways has the modernization process impacted upon the lives of older people in the UK?

Recent social changes, such as the spread of mass education and the introduction of new technologies, tend to impact negatively on the social status of older people as their traditional knowledge is no longer valued to the same extent. With the growth of industrialization, more people move from rural areas to cities in search of new jobs and it can mean that older people are left behind in rural communities. Thus, traditional patterns of caring may also be affected as extended family networks are broken. However, again we need to recognize that not all aspects of modernization and globalization have negative outcomes. Some older people in the majority world may benefit from improved standards of living and an enhanced economic status if welfare systems are also introduced. Consequently, we should explore the diversity of older age in different cultures rather than accept the taken-for-granted ideologies. In particular, we should consider the ways in which age intersects with gender, class, disability, ethnicity and geographical location (especially in urban versus rural locations), thereby producing a range of experiences for what it means to be old. Old age is a social construct that differs according to the meanings attached to the ageing process in a specific social and cultural context.

Old age and childhood in Britain

We have considered childhood and older age as being both social and cultural constructs. In this section we shall explore some of the broad similarities and differences of the treatment of children and older people in contemporary Britain. They are both marginal social groups whose lives vary according to class, gender, disability and ethnicity. Nevertheless, there are some general ways in which we can compare and contrast these two stages in the life course. These are summarized in Table 7.3 and then discussed in further detail.

Similarities of marginalized social groups

Both children and older people lack power, autonomy and independence in relation to the more dominant social category of adults (Hockey and James 1993). Children and older people are often perceived as being dependent on adults, in need of care, vulnerable and asexual. They tend to be seen as reliant on others,

Table 7.3 Comparing and contrasting old age and childhood in Britain

Similarities	Differences
Lack power	Temporality
Dependency	Length of time
Asexuality	Financial dependence
Voiceless	Negative stereotypes
Resistance	
Economic dependence	
Social exclusion	

sometimes described as burdens. Furthermore, they are often treated as if they are unable to speak for themselves. Their voices are silenced as adults take over and speak on their behalf. For example, during a visit to a health clinic, the parent is likely to discuss their child's illness with the doctor rather than allowing the child to speak directly for themselves. Similarly, at a residential care home, the adult son or daughter often speaks to the care staff on behalf of their older resident parent.

Despite lacking power in relation to adults, children and older people both have strategies of resistance to compensate for their relative powerlessness. They do not passively accept adult power and control over their lives. Such coping strategies may include feigning illness to avoid doing something they would rather not do and refusing food. For example, Waksler's (1996) research in the UK indicates that children may lie, fake illness, have temper tantrums and act cutely in order to cope with and control certain aspects of their lives. Reynolds' (1991) study of children in the Zambezi valley, Zimbabwe, refers to children's strategies of negotiating relationships in order to secure help for their future. She also highlights children's rebellion in defying adults' wishes, with reference to gambling, smoking and refusing to do certain tasks.

Alternatively, both children and older people may distance themselves from the role of 'cared-for': children look after younger children, and older people might care for those who are older than themselves. Hockey and James (1993) suggest that some older people use their actions and speech as a way of distancing themselves from their own frailty. For example, they resist referring to themselves as 'old' and, in some residential care homes, older women visit and help to care for other residents who are frailer than themselves. This then increases their sense of power as other people become dependent on them. Both age groups also have the power to shock. For example, older people might take delight in causing trouble in care homes, and young children may like the attention they get if they swear or say something rude at the family dinner table in front of relatives. These are forms of resistance used to counteract their lack of power in relation to more powerful adult social actors.

Both children and older people also experience economic dependence as their access to work is restricted. They are either excluded from work or, if not, their choice of work is limited to low-paid, low-status work, which is often irregular or temporary, such as doing a paper round or babysitting (for children) and gardening or domestic cleaning (for older people). This is because there is compulsory retirement for older people and compulsory schooling for children. Work shapes people's social identity and self-esteem, which means that exclusion from work can lead to social marginalization and economic dependency. Their limited incomes mean that they are less able to participate as active consumers in society. Furthermore, work provides access to social life and friendships, so both children and older people do not experience these additional opportunities for socializing. They tend to be confined to an age-based social life: children with their peers at school and older people in bridge clubs and bingo halls.

Differences of marginalized social groups

Perhaps the main difference between these two social groups is the temporality of childhood. Compared with old age, childhood is a transitory state as children grow out of dependency (Hockey and James 1993). In contrast, once older people move away from adulthood, their dependency is permanent and they remain on the margins of society. The length of time for these two stages in the life course may differ. At most, childhood tends to be perceived as finishing at 18 years of age, but old age could last for more than 40 years. Thus, old age can represent more than double the time span allotted to childhood. It is also worth bearing in mind that, as adults, we have all had experience of being part of the marginalized group of children, but as yet we do not have any personal experiences of being older, and this can affect how we understand the two groups.

The economic dependence of the two social groups is also different. Children are usually financially dependent on their parents, whereas older people are more likely to be dependent on their own savings or pensions. The final difference between childhood and old age as stages in the life course is that there appear to be more negative stereotypes about older people compared with children. Thus, although in Britain both groups are devalued in relation to adulthood, old age suffers greater denigration than childhood.

Summary

- Age is used in all societies to differentiate individuals in both positive and negative ways. For example, as Wilson (2007: 7) points out: 'Experiences of ageing can be disabling (we, who are old, cannot do this because we are old) or enabling (we, who are old, have experience and know better)'.
- The social significance attached to biological age is of interest to sociologists. Generally, in the UK and in much of the minority world, the ageing process is perceived negatively as something to be feared and avoided for as long as possible. However, although we define the later stage in the life course in negative terms, this does not mean that old age is universally perceived as having low status. We need to analyse critically different case studies rather than merely accept the values of our own culture.
- Childhood and old age in the minority world tend to involve a loss of autonomy, and these examples indicate that age is a social and cultural construction.
- Age is cross-cut by other forms of social differentiation, such as class, gender, ethnicity and disability.
- Age differentiation varies not only between different cultures but also within societies and throughout history. Therefore, the construction of age changes over time and place.

Links

The section on childhood and children's rights can be related to the discussion on child abuse in Chapter 11 (pp. 478–480).

The discussion of work and industrialization is developed in Chapter 12 (particularly pp. 492–493).

The discussion on childhood is relevant to the sections on child-headed households and siblings in Chapter 11 (pp. 457–458).

The section on childhood is linked to debates about the nature of children's lives in the majority world, which we address in Chapter 9 (pp. 393–401).

Further reading

Aitken, S., Lund, R. and Kjøholt, A. (eds) (2008) *Global Childhoods: Globalization, Development and Young People*, London: Routledge.
The changing nature of childhood is explored in this book, with a focus on three main issues: nation-building and identity, children's participation and globalization.

Hockey, J. and James, A. (2003) *Social Identities across the Life Course*, Basingstoke: Palgrave Macmillan.
This account shows how the ageing process throughout the life course shapes our sense of identity. It includes discussions of childhood, youth, middle age and older age.

Holmes, E.R. and Holmes, L.D. (1995) *Other Cultures, Elder Years*, London: Sage.
This book offers a comparative perspective on ageing by providing a range of cultural examples, including Inuit, Samoa, US and American ethnic groups.

Hunt, S. (2005) *The Life Course: A Sociological Introduction*, Basingstoke: Palgrave Macmillan.
This is a clear text that focuses on continuities and change across the life course, from infancy and youth to old age and dying.

James, A. and James, A. (eds) (2008) *European Childhoods: Cultures, Politics and Childhoods in Europe*, Basingstoke: Palgrave Macmillan.
This book explores the ways in which childhood is constructed through social policies and practices in different European countries, including Spain, Norway, Ireland, Denmark, Cyprus, Germany and the UK.

James, A. and James, A. (2004) *Constructing Childhood: Theory, Policy and Social Practice*, Basingstoke: Palgrave Macmillan.
This is a key book that considers the relationship between the social construction of childhood and social policy. It explores in detail the changes and continuities of childhood across time and space.

Maybin, J. and Woodhead, M. (eds) (2003) *Childhoods in Context*, Chichester: John Wiley & Sons.
A well-written, accessible and comprehensive book that explores childhood and family life, historical perspectives, youth transitions and the different arenas of school and work in both minority world and majority world contexts.

Panelli, R., Punch, S. and Robson, E. (eds) (2007) *Global Perspectives on Rural Childhood and Youth: Young Rural Lives*, London: Routledge.
This edited collection examines the sociocultural contexts and negotiations that young people face when growing up in rural settings across the world. The main themes addressed are identity, agency and power.

Qvortrup, J. (ed.) (2005) *Studies in Modern Childhood: Society, Agency and Culture*, Basingstoke: Palgrave Macmillan.
A variety of childhoods are explored in this book. Key contexts include children's work, child welfare and the media.

Vincent, J. (2003) *Old Age*, London: Routledge.
An excellent and up-to-date discussion of key concerns in relation to old age, including poverty, globalization, intergenerational conflict, consumerism, health and identity.

Websites

www.ageconcern.org.uk

Age Concern
This organization aims to improve the quality of life for older people in the UK. The website includes research, recent news and campaigns.

www.cpa.org.uk

Centre for Policy on Ageing
This organization is concerned with the analysis of public policy as it affects older people. The website offers relevant publications, research findings and an information service.

www.crfr.ac.uk

Centre for Research on Families and Relationships
This research centre has a main office at the University of Edinburgh, with partners at Glasgow Caledonian University and the universities of Aberdeen, Glasgow, and Stirling. The website provides many online reports and briefings of recent research projects that involve participants across the life course, from young children to older people.

www.savethechildren.org.uk

Save the Children
This organization aims to enhance children's rights and to improve the quality of life for children worldwide. The website is an extensive source of publications, research, policies and recent news relating to children's health, education, poverty and exploitation.

www.un.org/esa/socdev/ageing

United Nations Programme on Ageing
This website has useful information regarding the ageing of the world's population. It also provides a database on relevant policies and programmes.

Activities

Read the following two descriptions of different childhoods: 12-year-old Anna who lives with her mother, stepfather and stepbrother in a town in Britain and 13-year-old Edivaldo who has been running away from home periodically over the previous six years and consequently spent much time on the streets of Recife in northern Brazil.

Activity 1

A middle-class urban 'nurtured' British childhood

Interviewer: And what do you think it's like being a stepdad?

Anna: I think it must be quite good, because he treats me like his child and, like, I go to his family's house.
. . . And he gives me my pocket money and buys me Christmas presents, and just, like, normally treats me like my own Dad does. He disciplines me. And if I'm scared or something. He helps me with my homework if I don't understand something. [Section here on how she plays out with her mates.]

Interviewer: So you have a lot of independence?

Anna: Yes. My Mum doesn't mind where I go provided I tell her where I'm going. So if my friends I'm hanging round with say, Let's go down to [x], I either phone my Mum or I go home and ask my Mum if I can go and have some money to go with. And if she says, No, that means no – I'm not going; then I stay in and watch TV or just go out to play in my area, but if she says, Yes, I do, I get what I need and go to [x].

Interviewer: Do you get money regularly so you can go by bus and –

Anna: Yes.

Interviewer: Is that irrespective of what you might have to do?

Anna: I do housework, I clean dishes, do the Hoovering. But sometimes I get money for it, it depends on, if I've been really good the whole week. But occasionally if I need money my Mum will give it me if she's got it. But if she's got like £1 in her purse she'll say, OK take it. But I'll say, No, it's OK I'll stay in . . .

Interviewer: So do you get on with your Mum – cos you said you did with your, both your fathers?

Anna: Yes, she's my best friend.

Interviewer: What sorts of things do you do with her?

Anna: I go out with her, to visit friends. I went with her to see the *Titanic*. And when my stepdad's out, we watch videos, we move the couch in front of the TV and we get loads of snacks and we watch TV, stuff like that, we watch movies together. [Section about gender issues at school.] I like school, I love coming to school. I don't want to leave school ever!

Interviewer: Are there some things you specially like about school?

Anna: I like being with my friends. I like most of my lessons, but there's no particular. I like dance and PE [more about subjects at school, and afterschool clubs, and a homework club].

Interviewer: So school's an important part of your life?

Anna: Yes. Most people just go home after school. They think I'm mad because I stay on. But sometimes I walk home with my friends, and then I get all my homework done and then I go out. And, like, every night I get my bag ready, so when I get up I can just [set off to school with it].

Interviewer: Yes, so is it up to you how you arrange your time after school?

Anna: Yes, so long as I let my Mum know.

(Mayall 2002: 95–6)

Questions

1. What constraints and opportunities does Anna face in her everyday life?
2. In what ways does Anna indicate that she is a competent social actor, able to negotiate her autonomy and relationships on a daily basis?

Activity 2

A poor urban 'nurturing' Brazilian childhood

I only ran away from home because of my stepfather. He beat me with a wire cable, left me all cut up, then he threw water and a kilo of salt on me. When I would run away I'd go all over the place. I spent two days with a truck driver, then he said, 'Go away now,' so I left. I stayed in the city and met a lot of kids and that's how I started learning about street life.

I think I have way too much experience now. The street doesn't have anything to offer you except experience. In the street we learn how to live because at home we get spoon-fed everything. It's not like that in the street. In the street we have to work to have something. That's what the street teaches you.

Tobias: In the street, do you roam with a gang?

Edivaldo: If you hang out with a gang, it's worse than being alone, because, look, in a gang it's the strongest one who wins.
If I'm weak and, say, I steal a watch, the biggest guy in the gang is going to say, 'Hey, that watch is mine, I'm going to sell it.' That's why I prefer to roam alone.

I only went around with a gang once, because when I'm with a group, the group wants to fight to see who's strongest. If you get caught in the middle of something you're in trouble. The one time I was with a group I got stabbed.

I've run away from home twenty-nine times. I've always come to Recife when I run away from home. I'd get a ride with the trucks. Sometimes I'd hide under the spare tire. You know how trucks have that extra tire in case one pops? I'd hide back there and come to Recife all hungry.

The first time, I was seven years old. That's when I started learning about street life. My mother came to Recife and spoke with the police. She sent the police out after me, and she even offered a reward for the person who found me.

The second time I went to the Shopping Center in Boa Viagem. I asked a guy for money. He said he didn't have any and walked away. But then he came back and bought me food and asked if I wanted to work in his house. I said yes and I went to live there. I stayed for two days and then my mother found me. She got a whole bunch of kids together and gave them money so they would tell her where I was. I liked it there. I would have stayed. I went back twice [to see the man] but he already had another boy living there and when I went the third time he had left for São Paulo.

I went back to Caruaru and stayed for two months. Then I ran away again, but my mother didn't come to look for me. I stayed in the street in the center of the city for three days. Later I went home because I hadn't really learned what street life is about.

The fourth time was when I learned how to sniff glue. I got together with a bunch of kids and started sniffing, and I got used to it. So I just started running away from home to sniff glue. It's a vice, you know. It's not that I like it, you get to be a prisoner of glue.

Tobias: What do you mean?

Edivaldo: It's a temptation that hits you: 'Come on, sniff glue, sniff.' And you end up sniffing.

Tobias: And what happens when you sniff glue?

Edivaldo: You get high and start seeing things that aren't in front of you. That's what hooks you.

Tobias: What happens if you sniff every day and then all of a sudden you stop? How do you feel?

Edivaldo: You get a fever, a headache, you feel like dying.

Tobias: Does sniffing glue make you hungry?

Edivaldo: Yes, but only when you stop sniffing. Sometimes you sniff to kill the hunger, because when you're hungry and you sniff, the hunger goes away. But if you stop sniffing, the hunger gets you again.

Tobias: I've noticed that some kids sniff glue after eating. Why do they do that?

Edivaldo: It's so that you don't mess up your lungs, because if you eat and then sniff on a full stomach, it's not so bad for you. But if you sniff on an empty stomach, the air from the glue fills up your belly.

(Hecht 1998: 28–9)

Questions

1. What constraints and opportunities does Edivaldo face in his everyday life?
2. In what ways does Edivaldo demonstrate that he has developed coping strategies for managing his precarious life on the streets?
3. What are the similarities and differences of the two childhoods presented here?
4. Compare and contrast the two accounts in relation to the following themes: responsibility, autonomy, education, family life and adult–child relations.

Chapter 8

Disability

Kirstein Rummery

Deform'd, unfinish'd, sent before my time
Into this breathing world scarce half made up
And that so lamely and unfashionable
That dogs bark at me as I halt by them –
Why I, in this piping time of peace,
Have no delight to pass away the time
Unless to spy my shadow in the sun
And descant on mine own deformity.
(Richard III, Act 1, Scene 1)

. . . almost all studies of disability have a grand theory underpinning them. That grand theory can be characterised as 'the personal tragedy theory of disability'. (Oliver 1990: 1)

Key issues

- Is disability a product of biology or socially constructed?
- What key models and theories have informed our thinking about disability?
- What are the implications of the different models of disability for the way we treat disabled people in our society?
- What does being disabled mean in our society? Are disabled people unfortunate or oppressed, or both?
- How have different theories about disability shaped welfare policy?

Stop and think

- Think about how you would define 'disability' and 'disabled'.
- Make a list of words that you associate with these definitions. Now separate them into words that, for you, have negative connotations and words that are more positive. For example, in the first list you might have words such as 'dependent' and 'ill', and in the second list you might have words such as 'brave'.
- Did you find it easier to fill in the first or second column?
- When thinking about the second column, did you think primarily about the ways in which people 'overcome' disability? Why do you think this might be the case? Is it easier to think of this than try to find things about disability itself that are positive?

Introduction

Over recent years definitions of disability and attitudes towards disabled people in our society have changed dramatically. From being a group of people who invoke pity and were the subject of charitable campaigns, disabled people are now more likely to be the focus of equal rights legislation. The 1995 Disability Discrimination Act defined a person as disabled if they have 'a physical or mental impairment, which has a substantial and long-term adverse affect upon their ability to carry out normal day-to-day activities'. The Disability Rights Commission (now part of the Equality and Human Rights Commission) was established in 1999 to tackle discrimination against disabled people. In the first edition of this book, and in many other books on sociology, 'disability' did not feature as a distinct division in the same way as gender, age or 'race', but attitudes in sociology and society have changed. How we define 'disability', and how society views and behaves towards disabled people, are now the focus of much interest and debate. This chapter will start exploring some of these debates.

Disability is becoming more prevalent and more visible in our society than ever before. According to the Disability Discrimination Act definition, at least 10 per cent of the overall population is disabled – which means at least 6 million people in the UK of working age (ONS 2002); only three million of these people are employed (Disability Rights Commission 2002). Disabled people are at significant risk of experiencing poverty and of being excluded from mainstream society – in fact, the poorer you are and the lower your educational qualifications, the more likely you are to be disabled (Figure 8.1).

Conversely, the more disabled you are, the more likely you are to be living in poverty. The average take-home pay of a disabled worker is around 75 per cent of that of an able-bodied worker. Taking into account the extra costs associated with being disabled, and the higher risk of unemployment, disabled people's income falls to around 60 per cent of the average (Figure 8.2).

The 1995 Disability Discrimination Act makes it clear that anything that has a 'substantial and long-term effect' on your ability to carry out day-to-day activities can be classed as a disability; this includes a variety of conditions, such as mental health problems, learning

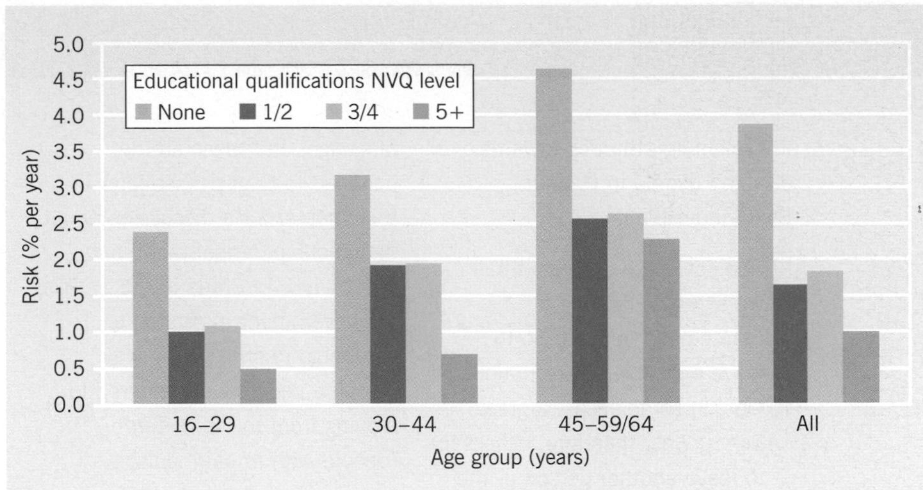

Figure 8.1 Risk of becoming disabled, by age and educational qualifications

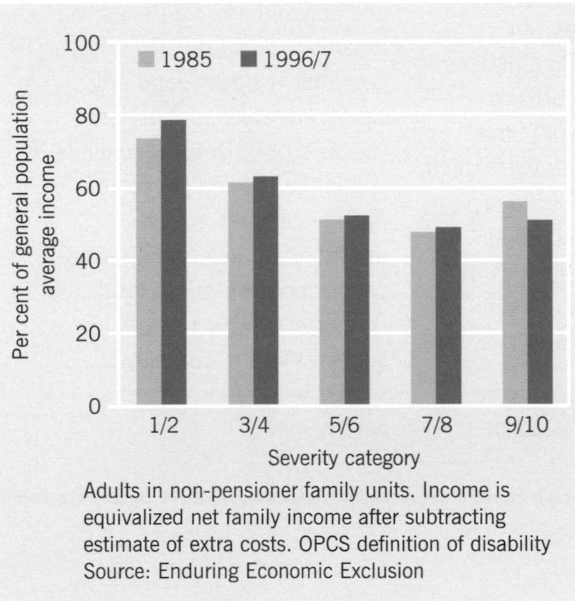

Figure 8.2 Disabled people's average income, taking account of extra costs

disability, physical impairments such as blindness, and long-term illnesses such as arthritis. Chapter 7 discusses how our likelihood of experiencing certain illnesses and long-term conditions rises significantly as we grow older: if you are not disabled now, then it is highly likely that you or someone you know (perhaps even someone you look after) might be considered as disabled at some point in the future. The links between disability and disadvantage are not only interesting in an abstract way for policymakers and sociologists; rather, they might actually affect you and your family directly at some point in your life.

Why are disabled people so much more likely to be disadvantaged in our society? Part of the explanation might be found in people's attitudes towards disability and disabled people. Several surveys of attitudes to disability undertaken within Western societies have found that people tend to think of disabled people as being passive, weak, dependent and needing help. People often react to disabled people with fear:

> **Just basically, I think that society tends to fear people when people are different, and disabled is no different than race or anything like that. People tend to fear them, if you can't communicate with someone, a lot of people with cerebral palsy and that type of thing, they can't communicate properly, I've got to get away from them. Then, there are those who are not right, somehow – you will see people in malls and stores who are talking to themselves and stuff. What do we do? We get right away from them too.**
>
> (Environics Research Group 2004)

This fear is echoed by this quote from a British woman:

> **When I was a child you didn't see disabled people. And when you did they weren't accepted. You looked on them with rather horror, perhaps fear.**
>
> (Grewal *et al.* 2000)

Negative attitudes towards disability and disabled people are not limited to our own society, as the next section shows.

A closer look

International attitudes to disability

The idea that disabled people are somehow different from, and of less worth than, non-disabled people is not limited to the UK or even to Western societies. For example, Owusu asserts:

> Throughout the ages in Ghana and Africa, disabled persons have been regarded with little appreciation. It has been erroneously assumed that disabled people are incapable of engaging themselves in any useful occupation, and therefore should be objects of sympathy and pity. Others considered disabled persons to be 'sick', thus encouraging a life of confinement or privacy in the home rather than participation in work and normal community activities.
>
> (Osuwu 1992: 57)

In explaining attitudes towards disabled people in Uganda, Bukumhe explains:

> The country had many tribal wars and a number of man-eating animals. So to leave a disabled person alone was, in some cases, a great risk. It was, therefore, necessary to leave another person in the home all the time to take care of the disabled person, or, alternatively, to carry the disabled child wherever one went. This was very inconvenient . . . So a disabled baby in the home became a great social problem in the family. The relatives who would, in other cases, rejoice and congratulate the mother on having a baby, instead came to mourn with the mother.
>
> (Bukumhe 1992: 74–5)

Attitudes towards disability can be reflected in debates about language, and these are not confined to English (see later in this chapter for a discussion about definitions of 'impairment' and 'disability'). In China in the 1990s, the government instigated a campaign to change the way disabled people were referred to, moving from the term *canfei* (people with impairments, a common and derogatory Chinese term translated as 'useless' or 'worthless') to the term *canji* (people with impairments, a new and neutral term, translated as 'disabled'), encapsulated in a government slogan *canji erbu canfei* ('disabled, not useless') (Stone 1999). Debates continue within the UK and US context about whether it is more appropriate to refer to 'disabled people' or 'people with disabilities' (the latter of which seems to suggest that the disability is somehow separate from the person).

Explanations for our views

Later in this chapter we will explore some of the social structures and policies that affect disabled people's lives. However, it can be difficult to understand how and why structures and policies operate the way they do without first understanding how our own individual views about disability are shaped, and how some of the social processes that affect our role in society actually happen.

This section looks at two different explanations for the way we think about and treat disabled people in our society. First we look at broad sociological accounts of chronic illness and disability, drawing on ideas that have come from writers such as Parsons (1951) on the social order and Becker (1963) on deviance. Then we look at two broad models or theoretical approaches to disability and discuss the implications of each model for the way we understand disabled people's role in society.

Sociological accounts of chronic illness and disability

In Chapter 13 we see how the work of Parsons (1951) has helped us to understand how social order and the stability of the social system are maintained through modern medical practice. Essentially, Parsons argued that, in order for society to function properly, everyone has to play their role appropriately to meet the needs of individuals and systems. Being healthy is regarded as being 'normal', because 'unhealthy' people disrupt society by being unproductive and dependent. The system therefore needs to manage unhealthy people so that they do not threaten the functioning of society as a whole.

Parsons' explanation for how the social system manages ill-health focuses on the 'sick role'. Individuals are 'allowed' to be sick, albeit temporarily and under certain conditions, as long as they conform to the 'sick role'. This role has two conditions attached to it:

- When someone gets sick, they must get confirmation of their illness from a medical authority, and they must cooperate fully with that medical authority in order to get better.
- The sick person has to agree that being sick is undesirable and must therefore want to get better.

If someone fulfils these two conditions, in return they receive two rights, or privileges:

- Once they have been diagnosed as sick by a medical authority, the individual is automatically relieved of all responsibilities and social expectations.
- Individuals are not held responsible for their illness, nor are they entirely responsible for their recovery.

Parsons' ideas attracted considerable criticism, but, for the purposes of this chapter, the most interesting critique of his approach was that the 'sick role' works only with episodes of acute, time-limited illness. Kassebaum and Baumann (1965) and others have pointed out that people with longer-term and chronic illnesses cannot easily 'recover' and return to 'healthy' status. Once it is recognized that the sickness is not temporary, writers such as Gordon (1966) argued that people fall into an 'impaired' rather than 'sick' role. People in an 'impaired' role do not receive the tolerance that those in the 'sick' role enjoy, and so they do not enjoy the same rights and responsibilities. The 'impaired' role is permanent, and people filling it must therefore accept social dependence and reduced income and resources (Barnes *et al.* 1999). So that the social order is not threatened, the 'impaired' role must be seen as undesirable.

This approach explains the powerful position that medical and rehabilitation professionals play in disabled people's lives. Many psychological and medical approaches to disability stress the importance of adjusting to changes in social and role expectations and the importance of grieving the 'loss' of the 'normal' (i.e. healthy) life; many social scientists have criticized these approaches for being rooted in the experiences of non-disabled rather than disabled people (Oliver 1996).

Stop and think

- Think about people you know who you think of as disabled. Do they fit into the 'sick role' or the 'impaired role'?
- What is it that makes you categorize them as one or the other? Is it the nature of their illness or injury, or is it how they have reacted to that illness or injury?
- What role have medical professionals played in their life? Have the opinions or actions of the medical professionals affected how you think about them? Has it affected whether you think they are 'sick' or 'impaired'?
- Do you consider yourself to be disabled? Why? What role have medical professionals played in deciding whether you are 'sick' or 'well' or 'disabled'?
- Do our attitudes towards 'sick' people explain our attitudes towards disabled people? Do they reflect our own fears about being unwell and being dependent on other people for help?
- As one of the first sociologists to examine the area of disability, Parsons' ideas are very medical in approach. What criticisms do you think have been made of his attempt to apply the 'sickness role' to people with disabilities? You may want to read the section on the 'social model' (pp. 344–347) before answering this question.

Several alternative social theories have sought to explain the way in which society treats disabled people. Many of these are based on Becker's (1963) ideas about deviance. Becker argued that people became classed as 'deviant' not as a result of their own actions but as a result of the application of rules and sanctions to those actions:

> **Deviance is not a quality that lies in the behaviour itself but in the interaction between the person who commits an act and those who respond to it.**
>
> Becker (1963: 9)

It is therefore not the actions or behaviour of people, but the way in which they are labelled, that decides whether society treats them as 'deviant' or 'normal'. Goffmann (1968) illustrated this in his work on stigma, which discusses the way in which society differentiates between those it considers 'normal' and those who have some kind of 'undesired differentness'. In the case of people who are chronically ill or impaired, their social identity is defined by the way in which 'normal' people treat them as stigmatized and 'not quite human' (Goffmann 1968: 15). In order to overcome this process of stigmatization, Goffmann asserted that people with chronic illnesses and impairments have three main strategies available to them:

- *Passing* – Whereby people control what information they choose to reveal about themselves, and particularly choose not to reveal information that may be 'discrediting' in some way. People may choose not to reveal that they have a 'hidden' condition such as epilepsy or mental health problems, and thus try to 'pass' for normal.
- *Covering* – Whereby the source of the stigma cannot be hidden but it is not allowed to dominate social encounters between 'normal' people and 'stigmatized' people. People may underplay their use of aids or support, or show that they have overcome their illness or impairment in a particularly able or heroic manner, by being brave or cheerful.
- *Withdrawal* – Whereby people who are stigmatized withdraw from social contact with 'normal' society altogether. People may choose to live in segregated communities or in isolation rather than be subject to the norms and expectations of 'normal society' (Goffmann 1968).

Case study

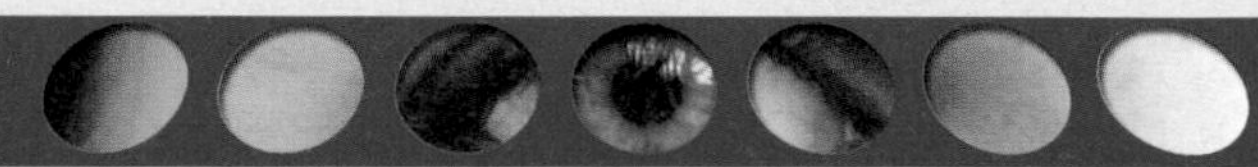

Franklin D. Roosevelt: disability, illness and power

Franklin D. Roosevelt was one of the most popular and longest-serving presidents in the USA, serving an historic four terms as elected president from 1933 to 1945, steering the USA out of the Great Depression and leading the country through the Second World War. In his inaugural address he coined the phrase 'We have nothing to fear but fear itself'. In 1921 he contracted poliomyelitis and thereafter was unable to walk unaided. He consciously downplayed his impairments when running for office, never allowing the public to see him being lifted into his wheelchair. He deliberately walked the 35 steps to the podium to deliver his inaugural address instead of using his wheelchair. Many biographers have portrayed him as a 'disabled hero' and a role model for disabled Americans because of his political achievements. John Duffy argues that Roosevelt manipulated his public image and portrayed himself as someone who was 'sick' rather than 'disabled':

> Roosevelt . . . hid the reality and manipulated [his] image . . . to enable FDR to obtain and retain political office. In 1912, when FDR experienced a bout with typhoid fever, he was presented to the public as a selfless public servant working from his sick bed against his doctor's orders. When FDR contracted polio in 1921, at first they said nothing, then said FDR was recovering from an illness, and finally admitted he had polio but stated FDR would experience no lasting injury. When they realized FDR was not going to recover soon, they laid down the rule that FDR was not to be carried in public. If FDR were to be seen as an invalid, it would ruin his political prospects . . . In his correspondence, FDR described his condition as one which was improving. He only permitted his condition to be seen under controlled positive conditions, avoiding any situation where the severity or permanence of his disability would become a matter of public knowledge. When running for public office, he campaigned hard and obtained the cooperation of the press in order to present himself to the public as a vigorous and healthy man – which he was – while, at the same time, hiding his disability. Once in office, he continued to be careful of his public image, presenting himself as a 'recovered cripple,' and he used a variety of special aids – some of which he had used as a wealthy private citizen – to deal with his functional problems.

Case study *continued*

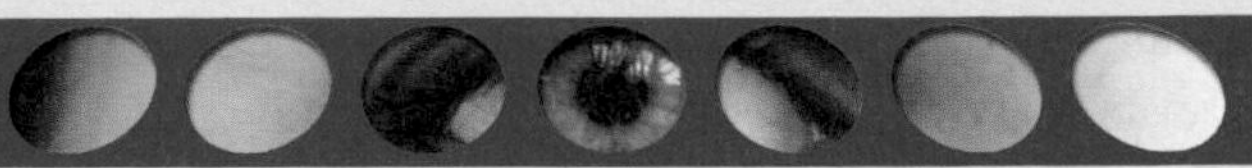

The vast majority of FDR's biographers make no distinction between illness and disability; they use the terms interchangeably, and they accept the view, which I do not, that FDR was concerned about the public perception of his health. Certainly questions about his condition were posed in terms of health, but I believe he defined the question in those terms so that is how the public and his biographers saw the question. A man regaining his health or who has recovered from an illness presents an acceptable public image; a cripple does not . . .

As I have mentioned before, it would have been fatal to Roosevelt's political ambition to have been perceived as permanently disabled. Yet, even after he obtained the Presidency, he still did not use his power and special knowledge to benefit the disabled. He could not have proposed such comprehensive legislation as the Rehabilitation Act of 1973, which forbids discrimination in federally funded programs. Such legislation could only have been advocated in an age concerned with civil rights. But he might have proposed legislation to eliminate physical and functional barriers that prevented persons with disabilities from using public housing, public buildings, trains and buses.

While President, he never attempted either directly or indirectly to promote legislation to benefit citizens with disabilities or to use his private influence to assist them. His failure to do so means that the disabled community is living in a society which is full of physical barriers instead of living in a society which is largely free of them. If he had acted, we would be living with greater understanding and less prejudice between citizens with disabilities and those without them.

(Duffy 1987: 113–35)

Questions

1. Why do you think Roosevelt made such an effort to present himself as 'sick' (and 'recovered') rather than disabled?
2. Do you agree with John Duffy's view that Roosevelt did disabled Americans a great disservice by attempting to hide the permanent nature of his disability?
3. To use Goffmann's terms, do you think Roosevelt was 'covering' up his impairment or 'passing' as a 'normal' person?

If, as Becker suggests, the treatment of disabled people is largely a product of social attitudes, then it is not surprising to find that these attitudes change from one society to another and over time. Rather than being able to predict narrow and mostly negative social responses to disability, this approach suggests that a wide variety of responses are possible. Kurz (1981) identifies at least ten popular images of 'mental retardation'. The limited amount of historical and anthropological research that has been carried out suggests that social attitudes towards disabled people range from the most negative, such as ostracism and death, through pity and tolerance, to admiration and reverence. From his research into cross-cultural attitudes towards mental disabilities, Edgerton has rejected the idea that social responses to disability are determined by the level of technical and economic complexity that a society has achieved ('simple people for simple societies'). He concluded:

> **Something more than a simplistic, environmental, deterministic formula must be involved to account for the differential treatment accorded the mentally retarded in the world's non-western societies. It is not simply that in some societies life is difficult whereas in others it is easy. Something far more complicated is involved; the answer must lie somewhere in the complex web that unites cultures and social organisations within the physical environment.**
>
> (Edgerton 1970: 547)

Oliver (1990) takes a more materialist view and argues that social attitudes depend in part on the mode of production (capitalist societies tend to marginalize and exclude the less productive members of society) but are also a response to prevailing ideologies. Adapting the work of Gramsci, he suggests that our ideas about disability have a certain amount of autonomy and that different societies (despite being at a similar stage of economic development) will have different moral, religious and philosophical traditions that encourage diverse ideological responses to disabled people. The value placed on religious or scientific discourse plays a major part in how societies view people with disabilities:

> **Disability is not defined or culturally produced solely in terms of its relationship to the mode of production. The core or central values are based upon magical, religious or scientific ways of thinking. Thus a society based on religious or magical ways of thinking may define disability very differently from one based upon science or medicine . . . in some societies, someone with polio may be seen as the victim of witchcraft, and someone with epilepsy as possessed by God or the devil. The important implication of this is that disability is not always defined as a personal tragedy with negative consequences: it may be seen as a sign of being chosen, as being possessed by a god, and consequently, the person may have their status enhanced.**
>
> (Oliver 1990: 22–3)

A contemporary example of conflicting ideological responses occurred in 2007, when a young girl was born in India with additional limbs. As she resembled the goddess of wealth, her parents named her Lakshmi. Unable to resist the medical challenge, doctors raised

Case study

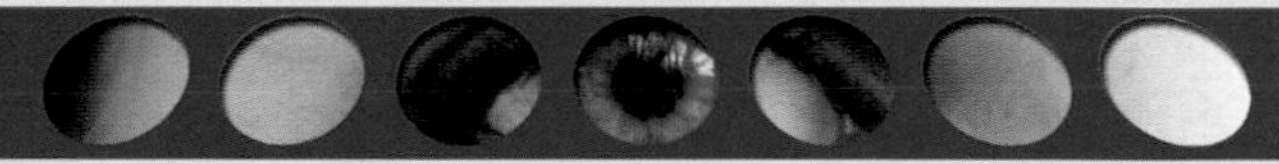

Disability, religion and culture: disability in Islamic texts

In exploring attitudes towards the economic status of disabled people in Jordan, Majid Turmunsani (2003) found that cultural attitudes towards disability were rooted in religious beliefs about society and roles:

> The concentration on a person's productivity and contribution to their family and society seems to reinforce that characteristic of Islamic society which accord status to a person, especially a man, according to his financial capability. However, generally speaking, Islamic society is characterized by conservative values, habits, attitudes and beliefs that influence the perception of disability amongst the population. The dominant Islamic faith and its teaching attributes everything that occurs, and all that exists in the world, to the will of God. Therefore, society tends to perceive disability as an act of God testing the faith of individuals to determine who is able to accept and tolerate their fate with gratitude and patience, and those who are not. Disability is looked at as a test or as the will of God and it is incumbent upon the person not to show any distress or bad feeling towards it. It has been mentioned in one of the prophet's traditions that there is a 'steadfast place' in Paradise for those parents to whom God has entrusted a disabled child who they have accepted without reservation . . .
>
> This perception of disability as the will of God and as a test of faith shapes attitudes towards disabled people to a large degree in Muslim societies of the majority world. Nevertheless, there is a tendency among many to distinguish between the causes of various types of impairment. For example, blindness is perceived to be an act of God and more divine power is attributed to the blind person. A common myth is that blind people are endowed with a sixth sense. However, deafness and 'retardation' are seen as an act of God with negative implications. For example, the notion that parents are being punished for their misdeeds and evil conduct is clearly associated with types of impairment.
>
> (Turmunsani 2003: 51–2)

Questions

1. How have your attitudes towards disabled people been shaped by your religious beliefs?

2. What parables or religious stories about disabled people do you know? What were you taught was the 'moral' of the story? What does that tell us about attitudes towards disabled people in your society?

£200,000 to pay for an operation for the girl, but many local people opposed the surgery, arguing instead for the erection of a temple to her miraculous birth. In an added twist to this story, her (extremely poor) parents resisted offers from a local circus to buy her for their 'freak show'.

Two opposing 'models' of disability

We can see that our attitudes towards disability and disabled people are shaped by the kind of society we live in, our own experiences and beliefs, our religious background, and whether or not disabled people behave 'appropriately' according to our values and beliefs. Within Western societies we often view disabled people as 'different' from the norm, as 'stigmatized' or 'deviant', because they can threaten our unspoken assumptions about the way our society should function and the roles that individuals should play within that society. We now return to the question that opened this chapter: how do we define disability? There are two main approaches to this question: the individual/medical model of disability and the social model of disability.

Barnes *et al.* (1999) describe two models of disability that stem from different understandings about the way in which we define disability and consequently the way in which we treat disabled people in our society. The first, dominant model within our society is the 'individual' or 'medical' model of disability. The second model has been developed by disabled campaigners and academics and has become known as the 'social' model of disability. There are strong similarities between this approach and C.W. Mills' insistence that the sociological imagination is necessary to help make sense of 'personal troubles' (see Chapter 1 and Barnes *et al.* 1999).

The individual model of disability

Definitions of disability that fall within the individual model of disability take as their starting point the idea that disability is caused by an 'abnormality' (such as a chronic illness or impairment) within a person. The most commonly used international definition of disability is that developed by the World Health Organization (WHO), which defines disability in the following way (WHO 1980):

- *Impairment* – Any loss or abnormality of psychological, physiological or anatomical structure or function.
- *Disability* – Any restriction or lack (resulting from an impairment) of ability to perform an activity in the manner or within the range considered normal for a human being.
- *Handicap* – A disadvantage for a given individual, resulting from an impairment or disability, that limits or prevents the fulfilment of a role (depending on age, sex, social and cultural factors) for that individual.

The WHO definition was part of its attempt to define and classify diseases in a systematic way that could be used by bureaucracies and administrators to distinguish between 'disabled' and 'non-disabled' people. Thus, legislation aimed at disabled people in the UK and the USA – such as the 1990 Americans with Disabilities Act and the British 1995 Disability Discrimination Act – take as their starting point definitions of disability that focus on the impaired nature of the individual compared with a 'normal' person.

Focusing on the individual in this way means that disability is seen as a personal tragedy affecting the individual and their family in a way that is unfortunate and undesirable.

Definitions of disability can influence the way in which non-disabled people respond to disabled people, and writers who adopt a social model (see pp. 344–347) have criticized the WHO definitions because they overlook the social aspects of disability by emphasizing the personal. This critical approach makes a much clearer distinction between impairment and disability, which is reflected in the individual and social models, respectively:

> **A disabled person is a person with an impairment who experiences disability. Disability is the result of negative interactions that take place between a person with an impairment and her or his social environment. Impairment is thus part of a negative interaction, but it is not the cause of, nor does it justify, disability.**
>
> ***Impairment*: an injury, illness, or congenital condition that causes or is likely to cause a loss or difference of physiological or psychological function.**
>
> ***Disability*: the loss or limitation of opportunities to take part in society on an equal level with others due to social and environmental barriers.**

(Adapted from *Fundamental Principles of Disability*, a pdf download at www.leeds.ac.uk/disability-studies/archiveuk)

Stop and think

- Do you see disabled people as being unfortunate and the victims of a personal tragedy? Why do you think such views are so prevalent in our society?
- Why do you think legislators are keen to use definitions of disability that are rooted in the 'medical' or 'individual' model of disability? What advantage does that give society and the state? How does it limit the kind of help that the state is obliged to offer disabled people?

The use of an individual model of disability places the location of the 'problem' clearly within the individual. While acknowledging that people with impairments experience a range of 'handicaps' in society (such as problems with access to physical spaces, problems in education and work, and increased risk of poverty), the individual model sees the cause of these problems as being the impairment or illness.

This approach has important implications for the way in which society treats disabled people. If the cause of disability is an individual's impairment, then society must concentrate its efforts in finding a cure for that impairment, or, failing that, a way of overcoming the impairment so that disabled people can be as 'normal'

Case study

The individual model of disability, medical power and personal tragedy

Many charities in the disability field rely on people donating money because they believe that disability is a 'personal tragedy' that can be overcome through research, professional interventions, therapies and rehabilitation. One example is conductive education, a system designed to teach people with spinal injuries to function without using special aids. Mike Oliver (1989) offers this critique of conductive education:

> The current fashion for conductive education has created a furore in the world of education . . . We have seen the creation of three new organisations aimed at furthering it, television programmes extolling its virtues, demonstrations at the House of Commons, picketing of the Spastics Society . . . it claims to be a method of enabling the motor impaired 'to function in society without requiring special apparatus such as wheelchairs, ramps or other artificial aids'. Well yes, but don't we all use artificial aids of one kind or another: try eating your dinner without a knife or fork or going to Australia without an aeroplane . . .
>
> Unsound ideology can quickly turn into oppression and Dr Hari's views are certainly oppressive to a large number of disabled people. In one example, she endorses . . . a way of teaching people with a spinal injury to walk, and adds that 'teaching must restore the will of the individual to do so.' As a person with a spinal injury, this view is oppressive to me, and other people with a spinal injury, in two ways. First, how dare she assume that our main goal is to walk, without consulting us in the first place. And second, how dare she imply that those hundreds of thousands of people with a spinal injury throughout the world are not walking because they lack the will to do so . . .
>
> . . . it is sad, but understandable that the parents of disabled children should clutch at the straw of conductive education as a means of resolving their own problems. To have a handicapped child in a society which has developed a fetishism for normality and which fails to even acknowledge the needs of these parents, let alone make any provision to meet them, is clearly is profoundly disturbing experience. But accepting the fetishism of normality can never even address these problems, let alone resolve them . . .
>
> The nightmare of conductive education is unachievable because nowhere in human history

Case study *continued*

have the different been turned into the normal and neither medical science nor other rehabilitative techniques or education interventions can assist in this process. The reason is simple: normality does not exist. Someone else, not very long ago, had a vision of normality associated with blond hair and blue eyes, and look where such a vision got him.

(Oliver 1989)

Questions

1. Do you agree with Mike Oliver that we live in a society that 'fetishises' the normal? What implications does this have on how we define disability?
2. It would seem self-evident that finding a 'cure' for illnesses and impairments would be desirable. Why do you think Mike Oliver finds it so disturbing in this example?

as possible. This means that resources must go into treatment and rehabilitation for disabled people, giving medical practitioners and charities an important role in the management of their lives.

The role of 'experts' in the individual model of disability is not confined to medical practitioners. Because the role relies on distinctions between 'disabled' and 'normal' people that are both socially created and reflect the values of society, the role of welfare professionals in defining an individual's needs and how those needs should be met is also important, particularly when deciding whether or not a person fits into a category that makes them eligible for welfare benefits and services (Albrecht 1976).

Therefore, 'individual model' policy responses to disabled people rely on medical and administrative definitions to define disability and decide on appropriate treatments, services and responses, without questioning the supposition that disability is a personal tragedy that must be 'overcome'. Disabled people are viewed as needing care and treatment and, in some cases, help to come to terms with the non-availability of care or treatment.

Throughout the 1970s and 1980s critiques of the individual model of disability began to be voiced, most particularly from disabled activists and their organizations, such as the Union of Physically Impaired People Against Segregation (1976), and then developed further theoretically by academic writers such as Oliver (1990), Finkelstein (1980) and Barnes and colleagues (1999). They pointed out several weaknesses and problems associated with the 'individual model'. First, it relies heavily on disability being defined by a dominant group in society ('non-disabled' people) with little or no experience of disability themselves. Second, it creates binary (either/or) distinctions between 'disabled' and 'normal' people without questioning what is 'normal' and without taking into account how our perceptions of 'normality' are framed by social forces.

Third, it sees disability as a static state and takes no account of the social context, particularly the way in which the organization of society can affect how 'disabled' a person is by his or her illness or impairment. This view of disability as a static state not only fails to reflect disabled people's experiences but also does not reflect the experiences of people who do not consider themselves to be disabled. For example, before the advent of technology to create vision-altering lenses in glasses, anyone with severe short- or long-sightedness would have been handicapped, particularly in situations where good vision was paramount to survival, such as hunting. Nowadays, access to glasses to correct vision impairments is so widespread that people wearing them are considered to be 'normal' – but ask anyone who loses their glasses to drive to work or read a book and you will soon discover how quickly 'normal' people can become impaired and disabled without their artificial 'aids'.

At the same time, social movements concerned with race and gender were heightening awareness that the inequality in society experienced by disabled people might be of a similar vein: that is, not a 'natural' result of biology but instead a more complex result of the social, political and economic organization of society (Driedger 1989). This combination of political and academic activity gave rise to what is now known as the 'social model' of disability.

Towards a social model of disability

In 1976 the Union of the Physically Impaired Against Segregation (UPIAS) produced a manifesto entitled *Fundamental Principles*, which argued that, instead of disability being caused by impairment or illness, it was in fact caused by the way in which society excludes and oppresses people with impairments and illnesses:

> **In our view it is society which disables physically impaired people. Disability is something imposed on top of our impairments by the way we are unnecessarily isolated and excluded from full participation in society. Disabled people are therefore an oppressed group in society.**
>
> (UPIAS 1976: 14)

Instead of the WHO's view that the source of the cause of disability was *internal* (i.e. the impaired body of an individual), UPIAS asserted that the cause of disability was *external* (i.e. society). It defined impairment and disability thus:

> ***Impairment*** **– Lacking part or all of a limb, or having a defective limb, organ or mechanism of the body.**
>
> ***Disability*** **– The disadvantage or restriction of activity caused by a contemporary social organisation which takes no or little account of people who have physical impairments and thus excludes them from participation in the mainstream of social activities.**
>
> (UPIAS 1976: 3–4)

A closer look

The individual versus the social model of disability

> Disability, according to the social model, is all the things that impose restrictions on disabled people; ranging from individual prejudice to institutional discrimination, from inaccessible buildings to unusable transport systems, from segregated education to excluding work arrangements, and so on. Further, the consequences of this failure do not simply and randomly fall on individuals but systematically upon disabled people as a group who experience this failure as discrimination institutionalised throughout society.
>
> (Oliver 1996: 33)

Oliver summarizes the key differences between the individual and social models of disability as shown in Table 8.1.

Table 8.1 Differences between the individual and social models of disability

Individual model	Social model
Personal tragedy theory	Social oppression theory
Personal problems	Social problems
Individual treatment	Social action
Medicalization	Self-help
Professional dominance	Individual and collective responsibility
Expertise	Experience
Adjustment	Affirmation
Individual identity	Collective identity
Prejudice	Discrimination
Attitudes	Behaviour
Care	Rights
Control	Choice
Policy	Politics
Individual adaptation	Social change

(Oliver 1996: 34)

The implications of the social model are that people with impairments are disabled by the social, attitudinal, physical and environmental barriers facing them in society. This means that, if the oppression of disabled people is to be addressed, then it is *external* factors – society – that must be changed. This is not to say that impairment itself is not acknowledged as being functionally problematic – writers such as French (1993) and Abberley (1987) have noted that, unlike the biological differences of sex and skin colour, impairment itself causes restrictions that are not entirely socially constructed, at least in part, leading to what Barnes *et al.* (1999) call 'internalised oppression'.

Shifting the focus from changing individual behaviour towards tackling oppression in society requires a fundamental change in attitudes and approaches. One example of how this change in perspective could make a significant difference is the way in which we define disability and view the source of the 'problem' and therefore the source of the 'solution'.

Stop and think

Look at Figure 8.3.

- If we use an individual model of disability, how and why is the man in Figure 8.3 'disabled'? What should we do about it? What's the 'problem' and what's the solution?
- Now think about using a social model of disability and asking the same questions: how and why is this man disabled? What should we do about it? What's the 'problem' and what's the solution?

Adopting a social model of disability means acknowledging that the various social, attitudinal and environmental barriers that are faced by people with impairments, rather than the impairment itself, are what 'disables' them. If we did accept this view, then we would have to change our focus away from helping

Figure 8.3 A man 'disabled' by the steps or by his inability to walk?

A closer look

Measuring disability and the OPCS surveys

Mike Oliver (1990) has argued that most large-scale government surveys designed to measure disability and its incidence in society have relied on an individual-model approach to defining disability. One of the largest surveys of the incidence of disability in the UK was that carried out by the Office of Population Census Survey (OPCS) in 1986 (Martin *et al*. 1988), which found that over 10 per cent of working-age adults were 'severely disabled'; this figure is used to calculate benefit rates today. Table 8.2 shows, in the left-hand column, the original individual-model questions used in the OPCS survey and, in the right-hand column, how Mike Oliver imagined these questions might look if they were rephrased to use a social-model approach.

Questions

1. If you can, get access to a claim form for a disability-related benefit or service (e.g. incapacity benefit, a 'handicapped parking' badge, an excuse form for work). How many of the questions are framed from an individual-model perspective?
2. What would the questions look like if they were reframed from a social-model perspective?
3. What would be the implications of this change of perspective?

Table 8.2

OPCS questions	Social model questions
Can you tell me what is wrong with you?	Can you tell me what is wrong with society?
What complaint causes your difficulty in holding, gripping or turning things?	What defects in the design of everyday equipment like jars, bottles and tins causes your difficulty in holding, gripping or turning them?
Are your difficulties in understanding people mainly due to a hearing problem?	Are your difficulties in understanding people mainly due to their inabilities to communicate with you?
Do you have a scar, blemish or deformity which limits your daily activities?	Do other people's reactions to any scar, blemish or deformity you may have, limit your daily activities?
Have you attended a special school because of a long-term health problem or disability?	Have you attended a special school because of your education authority's policy of sending people with your health problem or disability to such places?
Does your health problem/disability mean that you need to live with relatives or someone else who can look after you?	Are community services so poor that you need to rely on relatives or someone else to provide you with the right level of personal assistance?
Did you move here because of your health problem/disability?	What inadequacies in your housing caused you to move here?
How difficult is it for you to get about your immediate neighbourhood on your own?	What are the environmental constraints which make it difficult for you to get about in your immediate neighbourhood?
Does your health problem/disability prevent you from going out as often or as far as you would like?	Are there any transport or financial problems which prevent you from going out as often or as far as you would like?
Does your health problem/disability make it difficult for you to travel by bus?	Do poorly designed buses make it difficult for someone with your health problem/disability to use them?
Does your health problem/disability affect your work in any way at present?	Do you have problems at work because of the physical environment or the attitudes of others?

(Oliver 1990: 7–8)

impaired people to 'overcome' their illness or impairment towards changing the social environment to better accommodate the impairment or illness. Once example of how this might work in practice is discussed below.

Disability and social exclusion

The social model is not concerned simply with how we define disability or how it may be understood. It also examines the ways in which individual impairments may become transformed into social barriers by the discriminatory practices of the individuals and organizations with which disabled people come into contact. Following the work of Barnes and Mercer, it is argued that the traditional (medical) approach tends to explain the exclusion of disabled people in terms of their own impairments. In contrast:

> **the social model directs the analytical focus away from individual functional limitations to the barriers to social inclusion created by disabling environments, attitudes and cultures . . . It focuses on the exclusionary barriers that intersect disabled people's lives, such as inaccessible education, information and communication systems, working environments, inadequate disability benefits, discriminatory health and social support services, inaccessible transport, houses and public buildings and amenities, and negative cultural and media representations.**
>
> (Cunningham and Cunningham 2008: 67)

Barnes and Mercer (2003) argue that the patterns of exclusion and marginalization in these areas are so consistent over time that disability must be considered as a form of stratification in its own right, while Oliver (1990: 68) insists that disabled people must recognize their shared social position and 'reinterpret their collective experiences in terms of structural notions of discrimination and oppression rather than interpersonal ones of stigma and stigmatisation'.

In other words, just as quality of life and social opportunities can be affected by factors such as age, race, gender and social class, so disability may be regarded as another site of social discrimination and structural exclusion. Despite the general lack of sociological interest in this area, one writer was 20 years ahead of her time when she wrote:

> **Disabled people can be conceptualised as a disadvantaged or minority group because they have a great deal in common with the old, blacks, women, poor, and other minorities in that they are treated and reacted to as a category of people . . . The main reason for this similarity is the popular notion that disability, physical or mental (as well as old age, poverty, the female gender, or blackness of skin color), entails biological inferiority. Therefore, the disabled person is often considered to be less intelligent, less able to make the 'right' decisions, less 'realistic', less logical, and less able to determine his own life than a nondisabled person.**
>
> (Safilios-Rothschild 1981: 5)

It is not possible to cover all of the areas of social exclusion in the space available, but we discuss the key aspects below.

Employment and income

Consecutive UK governments have implemented policies designed to promote employment opportunities for disabled people and direct more resources to those in greatest need. But what impact have these policies had over the past 20 years? Tania Burchardt used nationally representative surveys to examine the past and present position of disabled people of working age in the income distribution and the labour market. The study found the following:

- Disabled people make up a large and growing proportion of the working-age population: between 12 and 16 per cent, depending on the definition used.
- Employment rates among disabled people are low, at around 40 per cent, and have remained stable. In 1999, disabled people made up half of all those who were not employed but said they would like to work, and one-third of those who were available to start working in a fortnight.
- Of those who become disabled while in work, one in six lose their employment during the first year after becoming disabled. By implication, improving retention could make a substantial difference to overall rates of employment among disabled people.
- Getting work is more difficult for disabled than non-disabled jobseekers, and one-third of disabled people who do find work are out of a job again by the following year.

- Half of all disabled people have incomes below half the general population mean (often taken as an indicator of poverty), after making an adjustment for extra costs. Even without adjustment, two in five are found to be in poverty – an increase of one-sixth since 1985 (Burchardt 2000; summary available at www.jrf.org.uk/knowledge/findings/socialpolicy/060.asp; see also the Equality and Human Rights Commission website at www.equalityhumanrights.com/en/Pages/default.aspx.

Education

Education is often touted as the key route into employment. It teaches the academic, technical and social skills required in the world of work and provides the qualifications necessary for vocational and academic progression. However, education also retains a selection function in a modern society characterized by a complex division of labour, which usually entails selective examination based upon ability (see Chapter 15). For people with disabilities, this selection function can act to exclude them from the world of education especially, where schools compete with one another and use league tables as a means of comparison. Consequently, educational provision for disabled children is often segregated, with 'special education' provided separately – a model found around the world. Special schools are often defended on the grounds that they are best suited to meet the needs of children with disabilities (especially those classified as special educational needs); however, the figures on achievement make gloomy reading and pupils tend to leave with low levels of qualification. Despite calls as far back as the 1970s for a more integrated approach (see Warnock 1978), many children with special needs are still educated separately; when they are schooled in the mainstream system, they are unlikely to be fully integrated or to have their needs properly addressed (Barnes and Mercer 2003: 43–6).

Barnes points out that, despite changes in education provision and government claims to make education available to all, children with disabilities are more than twice as likely than non-disabled children to leave school without any formal qualifications and that 'twenty five percent of disabled people of working age have no qualifications whatsoever' (Barnes 2008). This is supported by the Disability Rights Commission, which claims that 'disabled people are still only half as likely as non disabled people to be qualified to degree level and twice as likely as non disabled people to have no qualification at all'.

Leisure

As work accounts for more of our time than it used to, people in contemporary societies spend more money on leisure activities and define themselves in terms of what they do outside work. Whether leisure activities are home-based or in the community at a pub, a leisure centre or a football match, access to leisure activities can pose difficulties for disabled people, which means they may be excluded. In public and private facilities, issues of health and safety and the needs of other customers are often given as reasons to exclude people who may disrupt 'normal' enjoyment. This sometimes means that disabled people have to resort to the law to preserve their right to leisure; in one case, Raymond Crowe, a man with a facial disfigurement, was asked to leave a Belfast night club because he did not 'fit their criteria'. He was awarded £2500 in compensation, but the damage had been done. Mr Crowe has vowed not to return:

> **Now I just don't go out any more. I'm not going to let my wife go through what my friends did, I wouldn't let her go through the embarrassment of that.**
>
> (BBC News 19.12.07)

In some cases, as with education, provision of leisure facilities has been segregated for people with disabilities in day centres and special clubs. Disabled people are more likely to live alone and less likely to have contact with family, friends and neighbours compared with non-disabled people. Disabled people engage less in leisure activities that other people take for granted and are less likely to visit local shops. Unsurprisingly, disabled people often report being dissatisfied with their social lives and frustrated with the lack of opportunies to meet others and go out with friends. As expectations rise, surveys suggest that younger disabled people show the highest levels of dissatisfaction (Barnes and Mercer 2003: 54).

Another excluding factor is the level of hostility that disabled people face in a 'disabling society'. Disabled people are a target for verbal abuse and physical assault; recent reports have shown that this is more common than we may recognize. This is partly because such 'hate crimes' were not recorded as such until a change in the law insisted that 'disability-aggravated crime' be recorded as such. Since 2005, the Leonard Cheshire disability charity claims that one in five people with physical disabilities have been victimized; Mind suggests

Figure 8.4 Oscar Pistorius
MARK RALSTON/AFP/Getty Images

that people with mental health problems are at even greater risk, with 75 per cent reporting victimization within the previous two years (BBC News 2.12.07).

> **'You're not disabled by the disabilities you have, you are able by the abilities you have'**
>
> (Oscar Pistorius)

Oscar Pistorius (Figure 8.4) was born with a congenital disorder which led to both legs below the knee being amputated at the age of 11 months. He refused to allow this to interfere with his love of sport and played rugby, water polo and tennis at school as well as Olympic wrestling at club level. Following a rugby injury he took up running, using prosthetic legs. Some argued that this gave him an unfair advantage and in the run up to the 2008 Olympics he was involved in a legal battle as he fought for the right to represent South Africa in the Beijing games. He won the legal battle but was not selected. However, he scooped a hat trick of gold medals in the 100, 200 and 400 metres at the Paralympics which followed.

The built environment and transport

If we are to move from a disabling society to an enabling one, the physical barriers in the architectural environment that act as barriers to participation are crucial. Also, in a society where geographical mobility is part of the common experience, access to forms of transport is important. The issue of the physical infrastructure crops up again and again as a major concern for inclusion in the key areas of everyday life.

According to one survey, 181,000 households in the UK contain members with a disability or medical condition who are living in unsuitable accommodation, while around 70 per cent of buses are not regarded as 'accessible' for people with a disability (Cunningham and Cunningham 2008: 65). As Barnes and Mercer state:

> **Traditionally, urban infrastructures have been designed with little if any thought for the needs of people with impairments . . . An inaccessible built environment has a knock on effect for a wide range of activities, including the choice about where and when to work, type and location of housing, and participation in leisure activities. This in turn inhibits earning and shopping opportunities, while also often leading to higher travel costs and investment of more time in making the necessary or alternative arrangements.**
>
> (Barnes and Mercer 2003: 50)

Media representation and disability

In a society obsessed with appearance, the way in which disability is represented is important, particularly in terms of how disabled people see themselves and how they are seen by others. This is an area of significant study where the depiction of disabled people in literature, art, cinema and film reveals much about how disabled people are seen or ignored by those who produce media texts. We cannot generalize here, because the representation is partly a matter of who is producing the text (disabled/non-disabled), the mode of delivery (TV, cinema, etc.) and the purpose (entertainment, news, charity campaign, etc.), but it is difficult to disagree with Darke's conclusion that representations of disabled people over the years have been 'clichéd, stereotyped and archetypal' (quoted in Taylor 2008: 41). Representations are usually negative and tend to fit within one of the following categories:

A closer look

In an attempt to overcome the prejudices perpetuated by the media, a toy company has produced a range of 'disabled dolls' in the hope that they may provide more positive role models. This was not universally acclaimed and sparked a major debate. See www.timesonline.co.uk/tol/life_and_style/health/article4206469.ece.

Question

1. Do you think these images help or offend? Why?

- *Absence* – Disabled people are excluded from coverage and have no voice of their own, while issues of disablement and exclusion are overlooked. They are also underrepresented in popular culture as participants and members of the audience. How many disabled TV presenters can you think of?
- *Freaks* – In circuses first and then in film, disabled people were often exhibited for their abnormal appearance. For example, see Todd Browning's 1932 film *Freaks*.
- *One-dimensional* – Having limited lives in which they are 'dependent, unproductive and in need of care' (Barnes and Mercer 2003: 94). A walk-on part in *Casualty* may be as good as it gets.
- *Tragic victims* – Content analysis by researchers has demonstrated the popularity of coverage that emphasizes the personal struggle of plucky characters, eliciting feelings of pity or admiration but ignoring them as ordinary members of society (Barnes and Mercer 2003: 94). Charity organizations are often accused of exploiting this in their fund-raising campaigns.
- *Objects of fear* – When disabled characters do get to play centre stage, they are often portrayed as villains, criminals or monsters. You might consider the representation of physical disability in *Richard III*, *Dr Jekyll and Mr Hyde* and *Frankenstein*. The association between mental illness and evil is probably even more obvious; see, for example, *Psycho*, *Halloween* and *A Fatal Attraction*, and 'Images of madness in the films of Walt Disney' (downloadable from http://pb.rcpsych.org/cgi/reprint/20/10/618.pdf).

Commenting on the negative coverage of mentally distressed people in the news and, in particular, stories of violent assault, Philo concluded:

> **Media coverage [of the mentally distressed] does have a very important influence. Our study . . . of the content of press and television showed that this coverage had a major impact on audiences. Forty percent . . . believed that serious mental illness was associated with violence, while giving the media as the source of their beliefs. We have shown here that media images which stigmatise mental illness can also have a pervasive and damaging effect on users of services and on their immediate social relationships.**
>
> (Philo 1996: 112)

Challenges to the social model of disability

The implications of the social model are that disability is not fixed or binary (i.e. an either/or situation), but instead is a result of the social context: the social response to an individual with an impairment or chronic illness. This means that disability is seen not as a personal tragedy but as social, economic and political exclusion. In order to tackle disability, therefore, society rather than individuals needs to change: instead of rehabilitation and individual adjustment, the focus in the social model of disability is on collective action to instigate social change.

Although the social model of disability is now largely dominant in sociological thinking about disability, there are several challenges that need to be noted. Focusing exclusively on the external, social aspects to disability often has the effect of denying the subjective *experience* of chronic illness, impairment and how it affects everyday life. Morris asserts that:

> **There is a tendency within the social model to deny the experience of our own bodies, insisting that our physical differences and restrictions are *entirely* socially created. While environmental barriers and**

social attitudes are a crucial part of our experience of disability – and do indeed disable us – to suggest this is all there is is to deny the personal experience of physical or intellectual restrictions, of illness, of the fear of dying.

(Morris 1991: 10)

Medical sociologists such as Bury (1997) and Williams (1996) have also pointed out that the social model of disability tends to ignore the personal aspects of illness and impairment and presents an entirely 'social' account that focuses on the social, economic and political organization of society at the expense of more personalized accounts that reflect the reality of life for people with impairments. French (1993) has written about her own experience of blindness, the social awkwardness that comes from not being able to recognize people's faces and the social isolation she feels as a result of this. It is not easy to explain away her neighbour's reluctance to engage with her after repeatedly being ignored as simply the result of a 'disabling social attitude', and not a result of her own inability to recognize and respond 'appropriately' to people who should be familiar to her. Other writers, particularly those who focus on the sociology of the body (Doyal 1995), have echoed Morris's concerns that denying the link between impairment, illness and disability is just as oppressive as asserting that impairment and illness are the *only* cause of disability. Social theorists are struggling to assimilate these competing perspectives: the search is on for a theoretical explanation of disability that allows for the reality of the limitations caused by illnesses and impairments, and an understanding of the way in which social and physical barriers operate to exclude disabled people.

Stop and think

- Think about your experiences of chronic illness, disability and impairment. Have the problems you have experienced been the result of your illness or impairment, or of the way in which society has failed to respond adequately to your needs as an ill or impaired person?
- What other social theories can help us to understand disabled people's experiences in contemporary society?

Understanding disability in the context of welfare policy

In some respects, policy concerning the provision of services for disabled people reflects whether policymakers and service providers are using an individual or a social model of disability. Finkelstein (1994), a disabled academic, writes about two different experiences of accessing public space on his travels. In the first example, he visits the Peto Institute in Hungary, a location that Mike Oliver criticized for its focus on encouraging children with motor neuron illnesses to 'walk' rather than use artificial aids such as wheelchairs. Finkelstein found the experience uncomfortable: after using a lift to gain access to the upper floor of the building, he watched several children being forced to struggle up the stairs, taking half an hour or more to do the same journey that he had just effortlessly done in the name of achieving 'normality'. Why, he asked, is it 'normal' to use a lift but not 'normal' to use a wheelchair? He contrasted that with the experience of travelling in New York, where the ability to use wheelchair-accessible public transport meant that it was very easy for him to get around the city at the same pace as everyone else. He reflected on the importance for disabled people of having access to the same kinds of space and experiences as non-disabled people. In Hungary, an individual model of disability meant that policy and practice focused on helping individual disabled people to overcome their disabilities; in New York, a social-model approach to designing public transport made it more accessible for everyone and removed the onus on individuals to overcome their disabilities.

However, the different models of disability used by policymakers and practitioners (e.g. doctors, nurses, benefits advisors, social workers and care assistants who provide services to disabled people) only partly explain the approaches taken in providing services to disabled people. Finkelstein (1980) and Oliver (1990) have linked the rise of attention paid to disabled people as a 'social problem' with the changes to society that were the result of the growth of capitalism and the associated changes to the organization of society (see Chapter 12 for a fuller account of these and also Chapter 1, pp. 15–17). Oliver argues that

Changes in the organisation of work from a rural based, co-operative system where individuals contributed what they could to the production

> **process, to an urban, factory-based one organised around the individual waged labourer, had profound consequences . . . disabled people came to be regarded as a social and educational problem and more and more were segregated in institutions of all kinds including workhouses, asylums, colonies, and out of the mainstream of social life.**
>
> (Oliver 1990: 27–8)

How disabled people are viewed and treated within society is not only a matter of which 'model' of disability is used but is also related to the social, economic and political organization of the society and how it approaches the issue of 'welfare'. Within the UK the fundamental underlying principles of the provision of welfare support were enshrined in the Poor Law Amendment Act of 1834, which created a clear division between 'worthy' and 'unworthy' people living in poverty. 'Indoor relief' (provision of food and shelter) was available via the workhouse for those who were unable to provide for their own needs, but it was clear in policy aims that a distinction was to be made between the 'undeserving' poor – those for whom the expectation was that they should provide for themselves and their families through work – and the 'deserving' poor – those who were deemed to be unable to provide for themselves and their families through work.

This basic assumption that individuals should provide for their own needs continued until the establishment of the post-war welfare state, where the provision of free health services and education to all citizens and a comprehensive set of social security benefits to provide income when people were unable to work fundamentally changed the role that the state played in supporting individuals and families (Ginsburg 1992). Based on principles of universal social citizenship laid out by Marshall (1950) and Beveridge (1942), the political and ideological basis for the welfare state was that all citizens should be guaranteed basic social rights,

Case study

Community care

Since the 1990s the introduction of community care policies has meant that care is largely the responsibility of the family, and in particular women within the family. It has been estimated that between 30,000 and 100,000 children in the UK now care for elderly relatives. There are consequences for the quality of care, the impact on carers and family life.

Ten facts about caring in the UK

1. One in eight (1 in 8) adults are carers – around six million people.
2. Carers save the economy £87 billion per year – an average of £15,260 per carer.
3. Over 3 million people juggle care with work.
4. The main carer's benefit is £50.55 for a minimum of 35 hours, equivalent to £1.44 an hour.
5. 1.25 million people provide over 50 hours of care per week.
6. People providing high levels of care are twice as likely to be permanently sick or disabled.
7. Over one million people care for more than one person.
8. 58% of carers are women and 42% are men.
9. By 2037 the number of carers could have increased to 9 million.
10. Every year over 2 million people become carers.

(www.carersuk.org/newsandcampaigns/media/tenfactsaboutcaring)

Questions

1. How might these changes affect family life?
2. Why do you think more women than men end up as informal carers?
3. Find out how much informal carers get paid. Do you think this is adequate?

such as access to healthcare and education, regardless of their income or ability to pay (see also p. 177).

This 'universal citizenship' approach to welfare was challenged by the political and social changes that followed the economic crisis of the 1970s, and the election in 1979 of a British Conservative administration committed to reducing state expenditure on welfare. The Conservative government instigated a range of reforms, including the introduction of market-based systems into welfare services, the re-establishment of the importance of engaging in paid work, and the responsibility of families to provide help and care for those unable to undertake paid work.

The move to 'community care' was, on the face of it, a positive one – encouraging more independence and putting disabled people in charge of their own budgets – but in effect it transferred responsibility away from the state and on to the family and became a means of reducing costs (see Ferguson 2008). In this way, state care is replaced by a system of 'informal care' delivered by people who are often underpaid and poorly trained but with little choice in the matter (see Starkey 2007).

Welfare policies that have had a significant impact on disabled people concern not only the world of work but also the private world of the family and whoever provides 'care', help and support to disabled people. Community care policy, which began in the 1960s and 1970s in the UK with the closure of many long-stay residential care units for disabled people, has been a mixed blessing for many disabled people. On the one hand, most disabled people welcome the idea that they should be living in the community; as Finkelstein asserted in the example on transport above, it is an important part of not being 'excluded' from society that disabled people share in 'normal' social life. However, if there are not sufficient resources to support disabled people, then they will have to rely on their families and friends to provide the help they need. This means that disabled people can become trapped into relationships that Morris (1991) asserts are 'most exploitative', both for the person receiving the help (the 'disabled' person) and for the person giving the help (the 'carer'). Even where the state does provide help and resources, for example by giving disabled people home care assistants, evidence suggests that these services are not well organized to meet disabled people's needs: disabled people have very little control over the type and quality of help they receive and often have to wait for the service to be provided (Rummery 2002). Often the aims of such services are to help disabled people become 'independent': this seems to mean not needing or relying on anyone or anything for help. As Mike Oliver stated, try getting to Australia 'independently' without the use of an aeroplane – 'independence', as we commonly understand it, reflects an unrealistic ideal that policymakers do not often question. For disabled people, 'independence' can be more usefully defined as having control over the kind of help and support they receive (Morris 2004).

Some areas of community care policy have been welcomed as important gains for disabled people, allowing them to achieve 'independence' on their own terms. For example, within the UK it is now possible for disabled people to receive cash payments to directly employ personal care assistants, which allows them to exercise greater choice and control over the kind of help they receive, and thus enabling family members to choose not to be 'carers' (Rummery 2006). However, these developments have been argued to be popular among policymakers because they cost less than traditional community care services rather than because they give disabled people greater control over their lives. Welfare policy is shaped not only by overarching economic and political aims but also by values that come from policymakers' experiences and views of the world, and these are not necessarily likely to reflect disabled people's experiences. How many disabled politicians, journalists, teachers, professors and welfare practitioners are in a position to shape welfare policy for disabled people?

Summary

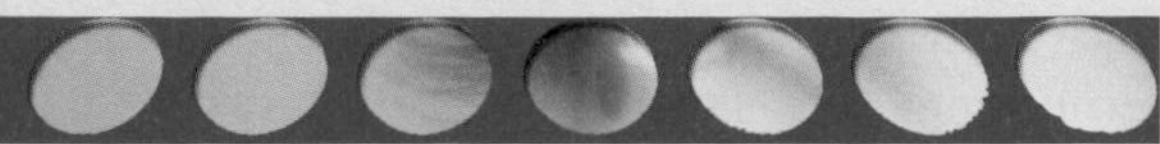

- Our beliefs about disability, and our attitudes towards disabled people, are shaped by our own experiences and by the social context in which we operate.
- Sociological explanations for our attitudes towards disabled people include accounts that explain our fear of illness and the way we treat people we consider to be deviant or different from 'normal'.
- Two main models of disability affect the way in which we define, and respond to, disability. The individual model sees disability as the result of chronic illness and impairment: the result of biology. The social model sees disability as the result of the way in which society responds to people with chronic illnesses and impairments: the result of social organization.
- Different models of disability give rise to different individual and collective responses to disabled people. Individual-model responses concentrate on rehabilitation, curing and helping disabled people to overcome their disability and fit into mainstream society. Social-model responses concentrate on changing the social environment to better accommodate the needs of people with chronic illnesses and impairments.
- Welfare policy for disabled people is a reflection not only of whether policymakers use an individual or a social model of disability but also of the ideology and aims underpinning welfare provision generally.

Links

Links to the chapters on Health as well as the concepts of Social inclusion/exclusion (see chapters on Stratification (Chapter 4) and Education (Chapter 15)) and the discussion of Identity (Chapter 1, pp. 27–29).

Further reading

Barnes, C. (1991) *Disabled People in Britain and Discrimination: A Case for Anti-Discrimination Legislation*, London: Hurst and Co.
A detailed study of social policy and disability in the UK, looking at education, employment, social security, health and social care, housing, leisure and political life.

Barnes, C., Mercer, G. and Shakespeare, T. (1999) *Exploring Disability: A Sociological Introduction*, Cambridge: Polity Press.
A detailed introduction to various sociological perspectives on disability.

Barnes, C. and Mercer, G. (2003) *Disability*, Cambridge: Polity Press.
A very useful overview of key concepts and perspectives.

Corker, M. and French, S. (eds) (1999) *Disability Discourse*, Buckingham: Open University Press.
An edited collection looking at personal narratives of disability, the social creation of disability identity and cultural discourses.

Hales, G. (1996) *Beyond Disability*, London: Sage.
A little dated now, but an interesting set of readings from a wide range of activists, researchers and practitioners.

Oliver, M. (1990) *The Politics of Disablement*, London: Longman.
A materialist perspective on disability in capitalist society, and one of the most important texts developing the 'social' model of disability.

Oliver, M. (1996) *Understanding Disability: From Theory to Practice*, Basingstoke: Macmillan.
A collection of essays detailing the development of the social model of disability.

Macionis, J. and Plummer, K. (2008) *Sociology: A Global Introduction*, Harlow: Pearson Education.
Chapter 14 touches on areas covered here but also includes a useful section on the disability movement.

Morris, J. (1991) *Pride Against Prejudice: Transforming Attitudes to Disability*, London: Women's Press.
An influential text drawing together feminist and disability theory.

Rummery, K. (2002) *Disability, Citizenship and Community Care: A Case for Welfare Rights?*, Aldershot: Ashgate.
Looks at how community care policy impacts on the citizenship of disabled people in the UK.

Swain, J., Finkelstein, V., French, S. and Oliver, M. (eds) (1993) *Disabling Barriers: Enabling Environments*, London: Sage.
An edited collection of essays detailing theoretical and empirical developments in disability studies from a social-model perspective.

Websites

www.leeds.ac.uk/disability-studies/archiveuk

Website for the Centre for Disability Studies. Full of information and updated regularly. Has some really useful material on social exclusion and social policy.

www.disabilityalliance.org

A charity whose main aim is to 'break the link between disability and poverty'. Offers advice and information, mainly of a practical nature. See also www.internationaldisabilityalliance.org.

www.mind.org.uk

MIND is the leading mental health charity in the UK. It promotes good mental health for all. The charity offers support and information for people interested in mental health issues.

www.carersuk.org

Carers UK is a campaign group representing the interests of carers in the UK. The organization provides practical help for informal carers, conducts research and publishes a range of fact sheets, booklets and reports, some of which are free.

Activities

Activity 1

Deaf activists in 'designer babies' storm

Controversy continues to rage over a clause in the Fertilisation and Human Embryology Bill currently going through parliament. The debate is particularly strong among deaf people – though other disabled individuals and groups have also objected to the clause. The bill says that, where embryos are being selected for IVF, those carrying no risk of genetic impairment must be preferred over embryos where the risk of impairment is present.

At the same time as objecting to this provision, deaf activists have also expressed serious concern over the press's presentation of the issues following stories asserting that significant numbers of deaf couples choose to have deaf 'designer babies.' Steve Emery of the Stop Eugenics campaign sets out to present the true position, arguing that the objections are to the ruling out of choice and the unequal treatment of one embryo over another on the grounds of disability. He also says that the numbers of people 'choosing' to have a deaf baby and deliberately setting out to do so are actually very small and the issue has been inflamed by sensationalist press coverage.

We were alerted to the HFEB Clause 14/4/9 when Baroness Deech, speaking in the House of Lords late last year, made a comment that the legislation would apply to deaf embryos. If an individual, through a particular type of IVF technique, had their embryos tested for the genes for deafness, and if there was a mix of deaf and hearing embryos, the hearing ones must be selected for implantation. On further investigation we also found, hidden in the explanatory notes accompanying the Bill, references that confirmed Deech's statement (note 109 to be precise); specific reference was made to those who would choose a deaf embryo. Interested to discover what consultation had taken place, we came across a Human Genetics Commission guideline document which recommended that no deaf embryos should be preferred over hearing ones.

This specific clause does not state what an 'abnormal' gene is; neither what a serious physical disability should be taken to mean; and therefore those applying the law will look for references. They will, we believe, be guided by those examples given and therefore include deaf embryos.

The legislation would specifically put into law a value judgement setting hearing as the norm and deafness (and disability), as a 'lesser state'. As such, this amounts to enshrining eugenics in UK primary legislation. Potential parents who want to try to ensure their baby is hearing can take a test through an additional step to IVF treatment called pre-implantation genetic diagnosis (PGD) and weed out the deaf embryo in favour of the hearing ones. There will be no objection to their doing so; it is already legally possible. If, however, a parent wants a deaf embryo to be replaced in the womb through the same technique, that opportunity is closed off if screening shows there are both deaf and hearing embryos. They would have to 'prefer' the hearing embryo, the deaf embryo could not be chosen.

There is no compulsion to take the test, and so those who do not care to select the hearing/deaf status of the embryo simply won't take it. Our concern, however, is that people who have a high incidence of deafness in their family or a good chance of conceiving a deaf offspring will feel compelled to take the test; given the way the medical profession generally perceives deafness as a serious deficit that should be cured or treated, there are fears people will be encouraged, if only by the influence of prevailing social attitudes towards deafness and disability, to be tested without being fully aware of the implications.

(Steve Emery, *Disability Now*, April 2008)

Questions

1. What does the story reported in *Disability Now* tell us about attitudes towards deaf people in contemporary society?
2. What sociological theories and models explored in this chapter help us to explain some of these attitudes?
3. If you were born deaf, would you prefer to have a deaf child or a hearing child? What factors do you think would influence your preference?

Activity 2

What's the problem? What's the solution?

Kirstein Rummery spent several weeks observing how social workers make decisions about what services and support to offer disabled people. She gives this example of a social worker's case:

> A practitioner returned from an assessment visit to discuss the results. Her client wanted to learn to play squash or tennis, but because of her medical condition she cannot stand up or feel the floor. The social worker and her supervisor felt that the client's desire to learn squash or tennis was unrealistic: the supervisor thought it was the result of the client failing to adjust to her lost mobility.
>
> (Rummery 2002: 63)

Questions

1. What model of disability were the social worker and her client using in this case?
2. What solutions to the client's problem do you think they will come up with?
3. How might they view the problem differently if they were using a different model of disability?
4. What social-model solutions to this problem can you think of?

Chapter 9

Global divisions

Globalisation, some argue, creates a world of winners and losers, a few on the fast track to prosperity, the majority condemned to a life of misery and despair.
(Giddens 1999: 15)

Key issues

- Why are Africa, Asia and Latin America predominantly poor? How can we account for global inequalities?
- What is development? Is development a wholly beneficial process, or does it have negative effects?
- What are the positive and negative consequences of globalization? Does everyone experience those outcomes in similar ways?
- What are the central issues in relation to gender and development?
- How do we understand childhoods in the majority world?

Introduction

When studying sociology, it is important to be able to consider a global perspective in order to recognize that what happens in our society, or even in other Western societies, is not necessarily the norm. Probably most of you reading this chapter stand among the most prosperous people in the world. If you are studying at a university in Europe, then you are likely to be among the privileged few in global terms. Certainly you will not be one of the many people in the world who are unable to get enough food and nutrition in order to survive healthily. Our position of advantage in the world means that we have better access to basic services such as electricity, drinking water, decent housing, education and health care than most of the global population. A sociological perspective reminds us that many of the achievements that we attribute to our personal abilities are also products of this privileged

Figure 9.1 In most countries a combination of tradition and modernity can be seen side by side
© Samantha Punch

position that we hold in the worldwide social system. The aim of this chapter is to enable us to consider the ways in which our life chances and our experiences of the social world differ dramatically according to the kind of society into which we are born. In particular, it may encourage us to reflect on our own location in the world and the nature of our relationships with distant others.

The chapter begins by defining the terms used to describe different areas of the world. It explores the nature of global inequalities by considering both economic and social differences. The historical background to global inequalities is highlighted with a discussion on colonialism, before outlining some of the more contemporary causes such as debt, aid and unequal global trading. The chapter then discusses the notion of development, looking at how different parts of the world have developed over time. Key sociological theories of development are presented, including the classical perspectives of modernization theory and dependency theory, and contemporary alternative approaches to development such as participatory development. The following section examines the multiple facets of globalization: economic, cultural and political. It discusses the extent to which processes of globalization are perceived to increase or decrease global inequalities. In order to fully understand both processes of globalization and of development, we need to consider the ways in which they impact on people's everyday life. For positive changes to take place, *all* people should have their needs taken into account and be given opportunities to participate in their own development. Consequently, the final two sections of the chapter focus on the roles and contributions of women and children in processes of development and globalization.

Stop and think

- What do you know about Africa, Asia and Latin America? What images do you have of these places?
- Consider the possible reasons why different parts of the world are so unequal.

Definitions: the majority and minority worlds

A range of different terms are used to describe different areas of the world. This chapter uses the recent terms 'majority world' (for the developing world) and 'minority world' (for the developed world) because they remind us that most people in the world live in the economically poorer continents of Asia, Africa and Latin America and that only a minority of people live in the wealthier areas of the world (Europe, Australia, New Zealand, Japan, the USA and Canada). The majority of the world's population live in the majority world, which also has a greater land mass. The minority world consists of fewer people and a smaller land mass, and generally refers to the minority of people who have more privileged lifestyles. The terms also invite us to reflect upon the global inequalities that exist between many of the people who live in Africa, Asia and Latin America compared with the rest of the world (see also Punch 2003).

These are relatively new terms that have come into use in the past ten years or so. The more traditional terms 'third world' and 'first world' have come to be problematic. As labels, 'third world' and 'first world' indicate some sort of ranking. Thus, 'third world' has become quite derogatory, implying that 'third-world' countries are in some way 'worse' than or 'inferior' to 'first-world' countries. This suggests that 'third-world' countries should be constantly striving to be what 'first-world' countries already are, as if our model of living in these richer countries is the norm to which all poorer countries should aspire. The traditional terms fail to recognize that the 'first world' is also undergoing a process of development and is by no means ideal, and they ignore the privileged historical background that has enabled richer countries to prosper. Other terms are used such as 'north' and 'south' and, more recently, the 'global north' and the 'global south'. These terms try to be more neutral by referring to the geographical distribution of the world's richer and poorer nations, but they are not always correct, as Australia and New Zealand are located in the south. Terms that are used to denote different parts of the world tend to have negative connotations for the poorer countries by emphasizing what they lack, for example develop*ing*, *less* developed, *low*-income, *un*developed. Although the terms 'majority world' and 'minority world' may seem confusing at first, they do make us stop and consider the unequal power relations between the two world areas.

Furthermore, as Panelli and colleagues point out, it is worth remembering that

> **. . . there are both limitations and benefits of adopting the terms Majority and Minority worlds. While providing useful conceptual tools, their potential drawback is that they divide global regions in an exclusive binary manner, when the world is not so neatly separated into clear cut and mutually exclusive categories.**
>
> (Panelli *et al.* 2007: 221)

There are increasingly a number of countries that fall in between the majority and minority worlds. Most notable are China, India and some Latin American countries, such as Venezuela, which are somewhere in the middle of the two polar ends. China, in particular, is an enormous and significant country that has the potential to reshape the world order. These intermediate countries are fast changing the picture of the world and challenge the majority/minority world divide. Nevertheless, while acknowledging this difficulty, this chapter broadly compares these two world regions, focusing on some of the key differences between poor and rich countries. The minority world is generally richer than the majority world, but we need to be wary not to overgeneralize and to recognize that both world areas are extremely diverse. However, to a certain extent, what it means to be poor in the minority world is different from being poor in the majority world, and that is what this chapter explores. Hence, although the chapter focuses mainly on the experiences of the majority world, it is important to remember that some very poor people in the minority world may live similarly impoverished lifestyles.

Global inequalities

Until recently, poor countries of the majority world have tended to be primarily agrarian societies, where most people lived in rural areas and worked in agriculture. Still today, almost half of the world's population lives in rural areas (Elliot 2006). Many people in the majority world continue to farm the land and survive from what they produce. This is known as subsistence farming. Agrarian societies in the majority world, such as Bangladesh, Bolivia, Cambodia, Vietnam and Indonesia, tend to have little industry. These countries rely more on a limited number of raw material products for export rather than on producing their own industrial goods. As Macionis and Plummer point out, poor countries in the majority world tend to maintain traditional lifestyles:

> **Kinship groups pass folkways and mores from generation to generation. Adhering to long-established ways of life, people resist innovations – even those that promise a richer material life. The members of poor societies often accept their fate, although it may be bleak, in order to maintain family vitality and cultural heritage. Such attitudes bolster social bonds, but at the cost of discouraging development.**
>
> (Macionis and Plummer 2008: 280)

This is changing, and poor countries are modernizing and developing local industries, but still many traditional ways of life continue to exist. The average number of children per family tends to be higher in the majority world. Partly this is because traditionally in subsistence economies, several children would be required to work on the family land in order to help farm what they need to eat, which would be a labour-intensive process. Another reason is because some of the children would not be expected to survive due to poor nutrition and a lack of adequate basic services (safe drinking water, sanitation, health centres), which meant that they could be vulnerable to disease and could die at an early age.

A key characteristic of the majority world is poverty, and as a result many people suffer from poor diets, insecure housing and vulnerability to illness and famine. Many are also illiterate and uneducated because of limited access to adequate schooling. In the minority world it can be very hard for us to grasp the extent of absolute poverty that many people in the majority world face. We sometimes get a glimpse of famine and starvation in countries such as Ethiopia and Zimbabwe, but it is hard for us to really understand how many people in the world have a daily struggle to survive due to constant poverty and extreme conditions. It is important to remember that many countries in the majority world have experienced the effects of colonialism, and this has tended to have a negative impact on their development. For example, most South American countries were colonized for over 300 years by Spain, and Brazil was colonized by Portugal. Poorer countries have been exposed to many years of exploitation at the hands of richer countries, and this has limited their ability to progress economically (for further details, see the section below on global divisions and the impact of colonialism).

A closer look

Table 9.1 Broad characteristics of the majority and minority worlds

Majority world	Minority world
Agrarian and rural	More urbanized
Limited industrialization	More extensive industrialization
More 'traditional'	More 'modern'
Large populations	Smaller populations
Poverty	Wealth
Colonized	Colonizers

Figure 9.2 Some women in India have to spend many hours of their time searching for firewood
© Samantha Punch

In order to highlight some of the stark contrasts between rich and poor parts of the world, consider for a moment how your life might have been different if you were born into a majority world country. For example, assuming that you were born in Europe or North America, compare your life chances with someone who was born in Sierra Leone, one of the poorest countries in the world today. Your life expectancy would be half of that in the minority world. Most people in Sierra Leone will not reach 45 years old: the life expectancy is 39 years for men and 43 years for women (CIA 2008).

In Sierra Leone, 157 children out of every 1000 die before their fifth birthday, which contrasts with 6 out of every 1000 children in the minority world. In Sierra Leone you would have only a 1 in 50 chance of going on to further education; if you are female, you would have virtually no chance, as 76 per cent of females in that country are illiterate. By contrast, in the UK almost every other person has some kind of further education. In Sierra Leone, there is only one television set per 60 people, compared with over two televisions for every three people in the UK. In Sierra Leone there is only one telephone line between 240 people. How would you cope with limited or no access to a television or telephone? Not only are media communications scarce in poor countries, but also many other basic services, such as sanitation facilities, safe drinking water, education and health care, are inadequate or lacking.

Many things that we take for granted in the minority world can be so different in other parts of the world. For example, if we want to drink water, we just turn on a tap inside our home, but in places such as rural India and Bangladesh people may have to travel long distances to reach a communal drinking well. Alternatively, they may have no access to safe drinking water and may simply get water from a nearby dirty river. They may not even be able to boil that water to purify it because they may have no gas or electricity. Many people in the majority world have to cook on open fires using firewood, which can be in short supply (Figure 9.2). Daily events such as eating and drinking can take up most of some women's day, because turning on a tap or a cooker are not options for them.

There are two key types of global inequalities that need to be considered: economic and social. Economic inequality refers mainly to levels of income. Worldwide there are an estimated 1.3 billion people living on less than $1 a day, which is approximately 20 per cent of the world's population (UNDP 2006). Of these 1.3 billion people in absolute poverty, the lives of at least 800 million are continually at risk. These people do not necessarily know where their next meal is coming from and are in an extremely vulnerable position. Absolute poverty refers to a lack of resources that is life-threatening, such as lacking the adequate nutrition necessary for long-term survival. People who are in absolute poverty may be relying on aid, food relief or their own meagre returns such as from scavenging on rubbish tips (Figure 9.3). Their lack of income means that they will not have access to adequate food, which in turn can lead to malnutrition. Malnutrition contributes to more than half of the deaths of children under five in the majority world. People in absolute poverty are also likely to be vulnerable to

A closer look

Children in the majority world

- Every day 30,500 children under five die from preventable diseases and illnesses.
- One million children die from measles each year.
- Each year nearly 12 million children under five die in the majority world; of these deaths over six million (55 per cent) are attributable directly or indirectly to malnutrition.
- Each year 1.8 million children die as a result of diarrhoea.

(Source: UNDP 2006)

Figure 9.3 Living a precarious existence in Calcutta, India
© Samantha Punch

Figure 9.4 Many houses in the majority world are insecure and unstable, made out of makeshift materials, and with whole families living cramped in one small room
© Samantha Punch

diseases; many of these diseases could be easily prevented with access to immunization and dehydration sachets, improved access to safe drinking water, better sanitation conditions and increased education.

People who live in economic poverty also suffer from social inequalities, including a lack of access to education and health care, inadequate access to safe water and sanitation, lack of adequate infrastructure

Case study

Inadequate access to basic services in rural Bolivia

This case study illustrates some of the ways in which a lack of resources and basic services can affect people's everyday lives. The two girls pictured in Figure 9.5, Marianela and Luisa, are nine and five years old and live in a relatively isolated rural community in southern Bolivia. They are small for their age as a result of poor diet and lack of adequate nutrition. They have to walk over an hour each way to school every day, but often they are unable to go because they are expected to contribute to the planting and harvesting of crops. They have five siblings so their parents cannot afford to send them all to school. The nearest town is five hours away by bus, but the local bus runs only on Mondays and Thursdays, so if they fall ill on another day of the week, the only means of transport is horseback to get to a doctor in the town.

In Figure 9.5 they are on their way to fetch water from the river, but it is dirty river water that they have to drink. In their community there are no toilets, no showers, no sewage systems, no electricity, no televisions and no telephone lines. It is interesting to compare this with rural Scotland, where even in the most isolated areas people have access to electricity and phone lines, and can even receive their post and have their rubbish collected on a regular basis.

Figure 9.5 Two girls on errands in Bolivia
© Samantha Punch

and inadequate shelter. Half of the population of the majority world, approximately 2.6 billion people, do not have access to basic sanitation:

> **Most of the 1.1 billion people categorized as lacking access to clean water use about 5 litres a day – one-tenth of the average daily amount used in rich countries to flush toilets. On average, people in Europe use more than 200 litres – in the United States more than 400 litres. When a European person flushes a toilet or an American person showers, he or she is using more water than is available to hundreds of millions of individuals living in urban slums or arid areas of the developing world. Dripping taps in rich countries lose more water than is available each day to more than 1 billion people.**
>
> (UNDP 2006: 5–6)

Therefore, global inequalities can be both economic (income levels) and social (access to adequate health services, housing, sanitation and education). The difference in under-five mortality rates between the majority and minority worlds has increased. As can be seen in Table 9.2, in sub-Saharan Africa 171 out of 1000 children die before they are five years old, compared with six in the minority world. If you are born into a minority world country, you can expect to live more than 30 years longer compared with people living in countries in sub-Saharan Africa. Latin America has higher literacy rates than Africa and Asia, where only 60 per cent of the adult population can read and write. Imagine what it would be like, as an adult, not to be able to read and write – 40 per cent of the population in Africa and Asia is in that position. Even when looking at life's little luxuries, such as owning a television, you can see even greater differences between the majority and minority worlds.

As shown in Table 9.2, Latin America fares better on every count compared with South Asia and sub-Saharan Africa. Latin America is more economically developed and industrialized than Asia and Africa. The economically poorest continent in the majority world is Africa. However, some poor countries in Latin America experience as much poverty as in Africa, so we need to remember that there are inequalities within continents. It is important to recognize that neither the majority world nor the minority world is homogeneous. There are also great differences between and within countries; for example, Brazil, Argentina, Chile and Venezuela are richer and more industrialized than Paraguay, Honduras, Peru and Bolivia. There can also be huge inequalities between people in the same country, such as between those living in rural and urban areas, or between the working and middle classes.

Global inequality is about an unequal distribution of wealth and inadequate distribution of resources. It is not about absolute shortages. For example, millions of people in India suffer from malnutrition, but India exports beef, wheat and rice. Therefore, India's malnutrition is not a problem of production, as there is enough food; rather, it is a problem of poverty, as many people cannot afford to buy the food that is available (Macionis and Plummer 2008).

We have seen that many people in the majority world are poor and undernourished, but it is worth remembering that many people in the minority world are overnourished; that is, we eat too much. On average in the minority world, in rich countries like ours, we consume about 3500 calories a day, which is more than we require to survive (Macionis and Plummer 2008). This excess can lead to obesity and related health problems, resulting in many people in the minority world spending large amounts of money on gym membership and specialized diets. In contrast, in the majority world, on average people consume fewer than 2000 calories a day. Many of them also engage in more physical labour than people do in the minority

Table 9.2 Economic and social indicators of poverty

Indicator	Sub-Saharan Africa	South Asia	Latin America	Minority world
GNP per capita	$611	$600	$3649	$32,232
Under-fives mortality rate per 1000	171	92	31	6
Life expectancy	46 years	63 years	72 years	79 years
Adult literacy rate	60%	58%	90%	98%
No. of TVs per 1000 in 1996	33	50	204	638

(Source: UNICEF 2006)

world, and so they require more calories. This means that people in the majority world are not consuming enough calories to maintain long-term survival.

Another grim thought to consider is this: in the time you spend at one university lecture of about 50 minutes' duration, about 1500 people in the world die of starvation. Approximately 15 million people die of starvation each year (Macionis and Plummer 2008). This emphasizes the extreme global divisions that exist. As well as being aware of the stark contrasts between the majority and minority worlds, we should also consider the interconnections:

> **For example, problems of 'over-development' in the industrialized countries, such as unhealthy diet and obesity, have complex socio-economic causes and effects. High consumption levels with their associated high CO_2 emissions in the industrialized countries not only have an impact on these countries, but also impact on developing countries through the global environmental effects of the emissions. Other examples of increasing interconnectedness between industrialized and developing countries are represented by the globalization of terrorism, security issues and pandemics (HIV/AIDS and avian flu for example).**
>
> (Sumner and Tribe 2008: 19)

On a global scale, the distribution of poverty between rich and poor continents can be seen clearly. Overall the majority world is much worse off both economically and socially than the minority world, but why is this the case? Why is the world divided up into such extremes of wealth and poverty? We may feel sorry for poor majority world countries in times of crisis, but perhaps we forget that our rich minority world countries have contributed to their economically poor status, both in the past and in the present. Historically colonialism initiated the patterns of global inequalities, and currently debts and the unequal global development of capitalism mean that the richer countries continue to exploit the poorer ones. The dominant role of the minority world has much to answer for in relation to the continued existence of global poverty, and it is to these issues that we now turn.

Global divisions and the impact of colonialism

The economic and social development of the majority world has been shaped to a large extent by its colonial past. It is interesting to note that nearly all the economically poor countries of the world were once colonies of the economically richer countries. It could be argued that rich countries, like most readers of this book are likely to be from, got richer as a result of making poor countries poorer. If we feel some form of moral outrage at the impoverished images of poor people living in the majority world, then it might be worth remembering that our societies in part created this poverty by extracting their riches and making them to a large extent economically dependent on the richer, more powerful countries of the minority world. The aim here is not to make you feel guilty for being born into a wealthy, privileged society, but to encourage you to reflect critically on the reasons for global inequalities.

McMichael (2000: 5) defines colonialism as 'The subjugation by physical and psychological force of one culture by another – a colonizing power – through military conquest of territory'. Colonialism was a way of controlling overseas territories in order to facilitate further development of capitalism in Europe (Bernstein 2000).

Main periods of colonialism

- *Latin America, 1500s–1880s* – Colonial expansion of the Portuguese in Brazil and the Spanish in the rest of Latin America was much earlier and lasted much longer than the colonization of Asia and Africa.
- *Asia and Africa, 1800s–1950s (sub-Saharan Africa 1880s–1960s)* – In Africa most colonial expansion took place between 1850 and 1900, which is the period known as the 'scramble for Africa' by different European countries (the UK, France, Germany, Belgium, Italy, Spain and Portugal).

Stop and think

➤ What are the advantages and disadvantages of colonialism that have impacted on the lives of people in the majority world today?

There were differences in the ways that colonial powers ruled and organized their colonies, but there were also some commonalities. The main aim of colonizers was to enhance their own financial positions and to search for goods to take back to Europe, rather than settling permanently or developing the colonized areas. Many resources were exploited, such as gold, silver and other precious metals, spices and opium. Natural resources were extracted, taken to the minority world, made into manufactured goods, and then sold back to the majority world at a far higher price. Consequently some local markets were developed in order to sell the imported manufactured goods from Europe, but it was only really the wealthy expatriates and indigenous elite who could afford them (Potter *et al.* 2008). Colonial territories were organized to produce cheap primary products at minimal cost, while simultaneously becoming an increasing market for industrial products (Bernstein 2000). This process reflects the minority world's control over global markets, which can still be seen today. Colonization thus impacted heavily on both economic and social life, and it has subsequently shaped and contributed to the majority world's poverty and economic dependency on the minority world.

Neo-colonialism

How does domination of the majority world by the minority world continue despite the fact that all the former colonies have now gained their political independence (most by the 1960s)? Why is global inequality getting worse rather than better? How can we explain why richer countries are getting richer and poorer countries are getting poorer? It has been argued that neo-colonialism is the process that continues to sustain the exploitation and poverty of majority world countries:

> **Neo-colonialism literally means a new form of colonialism, a form of socio-economic domination from outside that does not rely on direct political control.**
>
> (Webster 1990: 79)

A closer look

Characteristics of colonialism

Webster (1990) discusses three main features of colonialism that tended to apply to most colonial situations:

- *Control over agricultural production and mineral extraction* – Colonies were a source of cheap raw materials (crops and minerals) and provided a market for manufactured goods from Europe. The process of controlling agricultural production often affected traditional land-holdings, as the focus was on the production of cash crops such as coffee, cocoa, sugar and tea for export rather than on meeting the subsistence needs of local people. As a result, many people lost access to land of their own and had to sell their labour power by working on large plantations or in mines. As Potter *et al.* (2008: 65) point out: 'Colonies thus became associated with the production of one or two items, being forced to import whatever else was needed'.
- *The need for wage-labour* – Wage-labour was needed to work the mines and plantations. People had to work as many of them were now landless; they also had to earn money to pay taxes imposed by the colonizers. Forced labour (slaves) was used, and migrant labour was developed by encouraging people to move to areas where the mines and plantations were.
- *The imposition of a colonial system of law and order* – In order to control the colonies, the colonizers had to establish their authority and so they introduced a political, legal and administrative structure. This colonial administration was mainly in place to serve European interests and the development of capitalism in the minority world, rather than to develop the colonies themselves. Thus, internal markets were rarely developed as the emphasis was on production for export rather than on trying to serve local needs.

Colonialism had established international laws and regulations in relation to prices and banking systems, and most of these have continued to shape the world economy after colonialism (Webster 1990). Neo-colonialism refers to several things, including economic exploitation by transnational corporations (see the section below on the global economy), disadvantages of world trade, aid, loans and debt. Poorer countries find it increasingly difficult to compete in the global capitalist economy as they are not as able as the richer countries to develop large-scale capital-intensive industrialization. They tend to export raw materials but then have to import manufactured goods, which means that they receive relatively less for their exports while having to pay more for their imports.

Debt

Stop and think

➤ Did Live8 contribute positively towards alleviating debts in the majority world or, as some argue, was it a means for the rich to feel less guilty?

Majority world countries in the past have borrowed money from the richer countries of the minority world, and their levels of debt have increased so much because interest rates are so high. Every year (since 1983) poor countries pay out more money in loan repayments than the richer countries give in aid or invest in transnational corporations. In this sense the word 'aid' seems inappropriate, as the 'aid' that minority world countries are giving is much less than the loan repayment they are extracting. In recent years there have been many discussions about how to 'help' majority world countries to reorganize their massive debt repayments. In the 1980s the International Monetary Fund (IMF) and the World Bank (WB) were created partly to address this issue. Conditions were imposed surrounding how the money would be paid back, and these were known as structural adjustment programmes (SAPs). The SAPs imposed economic rules on poor countries as an attempt to enable them to save money in some areas so they were able to pay back their debts. SAPs consisted largely of controlling wages, devaluation of currency (to improve competitiveness of exports), cuts in public spending, especially on education and health, and promotion of the free market (Green 1997). The opening up of free markets was hugely unpopular and more likely to benefit the minority world. SAPs often had very negative impacts on social and environmental issues, in particular on human wellbeing. For example, many women and children had to enter the labour market to help their families to survive. Wages were reduced, while unemployment and poverty increased:

> **Throughout the developing world, especially Africa, structural adjustment programmes have destroyed jobs and public services, while shaping local economies to the demand of transnational capital.**
>
> (Potter 2000: 92)

Thus, most of the SAPs were not successful and, in the 1990s, the concept of debt relief emerged. Major development charities, such as Oxfam, petitioned world leaders in 1996 to cancel unpayable debts of the poorest countries under a fair and transparent process. It was the first ever global petition, with 24 million signatures, and it increased the public's awareness of majority world debt (Potter *et al.* 2008). As a result, the debt relief initiative of the Heavily Indebted Poor Countries (HIPC) emerged. In order to be eligible for relief, a country must be very poor as defined by the WB and IMF, have an unsustainable debt burden, and pursue good policies consistent with poverty reduction and sustained growth (World Bank 2001).

Therefore, in order to qualify for debt relief, countries now have to engage in poverty-reduction strategies (PRS), demonstrating how 'poverty reduction' is prioritized in government spending. They can use the funds that they would have used to pay off debts on their PRS, mostly targeting issues such as education, health, water and sanitation. Thus, if the HIPCs meet the requirements of the PRS, they no longer have to pay back their debts. However, this requires them to raise taxation and ensure that any revenue from productive activity is allocated to PRS. No additional resources are being provided to enable them to do this. Some writers argue that debt relief has only increased the levels of interference and policing of the majority world countries by the minority world:

> **The much vaunted debt cancellation that was rubber stamped at the G8 summit in Gleneagles in 2005 provided no new money or impetus for development for the developing world. In fact, debt relief has helped to entrench Western control,**

undermine democratic institutions and ensure that economic growth and serious development are not on the agenda for the countries most desperately in need of it.

(Dingle and Daley 2006)

Aid

Stop and think

➤ Is giving aid a good thing? Why do minority world governments give aid to the majority world? Can you think of any drawbacks or negative impacts of giving aid?

Aid is often seen as a way of helping poor countries to develop because they have been so crippled by their debts. Unlike a loan, aid does not have to be repaid. Different types of aid include short-term disaster relief, longer-term development aid and military aid. In 1970 the United Nations (UN) set out agreed targets for aid, suggesting that minority world governments should give 0.7 per cent of their gross national product (GNP) in aid. However, few countries have ever met this level of aid. For example, the UK gave 0.51 per cent of its GNP in 1979, but by 2000 this had fallen to 0.32 per cent (Regan 2002a). This figure is less than half what we should give according to the UN, although in recent years it has risen again. The USA is well below the recommended target, at 0.1 per cent. In 2005, only Denmark, the Netherlands, Luxemburg, Norway and Sweden had met or surpassed the recommended UN figure (Potter *et al.* 2008).

It is important to consider the reasons for giving aid and the motives of donor countries. Aid from governments in the minority world is supposed to be beneficial, but in the past it has often been 'tied aid', given on the condition that the recipient country buys specified goods from the donor country. For example, during the 1980s and early 1990s, 74 per cent of British bilateral aid was linked to contracts that involved buying British goods and services in return for the aid (Potter *et al.* 2008). Thus, the aid agreement becomes beneficial to Britain and increases the recipient country's dependency on a richer country. Parfitt (2002) refers to aid being used as a political bribe. Aid is often compromised by politics and may be given only to countries that adopt the 'correct' political position. This is often used to safeguard capitalism, and so aid from some parts of the minority world may be donated only to capitalist countries in the majority world.

Aid is given not only for humanitarian reasons but also as a way for richer countries to sustain their influence on ex-colonies or exert influence on new territories (Webster 1990). Thus, most aid has direct commercial benefit to the donor country and can be seen as both an economic and a political way of maintaining their dominant world position. Parfitt (2002) argues that aid is a form of violence and a destructive force because usually it is a top-down approach imposed on the majority world. In addition, local elites tend to keep aid as urban-centred – for bureaucrats, entrepreneurs, politicians and industrial

A closer look

Critiques of aid

There are two principal critiques of aid, which highlight the different negative impacts of giving money to poorer countries:

- *Liberal economic critique* – This sees aid as an obstacle to material progress because it is an unproductive and inefficient use of capital (in line with modernization theorists; see pp. 372–374).
- *Radical critique of aid* – This claims that aid increases dependency on foreign capital and ultimately services minority world interests as they are enabled to continue to extract majority world resources (in line with dependency theorists; see pp. 374–375)

Despite criticisms from both right and left, aid continues to be given by the minority world and continues to be requested by the majority world.

(Adapted from Webster 1990: 162–71)

A closer look

The case for and against aid

As we have seen, there is a debate around the extent to which providing aid is a beneficial or harmful process. Table 9.3 outlines the main advantages and disadvantages of the minority world giving aid to the majority world.

Table 9.3 Advantages and disadvantages of giving aid

Advantages	Disadvantages
Aid can provide useful emergency assistance and facilitate long-term development such as in health and education	Aid does not trickle down to the poorest of the poor and can be manipulated by majority world governments
Aid can contribute to a redistribution of global wealth, albeit in a limited way	Aid may divert attention from issues such as trade, debt and transnational corporations
Aid can help to initiate development projects by providing infrastructure and training	Aid may lead to majority world governments becoming dependent on support from the minority world
Aid can be an expression of humanitarian concern that enables people in the minority world to act on their concern	Aid is often 'tied', which forces the recipient country to buy goods or services from the donor country
Aid can create links between countries, which may facilitate mutual understanding	Aid distorts the free market, which, some argue, has negative impacts on economic development
Aid can transfer expertise and experience from the minority world to the majority world	Aid engenders feelings of superiority in the givers from the minority world and may perpetuate negative stereotypes of the majority world
Aid can foster relations of interdependence between the majority and minority worlds	Aid is used for economic and political reasons, resulting in continued patterns of global inequality

(Source: Regan 2002a: 127)

workers rather than for the mass of poor – and not much reaches isolated rural areas (Webster 1990). Furthermore, the consultants who undertake research into identifying what aid money should be spent on are often expatriates, living comfortably in urban areas, who go for brief field visits and fail to fully understand local situations and are conditioned by donor country approaches and priorities. It could even be said that aid creates jobs for European experts and expatriates still living in the ex-colonies.

Potter *et al.* (2008) argue that, if poverty is to be reduced, then there need to be improvements in both the quality and the quantity of aid. It has been suggested that aid should be aimed at the poorest people in the poorest countries, with a focus on health and education rather than on exports, with reduced costs of delivering the aid, better management by involving local communities and discussing their needs, and an aim to work towards sustainability in improving the quality of life. Similarly, Webster (1990: 171) suggests that perhaps 'aid should be given as advice/training for subsequent self-reliance so that rural and urban workers can *regain* control over their livelihoods'. Nowadays, in order to receive aid, governments have to demonstrate that they have effective social policies in place and engage in practices of good governance. The extent to which aid in the future will lead to more advantages than disadvantages for the majority world remains to be seen.

Sociology of development

We have seen that the relationship between the majority world and the minority world is complex. The sociology of development is about explaining these unequal global power relations. The term 'development' implies notions of growth, change, accumulation, progress or improvement (Regan and Ruth 2002). Initially development was 'the deliberate process to "develop" the "Third World" which began after World War II as much of it emerged from colonization' (Sumner and Tribe 2008: 10). Traditionally, when development studies emerged in the 1940s, the term 'development' tended to refer to the economic growth of the majority world, which was widely assumed to be a good thing. However, ideas about development have changed quite dramatically over time and there is a lack of agreement about what it is and what direction it should take. There is also the 'question of who decides what "development" consists of' (Sumner and Tribe 2008: 46). Generally development is about the process of improving people's standard of living, but we need to recognize that it is as much about social development as it is about economic development. Development is a contested, ambiguous and complex concept. Yet, despite a diversity of definitions, there is

> **. . . a general agreement on the view that 'development' encompasses continuous 'change' in a variety of aspects of human society. The dimensions of development are extremely diverse, including economic, social, political, legal and institutional structures, technology in various forms (including the physical or natural sciences, engineering and communications), the environment, religion, the arts and culture.**
>
> (Sumner and Tribe 2008: 11)

Over time, the notion of development has been questioned, particularly because the majority world continues to remain poor and arguably 'undeveloped'. Certainly there is a widening gap between the richest and poorest countries. As Chambers notes:

> **Development has been taken to mean different things at different times, in different places, and by different people in different professions and organizations. . . . Change is continuous in what changes and how it changes, and in what we see as good.**
>
> (Chambers 2005: 186)

A closer look

The meaning of 'development'

Table 9.4 outlines three different definitions of 'development'. The first is more historical, the second more related to policy and the third more ideological.

Table 9.4 Definitions of 'development'

Type of development	Characteristics of the development process
'Development' as a long-term process of structural societal transformation	A major societal shift with a long-term outlook, for example moving from a rural or agriculture-based society to an urban or industrial-based society (sometimes referred to as a shift from 'traditional' to 'modern' society)
'Development' as a short- to medium-term outcome of desirable targets	A focus on the outcomes of change, with a relatively short-term outlook; achieving goals that can be measured and compared with targets, such as poverty reduction or changes in income levels
'Development' as a dominant 'discourse' of Western modernity	A postmodern conceptualization of development based on a view that development has resulted in 'bad' change and 'bad' outcomes, which have been imposed on the majority world by the minority world. This has led to development being equated with 'modernity' and superiority. 'The "discourse" is socially constructed and places values on certain assets which the South does not have. Thus, it is argued, the South is viewed as "inferior"' (Sumner and Tribe 2008: 15)

(Source: adapted from Sumner and Tribe 2008: 11–16)

He emphasises that 'If development means good change, questions arise about what is good and what sort of change matters' (Chambers 2005: 184). Furthermore, development refers to values, aspirations and social goals and is also linked to ethical and moral ideas (Potter *et al.* 2008). This is why debates about development can be emotionally charged and linked to strong ideas about how the world should develop and progress.

Development theories

Competing theories of social change exist in relation to the ways in which the minority world has developed, such as the classic theories of Marx, Weber and Durkheim, followed by those of more modern social theorists such as Foucault, Parsons and Giddens (see Chapter 2). There are many social theorists, and they all have different views as to how and why societies have evolved and developed over time. It is unsurprising, then, that many different theories have been put forward to explain how the majority world has developed (or not developed) over time. Collectively, these are known as development theories, and within this large body of theory there are different schools of thought; the main ones are considered here.

Modernization theory

Modernization theory emerged in the 1950s around the time that the colonized countries were gaining their independence. There was much discussion about how these countries would develop and modernize. According to modernization theorists, development 'depends on "traditional", "primitive" values being displaced by modern ones' (Webster 1990: 49). Webster suggests that traditional societies have three key features:

- traditionalism is dominant (people are perceived to be tied to the past and not welcoming of new ideas);
- the kinship system is important (one's role and status in society is ascribed, not achieved);
- traditional societies have an 'emotional, superstitious and fatalistic approach to the world' (Webster 1990: 50).

This contrasts with modern societies, where people are more likely to progress culturally than hold on to traditional customs, where kinship is less important as status can be earned through achievement, and where people are forward-looking and willing to be innovative. Modernization theorists argue that tradition acts like a barrier to development and that poor

A closer look

Development theories over time

Classic development theories

- *1950s and 1960s: modernization theory* – After colonialism there was a perceived need for the majority world to 'modernize' and industrialize in similar ways to the capitalist progress of the minority world.
- *1970s: theories of underdevelopment: dependency theory and world systems theory* – These theories emerged as a critique of modernization theory, recognizing that it was too simplistic to expect the majority world to industrialize along Western lines when their historical development had been so hindered by colonialism.

Alternative development theories

- *1980s: sustainable development* – This is a call to ensure that processes of development are sustainable by not exhausting resources and not compromising the needs of future generations.
- *1990s: participatory development* – This reflects a recognition that, if development is to be successful, people should be given opportunities to participate and have a say in their own development. Effective progress cannot simply be imposed from above or from outside; rather, it needs to involve those at the grass-roots level.

Each of these accounts varies as to what the 'problem' of development is and what the possible solutions are.

countries can be too reluctant to change and modernize. For example, they suggest that rural peasants are perhaps too keen to hold on to their traditions rather than move forward and change to more modern lifestyles. Modernization theory claims that industrialization is the answer to accumulating wealth (see Rostow's model of economic development in the case study below). Poor countries in the majority world should follow the industrial model of the minority world, and their resulting economic growth would result in a decline in poverty. As we shall see later in this section, these ideas have been criticized for being too simplistic.

Hettne (1995) notes the strong role of dichotomy in early development thinking. For example, in modernization theory there is a juxtaposition of traditional versus modern societies that is often polarized as backward or primitive societies in contrast to advanced and civilized societies. It is often assumed that there is a dualism between the traditional, indigenous and underdeveloped majority world versus the modern, developed and Westernized minority world (Potter *et al.* 2008). Webster (1990) argues that, according to modernization theory, the history of development of industrialization in the minority world is the blueprint for majority world societies and that they should follow the same pathway. Thus, development can be achieved by imitating the Western model. In other words, modernization is often perceived as being the same as Westernization (Hettne 1995) and is also based predominantly on urban industrial growth. The minority world can help the majority world to develop in such a way by introducing ideas and technologies. Thus, the experience of the West can assist other countries in 'catching up' by sharing both capital and know-how (Potter *et al.* 2008).

Modernization theory perceives development to be a relatively straightforward, linear process. It recognizes that different societies are at different stages of development, and that some are more modernized than others, but if countries have the right values and ambition then underdevelopment can be overcome, especially by entrepreneurial innovations (Potter *et al.* 2008). The important characteristics are individual motivation and capital accumulation (Webster 1990). Thus, modernization theory provided:

> **. . . a great source of justification for the activities of development agencies. A whole range of policies were fostered by modernisation theory . . . They have included the injection of capital to aid both industrial 'take-off' and the commercialisation of agriculture, the training of an entrepreneurial elite in the values and motivations most likely to promote free enterprise, the expansion of educational programmes, and only assisting 'democratic' (or notionally democratic) countries.**
>
> (Webster 1990: 55)

Modernization theorists assume that developing the urban centre eventually leads to a 'trickling down' of growth to the more peripheral backward regions, so that it spreads from urban to rural areas. However, as we shall see in the following section, others strongly disagree with this view. According to modernization theory, these trickle-down effects are assumed to be

Case study

Rostow's *Stages of Economic Growth: A Non-Communist Manifesto*

Rostow (1960) developed a five-stage model of development, based on an analysis of the British industrial revolution:

1. The traditional society.
2. The preconditions for take-off.
3. Take-off.
4. The drive to maturity.
5. The age of high mass consumption.

According to Rostow the key features for success and development are entrepreneurial ambition alongside capital accumulation and investment. His model suggested that all countries have an equal chance to progress. The central argument was that the majority world needed to industrialize in order to develop (Potter *et al.* 2008).

inevitable (Hirschman 1958, cited in Potter *et al.* 2008). Hirschman's view is that governments should not intervene in order to reduce inequalities, as there will be spin-off effects of growth in peripheral areas. This goes hand in hand with the liberal model of 'letting the market decide'. Modernization theory, although academically criticized (see below), came to represent a framework for much development policy that focused on the expansion of manufacturing. However, it is worth recognizing that this is a top-down approach to development (Potter *et al.* 2008) that was strongly associated with the 1950s through to the early 1970s.

Dependency theory

Dependency theory emerged from Latin America in the 1960s as a way of explaining the continued failure of Latin American countries to develop economically. Its followers were also referred to as the Latin American structuralists because they focused on the unseen structures that may be held to mould and shape society (Potter *et al.* 2008). They argued that 'persistent poverty in countries like Argentina, Peru, Chile and Brazil was *caused* by exposure to the economic and political influences of the advanced countries' (Webster 1990: 85). This school of thought became globally popular in the 1970s, particularly the argument that the growth of the minority world led to the simultaneous underdevelopment of the majority world because the industrialized countries exploited the poorer countries and developed at their expense. It was recognized that the core (the privileged minority world) can learn from the periphery (the marginalized majority world) (Potter *et al.* 2008).

Thus, in the 1970s, dependency theorists argued that industrialization and economic development as encouraged by modernization theorists had not happened in the majority world. They explained that it would not happen because poor countries would not be able to follow the same path of industrial development as that of the richer countries. Dependency theory states that the colonial past of the majority world cannot be ignored and that the majority world continues to be dominated by the minority world in a form of neo-colonialism, as we saw earlier. Dependency theorists explain global inequality in terms of the historical exploitation of poor societies by rich ones, and argue that this unequal power relationship continues today in a variety of forms (debt, aid, transnational corporations, unequal global trading). According to them, this system of neo-colonialism makes poor societies poorer and more reliant on richer, capitalist societies.

Andre Gunder Frank's book *Capitalism and Underdevelopment in Latin America* (1967) was widely known for arguing that the continued poverty in the majority world was a reflection of its 'dependency' on the minority world. His key argument was that development and underdevelopment are opposite sides of the same coin, and both are the outcome of capitalism (Potter *et al.* 2008). *The Development of Underdevelopment*, which he wrote in 1966, summarized his approach: 'the condition of developing countries is not the outcome of inertia, misfortune, chance, climatic conditions or whatever, but rather a reflection of the manner of their incorporation into the global capitalist system' (Potter *et al.* 2008: 110). According to Frank (1966), underdevelopment is the direct outcome of development elsewhere. In other words, the advanced capitalist world both exploited the majority world and kept it underdeveloped.

Hettne (1995) points out that dependency theorists emphasize that the international division of labour is a key barrier to development rather than a lack of skill or capital. Frank (1967) argued that colonialism forced a specialization of production on majority world countries. This led them to mainly sell raw materials that the minority world needed and resulted in their production being limited, mostly specialized and export-oriented:

> **The Third World elites were incorporated into this system and could do little to establish a more diverse, independent form of economic activity. They became the mere intermediaries between the rich purchasers and the poor (peasant) producers. . . While the Third World elite enjoy a high standard of living from this relationship, the masses experience chronic deprivation as their surplus production is taken from them in the local rural region and transferred to the rich farmers and merchants in their own country and then on abroad.**
>
> (Webster 1990: 85)

Thus, Frank (1967) argues that there is a 'chain of dependency' going from rich countries (which he calls 'metropoles') to peripheral, subordinate areas ('satellites'). Then, within 'satellites' there are hierarchies running from rich merchants down to peasants. Hence, the process of subordination and exploitation operates both internationally and internally within countries, where backwardness results from

A closer look

The chain of dependency

Exploitative and unequal relations exist from dominant metropoles running down through a hierarchy of subordinate satellites. According to Potter *et al.*:

> 'The chain of exploitative relations witnesses the extraction and transmission of surplus value via a process of unequal exchange, extending from the peasant, through the market town, regional centre, national capital, to the international metropole . . . The terms of trade have always worked in favour of the next higher level in the chain.'
>
> (Potter *et al.* 2008: 112)

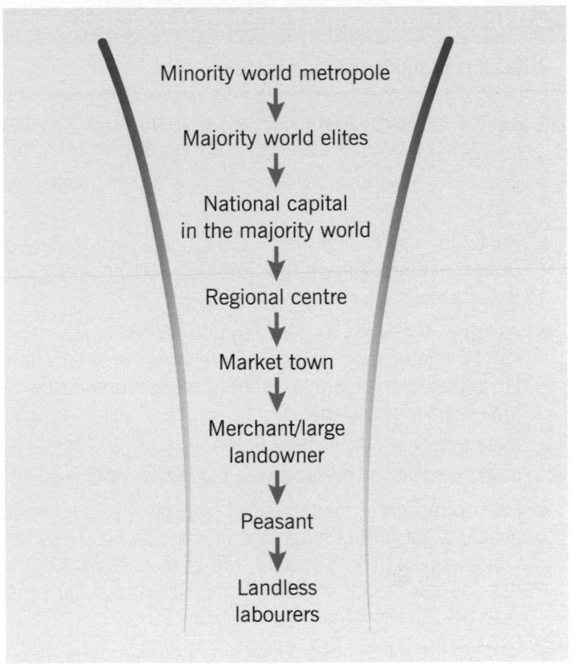

Figure 9.6 The chain of dependency

being at the bottom of the dependence hierarchy (Potter *et al.* 2008). Frank suggests that this means that the satellites are held back by the metropoles.

According to dependency theorists, the only way of stopping the exploitation is if the chain of dependency (Figure 9.6) is broken. The working class in the majority world could achieve this through a socialist revolution (Webster 1990). Thus, 'the development of young economies required withdrawal from the structure of exploitation that existed worldwide' (Regan and Ruth 2002: 31). The other alternative requires state intervention in order to weaken the dominance of the global system by imposing controls on trade and transnational corporations, as well as facilitating local production and indigenous development (Potter *et al.* 2008). Thus, dependency theory argues that the historical process of colonialism, and the continued existence of neo-colonialism, is of extreme importance in explaining global inequalities.

Alternative development

From the 1950s to the 1980s modernization and dependency theories dominated the discussions of development theorists. During the 1980s it was recognized that both of these theoretical positions were flawed and did not adequately reflect the contemporary processes of development. This led to the emergence of more context-specific micro-theories based on empirical research:

> **Modernization theories were criticized for their overriding belief in a linear, common path to development through economic growth and industrialization, especially as the environmental impacts of industrialization became more evident. There were also criticisms of a perceived over-emphasis on the 'macro' to the neglect of the 'micro'.**
>
> (Sumner and Tribe 2008: 87)

Thus, rather than having grand theories to explain the whole process of development, smaller-scale, context-specific theories were developed, such as participatory development (see below) and sustainable development (see Chapter 10). By the 1990s this new way of thinking about development became known as 'alternative development' or 'another development'. The approach was also referred to as 'development from below', 'grass-roots development' and a 'bottom-up

A closer look

Table 9.5 Criticism of modernization and dependency theories

Criticisms of modernization theory	Criticisms of dependency theory
• Failure to recognize the diversity of 'traditional' societies, e.g. tribal groups, feudal, caste societies, peasant societies • Focuses on the way societies develop rather than explaining *why* • Based too much on a linear and rational path to development, rather than recognizing that tradition and modernity can occur simultaneously • Assumes that with modernization extended family networks will be undermined, rather than recognizing that patterns of kinship may change and adapt to modern circumstances and may remain important • Fails to recognize that traditional roles could still be used in modern societies as resources, e.g. local crafts such as pottery • Fails to recognize that so-called 'conservative' and traditional peasants are often the most vulnerable groups in society, which makes them less able (rather than less willing) to take risks in order to progress economically; thus, their conservatism may be rational rather than illogical • Ignores the impact of colonialism and underplays the importance of history; needs to accept the role of external forces (i.e. the dominance of the minority world and its impact on development in the majority world) • Based on a minority world perspective of 'development'	• 'Dependency' as a concept is too vague and difficult to measure • Implies that the countries of the majority world are static and that all the surplus is taken out to the minority world so that no internal development is possible • Focuses on the exchange and transfer of surplus from satellites to metropoles, yet does not fully explain this process, denying that it may lead to some local development • Fails to analyse production relations properly, overlooking that there is potential for industrial growth in the majority world • Too economistic: suggests that the only way out is by delinking from the global economy, which nowadays is not particularly realistic • Fails to recognize the role of cultural processes, and that underdevelopment is also influenced and shaped by local cultures and local political structures • Fails to recognize that internal obstacles to growth are just as political as economic: the majority world is also at fault – majority world countries not only are passive victims but also must address internal problems, such as unstable governments, political in-fighting and corruption

(Source: adapted from Webster 1990)

approach'. The new paradigm emerged because 'development' had not really been working. Although some economic and social advances had been made, on the whole poverty in the majority world was not being alleviated and in some cases, such as sub-Saharan Africa, it was getting worse. Some argued that development was

> **. . . at best, an irrelevance which has failed to meet its own aims to improve standards of living and, at worst, has been a neo-colonial or western imposition on 'the Other' by claiming to 'know' about 'the Other' and what is good for 'the Other'.**
>
> (Sumner and Tribe 2008: 164)

Development was not trickling down to the poor, so there had to be a major rethink about what development entails. From the mid-1980s some anti-development thinking emerged, with talk of 'the end of development' (see Parfitt 2002) or being in an age of post-development. Thus, alternative approaches to development responded to this crisis by focusing on sustainability and participation as a possible way of avoiding some of the mistakes that had been made. It is thought that one of the key solutions to the problems of development is self-reliance:

> **The concept of self-reliance not only implies breaking the tie of dependency on the industrial**

centre but also an acceptance of the need to use available resources as efficiently and frugally as possible.

(Webster 1990: 181)

Sustainable development stresses the need for self-reliance and ecological sensitivity (this approach is discussed in detail in Chapter 10). Like sustainability, processes of participation are also central in recent approaches to development. The danger of development is that

> **. . . the poor are seen almost as passive victims and subjects of investigation rather than as human beings with something to contribute to both the investigation of their conditions and its alleviation. The poor often have quite different interpretations from outsiders about the particular problems they face. Rather than income levels or housing conditions, they place great importance on their vulnerability to sudden stress through insecurity.**

(Drakakis-Smith 2000: 133)

Participatory approaches: a way forward?

Frequently in the past 'outsiders', often from the minority world, assumed that they knew what poor people wanted. There is a more recent recognition that we need to understand and learn from indigenous knowledge: 'Participatory approaches essentially developed out of research techniques which sought to give citizens a greater voice in the decision-making processes affecting their lives' (Drakakis-Smith 2000: 178). This is much broader than merely listening to people's views; it is about empowering people to change their environment and to take action to improve their living standards. This kind of bottom-up development means 'facilitating a process through which the poor can begin to define and work towards their own development' (Parfitt 2002: 159). It is about providing projects that are more responsive to local people's needs and are less imposed from the outside. Local people are encouraged to identify and analyse their own problems and then to generate local knowledge on which appropriate action can be based (Parfitt 2002).

Robert Chambers (2005) is one of the key figures in promoting participatory development and is known for trying to put the last first (i.e. the poor before the rich). In particular he advocates trying to involve the most marginalized people, 'the poorest of the poor'. Shepherd (1998) reminds us that participation is also concerned with increasing local people's control over resources and is related to issues of equity and empowerment. Participatory development should involve collaborative planning, whereby a range of stakeholders are consulted, such as local government and policymakers, rich farmers who own much land, poor farmers who own little or no land, farmers' families, and young people. This enables issues relating to gender, age and generation to be taken into account, rather than focusing only on the perspectives of male adults. Excluding different groups such as women or children from development initiatives is detrimental not only to the young people or women concerned but also to development goals and the effectiveness of projects or relevance of policies (Chawla and Johnson 2004). This is a much more complex approach to development:

> **Consultation with groups who are likely to be principally affected (either positively or negatively) by a project, programme or policy can provide a basis for an enhanced positive impact, and/or a reduced negative impact . . . The process of consultation – or participation – can be used as a basis for the modification of the design of a project, programme or policy in order to make it more acceptable and more effective in achieving the objectives and priorities of communities.**

(Sumner and Tribe 2008: 142–3)

Participatory research has certainly increased our understanding about the complexity and diversity of poor people's livelihoods. However, there are different definitions of participation, which reflect the varying degrees to which people participate:

- Participation as a voluntary contribution, where people have some say and their voice is heard to some extent but they do not play a key role in shaping the development programme
- Participation consisting of people's involvement in decision-making processes, in implementing and evaluating the development programme
- Participation as organized efforts to control resources and be empowered
- Community participation as an active process whereby participants influence the direction, execution and outcomes of a development project (Parfitt 2002).

Different levels of participation range from being tokenistic, to being consulted and informed, to participating fully throughout the development process. There is a danger that development projects may only pay lip-service to notions of participation, and that groups are informed about proposed interventions, rather than becoming agents of their own development in a meaningful way: 'Often, however, the consultation process is restricted to "key" figures in the community with a corresponding limitation in beneficiaries' (Drakakis-Smith 2000: 180).

Meaningful participation is extremely difficult to achieve in practice and means changing existing power relations in decision-making and empowering those who previously have been ignored. As we have seen, participatory development is about increasing local people's control over resources; therefore, it is also linked to power relationships, because in order for effective participation to take place, a redistribution of power has to take place (Shepherd 1998). This has the potential to create conflicts as not everyone will be happy about redistributing power from the powerful to the powerless. Many people may find it threatening to their existing position in society.

Participatory development is not a straightforward process, but in order to facilitate hearing the voices of the most marginalized people a range of participatory techniques have been developed. Over the years different terms have been used to describe these methods: participatory rural appraisal (PRA), participatory action research (PAR) and rapid rural appraisal (RRA). The aim of participatory techniques is to bring insiders and outsiders to a closer understanding of each other. Visual and verbal tools are used to encourage local people to express their views and have their opinions taken into account when thinking about community planning and development (Shepherd 1998). The visual and accessible nature of many exercises enables non-literate people to participate.

Critiques of participatory development

It is important to be aware that, while there are strong arguments for participatory development as an appropriate approach to improving people's livelihoods, there are also many problems associated with it. It is extremely difficult to ensure that participation is approached in the right kind of way. Cooke and Kothari's book *Participation: The New Tyranny?* (2001) puts forward some very strong criticisms that challenge the claims of participatory development, particularly the assumptions about it being more effective than other approaches, and the often misplaced assumption that it always empowers poor people. Participatory development is highly complex and problematic to achieve effectively. McGee (2002) refers to this as being a predominance of rhetoric over authenticity; there can be more talk rather than action in relation to participation. She also recognizes that most participation on the ground is still just about people 'participating in projects' rather than becoming fully empowered and implementing change and improvements in their own livelihoods. Thus, we need to be aware that participation can be used superficially, insensitively and tokenistically.

As Shepherd suggests, there is a danger that it becomes a quick-fix solution, with the assumption that, just because participatory techniques are being employed, then the project must therefore be 'participatory'. He argues that 'Participation requires attitude change: understanding, humility, flexibility and patience' (Shepherd 1998: 182–3). Training in participatory methods is needed at all levels if people are to understand fully how they should work in practice. For example, if development workers are trained only briefly in PRA, then they may use the techniques ritualistically as a way of building rapport initially but then continue the project in a top-down way. Training needs to be continuous and reflexive, not just a one-off session at the start of a development project. Thus, participatory development can be an expensive, time-consuming and very small-scale approach. It involves great time commitments from farmers, development workers, researchers and other participants (Shepherd 1998). Furthermore, it can be a long time before changes emerge; much patience may be required to wait for results. If people do not see any tangible benefits for some time, then their motivation to continue to participate may decrease. Another problem is that enabling people to participate and have their voices heard may lead to unrealistic expectations of what participatory development can achieve.

Parfitt (2002) reminds us that outsiders need to learn from people on the ground, rather than overemphasizing their own views. Sometimes development practitioners impose their ideologies and definitions. Furthermore, many grass-roots people may not be used to criticizing the common discourses of the dominant elites. In addition, if care is not taken to enable the most marginalized people to participate, then it may be that the usual people take part – the most educated and the most articulate. Women, children,

A closer look

Key elements of alternative development strategies

- *Targeting the poor* – A bottom-up approach means starting with the poor and concentrating on meeting their needs.
- *Local small-scale projects* – Focus on community-based development projects where people live, involving relatively simple production techniques, using local materials and not requiring large capital investment.
- *Basic needs* – Food, clothing and housing should be the first priority.
- *Human-oriented frameworks* – An emphasis on human resource development, such as creating employment, rather than focusing only on economic growth.
- *Participation* – At local and community levels in order to involve people in the design and implementation of appropriate projects to meet their needs.
- *Self-reliance and appropriate technology* – Reducing dependency on the minority world and focusing on sustainability.

(Source: Brohman 1996)

disabled people, people from ethnic minorities and very poor people are likely to remain excluded if they are not prioritized (Shepherd 1998). It can be difficult to incorporate everyone's voices, to be sensitive to issues of gender and generation and to have a reflexive understanding of power and participation. As Parpart reminds us, the difficulties of truly listening to others in an open, interactive way should not be underestimated:

> **It requires the recognition that differences, and different voices, cannot just be heard, that language is powerful and that subjectivity (voices) are constructed and embedded in the complex experiential and discursive environments of daily life. Overcoming these barriers is not easy.**
>
> (Parpart 1995: 239)

However, despite all the problems, limitations and 'cautious optimism' associated with participatory development, McGee notes that the development agenda has now changed as a result of the participation discourse:

> **At the level of rhetoric, the participation orthodoxy no longer finds it sufficient to permit 'them' to participate in 'our' projects, but recognizes that 'our' projects are not going to change their lives much, and seeks to find out what 'their' projects of life might be, and how we – practitioners, academics, NGOs [non-governmental organisations], official agencies and partner governments – might most usefully participate in them.**
>
> (McGee 2002: 113)

For participatory development to be effective, a range of facilitating factors need to be in place: appropriate training, political support, decentralization, community organizations, availability of good leaders and managers, and technologies that promote self-reliance.

Thus, a bottom-up approach offers no easy solution, as it needs to be context-specific and linked closely to the particular sociocultural, historical and institutional conditions (Potter *et al.* 2008). For it to be effective, it should be based on the use of local resources, self-reliance, appropriate technology and participation. What is right for one country may not be right for another. The type of alternative development strategy that is applied needs to be tailored to the particular socioeconomic and cultural context.

Globalization

Stop and think

- Is globalization new? Or is it just an extension of earlier global processes?
- Is the world really becoming more uniform? Or are inequalities increasing?
- Will the benefits of globalization trickle down and improve the lives of the poorest people, or will there be increasing polarization between the rich and the poor?

Whether development is considered to have been successful in parts or a failure at times, there is little doubt that globalization is a fact of twenty-first-century life. Like the term 'development', globalization is also a highly contentious and contested concept. There are different definitions, many of which refer to the blurring of boundaries between the local and the global: 'a world in which societies, cultures, politics and economies have, in some sense, come closer together' (Kiely 1998: 3). Hence it is a stretching of social, political and economic activities across countries and continents, when 'the boundaries between domestic matters and global affairs become increasingly blurred' (McGrew 2000: 347).

A key feature of globalization is the notion of global interconnectedness (Sklair 1999): 'the free movement of goods, services, capital, information and, in some instances, people, across national boundaries' (Potter *et al.* 2008: 128). People increasingly talk about a 'globalizing world' and an era of global change. This is in relation to a range of changes, such as the notion of a global economy (trade and investment) and a global culture. It also includes recent developments in communications such as the Internet and email. New forms of communication and transport have led to the speeding up of global interaction: goods, ideas, information, capital and people can be linked up increasingly quickly. Globalization also applies to the way in which the effects of distant events can be felt locally:

> **. . . it refers to the ways in which developments in one region can rapidly come to have significant consequences for the security and well-being of communities in quite distant regions of the globe.**
>
> (McGrew 2000: 347)

What is happening in one part of the world can affect far away locations; local events can have global consequences. For example, the events of 11 September 2001 in New York had a big impact on global tourism as many people cancelled or postponed their travel plans. In London, some theatres had to close because they were not being attended by North American visitors, and even as far away as Hong Kong some tourist companies were struggling to get enough people to be able to organize day trips to local attractions.

There are some who connect the negative aspects of globalization to terrorism: 'The linking of globalisation, inequalities, division and danger in the post-11 September 2001 world is highly salient' (Potter *et al.* 2008: 169). Some writers argue that continuing exploitation and increasing global inequalities contribute to the creation and development of terrorist networks. The efficiency of contemporary technology enables such networks to spread throughout the world, so to some extent terrorism is also 'globalized'. As Cohen and Kennedy suggest in relation to the events of 11 September:

> **In the midst of their grief and anger, it may be that it was too much to expect that the American people would ask, let alone answer, this question: Does the growing inequality both within and between the nations of the world, coupled with a one-sided exercise of power by a few actors go some way towards explaining why violent and abusive acts are perpetrated by criminal and terrorist gangs against innocent citizens?**
>
> (Cohen and Kennedy 2007: 3)

'Globalization' is probably one of the most used and abused words in our vocabulary (Potter *et al.* 2008). Many things are blamed on globalization, and the world is now seen as more global. Many argue that globalization is not necessarily new, but that the rate and intensity of it have increased (McGrew 2000). Certainly the extent of global change is impressive when we consider the relatively recent advent of the Internet, email and mobile phones. Could you go back to 'surviving' without them? You might like to reflect on what changes you would have to make to your life if you no longer had such communication media.

Cohen and Kennedy point out that it is increasingly difficult to live without a global awareness of our connections with other people in distant places. For example, even in remote rural communities,

> **Jet planes and helicopters fly overhead, travellers appear as if from nowhere, roads are cut into the interior, mobile phones ring, the world's music pulsates from cheap transistor radios, while friends, neighbours and families share what they have seen on the ubiquitous TV screens.**
>
> (Cohen and Kennedy 2007: 7)

Even where there are no televisions or telephone lines, people can still be interconnected to the wider world to some extent. They may have more limited knowledge than people from other places, but they are likely to have some global awareness and information about life outside their community. Hence, a process that is related to globalization is 'globality':

> **Whereas globalization refers to the objective, external ties that bind us together, globality alludes to the subjective, personal awareness that many of us share, and are increasingly likely to share – a common fate.**
>
> (Cohen and Kennedy 2007: 7)

A key aspect of globality is reflexivity, and this is an important sociological concept. Reflexivity is the critical assessment of oneself and others. It is when we reflect on the consequences of our own and other people's actions, thereby having self-awareness and self-knowledge as we contemplate how our lives are changing. As we accumulate knowledge about how the social world works, we then revise our own behaviour in response to this new information (Cohen and Kennedy 2007). This happens all the time; for example, we become increasingly aware about using appropriate language in relation to changing understandings of social divisions such as race, disability and age. Older terms such as 'third world' become unacceptable, and new terms are introduced, such as 'majority world'. Thus, globality leads to us thinking about ourselves collectively. It means that we have a common interest in collective action to solve global problems, such as having an environmental awareness or a concern for human rights. Globality encourages us to be reflexive about social problems that affect others and not just ourselves. Thus, globalization refers to a series of changes that are taking place, and globality refers to our awareness of those changes.

A shrinking world?

One of the central aspects of global change is the compression of time and space, which makes it seem like the world is getting smaller (Allen 1995). The world is considered to be shrinking as distances are effectively decreased through faster and more efficient transport. Improvements in communications, such as cable, satellite and digital television, mean that we are informed of what is happening in the world more rapidly than ever before. As we are increasingly aware of what is happening in distant places, what are the social implications of this? These global changes call for a rethinking of our ethical and moral responsibilities to people who live far away, as we now are more aware of how they live their lives (Potter *et al.* 2008). However, it is worth bearing in mind that the mass media tends to refer to the majority world only when reporting bad news such as environmental disasters, riots and famine. There is a danger that we can be bombarded with images of poverty, particularly during a crisis, and we become hardened to it.

Even though the world is shrinking, not everyone shares the benefits of globalization. In some parts of the world, having a television is a luxury that is unaffordable for some people. Places that are not well connected to the global network are strongly disadvantaged. For example, it can be more expensive to fly from poorer countries to rich countries because of limited or less frequent links with other airports. Thus, the process of the shrinking world in terms of time and space can be experienced by people in different ways.

There is increased interconnectivity because of improvements in electronic communication, particularly the Internet and email, but also mobile phones, text messages and faxes. We now have the ability to move information and data quickly and cheaply. This is often referred to as the coming of the 'information society' (Castells 1996). This may offer poor countries new opportunities to be more globally connected. However, we need to be wary about assuming that the majority world can benefit from the spread of new technologies (Potter *et al.* 2008). The expansion of information technology has been highly uneven, creating an international 'digital divide'. Differences exist in the ability to access the Internet and in the skills required to use information technologies. Access to the Internet in many countries of the majority world is controlled by the state or is available only to a small minority who can afford it. Kiely points out:

> **At least 80 per cent of the world's population still lack access to the most basic communication technologies, and nearly 50 countries have fewer than one telephone line per 100 people. There are more telephone lines in Manhattan than there are in the whole of sub-Saharan Africa. While the United States has 35 computers per 100 people, even rapidly developing South Korea has only 9, while for Ghana the figure is as low as 0.11. Although the number of Internet users has expanded dramatically in recent years, its use is still largely confined to Western Europe and the United States.**
>
> (Kiely 1998: 5)

There is massive global inequality in access to telephones and even greater unequal access to computers. Thus, as Potter *et al.* (2008) remind us, the role of the Internet in improving the development of the majority world is based on misplaced optimism as poor people are likely to be further marginalized as a result of technical advances. Without wide access to phones and computers, majority world countries are going to be even less able to compete in the global economy. Therefore, expensive technologies mean that the relatively rich become the information-rich and that 'the digital divide is likely to exacerbate the differences existing between the world's haves and have nots in the twenty-first century' (Potter *et al.* 2008: 145).

It is recognized that the impacts of globalization are very uneven and vary from region to region and from one social group to another. The impacts, like the term itself, are highly debated, uneven and diverse (Hoogvelt 2001). However, we do have to be wary about our use of the term 'globalization'. It is a highly contested term in current social science thinking, and there are many different perspectives on it. Globalization is a complex process; the three main strands of globalization that we consider here are economic, cultural and political.

A global economy?

There are three key economic aspects of globalization that this section considers: global cities, transnational corporations (TNCs) and the new international division of labour (NIDL). The majority world experiences the fastest rates of urbanization (the proportion of a national population living in urban centres):

> **For much of human history, life was rural. In the year 1800, 97 per cent of the world's population lived in rural areas. Wind the clock on 200 years and we find that 254 cities each contained over one million people.**
>
> (Cohen and Kennedy 2007: 14)

One of the patterns of urban change in the majority world is that a high proportion of the urban population in some countries is concentrated in one or two major cities (Elliott 2006). 'Megacity' is a recent term used to describe a large sprawling urban complex with a population of more than eight million; many such cities are in the majority world. In contrast, 'global cities' or 'world cities' are those that dominate world affairs, and most of these are in the minority world; they include London, New York, Paris and Tokyo. Potter *et al.* (2008) argue that, despite this emerging network of world cities, these cities are highly centred and are not distributed evenly throughout the world. Most are located in the richer countries, although there are some important cities in certain parts of the majority world, such as Singapore, Bangkok, Johannesburg, Shanghai and Mexico. Overall most large cities in the majority world are not linked to global networks, compared with their counterparts in the minority world (Kiely 1998).

Friedmann (1995) argues that there are several key features of world cities that make them centres for capital accumulation. They have large populations and large manufacturing bases, they are finance and service centres, and they are a key link for transport to other places. Global cities are important as individual cities but also because of their relationship to each other. As Cohen and Kennedy point out:

> **Increasingly, many wealthier people living and working in global cities, or travelling there, find that they share conditions of life, attitudes, behaviour patterns and tastes with equivalent residents of other global cities. They lose their national culture or downgrade it in favour of an international and cosmopolitan culture.**
>
> (Cohen and Kennedy 2000: 17)

It is worth remembering that not only wealthy people live in such cities; many poor people can suffer greater marginalization and social exclusion as a result of living in world cities surrounded by so much wealth.

Transnational corporations (TNCs) are multinational firms that have the power to operate in more than one country. There has been capital investment from TNCs to the majority world, taking advantage of poorer countries being a source of cheap labour. The global economy is increasingly unstable because of fluctuations in commodity prices and exchange rates, and so TNCs have to cope with this uncertainty and take risks that majority world countries are less able to do. The location of TNCs in the majority world is limited geographically, focusing on South East Asia, South Africa, Mexico and parts of South America. Thus, like global cities, the distribution of TNCs is uneven and concentrated in particular areas. This can lead to increased inequalities between areas of the majority world. Some TNCs have annual turnovers that exceed the gross national products of some poor countries (Potter *et al.* 2008). TNCs represent the increasing concentration of capital on a world scale. Their growth is one of the key features of neo-colonialism as they exert control over the raw materials and labour power of the majority world.

There is a debate about the extent to which TNCs are beneficial or detrimental to the development of the majority world. Modernization theorists claim that multinational corporations will boost the host country's economic development and that there will be a trickle-down effect of wealth (Webster 1990). They argue that TNCs create many jobs for local people and introduce new technologies and foreign capital, and that this will lead to some industrial development locally. In contrast, dependency theorists argue that TNCs do not benefit the majority world, as they do not serve their long-term needs. They suggest that TNCs do not lead to a redistribution of resources; nor do they enhance majority world countries' capacity for self-determined development. Many of the benefits of TNCs are for the minority world companies themselves rather than for the host countries. For example, new production, innovations, capital and social surplus are unlikely to trickle down to the majority world (Potter *et al.* 2008).

Those in favour of dependency theory argue that multinationals only intensify global inequality, as they stifle the development of local industries that would provide a better source of local employment. Furthermore, TNCs tend to produce expensive consumer goods for export to rich countries rather than food and other necessities that local people need. Dependency theorists point out that TNCs set up in poor majority world countries because the cost of labour is so much cheaper there, and 'most transnational companies invest the bulk of their capital in their home country, and most of these same companies' foreign investment is in other "advanced" capitalist countries' (Kiely 1998: 11). Thus, TNCs move to poorer countries in order to exploit their cheap labour power, not to help them industrialize. Investment by TNCs in the majority world has often been justified in the name of development, claiming that TNCs create employment, provide investment of capital and introduce new technologies. However, others argue that TNCs do not provide majority world people with many new skills, as the jobs often involve menial repetitive tasks and only a limited amount of the profit goes back into the local economy (Kiely 1998). In many ways it could be argued from a perspective of dependency theory that TNCs increase global divisions rather than decrease them, although modernization theorists are likely to disagree with this view.

Furthermore, industrial growth is distributed unequally at a global level. Nowadays economic activity is more globalized, as production processes have become more mobile and dispersed. This is often referred to as the new international division of labour (NIDL), which is 'the shift from manufacturing in Northern countries to industrial production in the South where land and labour costs are cheaper' (Willis 2005: 175). This 'global shift' (Dicken 2003) came about partly because of reduced industrial profits in Europe and the USA due to increasing costs of wages and the need to meet environmental standards in the minority world. New manufacturing plants were set up in the majority world, where costs are lower:

> **In October 2003, HSBC Bank announced that it was going to cut about 4,000 jobs from call centres in the UK and move them to Hyderabad in India. The Indian city has a suitably-qualified workforce at a fraction of the cost of the British workforce. In addition, telephone charges between the UK and India have fallen greatly, so making this movement financially viable. Before January 2001 a call from India to the UK would cost about 48.0 rupees, but by October 2003 this had fallen to 7.6 rupees.**
>
> (Willis 2005: 176–7)

This process was also facilitated by the recent developments in communications technology and the increasing mobility and flexibility of financial services. The speed of financial transactions has increased enormously in recent years; money can now exist in electronic form only and can be sent around the world in seconds. For example, to send a Moneygram from a high-street travel agent in Scotland to a bank in Argentina, the money is guaranteed to be available for collection ten minutes after the transaction is completed. Thus, distance is now less important, as corporations and financial transactions move around in a 'borderless' world.

A global culture?

Stop and think

- To what extent can we talk about the existence of a global culture? If there is such a thing, whose culture is becoming more global?
- Are we increasingly becoming more similar in terms of cultural styles?

There has certainly been a rise of global corporations and marketing activities, and this has resulted in the availability of standardized products across the world.

For example, product names such as McDonald's, Coca-Cola, Nike and Levi can be seen everywhere. Even television programmes can become globalized, and series such as *Big Brother* and *Pop Idol* now appear in many different countries. Consequently some writers argue that, as a result of these global products and markets, places are becoming very similar but in a particular Westernized or 'Americanized' way. Minority world forms of consumption and lifestyles tend to be dominant, and it can be argued that cultural homogenization is a form of cultural imperialism:

> **Cultural imperialism is rooted in a common-sense notion many of us understand: that the reduction in cultural differences around the world – for example, that France does not seem as distinctive as it did 30 years ago – is *because of* the distribution by global corporations of commodified Western culture, a process which has *worked to the advantage* of the USA and Western nations . . . Cultural flows are profoundly imbalanced, and dominant cultures are seen as threatening more vulnerable cultures.**
>
> (Mackay 2000: 60)

Terms such as 'Hollywoodization', 'Coca-Colanization' and 'McDonaldization' reflect how this process tends to be an expansion of Western knowledge, capital and culture to the rest of the world (Tomlinson 1999). Some perceive this to be a negative process that encourages 'rampant individualism, the trivializing obsession with consumerism and the endless search for distracting entertainment . . . an empty materialism where money has become the sole measure of all things and people' (Cohen and Kennedy 2007: 5).

The increasing similarity in consumer preferences and habits is often referred to as 'cultural globalization' or 'global convergence' (Potter 2002). The mass media have a strong influence in this process, as television, newspapers and magazines spread their advertising campaigns. Those people most able to engage with this global culture are from the middle and upper classes. Many poor people in the majority world may not be able to afford to eat in McDonald's. However, although they may not be able to participate to the same extent as wealthier people in certain aspects of a globalized culture, they may take part at times, such as by owning a pair of jeans or drinking Coca-Cola. The capitalist system has a vested interest in globalizing the expectations of consumption aspirations and tastes so that more products can be sold (Potter *et al.* 2008):

> **Few individuals living under today's global condition can escape being influenced by glimpses of the dazzlingly seductive lifestyles lived by the world's celebrity figures, or by the temptations of other people's cultural repertoires. This is because of our ceaseless exposure to the flows of ideas and information through the media, or because of migration and the stories and souvenirs brought by returning travellers.**
>
> (Cohen and Kennedy 2007: 5)

However, we need to be wary about assuming that local traditions are being lost as a result of the invasion of outside influences and global images. The notion that the world is engaging in the same global culture is an exaggeration and an oversimplification. We may live in a more globalized world, where TNCs dominate world patterns of consumption and production, but this is not the same as becoming increasingly similar. Furthermore, global cultural processes can lead to new opportunities for cultural hybridization, as new and old processes are mixed, taking on new forms and being reinterpreted locally (Willis 2005). For example, Bollywood is India's own version of Hollywood, which illustrates that different meanings can be attached to minority world consumption and lifestyles in different places.

Thus, rather than serving to erode local differences, global culture works alongside them (Allen 1995). It is also important to recognize that, in relation to aspects of global culture such as fashion, music and tourism, it is not merely a one-way flow from the minority world to the majority world. Majority world products can also become popular and influential in the minority world, such as curries, reggae music and salsa dancing. Consequently, globalization increases the spread of cultures throughout the world, but it could be argued to lead as much to diversity and difference as to uniformity and sameness.

Global politics?

Processes of both economic and cultural globalization have led to changes in global politics:

> **It is apparent that the stretching of social relations across space is giving rise to new networks through which political demands and power are transmitted, and these may be both formal (for example, transnational governmental institutions such as the UN) and informal (for example, grassroots political**

communities such as the anti-globalization movement).

(Murray 2006: 169)

There are global links between national and international organizations. Murray (2006) explains that there are now three basic types of institution: national governments, international organizations (such as the UN, the World Trade Organization (WTO), the International Monetary Fund (IMF) and the World Bank) and transnational organizations (such as non-governmental organizations (NGOs), TNCs, environmental groups and international protest groups).

This has led to a debate over the role of the nation-state in contemporary societies. It can be said that globalization has, to some extent, eroded the role and power of the nation-state. States once held clear authority within their borders, as countries were clearly divided and protected by border controls. Now there is a notion of a more porous nation-state, partly because of the transnational movement of capital and uncensored forms of communication, like the World Wide Web. For example, it is very difficult for governments to control and police the Internet. Furthermore, there has been a rolling back of the state in relation to economic policies, as there has been a tendency to open up markets and have less state intervention:

> **The last two decades have witnessed a dramatic shift away from state intervention to the market as the emphasis upon deregulation, privatization and economic liberalization continue to make economies and societies more open to the world.**
>
> (McGrew 2000: 348)

There are two relatively polarized views on the extent to which globalization has affected the role of the nation-state. Waters (2001) argues that the 'modernizers' believe that globalization has led to the erosion of the nation-state as it now has less power and a smaller role compared with the past. Held (1991) asserts that cultural and economic processes along with increasingly powerful TNCs are reducing the power of nation-states. In contrast, more 'realist' thinkers such as Dicken (2003) argue that the role of nation-states is changing but that they are adapting and still hold an important regulatory role. Murray suggests that 'Nation-states remain active in the reproduction of cultural values and norms, and perhaps even more so in the era of accelerated globalization as they seek a distinctive place on the global stage' (Murray 2006: 185).

The anti-globalization movement

Unequal global trading and economic liberalization have brought a wave of anti-globalization and anti-capitalist protests:

> **The anti-globalization movement (AGM) is a nebulous term used to describe a wide range of protest, lobby and interest groups. Although the movement broadcasts its message through a variety of channels it is the proliferation of street protests, often planned to take place at the same time as important capitalist summits or events, that has brought the AGM to the attention of the world. Actions have been staged in places as diverse as Seattle, Genoa, London, Hyderabad and Wellington. Some see this 'globalized resistance' as a unified reaction/resistance to transnational regulatory processes from above.**
>
> (Murray 2006: 205)

World in focus

The war on terror

The war on terror instigated by the first George W. Bush administration (2000 to 2004) following the attacks of 9/11 is, arguably, shaping a new global geopolitical order. The USA and its major allies, including the UK, Spain, Pakistan and Australia, have undertaken both military and 'diplomatic' offensives in countries including Afghanistan, Iraq, Iran, Yemen, the Philippines, Indonesia, Syria, Sudan and Lebanon, in an attempt to neutralize the terrorist networks that were behind 9/11. Intelligence sharing at the nation-state level has also formed a central part of this 'war'. The principal target is al-Qaeda, an alliance of radical Islamic groups that have used

World in focus *continued*

terrorist and military tactics for over two decades to defend what they perceive as the oppression of Muslims. The group was formed in 1988 by Osama Bin Laden in order to expand the *mujahideen* resistance to the Soviet occupation in Afghanistan. Despite US backing for this movement in the context of the Cold War, the USA and its Western allies (including Saudi Arabia) became the group's principal targets in the 1990s, motivated principally by the West's intervention in the Gulf War of 1990 to 1991 and the ongoing Israeli-Palestinian conflict. The events of 9/11 represented the climax of this conflict and unleashed US efforts designed to remove the threat, although attempts to uproot the network, and to invade Iraq, were ongoing during the Clinton years and before. The rhetoric of al-Qaeda is that the West, led by the USA, is waging a new crusade in the Middle East designed to impose its will and culture, and as such the conflict has far deeper historical roots. The terrorist networks that have evolved, partly in *response* to the war, are thought to be truly worldwide in their extent and represent an amorphous and globalized target for the USA and its allies. In this sense the war is the first of its kind – fought against a group that is not spatially bounded and that does not identify itself with any one nation-state. The International Institute for Strategic Studies has estimated that al-Qaeda has over 18,000 militants at its disposal spread across sixty countries. Critics have argued that this greatly overestimates the true extent of the network and that such claims should be seen as part of the USA's wartime propaganda.

The rhetoric of the USA during this 'war' has been 'you are either with us or against us', an approach which seeks to draw new geopolitical lines in ways which echo the Truman Doctrine. Those who clearly demonstrate that they are with the USA can expect grand rewards, as the issuing of reconstruction contracts in Iraq following the 'end' of the war there in 2004 illustrated . . .

Is it possible that we are moving into other defining moments in global geopolitics in the post-Cold War world? The Washington Consensus of neoliberalism and good governance is certainly being eclipsed by simplistic notions of 'with us or against us'. If this were not the case, why has the West increasingly turned a blind eye to the most illiberal and undemocratic politics of Pakistan, Saudi Arabia and Indonesia, for example? What is clear is that, as always, the lines around which imagined global geopolitical divisions are drawn are contingent on the desires and needs of those who are most powerful.

What is for sure is that the broader war on terror has already been used as a means to promote the diffusion of neoliberalism . . . The challenge for the USA, as the hegemonic global force, is that it must have legitimacy in what it does – lest it fall prey to accusations of isolationism and self-interest. That the will of the United Nations was flouted in assembling the invasion of Iraq, that WMDs [weapons of mass destruction] were not found, and that some terrorist suspects have been held without trial in the US base Guantanamo Bay for over three years, has spurred on the global resistance movement which seeks to counter the unregulated and illegitimate actions of the US-led coalition. As it stands, however, it is probably most accurate to see the war on terror as an expansion of the post-Cold War order propagated by the world's only superpower in its efforts to spread neoliberalism and the political models that best support this.

(Murray 2006: 197–201)

Questions

1. What, if any, are the links between globalization and terrorism?
2. Could it be argued that increasing global inequalities contribute to the emergence of global terrorism? If so, what are the sociological explanations for this?

Protesters feel that 'a different world is possible' and that globalization should be shaped by human intervention to enable it to be more sustainable and empowering for everyone. Global controls, standards, policies and even taxes could be introduced to make globalization more effective at reducing inequalities rather than increasing them:

> **. . . global institutions will need to be reformed and strengthened in appropriate ways if they are to deal with the transnational flows of the contemporary world in an effective and equitable way. In this context, the reinvigoration of the United Nations is absolutely essential for global stability.**
>
> (Murray 2006: 217)

As Potter *et al.* (2008) point out, pro-globalists are in favour of global free trade but are far less global in relation to globally based taxes or the unrestricted movement of labour across borders. International migration can be beneficial and detrimental to both the sending and destination countries:

> **International migrants can bring highly motivated labour, economic skills and cultural renewal to many countries. They fill gaps in the labour market, particularly in affluent Western countries where the population is ageing and fertility is low. Nonetheless, they have managed to inflame public sentiments in many countries and politicians have consequently sought to control and restrict their movement.**
>
> (Cohen and Kennedy 2007: 11)

Minority world governments tend to maintain strict border controls and restrict access, particularly to people from the majority world. Some argue that the introduction of global taxes, such as on international financial transactions, could be used to decrease global poverty (Potter *et al.* 2008). Real efforts to strive towards a global redistribution of wealth seem sensible but have little support in practice. A global tax would also be difficult to monitor, collect and redistribute; but certainly, if the negative impacts of globalization are to be addressed, then some assertive action needs to be taken.

A globalizing world?

One of the key questions to consider in relation to globalization is whether we are living in a shrinking world or a more unequal world. As we have seen, 'the actual processes of globalisation that have occurred have been intrinsically uneven, unequal and unstable' (Kiely 1998: 11). The world may be getting smaller for those living in the minority world or the elites in the majority world, but for the majority of the world's population

A closer look

Managing globalization

According to McGrew (2000), there are three key strategies for managing globalization:

- '*Regulation* can mean developing states both attempting to reform the international institutions which embody the rules of the global system and trying to see those rules enforced favourably.' For example, the WTO is used by majority world countries to ensure that minority world countries abide by multilateral trade rules.
- '*Regionalism* replaces global solidarity among all developing countries with effective economic groupings on a regional basis.' For example, the North American Free Trade Area (NAFTA) and the South American Common Market (MERCOSUR) retain some protection from competition from minority world countries.
- '*Resistance* refers to challenges "from below" as social movements, citizen's groups and communities build transnational alliances to contest the neoliberal vision of globalization and promote an alternative programme.' For example, a global campaign consisting of social, environmental, women's and development movements joined forces to protest against the Multilateral Agreement on Investment (MAI), which then collapsed in 1998.

(Adapted from McGrew 2000: 360–64)

they may face greater vulnerability and exclusion as a result of global processes. Places are linked together in a globalizing world, but they are interrelated in very unequal ways. Given current patterns, inequality is more likely to increase rather than decrease. As Potter *et al.* (2008: 164) argue: 'globalisation is not leading to uniformity, but to heterogeneity and differences between places'. They suggest that, in the light of global norms of consumption, there is a tendency for convergence and increasing similarity. In contrast, in relation to production and ownership, there is a tendency towards divergence. There are increasing differences in ownership of capital and productive capabilities, which are spread unevenly and concentrated in specific world areas. Thus, it could be said that patterns of consumption are becoming more similar across the world, but patterns of production are becoming increasingly different.

> **In respect of homogenization–heterogenization, two generalized views have emerged concerning the relationships between globalization and patterns of development. The first view is the familiar claim that places around the world are fast becoming, if not exactly the same, then certainly increasingly similar . . . The second and far more realistic stance present almost the reverse view, that rather than uniformity, globalization is resulting in greater difference, flexibility, permeability, openness and hybridity, both between places and between cultures. Following on from this perspective, far from leading to a uniform world, globalization is viewed as being closely connected with the process of uneven development and the perpetuation of spatial inequalities.**
>
> (Potter 2002: 192)

As we have seen, globalization is a highly contentious issue. There are heated debates about the extent to which globalization has positive and negative effects. On the one hand, there are those who perceive it positively, as having the potential to make societies richer through trade and improved communication around the world. On the other hand, there are others who perceive globalization as contributing to the exploitation of the poor by the rich and as a threat to traditional cultures as the process of modernization changes societies. The rise of countries such as China and India raises questions of whether or not globalization and free trade can help solve poverty and inequality. The debate is torn between those who argue in favour of neoliberal globalization and free trade on the one hand and arguments for protectionism and regionalism on the other. For example, Wolf (2004) suggests that the growth of China illustrates that globalization and free trade are the answer, whereas authors such as Wade (2004) and Kaplinsky (2005) argue that China's recent development does not show this clearly. Thus, the changing world stratification complicates and alters the picture of global inequality.

Globalization theories

Different names have been given to globalization theories. They fall broadly into three categories: those in favour of ('globalizers') and those against ('sceptics') globalization, and a third approach ('transformationalist') that falls somewhere in between (Table 9.6).

Globalists

Globalists argue that international capitalism will generate more and more wealth, and ultimately more countries will be able to gain from it. They argue that, if globalization is well managed, then the benefits will outweigh the costs and will decrease world poverty in the long term. Thus, they tend to perceive globalization as a beneficial process that provides people with greater choices and better communications. From this modernization perspective, international competition is seen as a good thing and Westernization is seen as positive in spreading progress and development. Globalists generally believe that globalization will bring benefits to those in poverty. However, there are some globalists who are not quite so positive, seeing

Table 9.6 Globalization theories

Globalists	Modernization theorists support this view; also known as the neoliberal school, hyperglobalists, globalizers and modernizers
Sceptics	Dependency theorists support this view; also known as the radical school and traditionalists
Transformationalists	Also known as structuralists and neostructuralists

globalization as 'an inevitable development which cannot be resisted or significantly influenced by human intervention' (Cochrane and Pain 2000: 22).

Sceptics

The sceptics strongly disagree with the globalists and perceive globalization to have many negative impacts. Sceptics argue that globalization creates only a few winners but many losers and that ultimately it increases global inequalities (McGrew 2000). For dependency theorists who are sceptical about globalization, trade liberalization, the opening up of free markets and the minimization of the role of the state are likely to contribute to further exploitation and poverty at a global level. This negative view of globalization is similar to the negative perspectives towards the spread of capitalism. Rather than believing that this will lead to a more equal, more homogeneous world, it is feared that it may lead to greater inequalities and polarization between the majority and minority worlds (Potter *et al.* 2008):

> **. . . globalization as currently practised is exacerbating global inequalities, failing to raise people out of relative deprivation, and locking whole regions into an exploitative capitalist global economy.**
>
> (Murray 2006: 311)

The sceptics argue that there is room for economic independence and for a significant role for nation-states. Economic and social activity can be regional rather than global, and it does not have to be built on global interdependence. They also argue that the significance of globalization as a new phenomena has been exaggerated because 'in spite of increases in global flows of trade and money around the world, these are not substantially different to the economic and social interactions that have occurred between nations in previous historical times' (Cochrane and Pain 2000: 23).

Transformationalists

Transformationalists suggest that neither of the above two views is a sufficient explanation for recent global processes. They argue that globalization is creating a reordering of world relations (McGrew 2000). It is not about the minority world versus the majority world, as these divisions no longer make sense. Transformationalists point out that there are wealthy powerful elites in the majority world and there are poor, socially excluded people in the minority world. There are new complex patterns of global hierarchies, with new patterns of domination and subordination across, and within, regions. Transformationalists 'believe that globalization represents a significant shift, but question the inevitability of its impacts' (Cochrane and Pain 2000: 23). They acknowledge that important global changes are taking place, but they see the outcomes as being more complex, diverse and unpredictable than either the globalizer or the sceptical perspectives recognize.

Dimensions of globalization

Key aspects of globalization include economic, technological, social, cultural and political elements. Each of these dimensions reinforces and impacts on the others. However, we need to be cautious and critical about the extent to which globalization is happening. In particular, we should bear in mind that not everyone experiences the process of globalization in the same way and that it can have both positive and negative consequences:

> **. . . globalization is a highly uneven process: it results in clear winners and losers, not just between countries but within and across them. For the most affluent it may very well entail a shrinking world – jet travel, global TV and the World Wide Web – but for the majority of people it tends to be associated with a profound sense of disempowerment as their fate is sealed by deliberations and decision-making in chancelleries, boardrooms, and bureaucracies many thousands of miles away . . . For these reasons globalization has to be understood as a process which both unites and divides peoples and communities.**
>
> (McGrew 2000: 348)

Gender relations in the majority world

Stop and think

- What hinders women's participation in the process of development? What policies could be introduced to enhance women's contribution to development projects?

As we have seen, different approaches to development have been criticized over the years; in particular, past strategies of economic development have been heavily criticized as being inappropriate and too top-down. Another key critique that emerged in the 1970s was in relation to gender: development strategies were blamed for being male-dominated and gender-blind. Ideas about the importance of integrating gender took a while to be taken seriously, but by the 1990s it was recognized that gender analysis must be included in development thinking. A failure to include both women's and men's perspectives can lead to poorly developed strategies and less effective policies.

The first person to begin this process was Ester Boserup, with her work *Women's Role in Economic Development* (1970). She showed that women's agricultural production is critical in sustaining local and national economies but that women's work tended to be greatly undervalued. Women's subordinated status also means that their work tends to be degraded and has

A closer look

Feminist perspectives on development

A variety of feminist theories have emerged in relation to development. The main ones are outlined here:

- *Women in Development (WID)* – This was the first perspective to emerge in the early 1970s and is linked to modernization theory, which it sees as male-dominated. WID argues that the benefits of modernization have not reached women but it tends to see women as an undifferentiated category, overlooking diversity among women as a result of class, race and culture.
- *Women and Development (WAD)* – This perspective emerged in the mid-1970s and is linked to dependency theory, suggesting that women's inferior status is linked to their work roles. It argues that women's unpaid domestic and reproductive work is critical for capitalism, and it is this role that makes them vulnerable to exploitation in the productive sphere. It is a Marxist approach, which focuses on structural and socioeconomic factors, but it tends to concentrate on exploitation in productive, rather than reproductive, work.
- *Gender and Development (GAD)* – This theoretical perspective emerged in the 1980s and was influenced by socialist feminist thinking. It explores gender relations in both the productive labour force and the reproductive sphere. It is a more holistic perspective, which considers all aspects of women's lives. The key aspect of this approach is that, rather than just concentrating on women (as WID and WAD had done), it focuses on the social relations between men and women. Thus, gender relations are analysed rather than only seeing women as the category of analysis.
- *Women, Environment and Development (WED)* – This approach has been introduced by ecofeminists and stresses the need to incorporate women's voices on environmental issues, such as inequities of ownership and control of land and resources. It has been criticized for being over-romantic and for calling for a return to subsistence agriculture as the solution to women's problems. WED tends to emphasize the importance of women's role in managing natural resources, and this is criticized for being essentialist.
- *Development Alternatives for a New Era (DAWN)* – This approach emerged in the mid-1980s and, unlike all the other approaches, was initiated by women from the majority world. They challenged the universality of feminism by highlighting the significance of race, class and nation, thereby stressing the diversities among women. They preferred to focus on political consciousness-raising and popular education as much as on increasing women's income-earning opportunities. Fighting for greater gender equality and empowerment was as important as improving their work status and income.

(Source: adapted from Visvanathan 1997b)

little respect. Boserup increased awareness of women's marginalization; she provided evidence that women tended to lack access to technology and resources and that, if development was to be successful, then it must consider issues relating to women (Visvanathan 1997a). Since then aid agencies and NGOs have made efforts to integrate women into development planning and to create development programmes aimed at improving women's livelihoods.

Women in Development (WID) is the oldest and most dominant feminist perspective in development. It was very important in highlighting that women were being excluded from development and that modernization was impacting differently on men and women:

> **Instead of improving women's rights and status, the development process was at best bypassing them and at worst contributing to a deterioration in women's position in developing countries.**
>
> (Pearson 2000: 390)

WID argued that the experience and implications of poverty are different for men and women because they face different sets of constraints and responsibilities. The key goal for WID was to focus on improving women's lives and increasing their access to resources, rather than raising questions as to why women were subordinated in the first place. This is where Gender and Development (GAD) differed in its approach. GAD was particularly concerned with problematizing relations between men and women in a range of settings and highlighting the ways in which gender relations impact on development programmes. Young (1997a) argues that women are seen as agents of change rather than as passive recipients of development assistance. This does not assume that women have perfect knowledge or understanding of their social situation. They can be aware of their subordinate position but not necessarily of the structural roots of discrimination and subordination.

GAD is a holistic perspective that considers women's productive and reproductive roles:

> **In order to understand fully the nature of sex discrimination, women's wages, women's participation in the development process and implications for political action, analysts must examine the two areas of production and reproduction as well as the interaction between them.**
>
> (Beneria and Sen 1997: 49)

It goes beyond economic wellbeing to address individuals' social and mental needs. GAD recognizes that household conflicts can arise from both gender divisions and generational differences (Visvanathan 1997b). It stresses the importance of a gender analysis of distribution of power within households; that men, women, girls and boys have differential access to land and resources. As Young (1997a: 53) points out, 'GAD is much less optimistic about the role of the market as distributor of benefit'. GAD includes a definite role for the state in implementing development programmes that bring about equality between the sexes, in particular by focusing on strengthening women's legal rights (including changing inheritance and land laws). It strives to address existing power relations between men and women in society and also recognizes a need for organization. It emphasizes the need for women to organize themselves for a more effective political voice. It recognizes that patriarchy oppresses women and that there should be an emphasis on women's empowerment and male responsibility (Young 1997a).

In terms of gender planning in relation to development, Moser (1993) distinguishes between the needs of poor women and the issues relating to their gender subordination. She refers to these as practical needs versus strategic needs:

> **Practical gender needs are a response to immediate perceived necessity . . . and often are concerned with inadequacies in living conditions such as water provision, health care, and employment.**
>
> (Moser 1993: 40)

Women's needs are varied and depend on the particular context, but they may include an adequate food supply, convenient access to safe water, a steady source of income, availability of safe contraception, access to education, and access to training and credit. Moser contrasts practical needs with strategic interests:

> **Strategic gender needs are the needs women identify because of their subordinate position to men in their society . . . They relate to gender divisions of labour, power and control and may include such issues as legal rights, domestic violence, equal wages and women's control over their bodies.**
>
> (Moser 1993: 39)

Strategic needs enable women to achieve greater equality and challenge women's subordinate position, which may include male control of women's labour,

Case study

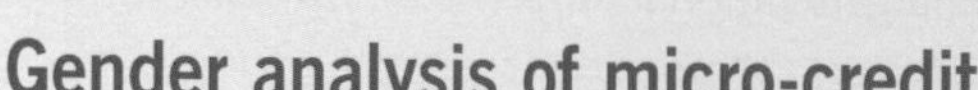

Gender analysis of micro-credit

Pearson (2000) explores the different WID and GAD approaches to development in relation to micro-credit. Giving small amounts of credit to poor farmers in rural areas became a popular tool of poverty alleviation in the 1990s. It was thought that lending small amounts of money would enable farmers to diversify their livelihoods and set up small-scale business to improve their income-earning potential and increase self-employment opportunities. One of the best known rural banks is the Grameen Bank, which began in 1976 in Bangladesh, with the aim of providing micro-credit for poor households.

WID sees this as an effective strategy for empowering women as it enables them to improve their productive economic activities (Pearson 2000). Most borrowers of the Grameen Bank are women, and this raises their involvement in income-generation, which in turn increases their status within families and communities. Women are regularly found to be more reliable as borrowers, as they are more likely to pay back the money and are more prompt with their repayments than men (Kabeer 2001). Furthermore, women are more likely to spend money on the general welfare of the family, especially on children (Kabeer 1994). As Pearson (2000) points out, this WID position focuses on targeting resources at women as a way of improving poor people's livelihoods, but the problem with such an analysis is that it ignores wider gender relations.

In contrast, the GAD approach considers the implications that such a development project may have on household relationships. It may lead to potential gender conflicts, as women have to juggle their new productive roles with other domestic reproductive work; when women gain greater access to financial resources, this can lead to difficulties within the household. For example, it has been found that in some cases women's access to credit does not increase their control over economic activities and the credit is used for activities controlled by men (Pearson 2000). The women may just end up having the responsibility of paying back the money, which means that it may actually increase women's dependence on men because of their responsibility for additional debts and the burden of repayment. It may affect the quality of relations between spouses because, as women gain more financial authority and increased assertiveness, this can in some cases lead to increased domestic violence if the husband feels threatened.

However, other research has pointed out that, in the long term, micro-credit increases women's voice in intra-household decision-making and may actually improve relationships between spouses and decrease family violence (Kabeer 2001). Hence, there are disputes over the extent to which this kind of project really does end up empowering women, and there are diverse experiences in different cultural contexts. Nevertheless, this case study illustrates that gender relations are an important factor in shaping the outcomes of development projects. Thus, relations between men and women must be taken into account, rather than only considering the position of women. The status and role of women need to be problematized and the gender implications of development programmes should be considered holistically.

women's restricted access to valued social and economic resources and political power, and issues of male violence against women (Moser 1993). Women's work is undervalued, but for it to be valued the pervasive ideology of male superiority has to be changed (Kabeer 1994).

However, most recent development strategies have recognized that in reality it is often very difficult to make distinctions between women's practical and strategic needs. It is now acknowledged that they are interlinked and that both need to be addressed. Women need to be empowered and there should be a commitment towards seeking gender equality, but also the basic needs of poor women should be met. One type of need should not be sought at the expense of the other: 'Women's interests span the household, workplace and community; women's issues are, therefore, public issues' (Wiegersma 1997: 363). Thus, women's perspectives should be seen as central to development programmes, as Young (1997b: 366) suggests: 'Planners have a great responsibility: both to listen to women and to build their vision into planning strategies'.

Nowadays it is widely recognized that women are potential beneficiaries of development and that their views have to be sought. However, we must bear in mind that women are not a homogeneous social category and we 'must take care not to misrepresent the diverse positions of different women . . . women's power is dramatically fractured by age and life cycle' (Pearson and Jackson 1998: 7–8). Women's conflicting and multiple interests should be taken into account, although Young reminds us that most feminists:

> **. . . whilst accepting and even emphasizing diversity, maintain that women share a common experience of oppression and subordination, whatever the differences in the forms that these take.**
>
> (Young 1997b: 372)

Nevertheless, empowerment is not only about economic conditions and improving women's income-generation or self-employment opportunities because: 'It also implies some degree of conflict: empowerment is not just about women acquiring something, but about those holding power relinquishing it' (Young 1997b: 372).

One of the key goals of feminists was to achieve 'gender mainstreaming', which meant that gender would be considered a central part of development processes:

> **The new strategy was to mainstream gender into general development policies, programmes and projects in order to counteract the tendency for women's concerns and gender issues to become marginalized, underfunded and ignored by the 'real' development experts and activities.**
>
> (Pearson 2000: 400)

Most recent discussions of gender and development have raised concern about ways of including men's perspectives of gender issues. Rather than merely seeing men as being part of the problem and the root cause of women's subordination, there is a shift towards considering how men can also be part of the solution. This requires the recognition that male domination is not necessarily universal; not all men try to oppress women. Furthermore, there are many different ways of being a man in the majority world, just as there are many different ways of being a woman. Men may experience social pressure to conform to dominant ideas about being a man, and this is often referred to as 'hegemonic masculinity'. Hence, the most recent recognition is that gender analysis is not only about women and their relations with men but also about men and issues of masculinity.

Childhoods in the majority world

Stop and think

- Do you think that child labour should be banned? What are the arguments for and against making child labour illegal?
- Should all children have primary and secondary education? Are there any reasons to suggest that forcing children to go to school is not a sensible strategy?

In the media, the conventional image of majority world children is that of starving, desperate, passive, exploited victims who evoke strong emotions of pity and concern. Such depressing photographs are frequently used in the minority world to elicit donations for charities. Yet, while they may facilitate the success of fundraising campaigns, such negative images only perpetuate the stereotypical notion that all majority world children are helpless and dependent. Majority world childhoods tend to be portrayed in stark contrast to minority world childhoods, where

> **The child is spared the responsibilities and anxieties of economic life, the world of work and the many worries which are to be inherited upon maturity. Childhood is a period of unconstrained freedom, a time for play, education and learning.**
>
> (Franklin 1986: 4)

This image of carefree childhood is perceived as the ideal to which all childhoods should aspire, and so there is a notion of a globalized model of childhood. However, this is based on minority world middle-class ideals (Boyden 1997). It is important to remember that the majority of the world's children live in the economically poor world regions of Latin America, Asia and Africa. Broadly comparing the majority and minority worlds, the most common type of 'childhood' is therefore that of majority world children (many of whom work). Yet paradoxically, majority world childhoods tend to be considered deviant when examined within the globalized model of childhood, which is based on a minority world perception that children should play and study but not work (Boyden 1997). Quantitatively, in global terms, it is more common for children to combine work and school rather than to have a childhood based on play and school (see also Chapter 7). We need to be wary about overgeneralizing in relation to different kinds of childhood, as children's lives are greatly varied in different geographical areas, according to the cultural, socioeconomic and historical context. Nevertheless, it can be argued that work is more commonplace and visible in majority world childhoods, whereas play tends to be considered more central to those in the minority world (James *et al.* 1998). Although not denying that some child work can be extremely exploitative, recent academic studies have shown that work is a key part of many majority world childhoods and that it is not necessarily detrimental, often having both positive and negative effects (Ansell 2005; Woodhead 1998).

There has been an ongoing debate about whether to use the term 'children's work' or 'child labour'. Some consider 'child work' to be acceptable, a social good and a positive form of socialization useful for the child's future. In contrast, 'child labour' is generally perceived as unacceptable, a social evil and a negative form of exploitation that is detrimental for the child's future (Ansell 2005). There may also be a distinction between two categories of child work: unpaid family work, and paid work outside the family circle. Recent thinking on children's work abandons the work/labour dichotomy and recognizes the complexity of the nature of child work.

Particular activities are perceived to be more appropriate, less harmful and even beneficial for child workers. Children working with family members, especially in rural environments, are less likely to be exposed to the same risk of exploitation as those working in labour-intensive industries or in urban areas. Boyden reported that in Peru domestic service and agriculture are legally considered more appropriate for children because

> **The assumption is that young people involved in non-waged activities, recruited into the labour market through kinship networks, or working in family enterprises, are in some way guaranteed protection. Exploitation is seen solely as a function of waged employment in large impersonal concerns.**
>
> (Boyden 1988: 199)

Nevertheless, it should not be assumed that child work is protected when it occurs within kinship relations. Exploitation may be more hidden and difficult to accept in family enterprises, but that does not mean that it is non-existent. Furthermore, it is often harder to intervene in cases of child exploitation when the child is dependent physically and emotionally on the exploiter. Domestic service is one of the main forms of child work but is also highly exploitative, as the child can be vulnerable to psychological, physical, verbal and sexual abuse. Paradoxically, it is one of the activities considered most appropriate and least harmful for children. Consequently, domestic service is often not included in legislation or is most lenient on the entry age of the child. It can lead to children being a source of cheap labour for wider family members. Ideologies of kinship should not lead to assumptions that kin relations are always based only on reciprocity and mutual support rather than exploitation and oppression (Boyden *et al.* 1998).

Similarly, it is wrong to assume that waged employment for children is necessarily exploitative. It can be positive, as it enables children to earn an income, however small, which enables them to support themselves or their families. Paid work can stimulate children's personal growth and development. By earning their own money, children have access to greater decision-making and bargaining power (Ansell 2005). In contrast, unpaid family work can reinforce children's economic dependence on their parents. Thus, some children prefer paid employment outside the home rather than engaging in unpaid 'taken for granted' family work. For example, children in Indonesia said they preferred to work for low wages in factories rather than for no wages within the family (Johnson *et al.* 1995). Some children say they prefer paid work because it has greater future prospects and is less exploitative.

It is too simplistic to assume that child labour in the urban world of business and industry is automatically exploitative, whereas child work in traditional occupations of farming and domestic service is a beneficial and essential form of socialisation (Boyden *et al.* 1998). White (1996) argues that children's work should be viewed on a continuum, rather than trying to categorize it as one of two extremes. UNICEF supports

Case study

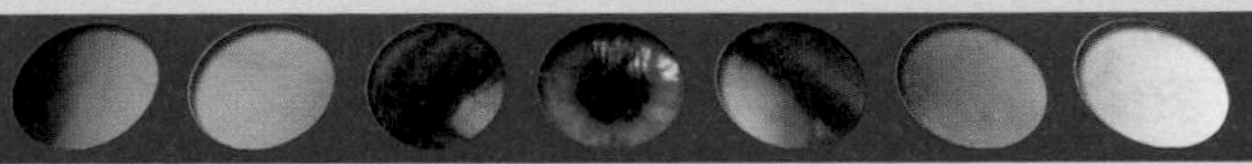

Primark: on the rack

In June 2008 the BBC1 documentary programme *Panorama* presented an investigation into the suppliers for the clothing shop Primark. *Panorama* had sent a team of reporters to pose as industry buyers in India in order to test out Primark's claim that it could provide cheap clothing without breaking ethical guidelines. During the programme it emerged that some garments were being produced using child labour that had been unofficially subcontracted without Primark's knowledge. Primark's response to the investigation was to sack three of its suppliers in India and announce that it would set up a 'Primark's Better Lives Foundation'. However, this sparked a debate about the ethics of Primark's reaction. Instead of trying to improve working conditions for the children and families involved, Primark took away a vital source of their income by placing a total ban on the use of child labour. Some of the children had been working at home, sewing garments by hand, alongside other family members. Denying them a source of income and somewhat naively labelling all child labour as unethical paradoxically may mean that some of these children end up working in more hidden, more exploitative forms of employment. *Panorama* revealed the minority world assumptions (underlying Primark's response) that all child labour is negative and should be banned without showing an understanding of the detrimental consequences of doing so.

the view that work is not just good or bad for children but moves on a continuum from best to worst:

> **At one end of the continuum, the work is beneficial, promoting or enhancing a child's physical, mental, spiritual, moral or social development without interfering with schooling, recreation and rest.**
>
> **At the other end, it is palpably destructive or exploitative. There are vast areas of activity between these two poles, including work that need not impact negatively on the child's development.**
>
> (UNICEF 1997: 24)

However, it is difficult to decide where particular employment should be placed along the continuum, since most work has both positive and negative effects simultaneously, both in the present and for the child's future. Children's work can be considered in either positive or negative terms:

> **For large numbers of children work is an ordeal, a source of suffering and exploitation, and a fundamental abuse of human rights. Often, child labour results in educational deprivation, social disadvantage and poor health and physical development. Yet child work can be an important element in maturation, securing the transition from childhood to adulthood. It can also be essential for family survival.**
>
> (Bequele and Boyden 1988: v)

Ways in which children are perceived to be 'exploited' vary and depend on one's definition of 'exploitation' (Bequele and Myers 1995). It can be considered in relation to the short-term or long-term detrimental consequences. Children's work can have many benefits for children themselves and their families. Woodhead (1998) found that children in Bangladesh, Ethiopia, the Philippines, Guatemala, El Salvador and Nicaragua demonstrated an ability to reason about which work was best for them. They considered a variety of advantages and disadvantages, including relative income, security, safety, hazard, exploitation, independence and autonomy. Woodhead also showed that children's perceptions of the benefits of their work, such as enhanced self-esteem and sense of responsibility, often outweighed the drawbacks, such as poor working conditions. Therefore, in order to reach an adequate understanding of the nature of children's work, one must take into account the long-term and short-term outcomes, the specific social and cultural environment, the historical and economic context, and both adults' and children's perceptions of their own situation (Woodhead 1998).

Whether children work is not a question of choice for many children or their families in the majority world. The causes of child labour usually stem from poverty and underdevelopment. However, children also work as a result of other structural constraints,

A closer look

Table 9.7 The advantages and disadvantages of children's work

Positive aspects	Negative aspects
Useful contribution to the survival of their household; may increase their status as a family member	Low pay, long hours
Work as a source of pride, satisfaction and self-esteem	Lack of legal protection
Moral value of work, giving children a sense of efficacy and responsibility	Sexual, physical or emotional abuse
Provides access to a wider social network	Slave-like or socially isolating conditions
Provides an income and enhances their ability to access consumer goods	Work that is mundane and repetitive
Personal autonomy: increases sense of independence and self-reliance	Health and safety risks of dangerous working environments
Enables the development of useful skills for their future	Use of unsafe tools and equipment
May enable them to pay for their own schooling	May have adverse effects on schooling

(Source: Boyden *et al.* 1998)

including the failure of the education system, the vested interests of employers, rapid rural–urban migration, lack of parental awareness of the implications for children's health and development, social and cultural attitudes, and lack of political will for effective action (Boyden *et al.* 1998; Panelli *et al.* 2007). It is worth bearing in mind that some children choose to work to help their families, to enhance their independence and competencies, to gain access to consumer luxuries, to gain useful skills, and as a means of self-actualization (Boyden *et al.* 1998). Family dynamics and household composition also influence whether children work. For example, Boyden *et al.* (1998: 138) observed that 'in many places, a disproportionate number of working children appear to be from homes headed by a single woman'. They noted that family emergencies, such as death or incapacitation of an adult earner, loss of a job, harvest failures and severe weather, may also increase the likelihood of children beginning to work.

Figure 9.7 Children face both physical and social dangers at work
© G.M.B. Akash/Panos Pictures

The UN Convention on the Rights of the Child states that exploitative child labour should be eliminated, but the Convention's recommendations 'may not be realistic for all countries, especially those whose economies and educational facilities are insufficiently developed' (Bequele and Myers 1995: 93). The International Labour Organization (ILO) has been striving to ban child labour since 1919. However, recent discussions of policymaking and legislation have shifted from a desire to ban all child labour to providing legislation to protect children from overexploitation. The illegal status of children's work forces it underground, to be denied by governments, employers, parents and the children themselves. Where it is concealed, it is not included in protective legislation, and it may be disguised as an 'apprenticeship' or 'training' when it becomes a convenient excuse to pay even lower wages. Illegal child labour tends to be confined to industrial or commercial jobs, especially factories, mines and other hazardous employment. Labour legislation prohibits children under a certain age, usually 12–14 years, from doing certain jobs, which

A closer look

Why do children work?

- On the demand side employers prefer to employ children as they can do labour-intensive tasks for lower wages than adults, they are a good source of casual labour, and they tend to be a docile labour force as they are unprotected by legislation and workers' rights.
- On the supply side, whether children work or not tends to depend on the wealth of the household, the employment status and wage rates of employable adults within the household, the availability and cost of schooling, and the social and cultural environment.

(Source: Bequele and Boyden 1988)

tend to exclude the agricultural and domestic sectors. However, Bequele and Myers (1995) argue that, even where comprehensive legislation exists, it is rarely enforced in the majority world. This is because there is a shortage of inspectors, who are poorly paid and often easily bribed. They also recognize that 'protecting children against a particular hazard, and making their work more tolerable, may encourage them to stay in it' (Bequele and Myers 1995: 156). There is no disputing that exploitative child labour conditions should be regulated, but the children's views, the context and the consequences should also be taken into account (Woodhead 1998).

Related closely to the debate on whether child labour can be regarded as exploitation or socialization is the discussion of the value of school versus work for children in the majority world. This debate considers which form of socialization is more appropriate or realistic for the child and household concerned: that of formal education at school, or that of unpaid work at home or paid work outside the household. For many children in the majority world, full-time, long-term schooling is not a readily available option because of both the direct and indirect costs of formal education. Direct costs of schooling include fees, uniform, school supplies and transport. Even where an official school uniform is not required, children still need reasonable shoes and clothing. Additional costs of board and lodging may occur where children have to migrate in order to continue their schooling. A major indirect cost of schooling is the labour or earnings lost while the child is at school. In some cases this can mean that hired help is needed to replace the child's labour.

The immediate costs of schooling are by no means the only reason why children may work (whether paid or unpaid, with family or non-kin) rather than attend school. The opportunities for attending school and the perceived returns from schooling relative to work are essential factors. Schooling does not always guarantee better employment prospects, and so it does not necessarily lead to a brighter future (Jeffrey and McDowell 2004). Consequently, parents may prefer their children to learn a trade, as they see little value in sacrificing limited resources to invest in formal education. Particularly in rural areas where children are thought most likely to end up working in traditional occupations of farming, parents are even more likely to consider school a pointless investment.

Thus, the main reasons why children do not go to school or why they drop out are the direct and indirect costs, limited access to schools, lack of available schools, the perceived returns of schooling, limited future working opportunities, and the poor quality of schools and teaching. Woodhead's (1998) research on children's perspectives of their working lives found that most children felt that combining work and school was their only feasible option. His study revealed that children saw both positive and negative aspects of education.

The benefits of schooling included:

- acquiring literacy and numeracy skills;
- improved work prospects;
- a sense of achievement and respect;
- making and playing with friends.

The negative aspects included:

- harsh and humiliating teaching methods;
- feelings of failure and boredom;
- teacher absenteeism;
- the costs of schooling;
- competing pressures of school and work.

It is recognized that children's views need to be taken into account when trying to weigh up the advantages and disadvantages of work versus school. In many cases,

Figure 9.8 Even in communities where schools exist, the enrolment rate can be low, as it can be considered tiresome and time-consuming to walk long distances to school © Samantha Punch

the decision as to whether a child should attend school or should work can be avoided by combining the two. The feasibility of this depends on the nature of the child's work, the distances and hours involved, and whether the two can be coordinated. A common, but ill-founded, assumption is that work that can be combined with school is more appropriate for children. However, combining school and work may be more of a burden for children, and so it should not be assumed simplistically that doing both is necessarily more beneficial to the child than doing work alone (Boyden *et al.* 1998).

It is no longer acceptable to consider development issues without including an analysis of the impact on women's and children's lives. In the past, development tended to be perceived from the perspective of adult

World in focus

Youth transitions: migration for work or education?

In many parts of the majority world, young people migrate in search of better opportunities for their future. Here we illustrate the dilemmas that children in 'Churquiales' (a pseudonym for a rural village in southern Bolivia) face when deciding whether to migrate in order to continue their schooling or whether to seek paid employment.

To a certain extent, children's experiences at school can enhance their social and intellectual autonomy. They learn basic literacy and numeracy skills, but this does not offer them a better social status and an alternative future livelihood. Young people from Churquiales are most likely to end up working in agriculture or the domestic service either within their community or in the migrant destinations of Tarija or Argentina. Only if they can continue on to secondary education and complete that cycle can they really expect a different sort of future livelihood. Such an option is not available to most rural children as it depends on economic resources, as well as supportive parents and the personal desire of the children themselves. In many cases secondary education is not a viable alternative to the more immediate material gains of work and migration . . .

This is partly because of their geographical location which, on the one hand, is in a relatively isolated, poor rural area with limited available agricultural land and a lack of employment prospects. On the other hand, it is relatively near the agricultural plantations in northern Argentina which require a large seasonal labour force. The higher wages and employment opportunities in Argentina thereby provide a logical alternative to the uncertainty, expense and perhaps wasted effort of pursuing education beyond primary school in Bolivia. Although migrant work is arduous and low skilled it offers more security and tangible benefits compared with the nebulous outcomes of following an educational pathway.

However, on the one hand, school acts as an important site of socialisation, providing children an opportunity to assert their social autonomy by socialising with their peers, especially in rural areas where they may otherwise lead relatively isolated lives. The importance of play at school should not be overlooked, since the enjoyment which children experience through having fun at school is a major reason for their enthusiasm in attending. On the other hand, there is a range of constraining factors including lack of resources, low wages, poor teaching quality, household work demands and climatic conditions which all lead to high rates of absenteeism, drop-out, repetition and failure. Such factors combine and result in a lack of confidence in the benefits of the formal education system. Paradoxically problems such as teacher absenteeism and poor training for the multi-grade system enable children to create opportunities for play. Yet ultimately this is at the expense of the quality of their education.

The structural constraints which surround teaching combined with household work demands and climatic conditions result in restricted educational choices for children in Churquiales. The drawbacks of primary education lead to a poor perception of schooling held by both parents and young people, diminishing the likelihood of pupils continuing to secondary education. Many children struggle to complete the six years of primary education, even though the community school is reasonably accessible in terms of both cost and distance. Some do not finish primary schooling, resulting in an early transition to work at 10 or 11 years old. Others feel that once they have completed those six years and have acquired the basic skills of literacy and numeracy it is time to move into the world of work

World in focus *continued*

either within or outside their community. The hurdle of completing secondary education is perceived, by many, to be unrealistic and extremely costly in both time and money. Consequently it is perhaps unsurprising that most major decisions about school-to-work are made on completion of primary school at 12–14 years of age. This relatively early and rapid transition from school into work contrasts with the delayed and extended youth transitions of much of the minority world (Wyn and Dwyer 1999) . . .

In such a context, seeking migrant work becomes an attractive opportunity for young people as it enhances both their economic and social capital, enabling them to be more flexible. They have the choice of continuing to migrate seasonally, to return to their community or to live more permanently in Argentina or Tarija. Migration is often used by young people as a bridge between being part of their parents' household and forming a new household of their own (Punch 2002a). It allows them to accumulate savings whilst also maintaining links with their families by sending remittances home. Furthermore, since young people's migratory experience is seasonal, it provides them with a sense of collective identity during periods spent within their home community. With better access to consumer markets, they return home with material goods and new clothes as their symbols of success and increased prestige. It is during this time that they meet and learn from one another's migratory experiences whilst also having a substantial impact on the social life of the community. This emphasises the importance and impact of informal social networks on young people's transitions to adulthood. Thus, migration, unlike education, offers young people a source of identity as well as enhancing their social and economic autonomy.

Therefore, in this rural community, migration rather than education is an important part of youth identity. On the one hand, migrants have significant social freedom during their time back home which is linked to their transitional youth status and their acquisition of greater independence. On the other hand, although they work extremely hard in Argentina, their migrant employment facilitates increased consumerism and enables them to continue to maintain interdependent family ties by contributing financially to their households (Punch 2002a). Furthermore since migrants return with their newly acquired material goods, they provide children with stronger role models than the exceptional few who have achieved academic success beyond primary level. The economic and social status attached to the migrant identity is particularly influential for children in the community who are more likely to want to follow in the migrants' footsteps rather than continue with secondary education. Therefore, the image of the young migrant representing economic success and social freedom should not be underestimated as a powerful mechanism in encouraging more young people to leave their community in search of work. However, this is not necessarily negative, particularly given the range of constraints associated with schooling, the limited agricultural land and the lack of employment opportunities in a country suffering from the ills of neo-liberalism and increased indebtedness (Green 2003). Thus migration for work, rather than for education, is perhaps a convenient and appropriate coping strategy for young people to pursue.

(Source: Punch 2004: 176–9)

Question

1. What are the possible constraints that young people in the majority world face when deciding whether to pursue secondary education? Consider a range of issues, including the impact of birth order, class, ethnicity, gender, household composition, and access to resources and work opportunities.

men, but now the views of women and young people must also be taken into account, as Ansell argues:

> **Since the 1980s, growing global economic inequalities have left many children in situations of worsening poverty. Yet, paradoxically, the neo-liberal policies that have fed poverty have also led to funds being directed away from government-led macroeconomic policies to an NGO sector that is highly concerned about development's negative impacts on children and youth. Only recently, however, have policy-makers and practitioners begun to recognise children and youth as subjects with their own ideas, able to act in their own interests. Increasingly it is recognised that failure to listen to young people's voices has often meant failure to address many of the issues that confront children and youth.**
>
> (Ansell 2005: 61)

Chawla and Johnson (2004) provide examples of projects that have installed water taps that are too high for children to reach and income-generating activities that result in children missing school to help their parents. They also argue that

> **. . . the basic needs that children express are conditions for well-being for all ages in society – such as safety, secure homes, adequate food and clean water, attractive environments, the protection of the natural world, education, fair livelihoods, friendly acceptance, and a hopeful future. Attention to children's needs also requires a timeframe that considers the consequences of decisions far into the future . . . Therefore development programmes that put children at the centre are well positioned to unify diverse groups and to build a strong foundation for broad alliances for progressive change.**
>
> (Chawla and Johnson 2004: 66)

In order to ensure that effective development policies for addressing global inequalities benefit all sectors of the population, issues of both gender and generation must be considered.

Summary

- Most poor countries in the majority world continue to have a subordinate role within the global economy. There is a widening gap between rich and poor countries, and this seems likely to increase as processes of globalization have uneven global impacts.
- Development theories explain how development has occurred and the directions it may take in the future. A range of different development theories exist, including the classics of modernization theory and dependency theory, and more contemporary alternative approaches such as participatory development and sustainable development. Each has its strengths and weaknesses in relation to offering effective explanations for processes of development.
- Issues of gender and generation are now central to development thinking. Relationships between men and women, and between adults and children, should be considered when developing policies and programmes to address global inequalities.
- The relationship between work and education for children in the majority world is a complex one. It is too simplistic to assume that school is beneficial and work is detrimental for children. The wider social, economic, cultural and historical context needs to be taken into account when weighing up the advantages and disadvantages of children's work and schooling.

Links

Issues in relation to alternative development link to the discussion of sustainable development in Chapter 10 (pp. 434–436).

The discussion of TNCs in the global economy section links to the globalization of economic life in Chapter 12 (pp. 507–509).

The section on gender relations in the majority world is related to issues discussed in Chapter 5 (pp. 219–221).

The section on childhoods in the majority world is linked to debates in Chapter 7 (pp. 314–321).

Further reading

Allen, T. and Thomas, A. (eds) (2000) *Poverty and Development into the 21st Century*, Oxford: Oxford University Press.
A key text that addresses both historical and contemporary topics in relation to global divisions. It is clearly written and provides an accessible overview of poverty and development in the majority world.

Ansell, N. (2005) *Children, Youth and Development*, London: Routledge.
A very accessible text that highlights the diversity of children's and young people's experiences in the majority world. It effectively draws on a wide range of examples from Africa, Asia and Latin America and includes chapters on health, education, street children, child soldiers, work and participation.

Cohen, R. and Kennedy, P. (2007) *Global Sociology,* 2nd edn, London: Macmillan.
This book covers a wide range of sociological topics from a global perspective, including globalization, work, nation-states, global inequalities, crime, migration, health, tourism, culture, the media, sport, religion and urban life.

Held, D. and Kaya, A. (eds) (2007) *Global Inequality: Patterns and Explanations*, Cambridge: Polity Press.
This is a challenging collection of papers that addresses the tough question: 'Has globalization affected inequality?'

Momsen, J. (2004) *Gender and Development*, London: Routledge.
A clear, broad overview of key gender issues in both rural and urban contexts, drawing on a wide range of case studies from Africa, Asia and Latin America. The text includes chapters on reproduction, health, violence, the environment and globalization.

Regan, C. (ed.) (2002) *80:20: Development in an Unequal World*, Wicklow, Ireland: 80:20 Educating and Acting for a Better World.
An accessible introduction to challenging development issues, such as human rights, colonialism, aid, debt, trade, participation, gender, HIV/AIDS, migration, transnational corporations and conflict.

Webster, A. (1990) *Introduction to the Sociology of Development*, London: Macmillan.
Excellent clear overview of key sociological issues in relation to development, including chapters on inequality, modernization theory, underdevelopment theories, education, aid and industrialization.

Websites

www.worldbank.org

World Bank
This site is useful for many issues related to global poverty, including up-to-date research, statistics and publications.

www.undp.org

United Nations Development Programme
A range of news stories and useful publications, such as human development reports, are available from this site.

www.foodfirst.org

Institute for Food and Development Policy (Food First)
The Institute for Food and Development Policy is concerned with analysing the root causes and injustices of global hunger, poverty, and ecological degradation.

www.dfid.gov.uk

Department for International Development (DFID)
The British government's development website, which includes many country profiles, case studies and publications relating to global inequalities.

www.opendemocracy.net/globalisation/index.jsp
Open Democracy
A discussion forum offering news and opinion articles from established academics and journalists covering contested debates about the effects of globalization.

www.worldwrite.org.uk/damned
Damned by Debt Relief
This website has a short version of the film *Damned by Debt Relief* and useful articles in relation to debt in the majority world.

www.younglives.org.uk
Young Lives
Young Lives is an international study of childhood poverty tracking the changing lives of 12,000 children in Ethiopia, India (in the state of Andhra Pradesh), Peru and Vietnam over a 15-year period. The website presents findings from the project, including children's views of their own experiences.

www.ilo.org
International Labour Organization

www.imf.org
International Monetary Fund

www.wto.org
World Trade Organization

www.un.org
United Nations

www.globalisationguide.org
Globalisation Guide

www.tni.org
Transnational Institute

www.oneworldaction.org
One World Action

www.plan-international.org/resources/development
Development dictionary

Activities

Activity 1

Applying development theories

Bolivia is one of the few countries of the world that does not have a McDonald's outlet. Imagine you are visiting Bolivia and your role, as chief executive of McDonald's, is to convince the Bolivian government to allow a branch of McDonald's to open in La Paz (the biggest city). Use modernization theory as a basis to put forward your arguments indicating that McDonald's would be beneficial to Bolivian development.

Now imagine you are the minister for development in Bolivia and are opposed to the introduction of McDonald's in your country. Use dependency theory as a basis to put forward your arguments indicating that McDonald's would be detrimental to Bolivian development.

Questions

1. Using globalization theories (the perspectives of globalists, sceptics and transformationalists), assess whether the introduction of McDonald's to Bolivia would be perceived as having positive or negative impacts on the lives of people in La Paz.
2. Consider your arguments from the perspectives of both rich and poor urban residents.

Activity 2

HIV/AIDS and development

Read the following extract from Regan (2002b: 190) and reflect upon the links between HIV/AIDS and development:

> According to the Joint United Nations Programme on HIV/AIDS (UNAIDS) poverty is the driving force of the AIDS pandemic in Africa: in poor communities men are forced to migrate to urban areas in search of work, which means that husbands may be away from their wives for a year or more and may seek extramarital relations. This is particularly true when they frequent bars, usually the only form of entertainment provided by their employers.
>
> At the same time, poor women are being forced into prostitution as the only means of earning an income to feed their children. As a result, southern Africa has become the global epicentre of the AIDS epidemic. One of the most high-risk groups is married women, who are often powerless in matters of sexual relations. In some communities, up to 48% of routinely tested pregnant women are HIV-positive.
>
> Despite decades of development in rural Africa most people still do not have access to clean water,

hygienic sanitation, electricity, affordable health care, education and food security. As a result of the AIDS crisis on already-weakened African economies, even the most modest development gains are being lost. People living with HIV urgently need all these things.

With access to clean water, timely treatment for opportunistic infections and a nutritious diet, people living with HIV can live healthy and productive lives for 10 to 15 years. In southern Africa, people are dying of AIDS within five years because they are poor and do not have the most basic food security.

The causes and consequences of the HIV/AIDS crisis are closely linked to wider development issues, including poverty, malnutrition, exposure to other infections, gender inequality and insecure livelihoods. The loss of labour to the epidemic cripples the household.

Questions

1. What are the social and economic consequences of the HIV/AIDS crisis?
2. Consider the different ways in which men, women, girls and boys within households may be affected when one or both parents are infected by HIV.

Part 3 Introduction to understanding social life

The heart of sociology is about the interpretation and critical analysis of social life. (McIntosh and Punch 2005: 9)

The sociological imagination can be applied to all aspects of our lives, from the extraordinary to the ordinary; from the most significant events to the everyday happenings; from the structures shaping our lives to our individual biographies. Indeed, sociology can act as a means for 'refining the knowledge we possess and employ in our daily life' (Bauman and May 2001: 166).

Each of the following chapters – on the environment, family, work, health and illness, and crime – focuses on a specific dimension of social life, but they also share some common themes:

- *Meanings* – We consider how we define the world around us. We do not often question the meaning of everyday terms such as 'the family', 'health' and 'nature' and why some definitions become accepted and others disregarded.
- *Social divisions* – We apply an understanding of social divisions to the areas of family, work, health and illness, and crime, and examine in more detail how inequality and power are formed and experienced in particular contexts. For example, in understanding the nature of work in a capitalist economy, many sociologists investigate the inequalities between social classes. In the study of crime, we question the extent to which crime is characteristic of particular social groups.
- *Social problems* – Although sociology does not always study social problems, the sociological imagination does offer insights into the way in which aspects of our lives are considered to be 'problems'; how problems are experienced; and the identification of these problems with particular groups in society. In these chapters we explore a range of social problems, including obesity, health inequalities, antisocial behaviour and domestic violence.
- *Personal issues* – Sociology enables us to understand the issues that affect us and to place them within wider social contexts. In doing so, it encourages us to critically reflect on our lives and the lives of those around us. In these chapters we address such issues as experiencing illness, intimate relationships, consumption and unemployment.
- *Social change* – Each chapter in this part explores processes of change and presents an understanding of how and why key changes take place. For example, how has waged labour changed as capitalism has developed? Why have family forms become more diverse? Why and in what ways has the environment become a sociological and a political issue?

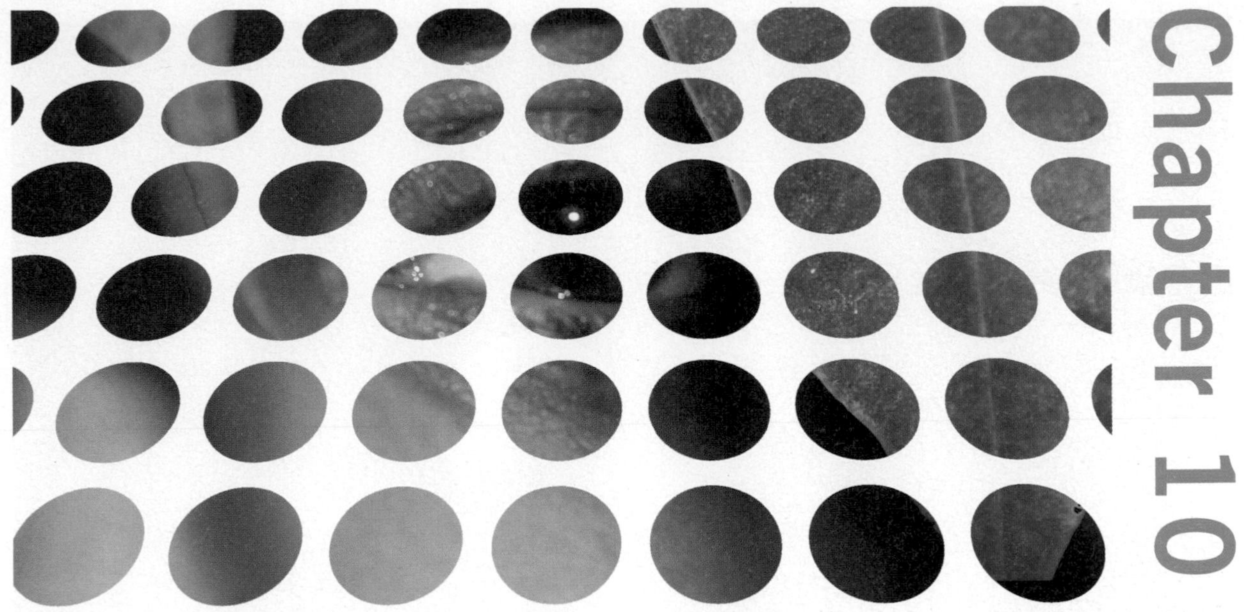

Environment

Eleanor McDowell

The degradation of the ecological and natural foundations of social life means that nature can no longer be understood outside of society or society outside of nature. The study of society must somehow incorporate an understanding of nature. (Beck 1992: 80)

Key issues

- What is environmental sociology? What is the value of an environmentally informed approach to sociology?
- What do we mean by the environment having an 'absent presence' within sociology?
- Why were sociologists called to embrace a 'new ecological paradigm'?
- What are the main theoretical developments in environmental sociology?
- Why are the principles underpinning sustainable development and environmental justice so important? What are the main challenges associated with these concepts? How do they relate to wider global environmental issues?

Introduction

The 'environment' is increasingly in the news. We hear of rivers being poisoned, species being wiped out, polar ice caps melting and vast areas of forests being cleared. The seasons appear out of kilter and floods, droughts and cyclones are considered less of a natural phenomenon. We are inundated with messages about greener lifestyles from politicians and celebrities, encouraged to switch to low-energy light bulbs, buy organic goods, recycle more, reduce waste, leave the car at home and avoid using plastic carrier bags when we go shopping. There are now hybrid cars, biodegradable laptops, Nike 'green' trainers, environmentally friendly holidays and even a new green nightclub (club4climate). Environmental issues are everywhere. What, however, do we mean when we refer to 'the environment', and what does it mean to you?

Figure 10.1 Earth from the Moon
© NASA

The natural environment, often termed simply 'the environment', refers to all living and non-living things that occur naturally on earth. 'Nature' in the broadest sense is equivalent to the natural world. It is everything not made by humankind, in contrast with the 'built environment', which is materially constructed for humanity's use. The impact of the environment is immeasurable. As a theme it is reflected in literature, art, photography, film and architecture. Environmental issues are taught in schools, colleges and universities; people work in a range of environmental occupations, and there are thousands of environmental groups and organizations worldwide. We acknowledge and discuss environmental issues overwhelmingly in physical terms – wildlife, species, habitats, landscapes, the atmosphere, oceans, pollutants and other types of environmental problems, such as rainforest destruction, the extinction of species and global warming. However, 'the environment' is more than simply physical. It also has important social, philosophical, cultural, economic, political and historical dimensions. Above all, the meaning of 'the environment' varies widely. It is viewed by some in a very instrumental sense, to be utilized for humanity's needs. In contrast, others recognize the intrinsic value of the natural world, stressing the interdependence and connection between all species and their environment. In the opening quote to this chapter, Beck suggests that the ecological and natural foundations of social life are fundamental to our existence – we shape the environment and the environment shapes us.

Stop and think

> You look at the river gently flowing by. You notice the leaves rustling in the wind. You hear the birds; you hear the tree frogs. In the distance you hear a cow. You feel the grass. The mud gives a little bit on the river bank. It's quiet; it's peaceful. And all of a sudden, it's a gear shift inside you. And it's like taking a deep breath and going . . . Oh yeah, I forgot about this.
>
> (Al Gore, former US vice-president, in the opening monologue of *An Inconvenient Truth*, a documentary film about global warming, released in May 2006)

Gore highlights how easy it is for us to be oblivious to the reality and impact of the natural world around us.

- ➤ As individuals, do we all have a responsibility towards protecting the environment? If yes, in what ways?
- ➤ Do environmental issues concern you? Reflect on how you and others feel about the environment. What shapes our views and attitudes on environmental issues?

What is environmental sociology?

The interrelationship between humanity, society and nature is a fundamental component of environmental sociology. As such, environmental sociologists aim to develop a critical and informed understanding of the complex interactions between societies and their respective environments. However, we might pause to ask why sociologists have been particularly negligent in terms of engaging with environmental issues in an academic capacity. Is the environment not the setting in which human action takes place? Is the environment itself not modified by human activity? These are important questions that we return to in more detail below, but it is fair to say that, until the late 1970s, sociology failed conspicuously to include environmental issues and analysis as a way of understanding and explaining various social phenomena. It is also arguable that humanity's part in creating environmental problems demands appropriate solutions to these problems. A sociological perspective can therefore help to identify not only the relationship between nature and wellbeing but also the manner in which social patterns can contribute to increasing stress on the environment along with society's response to these pressures. Thus, the broadening environmental agenda across local, national and global spheres provides sociologists with an opportunity to contribute to the complex dynamics of the environment and to consider the human and social context in which these occur.

By adopting an environmentally informed approach to sociology we can strive to:

- explore the interactions between the physical environment, economic and social organization and social behaviour;
- identify the manner in which environmental issues relate to specific political, cultural and economic arrangements;
- explore structural conditions, barriers and forms of risk, as well as positive characteristics regarding the environment;
- identify and monitor public views, attitudes and concerns about environmental issues;
- examine a range of strategies, theoretical paradigms and policy proposals.

This chapter considers the development of environmental sociology as an identifiable specialism within sociology and looks at the work of some of the main contributions in this field. Althought the scope of topics and theoretical developments is significant, a number of important questions nevertheless guide the approach of this work. When we view society through the lens of environmental sociology, we highlight the very nature of society itself. We consider the environmental implications of a vastly unequal society, and the effects of economic growth, mass consumption and technological development, and we question how these relate to notions of progress in an increasingly complex globalized world.

The role we play as part of the web of life is fundamental in our understanding of and response to environmental issues. For example, ecological Marxists take a critical view of industrial capitalism by forging links between accumulation and economic growth with environmental degradation. As we shall see, other theorists highlight the prevalence of a new stage of modernity associated with a so-called 'risk society' generated by large-scale technologies. Thus, there are various perspectives which view the dynamics of modern industrial-capitalist societies as having a tendency towards environmental degradation, including different forms of environmental or 'green' critiques, which, in their various guises, call for a more environmentally sound world.

There are other theorists, however, who take a more optimistic view. Ecological modernists argue that environmental improvements can result from appropriate technology, business enterprise and government intervention. In recent years, there has also been an increase in cultural debates around the socially created nature of scientific and environmental knowledge from social constructionists. In addition, we will consider important theories from ecological feminists, who view the patriarchal domination of women and other social groups as parallel to man's exploitation of the environment. In the course of this debate, we will also touch on some of the topics you will become familiar with while studying sociology generally. For example, ecofeminism is related to long-established debates in sociology around gender, power and equality issues. In the debate on environmental justice, we also consider time-honoured sociological topics such as class, race, poverty and inequality, when we look at why some people in society suffer from disproportionate levels of environmental degradation.

In the latter stages of this chapter, we will assess strategies for environmental development and reform by exploring the concept of sustainable development. Conceptually, sustainable development can be summed up as a long-term agenda for environmental action, which involves an improved level of cooperation within and between countries at different stages of their economic, social and environmental development. Before moving on to consider these themes in more detail, it is important to recognize that ideas and attitudes regarding the environment do not evolve in a vacuum; nor are environmental problems exclusive to contemporary society. In the section below, the debate is contextualized by highlighting a range of values and philosophical ideals that show significant links between society and nature at specific historical periods.

Historical views of nature

> **Nature is very tired.**
>
> (Luis Alfonso de Carvallo, Spanish monk, 1695)

It is often stated that our present ecological problems are completely unprecedented, but evidence suggests that this is not altogether true. Historical and archaeological evidence points to examples of overgrazing, deforestation, erosion and burning traced to ancient civilizations, the Middle Ages and other pre-industrial periods. Many ecological disasters, long understood as 'acts of God' or 'natural disasters', are in fact 'largely generated or substantially aggravated by collective and cumulative human behaviour' (Weiskel 1989: 98). For example, Easter Island, one of the most remote islands in the Pacific Ocean, was ravaged by complete deforestation by the time the first Europeans visited it in the eighteenth century. However, Easter Island is a place shrouded in mystery. How could islanders who lived a very primitive and squalid existence carve, construct and transport over 600 massive stone carvings over 20 feet high across the island? No one really knows, but anthropologists agree that the demands placed on the environment were catastrophic, leading to the island's demise. The Roman Empire's insatiable demand for grain also resulted in the destruction of North African provinces due to soil erosion and deforestation (Pointing 1991). There have also been periodic surges of concern throughout history over a wide range of environmental issues relating to air pollution and the protection of animals and birds, forests and historic monuments (Thomas 1983; Weiskel 1989). Environmental change is therefore a continual process that has been in operation since the earth first came into existence. By the same token, attitudes towards the environment have a very long tradition, with philosophical conceptions of nature in the early part of the sixteenth century based largely on *anthropocentric* views of the world.

In the past, many people justified their so-called 'rights of ascendancy' over the natural world with reference to classical philosophers and the Bible. The biblical account of creation was widely interpreted as humanity having God given dominion over all living things, stressing humans' superiority (White 1967). However, there were some exceptions to such views if we consider the sacredness of creation recognized by Celtic spirituality (Bradley 1990) and the views of St Francis of Assisi, who preached equality of all, 'calling creatures no matter how small, by the name of brother and sister, because he knew they had the same source as himself' (Linzey and Barsam 2001: 22). Anthropocentric notions were also formulated into a philosophy of science and progress by Enlightenment philosophers such as René Descartes (1596–1650), Francis Bacon (1561–1626) and Galileo (1564–1642). Descartes, for

A closer look

Anthropocentrism

Anthropocentrism is a world view regarding humans as the most important and central factor in the universe – one which is taken for granted by most Westerners. It sees humans as the source of all value i.e. It is they who bestow value on other parts of nature, since the concept of value itself is a human creation.

(Pepper 1996: 326)

Questions

1. Can you think of any examples whereby humans act as if nature were designed only for human purposes, such that they act superiorly towards and in charge of nature?
2. Do you think you have ever acted in an anthropocentric (human-centred) manner with respect to the environment?

example, viewed the universe as a giant mathematically designed engine and believed that the irrational and uncontrollable forces of nature could be 'mastered, managed and used in the services of humane life' (Porter 2001: 305).

Consequently, the intellectual and cultural environment of the Enlightenment, which stressed the control of nature as physical resource, was instrumental in shaping emerging capitalism, creating the moral justification for technology to exploit the natural environment and encourage capital accumulation – let the market do its work and emancipation and self-realization will follow. In many ways, industrial capitalism unleashed contradictory elements of progress and disruption, bringing increased prosperity, education and travel for some, while the majority of the labouring classes endured poverty, overcrowding, disease and the effects of poisonous air. Waste matter from the factories and mills of industrial Britain rendered their living conditions intolerable (Whol 1983). Friedrich Engels (1820–95), who formed an intellectual partnership with Marx, was one of the first writers to document the association between environmental degradation, poverty and ill-health in his study *The Condition of the Working Class in England*. In the following extract Engels reflects on the horrendous conditions in the old town of Manchester:

> **If any one wishes to see in how little space a human being can move, how little air – and *such* air! – he can breathe, how little of civilization he may share and yet live, it is only necessary to travel hither. True, this is the *Old* Town, and the people of Manchester emphasize the fact whenever anyone**

A closer look

The Enlightenment

The main era of the Enlightenment was the second half of the eighteenth century, when European thought became concerned with reason, experience and scepticism of religious and traditional authority. The eighteenth century was a time of tremendous change as European thought became significantly mechanistic and the natural philosophy of Isaac Newton was applied to the natural and social sciences. Key thinkers associated with the Enlightenment include Kant (1724–1804) in Germany, d'Holbach (1723–89) in France and David Hume (1711–76) in Scotland.

The growth of ideas leading to the Enlightenment began in the seventeenth century, with Francis Bacon's (1561–1626) use of scientific method and René Descartes' (1596–1650) critical rationalism.

> **mentions to them the frightful condition of this Hell upon Earth; but what does that prove? Everything which here arouses horror and indignation is of recent origin, belongs to the *industrial epoch*.**
>
> (Engels 1845: 48–53)

From 1500 to 1800 there was a very gradual weakening of the belief in humanity's unquestioned ascendancy over the natural world (Thomas 1983). The growing interest in the scientific study of natural history, the development of humanitarian values towards other species and the growth of Romanticism helped to discredit previously held anthropocentric assumptions. Little wonder, then, that the 'soullessness' of industrialism and associated problems of squalor and pollution were among the most significant consequences of industrial society. The relationship between Romanticism and nature is vast and can only be touched on here, but it is clear that the Romantics cultivated an immense sensitivity to nature and believed that the built environment was foreign and alienating.

A closer look

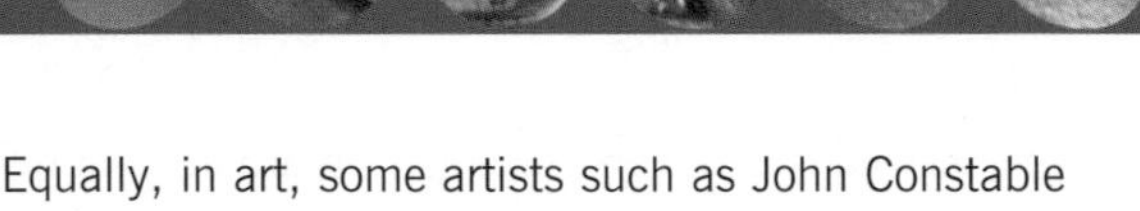

The Romantic movement

The Romantic movement was formed from an intricate group of artistic, literary and intellectual figures during the second half of the eighteenth century in Western Europe. The movement gained momentum during the rise of the Industrial Revolution, when its main protagonists rejected the dispassionate, mechanical and scientific view of nature; for them, the conquest of nature resulted in corruption of the human spirit – a fall from grace. Thus, the Romantic poets such as Blake, Shelley, Wordsworth and Keats sought a deep relationship with nature and viewed it as a source of revelation and wisdom. In his celebrated work 'Above Tintern Abbey', Wordsworth illustrates his love for nature as a place of splendour and solace, which the city was incapable of providing.

> But oft, in lonely rooms, and 'mid the din
> Of towns and cities, I have owed to them
> In hours of weariness, sensations sweet,
> Felt in the blood, and felt among the heart;
> And passing even into my purer mind,
>
> Therefore am I still –
> A lover of the meadows and the woods,
> And mountains and all that we behold –
> The anchor of my purest thoughts, the nurse,
> The guide, the guardian of my heart, and soul
> Of all my moral being.
>
> (Extract from 'Above Tintern Abbey', William Wordsworth, *Lyrical Ballads*, 1798)

Equally, in art, some artists such as John Constable (1776–1837) conveyed a reciprocal and harmonious relationship between God, humanity and nature in works such as *Salisbury Cathedral from the Meadows* (1831), while other Romantic artists such as Caspar David Friedrich (1774–1840; Figure 10.2) viewed nature as sublime, awesome and mysterious.

Figure 10.2 Caspar David Friedrich (1774–1840): *Wanderer above the Sea of Fog*, 1817
Bridgeman Art Library Ltd

Stop and think

Nature has been conveyed culturally in a variety of forms throughout the ages. For example, the central principles of design in the work of American architect Frank Lloyd Wright (1867–1959) were drawn from the natural world.

- Can you think of any other examples from contemporary culture, paintings, poems, books or films that convey a concern or appreciation for the environment?
- Do you think cultural portrayals of the environment in society influence our views and perspectives on the environment issues? If so, in what way?

Thus, the lure of rugged scenery was galvanized by the Romantic movement, but it was the late Victorians who campaigned relentlessly to retain open spaces; protect birds, animals and wild plants; preserve historic buildings; tackle pollution; and improve the environment through efficient town and country planning (Park 1976). The naturalist writings of John Ruskin (1819–1900) and Henry David Thoreau (1817–62) also transformed their appreciation of nature into a dominant political message that can be traced throughout ecological thought to the present day (Smith 1998). In North America, John Muir (1838–1914) chronicled the loss of wild areas of the American West in the late nineteenth century and pioneered ecological responsibility with the founding of the Sierra Club in 1898. Equally, Aldo Leopold's (1887–1948) revolutionary call for a new 'land ethic' in his classic *A Sand County Almanac* signalled a new form of morality regarding the environment in the twentieth century, based on a *social model* of nature where human beings are citizens of a wider 'biotic community'. In *Black Elk Speaks* (1932) the poignant transcripts from John Neihardt's interviews with Black Elk (1862–1950), a native Lakota Indian, provide a powerful insight into the symbolism and centrality of nature as a holistic *family model* of environmental ethics. Thus, 'is not the sky a father and the earth a mother, and are not all living things with feet or wings or roots their children?' (Callicott 2001: 152).

In the foreword to *Seeing Green* (1984), Jonathan Porritt, a longstanding spokesperson for the environment, aptly described the contemporary green movement as the 'rediscovery of old wisdom made relevant in a very different age'. If we consider Porritt's analysis of 'criteria for being green' these include:

> **. . . a reverence for the Earth and all its creatures; a rejection of materialism and the destructive values of industrialism; an emphasis of personal growth and spiritual development; a respect for the gentler side of human nature and an emphasis on self-reliance and decentralized communities.**
>
> (Porritt 1984: 10)

It is not difficult, therefore, to forge a link between the philosophy and ideals found in earlier periods with an ecological approach in contemporary society. Thus, the meaning of the environment varies widely. It is a contested and shifting concept open to a range of ideas, values and classifications, particular to changing cultural and structural developments at given points in history (Sandbach 1980; Palmer 2001). The severity of environmental problems has also resulted in a number of individuals and groups endorsing a variety of theories and actions as correctives to environmental

A closer look

Environmentalism and ecologism

Environmentalism argues for a managerial approach to environmental problems, secure in the belief that they can be solved without fundamental changes in present values or patterns of production and consumption.

Ecologism holds that a sustainable and fulfilling existence presupposes radical changes in our relationship with the non-human natural world, and in our mode of social and political life. For example, the Queen does not suddenly convert to ecologism by having her fleet of limousines converted to lead free petrol.

(Dobson 1995: 1)

problems. However, it is important to recognize the heterogeneous dimension of environmentalism, for it is not uncommon, even among 'green-minded' individuals and groups, to have conflicting environmental perspectives. Although these perspectives recognize the existence of environmental problems and have a common concern for the environment, they differ fundamentally in their basic ideological standpoints and tactics in dealing with them.

The distinction between 'shallow' and 'deep' ecology was first made by the prominent environmental philosopher Arne Naess in the early 1970s. Since then, deep ecology has also been referred to as 'ecocentricism' (Eckersley 1992). Deep ecology is fundamentally based on a holistic view that all organisms have intrinsic value, are intrinsically related and are of equal value – thus, 'all life is fundamentally one' (Naess 1973: 8). Although Naess produced a strong theoretical foundation in rejecting anthropocentric (human-centred) paradigms and the dualistic nature of humans and nature as separate and different, his work has attracted its share of critics, who have denounced deep ecology as lacking a concrete and sustained set of policies to move from theory to practice (Frankel 1987). However, there are some organizations such as Earth First! that follow deep green philosophical views with respect to their approach of direct action (Foreman 1998).

Stop and think

At a fundamental level, environmental sociology should help us to examine and understand the social response to environmental problems and environmental issues.

➤ Do you think a radical approach is necessary in order to tackle environment problems? For example, when environmentalists first called for a 'green' shopping day, anti-consumerist greens called for a 'no shopping day'. Try to support your answer by using explanations and examples.

At this point we turn towards developments associated with the rise and development of modern environmentalism. This leads on to a discussion about sociology having an 'absent presence' with respect to its engagement with environmental issues, resulting in calls for sociology to embrace a 'new ecological paradigm'.

Modern environmentalism

They took all the trees
Put 'em in a tree museum
And they charged all the people
A dollar and a half just to see 'em

Don't it always seem to go
That you don't know what you've got till it's gone;
They've paved paradise,
Put up a parking lot.

Hey farmer farmer
Put away that D.D.T. now
Give me spots on my apples
But leave me the birds and the bees
Please!

(Joni Mitchell, 'Big Yellow Taxi', 1969; released on *Ladies of the Canyon*, 1970)

As discussed above, environmental consciousness and environmental issues have a long historical tradition. However, the era of modern or 'new environmentalism' evolved largely during the 1960s (McCormick 1995). Although the growth of the environment as a new social movement (NSM) and the rise of green parties is outside the scope of this chapter (see the list of further reading at the end of this work), the growth of 'new environmentalism' was viewed not as an organized phenomenon but as an 'accumulation of organisations and individuals with varied motives and ideals, with roughly similar goals but often different methods . . . anarchism, evangelism, social reform, political reform and hard science (McCormick 1995: 57). The increasing importance of scientific and environmental knowledge and society's response to them had important ramifications, as the concerns and threats were understood not exclusively as an environmental crisis but as a crisis for humanity itself. This issue will be developed further when we come to look at the debate on environmental risk.

During this period of increased environmental consciousness, alarm was directed towards world population growth, increasing levels of pollution, use of pesticides, dependence on fossil fuels and the depletion of non-renewable natural resources. Environmentalism in the late 1960s and early 1970s was characterized by warnings of imminent ecological disaster and demands for urgent, often drastic, measures to avert this fate (Elrich 1968; Hardin 1968; Goldsmith *et al.* 1972).

In *Silent Spring* (1962), American biologist Rachel Carson (1907–64) warned the public about the long-term effects of indiscriminate spraying of DDT (technically known as dichloro-diphenyl-trichloroethane) and other synthetic pesticides on the natural ecosystem. The book has been credited as marking the beginning of the 'environmental revolution' (McCormick 1995: 67). Carson documented the threat to birds and wildlife, resulting in the potential loss of the dawn chorus – a silent spring:

> **Dead birds found in treated areas had absorbed or swallowed the poisons. Species that live on the ground or frequent low vegetation suffered 100 per cent mortality, even a year after treatment, a spring die off of songbirds occurred and much good nesting territory lay silent and unoccupied.**
>
> (Carson 1962: 151)

Despite fierce criticism and threats of lawsuits from the chemical industry, Carson's work was instrumental in leading to a ban on national pesticide policy in the USA and instrumental in the creation of the Environmental Protection Agency. After a long battle with cancer, Carson died just two years after the publication of *Silent Spring*. (See www.rachelcarson.org for more details.)

The Limits to Growth (Meadows *et al.* 1972) was another seminal text, which produced a controversial response from various economists, industrialists and politicians, collectively known as the Club of Rome. The book's authors argued that unchecked growth on our finite planet was leading to ecological 'overshoot' and pending disaster. Now, over 30 years on, Meadows *et al.* (2002) continue to argue that population growth and material consumption must be radically reduced. The 1970s also witnessed the first Earth Day, the growth of groups such as Greenpeace (which used high-profile tactics to draw attention to environmental issues), the development of green parties, and concern over issues such as nuclear power, acid rain and recycling.

James Lovelock (1979) produced the influential 'Gaia theory', named after the Greek earth goddess, which promoted a holistic view of the world where all life on earth interacts with the physical environment to form a complex system, a single super-organism. This view of the earth took on a great significance following the space flights in the 1960s, which allowed the earth to be viewed as a complete entity for the first time (as depicted in Figure 10.1 at the start of this chapter). By the mid- to late 1970s few countries could dismiss environmental issues or be unaffected by them. The United Nations Conference on the Human Environment, held in Stockholm in 1972, was another major environmental landmark as the first of a series of world environmental conferences. As McCormick (1995: 107) suggests, the Stockholm conference marked an important transition from 'the emotional and occasionally naive New Environmentalism of the 1960s to the more rational, political and global perspective of the 1970s'.

By the late 1980s the environment moved from a marginal position into the realms of mainstream

A closer look

Bhopal

The Union Carbide pesticide plant in the province of Madhya Pradesh in Bhopal, India, gained worldwide attention due to a catastrophic chemical disaster on 3 December 1984. The release of lethal gas resulted in over 3000 deaths and the serious injury of over 100,000 people concentrated in the poorest and most crowded areas of the city (Gupta 1998). Fierce controversies and legal battles regarding the cause of the accident are still being fought. It is understood that water got into the main tank, but how this happened still remains a mystery. Union Carbide, a subsidiary of the United States Dow Chemical Industry, suggests that the accident was caused by an act of 'sabotage'. However, the sabotage theory is strongly contested not only by official Indian reports but also by Bhopal victims who hold Union Carbide culpable of gross negligence due to a lack of maintenance of the plant. According to Amnesty International (2004), despite the determined efforts of survivors to secure justice, the large numbers affected have received inadequate compensation and medical assistance.

society. This striking shift in awareness elicited a series of pragmatic responses from various quarters, such as governments, industry and commercial interests. In addition, a series of spectacular environmental issues and incidents exploded in the media. Although decreases in the ozone layer had been predicted from the late 1970s, these were widely reported from the mid-1980s as forming a 'hole' over the earth's polar regions. In 1984 the world's worst industrial accident also occurred, in the Indian city of Bhopal, followed by the world's worst nuclear power catastrophe, at Chernobyl in 1986.

Sociologically, the Bhopal tragedy raises a number of crucial questions. The tragedy dramatically exposed the human costs of globalization, illustrating the ineffectiveness of law and science to restore order when radically different cultures of knowledge and justice were joined in this unplanned and unmitigated confrontation. In Jasanoff's analysis of Bhopal, she argues that 'the insufficiency of scientific knowledge is inseparable from the inadequacy of justice' (Jasanoff 2007: 6). This view supports survivors' claims that the multinational Union Carbide company and the Indian state were both 'implicated in equally reprehensible acts of denial of knowledge as well as legal responsibility' (Jasanoff 2007: 6). Furthermore, the location of a toxic chemical plant in the heart of a built-up, low-income community, the lack of information regarding the potential risks for workers and the general disregard for victims' 'self-knowledge' following the accident link directly to a number of important sociological debates and raise questions on the nature of manufactured risk in society, the construction of scientific knowledge and the demand for environmental justice (these issues are developed further below).

Stop and think

In sociology it is very important to understand structures of power.

➤ Why do you think the victims of Bhopal felt so helpless and powerless in the aftermath of the chemical industrial accident?

While the human and environmental consequences of Chernobyl are catastrophic, it is also the case that the political and symbolic repercussions following Chernobyl cannot be overstated. The communist

A closer look

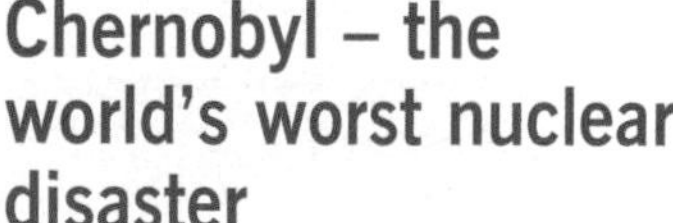

Chernobyl – the world's worst nuclear disaster

In the early hours of 26 April 1986, one of four nuclear reactors at the Chernobyl power station exploded. The disaster happened due to an experiment associated with the deliberate switching-off of safety systems, resulting in over 30 deaths and around 200 people affected by radiation sickness (McCormick 1995). The Chernobyl disaster released at least 100 times more radiation than the atom bombs dropped on Nagasaki and Hiroshima in the Second World War. Much of the fallout was deposited close to Chernobyl, in parts of Belarus, Ukraine and Russia. Hundreds of towns and villages were evacuated, and in the aftermath of the accident traces of radioactive deposits were found in nearly every country in the northern hemisphere, highlighting the impact of the disaster far beyond national boundaries. The number of people who could eventually die as a result of the Chernobyl accident is distressing. At least 1800 children and young people in the most severely contaminated areas of Belarus have contracted cancer of the thyroid because of the reactor disaster. It is feared that the number of cases of thyroid cancer among those who were children or young people when the accident happened will reach 8000 in the coming decades. There have also been rises in many other types of cancer, diabetes, heart disease, respiratory and digestive problems, birth defects, and psychological disorders, along with the permanent contamination of millions of acres of land (Shrader-Frechette 1999; UNDP 2002).

system, unlike the Western capitalist model, was constructed on the principle that technological production, not guided by profit motives, would subsequently be in society's best interest. Yet, the tragic circumstances of Chernobyl are shrouded in 'cover up and denial' regarding the consequences of the disaster resulting in another classic case of environmental injustice for the victims and dispersed pattern of damage, cross-border through climatic effects (Shrader-Frechette 1999).

Stop and think

The Chernobyl disaster resulted from technical mismanagement and led to the contamination of the global environment.

- In what way did the events of Chernobyl highlight new levels of people's experiences or awareness of risk in late modernity?
- As a society, what do you think we can learn from catastrophic incidents such as Chernobyl?
- Can you think of any other examples where human activity has resulted in serious environmental damage?

By the mid-1980s the highly influential report of the Brundtland Commission, *Our Common Future* (World Commission on Environment and Development 1987), signified the global nature of environmental problems and the need for all nations to establish policies for sustainable development (see pp. 434–436). Media coverage during this time was also notable for its depiction of the appalling levels of devastation brought about by famine affecting various African countries, resulting in high-profile Band Aid recordings in 1984, 1989 and 2004, the Live Aid concert in 1985 and the Live8 concert in 2005. Although the effects of environmental degradation as a contributory factor in the famine/drought were generally overlooked, there was a growing awareness that development policies over the previous two decades required a rigorous re-examination (McCormick 1995) (see Chapter 9 for further details).

A persistent problem is that burdens of environmental degradation rarely fall directly upon those who are responsible for causing them (see pp. 437–439). The polluted living conditions of disadvantaged communities, the impact of Bhopal and Chernobyl on the blameless masses, and the transportation of toxic waste to developing countries are but a few examples of disproportionate burden imposed on more marginalized communities. Important issues must be addressed in confronting the environmental demands of affluent nations (with high and rising levels of mass consumption) and the needs of poor nations struggling in some of the world's most environmentally fragile areas. The sad truth is that poverty can accelerate ecological deterioration by forcing poor people to destroy potentially renewable resources such as soils, forest and wildlife for survival (Satterthwaite *et al.* 1996; Human Development Report 1992).

A small share of the earth's population in the developed world consumes most of its energy and produces the bulk of its pollution. In marked contrast, over one billion people live in cities where air pollution is below World Health Organization (WHO) standards, and each day 35,000 children die from environment-related diseases attributable to pollution and unsafe water (UNCED 1992; Satterthwaite *et al.* 1996). These shocking statistics are just a sample of the data that formed the backdrop to the meeting of the UN Conference on Environment and Development (UNCED) in Rio de Janerio in 1992, often referred to as the Earth Summit (www.earthsummit.info). The signing of a series of conventions by 152 world leaders at the Earth Summit and the agreement to a UN Commission on Sustainable Development (www.un.org/esa/sustdev/csd/csd11/CSD11.htm) signalled a growing recognition of the need for cooperation within the international community in the support of global environmental goals.

Stop and think

By the start of the 1990s, the first assessment report for the United Nations Framework Convention on Climate Change (UNFCCC 1990) was put into force. This was followed by the infamous 'World scientists warning to humanity' broadcast in 1992, highlighting the threat to the planet due to humanity's failure to address growing environmental degradation. The warning was transmitted by 1670 scientists, including 110 of the 138 living winners of Nobel Prizes in the sciences:

> We are fast approaching many of the Earth's limits. Current economic practices which damage the environment cannot continue. Our massive tampering could trigger unpredictable collapse of critical biological systems which are only partly understood. A great change in our stewardship of the Earth and the life on it is required if vast human misery is to be avoided and our global home on this planet is not to be irretrievably mutilated.
>
> (Bruges 2000: 6)

This begs some crucial questions regarding global risk:

- Are we *all* in the same boat?
- Who would be hit the hardest, and why?

The effectiveness of international cooperation is, however, determined largely by the strength of commitments from national governments, with a view to taking corrective action. Although the Montreal Protocol (1989) was instrumental in reducing the number of substances believed to be responsible for ozone depletion, particularly chlorofluorocarbons (CFCs), a different situation emerged regarding a collective response to climate change.

Climate change

Although climate change has been a natural phenomenon since the earth's existence, the rate of change is now accelerating and having a major impact on the earth's surface. The warming of the earth's surface (global warming) is believed to result from the concentration of *greenhouse gases* – a series of gases, such as carbon dioxide, methane, nitrous oxide and CFCs, in the atmosphere. We can imagine these gases as a blanket around the earth, insulating the earth from escaping heat and remaining at a constant concentration for thousands of years. However, the rate of synthetic greenhouse gases has accelerated dramatically due to industrial production (the burning of fossil fuels) and daily use of energy (oil, gas, coal) in addition to other forms of human activity such as tropical deforestation. This type of activity has led to the sun's energy being trapped in the atmosphere by a bigger 'blanket', which has caused the earth's temperature to increase more rapidly than it has for thousands of years.

The Intergovernmental Panel on Climate Change (IPCC 1990, 1995, 2001, 2007) (www.ipcc.ch) and the Stern Report (Office of Climate Change 2006) commissioned by the British government (www.occ.gov.uk/activities/stern.htm) report that evidence on the planet's warming is now 'unequivocal', revealing that 11 of the past 12 years rank among the warmest since 1850, with a temperature increase of almost 1 °C. The likely trend of emissions of greenhouse gases over the next few years suggests that another 1 or 2 °C rise will be difficult to avoid, even if we take responsible action. Melting glaciers, sea-level rises, altered ecosystems and patterns of extreme weather events indicate that we are already experiencing global climate change. As a consequence, places, ecosystems and people are all vulnerable to the threat of human-induced global warming. Climate variability holds great risk, particularly for people who live in the developing world, where marginalized groups are already exposed to poverty, debt, and food and water shortages. There is also a greater exposure to droughts and floods in areas of economic and political instability, leading to the displacement of people and communities (Adger *et al.* 2006). Reports claim that a 'business as usual' or 'wait and see' response could lead to the probability of much higher temperature increases, which could disastrously transform our planet (UNICEF 2008: 1).

In response to the Stern Report, the then UK prime minister Tony Blair said the consequences of inaction for the planet were 'literally disastrous' and the then chancellor of the exchequer Gordon Brown claimed:

> **In the 20th century our national economic ambitions were the twin objectives of achieving stable economic growth and full employment. Now in the 21st century our new objectives are clear, they are threefold: growth, full employment and environmental care.**
>
> (http://news.bbc.co.uk/1/hi/business/6096084.stm)

Stop and think

- Do you think the consequences of our 'national economic ambitions' in the twentieth century resulted in 'inevitable' environmental damage?

New proposals for halving global emissions by 2050 were hailed as 'major progress', by UK prime minister Gordon Brown at the 2008 G8 Summit in Hokkaido, Tokyo. The G8 comprises the eight leading industrialized nations, namely the USA, Canada, the UK, France, Germany, Japan, Italy and, most recently, Russia. They meet annually to discuss global economic issues. While leaders from the G8 and the so-called G5 (five of the largest emerging countries – Mexico, Brazil, China, India and South Africa) agreed they had established a 'shared vision' on climate change, they failed to bridge important differences between rich and emerging countries on the scale of change required. In particular, the G5 countries believed that the proposal to reduce carbon emissions by 50 per cent did not go far enough and wanted the G8 to cut emissions by more than 80 per cent.

This marked the final major summit attended by US president George W. Bush. The USA is one of the world's main oil producers and the largest per-capita contributor to carbon emissions. The USA is also the most significant country failing to ratify the Kyoto Protocol to cut carbon emissions to the levels recorded in 1990, despite being a signatory to it. The Kyoto Protocol was adopted in 1997 and took effect in 2005, but it remains non-binding on the USA. Neither President Clinton nor President Bush ratified the protocol. President Bush stated that this was because of the exemption granted to China (the world's second-largest contributor to greenhouse gases by volume) and the economic costs that he believed would follow. At the Tokyo Summit in 2008, President Bush ended a private meeting of G8 leaders with a joke about the USA's record: 'Goodbye from the world's biggest polluter' (www.telegraph.co.uk, 11 July 2008).

Monbiot (2006: xii) argues that rich nations (the G8) are in no position to 'preach restraint' to poorer countries based on the following data:

- China's emissions have been rising by 2 per cent a year.
- A citizen of China produces on average 2.7 tonnes of carbon dioxide a year.
- A citizen of the UK produces 9.5 tonnes of carbon dioxide a year.
- A citizen of the USA produces 20 tonnes of carbon dioxide a year.

An analysis assessing the challenge of 'fairness in adaptation to climate change' (Adger *et al.* 2006: 227) also highlights the 'justice dilemmas', which include critical questions including:

- Responsibility for climate change impacts;
- The level and burden of assistance to developing countries for adaptation;
- Distribution of assistance between countries and adaption measures; and
- Equal participation in planning and decisions on adaptation.

There are some positive indicators that the importance of global warming is being heard in society. The IPCC and Al Gore were awarded the Nobel Peace Prize in 2007 for their efforts to build up and disseminate greater knowledge about man-made climate change (see www.climatecrisis.net).

In 2012 the Kyoto Protocol to prevent climate change and global warming runs out. The parties of

A closer look

The environment and President Obama

With Barack Obama's historic election victory in November 2008, there is a renewed sense of optimism within and beyond North America. Although no incoming president in recent times has aroused such hope, few have faced such serious political, economic and social challenges. With respect to climate change, Mr Obama has called for a 'crash programme' of research and development into new technologies to help make the US independent of imported oil within a decade. More immediately, attention will focus on whether the US will agree to sign up to a new treaty on climate change when the Kyoto agreement expires.

In a Gallup poll (November 2008) a sample of 1010 Americans were asked if they thought an Obama administration would be able to achieve 16 policy objectives. Two of these relate to the environment: by a margin of 70–28 per cent, respondents expected the new administration to 'improve the quality of the environment' while a majority (57%) expected it would be able to 'reduce US dependence on oil' (and 41% expected it would not).

A closer look

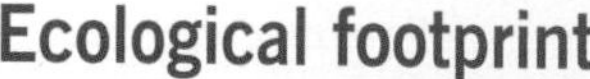

Ecological footprint

The metaphor 'ecological footprint' is used to mean a measure of human demands on the environment at a personal level (e.g. energy consumption, car use, air travel) and in terms of inequalities and resources at a wider global level.

The band Radiohead recently asked fans to take public transport to their concerts, and the organizers of the festival T in the Park promoted the biggest carbon-neutral music festival in the world, with its 'Cut the Carbon' campaign.

Questions

1. **Do you think it is a good idea for musicians to get involved in environmental issues? Try to support your answer with explanations.**
2. **Have you ever considered the impact of your own ecological footprint?**
3. **In what ways do you think you could lower your own ecological footprint on the planet?**

To calculate your own carbon footprint, go to www.google.co.uk/carbonfootprint/index.html.

the UNFCCC will meet in Copenhagen during 2009 for the last time at a government level before the climate agreement needs to be renewed.

Stop and think

The G8 Summit in Hokkaido, Tokyo, in June 2008 was hosted at the luxury Windsor Hotel amidst high security at a cost of £238 million.

- With extreme levels of poverty and inequality in the world, do you think the cost of this kind of international summit can really be justified?
- Can you think of reasons why there are increasing levels of disillusionment, especially among young people, in terms of their involvement in the democratic process, e.g. willingness to vote, and yet movements such as anti-globalization protests indicate growing concerns about social, political and environmental issues?

With the growing awareness of environmental issues, sociologists have only recently jumped on to the green academic bandwagon. Why is this the case? As an academic discipline, sociology has been taken to task for its lack of attention regarding the environment. In the next section we consider this position, before moving on to discuss some of the more recent theoretical developments in the field.

Environmental sociology: an 'absent presence'?

> **When Earth Day inaugurated the 'Environmental Decade' of the 1970s, sociologists found themselves without any prior body of theory or research to guide them towards a distinctive understanding of the relationship between society and the environment.**
>
> (Hannigan 1995: 5)

Although the environment forms an integral backdrop to societal and human relations, at a sociological level it could be termed as having an 'absent presence'. The theoretical vacuum associated with sociology's past neglect of the environment reflects not only its late entry into the field but also what Newby (1997) has referred to as the 'intellectual inheritance' of sociology – that is, what sociology as a discipline actually *defines* as sociological. Perhaps sociological insights were never adequately brought to the fore, largely due to translators who focused more on social phenomena over physical or environmental insights (Buttel 1986: 338). It is certainly the case that geographical perspectives on society and nature by theorists such as Henry Thomas Buckle and Ellsworth Huntington were influential in intellectual circles during the nineteenth century; hence, the natural world was viewed through a lens of 'geographical determinism' or by means of Darwinist principles – evolution, natural selection and the survival of the fittest (Hannigan 1995: 6–7). By the 1920s many sociologists embraced psychology, rather than physics or biology, as the theoretical foundation for sociology. This social-behaviourist approach is reflected in Charles Cooley's *Looking Glass Self*, with an emphasis on introspection and imagination, developed in his classic work, *Human Nature and the Social Order* (1902). George Herbert Mead (1934) also aimed to build a general theory of 'mind, self and society', highlighting the reflexive nature of the self, particularly through language, symbols and communication.

Classical thinkers and the environment

As noted above, there has been general agreement among environmental sociologists that the classical sociological tradition has been generally inhospitable to the nurturing of an ecologically informed sociological approach (Buttel 1986; Dickens 1996). One explanation for this could be the anthropocentric legacy of the classical theorists – an emphasis on a human-centred rather than ecological view of the world. Thus, the emphasis on social phenomena, to the neglect of ecological phenomena, may have encouraged contemporary sociological theory to follow in a similar path. The rise of an industrial economy, the growth of cities and the emergence of new political ideas focused the attention of the early sociologists on the operation and organization of society. In their various guises, they reflected on individualism, patterns of social solidarity, isolation and forms of detachment. Although the classical theorists were deeply concerned about the disruptive and dehumanizing effects of industrialism, for Marx the central issue was the dehumanization of man (*alienation*) generated by the capitalist mode of production (see Chapter 12 for a fuller discussion).

In Marx's early *Manuscripts* (1844) he recognized the alienation of people from nature under modernity and nature as integral to human wellbeing (for further explanations of Marxist theories and concepts, see Chapter 2). Societal relations came to be dominated by instrumental rationality – the calculation of the most efficient means to the achievement of economic goals of industrial society (Bottomore 1963; Parsons 1977). Clearly, both Marx and Engels understood the social and environmental mayhem resulting from capitalist development, evidenced by their commentaries on the effects of poisonous air on the health of the workers. Not for nothing were the industrial and mining parts of the West Midlands called 'the Black Country' (Whol 1983). Although Marx and Engels argued for a new relationship between people and nature, there was a lack of direction over the exact form this would take. As O'Connor suggests:

> **While Marx and Engels were master theoreticians of the social havoc caused by capitalist development, neither put ecological destruction at the centre of their theory of capitalist accumulation and socioeconomic change. They underestimated the extent to which the historical development of capitalism as a mode of production has been based on the exhaustion of resources and degradation on nature.**
>
> (O'Connor 1998: 124).

It is also the case that Marx referred to aspects of agricultural production, but there was no explicit formula for a theoretical ecological framework (O'Connor 1998). Perhaps the lack of consideration about the ecological impacts of these developments was due to the fact that they were writing at a time when, for many, survival was the factor – accumulation crises were more pressing than environmental crises.

Ecological Marxism

In recent years, Marxist writings have developed to have an important influence on contemporary environmental theories, which highlight the impact of capitalist economic systems in exacerbating ecological degradation. Among other things, eco-Marxists view the relationship between nature, the economy and society as laying bare the contradictions, crises and environmental degradation synonymous with capitalist production, distribution, exchange and consumption (Benton 1996; Harvey 1996; O'Connor 1996, 1998). Essentially, humans may seek to master nature, but in doing so they are constantly forced to come to terms with the unintended environmental consequences of their actions. The early work of Marx and Engels has had an important influence on a range of contemporary neo-Marxist literature, including theoretical insights that identify the effect of capitalism in exacerbating environmental degradation and the commodification of nature. When we refer to the 'commodification' of goods, we mean the manner in which goods are produced for exchange, as goods that were previously used for subsistence now have a new value, a market (monetary) value. In Schnaiberg's compelling study *The Environment: From Surplus to Scarcity* (1980), a tension is identified between the creation of profit, increasing consumer demand and calls for environmental protection.

Both Emile Durkheim and Max Weber distanced themselves from notions of biological determinism in their general methodological approach. This view of the world explained social or cultural phenomena in biological terms. For example, Darwin's theory of evolution and natural selection was very influential at this time. Durkheim saw industrialization as a threat to social order through a breakdown of normative consensus (*anomie*). Durkheim's (1964) emphasis on 'social facts' in the *Rules of Sociological Method* stressed the 'social' causes of complex social phenomena. However, it is possible to trace the impact of increased population, rural–urban migration and the struggle over scarce resources in the transition from 'mechanical' to 'organic' society (see Chapter 2 for further explanation). According to Dunlap *et al.* (2002: 40), such work bears a resemblance to 'modern notions of human ecology'. It is reasonable to suggest that, due to his general focus on social action and human motivation, Weber is rarely thought of as an ecological theorist. Nevertheless, more recent scholars such as West (1984) have drawn upon Weber's account of religion and ancient societies in an effort to extrapolate a human–ecological dimension. Similarly, neo-Weberian theorists such as Raymond Murphy (2002) have revised aspects of Weber's rationalization theories, leading to the concept of 'reflexive alienation'. In effect, the cumulative growth of scientific and technological knowledge (primary rationalization) that led to the separation and mastery of nature, and our alienation from it, has also resulted in a gradual recognition that humans have to confront the environmental consequences of their actions.

On reflection, the charge against the limitations of the classical thinkers regarding environmental issues is partially fair. It is important to acknowledge the historical and ideological influences surrounding the development of sociology during the nineteenth and twentieth centuries as well as the complex structural transitions affecting the growth and development of society. Indeed, there is a view that other dominant forms of sociology (functionalism, post-industrialism, modernization theory, pluralism) were even less anchored in the 'natural' world (Dunlap *et al.* 2002: 42). However, as Sutton (2004: 92) points out, 'it may be more productive to examine some of the more recent sociological theories which try to tackle environmental issues head on.'

Environmental sociology: new beginnings

> **Environmental problems are problems for society, and as people create environmental problems, it is people who must resolve them, and for that, among other things, we need sociology.**
>
> (Mayerfield-Bell 1998: 2)

Sociologists, like many other members of the public, are now recognizing that society is threatening the very conditions of its existence. Environmentalism slowly but surely brought into sharp focus the need for sociologists and others to revisit the assumptions made about how social and economic progress have been perceived – that the post-war Western experience of economic growth and prosperity is both exceptional and contingent, as there is no continuous linear development guaranteed for modern society, and nor is this development necessarily harmonious. In a world of global environmental degradation and uneven consumption patterns, the conflict between human interests and environmental interests becomes glaringly exposed, and the conventional ways of one era are not necessarily applicable in the next.

In a variety of works from the late 1970s, demands for sociology to embrace a 'new ecological paradigm' were heralded by North American rural sociologists William Catton and Riley Dunlap (Catton and Dunlap 1978; Dunlap 1980; Dunlap and Catton 1980). In essence, Catton and Dunlap argued that most sociologists viewed human societies as 'exempt' from ecological principles, exemplified by the narrow anthropocentrism (human-centred) view of classical sociology. This pioneering approach called for a transition towards a more ecocentric view of nature, stressing the interconnectedness of the human–environment condition, that everything is connected to everything else.

Stop and think

- If sociology helps us to understand the world we live in, then how might environmental sociology contribute to a better understanding of environmental issues, set within a social context?

A closer look

A new ecological paradigm (NEP)

Dunlap and Catton's (1980: 15–47) critique of existing sociology had four basic features:

- People continued to be seen as completely distinct from other creatures/had domain over them.
- People were wholly in control of their own destinies.
- The planet and its resources are vast and provide unlimited resources for human beings.
- The history of humanity is one of progress: for every perceived problem, there is a solution and progress will never cease.

Such assumptions were fundamentally unecological.

In contrast, the new ecological paradigm (NEP) would recognize continuities between people and other species. The NEP would also reject the view that sociology is distinct from other disciplines such as biology and consider whether the human potential for creative thinking could lead to greater environmental awareness, solutions to problems and less destructive action.

Modern societies that have preoccupied sociology have undergone tremendous change, involving great technological and scientific developments. However, to what extent have these developments been at the expense of the environment? Has unrestrained economic growth been the cause of or the solution to environmental problems? When we talk of 'progress', what type of progress are we actually referring to in an age of nuclear, chemical and genetic technology? The capacity for humans to be both highly creative and destructive was illustrated dramatically in photographs of the earth taken by the space shuttle Discovery in 1988, depicting rising smoke from fires clearing vast areas of rainforest in the Amazon basin. Thus, technological conquest led to exploration in space, but paradoxically it exposed the fragility of the earth along with our capacity to put the planet at great risk. The quote below is based on an observation of the earth from space, from Russian astronaut Aleksei Leonov:

> **The Earth was small, light blue, and so touchingly alone, our home that must be defended like a holy relic. The Earth was absolutely round. I believe I never knew what the word round meant until I saw Earth from space.**
>
> (Aleksei Leonov, www.solarviews.com/eng/earthsp.htm)

We might ask ourselves whether the benefits of late modernity outweigh the risks that are often associated with technological progress and advances in science. One of the key features of the new phase is the significance of ecological destruction and large-scale hazards in the transformation of the social world we inhabit. The section that follows focuses more specifically on the environmental dimension of risk, drawing particularly on Ulrich Beck's analysis of a 'risk society'.

Risk society

> **'Risk Society' means an epoch in which the dark sides of progress increasingly come to dominate social debate.**
>
> (Beck 1995: 2)

Sociologists Ulrich Beck (1992, 1994, 1995) and Anthony Giddens (1990, 1991) are best known for their insights and analysis of modernity, whereby the institutional, cultural, social and political identity that characterized earlier phases of modernity are in the process of being displaced. The practice of reflexivity leads us to reflect upon the behaviour of ourselves and others promoted by the social conditions and experiences of late modernity. In his theory of 'risk society', Beck claims that new technologies and their associated risks are creating a new era, an advanced stage of modernity that is 'freeing itself from the contours of the classical industrial society and forging a new form – "risk society"' (Beck 1992: 9). However, a 'risk society' is not intended to imply simply an increase of risk but rather a society that is organized in response to risks. Risk is defined as 'a systematic way of dealing with hazards and insecurities induced and introduced by modernization itself' (Beck 1992: 21).

Arguably, humans have always been subjected to different levels of risks, for example plagues, famines, natural disasters, road accidents and smoking. However, Beck's notion of a 'risk society' is concerned predominantly with 'manufactured risk', such as nuclear power, nuclear weaponry, chemical and biotechnical production, genetic engineering, genetically modified foods and global warming – risks that are more global in character and fail to respect conventional boundaries between the powerful and the powerless, between rich and poor. Beck's analysis of global hazards struck a responsive chord in society, particularly in light of catastrophic incidents such as Bhopal and Chernobyl (see pp. 415 and 416), resulting in a wavering trust in industry, government, science and the secure knowledge of 'experts' (Giddens 1990). Thus, a greater awareness of risk has 'become central to the way in which human agents and modern institutions organize the social world', but it can also undermine our confidence in different systems of knowledge, expertise and forms of social organization (Elliot 2002: 299).

According to Beck (1992), widespread risk contains a 'boomerang effect' as individuals producing risk also become exposed to it. For Beck, the key point is knowledge – if you are unaware of the risk, then your economic status is irrelevant. According to Beck (1992), the hazards of 'risk society' are qualitatively different from those of simple modernity and have been summarized by Benton (2002: 261) in the following way:

- They are unlimited in time and space, with global self-destruction now a possibility (e.g. climate change).
- They are socially unlimited in scope: potentially everyone is at risk.
- They may be minimized, but not eliminated, so that risk has to be measured in terms of probabilities.
- They are irreversible.
- They have diverse sources, thus traditional methods of assigning responsibility do not apply.
- They are literally incalculable on such a scale that they exceed the capacities of state or private organizations to provide compensation and/or insurance.
- They may be identified and measured only by scientific means. Consequently, the contesting of scientific knowledge and public cynicism about science are key aspects of the 'reflexivity' of the risk society.

Thus, what was once obvious and calculable now has a more insidious aspect. Currently, the more sinister dimension of risk relates to the unseen, unknown quantity of the nature, time and duration of risk.

Risk society: the death of class?

> **The driving force of the class society can be summarized in one phrase: I am hungry! The movement set in motion by the risk society, on the other hand, is expressed in the statement: I am afraid.**
>
> (Beck 1992: 49)

Beck and Giddens both agree that, although material inequalities continue to exist within the context of a 'risk society', the political agenda is nonetheless changing from conflict over class distribution of goods to conflict over the *non-class distribution of 'bads'* – environmental problems resulting from the industrial and technological expansion of modernity. Thus, global risk cuts across patterns of class and national society, summed up in the formula 'poverty is hierarchic, smog is democratic' (Beck 1992: 36). Although *Risk Society* and subsequent writings became a catalyst for innovative thinking and a framework for a range of sociological debates, it is has not been without its critics. Turner (1994) questions the fundamental notion of 'risk' per se as the ultimate concern in contemporary culture, drawing upon earlier periods in history that demonstrate 'profound uncertainties about life'. A number of theorists also challenge Beck on his general neglect of risk with respect to forms of 'symbolic' meaning. This alludes to the way in which meanings around notions of risk emerge and are produced through societal interaction and can be distinguished as an aesthetic, psychological and cultural process through which risk is conducted, perceived and monitored in contemporary society (Elliott 1996, 2002; Lash and Urry 1994). There are also concerns around Beck's 'restricted' analysis of exactly how we moved into an age of reflexivity (Elliot 2002). In addition, Beck's views on class, his vision of a reorganized 'sub-politics' and his account of the equal distribution of 'bads' contradicts theoretical and empirically based evidence correlating the proximity to environmental degradation with an individual's or group's social class, ethnic status and geographical location (see below). For Benton:

> **concern about the most basic conditions for survival itself, poisoning of food and water supplies, the danger of industrial accidents, the unpredictable**

alteration of global climates and so on could hardly be more materialist.

(cited in Dunlap *et al.* 2002: 264)

Finally, why do we find reflexivity in some sectors of socioeconomic life and not in others? Elliot (2002: 303) suggests that 'against the backdrop of new communication technologies and advances in knowledge transfer, vast gaps in the socio-cultural conditions of the wealthy and the poor drastically affect the ways in which individuals are drawn into the project of reflexive modernization'. The appalling lack of knowledge transfer, practices of denial and cover-up associated with the Bhopal and Chernobyl disasters are a case in point.

Stop and think

Friedrich Engels (1820–95), nineteenth-century philosopher, socialist and co-founder of Marxism, suggested that 'nature has ways of ultimately taking its revenge on human societies' apparent victories over it'.

- What do you think Engels meant by this statement?
- Do you think that this comment by Engels has any relevance in today's society?

Try to support your views with examples and explanations.

As we noted above, for Beck (1992) modern society is associated with new forms of risk, increasingly at a globalized level. As competent reflective individuals in society, we are progressively more sensitive to the various forms of risk that have a bearing on our everyday lives. However, is it possible, through social or technical innovation, to find our way out of the environmental crisis without undermining the existing social structures and processes? Other theorists, known as ecological modernists, advocate what appears to be an alternative approach to risk society theory with respect to the *positive* benefits of science and technology.

Ecological modernization

The concept of ecological modernization (EM) proposes that policies for economic development and environmental protection can be combined in a more progressive manner. Thus, EM theorists suggest that economic and environmental goals can be integrated within the framework of an advanced industrial economy (Spaargaren and Mol 1992; Garner 1996). In this way, economic growth need not result automatically in higher rates of environmental degradation. For example, new, clean technologies and greater energy efficiency could address energy crises, waste could be reduced and a higher level of materials could be recycled, while genetically modified crops could help to solve hunger. As a theory, EM sought to take account of patterns identified in Western Europe in the late twentieth century that showed improvements in environmental quality. However, as Mol suggests:

a distinction should be made between ecological modernization as a *theory* on social continuity and transformation and ecological modernization as a *political programme* for environment-inspired reform of contemporary industrial society.

(Mol 1997: 140)

For the most part, critiques against EM derive from its 'prescriptive undertones', for example the feasibility of EM as a normative proposition, in terms of what governments and institutions ought to do in order to address environmental problems (Mol 1997). The debates on EM are essentially linked to the nature of progress in the twenty-first century: questions of growth and the role of technology as well as the role of the state. Whether capitalism can accommodate the environmental challenge and the extent to which sustainable economic growth is possible are topics of ongoing debate, largely for the following reasons:

- EM is questioned over its capacity to address questions of social change and social justice.
- The potential of new technologies such as clean technology and energy have not been sufficiently explored.
- Environmental degradation (waste/pollution) has effectively been exported.
- The progress of EM has not been uniform across countries.
- Government policy at a macro-level is often short-term, e.g. in a reaction to a crisis.
- Alliances between government and industry can constrain new approaches to policy.
- There may be too much reliance placed on industry's ability to produce a technological 'fix'.

- There is evidence of a lack of information, risk assessment and managerial capacity to accommodate EM.
- New approaches to policy are required if EM is to be encouraged.
- Behavioural changes are still needed until technology offers better solutions (even within an EM paradigm).

Despite the critical references to EM, as a theory it clearly identifies modern science, technology and the state as key institutions in the dynamics for ecological reform, including the role of innovators, entrepreneurs and others as agents of ecological restructuring. Mol (1997: 141) also suggests that EM adheres to the Brundtland Commission's concept of sustainable development in rejecting the 'fundamental opposition between economy and ecology'. (For further details on Brundtland, see pp. 434–436.)

Stop and think

The two global approaches in environmental sociology – risk society and ecological modernization – focus on the potential role of modern technology for either:

(a) overcoming environmental degradation, or

(b) exacerbating environmental degradation.

- Do you think environmental modernization can transcend the traditional antagonisms between economic progress and responsible environmental management?
- Ecological modernists claim that technology and improved design can achieve gains in ecological sustainability, for example renewable energy and hybrid cars. What other examples of new technology or innovations in society might benefit the environment?

During the past decade, debates around risk, science and technology have resulted in the emergence of a range of environmental narratives. Clearly not all environmental problems cause the same levels of concern: why might this be the case? We might speculate on the extent to which attitudes and views regarding the environment are shaped and influenced through human processes such as scientific knowledge, activists' efforts and media attention. In a sociological sense, this debate is important, as it lends itself to understanding various cultural manifestations, definitions, interpretations and 'constructs' of environmental issues and problems that are bound up with wider dimensions of living in late modernity. Postmodernists and poststructuralists (see Chapter 2) would generally be wary of claims about an 'essential' nature, in a pluralistic and diverse society. Thus, nature would be seen as a social construct and relations between humans and nature could have unbounded limits (Cheney 1989).

The social construction of environmental issues

> **Environmental problems do not materialize by themselves, rather they must be 'constructed' by individuals or organizations that define pollution or some other objective condition as worrisome and seek to do something about it.**
>
> (Hannigan 1995: 2)

As other examples in this book demonstrate, a social constructionist approach aims to understand how people assign meaning to their world. We only have to look at areas such as gender, age, disability and race to see how the socially created nature of our social world takes effect. Sociologists also question the extent to which environmental problems are 'constructed' through the interpretation and activities of groups of different social actors in society, including the mass media, activists and scientific communities.

The main objective of social constructionists is not to undermine environmental claims or the actual reality of environmental problems but rather to understand the manner in which they are constructed and legitimated. For example, what is the true nature of the problem? Is it local, national or global? Who and where does the issue affect? Who is interested in the issue, and why do some environmental issues get on to the political agenda or gain a high level of media attention while others do not? Who has the most or least at stake in resolving environmental problems and reducing risk?

The kind of language, rhetoric and imagery used to form, interpret and convey the issue is also important. When scientists referred to the 'hole' in the ozone layer, it was actually a 'thinning in concentration', but the former depiction invariably had a more dramatic impact on the public imagination (Hannigan 1995: 30).

Therefore, a range of environmental problems are shaped and determined by the cultural processes of human action, judgement and social recognition, leading to questions about what is actually classified as an environmental problem in the first place (Yearley 1991). This, in turn, can be linked to levels of environmental consciousness, concern and activity. In an effort to understand why some environmental issues attract more public attention than others, Hannigan (1995: 55) reveals the manner in which environmental claims are presented by a limited number of interest groups in society. The following 'range of necessary factors' account for the social construction of environmental problems:

- Scientific authority for and validation of claims
- Existence of 'popularizers' who can bridge environmentalism and science
- Media attention in which the problem is framed as novel and important
- Dramatization of the problem in symbolic and visual terms
- Economic incentives for taking positive action
- Emergence of an institutional sponsor who can ensure both legitimacy and continuity.

However, it is important to identify the contested nature of science itself. As Yearley (1997: 223) points out, 'science is not a neutral medium, not only because of the contingent nature of scientific knowledge, but because environmental controversies have moral and political components that cannot be resolved by scientific inquiry'.

The realist approach

In contrast to the social constructionist approach, the realist perspective advocates that, while we can only grasp nature through our language and culture, we can still treat the structures and properties of natural objects as real. To draw on a literary analogy, in the backdrop to Shakespeare's *Romeo and Juliet*, the ancient grudge between the households of Montague and Capulet brings Juliet to question, 'What's in a name? That which we call a rose by any other word would smell as sweet.' By the same token, Dickens (1992) makes the point that turbulent water involves real forces at work and causes physical damage, regardless of whether we interpret it as a storm or hurricane. Despite an ongoing debate between the 'constructivist' and 'realist' camps, the two sides have found some common ground, as both accept that, although most environmental problems have a material reality, they nonetheless become known as a result of human processes, interpretation, knowledge and dissemination of information. The social construction of environmental issues offers a range of important theoretical insights, but traditional sociological concepts of power and authority in evaluating why some environmental issues are accorded legitimacy, and others are not, must also be recognized. In many ways social constructivism reflects the political nature of agenda-setting, which can be at the expense of more marginalized groups. For example, during a lengthy campaign to tackle damp housing on a peripheral housing estate in Glasgow, local residents eventually secured a unique sustainable initiative, the first ever tenant-led passive solar energy demonstration project (McDowell and Chalmers 1999). However, the need for residents to voice their own views and opinions was palpable:

> **Hey look . . . we are not daft; we know how we want to live. We only need an opportunity like this to get our ideas and solutions on the drawing board, in a way that enables these people (other professionals) to understand that we have our own form of expertise.**
>
> (Quoted in McDowell and Chalmers 1999: 86)

It is equally true that there has been a range of symbolic 'gender–nature' constructs, which naturalize women and feminize nature through negative connotations and sexist language. For example, women have been described in a derogatory manner in animal terms: as 'cows', 'chicks', 'bitches', 'old bats', 'birdbrains' and 'hare brains'. Equally, nature has often been described in female and sexual terms – 'virgin timber', 'fertile soil' and 'barren land' – or by references to nature being 'mastered', 'raped', 'conquered' or 'controlled' (Warren 1998: 268). In the section that follows, we continue with a gender dimension to environmental issues with a consideration of ecofeminism.

Stop and think

- In what ways are environmental issues a product of the culture that produces them?
- Can you think of environmental issues that receive more prominence and attention than other issues? If so, why?

Ecofeminism

In the course of discussing environmental sociology in undergraduate seminars, there was often a lively exchange among students when issues regarding gender and the environment came up. I recall one student stating that, if women were in charge of world affairs, then the environment would be in better shape; another insisted that, given that they were not – nor likely to be in the near future – we would never know. Some commented on high levels of consumerism in society, with one student referring to his girlfriend's surplus of shoes as a prime example of 'women's overindulgence'. Some also argued that men and women both suffered from the effects of environmental degradation: both were culpable in terms of causing environmental damage and both should be recognized for their efforts to protect the environment. For varied reasons, others believed that women were more nurturing (like Mother Earth), but there was never a consensus on the issues. At the heart of this debate are questions around the extent to which a feminist analysis could contribute to our understanding of a more sustainable and just society. Like other perspectives, such as deep ecology and ecological Marxism, ecofeminism can be viewed as a reaction to the severity of environmental issues, resulting in theories and actions as correctives to environmental problems.

> **Ecofeminism is an umbrella term which captures a variety of multi-cultural perspectives on the nature of the connections within social systems of domination between those humans in subdominant or subordinate positions, particularly women, and the domination of non-human nature.**
>
> (Warren 1994: 1)

Ecofeminism is a relatively new part of the feminist tradition, evolving out of political activism over the past three decades – movements around peace, anti-poverty, anti-nuclear, environmental and animal liberation issues raised the consciousness of various individuals and groups, seeking new power relations in different aspects of society. In their different guises, ecofeminists believe that the domination of women and the domination of nature are directly connected. What makes ecofeminism *ecological* is a focus on the importance of valuing ecosystems and the need for an environmental dimension to feminism or feminist philosophy. What makes ecological feminism *feminist* is a commitment to eradicate male-gender bias and the development of policies and theories that challenge sexist oppression (Warren 1994). Ecofeminism emerged in the 1970s with an increasing awareness of the relationship between women and nature. This is not to say that 'women–nature' connections were unproblematic or absent before this, as women have been identified variously with nature and constructed as equivalent throughout different historical periods. For example, before the Bronze Age, ritual figurines of females with the head of a bird were symbolic of the sacredness of the women–nature connection. In contrast, with the transition from an organic to an instrumental view of nature in the early seventeenth century, nature and women were mutually constructed as disorderly and chaotic and as such had to be 'controlled' and 'tamed' (Merchant 1989).

Raising the question of women's relationship to nature is inherently problematic for feminists who have long sought to distinguish between sex and gender due to a 'perceived biological limitation and "weakness" of being female that has denied women political and social rights' (Mellor 1997: 195). However, feminist environmentalists view sexism and exploitation of the environment as parallel forms of domination. Currently ecofeminism embraces an interdisciplinary approach, making a range of important contributions to debates on environmental theory, philosophy, sociology, ethics, spirituality, politics, poetry, nature and history. Although the movement has grown significantly since the term was introduced by Françoise d'Eaubonne in her pioneering work *Feminism or Death* (1974), issues of patriarchy, power and subordination are still fundamental aspects of the ecofeminist philosophy. Consequently, for many ecofeminists, the present environmental crisis is not simply a crisis of environmental degradation (ozone depletion, deforestation, species loss, oil spills or global warming) but also a crisis of the 'dominant male ideology' associated with aspects of political wrangling, power, institutional and bureaucratic arrangements, and the cultural conventions that generate conditions of environmental destruction. In Joni Seager's hard-hitting book *Earth Follies* (1993), the roles of governments, militaries and multinational corporations come under the spotlight as primary agents of environmental destruction (see Chapter 9 for more discussion on the role of transnational corporations). Thus, the institutional culture that is responsible for most of the environmental calamities of the past century is a

A closer look

Ecofeminism: essentialist (biological determinism) versus constructionist views

Essentialists take the view that women are closer than men to nature and that this innate quality should be recognized and celebrated. As noted previously, both women and nature are often viewed as irrational, uncertain, hard to control, chaotic and more mysterious in motivation than men. Thus, for some ecofeminists, the basis for the closeness and affinity to nature is based on biological determinism – women's experiences of reproduction and child-bearing, which forge a sense of connection with the natural world:

> Nothing links the human animal and nature as profoundly as woman's reproductive system which enables her to share the experience of bringing forth and nourishing life with the rest of the living world.
>
> (Collard 1988: 102)

Associated with this view is that female values, traditionally undervalued by patriarchy, require a more positive re-evaluation, a special feminine connectedness with nature. It draws upon ancient myths of women and nature/mother and earth in a nurturing cooperative relationship. Collard (1988) associates earth goddess worshipping and non-hierarchal matriarchies with 'traditional' or 'primitive' societies. Maori women, for example, bury their afterbirth in the earth as a symbolic link between women as life-givers and the earth as the fount of life (Dobson 1995). Thus, the closeness to nature is biology – and it is difficult to deny a sense of connection with the natural world due to the life-giving reproductive cycle.

In contrast, social constructionist or cultural ecofeminists view this stance as extremely offensive and long used by men to keep women in subjugation. For ecofeminists such as Val Plumwood (1988), when women are identified biologically with nature, men are inclined to appropriate the realms of science and rationality for themselves. The social constructionist view strongly refutes the notion that women's biology renders them intellectually and morally different from men. According to Plumwood, the whole idea of women as 'earth mothers' due to the belief that they are naturally closer to nature is

> Regressive and insulting, portraying women as passive, reproductive animals immersed in the body in an unthinking experience of life.
>
> (Plumwood, cited in Pepper 1996: 107)

Plumwood goes on to suggest:

> What is common to ecological feminisms is no more than a rejection of the belief in the inferiority of the sphere of women and of nature.
>
> (Plumwood 1993: 33)

'masculinist' culture – the 'expert' culture of scientists, decision-makers and bureaucrats.

Ecofeminist theoretical positions are as diverse as traditional feminist philosophies and include liberal, Marxist, cultural and social variations (Merchant 1992). Warren's (1998) review of 'women–nature connections' provides further theoretical insights. However, there are two prominent controversial debates within ecofeminism, which revolve around essentialist versus constructionist theories.

Stop and think

- To what extent do you agree that women are inherently closer to nature as a result of their biology?
- How do power and control in society impact on the environment, and how does this relate specifically to gender?
- What focus is needed on specifically male patterns of belief and behaviour in this regard?

Consider explanations for your answer.

Clearly, not all ecofeminists agree with the biological difference view. Some argue that if women are more caring, less aggressive and less power-hungry than men, then it is due to social conditioning rather than innate differences (Gray 1981; Griffin 1978; Plumwood 1991). In her later work, Shalleh (1992) moved towards a greater stress on the links between women's prescribed roles and lived experiences, for example as mothers and carers. Therefore, by virtue of these experiences, she suggests that women form a more empathic relationship with nature. Ecofeminism, therefore, is part of the green movement, which, like most other political movements, incorporates a variety of viewpoints and has internal as well as external divisions, including some men identifying with ecofeminism (Swimme 1990). Although ecofeminism comprises a wealth of diverse analyses, it is distinctly ecological, asserting the fundamental interconnectedness and interdependence of nature, including humanity. While there are theoretical overlaps between ecofeminists and deep ecologists, the seemingly androcentric (male-centred) approach of deep ecologists has been viewed by a number of ecofeminists as failing to address the multiple dimensions of related oppressions, in particular female exploitation (Shalleh 1992).

Ecofeminists have also been challenged over various aspects of their theoretical standpoints, including what is viewed as their capacity to exaggerate the logic of domination in aspects of Western ideology. Are other cultures (e.g. Eastern cultures) not capable of dominating nature? Did the former Soviet Bloc not cause extensive environmental damage in its labour-intensive modernization process? Equally, are men not also linked with nature if we consider notions of 'Father Sky', 'Sun God Apollo' and 'Ocean God Poseidon', and are women not capable of exploiting the earth? It is certainly the case that not all women feel connected in some way to the earth. There are also questions over the extent to which the dynamics of class and race are considered as sufficiently as other causes of domination within ecofeminism. It would appear, then, that there are various unresolved contradictions; despite obvious divisions, however, ecofeminist philosophers offer valuable insights into the overall feminist analysis, extending the study of domination to include critiques of colonial and capitalist exploitation of women and nature in developing countries (Shiva 1994). (For a closer look at neo-colonialism and debates on women, environment and development issues, see Chapter 9.) Ecofeminists, therefore, are keen to stress the interconnectedness of life with a focus on a non-hierarchical, decentralized, global approach.

Challenges from the grass roots

It is reasonable to suggest that there has always been a human dimension to environmental issues and problems. Currently, some of us might be acting in an environmentally responsible manner, recycling, reducing waste, buying green goods or using public transport rather than the car. Other members of the community might challenge decisions affecting their local communities, for example motorway extensions or new airport runways and terminals. This can happen in the face of strong opposition, as many local conflicts have to confront a range of powerful opponents, such as developers, government departments and transnational corporations. Within this context it is useful to note that Principle 10 of the Earth Charter, included in Agenda 21 (an action plan for sustainable development), asserts that environmental issues are best handled with the participation of all concerned citizens, at the relevant level (UNCED 1992). This reinforces the point that people have a right to be involved in their 'local patch' on issues that affect them directly. Indeed, we are actively encouraged to 'think global and act local'. However, as Selman (1996) articulates, this principle is built around assumptions that governments would be willing to disperse power away from the centre and that citizens would be inclined to participate actively in addressing environmental issues.

In certain circumstances, people's principles can be put unswervingly to the test, particularly in developing countries, where there are significant imbalances of power and issues of survival are at the forefront of environmental campaigns. In an age of greater fragmentation and individualism, some theorists argue that we are living in an era of 'civic sclerosis', with few people willing to act as 'community champions' (Alinski 1972). Sociologically, such issues are significant as they encourage us to consider our role as active citizens (our agency in society) in conjunction with the wider mechanisms or social structures that could support the pursuit of local sustainability. Throughout history, both men and women have been ardent defenders of the environment. Here are a few examples of individuals who, in the face of fierce opposition, defended the causes they deeply believed in:

- *Chico Mendes* (1944–88) became a rubber tapper (extracting latex from rubber trees) in Brazil at the age of nine. Many rubber tappers were brutally exploited and evicted by local merchants or ranchers who cleared forests for cattle. Mendez founded the National Union of Rubber Tappers in the early 1970s, proposing an equitable and environmentally sustainable policy of 'extractive reserves' for people to live and work on the land. He became a prominent figure, negotiating with various governments and the World Bank, and he received international awards for his environmental campaigning. In 1988 he was assassinated by ranchers opposed to his activism. Although there are now over 20 extractive reserves established in seven states in Brazil, illegal logging is still a major problem and the degradation of Amazonia continues (www.rainforestfoundationuk.org).
- *Ken Saro-Wiwa* (1941–2005) was a businessman, novelist, television producer and environmental campaigner. He was executed in November 1995 by the Nigerian state for campaigning against the devastation of the Niger Delta by oil companies, particularly Shell and Chevron. Focusing on his homeland of Ogoni, Saro-Wiwa launched a non-violent movement for social and ecological justice. By 1993, the oil companies had to pull out of Ogoni, but this cost Saro-Wiwa and eight other Ogoni supporters their lives. There was international condemnation and outrage against both the military junta and Shell, resulting in the strengthening of limited sanctions and the suspension of Nigeria from the Commonwealth.
- *Sister Dorothy (Dora) Stang* (1931–2005) was an American Dominican nun and prominent Amazonian rainforest activist in the vast Pará region of Brazil. Dora received various death threats from loggers and land owners after denouncing environmental and human rights abuses. For more than 20 years she had been involved in social projects helping poor people in the region. In February 2005, while reading her Bible, she was shot repeatedly at point blank range by illegal loggers. She received a posthumous award of Defender of Human Rights in 2006 from the Brazilian president.

Stop and think

Can individuals really make a difference to the state of our planet? A panel for the *Guardian* newspaper, taking nominations from key environmental figures, compiled a list of 50 people who are considered 'green heroes' (www.guardian.co.uk/environment/2008/jan/05/activists.ethicalliving). Although 19 nationalities are represented, one in three is from a developing country.

- What do you think about this list of nominees?
- What is notable about their environmental contributions?
- Does this suggest that grass-roots resourcefulness will be as important as money and technology in the future?
- Should such a list make us more positive about society's potential for environmental progress?

Equally, at a grass-roots level, numerous local people (many of them women) have campaigned tirelessly in their communities for environmental and social justice:

- In 1977 in the USA, *Lois Gibb* was instrumental in founding the Love Canal Homeowners Committee in New York after houses in her working-class district were found to be built on top of 22,000 tons of discarded chemical waste. Residents found their basements full of noxious liquids that caused serious health effects on resident children. The Love Canal campaign, along with struggles in Warren County, North Carolina, opposing the disposal of toxic waste in landfills in a predominately African–American area, led to the rise of the Environmental Justice Movement in the USA (see p. 437 for further details).
- In India *Medha Patkar* led a ten-year struggle against the Narmada River Dam Projects, while at Greenham Common in the UK the anti-nuclear movement was dominated by women challenging the dominance of nuclear weaponry.
- *Erin Brokovich*, a film with Julia Roberts in the lead role, tells the true story of an unemployed single mother who almost single-handedly brought down a Californian power company accused of polluting a city's water supply. Despite the lack of a formal law school education, Brokovich successfully brought a

Figure 10.3 Chipko activists
Rod Johnson/Panos Pictures

case against the Pacific Gas and Electric Company of California in 1993, and settled three years later for $333 million. This was the largest settlement paid in a direct-action lawsuit in US history.

- The Chipko movement was a global grass-roots movement advanced by rural Himalayan hill people, particularly women, who campaigned to stop forest destruction by issuing a call to 'hug the trees' (Figure 10.3).

A key theme running through these examples is that, despite the unyielding power behind many male-dominated areas of government, industry and business, a few have been held to account by ordinary local people, driven by a sense of injustice and desperation for survival. The Chipko movement has subsequently been referred to as both ecological and feminist (Shiva 1989). Although both men and women were part of the Chipko movement, it was women who were worst hit by the loss of fuel at a domestic level and who fought against deforestation for this purpose. The women also successfully challenged the government over its initial failure to involve them in the consultation process. As the box opposite suggests, local women, who were normally confined to household work, became a real force to be reckoned with and gained international recognition through non-violent direct action. The movement also gave the women grounds for a new form of identity, founded on respect for the environment and each other.

Stop and think

- Why would the Chipko movement be referred to as both 'ecological' and 'feminist'?
- The Chipko movement was focused on passive resistance. Why do you think forms of passive resistance such as tree-hugging could be such a powerful mechanism for social change?

World in focus

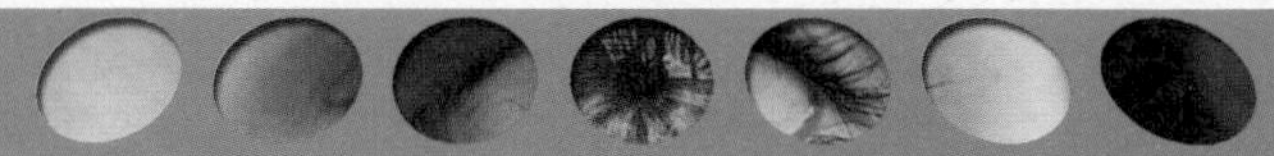

The Chipko movement

The Earth provides enough to satisfy every man's need, but not every man's greed.

(Gandhi)

Mahatma Gandhi's concept of Gram Swarajya (village self-rule) aimed to create egalitarian, self-sustaining communities within a non-violent society. To work toward that goal, a group of people established the Dasholi Gram Swarajya Mandal (Dasholi Village Self-Rule Organization) or DGSM at Gopeshwar, India, in 1964. In 1970, a massive flood hit the Alaknanda basin in Uttar Pradesh, devastating lives and destroying property. The government labelled the flood 'a natural calamity'. However, the relief workers of DGSM refused to accept that characterization, because for the previous twenty years they had seen the plight of forests in the watersheds where the flood originated.

Then, in 1973, while the memory of the 1970 flood was still fresh, a sporting goods company was given permission to harvest ash trees from the Mandal Forest near Gopeshwar. There was only one option: We decided to cling to the trees (chipko) that were marked for felling and prevent the lumberers from axing the trees without cutting us first.

The spread of the movement

Mandal Forest was the starting point of people's non-violent resistance to commercial exploitation of forests in the region. Seeing the massive participation of the people, the contractor retreated. When a subsequent contract was awarded to a lumberer in the Mandakini Valley, the contractor again faced the people's resistance.

After the Mandal Chipko action, DGSM volunteers fanned out into all potential lumbering areas to educate and warn the people about the possible threat. The turning point came in 1974, when lumbering rights in the Rani forest were auctioned off. Chipko workers, local people and students got involved in the movement, demonstrating against the arrival of lumberers in the sensitive catchment area of the Rishi Ganga River near Reni village.

The protest resulted in a dramatic victory. One day, only the women remained in the village: twenty-seven small bodies against many professional axe-men. Not worried about the odds against them, the women rushed to the felling site and clung to the marked trees while angry lumberers threatened them with their glistening axes. They remained in the forest for the entire day despite the overwhelming odds. The next day, their numbers increased as the women and men of about a dozen villages arrived at the site to join them.

The women of the region, who were usually confined to household work, began to take the lead because they were the worst hit by the decline of the forests since collecting fuel and fodder for their domestic needs had become more difficult. The women's leadership proved a decisive blow to the contractors, who came to realize that their objectives could not be achieved. The Reni vigil continued for three years until 1977, when the Reni Chipko Committee appointed by the Uttar Pradesh Government in 1974 recommended a complete ban on logging in the area.

The movement spread into Bhyundar Valley, the lower part of the celebrated Valley of Flowers. Despite heavy snowfall there, the local women saved the trees. Then, in 1980, another village in the Chamoli district, Dungri-Pantuli, took up the Chipko task. The women put up brave and determined resistance and questioned the government officials about their failure to consult the village's women before felling. This was a major victory for the Chipko movement and built the organizing capacity of the hill women. As the movement gained momentum, it won sympathy from various people in the region and beyond. Institutes like the Gandhi Peace Foundation and the media gave significant coverage in the national and international press.

World in focus *continued*

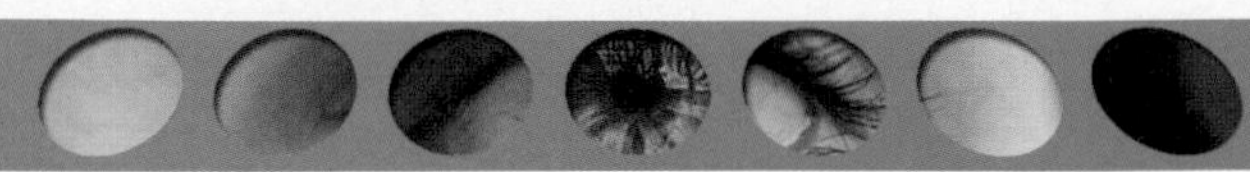

Goals and outcomes

Chipko's goal was to prevent commercial felling of forest crops, while safeguarding the traditional rights to the forests in the river basin. An important outcome was conducting eco-development and environmental conservation camps in the Upper Alaknanda basin for the past 30 years, with overwhelming participation of the local people, particularly the women.

Empowerment

The movement, which began with saving the forest from commercial exploitation, became a symbol of the fight against social injustice, improper developmental planning and faulty environmental policies. Rural hill people who had been mere spectators of government policies became a force to reckon with. There are innumerable village level women organizations called Mahila Mangal Dals (Organizations for Women's Development).

Commercial forest felling is completely banned in the Alaknanda basin where the Chipko movement started and in the entire Central Himalaya region. A movement that started from the sheer need for survival became the mouthpiece of the local people, who could now think, plan, and undertake programmes to meet their needs and pool their collective energy to save the terrain from further calamity.

(Source: this case study is based on extracts taken from 'The Chipko Movement', a paper given by Chandi Prasad Bhatt at the Orissa conference on Nonviolence and Social Empowerment in 2001, translated from the original Hindi)

The way forward? Sustainable development and environmental justice

Sustainable development

> **Sustainable development is a hollow concept if limited to the rich world while forgetting the poor, or focused on the future while forgetting the present.**
>
> (Lomborg 2002: 21)

The concept of sustainable development is now fashionable in environmental and mainstream discourse around the world. The term was first coined at the 1980 World Conservation Strategy but gained more attention through the 1987 World Commission on Environment and Development report *Our Common Future*. The latter is more commonly known as the *Brundtland Report*, after the Commission's Chair, Gro Harlem Brundtland, then Prime Minister of Norway. Sustainable development means different things to different people, but the most frequently quoted definition is:

> **To meet the needs of the present without compromising the ability of future generations to meet their own needs.**
>
> (World Commission on Environment and Development 1987: 8; to access the full report, see www.un-documents.net/ocf-02.htm#I)

The Commission's report identified two key concepts related to the sustainable management of the earth's resources:

> 1. **The basic needs of humanity must be met. This involves giving priority to the unmet needs of the world's poor.**
> 2. **The limits to development are not absolute but are imposed by present states of technology and by social organization and by the impacts upon environmental resources and upon the biosphere's ability to absorb the effect of human activities. But technology and social organization can be both managed and improved to make way for a new era of economic growth.**
>
> (World Commission on Environment and Development 1987)

The need to balance environmental and development needs are central to most definitions of sustainable development (SD). In simple terms:

- SD is usually regarded as a marriage of environmental, social and economic concerns, a form of development that does not cause environmental damage.
- SD focuses on improving the quality of life for all of the earth's citizens without increasing the use of

natural resources beyond the capacity of the environment to supply them indefinitely.

- SD is about taking action, changing policy and practice at all levels, from the individual to the international level.

Although sustainable development is a term much used in academic and policy circles, there is nevertheless a great deal of confusion and controversy regarding its meaning and value (Fitzpatrick 1998; Chatterton and Style 2001). The proliferation of views and definitions surrounding sustainable development highlight its contestability as a term that is 'up for grabs' (Fritsch *et al.* 1994; Jacobs 1999). This is hardly surprising, as sustainable development has multiple meanings that embrace physical, cultural, economic and social elements between humans and ecosystems (Fitzpatrick 1998). The controversy over definition is replicated in the debate about whether or not present-day societies can become sustainable. In this debate, sustainable development is taken as something real, or at least potentially so. In summary, we can think of the sustainable development model as offering a new approach, which focuses on the ability to coexist in a way that maintains the natural environment and economic wellbeing and offers an equal opportunity for all people to benefit from a better quality of life now and in the future.

The United Nations (UN), in particular, has played a significant role in promoting the model of sustainable development through the establishment of various agencies and institutions at a civic, business and political level, the organization of several world summits and the development of legally binding agreements (Baker 2006).

Modern environmentalism emerged as a critique against the broad assumptions of the dominant Western development model, in particular the instrumental approach to nature and natural resources – a 'human-centred' approach, with notions of 'progress' based on the domination of nature, not only in Western society but also in many developing countries. Other characteristics of the current framework are an emphasis on economic growth, consumption and traditional patterns of authority, governance and policymaking (Baker 2006).

Constraining the progress of 'sustainable development' by narrowing its definition in such a way as to make it a factor in a preoccupation with competitive economic growth is an issue of ongoing

A closer look

The Rio Declaration

The Rio Declaration, a set of 27 principles agreed at the United Nations Conference on Environment and Development (UNCED) in 1992, underpinned the global partnership for environment and development. Many of these principles involved the roles, rights and responsibilities of signatory states, including a series of *normative principles* – moral statements that guide or mould attitudes and behaviour. A few examples of an attempt to create a 'charter for the earth' are given below:

- *Intergenerational equity (futurity)* – Requires that the needs of the present are met without compromising the ability of future generations to meet their own needs.
- *Intragenerational equity* – States that all people currently alive have an equal right to benefit from the use of resources, both within and between countries.
- *Subsidiarity* – Environmental issues are best handled with the participation of all concerned citizens, at the relevant level.
- *Developing countries* – The special situation of developing countries, particularly the least developed and those most environmentally vulnerable, shall be given special priority.
- *Women and development* – Women have a vital role in environmental management and development. Their full participation is therefore essential to achieve sustainable development.

For full details on all 27 principles, see www.un.org/documents/ga/conf151/aconf15126-1annex1.htm.

concern. Friends of the Earth (2002) and Porritt (2005) have commented on the overbearing interest in the economy and the needs of business at the expense of progressive sustainable policy incorporating a stronger quality of life. As one starts to dig below the surface of public rhetoric, a number of questions emerge about general acceptance of the concept. Bureaucrats may argue that the terms 'sustainability' and 'sustainable development' are too vague or ill-defined to be of any use in practical decision-making and real-life policy. In the same vein, we often hear the warning that aims such as sustainability 'are lightly professed in theory without looking at all at practical realization' (Achterhuis 1994: 198). For example, what do we really mean by 'development'? Whose 'needs' are we really talking about? (See Chapter 9 for a discussion on the sociology of development.) Sustainable development can be viewed in terms of a continuum from 'weak' to 'strong' or 'ideal' forms, indicative of a 'ladder of sustainability'. It is also the case that not all environmentalists endorse the Brundtland formulation of sustainable development: for some it is too anthropocentric (human-centred), while for others it is either too radical or not radical enough (Baker 2006).

The Brundtland Commission report suggests that sustainable development at a global level can be achieved only through major changes in governance. If sustainability is to mean anything, then ordinary people must also play an active part in delivering sustainable initiatives relative to the needs, circumstances and aspirations of their own communities. Sustainable communities therefore depend on effective governance and the empowerment of communities in civil society to participate in the decisions that affect their lives (see Chapter 9). The implementation of Agenda 21 was intended to involve action at international, national, regional and local levels (http://worldinbalance.net/agreements/1992-rio-agenda21.html).

Sustainable development, therefore, cannot be viewed as a fixed state but rather is a dynamic process of change. The UK Sustainable Development Commission, established in the first term of the Blair government, identifies the concept as the organizing principle for all democratic societies. However, the generality of the concept contradicts the true cost of implementation. As Redclift suggests:

> **Like motherhood and God, it is difficult not to approve of. At the same time, the idea of sustainable development is fraught with contradictions.**
>
> (Redclift 1997: 438)

With reference to sustainable development in the developing world, Elliot (1999: 43) argues that 'immediate survival needs, such as fuel, access to clean water and sanitation, restricts options in terms of resource management'. Baker outlines a series of policies and processes that are central to the building of sustainable development in the developing world, summarized under the following five key headings:

- Setting a relevant policy agenda
- Dealing with gender specific dimensions
- Recognizing the negative relationship between the current global free trade regime and the promotion of sustainable development
- Admitting the power base of science, while acknowledging the validity of different types of knowledge, as well as recognising that indigenous knowledge sources can have a role in the promotion of a sustainable future
- Reforming the institutions that finance the promotion of sustainable development (Baker 2006: 184).

Despite its complexity, Brundtland's formulation of sustainable development has obvious strengths. It draws diverse interests towards a common cause, with an aim to advance the balance between social, economic and environmental aspects of development. This allows for a framework for the integration of environmental policies and development strategies into a *new development paradigm* – one that breaks from the perception that environmental protection can be achieved only at the expense of economic development. Symbolically and politically this is highly significant, underpinning Brundtland's 'authoritative status' (Baker 2006: 17).

Stop and think

- The Brundtland approach to sustainable development offers guiding principles for social and environmental change. What existing patterns of human and social activity would you consider to be unsustainable? Why?
- What are the likely consequences if such unsustainable activity continues?
- How optimistic are you that new forms of sustainable development can be achieved in society?

Environmental justice

> **While money moves upward, pollution moves downwards.**
>
> (Bryant 1995: 8)

Various studies alert us to the fact that, when it comes to analysing distributional consequences, both social and spatial, lower-income groups are more prone to experiencing environmental problems, unwanted development, and a lack of consultation in the overall decision-making process. Despite significant improvements in environmental protection, many people continue to live in unsafe and unhealthy physical environments. Over the past decade there has been a substantial rise in evidence correlating the proximity to environmental degradation with an individual's or group's social class, ethnic status and geographical location (Bullard 1990; Burningham and Thrush 2001; Agyeman and Evans 2004).

The movement for environmental justice grew as a reaction to the limitations of mainstream environmentalism, which was viewed as being dominated by elitist, white, upper-class environmental individuals reflecting a narrow range of views. Further, many writers argued that the traditional environmental movement was not adequately addressing issues such as race, power and inequality (Bullard 1990). In the USA, the movement for environmental justice has become a significant political force. Over 7000 grass-roots groups are now actively fighting environmental threats, raising the call for environmental justice and a shared role in decisions that shape their communities. The drive for environmental justice extends the quest for basic civil rights. Actions taken by grass-roots activists to reduce environmental inequalities are consistent with the struggle to end other forms of social injustice found throughout society – in housing, education, employment, health care, criminal justice and politics.

The first National People of Color Environmental Leadership summit was held in Washington, DC, in October 1991. At this summit, 17 key principles were established that serve as a defining document for the growing grass-roots movement for environmental justice (www.ejnet.org/ej/principles.html). The central principles incorporate the need to redress unfair and inequitable distributions of *environmental burdens* (pollution, industrial hazards, crime, poor quality of life) and access to *environmental goods* (clean air, water, transport, parks, recreation, safe jobs, health care, education) in a variety of situations and social contexts.

Some of the key concepts associated with this debate are clarified below:

- *Environmental racism* focuses on the disproportionate impact of environmental hazards on minority ethnic and low-income communities.
- *Environmental equity* refers to the equal protection by environmental laws to ensure the proper siting, clean-up and regulation of pollution, regardless of the racial and economic composition of the community.
- *Environmental justice* is broader in scope, referring to cultural norms, values, rules, regulations, behaviours, policies and decisions to support sustainable communities, where both cultural and biological diversity are respected and where distributive justice prevails.
- *Distributive justice* refers to principles specifying the just distribution of benefits and burdens. This is important because of the extent of unequal distribution of wealth and the unfair distribution of toxic exposure throughout society.

According to Wright (1995: 58), in the USA neighbourhoods comprised of predominantly poor and minority groups have been 'prime targets for the most non-desirable but "necessary" by-products of an industrial society'. Such communities are considered 'paths of least resistance' and thus more likely to be targeted for pollution. Indigenous people have also suffered disproportionate environmental impacts. For example, given the economic vulnerability of many indigenous communities, economic blackmail has often been used by private waste-management companies to permit the siting of landfill and incinerator facilities on indigenous land (Goldtooth 1995). Subsequently:

> **doing battle with the lack of self-respect that comes from 'being associated with trash' lends a very emotive symbolic angle to the discourse and highlights the racial and discriminatory aspects of the problem.**
>
> (Harvey 1996: 387)

Evidence from Friends of the Earth (England, Wales and N. Ireland) revealed that many of the more deprived communities in England experienced serious effects of factory pollution. Their study *Pollution and Poverty: Breaking the Link*, which focused on chemical air emissions recognized as being carcinogenic (cancer-causing), found that factories in predominantly more deprived local authority wards in England had the worst

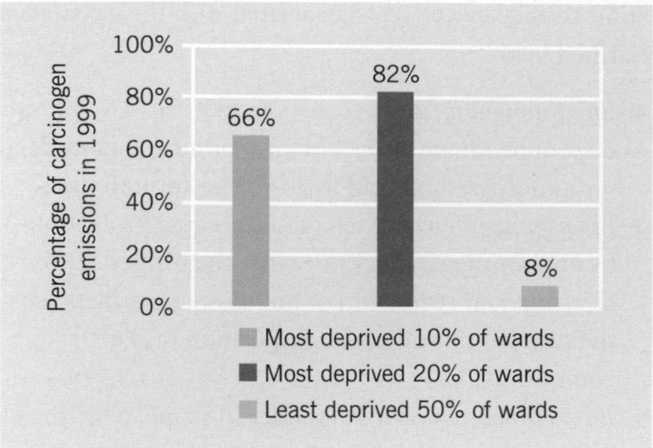

Figure 10.4 Pollution from factories and deprivation in England
Source: Friends of the Earth 2001

Figure 10.5 Another form of recycling as children scavenge for plastic
STILL Pictures The Whole Earth Picture Library

pollution. Friends of the Earth found that 660 of these factories were situated in areas where the average yearly income was around £15,000, whereas only five were situated in areas where the average yearly income was around £30,000 (Figure 10.4) (Friends of the Earth 2001).

Of over 11,000 tonnes of carcinogenic chemicals emitted to air in England in 1999:

- two-thirds (66%) of carcinogen emissions were in the most deprived 10 per cent of wards;
- four-fifths (82%) of carcinogen emissions were in the most deprived 20 per cent of wards;
- less than one-tenth (8%) of carcinogen emissions were in the least deprived 50 per cent of wards.

Similarly, in Scotland, environmental problems are clearly associated with social exclusion, inequality and deprivation. People living in the most deprived areas have been found to be more likely to live next to long-term derelict sites, multiple derelict sites, seriously polluted rivers and industrial quarries compared with those living in the least deprived areas (Dunion 2001; Fairburn *et al.* 2005). Despite growing awareness that environmental justice could play a role in existing policies for sustainability and social exclusion, evidence of environmental inequalities draws attention to where sustainable polices could be more effective.

Over the years, the environmental justice movement has become global, comprising groups from different countries, including members of diverse ethnicities, ages, class backgrounds and genders. However, despite advances in technological and scientific knowledge, environmental injustices continue to exist in society. Many injustices disproportionately affect more marginalized groups, such as the Bhopal industrial disaster (highlighted above). According to Ted Benton:

> **. . . in societies governed by deep inequalities of political power, economic wealth, social standing and cultural accomplishment, the promise of equal rights is delusory, with the consequence that for the majority, rights are merely abstract, formal entitlements with little or no de facto purchase on the realities of social life.**
>
> (Benton 1993: 144)

The condition of developing countries with problems of rising poverty and mounting debt brings into sharp focus the divide between the rich and poor in the world. The UNICEF report *Our Climate, Our Children, Our Responsibility: The Implications of Climate Change for the World's Children* (2008) (www.unicef.org.uk/publications/pdf/climate-change.pdf) highlights the serious and detrimental impacts of climate change, particularly upon vulnerable children. The report argues forcefully that both mitigation and adaptation are necessary as advised by the UK Stern Review (Office of Climate Change 2006) and the IPCC. The Stern Review advised that global warming could shrink the global economy by 20 per cent, but taking action now would cost just 1 per cent of global gross domestic product.

For the vast majority of people in developing countries, the impact of climate change means a greater risk of insecurity in terms of losing their homes and livelihoods, with higher levels of disease and mortality (see Chapter 9 for a discussion on global inequalities). Children in the world's poorest communities are more susceptible to the effects of global climate change through malnutrition, disease, poverty, inequality, increasing risks of conflict and ultimately increased child mortality rates (UNICEF 2008).

Stop and think

- Why do some communities and countries suffer a disproportionate amount of environmental degradation compared with others?
- How are issues such as power, inequality and discrimination related to the concepts of sustainable development and environmental justice?

How might the environmental justice movement move forward in a more progressive and just manner? Harvey (1996) suggests that the environmental movement requires a 'universal solution' to solving environmental injustice, not simply parts of the movement challenging injustices in particular communities. This collective approach would 'pull together' all its disparate parts in an effort to the 'challenge the processes (and their associated power structures, social relations, institutional configurations and discourses and belief systems) that generate environmental and social injustices' (Harvey 1996: 401). Although there is no specific definition of what constitutes an environmental justice movement, the range of principles associated with it – including ecological wisdom, grass-roots democracy, egalitarianism, a respect for diversity, a focus on the future and global responsibility – do convey a synthesis between human and environmental welfare. The dividing line is how to deal with the underlining problems.

Environmental justice also depends on effective governance, a willingness to tackle issues of disempowerment and deficiencies in the decision-making system (Dunion 2003). The need for effective dialogue at an international level is also fundamental. At discussions during the June 2008 G8 summit in Tokyo, the proceedings were dominated by leaders from the world's richest nations. The absence of countries whose global significance has grown since the mid-1970s means that the discussions and conclusions are essentially one-dimensional. The growing complexity, fragility and interconnectedness of the world call for an international forum reflecting this reality in an institutional framework, rather than one dominated by Europe, North America, Russia and Japan. The G5 Group (China, India, Brazil, South Africa and Mexico) were invited to join discussions only on the last day of the summit.

At a time when energy, food and raw materials costs are soaring, the major oil producers and African nations rich in mineral resources should be around the table, along with Brazil, which is currently at the centre of the global biofuels debate. Biofuels are an organic source of alternative fuel derived from agricultural crops. Brazil is one of the world's largest exporters of ethanol, which is derived from sugar cane. However, there are concerns that increased production of crops for ethanol and biodiesel is driving out production of food crops, causing a surge in global food prices and pushing cattle ranchers and farmers further north in Brazil, contributing to the destruction of the Amazon rainforest. Some of Brazil's neighbours, led by oil-rich Venezuela, have warned that biofuels could increase malnutrition in Latin America. A shift from agricultural fuels to products normally used for waste and landfill may be one solution. However, if aspects of development are to be reconciled with environmental justice, then such issues give cause for serious consideration.

Stop and think

- As citizens in a complex and dynamic world, how do environmental issues reflect our shifting responsibilities in society? For example, this might relate to the type of goods and products we buy as consumers or the manner in which goods are produced, transported, consumed and disposed of. Other responsibilities also relate to our wider relationship between human and non-human nature. Try to think of examples to support your answer.

Environmental sociology: beyond an 'absent presence'

Sociological research has a long way to go before it can explain adequately humanity's part in a complex ecological system. Despite such slow beginnings, there is a growing awareness of the value of an ecologically informed sociology and a growth in scholarship within a variety of conceptual and empirical approaches. The ubiquitous nature of environmental issues cannot be overstated. We are living in times of great change shaped by new information and technology, globalization and unprecedented environmental change. However, sociology must constantly recreate itself if it is to fully understand the society it reflects, and new paradigms must be established to convey the complexity of the social world we inhabit.

Both analytically and theoretically, environmental sociology has provided fuller insights into, and understanding of, a range of themes characteristic of traditional sociological enquiry. The following are indicative rather than definitive: race, class, gender ethnicity, communities, globalization, inequality, consumerism, technology, risk, health, organizations, science, power, justice and development. By the same token, environmental sociology has galvanized interest in new areas of sociological enquiry, including ideas and cultural constructions around the environment; 'expert' knowledge and the role of science; the relationship between ecology, society and the economy; notions of progress and development; green critiques; theories on risk; gender and the environment; the role of the state; and the rise of environmental consciousness, mobilization and strategies for change. There is also plenty of scope for sociologists to apply their sociological imagination in ways that inform public debate, improve public policy and stimulate greater theoretical and empirical insights within this field.

The phenomenon of globalization reflects the increasing interconnectedness of different parts of the world, and yet there is a lack of sociological research into humanity's relationship with nature over time in different cultural and social contexts. Equally, greater insights are needed regarding the effects of global warming as a driver for social change, including forced displacement, international migration and growing conflicts over scarce resources. Thus, we have entered a new era of global environmental problem-solving and, as such, sociologists have a part to play in offering critical insights and contributions to ongoing debates.

Riley Dunlap reflects on recent developments in sociology in this way:

> **It seems clear to me that sociology in general and sociological theory in particular are paying far more attention to the environment nowadays than was the case in the 1970s. The steady decline in defenses of exemptionalist thinking, are coupled with growing theoretical and empirical attention to environmental phenomena. For a discipline that was virtually blind to the biophysical environment in the early 1970s, this is a monumental change. Whether it creates a true paradigmatic shift within sociology will no doubt continue to be the subject of debate.**
>
> (Dunlap 2002: 345–6)

When Dunlap and Catton called for a new ecological paradigm back in the early 1970s, they recognized the first law of ecology – that everything in nature is connected to everything else. There can be no other conclusion, therefore, but to agree with Beck's declaration in the opening lines of this chapter, stressing the importance of 'the ecological and social dimensions of our existence' (Beck 1992: 80). If we start from the principle that our relationship with nature (and each another) needs to be based on mutual respect, then we may be able to provide a more just and sustainable existence for ourselves and future generations. This approach is inherently complex as it challenges our basic anthropocentric assumptions, and concern for the environment raises fundamental issues about the kind of society we wish to create for ourselves and our descendants.

Although there are ongoing and complex debates weighing up the extent of the crisis and the progress already made, one thing is certain: the environment is one of the most pressing issues of our time. On a positive note, there is greater awareness about environmental issues in society than there has ever been. Some countries are rising to the challenge: New Zealand has announced its ambition to become the world's first truly sustainable nation as it aspires to be carbon-neutral, while Malmö in Sweden aspires to be the world's first carbon-neutral city. At a national and international level, regulatory frameworks and economic and fiscal policies need to provide positive incentives for sustainable behaviour. However, the challenge involves more than an institutional or technical response: current levels of environmental degradation and social inequality must reinforce the point that a sustainable future depends as much on our moral resources as on our physical or sociological resources.

Summary

- The interrelationship between humanity, society and nature is a fundamental component of environmental sociology.
- The environment is a contested and shifting concept open to a range of ideas, values and classifications throughout different historical periods.
- Sociology's past neglect of the environment can be referred to as an 'absent presence'.
- Sociologists are now called to embrace a 'new ecological paradigm' stressing the interconnectedness of the human–environment condition.
- Two global approaches in environmental sociology, risk society and ecological modernization, focus on the potential role of modern technology for either exacerbating or overcoming environmental degradation.
- Ecofeminists, in their various guises, believe that the domination of women and the domination of nature are directly connected.
- The need to balance environmental and development needs are central to most definitions of sustainable development. Although this is a complex and contested concept, the Brundtland Report offers guiding principles for social and environmental change.
- The proximity to environmental degradation can be correlated with an individual or group's social class, ethnic status and geographical location. The quest for environmental justice extends the quest for basic civil rights.
- Environmental sociology is now a valued and recognized subdiscipline of sociology. It offers a critical and informed understanding of the complex interactions between societies and their respective environments.

Links

The discussion of Marx's early work links with the section on Marxism in Chapter 12 (pp. 486–487).

The section on ecofeminism links with discussions in Chapter 5 (pp. 222–227).

The discussion of sustainable development is related to the section on alternative development in Chapter 9 (pp. 375–379).

Further reading

Baker, S. (2006) *Sustainable Development*, Abingdon: Routledge.
An excellent insight into the different theories and challenges surrounding the concept of sustainable development. A series of global case studies also highlight the promotion of sustainable development in different social, political and economic contexts.

Dunlap, R.E., Buttel, F.H., Dickens, P. and Gijswijt, A. (eds) (2002) *Social Theory and the Environment: Classical Foundations, Contemporary Insights*, Oxford: Rowman & Littlefield.
This book brings together a number of prominent theorists who explore the relevance of classical and contemporary social theory in terms of issues pertinent to environmental sociology.

McCormick, J. (1995) *The Global Environmental Movement*, 2nd edn, Chichester: John Wiley & Sons.
This text provides a valuable and informative overview of the growth and development of the global environmental movement, covering the rise of the greens along with various prominent environmental issues and events.

Palmer, J. (ed.) (2001) *Fifty Key Thinkers on the Environment*, London: Routledge.
A fascinating guide to some of the most influential environmental thinkers across the world, spanning various historical and contemporary periods.

Redclift, M. and Woodgate, G. (eds) (1997) *The International Handbook of Environmental Sociology*, Cheltenham, Edward Elgar.
This text is not aimed at an introductory level. However, the authors provide a comprehensive range of important concepts, theories and issues, including international perspectives, on key aspects of environment and society.

Sutton, P.W. (2004) *Nature, Environment and Society*, London: Palgrave Macmillan.
An interesting and accessible introduction that considers sociology's response to the challenge of environmental issues. Key themes include risk, interpretations of nature, environmental realism and ecological modernization.

Warren, K.J. (1990) 'The power and the promise of ecological feminism', *Environmental Ethics* 12(2): 125–46.
This article gives important insights into both the logic of domination and the social construction of nature.

Websites

www.ipcc.ch

The Intergovernmental Panel on Climate Change. These reports offer a broad scientific consensus on the causes and effects of global warming. Hundreds of experts from all over the world contribute to the detailed preparation of IPCC reports as authors, contributors and reviewers. Reports are published in several volumes, one for each of the Working Groups of the IPCC. The Assessment Reports are as follows: *The IPCC First Assessment Report: Climate Change 1990*; *The IPCC Second Assessment Report: Climate Change 1995*; *The IPCC Third Assessment Report: Climate Change 2001*, followed by the most recent, *IPCC Fourth Assessment Report: Climate Change 2007*, which is composed of four volumes with various contributions, launched in November 2007. All reports are available online at: http://www.ipcc.ch/ipccreports/assessments-reports.htm.

www.occ.gov.uk/activities/stern.htm

The Stern Review on the Economics of Climate Change (2006) commissioned by the UK government looks at climate change projections for the UK, including the economic costs and benefits of various responses.

www.guardian.co.uk

The website of the *Guardian* newspaper is an excellent source for up-to-date environmental news and coverage of key environmental issues and events.

www.earthsummit.info

This is one of the most comprehensive sources of environmental information on the major world/Earth Summits, with over 600 links covering a wide range of environmental issues, reports and studies.

www.foei.org; www.foe.co.uk

Friends of the Earth websites are very informative and accessible, covering a broad range of important environmental issues, such as biodiversity, climate change, trade, environmental justice, transport, renewable energy and waste. Downloads include annual reports and various briefing papers.

www.greenparty.org.uk/news; www.scottishgreens.org.uk

These are some examples of Green Party websites to give a sense of the party's current issues, objectives and reports.

Activities

Excess and deficiency are equally at want.
(Confucius: XI.15)

From the late 1970s onwards a growing minority of consumers became more interested in the goods they could buy with a clear conscience, even if they were not the cheapest. Sometimes this worked in a positive way, as with cosmetics that had not been tested on animals; or the choice was based on boycotting specific companies, such as those that were tangling dolphins in tuna nets. From a slow start, interest in green consumerism grew. In 1959, Oxfam pioneered a fair trade scheme by selling pincushions made by Chinese refugees to the UK public. There are now around 1500 Fairtrade product lines, stocked by numerous retailers. However, as things stand, the major weakness of 'fair trade' is its voluntary nature. Fair trade relies heavily on ethical persuasion, not legal obligation, from market actors. While some Western consumers may also be willing to pay extra for Fairtrade products, not all consumers are in a position to do so, even if they would like to.

The rise of green consumerism was reflected in the success of Body Shop, which set up cruelty-free cosmetics in 1976. By 1990 it had 150 shops in Britain and 338 abroad. Another milestone was the publication of *The Green Consumer Guide* in 1988 by John Elkington and Julia Hailes. For the first time, a book that made the best-seller list suggested that buying green could have a bearing on the future of the planet. The growth in green-consciousness suggests that people want change, and the corresponding change in corporate behaviour suggests that companies are more than eager to flaunt their green credentials and products. But is buying organic socks from M&S enough? The fact remains that over one billion consumers use the majority of the world's resources and create the bulk of carbon dioxide (CO_2) emissions.

Activity 1

Green values and behaviour

Environmentally conscious citizens can adopt more sustainable lifestyles:

- as consumers;
- as investors (e.g. ethical banking);
- as commuters (e.g. using public transport, cycling, walking);
- by conservation (e.g. water, energy);
- by waste reduction (e.g. food);
- by recycling used materials.

Questions

1. **To what extent do you purchase from an environmental or ethical standpoint?**
2. **Do you buy Fairtrade goods, local produce, and organic or recycled goods? Do you avoid using plastic bags?**
3. **Do you recycle unwanted packaging, paper, plastic, cans and bottles?**
4. **Do you walk, cycle or use public transport, as opposed to driving a car?**
5. **Do you actively try to conserve energy, water and other resources?**
6. **What would make it easier for more people to do some of these things – and where does responsibility lie?**
7. **If you actively engage in 'green' forms of behaviour, what is your overall motivation for doing so?**
8. **Are there some forms of green activity that you consider to be more important, effective or feasible than others? If yes, explain why.**

Consider the extract below, by writer and environmentalist George Monbiot:

> **Ethical shopping is just another way of showing how rich you are.**
>
> (Monbiot 2007)

> **The middle classes rebrand their lives, congratulate themselves on going green, and carry on buying and flying as much as before. It is easy to picture a situation in which the whole world religiously buys green products and its carbon emissions continue to soar. Ethical shopping is in danger of becoming another signifier of social status. I have met people who have bought solar panels and wind turbines before they have insulated their lofts, partly because they love gadgets but partly, I suspect, because everyone can then see how conscientious and how rich they are. We are often told that buying such products encourages us to think more widely about environmental challenges, but it is just as likely to be de-politicizing. Green consumerism is another form of atomization – a substitute for collective action. No political challenge can be met by shopping.**
>
> (www.monbiot.com)

Question

1. **To what extent do you think ethical shopping is in danger of becoming merely another signifier of one's social status rather than a force for change?**

Activity 2

'The false logic of material consumption'

Anti-consumerist greens argue that green consumerism reinforces a focus on material acquisition, which leads to one-sided human development (acquisition and materialism) rather than non-material spiritual, cultural and intellectual development. Although individual actions are very important, some people (including deep greens) argue that the wave of green advertising urging us to save the world by simply consuming greener is not enough to avert the ecological crisis – the real issue for them, therefore, is to consume less because green consumerism is effectively still consumerism.

Anti-consumerist greens also highlight the *false logic of material consumption* – the influence of seductive advertising and social pressure, which they claim leads consumers into a spiral of competitive purchasing. In order to pay for goods, you have to work harder, over longer hours, and have less time to enjoy life, resulting in more stress and ill-health. We should ask ourselves *why* we purchase the goods we buy, as the materialism of modern life is often accelerated by social-psychological desires for status and social approval. Finally, it is important to note that increased consumption and materialism broaden the gulf between the affluent and those in poverty. Wealth that does exist is often concentrated in the hands of relatively few.

Questions

1. **Given the relentless focus on consumerism in society, do you think it is realistic to expect people to cut down on their consumption of goods?**
2. **Would you consider consuming less in an attempt to have a less materialistic approach to life? If yes, what steps would you consider taking?**
3. **To what extent do you agree with the notion of the 'false logic of material consumption'?**

Chapter 11

Families and households

Although there is, today, greater acceptance and recognition of the diversity of family forms, it is also the case that strongly held ideas of families and family life continue to shape our expectations and experiences . . . The family remains a strong institution that forms one of the foundations of the world in which we live. (McKie *et al.* 2005: 10)

'Family' is a powerful and pervasive word in our culture, embracing a variety of social, cultural, economic and symbolic meanings; but traditionally it is seen as the very foundation of society. It is also a deeply ambiguous and contested term in the contemporary world, the subject of continual polemics, anxiety, and political concern about the 'crisis of the family'. (Weeks *et al.* 2001: 9)

Key issues

- What do we mean by 'the family'?
- In what ways have family structures changed in recent decades?
- What are the key features of contemporary intimate relationships?
- How can we reach a sociological understanding of singlehood, parenting, grandparenting and sibling relationships?
- Are family relationships based on democracy and equality, or is this a myth?

Introduction

Stop and think

- What is a family? What does family mean to you?
- What problems might we encounter if we try to develop a universal definition of the family?

Families can be sites of conflict, tension and arguments, and yet they may also be sources of love, care, support, affection, commitment and a sense of belonging, as well as involving relations of responsibility, obligations and duties. Thus, family living can be both positive and negative and often provokes ambivalent feelings and emotions in all of us. We all have a common-sense understanding of what a family is, but do we all share the same definition? The family has always existed in some form throughout history, and variations of the family can be found in all societies. However, we must not assume the family to be a 'natural' unit. As sociologists we need to problematize it because the ways in which the family is understood change at different points in history and in different cultures. Thus, the family is a social construction that changes across time and place. There are many different ways of being a family, and this chapter explores this diversity in relation to family form and the experience of family life.

A traditional, ideological view of the family is a father who goes out to work and a mother who stays at home to care for her husband and two children. However, this idealistic notion of a 'typical' traditional family is somewhat mythical, and in contemporary society a range of different family types exist. Soap operas on television, such as *Eastenders* in the UK, portray many family forms, including step-parents, step-children, half-brothers, half-sisters, lone parents, and extended and nuclear families. Even the British royal family consists of divorces, remarriages and co-parenting. As Cheal points out, their family lives have become closely scrutinized:

> **Inside information, or rumours, about the personal lives of royalty has helped to sell huge numbers of newspapers, magazines and books. Today, the details of family life are often public business on a grand scale.**
>
> (Cheal 2002: 16)

There is also much diversity within celebrity families, as we hear about Paul McCartney's high-profile divorce from Heather Mills and Madonna's adoption of David from Malawi. The Hollywood duo 'Brangelina' have their own children Shiloh and twins Knox and Vivienne, as well as three adopted children: Maddox from Cambodia, Zahara from Ethiopia and Pax from Vietnam. Brad Pitt has famously said that he will not marry Angelina Jolie until the restrictions on who can marry whom are dropped. Can you think of other celebrity unions that reflect a range of family forms?

Back in 1982, Barrett and McIntosh (1982: 9) highlighted that 'the family is a contentious and emotive subject'. The family often emerges within political rhetoric and policy as a social institution that is beneficial and positive in many ways. Yet some

Figure 11.1 The British royal family

Figure 11.2 The BBC's Royle family
BBC Photo Library

would argue that recently we are considered to be in a time of family crisis, as the family is blamed for a variety of social problems, such as youth crime, teenage pregnancy and truancy. Traditional family values have often been emphasized by conservative governments and recently have been echoed by the Labour government in the UK:

> **We cannot say we want a strong and secure society when we ignore its very foundations: family life . . . Every area of this government's policy will be scrutinized to see how it affects family life. Every policy examined, every initiative tested, every avenue explored to see how we strengthen our families.**
>
> (Tony Blair's first major conference speech, *Guardian*, 1.10.97)

> **My father and my mother taught me about family and the great virtues of hard work, doing your duty and always trying to do the right thing . . . I stand for a Britain where all families who work hard can build a better life for themselves and their children.**
>
> (Gordon Brown's first major conference speech, *Guardian*, 24.9.07)

In his first conference speech, Gordon Brown went on to recognize that contemporary British society includes a wide variety of family forms:

> **And I say to the children of two-parent families, one-parent families, foster-parent families; to the widow bringing up children: I stand for a Britain that supports as first-class citizens not just some children and some families but supports all children and all families.**

Recent changes in family living include increasing cohabitation and divorce, remarriage (serial monogamy), reconstituted or step-families, lone parents, joint custody, same-sex couples, abortions and two-career households (Jagger and Wright 1999). As we shall see in this chapter, such changes in family structure can create demands for new government policies, and the increased diversity of family forms often sparks intense public and academic debate.

This chapter continues by exploring definitions of families and households. The following section looks at changes in family structure, including marriage, divorce and cohabitation; singlehood; step-families; and families in other cultural contexts. The chapter moves on to explore recent sociological debates about intimate relationships, focusing on parenting, fatherhood, homosexual families, sibling relationships and grandparenting. The final section discusses social problems in relation to families, including domestic violence and child abuse.

Defining families and households

Even though 'the family' is a taken-for-granted term used in everyday language, it is difficult to define, as it can vary so much both within societies and across cultures. Gittins (1993) argues that we should not refer to 'the family' in the singular, but use the plural term 'families' in order to reflect the variety of family living. This is useful, but, although recognizing the diversity, it is also important to consider what is meant by the dynamic and complex term 'family'. In the social sciences there are different definitions of 'family', and these can be contested. Even sociologists differ slightly in the definitions they use, for example:

> **The family has been seen as a social institution that unites individuals into cooperative groups . . . Most families are built on kinship, a social bond, based on blood, marriage or adoption, that joins individuals into families.**
>
> (Macionis and Plummer 2002: 436)

> **A family is a group of persons directly linked by kin connections, the adult members of which assume responsibility for caring for children.**
>
> (Giddens 2001: 173)

Case study

The royal family: divorces, single mothers, reconstituted families

Three of the Queen's four children are divorced (Table 11.1). Two of the divorces led to Princess Diana and Sarah Ferguson being single mothers, but, because of their privileged lifestyles, we are likely to forget about their lone-parent status.

Table 11.1 The British royal family

Queen's child	Marriage status	Children and step-children
Charles, Prince of Wales	Divorced Lady Diana Spencer in 1996 and remarried Camilla Parker Bowles	Charles has two children: Prince William and Prince Harry. He now also has two step-children from Camilla's first marriage: Thomas Henry and Laura Rose
Anne, Princess Royal	Divorced Captain Mark Phillips in 1993 and remarried Commander Timothy Laurence	Anne has two children, Peter and Zara, from her first marriage but none from her second marriage
Andrew, Duke of York	Divorced Sarah Ferguson in 1996	Andrew and Sarah have shared custody of their two children, Princess Beatrice of York and Princess Eugenie
Edward, Earl of Wessex	Married Sophie Rhys-Jones	Edward and Sophie have two children: Lady Louise Windsor and James Alexander Philip Theo

Thus, there is no agreed definition of the family, and recent definitions tend to be broad in order to recognize the growing complexity of different family forms, including lesbian and gay families:

> **A household is a residential group whose members usually share some basic tasks (like cooking). A family may or may not also be a household, but is usually distinguished by formal ties of 'blood' and marriage. However, 'family' also connotes ties of love and affection, commitment, and obligations whether these are formally recognised or not.**
>
> (VanEvery 1999: 178)

As VanEvery suggests it can be useful to make a distinction between 'family' and 'household'. Young adults increasingly spend periods of their lives sharing households, especially as students or before they can afford a house on their own or in a relationship. Thus, financial reasons or delayed marriage or forming of partnerships result in young people living in shared households.

Families are not only about who they are but also about what they do, such as caring, sharing resources, meeting responsibilities and fulfilling obligations (Silva and Smart 1999). Bernardes (1997) emphasizes that families are constructed, the result of everyday lived realities. Such a view is similar to the family practices discussed by Morgan (1996), who argues that families are a product of daily interactions, routines and transactions that may be both enabling and constraining. Thus, our family relationships can be experienced as a mixture of love and hate, burden and duty, care and protection, approval and disapproval.

Changes in the family have led to an increased focus on relationships rather than seeing the family as a social institution (Morgan 1996). Given that it is recognized that there are diverse ways of 'doing family', sociologists now explore what family means to people at different stages in the life course. More recently, Finch has introduced the concept of 'display' as a new way of understanding the diversity and fluidity of contemporary family relationships; she defines 'displaying families' as:

> **The process by which individuals, and groups of individuals, convey to each other and to relevant others that certain of their actions do constitute 'doing family things' and thereby confirm that these relationships are 'family' relationships.**
>
> (Finch 2007: 73)

She argues that 'displaying' family is as important as 'doing' family. There is a need to 'display' family in order to demonstrate to others that one's actions and interactions are family practices that are recognized as such by others. This can be more important where relationships take a non-conventional form in 'families of choice', such as same-sex partnerships or people who live alone but have intimate relationships with others. She also argues that the need for display will vary over time, as relationships are renegotiated at different stages in the life course or according to changing circumstances. The concept of display thus coincides with perceiving families as a qualitative relationship 'rather than a thing' (Morgan 1996: 186). This emphasizes the contingent nature of contemporary family relationships, which need to be both 'done' and 'displayed' in order to recognize their family-like quality:

> **It is precisely because relationships are both defined and experienced by their quality – not simply their existence – that family relationships need to be displayed as well as 'done'. Displaying families confirms the qualitative character of a given relationship, at a particular point in time, as 'family'. In itself this requires a message to be conveyed that this relationship 'works' as a family relationship. If it does not work, then its existence as a family relationship is called into question . . .**
>
> (Finch 2007: 79–80)

Therefore, we can conclude that families are both socially and culturally constructed. The way we understand 'the family' changes over both time and space, both within and between different societies. As Jagger and Wright remind us:

> **The groupings that are called families are socially constructed rather than naturally or biologically given. Families and family relations are, like the term itself, flexible, fluid and contingent. They encompass a whole variety of historically and culturally specific types of domestic arrangements and kinship systems.**
>
> (Jagger and Wright 1999: 3)

The dominant sociological theory in relation to the family until the 1960s was functionalism:

> **Functionalism is a theoretical approach which stresses the positive benefits of families. Families are therefore often described as adaptive systems, which respond creatively to the stresses that are caused by unmet needs. Functionalist sociologists also argue that the reason why families exist is because of the functions which they fulfil . . . According to this point of view, families are thought to be still evolving today in order to help us cope with our changing economic and social environments.**
>
> (Cheal 2002: 8–10)

Functionalists argued that the family's key role was to perform certain functions: to socialize its family members, maintain social order and work as an economic unit, enabling the functioning of capitalist market forces. Murdock (1949) suggested that the family fulfils four basic functions: sexual, reproductive, economic and educational. Similarly, Parsons argued that two of the key roles of the family were the socialization of children and personality stabilization (Parsons and Bales 1956). Individual members are supposed to fulfil their family obligations and be controlled within the bounds of the family unit. In some respects, this view has not changed, as the family is still perceived to be an important social institution that helps to maintain social order. When there is social disorder, such as youth homelessness or youth crime, it is considered that the family is no longer performing its duties. The family is often blamed for not being able to ensure that its members are adequately socialized and educated.

The traditional nuclear family consists of a mother and a father raising their own biological children (Almond 2006: 98). From a functionalist perspective, this traditional family form was reinforced by the state for many decades because it performed functions and transmitted values that were important to the state. However, functionalist theories of the family failed to recognize that families can be sites of conflict and are not always harmonious units. The ideal of the conventional family was based on idealistic private domestic life, where the man worked as the breadwinner in the public sphere and the woman stayed at home in the private sphere to care for the home and children (Barrett and McIntosh 1982). It is worth bearing in mind that this construction of the family is based on white Western middle-class ideals and norms. Hence, the underpinning assumptions of this family ideology could be argued to be classist, sexist, homophobic and racist, by presenting it as the 'best' family form. Nevertheless it existed unproblematically until the late 1960s and early 1970s, when feminist

Figure 11.3 The traditional extended family
© Jose Luis Pelaez, Inc./CORBIS

critiques challenged the role and function of the traditional family.

Feminist perspectives then dominated the sociology of the family during the 1970s and 1980s. Feminists argued that the conventional family was an ideological and historical creation. They pointed out that most families' everyday lived experiences did not match the harmonious ideals of the traditional family. They challenged the conceptualization of the family as a universal, natural unit by highlighting that there was a diversity of family forms. There was a need for public recognition that there were many different experiences in relation to being a family, such as same-sex unions, reconstituted families and single-parent households.

One of the key aims of feminist approaches was to draw attention to the unequal power structures within the family, particularly between men and women but also between adults and children. Feminists argued that patriarchy, male domination and the oppression of women could lead to the potential for violence in the domestic sphere. In particular, given that the modern family was a private sphere separated from public social worlds, feminism raised public awareness about the negative consequences of shutting women and children out of the public life of society, isolated behind closed doors. This deconstruction of family life questioned the notion of the family as a safe haven, showing that the ideology of the traditional family did not necessarily reflect lived realities. Thus, feminists highlighted the potential for women's oppression in the family and the need to develop family policies that recognized the changes in family forms. There were different strands of feminist perspectives on the family, as Barrett and McIntosh indicate:

> **Many feminists identify the family as a primary site, if not *the* primary site, of women's oppression and seek to abolish it . . . Many others argue that feminism must recognize that the majority of women are not helplessly trapped in the family but have willingly identified marriage, children and a family with their own happiness, and it is to this reality that feminism must be made relevant.**
>
> (Barrett and McIntosh 1982: 20)

Despite all the critiques of the conventional family, there are still collective views of what families should look like that dominate in many ways today:

> **An *ideology* provides collective definitions of what a 'normal' family is thought to be, what is a 'proper' marriage, and what it means to be a 'good mother' or a 'good father'. Family ideologies are held out as ideal ways of living.**
>
> (Cheal 2002: 72)

As Gittins points out, ideas about the 'ideal family' are not unfamiliar to most people:

> **It manifests just enough similarity to people's life situations to make it seem tangible and real to most. Thus the never-married, the divorced, and the child-less can at least identify part of the 'ideal family' with a past childhood or family distorted in memory, and feel that their own 'failure' has been an individual failing rather than an unrealistic ideal.**
>
> (Gittins 1993: 165)

Several institutions are responsible for shaping a particular ideology of the family, including the state and the media. As Coppock (1997: 75) argues: 'It is this gap between ideology and reality which signifies the assumed "crisis" in the family'. British government policies at the beginning of the twenty-first century have placed both the family and paid employment centre stage as moral driving forces behind strong communities. Government discussions about respect and community enable issues such as antisocial behaviour to be addressed. The family is put forward as the foundation of community, with parents being responsible for the nurturing of well-socialized adults who will become good citizens (Wyness 1997). At the same time, paid employment is identified as the path to opportunity and out of poverty. However, this can lead to tensions between the dual aims of building a community based on work and one based on the strong family. This means that often contradictory demands are made on families. As we shall see later in this chapter, researchers are increasingly illuminating the challenges, contradictions and inconsistencies facing working parents trying to achieve a work–life balance (Backett-Milburn *et al.* 2001; Duncan and Edwards 1999; Mauthner *et al.* 2001). These are especially acute for low-income families, who may also experience considerable movement in and out of low-paid employment (Kodz *et al.* 2002). It is recognized that there is a need to support working families, and policy initiatives have been introduced with this aim, such as the National Childcare Strategy and the Scottish Executive Working for Families Fund.

Thus, over the past 20 years or so, there has been much debate about the decline of the traditional family and its values, and the family has been increasingly recognized as a flexible social category (McKie *et al.* 2005). In spite of the growing acknowledgement that families have changed, certain assumptions continue to prevail, such as assuming that families share similar aims and objectives or that they tend to consist of two heterosexual adults with children (Bourdieu 1996). The following section explores the most recent changes in family types and in attitudes to family life.

Changes in family structure

Stop and think

- What are some of the recent changes that have occurred in relation to family structures in your country?
- Why might some of these changes in family forms give your government a cause for concern?

Marriage, divorce and cohabitation

In Western societies in the twentieth century there were two key changes that affected the structure of families: the increase in divorce and the rise of cohabitation. Until the 1970s divorce and births outside marriage were relatively rare. In the twenty-first century heterosexual and same-sex couples who are not married but are in long-term partnerships are increasingly being accepted as family relationships (Weeks *et al.* 2001). The boundaries between who counts as family, and who does not, are becoming increasingly blurred (Jamieson 2005). There is no longer the same stigma attached to living together without being married; it is now rarely referred to as 'living in sin'.

In Britain there was a steady increase in the divorce rate since the Second World War, until it peaked in 1993. In 1971 there were just under 80,000 divorces; this figure rose to 180,000 in 1993 (ONS 2004). While the divorce rate increased, the number of marriages fell, from around 459,000 in 1971 to just over 286,000 in 2001. As a result of fewer marriages taking place, the number of divorces began to drop in the 1990s, falling by 13 per cent to 157,000 in 2001 (ONS 2004). It could be argued that serial monogamy is a more appropriate way of describing the pattern of many British relationships. Similar trends of declining marriage rates and the prevalence of divorce and cohabitation are evident throughout Europe. However, there is some variation. For example, Denmark had the highest marriage rate at 6.6 marriages per 1000 people in 2001, while Sweden had the lowest rate of four marriages per 1000 people (Table 11.2). The different divorce rates across Europe are due mainly to religious, social, cultural and legal differences. In 2001, countries in

Table 11.2 Marriage and divorce rates: EU comparison, 2001

	Rates per 1000 population	
	Marriages	Divorces
Denmark	6.6	2.7
Portugal	5.7	1.8
Greece	5.4	0.9
Spain	5.2	1.0
UK	5.1	2.6
France	5.1	2.0
Irish Republic	5.1	0.7
The Netherlands	5.1	2.3
Italy	4.9	0.7
Finland	4.8	2.6
Germany	4.7	2.4
Luxembourg	4.5	2.3
Austria	4.2	2.5
Belgium	4.2	2.9
Sweden	4.0	2.4
EU average	5.1	1.9

(Source: ONS 2001b)

northern and western Europe typically had the highest divorce rates, while the Irish Republic and Italy had the lowest divorce rates.

In the past, material interests played a greater role in marriage, whereas now marriage is concerned more with romantic love. Thus, the satisfaction of personal needs and desires can become more important than cultural tradition or religious codes of conduct. In pre-industrial times couples married in order to gain economic security and domestic survival. Gendered roles were clearly marked, as men met the productive household needs and women attended to the reproductive needs of the household. Love was not the central concern, but more recently there has been a marked shift to individual fulfilment: 'Much of the commentary on family change has emphasised the part played by the pursuit of self-fulfillment and individual happiness over and above regard for marriage vows' (Lewis 2001: 3). The promise of ''til death do us part' is no longer strictly adhered to. Nevertheless, although traditional conventions have decreased, they are still important:

> **Despite the increased prevalence of cohabitation, weddings remain important to many people in many places because they provide the opportunity to publicly demonstrate a private commitment to a long-term relationship.**
>
> (Cheal 2002: 55)

As Dimmock points out:

> **Despite the current concern about the uncertain future for marriage and the family, statistics suggest the majority today still seek a union of two people – 80% wanting children – ideally for many years.**
>
> (Dimmock 2004: 193).

However, it is worth bearing in mind that 'divorce rates might be high but we have no idea how stable cohabitation is' (VanEvery 1999: 179). There is an assumption that cohabitation is more unstable than marriage:

> **The concern that cohabitation may be increasing at the expense of marriage has been heightened by concern that it appears to be relatively impermanent and a less 'committed' form of relationship, with higher rates of dissolution.**
>
> (Lewis 2001: 38)

Yet some regard cohabitation as a 'trial marriage' and, after a few years of living together, many couples do go on to get married:

> **The reality is that 70 per cent of first partnerships are cohabitations lasting on average two years, while 60 per cent of all cohabitations moved into marriage. In 1980, 2 per cent of women had children whilst cohabiting. In 1997, the figure had risen to 22 per cent.**
>
> (Hunt 2005: 135)

Thus, there are different types of cohabiting couples: those who go on to get married, those in a long-term relationship with no intention of ever marrying, and more casual or short-term relationships with less long-term commitment. The increased rate of cohabitation partly explains why the average age of marriage has risen to 30 years for men and 28 years for women, compared with 24 years for men and 22 years for women in 1971 (ONS 2004). Nevertheless it is worth remembering that, despite the changes to household forms, married couples are still the most common form of household. There is a degree of continuity within the recent changes that have occurred.

Single-person households

In developed countries, a growing alternative to either marriage or cohabitation is to live alone. There are growing numbers of people living by themselves as a result of not being married or having a partner, or their partner living elsewhere, or because they are divorced, separated or widowed. Hunt suggests:

> **a new group of divorced men under the age of 65 has become the second biggest group to live alone: there were two and a half-times the number of men living a single life in 1996 than in 1971.**
>
> (Hunt 2005: 135).

Between 1971 and 2001 the number of one-person households almost doubled, from 17 to 31 per cent (ONS 2001b), and it is predicted to increase to 36 per cent in 2016. Wasoff and Jamieson point out:

> **The increase in people living alone may mean a redrawing of boundaries around 'family' and 'household'. Although those who live in one person households are, by definition, not in 'family households', this does not mean most solo livers see themselves as outside family boundaries. In fact, most remain family connected, keeping regular contact with relatives.**
>
> (Wasoff and Jamieson 2005: 222)

The recent growth in 'singletons' is reflected in films and books, such as *Bridget Jones' Diary*. Single people

Case study

Changes in household composition

> Between 1971 and 2001 the overall number of one person households, cohabiting couple households and lone parent households increased, while multi-family households – i.e. those comprising more than one family (one-third of lone parents in multi-family households in 1971) – and married couple families declined.
>
> (Williams 2004: 12)

This is illustrated in Table 11.3, while Table 11.4 indicates the changes in family forms,

> showing a reduction in families headed by a married couple and in widowed lone parents, and an increase in the number of families headed by a separated, divorced or single lone parent and in cohabiting couples.
>
> (Williams 2004: 13)

Table 11.3 Changes in household composition, 1971–2001 – England and Wales

Household composition	1971	2001
Married couple	68% (no separate figures until 1979)	45%
Cohabiting couple		8%
Lone-parent household	6%	10%
Other (shared accommodation/ multi-family)	8%	7%
One-person households (pensionable age)	12%	14%
One-person households (under pensionable age)	6%	16%

Table 11.4 Changes in family forms, 1971–2001 – UK

Families with dependent children	1971	2001
Married couple	90% (no separate figures until 1979)	64%
Cohabiting couple		12%
Other (multi-family households)	3%	1%
Lone parent – single	1%	10%
Lone parent – divorced	2%	9%
Lone parent – separated	2%	3%
Lone parent – widowed	2%	1%

A closer look

Concern over increasing singledom

While the everyday experiences of living alone have not yet been researched extensively by sociologists, Chapman (2004) reminds us that the position of single people in society is high on the political agenda for the following reasons:

- Governments are becoming increasingly concerned about the growing number of single people who may become dependent on the state later in life.
- Governments have recognized that increased divorce rates and the breakdown of long-term cohabiting couple relationships are producing higher levels of state dependence for single-parent families.
- Governments have been alerted to the fact that the breakdown of relationships can produce social problems, including marital violence, homelessness, and alcohol and drug abuse, which has put more pressure on law enforcement, housing and health services (Chapman 2004: 159–60).

tend to have stronger networks of friends, and it may be argued that friendship is the new family for people living on their own. As Williams (2004: 49) suggests, 'For many people, then, friends play an important, even central role in their commitments and sense of belonging'. There may even be a blurring of the boundaries between friends and family. Furthermore, a new family form has emerged: couples who are living apart together (Levin 2004). A heterosexual or same-sex partnership does not have to share a household together in order to be perceived as a couple. Thus, it is important to remember that, just because someone may choose to live alone, this does not necessarily mean that they are not in a long-term or casual relationship. There are a variety of reasons why couples may choose to live apart in two separate households rather than move into one household together. Levin (2004) outlines the reasons as follows:

- *Commitments to already existing relationships*, such as children or grandchildren from previous relationships or caring for older parents.
- *Career opportunities* would diminish if one half of the couple relocated to be with the other. This may be temporary in the case of students who study in different places or more long-term for those who have jobs and friends in different locations.
- *Choosing to avoid the potential boredom of everyday living together* – Some couples live in separate households in order to avoid another painful break-up, either as a strategy to maintain interest in the relationship or to avoid making the same mistake twice.
- *Changes in technology* enable people to communicate more easily and maintain a relationship at a distance. IT communication may also be the medium through which couples meet, due to the increase in Internet dating.
- *Deciding to live apart after previously living together* – For some couples experiencing difficulties in a current relationship, a solution may be to save the relationship by living nearby instead of together.
- *Holiday and work-related travel* mean that people meet others living at a distance and may decide to continue in a relationship without relocating.

Trends in child-bearing

According to the Office for National Statistics (2004), in 1980 nearly 12 per cent of all births were outside marriage, but by 2002 the figure had reached 41 per cent. However, as Denscombe (1998: 20) points out, four out of five such births are registered with both parents identified and, in most cases, with both parents living at the same address. As well as the increasing proportion of children born outside marriage, more women are deciding not to have children, to have children later in life and to have fewer children. Recent figures show that only 11 per cent of women born in 1925 were still childless by age 35, but this increased to 25 per cent of women aged 35 who were born in 1965 (ONS 2004). This pattern is expected to continue and is linked to women's increased participation in the education and labour market as well as the wider choice and effectiveness of contraception.

Technological changes in fertility treatment have led to an increase in older women having children. Advances in reproductive technology, such as in vitro fertilization (IVF) treatment, also mean that women can have children without being in a relationship with a man. According to British government statistics, the conception rate for mothers aged between 40 and 44 reached its highest, at 12.2 per 1000, in 2006, which was a 6 per cent increase from 2005. Nowadays more women are having children in their forties; for example, Madonna had her second child Rocco at 41, Cherie Blair gave birth to her fourth child Leo at 45, and Nicole Kidman was pregnant for the first time at 41. Delays in starting a family, particularly for women with careers, are now more socially acceptable.

There has been a decline in the birth rate in Britain, falling to an average of approximately 1.8 children per family: 'The proportion of women having three or more children has fallen, from nearly four in ten women born in 1941 to only three in ten women born in 1961' (ONS 2007). Practical reasons for this include access to contraception and abortion. Another key reason is that children are becoming expensive to raise. Specialized markets target children and put increased pressure on parents to meet their children's consumption wishes. Children in developed countries are expected to attend school and not engage in paid work, thereby becoming an economic liability rather than being able to financially contribute to their households (see Chapter 7 for more in-depth discussion of the sociology of childhood). Compulsory education also means that this period of economic dependence upon parents is extended until at least 16 years of age, and several years longer for those who continue in further or higher education. Consequently, childlessness has been on the increase in recent years. According to the Office for

National Statistics (2007), 'Nearly one in five women born in 1961 was childless, compared with one in ten women born around 1941'.

While some couples choose to be childless, it is important to remember that there are many people who would like to have children but are unable to, as Beck-Gernsheim outlines:

> **In recent years, a wide range of more or less intricate procedures have been developed in reproductive medicine to offer help to those who are childless but would like to have children. The best known of such groups are couples who suffer from some biological impediment, but there are also newer groups, less present in the public mind, who have increasingly appeared with the pluralization of lifestyles and for various reasons demand medical assistance to fulfil their wish for a child. These are women and men who once got sterilized and now regret the decision (for example, in the context of a new relationship); women who are already past the menopause but hope to become mothers through an egg donor; gay and lesbian couples who wish to become parents; and single persons who, though without a partner, do not wish to be left without a child.**
>
> **However different these motives may be, they all point towards the 'technically assisted reproduction' which is covertly as it were, clearing the way for new forms of parenthood.**
>
> (Beck-Gernsheim 2002: 97)

Advances in reproductive technologies open up many new possibilities, such as having two 'biological' mothers, and can also mean the separation of biological and social parenthood. This raises many social and ethical questions around the circumstances in which people can decide to create a family of their own choosing (Almond 2006). Do you think that all men and women have the right to have a child, or are there any situations when this might not be appropriate? Does everyone have the right to donor-assisted reproduction? Almond indicates that this issue tends to divide people's opinions:

> **As a new era of reproductive choice opens up, it raises many questions about where this expansion of possibilities may be leading. Some see a need for caution and would prefer to hold back on institutionalizing the untested social experiments made possible by novel progenitive procedures. Others welcome them as offering a new dawn for the family, which, they believe, has not been diminished, but renewed and regenerated in myriad new forms.**
>
> (Almond 2006: 98)

She calls attention to the particularly interesting issue of the rights of the 'donor-conceived' child. Should the child have a right to choose whether to know about their parentage, or should this be concealed from them? Almond (2006) reminds us that new reproductive technologies have created both new risks and new rights that need to be considered with care.

Step-families

Family policy and law shape the ways in which family life is understood. In Britain there has been a shift towards emphasizing the importance of biological parenthood in a context of increasing divorce, remarriage and reconstituted families. This raises questions in relation to the role and expectations of step-families. Like other family forms, there are definitional difficulties as to what exactly constitutes a step-family. Since members can cut across several

A closer look

The role of fathers in fertility treatment

In May 2008 British MPs voted to remove the requirement that fertility clinics consider a child's need for a father. The new Human Fertilisation and Embryology Bill will no longer require that fertility clinics take account of the 'need for a father' when assessing women for treatment. This rule has been replaced with the 'need for supportive parenting'. This means that single women and lesbian couples have greater parental rights as they cannot be rejected as potential parents on the basis that their children will not have a father or male role model. Opponents of the new law say that it denigrates the role of a father in a child's life.

different households, and boundaries may be blurred, there can be differing perspectives of who counts as family. For example, as Ribbens McCarthy *et al.* (2003) point out, a new step-family may include a non-resident parent and their partner, step-grandparents and other kin. Furthermore, some people may not readily recognize themselves as being part of a step-family.

Allan and Crow (2001) argue that, as distinct family histories are brought together, the sense of solidarity and unity can be more complex to develop compared with families based purely on blood ties. This can lead to divided loyalties and perceived interventions from 'outsiders'. Bernardes summarizes some of the key tensions that may have to be resolved in step-families:

> **There may be conflicts between children and their stepparent, especially revolving around the extent to which the child and stepparent 'accept' each other and how far the child 'accepts' the adult taking on the role of 'mother' or 'father'. There may be disputes between the new partners in which children manipulate loyalties; there may be disputes between different 'classes' of children. Beyond this, there may be dispute and confusion about the roles of grandparents and previous spouses.**
>
> (Bernardes 1997: 164–5)

Thus, relations with step-families can be difficult to manage. Issues of time and attention, financial resources and contact with a non-resident parent may arise. In addition, attempts to work out these issues may be exacerbated with intensified emotions of resentment and jealousy on behalf of the parent or child concerned. Step-parenting can be a difficult role to negotiate and may include heightened tensions in relation to the appropriate manner of child-rearing, especially disciplinary issues. Research has shown that different strategies can be employed. Some step-parents try to replace the non-resident biological parent, whereas others do not attempt to do so. However, not only is there limited research on this aspect of family living, but also step-families lack normative role models and can be ill-prepared for the re-parenting role (Bernardes 1997).

Thus, step-families can be based on contradictory expectations and tend to be contingent relationships dependent on the ways in which individuals manage their new roles. Members of step-families are not automatically accepted on the basis of the legal context of remarriage but have to 'earn their place' and negotiate good relationships achieved through social practices rather than ascribed by formal status (Ribbens McCarthy *et al.* 2003). In their research on step-parenting in the UK, Ribbens McCarthy and colleagues were somewhat surprised to find that, rather than defining themselves as a different and new form of family, many step-families sought to develop traditional family ties. Most rejected the term 'step-family' and placed continued importance on the 'family' consisting of responsibility, team effort, togetherness and commitment. It was felt that the investment of time and fairness towards all family members would encourage the creation of solidarity. Thus, in their study, family 'may be seen as fixed by blood or marriage ties, or as something that develops over time' (Ribbens McCarthy *et al.* 2003: 50). Their research also found consistent class differences: middle-class step-families revealed that they perceived biological parental ties as being crucial, whereas in working-class step-families the social practices of the current household were more important than biology. The study emphasized the continued importance of the family that is cross-cut by notions of class, gender and generation.

There are many different ways of being a step-family, so we need to refer to 'step-families' rather than 'the step-family' (Ribbens McCarthy *et al.* 2003). Certainly not all step-families are problematic, and many of the tensions and difficulties that they face are not necessarily very different than those of intact families, but they may become more intense and complex:

> **It can be recognised that within stepfamilies the interests of the different members are less uniform; the sets of relationships which need to be managed are broader; and the sense of family cohesion is less secure than in natural families. Equally, some stepfamilies 'work' much better than others.**
>
> (Allan and Crow 2001: 161)

Reasons for changes in family patterns

Several reasons account for the contemporary changes to family forms. An increase in life expectancy has led to people living longer and having more time to become dissatisfied within their marriage and seek new partners. As Levin states:

> **Previously, when marriages were shorter, death occurred before couples had time to divorce. In our day, divorce has replaced death as one of the main reasons for the dissolution of marriage.**
>
> (Levin 2004: 224)

It is now quicker and cheaper to seek a divorce, and there is less social stigma attached to it. Legal changes enable divorce to be obtained more easily, and this reflects that divorce has become more socially acceptable. The decline in religious beliefs also means that divorce is less likely to be perceived as morally wrong. Similarly, social attitudes towards cohabitation and lone parenthood have also changed. There is less social stigma attached to living together or having children outside marriage.

Importantly, recent improvements in gender equality have led to changes in family structures. For example, more women go out to work and are more financially independent than in the past. The full-time housewife is far less common nowadays, as many European households are based on dual income. Women are also working more throughout their lives, in particular after having children. Gendered family roles have become more fluid, diverse and negotiable (Chapman 2004). This may mean that some women are less prepared to tolerate a deteriorating relationship, which perhaps their mothers or their grandmothers might previously have remained trapped within. People now have higher expectations of marriage and are more likely to end an unsatisfactory relationship. It is no longer necessary for women to be married in order to achieve financial security. However, some caution needs to be exercised when considering greater levels of gender equality because, although changes have taken place, continuities also exist. In addition, it is important to recognize that attitudes change more quickly than behaviour, and so only over time will actions become more in line with beliefs (Dermott 2008: 22).

A closer look

Gender equality within families?

Despite recent improvements in levels of gender equality, many inequalities continue to exist:

- Women's careers are more likely than men's to be disrupted when they have children. More women than men work part-time in jobs that can be combined more easily with child care.
- Women continue to do more housework and child care than men.
- Women do more emotional labour (listening to, talking with and supporting family members) than men.
- Women are more likely than men to make financial and time sacrifices in order to meet their children's needs.

World in focus

Child-headed households

Child-headed households (CHHs) are a relatively recent concept on the academic stage. Early recorded observations of them date back to the late 1980s and early 1990s, and research on CHHs has since been conducted in countries including, but not limited to, Zambia, Zimbabwe, South Africa, Kenya, Namibia, Rwanda and Uganda (e.g. see Ayieko 2004; Foster 1997; Graham 2007; Payne 2007; Walker 2002). CHHs have come to light in the wake of the HIV/AIDS pandemic and discussions of an 'orphan crisis' (Bray 2003) in Africa. This is because CHHs are generally, but incorrectly, perceived to be synonymous with orphan-headed households. Moreover, they are frequently characterized as one of the most worrying and visible manifestations of extended family breakdown (Barnett and Whiteside 2002). There is evidence to support claims that CHHs constitute an especially vulnerable group. For example, Foster (1997) argues that children within CHHs are more likely to have early sexual experiences and are especially vulnerable to sexual and economic

World in focus *continued*

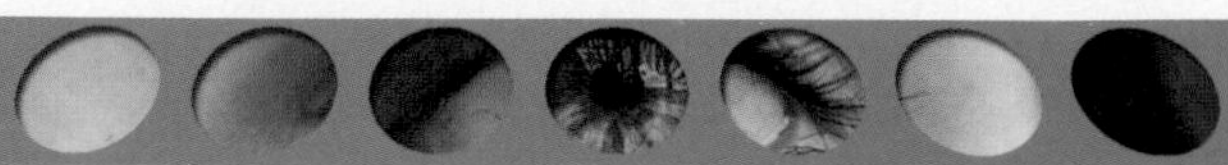

exploitation, while Walker (2002) suggests that CHHs experience more limited access to the usual safety nets provided by extended families and communities than non-CHHs. Consequently, they are rapidly becoming a target for international development agencies and non-governmental organizations (NGOs) concerned with the provision of assistance to orphans and vulnerable children, although such mechanisms of support remain in their infancy. Furthermore, despite proliferation in the use of the term 'child-headed household' in recent years, there remains little conceptual understanding of it at either academic or practitioner level and there exists little qualitative documentation of the ways in which such households are coping, surviving and experiencing day-to-day life (Bray 2003).

Definitions of CHHs are hotly contested, but they are largely recognized to be households

> **in which the caregiver responsible for the day-to-day supervision of younger children (including bathing children, dressing them, preparing meals, dealing with minor illnesses etc) is under the age of 18 years but is not their biological mother or father.**
>
> (Foster 1997: 4).

However, Foster (1997) acknowledges that, in some CHHs, adults may also be present but not functioning as the caregiver due to reasons such as terminal illness, disability or mental incapacity. Likewise, research in Zambia investigated CHHs in which parents or guardians were either completely absent or not 'fully functioning' in terms of providing for the material and emotional needs of children (Payne 2007). This research, therefore, also embraced households where children are living with parents and adult relatives unable to adequately care for them. Moreover, it revealed the complex mix of factors that both initiate and sustain child-headedness, including, but not restricted to, alcoholism, illness, disability and death of adult caregivers, abandonment by parents, early marriage of siblings and poverty.

CHHs are recognized to be inherently fluid entities, given the eventual transition of child household heads to the social position of adulthood. This is acknowledged internationally to begin upon reaching 18 years of age (United Nations 1989), although local traditions and understandings of such constructs differ widely. CHHs present further challenges to conceptualizations of 'childhood' and 'adulthood', because of the tendency for household members to perform both identities simultaneously, according to the different roles and responsibilities each undertakes at different times as de facto 'parent', caregiver, role model, advisor or breadwinner (Payne 2008). Consequently, CHHs constitute sites for growing up in new and unexpected ways involving the (re)construction of family relationships, household patterns, roles and responsibilities and the carving out of alternative pathways to adulthood in which traditional customs are being recast by young people. As Payne (2008) argues, CHHs are also dynamic in response to the often rapidly changing circumstances of their members relating, for example, to the income-earning opportunities, health and mobility patterns of household members and overall household structure according to age, gender and sibling composition, which may invoke a period of temporary child-headedness. CHHs disrupt normative understandings of 'household' and 'family' by challenging us to consider these terms in different ways. It is widely recognized that households and families are both diverse and fluid entities with formations and compositions shifting through time and space (Young and Ansell 2003). Consequently, CHHs can be conceptualized as a powerful form of the evolving family and positioned within a context of changing families, households and kinship patterns rather than simply illustrative of 'extended family breakdown'.

(Source: Ruth Payne, Royal Holloway, University of London)

(For more information see www.streetchildafrica.org.uk/research.)

Question

1. **Consider some of the ways in which growing up in a CHH disrupts conventional understandings about families and households. For example, in what ways do CHHs constitute a challenge to understandings of the 'traditional extended family'?**

Families and diversity

As we have seen, there are a range of family forms within Britain and Europe. If we look at other cultures, further patterns of family diversity emerge. For example, Asian families tend to be more extended, based on strong ideas of honour and family loyalty, and are structured around male networks. In contrast, African-Caribbean families tend to be headed by women and revolve around female networks. However, we need to bear in mind that we should not overgeneralize about different cultures' family structures. Reynolds (2002) reminds us that African-Caribbean family forms often include single mothers, common-law joint residence couples, married couples and visiting relationships (where the male partner does not live permanently in the household). These diverse family forms are also reflected in African-Caribbean families living in Britain:

> **The Black family offers one example, among many in Britain, of a social and cultural group that has many diverse family structures and household arrangements. Yet traditional definitions of the Black family in Britain and the USA present the female-headed household as a fixed and a unitary Black family structure. In reality, however, this household structure is one of the many stages of family life that Black women continue to move through during their lifetime.**
>
> (Reynolds 2002: 75)

An increase in international migration has meant that family cultures may adapt or change in the migrant destination. 'Transnational families' are a relatively new type of family, emerging in the context of globalization and the search for new global opportunities across borders. Bryceson and Vuorela (2002: 3) define them as 'families that live some or most of the time separated from each other, yet hold together and create something that can be seen as a feeling of collective welfare and unity, namely "familyhood", even across national borders'.

Britain is a multicultural society (see Chapter 6), but at times there are tensions between the younger and older generations in relation to family values and expectations. For example, in South Asia arranged marriages are common, but some young Asians living in Britain wish to choose their own partners and reject their parents' plans for an arranged marriage. This can cause conflicts, particularly in relation to forced marriages, which have received media attention

A closer look

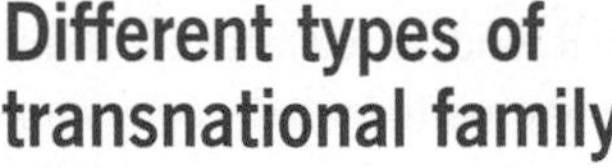

Different types of transnational family

Bryceson and Vuorela's (2002) edited collection on transnational families in Europe identifies several different types of transnational living arrangements:

- Refugee families who have to learn new languages and face constraints of hostile labour markets
- Tightly knit migrant communities who retain many aspects of their identity and culture in the place of destination
- Migrant families who experience intergenerational conflict of family cultural values, as the younger generation grow up in the migrant destination
- Transnational elites who have moved for financial or status reasons, seeking international careers and networking through choice rather than necessity.

> The many permutations that families and networks take as people relativize their familial and associational ties in new cultural surroundings and material circumstances testify to the impossibility of identifying any simple categorizations or tendencies. The motivation for the spatial movement of transnational family members in the first instance tends to be welfare-enhancement, but the actual form and dynamics of transnational families are part of a creative social process that is impossible to predict. The unknown frontier is a mixture of cultural, social, economic and political horizons that are constantly being mapped, then remapped.
>
> (Bryceson and Vuorela 2002: 266)

recently. Arranged marriages are based on the economic and social suitability of the tie, with a belief that love emerges within the marriage rather than acting as the key motivation for the union. Despite some changes, such as young people wanting more involvement in their choice of partner, South Asian families in Britain tend to have strong familial bonds and lower divorce rates.

World in focus

The impact of globalization on family life in India

The postindustrialization period in the West led to dramatic changes in religious beliefs, family structures, family size, work ethic, morals, economics, education, literature, health, politics, human rights, medical and scientific research, and several other areas of human concern . . .

It has been argued that globalization will lead to a process of Westernization and modernization and that all the developing countries will eventually come to imbibe the Western values of individualism, rationalism, humanism, empiricism, and secularism, thus becoming ultimately indistinguishable from the Western countries . . .

That certain Western values, as a result of globalization, will impinge on the people of Asian cultures is inevitable. Insofar as economic affluence is concerned, this is already evident by the significant changes that are noticeable in India. Affluent Indians in the urban areas of India have begun to adopt Western ways of living, including living in high-rise blocks, condominiums (with swimming pools and tennis courts), furnishing their homes in modern Westernized styles, membership in exclusive Western-type clubs, Western culinary preferences, modes of dress, artistic and other esthetic preferences, driving imported luxury cars, increasing use of communication and information technologies, and last but not least, foreign travel . . .

However, as soon as one starts to dig deeper and observe the day-to-day lives of families at home, the picture changes; the observable similarities, so easily noticeable from the outside, seem merely cosmetic – not unlike a new, conspicuous patchwork on an ancient family heirloom. The house, although furnished in modern Western style, is still dominated by a temple or a shrine. The family members, one finds, usually eat their meals together, the home-cooked food often conforms to the families' indigenous regional culinary habits, family life still tends to operate on a hierarchical order. Although children 'enjoy' a certain degree of latitude in expressing their views and opinions, and although the children are not any the less indulged than they were in the past, deference to the views of the elders to a large extent is taken for granted and remains unquestioned. Collective activities, in which all family members are expected to participate – visiting relatives, entertaining relatives, performing prayers and *pujas*, participating in all the religious rituals (e.g., the mundan ceremony [tonsure ceremony], the sacred thread ceremony, betrothals, marriages, and festivities), are still are an integral part of family life.

One of the most important factors that distinguishes Indian families from Western (English or American) families is the fact that children (sons), upon reaching maturity, are *not* expected to leave home and set up their own lives.

(Laungani 2005: 100–101)

Questions

1. What kinds of collective activity did you participate in with your family when you were a child? To what extent do you still engage in family events?

2. What impact do you think recent social changes have had on contemporary family practices? For example, in what ways have modern technologies (e.g. microwaves, DVD players, mobile phones) and changing working patterns (e.g. more women participating in the labour market) shaped family life?

Intimate relationships

Since the well-known sociologist Anthony Giddens wrote the book *The Transformation of Intimacy* (1992a), there has been a shift to considering the ways in which the everyday experiences of intimacy affect family practices. In particular, there has been a move to focus on 'cultures of intimacy and care' (Roseneil and Budgeon 2004) rather than a more narrow concern with 'the family'. This includes research with non-cohabiting partners, intimate friendships and 'families of choice' (Weeks *et al.* 2001). A change in emphasis to studies on personal relationships reflects the recognition that there is a

> **. . . blurring of the boundaries, and movement between, friendship and sexual relationships which often characterizes contemporary gay and lesbian intimacies. Friends become lovers, lovers become friends, and many have multiple sexual partners of varying degrees of commitment.**
>
> (Roseneil and Budgeon 2004: 138)

Giddens argues that in the late twentieth century people became more aware of the need for a fulfilling relationship based on 'confluent love' that is active and contingent. This contrasts with marriage, which, in pre-industrial times, was often linked to economic purposes and, since the nineteenth century, was based on romantic love that tied a person to a lifelong relationship with one other person. The more recent development of 'plastic sexuality' (Giddens 1992a) refers to sex as being separated from reproductive needs, partly because of improved contraception and partly because of greater choice over sexual partners.

Thus, there is a stronger emphasis on the quality of relationships, which is perceived to be something that has to be achieved rather than taken for granted. Giddens (1992a) refers to this as a 'pure relationship' that is not bound by traditional notions of duty and obligation. Intimate relationships now tend to be based more on sexual and emotional equality between men and women (Roseneil and Budgeon 2004). As Jamieson comments:

> **Commitment does not mean an obligation to stay together for life . . . what subsequently sustains the relationship is a mixed repertoire of practices of intimacy and processes that subsequently institutionalise the relationship.**
>
> (Jamieson 2005: 201)

Contemporary intimate partnerships are contingent upon each half of the couple benefiting from the relationship, where 'communication and negotiation become central to this achievement and success cannot be guaranteed' (Williams 2004: 17).

Beck and Beck-Gernsheim argue:

> **. . . it is no longer possible to pronounce in some binding way what family, marriage, parenthood, sexuality or love mean, what they should or could be; rather these vary in substance, exceptions, norms and morality from individual to individual and from relationship to relationship. The answers to the questions above must be worked out, negotiated, arranged and justified.**
>
> (Beck and Beck-Gernsheim 1995: 5)

Love is complex, fluid and changing. In contemporary society it can be argued that family relationships are chosen rather than given. Bauman (2003) suggests that the increased flexibility to choose relationships and not remain bound to one person can lead to tensions between security and freedom. Zygmunt Bauman is a prolific writer in sociology and one of his books, *Liquid Love* (2003), highlights the frailty and impermanence of human bonds, which can create uncertainty and anxiety. Greater individual choice over partners means that relationships have to be worked at and are 'open to this constant re-evaluation and potential cessation' (Dermott 2008: 239).

Beck and Beck-Gernsheim (1995), Bauman (2003) and, to some extent, Giddens (1992a) have based their arguments on the individualization thesis. This thesis argues that class is now less important in structuring people's lives as 'individuals are left to shape their own destinies' (Brannen and Nilsen 2005: 15). The above authors apply this to family relationships and have been criticized for overemphasizing the role of individual agency and downplaying key structural factors such as class and gender as well as overlooking the nature of power and intergenerational relationships (Jamieson 1998; Ribbens McCarthy *et al.* 2003; Smart 2007). Brannen and Nilsen (2005) warn that, by focusing on individualization and individual choice in relationships, the ways in which people continue to connect and depend upon each other are ignored.

In her book *Researching Intimacy in Families*, Gabb (2008: 1) states that: 'Intimacy is about our everyday relationships and affective interactions . . . It now symbolises an emergent intellectual framework around the detraditionalization of interpersonal exchanges and kin formation'. Her research aims to increase understanding of the ways in which families show love and affection, both within and across generations. Jamieson's (1998, 2005) work has also been central to the ongoing debates about intimacy and family relationships. She defines intimacy in the following ways:

> **In everyday current usage, intimacy is often presumed to involve practices of close association, familiarity and privileged knowledge, strong positive emotional attachments, such as love, and a very particular form of 'closeness' and being 'special' to another person, associated with high levels of trust. Recent discussions of intimacy emphasise one particular practice of generating 'closeness' above all others, self-disclosure. Intimacy of the inner self, 'disclosing intimacy' or 'self expressing intimacy' has become celebrated in popular culture as the key to a 'good relationship' although some academic work has suggested that this type of intimacy may be more of an ideological construct than an everyday lived reality.**
>
> (Jamieson 2005: 189)

Intimacy depends on keeping 'others' at a distance and requires a level of communication between partners, which needs to be renegotiated over time. Recent research focuses on the ways people 'do intimacy' and recognizes that there are now a multiplicity of living arrangements and different types of relationship that could be considered to be 'family-like'. Jamieson (1998) reminds us that, even though we are living in a period of intense social change, contemporary intimate relationships are not necessarily equal and democratic and gender inequalities continue to prevail. A 'good' relationship is not always a reflection of equality and may not be permanent. However, this fragility of intimacy is less likely to apply to the parent–child relationship, which we explore in the following section.

Carol Smart has worked for many years within the sociology of the family, and has suggested that the way forward for this field is a sociology of 'personal life' (2007). She does not mean this to replace the terminology of 'family', but rather she uses it as an inclusive concept that reflects the complexity and ambiguity of relationships and intimacy. She explains:

> **'The personal' designates an area of life which impacts closely on people and means much to them, but which does not presume that there is an autonomous individual who makes free choices and exercises unfettered agency. This means that the term 'personal life' can invoke the social, indeed it is conceptualized as always already part of the social. This is because the very possibility of personal life is predicated upon a degree of self-reflection and also connectedness with others.**
>
> **. . . The term is also appropriately neutral in that it does not prioritize relationships with biological kin or marital bonds. Such a landscape of personal life does not have hierarchical boundaries between friends and kin. This means that there is more open conceptual space for families of choice, same-sex intimacies, reconfigured kinship formations and so on.**
>
> **. . . Finally, personal life as a concept does not invoke the white, middle-class, heterosexual family in the way that, historically at least, the concept of 'the family' has. This means that important dimensions of class, ethnicity, religion, sexuality, gender, and disability can be written through the narrative and given significance.**
>
> (Smart 2007: 28–30)

The key limitation of this term is that it is perhaps too wide a concept that 'can appear to include anything and everything that pertains to a person' (Smart 2007: 30). It remains to be seen whether it will become a popular lens for exploring family life. The concept of 'personal life' certainly encapsulates a sense of fluidity and diversity, connecting the family with other spheres such as work, education and leisure.

Parenting

Being a parent and having parental responsibility is by no means an easy task. As Ribbens McCarthy *et al.* (2003: 145) point out, 'In Britain, parenting is a privatised, individualised responsibility'. However, there are many public discourses in relation to being a 'good parent', which adds a moral dimension to parenting as the implication is that parents *should* be raising their children in a certain manner. Parents may feel pressure that they *ought* to be doing particular things, such as being highly involved with their children's education or enabling them to undertake activities such as music lessons, sport or dance classes. There is a potential conflict between private and public spheres as parents take on responsibility for children; much of this 'work' takes place in the private sphere, and yet, increasingly, expectations about parenting extend into the public sphere, such as health discussions around obesity (see Chapter 13). Public discourses, including policy,

A closer look

Changing theoretical perspectives on families

As we have seen throughout this chapter, different terms for the 'family' and theoretical stances on the family have changed over time (Table 11.5).

Table 11.5 Changing theories and terms for the family

Period	Theory	Key authors	Key terms used
1950s to 1960s	Functionalism	Parsons and Bales	'The family' as a social institution
1970s to 1980s	Feminist theories	Barrett and McIntosh, Gittins	Household or private sphere; families (not 'the family')
1990s	Individualization thesis	Bauman, Beck and Beck-Gernsheim, Giddens	Family practices (Morgan 1996); families of choice (Weeks *et al.* 2001)
2000s	Intimacy	Jamieson	Displaying families (Finch 2007)
Way forward?	Connectedness thesis	Smart	Personal life (Smart 2007)

political and cultural discourses, can affect how all parents see themselves and other parents. However, this may be felt even more strongly in working-class 'problem' families, where there tends to be more direct intervention from the public sphere, such as health-care professionals or social workers:

> **Parenting is no longer accepted as an interpersonal bond characterised by love and care. Instead it has been re-framed as a job requiring particular skills and expertise which must be taught by formally qualified professionals. Working class mothering practices are held up as the antithesis of good parenting, largely through their association with poor outcomes for children.**
>
> (Gillies 2007: 2)

Thus, the moral dimension of parenting tends to have class undertones. For example, there is an assumption that, in working-class families, children are less likely to be engaging in constructive activities, such as chess or ballet classes, and are more likely to be making less constructive use of their time in front of the television or video games. The television programme *Wife Swap* often illustrates different modes of parenting and the diversity of family forms. There tends to be a class element attached to the two families that are juxtaposed in the same programme. This reminds us that not all families have the same degree of choice in their parenting and child-rearing strategies. Gillies' research on working-class experiences of parenting illustrates the daily 'struggles to cope with financial constraint, vulnerability, insecurity, limited power and disrespect' (Gillies 2007: 144). She argues that, instead of blaming working-class mothers for not conforming to parenting standards that are grounded in middle-class advantage, there should be a case 'for replacing coercive "skills" training and other forms of regulation with real financial, practical and material support' (Gillies 2007: 145). However, many parents, not just those of working-class background, may find themselves in a peculiar position between the individualized, private space of the home and the public discourses that construct appropriate models of acceptable family life.

As we have seen earlier in this chapter, there has been an increase in divorce, remarriage and reconstituted families. This means that many children are likely to spend parts of their life living away from one of their parents. However, some commentators have argued that parent–child relationships are perhaps more permanent and reliable than marriage (Beck and Beck-Gernsheim 1995; Gabb 2008). Jensen and McKee note:

> **Modern childhood is often portrayed in terms of enhanced democratic relationships between parents and children, with the assumption that children's negotiating power has increased over time. The**

A closer look

Scottish Schools (Parental Involvement) Act 2006

This act modernizes and strengthens the framework for supporting parental involvement in school education. It aims to help schools, education authorities and others to engage parents meaningfully in the education of their children and in the wider school community. It requires Scottish ministers and education authorities to promote the involvement of parents in children's education at publicly funded schools. It aims to help all parents to be:

- involved with their child's education and learning;
- welcomed as active participants in the life of the school;
- encouraged to express their views on school education generally and work in partnership with the school.

Question

1. To what extent do you think the state should play a role in shaping the nature of parenting? In what areas do you think the state should intervene or offer guidance for parents?

(Source: Scottish Government 2006; www.scotland.gov.uk/Publications/2006/09/08094112/0)

suggestion is that families today permit more individual choice and facilitate negotiated relationships.

(Jensen and McKee 2003: 1)

Research in the sociology of childhood provides empirical evidence that children are social actors who participate in and actively construct their everyday experiences and relationships, both within and outside the family (James *et al.* 1998; Mayall 2002). However, Jensen and McKee also comment that we need to be wary about the extent of children's ability to negotiate with more powerful adult social actors, such as their parents:

> **Within a market society themes of self-actualization, individualism and the ideology of personal choice may be masking persistent inequalities between children and adults, and children and parents.**
>
> (Jensen and McKee 2003: 167)

Thus, although society may be more aware of children's rights and more child-centred, there are limitations on the ways in which children can influence and shape their daily lives (see Chapter 7 for further discussions on some of the opportunities and constraints that structure children's lives).

Furthermore, Solomon *et al.* (2002) illustrate that communication between children and parents can be problematic. Information-seeking, intended by parents as developing closeness with their teenage children, can be perceived as a controlling strategy by the young people themselves. Open communication between children and parents can reflect intergenerational power struggles (see also Punch 2005):

> **For parents, information gain means the retention of power and control, while for teenagers, withholding information from their parents ensures their privacy, power and identity.**
>
> (Solomon *et al.* 2002: 965)

Thus, even though contemporary families are considered to be more democratic and equal, mutual disclosure of honesty and openness between children and parents is not necessarily a reality. It is increasingly recognized that family relationships between generations (for example, between siblings or between male and female partners) and across generations (between parents and children or between grandparents and grandchildren) are subject to negotiation and compromise. Households are neither totally consensual units nor entirely sites of conflict. Household relations include a mixture of cooperation and competition (Punch 2001a). On the one hand, households function as units of mutual support and solidarity, where moral obligations and expectations are fulfilled. On the other hand, these are the result of long-term relationships built up over time and are subject to negotiation, tension and conflict (Finch and Mason 1993). People work out responsibilities and commitments in everyday interactions: 'Family responsibilities thus become a matter for negotiation between individuals and not just a matter of following normative rules' (Finch and Mason 1993: 12). Thus, household relationships are constantly being renegotiated through sibling negotiation and parent–child negotiation (Punch 2001a).

Ribbens McCarthy *et al.* (2003: 17) point out that 'Gendered divisions in parenting roles remain considerable in British families, despite mothers being more involved in paid work outside the home'. Mothers tend to have the main responsibility for the domestic life and the everyday care of children after separation or divorce. While it is acknowledged that there is not a fixed model of good mothering, many mothers do feel pressure to live up to an ideal of a 'good mother'. Hunt points out that motherhood can produce a mixed response from women in contemporary society particularly when surrounded by conflicting expert advice on child-rearing practices:

> **Some women complain of being trapped by the motherhood role or at least display mixed emotions about raising children. Paradoxically, the decision to opt for motherhood now brings even greater demands.**
>
> (Hunt 2005: 73)

Furthermore, it is recognized that a father's relationship with his children tends to be mediated through the mother. Lone parenthood is more likely to consist of a single mother rather than a single father. In Britain there were around 1.5 million lone parents bringing up 2.3 million children, which totalled just over one-fifth of all households with dependent children (Daniel and Ivatts 1998). The 2001 General Household Survey indicated that the number of lone parents bringing up children almost doubled from 12 per cent in 1981 to 23 per cent in 2001 (ONS 2001b). Younger parenting is also a feature of single parenthood. According to the Office for National Statistics, births outside marriage are more likely to take place at a younger age than those inside marriage. For example, in 2000 'women giving birth outside marriage were more than four years younger than their married counterparts' (ONS 2001a).

Kiernan (1992) argues that young people are more likely to leave lone-parent households and step-families at a younger age than those living in traditional nuclear families. She also suggests that they are more likely to have children earlier, have lower educational attainment and have less employment prospects. Dimmock (2004) states that in Britain approximately 25 per cent of children under 16 years of age experience their parents' divorce. It is worth remembering that changes to family structure, such as divorce, are likely to have different impacts on different family members, and they may experience a combination of both positive and negative effects. For example, as Jensen and McKee (2003: 1) illustrate: 'divorce may provide a positive outcome to an unsatisfactory marriage for one (or both) adults, while leading to a deterioration of economic security either for one of the adults involved and/or for the children'.

More recently there has been some research that explores children's perspectives of their parents' divorce. Moxnes' (2003) study showed that in Norway, after a divorce, children found that a decline in household income, change of residence and having step-parents were difficult and stressful processes but that, with sufficient time and support from their parents, they learned to cope. In contrast, children who felt they were not listened to or involved in any of the negotiations felt increasingly vulnerable and lonely. Similarly, in Robinson *et al.*'s (2003) research in the UK children were discovered to be resilient and able to cope but that they needed adequate information in order to help them to understand and adapt to the new situation. The children in their study said that they experienced their parents' divorce as a period of emotional turmoil and upset, but that they appreciated being actively involved in managing post-divorce changes. Co-parenting is increasingly perceived as an appropriate way of enabling children to maintain regular contact with both parents. However, the sharing of child care forces separated parents to continue to cooperate and work together, which can be emotionally problematic after divorce (Allan and Crow 2001). Furthermore, children can experience the moving between two households as tiring, time-consuming, and requiring much emotional and practical effort in order to maintain competing demands on their use of time and space (Robinson *et al.* 2003; Smart *et al.* 2001).

Fatherhood

Stop and think

- What do we mean by the 'new man', and how does this reflect his changing role within families?
- Can you think of any distinctions between 'new man', 'new lad' and 'new dad'?

Partly as a result of some increases in gender equality over the past two decades, there has been a growing interest in the nature of contemporary fatherhood (Lupton and Barclay 1997). Dermott points out:

> **Questions such as what involved fathering entails, whether the absence of fathers from families is problematic, whether breadwinning is an essential component of good fatherhood and if mothering and fathering are equal, all remain key areas of debate.**
>
> (Dermott 2008: 2)

In her book *Intimate Fatherhood*, Dermott (2008: 4) recognizes that fatherhood is a controversial political issue that is often polarized by either 'condemning fathers or claiming that they are oppressed'. Traditionally the family is perceived to be more a mother's domain, as 'a woman's place is in the home', whereas men's status was linked to the masculine role of breadwinning (Chapman 2004: 59). This partly explains why fatherhood has emerged only recently as an interesting area of sociological concern:

> **Fatherhood, then, is perceived as more marginalized, reinforcing the idea that men's identity comes largely from the public sphere of paid work . . . The major image of father in the traditional appraisal was of the aloof, distant breadwinner . . . Typically, a father was respected but feared by his children, with a relationship that was emotionally remote. His interaction with his children was characterized as restricted to a brief interaction at bedtime, typically masculine work activities in the home at the weekend, Sunday outings, and the annual summer two-week vacation.**
>
> (Hunt 2005: 77)

However, in the past couple of decades some men have become more actively involved in parenting, reflecting the emergence of the 'new man': 'the sensitive, caring male who seeks to escape the restrictive and dominating traditional masculine role' (Hunt 2005: 78). In particular, there is an interest in the extent to which fathers are involved in child care and balance their role as 'father' and 'worker'. Increased opportunities for fathers to take paternity leave from their employment reflects recent changes in attitudes towards fathering. Dermott (2008) argues that, although some fathers are spending more time with their children and making more of an effort to have an emotional connection with them, this does not necessarily lead to an increase in child-care responsibility or more equal parenting. It does appear that a new type of fatherhood is emerging as being more child-centred, resulting in more time being spent between fathers and their children, but perhaps equality of co-parenting roles and responsibilities has yet to evolve.

Politicians and the media often raise concerns over 'absent fathers'. In the UK over 25 per cent of children are growing up without a father at home (Hunt 2005: 79).

> **The 'absence' of fathers can have a number of dimensions: the physical absence of men from the households in which their children live; an emotional distance from children's lives; a relinquishment of the role of financial provider and thereby economic absence. In effect, what is usually being spoken about is the absence of fathers from the households in which children live on a permanent basis, in response to relationship breakdown. This, in turn, is viewed as impacting on the ability of men to be involved with their children in other ways. Fatherlessness, as it has been termed, has been identified as the cause of a whole range of social problems for children, from low educational achievement to childhood delinquency, gun crime to promiscuity.**
>
> (Dermott 2008: 15)

Thus, fatherhood is more likely to be fragmented as fathers may not be constantly involved in their children's lives. Furthermore, given the rise in divorce and reconstituted families, more men are becoming social fathers rather than, or as well as, biological fathers. This means that being a step-father has to be 'achieved' and earned through social practices rather than being an assumed status (Ribbens McCarthy *et al.* 2003). As Dermott (2008: 26) reminds us, 'fathers are now more likely to experience more than one family type over their lifecourse'.

Another issue to recognize is that, although comparatively rare, there is also an increase in single fathers and house-husbands who stay at home to care for the children while their female partners engage in full-time paid work. However, despite recent changes it has to be recognized that:

> **Society limits fathers by the influence of employment, care-giving arrangements, the economics of unequal salaries, infant activity, and residual social attitudes about men's roles. This may leave fathers feeling inadequate caregivers compared to mothers.**
>
> (Hunt 2005: 80)

The key point to remember is that fatherhood, like motherhood and grandparenthood, is diverse. Contemporary fathers may be more loving, involved and non-authoritarian compared with the more emotionally distant fathers of the past, but there are many different ways of 'doing' fatherhood (Dermott 2008).

Negotiating a balance between work and family life

The recent changes in family structure and increases in gender equality have led to challenges regarding the balancing of work, family life and child care. Cheal (2002) suggests that parents with children adopt a range of strategies in order to enable them to combine employment and family life, including the following:

- employment at home;
- working non-standard hours;
- altering work practices and conditions of employment;
- reducing the amount of paid employment;
- reallocation of labour within the household and between kin;
- use of commercial or state child-care services.

Women in particular may choose a type of employment that is easier to manage alongside parenting, such as part-time work. However, it is worth remembering that the part-time working model adopted by many mothers in the UK is not consistent across Europe. It is a model of working that is influenced by social policies such as the availability of affordable and decent child care as well as personal preferences. For example, Scandinavian countries have innovative child-care policies that even include cash payments for home-based care.

Cunningham *et al.* (2005) found that working mothers in the UK strived to separate home and work as a strategy that facilitated the balancing of their caring and providing roles. This enabled them to maintain their identities as both mother and worker. Nevertheless, it was also recognized that:

> **No matter how much a mother in paid work outside the home might wish to prevent work intruding on family or family on work, this will happen at some time, no matter how carefully she has tried to separate the two through careful boundary construction and maintenance. Flexibility may be necessary within each sphere . . .**
>
> (Cunningham *et al.* 2005: 32)

Case study

Working from home or living at work?

The discourse of the work–life balance focuses on the ability of adults to manage paid employment with what they consider to be a 'proper' family life. Much paid employment occurs in a separate location from that of the home, but there is an increasing recognition of the single location home/workplace and that it may be a site of deliberate choice for some workers. Seymour's (2005, 2007) work on families living in family-run hotels, pubs and boarding houses looks at an extreme case of people operating a business in the same space in which their domestic life occurs and thereby makes transparent lay assumptions about family life that are often not made explicit.

Key definitions that emerged in interviews with parents and children about a 'proper' family life were:

- time together with *all* family members, especially at mealtimes;
- undisturbed family time;
- the ability to give children attention;
- the freedom of the family home (spatial, aural, psychological);
- celebrating public holidays with only the family.

Seymour's research explores whether living in a location that combines business and home helps or hinders the achievement of the 'imagined' or ideological family life. She shows how families are able to 'do' family in the single-location home/workplace through spatial, temporal and relationship practices. The work shows the creative strategies that adults and children employ to aim for the family life they are seeking, but it also reminds us that the reality of family life (in any location) rarely matches that of the ideology.

Thus, the spheres of work and home are interrelated and one impacts upon the other (see also Chapter 12). Nowadays more people are working from home due to the availability of computer-based technologies such as email and the Internet. Furthermore, since women are engaged in paid work more than in the past, there has also been some increase in men's involvement in child care and domestic work. However, while some changes are evident, continuities in the traditional domestic division of labour continue to prevail:

> Reallocation of domestic labour within the family can be one way of ensuring that an employed mother's burden of childcare and housework is not overwhelming.
>
> In nuclear families, the possibilities for reallocation of labour are typically rather limited. Career-oriented wives must call upon their husbands to do more housework and to take equal responsibility for raising children. Many husbands have been slow to respond to their wives' demands, partly because they face career pressure of their own.
>
> (Cheal 2002: 123)

For some women, their increased participation in the labour market may mean they face a heavier burden of trying to combine their paid work with their domestic and caring work. There is evidence that men are contributing more to housework in contemporary society, but still women tend to do between one-third and one-half more domestic work than men (Chapman 2004). Negotiations around the allocation of domestic division of labour continue to cause tensions and conflict in households.

Stop and think

- Consider the levels of equality in the domestic division of labour in the household you live in or in your parents' household. Who is most likely to do the cooking, ironing and shopping? Who cleans the toilet and washes the kitchen floor?
- To what extent do gendered divisions of domestic labour persist, and how does this relate to perceptions of masculinity and femininity?

Case study

'Changing Lives and Times: Relationships and Identities through the Life Course'

'Changing Lives and Times: Relationships and Identities through the Life Course' (known as 'Timescapes' for short) is the first major qualitative longitudinal study to be funded in the UK. This research involves a consortium of five universities from across the UK and is funded for five years from February 2007 by the Economic and Social Research Council (ESRC). The Timescapes study follows people over time, investigating the ways in which their personal relationships and identities unfold over the life course. The focus is relationships with significant others: parents, grandparents, siblings, children, partners, friends and lovers. Timescapes is based on seven empirical projects that span the life course: two on young lives (siblings and friends, the changing lives of teenagers), three on mid-lives (motherhood, fatherhood and work–life balance) and two on older lives (grandparenthood and the oldest generation). The aim is to track individuals and family groups over time in order to document changes and continuities in their relationships and identities. Timecapes explores how contemporary relationships are 'worked out' in different socioeconomic, historical and cultural contexts.

One of the Timescapes projects is 'Work and Family Lives: The Changing Experiences of "Young" Families', being conducted by researchers from the University of Edinburgh and Napier University. The study focuses on the ways in which families reconcile their work and family lives over time and looks in detail at the ways that tensions between work and family are manifested in the everyday lives of parents and children. The study investigates areas that have thus far been neglected by research, such as processes of negotiation between parents and children in addressing issues raised by working parenthood, the ways in which such issues impact on everyday family practices, and the ways in

Case study *continued*

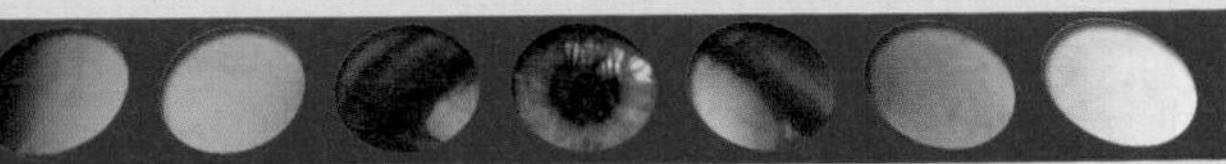

which family practices may change over time in response to changes in work and family circumstances, including those in the children's lives.

The study aims to deepen understandings of how work and family issues are constructed and 'worked out' by parents and children living under different socioeconomic and labour market conditions by following and comparing the experiences of ten low-income families and ten more affluent families. The three waves of data collection involve repeat individual interviews with parents and children (aged between 9 and 12 years) as well as 'family' group interviews. These methods are being used to explore mothers', fathers' and children's accounts of their families' everyday lives and to unpick the ways in which children describe their own lives and concerns within the temporal, spatial and financial structures of their parents' working or non-working lives.

(Source: Alice MacLean, Centre for Research on Families and Relationships (CRFR): for more information, see www.timescapes.leeds.ac.uk)

Gay and lesbian partnerships

VanEvery (1999) reminds us that, although sociologists have explored many aspects of modern nuclear families, we know comparatively little about other family structures. Recent research has begun to address this gap (e.g. O'Donnell 1999; Ribbens McCarthy *et al.* 2003; Silva and Smart 1999):

> **Sociology continues to marginalise the study of love, intimacy and care beyond the 'family', even though it has expanded the scope covered by this term to include a wider range of 'families of choice'.**
>
> (Roseneil 2005: 243)

Lesbian and gay families present a key challenge to traditional family life as they clearly depart from the norm of the heterosexual ideal (O'Donnell 1999). Furthermore, as Allan and Crow point out:

> **Indeed many gay couples, whether male or female, actively strive for relationships which are marked by *difference* from dominant heterosexual patterns.**
>
> (Allan and Crow 2001: 106)

First, lesbian and gay relationships are often constructed as 'families of choice' (Weeks *et al.* 1999), whereby a sense of belonging and long-term companionship is created. However, because such relationships are not bound by conventional understandings of marriage, they are more contingent upon continuing satisfaction, which tends to result in more reflexivity and negotiation around commitment and responsibility (Allan and Crow 2001).

Second, same-sex relationships are not constrained by the norms and assumptions associated with traditional gender roles. For example, Dunne (1999) argues that, while lesbian couples still have to negotiate their relationships in order to avoid inequalities, they can work towards a more egalitarian social world where power is not rooted in conventional roles and expectations of gender. Similarly, Weeks *et al.* (1999) discuss the ways in which same-sex relationships enable men and women to express their masculine and feminine identities in alternative ways. However, Silva and Smart (1999: 8) suggest that the distinctiveness of same-sex relationships that Weeks *et al.* and Dunne discuss may 'increasingly be shared by newly emergent patterns in heterosexual relationships where commitment may be a matter of negotiation, rather than ascription'.

One of the important points to remember is that homosexual families, like heterosexual families, are diverse. Yet most non-heterosexuals continue to experience 'some form of informal discrimination, ranging from enforced self-censorship to physical attack' (Weeks *et al.* 1999: 97). Some same-sex couples seek the same rights of social recognition as heterosexual couples (including pension rights, inheritance and civil partnership), while others fear that legal recognition may impinge on the flexible and egalitarian nature of their relationships, resulting in unnecessary power struggles (Cheal 2002). Thus, some gays and lesbians would like to be able to marry, and others prefer to retain their status of difference.

A closer look

Civil partnerships

In Britain a Civil Partnership Act was passed in 2004 to enable same-sex couples to have the legal rights equivalent to those of married couples, in relation to property, inheritance, pensions and welfare benefits. The first civil partnerships were celebrated on 22 December 2005, including that of Sir Elton John and David Furnish. According to the Office for National Statistics (2008) the total number of partnerships formed since the Act came into force in December 2005 is 26,787. Civil partnerships, like marriage, can only be dissolved through a divorce.

Figure 11.4 Civil partnership ceremony
Jim West/Alamy

Tasker and Golombok (1991) remind us that gay and lesbian parenting is no more damaging than heterosexual parenting, yet often this evidence tends to be disregarded in the legal process. As O'Donnell argues:

> **Although some changes in the legal perspective can be identified, such as an increased willingness to recognise parenting existing outside marriage, the law still tends to emphasise traditional concepts in its construction of the family and thus adopts an exclusive approach to its construction of the family, denying recognition and validity to what are perceived to be 'abnormal' forms. The emphasis placed upon marriage as the source of family status excludes homosexuals (and transsexuals) who cannot validly marry and whose relationships with each other are devalued.**
>
> (O'Donnell 1999: 94–5)

Adoption policies vary in different countries; for example, currently in the Netherlands, Sweden and the UK it is possible for same-sex couples to adopt children; while in Denmark and Germany a person may adopt the child of their same-sex partner (Almond 2006). Thus, there has been an increasing, if somewhat reluctant, recognition of homosexual relationships as an alternative family form, but public debates about non-heterosexual marriage, parenting, custody and adoption continue to be highly contested.

Sibling relationships

Most research on siblings has been conducted in psychology; there has been a paucity of sociological research on sibling relationships until recently (see Brannen *et al.* 2000; Edwards *et al.* 2005, 2006; Mauthner 2002, 2005; Punch 2005, 2008a). As Mauthner (2005: 623) notes, 'the experience of being a sister or a sibling is largely absent from social research on family life'. Sibling relations are multifaceted and diverse, entailing a 'complex interplay of co-operation and conflict' (Allan 1996: 64) and shaped by a range of factors, including gender, age, birth order, class and social context (Edwards *et al.* 2006; Mauthner 2002). Sibling interactions are often characterized by dynamic power struggles that involve a mixture of negotiation, compromise and resistance (McIntosh and Punch 2009).

> **On the one hand, since siblings share much time and space together as well as knowledge of each other, this combination means that sibship is likely to be an intimate, close relationship, forming a bond between them. On the other hand, because siblings share almost too much time together in a relatively small space and know much about each other's bad habits, the sharing of time, space and knowledge can create conflicts. Hence, sibship tends to be a dynamic relationship which can switch almost simultaneously between being a positive and negative experience.**
>
> (Punch 2008a: 342)

Psychological literature has tended to perceive siblings in relation to the roles and expectations of their birth order position. Until recently, the status hierarchy of the birth order has often been assumed to be ascribed and fixed rather than socially constructed. Edwards *et al.* (2005) emphasize the importance of social context and children's own understandings of the sibling order. Power is negotiated in interactions between siblings and is not simply the product of birth order (McIntosh and Punch 2009). Punch's research (2008b) on siblings in Scotland illustrates how birth order can, at times, be experienced as a constraint on sibling behaviour and at other times as a resource that can be utilized in a dynamic and creative manner. Thus, although birth order is important in shaping children's experiences of sibship, relative benefits have to be actively maintained, and limitations of each position in the sibling order are not passively accepted and are often contested.

Similarly, Brannen *et al.* found that children's sibling relations were shaped by the hierarchies of age and birth order, and that 'Sometimes they challenged and sometimes they invoked these social hierarchies, depending upon their position within them, and their ability to negotiate them' (Brannen *et al.* 2000: 129). Sociological research has found that children can have a clear understanding of the stereotypical expectations, roles and power hierarchy in relation to birth order, and yet they also recognize and demonstrate that in practice the roles and power of their birth order positions are not static but can be negotiated and transformed. Mauthner (2002), in her research on sistering, describes this as a *shifting positions* discourse, where role reversals take place between the 'big sister' role of carer and the 'little sister' position of being cared for. Edwards *et al.* (2005) also observed that children's birth order hierarchy could be questioned, mainly in relation to issues of care and protection, such as when a sibling was ill or being bullied, or in relation to the perceived (im)maturity of their sibling.

It is also worth bearing in mind that sometimes children accept their sibling status position and do not try to compromise or choose not to resist. Just as Finch and Mason (1993) argued that responsibilities and notions of reciprocity are worked out rather than fixed in *inter*generational family relationships, processes of negotiation within *intra*generational family relationships are also more important than normative rules. Hence, there are no set rules regarding the ways in which siblings' experiences of birth order are worked out in their everyday lives (Edwards *et al.* 2006). The characteristics of the different sibling order positions are diverse and complex: they may be enabling or constraining or both, but they are not fixed. The sibship issues described in this section apply to adults as well as children. Thus, birth order and age are flexible and dynamic hierarchies, which can be subverted, contested, resisted and negotiated in children's and adults' everyday lives.

Stop and think

- To what extent are your relationships with your partner, parents, grandparents, siblings and friends similar or different? In what ways can you compare and contrast the intimate personal relationships in your life?

Grandparenting

Given the recent changes in family patterns, the sociology of sibling relations remains an area to be explored further, as does the sociological significance of grandparenting. Ferguson (2004) illustrates that there is a diversity of grandparenting, which depends on a variety of factors, such as geographical distance, the quality of the parents' relationships with the grandparents, the age of the grandparents and grandchild and the differences between grandmothers and grandfathers. This intergenerational relationship is often linked to grandparents providing emotional, financial and instrumental support for their grandchildren. A more mutual aspect of their relationship is intergenerational learning, which means that both grandchildren and grandparents can have an educational impact on each other.

Ross *et al.* (2005) found that both grandparents and grandchildren expressed a general sense of obligation towards each other. Grandparents would sometimes act as useful mediators between the grandchildren and their parents. This grandparenting study emphasizes young people's capacity to have independent relations with their grandparents and highlights the importance derived from the perceived connectedness of the relationship. Similarly, Brannen (2003) argues that grandparents are increasingly providing child care for their grandchildren, particularly after a divorce. As people move through the life course and experience new situations, the nature of their family relationships changes and needs to be renegotiated accordingly.

Case study

Grandparents and teenage grandchildren: an examination of intergenerational relationships

This grandparenting project was conducted by researchers at the Centre for Research on Families and Relationships (CRFR). The UK study adds to our understanding of grandparent–grandchild relations by placing particular relationships in the context of family and peer relations. The main findings are as follows (Ross *et al.* 2005):

- Grandparents generally spoke positively about becoming and being a grandparent, using terms such as 'love', 'enjoyment' and 'happiness'.
- Some grandchildren saw their grandparents as fitting stereotypical images of older people, as frail or out of touch, but others said they were 'modern', describing them as 'fun', 'caring', 'active' and 'up to date'.
- Both generations described how grandparents often played a key role in listening to grandchildren.
- Many young people said they could share problems and concerns with their grandparents and referred to the way grandparents would sometimes act as go-betweens in the family, particularly when there were disagreements between themselves and their parents.
- More young people said they were closer to grandmothers than grandfathers, and especially to their maternal grandmother. The relationships were influenced by past contact and care, geographical distance, frequency of meeting, feelings of connectedness, and overlaps in interactions between family and friends.
- The dynamic nature of grandparent–grandchild relations was affected by stage of life and changing circumstances, such as death, divorce and separation within families.
- Divorce and separation affected contact with those grandparents who were related through the non-resident parent, with bonds more likely to continue if a good relationship had existed between the parent and the grandparents before the separation, if there was recognition of shared experiences, and if it was believed that continued contact was important.
- Some grandchildren suggested that close involvement with grandparents affected their views of older people in general, usually in a positive way.
- A few grandparents reported that they had more responsibilities for care of their grandchildren than they desired.

A closer look

Brannen (2003) suggests that in the UK our families are now best described as narrow 'bean-poles' rather than as having larger family 'trees'. The 'bean-pole family' (Figure 11.5) consists of an extended family of different generations but is 'leaner' due to the reduced numbers of siblings per family compared with the 'broader' family trees of the past, which included greater numbers of aunts and uncles. This is partly because people are living longer as a result of improvements in health and medicine (see Chapter 7), and partly because couples are having fewer children. Families with three or four generations are now relatively common.

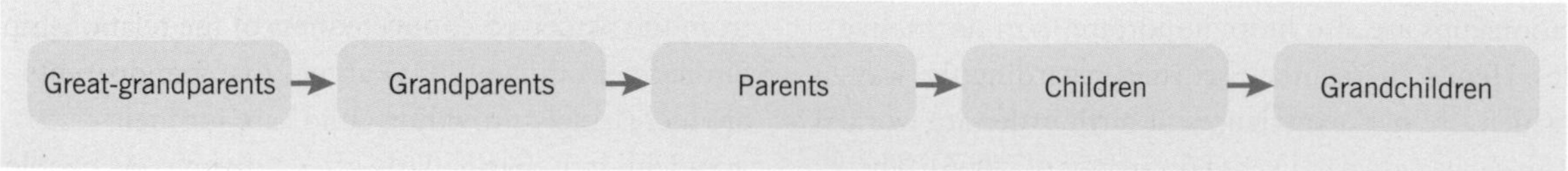

Great-grandparents → Grandparents → Parents → Children → Grandchildren

Figure 11.5 The 'bean-pole family'

Families and social problems

In Western society we tend to assume that the family is a good thing. It can be difficult for us to question the family when we take for granted that it is a positive aspect of our lives:

> **Typically, family life is thought to be warm, intimate, stress reducing, and the place that people flee to for safety. Our desire to idealize family life is partly responsible for a tendency either not to see family and intimate violence or to condone it as being a necessary and important part of raising children, relating to spouses, and conducting other family transactions.**
>
> (Gelles 1997: 1)

Partly this is linked to a reluctance to accept that the family can be simultaneously a site of violence and of love, and partly there is a notion that we should not intervene in the private world of the family. The discourse of family privacy can lead to family problems being perceived as personal troubles for individuals to sort out rather than as public issues that the state should address (see Wright Mills 1970).

Since the 1990s we have often been considered to be in a time of family crisis, which politicians and the media have referred to as the 'breakdown of the family'. The family becomes a social problem when it presents a threat to the dominant values and interests of society. Certain types of family can be used as scapegoats for this decline of the family, and they become labelled as 'problem' families or 'dysfunctional' families, threatening the values and morality of society. It has been argued that the decline of the traditional family led to the creation of an underclass dependent on state welfare. This in turn resulted in social ills such as youth crime, homelessness and teenage pregnancy. Right-wing

Case study

Why are poor families more likely to be labelled as 'problem' families?

Single parenthood

- The middle-class single mother: personal trouble.
- The working-class single mother: public issue.

Some family problems are constructed only as a problem for certain sectors of the population and not for others. As we have seen, the traditional two-parent family has been considered as most compatible with capitalist society as one parent (usually the father) undertakes paid work while the other parent (usually the mother) cares for the family. The decline of this traditional family is thus seen as a threat to the success of the objectives of the capitalist market. The one-parent family is less likely to contribute to the goals of the market economy and more likely to have to rely on state intervention and welfare benefits. This can lead to social and political reluctance to accept some family types. However, it is interesting to see why single parenthood becomes a social problem when it involves the working classes but not when it happens in middle-class families. It is useful to use Wright Mills' (1970) distinction of personal troubles and public issues to explore this:

- If the single mother has the social and economic resources to continue caring for her child without state intervention, then it is not considered to be a social problem. For example, if she has a good enough job to pay for private child care or receives sufficient maintenance from her ex-partner to cover child care or to enable her not to have to work herself, then she is perceived to be solving her individual problem herself. Hence, the middle-class woman as a single mother is a personal trouble, as it is an individual problem that she addresses.
- If the single mother lacks economic resources and cannot afford child care, then she may become reliant on state benefits. She is seen as part of the social problem of lone parents. The working-class woman as a single mother is a public issue as her individual problem becomes a social problem that society has to deal with because the state has to intervene and provide a collective solution, in terms of welfare benefits.

Therefore, single parenthood in itself is not problematic. It is perceived as a threat to society only when the lone parent is unable to perform traditional family functions self-sufficiently and has to rely on state intervention.

politicians have claimed that children who were brought up by single mothers with no fathers were more likely to engage in antisocial and criminal behaviour as they needed to be socialized and disciplined by their fathers. Mothers were also blamed for being out at work instead of caring for their children.

The state thus constructed the idea of the 'normal' versus the 'abnormal' family, or the functional family versus the dysfunctional family. The idealization of the conventional family led to understanding any negative experiences within families as individual problems, rather than seeing them as resulting from the ways in which the family is constructed as a social institution based on unequal power relations. If the family was seen as a problematic institution, then difficult or negative occurrences would become public issues rather than personal troubles (Wright Mills 1970). However, the state has an interest in trying to define problems as individual ones rather than as social problems so that it can blame individual families rather than the structures of society. For example, the ordinary and routine incidence of adult (usually male) power and violence within the family is perceived as deviant behaviour carried out by pathological individuals rather than as a consequence of the normalization of unequal power relations in the family.

Family ideology presents us with one ideal type of family form: the heterosexual couple who are married with two children. This ideology of the nuclear traditional family fails to recognize that most people nowadays do not choose, or are not able, to live their lives according to this ideal family type. It also serves to legitimize male dominance in the private sphere and neglects to recognize the existence of structural inequalities. Hence, the idealization of the traditional family disguises the reality of adult power, especially adult male power, in all families.

When considering social problems in the family, there are two types of inequality to bear in mind: inequality between families (the opportunities and constraints available to working-class versus middle- or upper-class families) and inequality within families (adult power over children, and male adult power over women and children). Family problems such as domestic violence, youth homelessness and child abuse are frequently constructed as being problems of working-class families, but this is not necessarily the case. Poverty may be part of the underlying causes of such problems, but it is important to remember that these problems do not occur only in poor families. What often happens is that these problems can be more visible in working-class families, as such families may have to rely on state funds for help with child care or youth therapy. In contrast, when the same problems occur in richer families, the families are more likely to be able to hide the problems by paying privately for services such as nannies or attending private family counsellors rather than needing the state to intervene. Thus, social problems become less visible in wealthier families. We need to be wary about unproblematically linking family problems to being problems of working-class families without recognizing the political, social and structural causes of such problems. Individuals in poor families can be labelled as being deviants where their problem conveniently becomes defined as an

A closer look

Social problems in the family occur across all classes

In 1997 the British home secretary, Jack Straw, took his 15-year-old son, William, to the local police station to give a statement about allegations that William supplied cannabis to an undercover newspaper reporter. Mr Straw's son was cautioned, but it was a bit ironic given that, as home secretary, Mr Straw was responsible for the nation's law and order.

In July 2000, prime minister Tony Blair's 16-year-old son Euan was arrested for being drunk and incapable. The teenager, who was celebrating the end of his GCSE exams, was found by police officers in Leicester Square, London. In a speech shortly afterwards, Tony Blair said: 'Being a prime minister can be a tough job. Being a parent is probably tougher, and sometimes you don't always succeed. But the family to me is more important than anything else.'

individual rather than a social problem that requires a political and social solution. Thus, they become individual scapegoats for social problems that need a collective response.

Stop and think

- What things might you do in the privacy of your own home that you would not consider doing in the public sphere? Why might this be the case, and what are the boundaries between public and private behaviour?

Family violence

Despite continued assumptions that families are a good thing, it is interesting to note that, statistically speaking, the family can be a dangerous place to be. For example, according to Home Office (1992) statistics, in England and Wales, each year 45 per cent of female homicide victims are killed by their present or former male partners. This equates to an average of two women per week who are killed by their partners/ex-partners. More than one child a fortnight is killed by their parents; babies are most at risk: 'Every ten days in England and Wales one child is killed at the hands of their parent' (Coleman *et al.* 2007). In just over half (52%) of all the cases of children killed by another person, the parent is the principal suspect. These figures contrast with the very small numbers of children at risk from 'stranger danger'. For example, according to the the Bureau of Justice Statistics (BJS 2007), in the USA, of all children under five murdered between 1976 and 2005:

- 31 per cent were killed by their father;
- 29 per cent were killed by their mother;
- 23 per cent were killed by a male acquaintance;
- 7 per cent were killed by another relative;
- 3 per cent were killed by a stranger.

There are several reasons why families can become sites of violence. First, family members spend large amounts of time together, and so the emergence of conflicting interests is almost inevitable at times. This is especially the case where limited resources have to be shared by all the family. For example, having only one television in the household may lead to arguments and tensions over which programme is to be watched. Stress, especially if arising from poverty, impacts upon the ways in which family members relate to each other. For example, if one family member is stressed due to being unemployed, then this is likely to have a negative effect on others in the family.

Furthermore, family members have ascribed hierarchical roles based on age and sex, which reflect an unequal structure of power, as the adult male tends to hold most power. Families tend to be created through involuntary membership as we cannot choose which family we are born into. Perhaps one of the key reasons why violence may take place within the family is because of privacy. The family is a private institution, which is protected from the gaze of wider society. People can behave differently in the privacy of their home, behind closed doors, compared with how they act in the public sphere, and this can be the same with violence.

A man who hits his wife might never dream of hitting anyone else, but in the privacy of his own home he might break the rules of wider society. Similarly, a parent may consider it to be acceptable to smack their own child, but if someone else, such as a teacher, smacked their child they might object strongly.

However, there can be a fine line between appropriate discipline and unacceptable physical punishment.

For these reasons, personal violence in intimate relationships is tolerated more than violence outside the home. This does not mean that violence is appropriate but that it can be more likely to happen in the private domestic sphere than in the public domain.

As we saw earlier, feminists have largely been responsible for raising public awareness of the potential for women's and children's oppression in the family.

> **The policy of promoting the nuclear family as the source of social justice and social cohesion is flawed. It fails to recognise that this kind of family is in fact a site of disadvantage, subordination and oppression for its members, particularly women.**
>
> (Bilton *et al.* 2002: 245)

In the 1970s and 1980s, feminists exposed the possibilities for conflict, violence and inequality in the family, thereby challenging the myth of family ideology and the notion of the 'family as a safe haven'. They argued that the existence of unequal power structures within the family could lead to male physical and sexual violence against women and children (Fiorenza and Copeland 1994). For feminists, the legitimization of male dominance in the private sphere can result in the normalization of violence within the home. They argue strongly that issues such as domestic violence and child abuse are thus social problems that reflect structural inequalities of power within the family. However, as we shall see in the following sections, others argue that these are individual problems occurring only in certain pathological or 'dysfunctional' families (Jamrozik and Nocella 1998). This debate of the extent to which family problems are personal troubles or public issues is key to understanding the different ways in which domestic violence and child abuse have been explained.

Domestic violence

Domestic violence has emerged only relatively recently as a social problem. Before the 1970s, it had been seen as a private individual family problem, something that occurred behind closed doors. Okun (1986) suggests that a husband having the right to physically punish his wife dates back to Roman times, when a man could legally beat his wife with a rod, as long as the rod was no thicker than his thumb. This was known as the 'rule of thumb' of English common law. A husband's domination over his wife was also supported by the Church, as this quotation by a friar in the fifteenth century illustrates:

> **When you see your wife commit an offence, don't rush at her with insults and violent blows . . . Scold her sharply, bully and terrify her. And if this still doesn't work . . . take up a stick and beat her soundly, for it is better to punish the body and correct the soul . . . Readily beat her, not in rage but out of charity . . . for [her] soul, so that the beating will redound to your merit and her good.**
>
> (Friar Cherubino of Siena, cited in Okun 1986: 3)

Intervening in the private domain of the home has traditionally been seen as a controversial issue, as what went on behind the closed doors of the family was perceived to be nobody else's business.

There have been several different ways of defining family violence, resulting in the use of a variety of terms, such as 'wife battery', 'woman abuse', 'wife assault' and 'violence against women'. Recently, the more gender-neutral terms 'domestic violence' and 'intimate partner violence' have been used, recognizing that men can also be battered. Such terms can refer to different types of abuse, including physical, sexual and emotional abuse. Nevertheless, Dobash and Dobash (1992) argue that violence between adults in the home is systematically and disproportionately directed at women and that such violence is the extension of a husband's control over his wife:

Figure 11.6 Domestic violence

> **Within the family the use of physical force and violence has traditionally been a prerogative of men who were given the rights and responsibilities over all members of households, including women, children.**
>
> (Dobash and Dobash 1992: 267)

Thus, this control is historically and socially constructed. In other words, violence against women in the home can be explained by looking at the history of the family and the status of women in society. Therefore, although battered husbands also exist, 'wife beating' is comparatively more common.

Given that studies may use different definitions to describe different types of domestic violence, it can be problematic to compare research and estimate the extent of family violence. It is also difficult to measure something that is frequently underreported. Methodological difficulties, such as accessing victims and sampling techniques, mean that statistics on the incidence and prevalence of domestic violence may be unreliable and vary considerably. For example, much initial research was carried out by interviewing samples of women at shelters for battered wives. This tended to lead to a focus on the more severe cases of women who had left their homes, but little was known about those who did not come forward and identify themselves as abused. Estimates have varied from figures of about 5 per cent of female partners to claims that family violence was an epidemic and perhaps nearly 50 per cent of all female partners were abused. A Home Office (2008) report indicated that findings from the British Crime Survey reveal that 28 per cent of women and 18 per cent of men aged between 16 and 59 years report that they have been victims of domestic abuse at some point in their lives. The purpose of trying to estimate the incidence of abuse is to maintain public interest in the problem so that something can be done about it. However, ultimately there is such a wide range of estimates that policymakers tend to feel that the real magnitude of family violence remains unknown.

In the past, cases of domestic violence (referred to as 'domestics') were not always taken seriously by the police, who tended to consider wife-battering as a private family matter rather than a criminal offence (Foreman and Dallos 1993). Police rarely arrested batterers, and the court system rarely convicted them. There was even a certain amount of victim-blaming, whereby the victims of domestic violence were perceived as weak individuals who allowed the abuse to take place or it was assumed that they provoked or even perhaps deserved the violence (Gelles 1997).

Thus, there was a traditional denial of the problem until the 1970s, when the feminist movement played a key role in defining the issue of domestic violence as a social problem that required a collective solution. Feminists perceived domestic violence as being based on the unequal power relationships between men and women in society, as reflected in family structures (Fiorenza and Copeland 1994). Their initial response was to provide immediate help and shelter for battered women by providing refuges as a place of safety (Dobash and Dobash 1992); the first refuge was founded in 1972 in Chiswick in the UK. The broader aim was to raise public awareness of male violence in the family, which gradually began to filter through to policies of intervention and popular consciousness (Foreman and Dallos 1993).

In contrast, the government has preferred to define the problem of domestic violence as a psychological rather than as a sociological problem, using causal models to explain it as being as a result of individual character disorders rather than having structural causes (Jamrozik and Nocella 1998). The state has defined domestic violence as a problem caused by pathological individuals, often as a result of drug or alcohol misuse. Thus, the state's response has been to provide much larger 'service' centres run by a range of different professionals, which also offer services for batterers, such as drug and alcohol treatment and psychiatric counselling. Their aim is to work towards family reunification and they have tended to individualize the problem.

As we can see, the way in which a particular group defines a problem, and the particular explanation they give for it, affects the kind of action they propose as a solution. Refuge shelters began with a commitment to radical social change but became transformed into professional services dealing with individual problems, which led to a redefining of the image of domestic violence. Thus, using the terminology of Wright Mills (1970), we could say that, before the 1970s, domestic violence had always been considered a private trouble; subsequently, the women's movement identified it as a social problem and for just over a decade it was a public issue. However, once the state became more involved, it was redefined as a personal trouble in order to avoid the creation of a large-scale moral panic about the potential for male violence in a male-dominated society.

In the decade following the emergence of wife battery as a social problem, there was a large increase in the number of shelters for victims and a rise in public funds spent on the issue. Eventually, there were some legal changes and an increase in police cooperation, which has resulted in more protection for victims and the recognition of domestic violence as a crime. Rape in marriage became classified as a crime in Britain in 1991. However:

> **There is little real commitment to relieving some of the stresses, financial, occupational, and/or housing, that families experience and which can contribute to violence. Likewise, encouragement and opportunities for women to escape from violent relationships are lacking. Instead, most women are still likely to feel the situation would have to be very dire before they would choose to escape.**
>
> (Foreman and Dallos 1993: 34)

Consequently, on the one hand, the feminist movement was successful: public awareness was raised and action was taken. On the other hand, it was only a partial victory because their initial aims of addressing the issue of male domination in society became lost as the state reinterpreted the problem as an individual, pathological one rather than as a structural, societal one (Jamrozik and Nocella 1998).

Child abuse

Society's views of what is considered to be child abuse change over time, according to shifting definitions of the value of children and the changing social response to perceptions of appropriate parental behaviour. For example, there has been much debate about the legality of smacking. Currently, there is not an outright ban on smacking in Britain: mild smacking is permitted if it is 'reasonable chastisement', provided it does not cause harm such as bruising, scratches or reddening of the skin. Meanwhile, children's organizations concerned with children's rights, such as the National Society for the Prevention of Cruelty to Children (NSPCC) and Save the Children, continue to campaign for a complete ban on all forms of physical punishment against children.

Notions of what constitutes child abuse change not only over time but also over place. What one culture regards as appropriate may be unacceptable in another culture. For example, smacking has been totally banned in Norway, Austria, Denmark, Finland, Latvia, Sweden, Croatia and Cyprus. If a parent were to smack a child for any reason in one of these countries, it would be considered a form of child abuse. Therefore, we can say that child abuse is socially constructed, because the way we understand it changes over history and in different cultures. Abusing parents are ever present, but what changes are the definitions of cruelty and abuse and the public interest in the problem, rather than the abuse itself.

It is likely that child abuse has always existed, but it was not publicly discussed until the end of the nineteenth century. Before the 1870s, child-rearing decisions were considered the prerogative of parents. In order to bring a problem to light, a group in society needs to define it and take action. In relation to child abuse, that group was the NSPCC, which was formed in 1884. The NSPCC raised public awareness about the issue of cruelty to children, leading to increased state intervention based on the notion of rescue: saving children from damaging environments or cruelty by placing them into institutional care.

Public interest diminished in child abuse as a social problem from the early 1900s until the 1960s. The silence of this 60-year period is hard to explain: child cruelty was known to exist and did not suddenly cease, but there was little public awareness about it. Public and professional anxiety about child abuse then re-emerged in the 1960s, when Dr Henry Kempe wrote an article called 'The battered-child syndrome', published in the *Journal of the American Medical Association* in 1962. Stories in popular magazines also emerged, and child abuse began to be seen as an urgent problem. Until then, professionals had been cautious in recognizing that some parents violently assaulted their children, mainly because their behaviour departed so radically from the ideal.

Dr Kempe and his paediatrician colleagues offered a medicalized account of the 'battered child' and were the first group since the end of the nineteenth century to highlight the issue of child abuse. The term 'child abuse' has been used since the 1970s because it broadens the scope of what is included as abuse. Rather than referring only to physical abuse, the term 'child abuse' also includes physical neglect, sexual abuse and emotional abuse. However, this also means that it is a vague and ambiguous category, and it may be unclear as to what constitutes abuse.

It is difficult to estimate the number of child-abuse cases because, as well as depending on the definition used, it also depends on how the information is obtained (Saraga 1993). How do we count something that is often not reported? Difficulties with definitions

A closer look

Rediscovery of child abuse since the 1960s

- *1960s* – The battered baby syndrome
- *1970s* – Child abuse
- *1980s* – Child sexual abuse
- *1990s* – Paedophilia
- *2000s* – Paedophiles, child abuse and the Internet

Case study

Victoria Climbié and the creation of a moral panic

In 2000, the case of Victoria Climbié became a major media issue, and a public inquiry was set up. Victoria was born near Abidjan in Ivory Coast on 2 November 1991. She was the fifth of seven children. In October 1998 Kouao, her great-aunt, came to Abidjan and offered to take Victoria to live with her in France, where she promised to provide her with an education. Victoria's parents agreed and Victoria lived with Kouao in France until 24 April 1999, when the two of them travelled to England. Victoria travelled on Kouao's French passport, named as her daughter. On their second day in the UK, Kouao and Victoria visited the homeless persons' unit in the London borough of Ealing. In the months that followed, Victoria was known to no fewer than four social services departments, three housing departments and two specialist child protection teams of the Metropolitan Police. Furthermore, she was admitted to two different hospitals because of concerns that she was being deliberately harmed and was referred to a specialist children and families centre managed by the NSPCC, all between 26 April 1999 and her death in England on 25 February 2000. According to the inquiry, 'What transpired during this period can only be described as a catalogue of administrative, managerial and professional failure by the services charged with her safety.'

It emerged that Victoria had spent the cold winter months bound hand and foot, in an unheated bathroom, lying in a cold bath in a plastic rubbish bag. At the time of her last admission to hospital, her body temperature was so low that it did not register on a standard thermometer and her legs could not be straightened. Eight-year-old Victoria had 128 injuries on her body through being beaten and burned with cigarettes. She died suffering from hypothermia and malnutrition. The reaction to the case and the events that followed signified a dramatic event that took on the proportions of a moral panic. In Stanley Cohen's book *Folk Devils and Moral Panics* (2002), he outlines four key stages in the development of a moral panic, which can be related to the events surrounding the death of Victoria Climbié (Table 11.6).

Table 11.6

Stage of moral panic	Characteristics	Case of Victoria Climbié
1. Warning	Difference noted and apprehensions present	Fear of paedophilia enhanced public awareness of the social problem of child abuse
2. Impact	Media coverage of a particular event; 'folk devils' are often identified and demonized by the media	Victoria Climbié's death on 25 February 2000 and subsequent media coverage and public outrage; the 'folk devils' were her abusing guardians and the welfare professionals, as their incompetence was said to have 'allowed' it to happen
3. Inventory	Experts' commentary	Medics, academics and politicians all gave their views on the issue; child abuse was linked to wider concerns of society, such as criminality, drugs and other social anxieties that pointed to the erosion of family values; a public inquiry into Victoria Climbié's death was published in January 2003, and this was crucial in re-establishing the issue of child abuse as a major social problem
4. Reaction	Solutions (laws/policy changes)	Marie Therese Kouao and her boyfriend Carl Manning were sentenced to life imprisonment for Victoria's murder; two social workers were sacked for gross misconduct; child abuse became a political issue in need of a collective solution; the public inquiry into Victoria Climbié's death introduced fundamental changes in policy and practice; a ministerial children and families board was established in the British government; area child protection committees were replaced by a new national agency for children and families, with powers to ensure that all of the key services carry out their duties in an efficient, effective and accountable way

For more information see www.victoria-climbie-inquiry.org.uk

and measurement have led to a wide range of estimates of the size of the problem (see Gelles 1997). Comparing different research is also problematic because some studies count the number of deaths from abuse, others the number of physical injuries and others the number of reports of sexual abuse.

Like domestic violence, there are alternative accounts of child abuse, and different explanations lead to different suggestions of ways to solve it. One of the key issues is the extent to which the actions of the perpetrator are seen as deliberate. In other words, are the perpetrators individually responsible for their actions, or are the social structures of society to blame in any way? Different theories have been put forward to explain child abuse, and they fall mainly into three categories: medical, psychological and sociological. The medical explanation emerged in the 1960s by paediatricians who defined the battered baby syndrome (Parton 1985) and related it to the individual illness of the perpetrator. With this medical view, the problem was seen to be behavioural and the explanation was thought to be found in the personality and family background of the abuser. The paediatricians emphasized the individuality of the perpetrator, the 'diseased' person who could perhaps be cured by therapy (Saraga 1993). This disease model suited the paediatricians because they could offer a solution based on treatment and there would be a crucial role for doctors. Hence, there was a certain amount of professional self-interest in defining the problem in this way (Parton 1985).

Psychologists also put forward an individualized explanation, but their views were linked to the intergenerational transmission of violence, often known as 'the cycle of violence' (Gelles 1997). This is when it is thought that people who are victims of child abuse are disproportionately more likely to become abusing parents themselves. In contrast, sociologists would say that these are inadequate explanations of child abuse. Sociologists would argue that child abuse is a social and political issue rather than one of individual or family pathology. For example, the social structural model suggests that physical child abuse is linked to stress caused by poverty and material deprivation (Corby 2000). This is not to say that poverty directly causes abuse, and we need to recognize that abuse also occurs in affluent families. However, as Saraga (1993) argues, people who live in poverty are more likely to experience economic and social stress, which may lead to parents taking out their frustrations on their children.

Another sociological view is the social cultural perspective, which emphasises the importance of unequal power relationships, highlighting the generally low and oppressed status of children in society. Children are subordinated and there is a routine use of power by adults over children. Children are relatively powerless and can be considered as the 'property' of parents (Saraga 1993). As a result, violence against children can become normalized and accepted in society: 'violence is a socially sanctioned general form of maintaining order and . . . is approved of as a form of child control' (Corby 2000: 147). Thus, some commentators suggest that the protection and reinforcement of family values is problematic in that it reinforces the very institution that is the source of conflict. A potential solution would be to address the power structures of society and take seriously the issue of children's rights, such as by banning all physical punishment of children, including the use of smacking. This perspective suggests that a broad change is needed in the way we treat and control children in society (Corby 2000).

As we have seen, there are a range of possible interpretations for explaining child abuse, and we need to bear in mind that there are most likely diverse causes that are to blame. While certain factors, such as the inequalities of social structure, are important, they do not provide adequate explanations on their own, as not all powerful adults abuse less powerful children. Thus, rather than focus on single-factor explanations, it is necessary to consider a combination of factors because problems such as child abuse and adult domestic violence are complex issues.

The interesting point to note is that, if problems such as child abuse and domestic violence are individualized, then the abuser is blamed, rather than 'normal' attitudes in society towards women and children being blamed. Individual responses to social problems lead to the maintenance of existing power relations. Furthermore, it is worth remembering that problems are more likely to be seen as individual when the group with the problem is more powerless and less able to contest the definition of their problem (Jamrozik and Nocella 1998). In contrast, if a problem is acknowledged as a public issue, then a collective response is required to address the power inequalities that may underlie the abuse. However, the extent to which a problem may be seen as individual or collective will vary not only across time and place but also according to who is defining or interpreting it.

Summary

- Families and households are diverse. The ways we understand the terms 'family', 'marriage', 'motherhood', 'fatherhood' and 'childhood' vary over time and space.
- There are both changes and continuities in relation to family patterns throughout the world. Over the past three decades in Britain, there have been many changes in family structure, with increases in divorce, cohabitation, single-person households and reconstituted families, while both birth and marriage rates have declined.
- Despite some weakening of bonds, personal intimate relationships, such as with parents, siblings and grandparents, continue to be an important source of support, care and identity. Some aspects of motherhood and fatherhood may be changing, but parenting is still crucial for nurturing children, whether that be in single-parent households, post-divorce parenting or gay and lesbian partnerships.
- Understanding the family as a social problem involves a consideration of the extent to which problems such as domestic violence and child abuse are interpreted as private troubles or public issues.

Links

The section on feminist approaches is related to issues discussed in Chapter 5 (pp. 222–226).

The section on balancing work and family life can be related to issues raised in Chapter 12 (p. 507).

The sections on child-headed households and siblings are relevant to the childhood section of Chapter 7 (pp. 313–321).

The section on child abuse can be related to the discussion of childhood and children's rights in Chapter 7 (pp. 313–316).

Further reading

Allan, G. and Crow, G. (2001) *Families, Households and Society*, Basingstoke: Palgrave.
Written in a very accessible style, this book explores key changes in relation to family living, including leaving home, demographic changes, cohabitation and marriage, lone-parent families and divorce, step-families and households in later life.

Cheal, D. (2002) *Sociology of Family Life*, Basingstoke: Palgrave.
An extremely clear and well-written text that brings to life key issues in the sociological study of family life, drawing on a range of cross-cultural examples.

Jagger, G. and Wright, C. (eds) (1999) *Changing Family Values*, London: Routledge.
Based on feminist perspectives, this book examines contemporary issues in relation to family values, including single mothers, masculinities, same-sex families and implications for social policy.

Layard, R. and Dunn, J. (2009) *A Good Childhood: Searching for Values in a Competitive Age*, London: Penguin.
This book is based on a report commissioned by The Children's Society as the UK's first independent national inquiry into childhood. Its aims were to renew society's understanding of modern childhood by discussing the problems children face such as the pressures to drink or the stress of exams. The book explores whether life really is more difficult for children than it was, and if so why. See also The Children's Society webpage: http://www.childrenssociety.org.uk/default.asp.

McKie, L. and Cunningham-Burley, S. (eds) (2005) *Families in Society: Boundaries and Relationships*, Bristol: Policy Press.
This edited collection considers families as relationship processes and has useful chapters on work–life balance, children in families, family violence, intimacy, solo living and homosexual relationships.

Scott, J., Treas, J. and Richards, M. (eds) (2007) *The Blackwell Companion to the Sociology of Families*, Malden, MA: Blackwell.
This book covers a wide range of topics relating to the sociology of families and provides many European and North American examples. It discusses multicultural families, social inequality, parenting practices, gay and lesbian families, children's work and immigrant families.

Williams, F. (2004) *Rethinking Families*, London: Calouste Gulbenkian Foundation.
Changes in family patterns and structures are highlighted in this book. It discusses how people deal with these recent changes and considers the implications for social policy. It illustrates the connections, commitments and care responsibilities that families continue to manage.

Websites

www.crfr.ac.uk

Centre for Research on Families and Relationships
This research centre has a main office at the University of Edinburgh, with partners at Glasgow Caledonian University and the universities of Aberdeen, Glasgow and Stirling. The website provides many online reports and briefings of recent research projects.

www.socialsciences.manchester.ac.uk/morgancentre

Morgan Centre for the Study of Relationships and Personal Life
This website has information on the centre's research activities and key findings relating to a wide range of projects based at the University of Manchester.

www.lsbu.ac.uk/families/index.shtml

Families and Social Capital ESRC Research Group, South Bank University
This research group has a wide range of online publications relating to the dynamics of family change.

www.sps.cam.ac.uk/cfr

Centre for Family Research, University of Cambridge
This research centre conducts a variety of research on parenting, children and family relationships, including a focus on non-traditional families such as lesbian-mother families, solo-mother families and families created by assisted reproduction.

www.familyandparenting.org

Family and Parenting Institute
The Family and Parenting Institute carries out research that aims to influence policymakers and improve the services that families use.

www.dcfs.gov.uk/childrenandfamilies

Department for Education and Skills
This government website offers information on a range of family issues, including child protection, family policy and teenage pregnancy.

www.statistics.gov.uk

National Statistics
This website is an invaluable resource of a range of statistics indicating the changing nature of different family structures.

Activities

Activity 1

Read the following quotations from Scottish children about their sibling relationships. Consider the quotations in relation to your own experiences of growing up within your family:

> **Because they think that our mum and dad are the boss and because they're adults, they should be in charge. But when my mum goes in the garden and my dad's at work, I've got to be in charge because I'm normally told to be but they don't like listening to me. So when I tell them to get out of the bath or something, they don't do it, they only do it when an adult says so.**
>
> (Helen, 10, oldest sibling)

> **I behave much better with my mum and dad . . . Like I just behave much better, like I just sit down with my mum and dad, whereas with Richard and Ian**

they just come up and annoy me. Richard comes up and annoys me and then I go and annoy Ian, and then we all start in a fight.
(Angus, 13, middle sibling)

Ashley thinks it's bad being the oldest because you get all the responsibility. Beatrice thinks it's bad to be the bottom because you're the ones who gets bullied but being in the middle I reckon's the worst because you're getting annoyed by your little sister and bullied by your big brother so you're getting both annoyed and bullied at the same time. And if both are in the same room Beatrice is fussing about can she play with something and Ashley's sometimes bullying me. And Ashley I reckon thinks it's good to be the oldest because he always pretends to be a grown up like telling me off as though he thinks he's a grown up. And Beatrice thinks it's good to be the little one because she gets good excuses for everything, she always gets let off.
(Barry, 9, middle sibling)

Sometimes it's annoying 'cos like things I didn't get to do until I was say 11, they get to do when they were younger. I sometimes find that really annoying. And you can start saying 'well I didn't get to do that when I was their age' and they'll [parents] say 'well you're not him are you?' And I find that so annoying.
(Samuel, 16, oldest sibling)

Well, you get to like stand up for them and that and that's OK, you get to help them with things and that's good and they look up to you a lot so you've got to do the right thing with them. 'Cos if you do the wrong thing they'll like copy, especially Alison, she's younger.
(Lisa, 16, oldest sibling)

I think it's quite hard for James, I feel quite sorry for him because he's the oldest one and he's like always the one responsible for us. And like he most of the time gets into trouble . . . he's always the one that gets blamed for it when we get hurt, he's always responsible for it.
(Becky, 8, middle sibling)

Although sometimes people think being the youngest is easiest I find it quite hard because everybody's older . . . The good thing is that their friends might look out for me and make sure that I might not be getting bullied.
(Mandy, 11, youngest sibling)

Questions

1. What different aspects of intragenerational relationships can you see within the above quotations? For example, to what extent are the siblings' comments related to issues of conflict, rivalry or support? What other issues emerge from the quotations in relation to children's roles, responsibilities and status within the family?

2. Recent sociological research on sibling relationships shows that birth order is socially constructed rather than ascribed and fixed:

> . . . birth order and age can be experienced at times as a constraint on sibling behaviour and at other times as a resource that can be utilised in a dynamic and creative manner. Thus, although birth order is important in shaping children's experiences of sibship, relative benefits have to be actively maintained and limitations of each position in the sibling order are not passively accepted and are often contested . . . birth order and age are not fixed hierarchies but can be subverted, contested, resisted and negotiated through children's everyday experiences of family life.
> (Punch 2008b: 30)

Consider the above extract in relation to your own experiences of being an older, middle or younger sibling. To what extent are the advantages and disadvantages of your birth order position negotiated in your interactions with your siblings? If you are an only child, what do you perceive to be the benefits and limitations of not having any siblings?

Activity 2

Read the three extracts below and consider them in relation to your own past and current relationships:

> Love is a mortgage loan drawn on an uncertain, and inscrutable, future . . . the temptation to fall in love is great and overwhelming, but so also is the attraction of escape. And the enticement to seek a rose without thorns is never far away and always difficult to resist.
> (Bauman 2003: 8–9)

> The meaning of love, of togetherness, is always at risk, another proof of its secular nature. One main threat in this system lies in who decides whether

> togetherness should continue, and if so in what form. The lovers have two levers to two trap-doors: the end can come very suddenly, on the decision of the other, and there is no appeal. The criteria are ultimately subjective feelings, and how each perceives the relationship in terms of his/her dreams (or competing offers which are waiting in the wings).
>
> (Beck and Beck-Gernsheim 1995: 193)

> A pure relationship . . . refers to a situation where a social relation is entered into for its own sake, for what can be derived by each person from a sustained association with another; and which is continued only in so far as it is thought by both parties to deliver enough satisfactions for each individual to stay within it. Love used to be tied to sexuality, for most of the sexually 'normal' population, through marriage; but now the two are connected more and more via the pure relationship.
>
> (Giddens 1992a: 58)

Questions

1. Do you agree that contemporary intimate relationships are fragile, impermanent and easy to dissolve? Consider the reasons for your decision.
2. Is marriage a thing of the past, or does it still have validity in contemporary society?

Chapter 12

Work

Ian McIntosh

People who speak grandiosely of the 'meaning of work' should spend a year or two in a factory. (Fraser 1968: 12)

Key issues

- ➤ What are the difficulties involved in defining 'work'?
- ➤ How has wage labour changed with the development of capitalist societies?
- ➤ Why have certain areas of employment expanded and others declined?
- ➤ What impact have these changes had on the structure of the labour market and on the role of trade unions?
- ➤ What effects has unemployment had on different groups in society?
- ➤ To what extent has capitalism become a global phenomenon?

Introduction

'So, what is it that you *do*?' This is a familiar question that you will no doubt have been asked on many occasions. Although it is a question that seems obvious and commonplace, it is worth some reflection as it makes huge assumptions about the way we live, our place in the world and the knowledge we have of that world. The answer to this question, as we all instantly recognize, is to do with work. Work is, of course, a cornerstone of our individual and collective identities, crucial to how we see ourselves. The work we do can define in large part who we are, and changes to the form and type of work we do can thus have powerful implications for our sense of identity (Strangleman and Warren, 2008). But what kind of work? Housework? The work we carry out as part of our hobbies or leisure activities? The work of caring for relatives or children? No, generally not. Almost always we tell people about our paid employment, the work for which we receive a regular income; people without such work might reply that they are currently without work or that they are 'not doing anything at the moment'.

Paid employment is, of course, by no means all that we do, and people who are unemployed do not suddenly cease to exist – even if they may feel, and get treated, as though they do. Delineating the boundary between work and non-work is an extremely difficult thing to do. Imagine you come across someone sawing a piece of wood. They could be doing this as part of a hobby or doing it for a friend for a 'payment' of some kind. Perhaps the person involved is a joiner or maybe they are being forced to do it at gunpoint! The point is that simply observing a task will not serve as an accurate guide as to whether or not it will count as work. What is crucial is the context within which the activity takes place (Figure 12.1).

Stop and think

- Identify two activities that are conventionally seen as (a) work; and (b) non-work.
- What are the characteristics that distinguish them?
- What activities are seen as both work and non-work within different contexts (consider, for example, Figure 12.1)?

In a society such as ours, paid labour is most often equated with work – in the above example, only the person sawing the wood as a joiner would be seen to be 'at work'.

Figure 12.1 Teaching a child to read may be seen as work when done by a teacher and non-work when done by a parent

The contemporary centrality of wage-labour in many societies cannot be assumed and is in no sense a 'natural' or fixed state of affairs. That it often appears to us in this way is the outcome of a complex mix of social and economic changes, upheavals and struggles played out over a long period of time (Marx 1970). But in an 'advanced' capitalist society such as the UK, it is paid employment that has come to form the basis of many people's lives, their sense of self and wellbeing, and the nucleus around which the bulk of wider social relationships gravitate. Given this, it is justifiable to begin with the classical analysis of wage-labour within capitalism, that of Karl Marx.

Marx and the labour process within capitalism

For Karl Marx (1818–83), labour was the quintessential human activity, not in the narrow way in which we have come to understand labour today but labour in the broadest sense – a purposeful and sensuous interaction between people and nature. How people organized themselves in the act of production was the starting point for Marx's materialist method: 'Thus the first fact to be established is the physical organisation of these individuals and their consequent relation to the rest of nature' (Marx 1967: 42). Individuals, for Marx, 'begin to distinguish themselves from animals as soon as they begin to produce their means of subsistence' (Marx 1967: 42). The manner in which people 'produce their means of subsistence' forms the basis of Marx's basic unit of historical categorization, the *mode of production*.

It is only within the *capitalist mode of production* (CMP) that *wage-labour* comes to predominate. Essentially, within capitalism *labour power*, the mental and physical ability to labour, becomes all that a property-less working class has to sell to those who own the means of production – the ruling or capitalist class. Within the CMP, labour itself becomes a commodity. For an agreed period of time, a worker relinquishes control of his or her labour power to the capitalist, who will then put it to use in an attempt to create surplus value and realize a profit in the marketplace. The CMP is thus an inherently exploitative, antagonistic and class-ridden socioeconomic formation, and it is within CMP that *alienation* becomes endemic to wage labour and a perennial condition and experience for workers (see pp. 60–63 for an elaboration of these concepts). As Marx (1967: 571) states, 'The whole

A closer look

The mode of production

This has two key components:

- *A labour process* – The manner in which purposeful human activity fashions objects and the tools (often referred to as the means of production) with which this is done.
- *The social relations of production* – The relationships that form within and around the labour process.

system of capitalist production is based on the fact that the workman sells his labour power as a commodity'.

Braverman and *Labour and Monopoly Capital*

Harry Braverman (1974) attempted an extensive application of the Marxist analysis of the labour process for the twentieth century in *Labour and Monopoly Capital* (*LMC*). He argued that work in the twentieth century was undergoing a process of debasement and *deskilling* – hence the subtitle of the book, 'The degradation of work within the twentieth century'. In the era of 'monopoly capital' there was an intensification of the *division of labour* – the tendency towards a specialization of tasks – and the systematic, rational and 'scientific' application of managerial methods to work.

Taylorism

The most important catalyst and representative statement for such a management approach, according to Braverman, was to be found in F.W. Taylor's book *The Principles of Scientific Management* (1967; first published 1911). For Taylor, management's problem was essentially exerting total, or 'direct' (Friedman 1979), control over the workforce. Taylor reasoned that a workforce could not be trusted to maximize its output and efficiency on its own. 'Skill' represented something of an unknown to management and offered the workforce many opportunities to limit its output and subvert and deflect managerial authority. The following comment from Taylor is indicative of his perspective:

> **hardly a competent workman can be found in a large establishment, whether he works by the day or on piece work, contract work or under any of the ordinary systems of compensating labour, who does not devote a considerable part of his time to studying just how slowly he can work and still convince his employer that he is going at a good pace.**
>
> (quoted in Braverman 1974: 98)

Thus, Taylor believed that skilled tasks had to be broken down into simple and more 'manageable' operations and subjected to detailed and intensive timing – via time-and-motion study – and monitoring. An essential part of this was to ensure that 'All possible brain work should be removed from the shop and centred in the planning department' (Braverman 1974: 113). This was a process that Braverman laid great stress on and described as the 'separation of conception from execution'. He thought that this systematic 'deskilling' was inevitable within twentieth-century capitalism and would extend to all types of occupation throughout the economy. Thus, the future for 'skilled' work and workers themselves within capitalism looked bleak.

Braverman and the labour process debate

Braverman's book continues to be extremely influential and was the catalyst for what was to become known as the *labour process debate* (R. Brown 1992; Thompson 1989; Grint 2005). As a result of this debate, *LMC* has been subjected to an intense and prolonged critique. However, the subsequent elaboration and further discussion of *LMC*'s omissions and perceived shortcomings have greatly enhanced our understanding of work and employment. It is therefore worth

Case study

Factory time

I work in a factory. For eight hours a day, five days a week, I'm the exception to the rule that life can't exist in a vacuum. Work to me is a void, and I begrudge every precious minute of my time that it takes. When writing about work I become bitter, bloody-minded and self-pitying, and I find difficulty in being objective. I can't tell you much about my job because I think it would be misleading to try to make something out of nothing; but as I write I am acutely aware of the effect that my working environment has upon my attitude towards work and leisure and life in general . . .

After clocking-in one starts work. Starts work, that is, if the lavatories are full. In an hourly paid job it pays to attend to the calls of nature in the firm's time. After the visit to the lavatory there is the tea-break to look forward to; after the tea-break the dinner-break; after the dinner-break the 'knocking-off' time. Work is done between the breaks, but it is done from habit and is given hardly a passing thought. Nothing is gained from the work itself – it has nothing to offer. The criterion is not to do a job well, but to get it over with quickly. Trouble is, one never does get it over with. Either one job is followed by another which is equally boring, or the same job goes on and on for ever: particles of production that stretch into an age of inconsequence. There is never a sense of fulfilment.

Time, rather than content, is the measure of factory life.

Time is what the factory worker sells: not labour, not skill, but time, dreary time. Desolate factory time that passes so slowly compared with the fleeting seconds of the weekend. Monday morning starts with a sigh, and the rest of the working-week is spent longing for Friday night. Everybody seems to be wishing his life away. And away it goes – sold to the man in the bowler hat.

People who speak grandiosely of the 'meaning of work' should spend a year or two in a factory.

(Fraser 1968: 11–12)

Questions

1. Can we draw any parallels between this type of factory work and other forms of work?
2. What do you think are the social, personal and economic consequences of the types of feelings described in the passage?

spending some time reviewing some of the more pertinent criticisms of *LMC*.

Braverman and skill

Given that Braverman's work has often been given the shorthand label of the 'deskilling thesis', and that the notion of skill obviously figures centrally within his investigations, it is somewhat surprising to find that nowhere in *LMC* does he systematically define, or even take to task, what 'skill' actually is or how it can be recognized. Braverman talks of 'skill' as though it were an axiomatic and unproblematic category that we all understand in a similar way. We should in no way dispense with the category of skill or portray it as being in some way false or illusory. However, it is important to bear in mind that the notion of skill is a socially and historically specific category that requires close sociological and empirical investigation.

Stop and think

- What do you think constitutes 'skill'?
- Why do you think the work that women do is often not seen to be skilled?

The creation of skill operates within relations of power and influence. Think of the ways in which trade unions and professional bodies struggle to get their work defined as being 'skilful' in some way. We should reflect on why it is that the work that women do (very often work that is extremely similar to that of men) is often not defined as being 'skilled', has less status and consequently is not so well rewarded financially. Much work away from the 'formal' sector of paid employment, especially domestic labour, is not regarded as being skilled or even 'proper' work. However, consider how much knowledge, physical effort and manual dexterity are involved in preparing, cooking and serving a meal for a group of people day after day. (If you doubt that there is any great skill involved in such a task, then try it some time!) That most of the work done that is regarded as skilled or of high status is generally carried out by men, often from a middle- or upper-class background, is not a mere coincidence and requires some explanation.

The implicit datum from which Braverman judges work in the twentieth century is a romanticized 'golden age' of skilled craft workers, a masculine world of artisans using a creative combination of hand and brain to fashion intricate goods and artifacts. This is an accusation Braverman refutes without any real conviction: 'I hope that no one draws . . . the conclusion that my views are shaped by nostalgia for an age that cannot be recaptured' (Braverman 1974: 6–7). This is not to say that such workers never existed, or do not exist now, and that we should not lament their 'deskilling', but Braverman offers little proof that this was ever the work experience for the vast majority. Braverman does not operate with the norm or average from the past, given that in the history of human toil it is probably fair to say that most people have been employed to pick things up and put them down again! Braverman also ignores the way in which new 'skills' are created and have emerged throughout the twentieth century – for example, think of those people who work in the telecommunications industries, with information technologies or computer programming and in the new service industries, to name but a few. Throughout the CMP the creation and recomposition of skills has always provided something of a counterbalance to the destruction of skills – however we define skill.

Braverman and the influence of Taylorism

Braverman's assumption about the widespread influence of 'Taylorism' has also been cast in doubt (Burawoy 1985; Littler 1982; Wood 1982). It is by no means clear that Taylor and his writings had the profound impact on management practice that Braverman assumed to be the case. There was much resistance to Taylorist forms of management at all levels within many organizations. Leaving aside the huge amount of effort that a Taylorist 'direct control' strategy requires on the part of management, there is no reason why the same principles of 'scientific management' could not be turned on management themselves – especially middle management. Braverman's rigid and dogged use of 'Taylorism' as a coherent and dominant set of practices also greatly underestimates the variety and range of managerial methods employed in workplaces to best ensure efficient production and maintain 'acceptable' and 'realistic' levels of control over the workforce. As Grint says:

> **Taylorism, at least in its total form, as a unique and discrete managerial strategy, rather than just one more form of an increasingly rationalized approach to management, had a very limited application anywhere.**
>
> (Grint 2005: 177–9)

In many ways, Taylorism can best be understood as a metaphor for the widespread intensification of the division of labour and the minute detailing of tasks in many workplaces in the twentieth century, part of Max Weber's all-pervasive rationalization of many areas of social and economic life in capitalist societies (Gerth and Mills 1991).

Braverman and workers' resistance

Another rather glaring omission from *LMC* revolves around Braverman's 'heroic' admission that 'no attempt will be made to deal with the modern working class on the level of its consciousness, organization or other activities' (Braverman 1974: 27). Braverman admits that this is a 'self-imposed limitation to the objective content of class and the omission of the subjective' (Braverman 1974: 27). Not to include an appreciation and discussion of workers' 'subjectivity' and 'agency' in his discussion of the development of the labour process greatly undermines the authenticity and power of Braverman's analysis. It is also something of a surprise, to say the least, for someone who was such a committed Marxist. The history of wage-labour within capitalism is fundamentally a history of struggle, resistance, subversion and sheer bloody-mindedness as well as being about domination, complicity and subordination. If we accept the Marxist understanding of the labour process outlined above, then it could hardly be otherwise.

A closer look

Resistance

The women protested and resisted the target and grading system, individually and collectively, on a day-to-day basis. The work-study analysts were often marked out as the main enemy and were constantly discussed – at times, more vehemently than higher levels of management. These women were seen as the perpetrators of a system which presented to the shopfloor targets which could not be reached, let alone surpassed to allow for a bonus to be earned. It is the encounter between the work-study analyst and the shopfloor worker which encapulates the collision between labour and capital, as this is the point at which the contract for the sale of labour power is realised and where labour power is turned into labour time and, thus, profits for the company . . .

[One] timed a woman and didn't ask if she could bring the clock out. It's against the rules. The girls are only timed if they agree to the clock coming out and it has to be visible to the girl. Well, this time it wasn't. She did it on the sly and when the girls found out they walked off the job. The nearest thing we've had to a strike here. We had to get John to sort it out. They have no idea what they are doing with their clocks and their minutes.

Outside the coffee bar, a row was developing which looked as though it might erupt into a walk-off. Gillian's unit had just been given minutes for making a baby garment – a tee-shirt which was edged, and had pants to match. Gillian was looking distraught and said: 'I hate this minutes thing; it's the worst part of my job. I feel sick, I've got a headache. Every time the minutes are given there is a row, every time.' Lisa, the assistant supervisor, was also looking very worried as the fury from the women grew. Some sat defiantly with arms folded while others talked together in small groups. The unit had disintegrated.

(Westwood 1983: 49–51)

Resistance from the workforce can materialize in a variety of ways. Strikes, walkouts, go-slows and works-to-rule are only the most visible, and organized, instances of workers' resistance. Less obvious, but at least as significant when taken in aggregate, are the countless occasions when workers deliberately, and often literally, 'put a spanner in the works' and subvert, renegotiate and reorder managerial authority through their own 'subcultures' (Roy 1954). Willis put it well when he wrote that people 'thread through the dead experience of work a living culture which isn't simply a reflex of defeat' (quote in Clarke *et al.* 1979: 188). Workers can sabotage machinery, limit their output, deceive the person from 'time and motion', hide in the toilets, go 'on the sick', jam the photocopier, break the drill, destroy the accounts, stop for a 'ciggy'. All these actions, and a million others, have to be coped with in some way by management. Therefore it is crucial that we take into account the subjectivity of the workforce to properly understand the development of the labour process within capitalism (Littler 1982; Jermier *et al.* 1994). Resistance is not only derivative but also determinative of the labour process (Burawoy 1985).

The organization of work

We have seen that maintaining control over a workforce is no easy task. Such a recognition has been the catalyst for a huge effort on the part of managers and a whole host of analysts, consultants and academics to devise ever-more efficient methods to organize, control and increase the productivity of a workforce. Evidence of this can be seen in the seemingly never-ending stream of 'new' managerial methods and techniques, the impressive edifices of management and business schools seen in many large cities, and the appearance on bestseller lists of 'management books' (Peters and Waterman 1982; Peters and Austin 1985). A former chairman of ICI, John Harvey-Jones, even fronted a popular TV series in the guise of a managerial 'troubleshooter'. In the space available we can only

A closer look

Managerial strategies

- *Simple control* – Management control via open displays of power and the personalized imposition of control and order.
- *Technical control* – An intensive division of labour and the pacing of work via machinery (classically, the assembly line).
- *Bureaucratic control* – Managerial authority becomes increasingly depersonalized and diffused through a hierarchical system of impersonal rules and procedures. Companies use internal career ladders and labour markets to reward workers' commitment to the ideals and aims of the company. Control here is embedded in the social and organizational structure of the firm.

outline some of the more influential discussions, managerial strategies and techniques of work redesign (Thompson and McHugh 2003).

Bureaucratic control

R. Edwards (1979), in an influential study, offers a framework for understanding the development of managerial strategies in the twentieth century. This involves three stages (see above).

Although Edwards provides a useful shorthand account of attempts to exert control over the labour process, he has been taken to task over how prevalent such a system of bureaucratic control is (Grint 2005) and how successful it is in overcoming resistance and 'incorporating' the workforce. Rules and procedures, no matter how detailed, rarely cover every potentiality; control can never be that absolute. Further, rules can be subverted or they can be kept to rigidly – the basis of the long-established tactic of 'work-to-rule' – in such a way that the 'system breaks down'. The inflexible nature of bureaucratic and rigid systems can often be their Achilles' heel and, when workers stop giving of themselves, organizations can often shudder to a halt (Gorz 1979).

Giving the workers some 'responsible autonomy'

Friedman (1979) points out the limitations, some of which were discussed above, of *direct control* (DC) methods (exemplified by Taylorism). He suggests that managerial strategies have emerged to overcome these limitations and increasingly involve giving the workforce a measure of what he terms 'responsible autonomy' (RA); we can also understand these changes as being part of a move from 'low trust' to 'high trust' systems (Fox 1974). RA methods seek to empower workers by giving them some degree of control and decision-making in the process of production and attempt to incorporate the 'subjectivity' of the workers through aligning them more closely with the goals and aims of the company. This has been part of a long-standing interest in the *humanization* of work.

Work humanization and redesign

Two main techniques of work redesign are job rotation and job enlargement. *Job rotation* does nothing to change particular work tasks but entails moving workers around a number of jobs at regular intervals in order to reduce boredom and stimulate some interest through variety. *Job enlargement* involves merging together a number of work tasks to form a more complex and extended single operation. Obviously, these methods carry with them dangers of having the opposite effect of that intended, as both could lead to an intensification of tasks and a deterioration of working conditions.

Job enrichment revolves around an attempt to empower workers by giving them, in a way antithetical to the doctrines of Taylorism, not only a variety of work tasks but also an element of control and planning. Many repetitive and simplified production jobs could possibly be enriched 'by the inclusion of tasks such as machine maintenance, elements of inspection and quality control, or machine setting' (Fincham and Rhodes 1994: 207). Again, such methods have met with mixed success. As one worker memorably put it:

World in focus

Quality circles

An aspect of the Japanese model that receives attention is *ringi seido* or bottom-up management, which is operationalized through the use of quality circles. Quality circles involve small groups of between five and ten employees who work together and volunteer to meet regularly to solve job-related problems. Usually meetings take place during company time, but the frequency varies; some are weekly while others are monthly. Normally though not always led by supervisors, circles aim to improve quality, reduce production costs, raise productivity and improve safety.

Specific characteristics distinguish quality circles from other managerial techniques such as project groups, joint problem solving and job laboratories. Firstly, quality circles have a permanent existence and meet regularly, and are not *ad hoc* creations to solve specific problems. Secondly, participants decide their own agenda of problems and priorities. Finally, all circle members are trained to use specialized tools of quality management which include elementary statistics.

Three important assumptions underlie quality circles: one, all employees, and not just managers or technical experts, are capable of improving quality and efficiency; two, among employees there exists a reservoir of relevant knowledge about work processes, which, under conventional work practices, is difficult to tap; three, quality is an integral part of the entire production process. It is not an adjunct but the responsibility of every employee.

(Clarke *et al*. 1994: 364)

> **You move from one boring, dirty monotonous job to another dirty, boring monotonous job and somehow you're supposed to come out of it all 'enriched'. But I never feel 'enriched' – I just feel knackered.**
>
> (Beynon and Nichols 1977: 16)

Variants of *team working* have been tried within a wide range of organizations. *Quality circles* are the best-known method of team or group working and are associated most closely with work experiments in Japan. In the mid-1980s, quality circles were found in at least 400 UK companies (Clarke *et al.* 1994). Organizing workers into collaborative work groups obviously represents a major break from the assumptions about workers' behaviour implicit within Taylorist or DC methods. Workers themselves can decide how to overcome production problems and reach production targets instead of all such responsibility being delegated to management; in some cases, workers even have the power to stop the production line. At a company level, there has been a move away from the classical bureaucratic and hierarchical firm, characterized above by Edwards, towards much 'flatter' and less stratified organizations, with fewer layers of middle management between the workforce and top-level management. US computer giants IBM and Compaq are examples of 'flat' organizations that also utilize team working.

Stop and think

- Consider the following occupations:
  - (a) shop assistant;
  - (b) waiter;
  - (c) teacher; and
  - (d) cleaner. How might 'job enrichment' be applied to these jobs?
- What problems might arise from this?

Industrialism and de-industrialization

The march of industrialism halted?

For a long period, particularly after the Second World War, capitalism and 'industrialism' were increasingly seen as panaceas for the ills of all societies. *Convergence theory* explained how many previously diverse societies, particularly those from the Eastern bloc and the Western industrial societies, were travelling along a basically similar trajectory of social and economic development (Kumar 1978). The USA, in particular, was seen to be at the end of this long evolutionary path (Burns 1969; Kerr *et al.* 1962; Rostow 1960). The development of industrial societies in the post-war period was linked with powerful notions of 'progress' and 'modernity', and it seemed that most of the major social and economic problems in the industrialized world either had been solved or were about to be. Such extravagant claims were not solely down to the apologists for the capitalist system, as the advanced industrialized nations had indeed experienced some remarkable social changes. Unemployment had to a large extent been contained (especially when compared with the misery of mass unemployment in the 1920s and 1930s), economic growth had increased consistently, and wage levels and spending power had reached unprecedented levels for many millions of people across the Western world. For the first time, travel abroad became a realistic possibility for many, as did the purchase of, among many other things, cars, washing machines, television sets and record players.

To all intents and purposes, capitalist industrialism, and the huge surpluses created by the manufacturing sector in particular, were seen to have solved most of the pressing social and economic problems encountered in the Great Depression of the 1920s. However, as the 1970s wore on, the industrial world appeared to be undergoing a series of far-reaching changes. Prime among them was the onset of *de-industrialization* – the reduction, in terms of employment and output, of the manufacturing and extractive industries. Such was the importance attached to successive developments that some thought that we were on the threshold of another 'Great Transformation' (Kumar 1978).

World in focus

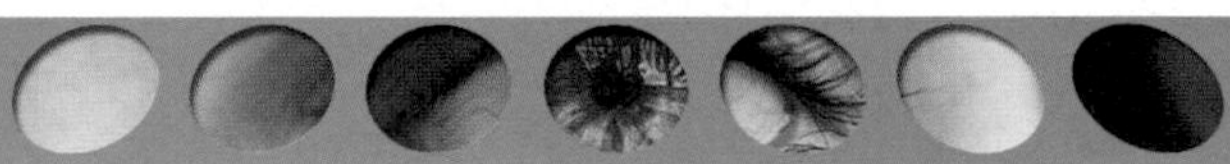

Japanization and 'lean production'

Japanese work organization and associated methods of *lean production* created a great deal of interest in the Western industrial world in the 1970s and early 1980s (Delbridge 1998; Sayer and Walker 1992; Thompson and McHugh 2003). At that time many envious corporate eyes were casting anxious glances to the 'East' and the spectacular growth of the Japanese economy and the success of companies such as Toyota and Nissan. Such was the impact of a fact-finding visit to Japan in 1980 on the head of Ford Europe (Bill Hayden) that it led to the company establishing a new calendar, replacing AD with AJ – 'After Japan'.

Japanization and lean production (the terms are often used interchangeably) defy precise definition being catch-all terms which describe a range of methods and production techniques, none of which are particularly original when taken in isolation. Essentially they involve a combination of the 'holy trinity' of flexibility, quality and teamwork. These elements are central to the work organization most closely associated with Japanization and lean production, also known as the *just-in-time* system (JIT). Put simply JIT 'is a system for delivering the exact quantity and defect-free quality of parts just in time for each stage of production' (Fincham and Rhodes 1994: 350). Such a system relies upon *total quality management* (TQM) whereby components must have 'zero defects' to ensure that production is not interrupted while faulty parts are being replaced. Systems of *kanban*, where components are instantly replenished when required, and of *zero stocks*, not holding 'buffer stocks' of components or partially completed assemblies, are also crucial to the smooth running of the JIT system. Work innovations such as quality circles (QCs) are used to help to ensure that production is closely monitored by workers and total quality can be maintained. Flexibility of labour is also a crucial requirement and JIT is a

World in focus *continued*

system that often entails the reworking of 'traditional' union practices (McIlroy 1995).

It is important, however, not to exaggerate the importance of Japanization within Western economies. In the UK (1996) there were 216 Japanese owned companies employing around 73,000 people (Delbridge 1998) compared with the half a million employed in 5,600 US companies. Also the take-up of a Japanese model by Western companies has been patchy and not enthusiastically embraced (Delbridge 1998; Thompson and McHugh 2003). Implementing QCs and JIT systems operate best within workplaces that are characterized by cultures of 'high trust' as opposed to cultures of 'low trust' – essentially the culture of 'us-and-them' – that are typical of many UK working environments. In many ways the rhetoric associated with Japanization and lean production systems operates most powerfully as a 'motivating' force for Western management and workers as companies strive to meet the challenges of a global economy. The terms also often serve as a summation of 'best practice' and a datum by which we should measure ourselves.

(Bradley *et al.* 2000)

De-industrialization

Most advanced capitalist societies have apparently been undergoing some form and degree of de-industrialization. Although we have to be extremely careful how we measure de-industrialization (Allen and Massey 1988) – for example, employment can decline while output can actually increase in many industries – it seems to be the case that the composition of the workforce has changed dramatically in the postwar period. Certainly the statistics make for dramatic reading. In the UK in 1946, the manufacturing, construction and mining industries employed about 45 per cent of the labour force. By 2007, this had dwindled to around 18 per cent. The teaching profession now employs more people than do the mining, steel and shipbuilding industries combined.

To take the example of Scotland, one of the first industrialized nations, employment levels in a variety of occupational categories seem to show a marked shift away from the 'industrial sector'. In 1911, 183,000 people were employed in the metals, minerals and chemicals industries; by 1993, this had declined to 36,000 people. During the same period, employment in banking, finance, insurance and business services rose from 23,000 people to an astonishing 204,000 people (Lee 1995). A similar statistical profile can be shown for the UK as a whole and for other advanced industrial societies; for example, the numbers employed in UK manufacturing and services in 2005 were 3.1 million and 28.8 million, respectively (Noon and Blyton 2007). The question arises, given the collapse of manufacturing employment and the general shrinking of industry (whatever definition we care to use), as to what extent can we continue to call a society such as the UK 'industrial' in any meaningful sense? This is a question of great importance given that many of the occupations that are now disappearing were often the ones that were considered to be 'real' or 'proper' jobs. The trades, skills and work that made up these jobs – for example, in mining, shipbuilding and engineering – were of course male-dominated and classic sites of masculine occupational cultures and key for the development and maintenance of working-class male identities (Clarke *et al.* 1979; Morgan 1991; Strangleman and Warren 2008). The iconography, meanings and powerful imagery of such occupations in many ways became synonymous, within industrial societies, with work generally and were often used erroneously as templates for all work, something, incidentally, that much 'sociology of work' – not long ago subsumed under the general heading of 'industrial sociology' – has done relatively little to counter. This is why 'de-industrialization' is about more than simply the demise of particular jobs but involves, among other things, the dismantling of social and cultural relations and a renegotiation of the meaning of work itself – particularly as a vehicle for masculine identities.

At a broader level, de-industrialization, given the spatial division of labour (Massey 1994), varies across geographical areas. This means that the social fabric and economies of certain regions can be affected particularly badly. This is evidenced in the UK in the huge pools of unemployed labour and industrial collapse of areas such as north-east England, Clydeside and South Wales, as they deal with, often painfully felt, social and economic restructuring (Allen and Massey 1988; Massey and Allen 1988).

The coming of post-industrial society?

Some writers observed the changes that were taking place within many advanced industrial societies differently and in an altogether more positive and optimistic light. The collapse of employment in industry, or the manufacturing and the extractive industries to be more accurate, has been seen as symptomatic of the emergence of a new order. In particular, the growth of employment in the service sector is seen to be a development of great significance. Some commentators have argued that we are witnessing, and living through, the emergence of a new social formation – a break from previous societies that is as clear and revolutionary as the break between agricultural and industrial society.

The best-known and most influential statement of this *post-industrial* thesis or vision was put forward by Daniel Bell (1973) in *The Coming of Post-Industrial Society*. For Bell, the type of employment that is most common becomes a central and defining feature of society. Agricultural employment predominates in pre-industrial societies, factory work is the norm in industrial society, and, Bell argues, employment in the service sector becomes the largest occupational category of post-industrial society.

In industrial society, the rational pursuit of economic growth was the 'axial principle' around which large swathes of social and economic life were organized. People were now, according to Bell, less involved in the 'fabrication' of things and more involved in the manipulation, storing and processing of information and knowledge. For Bell, post-industrial society was also the 'information society'; information processing and knowledge generation have become the 'axial principle' of post-industrial society.

The huge advances in information technologies and global communications networks had provided the catalyst, and offered the opportunities, for a revolution in the workplace. The new types of work that people do will involve less capitalist rationalization and control and will be less alienating than the jobs associated with 'industrial society'. 'White-collar' (as opposed to 'blue-collar') and professional jobs would become the norm. Knowledge and 'professional elites' will hold power and influence in society and will replace the marginalized and anachronistic industrial ruling classes. Indeed, given that the old industrial working class would wither away, so too would class lose its importance as a major social divide and source of collective identity. Centres of information, knowledge, innovation and dynamism, such as universities and centres of research and development, will become the nerve centres of post-industrial society, not the factory or the industrial complexes of old. The new knowledge elites could utilize the available new technologies to plan and forecast the future more effectively, thus freeing society from the fluctuations and cyclical uncertainties of the old industry-based economy. Generally, post-industrial society would be a more stable and harmonious society in which there would be more time for creative and leisure pursuits. The drudgery of most people's work would be alleviated through the sensitive and systematic application of new technologies.

All versions of post-industrial theory (Touraine 1971) have been subjected to a sustained and thorough critique (Hall *et al.* 1992; Kumar 1978, 1995; Webster 2002), but they continue to display a remarkable longevity and resilience. Perhaps this is because they tap into widely held notions and fears about the pace of change of social and economic life and the ambiguous role of the bewildering range of new technologies. Post-industrial visions paint a generally positive and possibly comforting picture that many people find appealing and are wont to cling to. However, the shortcomings of 'post-industrial' theory are many and far-reaching.

The difficulty of defining services

The move to a service economy and the growth of people working in service occupations are central to discussions about post-industrial society and are used as incontrovertible evidence that we are undergoing a change of great significance. However, the definition of a service occupation or the service sector is notoriously difficult to achieve (Massey and Allen 1988). 'Services' are sometimes described as being 'anything that cannot be dropped on your foot', the absence of a physical product being crucial. However, we immediately run into problems, given that a wide variety of tasks that are generally included in most classifications of the service sector, such as catering, laundering and many financial services, very often do deal with a tangible product or 'thing'.

The problem of operating with a 'service sector' and 'manufacturing sector' distinction is that it blinds us to the interdependent and hugely complex nature of modern economies and the division of labour – something that Durkheim brought to our attention a long time ago. The use of labels such as 'services' and 'the service sector' tends to homogenize a heterogeneous group of activities. This is sociologically and empirically problematic as it glosses over a myriad of different labour processes, work environments and experiences. The term 'services' is a highly unsatisfactory social construction. However, it is probably unrealistic to expect people to dispense with the term completely, although we have to treat it with great caution. The 'service sector' is a 'rag-bag of industries as different as real-estate and massage parlours, transport and computer bureaux, public administration and public entertainment' (Jones, quoted in Webster 2002: 42). It is difficult to see how such a definite and crucial change as the move from industrial to post-industrial society could be based on such a flimsy and fractured foundation.

Post-industrialism: a radical change?

The extent of the change brought about by the developments discussed above is a matter of some controversy. Commentators such as Toffler (1970, 1980) maintain that we are witnessing nothing short of a revolution. However, as Kumar (1978, 1995) notes, service jobs have long been critical to any capitalist society; in fact, Scotland's 'service sector' was the major employer as long ago as 1900. No capitalist nation in fact has ever had the majority of its workforce employed in the manufacturing sector – with the exception, for a brief time, of the UK (Webster 2002). Also, post-industrial theorists give no compelling reasons as to why the decline in manufacturing jobs is such a cataclysmic change anyway. Why not, for instance, highlight the collapse of employment in agriculture and forestry? We have given some statistics that highlighted the decline of manufacturing in Scotland (see p. 494). Over the same period, employment in agriculture and forestry plummeted from 238,000 people in 1911 to only 27,000 people in 1993 (Lee 1995). As Kumar suggests, if there has been a startling change in the structure of capitalist societies, then it has been one from agricultural employment to service employment (Kumar 1978). However, we rarely hear of discussions about a 'post-agricultural society'.

Wage-labour (for Marx, the basis of the whole system of capitalist production) is still of course the predominant employment relationship. Many types of work often included within the service sector, such as

A closer look

Services

There are four different uses of the term 'services':

- *Service industries* – These make up the service sector.
- *Service occupations* – These are present in all sectors of the economy and alert us to the fact that clerks, accountants, cleaners, catering staff, among others, are common and integral to many different industries and organizations, whether they be engineering plants or advertising agencies.
- *Service products* – These refer to the fact that even manufacturing firms produce these in terms of 'follow-up services', service contracts, information services, etc.
- *Service functions* – This category draws attention to the ways that many manufactured goods provide a 'service' to some degree, e.g. TVs and videos provide a 'home entertainment' service and washing machines and irons service people's laundry needs.

(Gershunny and Miles 1983)

World in focus

McDonald's

The sheer number of fast-food restaurants has grown astronomically. For example, McDonald's, which first began franchising in 1955, opened its 12,000th outlet on March 22, 1991. By the end of 1991, McDonald's had 12,418 restaurants. The leading 100 restaurant chains operate more than 110,000 outlets in the United States alone. There is, therefore, 1 chain restaurant for every 2,250 Americans.

The McDonald's model has not only been adopted by other hamburger franchises but also by a wide array of other fast-food businesses, including those selling fried chicken and various ethnic foods (for example, Pizza Hut, Sbarro's, Taco Bell, Popeye's, and Charley Chan's) . . .

This American institution is making increasing inroads around the world as evidenced by the opening of American fast-food restaurants throughout Europe. (Not too many years ago scholars wrote about European resistance to fast-food restaurants.) Fast food has become a global phenomenon; consider the booming business at the brand-new McDonald's in Moscow where, as I write, almost 30,000 hamburgers a day are being sold by a staff of 1,200 young people working two to a cash register. There are plans to open 20 more McDonald's in the remnants of the Soviet Union in the next few years, and a vast new territory in Eastern Europe is now laid bare to an invasion of fast-food restaurants.

Already possessing a huge Kentucky Fried Chicken outlet, Beijing, China, witnessed the opening of the world's largest McDonald's, with 700 seats, 29 cash registers and nearly 1000 employees, in April 1992. On its first day of business, it set a new one-day record for McDonald's by serving about 40,000 customers. In 1991, for the first time, McDonald's opened more restaurants abroad (427) than in the United States (188). The top 10 McDonald's outlets in terms of sales and profits are already overseas. By 1994, it is expected that more than 50 percent of McDonald's profits will come from its overseas operations. It has been announced that starting in 1992, McDonald's will start serving food on the Swiss railroad system. One presumes that the menu will include Big Macs and not cheese fondue.

(Ritzer 1993: 2–3)

Questions

1. How far do you think a society such as the UK shows evidence of 'McDonaldization'? Give examples.
2. What spheres of work and employment do you think would be impossible to 'McDonaldize'?

Figure 12.2 McDonald's in Eastern Europe: evidence of the global community
Sean Gallup/Newsmakers/Getty Images

work in the tourist industry, catering and cleaning, are poorly paid, casualized, characterized by insecurity and subject to the same kinds of rationalization and control that were supposed to be the preserve of industrial work.

Certainly 'fast food' restaurants, to take one example from a growing sector of employment, often display a level of control and systematization that Ford and Taylor would have been proud to have achieved. At McDonald's we are told that a 'quarter pounder is cooked for exactly 107 seconds. Our fries are never more than 7 minutes old when sold . . . [we] aim to serve any order within 60 seconds' (quoted in Abercrombie and Warde 1992: 180).

As Beynon suggests,

> **If we take industrialisation to mean the production of commodities through the use of machinery aided with rational systems of organisation, the post war period can be seen as one in which areas of life hitherto un-affected by the march of capital were subjected to this process . . . Add to this the mechanisation of banking, transportation and the home and we have the bones of an on going industrialisation thesis and the *extended* rather than the *post*-industrial society.**
>
> (quoted in Abercrombie and Warde 1992: 180)

Certainly Beynon's analysis can be further supported if we look at the growth of industrialism as an international rather than a national phenomenon. Countries such as Taiwan, South Korea, Indonesia and Brazil are all experiencing rapid economic growth, which is based on an unbridled capitalist industrialism. So, the case for post-industrialism becomes even more difficult to sustain if we look at the global picture (Webster 2002).

Fordism and mass production

More than anything else, the image of people working on an assembly line (immortalized in Charlie Chaplin's film *Modern Times*) epitomizes the way in which many of us think about work in the twentieth century. Henry Ford's creation – the Model T – became the emblem of *mass production*. Ford pioneered the organization of mass production (within which the assembly line was only *one* element) for the production of complex commodities such as the Model T.

Of course, the production of vast quantities of identical, or similar, commodities is pointless if they do not meet a demand in the marketplace. One answer was to increase the purchasing power of the workforce. This was done at Ford in 1914 through the introduction, in a qualified and partial way, of the (in)famous 'five dollar day' (Meyer 1981). It is unclear whether the introduction of the five-dollar day really was a deliberate attempt to increase the spending power of the Ford workforce or, as seems more likely, was done in order to 'buy off' any organized resistance to the intense pace of work within the Detroit plant and reduce the number of employees leaving the company. Ford plants had exceptionally high levels of labour

A closer look

Fordist mass production

Sabel (1982: 210) describes this as 'the efficient production of one thing'; it operates along the following principles:

- long runs of standardized commodities, the Model T being the classic example;
- the use of fixed or dedicated machinery tooled up to produce many thousands of identical components;
- the widespread use of unskilled labour within the production process;
- an intensive and extensive division of labour.

With the systematic application of these fairly simple principles the Ford Motor Company was able to achieve incredible levels of relatively low-cost production, and Ford's plant in Detroit was quickly churning out vast quantities of cars; by 1913, Ford was producing around 180,000 vehicles a year, more than three times the output of all British companies (McIntosh 1991).

turnover: in 1913 Ford required around 13,000 workers to operate his plants and in that year alone around 50,000 workers quit (Beynon 1975: 19).

However, the growth of purchasing power for a large section of the working class during the Fordist era came to be seen as part of the Fordist 'bargain' – 'high' wages and spending power and continuous employment in return for putting up with alienating and repetitive work conditions.

Mass production thus required a corresponding *mass consumption*. Mass marketing and the mass media were used to create demands for a bewildering array of products and commodities. Mass unionism, a state-regulated industrial relations framework and, in the realm of politics, general cross-party support over several key objectives – a commitment to full employment being central – provided the essential regulatory mechanisms (often referred to in the UK as the 'post-war consensus') to keep the economy in dynamic equilibrium. Such a series of social and economic arrangements were thought to be particularly prevalent during the classic era of Fordism – roughly the post-war period up to the early 1970s.

'Fordism' has come to refer to more than the mass production of particular commodities and is used as a shorthand way to characterize the organization of a whole social system and a particular historical time period or epoch – the 'Fordist era' (Allen *et al.* 1992; Gramsci 1971; Harvey 1990). Many areas of social life and a host of activities are said to have been Fordized. Symbols of Fordism are not only automated factories, typing pools and people working 'on the line' but also large housing estates such as Drumchapel in Glasgow and Hulme in Manchester, holiday camps, tower blocks and, more grimly, Nazi concentration camps, which were organized to mass-produce death (Bauman 1989).

The limits of Taylorism and Fordism: Fordism in crisis?

However, in the late 1960s and early 1970s it appeared that Fordism was showing signs of stress and breakdown. There were a series of shocks to the Fordist system, culminating in the 1973 oil crisis. Many Western economies were showing signs of a slowdown in economic growth and a falling away of levels of labour productivity and profits. The long and stable post-war boom was apparently coming to an end. Why? An important reason was to do with the apparent inability of the Fordist labour process to secure further increases in productivity within the manufacturing sector and the inapplicability of Fordist methods to other sectors of the economy, especially the 'service sector'. The technical limits of Fordism had been reached. Waves of strikes across the Western world and apparently chronic and endemic, problems, with workforce resistance and unrest, seemed to suggest that workers had also reached their limits within Fordized workplaces. The very inflexibility of the Fordist labour process was showing itself to be an unforeseen Achilles' heel. Consumers were increasingly making demands for individualized goods. Newly emerging social developments such as youth and pop cultures and styles, and shifting patterns of taste and demand, exposed the rigidity of Fordism. The stability of the Fordist global system, underwritten and maintained by the huge economic, financial and military might of the USA, was being challenged by the rise of other economies, especially in West Germany and Japan.

Post-Fordism and flexibility

Given the break-up of mass production, mass markets and mass consumption, some commentators have argued that we are witnessing a widespread move towards *post-Fordism* (Hall and Jacques 1989; Hall *et al.* 1992). The key term here is 'flexibility'. As with the post-industrial discussion, there is an important role for new technologies such as computer-integrated manufacturing systems and new social innovations at work, such as less hierarchical organizations, team working, flexitime and a range of more flexible work practices – some of which were discussed above, particularly in relation to Japanization and lean production (see pp. 493–494).

Some commentators see these tendencies coming together in the form of the *flexible firm*, of which the best-known and most influential discussion is that of Atkinson (1984), shown in Figure 12.3. Here, management is able to 'flex' production up and down in order to meet changes of demand in the marketplace. This is achieved through a reorganization of working practices, increased subcontracting, use of agency workers and employing workers on a range of different contracts of employment. This leads Atkinson to make a distinction between a group of 'core' workers, who are multiskilled and therefore have 'functional flexibility', and a 'peripheral' group, who are employed variously

A closer look

Post-Fordist production

The following are the key elements of a post-Fordist labour process:

- Flexible production systems
- A move from economies of scale to economies of scope
- Flexible work organization – for example, team working and JIT – and a concomitant restructuring of union practices and collective bargaining
- A decentralization of production into more spatially diverse and smaller units
- Niche versus mass marketing.

on a part-time, seasonal or casual basis and can be hired and fired when required. This latter group Atkinson describes as having 'numerical flexibility'.

Flexibility has become a buzzword for managers in a range of different workplaces and environments. Many areas of local government, for example, are seen to be reorganizing along more flexible and post-Fordist lines (Stewart and Stoker 1989; Burrows and Loader 1994). As a supervisor in a council cleansing department indicates, the 'new' world of flexible working practices can take its toll on workers and managers alike:

> **We have had to become more 'business like' if you know what I mean, we have to price jobs up and be more careful in what we do . . . we have to respond more quickly and we have to be flexible and be able to respond immediately. Before you could leave things to the next day. Labour has to be far more flexible, work has to be done on the same day so it's important that they go out and do it and don't come back until it's finished.**
>
> (McIntosh and Broderick 1996)

Stop and think

➤ How might 'flexible' work practices benefit or disadvantage (a) management; (b) workers; and (c) society as a whole?

The whole notion of 'flexible' working practices as a desirable, new and widespread phenomenon has come under much scrutiny (Pollert 1988a,b). The bandying around of the terms 'flexibility' and 'flexible specialization' (Piore and Sabel 1984) often serves to give a gloss of sophistication to many changes that are taking place in UK workplaces. Basically, 'flexibility' often amounts to the very unsophisticated and long-established practices of shedding labour, increasing workloads and employing workers on a variety of seasonal and temporary contracts.

Similarly, the notion that post-Fordism represents a radical break from Fordism has been questioned (Hall *et al.* 1992; Kumar 1995; Sayer and Walker 1992; Webster 2002). To begin with, we have to question whether Fordism as it is often portrayed is a valid construction in the first place. Companies such as Ford have long been able to change production in order to meet changes in demand and have always hired and fired workers in order to maintain some flexibility in working arrangements. As one man who worked at Ford's Manchester plant in the 1920s says: 'If they got a bit slack they fired people and if they got a bit busy they took them on' (McIntosh 1995: 75).

Talk of Fordism's demise is also seen to be wide of the mark. Williams *et al.* (1987) point out that techniques of mass production are still very much in evidence. A whole range of more recent commodities, such as CD players, dishwashers, flat-pack furniture, TVs and camcorders, are still mass-produced and 'consumed' in their millions.

As with discussion of industrial and post-industrial society, debates around the move from Fordism to post-Fordism operate with sharply drawn 'binary histories' (Sayer and Walker 1992). Such a perspective can easily lead us to construct erroneous dichotomies into which we force 'relevant' bits of evidence. Underlying continuities get lost in the attempt to perceive dramatic change. The 'reality' is that Fordism and a range of flexible working practices can operate quite happily side by side – Japanese methods are a good example of this – and capitalism has long displayed an ability to adapt to changing socioeconomic environments and pressures.

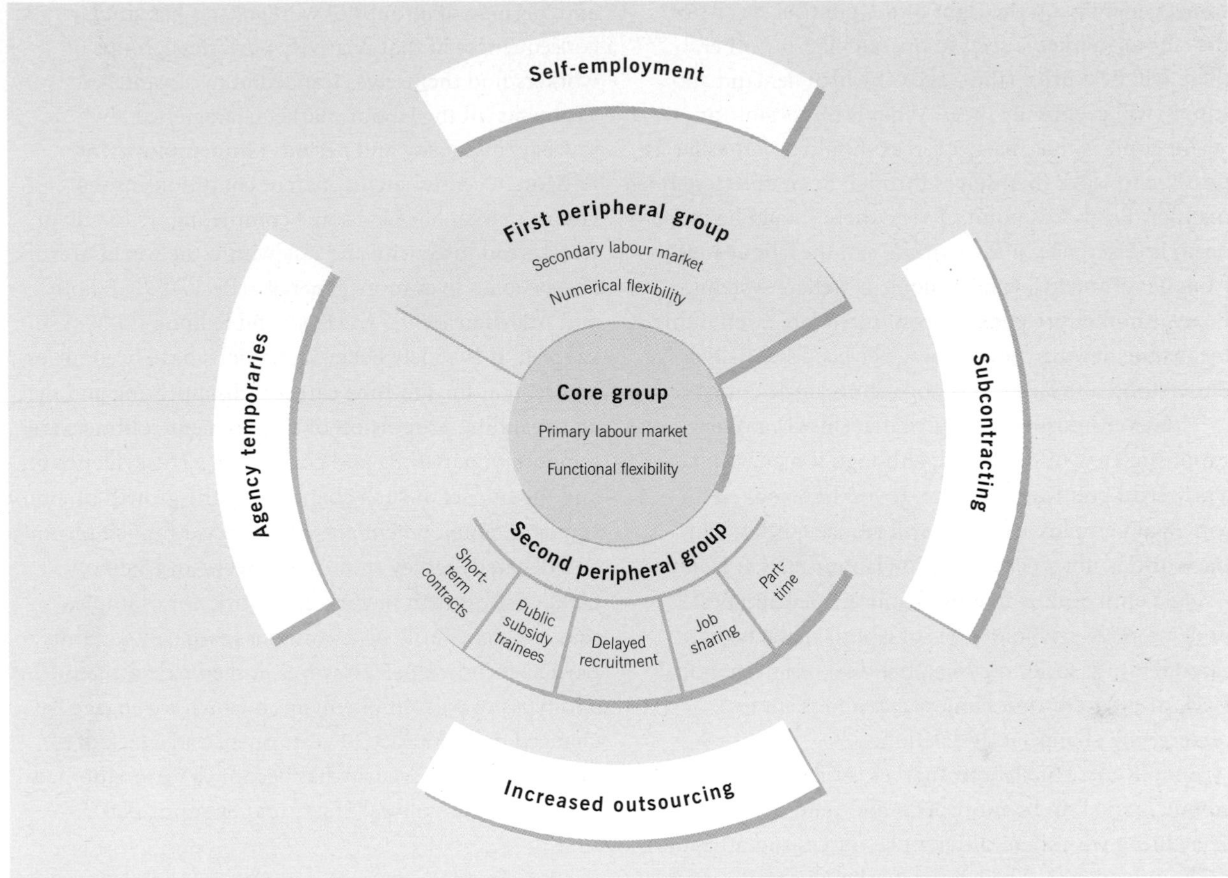

Figure 12.3 The flexible firm
Source: Atkinson 1984

The labour market

When people look for employment, they become involved in the *labour market*. It is through the labour market that people secure employment. We cannot understand this as a single market located at a particular place at a certain time. We have to think of the labour market in the abstract, a label attached to a hugely complex set of relationships.

An understanding of the workings of the labour market can have crucial implications for the way you come to view the world of work and paid labour. For

A closer look

Labour market

Fevre (1992) has identified five functions served by the labour market:

- *Informing employers* about the availability of workers for employment
- *Informing workers* about what jobs are available, through job centres, word of mouth, newspapers and other means
- *Screening workers* in order to identify what skills and attributes workers have and how much or little they are prepared to work for
- *Screening employers* in order to find out what the job pays and involves and how secure it is
- *Making an offer of employment*, which may or may not be bound up with a contract of employment.

some, generally on the right of the political spectrum, the labour market is seen to operate like any other: there will be a price (the wage) at which demand and supply will eventually meet. What is important for such people is that market forces should be left as far as possible to work themselves through in an unfettered manner. From this point of view there should be little or no interference in the workings of the labour market from governments, trade unions or welfare systems. People should 'price themselves into a job', even if this means the driving down of wage levels. Essentially it is understood as a largely homogeneous single entity.

However, most would agree that this is a rather simplistic view of the world, although it may well have a powerful political influence. If you have looked for some paid employment you will realize quickly that the world is not so clearcut. The labour market is not a single entity but is fractured and divided and best understood as a whole series of labour markets that can operate at local, regional, national or international levels at different times and places and is always undergoing change and variation.

People enter the labour market (or a particular labour market, to be more accurate) on different terms. They bring with them different resources and attributes, skills and abilities. The labour market does not operate in a vacuum but is inextricably interlinked within the society in which it operates. Thus, if in society at large we see people divided and discriminated against along lines of class, gender, ethnicity or religion, then it should come as no surprise to see such prejudices at work or emerging within the labour market. Sexism and racism limit the entry of women and black people into the labour market and proscribe the kind of employment they can obtain; similarly with people with disabilities. This is evidenced in terms of the jobs that people do and the rewards they can get. For example, women on average earn about 75 per cent of the wages that men get, even if they do similar types of work. The sexual division of work is extremely pronounced in the UK: women and men are segregated into occupations that are seen to be 'appropriate' for the genders; for example, the vast majority of clerical workers, nurses and canteen assistants are women (see pp. 237–246 for a fuller discussion of the gendered division of labour).

To take such factors into account, and to acknowledge people's differential access to the labour market, notions of the *dual* or *segmented labour market* have been put forward (Massey and Allen 1988). This corresponds closely to previous discussions of 'core' and 'peripheral' groups of workers and has similar consequences in that relatively powerless groups of workers find themselves trapped in disadvantaged 'segments' of the labour market characterized by low pay, insecurity and periods of unemployment.

More recently, such apparent conditions in the labour market have led some commentators to talk of widespread insecurity and risk within the world of work and people's lives more generally (Beck 1992; Elliott and Atkinson 1999). As Heery and Salmon (2000: xi) suggest, 'It is widely believed that jobs have become less secure, that the life-time career is disappearing and that an expanding proportion of employment contracts are temporary, part-time and contingent'. The evidence for and the impact of such changes and the growth of 'non-standard' employment are the subjects of much scrutiny and debate (Bradley *et al.* 2000; Heery and Salmon 2000). The growth in part-time work, for example, may not necessarily be a cause for insecurity for any particular individual. However, it seems clear that forms and types of paid employment in which we engage have changed over the past 30 years or so, and a lack of permanence and security has become a feature of many people's working lives (Heery and Salmon 2000).

Unemployment

Given previous discussion about what we actually count as being 'proper' work, it follows that what 'unemployment' means is not as straightforward as we might at first assume (Whiteside 1991; Gallie 1989; Gallie *et al.* 1993). Unemployment is generally understood as referring to people out of paid employment, which as we know is a limited understanding of the notion of 'work'. Many people who are not directly involved in the formal economy often 'work' extremely hard – for example, people (mainly women) who carry out the huge numbers of domestic tasks in the home, caring for children, elderly or sick relatives, people who might 'work' constantly on hobbies or who put in thousands of hours of voluntary work. Most of this work is generally ignored in discussions of unemployment.

However, not being part of the world of the formal economy and paid employment is most often for people a miserable state. Given the aforementioned centrality of work and the way that it can be a central source of our identity and sense of self, it should come as no surprise that to lose a job can be a devastating experience for

A closer look

Table 12.1 International gender pay gap, 2002

	Female earnings as % of male earned income	Female economic activity rate (as % of male rate)
Argentina	37	48
Armenia	69	88
Australia	71	78
Bangladesh	56	76
Belgium	50	67
Brazil	42	52
Cambodia	77	97
Canada	63	83
Czech Republic	56	83
Ghana	75	98
Hungary	59	72
Ireland	40	53
Italy	45	59
Japan	46	68
Korea, Republic of	46	71
Lebanon	31	39
Malawi	68	90
Malaysia	40	62
Malta	37	38
Oman	22	26
Pakistan	33	44
Peru	27	44
Russian Federation	64	82
Saudi Arabia	21	29
Senegal	55	72
Singapore	50	64
Sweden	83	89
Uganda	66	88
UK	60	75
USA	62	82
Vietnam	69	91
Zambia	55	74

(Source: created from ILO & UN statistics at Human Development Reports, http://cfapp2.undp.org/statistics/data.cfm)

many people (Gallie and Paugam 2000). Employment helps to provide a temporal structure, without which many people become lost and stupefied. As one man says:

> **I spend the odd hour or two walking up and down the stairs, counting each step. I still manage to read but my concentration is almost shot. In fact, half the time I am unable even to think. . . . I am six stones overweight and pulling my brain and fat together isn't easy.**
>
> (*Independent* 9.2.94)

The loss of social contacts and being forced into a kind of semi-isolation is also a major problem for people who lose their jobs. Unemployment can also adversely affect people's health and wellbeing and plunge them into a state of grinding poverty.

Official classifications of unemployment have shown a great deal of flexibility over the past 20 years. For example at least 14 changes were made to official definitions of unemployment in the period 1982–86. This had the effect of removing about 400,000 people from the total (Whiteside 1991; Gallie 1989; Gallie and Paugam 2000). Thus, the 2008 'official' figure for unemployment of 1.64 million, or 5.3 per cent of the workforce (National Statistics Online, www.statistics.gov.uk), has to be understood as just one of a variety of ways in which to measure unemployment in the UK (Centre for Economic and Social Inclusion, www.cesi.org.uk).

In addition, unemployment levels display great regional disparities. This should come as no surprise, given the variable nature of economic restructuring and processes of de-industrialization discussed above. So, in 2007 Scotland had 5.1 per cent of its workforce unemployed, while the figure for the south-east of England was 3.8 per cent and for the north-east 6.8 per cent (National Statistics Online). These figures, which are still for large geographical areas and large populations, tend to average out the effect of unemployment on particular localities in the UK where almost no one works in full-time employment.

Unemployment also impacts differently upon different groups within society. The unemployment rate in relation to ethnicity in the UK shows a wide variation, being 4.7 per cent for white people, 13.8 per cent for black people and 22.9 per cent for Bangladeshi people. Again, this draws our attention to the way in which discrimination can be structured into the workings of the labour market and employers' strategies. Young people are often particularly affected by unemployment, as the 2003 unemployment rate of 14.6 per cent for the 16–24 years age group indicates; nearly three times greater than the overall rate of 5 per cent.

We now face the very real prospect that, for the first time in the post-war period, a large number of people may never be in full-time and permanent employment. Thus, whereas in the not so distant past 'full employment' was seen to be a key objective of all British governments, now the very notion seems to have a rather utopian ring to it. Unemployment is in fact seen by many to be an unfortunate but unavoidable problem within modern societies. This, however, ignores the way that 'employment' and 'unemployment' are social and political categories, not timeless or immutable, and 'work' itself can be reorganized economically and reinterpreted socially and culturally in such a way that 'full employment' need not be such an unattainable goal (Dickens *et al.* 2004).

Stop and think

- How might employment be reorganized in order to reduce levels of unemployment?
- What would be the likely obstacles that would prevent such a reorganization taking place?

Trade unions

Millions of workers around the world are members of trade unions. Although the structure, size and power of unions show considerable variation, all unions attempt to provide workers with a degree of collective strength and to defend the interests of their members in relation to management and capital. In the UK, which has the world's oldest unions, they are a familiar part of the social, economic and political landscape. Unions and their activities are a constant source of copy for newspapers and the centre of endless discussions about their appropriate position and place within public life. Unions themselves often appear not to have a clearly defined role: are they defensive and sectional organizations concerned only to look after their members' pay and conditions, or can they have a more 'progressive' role in terms of being vehicles implementing partial, or even revolutionary, social change? This is something of an ongoing dilemma for many unions that has never been satisfactorily resolved.

Unions and social and economic change

As McIlroy (1995: 1–2) says, 'Trade unions are inseparable from the society in which they are created and recreated'. Unions have been affected by, and have had to adapt to, contemporary changes to employment such as those outlined above. Membership of trade unions in the UK grew steadily through the post-war period, and union density (the proportion of employed

World in focus

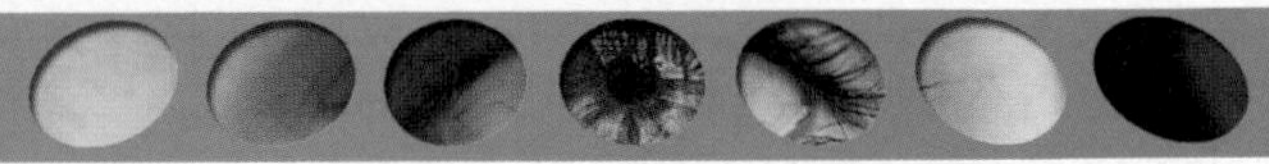

Work and employment in the developing world

Unemployment in the developing world is frequently viewed as a symptom of unequal and inadequate development, but attempting to identify the 'unemployed' remains a highly controversial task . . . difficulties arise as attempts to measure categories of employment are generally constructed around Western concepts of work (Pahl 1988). Western theories of urban economic structure and labour force segregation have failed to adequately analyse and explain the structure of the urban labour force in developing countries. One issue which is widely agreed upon is the pressing need to work. A subject which is less clear centres on the definition of the boundary between work and employment in the developing world context.

Work undertaken outside the realms of officially accounted employment is prevalent in the urban economies of developing countries. Much productive work is undertaken outside the confines of the formal waged economy; indeed many household productive and reproductive activities are unremunerated. Informal activity, self-employment, casual work and home-based production have provided alternatives to formal employment for decades. It is important therefore to expand Western notions of work to include a wider range of social and economic activities which, due to their unregulated nature, often have most salience in urban areas.

There is also the problem of definition (Gilbert and Gugler 1992). The ILO defines the unemployed as those who are without work but who are actively seeking it. It is widely argued that the true unemployed are not amongst the urban poor. As far back as 1968 Myrdal argued that unemployment is a luxury few can afford in such circumstances . . . due to the absence of social security only educated professionals, such as white-collar workers or public sector executives, or possibly new entrants to the labour market who are able to rely on family support, contribute to the true 'unemployed' in most developing countries. As a result, Udall and Sinclair (1982) argue that the unemployment figures published by official agencies are meaningless and inappropriate, for they fail to provide a clear picture of the true structure of employment . . . Due to the inadequacy of the term 'unemployment', it is now widely recognized by researchers and academics that underemployment provides a better indication of the employment problem.

(Adapted from Potter and Lloyd-Evans 1998)

Questions

1. Consider the ways in which the categories of work, employment and unemployment are socially constructed and specific to particular societies.
2. In what way does considering the above passage make us question the relation and boundary between employment and unemployment?
3. Consider the relevance of using the term 'underemployment' within the context of Western economies.

workforce in unions) peaked in 1979 at 55 per cent – a total of just over 13 million people. In 2006, 6.5 million people were members of unions, and union density has now dropped to just over 28 per cent. Such a figure means that the UK is still one of the most highly unionized countries in the world (in the USA, union density is around 13 per cent), although it is a long way behind Scandinavian countries such as Sweden, which has a union density of 75 per cent. Much of the fall in union membership can be accounted for by the impact of de-industrialization and the collapse of the manufacturing sector. Some of the UK's once-largest and most powerful unions have fallen away drastically. The most dramatic example is that of the miners' union, the NUM, whose quarter-of-a-million membership in 1979 crumbled in 1998 to a mere 8500 – a figure dwarfed by membership of the actors' union Equity, which is estimated to be around 36,000. It is worth bearing in mind, however, that in 2006 around 47 per cent of UK workers were employed in a workplace where there was union representation of some kind.

Generally the industries that have contracted – such as mining, engineering and shipbuilding – were those that had high union densities. A number of unions have maintained their membership at consistent levels – UNISON has a membership of 1.3 million. However, the restructuring of the economy and occupational changes have to a large extent altered the face of British trade unionism. The gender landscape of unions has changed as women are now as likely as men to be members of a trade union, with union density for both at about 29 per cent (www.berr.gov.uk). This challenges long-held notions that women are not 'interested' in union matters (Cockburn 1983). Women are still, however, underrepresented at the top levels of union organization.

Unions themselves are having to adapt to the new labour market environment, given that the classic location for union organization was within the masculine work environments of the manufacturing industries. The post-war stability of the 'traditional' industries allowed for the development of powerful occupational cultures that provided the necessary social organization and networks and cultural resources that are crucial for the development of grass-roots unionism. This form of unionism became the template for union organization in the UK, and unions are now faced with the difficult task of reorganizing and rethinking their practices in order to meet the demands of a post-industrial society, a fragmented workforce, the decline of full-time male employment, disparate working environments and the dispersal of plants away from the traditional urban base of British trade unionism. Lane (in Allen and Massey 1988) notes that a typical large company now has around 100 plants dispersed around a number of 'greenfield' sites; the largest plant could employ up to 1000 workers and the smallest around 15. Many 'service' sector jobs (retailing, catering, tourism), all of which having been growing in employment terms, have proved difficult to unionize. Such 'industries' are characterized by high labour turnover, part-time work and short-term contracts, and a lack of a 'union culture'. The Union of Shop, Distributive and Allied Workers (USDAW) has a membership of which 40 per cent are part-time, and around 30 per cent leave the union each year. The proportion of full-time employees belonging to a trade union stands at about 32 per cent compared with 21 per cent for those working part-time (www.berr.gov.uk).

Trade union power and ability to organize were severely curtailed through the efforts of the Conservative government of 1979–97, which was fundamentally hostile to unions. Unions in the UK have no direct or 'legitimate' role to play at a national level in terms of exerting an influence on government thinking or economic policy. Throughout the 1980s and 1990s, a range of sweeping legislation – for example, the Employment Acts of 1980, 1982 and 1988 and the Trade Union Act 1984 – were passed with the aim of limiting the effectiveness of unions in defending their members' interests. What constitutes a 'proper' and 'lawful' trade union dispute has been limited, time off from work for union representatives has been reduced, all secondary action is now unlawful, seven days' notice is now required for industrial action, and a host of other attacks (McIlroy 1995) on union power have severely limited their range of operation (Gospel and Wood 2003).

Unions have also had to face the might of giant transnational corporations, which can move production around the globe and set up plants in a number of different countries. Multinational companies can thus undermine national agreements and put immense pressure on unions to meet their demands for accepting no-strike deals, single-union agreements and flexible work practices. If unions do not accept such conditions, then these giant enterprises can simply build their plant somewhere else. Ford did exactly this when it laid down a variety of conditions to unions before commencing building a factory in Dundee in 1987; when the unions involved failed to reach an agreement, Ford built the proposed Dundee plant in Portugal.

Unions, then, face difficult times, but their resolve and importance – at least as defensive organizations – should not be underestimated. There has been very little decline in union organization in workplaces where collective bargaining was already well established, and workplaces with over 200 employees largely continue to keep union recognition and organization (*Socialist Review* March 1995). According to numerous opinion polls and surveys, unions are regarded in an overwhelmingly positive manner. Eight out of ten people see unions as being essential for defending workers' rights, and only a minority of people think that unions have 'too much power' (McIlroy 1995). Thus, despite the formidable challenges to unions, it is clear that they will continue to play a crucial role in millions of people's working lives (Gospel and Wood 2003).

Stop and think

- What do you think are the benefits of a union organization for a workforce?
- How might the developments mentioned above provide major obstacles to effective unionization?

Working at home?

The wide-scale prevalence, in some countries at least, of information technologies, computers and innovations such as the Internet has raised possibilities for people to increasingly 'work at home'. It is worth bearing in mind that homeworking is a very old form of labour, although it seems that it is growing on a global scale (Burchielli *et al.* 2008). It can be useful to make a distinction between those who 'work from home' and homeworkers. The former category are often well-paid professionals who can take advantage of information and communication technologies such as the Internet, email and often a spare room at home to set up an 'office' in order to organize work and home (in particular, child care) commitments into a satisfactory work–life balance. Homeworkers, on the other hand, are generally a category of workers who carry out their paid employment at home. This may or may not involve new technologies, but it often involves work that is poorly paid and takes place in less than ideal conditions (Bradley *et al.* 2000; Edgell 2006). However, according to some researchers, the picture is complex, and they argue that in the UK the person who does all or a significant amount of their employment at home is now on average better qualified and better paid than the rest of the UK workforce. The extent of homeworking is difficult to quantify; according to one source, in 2000:

> **Over 25% of the UK workforce 'sometimes' work at home. But the number of people working 'mainly' at home is 2.5% of the workforce – 681,000 – though that is almost a doubling of the number who did so in 1981 (346,000).**
>
> (Felstead *et al.* 2000)

The bulk (80 per cent) of this work done at home in the UK is non-manual and most involves access to a computer. As Felstead *et al.* (2000) point out, '61.2% of those working at home at least one day per week use a telephone and computer to do so; 49.5% of those who work mainly at home use a computer to do so'. Felstead and colleagues suggest that there is a marked gendered division of labour for those who work mainly at home, as around two-thirds of these workers are women; the situation is almost reversed for those who work at home only partially. It seems to be the case that, despite the continuation of well-established patterns of homework being low-paid and low-skilled, many households are utilizing opportunities offered by information technologies to find a more convenient and, for some, rewarding work–life balance.

The globalization of economic life

The world, it is often said, is getting smaller, or, as Harvey (1990) would have it, we are witnessing 'time–space compression'. This certainly seems to be the case in respect of the movement of capital around the world. Capitalism has long operated at an international level (Hirst and Thompson 1996). However, capitalist economies since the late 1960s have become increasingly integrated, encouraging talk of a 'global capitalist system' or a 'world economy' (Frobel *et al.* 1980). Production, trade and finance, with the aid of new information technologies, satellite and telecommunication systems, can now be organized at a global level rather than at a national or even international level. The most obvious protagonists of this capitalist world system are the multinationals or, more recently, transnational corporations (TNCs). TNCs are the linchpins of what Frobel *et al.* (1980) call the 'new international division of labour'. Car firms such as Ford in the early 1970s began the production of their 'world car', the Fiesta, and reorganized production around the globe. Carburettors and distributors were built in Belfast, axles were built in Bordeaux and various bits of assembly were put together in plants in the UK, Spain and Germany. The world market allows TNCs such as Ford to distribute and sell products to all corners of the globe. Although it is important to note that most of the investment by TNCs is within the 'industrialized' nations, production can also be relocated in order to tap into cheap, and generally non-unionized, pools of labour in many developing countries. The breakdown of production processes means that each operation can be done with minimal levels of skill, and so labour need have few industrial skills.

Such a relocation and restructuring of capital has huge implications for work and employment in the 'old' centres of production and industry such as the UK. Increased competition from around the world and the movement of sites of production can accelerate the process of de-industrialization and decimate regional economies; we have only to think of the catastrophic impact of global competition in the shipbuilding industry on regions in the UK such as Tyneside and Clydeside.

It is also increasingly difficult to think of these vast organizations as actually 'belonging' to a particular country in any meaningful way. One of the flagships of UK multinational capital, ICI, employs more people in its plants outside the UK than it does within the UK. Thus, to what extent we can still apply a 'British' tag to a company such as ICI, or BP for that matter, has to be cast in some doubt; indeed, firms such as ICI and BP *prefer* to be known as 'international companies'.

Some sectors of the UK economy, and thousands of jobs, are very dependent on and integrated into the global economic system. This is most obviously the case with the vast array of financial institutions and companies that comprise the City of London. London is one of the big-three financial nerve centres of the global economy; New York and Tokyo are the others. London has more than 30 per cent of the world's foreign exchange business (nearly twice that of New York) and has more US banks than New York and more German banks than Frankfurt; 375 of the biggest 500 companies have offices in London (*Europe: Magazine of the European Union* 1999, www.eurunion.org/magazine/home.htm).

Although not all parts of the UK economy are as globalized as the City of London, hundreds of thousands of jobs in the UK are linked closely to a global economy, a situation that brings both benefits and costs. The movement of UK call centres to Asia (Figure 12.4) has highlighted the precarious nature of this connection. Over 10,000 jobs have been relocated to Asia (out of a UK total of 800,000), and this figure is expected to grow dramatically; in the USA, half

Figure 12.4 A call-centre operative in India
© Sherwin Crasto/Reuters/Corbis

a million jobs in the financial sector have been 'offshored', mainly to the Philippines and India (*Sunday Herald* 30.11.03). The major reason given for this is cheaper costs due to the ability to pay lower wages in these countries. Some commentators note that such developments can put increased pressures on workers to be more flexible in relation to working practices, in ways discussed above. As Castells notes:

> **Induced by globalization . . . and facilitated by information/communication technologies, the most important transformation in employment patterns concerns the development of flexible work, as the predominant form of working arrangement.**
>
> (quoted in Edgell 2006: 190)

TNCs are huge; financially relatively few countries are bigger than the largest TNCs. The revenues of the top 500 global companies (cf. *Fortune* Global 500, www.money.cnn.com/magazines/fortune/fortune500) amount to over $11 trillion (11 thousand billion), their assets exceed $32 trillion and they employ around 35 million people (Sklair 2001). By way of comparison, the combined GDP of New Zealand, Greece, Egypt, South Africa, Czech Republic and Israel was $540 billion in 1998 (Held 2000). Indeed, of the largest 100 'economies' in the world, 51 are global corporations and only 49 are countries. The immense economic power of TNCs means that they set the tone in terms of pricing, market innovation and leadership, and control of subsidiaries. Given the gargantuan size, huge resources, and economic, political and financial power of TNCs, it is debatable as to what extent we can still meaningfully talk about 'national economies'. The managements of TNCs are not noted for paying too much attention to the dictates of 'national economic policy' – if nations do not want them to locate production on their territory (very unlikely, given that most national governments actively compete with each other to offer the most attractive packages for TNCs to locate production within their borders), then they can move to another, more amenable, part of the globe. Other supranational organizations such as the World Bank, the European Community (EC) and the International Monetary Fund (IMF) have all had the effect of eroding the sovereignty of nation-states and limiting their ability to withstand worldwide competitive pressures and offer protection to national industries and jobs.

However, it is important not to exaggerate the ability, or desire, of huge companies to move freely around the globe. TNCs originate in a relatively limited number of wealthy countries (in particular, Japan and the USA) and, although they account for about 25 per cent of world production, the vast bulk of their global trade, jobs and profits are shared between these already rich and powerful nations (Cohen and Kennedy 2000; Hirst and Thompson 1996). But there is little doubt that increasing processes of globalization will continue apace and the capitalist global economy looks set to wield its immense power over us for some time to come (Bauman 2000).

Summary

- Defining precisely what constitutes 'work' is problematic. 'Wage-labour', or 'paid employment', is often equated with work generally, but much unpaid and largely unacknowledged work gets done in contemporary societies.
- The classical and most influential discussion of wage-labour within capitalism is that of Karl Marx.
- Braverman (1974) utilized and extended Marx's analysis of the labour process and applied it to work in the twentieth century. Braverman thought that work had undergone a process of 'deskilling' and that the main catalyst for this was attempts by management to exert total control over the workforce. Taylorism exemplified this managerial strategy.
- Braverman has been strongly criticized on a number of points. The widespread influence of Taylorism has been questioned. Braverman's understanding of 'skill' was seen to be lacking, and he failed to take adequate account of workers' resistance.
- A wide range of managerial strategies have been developed to control and maximize the productivity of a workforce. This has included giving the workforce some 'responsible autonomy', 'humanizing' work tasks and the reorganization of work through team working and 'Japanese' methods.
- Industrialization was seen by many to be an inevitable tendency for most countries of the world; however, this was put in doubt with the emergence of 'de-industrialization' and the decline of employment in a number of sectors of industry.
- Writers such as Bell (1973) foresaw the emergence of a 'post-industrial' society based on an economy where employment in the 'service sector' was dominant. Such ideas have been criticized as being overly optimistic, inaccurate and based on an erroneous interpretation of changes taking place within many capitalist societies.
- 'Fordism' is a term used to describe a socioeconomic system based on mass production and mass consumption, which was seen to be dominant during the post-war period. It is argued that Fordism reached its limits in the early 1970s and was increasingly replaced with more flexible methods of production and work organization. The term 'post-Fordism' is often used to describe these changes. The distinction between Fordism and post-Fordism has been criticized for being too polarized and based on an empirically weak foundation.

Summary *continued*

- Labour markets are where employers and prospective employees can 'meet' and/or gather information about each other. Labour markets can often display similar patterns of racism and sexism that are present within wider society, to the extent that we can talk of dual or segmented labour markets.
- Unemployment is a feature of many modern societies and is generally experienced as a profoundly depressing and miserable state for most individuals. Rates of unemployment vary for different regions and for different groups of people.
- Trade unions are a crucial part of our society. Unions have had to adapt to a changing socioeconomic environment brought about by de-industrialization, falling membership, hostile legislation and transnational corporations, but they still provide an important function for millions of workers.
- Capitalism has to be understood as a world phenomenon. Production, trade and finance, with the aid of new information technologies, satellite and telecommunication systems, can now be organized at a global level, and massive transnational corporations wield enormous power and influence around the world.

Links

The section on Marx and the labour process within capitalism can be related to the discussion on Marx's analysis of capitalism in Chapter 2 (pp. 54–63).

The discussion of the globalization of economic life is developed in Chapter 9 (pp. 382–383).

Further reading

Braverman, H. (1974) *Labour and Monopoly Capital: The Degradation of Work within the Twentieth Century*, New York: Monthly Review Press.
Still regarded as a classic Marxist analysis of work in the twentieth century.

Bradley, H., Erickson, M., Stephenson, C. and Williams, S. (2000) *Myths at Work*, Cambridge: Polity Press.

Edgell, S. (2006) *The Sociology of Work: Continuity and Change in Paid and Unpaid Work*, London: Sage.
A very good further exploration of many of the issues discussed in this chapter.

Gospel, H. and Wood, S. (eds) (2003) *Representing Workers: Trade Union Recognition and Membership in Britain*, London: Routledge.
A comprehensive look at contemporary trade unions in the UK.

Grint, K. (2005) *The Sociology of Work*, 3rd edn, Cambridge: Polity Press.
Concise introduction to the major issues in the sociology of work.

Kumar, K. (1995) *From Post-Industrial to Post-Modern Society*, Oxford: Blackwell.
Balanced discussion of post-Fordism, the 'information society' and postmodernism.

Noon, M. and Blyton, P. (2007) *The Realities of Work: Experiencing Work and Employment in Contemporary Society*, 3rd edn, Houndmills: Palgrave Macmillan.
An accessible account of key contemporary issues in work.

Strangleman, T. and Warren, T. (2008), *Work and Society: Sociological Approaches, Themes and Methods*, London: Routledge.
An excellent and innovative introduction to the sociology of work.

Thompson, P. and McHugh, D. (2003) *Work Organisations,* 3rd edn, London: Palgrave Macmillan. The third editon of a text that continues to provide a clear guide to major changes taking place in work organizations.

Webster, F. (2002) *Theories of the Information Society,* 2nd edn, London: Routledge.
Contains critical discussions of post-industrialism and post-Fordism and the role of information technologies within work.

Websites

www.globalisationguide.org/09.html

Globalisation Guide
A useful source of information on various issues to do with globalization. Also has numerous helpful links to other sites.

www.statistics.gov.uk

National Statistics Online
An invaluable and huge source of information on many aspects of UK employment, unemployment, the labour market and much more.

www.tuc.org.uk

Trades Union Congress
A good source of information on trade unions.

Activities

Activity 1

'The corrosion of character?'

The title of this activity and the extract below are taken from Richard Sennet's influential book that looks at the impact of changing forms of work on individuals and their sense of self.

> Th[e] emphasis on flexibility is changing the very meaning of work, and so the words we use for it. 'Career', for instance, in its English origins meant a road for carriages, and as eventually applied to labor meant a lifelong channel for one's economic pursuits. Flexible capitalism has blocked the straight roadway of career, diverting employees suddenly from one kind of work into another. The word 'job' in English of the fourteenth century meant a lump or piece of something which could be carted around. Flexibility today brings back this arcane sense of the job, as people do lumps of labor, pieces of work, over the course of a lifetime.
>
> It is quite natural that flexibility should arouse anxiety: people do not know what risks will pay off, what paths to pursue. To take the curse off the phrase 'capitalist system' there developed in the past many circumlocutions, such as the 'free enterprise' or 'private enterprise' system. Flexibility is used to day as another way to lift the curse of oppression from capitalism. In attacking rigid bureaucracy and emphasizing risk, it is claimed, flexibility gives people more freedom to shape their lives. In fact, the new order substitutes new controls rather than simply abolishing the rules of the past . . .
>
> How do we decide what is of lasting value in ourselves in a society which is impatient, which focuses on the immediate moment? How can long-term goals be pursued in an economy devoted to the short-term? How can mutual loyalties and commitments be sustained in institutions which are constantly breaking apart or continually being redesigned? These are the questions about character posed by the new, flexible capitalism.
>
> (Sennet 1998: 9–10)

Questions

1. Do you agree with Sennet's generally negative portrayal of the consequences of more flexible work forms?
2. Do you think that the demise of the 'job for life' will have negative consequence for communities and society more generally?
3. Do you think that Sennet exaggerates the importance of paid employment in people's lives and their sense of identity and who they are? If so, what else can be a key source of identity for individuals?

Activity 2

Working in a nursing home

This article is drawn from ethnographic doctoral research undertaken in two homes for older people in south-west England.

The bedroom job

The bedroom was the main site of work for the auxiliaries and most of the patients' time in the home was spent there. Morning work was virtually all bedroom work and was officially begun by the auxiliaries entering patients' rooms on the tea round. This was a point of the day at which cups of tea were served and bottoms were washed. It was customary to present the patients to the new shift intact, clean and quiet in their rooms for 8am. Presenting well-ordered bodies seemed to symbolise the job properly done. The next shift spent all the morning in the bedrooms, washing and dressing patients. The workers spent most of the morning getting patients ready, then taking them down to the lounge. By lunch time they were all down, but straight after lunch it was time to put them back to bed for a nap and later get them up again.

In the evenings work again revolved around the bedrooms as staff got patients ready for bed. By the time the night shift came on all patients were in bed. In this way the auxiliaries' work could be said to revolve around the bedroom. And it was in this private world that they were able to decide the rules and had total hidden control.

Making jokes at the patient's expense was seen as 'having some fun with the patients' (Vera) and workers argued it involved patients in some way with the work. For example, patients who could not walk properly were told to 'race' down the corridor, and jokes would be made about Nigel Mansell etc. Patients who were crying in pain would be told to buck up and smile. Mimicry was also common, with staff copying the words of confused residents. Most patients either could not hear, see or understand jokes that the workers made at their expense, while others became distressed at them. But 'joking' appeared to help auxiliaries get through the work; it broke up the stress and gave them some sort of control.

The hard culture

Auxiliary work in nursing homes is hard work: low paid, low status, dirty, physically back-breaking and tiring. However, far from complaining about the conditions of their work the nursing auxiliaries appeared to have elevated the notion of personal hardship with their subculture. Personal hardship and hard behaviour towards patients seemed central to auxiliaries' understanding of what they were supposed to do. They spoke about others, such as residential home workers, and trained staff, as too 'soft'. A strong emphasis was placed upon coping and getting on with the work, even avoiding the use of hoists and aides, despite a frequency of serious back problems. Auxiliaries were not only trying to make sense of their work, given the poor working conditions, but also to make it easier and give themselves a clear role and place in relation to trained nursing workers. In response to this the auxiliaries at Cedar Court became the 'hardest' workers.

(Lee-Treweek 1994)

Questions

1. The jobs discussed in the above extract are ones that are generally considered to be part of the 'service sector'. Do you think that they fit well into Bell's vision of 'service employment' in a 'post-industrial' society?

2. Can we draw any parallels between the work discussed by Lee-Treweek and work that takes place in other environments such as industry? You should have another look at the case study 'Factory time' on p. 488.

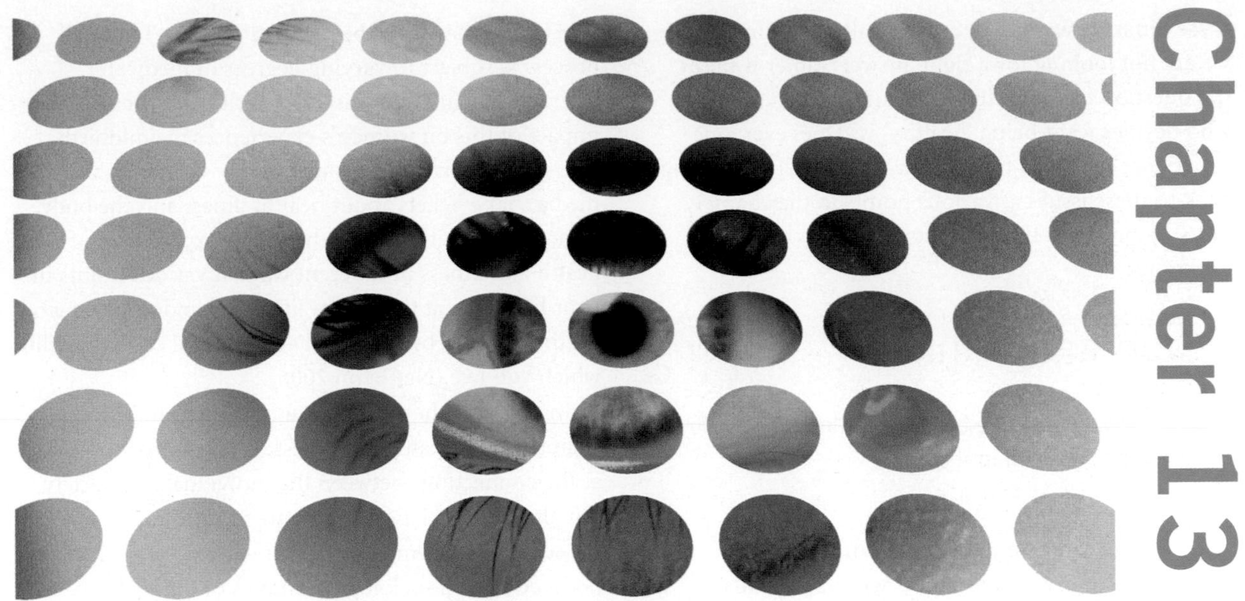

Chapter 13

Health, illness and the body

To be human is to be concerned with health and illness. (Bury 1997:1)

Key issues

- How can health, illness and the body be understood as social as well as biological phenomena?
- How is medical knowledge socially constructed?
- How are lay ideas about health and illness developed?
- How are health and illness experienced, and how does your position in society shape these experiences?
- How do the sectors of health care – professional, popular and folk – relate to each other?

Introduction

Health and illness are part of our everyday lives. You have probably had contact with health professionals, for example doctors, dentists and nurses, regularly or at certain stages in your life. You will have taken decisions about your health, for example in deciding whether to take home treatments such as headache tablets, choosing to diet or exercise or seeking treatment from an alternative practitioner. Even when health is not the focus, what you do in your everyday life has an impact on how you feel. There is often discussion in the media about the 'choices' we make in our behaviour, our actions, and the impact these have on our health. For example, poor eating habits are blamed for the rise in obesity in many Western societies.

Sociology raises many questions about health and illness and gives us the tools to understand an area of our lives that many of us take for granted. Health and, for some people, illness are so much a routine part of our daily lives that it may seem strange to question what we mean by health and illness or how we can define health and illness. Some people may answer that being healthy is not being ill. For another person, being healthy may entail feeling good, both physically and mentally. Yet another definition may relate to what we can do – we are healthy if we can carry out our normal daily activities and we are ill if we cannot. In presenting these different ways of defining health and illness, we are not looking for a right answer; rather it raises the question of where these definitions come from – who decides what being 'healthy' is? Does everyone experience health in the same way? We will be coming back to these issues at various points in the chapter, but stop now and think about your views on these questions.

Stop and think

- How do you define health and illness? Why do you define them in that way?

Sociology can help us to place our views and experiences of health and illness within particular contexts. Health and illness are often considered to be very individual concerns – you become ill because of a germ, virus or hereditary condition that makes your body 'fail'; and you stay healthy because you make 'good' decisions about your lifestyle and about how your treat your body. Sociology looks at where these ideas come from and whether they tell the whole picture. Throughout the life course, social processes affect your health. The social class of your parents will affect your chances of being born healthy. The birth process is subject to varying degrees of medical intervention, and feminists have critiqued the negative impact of this on women's experiences in childbirth. The society you live in, your family, your peers and the media shape beliefs about health, illness and the body. Your self-identity may be shaped by experiences of health and illness in different ways at various points in your life. Even at the end of life, your understanding of death is shaped by the social and cultural context within which you live (Nettleton 2006).

In applying the sociological imagination (see Chapter 1) to health and illness, it is essential to look at the connections between the individual and society but also at the relationship between the biological and the social. This is most apparent when considering the body. Although sociological studies of the body go beyond a focus on health and illness, it is difficult to separate the two areas. When we think about health and illness, we are automatically also thinking about the body. When we are defining health and illness, we are also defining healthy and ill bodies, and at times we are questioning the relationship between the body and the mind. When we are experiencing health and illness, we are also experiencing healthy or ill bodies. When doctors are treating patients, their treatments are based

A closer look

Body awareness

Just think for a moment about your own body. Where do you start? With your appearance (the spot that has materialised from nowhere, the bad hair day)? With its shape and size (the diet you keep meaning to go on)? With its aches and pains and reminders of daily physical struggles? How do you feel about your own body? Are there parts you would like to change? Do you feel the need to keep in shape, or try to be healthy? Are you more aware of your body at some times rather than others, such as when you trip over your feet in a crowded room, belch unexpectedly or break wind in company? How do you feel when you become aware of your body in these circumstances? Now think about the bodies of other people. What seems most obvious to you is probably the appearance of others – how people look – but think harder and soon you will find that the bodies of other people become conspicuous in other ways – smell, size and shape, personal habits. Many of us expect people to smell 'fresh' or be devoid of odour, to refrain from touching us until we feel we know them sufficiently well and to demonstrate 'good manners' in public places. When you stop to think about it, it isn't hard to become conscious of the human body, yet in much of our daily life we tend to take our own bodies and the bodies of others for granted.

(Howson 2004: 1)

Table 13.1 Key sociological theories in relation to health and illness

Theory	Key points	Theorists
Functionalism	Health is essential to the functioning of society, and illness is dysfunctional; the relationship between patients and the medical profession is based on consensus and shared values	T. Parsons
Marxism	Marxists argue that health is related to the capitalist economic system and the medical system reinforces existing inequalities	V. Navarro
Conflict	The medical profession acts, as a professional group, to protect its own position, and this can lead to conflict with other health-care providers and with patients	E. Friedson
Interpretative	The focus is on interactions, meanings and experiences within health and illness	M. Bury
Social constructionist	The construction of medical knowledge as 'fact' is questioned; knowledge is understood as developing within particular social contexts and as the product of social relations and of discourses.	M. Foucault

on particular beliefs about how the body works. Therefore, health and illness are 'embodied' and yet we are often very unaware of our bodies. For example, if you have a bad cold, you may feel shivery or have a sore head and be very conscious of how your body feels; but, when you recover, your awareness of your body may not be as apparent.

This chapter provides you with opportunities to consider your experiences in relation to health and illness; to question your assumptions; and to reflect on the bodily aspects of health and illness. The chapter is divided into four sections. In the first section, we explore definitions of health, illness and the body, and the social contexts in which these ideas arise and develop. In the second section, we consider the different arenas in which health is experienced – professional, popular and folk – focusing on the ways in which beliefs about health and illness are contested within and between the three sectors. In the third section, we look at the experience of illness in relation to chronic illness, dying and health inequalities. In the final section, we turn our attention to recent technological developments and their impact on our understanding of health, illness and the body. Throughout the chapter we consider a range of theoretical approaches (see Chapter 2 for more detail on the theories). A summary is provided in Table 13.1.

The social construction of medical knowledge

By reflecting on how we define health and illness and how they are embodied, we are also beginning to question how beliefs about health and illness are formed. Sociologists question the idea that the beliefs or knowledge that we have about health, illness and the body are 'facts'. Rather, they are interested in exploring the contexts within which ideas emerge and develop. What is the most common understanding of health, illness and the body in our society, and where did those ideas come from?

The biomedical model

The dominant set of ideas for understanding health, illness and the body in Western societies is often called the biomedical model. It is so much a part of our lives that we have come to think of it not as *a* way of thinking about health, illness and the body, but as *the* way. Mishler (1981) refers to the features of the biomedical model as 'silent assumptions'.

Features of the biomedical model

- *Mind/body dualism* – The mind and the body can be treated separately.
- *Mechanical metaphor* – The body is likened to a machine that, when ill, breaks down. Doctors then take on the role of engineer to repair the machine. Scientist and writer Buckminster Fuller described the human body as

> **a self balancing, 27 jointed adapter-base biped, an electrochemical reduction plant, integral with the segregated stowages of special energy extracts in storage batteries, for subsequent actuation of thousands of hydraulic and pneumatic pumps with motors attached: 62,000 miles of capillaries, millions of warning signals, railroad and**

> **conveyor systems; crushers and cranes . . . and a universally distributed telephone system needing no service for 70 years if well managed; the whole extraordinary complex mechanism guided with exquisite precision from a turret in which are located telescopic and microscopic self-registering and recording range-finders, a spectroscope, et cetera.**
>
> (cited in Osherson and Amara Singham 1981)

- *The role of technology* – There is an emphasis on technology in defining and treating illness at the expense of the experience of the patient.
- *Biological focus* – There is a search for a specific identifiable cause for disease, for example a virus. This is known as the 'doctrine of specific aetiology'.
- *Scientific neutrality of medicine* – Medicine is presented as being objective and neutral, which in turn enhances its claims to discovering the 'truth' about the body, health and illness.

We will come back to the specific aspects of the biomedical model at various points in this chapter. Here, we concentrate on where these ideas come from and to what extent we can see them as the truth about health and illness or simply as one model for understanding these issues. It is easy to consider the dominant way of thinking about health, illness and the body in our society – the biomedical model – as 'right' because it works. Think of the advances that medicine has made in the eradication, cure or management of many diseases. Indeed, medical science is characterized by the belief that there is a continual progression towards new treatments and new cures for illness. Sociologists challenge these assumptions and view medical knowledge as socially constructed.

> **Medical knowledge is regarded not as an incremental progression towards a more refined and better knowledge, but as a series of relative constructions which are dependent upon the socio-historical settings in which they occur and are constantly renegotiated.**
>
> (Lupton 1994: 11)

So, the social constructionist approach (see Chapter 2) does not take medical knowledge as given, or as separate from society. How it is formed and by whom are considered to be reflections of wider social relations within any particular time and place (Wright and Treacher 1982). There are three dimensions to the social constructionist approach to understanding medical knowledge, which we will consider in detail below:

- Sociologists address the question of what is considered to be 'reality' in discussing health, illness and the body.
- Medical knowledge is understood as arising within particular social contexts.
- Medical knowledge cannot be isolated from the social relations within which it exists.

Problematizing 'reality'

Perhaps the most 'real' aspect of health and illness is the body itself. Within the biomedical model, the body is a machine to be analysed, understood and fixed when broken. However, sociologists would argue that the body is not simply a biological object. Rather, it is a 'simultaneously social and biological phenomenon' that changes through our life, shaped by social factors and experienced through particular social relations (Shilling 1993: 199). While the body is a physical thing, made of flesh and bones, these physical elements are constantly changing, and this process of change is one that is shaped by wider society. For example, boys and girls are expected to demonstrate different bodily behaviour.

Stop and think

> Think about the way you move, for example when walking, sitting and running. Are there differences between women and men in how their bodies move? If so, why do you think there are differences? Do you think this changes with age?

It is not just the idea of the body that is questioned as a fixed biological thing. The biomedical model presents diseases as having specified causes, symptoms and outcomes. Sociologists argue that the categories we use to describe diseases are created in a social context. This is not denying that there may be a biological basis to illness, or that it can involve physical pain. Rather, it is argued that aspects of our life that we may consider to be a straightforward product of nature should also be considered as the products of social activities and not simply biological facts. This can be seen by looking at how a form of behaviour can be categorized as illness/disease. For example, the medical labels 'hyperactivity' and 'attention deficit disorder' are applied to children who behave in ways that would previously have been regarded as 'disruptive' or 'naughty'. Moreover, there is disagreement among the medical profession about what the condition 'hyperactivity' involves, and many different terms are used to label the same set of 'symptoms' (Conrad 2006: 54).

The first aspect of understanding medical knowledge as socially constructed concerns the questioning of what may be considered 'reality', including our understanding of the body and the labelling of illness. This leads us to question how we can understand the development of medical knowledge.

Medical knowledge and social context

The biomedical model presents medical knowledge as formed through objective, neutral, scientific evidence, but this tells us little of the social context within which such knowledge has emerged, who had a stake in the development of these ideas, and how the knowledge has been used. Some sociologists explore medical knowledge as a discourse (ways of talking and thinking that we use to make sense of the world and to communicate with one another). Most influential here is the work of Foucault (1976), who argued that disease and the body are created through medical discourse that defines, organizes and controls the human body. Foucault looked at historical developments in France – though his ideas have been applied more widely to an understanding of the development of Western medical knowledge more generally – in order to understand the contexts within which biomedicine developed.

The biomedical model began to take shape in the eighteenth century and was fully developed by the end of the nineteenth century. If we look at ideas and practices about health, illness and the body before this time, we can see a very different picture. In the sixteenth and seventeenth centuries, healing was carried out by many different groups, and practices ranged from the use of herbs to draining blood through leeching; illness was often viewed as arising from a spiritual cause. The medical profession as we know it today did not exist, and ideas about the body and how illness formed were very different from those adopted by modern medicine. The most popular beliefs were based on the writings of Galen, a Greek physician, who considered the body to be made up of four fluids (*humors*) – phlegm, black bile, yellow bile and blood – which, when unbalanced, led to illness. His ideas were considered to be so important that any new ideas that challenged them were ignored or discredited by the Church and the medical establishment. In Rome in 1600, Giordano Bruno, a philosopher and mystic, was burned at the stake for contradicting Galen's ideas by claiming that blood moves around the body as the planets move around the sun (Woolley 2004: 67).

During the eighteenth and nineteenth centuries, huge economic and social changes began to take place, reflected in and pushed forward by changes in the world of ideas. Can you imagine a world in which science did not have a central place? Our world is influenced heavily by science, which gives us a way of understanding our history, our present lives and our future. It was at this time of change that science and scientific practices began to dominate within intellectual circles. This involved a belief in the objective neutral description of the world and a move away from religious beliefs and explanations. Within medicine this led to a belief in the process of observation and interpretation – the 'clinical gaze'. This provided doctors with a way of thinking and talking about bodies and health and illness (Foucault 1976). It involved viewing the signs and symptoms of disease and tracking the course of disease within the body. Fundamental to this process was the mapping of the body, the description of the body through diagrams and pictures, through the development of what Foucault (1976) called the 'anatomical atlas'. Such images are now commonplace and are familiar to us even though we are not students of anatomy.

It may seem that what developed was a 'better', more 'systematic' way of understanding the working of the body. This period certainly did reveal more detail about the human body, particularly through the increased use of dissection. You can see the far greater internal detail in the modern anatomical picture. However, if we think of the body as more than a biological fact to be observed and described, what else can we say about this process? Social constructionists argue that the body as we know it came into existence only when defined by the anatomical atlas. Although obviously bodies existed before this – people walked around, talked, ate, became ill and died – it is argued that our understanding of the body is formed by *how we learn to look at bodies*. So, at this time, the drawings of the body were not simply showing the body as it was; they also shaped the way doctors viewed and understood the body: 'What the student sees is not the atlas as a representation of the body but the body as a representation of the atlas' (Armstrong 1983: 2). From Foucault's perspective, the discourses (reflected, in this case, in the pictorial representations of the body) were not simply a reflection of ideas but were actually shaping the development of ideas.

Today a new anatomical atlas sits alongside the traditional model. The image of the body as reflected through its genetic makeup, its DNA, is now a very familiar image but is one that presents the body very differently from the traditional anatomical atlas. It is the same body that is being described or represented at a more micro-level, but the image itself acts to shape our understanding of how bodies work and so also our understanding of health and illness. We will come back to the wider implications of genetic research later in this chapter.

The biomedical model makes sense within the context in which it emerged and continues to develop in many Western societies. The importance of understanding medical knowledge in context can also be seen when we look at differences between cultures. There are many different models for understanding health, illness and the body across the world. Cross-cultural examples may seem bizarre or irrational because they offer very different ways of thinking about health, illness and the body. Nevertheless it is important to be mindful of ethnocentrism – the assumption that our own practices are correct and others misguided. A focus on what is apparently right or wrong does not offer us a full understanding of where knowledge comes from and how it is used. We can also look to contemporary examples from our own society to see very different models of understanding through the practice of complementary and alternative medicines (CAMs). In acupuncture, for example, it is believed that the needles, inserted in specific locations in the body, realign the energy flow within the body. There is a more detailed discussion of CAMs later in this chapter, when we look at the way health and illness are worked out in different sectors of health care.

The social context within which medical knowledge emerges is central to an understanding of the ideas themselves. However, we cannot fully grasp the significance of these contexts without an understanding of the social relations that form them.

Medical knowledge and social relations

Disease categories are not simply a result of scientific research; they also reflect and often hide wider social relations. Medical knowledge is not only a description of, or an attempt to treat, disease and illness; it may also be used to reproduce and reinforce existing social relations. What may be claimed to be the 'truth' is never neutral but always acting in the interests of someone. For example, medical knowledge was used to justify the system of slavery by medicalizing the behaviour of slaves who threatened to undermine the system. New conditions such as 'draeptomania' (running away from a master) were created (cited in Ahmad and Bradby 2007).

From the perspective of historical sociology, the construction of categories of disease and deviance appears to be closely related to the

A closer look

Seeing the body: changing anatomical atlases

From Figures 13.1 to 13.3 we can appreciate how ways of seeing the body change through time. The first drawing is from the fifteenth century, when medicine was influenced by Galen (see above) and there was limited knowledge of the internal body. The second picture is a modern medical anatomy drawing of the kind Foucault (1976) referred to when discussing the anatomical atlas. Far greater knowledge of the internal body was presented in the detailed labelling of all body systems. The final picture may not seem to show a body at all – it shows a double helix, strands of DNA wound together. This image not only represents new scientific knowledge but also shapes the way we think about the body, not simply as the physical parts that we can see and feel but as the genes that make us who we are.

A closer look *continued*

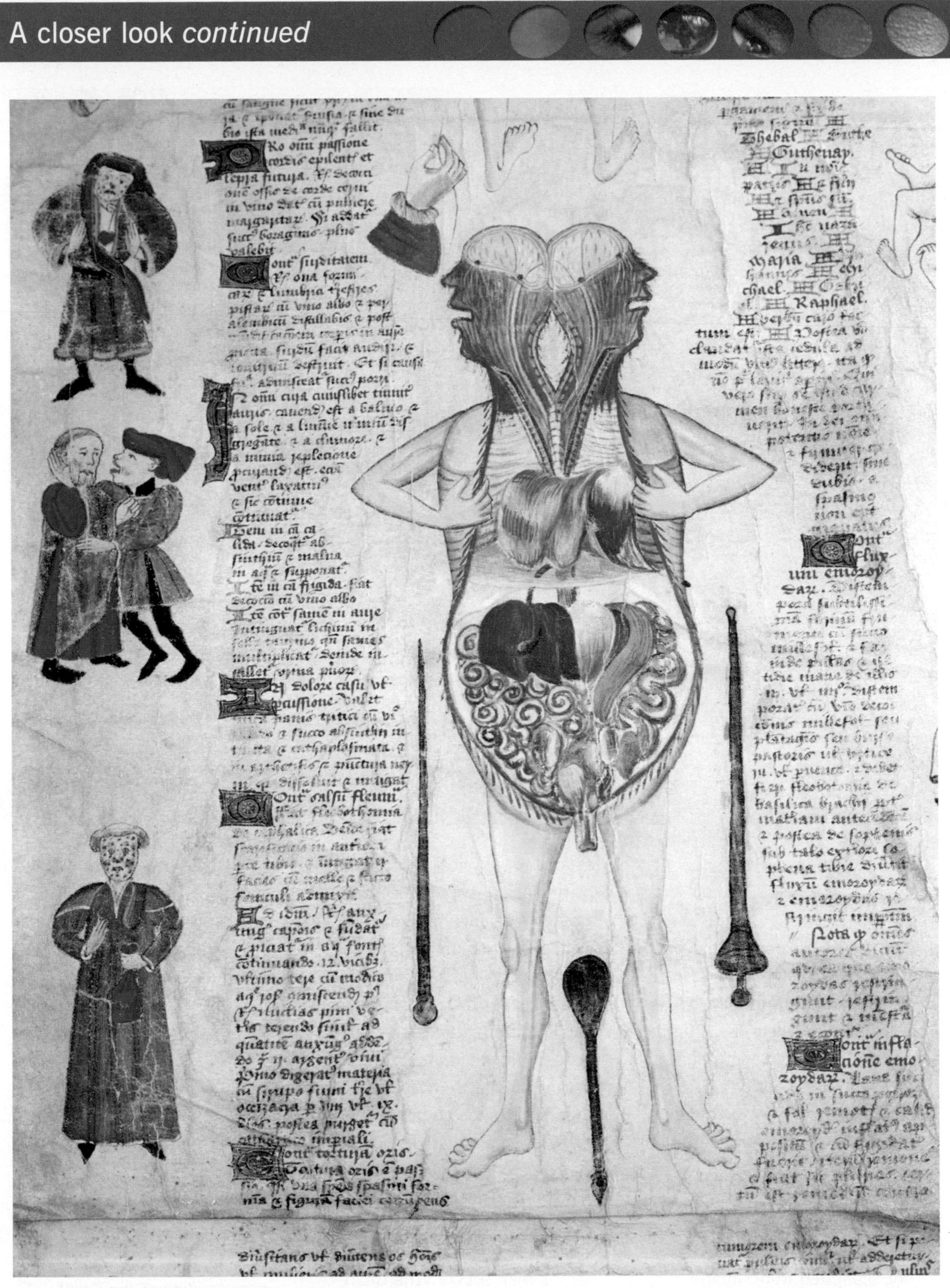

Figure 13.1 The medieval body
© The Bridgeman Art Library/Getty Images

A closer look *continued*

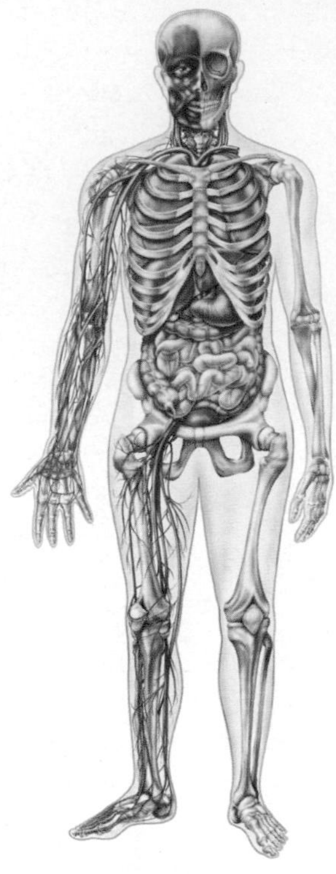

Figure 13.2 The anatomical atlas
Miles Kelly Art Library/Wellcome Images

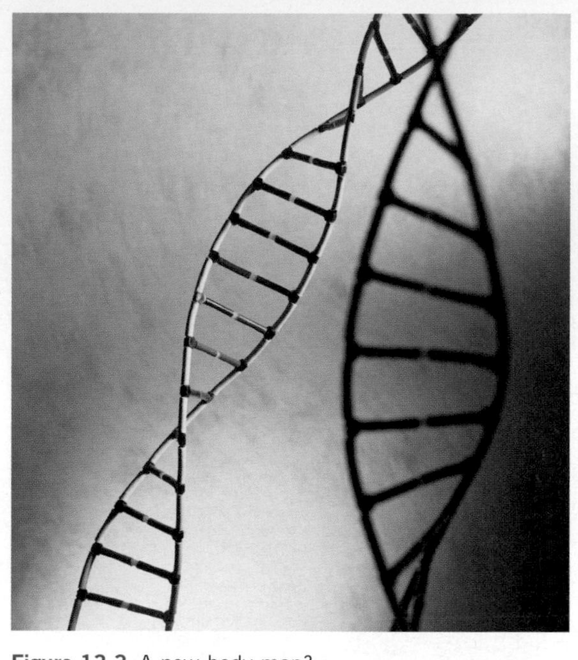

Figure 13.3 A new body map?

World in focus

The Gnau of New Guinea

Anthropologist and doctor Gilbert Lewis studied the Gnau of New Guinea and his work gives us a detailed insight into a way of thinking about health, illness and the body that is very different to our own (Lewis 1986). The word for illness, 'wola' also means 'bad', 'evil', 'wretched', 'harmful', 'forbidden' and 'potentially dangerous'. Illness is therefore not separated from other negative happenings in their lives and is not viewed primarily as a set of physical or psychological symptoms. Illness is often explained in terms of evil spirits or ancestors, magic or sorcery. When a Gnau is sick s/he does not tell anyone they are ill and does not seek help. Instead, the illness is displayed through changed behaviour – shunning company, not eating, speaking in an altered voice – intended to deceive the evil spirits. This change of behaviour is then interpreted by relatives as meaning illness and help is then sought. The Gnau have no specific healers and any adult, though usually a senior man, can assist in treatment. Treatment involves various rituals to rid the sufferer of the evil spirit and would be carried out in the home.

(Stacey 1988)

Questions

1. How does the Gnau understanding of health and illness differ from the biomedical model in terms of defining and treating illness?
2. Do you think there would be any limitations to Gilbert's understanding of the Gnau beliefs and practices?

> **problem of the definition of social membership. Patterns of membership determine access to resources, of which power is the most significant component. We can argue that the social struggle over deviance and disease is a political conflict over the distribution of power.**
>
> (Turner 1987: 84)

In the case of slavery, the distribution of power was very explicit and was clearly reflected in the creation of disease categories. We can look at a somewhat less explicit example of the way in which medical knowledge reflected and reinforced the power of certain groups in society in relation to male and female bodies. Today, we distinguish very clearly between male and female bodies, most notably in terms of differences in reproductive organs. But were such differences always given significance? Lacqueur points out that this was not the case, but interestingly the denial of difference did not arise from ignorance: 'Ideology not accuracy of observation, determined how they were seen and which differences would matter' (Lacqueur 1990: 88). By 1800 writers began to argue that men and women were opposites, both physically and morally. Women's biological role in reproduction was considered to present dangers, leading them to potential animalistic behaviour from which they must be protected.

Common diseases among women at that time reflected such ideas. Hysteria, coming from the Greek for uterus, was common in the nineteenth century, involving emotional outbursts and fainting. Women not fulfilling their biological destiny and associated social roles – widowed or single women – were seen as particularly prone. This was also the case with nymphomania, the inappropriate signs of sexual desire in women.

Neither disease is now recognized in official disease classifications, although emotional behaviour, fainting and sexual desire are still symptoms that women (and men) may experience at some point. We have to understand the construction of these diseases as part of wider gender relations in the nineteenth century. Women, particularly those from the middle class, were confined to roles associated with their biology – child-bearing, child care and domesticity. Medical knowledge was formed as part of these ideas but also served to reinforce them, as it was used to support arguments against women's involvement in higher education and against voting rights.

Stop and think

- Hysteria is no longer a recognized disease, but today premenstrual tension/syndrome (PMT/PMS) has similar symptoms. How has PMT/PMS been used by particular groups (e.g. men, women, employers) to support their arguments?

In this section we have considered medical knowledge to be socially constructed. By doing this, sociologists are not denying the fact that people get ill and may suffer great pain and discomfort. It is important to recognize that our understanding of health and illness is formed through social activity and is shaped by the society within which it exists. This also means that the biomedical model itself is not static or fixed. Key changes in the patterning of illness, public health agendas addressing the social contexts of health and illness, and new developments in medical knowledge, particularly in the field of genetics, have all shaped the form that the biomedical model takes and its social implications. These changes will be considered at various points within this chapter. We now go on to look at the sectors within which health and illness are defined and experienced. In doing so, we consider the ways in which the biomedical model is developing and is being challenged.

Sectors of health care

You might associate health care with hospitals or your general practitioner's (GP) surgery, and perhaps less so with the home and the family. Some people may frequently use alternative practitioners and so link health to these visits. There are a number of places involving a range of different roles within which health and illness are experienced. Kleinman (1980: 50) combines these and describes them as 'a local cultural system composed of three overlapping parts: the popular, the professional, and folk sectors' (Figure 13.4). In this part of the chapter we look at how health and illness are constructed in each of these sectors, at the dynamic nature of each sector and at how the sectors relate:

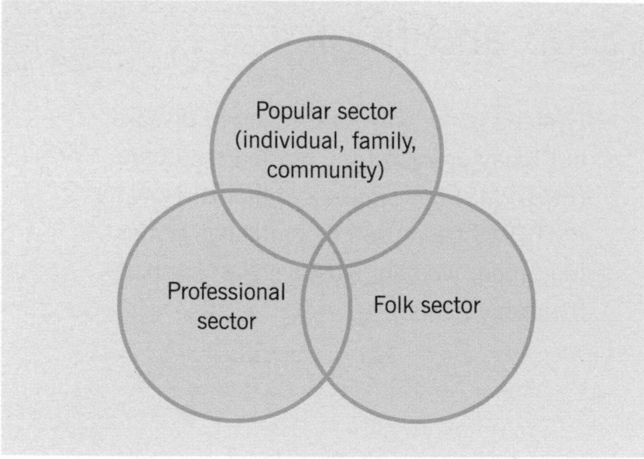

Figure 13.4 Kleinman's model of health-care sectors

- The *popular sector* refers to the lay, non-professional, non-specialist arena.
- The *professional sector* refers to the organized healing professions.
- The *folk sector* is the non-professional, non-bureaucratic, specialist sector.

The professional sector

In the last section we noted the development of the biomedical model in the eighteenth and nineteenth centuries in Europe, as a set of ideas about health and illness. This development was not only about ideas; it was also the dawning of the medical profession as the dominant force in the provision of health care. This was in stark contrast to the earlier pluralistic model, in which a profusion of different healers offered a range of types of treatment. The medical profession was very successful in establishing its position and in challenging others who lay claim to a similar role.

The power of the medical profession was based on the exclusion of certain groups, in particular women (see Chapter 5 for a wider discussion of gender inequality in paid labour). We have to understand the gendered composition of the medical profession in terms of exclusionary strategies: the process by which an occupational group tried to secure its privileged position through the subordination of others (Witz 1992). In the UK, the 1858 Medical (Registration) Act unified medical practitioners (including physicians, surgeons and apothecaries) into an alliance and was a key point in the formation of the modern medical profession. Other healers were not banned, but they were not permitted to register as medical practitioners, and so their work was restricted. Nothing within the act specified that women were excluded. However, by stating that only those with an approved degree in medicine could practise, women were in effect excluded because they were denied access to higher education at that time. By the mid-nineteenth century, medical diagnosis and treatment were carried out exclusively by men, and women were restricted to care of the sick, primarily through their role in nursing.

Sociologists have explored the ways in which the medical profession maintained professional dominance over other health-care providers and maintained control over its work (professional autonomy). The medical profession, in Western societies, has been incredibly successful in both of these aspects. There is a clear hierarchy in the health-care sector, with doctors firmly placed at the top of the hierarchy above nurses and allied health professionals. It has also maintained tight control over its work practices through the protection of the knowledge associated with clinical expertise. In the UK, the medical profession is organized in royal colleges, for example the Royal College of Surgeons, and the General Medical Council (GMC). Questions have been raised in recent years about whether a more independent group should perform these roles. These bodies regulate entrance to, and the work of those within, the profession. Can a profession police itself? In contrast to the UK, in Sweden and Norway the medical profession's organization and control have been tied closely into the state since the mid-nineteenth century (Erichsen 1995).

The hospital

For many of us, hospitals are a recognized aspect of health-care provision or simply a feature of the landscape of our cities and towns. For some people, visits to hospital clinics may be a regular feature of life in treating an enduring illness. For all of us, hospitals are taken for granted – and yet we can look back to a time when hospitals did not exist. Indeed, the development of hospitals in Western Europe during the eighteenth and nineteenth centuries was crucial to the rise of clinical medicine and the medical profession. By concentrating care in central locations, it meant that a large number of patients could be observed, diagnosed and monitored. This allowed doctors to collect evidence to support their ideas about the body. Examining many cases enabled a good mapping of diseases and the ability to develop specialised treatments and routines. By the twentieth century, hospital-based medicine was

World in focus

The professional sector: global comparisons

While the medical profession holds a powerful position in the provision of health care in most Western societies, globally, most care takes place in the popular or folk sectors. The World Health Statistics report (WHO 2008) compares the availability of health personnel between the world's regions (Table 13.2).

Table 13.2 Global distribution of health workforce

Region	Health workforce 2000–2006 (density per 10,000)		
	Physicians	Nurses and midwives	Dentistry personnel
Africa	2	11	< 1
Americas	19	49	11
South East Asia	5	12	< 1
Europe	32	78	5
Eastern Mediterranean	10	15	2
Western Pacific	14	20	2

(Source: WHO 2008)

dominant in most Western European countries. As a result, hospital consultants became the core of the medical elite, and hierarchies within the medical profession were established.

The rise of hospitals was also central to the changing relationship between doctors and patients. Jewson (1976) referred to changing 'medical cosmologies', or ways of interacting that shaped the formation of medical knowledge. He characterized earlier eras as having a 'person-oriented cosmology' within which physicians were dependent on the patronage of their clients and, without many firm ideas about health and illness, were dependent on the subjective opinions of the patient and on an understanding of their health as a whole. As biomedicine developed and hospitals became the centres of health care, so the medical cosmology changed to an 'object-oriented cosmology'; people became cases and the focus was firmly on the disease and not the person. Hospitals became the institutional site within which the biomedical model was practised.

Implications of the medical profession's power

Sociologists hold different views about the role that the medical profession plays in society and so about the implications of their power. Some have focused on the role of the profession in social control, though this can take different forms. Marxists, for example Navarro (1978), argued that doctors engage in a form of social control on behalf of capitalism by keeping the workforce healthy so they can create greater profits and by mystifying people as to the real causes of illness in the world. The profession acts as an agent of social control by translating the collective and political problem of health and illness into an individual one. From this perspective, the power of the medical profession has negative implications because it reinforces existing inequalities. Addressing the issue of social control somewhat differently, functionalists, most notably Talcott Parsons (1951), argued that illness is deviant and so detrimental to the functioning of society. Doctors perform a key role in minimizing this impact and so maintaining the balance and consensus in society.

Strong (1979a,b) used the term 'medical imperialism' to refer to the fact that Western medical systems are characterized by the dominance of the medical profession. Many of the issues he raised relate to a key concern about the impact of medical power – medicalization. Zola (1972) pointed to medicalization as the process by which medicine expands into new areas of our lives, for example the screening of people who are well. This medicalization has been argued to have implications for individual patients and for society as a whole. Illich (1976) argued that medicine itself can often be the cause of problems. This is what he called iatrogenesis – medically induced illness – and refers primarily to the potential harm caused by medical treatment, for example the side effects of drugs or the risks of hospital-based infections. Medicalization is a reflection of, and also reinforces, the power of the medical profession. However, increasingly the role of the medical profession, its expert status and indeed its powerful position is seen to be challenged.

Power in decline?

Marxist writers in the USA have argued that the medical profession has undergone a process of 'proletarianization' as its control over aspects of its work is undermined by the move from self-employment to corporate medicine (McKinlay and Stoekle 1988). However, unlike in the USA, the medical professions in many countries within Western Europe have a long-established relationship with the state. For example, in the UK, doctors have been employed by the state since the onset of the National Health Service (NHS). Although the private sector is now flourishing, there are still obligations to work within the NHS upon qualification and for a portion of their time thereafter. In the UK and in many other European countries, the profession and the state are in a symbiotic relationship. This means that both the medical profession and the state have to work together in order to resolve any issues of conflict (Light 1995: 31). Despite working within state structures, the medical profession in Europe has retained a powerful position.

Nevertheless, recent changes within many countries have begun to threaten this position. Wider political changes since the 1980s have resulted in attempts to introduce more market-focused health-care systems.

> **Pressures derive from the concerns of government in capitalist societies. Governments are concerned to cut health service expenditures, to curtail the demand for services and obtain value for money.**
>
> (Allsop 1995: 76)

These changes 'represent a shift from protected professionalism to contracted professionalism, from autonomy and authority to accountability and performance, with managers in a pivotal middle position' (Light 1995: 31).

However, doctors still enjoy what Freidson (1970) calls a 'zone of discretion' arising from their monopoly over skills and the levels of uncertainty that are an inevitable part of medical practice. There are limits to the degree of control that could be exerted over medical work. Freidson also makes the point that we should be wary of discussing the question of power in terms of the medical profession as a whole. It is important to recognize the hierarchies within the medical profession. Specialization in medicine is regarded as higher-level work than general medicine, and as a result it tends to be hospital consultants that form the medical elite in Western medicine. As organizational changes occur within health services, it may well be that they will impact upon the work of some more than others. For example, within the UK, in 2008 changes were imposed on the work of GPs, traditionally lower in the medical hierarchy, by the government. GPs were asked to choose between the government's two alternative models of extended working hours arrangements, neither of which was regarded by GPs as acceptable.

Changes are also shaping the composition of the medical profession. While medical professions in Western Europe were once predominantly male, they are now experiencing a process of feminization, with increasing numbers of women entering medicine. It is too early to say how this trend will affect the status and power of the medical profession. However, when comparisons are drawn with already feminized medical professions in Eastern Europe, we see a very different professional group, with much lower status than in the West. There are obviously complex factors that shape a professional group's status, but gender is a significant part of this process (Harden 2001). We can already see some similarities emerging in the form of a dual labour market – female doctors are concentrated in primary care and in low-paid areas of the profession. These changes raise questions about the nature of the power of the medical profession. Indeed, feminization

> **raises the possibility that power in medicine resides not so much within the legitimacy (and supposed sanctity) of the clinical (physician–patient) encounter but rather within the structure of gender relations and within the relationship of organised medicine to other organisational entities, including the state.**
>
> (Hafferty and McKinlay 1993)

Therefore, the medical profession remains the dominant group within health care in all Western societies, but challenges to that position are coming from changing political and economic priorities, and from internal changes to the composition to the profession. From a different angle, it has been argued that there is a decline in the cultural status of medicine and its monopoly over health-related knowledge. This process of 'deprofessionalisation' (Haug 1973) has arisen most notably from increased lay knowledge about health in the context of more critical public attitudes to professional expertise. Particularly important in this respect are the media and easy access to medical and lay views on a range of health issues via the Internet. It has been estimated that between 40 and 60 per cent of adults in Europe seek online health advice. However, it cannot be assumed that increased knowledge will automatically result in a decline in confidence or belief in the expertise of the medical profession. Research with users of online health advice indicates that it is often seen as a useful source but that the medical profession is still considered to be the most important source of information (Sillence *et al.* 2007).

The media, both online and offline, have also had an impact on the status of the profession by publicising concerns about the potential negative implications of medical power and of medicine (see Chapter 17 for a wider discussion of media influence). High-profile cases of malpractice have undermined the idea of the trustworthy doctor; for example, in the UK, the case of the GP Harold Shipman who was found to be murdering his older patients; and the unethical removal and retention of children's organs at Alder Hey in Liverpool. These cases are not typical, but they do raise the questions of trust in the medical profession and point to an undermining of the acceptance of medical knowledge as truth. We will explore these issues in more depth when we look at doctor–patient relations. Before that, we will look at the second key sector within which health and illness are defined and experienced – the popular sector.

The popular sector

In this discussion of the popular sector we refer to lay views, meaning the perspectives of the non-professional or non-expert, though, as we shall see, these terms cannot be applied unproblematically. Why are sociologists interested in lay views? By studying lay understandings of health and illness, sociologists come to understand how our views and our actions are embedded in the society within which we live, and our place within that society. Lay views about health and illness do not simply duplicate the biomedical view (Nettleton 2006). We adopt aspects of 'expert' knowledge but reflect on these through our own personal experiences. Research by Hansen *et al.* (2007) in Australia found that patients suffering from the lung disease chronic obstructive pulmonary disease (COPD) were sceptical about the medical assertion that it was caused by smoking. They questioned the link, citing evidence of those who smoke but do not develop COPD. Instead, they explained the illness through working conditions and family history. As Hansen *et al.* note:

> **it is not surprising that participants constructed explanatory narratives that placed varying degrees of emphasis on factors such as the workplace, their family and significant events. Lay explanations for COPD, as with explanations for other chronic illnesses, reflect how a person perceives their illness in the wider context of their biography.**
>
> (Hansen *et al.* 2007: 742)

This does not mean that lay views are wrong or weaker versions of the 'real thing' (medical knowledge). These views, even when at times contradictory, are central to an understanding of how and why people behave in particular ways in terms of their health.

The way we think about health, illness and the body is shaped by our personal experiences, our social identity, our structural location and the wider cultural context. For example, research has shown that class location shapes the way that health and illness are defined. Pill and Stott (1982) found that working-class women were more likely to hold a functional definition of health – that is, that being healthy entails being able to participate in normal social roles. As one mother said, 'I haven't got time to worry about anything being wrong. Not only that, I think with a family you can't afford to be ill.' Cornwell found that gender was a significant factor in health definitions. One respondent in the study noted the differences between men and women in terms of time off work:

> **Men, they are like babies. You don't know what I put up with from him. Women, they get on with it . . . I'd say women have more aches and pains than men but as I say, when you've got a family you will find a woman will work till she's dropping. But she'll do what she's got to do and then she'll say, 'Right I'm off to bed'. Whereas it's all right for a man. If he's ill he's got nothing to do, he just lies there doesn't he?**
>
> (Cornwell 1984)

Stop and think

➤ Think about your position within society – your social class, gender, ethnicity, age. Are there ways in which these have shaped the way you define and experience health and illness?

Responsibility, lifestyle and risk

Lay concepts of health and illness are culturally framed within wider systems of belief. In Western societies, individualism is a very powerful ideology and is apparent in health beliefs and practices, with value given to responsibility for the self, and in particular for the body, through lifestyle choices and minimizing risks. In recent years there is increasingly an expectation that people should participate in their health care by taking responsibility for their health. Within the UK this is part of a wider raft of policies that reflect the concept of 'active citizenship' that, in relation to health, moves away from the idea of the passive reactive patient towards the proactive health consumer (Low and Murray 2006). Health is redefined as a personal goal to be achieved rather than a physical or psychological state of being. This not only shifts attention away from the structural inequalities in health but also gives it a moral dimension – indicating how people *should* behave. Crawford (2006) refers to 'healthism' to reflect the fact that achieving health is now deeply embedded in Western culture.

> **In a health valuing culture, people come to define themselves in part by how well they succeed or fail in adopting healthy practices, and by the qualities of character or personality believed to support healthy behaviours. They assess others by the same criteria. Accordingly, both the conventionally understood means of achieving health and the social state of being designated as 'healthy' are qualities that define the self. They become features of modern identity.**
>
> (Crawford 2006)

Stop and think

➤ What actions do you take that you would consider as 'taking responsibility' for your health? Is everyone equally able to do this?

We can see evidence of the centrality of 'responsibility' in health beliefs in the research findings of Blaxter (1997) and Popay *et al.* (2003). They found that, when asked directly, there was a general denial of the connection between poverty and ill-health among the working-class women they interviewed. Instead, importance was given to individual responsibility. However, when talking more specifically about their own lives, many references were made to the links between poverty and ill-health. In both studies, the conclusion was drawn that the denial of the connection related to the fact that the women did not want to appear to be shirking responsibility for health by linking illness to poverty.

A key part of individual responsibility for health involves behaving in appropriate ways, often referred to now as choosing an appropriate lifestyle. The most commonly discussed aspects of lifestyle that impact on health are smoking, drug and alcohol use, diet and exercise. All of these activities involve consumption, the purchase of a product or service, and we are expected as health consumers to make the 'right' choices. A vast array of health advice and warnings is reflected in the media, government policies, health education, and the wide range of health-related products available in order to help us in making our choices. Making the 'wrong' choice can result not only in poor health but also in public condemnation.

In the difficult economic context within which all health-care systems currently function, discussions around responsibility for health inevitably lead to debates about the economic implications of conditions attributed primarily to particular lifestyles. In the UK, the Wanless Report (2004) addressed the implications of health behaviour patterns for the NHS:

> **With the increase in chronic diseases has come an attendant focus on the factors that can be modified to reduce the risk of such diseases. The promotion of exercise, healthy eating and smoking cessation has therefore risen up the health agenda. These are predominantly factors linked to personal behaviours; consequently, modifying individual-level behaviour has become a focus for improving health at the population level. This situation forces consideration of individual choice alongside society's concern for improving the health of the population. It is necessary to consider the roles and responsibilities of all sectors of society. Sufficient account must be taken of all the benefits and costs,**

A closer look

Obesity: blame the parents

Below are extracts from the Sky news online forum discussing childhood obesity. The participants' comments highlight the issue of responsibility and blame tied into the notion of being a health consumer. The language of the participants has not been changed.

> It is a parents responsibility to keep there child healthy its just common sense those who have obese children obviously let them eat rubbish they haven't got that way eating veggies have they.
>
> I have two children 9 and 11 both enjoy computer games and TV and going out to play – a healthy balance. They are as slim as whippets this is because they have a healthy home cooked meal every evening and do not stuff themselves with sweets cakes or fizzy drinks. I'm not mean I let them have chocolate and sweets sometime and they never nag me for them. Its a parents responsibility to bring their children up with a healthy attitude towards diet from day one.
>
> We live in a lazy society. You can't blame a child for being overweight – parents nowadays take the easy way out and push their kids in front of the TV or computer rather than spend quality, outdoors time with them. Others can't be bothered or don't want to learn how to cook healthy meals for their kids – instead plying them with snacks and ready meals . . . I acknowledge that todays life is much faster, and parents have less time on their hands – however they made a conscious choice to have kids and should therefore make conscious and positive choices aimed at avoiding issues such as obesity.
>
> This is one of those areas where it is the parents fault, and only the parents fault. The parent dictates how much time a child plays outside. 'It's not safe enough' does not wash. If it is not safe for a child to play in the street – then go for a walk with them.

(Source: Sky News Forum http://news.sky.com)

Questions

1. What are your views on childhood obesity?
2. To what extent do you think parents are to blame if their children are overweight?
3. What other factors should be taken into account?

of the impact on individual liberty and of the ability of any policy to facilitate healthy behaviours as directly as possible.

(Wanless 2004)

Stop and think

- Should patients be refused treatment on the NHS for the following?
  - (a) lung cancer caused by smoking;
  - (b) illness relating to obesity;
  - (c) sports injuries.

In the section on health inequalities, we will question whether 'lifestyle' is an adequate explanation for understanding ill-health and whether the notion of choosing lifestyles takes into account the fact that our choices may depend on a range of factors, including levels of poverty. Certain lifestyles are considered to be problematic for the individual, and for wider society, in terms of the risks they pose to health. For example, as we saw above, children's diet and exercise are regarded as key to minimizing the risk of obesity. We are expected to take responsibility for our health through our actions as health consumers, and this consumption involves taking stock of a range of risks that may impact upon our health.

Self-care

An understanding of lay conceptualizations of health, illness and the body has significant practical implications. Most health care is not carried out in formal health-care settings by health-care professionals. Instead, it takes the form of self-care carried out by lay people in their everyday lives. Think of how often you

Case study

HIV and AIDS

The concepts of 'choice', 'responsibility', 'lifestyle' and 'risk' are often evoked in discussions around HIV/AIDS. For example, health-promotion messages centre on acting responsibly by having 'safe' sex. But can we really understand HIV/AIDS as the result of individual behaviour and choice? When the patterning of the disease both within the UK and globally is assessed, it is clear that it is the poor and disadvantaged who are most at risk. An estimated 38.6 million people worldwide were living with HIV in 2005. Of these, 24.5 million live in sub-Saharan Africa and 2 million in North America and central and western Europe.

Hart and Carter (2000) point to three levels of understanding of HIV risk behaviour:

- The *macrosocial level* addresses the wider societal influences that shape individuals' 'choices'. For example in sub-Saharan Africa, patterns of work result in many men working away from home for long periods, which in turn has an impact on the family's resources and contributes to prostitution among women.
- The *mesosocial level* looks at the community and its impact on health behaviour, such as through education in schools or health care. For example, Bravo *et al.* (2007) discuss the impact of needle-exchange schemes in Spain in reducing the number of new intravenous drug users and so limiting the spread of HIV/AIDS among this group.
- A microsocial analysis focuses on the meanings of health and illness and of the specific HIV-risky behaviours. Ridge *et al.* (2007) explored views about sexual relations among HIV-positive men and women in order to understand how people manage the risks involved.

By examining HIV risk behaviour at all levels, it is possible to contextualize and so provide a more complete understanding of individual behaviour. This type of analysis could also be applied to an understanding of other risk behaviours, such as smoking or poor diet (Nettleton 2006).

Question

1. **Apply this form of analysis to another area of health behaviour, for example diet. What do you think would be macro-, meso- and micro-issues in relation to dieting?**

have asked for the opinion of friends and family about the state of your health and whether, for example, to seek medical help. These 'lay consultations' (Scambler *et al.* 1981) are about more than the physical symptoms. They are shaped by the relationship between the ill person and their 'consultant', and the meaning they give to health and illness. Rappley's research on decision-making gave the example of a women faced with the high risk of stroke. She was reluctant to discuss her concerns with the doctor but had sought advice from her friend:

> **Me friend said 'have you never been on aspirin Anne'. I says, 'no I haven't'. She says 'eeh well I take aspirin every day' she says, 'because that thins your blood and everything and that'. I says, 'no I've never been on' I says, 'they said to go on warfarin' and she says 'probably that's the same' but she says, 'I've been on aspirin'.**
>
> (Rappley 2008: 435)

It is not necessarily that lay consultations replace medical advice, but rather that the decisions patients make are 'developed in, shaped by and then revisited in the unfolding trajectory of a series of medial and non-medical encounters' (Rappley 2008: 433).

Lay consultations construct health and illness in the popular sector and are shaped by wider discourses. This is clear in cases of illness that has no obvious identifiable cause (idiopathic illness) or is not readily diagnosed, particularly mental health problems that manifest themselves through behavioural change. Research with parents of teenagers with mental health problems found that changes in their child's behaviour

A closer look

Lay views and trust

The MMR (measles, mumps and rubella) immunization is a recent example of lay challenge to medical knowledge. The MMR is used in most European countries, but in the UK there has been considerable discussion in the media about the possible link to autism. Despite medical reassurances that there is no valid evidence to support such a claim, concerns have led to fewer children being immunized. To what extent is this evidence of the decline in trust in the authority of medical expertise? Brownlie and Howson (2005) researched parents' attitudes towards MMR immunization. They argue that parents' responses to the risks associated with the MMR were based in part on knowledge acquired by themselves and through the medical profession. Knowledge alone was not sufficient to make the decision on immunizing their child, as outcome about the uncertainty remained. Parents had to make a 'leap of faith' by trusting medical advice. This 'leap of faith' rested on the trust they placed in their doctors, not necessarily just as medical experts but as parents. As one parent said:

> If the health professional were to say 'I would have no hesitation to have my own children vaccinated' well then, I would trust their decision, but to just blindly say it's safe because they told me about this research, well who's to say that this research is accurate.
>
> (Brownlie and Howson 2005: 230)

This need to build trust by personal example was clearly not recognized by former British prime minister Tony Blair, who, despite advocating the MMR, refused for many months to say whether his son Leo had been given the injection.

were often explained by friends and family as hormonal or teenage moods, reflecting discourses of 'normal' teenage development. It was also the case that, even when a medical diagnosis was given, lay consultants often did not accept it and maintained that the problem would disappear with age (Harden 2005). Again, this shows that an understanding of lay views is essential to allow us to grasp the way health and illness are constructed by individuals and through their relations with others.

Lay views and experiences form a central part of our understandings of health and illness and of our actions. While we have looked at these within the popular sector, as the overlapping circles of Kleinman's model indicate, lay views are not formed or experienced within isolation. It is to the overlap between the popular and professional sector that we will now turn in a consideration of doctor–patient relationships.

Doctor–patient relationship

Sociology has offered many different ways of reflecting on the relationship between doctors and patients. Parsons' (1951) functionalist account emphasized the importance of understanding the roles that doctors and patients perform as part of the wider functioning of society. He argued that there was a shared consensus around the rights and obligations associated with the status of being either a doctor or a patient. Doctors are obliged to help patients regain their health through applying their knowledge and expertise; to be altruistic and forgo self-interest; to be objective and emotionally detached; and to be guided by a professional code of ethics. If they fulfil these obligations, then society grants them the right to examine patients, the right to autonomy in their practice and the right to occupy a position of authority.

Patients took on what Parsons (1951) referred to as 'the sick role'. Parsons considered ill-health to be dysfunctional for society as it resulted in the withdrawal from normal social roles. Patients were therefore obliged to seek professional help in order to allow them to recover as quickly as possible. In doing so, they were granted the right to exemption from their normal social roles and exemption from blame for their illness. For Parsons, the goal of the doctor–patient relationship was to ensure that the state of sickness is temporary and to reintegrate the person into their normal social roles as

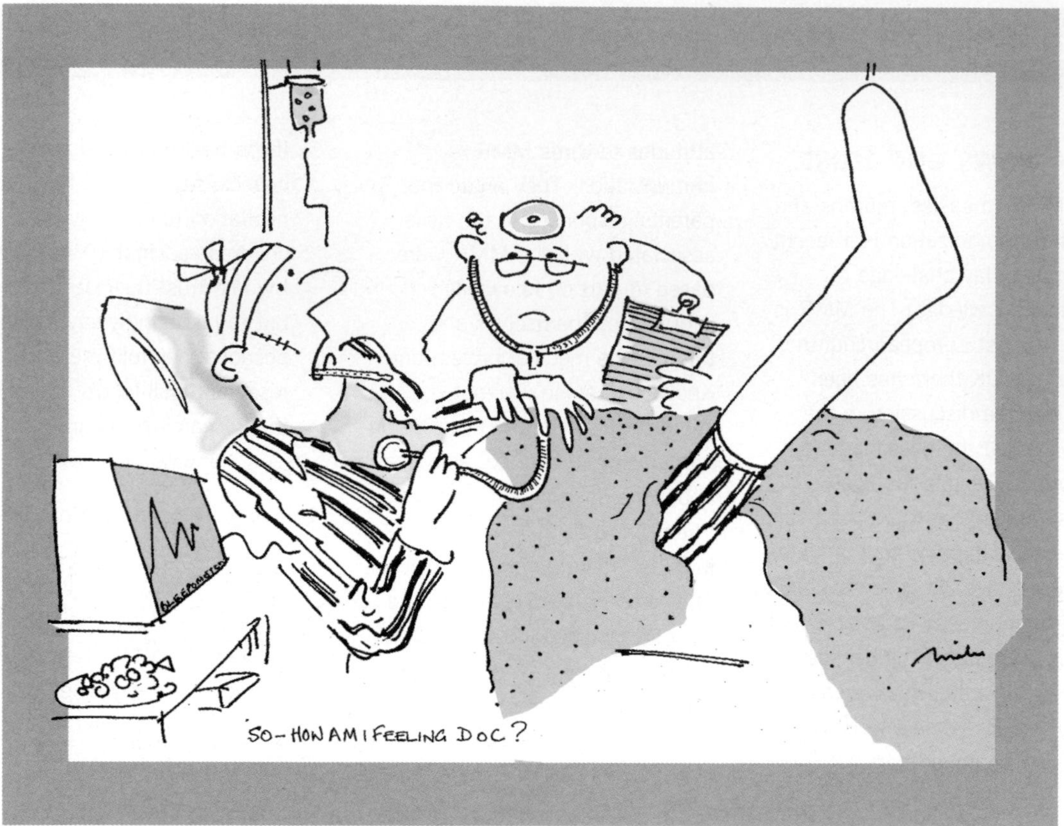

Cartoon by Mike Keating

quickly as possible. In this context, doctors act as gatekeepers, giving formal recognition of illness. For example, students and employees may be required to show medical evidence for absence due to illness.

However, the notion of sickness as a temporary phenomenon does not apply to much illness today, reducing the relevance of Parsons' work. Nettleton (2006) also pointed out that entry to the sick role is not as simple as Parsons implied. As we saw above, we often carry out lay consultations, and the views of those around us can shape when or indeed whether medical attention is sought. In addition, value judgements are part of medical practice, and these values often become part of the application of the 'sick role'. For example, Waldby (1996) argued that, in the early days of AIDS and HIV, medical knowledge was limited and cultural assumptions and value judgements around sexuality were a central part of the diagnostic process.

Parsons' work has also been criticized for neglecting the potential for conflict within the doctor–patient relationship (Waitzkin 1991). He argued that, although it is a two-way relationship, it is not equal – professionals are granted power, status and prestige. From a functionalist perspective, this hierarchy has positive consequences: those with knowledge and ability will gain rewards and so want to enter the profession, and patients will trust the trained professionals. Waitzkin (1991) looked at this from a Marxist perspective: he argued that, rather than there being a sense of shared values, the doctor–patient relationship served to reinforce the dominant ideologies of the capitalist system by presenting illness as an individual matter rather than focusing on the social and economic causes. Indeed, the role that Parsons understood that doctors play in determining whether sickness is genuine or not can be viewed not as a form of social control that benefits everyone but as a way of meeting the needs of the capitalist system, ensuring maximum productivity among the workforce. Doctors themselves often feel uneasy in this role. One GP in the UK said, 'GPs want to treat genuinely ill patients and don't want to act as policemen, identifying those who are claiming bogus sick notes' (www.countrydoctor.co.uk).

From a different perspective, though still looking at conflict, Freidson (1970) argued that the relationship was structured around medical dominance. He believed that, although doctors are concerned with the disease, patients are focused on their experience of the illness and that these different standpoints lead inevitably to conflict. Similarly, Bloor and Horobin (1975) argued that doctors expect patients to have thought about what is wrong before visiting them, but they still expect patients to defer to their knowledge and expertise. This contradiction leads to conflict in the relationship between doctors and patients. For example, a mother may have assessed the health of her child through lay consultations with friends or family or through Internet sites and decided to visit the doctor. Upon visiting the doctor, that knowledge and those beliefs can cause conflict if they are not in agreement with the doctor's views.

While it is important to look at the conflict that can arise in medical encounters, others have questioned whether this conflict is inevitable. Sociologists interested in the micro-aspects of relationships have looked at the ways in which the doctor–patient relationship is negotiated. This negotiation is dependent on many factors, including the nature of the illness, the stage of the illness, the health-care setting and the structural characteristics of the patient. For example, the relationship between a doctor and a patient is likely to change through the course of a chronic illness; the relationships will differ between the patient and their GP and consultant; and it will be shaped by the social class, age and ethnicity of the patient and the doctor. This does not mean that all doctor–patient relationships are individual, but that it is important to look in more detail at how both parties play an active role in shaping the nature of the encounters.

Strong (1979a,b) studied consultations between doctors and parents of young children. He describes the relationship as a form of ceremony, the main feature of which was the doctor's control over the consultation. The key characteristic of doctor-centred style of interaction was information-gathering. Doctors are aiming to diagnose and treat illness and so structure the consultation in a question/answer format in order to achieve that. From this, it may seem that patients are entirely passive and powerless in the relationship with doctors, but this is not necessarily the case. Patients may not always directly challenge doctors, but there are more subtle ways in which we can see evidence that patients play an active part in the consultation. Before the consultation, patients often prepare what they will say and so have some control at the start of the process. During the consultation, patients can shift the focus by introducing a second health concern not mentioned initially (Campion and Langdon 2004). Although patients are not able to determine the outcome of a consultation, they may be able to control some aspects of the event as it happens or regain control by the way they retell the event – recounting stories of the consultation to friends can allow them to shift the balance of power in their favour.

Stop and think

- Think about the last time you visited the doctor. Who do you think was in control of the consultation? How did that make you feel?

Changes to the doctor–patient relationship

The form that the interaction between the professional and popular sector takes, in particular that of the doctor – patient relationship, is constantly changing. While doctors are still in a powerful position as medical experts, the challenges to this directly impact on the relationship between the two sectors and, in particular, between doctors and patients. Lay views and experiences are now high on the agenda for improving health care throughout Europe. For example, as part of the 'Better Together: Scotland's Patient Experience' programme, a centre has been set up to coordinate feedback from patients. Self-care has also been given a high profile in recent UK health policy. The Expert Patients Programme (EPP) was launched by the Department of Health in England in 2001 with the aim of establishing lay-led self-management programmes in the NHS. The EPP entails patients undertaking a training programme in order to enable them to have a better understanding of their condition and so to manage it most effectively. The reasons for the introduction of the EPP may in part be economic; as the NHS struggles to survive, it would appear to make economic sense to encourage patients to carry out their own care where possible. However, evidence suggests that, while offering some benefit to patients in terms of confidence and psychological wellbeing, participation in the EPP does not reduce use of formal health care (Griffiths *et al.* 2007).

The notion of patients as experts or partners in their care links into the idea of patient choice in health care. In the UK, the Patients' Charter (1991) positions patients as 'consumers' and outlines the rights of patients to a say in their own health care. This links to the wider changes towards more market-oriented health-care systems that we discussed earlier. In this context, Giddens (1991) refers to the possibility for reskilling of the lay public. He gives the example of a woman with back pain. She may visit her doctor, who might refer her to a specialist, but she may not be satisfied with the outcome and may decide to visit an alternative therapist. She might inform her choices by finding information on back pain or by joining a support group (Giddens 1991). The choices patients can make as 'health consumers' have now extended beyond national borders as some patients choose to undergo health care abroad.

The trend towards health tourism indicates that, for some, the notion of the health consumer is very real. However, a different side is presented when we consider the UK government's attitude towards foreign nationals coming to the UK in order to benefit from free health care. In response to this growing trend, the government has charged GPs with the task of ensuring that patients are eligible before any referrals to hospital consultants are made. This illustrates that the notion of consumer choice within health care is relevant only to those with the money to pay for that status.

We can also question whether we are all happy to be health consumers. Do we want the responsibilities that come with choosing between an array of health products and health advice? There seems to be an expectation that the model health consumer is 'a self who acts in a calculated manner to engage in self-improvement and who is sceptical about expert knowledges' (Lupton 1997: 373). However, this is more of an ideal type and people are more likely to behave in contradictory ways, at times taking on the role of the active health consumer and at others being the passive patient. Henwood *et al.* (2003) found that the women they interviewed about hormone replacement therapy preferred to trust their doctor and did not want the responsibility of making health decisions for themselves.

Case study

Health tourism

Health tourism is becoming increasingly popular as patients in Western Europe become dissatisfied with public health services and shop around internationally for the best deal in private health care treatments. One man, George Marshall was told he would have to wait six months for a heart bypass or pay £19,000 for an immediate private operation. Instead, he chose to pay £4,800 to have his surgery in Bangalore, India. He researched the options through internet sites and contacted the hospital by email to discuss the operation. He said,

> Once I knew others had come I thought, why not? In Europe hospitals in Germany and Belgium would do the operation for less than doctors in Britain. But Europe was still more expensive than here. And the staff speak English in India.

George was wary about coming to India and was shocked when he first arrived. However once he was settled with a room providing air conditioning, cable television and personalised nursing, he relaxed, stating that . . . 'really I don't have to deal with what's outside'.

Critics complain that the private medical industry does not benefit the people of India. The country has less than one hospital bed per 1,000 people, compared with more than seven in first world countries. There are just four doctors in India for every 10,000 people, compared with 18 in Britain.

Ravi Duggal, a health researcher said, 'The poor in India have no access to healthcare because it is either too expensive or not available. We have doctors but they are busy treating the rich in India'. He went on to note 'Now we have another trend. For years we have been providing doctors to the western world. Now they are coming back and serving foreign patients at home'.

(Adapted from Ramesh 2005)

Questions

1. How did Mr Marshall make the decision to have treatment in India? Is his choice any different than choosing between consultants in the UK?
2. What conclusions can you draw from this about the idea of patients as health 'consumers'?

It also remains to be seen whether policy initiatives on partnerships of care are more rhetoric than reality. The medical profession may want to engage patients in their own care, but would this really be an equal partnership? As a professional group, the medical profession would still distinguish between their expert view and the patients' lay experiences.

What happens when the relationship goes sour? The potential to make doctors more accountable by using, for example, league tables for hospitals and consultants in combination with an increased emphasis on patient (consumer) rights will inevitably have an impact on the doctor–patient relationship. We may be moving towards a claims culture in which patients are more willing to take legal action if they are not satisfied with their care and doctors begin to make decisions based not solely on clinical judgement but also on potential legal implications. However, the question remains: to whom are doctors accountable? Do patients really have any power in this context? In the UK, the medical profession may be accountable to managers within the NHS, but ultimately judgements on practice are still decided internally through the General Medical Council.

It is important to avoid taking for granted the key terms – 'responsibility', 'choice', 'consumer' and 'expertise' – that are used in government policy, media discussion and everyday lay commentary. Sociology encourages critical thinking around these issues and so enables you to deepen your understanding of doctor–patient relations.

The folk sector

The final sector of health care to explore is the folk sector. In doing so we discuss the nature of this sector in Western health care and its relationship to the popular and professional sector. Although the biomedical model is dominant in our society, it is being challenged by the increasing popularity of alternative models for understanding the body, health and illness. Many terms have been used to classify this type of medicine, including 'unconventional', 'alternative', 'complementary', 'holistic', 'traditional' and 'natural'. Here we will use the umbrella term 'complementary and alternative medicines' (CAMs). These can be defined as:

> **a broad domain of healing resources that encompasses all health systems, modalities, and practices and their accompanying theories and beliefs, other than those intrinsic to the politically dominant health systems of a particular society or culture in a given historical period.**
>
> (Cochrane Collaboration, cited in House of Lords 2000)

This definition is useful because it indicates that the identification of a model of health care as CAM does not necessarily reflect the ideas or treatments themselves but rather their relation to the dominant model in society. As Bakx (1991: 35) argues, 'Culture is never static, what is unorthodox today may become the orthodoxy of tomorrow'. For example, in the USA osteopathy is considered part of conventional medicine and requires full medical training, while in the UK it is still regarded as a CAM – though as we shall see shortly this may be changing. In India, Ayurvedic medicine and 'Western' medicine are practised together by the same doctors, but in the UK Ayurvedic medicine is considered one of the more marginal CAM therapies.

The umbrella term 'CAM' disguises huge differences between the therapies available. In 2000, the House of Lords Science and Technology Committee report categorized CAMs into three groups:

- *Professionally organized therapies* – Sometimes referred to as the 'big 5', these include acupuncture, osteopathy, herbal medicine, chiropractic and homeopathy.
- *Complementary therapies* – These include aromatherapy and reflexology.
- *Alternative therapies* – These include traditional Chinese medicine and crystal healing.

CAMs are becoming increasingly popular, and there are 50,000 CAM therapists working in the UK (House of Lords 2000). It is difficult to get accurate statistics on the numbers of people consulting CAM practitioners; figures range from 10.6 per cent to 20 per cent of the population. Estimates of the expenditure on CAM range from £108 per person, or a total of £450 million in England and Wales per year, to £163 per person, or a total of £1.6 billion, 90 per cent of which is privately funded. Patient surveys suggest that patients increasingly want CAM therapies provided on the NHS.

Stop and think

- ➤ Why do you think CAMs are becoming more popular? Do you think CAMs should be available within the public health-care system?

There are many explanations given by sociologists as to why CAMs are growing in popularity over recent years. The most significant factor is dissatisfaction with biomedicine. There are many chronic conditions that biomedicine cannot cure and for which it can offer only limited forms of relief. In these cases, patients turn to CAMs as another avenue to explore. Patients are also concerned about the potential side effects of conventional treatments; CAMs are often considered to be more 'natural' and less invasive in their treatments. Patients who turn to CAMs are also dissatisfied with the traditional medical consultation during which they feel their views are not valued and they are given only limited time to fully explore the health concerns they have. CAMs are believed to offer a more patient-centred approach (McQuaide 2005).

We are expected to be committed to and constantly seeking to improve our health. Coward (1989) found that alternative therapies cater for this change in the role of our health and that CAMs allow even the 'worried well' (people who are healthy but are concerned about maintaining health) to feel they are doing something positive for their health.

> **Frequently the criticism of society expressed in alternative therapies turns into a nostalgia for an imagined wholeness and health, for what has been destroyed by modern society. The health of the body is presented as the vital front line by which the individual can counter the excesses of 'modernity', of 'industrialization' and impersonality.**
>
> (Coward 1989: 202–3)

With responsibility for health an accepted part of our culture, shopping around for new forms of health care is increasingly popular. The holistic ethos of many CAMs, giving attention to the 'whole' person's wellbeing, fits with this focus on individual responsibility for health (Hughes 2004) and indeed is for some a key part of the attraction. But there is also a danger that this contributes to an individualization of health, shifting responsibility to the individual and neglecting the wider social dimensions of health. It is also important to remember that the majority of CAM provision is available only privately in most European countries, making the status of health consumer applicable only to those with the money to spend. For example one chiropractic treatment in the UK costs about £30–40.

This would indicate that CAMs are linked into wider social changes. Bakx (1991) argued that the increasing popularity of CAMs (what he calls 'folk medicine') reflects wider cultural and economic changes. Specifically, Bakx locates the rise in popularity of CAMs within a modern economic context in which the emphasis is on consumption and choice. Bakx claims that 'modernism, biomedicine included, has become politically and culturally out of synch with a growing section of the population' (Bakx 1991: 25). We now have a vast array of health products and practitioners to potentially choose between, and this places CAMs and biomedicine in direct competition (McQuaide 2005).

Does the rise in CAMs really indicate a wider cultural movement and change that includes the rejection of orthodox medicine by large sections of population? While there has been a dramatic rise in the use and practice of CAMs, and while these therapies may potentially represent a challenge to the medical profession and the dominant biomedical model, the research indicates that there may be more orientation towards using them as additional modes of treatment rather than as direct alternatives to biomedicine. As we have seen, lay beliefs about health, illness and the body do not simply reproduce the dominant biomedical model. They are multidimensional, dynamic, contradictory and often dependent on both cultural and individual contexts. This makes Bakx's (1991) understanding of a cultural shift from biomedicine to CAMs too simplistic. It is far more likely that lay views simultaneously reproduce and refute aspects of both. For people who can afford them, CAMs form part of the health choices made, and it is interesting sociologically to understand the ways in which those choices reflect the wider cultural beliefs we addressed earlier – the health consumer and responsibility for health.

The reaction of the medical profession

How has the medical profession reacted to the increasing popularity of CAMs? For a long time, the official position of the medical profession was very negative towards CAMs. In 1986 a British Medical Association (BMA) report *Alternative Therapy: Report of the Board of Science and Education* was very dismissive of CAMs, describing them as 'doctrines embracing superstition, magic, and the supernatural'. In the UK in 1989, the Campaign Against Health Fraud (CAHF), later renamed Health Watch, was created, with the aim of protecting sick and vulnerable people from being exploited by those making claims on unproven or dangerous cures.

Although remaining sceptical, the views of the medical profession have begun to shift and there is now a partial recognition that some aspects of CAMs are useful for particular conditions and that their practice is acceptable as long as they cause no harm. A later BMA (1993) report, *Complementary Medicine: New Approaches to Good Practice* used the term 'complementary' rather than 'alternative' for the first time and acknowledged a limited use of CAMs alongside traditional medicine in treating certain conditions. This has led to calls for the integration of CAMs into the NHS and into medical practice. The House of Lords report ended with a plea:

> **We urge CAM practitioners and GPs to keep an open mind about each other's ability to help their patients, to make patients feel comfortable and about integrating their health care provision and to exchange information about treatment programmes and their perceptions of the healthcare needs of patients.**
>
> (House of Lords 2000)

In a broader context, the World Health Organization (WHO) defined its objectives concerning the integration of traditional medicine (TM) and CAMs with conventional medicine to

> **integrate TM/CAM with national health care systems, as appropriate, by developing and implementing national TM/CAM policies and programmes.**
>
> (cited in Dixon 2008: 5)

A key part of the recommendations of integration, at both national and international levels, involves greater regulation of training and organization. Within the UK the Group 1 therapies stand apart from the others in terms of their level of professionalisation and in the regulation of training. For example, osteopathic training is now university-based and subject to statutory regulation. This gives validation to the expertise of the therapists and makes it easier to envisage integration of some CAMs with conventional medicine. However, the terms of this integration are quite limited. In the UK the intention is to bring certain CAMs under the NHS umbrella with referrals coming from GPs and judgements about the suitability of use resting firmly in the hands of the medical profession.

The professionalization of some CAM therapists also indicates a blurring of the boundaries between conventional medicine, situated in the professional sector, and CAMs, situated in the folk sector. When does a CAM become conventional? This should be understood in terms of the relations between and

Case study

The reaction of the medical profession to acupuncture

Mike Saks (1992) set out to explain changing attitudes of the medical profession to acupuncture. He noted two phases. Before the 1970s the medical profession was opposed to acupuncture by medical or lay practitioners. Saks suggests that this rejection was based upon the self-interest of the medical profession because lay practice of acupuncture (based on an oriental philosophy) challenged the knowledge base of the medical profession. Acupuncture contradicted the biomedical understanding of health, illness and the body by focusing on the energy flows within the body, which the needles can help to realign.

Since the mid-1970s there has been a focus on incorporating acupuncture into medical practice. However, this incorporation is limited both in its understanding of how acupuncture works and in terms of who should practise it. The philosophical elements of acupuncture are rejected in favour of neurophysiological explanations that are more compatible with the biomedical model, and lay practice is rejected in favour of medical practice. Although taking a different form, Saks argues that incorporation, like rejection, was shaped by professional self-interest. This leads to a 'paradox of incorporation': the response of the medical profession may have changed, but the motive behind it has remained in place.

Question

1. Why do you think the medical profession's incorporation of acupuncture is limited?

within professional groups. The concept 'boundary work' refers to the way in which professional boundaries are established and maintained by those involved. Adams (2004) researched GPs who use CAMs and found that they draw boundaries between their work and the work of CAM therapists. They argued strongly that only medical doctors can carry out thorough diagnoses and that, while CAM therapists may usefully treat illnesses, this should happen only once the patient has been diagnosed through medical care. In this way GPs were stamping their authority over the use of CAMs by reinforcing the idea that responsibility for decisions around care, particularly in relation to diagnosis, should lie with the medical profession.

In this section, we have looked at the arenas in which health and illness are acted out and the people involved in that process. From this discussion we can see that that we can only understand the nature of the three sectors – popular, professional and folk – within specific social and cultural contexts. What is considered to be 'folk' medicine in one society may well be regarded as 'professional' in another. In some societies there is far less distinction between the popular and professional sectors. Within societies, the sectors are constantly shifting and contested, and the boundaries between the sectors are fluid and increasingly blurred.

Experiencing illness

We have all been ill at some point in our lives, whether with a short-term viral infection, a serious acute illness or a life-changing chronic illness. Being ill does not simply involve the biological process of what is happening in the body. The study of illness illustrates the close connections and interaction between the body, the individual and society. The symptoms of an illness may be predictable, but how, when and why they are experienced may depend on our social location. Our chances of becoming ill or of dying young are shaped by our social location. In this section we look at three dimensions of the experience of illness: chronic illness, dying and health inequalities.

Chronic illness

For those of us without any significant enduring conditions, temporary illnesses such as a simple cold may limit our normal everyday life. However, in this situation, the symptoms, and so their impact, are known to be temporary. It can even be quite nice having a couple of days off!

Stop and think?

➤ How do you think you would respond to a set of symptoms that interrupt your everyday routine permanently? Think about how it might make you feel about yourself; the impact on your relationships; and the effect on your family, friends and colleagues. If you have a chronic illness, then think about how you feel when those who are 'healthy' complain about short-term non-serious conditions.

In Western societies, medicine is increasingly able to cure or manage previously fatal conditions. As a result, life expectancy has risen; but at the same time, the prevalence of chronic illness has increased. Attention has turned in many areas, not only within sociology, towards understanding the experiences of those with chronic illness. Chronic illness by its very nature is likely to be experienced very differently from short-term illness. Much sociological work in the understanding of the experience of illness comes from interpretivist sociologists. They are interested in the micro-level of society and in understanding how the meaning of illness is formed and experienced, and how it is shaped through interactions with others – in short, how people make sense of illness.

According to Bury (1982) the onset of illness exposes us to changes that can alter how we feel about ourselves (our self-identity) and throw our lives into chaos. The term 'biographical disruption' is an expression of these processes.

> **Treating chronic illness as a disruptive event in this way allows for its meaning to be situated in temporal and life course contexts. Changes in the body and the onset of symptoms simultaneously involve an alteration in the person's life situation and social relationships.**
>
> (Bury 1997: 124)

It is not only the tangible aspects of people's lives that are shaken by illness. Charmaz (1983: 168) argues that chronically ill people experience 'a loss of self' and 'a crumbling away of their former self images'.

These forms of understanding of the experience of chronic illness go far beyond a medical definition of the illness and its impact on the body. They provide a more rounded picture of the illness and the meanings given to it. In part, this focus on meanings concerns how people adapt to having illness in their lives. Corbin and Strauss (1991) identified the process of what they call 'comeback': achieving a satisfactory life in the face of illness. This can involve adjustment to physical aspects of an illness or associated treatments, but it can also relate to more biographical dimensions of the person's life. Williams (1984) argued that, when faced with a chronic illness, people establish a 'narrative reconstruction' of events leading up to and through the illness. Patients and their carers tell their own version of how and why the illness developed and what it means for them (Harden 2005). They tell a 'story' of their illness in order to enable them to make sense of it in their lives. Often this involves a rethinking of their past, present and future life and can be considered to be a means of coping with the disruption that chronic illness may bring.

Is illness always disruptive?

Biographical disruption has been a central concept in sociological understandings of chronic illness, and its influence has also spread to other disciplines, such as psychology and nursing. But is illness always a disruptive event? Williams (2000) warns that we should be wary of assuming biographical disruption in all contexts. This model was developed primarily to understand the impact of chronic illness among adults whose lives, their biography, was well established. Its relevance to an understanding of the lives of children born with or developing a chronic illness at a young age may be less apparent. If an illness has always been part of a person's life, then we may need to find ways to understand illness as continuity rather than disruption. Or we may need to think of biographical disruption in a different light – it may be that any disruption is not temporal in terms of the before and after the illness but is more comparative viewed through the lives of others.

There are also problems with prejudging the issue of illness as biographical disruption without considering other aspects of a person's biography. Carricaburu and Pierret (1995) found differences between people who contracted HIV through gay sex and haemophiliac people who contracted HIV through blood transfusions. The haemophiliacs saw the illness as *biographical reinforcement* rather than disruption, since they already tended to view their lives in terms of their illness. Ciambrone (2001) also found that the effects of HIV

A closer look

Motherhood, chronic illness and biographical disruption

Sarah Wilson (2007) carried out in-depth biographical interviews with 12 women with HIV. She found that their experiences and the meaning given to their illness were shaped by the relationship between the illness and their identity as mothers. The illness was perceived as a threat to their identity as mothers, both through the potentially fatal outcome associated with HIV and through the stigma with which it is attached. These threats can be understood as a form of biographical disruption.

The illness shaped the women's experiences as mothers. One woman talked about her experience of giving birth: 'Staff make it very clear that they have an opinion towards you . . . basically scum . . .' It also changed how they related to other people. For example, this woman spoke about stepping back from a new relationship because of her worries about telling her new partner and his family about the HIV: 'It's hard to bring new people into my life because then they're just going to get hurt'.

Through the interviews, the women often reinforced that they were good mothers and placed the needs of their children first. This was most evident in the mothers' references to trying to stay alive for their children's sake, but was also seen through their attempts to create a 'normal' life for their children.

This research brings insight into the experience of suffering from a chronic illness and the ways in which illness and identity relate.

on women with a history of drug use, prostitution and poverty were not viewed as disruption because their lives were full of crises and disruption already. In this case, the illness experience could be understood as biographical anticipation rather than disruption. It may be that a sense of disruption is more prevalent among the more privileged classes, who engage in life-planning and who have a sense of control over their lives. Similarly, with old age, there is more of an expectation that illness may form part of our lives and so may be anticipated rather than considered primarily as a disruption (Sanders *et al.* 2002). This is not to say that all older people will anticipate illness or that it is not disruptive beyond a certain age, but it does indicate that we cannot assume the nature of the meanings given to the illness experience.

Chronic illness is increasingly a feature in the Western world: as the population ages, the level of morbidity (illness) has risen. The boundary between fatal and chronic conditions has also become more blurred, as some previously fatal conditions, such as HIV, have become more controlled and the lifespan of patients extended. The next section explores the experience of fatal illness, considering the cultural construction of death within society and the experience of dying.

Death and dying

The place that death has in society, and the way it is perceived, reflects the wider belief system within a society. We can see very different attitudes compared with our own if we look back within our own history or if we compare our society with others. Death was viewed for a long time as unpredictable, inevitable and the will of God. Attention was focused on the soul of the dying person rather than the body. With the biomedical model of illness and the body, the attitude to death changed markedly. Death was rooted very much in the body and its failure, and so attention focused on attempts to 'repair' the body and to avert death (Kastenbaum 2004). Death became a medical concern, and this has continued to shape our attitude to, and experience of, death and dying. Where death occurs, when death occurs, what defines death, who decides what has caused death and the nature of dying are all decisions with which the medical profession is involved. We view death and dead bodies through the biomedical framework, and it is the medical profession that acts as the 'gatekeeper' between life and death (Howson 2004).

Institutionalization of death

Since the early to mid-twentieth century, the majority of deaths in Western societies have occurred in hospitals. This is in part a reflection of the control over the process of dying by the medical profession and the extent to which death can be regulated. It can also be seen as part of the hiding away of death and dying. For Ariès (1981), the main feature of death in modern society is that it is hidden; it is a taboo. Similarly, Elias (1985) argued that a feature of modern society is the screening off of the more troublesome parts of life, including death. Hospitals are part of the process of establishing and maintaining the boundary between life and death.

A closer look

Viewing death and dying

'Death is a test of one's maturity. Everyone has to get through it on their own', says Frau Clavey.

> I want so very much to die. I want to become part of that vast extraordinary light. But dying is hard work. Death is in control of the process, I cannot influence its course. All I can do is wait. I was given my life, I had to live it, and now I am giving it back.
>
> (Edelgard Clavey)

These are the words of one of the people photographed by Walter Schels as part of his 'Life after Death' series. The photos capture the image of terminally ill people while dying and in the moments after their death. Have a look at the photographs at www.lensculture.com/**schels**.html. How do the pictures make you feel?

Technological regulation of death

We saw earlier that one of the characteristics of the biomedical model is a reliance on, and belief in, the role of technology in health care. This is very apparent in relation to death and dying. Before the development of modern technology, death was determined by the doctor by such measures as the taking of a pulse. At times this did lead to mistakes. Mark Twain, in *Life on the Mississippi*, recorded his feelings on visiting a 'dead house' (mortuary) in Munich in 1883:

> **Around the finger of each of these fifty still forms, both great and small was a ring; and from the ring a wire led to the ceiling, and hence to a bell in a watch-room yonder, where day and night a watchman sits always alert and ready to spring to the aid of any of that pallid company who, waking out of death, shall make a movement – for any, even the slightest movement will twitch the wire and rings that fearful bell. I imagined myself a death-sentinel, drowsing there alone, far into the dragging watches of some wailing, gusty night and having in a twinkling all my body stricken to quivering jelly by the sudden clamour of that awful summons!**
>
> (cited in Kastenbaum 2004: 51)

Technology now allows for the detailed monitoring of all bodily functions and for 'life' to be maintained in the context of bodily failure. However, this raises questions of how death is defined. The most widely accepted criteria for defining death in Western medicine are the Harvard Criteria: death is determined when the following criteria are met:

- Unreceptive and unresponsive
- No movements and no breathing (spontaneous)
- No reflexes
- Flat electroencephalogram (EEG; measurement of electrical activity produced by the brain)
- No circulation to or within the brain (Kastenbaum 2004: 54).

However, even such an apparently clearcut set of criteria can be flawed. A woman who suffered internal bleeding in the brain was pronounced clinically dead but later revived and was considered a 'miracle patient'. She uses her experience to challenge doctor's decisions to remove life support or to take organs from brain dead patients: 'Unconscious or dying people are not people of lesser value. More and more ethicists, philosophers and churches are rejecting brain death specifically for that reason' (Kennedy 1999, cited in Lock 2002: 363).

Harvey (1997) studied processes within an intensive care unit (ICU) and found several ways in which death was regulated through technology by the medical profession.

- *Time* – The work of the hospital and so the lives of patients are highly structured around time. Observations are recorded at set times, and time limits are set for improvement or change. This indicates that the body is viewed mechanically and its performance measured quantitatively.
- *Withdrawal of support* – The process of withdrawal is highly regulated and makes the process of dying very visible. As one nurse said:

  > **It is very strange really . . . you can watch the blood pressure, watch the heart rate, see everything that happens . . . you just can't take them off the ventilator really. So I was quite fascinated in a way to see how people could die.**

  Harvey argues that the oscilloscope has become a cultural image for death – the sound of the constant tone and the sight of the flat line on the screen.

- *Impression management of death* – Decisions around how to manage the death of patients in the ICU were about the impression of death to the relatives. As one consultant said:

  > **I think its better to take things away slowly rather than switch things off . . . If you're withdrawing something they're on, it's not the same as switching things off. They usually ask you about this. They say, 'Are you going to switch the ventilator off?' We say, 'No we're not'. Because that's a very positive act, as near to pointing a gun at someone and shooting them. You've not only made the decision to withdraw treatment, you've actually done it and so it's a withdrawal process.**

- *Bureaucratization of death* – All procedures must be recorded and certain procedures must take place in a particular way. What is regarded as being an acceptable death is defined legally and organizationally.

Stop and think

Supporting life through technology raises many ethical issues. Consider the medical, social and ethical aspects of the following:

- If family members agree that the life-support machine should be withdrawn because the patient is unresponsive and has no apparent chance to recover, then would pulling the plug be murder or is the person already dead?

The Harvard Criteria imply that there is an objective division between life and death and that this is rooted within the body. However, there are instances when an illness, such as Alzheimer's disease, results in such dramatic changes to the personhood of the sufferer that it could be argued that, although the person is physically alive, their self is dead – that is, their identity and their relationships no longer exist and, as such, they have suffered a social death.

The experience of dying

We are no longer as concerned about the after-life – what happens when we are dead – as with what happens when we are dying. Sociological research has explored the impact that medical control over dying has had on the experience of dying. Glaser and Strauss (1965) refer to 'closed awareness' situations in some hospitals, where staff hide awareness of dying from the patient. More recently, work has focused on the experience of dying and the idea of the 'good death'. Based on his research with people dying of cancer, Kellehear (1990) developed an 'ideal type' model of the good death, involving the following:

A closer look

Alzheimer's disease: a social death?

Alzheimer's disease is the most common form of dementia, affecting over 400,000 people in the UK. It is a progressive illness that gradually destroys the brain, resulting initially in confusion, memory loss, personality change and mood swings; in later stages, it can cause incontinence, inability to talk, eat or walk, and finally death. It is perhaps the changes in mental capacity, the gradual loss of ability; or, as the author Iris Murdoch described it, 'sailing into darkness', that is the most alarming aspect of the disease for patients and carers. The person is still present physically but the sense of who they were has changed or gone completely. Aware of this, Terry Pratchett (author of the Discworld novels), when announcing his diagnosis of Alzheimer's disease, said 'I am not dead. I will of course be dead at some future point, as will everybody else.'

It is newsworthy to document the lives of famous authors, and there is no denying that those who work with words will suffer when unable to do so, but the pervasive destruction of Alzheimer's disease is a devastation to all concerned. Ian Hulme, suffering from the disease, shows the disconnection that Alzheimer's brings:

> Am I alone or not? No one comes, no one cares. I am really all alone. I think someone came yesterday but then again I'm not sure. Did somebody call my name or was it someone else? Is today Tuesday or Wednesday and is it morning or night? I think I am a bit confused OK then so what's new? . . . The doctor says I have Alzheimer's and it's hard to understand that one day I will know who you are and the next day I know no-one. I'd love to remember who I am and who you are too but I can't remember this morning let alone yesterday. I think I loved you at some time but I'm not that sure. Please will you remember for me the things we used to do. Do not forget all the happy times and some sad ones too. I still love you with my heart . . . at least I think I do.

To read more stories from patients and carers, visit the Alzheimer's Society website at www.alzheimers.org.uk.

- *Awareness of dying* – More openness about the prognosis.
- *Personal preparations and social adjustments* – Time to resolve any personal matters and to prepare those around you.
- *Public preparations* – Arranging documents such as your will and arranging your funeral.
- *Relinquishing of responsibilities* – Stepping back from responsibilities in areas such as work.
- *Farewells* – Formal and informal.

Lawton (1998) looks at the process of dying and points out that we should be wary of using the homogeneous category – the dying patient. Experiences vary between people, between illnesses and across time. Lawton focuses on the body of the patient, the disease processes taking place within it, how the disease becomes visible outwardly, and the impact these have on the process of dying. She notes the perceived importance of retaining a 'bounded' body; one that did not 'leak' (particularly in cases of double incontinence) as central to maintaining a sense of self. This also links back to Elias's (1985) notions of hiding away our bodily functions within our 'normal' lives. For many of the carers in Lawton's study, it was at the point when this was no longer possible, when the body began to 'leak', that the dying person was admitted to a hospice. The hospice then becomes a 'no place', a 'space within which the taboo processes of bodily disintegration and decay are sequestered' (Lawton 1998).

Cheating death

Medicine has made some amazing breakthroughs with cures for diseases and increasing our understanding of genetics. This may lead us into feeling that medicine will provide a cure for everything – that we can have Star Trek devices that we just sweep over the body and everything is sorted. Our desire to cheat death takes many forms. Bauman (1992) refers to this as 'survival strategies' – attempts to keep death away by making choices in how we live our life and how we treat our body. In the end, this is of course a futile attempt, as Bauman notes:

> **. . . the ultimate meaning of staving off the danger of dying of cause A is the increase in probability that my death, when it comes, will be described by cause B, C . . . Z. 'I do not want to die' always translates, in its pragmatic conclusions, into 'I would rather**

Case study

The right to die?

The 'right to die with dignity' movement argues that dying people should have the right to choose when to end their life, even if medical treatment could still prolong it. Dying patients' basic human rights are seen to be violated when there is a lack of knowledge or power to make decisions around the dying process, particularly around when to die. There is considerable debate within and between the countries of Europe on this issue. In strongly Catholic countries, such as Italy, Spain and Poland, all forms of euthanasia are illegal. In other countries, such as Sweden and the UK, passive euthanasia (withdrawal of treatment leading to death) is tolerated. The Netherlands was the first country in the world to legalize active euthanasia (taking deliberate action to end a person's life) in 2002, followed by Belgium later that year.

Some patients are beyond being able to help themselves and raise the issue of family or friends becoming involved in assisted suicide. In the UK, Diane Pretty wanted to die but, due to her illness, she was unable to move and so unable to take her own life. She took her case to the European Court of Human Rights in order to allow her husband to help her to die, without him then being charged with murder. She lost her case and died naturally a few months later. In Switzerland, the organization Dignitas, staffed by volunteers, helps terminally ill people to end their life. This is a form of assisted suicide and is illegal only if done for self-gain.

Question

1. Do you think carers – doctors, family, friends – should be allowed to help others to die?

> **die of that rather than this'. As the 'that' cannot be exhausted, the truth of this translation must not be admitted into consciousness, and this requires that survival effort scores ever new successes. Survival needs constant reassurance; and the only convincing reassurance is the death of others: *not me*'.**
>
> (Bauman 1992: 10)

We have seen that the issues of death and dying raise many questions about the nature of bodies, how we view the relationship between bodies and our selves, and how we strive in some ways to control the experience of dying and the timing of death through technology. We all die eventually, but our chances of dying young, and the cause of our death, are related to social and cultural factors. This is also true of health and illness in our daily lives. We will now go on to explore how our experiences of health and illness, and indeed our chances of dying young and dying from particular conditions, are shaped by our social position – our social class, gender and ethnicity.

Health inequalities

In the biomedical model, illness is regarded as predominantly an individual and biological phenomenon – a person is ill perhaps because of a virus that attacks the body. While this is certainly part of our understanding, it is not the whole story. Health and illness are not distributed randomly across the population, with everyone having the same chance of being healthy or being ill. Social class, gender and ethnicity shape your chances of being healthy or ill: health and illness are socially patterned (for a broader discussion of these concepts, see Chapters 4, 5 and 6).

Health, illness and social class

There have been many reports that indicate a clear link between social class and health – the lower the social class group, the higher the chance of illness and early death:

> **At the start of the 21st century, all European countries are faced with substantial inequalities in health within their populations. People with a lower level of education, a lower occupational class, or a lower level of income tend to die at a younger age, and to have a higher prevalence of most types of health problems.**
>
> (Mackenbach 2006)

Mortality

Sir Donald Acheson led a systematic review of research on health inequalities to report on patterns of inequality and change within the UK. The Acheson Report (1998) highlighted that the overall death rate for people aged 35–64 years fell in the period studied, but the gap between the highest and the lowest social classes increased by 15 per cent among men and by 5 per cent among women. Within particular areas of the UK, the differences between classes are even more marked. In Scotland, male life expectancy in the 10 per cent most deprived areas is 13 years lower than that in the 10 per cent least deprived areas. These differences are increasing – the life expectancy gap between best and worst constituencies was 7.8 years in 1991 and 13.7 in 2001 (Scottish Government 2007).

Providing an overview of mortality patterns in Europe, Mackenbach noted:

> **Rates of mortality are consistently higher among those with a lower, than among those with a higher socio-economic position. Not only is the size of these inequalities often substantial, but inequalities in mortality have also increased in many European countries in the past decades. Inequalities in mortality:**
>
> - **start early in life and persist into old age,**
> - **affect both men and women, but tend to be larger among men,**
> - **are found for most but not all specific causes of death.**
>
> (Mackenbach 2006)

Morbidity

In relation to self-reported long-term illness, it was noted in the Acheson Report that 'socioeconomic differences are substantial'. In 1996 among the 45–64 years age group, 17 per cent of professional men reported a limiting long/standing illness compared with 48 per cent of unskilled men. Among women, 25 per cent of professional women and 45 per cent of unskilled women reported such a condition.

> **Inequalities in morbidity are found for many morbidity indicators:**
>
> - **prevalence of less-than-'good' self-assessed health,**
> - **incidence and prevalence of many chronic conditions,**
> - **prevalence of most mental health problems, and**
> - **prevalence of functional limitations and disabilities.**

Table 13.3 Global comparisons: mortality and morbidity

Region	Life expectancy at birth (2006, both sexes)	Under-5 mortality rate (2006, both sexes) (probability of dying by age 5 per 1000 live births)	Healthy life expectancy at birth (2002, both sexes) (years living without serious illness)
Africa	51	157	41
Americas	75	21	65
South East Asia	64	69	54
Europe	74	16	65
Eastern Mediterranean	64	84	54
Western Pacific	74	24	65

(Source: adapted from information from the World Health Statistics Report 2008, www.who.int/whosis/whostat/EN_WHS08_Table1_Mort.pdf)

> **As a result, people with lower socio-economic positions not only live shorter lives, but also spend a larger number of years in ill-health.**
>
> (Mackenbach 2006)

Although the statistics given above relate to comparisons between groups within a particular society, it is also possible to look at inequalities on a global scale. Table 13.3 compares mortality and morbidity between the main regions of the world.

Stop and think

- What factors are significant in explaining these patterns of health inequality? Why do you think there are such differences between world regions?

This information gives a clear indication of the connections between social class position and health and illness. Nevertheless, we also need to look at the explanations for why these patterns exist within our society. Attempts to understand, and so to be able to tackle, health inequalities have been ongoing for many years. One of the most significant reports on this was the Black Report 1980. This report was considered politically sensitive at the time, because its focus on poverty as the root cause of health inequalities was so at odds with the incoming Conservative government's policies. As a result, the report was deliberately released over the August public holiday weekend, to minimize interest, and only 260 copies were made. This gagging strategy did not work, and the report remains influential to this day. It examined four types of explanation for health inequalities: the artefact explanation, the social selection explanation, the cultural/behavioural explanation and the material deprivation explanation. By looking briefly at these explanations, we can see that, although this report was written some time ago, many of the issues raised are still relevant and lie at the heart of debates today.

The artefact explanation

Artefacts are things made by people. In this context, it is argued that class-based health differences are a statistical fiction, created by the way the data are gathered and analysed. There are many different measures that can be used to define 'health', leading to difficulties in comparing studies using different terms. At the same time, social class is often defined in terms of occupation, leading to problems when drawing comparisons over time when the occupational structure has undergone significant changes. It has been argued that comparing the bottom social class (V) over time is problematic because the number of people in this class has declined so greatly that comparisons are not valid (Bury 1997: 61). The issues raised in these discussions continue today as researchers debate the best ways to measure health and class and the relationship between them. It is important to draw attention to the methodological concerns in this area of research, but this alone does not help us to understand the nature of health inequalities in society.

The social selection explanation

This approach argues that good or bad health determines class position rather than vice versa. For example, having a long-term illness may limit a person's career opportunities. However, critics have argued that, although illness may have an impact on life chances, it is not always the case that illness leads to downward mobility. This explanation also offers little understanding of inequalities in infant health. It is now becoming possible, through longitudinal studies such as the British Birth Cohort and the Growing Up in Scotland (GUS) study, to trace people's lives from birth through to adulthood and so to look at the impact of health on life chances.

The cultural/behavioural explanation

This is a broad explanation that relates health to cultural practices and beliefs. It suggests that different social classes behave in different ways – the poorer health of people in lower social classes is caused by their behaving in ways that are more likely to damage their health, for example eating a poor diet, smoking and consuming alcohol. This kind of explanation can be very simplistic and confrontational – blaming the individual for their own ill-health. However, it can also be viewed in relation to discussions of class culture. Shilling (1993), building on the work of Bourdieu, argues that the production of physical capital – the way we shape our bodies through exercise, food, etc. – varies by social class. The lower social classes tend to see the body in terms of what it enables them to do, for example work or look after children. Behaviour that will have a long-term impact on health may not be considered as problematic if the body continues to function as normal. The higher social classes treat the body as an end in itself, as something to be worked on, and place a higher value on taking care of it and preventing illness.

The focus on culture and behaviour is politically very relevant, but is it convincing as an explanation of health inequalities? It is certainly evident that 'bad' health behaviour, such as smoking, is more prevalent in lower social classes and that this in part may be explained in terms of class culture. However, these behaviours may also be explained as rational responses to living in difficult circumstances. If you live in poverty, in poor housing, struggling with everyday life, then 'bad' behaviours for health can be seen as means of coping or as a form of luxury. For example, having a drink or smoking a cigarette may be enjoyable activities in the context of otherwise difficult lives. The meanings behind these 'bad' behaviours are often hidden within common sense and political discourses such as 'we can all choose' and 'no one makes you smoke'. What is important, therefore, is to understand the contexts within which people make 'choices' that impact on their health and wellbeing. Significantly, we can also question the extent to which choice is a reality for many people, and this leads on to the final explanation discussed in the Black Report.

The material deprivation explanation

It is argued that people's material situation, the conditions within which they work and live, is an important factor in determining their health and the choices they have. There are a number of key issues that are significant here:

- *Poverty* – Being on a low income can impact on health in a number of ways. Lack of resources for adequate food or shelter can make you vulnerable to physical illness. Lack of control over the circumstances in which you are living can be psychologically damaging.
- *Employment* – Lower-status jobs are linked with higher rates of illness and mortality, due in part to higher incidents of accidents and injury in manual jobs (Nichols 1999). Lower-grade non-manual work can also bring health risks in relation to such issues as the amount of control over work. There are also greater stresses from unemployment, experienced more by people in the lower social classes, which in turn has an adverse affect on health.
- *Housing* – This can have a direct impact on health in a number of ways. The location of housing can create problems with crime, noise levels, pollution and availability of services. The design and maintenance of housing brings issues of availability of safe places to play, cost of heating, incidence of damp, infestations and risk of fire. People on low incomes are more likely to be exposed to these risks, since they have less choice of housing.
- *Access to care* – We can question whether different classes have different access to care or make use of services in different ways. Factors such as where you live, whether you own a car and working hours can all affect access to care. Recent reports in the UK of people removing their own teeth with pliers because of the lack of free care from NHS dentists is a graphic example of this problem (Figure 13.5).

Combining explanations

The discussion of the issues raised through these explanations should highlight that there is no simple single answer to understanding the links between social class and health. To address the complexities of the issues involved, the Acheson Report (1998) adopted a socioeconomic model of health and inequalities

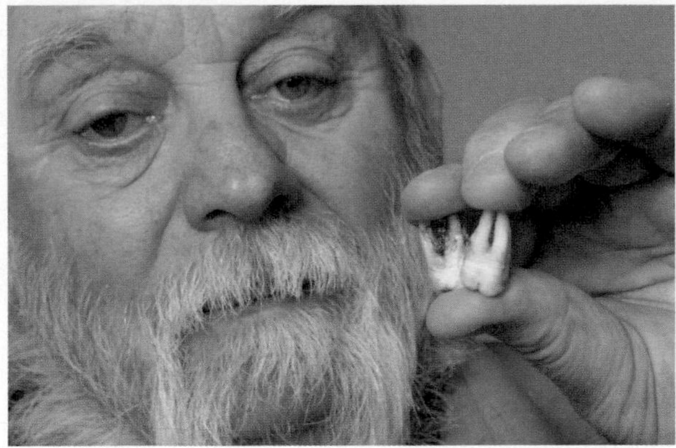

Figure 13.5 Arthur Haupt, who removed some of his own teeth with pliers
PA Photos

(Figure 13.6). At the centre are individuals characterized by age, sex and constitutional factors that influence health potential but that are fixed. Surrounding the individuals are layers of influence that can change. The innermost layer refers to personal behaviour and the way of life adopted by the individual, for example smoking. But individuals do not exist in a vacuum – they interact with friends, relatives and their immediate community, and so they come under the social and community influences of the next layer. The wider influences on a person's ability to maintain health, for example their living and working conditions, are contained in the third layer. Finally, the economic, cultural and environmental factors of society are in the outer layer.

Stop and think

➤ Place yourself in the middle of the rainbow model in Figure 13.6 and fill in those factors that have affected your health.

However, this model does not necessarily address the connections between the different aspects contained within the layers, and the complexities of the connections between them. Many sociologists argue that the focus should not be only on determining cause and effect in relation to health inequalities. Rather, we should seek to understand the meanings given to health and health inequalities and the ways in which these are experienced. This links back to the earlier discussion on the importance of understanding lay perspectives.

Gender differences and health

For a long time, women in many Western societies lived on average five years longer than men, though the gap is now narrowing (Scottish Government 2007). Although women tend to live longer than men, they also tend to experience more illness – the *healthy* life expectancy of females is only two to three years more than that of males (Acheson 1998). Although there are obvious biological differences between men and women, such

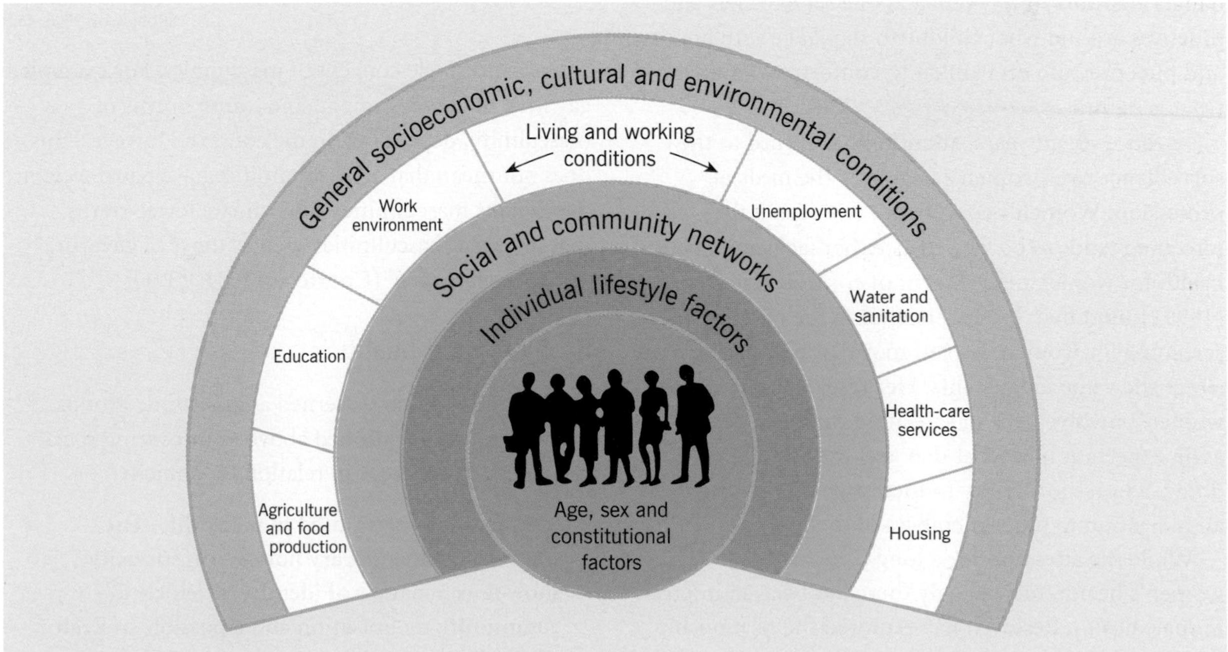

Figure 13.6 The rainbow model of socioeconomic factors

differences offer limited understanding of differences in health, and it is important to address the social issues relating to gender and health. Researchers have linked gendered patterns in health to cultural images and expectations around gendered behaviour. For example, pressures on women to be slim can contribute to eating disorders and make women who smoke reluctant to give up for fear of putting on weight. However, attention is also paid to the significance of material factors. Women are the primary carers for children and older relatives, and this responsibility may contribute to physical and psychological illness. Women's poor health may also be connected to poor employment conditions. A large percentage of women in paid employment do part-time work, which is more likely to be poorly paid, be of low status and with little control (see Chapter 5 for more detail on gender segregation in employment).

Gendered health inequalities also relate to women's experience of health care. The focus of research for many years was on the medicalization of many natural aspects of women's lives relating to reproduction. Oakley (1984) argued that women's experience of childbirth was tainted by the doctor's overriding concern with the risks involved. Such concerns fuelled calls for a return to 'natural childbirth', giving women control over the planning of the birth of their child, where the birth would take place and with a reduction in the level of medical intervention. However, there is a danger that this simply replaces one set of beliefs and practices around what childbirth *should* be with another and puts pressure on women to conform to an image of what is natural.

In more recent years, attention has turned to the surveillance over women's health by the medical profession. Women's compliance with cervical screening tends to be viewed as either facilitating better health for women or as a form of control. Howson (1999) found that, by understanding the meaning of screening for women, we can move away from the more simplistic value judgements. Her research showed that women's involvement in screening can be understood as an expectation of what they feel they should be doing, as a responsibility to their own bodies, and as an obligation to other members of their family.

While the attention for a long time has been on women's health, increasingly there has been an interest in male health. Research has explored the relationship between men's health behaviour and masculinity. Charmaz argues that men use health beliefs and health behaviours to demonstrate dominant masculine ideals that clearly establish them as men and avoid behaviours that challenge their masculinity. Masculinity is associated with a denial of weakness or vulnerability making illness particularly problematic. Illness 'can reduce a man's status in masculine hierarchies, shift his power relations with women, and raise his self-doubts about masculinity' (Charmaz 1995: 268). Gender constructions around masculinity also lead men into dismissing their health-care needs. For example, the use of sunscreen to protect again skin cancer challenges a number of constructions around masculinity, health and illness and the body:

> **. . . masculine men are unconcerned about health matters; masculine men are invulnerable to disease; the application of lotions to the body is a feminine pastime; masculine men don't 'pamper' or 'fuss' over their bodies; and 'rugged good looks' are produced with a tan. In not applying sunscreen, a man may be simultaneously demonstrating gender and an unhealthy practice.**
>
> (Courtenay 2001: 1389)

Robertson has argued that we should avoid assumptions that men do not care about health:

> **[there is a] diverse and complex relationship between 'masculinity' and 'health' in everyday life, and this is mediated through other aspects of identity.**
>
> (Robertson 2006: 452)

There is no single concept of masculinity. For example, gay men may use 'straight' and 'camp' forms of masculinity, depending on the context. However, this does not mean that all masculinities have equal weight: 'Dominant masculinities subordinate lower-status, marginalised masculinities such as those of gay, rural or lower-class men' (Courtenay 2001: 1391).

Ethnicity and health

Health status is also patterned across ethnic groups. The difficulties mentioned above in measuring social class are also apparent in relation to ethnicity:

> **'Ethnicity' is a term used in many different ways . . . Contemporary notions of 'ethnicity' show it as a marker of identity, a vehicle of community mobilisation and a possible indicator of disadvantage, discrimination or privilege.**
>
> (Ahmad and Bradby 2007: 796)

Despite this it is noted that 'Ethnic identity can be powerfully related to access to resources such that the formation, maintenance and transformation of ethnic relations is crucial to wellbeing' (Ahmad and Bradby 2007: 797).

It is also difficult to specify which groups are referred to when discussing ethnicity and issues of health. Studies initially focused on the health status of ethnic minorities within a country's population, but increased migration within Europe in recent years has led to growing concerns about ethnic minorities within migrant populations. A conference on health and migration was held to mark the Portuguese presidency of the EU, at which it was noted that 'migrants experience increased health risks, frequently similar to those of the disadvantaged groups'. Questions around ethnic identity have been part of the Census in the UK since 1991, and discussions around the categories are under way for the next census in 2011, taking into account the diversity of nationalities represented within the UK in order to give a more accurate picture.

Differences in mortality rates are often difficult to determine because the information required is limited and has only been recorded in recent years. Nevertheless, statistics indicate higher rates of early mortality among men and women born in Africa and the Indian subcontinent and now resident in the UK. Among mothers who were born in countries outside the UK, those from the Caribbean and Pakistan have infant mortality rates almost double the UK national average. There are also indications of high rates of illness among people of ethnic minorities. People of Pakistani or Bangladeshi origin have the highest rates of limiting longstanding illness (Acheson 1998).

As with gender and social class, there are a number of explanations that address these inequalities. Cultural explanations focus on the behaviour linked with certain ethnic groups. This is a similar argument to social class explanations in health patterning. It suggests that the way of life of people from different ethnic groups affects their chances of staying healthy or becoming ill. This type of view tends to be based on assumptions about ethnic cultural inferiority rather than on real facts about cultural practices. Ahmad and Bradby (2007) note that racial categorization is not used explicitly but that the notion of fixed, innate differences has shifted on to the concept 'ethnicity'. Initially, interest in the UK in minority ethnic health came from public health and tropical medicine specialists, with a focus on protecting the British population from diseases brought into the country by an immigrant population. This was followed by an interest in diseases specific to certain minorities and led to a neglect of most common diseases and to cultural stereotyping. For example, vitamin D deficiency, leading to rickets, was common among children in the UK in the mid-twentieth century and was eradicated by, among other things, the introduction of fortified margarine. When rickets appeared in immigrant South Asian children in the UK in the 1970s, it was attributed to 'exotic' diet, codes of gender and dress (inhibiting exposure to sun), and pigmentation of the skin (reducing the production of vitamin D in the body). Yet the obvious solution – fortification of a staple food item with vitamin D – was not considered appropriate for a long time. Ahmad and Bradby (2007) argue that in this case ethnicity led to stereotyping and so to differential treatment.

Explanations also focus on the material circumstances within which people live, including income, housing and employment. The impact of these on health is discussed above in the section on social class. Why are these problems for particular ethnic groups? It is suggested that racism and racial discrimination are a significant part of this explanation (Karlsen and Nazroo 2002). Racism can lead to the concentration of ethnic minorities in types of work associated with ill-health and to higher chances of unemployment. Investigations into ethnicity and housing reveal that people of some ethnic minorities are more likely to live in poorer accommodation and in poorer inner-city areas. Racism can also lead to attacks, abuse and thus physical and mental harm. Racism may also shape the experience of ethnic minorities within the health-care system. Bowler (1993) studied maternity wards and midwives' attitudes to patients from ethnic minorities and found evidence of racial stereotyping.

Our health, and the way that we experience health, illness and the body, are shaped in part by our position in society – our class, gender and ethnicity. This does not mean that our lives are predetermined before birth and that we have no impact on this, but when we often hear about health in the context of discussions around responsibility and choice, it is important to think critically about the notion of choice. While our individual actions in choosing, for example, what we eat, how much alcohol we drink, and whether or not to take illegal drugs, will impact upon our health, is it possible to understand these actions in isolation? Sociologists argue that our behaviour as individuals can be understood only through an understanding of the wider social contexts within which we live. This is also a key point in reflecting back on this section of the chapter as a whole. In seeking to understand the experience of illness, we have looked at chronic illness, at the process of dying and at health inequalities. In each case, we have pointed to the importance of looking critically at taken-for-granted concepts and at questioning the notion of illness as an individual phenomenon. While we may experience illness individually, through the particular features of our own lives, we are also simultaneously part of a wider society that shapes those experiences.

The body, technology and change

Technology offers us new possibilities and opportunities in all areas of life, including in relation to the body, health and illness:

> **Open a paper, turn on the television, listen to the radio or surf the Internet, and there, ready and waiting for you, are an array of amazing, bewildering, dazzling or terrifying tales of these 'cutting-edge' technologies.**
>
> (Williams 2003: 154)

However, the control that technology offers also poses questions about the nature of the human body and its boundaries. What does it mean to be human if parts of your body are non-human? Are we now becoming 'cyborgs' as the boundary between humans and machines becomes more blurred? What does it mean to the notion of the self if parts of your body previously belonged to someone else or to another species?

Technological advances mean that we are now capable of reshaping the human body. Cosmetic surgery has never been more popular, and even major surgical procedures have been normalized through makeover programmes and the celebrity lifestyle influence. The number of cosmetic surgical procedures in the UK rose by 47 per cent between 2005 and 2007. The number of anti-ageing procedures increased the most, rising by 36 per cent between 2006 and 2007. The most popular procedure is breast augmentation, with 6497 such operations being carried out in 2007 (British Association of Aesthetic Plastic Surgeons 2007). Breast augmentation involves the insertion of implants to increase breast size and is an example of the fusion of technology within the body. The use of pacemakers and eye and ear implants may be for a very different purpose, but they raise the same issue concerning the nature of the human body when it becomes shaped by, and dependent upon, technology.

The potential to change human bodies is also apparent in developments in the field of organ transplantation. The first heart transplants took place in 1967 and, though still a complex procedure fraught with risks, heart transplantation is now relatively common. In 2005 the first face transplant was performed, in France, on a woman, Isabelle Dinoire, who had been disfigured after an attack by a dog (Figure 13.7). Face transplants raise the issue of the implications of merging bodies more explicitly than other forms of transplants. In the process of transplantation, the bodily organs lose their connection to the whole; they become parts of the machine that can be transferred from one to another, hidden beneath the surface of the body. Yet, with face transplants, the transfer is a highly visible process. The face is our primary physical identifier, and so what does it mean to take on the face of another person? The surgeons reported that the woman in France will have a 'hybrid' face looking like neither the donor nor herself before the accident. But this still leaves the question of what this process means for the notion of the self and identity reflected in and experienced through the body.

Stop and think

- Is there something qualitatively different about the removal of a face, even after death, than the removal of other body parts, for example the liver?

The technological potential to transplant organs and body parts also raises the question of the donation. There are many ethical issues raised in relation to the 'harvesting' of body parts from those who have died, but it is particularly controversial in cases of brain death. Indeed, some argue that the concept of 'brain death' describes a bodily state but that it is only because the word 'death' is used that we think of the person as being dead. This is a very modern form of death, and one that some would argue is not appropriate or accurate. Lock (2002: 374) argues that the invention of the term 'brain death' was a 'political act' connected to the need for organs. To maintain the highest chance of acceptance of organs into a new body, the donor's body

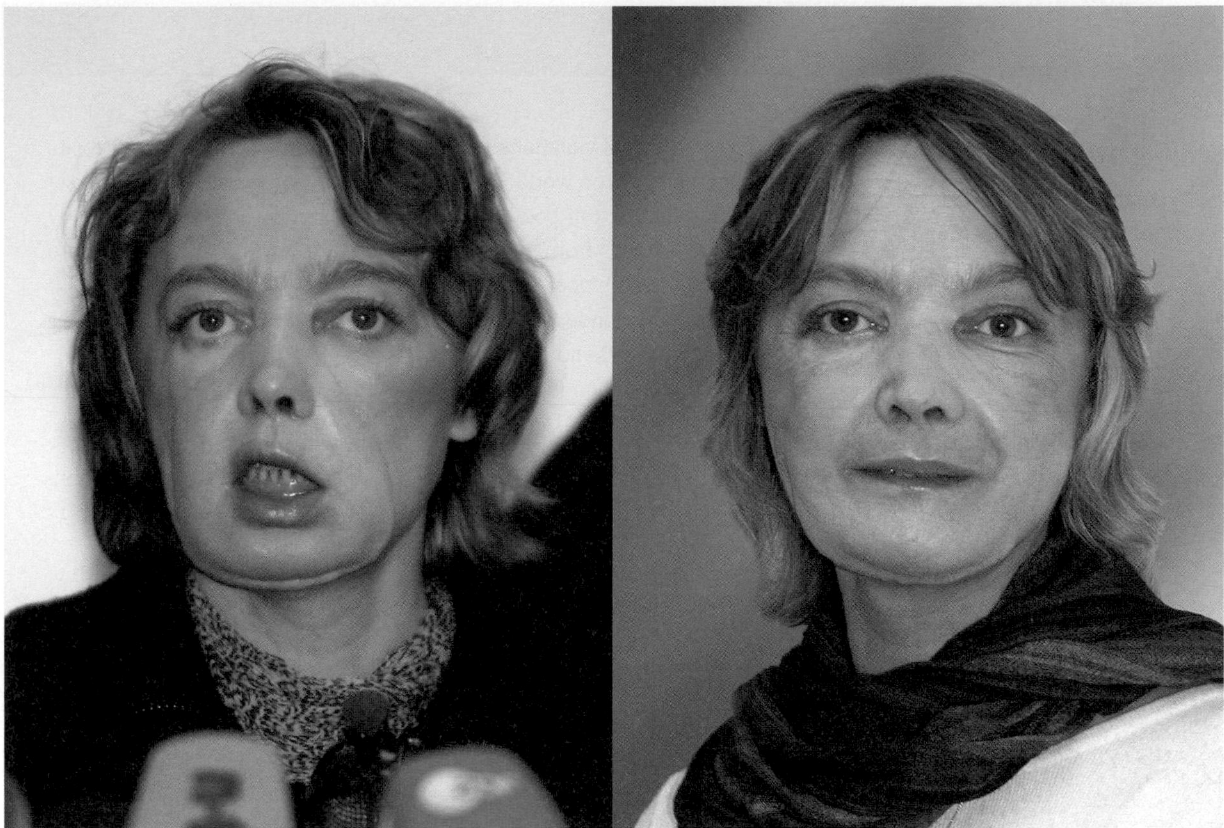

Figure 13.7 Isabelle Dinoire, the French woman who received the world's first face transplant, in June 2001
DENIS CHARLET/AFP/Getty Images

is often treated with drugs and must be kept ventilated until the body parts can be removed. This has led some to critique the treatment of people in this state as unethical because their bodies are being manipulated rather than allowed to die a 'natural' death. This ongoing debate highlights that death, though a biological reality for us all, is also socially constructed.

The lack of human body parts to meet the demand for transplantations has led medical science to pursue other possible sources. Xenotransplantation refers to the use of animal organs or cells for human transplants. In 1995 Imutran created a pig, Astrid, designed with organs less likely to be rejected by humans. This raises many questions about species boundaries. In our society, pigs are often culturally or religiously defined in negative ways, and the word 'pig' may be used to denote a person who is unclean or rude. How then would you feel about having a pig's organ to replace your own?

More recently, attention has turned to manufacturing organs and tissues from stem cells. Stem cells are cells that are at an early stage of development, with the potential to turn into many different types of cell. Scientists believe that it should be possible to use stem cells as the basis for repairing the body. However, the use of stem cells is controversial. The best form of stem cells is found in human embryos, and stem-cell research involves taking cells from embryos just four or five days old, created in the laboratory. Pro-life campaigners argue that all embryos are potential human beings, and so it is morally wrong to carry out such experiments on them. There is also controversy when human and animal cells are combined to produce hybrid embryos. Cardinal Keith O'Brien referred to these experiments as being of 'Frankenstein proportion' and called the proposed Human Fertilisation and Embryology Bill a 'monstrous attack on human rights, human dignity and human life' (Times online 22.3.08).

Genetic technology

Perhaps the most widely discussed technological development within medical science in recent years has been in the field of genetic research, with the mapping of the human genome in 2001 and the sequencing

World in focus

Organ donation

With advancements in technology, the demand for organs to transplant has increased. Recent debates around the move to an opt-out scheme for organ donation within the UK, to replace the present opt-in process that is currently used, reflect this demand. In the context of global capitalism, body parts have now become big business involving the international trafficking and even ordering of parts. Studies by a group in California – Organs Watch – have found evidence of ethical, moral and legal violations in many parts of the world. These include the theft of body parts such as kidneys from vulnerable patients, mostly poor and female, when undergoing routine surgery; and coercion in kidney donation in countries such as India, for example through offers of lower sentences to prisoners. The tightening up of laws on the purchase of body parts, in Western societies such as the UK, may reduce the demand for organs.

(Source: Organs Watch, http://sunsite.berkeley.edu/biotech/organswatch/pages/hot_spots.html)

See also the BBC *Horizon* website on body parts, which allows the reader to find out how much body parts are worth and what they are used for:

www.bbc.co.uk/sn/tvradio/programmes/horizon/broadband/tx/bodyparts/values/.

Question

1. In which regions of the world are moral and ethical violations on the use of body parts most likely to take place and why? After considering this question, look on the 'hot spots' section of the Organs Watch website. How did the information provided there compare to your ideas?

of the entire DNA code in 2003. The purpose of the Human Genome Project was to find a genetic base for the 4000 or so genetic diseases in order to eventually develop cures. Genetics is a rising paradigm in medicine and science. Tony Blair, former British prime minister, in the foreword of a White Paper on genetics in 2003, said:

> **The discovery in Britain of the structure of DNA 50 years ago – perhaps the biggest single scientific advance of the last century – marked the beginning of a golden age of bio-science in Britain which continues today. It is likely to have as big an impact on our lives in the coming century as the computer had for the last generation.**
>
> (Department of Health 2003: 1)

Despite this genetic 'revolution', there is a very close fit between this way of understanding the body, health and illness and the biomedical model (Conrad and Gabe 1999). This in part explains why genetics has been so readily accepted by the public and within the scientific community – it is a complementary rather than a challenging model. The genetic paradigm does not undermine the view of the body as a machine. Genes can be understood as representing a blueprint of the body, offering a closer look at the workings of the machine, and the implications in popular understandings is that faulty genes can be 'fixed'. Like the traditional biomedical model, genetics focuses on specific aetiologies and on the biological, internal cause of disease, neglecting the social context. The acronym O-GOD (one gene, one disease) reflects this idea. As we saw earlier, genetics has offered us a new discourse with which to talk about the body, health and illness; as part of this, we also have a new set of images – the new 'anatomical atlas'.

Genetics is not simply about the discovery of the human genome, a scientific procedure involved in addressing bodily problems. Cultural assumptions shape what kinds of questions scientists ask, where they look for answers and how they interpret their data (Conrad and Gabe 1999). Cunningham-Burley and Kerr (1999) looked at the scientific discourses around genetics and at how these discourses both reflect and produce the status of scientific knowledge and of the scientists themselves. As the potential for discovery within the field of genetic research expands, so too does the potential for gain, in both a financial and a professional sense. The mapping of the genome is often referred to as a 'race', with different teams competing, and each new discovery is often characterized in this competitive light. In 2005 it was discovered that a South Korean scientist had fabricated claims about advances in embryonic cloning.

However, it is not only within scientific circles that knowledge about genetics is produced. The media is a key player in shaping our understanding in this field of medical science. The mapping of the genome has been referred to within the media under a range of dramatic headings – 'the Holy Grail', 'the essence of life', 'the book of life'. It has become something of a cultural icon, and its impact is extending way beyond science. Media discourse on genetics is not always in step with scientific reality and tends to reproduce the idea that genetic causes and cures are simply awaiting discovery, often misrepresenting the complexity of the disease aetiology and the possibility of genetic treatment.

The meanings that people give to genetics are shaped by scientific and media discourses, but also by their own experiences and contexts. In the case of Huntington's disease (a neurological disorder), a genetic cause has been identified, enabling families with a history of the disease to take a predictive test. Cox and McKellin found that the meaning that families give to this genetic link is based not only on medical knowledge, giving an 'objective' indication of the risk that they may have inherited the disease, but also on their social relationships:

Case study

Is 'Eve' the world's first clone?

The birth of the world's first cloned human was condemned by British scientists today as another example of the 'sordid depths' to which maverick physicians will sink. The claim by Clonaid announcing Boxing Day's arrival of a baby girl called Eve, born by Caesarean section, will prompt 'revulsion and disgust' throughout the world and will see 2003 go down in history of mankind as the Year of the Clone, Dr Patrick Dixon claimed.

Dr Dixon, a leading expert on the ethics of human cloning, described today's news as 'totally inevitable', with separate US and Chinese teams also claiming that they have created large numbers of human-cloned embryos for medical research (see below). He warned that it would all mark a watershed when the world would suddenly realize that science is spinning out of control.

'We don't know yet . . . whether the claim about Eve is fact or fraud but one thing is clear. There's a global race by maverick scientists to produce clones, motivated by fame, money and warped and twisted beliefs,' he said. 'Today's announcement is totally inevitable and we can expect a number of other births of clones to be announced over the next few weeks.'

He said that physicians across the world were propelled by 'private passions and weird emotions' with the determination to deliver a cloned baby to any man or woman who wished to 'duplicate themselves or recover the dead'. The cloning industry, and today's announcement, was worth tens of millions of pounds, he said.

Dr Dixon added:

> 'The baby born has been born into a living nightmare with a high risk of malformations, ill-health, early death and unimaginable severe emotional pressures. We should be very concerned for Eve's welfare.
>
> Can you imagine what it will be like for a 12-year-old daughter to look at her mother and realise she is seeing her own sister? For Eve to look at her own grandparents around the Christmas table and to see her parents? Can you imagine what kind of freak show she will be regarded as for her entire lifetime?
>
> What will it do to her sense of personal identity, knowing that she's only a copy of someone else who is much older?'

To read more about this debate follow the links at www.globalchange.com/eveclone.htm.

Question

1. What might be the implications for personal identity formation of knowing that one was a clone?

> **Factors such as geographic and social proximity to an affected family member are as important as biological ties in explaining test candidates and their families' intersubjective constructions of hereditary risk.**
>
> (Cox and McKellin 1999: 641)

Developments in genetic research have wider implications than the potential to treat or cure disease. Disability groups have particular concerns about the use of genetic research. Issues have also been raised about the potential this technology offers for surveillance and control. The UK Biobank has been created, storing genetic and personal medical information (www.ukbiobank.ac.uk), but its creation has been controversial. There are concerns about confidentiality and surveillance, and questions are raised about how the data will be used. This relates to issues mentioned earlier around public confidence in medicine and medical science, as the role that medicine plays in healing and social control becomes increasingly blurred (Peterson 2005).

As with all the topics we have discussed in this chapter, the contexts within which health, illness and the body are experienced in the private sphere, and debated in the public sphere, are constantly changing. The sociological imagination gives us the tools to understand these changes and so to reflect on our own lives.

Summary

- Biomedicine is the dominant model for understanding health and illness in Western societies. Its emergence was part of the rise of scientific thought more generally, and it served as the foundation for the development of the modern medical profession.
- Biomedicine is not the only way of thinking about health, illness and the body. There are many examples of different models from other cultures. Within Western cultures, lay beliefs often challenge the biomedical model. Challenges also come from complementary and alternative medicines offering different forms of healing.
- Health, illness and the body are both biological and social phenomena. For example, illness is not only a biological condition within the body; it is also experienced through the changes to a person's life.
- Health and illness are structured by social location. Social divisions are reflected in varying health chances between social classes, between ethnic groups and between men and women.
- Technology offers us possibilities to develop new cures, to extend life and to change bodies. Such developments also present many complex ethical and moral issues and raise questions about the role of medicine in society.

Links

The theoretical approaches referred to in this chapter are discussed more widely in Chapter 2.

The section on health inequalities links to the coverage of social stratification in Chapter 4 and to the discussion of global inequalities in Chapter 9 (pp. 360–368).

The section on gender differences and health relates to the discussion of gender in Chapter 5.

The ethnicity and health discussion relates to the discussion of 'race' and ethnicity in Chapter 6.

The discussions on the experience of chronic illness and on genetics relate to issues of disability considered in Chapter 8.

Websites

www.bma.org

British Medical Association (BMA)
The BMA website gives information on issues affecting doctors, such as violence at work and working hours. It also provides official statements on key health issues.

www.dh.gov.uk

Department of Health
This government website provides links to key health-policy publications and statistics.

www.englemed.co.uk
www.reutershealth.com

Two useful sites providing up to date reports on health related news.

http://sunsite.berkeley.edu/biotech/organswatch

Organs Watch
This website provides information and debate from a team of researchers from the University of California, Berkeley, exploring the social and economic context of organ transplantation. It focuses on the human-rights implications of the worldwide search for organs.

www.who.int

World Health Organization (WHO)
This website provides interesting and useful information and reports on global health issues from the United Nations' health organization.

Further reading

Bury, M. and Gabe, J. (eds) (2004) *The Sociology of Health and Illness: A Reader*, London: Routledge.
A collection of classic and contemporary readings on health beliefs, inequalities, professional–patient interactions, chronic illness and the politics of health care.

Bartely, M. (2004) *Health Inequality: An Introduction to Theories, Concepts and Methods*, Cambridge: Polity Press.
A very thorough but accessible discussion of key issues in understanding health inequalities.

Kleinman, A. (1988) *The Illness Narratives: Suffering, Healing and the Human Condition*, New York: Basic Books.
A fascinating look at the illness experience, expressed through a range of narratives.

Lupton, D. (2003) *Medicine as Culture*, London: Sage.
This book focuses on a social constructionist approach to understanding health and illness.

Nettleton, S. (2006) *Sociology of Health and Illness*, Cambridge: Polity Press.
A very accessible but in-depth text covering all key aspects of contemporary debates around health and illness.

Williams, S. (2003) *Medicine and the Body*, London: Sage.
A very interesting look at the embodied aspects of health and illness from an influential sociologist within the field of health and illness.

Activities

Activity 1

Women's smoking: government targets and social trends

The patterns of women's smoking

> There has been a steady decline in the prevalence of women's smoking in Britain. However, this decline has been accompanied by a rapid change in the social distribution of cigarette smoking and has been less steep for women than men. Cigarette smoking in Britain is becoming increasingly linked to being a woman and to being working class.

Social class and smoking

> . . . Among the factors explaining the gender and class differences in smoking, ignorance of its harmful effects is no longer considered to be a major factor. Most smokers are aware of the health-risks of smoking both for themselves and for their children.

Why women continue to smoke

> . . . Smoking among white women is not only associated with more caring responsibilities, it is also associated with living on less income . . . Few studies have asked women about why caring for others and living in poverty makes it harder to give up smoking.

The limited evidence suggests that cigarette smoking is deeply woven into the strategies women develop to cope with caring and to survive in circumstances of hardship. For women in paid work, cigarette smoking can similarly provide a way of structuring time and coping with stresses and pressures of the job. 'I smoke when I'm sitting down, having a cup of coffee. It's part and parcel of resting' [a mother].

In talking about smoking in the context of poverty, material hardship gives them and their children little opportunity to take part in the lifestyles that others take for granted . . . In a lifestyle with little style left in it, smoking cigarettes can be the only item of personal spending and the only luxury. 'I try to cut down on cigarettes to save money but cigarettes are my one luxury, and at the moment they feel a bit of a necessity' [a mother].

(Source: Graham 1993)

Questions

1. What reasons are given in the article for continued smoking?
2. How do these reasons relate to the cultural/behavioural and material/structural explanations for health inequalities? Which do you find most convincing and why?

Activity 2

Obesity: a sociological issue

A WHO report in 2007 stated that 'the prevalence of obesity has risen threefold or more since the 1980s, even in countries with traditionally low rates . . . If no action is taken and the prevalence of obesity continues to increase at the same rate as in the 1990s, as estimated 150 million adults [within Europe] will be overweight or obese by 2010. The epidemic is progressing at especially alarming rates among children. For example, overweight among children increased from 4% in 1960 to 18% in 2003 in Switzerland and from 8% in 1974 to 20% in 2003 in England'.

(Branca *et al.* 2007: 2)

Nick Crossley (2004) has made the point that 'fat is a sociological issue'. One way in which sociology can help us to understand obesity is by doing research with people about weight. The following extract is taken from research carried out by the Research Unit for Health and Behavioural Change, University of Edinburgh. The researchers were interested in young people's perceptions of their own and other's bodies in relation to weight.

The young teenagers who were BMI-defined as being overweight or obese often talked in contradictory and complex terms about their weight and body size. Three quarters of these teenagers either had positive things to say about their weight, body size or parts of their body, or reported being comfortable with their body's size or shape. Nicole, for example, who was BMI-defined as obese, liked looking at herself in the mirror, particularly as she perceived herself as being thinner than a year ago:

Nicole: In primary school I was as fat as anything, in first year [at secondary school] I was not bad, but now I feel for the last couple of years I was as podgy as anything, fat arms, and see now? When I look in the mirror at myself, ken [Scottish term meaning 'you know'], I used to hate looking in the mirror when I was fat, I used to hate looking in it, but now I look in it every day, my wee favour.

Interviewer: Yeah? It makes you feel good?

Nicole: Aye. (Aged 13; Obese).

(Wills *et al.* 2006: 399)

Questions

1. Why is it important to understand the perceptions of young people about weight and health?
2. How else could sociology contribute to our understanding of obesity? Think about the social factors raised in discussions about obesity.
3. In this chapter we looked at the social construction of medical knowledge. In what ways can 'obesity' be seen as socially constructed?

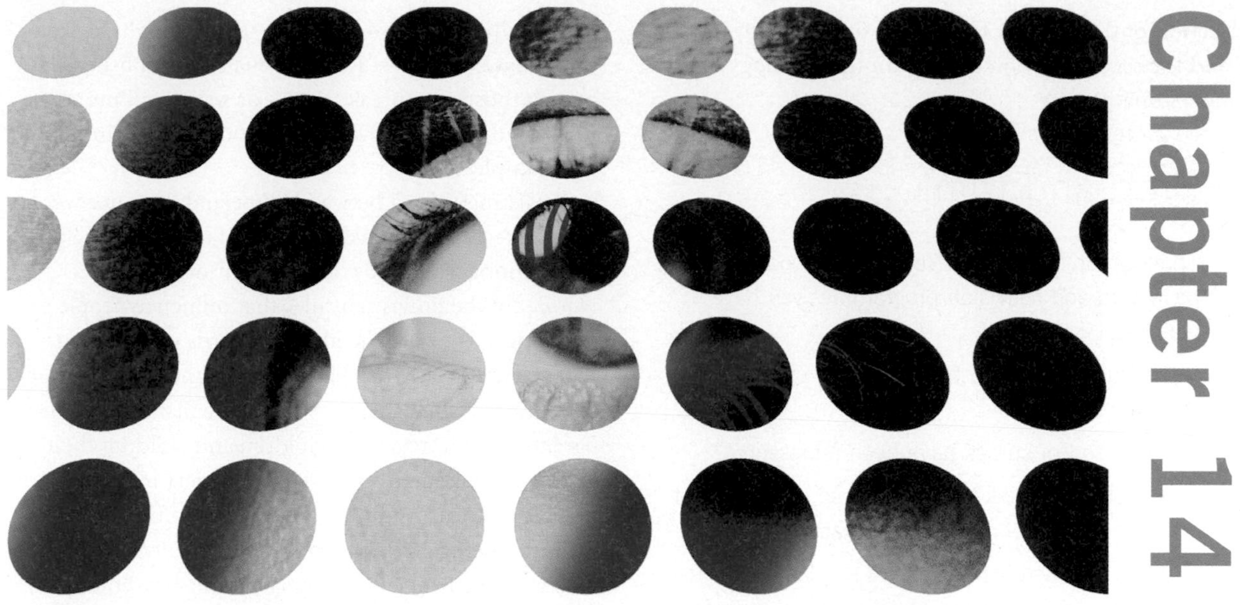

Chapter 14

Crime and punishment

The study of crime begins with the knowledge of oneself. (Miller 1970 [1945])

The standards of a nation's civilisation can be judged by opening the doors of its prisons. (Dostoevsky 1962 [1860])

Key issues

- How has crime been defined and measured?
- How have sociologists tried to explain crime?
- To what extent is crime characteristic of particular social groups?
- What are the main aims of punishment?
- How have sociologists explained the role of punishment in society?

Introduction

Unconventional and criminal behaviour fascinates people. Many popular TV programmes, successful films and bestselling books are about crime and criminals, both 'real life' and fictional. Our interest is in criminal behaviour – what it involves and how it is done – and in what happens to the criminals – whether they 'get away with it' and what happens to them if they do not. However, while we like to watch and read about crime, and many of us break laws from time to time, relatively few of us will have been caught and prosecuted for our lawbreaking behaviour, and even fewer will make crime a way of life and become professional murderers, smugglers or fraudsters.

This chapter looks at both crime and punishment, at the extent of crime, why some people and social groups are more likely to engage in criminal behaviour than others, how society controls crime and how it deals with those people who are caught. The role of the police in enforcing the law and the debates surrounding punishment of offenders are discussed. Punishment is examined as a key element of the sociology of crime; this is evident in the work of Durkheim, the major 'classical' theorist in this area. Durkheim highlighted the importance of crime for maintaining the collective conscience of society and emphasized how punishment exemplified this collective conscience at work. The first section of this chapter focuses on the sociology of crime and the second section centres on the sociology of punishment.

Stop and think

Think of the films you have seen, the books you have read and television programmes you have watched recently.

- How many of them have included examples of criminal behaviour?
- What sort of crimes have been represented?
- Why do you think that there is so much interest in all aspects of crime in the mass media?
- What are the differences and similarities between the depiction of fictional and real-life crime on television?

The sociology of crime

The relationship between crime and deviance

Before looking at sociological work on crime, we need to define and clarify our subject matter, particularly as crime is often examined as part of the broader field of the sociology of deviance and the terms 'crime' and 'deviance' are sometimes used interchangeably. Unconventional behaviour fascinates people; such behaviour might involve breaking the law or might fall just outside the commonly held definition of what is normal and reasonable. This distinction helps us to distinguish crime from deviance.

Crime may be defined as an act that breaks the criminal law; it can be followed by criminal proceedings and formal punishment.

Deviance is a less precise concept than crime: deviance means any behaviour that differs from the normal. Thus, deviant behaviour could be uncommonly good or brave behaviour as well as unacceptable behaviour, such as theft or vandalism. It could also be eccentric or bizarre behaviour, such as talking loudly to oneself or to no one in particular in public places. However, deviance generally refers to behaviour that is disapproved of and subject to some form of punishment; behaviour that is outside the rules of society and leads to a hostile and critical response from 'conventional society'. These rules might be legal rules – laws that have specific penalties established to punish those who break them – or social and moral rules – rules about how people should behave in public, for example.

In distinguishing between crime and deviance we have talked about breaking laws and not following conventional standards of behaviour or norms. *Norms* are the unwritten rules that influence people's behaviour. They are the ideal standards of behaviour that members of a social group share and form part of the culture of that society, such as the manner in which parents should treat their children and children their parents. Different groups within a society may have their own norms. While it is the norm in the UK to eat meat, being a vegetarian is not generally seen as unacceptable behaviour. Young people may hold quite different norms from older people, and particular youth groups have norms that are distinct from other groups.

The definitions of crime and deviance as behaviour that is outside the laws or norms of society emphasize the importance of the reaction of others; such behaviour will usually produce some form of critical or hostile response from the wider society. However, laws and norms are not fixed; they vary from time to time and from place to place. Therefore, behaviour that breaks them will also vary. So crime and deviance are *relative concepts*, which vary according to the particular social situation. Behaviour that is criminal in one country can be acceptable in another, for example drinking alcohol or having several spouses at the same time. Certain types of behaviour have been criminal at one period of time but not at others; homosexuality, for instance, has been decriminalized in many countries but still carries the death penalty in Iran.

Social reaction is of central importance in determining whether behaviour is categorized as criminal or deviant. No action is criminal or deviant in itself; it becomes so only if the society defines it as such, through the legal system or through the general acceptance of certain norms of behaviour. In modern societies, killing is usually seen as the most serious of offences, but in the context of war killing can be seen as heroic and people may even be punished for not wanting to take part in killing, as happened to the conscientious objectors who were imprisoned in the First World War.

Crime is behaviour that deviates from conventional, accepted behaviour and can lead to formal punishment. Many other forms of behaviour contravene norms without actually breaking the law and becoming criminal. Transvestism is not a crime but may be considered deviant. While deviance is a broader concept that encompasses crime, criminal behaviour is not always seen as deviant. Making private phone calls on an office telephone is, strictly speaking, theft and yet may be widely accepted as a 'perk' of the job.

The sociological study of crime

Crime encompasses such a vast range of activities that its sociological study is a massive and uncertain task. An unquantifiable, but clearly large, amount of crime is not generally known about. Burglars and fraudsters may not be caught; assaults, prostitution and illegal drug use occur on a far wider scale than is officially recorded. People who break the rules of society tend not to advertise themselves, which makes the study of this sort of behaviour more problematic than many other areas of sociological study. Some criminals do appear to enjoy publicity, but the majority of those who commit criminal actions attempt to conceal themselves.

The secretive nature of crime raises a number of problems for those wishing to study it. Initially, the researcher needs to find the subjects for study. How do we go about locating a group engaged in forgery, for example? Crime often occurs in conventional situations and the researcher has to be alert to this. In *Cheats at Work*, Gerald Mars (1982) studied the variety of crime in everyday work situations and found that fiddling and thieving were accepted practices in many occupations. One example that Mars cites involved 462 watch repairers being presented with an identical problem: a watch in perfect condition except for a small fault, a loose screw that could be easily tightened and that would be obvious to a scarcely trained repairer. Nearly half the sample (226 repairers) responded to this 'problem' with diagnoses that lied, overcharged or suggested extensive and unnecessary repairs; many of the repairers suggested that the watches needed a clean and overhaul, in spite of their pristine condition. Mars called this the exploiting of expertise, when one person (the expert) has knowledge that others (the customers) do not have access to. Although not rare, employee theft is usually hidden, which raises problems for research.

Once a group or individual has been located, it is necessary to convince them that they can safely discuss their criminal behaviour with the researcher. Their confidence has to be gained, and it can take months to gain the trust of a professional criminal. Research into crime is thus likely to take comparatively longer and be more expensive than research into other areas of social behaviour. Other practical problems include the potential (physical) danger faced by researchers who investigate certain types of criminal behaviour and criminals – most obviously, from violent criminals – and the fact that criminals are perhaps particularly likely to give false information – although this is not to suggest that lying is limited to criminals.

As well as practical difficulties, researching into criminal behaviour causes ethical problems. The behaviour being studied is often widely condemned, which can cause moral dilemmas for the researcher over whether to reveal information that might help the authorities and could, perhaps, help to prevent others getting hurt. This problem is faced by other people who are entrusted with confidential information, such as doctors, lawyers and priests. Finally, it is not always easy for researchers to remain neutral and objective; they may feel sympathy or disgust, depending on the particular topic being studied.

Stop and think

- In view of the problems that the sociological study of crime faces, which methods of research might be most appropriate for investigating such behaviour? Why would they be appropriate?
- What particular problems would be faced by the different methods?

Why do most people conform?

Although many people break the law, few become regular offenders and most people are never found guilty of criminal offences. So why does the majority conform to the generally accepted standards of behaviour? This question can be answered by referring to two basic types of social control or restraint:

- *Informal mechanisms of control* centre around the socialization process: children learn that stealing, cheating and so on are wrong.
- *Formal mechanisms of control* involve legal and formally established sanctions, such as the law, the police and the punishment system.

These control mechanisms do not exert a uniform influence on all individuals or groups. This can be

Case study

Crime and deviance: cultural and historical relativity

It is easily observable that different groups judge different things to be deviant. This should alert us to the possibility that the person making the judgement of deviance, the process by which the judgement is arrived at, and the situation in which it is made will all be intimately involved in the phenomenon of deviance . . .

Deviance is the product of a transaction that takes place between a social group and one who is viewed by that group as a rule breaker. Whether an act is deviant, then, depends on how people react to it . . . The degree to which other people will respond to a given act as deviant varies greatly. Several kinds of variation are worth noting. First of all, there is variation over time. A person believed to have committed a given 'deviant' act may at one time be responded to much more leniently than he would at some other time. The occurrence of 'drives' against various kinds of deviance illustrates this clearly.

(Becker 1963: 4–12)

Figure 14.1 Witches in Europe
The Bridgeman Art Library/Getty Images

Witches in England

Witchcraft was not made a capital offence in Britain until 1563 although it was deemed heresy and was denounced as such by Pope Innocent III in 1484. From 1484 until around 1750 some 200,000 witches were tortured, burnt or hanged in Western Europe. Most supposed witches were usually old women, and invariably poor. Any who were unfortunate enough to be 'crone-like', snaggle-toothed and having a hairy lip were assumed to possess the 'Evil Eye'! If they also had a cat this was taken as proof, as witches always had a 'familiar', the cat being the most common. Many unfortunate women were condemned on this sort of evidence and hanged after undergoing appalling torture. The 'pilnie-winks' (thumb screws) and iron 'caspie-claws' (a form of leg iron heated over a brazier) usually got a confession from the supposed witch . . .

In August 1612, the Pendle Witches, three generations of one family, were marched through the crowded streets of Lancaster and hanged.

(www.historic-uk.com)

Questions

1. Alcohol drinking and bigamy illustrate the relative nature of crime and deviance. List other types of behaviour that have been categorized as criminal or deviant in one society but not another.

2. Give examples of behaviour that has been criminal or deviant at different periods of time in the same society.

3. In looking at responses to crime and deviance, Becker refers to 'drives' against certain types of behaviour. What types of crime or deviance have been subject to such drives in recent years in the UK?

illustrated by considering your own behaviour. Why do you follow the laws of society? If you follow laws because you agree with them and feel them to be right, then this indicates the influence of informal control mechanisms. If you follow laws because of a fear of being caught and punished, then the influence of formal control mechanisms is greater. Would you steal from shops if it could be guaranteed that you would not get caught? Answers of 'yes' to this question would suggest that formal control mechanisms are the major determinant with regard to shoplifting, rather than a belief that the behaviour is wrong in itself.

Clearly it is not always easy to pinpoint exactly why we do or do not follow any particular action. Often the reasons reflect a mixture of informal and formal social controls, their relative importance varying with different circumstances. It might be very easy to steal from a family member or friend and not get caught, but most people would feel this to be wrong. Such feelings of disapproval would perhaps not exert such a strong influence over decisions as to whether to steal from less personal, larger victims. Stealing from a small corner shop may seem more personal than stealing from a supermarket that makes vast profits and expects a certain amount of theft or 'stock shrinkage'. However, it is more 'dangerous' to steal from a supermarket in that the chances of getting caught and prosecuted will be greater in the larger store.

Explaining crime

Explanations for why people break laws are of great public interest. Over time, a vast array of possible causes of crime have been suggested, such as inherited personality traits, poor housing, getting in with the 'wrong crowd' and inadequate parental control. More recently, there has been considerable controversy over the possibility raised by some scientists that individuals might have a genetic or inherited predisposition to certain types of behaviour and feelings that are more likely to result in criminal acts. But even these deterministic approaches do not deny the importance of environmental factors such as nutrition and deprivation.

Sociological theories of crime emphasize the importance of the social context: crime and criminals are viewed in relation to specific social conditions and opportunities. The review of theories in this section follows the conventional division of functionalist, interactionist and conflict-based approaches; these are broad schools of thought containing many variations, and particular studies may not fall neatly into one perspective. Nonetheless, this division does enable sociological theories to be discussed in a chronological sequence. At the risk of oversimplification, functionalist approaches were taken issue with by interactionist and conflict theories in the 1960s and 1970s. More recent theoretical approaches have included elements of the interactionist and conflict perspectives in an attempt to avoid the limitations of one particular theoretical position.

We will start, though, by considering classical criminology and how it influenced the early sociological theorizing about crime.

Classical criminology

Sometimes known as classical jurisprudence, classical criminology emerged from the period known as the Enlightenment and was developed by penal reformers in the later eighteenth and early nineteenth centuries who wanted to create a fair and legitimate criminal justice system based on equality. The intention was to develop a rational and efficient means of delivering justice in place of previous arbitrary, corrupt and prejudiced forms of punishment. Classical criminology was based on the notion that individuals had free will and made rational choices about the way in which they would behave. People, including those who commit criminal acts, have to be considered as rational, and so an individual's behaviour will be based on a rational calculation of the consequences. The major control over a person exercising their free will is fear – particularly fear of pain. The fear of pain, in the form of punishment, would then deter an individual from criminal activities and act as a control on their behaviour.

The two Enlightenment philosophers most associated with developing this approach were Cesare Beccaria and Jeremy Bentham.

Beccaria was an Italian university professor who, at the age of only 26, wrote an essay on punishment entitled *Dei Deliti e Delle Pene* (*On Crimes and Punishment*) that was published in 1764. This book, which was written at a time when severe and barbaric punishments were the norm, caused something of an outcry with its rational approach to punishment – although condemned by the Roman Catholic Church, it was widely read and translated into 22 languages. Essentially Beccaria advocated a reformed system of criminal justice that provided a more logical and rational approach to the punishment of crime.

Many of Beccaria's ideas have formed the basis of modern criminological theorizing. In discussing the ranking of crimes within society, Beccaria acknowledges and highlights the relative nature of crime and the social reaction to it – a notion central to the work of the interactionists, labelling theorists whose work became very much in vogue in the sociology of the 1960s and 1970s (see pp. 563–564):

> **Whoever reads, with a philosophic eye, the history of nations, and their laws, will generally find, that the ideas of virtue and vice, of a good or bad citizen, change with the revolution of ages, not in proportion to the alteration of circumstances, and consequently conformability to the common good, but in proportion to the passions and errors by which the different lawgivers were successively influenced. He will frequently observe that the passions and vices of one age are the foundation of the morality of the following . . . Hence the uncertainty of our notions of honour and virtue; an uncertainty which will ever remain, because they change with the revolutions of time . . . they change with the boundaries of states.**
>
> (Beccaria 1963 [1764])

In particular, Beccaria is known for his advocating of a utilitarian approach to the law and punishment, arguing that, although the laws of a society might affect the liberty of a few, they would be acceptable if they resulted in the greater happiness of the majority. He believed that human behaviour was essentially rational and based on the pleasure–pain principle. As regards punishment, the pain of punishment should be greater than the potential pleasure resulting from the criminal act – so the punishment should be proportionate to the harm done to society by the crime.

In a similar vein, Bentham promoted the utilitarian approach, and argued that punishment should be calculated carefully to inflict pain in proportion to the harm done to the public by the particular crime. This sort of argument was based on the notion that criminals and non-criminals were similar in that criminals were reasoning individuals who had made an error of judgement in committing a crime; and that rational, swift and certain punishment was the best way to stop such behaviour recurring. Influenced by Beccaria, Bentham believed that people behaved rationally and would seek pleasure and aim to avoid pain. So punishment must outweigh any pleasure that might be derived from criminal behaviour. Bentham claimed that all law and punishments should be based on the utilitarian principle of 'the greatest happiness of the greatest number' and on calculating degrees of pain and pleasure – so the pain of punishment could be justified only if it prevented more and greater pain.

Classical criminology certainly seemed to offer a much fairer and more open philosophy and system of punishment than the previous cruel and harsh systems. However, in emphasizing the free will and rationality of individuals, it did not consider issues of social inequality that might encourage certain individuals to commit crime, and it assumed there was a generally agreed set of values or goals in society, ignoring the conflicting aims and goals of different groups.

Functionalist theories

Durkheim

Of the founding 'classic' sociological theorists, it was Emile Durkheim who wrote most on crime (and punishment), and his work formed the basis for the functionalist school of thought in sociology.

The underlying characteristic of all functionalist-based theory is the importance of shared norms and values that form the basis of social order. Durkheim argued that deviance, and crime in particular, was a normal phenomenon in society, an 'integral part of all healthy societies'. Given that crime involves breaking laws, it might seem odd to argue that it is necessary for society. The emphasis of Durkheim's argument is that crime is inevitable and can be functional. His work is looked at in more detail in relation to the punishment of crime (see pp. 589–591). The case study opposite illustrates how crime can not only encourage social change but also strengthen the generally held values and rules of a society.

The Chicago School

Durkheim's early sociological theorizing on crime has been developed in a number of directions by later social theorists and criminologists. Here we will look at the work of the Chicago School on the relationship between increasing social disorganization and criminal behaviour and, in the next section, at the argument of Robert Merton linking anomie with criminal behaviour. The notion that modern, industrializing and urbanizing societies would bring with them greater social disorganization and therefore

Case study

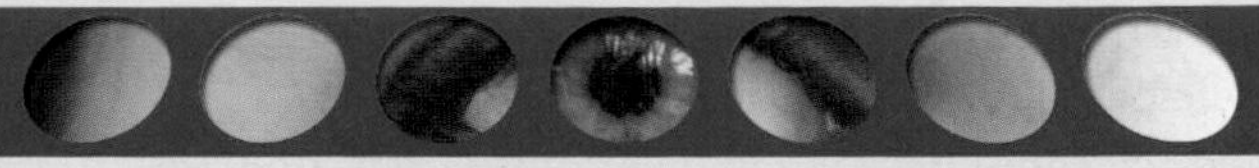

Crime and the collective conscience

In the first place crime is normal because a society exempt from it is utterly impossible. Crime consists of an act that offends certain very strong collective sentiments . . . Imagine a society of saints, a perfect cloister of exemplary individuals. Crimes will there be unknown; but faults which appear venial (trivial) to the layman will create there the same scandal that the ordinary offense does in ordinary consciousness. If this society has the power to judge and punish, it will define these acts as criminal and treat them as such. For the same reason, the perfect and upright man judges his smallest failings with a severity that the majority reserve for acts more truly in the nature of an offense . . .

Crime is, then, necessary; it is bound up with the fundamental conditions of all social life, and by that very fact it is useful, because these conditions of which it is a part are themselves indispensable to the normal evolution of morality and law . . .

Crime itself plays a useful role in this evolution. Crime implies not only that the way remains open to necessary changes but that in certain cases it directly prepares these changes. According to Athenian law, Socrates was a criminal. However, his crime, namely, the independence of his thought, rendered a service not only to humanity but to his country . . .

Nor is the case of Socrates unique; it is reproduced periodically in history. It would never have been possible to establish the freedom of thought we now enjoy if the regulations prohibiting it had not been violated. At that time, however, the violation was a crime . . .

From this point of view the fundamental facts of criminality present themselves to us in an entirely new light. Contrary to current ideas, the criminal no longer seems a totally unsociable being, a sort of parasitic element. On the contrary, he plays a definite role in social life.

(Durkheim 1964: 67–72)

Questions

1. What are the positive and useful functions of crime suggested by Durkheim?
2. Suggest any other social functions that crime might perform.
3. Look at press and/or television reports of a recent criminal trial and suggest (a) the values reinforced by the crime; and (b) the possible social changes that might follow from that case.

a growth in social problems, including crime, underpinned the work of sociologists at the University of Chicago in the 1920 and 1930s. The approach and theorizing of these sociologists has become known as the Chicago School.

Based on Durkheim's work, the Chicago School saw crime as a social, rather than an individual, phenomenon. They argued that social life in certain areas and neighbourhoods was chaotic and pathological and that in such situations crime was an expected and normal response. This view was coloured with a degree of optimism in that it was felt such a situation was only temporary due to the rapid social changes brought on by industrialization and urbanization and that in this context a certain amount of crime was inevitable and of no particular threat to the basis of society. A key figure in establishing the reputation of the Chicago School was Robert Park. He believed, that in order to study crime, sociologists should actually go out into the city and engage in first-hand research – a view that encouraged the development of a number of important and renowned ethnographic research studies by sociologists at the University of Chicago. Park and colleagues argued that cities should be considered as ecological systems, with different areas and neighbourhoods within them developing at different times and in specific ways.

Ernest Burgess, another leading Chicago School sociologist, developed this 'ecological' approach by mapping out the different 'zones' of Chicago, which formed five concentric circles covering the whole city. At the centre there was a business area of banks and offices and outside were different residential zones – what was termed the 'zone of transition' just beyond the central business zone, then the zone of what he called workingmen's homes, the residential zone and the commuters' zone. The zone of transition was where most crime and other social problems occurred. Clifford Shaw and Henry McKay, two researchers associated closely with the University of Chicago Sociology Department, developed Burgess's approach to examine patterns of juvenile crime in Chicago. In this zone the housing was typically run-down, and the inhabitants were often new immigrants and others lacking the means to live elsewhere in the city. They found that, in this deprived area with a transient population who were unable to put down roots, the values and norms that led to criminal behaviour were most likely to be found.

> **The high rates of juvenile crime found in the zone of transition were said to be linked to the social disorganisation in those areas. In the absence of strong normative controls from the family and the community, juveniles were likely to engage in delinquent activities.**
>
> (Tierney 1996: 91)

Structural and subcultural adaptations

Durkheim's argument that crime is inevitable and functional does not explain the causes of crime or why certain people are more likely than others to engage in criminal activities. More recent functionalist theories, based on the notion of there being a general consensus of values and norms, have focused on and tried to explain the *causes* of criminal behaviour.

Robert Merton (1938) suggested that, in situations where there is a strong emphasis on particular goals but the means for achieving these goals are not available for certain groups or individuals, *anomie* will result. This means that the rules that normally govern behaviour lose their influence and are liable to be ignored: the shared values and norms no longer determine behaviour. Merton explains criminal behaviour as resulting from a contradiction between the aspirations into which society has socialized people (the goals – in Western society, material success is a generally held goal) and the ways that are provided for the realization of these aspirations (the means). In devising ways of adapting to this contradiction between what they want from society and the means they have available to get it, some people will turn to criminal behaviour, such as theft. This approach explains crime in terms of the structure and culture of society, rather than in terms of the individual; it laid the ground for explanations based on the notion of subculture and the argument that certain groups will be more liable than others to engage in criminal behaviour.

Albert Cohen's (1955) study *Delinquent Boys* is generally seen as the starting point for subcultural theories. Cohen takes issue with the view that delinquent behaviour is caused directly by the desire for material goals. Although some forms of crime and delinquency are centred on acquiring goods or money, a large amount of it is expressive (e.g. vandalism) rather than concerned with materialistic gain.

Cohen's explanation turns to the educational system. Schools, he argues, are middle-class institutions that embody middle-class values and goals. Individuals brought up in a working-class environment will be likely to desire the generally held goals but will have less opportunity to achieve them due to educational failure. Seeing the avenues to success blocked will lead to working-class boys suffering from what Cohen termed 'status frustration'. They will be likely to reject the school system and form a delinquent subculture. Delinquent subcultures, according to Walter Miller (1958), are based on a number of 'focal concerns' that reflect the values and traditions of 'lower-class' life; these focal concerns include 'toughness', 'excitement' and 'smartness'.

The subcultural approach stresses the collective response as crucial, rather than seeing criminal behaviour as an individual response to failure, as Merton argued. As Cohen puts it:

> **Delinquency, according to this view, is not an expression or contrivance of a particular kind of personality; it may be imposed upon any kind of personality if circumstances favour intimate association with delinquent models. The process of becoming a delinquent is the same as the process of becoming, let us say, a Boy Scout. The difference lies only in the cultural pattern with which the child associates.**
>
> (Cohen 1955: 13–14)

Another subcultural theory that stresses deprivation and develops from the work of Merton and Cohen is that of Cloward and Ohlin (1961). They argue that there is greater pressure to behave criminally on the working classes because they have less opportunity to 'succeed' by legitimate means. Working-class boys are liable to form and join delinquent subcultures, but there is more than one type of subculture. Cloward and Ohlin define these as:

- a *criminal subculture*, where delinquency is closely connected with adult crime;
- a *conflict subculture*, which develops where links with adult crime are not well established;
- a *retreatist or escapist subculture*.

Subcultural theories suggest that crime and delinquency can, ironically, represent conformity. In modern society there are a range of subgroups with their own subcultures that include norms, values and attitudes that differ from and conflict with those of the rest of society. Conformity within such subgroups will involve some form of deviance from and conflict with the wider society.

Stop and think

➤ Delinquent subcultures are typically described as male and working-class. Can you think of examples of criminal, delinquent subcultures that do and do not fit this stereotypical picture, in terms of both class and gender?

➤ Cloward and Ohlin refer to criminal, conflict and retreatist subcultures. Give an example of each type.

Functionalist theories can be criticized for offering explanations of crime that are too generalized. Characteristics that are common to the working class as a whole are used to explain crime. Merton (1938) highlighted the importance of restricted opportunities to achieve material goals; however, restricted opportunities are very common and most people who suffer from them do not turn to crime. A similar point can be made with regard to Cohen's (1955) notion of status frustration and Cloward and Ohlin's (1961) explanation of delinquent subcultures.

Interactionist theories

Functionalist theories of crime tend to assume that there is a general consensus within society over what is right and wrong behaviour. The interactionist approach questions this assumption; it does not see criminals as essentially different from so-called 'normal' people. Many people commit criminal actions, and it is therefore not easy to maintain a clear distinction between the criminal and non-criminal in terms of particular personal characteristics.

Labelling

Labelling theory is perhaps the key aspect of the interactionist perspective. The criminal is an individual who has been labelled so by society, and interactionist theory centres on the relationship, or interaction, between criminals and those bodies or individuals who define them as such.

Howard Becker's (1963) study of deviance, *Outsiders*, contains one of the most quoted statements on the labelling perspective:

> **Social groups create deviance by making rules whose infraction constitutes deviance and by applying those rules to particular people and labelling them as outsiders. From this point of view deviance is not a quality of the act a person commits, but rather a consequence of the application by others of rules and sanctions to an offender. The deviant is one to whom that label has been successfully applied; deviant behaviour is behaviour that people so label.**
>
> (Becker 1963: 9)

Thus, labelling is a process by which individuals or groups categorize certain types of behaviour and certain individuals. A deviant or outsider is a person who has been labelled as such, which raises the question of 'Who does the labelling?' The actions and motives of those doing the labelling are of as much, if not more, concern as those of the labelled. The focus on the process of labelling raises the issue of who has the power to define and impose their definitions of right and wrong on others. Giddens puts the interactionist position succinctly:

> **The labels applied to create categories of deviance thus express the power structures of society. By and large, the rules in terms of which deviance is defined, and the contexts in which they are applied, are framed by the wealthy for the poor, by men for women, by older people for younger people and by ethnic majorities for minority groups.**
>
> (Giddens 1993: 128)

The emphasis on labelling is due, in part, to the interactionist interest in the political nature of crime and deviance. Laws are essentially political products that reflect the power some groups in society have, a power that enables them to impose their ideas about right and wrong, normality and the like on the rest of society. Although the law applies to everyone, including the powerful, interactionists suggest that it is applied less frequently and vigorously to some people and groups: there is a selective enforcement of the law and a selective application of criminal labels.

The selective enforcement of the law was examined by Cicourel (1976) in his study of the way in which juvenile justice is administered in the USA. Cicourel found that particular groups are selected, processed and labelled as delinquent. White middle-class youths are less likely to be identified by police and probation officers as being potential delinquents. The police are more liable to react towards those groups and individuals whom they see as being especially prone to engage in delinquent behaviour, often labelling such individuals before the actual committing of any act.

Labelling individuals will tend to mark them out. The knowledge that someone has been convicted for a violent crime, for instance, might well influence how you react to that person. Furthermore, individuals who have been labelled tend to view themselves in terms of the label and act accordingly. This produces an amplification or snowballing effect: the label becomes fixed more firmly and the person becomes more attached to it. Interactionists argue that the social reaction, in terms of labelling, can actually increase or 'amplify' the criminal behaviour of the labelled individual.

This amplifying or snowballing effect can also occur at a wider, societal level, as well as at an individual level. Jock Young's work on hippies and the police in London during the 1960s and 1970s illustrated this wider application. Young (1971) found that the harder the police tried to stamp out drug use among hippies, the more it actually grew. He suggested that the police acted as amplifiers of this illegal behaviour. The police attempted to control drug use through the formation of drug squads; however, this had the effect of spreading and amplifying such drug use. The drug squads discovered more cases of drug use because that was what they were searching for; this led to more police time and money being invested in dealing with it; this led to even more drug use being discovered – in other words, there was a 'spiral of amplification'. Furthermore, Young argued that the way in which the police acted against hippies, stereotyping them as dirty, idle, drug fiends and harassing them, helped to unite drug users and led to the development of a sort of group identity and ethos, 'drug taking becomes of greater value to the group as a result of the greater police activity'.

A more general criticism of labelling theory is that it pays little attention to the original causes of crime and deviance. If crime and deviance are the result of labelling by others, then how does 'primary deviance' occur. In other words, an initial deviant action could be seen as 'unlabelled deviance' (Tierney 1996). Tierney argues that, although a rule or law might have been broken, the individual has not yet been labelled and so how can that action be deviant? In response, it could be argued that deviant and criminal behaviour are actions that break established laws or rules and that the labelling of a particular individual need not occur in order for crime or deviance to exist. In other words, it is quite possible for a 'secret deviant' to exist.

The interactionist, labelling approach has also been criticized for focusing on the rules and laws themselves. Interactionists place great stress on social reaction; however, they do not really attempt to explain why certain actions and not others are labelled as crimes. There is little examination of who makes the rules. The relationship between power and crime is raised with regard to the selective nature of labelling but is not really explored. Interactionism concentrates on the specific interactions between people, on the 'drama' of the police station and courtroom, without investigating the importance of the social system itself. Interactionists look at criminals, the police and the legal system without examining the power underlying the system, without examining how power and decision-making are distributed. These issues are central to the conflict explanations of crime.

Conflict theories

'Classical' Marxism

Marx did not write in detail or theorize about crime, but later writers working within a Marxist framework have developed a Marxist theory of crime. From this perspective, crime is seen largely as the product of capitalism, with criminal and antisocial behaviour indicative of the contradictions and problems inherent in the capitalist system. The basic motivations of capitalism, such as the emphasis on materialism and self-enrichment, encourage self-interested, antisocial and, by implication, criminal behaviour.

With regard to the control of crime, Marxists argue that the law expresses and reflects the interests of the ruling classes. Furthermore, there has been a great increase in the range of behaviour that has come under the control of the law. In their introduction to *Critical*

Case study

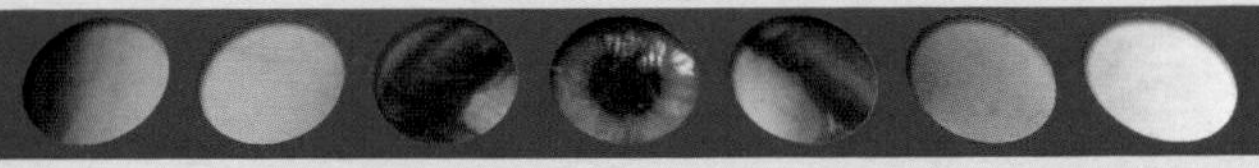

High jinks and hooliganism: having a smashing time

It was a lovely evening. They broke up Mr Austen's grand piano, and stamped Lord Rending's cigars into his carpet, and smashed his china, and tore up Mr Partridge's sheets, and threw the Matisse into his water-jug; Mr Sanders had nothing to break except his windows.

Evelyn Waugh's account of the activities of the Bullingdon Club at Oxford University was written in the 1920s. The recent antics of James Sainsbury and other Oxford undergraduates suggest that little has changed since then. Sainsbury, heir to £124 million-worth of his family's grocery business, went out to dinner in June at Thatcher's restaurant, near Oxford, with fellow members of the Assassin's Club. They set fire to the table cloths, smashed crockery, threw food at the walls, vomited on the carpet and tore curtains down. Sainsbury was fined £25 last week.

If James Sainsbury's hooliganism was in keeping with the traditions of his university, so was the gentle punishment which he received for his misdeeds. (When asked if he could afford the £25 fine and £25 prosecution costs, he replied: 'I expect I can manage it'.) Sean Paton, co-editor of the student newspaper *Isis*, thinks that too much fuss has been made about the Sainsbury case. 'James Sainsbury's a pretty harmless bloke,' he told me. 'He just does silly things when he's drunk. To his friends he's a pretty reasonable bloke.' Paton adds: 'I think it's all high jinks.'

Indeed, some upper-class and upper-middle-class parents actually approve of 'horseplay' (a word which is applied only to their class; when working-class youths behave in a similar manner they are called juvenile delinquents).

(Wheen 1982: 9)

Rules tend to be applied more to some persons than others. Studies of juvenile delinquency make the point clearly. Boys from middle-class areas do not get as far in the legal process when they are apprehended as do boys from slum areas. The middle-class boy is less likely, when picked up by the police, to be taken to the station; less likely when taken to the station to be booked; and it is extremely unlikely that he will be convicted and sentenced.

(Becker 1963: 12–13)

Questions

1. Why might upper-class hooliganism be responded to in a different manner from working-class hooliganism, and by whom?
2. Becker and Cicourel highlight social class as a factor that influences whether or not a person is defined as criminal. What other social factors might influence such definitions? How might they do so?

Criminology, Taylor *et al.* (1975) point out that old laws have been reactivated and new laws created in order to control and contain an increasing range of behaviour seen as socially problematic. The legal system is seen as reflecting economic interests; it is seen as an instrument that supports the powerful groups in society against behaviour that threatens or interferes with their interests.

An example of the way in which the law reflects the interests of the powerful is the way in which the 'crime problem' tends to be equated with working-class crime, often of a fairly trivial nature, rather than the more significant, at least in financial terms, business and white-collar crime. Marxists argue that business crime is largely ignored by the legal system. There are some well-publicized exceptions, but these tend just to reinforce the impression that criminals are mainly from the working classes and that business criminals are not 'real' criminals – they are just doing 'what everyone else does'.

The way in which the legal system reflects economic interests is also illustrated by the relative power that different groups have to impose rules and their own definitions and interpretations of them on others.

When, for example, is a particular behaviour – like drinking liquor or smoking pot – defined as deviant or illegal and when is it viewed as an 'alternative life-style' that individuals are free to accept or reject?

Case study

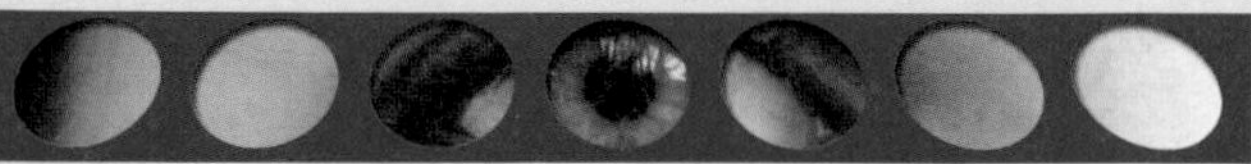

Criminal law

The Criminal Justice and Public Order Act 1994

This Act brought massive changes to the criminal justice system. Essentially, it was an attempt by the then home secretary, Michael Howard, to deal with all the outstanding problems of criminal justice as he saw them. Not surprisingly, then, the provisions of the Act were wide-ranging. Among other things, the principle of a defendant's 'right to silence' was withdrawn and the power of the police to stop and search and to take intimate body samples was extended. Part Five of the Act dealt with public order offences. A series of clauses in the Act have effectively criminalized sections of the community that the government felt to be 'antisocial'. It became an offence to take part in a gathering of more than 20 people on a highway or any land without the owner's permission. Hunt saboteurs and squatters were criminalized, raves were banned and New Age travellers had their sites taken away. This Act was a central plank of the Conservative government's policy on crime; indeed, the Conservative Party's campaign guide in 1994 talked directly about a 'crackdown on squatters, "ravers", "New Age travellers" and hunt saboteurs'.

The Crime and Disorder Act 1998

One of the key elements of the subsequent Labour government's thinking and policy towards crime and its reduction is an emphasis on 'community safety'. This is reflected in the Crime and Disorder Bill that it introduced in 1997 and that became law in 1998. This legislation required local authorities and other responsible agencies to formulate and implement strategies for reducing crime and disorder in their areas. It was the first opportunity for the (New) Labour government to implement its pre-election pledge to be 'tough on crime and tough on the causes of crime'. In particular it adopted a tough approach to youth offending. The proposal for curfews, for instance, exercised greater control over the behaviour of young people, while the legal powers introduced to deal with behaviours not previously seen as criminal, termed 'ASBO' (antisocial behaviour order), widened the criminal net. Although there is no detailed definition of 'disorder', it would seem that it was being equated with antisocial behaviour and would be interpreted by local authorities to cover the things that people complain about, such as noise, litter and young people hanging about.

The Criminal Justice Act 2003

The Criminal Justice Bill was introduced by the government in November 2002 and became law in 2003. The focus of the Act is on the reform of sentencing arrangements and criminal procedures. The Home Office described it as 'an integral part of the government's commitment to modernise the criminal justice system which at present is not bringing enough offenders to justice'. In attempting to do this, new types of sentences were introduced in order to protect the public from dangerous offenders, including 30-year minimum sentences for some crimes. The length of prison sentences that magistrates can mete out rose from 6 to 12 months. Such new provisions are likely to lead to an increase in the already record prison population as magistrates adopt a tougher approach to sentencing.

Key points of this new Act include:

- changing the rules of evidence in order to allow the use of previous convictions where relevant and to allow reported (hearsay) evidence where there is a good reason why the original source cannot be present;
- making retrials of acquitted defendents possible in serious cases if there is new and compelling evidence;
- new, longer sentences to ensure that dangerous offenders remain in custody for as long as they remain a threat to the community, new community sentences, and new custodial sentences with periods of supervision in the community.

Questions

1. The pieces of legislation introduced above aim to tackle offending behaviour more effectively and to reduce crime. To what extent do you think they will be successful?
2. How might a Marxist perspective 'interpret' them?

> **Formal and informal social power play major roles in this definitional process.**
>
> (Persell 1990: 159)

The Marxist argument that the legal system works in the interests of the powerful and against those of the working classes is returned to in our examination of theories of punishment (pp. 591–594).

New criminology and recent conflict approaches

Marxist explanations suggest that capitalism produces the conditions that generate criminal behaviour. Crime occurs because of economic deprivation and because of the contradictions that are apparent in capitalist societies. Working-class crime is a 'rebellion' against inequality and against a system that uses the legal process – including the law, the police, courts and prison – as weapons in a class war.

A number of writers who adopt a broadly conflict perspective have criticized the 'left idealism' of the basic Marxist approach and have developed a realistic approach to law and order. The left idealist position has been criticized for its apparent lack of interest in issues of policy. Lea and Young (1984), for instance, argue that, in contrast to the left idealist view, crime really is a problem for the working classes – and a problem that needs tackling with realistic policies and practices. This is not to deny the impact of crimes of the powerful, but to suggest that the working classes are most often the victims of crime – both crimes of the powerful and working-class or 'street' crime. In street crime there is an overlap between victims and offenders, with the working class forming the great majority of both groups. As Young (1992: 146) suggests, 'it is difficult to romanticize this type of crime as some kind of disguised attack on the privileged'. In her discussion of realist criminology, Croall (1998) emphasizes how, in its attempt to understand crime, the left realist approach advocates the exploration of all the dimensions of crime – offenders, victims, the public, and the state and its agencies, and the interrelationship between them. This provides a broader view of crime than other theories, in particular through recognizing the victim. The 'left realist' approach also highlights the widespread consensus there is about crime. Most people of all social classes are offended by rape, robbery, drug smuggling and so on; there is little evidence that the working classes see crime as a rebellion against the inequalities of capitalism.

Although rejecting any single cause of crime, the left realist approach does emphasize the role of relative deprivation. While there is no clear evidence that deprivation in itself produces crime, deprivation is a relative concept in that people have different expectations about what they deserve. As Croall puts it:

> **They may compare their situation with others whom they would expect to equal – to a reference group. If these expectations are not met they may feel deprived – not absolutely but relatively. Unemployed youth may feel relatively deprived compared with employed youth and feel frustrated because they feel their unemployment is not their fault. Young members of ethnic minorities may experience deprivation in comparison to white youth . . . Members of some occupational groups feel deprived in comparison to others whose jobs they feel are of equal value. The executive may feel relatively deprived if denied the chance of promotion.**
>
> (Croall 1998: 78)

While not all of these feelings of deprivation will lead to crime, they may do so in situations where legitimate ways of pursuing grievances are not available. This is perhaps particularly likely to be the case for groups or individuals who are socially or politically marginalized – such as the young unemployed or ethnic minorities.

Young and Mathews (1992) distinguish between what they term the 'realist' and the 'radical' positions. The classical Marxist approach is linked with radical notions that the criminal justice system does not work in the interests of the mass of working people and should therefore be abolished. A more accountable and efficient system of justice is not possible; nor is it really desirable – the legal system is just another aspect of ruling-class domination that should be smashed.

This left radical view has been attacked by sociologists and criminologists writing from the left realist position. Left realists point to the injustices that marginalize sections of the population and encourage crime. However, they realize that there are no magical solutions. Only socialist intervention will reduce the causes of crime fundamentally, as these causes are rooted in social inequality; only a genuinely democratic police force will provide greater safety in the community. Young and Mathews (1992) point out that poor people pay dearly for inadequate protection; there is a need for an adequate criminal justice system that

Case study

White-collar crime

The term 'white-collar crime' is usually associated with scandals in the business world and sophisticated frauds. Croall (1992) adopts a broad definition of white-collar crime as 'the abuse of a legitimate occupational role which is regulated by law'. This includes occupational crimes committed by employees and corporate crime, where businesses or corporations exploit consumers and workers.

There are regular examples of notorious white-collar crimes such as the Guinness takeover in 1990, the collapse of the Bank of Credit and Commerce International in 1991 and the 'breaking' of the City of London's oldest merchant bank, Barings, in 1995. The Barings case involved Nick Leeson, one of the bank's general managers and the head of its futures operation in Singapore, allegedly entering into a series of fraudulent trades involving fictitious client accounts to try to cover up for substantial losses he had made on behalf of Barings. White-collar crime can also encompass 'accidents' such as the sinking of the ferry the *Herald of Free Enterprise* in 1987. The ferry had sailed from Zeebrugge with its bow doors open – something that should have been checked before the ship left port – and 193 people were drowned when it sank. The ferry's owners, Townsend Thoresen, had a poor safety record. Although it could be argued that these kinds of crime are more serious and damaging to society than conventional crimes such as burglary, white-collar crime tends not to be seen as part of a 'crime problem'. The public are more concerned about and afraid of being mugged or burgled than they are of being misled by bogus adverts or killed on a ferry. This is not to say that white-collar crime is ignored, but the media and public focus tends to be on the more spectacular frauds involving millions of pounds or on cases involving well-known personalities (e.g. Ken Dodd and Lester Piggott).

Croall (1992) describes the considerable scope of fraud:

- Tax evasion is commonly referred to as a 'perk'. Often law-abiding taxpayers condone tax evasion by paying for services 'cash in hand'.
- Trade description offences include the false description of goods, misleading bargain offers and other deceptive practices.
- Weights and measures offences include deceptive packaging and short measures.
- Food and drugs offences include selling 'unfit' food.

Although we are unaware of it, most of us are probably multiple victims of white-collar crime. Many offences are commonplace and there is a thin line between normal trading and fraud and deception.

Questions

1. How does the relative power of different groups in society influence the way in which the following activities are viewed:
   (a) prostitution;
   (b) social security fraud;
   (c) providing false information to tax inspectors.
2. Why might business crimes and criminals be treated differently from other forms of crime?
3. Give an example of each type of fraud listed by Croall:
   (a) tax evasion;
   (b) trade description offences;
   (c) weights and measures offences;
   (d) food and drugs offences.
4. How often have you or your family been victims or perpetrators of these frauds?

works in the interests of all social groups. Left realism is advocated as a social democratic approach to the analysis of crime and the development of effective policies to control it.

Left idealism is often contrasted with left realism – indeed left realism was essentially a reaction to what was felt to be the tendency for Marxist criminologists to idealize and romanticize the

working class criminal and not take enough account of the effect of crime on working class people and communities. However a number of British criminologists (including Gilroy, Scraton, Sim and Gordon amongst others) did not accept this left realist argument. They felt that left realism over-simplified the idealist position. Left idealists supported practical action by community groups to change and reform the criminal justice system – and supported those who questioned the way the criminal justice system operated. In Britain, they have supported and worked with groups involved in major political issues such as the Hillsborough disaster of 1989 and the Inquiry into the death of Stephen Lawrence.

(MacPherson 1999)

Stop and think

- How might left realists and left radicals respond to initiatives such as neighbourhood watch schemes and community policing?

In this section on 'explaining crime' we have introduced a number of theories. All of them contain important insights and elements of 'truth', but it is unrealistic to expect to discover an ultimate explanation for such behaviour given the diverse range of activities encompassed by the term 'crime'. Why should an explanation for fraud by wealthy business people also provide an explanation for football hooliganism or burglary committed by drug addicts, for example?

The extent and pattern of crime

Official crime statistics in Britain are published by the Home Office and provide data on criminal offences recorded by the police (Table 14.1). They play an important part in influencing government policies towards crime and its treatment. This section begins with a brief review of the trends in officially recorded criminal behaviour and then examines some of the problems associated with the use of crime statistics.

What do official crime statistics measure?

There are hundreds of possible offences, ranging from murder to not paying one's TV licence. Recorded offences generally include only *notifiable offences*. These are the more serious offences; illegal parking, minor assaults, licence evasion and speeding, for example, are not notifiable. Notifiable offences are a measure of the number of crimes that are recorded by the police. It is not a measure of the real level of crime: many offences are not reported to the police, while others are not recorded if the police do not feel that there is enough

A closer look

Globalization and crime

Globalization can be used to refer to the notion of a global economy and world financial markets (see Chapter 9). It can also be applied in a much broader manner to the blurring of the boundaries between nation-states. As regards crime, it can be applied to the increasingly transnational character of organized crime. Technological developments in communication and transportation networks allow criminal operations to develop global networks and alliances. The old notion of crime being a local issue and problem is replaced with the need to understand 'the global contours of crime' (Burke 2005). However, Burke warns against over-romanticizing the past and points out that a good deal of crime in the past also relied on international markets and contacts – including slave and drug trading throughout history. Indeed, the adage that 'there's nothing new under the sun' has always had a strong resonance in study of crime.

Of course, drug trafficking and pornography have been transformed by global transport and communications – including the World Wide Web – and new crimes such as e-piracy have appeared. Meanwhile, old crimes have been updated – piracy is a crime that conjures up images of sailing ships and the Middle Ages, but such a crime continues.

Table 14.1 Crimes recorded by the police, by type of offence, 2005–06

	Percentages		
	England and Wales	Scotland	Northern Ireland
Theft and handling stolen goods	36	34	24
Theft of vehicles	4	3	3
Theft from vehicles	9	6	4
Criminal damage	21	31	28
Violence against the person	19	2	25
Burglary	12	7	10
Fraud and forgery	4	3	4
Drugs offences	3	11	2
Robbery	2	1	1
Sexual offences	1	1	1
Other offences	1	10	3
All notifiable offences (= 100%) (thousands)	5557	418	123

(Source: *Social Trends*, 37, 2007)

Table 14.2 Comparison of homicide in selected cities, 1997–99

	Total homicides during 1997–99	Homicide rate*
London	539	2.36
Belfast	45	5.23
Edinburgh	29	2.15
Paris	139	2.21
Berlin	333	3.23
Dublin	76	2.37
Moscow	3863	18.20
Sydney	200	1.70
Tokyo	420	1.17
Pretoria	1512	27.47
New York city	2074	9.38
Washington, DC	802	50.82

*Murders per 100,000 population of the city, average per year from 1997 to 1999

(Source: international comparisons of criminal justice statistics, Home Office 2001; adapted from Denscombe 2002)

evidence that a crime has been committed. Unrecorded crime is known as the 'dark figure of crime'. So, official crime statistics provide only a partial picture of crime committed. Crime recording can start only when someone reports an offence to the police or when the police themselves discover an offence.

The official statistics indicate that there is an ever-increasing rate of crime. Recorded offences in England and Wales rose from around 3 million in 1981 to over 5.5 million in 2005–06 (ONS 2007b).

The increase in recorded crime is not a recent trend. Radzinowicz and King (1977) found that the police in England and Wales recorded fewer than three crimes per 1000 of the population in 1900; by 1974 they recorded four crimes per 100 of the population – a 13-fold increase in just over 70 years. Although the increases in crime appear startling, it is important to bear in mind that concerns over 'crime waves' are not new. The streets of London and other cities in the mid-nineteenth century were not havens of safety, ideally suited for a night-time stroll. Robbery and violence were commonplace, as the stories of Charles Dickens and other writers illustrate. Although official statistics demonstrate a rapid increase in crime, violent crime is not a modern problem.

As long ago as 1195 Richard of Devizes, in describing the London of his time, stated that

> **No one lives in it without falling into some sort of crimes. Every quarter of it abounds in grave obscenities . . . If you do not want to dwell with evil-doers, do not live in London.**

However, while crime is not new, the explosion in the data and information we now have about crime is. In contrasting the kinds of information available to criminologists today compared with 50 or so years ago, Maguire (2002) points out that virtually the only source of systematic information about crime in the 1940s and 1950s was the annually published Criminal Statistics. Since then, the research capacity of the Home Office has expanded rapidly, as has the number of criminological researchers in general. In addition, there are now massive electronic datasets, such as the British Crime Survey and the Offenders Index.

Just as crime is not a modern phenomenon, it is not particular to any one country. As Table 14.2 demonstrates, Britain is by no means the most crime-prone nation in the world.

Problems with crime statistics

Although official crime statistics do not measure the real amount of crime, they are the basis for people's ideas about crime and criminals. The 'facts' about crime quoted in the media are assumed to provide an accurate picture of the extent of criminality. As Maguire puts it,

> **despite the warnings of criminologists and government statisticians . . . these statistics are still treated by many politicians and journalists as an accurate 'barometer' of crime, and any sizeable rise in the figures they produce tends to receive widespread publicity and spark off arguments about police or government ineffectiveness or the need for sentencing changes.**
>
> (Maguire 2002: 334)

The official statistics are the end result of a series of decisions by victims, the police and the courts about what action to take in particular situations; they are 'socially constructed'. The relationship between the real and recorded rates of crime is complex. Some indication of the gap between them can be seen by contrasting the official figures with those provided by the British Crime Surveys, which ask people, among other things, whether they have been victims of crime and, if so, what crimes. The British Crime Survey began reporting in 1982 and produced its ninth survey in 2001 – since then a report has been published annually. It is estimated that a total of just over 19 million crimes were committed in 1995, of which 41 per cent were reported to the police. While this might seem alarming, the main reason people gave for not reporting offences to the police was that they considered them too trivial to waste police time. It is reasonable to assume that a much higher proportion of serious offences is known about by the police and included in the official statistics. The degree to which official statistics underestimate the actual level of crime depends, therefore, on the particular category of crime. Virtually all stolen cars are reported for the simple reason that this is the only way owners will get insurance compensation.

Stop and think

- Reasons why the official statistics underestimate the amount of criminal activity include:
  - (a) victims being unaware that they are victims of specific crimes;
  - (b) victims feeling that there is no point in informing the police;
  - (c) victims dealing with the matter informally, outside the legal system;
  - (d) victims' embarrassment;
  - (e) victims (or witnesses of a crime) not liking or trusting the police;
  - (f) crimes without victims – all parties involved in a crime not wishing the police to know about it.

  Give an example of a criminal activity that is liable to be unrecorded for each of these reasons.
- Why are the following offences unlikely to become official statistics:
  - (a) fraud;
  - (b) drug dealing;
  - (c) incest?
- What problems might there be with the use of crime surveys to find out about rates of crime?

The social incidence of crime

Official statistics indicate that criminal behaviour is not distributed randomly throughout the whole population; some social groups commit more crime than others. In particular, crime is committed predominantly by young people and males. In 2005, 1.8 million offenders were found guilty of, or cautioned for, criminal offences in England and Wales – most of these were male (79 per cent), with about 12 per cent aged 17 and under (ONS 2007) (Figure 14.2). With regard to age of offending, the number of offenders as a proportion of the population is highest for males aged between 10 and 17. In 2005, 6 per cent of all males aged 17 were found guilty of, or cautioned for, indictable (more serious) offences, the highest rate for any age group – this contrasts with a figure of less than 1 per cent of men in age groups over 43 (ONS 2007). Data on the social incidence of crime indicate a clear relationship between crime and gender and crime and ethnicity – issues that are looked at in the following two sections.

Stop and think

- Summarize the patterns for the relationship between crime and age and crime and gender in Figure 14.2.
- What explanations can you offer for these relationships?

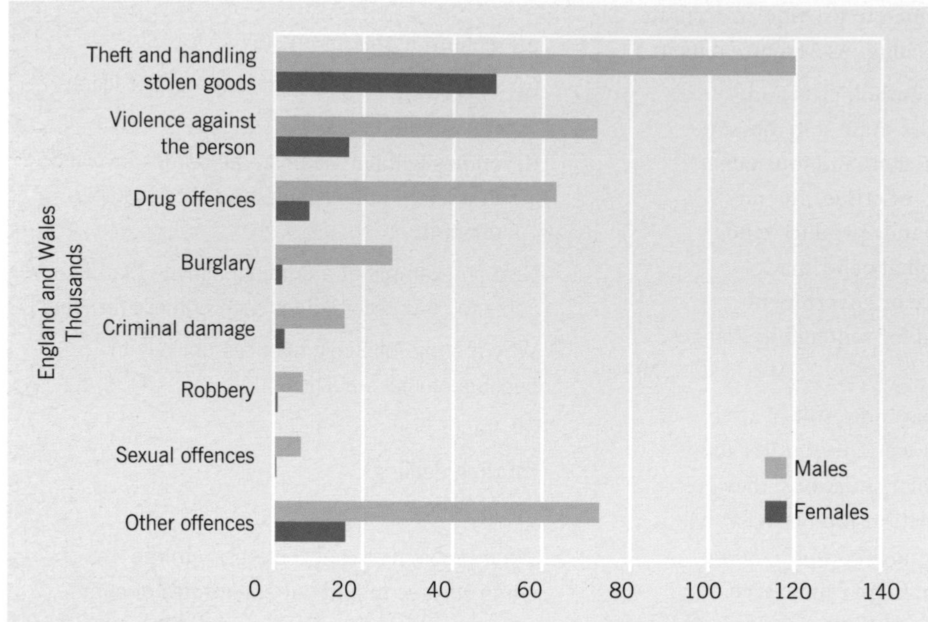

Figure 14.2 Offenders found guilty of, or cautioned for, indictable offences, by sex and type of offence, 2005

Crime and gender

There is a strong link between gender and both the rate of recorded crime and crime survey data. All the data indicate that crime is an activity carried out mainly by males. About 80 per cent of people convicted of serious offences in England and Wales are males (ONS 2007). While women commit all types of offence, the proportion of male and female offenders varies according to the offence. Women outnumber males in only two offence groups: prostitution and failing to pay for a TV licence. Although sexual offences, which include rape and indecent assault, are overwhelmingly committed by males, prostitution is generally defined as a female offence. The fact that women are more likely to be found guilty of not paying TV licences is due partly to women being more likely to answer the door to enforcers. Aside from these examples, men are more likely to commit every other category of offence (Croall 1998, citing Coleman and Moynihan 1996). The most common offences for both sexes are thefts. Shoplifting is often thought of as the 'typical' female crime, but more males than females are convicted of it: '40 per cent of the convicted are female [but] many more women than men are shoppers, so that the proportion of women shoppers who shoplift is smaller' (Hart 1985: 299). Women commit fewer crimes of violence. In 2001, 47,000 males were found guilty of, or cautioned for, crimes of 'violence against the person', compared with under 8000 women (ONS 2003c). With regard to imprisonment, the differences between men and women are even greater. In October 2005, the British prison population stood at (another) new high of 77,774; of this number, 4621 were females (National Offender Management Service data). So, women make up roughly 6 per cent of the total prison population. However, the rate of female imprisonment has risen fairly dramatically in recent years – the number of female prisoners has increased by 175 per cent since 1992, compared with a corresponding figure of 50 per cent for men.

Women are also underrepresented in the criminal justice system. As Table 14.3 shows, women made up less than a quarter of the number of police officers in England and Wales in March 2006. In a similar vein, senior British judges are still overwhelmingly male. Of the first 85 judges appointed since the Labour Party were elected to power in 1997, only seven were women.

Why do women commit less crime?

Heidensohn (1989) points out that, in spite of the clear and persistent differences in rates of male and female criminality, it is only since the 1970s that sociological and criminological attention has turned to this issue.

Before this, explanations focused on the biological and/or psychological makeup of women. These studies, often written by men, argued that female biology determines women's personality and makes them more

Table 14.3 Police officer strength, by rank and sex, 2005–06

United Kingdom	Numbers		
	Males	Females	All
ACPO ranks	230	32	262
Chief superintendent	708	61	769
Superintendent	1056	101	1157
Chief inspector	2081	261	2341
Inspector	7534	983	8517
Sergeant	21,483	3491	24,974
Constable	97,276	31,879	129,156
All ranks	130,368	36,807	167,174
Police staff	42,003	50,904	92,907
Police community support officers	3936	2833	6769
Traffic wardens	847	567	1414
Designated officers	778	550	1328
Total police strength	164,925	88,025	252,949
Special constabulary	10,210	5104	15,314

(Source: *Social Trends*, 37, 2007)

passive and timid and therefore less likely to commit crime, which is an aggressive activity. The relatively few female criminals were seen as suffering from some sort of physical or mental pathology. In 1895 Lombroso and Ferrero argued that women were naturally less inclined to crime than men, and that those women who did commit crimes were not 'really' feminine. Explanations emphasizing the physiological bases for females' criminality remained popular up to the 1960s (Cowie *et al.* 1968), and their influence can still be seen in the tendency to view women who commit crimes, and especially the more serious crimes, as 'abnormal' or pathological in a way that male criminals are not viewed.

Sociological explanations have argued that gender differences in crime cannot be 'reduced' to biological differences alone. As large numbers of women do commit crime, it is difficult to maintain that females are innately less disposed to crime than males.
In attempting to explain the gender gap in crime, sociologists have focused on the expectations and constraints that are placed on women by society and how the different role expectations for women and men lead to different patterns of socialization. This 'sex role theory' approach sees crime as more consistent with male roles – men, rather than women, learn the

Figure 14.3 Boy playing with toy gun, Corsica. It has been argued that boys are more likely to be socialized for active and aggressive behaviour
Imagebroker/Alamy

skills that are usually connected with certain types of criminal activity. Boys play with guns (Figure 14.3), learn how to fight and are more likely to be socialized for active and aggressive behaviour. Burglary, for example, is an untypical female crime. It requires the criminal to be out alone on the streets at night and to possess 'masculine skills' associated with being able to force an entry. However, 'women have got sufficient strength and skills to commit all sorts of offences which they hardly ever do commit. One does not need much strength to mug a small and frail old lady' (Hart 1985: 299).

A different approach to female criminality has been to focus on conformity and the pressures on women to conform. It has been argued that women, and girls in particular, are subjected to stronger social control than are men and boys. Girls are 'taught law-abiding behaviour and are expected to be non-violent, co-operative and docile' (Hart 1985: 300). Girls are expected to conform to a stricter morality by their parents and also by their peers (girls have to keep their 'reputations' in a way that does not apply to boys). Adolescent girls are likely to be allowed less freedom to go out and stay out than are their male peers. This will limit the opportunities they have to become involved in criminal and delinquent behaviour. As with the 'sex role theory', the argument that women are subject to more restrictions and greater control is difficult to substantiate and is based on rather stereotypical notions about gender and appropriate behaviour for females and males.

Heidensohn (1989) summarizes the impact of feminist criminology on the study of women and crime. A major area of interest has been the criminal justice system and the alleged bias in favour of women – the 'chivalry' idea that male police officers and judges treat female offenders more sympathetically than they do male offenders. Heidensohn dismisses this idea and suggests that women offenders are more stigmatized than men. She argues that the much lower levels of women's recorded criminality compared with men's has significant consequences for those women who do offend (Heidensohn 2002). They are seen to have broken gender norms as well as social norms and the courts treat them as doubly deviant – as being both unfeminine and criminal by breaking laws. The social consequences of this can be women offenders losing their children, homes and partners. In examining reasons for the low rate of female crime, feminists have warned of the dangers of looking for all-embracing explanations. Women's criminality, like men's, is mainly instrumental and related to economic goals; women can and do commit all crimes, including very serious, sometimes horrific, crimes such as terrorism and child murders.

An important feature of feminist work on gender and crime has been an emphasis on women's victimization. This is not to deny that men are victims but to highlight the different experiences of victimization according to gender. As Croall puts it:

> **Men and women have different experiences of victimization. In respect of violent crime, for example, it has been seen from victim surveys that while men are more likely to be victimized in public spaces, women are more likely to be victimized at home.**
>
> (Croall 1998: 138)

On the whole, domestic violence is perpetrated by men against women and children. Awareness of the problems of wife battering, child abuse and sexual assault has grown in the 1990s due in part to the work of feminist sociologists (see pp. 475–477). There has also been concern about the different ways in which women and men are treated by the courts; for example, men who kill a 'nagging' wife have been given derisory sentences in comparison with women sentenced to life imprisonment for killing long-term violent husbands.

In concluding her review of gender and crime, Heidensohn (2002) suggests that those studying this area perhaps need to ask different questions. Rather than trying to explain why women's commit rate is so low, the emphasis should be on why men's is so high. Research into the relationship between masculinity and crime is a fast-developing area. Feminists have argued that the aggressive and violent behaviour of men should be viewed as normal rather than unusual or abnormal in criminological theorizing. As Newburn and Stanko (1994a: 4) put it in their introduction to an edited collection of papers on masculinities and crime, 'The task is to use the developing understanding of masculine identities to make sense of male over-involvement and female under-involvement in criminal activities'.

Stop and think

- Do you agree that girls are subject to stricter social control than boys by their families?
- Give examples from your own experiences.
- Does this continue into adulthood?
- Look at press or TV reports of recent criminal trials. What evidence can you find of the different treatment of women and men? To what extent does it support the 'chivalry' idea?

Crime and ethnicity

Official Home Office statistics on race and the criminal justice system are produced annually under Section 95 of the Criminal Justice Act 1991, which states that 'The Secretary of State shall in each year publish such information, as he considers expedient for the purpose of . . . (avoiding) discriminating against any persons on the ground of race or sex or any other improper ground.' These statistics provide a wealth of information across a range of areas, including stop-and-search rates, arrest rates, prosecutions and imprisonment, as well as detailing the numbers and proportions of ethnic minority practitioners working in the different criminal justice agencies. In a report referring to figures for 2003–04 in England and Wales, the 2001 census figures are used to determine the percentages of the population from different ethnic groups: 2.8 per cent of the general population black, 4.7 per cent Asian and 1.2 per cent 'other'. These proportions need to be kept in mind when looking at the proportions of different ethnic-minority groups involved with crime and criminal justice. There were 738,016 stop and searches recorded by the police in 2003–04, of which 15 per cent were of black people, 7 per cent of Asian people and 1 per cent of 'other' ethnic origin; so relative to the general population figures, black people were 6.4 times more likely to be stopped and searched than white people, and Asian people twice as likely. Of 1.33 million arrests for notifiable offences, 9 per cent were recorded as being of black people, 5 per cent Asian and 1 per cent 'other', with black people over three times more likely to be arrested than white people.

The report also breaks down these arrest figures for different offence groups, which shows that the main differences between ethnic groups was a greater tendency for white people to be arrested for burglary and criminal damage, black people for robbery, fraud and forgery, and Asian people for fraud and forgery.

The proportions of ethnic minority groups in prisons (Table 14.4) are massively greater than would be expected by the general population figures. In February 2003, black and minority ethnic groups accounted for 24 per cent of the male prison population (16% black, 3% Asian, 5% 'other') and 31 per cent of the female prison population (25% black, 1% Asian, 5% 'other'). However, these figures included foreign nationals, who made up 12 per cent of the male and 21 per cent of the female prison populations.

Stop and think

- Summarize the information in Table 14.4 and try to explain the overrepresentation of certain ethnic minority groups in prison. In particular, consider the discrepancy in the prison figures between (a) black and white populations and (b) black and Asian populations.
- Why do you think that such a high percentage of female prisoners are black?

Finally, with regard to people working in the criminal justice system, the most obvious finding is the underrepresentation of ethnic minority groups. While these figures do not relate to black and non-white people committing crime, they are worth mentioning in relation to the treatment and perceptions of treatment of ethnic minority groups by the criminal justice system, and to the related issue of bias (or not) within the system. The proportion of black and ethnic minority officers with the 43 police forces in England and Wales was 3.5 per cent as at 31 March 2005; however, the figure dropped to 2 per cent for those at inspector or chief inspector level. Nonetheless, this was an increase on previous years, and a similar increase was found in the number of black and ethnic minority prison officers, with 4.1 per cent now from black and minority ethnic backgrounds. However, the number of non-white people reaching the more senior positions in the judiciary is virtually non-existent. Of the 105 high court judges and 36 lord chief justices, none was from

Table 14.4 Prison population in England and Wales by self-identified ethnic group and gender (30 June 2005)

	Males (numbers and % of total male prisoners)	Females (numbers and % of total female prisoners)	All (numbers and % of total number of prisoners)
White	53,607 (74.8%)	3217 (71.3%)	56,824 (74.6%)
Black or black British	10,294 (14.4%)	875 (19.4%)	11,170 (14.7%)
Asian or Asian British	4459 (6.2%)	104 (2.3%)	4564 (6.0%)
Mixed	1934 (2.7%)	223 (4.9%)	2157 (2.8%)
Chinese or other ethnic groups	790 (1.1%)	73 (1.6%)	862 (1.1%)
Not recorded	592 (0.8%)	22 (0.5%)	613 (0.8%)

(Adapted from *Statistics on Race and the Criminal Justice System 2005*, London: HMSO)

an ethnic minority background; among the 564 circuit judges, one was black and three were Asian.

As a final comment on ethnicity and criminal justice, in the USA, 36 states have executed people since the death penalty was reinstated in 1977. Black people are much more likely to be executed than whites. Although only 12 per cent of the US population is black, 42 per cent of the nation's condemned prisoners are black (Amnesty International: www.amnesty.org), and 290 of the 845 people executed since 1977 were black – roughly 35 per cent.

Explanations for the relationship between crime and ethnicity

Historical background

Bowling and Phillips (2002) argue that a historical perspective is necessary in order to understand current links between ethnicity and crime. Supposedly 'scientific' ideas about 'race' developed in the seventeenth-century period of the Enlightenment through the work of philosophers such as Kant and Hume. This period was seen as the 'age of reason', with civilization and progress associated solely with white people and, specifically, northern Europe. Those people of other ethnic and cultural origins were seen as less rational, less moral and inferior. These notions of white supremacy encouraged the practice of slavery, and, although slavery ended in the early nineteenth century, the ideas of racial superiority and inferiority were embedded in British imperialism and colonial policies. It was a short step from these ideas to link 'race' with crime, and Lombroso's work became representative of a new 'scientific criminology'. In his study *The Criminal Man* (1876) he argued that 'many of the characteristics found . . . in the coloured races are also to be found in habitual delinquents'.

Sociological explanations

First, some of the difference in crime rates between white and black people may be due to *demographic factors*: there is a greater proportion of young people among ethnic minority populations, and black people are more likely to live in poor inner-city areas. However, research that has isolated age and socioeconomic variables has indicated that such factors cannot be used to explain the higher rate of crime among West Indians (Stevens and Willis 1979, cited in Moore 1988).

Second, there may be some *racial prejudice within the police*, but this could not completely explain differences

Case study

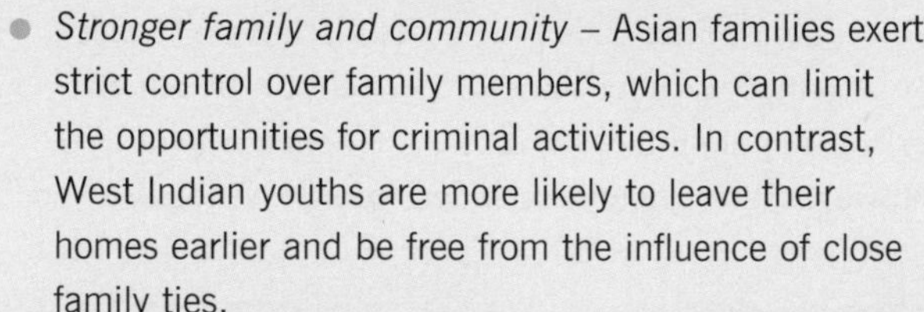

Crime and different ethnic minority groups

The sociological study of crime and ethnicity should acknowledge that different ethnic minority groups have varying propensities to offend and differing relationships with the criminal justice systems. Most discussion of the crime and race issue has concentrated on Afro-Caribbeans and ignored people from other ethnic minority groups. Moore (1988) summarizes explanations for the low levels of criminality in Asian groups:

- *Greater economic success* – Asians, particularly Indians, have been relatively successful in business and commerce in Britain and are more likely to be in employment. Therefore, they suffer less from the marginality experienced by young black people.
- *Stronger family and community* – Asian families exert strict control over family members, which can limit the opportunities for criminal activities. In contrast, West Indian youths are more likely to leave their homes earlier and be free from the influence of close family ties.
- *Different cultures* – Asian cultures are clearly distinct from mainstream British culture, and Asians are perhaps less likely to feel resentful about the difficulties they face in becoming part of this mainstream culture. Lea and Young (1984) argued that young West Indians feel more bitter when they are not accepted by the wider culture and are consequently more likely to turn to crime.

Question

1. To what extent do you feel that these explanations for lower levels of Asian crime hold good today?

in police arrest rates. The fact that the vast majority of serious crimes are reported by the victims rather than initiated by the police will limit the police's influence on reported crime rates.

Third, *race and political struggle* are rooted in Britain's colonial history. Britain controlled its colonial populations through force, slavery and 'education'. When immigrants from the former colonies were recruited to work in Britain in the 1950s, the conditions of the colonies were reproduced in the British inner cities. Black crime is seen as a continuation of the struggle against colonialism; the activities of young blacks are a form of rebellion. Crime is, then, a form of politics, a form of organized resistance (Moore 1988). However, there is little evidence that black people commit crime as a form of political struggle. Black youths appear to be as conformist as other young people to the values of the wider society. As Moore (1988) puts it, 'One must be suspicious when "experts" can read meaning into behaviour that the actual participants are totally unaware of.'

Fourth, black people have been *marginalized* due to their lack of opportunities to achieve financial success; this encourages some of them to turn to crime. Cashmore (1984) argued that young black people faced a situation where their aspirations (for consumer goods) were not matched by the reality of their economic situation (high unemployment rates). The outcome is that they are drawn into criminality. Again, this explanation lumps together all young black people and does not take account of the variety of responses; only a small proportion of those who cannot achieve financial success turn to crime.

Having looked at possible explanations for crime and the extent and distribution of recorded crime, we shall now focus on the control of crime; we shall look briefly at the role of the police before examining in greater detail the punishment of crime.

Controlling crime: law enforcement and the role of the police

In looking at why most people conform, we discussed two basic types of social control – informal and formal social control (see pp. 557–559). The police are part of the formal control mechanisms of modern society. They are not the only agency of formal control; customs and excise, private security firms, store detectives and regulatory bodies such as factory inspectorates are all able to exert formal control over others. However, the police have a decisive role as the 'last resort' in the process of social control. The police tend to be seen, and to see themselves, as the 'thin blue line' protecting the majority of respectable citizens. The division between informal and formal social control is not absolute; although the police are the most visible agent of formal social control, much of their work is carried out in an informal manner. There is a considerable degree of flexibility and discretion in police work. As well as being perhaps the most visible agency of social control, the police are also the most expensive element of the criminal justice system. Around two-thirds of the £14 billion public expenditure on the criminal justice system in England and Wales is on the police compared with around a sixth on prisons.

The police and the public

The police are a segregated group in society. Public opinion varies from suspicion to hostility, and a major police problem appears to be relations with the public. The Policy Studies Institute (PSI) report *The Police and People in London* (1983) indicated that roughly half of the London population had serious doubts about the standard of police conduct. Everyday interaction between the police and the public tends to do little to improve relations. Traffic patrol, for instance, provides many people with their only direct contact with the police; the attitude that 'they should be catching criminals, not bothering me' would seem to be widely held.

In examining what he terms 'cop culture', Reiner (1992) found that many police officers report difficulties in mixing with members of the public in everyday life. This relative social isolation encourages strong intergroup solidarity and mutual dependence, which tends to further their segregation. Occupational groups often mix together and have some measure of self-identification, but the police have a particularly high degree of occupational solidarity. This segregation encourages the development of a special code and subculture within the police, which we examine in the case study below.

As well as conflict with the public, relations between the police and the legal system are not always easy. The British legal system depends on the rule of law and the supremacy of Parliament (which makes the laws), and the police are required to maintain order under the rule of law. There is, though, a basic tension between the concepts of order and legality. Criminal law presumes

A closer look

The clearance rate

The clearance rate is the percentage of crimes solved out of those reported. It is an official means of measuring the success and efficiency of the police and of comparing different police forces. If a particular police force or division had a 50 per cent clearance rate, then it would be solving ('clearing up') 50 per cent of the crimes reported to it. Thus, the higher the clearance rate, the more efficient that police force is seen to be.

Questions

1. The clearance rate varies from offence to offence. What kinds of offences will have the highest clearance rates and what kinds the lowest? Give reasons for your answers.
2. What problems are there with using clearance rates as a measure of police efficiency?

innocence until guilt is proved. The police, however, tend to presume guilt. When arresting someone, the police officer will believe the suspect to be guilty. Furthermore, the police are likely to feel that the legal process makes their task increasingly difficult. The presumption of innocence is the first in a series of restrictions: the police are interested in actual guilt, which they believe they can recognize, rather than legal guilt. Court decisions to dismiss charges are especially likely to annoy the police, who will have spent time and effort bringing the case to court. When in court, police officers face something of a role reversal in that they are subject to cross-examination, whereas they are usually questioning suspects themselves.

Case study

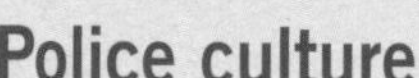

Police culture

The first extract below summarizes some of the main findings of the Policy Studies Institute (1983) report into the Metropolitan Police Force: a detailed examination of the world of the police officer in London. The second extract is taken from Robert Reiner's discussion of 'cop culture' in his study *The Politics of the Police* (1992).

The police and people in London

In contrast to the image of police work as exciting and dangerous (an image which the police themselves tend to stress), for most police officers, patrolling was invariably boring and somewhat aimless. A considerable amount of police behaviour can best be understood as a search for some interest or excitement. Officers on patrol might spend whole shifts without doing any police work apart from providing simple information. Even car patrolling might involve hours of doing nothing while waiting for calls. Occasionally a patrol car will be rushing from one call to another, but such occasions are unusual. This boredom and aimlessness is not apparent in popular portrayals of police work in the media, where there is a natural concentration on the interesting bits.

The desire for action is illustrated by the comment of one officer, who recounted how much he enjoyed the Southall race riots of 1981:

> It was a great day out, fighting the Pakis. It ought to be an annual fixture. I thoroughly enjoyed myself.

While some of this talk might be exaggerated, many police officers do not appear to object to occasional violent confrontations. And the comment on Southall illustrates another aspect of police culture – racism.

Racism

Racialist language was used by the police in a casual, almost automatic way and was commonly

Case study *continued*

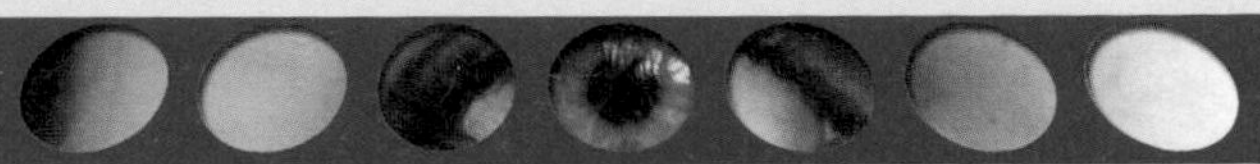

used over the personal radio. The report's authors heard one inspector say over the radio, 'Look I've got a bunch of coons in sight'. The report found that black people (but not Asians) were much more likely to be stopped by the police than white people.

Masculinity

The report describes a 'cult of masculinity' in the police force which has a strong influence on police officers' attitudes to women and toward sexual offences. Most of the women police officers interviewed felt that there was a prejudice against them; they felt that the importance of physical strength in police work was greatly over-emphasized and that they were regularly excluded from more interesting kinds of police work. Many of the women officers have had to accept these attitudes. One recounted how an inspector at training school had said to her, 'Why don't you admit it, you're only here to get a husband, aren't you?' She had 'let it run off her back'.

Solidarity

There is a strong sense of solidarity among police officers and particularly among the small groups who work together. Calls for urgent assistance from police officers are always met with a massive and immediate response – all available cars would dash to answer such calls. However, this solidarity encourages officers to cover up for colleagues. On being asked whether he would 'shop' a colleague who had seriously assaulted a prisoner, one sergeant responded:

> No, I never would. If one of the boys working for me got himself into trouble, I would get us all together and I would literally script him out of it. I would write all the parts out and if we followed them closely we couldn't be defeated. And believe me, I would do it.

When questioned a bit further on his attitude, he said that the disciplinary system was unfair and he wouldn't stand by and let someone lose their job.

(Smith and Gray 1983)

'Cop culture'

The core of the police outlook is this subtle and complex intermingling of the themes of mission, hedonistic love of action and pessimistic cynicism. Each feeds off and reinforces the other, even though they may appear superficially contradictory. They lead to pressure for 'results' which may strain against legalistic principles of due process . . .

Suspicion

Most policeman are well aware that their job has bred in them an attitude of constant suspiciousness which cannot be readily switched off . . . Suspiciousness is a product of the need to keep a look-out for signs of trouble, potential danger and clues to offences . . .

Isolation/solidarity

The them and us outlook which is a characteristic of police culture makes clear distinctions between types of 'them' . . . The crucial divisions for the police do not readily fit a sociologist's categories of class or status. The fundamental division is between rough and respectable elements, those who challenge or those who accept the middle-class values of decency which most police revere . . .

Police conservatism

The evidence we have of the political orientations of police officers suggests that they tend to be conservative, both politically and morally. Partly this is a function of the nature of the job. The routine 'clients' of the police are drawn from the bottom layers of the social order . . . Furthermore, the force has from the start been constructed as a hierarchical, tightly disciplined organisation. Thus the police officer with a conservative outlook is more likely to fit in.

(Reiner 1992: 114–22)

Questions

1. How might the sort of police culture described above influence (a) the way the police carry out their job; and (b) their relations with the public?
2. Do you think police officers should be subject to stricter rules of behaviour than other people?

The organization of modern policing

Effective policing depends on receiving information: the vast majority of recorded crimes are reported to the police by the public. The investigative policing common on TV portrayals is not the norm. However, the extent to which the police and public work together varies according to the style of policing; since the 1970s there have been two distinct styles, which seem to pull in opposed directions.

Community or consensus policing

The community sees the police as doing a socially useful job and supports them. This style is characterized by foot patrols, juvenile liaison schemes, neighbourhood watch and a generally 'softer' approach from the police. Here, the police are likely to receive useful information from the public.

Military or 'fire-brigade' policing

Essentially this style of policing is without consent and with some hostility from the community. It is reactive and involves the use of guns, CS spray, surveillance technology and so on. The flow of information to the police is likely to be minimal, and an important part of police activity will be random stopping and questioning. The police tend to concentrate on those people they feel to be 'typical criminals'; they make maximum use of stereotypes.

In the past 50 or so years, and particularly since the 1960s, there has been a changed context of policing, with a number of factors combining to distance the police from the public. These factors include the increased use of technology by the police, initially the use of mobile patrols and radios, reducing the need for so many police officers 'on the beat'. There were growing concerns over police corruption and scandals, as a result of the exposures of senior police officers in the 1970s, which indicated systematic and widespread malpractice. The heavy-handed policing of demonstrations, including anti-war demonstrations in the 1960s and industrial disputes in the 1970s and 1980s, alienated sections of the population, most dramatically evidenced in the miners' strike of 1984–85, which polarized the police from large sections of the working population in the areas threatened with pit closures. The inner-city riots in the early 1980s in Brixton (London), Toxteth (Liverpool), Moss Side (Manchester) and elsewhere reflected an increased deterioration in the relationship between the police and sections of the population, in particular the young black population. Finally, the style of policing in Northern Ireland has affected attitudes across the UK: the images of a routinely and heavily armed police force there has helped to undermine traditional notions of the British police. Waddington (1993) highlights how such pressures have tended to push contemporary policing towards the military style. It is difficult to prevent the continuation of 'fire-brigade' policing due to the subcultural emphasis on action and excitement, while 'the police persist in rushing from one reported incident to the next and spend little time in the proactive business of fostering links with the community' (Waddington 1993: 18).

Stop and think

- We have suggested that the police tend to have a picture of the stereotypical criminal. What sort of person do you think the police see as the 'typical criminal'?
- What is your attitude to the police? Is it based on stereotypes?

The sociology of punishment

In this section we look at the relationship between crime, punishment and society. The examination of punishment as a social phenomenon provides a broader approach than that of 'penology', which focuses on the workings of specific institutions of punishment. Although punishment occurs in various social contexts – in the family, at school and at work, for instance – our focus is on punishment in the legal system.

The legal punishment of offenders is a complex process that involves law-making, conviction, sentencing and administering penalties. The sociological examination of punishment has, therefore, to be wide-ranging. Legal punishment can have various aims, although its major purpose is to reduce the rate of crime. Punishment is seen as a means to an end, of controlling crime. Given that crimes still occur, and in ever-greater numbers, it could be argued that punishment has 'failed', but it is probably unrealistic to expect punishment to control crime.

Until the mid-twentieth century the main aim of punishment was to punish wrongdoers and there was little attempt to reform those who had offended. Punishments tended to be quick, harsh and public, with little pity wasted on law-breakers.

During the 1950s and 1960s in Britain, reform and rehabilitation became key elements in what Garland (1990) has termed the 'ideological framework' of punishment. They provided a sense of purpose and justification for punishment, reflected in the introduction of a number of a new methods of punishment. Parole and suspended prison sentences were established by the Criminal Justice Act 1967 and community service orders and day training centres by the 1972 Act. These measures greatly extended the role of the Probation Service, which played a major role in many of the new initiatives that aimed to reduce and avoid custodial punishments: probation officers were responsible for supervising offenders on probation, parole, suspended sentences and community service orders.

In the 1970s optimism gave way to a general scepticism. Rising crime rates and the high percentage of criminals who reoffended raised doubts about the efficiency of 'modern' punishment. The emphasis moved away from reform; in 1980 'short sharp shock' sentences were introduced in detention centres and senior politicians advocated a hard-line approach to punishment.

Such initiatives have had little effect on the size of the prison population or on rates of recidivism. After a slight dip in the late 1980s, the prison population in Britain has continued to rise pretty steadily, with over 83,000 people in Prison Service establishments in September 2008 (www.hmprisonservice.gov.uk). The number of people given immediate custodial sentences in 1999 was over 105,000 compared with just under 80,000 four years previously (Home Office 2002). The reason why the number of people sent to prison each year is greater than the prison population reflects the fact that most prisoners are sentenced to short sentences of less than one year and so not all would be in prison when the annual figure is calculated. With regard to repeat offenders and the rate of recidivism, it would seem that a relatively small number of offenders are responsible for a large proportion of offences. Of the 97,800 males who entered prison in 1999, almost 68 per cent had had previous convictions for 'standard list offences' (which includes all indictable offences plus some of the more serious summary offences), with 46 per cent having had three or more previous convictions (Home Office 2002).

Case study

The politics of punishment: hard versus soft approaches

In the political arena, the debate about punishment has tended to polarize around the 'hard' versus 'soft' positions. Former Home Secretary Michael Howard was a strong advocate of the 'hard' position:

> Prison works . . . it makes many who are tempted to commit crime think twice . . . This may mean that more people will go to prison. I do not flinch from that. We shall no longer judge the success of our system of justice by a fall in our prison population.
>
> (Michael Howard, Conservative Party Conference, October 1993)

As well as being out of line with his Conservative predecessors as home secretary – Kenneth Clarke, Kenneth Baker, David Waddington, Douglas Hurd, Leon Brittan and William Whitelaw all favoured a reduction in prison sentences, for minor offenders at least – Howard's comments were criticized by those centrally involved in the running of our prisons. The former Lord Chief Justice, Lord Woolf, said that sending more people to prison is the easy answer to concerns over increasing crime and would increase the likelihood of prison disturbances and riots. The former director general of the Prison Service, Derek Lewis, criticized Michael Howard's call for stricter, more austere prisons and stated that he would not abandon the rehabilitative role of prisons.

This hard-line approach tends to be popular with the general public and with certain sections of the mass media. Perceived 'softness' on crime tends to be seen as a sign of political weakness. In the face of the evidence (and reporting) of horrific crimes, it is easy to see how hard-line, 'hang 'em high' approaches to punishment gain considerable sympathy and support.

Case study *continued*

The hard-line approach to punishment was highlighted by former prime minister John Major's comment on the supposedly lenient treatment of juvenile offenders serving custodial sentences, that 'we should understand a little less and condemn more'.

This approach appears to have been continued by the Labour administration since 1997 with its oft-repeated promise to be 'tough on crime and tough on the causes of crime'. The Crime and Disorder Act 1998 included proposals for selective curfews on young people in high-crime areas, which suggests that regimes of routine and control will become regular features of life in poorer working-class areas.

The debate between the 'hard' and 'soft' positions can be illustrated by the comments made by Lord Woolf in December 2002, when he told judges and magistrates that burglars facing a sentence of up to 18 months should not go to prison but should be given a non-custodial sentence and that, even where a prison sentence was imposed, it should be no longer than necessary. This 'soft' position led the leader of Britain's chief constables, Sir David Phillips, to say that such a move would undermine the morale of the police who had successfully focused on burglary for a number of years, while the Police Federation, which represents rank and file officers, felt that such comments would encourage burglars.

Questions

1. **Make a case for and against sending more offenders to prison. What are the arguments for and against alternative methods of punishment to prison?**

2. **Look at the quote from Dostoevsky on p. 555. Do you think that the way in which law-breakers are punished tells us something about a society? Give reasons for your answer.**

These kinds of figures and the concerns they raise about the punishment of offenders have highlighted questions about the aims of punishment, which we look at in the following section.

The aims of punishment

We shall discuss five aims of punishment:

- Deterrence
- Retribution
- Rehabilitation
- Incapacitation
- Reparation.

Deterrence

The utilitarian approach to punishment focuses on its 'usefulness' for society (utilitarianism is a doctrine that the value of anything is determined solely by its utility). If punishments deter offenders from reoffending or discourage other people from offending in the first place, then their utility is apparent. There are two basic ways in which deterrence can work, described by Cavadino and Dignan (1993) as individual deterrence and general deterrence. *Individual deterrence* is when offenders find their punishment so unpleasant that they never repeat the offence for fear of that punishment. *General deterrence* is when offenders are punished not only to deter them from reoffending but also to encourage others not to commit similar offences. As the focus of deterrence is on frightening people into not offending, it is associated with severe penalties, such as long prison sentences.

While the theory of individual deterrence – that people 'refrain from action because they dislike what they believe to be the possible consequences of those actions' (Walker 1991) – seems plausible, it does not work well in practice. Offenders who have been subjected to harsh punishments should, in theory, be less likely to reoffend than similar offenders who received a less severe punishment. In practice, the reverse seems to occur. The introduction of much stricter regimes in detention centres in the early 1980s had no effect on the reconviction rates of young offenders. Cavadino and Dignan (1993: 34) point to research that suggests that offenders who suffer more severe penalties are more likely to reoffend: 'harsher penalties . . . could help foster a tough, "macho" criminal self-image in the young men who predominate in the criminal statistics'. This is not to argue that no offender is ever deterred by a harsh punishment but that there are other effects of punishment that will have a greater influence on offenders.

Walker (1991) suggests that the notion of deterrence with regard to punishment is imprecise. Are individuals deterred if they refrain from committing an offence at one time but then commit the same offence later, or in another place? The sight of a police car might deter the burglar for that particular night, or the burglar might move to another street. Whether this sort of 'displacement' could be classified as deterrence is, Walker argues, rather doubtful.

The potential punishment is not the only factor influencing the would-be offender. Walker suggests that 'on-the-spot deterrents' that pose practical difficulties, such as effective security, high walls, large dogs and the like, will have a greater deterrent effect. More remote consequences, such as the 'stigma' of being known as a shoplifter, may also be deterrents.

Deterrence involves the individual weighing up a range of possible consequences of committing an offence, but it would 'work' only if that individual was tempted to offend in the first place; a person who is not tempted cannot be deterred. Walker (1991) argues that the key factor in assessing the effectiveness of deterrent punishments is that the person believes in the deterring consequences; some people will be deterred by quite remote possibilities. Walker uses the example of many parents not immunizing their children against whooping cough because of a minimal risk of brain damage. The effectiveness of deterrence can vary as the individual's state of mind varies. Normally law-abiding people might become undeterrable when sufficiently angry, drunk or jealous, and commit offences from which they would usually be deterred.

The fear of being caught and stigmatized is enough to deter some people from committing any offence, and the degree of harshness of the punishment attached to an offence is irrelevant. Others see punishment as part of the risk: 'If you can't do the time, don't do the crime.' Punishments can have some deterrent effect. If life imprisonment was the standard sentence for shoplifting or exceeding the speed limit, then the rate of such offences would probably be reduced significantly. Cavadino and Dignan (1993) refer to the deportation of the entire Danish police force by the German occupiers for several months during the Second World War, leading to a spectacular rise in rates of theft and robbery in Denmark. However, aside from such extreme examples, there is little evidence that the type or severity of punishment has much influence as a general deterrent. This argument is supported by the example of a Birmingham youth receiving a 20-year detention sentence for a mugging offence in 1973.

This exceptional punishment attracted plenty of media attention, and yet research comparing rates of mugging before and after that sentence, in Birmingham, Liverpool and Manchester, found that it had had no effect on the rate of such offences.

Stop and think

- Do exemplary sentences work?
- Which of the following crimes have you committed?
  (a) theft of stationery or similar from the workplace;
  (b) using TV without a licence;
  (c) possession of illegal drugs;
  (d) buying goods that may have been stolen;
  (e) theft of a car;
  (f) drinking in a pub while under age.
- What would deter you from committing such crimes?

The old saying 'might as well be hanged for a sheep as a lamb' suggests that too severe a punishment for a relatively minor offence might drive the offender into committing more serious offences. Although offenders always run the risk of being caught, the chances of getting away with an offence (the amount of unrecorded and unsolved crime indicate these chances are pretty good) will greatly weaken the deterrent effect of any punishment.

The probability of conviction – the offender's own estimate of whether they will 'get away with it' – is a key influence on whether a particular offence is committed. The actual punishment seems to have less influence as a general deterrent than the offender's estimation of the likelihood of detection.

Capital punishment

Capital punishment is often seen as the ultimate form of deterrence. Those who advocate the reintroduction in Britain of capital punishment for murder have argued that the death penalty would have a deterrent effect and lead to a reduction in serious crime. The view that capital punishment must be a better deterrent than any other penalty presupposes that the potential murderer rationally calculates the advantages and disadvantages of murder and is therefore deterrable. However, an estimated three-quarters of murders are committed on impulse, perhaps in a fit of rage or during a fight. Furthermore, it is questionable whether the supposedly rational murderer – for instance, the terrorist or armed robber – is so easily deterrable. They will tend to think that they have a good chance of getting away with their crime, and, particularly in the case of politically motivated murderers, they will often have some form of organization to help them escape detection.

It is possible that capital punishment does act as a deterrent in some cases, but it is difficult to recognize when deterrence works. There is little evidence that long-term imprisonment deters would-be murderers any less than capital punishment. There are other arguments concerning capital punishment that have nothing to do with its deterrent potential, including the belief that murder is so wicked that the death penalty is the only proper response, which illustrates the retributionary aim of punishment (see below). These beliefs may account for the fact that in a MORI poll carried out in 2002, over half (56 per cent) of respondents were in favour of reintroducing the death penalty.

Retribution

Retribution is based on the revenge motive 'an eye for an eye and a tooth for a tooth'. It originally meant the paying back of a debt and in the penal context refers to deserved punishment. It is often seen as the most important aim of punishment: certain offences deserve certain punishments and, if criminals do not receive 'proper' punishment, then law and order will break down. Linked with retribution is the belief that punishment should demonstrate society's condemnation of particular offenders; offences that excite the strongest condemnation merit the severest punishments. Although punishment cannot undo the harm done, it can make the victims of crime feel better and help people to make sense of the senseless (in cases such as child abuse). Retribution emphasizes the denunciation aspect of punishment. The passing of a sentence acts to denounce the particular offence and can be seen as a public statement of disapproval; the severity of the actual punishment demonstrates the extent of this disapproval.

The death penalty is a retributionary punishment that meets the desire for revenge. It can be argued that people who kill deserve to be killed themselves; crimes that are totally condemned by society are seen as requiring the severest possible punishment. However, retribution is not generally put forward as the most important argument for reintroducing capital punishment; rather, the debate has focused on its deterrent effect (pp. 582–583).

Stop and think

- Would a return to retributive punishment lead to televised executions?
- Suggest arguments for and against televised punishments.

Walker (1991) sees retribution as promising the certainty that the notion of deterrence and the utilitarian approach cannot provide. The retributive justification for punishment is based clearly on what a person has done. The idea of deserved punishment implies that the gravity of the offence should determine the severity of the penalty. However, the extent to which harm was intended is a variable that affects the sort of punishment received: an accidental killing is not punished as if it were murder, even though the end result is the same. Furthermore, some offences might cause only a minimal degree of harm and yet be seen to merit severe punishment: an attempted murder may do no actual harm and yet be punished almost as severely as a successful murder. As Walker (1991) puts it, 'incompetence does not mitigate'.

Some physical harms are clearly greater than others: injuries that lead to permanent disability are obviously distinguishable from minor cuts and bruises. The psychological harm caused by offenders is less easy to quantify. In the case of theft, the amount of money lost is not the sole factor: victims deprived of all their savings, whatever the total sum, will suffer far more than better-off victims who lose a similar amount. The feeling of violation following a burglary in one's home or a personal attack can be long-lasting, while shoplifting from large stores is liable to cause little personal suffering.

World in focus

Capital punishment: China and the USA

During 2002 at least 1526 prisoners were executed in 31 countries and at least 3248 people were sentenced to death in 67 countries. Of the executions in 2002, 81 per cent took place in China, Iran and the USA.

China outstrips world on executions

China executed more people in the last three months than the rest of the world did in the past three years, the human rights group Amnesty International says . . . The London-based group said China has put people to death not just for violent crimes, but also for offences such as bribery, embezzlement and stealing gasoline.

Using figures tallied from publicly available reports, Amnesty International said since an anti-crime campaign, Strike Hard, was launched in April, China has carried out at least 1781 executions. In contrast, Amnesty International counted 1751 executions in the rest of the world over the past three years. But only a fraction of death sentences and executions in China are publicly reported and the actual number of people put to death is far higher . . .

Most executions in China take place after sentencing rallies in front of massive crowds in sports stadiums and public squares. Prisoners are also paraded through the streets past thousands of people on the way to execution by firing squad in nearby fields or courtyards.

(BBC News Online 6.7.03)

Figure 14.4 Awaiting execution
AP Photo/Vincent Yu

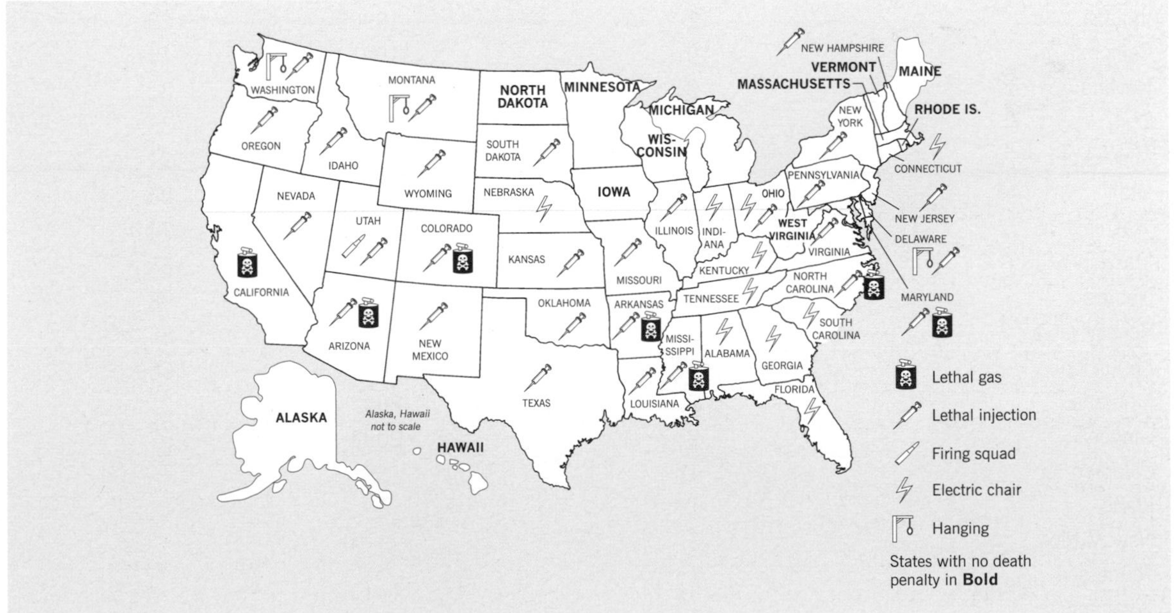

Figure 14.5 US states that have the death penalty
Note: Since the Supreme Court overturned the ban on the death penalty in 1976, 36 states have executed people
Source: Adapted from the *Guardian* 8.4.95 – this was still the case in 2008 with 36 states having the death penalty and 14 not

World in focus *continued*

The death penalty in the USA

Seventy-one prisoners were executed in the USA in 2002, bringing to 820 the total number executed since the death penalty was resumed in 1977.

Over 3700 prisoners were under sentence of death as of 1 January 2002.

Thirty-eight of the 50 US states provide for the death penalty in law.

(Amnesty International 2003 – www.amnesty.org/en/death-penalty)

Table 14.5 US execution statistics by state and year (as at 10.03.03)

State	No. of executions	Year	No. of executions
Texas	310	1976	0
Virginia	89	1977	1
Oklahoma	69	1978	0
Missouri	60	1979	2
Florida	57	1980	0
Georgia	33	1981	1
Alabama	28	1982	2
South Carolina	28	1983	5
Louisiana	27	1984	21
North Carolina	27	1985	18
Arkansas	25	1986	18
Arizona	22	1987	25
Delaware	13	1988	11
Illinois	12	1989	16
Indiana	11	1990	23
California	10	1991	14
Nevada	9	1992	31
Ohio	8	1993	38
Mississippi	6	1994	31
Utah	6	1995	56
Washington	4	1997	74
Maryland	3	1998	68
Nebraska	3	1999	98
Pennsylvania	3	2000	85
Kentucky	2	2001	66
Montana	2	2002	71
Oregon	2	2003	57
Colorado	1		
Idaho	1		
New Mexico	1		
Tennessee	1		
Wyoming	1		
Total executions since 1976	877		877

(Source: http://smu.edu/pages/people.asp)

Figure 14.6 Eye for an eye in the Taleban's Kabul. Bahram Khan, 29, an accused murderer, kneels in the centre of Kabul's football stadium moments before being shot. At least 35,000 people turned out for the execution
© Zaheerudin/Webistan/Corbis

Stop and think

- Although incompetence may not be seen as a mitigating factor (something that might be taken into account to lessen the normal penalty), there are other factors which influence the punishment received. List as many factors as you can that you feel sentencers should take into account when punishing offenders.
- Suggest reasons for and against these factors affecting a sentence.

Harm done is not the only factor that causes difficulty in applying the retributive idea to punishment. Assessment of the offender's character is often problematic. Walker (1991) refers to a case where the Court of Appeal reduced the prison sentence given for a serious insurance fraud because the offender, while on bail, had jumped into a canal to save a drowning boy. He suggests that 'spectacular behaviour seems to influence courts more than unobtrusive decency'. We have seen that it is difficult to quantify the suffering experienced by victims. A by-product of punishment is that people other than the offender will often unintentionally suffer from that punishment. If the offender has a family, then imprisonment or fines will usually cause distress and hardship for innocent partners and children.

Rehabilitation

Rehabilitation is based on the belief that people can change: they are never beyond reform. Thus, offenders can be taught how to be 'normal' law-abiding citizens; their punishment will make them less likely to reoffend. We shall use the terms 'rehabilitation' and 'reform' interchangeably, although strictly speaking *reform* refers to individuals being persuaded and given the space to change themselves, while *rehabilitation* involves a more planned and regulated treatment, for example a supervisor finds employment for offenders and monitors their progress. The focus is on how punishment can be used to 'correct' an offender's behaviour (indeed, Walker uses the term 'correction' in preference to rehabilitation or reform).

Religious influence has usually emphasized the correction of the offender, but religiously motivated attempts at reform have often caused as much hardship as the methods that they aimed to replace. Victorian reformers believed that prison should be a place where the offender might become a reformed person; they advocated long periods of solitary confinement, during which time prisoners could examine their soul and conscience, spend hours in prayer and emerge purified; Bibles were made available in all cells.

With the growth in the study of crime, there have been strong arguments for more constructive and humane punishments, supported by groups campaigning against unjust and inhumane punishments, such as Amnesty International and the Howard League. However, revenge and deterrence justifications for punishment are still supported widely, and public anxiety is easily aroused about the supposed softness of modern punishments. Whenever there are moves to release, or even discuss the release, of widely condemned prisoners, there is immediately a massive media and public outcry. Before her death in November 2002, any consideration of parole for Myra Hindley, the Moors murderer, caused such widespread public and media anger that it was unlikely any government would have ever contemplated it.

In practice there has tended to be a balance between reform and retributivist themes; one or other theme becomes fashionable at particular times. Cavadino and Dignan (2002) suggest that there has been a revival of the rehabilitative approach in recent years, although the idea that methods of punishment could 'work' almost independently of the offenders having been replaced with an emphasis on how a specific punishment can be used to help offenders improve their behaviour. These newer approaches often centre around confronting offenders with the consequences of their behaviour in the hope that they will choose to change both their behaviour and their attitudes towards offending. These ideas characterize the notion of restorative justice, which is considered below.

The contradiction between reform-based and retribution-based punishments is a basic problem that faces any system of punishment. The lack of success of harsh punishments encourages reform measures, but these are felt by many people not to be a proper response to the harm caused by offenders.

In assessing the extent to which rehabilitation 'works', Walker (1991) points to the difficulty of ever being sure why a particular offender ceases to offend. It may be the stigma, the unpleasant memory of the punishment, or the influence of family, friends or social workers. Even offenders who appear to be successfully corrected may still be involved in crime but have not been caught again. The difficulty in assessing reform-based punishments does not mean that 'nothing works'; some approaches may work with some offenders but not with others.

Uncertainty over the extent to which rehabilitation works led to the emergence of a justice model of punishment in the 1970s. Rehabilitative, treatment-based approaches included indeterminate sentences, based on the notion that when the treatment worked the punishment could end. However, the *justice model* argued that this gave too much discretion to 'experts' working in the criminal justice system and that punishment should be based on the seriousness of the offence; the rehabilitative approach was inherently unfair in that it treated similar offences in very different ways. Cavadino and Dignan (2002) highlight the abolition in 1982 of the indeterminate borstal sentence for young offenders (who were released at any time between six months and two years according to how they had 'responded' to their punishment) and its replacement with a fixed-term sentence as evidence of the impact of the justice model on penal policy in Britain.

Incapacitation

Incapacitation means that offenders are prevented from reoffending, either temporarily or permanently, by the punishment they receive. In some societies this has taken the form of preventive detention, whereby people who are perceived as potential offenders or a political threat are imprisoned. This is clearly opposed to the basic notions of individual freedom. Milder forms of incapacitation can result from a range of punishments. Banning people from driving should prevent them from repeating motoring offences. Any form of detention or imprisonment ensures that the offender is unable to commit certain offences, at least for the duration of the sentence.

Reparation

Another aim of punishment is *reparation* or *compensation*. Reparation is based on the principle of *restorative justice* and the notion that crime affects communities and victims, who should therefore have a part to play in administering justice. This approach to punishment usually involves the offender being confronted with what they have done by being brought face to face with those they have harmed. Charles Pollard, former chief constable of Thames Valley Police, saw this as a

> **. . . hugely powerful thing. There is nowhere for them to go. There is no defence lawyer giving lots of mitigation and trying to minimise the responsibility for what they have done . . . This is about coming face-to-face with the harm they have caused, and that has the impact of shaming the offender. But what's important is that it is in private and is what we call *reintegrative shaming* which means that once that person has really understood the impact they have had on others they are very ready to really think about how they are going to change their behaviour in the future. They are ready to think about how they are going to repair the damage to the people they have harmed whether by compensation, certainly by apologising, maybe doing some work for them.**
>
> (Pollard 1998)

Pollard (1998) went on to point out that the criminal justice system does not have a mechanism for people to apologize for their behaviour, and that an apology has to be the first and most important part of any form of reparation. In discussing the community conferencing scheme used in Thames Valley, he emphasized how restorative justice gives victims 'a part to play in the system'.

If there is not an individual victim or identifiable victim for the offender to compensate, then reparation could be made to society through some form of community service or by paying a fine into public funds. However, reparation is difficult to apply. Often the offender will not have the means to repay the victim; if a youngster commits an offence, then it is debatable whether the parents should be responsible for compensation. Nonetheless, in a high proportion of offences, the offender and victim know one another; if they are brought together to arrive at a settlement, then it can be better and quicker for all parties, as well as cutting down on court workloads. Such an approach is generally seen as particularly suitable for minor offences such as car crime and damage to property. However, like other new methods, it tends to be seen by many as too soft a response to crime.

Sociological theories of punishment

Although punishment and justice have not been a major area of sociological enquiry, certain theoretical approaches provide the basis for the sociological study of punishment:

- *Punishment and social cohesion* – Durkheim
- *Punishment and class control* – Marxism
- *Punishment, power and regulation* – Foucault.

Sociologists have examined punishment in social terms rather than as crime control. Garland (1990) points out that institutions of punishment such as prisons or community service orders are social artefacts reflecting cultural standards. Just as styles of building or music cannot be explained solely in terms of their obvious purposes of providing shelter or entertainment, so punishment has to be considered in historical, cultural and social contexts.

Stop and think

- What social purposes other than the control of crime might punishment have?
- What specific penalties might achieve these purposes?

Punishment and social cohesion: Durkheim

In Durkheim's sociological analysis, punishment represented the 'collective conscience' of society at work, and the examination of punishment would provide an insight into the moral and social life of the society. Durkheim believed that social order was based on a core of shared values and moralities (see pp. 47–49). Punishment provides a clear illustration of the moral nature of social order; it is not just about controlling crime. In Durkheim's *The Division of Labour in Society* (1960 [1893]), changes in the nature of punishment were seen as reflecting changes in the nature of social morality and social solidarity.

Durkheim emphasized the relationship between the punishment of crime and the maintenance of moral and social order. Crimes are moral outrages that violate a society's collective conscience; this violation produces a punitive reaction. As Durkheim puts it, 'crime brings together upright consciences and concentrates them'; crime provides an occasion for the collective expression of shared moral feelings (see p. 560).

The existence of social morality and social solidarity makes punishment necessary, in that it reaffirms moral and social bonds. Of course, punishment is not the only social institution that reinforces social morality and solidarity. Religion, education and family life all help to strengthen the collective conscience and to promote social cohesion; however, formal punishment enjoys a special place in Durkheim's work.

Durkheim acknowledged that the nature of punishment changes as society changes; he saw punishment as more important as a means of reinforcing moral and social order in less complex societies with a less developed division of labour. However, while methods change, the functions of punishment remain constant. Although people are outraged by different activities over time, punishment as a social process has an unchanging character.

In contrasting simpler societies based on mechanical solidarity with modern societies based on organic solidarity, Durkheim suggested that the former are characterized by more severe and intense punishment. The intensity of the collective conscience in simple societies is reflected in the intensity of punishment. In modern, advanced societies, collective sentiments are less demanding; there is more scope for diversity and interdependence, and so punishment for violations of the collective conscience is more lenient. The intensity of punishment reflects the nature of the collective conscience; as society develops, the severity of punishment diminishes.

The link between punishment and morality is the key element of Durkheim's sociology of punishment. Punishment helps to prevent the collapse of moral authority and demonstrates the force of moral commands; its primary function is the reassertion of the moral order of society. Punishment is not an instrument of deterrence; the threat of unpleasant consequences just presents practical problems that stand in the way of the criminal's desires. Although in practical terms punishment has to be unpleasant, Durkheim saw this as incidental. The essence of punishment is the expression of moral condemnation.

Rituals of punishment

Durkheim believed that it was the rituals associated with punishment that specifically conveyed moral messages and helped to maintain social order. These rituals tend nowadays to centre around the courtroom drama. They include the wearing of wigs and gowns, the process of the trial, the passing of a sentence (guilty or not) and the meting out of punishment. The focus on the courtroom is due in part to the decline in public, and therefore visible, punishments, such as public floggings and executions. Prisons and other institutions responsible for punishment tend to be closed to the public and the media. Of course, there are rituals associated with imprisonment; in his famous study of total institutions, Goffman (1968) highlighted the rituals of initiation that serve to 'mortify the self', including the replacing of the prisoner's name with a number, the issuing of prison clothing, the shaving of the prisoner's head and the restrictions on contact with the outside world. However, these rituals are undertaken to maintain the institution itself; they are done for an internal audience. As a consequence of this decline in public punishment, the focus of public and media interest tends to be on the trial of offenders and on 'who gets what' rather than on the detailed workings of the processes of punishment. Durkheim's emphasis on the rituals of punishment can be compared with his study of religion: it does not matter whether or not a particular doctrine is true; the importance is the faith and the rituals that have social functions (see pp. 655–657).

Stop and think

- Which criminal trials have received detailed media coverage recently?
- How have the media reported these trials? How did it make you feel?
- To what extent might such trials strengthen the 'collective conscience'?
- Court cases and punishments can provoke a range of responses as well as social solidarity. What other responses might these trials have provoked?

Comment and criticism

Just as Durkheim's description of simple societies, characterized by mechanical solidarity, and advanced societies, characterized by organic solidarity, has been criticized as oversimplistic, so his history of punishment has been similarly criticized. Garland (1990) suggests that the historical transition from simple societies characterized by severe punishments to advanced ones characterized by lenient punishment is not really demonstrated by Durkheim; no account of any intermediate stages is given.

Garland also criticizes Durkheim's application of the notion of the collective conscience. A certain degree of order in society does not necessarily indicate a general commitment to shared moral norms; many people follow laws for practical reasons, to avoid punishments rather than because of moral commitment. This raises the question as to whether violations of the criminal law do really break genuinely held moral sentiments. Clearly there is some link between the law and popular sentiment; the laws protecting property and personal safety, for instance, are supportive of widely shared values. However, while there may be general agreement that rape and burglary are morally repugnant, there is considerable disagreement over the 'proper' punishment for such behaviour. And there is even less agreement over criminal offences which do not offend such strongly and widely held sentiments – crimes such as tax evasion or infringing copyright laws, perhaps. Punishments that deal with the most serious and shocking crimes – child murder, for example – provoke the strongest feelings and the greatest moral outcry.

It seems clear that the punishment of crime produces emotional responses. Garland refers to the philosopher Nietzsche, who suggested that positive pleasure can be gained from punishment; it can gratify impulses of sadism and cruelty. The fascination with crime and criminals – witness, for example, the popularity of films, books, magazines and TV programmes on serial killers – can be seen as a gratification of repressed aggression as well as a reflection of horror and repugnance.

Stop and think

- Which crimes excite the greatest moral repugnance? Why?
- What forms of punishment express this moral condemnation and repugnance?

To what extent, then, is punishment functional for society? Certainly it performs some functions – restraining some types of behaviour and legitimizing some forms of authority. However, what is functional from one point of view may be dysfunctional from another. This is a criticism that is often made of functionalist work, which implies that there is a general agreement over what is functional or not and what should and should not be valued and appreciated. It could also be argued that punishment has dysfunctional as well as functional consequences. The fact that crime does produce emotional responses can encourage societies to direct their punishments towards the denunciation of particular criminal individuals rather than doing anything about wider social conditions that may give rise to crime. In addition, directing anger and punishment solely at the individual may also encourage the scapegoating and potential for harassment of specific groups of people.

The emphasis on general agreement ignores the obvious power differentials in the maintenance of order in society. Durkheim's work seems to ignore or at least underplay the fact that people are members of groups that can have opposed interests and to neglect the conflict between interest groups. Garland also questions whether Durkheim's theory is relevant to modern, advanced societies with a complex division of labour and where the moral order is not necessarily universal.

Durkheim's work has encouraged examination of the social processes of punishment; his work introduced the symbolic and emotional elements of punishment rather than just the narrow technical side. In arguing that punishment was necessary and functional for society, Durkheim realized that it had only a very limited ability to control criminal behaviour. It was this apparent contradiction – that punishment was politically and socially functional and yet had little effect on actual criminal behaviour – that Garland argues is the crucial characteristic of punishment:

> **This sense of being simultaneously necessary and also destined to a degree of futility is what I will term the *tragic* quality of punishment.**
>
> (Garland 1990: 80)

Punishment and class control: Marxism

Neither Marx nor Engels analysed the practices and institutions for the punishment of offenders; they wrote very little on crime and criminals and did not develop a theory of crime. Thus, we have to look at the writing of later Marxist writers to provide us with a Marxist analysis of punishment.

The basic Marxist approach sees the economy as the key locus of power in society. The economic system determines all other areas of social life, including the legal system. Those groups that have economic power are able to ensure that social institutions work in a way that is consistent with their interests. Thus, the institutions of the law and punishment come to reflect the interests of the dominant economic groups. Marxist analysis of punishment has tended to focus on the way in which elements of the superstructure support ruling-class power. The law works in the interests of some groups more than others: 'there's one law for the rich and one for the poor'.

Garland suggests that the Marxist analysis of punishment centres on the notion of class struggle and the ways in which the relationship between social classes shapes the form of punishment in a particular society. He highlights the work of Rusche and Kirchheimer as the best example of the Marxist interpretation of punishment. Rusche and Kirchheimer's major text, *Punishment and Social Structure* (1968 [1939]), was not widely read when first published and it is only since its reissue in 1968 that their work has been taken up by Marxist criminologists and become more widely known.

Rusche and Kirchheimer provide a detailed history of punishment that emphasizes how the economy and, in particular, the labour market influence the methods of punishment in society. An illustration of their basic argument is provided by their account of the development of punishments such as galley slavery, transportation and hard labour. These 'new' punishments emerged in the sixteenth and seventeenth centuries alongside the early developments of a capitalist economic system. Labour power increasingly came to be seen as a vital resource, and harsh physical punishments, such as whipping, branding and execution, were replaced by punishments that involved productive, hard labour and particularly work that 'free' people were unwilling to undertake. During this period there were vast amounts of land in the colonies that needed to be worked, and the penalty of transportation was used to develop these areas. Transportation was initially offered as a commutation of capital punishment, but by the early 1700s it was regularly used as a sentence for a range of minor offences. By the end of the eighteenth century, the growing prosperity in the colonies led to the decline of this form of punishment; the free immigrants to Australia and elsewhere were not happy about criminal labour and convicts undercutting

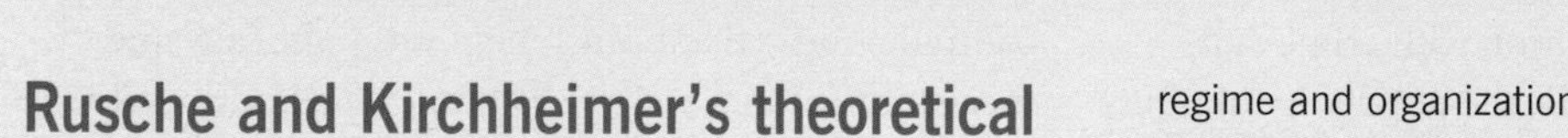

Rusche and Kirchheimer's theoretical approach to punishment

- Punishments have to be viewed as historically specific phenomena that appear in particular forms at different periods. This principle of historical specificity distinguishes Marxist accounts from Durkheim's view of punishment as something that performed essentially similar functions in all societies.
- The mode of production is the major determinant of specific penal methods in specific historical periods. Different systems of production will produce different methods of punishment.
- The particular forms of punishment are, therefore, social artefacts or constructions.
- Penal policy is one element within a wider strategy for controlling the poor. Punishment is seen almost exclusively as aimed at the control of the 'lower orders'. Rusche and Kirchheimer suggest that there were clear similarities between the way criminals were treated and the policies aimed at controlling the labouring masses. In the early industrial period the regime and organization of prison life was similar to the way workers were treated in factories and beggars and vagrants in workhouses.
- Punishment is a mechanism deeply implicated within the class struggle: 'the history of the penal system is the history of the relations between the rich and the poor' (Rusche (1980 [1933]).
- Although punishment is generally and conventionally seen as an institution which benefits 'society as a whole', for Marxists, in reality it supports the interests of one class against another. Punishment is (another) element and example of control that is hidden within ideological veils.

(Adapted from Garland 1990: 90–92)

Questions

1. What do you think were the main similarities between prison and factory life in the early industrial period?
2. Think of examples of how 'different systems of production will produce different methods of punishment'.

their wages, while the authorities felt that transportation was becoming little deterrent to criminals.

Comment and criticism

The priority given to economic explanations by Marxist writers such as Rusche and Kirchheimer has been criticized for understating the importance of political and ideological factors; religious and humanitarian influences on the development of punishment are accorded only secondary importance, for example. Furthermore, the emphasis given to class and class relationships tends to ignore popular attitudes to punishment. There is widespread support among the working classes for harsh punitive policies and little evidence that the working classes support criminals any more than other social groups, which Garland suggests casts doubt on a simple class conflict approach to punishment.

However, these comments do not refute Rusche and Kirchheimer's argument that economic relationships and the labour market can exert an important influence on penal policy and that the institutions of punishment can be seen as part of a wider strategy for managing the poor and working classes.

The essence of the Marxist approach is that the approach to, and form of, punishment is influenced by the strategies that the dominant, governing groups adopt towards the working classes. Punishment is shaped not merely by patterns of crime but by the perception of the working class, and the poor in particular, as a social problem. Rusche and Kirchheimer argue that the working classes have little commitment to the law or to the dominant moral order in general and that it is therefore important for the criminal law and the punishments associated with it to make sure that crime does not pay. Punishments have to be severe and institutions of punishment such as prisons have to be unpleasant; indeed, they have to be more unpleasant than the conditions that the worst-off 'free' people are able to live in.

Stop and think

Think of some recent criminal cases that have received a lot of publicity.

- To what extent does class play a part in the way that the public reacts to crime and criminals?
- How fair is it for Rusche and Kirchheimer to suggest that the working classes have little commitment to the law?

Case study

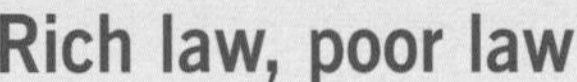

Rich law, poor law

The sociological study of white-collar crime lends support to the idea that the extent and severity with which the legal system is applied varies between different social groups. Dee Cook (1989) examined the different responses to tax and supplementary benefit fraud. She cited examples of judicial responses to defrauding the public purse by two different means – by defrauding the Inland Revenue by evading tax and defrauding the DHSS by falsely claiming supplementary benefit:

> Two partners in a vegetable wholesalers business admitted falsifying accounts to the tune of £100,000. At their trial the judge said he considered they had been 'very wise' in admitting their guilt and they had paid back the tax due (with interest) to the Inland Revenue. They were sentenced to pay fines. A chartered accountant who defrauded taxes in excess of £8,000 was sentenced to pay a fine as the judge accepted, in mitigation, that his future income would be adversely affected by the trial.
>
> An unemployed father of three failed to declare his wife's earnings to the Department of Health and Social Security (DHSS). He admitted the offence and started to pay back the £996 he owed them by weekly deductions from his supplementary benefit. He was prosecuted a year later and sentenced to pay fines totalling £210, also to be deducted from his benefit. Magistrates told him that 'this country is fed up to the teeth with people like you scrounging from fellow citizens'. A young woman defrauded the DHSS to the tune of £58: she served three months in custody as magistrates said she 'needed to be taught a lesson'.
>
> (Cook 1989: 1)

Case study *continued*

In looking at why the law does not treat white-collar crime in the same way as conventional crime, Hazel Croall (1992) points out that white-collar crime is subject to different regulatory arrangements and these tend to be more lenient than those of the criminal justice system; regulatory bodies are less worried about securing convictions and more keen on settling disputes with a minimum of fuss and, often, publicity. This point is supported by Steven Box's (1983) comments on the deterrents for would-be corporate criminals:

> For the most part corporate crimes are not/do not fall under the jurisdiction of the police, but under special regulatory bodies . . . In the UK, there are numerous inspectorates, commissions and government departments . . .
>
> Although they all have powers either to initiate or recommend criminal prosecution, they are primarily designed to be regulatory bodies whose main weapon against corporate misbehaviour is administrative, i.e. (occasional) inspection coupled with (polite) correspondence. Corporate executives contemplating the possibility of being required to commit corporate crimes know that they face a regulatory agency which for the most part will be unable to detect what is going on, and in the minority of cases when it does, it will have no heart and few resources to pursue the matter into the criminal courts . . .
>
> Criminal laws aimed at regulating corporate activities tend to refer to a specific rather than a general class of behaviour . . . they focus purely on the regulation broken and not on the consequences of that broken regulation. Thus the company responsible for the hoist accident at Littlebrook Dee power station were not prosecuted for the fact that five men died, but for the fact that the machinery was not properly maintained or inspected. For this they were fined £5000. In conventional crime . . . a person is charged with the consequences of his/her action; if someone dies as a consequence of being stabbed, the assailant is more likely to be charged with a homicide offence rather than 'carrying an offensive weapon'. The point of this fracture between the regulation broken and its consequences is that it facilitates corporate crime; executives need only concern themselves with the likelihood of being leniently punished for breaking regulations.
>
> (Box 1983: 44–58)

Questions

1. What are the key differences between corporate and conventional crime?
2. To what extent do they provide a justification for the differential treatment of white-collar and business criminals?

In contrast to Durkheim's view that punishment expresses the interests of society as a whole, the fairly simplistic review of the Marxist approach to punishment that we have presented here sees punishment as expressing ruling-class interests only. Although the criminal law and punishment does provide protection for the working classes as well as the ruling classes – protection against assault and burglary, for instance – it does not, according to Marxists, 'protect' against economic domination and oppression.

Punishment, power and regulation: Foucault

Foucault's (1977 [1975]) *Discipline and Punish* has become one of the key texts in the sociology of punishment. Foucault sees punishment as a system of power and regulation that is imposed on the population – an analysis that overlaps with the Marxist approach and contrasts with Durkheim's argument that punishment is embedded within collective sentiments and therefore conveys moral messages. Foucault, however, focused on the specific workings of penal institutions – how they were structured and how they exercised control. This approach moves away from the examination of society as a coherent whole that can be analysed by structural methods, and to that extent Foucault's work could be described as phenomenological rather than Marxist (see pp. 96–100 on post-structuralism).

The historical issue that Foucault sets out to explain in *Discipline and Punish* is the disappearance of punishment as a public spectacle of violence and the emergence of the prison as the general form of modern punishment – hence, the subtitle of the book 'The birth of the prison'. This change in the basic form of punishment took place between 1750 and 1820, when the target of punishment changed, with an emphasis on changing the soul of the offender rather than just the body, on transforming the offender rather than just avenging the crime. Foucault sees these developments as reflecting how power operates in modern society with open physical force and ceremonies associated with it replaced by more detailed regulation of offenders; troublesome individuals are removed from society rather than destroyed; they are resocialized.

Foucault goes on to consider why imprisonment so quickly became the general method of legal punishment. He saw the development of the prison and imprisonment in relation to the growth of the human sciences. The prison practice of isolating and monitoring inmates ensured that they were studied as individuals with their own characteristics and peculiarities. To an extent, prison led to the discovery of the 'delinquent' – a person distinct from the non-delinquent – and, according to Foucault, to the rise of the science of criminology.

Foucault also argues that the creation of delinquency has been a useful strategy of political domination by dividing the working classes, enhancing fears of authority and guaranteeing the power of the police. Delinquency, which generally consists of relatively minor attacks on authority, is not a particular political danger and can, within limits, be tolerated by the authorities; furthermore, it produces a group of known habitual criminals who can be kept under surveillance.

Although Foucault did not develop a 'grand theory' in the manner of classic social theorists, such as Karl Marx, as mentioned above his work shares a Marxist appreciation of the importance for capitalism of labour power. In the context of punishment, he considered how methods of punishment could be used to turn rebellious subjects into productive ones. For instance, in charting the emergence of prisons and prison regimes in the nineteenth century, he emphasized how they produced a new kind of individual 'subjected to habits, rules and orders'. This investigation of the development of prisons in the early nineteenth century was used by Foucault to help him explore the general themes of domination and how that is achieved and of how individuals are 'socially constructed'.

Foucault saw an extension of power and domination occurring through the methods of surveillance that were part of the design of the new prison buildings of this time. The panoptican designed by Bentham was a prison building constructed so as to allow for the constant observation and monitoring of 'progress' of all its inmates – essentially, it was a circular building built around a central axis that allowed the guards to observe the inmates without themselves being observed. The aim of this design was to induce in the inmates the belief that they were under constant surveillance; although that classic sort of panoptican was never fully instituted, the ideas and basic approach behind it were integrated into the architecture of the new nineteenth-century prison buildings. Foucault saw the prison as illustrating the basic principle of punitive and disciplinary power:

> **The perfect disciplinary apparatus would make it possible for a single gaze to see everything constantly . . . the major effect of the panoptican: to induce in the inmate a state of conscious and permanent visibility that assumes the automatic functioning of power.**
>
> (Foucault 1977: 173–201)

Stop and think

- In spite of the problems with prisons, Foucault suggests that prisons have important political effects at a wider social level. What do you think these effects might be, and how might they work?
- Foucault argued that observation could be used as a means of regulation and control. Give examples of how this might happen.

Punishment in modern society: the rationalization of punishment

Over the past 200 or so years, makeshift forms of punishment have been replaced by centrally administered arrangements, with greater uniformity in punishment and the development of a penal infrastructure, due in part to the growth in population since the eighteenth century and the rising rate of crime. The range of professional groups working in the penal system – social workers, probation officers, psychiatrists, prison officers and governors – tend to see prisoners in terms of whether they are good or bad inmates on account of their institutional conduct, rather than as evil or wicked on account of the crimes for which they are being punished. The punishments are administered by paid officials rather than the general public or, indeed, those personally affected by the offenders' actions.

This 'professionalization of justice' (Garland 1990) has altered the place and meaning of punishment in modern society. The institutions of punishment have become less accessible and more secretive as specialized professions have become involved. This trend toward rationalization runs counter to Durkheim's emphasis on the emotional nature of punishment – as reflecting an outrage to generally held moral sentiments. Indeed, this may help to explain why the public often feels frustrated by moves to release criminals 'early' – as evidenced by the campaign to ensure that the two ten-year-old boys who abducted and killed toddler James Bulger in 1993 remain in prison for many years and the opposition to periodic suggestions that, before her death in 2002, Moors murderer Myra Hindley (imprisoned in 1965) be considered for release on parole.

No method of punishment has ever managed to control crime or to achieve high rates of reform of offenders; it is unrealistic to hope that any methods will. Punishments fail because they can never be any more than a backup to the mainstream processes of socialization. A sense of duty and morality, acceptable standards of behaviour and so on have to be learned and internalized; they cannot be imposed. 'Punishment is merely a coercive back up to those more reliable social mechanisms, a back up which is often unable to do anything more than manage those who slip through these networks of normal control and integration' (Garland 1990: 289).

Garland suggests that we should expect less from penal policy. Although sometimes necessary, punishment is beset by contradictions and irresolvable tensions:

> **However well it is organized, and however humanely administered, punishment is inescapably marked by moral contradiction and unwanted irony – as when it seeks to uphold freedom by means of its deprivation or condemns private violence using a violence which is publicly authorized.**
>
> (Garland 1990: 292)

Summary

- Crime is behaviour that breaks the criminal law and, if detected, may lead to criminal proceedings and formal punishment; it is distinct from the broader area of deviant behaviour.
- Those who commit crimes generally wish to keep their criminal behaviour secret. The methodological problems for the sociological study of crime include the difficulty of gaining access to such behaviour and of collecting reliable data from law-breakers and the moral dilemmas that can face researchers who are confronted with behaviour that may, for instance, cause suffering to innocent victims.
- Crime has always fascinated people and explanations for it have been wide-ranging. Sociologists emphasize the specific social conditions and opportunities that are available to different groups. However, there is no one sociological position on crime.
- Crime has been seen as a response to the frustration felt by those who cannot achieve the 'success goals' of society (Robert Merton and Albert Cohen, for example); as a consequence of society, and particularly the agencies of social control within it, labelling certain forms of behaviour and groups of people as criminal (interpretativist approaches); and as a result of the power of the ruling, dominant groups to impose their standards of appropriate and inappropriate behaviour on other, less powerful groups (critical, Marxist theories).
- Criminal statistics indicate that crime grew spectacularly in the twentieth century. However, these statistics have to be treated with caution: the extension of formal control mechanisms, such as more and better-equipped police officers and more laws, will clearly influence the amount of criminal behaviour that is

Summary *continued*

known about. Criminal statistics also show that crime is a largely male preserve and that people from ethnic minorities, and especially black males, are more likely to be convicted and punished for criminal behaviour than other social groups.

- The police are the most visible formal agency of social control; the relationship between the police and public is of crucial importance in the control and subsequent punishment of criminal behaviour. A 'police culture' has helped to segregate the police from certain sections of the wider public, particularly young black people.
- Legal punishment is the ultimate form of social control. There are different opinions over what should be the 'aims of punishment'. Deterrence, retribution and rehabilitation are three major aims that have been given more or less support and credibility by both government and the public at different periods of time.
- There are various sociological explanations of the role of punishment in society. The Durkheimian approach sees punishment as helping to maintain social cohesion through strengthening the moral and social bonds of a society; the work of Foucault and the Marxist approaches have focused on punishment as a formal means for regulating the mass of the population and for supporting the power of the ruling classes.

Links

The section on explaining crime (pp. 559–569) includes different theoretical approaches that are examined more generally in Chapter 2.

The discussion of policing (pp. 577–580) touches on the issues of racism and policing considered in Chapter 6.

Further reading

Becker, H.S. (1963) *Outsiders: Studies in the Sociology of Deviance*, New York: Free Press.

Cohen, A.K. (1955) *Delinquent Boys: The Culture of the Gang*, New York: Free Press.

Pearson, G. (1983) *Hooligan: A History of Respectable Fears*, London: Macmillan.

Young, J. and Mathews, R. (eds) (1992) *Rethinking Criminology: The Realist Debate*, London: Sage.

There is nothing like the 'real thing', and many of the original sources referred to in our examination of theories of crime are most accessible.

Cavadino, M. and Dignan, J. (2002) *The Penal System: An Introduction*, 3rd edn, London: Sage.

As well as looking at justifications and explanations for punishment, this book examines the specific elements of the penal system of England and Wales, including sentencing practices, imprisonment, non-custodial penalties and issues of bias within the criminal justice system.

Croall, H. (1998) *Crime and Society in Britain*, Harlow: Addison Wesley Longman.

Marsh, I., Melville, G., Morgan, K., Norris, G. and Walkington, Z. (2006) *Theories of Crime*, London: Routledge.

Valier, C. (2002) *Theories of Crime and Punishment*, Harlow: Longman.

These three texts provide clear comprehensive introductions to the sociology of crime. Croall's text analyses and describes various kinds of crime, including violent and sexual crimes, organized and corporate crime, and crimes of the state. The book by Marsh and colleagues examines biological, psychological and sociological theories of crime and considers explanations for the criminal behaviour of women and people from ethnic minority groups. Valier's study covers sociological theories of both crime and punishment.

Garland, D. (1990) *Punishment and Modern Society: A Study in Social Theory*, Oxford: Clarendon.

A comprehensive introduction to the sociology of punishment.

McLaughlin, E. and Muncie, J. (eds) (2001) *Controlling Crime*, 2nd edn, London: Sage.

Newburn, T. (2003) *Crime and Criminal Justice Policy*, 2nd edn, Harlow: Longman.
Two up-to-date overviews of the criminal justice system that include coverage of future policy issues such as the implications of privatization.

Maguire, M., Morgan, R. and Reiner, R. (eds) (2007) *The Oxford Handbook of Criminology*, 4th edn, Oxford: Clarendon.
Comprehensive and up-to-date readings by key writers and researchers on criminology and the criminal justice system.

Marsh, I., Cochrane, J. and Melville, G. (2004) *Criminal Justice: An Introduction to Philosophies, Theories and Practice*, London: Routledge.
Part 1 of this book provides an overview of the major philosophical aims and sociological theories of punishment and the developing perspective of victimology, while Part 2 focuses on the main areas of the criminal justice system, including the police, the courts and judiciary and prisons.

Walker, N. (1991) *Why Punish?*, Oxford: Oxford University Press.
This short, thought-provoking book looks at the justifications for, and aims of, punishment, grappling with the moral issues and dilemmas that they raise.

Websites

www.homeoffice.gov.uk

This is a major site that has substantial sections on crime and policing and justice and victims. It also includes a mass of statistics and research findings relevant to crime and its punishment.

www.crimetheory.com

As well as highlighting recent research on criminological theorizing, this site has an excellent archive of historical texts on the theory of crime – including Beccaria, Lombroso and Merton.

Activities

Activity 1

Explanations of crime

Rather than focusing on the individual characteristics of criminals, sociological theories of crime emphasize how the characteristics of the particular society play an important part in the explanations for crime. The following extract is from American sociologist Jack Levin (1993), who describes how the sociologist's 'eye' on crime differs from biological, psychological and common-sense explanations.

> Watching the evening news on television, I learn that a 35 year old man has murdered 23 people at a Luby's Cafeteria in Killeen, Texas. I read in the paper that a 'cannibal killer' in Milwaukee has strangled and dismembered 17 men. Then, I discover that the cities are burning again. The city of Los Angeles has gone up in flames following days and nights of rioting, looting and killing. Everyone is eager to understand why. So they consult the experts.
>
> Biologists and psychologists find their answers in the offenders themselves. Perhaps the mass murderer in Killeen had an undiagnosed tumour; maybe he had experienced severe blows to the head as a child. Perhaps the cannibal killer had been abused or neglected. He certainly had to be 'crazy', didn't he? And, the rioters must have been 'just plain rotten.'
>
> . . . [Sociologists] look at the structure and changes in American society that are possibly responsible for our growing problem of discontent and violence . . . the breakdown in rules and regulations concerning moral behaviour, the high divorce rate and residential mobility . . . a high unemployment rate and a stagnant economy, and a collective belief that the ordinary American is powerless to control his or her destiny.
>
> Biological and psychological explanations are not necessarily incorrect. In fact, many serial killers may suffer from bad childhoods. Some rioters may have had brain disease. [But] someone looking only for psychological or neurological causes will focus on the perpetrator alone: Send him to prison, put her in the chair, give him surgery, treat her with anti-convulsant drugs, or see that he receives psychoanalysis or electro-shock therapy. From this viewpoint, only the perpetrator needs to change; the rest of us don't have to do anything.

The sociological eye sees things differently. It does not deny the need to punish or rehabilitate violent offenders, but it also focuses our attention on ourselves and, so takes a much broader view. To reduce the level of violence, for example, we might consider changing laws, modifying the distribution of wealth, improving education, providing jobs that lead to upward mobility, reducing discriminatory practices, lowering the level of isolation in our major cities, improving our criminal justice system, or possibly even changing our values. As a society, as a community, as a group, we must make at least some changes, too.

(Levin 1993: xvi–xvii)

Questions

1. The notion of the 'criminal type' is still held widely. What sort of characteristics form the common perception of the 'criminal type'?

2. Take an example of one particular criminal activity. What kinds of explanation for this would be offered by the different theoretical perspectives we have looked at?

Activity 2

Crime and punishment

The second extract below, 'Prison inspections', is taken from a review of reports into particular prisons that are published in the *Howard Journal of Criminal Justice*. They suggest that some aspects of prison life have changed little since the nineteenth century, when Dostoevsky (the source of the first extract) was writing. The final two extracts illustrate quite different views of prison life as reported in national newspapers.

Those first few weeks, and indeed all the early part of imprisonment, made a deep impression on my imagination. The following years, on the other hand, are all mixed up together, and leave but a confused recollection. Whole periods, in fact, have been effaced from my memory. Generally speaking, however, I remember life as the same – always painful, monotonous and stifling. What I experienced during the first few days of my imprisonment seems to me as if it took place but yesterday. Nor is that unnatural. I remember so well in the first place my surprise that prison routine afforded no outstanding feature, nothing extraordinary, or, perhaps I should say, unexpected . . .

I experienced, moreover, one form of suffering which is perhaps the sharpest, the most painful that can be experienced in a house of detention cut off from law and liberty. I mean forced association. Association with one's fellow men is to some extent forced everywhere and always; but nowhere is it so horrible as in a prison, where there are men with whom no one would consent to live. I am certain that every convict, unconsciously perhaps, has suffered from this.

(Dostoevsky 1962: 21–3)

Prison inspections

The unannounced, follow-up inspection of HMYOI (Young Offenders Institution) Reading was critical, and the Chief Inspector (Ms Anne Owers) comments on the institution's failure to provide 'the environment that its young men needed'. There were dirty and cold cells, showers were in an appalling state and there was an ineffective incentives and earned privileges scheme. And, echoing a theme throughout the previous reports during this period, there was inadequate purposeful activity with little meaningful work that resulted in prisoners spending long periods in their cells. Crucially, Ms Owers also identifies 'an institutional and systematic lack of respect' between staff and prisoners.

(*Howard Journal of Criminal Justice* 2002 41(5): 490)

Now prisoners get to watch TV to save distress

Prison bosses were criticised yesterday for spending thousands of pounds on an information service designed to stop inmates suffering 'emotional distress'. Rapists, murderers and paedophiles waiting to be locked up at Pentonville jail will be comforted by a state-of-the-art TV providing information on prison life. The Ministry of Justice said it wanted to stop 'boredom' and 'emotional distress', as well as lessening the risk of self-harm.

The decision to install the flatscreen TV . . . was slammed as a waste of taxpayers' money and an insult to crime victims. Blair Gibbs, spokesman for the Taxpayers' Alliance, said: 'If they can spend money on this, why can't they build prisons'. A Spokeswoman for the Ministry of Justice said: 'The last report by the Chief Inspector of Prisons criticised Pentonville for holding prisoners in the reception area for long periods of time with no distractions which led to boredom and emotional distress . . . This will be paid for out of the prison's annual budget.'

(*Daily Express*, 2.7.07)

Prison wing 'unfit for animals' closed down

A damning report from environmental health inspectors has led to the closure of a prison wing after inmates threatened the Prison Service with a high court action. The last of 80 prisoners from Gurney wing at Norwich prison were moved to other jails this week as the 81,333 prison population in England and Wales was expected to reach record levels today . . .

The wing was originally scheduled for closure in January after the Independent Monitoring Board declared it was 'unfit for animals', but it was reopened after three days because of overcrowding. The Prison Service only put inmates in cells certified as fit for habitation, but prisoners complained they were living next door to uncertified cells which had broken soil stacks, mould on walls, nesting pigeons, rodent infestation and a terrible stench. Environmental health inspectors found that cells on Gurney wing were between 50 and 75 times more hazardous to inmates' health than normal housing conditions.

(*Guardian*, 5.10.07)

Questions

1. What do you think may be the long-term effect on prisoners, prison warders and society as a whole of experiences and institutions such as these? How do you think they might affect you?
2. How might those who favour (a) retribution and (b) rehabilitation respond to these extracts?
3. What explanations can you think of the quite different pictures of prison life illustrated by the extracts from the *Daily Express* and the *Guardian*?

Part 4 Introduction to knowledge and power

[The sociology of knowledge is] that branch of sociology which is used to examine the social origins of knowledge and the way in which individuals and social groups claim to know and believe something, despite the variety of alternative ways of seeing the world. (Boronski 1987)

It has been said that the concept of knowledge is as fundamental to the discipline of sociology as that of attitude is to psychology. While theologians and philosophers attempted to establish the criteria by which reality can be known, sociologists by and large have rejected the idea of absolute and universal truths and argued that knowledge is relative to historical period, culture and social structure. What people believe about the nature of reality is to some extent conditioned by their experiences, social position and the social organizations to which they belong. Some writers, such as Durkheim, Marx and Mannheim, took a hard line on this, arguing that knowledge is determined by social structure and power relations, while Berger and Luckman took a more flexible view that allowed for the influence of the individual in the shaping and transmission of ideas. In Foucault's work, knowledge itself is seen a source of power in society. Despite their theoretical differences, these writers all seem to share C. Wright Mills' idea that knowledge is framed by the individual's interaction with society and history. In this process, some forms of knowledge are legitimated over others to establish a 'universe of meaning'.

In the previous parts of this book, the connections between knowledge, society and power are recurrent themes. In Part 1 we considered the attempts by sociologists to create a sociological imagination that has some claims to scientific rigour and superiority over 'common sense' (Chapter 1). In Chapter 2 we examined theories of society and the focus was on epistemology (what we think we know), while Chapter 3 was concerned more with methodology (how we test what we think we know).

In Part 2 we looked at various ways in which social division and inequality may affect the way we perceive the world and the impact of, for example, class, gender and race on our ideas of who we are in relation to others. If our identities are linked to such ideas, then where do we get these ideas from?

In Part 3 we examined the understanding of everyday life. Again, the everyday knowledge that we use to make sense of family life, work, health and what is deviant is explored and challenged. The way in which our understanding of what these things mean can change over time is also considered.

In Part 4, we are more interested in how social knowledge is produced, who produces it, how it is disseminated and how it is used. We also consider the extent to which such influences may be negotiated by social actors. The three remaining chapters look at institutions that play or have played a key role in the creation and dissemination of ideas: religion, education and the media. Again, many of the previous themes emerge, such as the creation of meaning, identity formation and the impact of social change in all three areas. We also consider issues of ideology, power and social control in the production and creation of knowledge. At the beginning of the twentieth century Durkheim was convinced that the decline of religion would have serious consequences for the stability of society and hoped that education might provide an alternative source of social cohesion. In the twenty-first century the role of the media in the production of attitudes and ideas seems to have taken centre stage.

Chapter 15

Education

Janet McKenzie

School and schooling is experienced as something 'done to' the children, legitimized by a discourse which prioritizes adult/future-oriented needs and expectations over present lived experience. The emphasis lies with the preparation of children as future citizens, equipped with the skills (productivity, competitiveness, comportment and control) to contribute as adults to the needs of modern industrial/postindustrial society. (Devine 2002: 312)

Key issues

- How have systems of education been influenced by the distribution of power?
- What are the main sociological approaches to the study of education, and what problems do they identify?
- How has the sociology of education helped to inform education policies?
- In what ways do social class, gender, ethnicity and special educational needs affect experiences of education and educational achievements?

Introduction

The opening words for this chapter refer to the relative powerlessness of schoolchildren in education systems that have been designed and administered by adults. Since 1989 most countries in the world have been expected to follow Article 31 of the United Nations Convention on the Rights of the Child, which emphasizes rights to have rest, leisure and play. However, some critics claim that such rights have not been applied to school activities and that childhood may even be 'lost' (Primary Review 2007) amid the never-ending demands of credential inflation and resulting 'immiseration' of education (McKenzie 2001). This means that, as more people get more qualifications, the qualifications needed in order to get a job are raised higher and higher, and pressures on pupils and students increase. At the same time, dominant Western discourses about education emphasize the importance of satisfying 'consumer' choice, while the reality is that those who are making the choices about schooling are parents of the genuine consumers. Devine (2002) suggests that schooling is something that is 'done to' children in an environment that some writers (e.g. Summit 1984) have related to 'adocentrism' (adults being at the centre of decision-making processes). This means that, although our common sense suggests that education has only positive benefits, sociologists have also recognized its negative aspects. Education can be seen as potentially empowering, liberating and fulfilling but also as potentially disempowering and frustrating. Knowledge can be seen as enlightening and life-enhancing, but it must be appreciated that it is also relative to its cultural environment. Our individual efforts and competencies are still important, but what we learn and how we learn emerge from circumstances that are beyond our own choosing. Sociologists can therefore argue that educational experiences are influenced heavily by social contexts, and it is this relationship that we are about to explore.

> **I regard as the prime postulate of all pedagogical speculation that education is an eminently social thing in its origins as in its functions, and that, therefore, pedagogy depends on sociology more closely than any other science.**
>
> (Durkheim 1956: 114)

Sociologists commonly use a wide definition of education, to include informal learning in the home and elsewhere. As education is part of the process of socialization, and influenced by other agencies of socialization, studies that separate it from other parts of society are severely limited. In Chapter 11 we saw how important the family is to our whole experience of life, and the influence of the family on our educational experiences can hardly be overestimated. However, sociologists are likely to reject claims that intelligence is primarily innate and inherited biologically from our parents. Instead, they will emphasize the ways in which families influence educational achievement after birth and the social labelling of children according to their background.

Sociologists show us that individual 'failures' or 'successes' are socially as well as personally constructed, that knowledge is socially constructed, and that the identification of intelligence is a social and subjective process. We should, for example, be aware that there are many types of intellect (such as a quiz champion who cannot cook a meal, and an autistic child who can make rapid mathematical calculations) and a wide variety of educational experiences and outcomes. Howard Gardner (1983, 1993) challenged the notion of a single type of intelligence by writing about multiple intelligences: those that are typically valued in schools (linguistic, logical-mathematical), those associated with the arts (musical, bodily-kinesthetic, spatial) and 'personal intelligences' (interpersonal, intrapersonal).

Schooling also includes hidden messages or unofficial rules that must be understood if we are to succeed. Jackson (1968) called this unofficial learning the 'hidden curriculum', and Hargreaves (1978) described it as the 'paracurriculum'. Aspects of this unofficial learning and personal experiences of education can teach us that we are valuable, intelligent individuals, or that we are worthless and 'dim'. Sociologists sometimes talk about personal aspirations being 'warmed up' or 'cooled down'.

Stop and think

- Think of illustrations of your personal 'growth' or 'regression'. Do you perceive your own experience of schooling mainly as a process of 'warming up' or 'cooling out', or neither? Was this process straightforward?
- Interview another student about his or her experiences.
- To what extent can we associate the roots of these positive and negative educational processes with individual action or with the social structure?

We will now consider types of education systems, how they are governed and regulated, and how they are influenced by the apparently universal problem of credential inflation. Then we will look at how sociologists have used various perspectives in their critical analyses of education and social inequalities. Here we can get an impression of some of the problems associated with education, and often the sociology of education has stopped at this point. Some theorists have felt that their role was to describe what existed, and not to concern themselves with what 'could be'. However,

A closer look

The problem of credential inflation

College degrees, once the possession of a tiny elite of professional and wealthy individuals, are now held by more than a fourth of the American population. But as education has expanded, the social distinctiveness of the bachelor's degree and its value on the marketplace have declined – in turn, increasing the demand for still higher levels of education. In fact, most problems of contemporary universities are connected with 'credential inflation'.

In 1910, less than 10 per cent of the population obtained, at most, high school degrees. They were badges of substantial middle-class respectability; until mid century, conferring access even to the managerial jobs. Now, a high school degree is little more than a ticket to a lottery in which one can buy a chance at a college degree – which itself is becoming a ticket to a yet higher lottery.

Such credential inflation is driven largely by the expansion of schooling – like a government's printing more paper money – rather than by economic demand for an increasingly educated labor force. Our educational system, as it widens access to each successive degree, has been able to flood the market for educated labor at virtually any level.

Many people believe that our high-tech era requires massive educational expansion. Yet the skills of cutting-edge industries are generally learned on the job or through experience rather than in high school or college. Compare the financial success of the youthful founders of Apple or Microsoft, some of them college dropouts, with the modest careers of graduates of computer schools.

Furthermore, a high-tech society does not mean that a high proportion of the labor force consists of experts. A more likely pattern – and the one we see emerging today – is a bifurcation of the labor force into an 'expert' sector – perhaps 20 per cent – and a much larger range of those with routine or even menial service jobs.

(based on Collins 2002)

Questions

1. Have you any personal experience of credential inflation?
2. What problems in universities could be caused by credential inflation?
3. Do you agree with Collins' claim that qualifications have become tickets in a lottery?
4. What arguments can be made for and against the claim that 'our high-tech era requires massive educational expansion'?

contemporary studies of education are often concerned just as much with prescription as with description. Debates about how many of these problems could be tackled via educational policies are in many ways more constructive and positive, but they do tend to highlight even more difficulties than those initially identified.

Education systems

The organization of formal educational provision within any one country can often seem confusing, and so you may expect comparisons between various systems to be even more confusing. However, we will make such comparisons by asking simple questions such as 'How many years of education are provided?', 'Who is included and excluded from educational decision-making?', 'In what ways is knowledge identified and measured?' and 'How are teaching standards monitored and controlled?' All of these questions relate to how systems of education are socially constructed within particular structures of power.

How many years of education are provided?

At a very basic level, social influences on education can be seen in access to a certain number of years of

A closer look

Influences on different national education systems

- *Different economic structures* – including systems of skills formation and numerous economic indicators, such as unemployment, income distribution and wage costs.
- *Different geopolitical and geocultural influences* – 'the broad cultural traditions in the major regions of Europe, stereotypically represented as universalism in France and southern Europe, cultural particularism in Germany and the German-speaking states, communitarian solidarity in Scandinavia and liberal individualism in the UK and Ireland' (Green *et al.* 1999: 26).
- *Different labour market organization* – for example, the influence of trade unions and other trade groups.
- *Different political and institutional traditions* – France and southern European states are seen as having state-centred policies and relatively centralized forms of educational admission; German-speaking states as having more decentralized or federal systems, with an emphasis on regional control of education and well-defined roles for employers; the Scandinavian states as being influenced by neo-corporatist and communitarian ideas, resulting in a shift towards local control of education; and England (and, to a lesser extent, other UK countries) as being influenced by laissez-faire liberal traditions, weak social partnerships, and a history of voluntarism and local autonomy in education.

(Adapted from Green *et al.* 1999: 25–6)

Questions

1. How do these four features influence your national system?
2. How might these features reflect dominant power relationships in your country?

schooling and opportunities vary from country to country. In countries in the Organization for Economic Cooperation and Development (OECD), the average age at which primary, secondary and higher education ended ranges widely – from 12.9 years in Mexico to 21.2 years in Australia (cf. 20.4 years in the UK). Many other states do not provide any formal system of education, and arrangements for the provision of education within an individual state vary according to constantly changing political, economic and social contexts.

Who is included and excluded from educational decision-making?

To tackle this question, some analysts have studied various types of regulation and governance. By 'regulation', we mean the ability to determine policies and sanctions; in other words, the ability to make rules affecting education. 'Governance' includes processes of coordination and collective decision-making that impact upon education. In Table 15.1 you can see that an education system can be controlled primarily by the state, by a market system, by community organizations or by a combination of all three.

An education system that is governed by the state is funded by taxation, ruled by laws of the state and delivered to people who are labelled as state citizens. When an education system is dominated by theories about an open market, it is privately financed (typically by parents, students or commercial companies), which means that there may be an emphasis on deregulation in order to remove barriers to trade, and it is delivered to people (typically parents) who are seen as consumers. An education system that is governed by communities is funded by various organizations (often churches), follows organizational rules and is delivered to people who are labelled as members.

This identification of three types of governance provides a useful analytical tool but, when we consider individual countries, we can see that sometimes an education system includes a combination of institutions governed and regulated by the state, the market and communities. There seems to have been a shift in that direction among OECD states, and this sort of pattern can be seen in the UK, where

Table 15.1 Simple representation of the governance of education

Governance activities	Coordinating institutions		
	State	**Market**	**Community**
Funding by	Taxation	Private	Organizations, e.g. churches
Regulation	Rules, laws, state control	Deregulation, removing barriers	Organizational rules
Provision/delivery to	Citizens	Consumers	Members

(Source: Dale 1997, Table 17.1)

most children are educated in state schools but some state schools are funded partially by private sponsors, many children attend schools that are funded by churches and other religious organizations, and increasing numbers of children attend schools that are funded by private finance (from commercial enterprises or fees paid by parents). Having already read about influences on different national education systems, you should now be able to appreciate how this fragmented pattern in the UK has been influenced by 'laissez-faire liberal traditions, weak social partnerships and a history of voluntarism and local autonomy in education' (Green *et al.* 1999).

A closer look

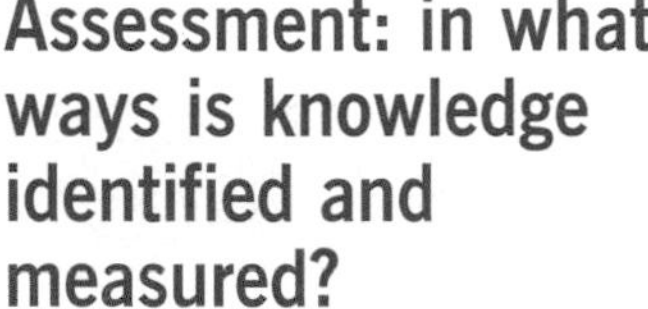

Assessment: in what ways is knowledge identified and measured?

To start we could ask whether the purpose of the assessment is 'summative' or 'diagnostic'. *Summative assessment* aims to describe an individual's current intelligence/knowledge/ability. This may lead to a grading, or some other type of summary or label, for example a second-class honours degree. Yet, even a descriptive assessment of this kind can lead to a variety of results. Objectivity is very difficult to achieve, and examiners may disagree about what questions should be asked, what skills should be tested, and how results should be interpreted. *Diagnostic assessment* is likely to include a summative assessment but will go further by providing an indication of what the next stage of the learning process should be, for example by identifying special educational needs. Positive action can be taken, but again we can reasonably ask how objective the assessor's recommendations can be.

The degree of objectivity must also be considered in the selection of a standard, or standards, against which individuals are to be judged. When *criterion-referencing* is used, there is some sort of list of criteria available to provide guidance concerning the standard that has been reached. An individual is assessed according to how the criteria have been satisfied, and the assessment can be made by a tutor or by the student, for example self-assessment using a tutorial on computer. When *norm referencing* is used, the performance of one individual is ranked in comparison with that of others. Usually the aim of this approach is to ration the number of 'passes' or qualifications, for example in the use of an 11+ examination to allocate children to a limited number of grammar-school places.

Questions

1. What type of assessment is most likely to be used for the following?
   (a) a driving test;
   (b) admission to a university;
   (c) music grades;
   (d) qualifications at school-leaving age;
   (e) assessment of students' knowledge of sociology.
   Give reasons for your answers.
2. Do you think the types of assessment are appropriate and fair?

In what ways is knowledge identified and measured?

In sociology, even the use of concepts such as 'intelligence', 'knowledge' and 'ability' is regarded as problematic. Our common sense may tell us that such things can be identified and measured, but those professionals with a responsibility for their measurement are often acutely conscious of the practical problems involved, and relevant decisions have to be made in any education system:

> **How a society selects, classifies, distributes, transmits and evaluates the educational knowledge it considers to be public, reflects both the distribution of power and the principles of social control.**
>
> (Bernstein 1971: 47)

In order to gain an insight into how complex this topic is, we now take a closer look at how the purpose of assessment influences the methods used (see Box on p. 607).

How are teaching standards monitored and controlled?

Processes of accountability are often anything but straightforward, and it would be a daunting task to make comparisons between countries. In this chapter we will therefore draw on just one trend that is impacting on many countries. Performativity is sometimes seen as a powerful culture influencing a whole system of education, its forceful presence being such that it is individual teachers who monitor themselves most harshly. Although it may still be possible for teachers to subvert bureaucratic control, they are aware that their performance is being watched and evaluated, and that they may be judged harshly. This is similar to what Foucault (1977) had to say about discourse, surveillance and disciplinary power. In the next part of this chapter, we will move on to some of the main sociological perspectives and apply them to education, including Foucault as we do so.

A closer look

Performativity in education

Ball described 'performativity' as a

> . . . technology, a culture and mode of regulation, or even a system of 'terror' in Lyotard's words, that employs judgements, comparisons and displays as a means of control, attrition and change. The performances of individual subjects or organizations serve as measures of productivity or output, or displays of 'quality', or 'moments' of promotion or inspections. They stand for, encapsulate or represent the worth, quality or value of an individual or organization within a field of judgement.
>
> (Ball 2004: 143)

The strength of performativity is in its ability to incorporate the people being watched so that they continually monitor and criticize themselves. A teacher quoted by Jeffrey and Woods said:

> I don't have the job satisfaction now I once had working with young kids because I feel every time I do something intuitive I just feel guilty about it. 'Is this right; am I doing this the right way; does this cover what I'm supposed to be covering; should I be doing something else; should I be more structured; should I have this in place; should I have done this?' You start to query everything you are doing – there's a kind of guilt in teaching at the moment. I don't know if that's particularly related to OFSTED but of course its multiplied by the fact that OFSTED is coming in because you get in a panic that you won't be able to justify yourself when they finally arrive.
>
> (Jeffrey and Woods 1998: 118)

Question

1. **Discuss the effectiveness of performativity as a way of monitoring and improving teaching standards.**

Sociological explanations and theories about education

We now consider the main sociological approaches to the study of education and the problems they identify. Sociological perspectives (see Chapter 2) can help us to make sense of educational provision and processes, but critical analyses of education have often limited themselves to describing problems, without concerning themselves with solutions. We shall follow this application of familiar sociological explanations and theories with a short analysis of themes that are more particular to the study of education policies.

As the aim here is to follow a basically developmental approach, we shall start, as early sociologists tended to start, with an emphasis on the social structure. Writers such as Durkheim were concerned with establishing the relatively new study of society and with arguing the merits of a sociological study of education at a time when education was largely seen as a matter for individuals only. This structural approach emphasizes the role of education in maintaining consensus and continuity in society, and is often primarily descriptive. However, other writers, from Karl Marx onwards, have emphasized the use of education as a means of perpetuating or shifting structural inequalities within society, focusing their attention on education as a source of not only continuity but also conflict and change.

These structural concerns could be viewed as overdeterministic if they ignore the reactions of individuals to their educational experiences. We have already noted that some individuals can subvert or be incorporated into a culture of performativity. This emphasis on interaction will be considered in more detail when we look at interpretative approaches. The dynamic relationship between structural and interpretative approaches will be acknowledged when we look at recent movements towards a synthesis of these theoretical positions.

Structural explanations: consensus and continuity

Consensus perspectives emphasize the important role of education in socializing the individual to fit into,

Case study

Durkheim: education and sociology

In sum, education, far from having as its unique or principal object the individual and his interests, is above all the means by which society perpetually recreates the conditions of its very existence. Can society survive only if there exists among its members a sufficient homogeneity? Education perpetuates and reinforces this homogeneity by fixing in advance, in the mind of the child, the essential similarities that collective life presupposes. But, on the other hand, without a certain diversity, would all co-operation be impossible? Education assures the persistence of this necessary diversity by becoming itself diversified and by specializing. It consists, then, in one or another of its aspects, of a systematic socialization of the young generation. In each of us, it may be said, there exist two beings which, while inseparable except by abstraction, remain distinct. One is made up of all the mental states which apply only to ourselves and to the events of our personal lives. This is what might be called *the individual being*. The other is the system of ideas, sentiments, and practices which express in us, not our personality, but the group or different groups of which we are a part; these are religious beliefs, moral beliefs and practices, national or occupational traditions, collective opinions of every kind. Their totality forms the *social being*. To constitute this being in each of us is the end of education.

(Adapted from Durkheim 1956: 114–16)

Questions

1. Can you find any examples of education policies that have as their 'principal object the individual and his interests'?
2. Why did Durkheim regard diversity (and the provision of diversity via education) as necessary in order to promote social cohesion? (See Chapter 2 for guidance.)

and perpetuate, the social system. Individuals are seen as being born into a society that already has an identity of its own, and education as serving the function of passing on the collective consciousness, or culture, of that pre-existing society. This approach is associated most commonly with functionalist perspectives and Emile Durkheim, who urged his readers to accept a relatively unorthodox idea at the time – that education had a social, rather than just an individual, reality.

As a socialist, Durkheim was concerned about social inequality, but as a positivist, he also believed that the role of sociology was to describe society without aiming to change it. Functionalist approaches to education have therefore been portrayed by their critics as being rather conservative: analysing the functions of education in maintaining an efficient and stable social order. They have also tended to adapt to the context of the time, more recent writers focusing on the study of classrooms and schools as social systems.

Parsons, for example, was concerned primarily with the problem of

> **how the school class functions to internalize in its pupils both the commitments and capacities for successful performance of their future adult roles, and second of how it functions to allocate these human resources within the role structure of the adult society.**
>
> (Parsons 1959: 297)

Parsons was aiming to integrate structural and interpretative approaches by emphasizing how the social structure influences the roles of individuals within the education system. His work is relevant in both sociology and psychology and is an example of how unrealistic it is to make sharp distinctions between structural and interpretative approaches. Nevertheless, Parsons' work is more often cited in the sociology of education as a 'structural functionalist' approach simply because he did not emphasize the routine small-scale classroom interactions that provide a focus for interpretative approaches. He was interested in the 'patterned expectations' (rules and regulations) governing how individuals should behave in order to maintain social order and continuity. More specifically, he saw education as serving the four functional requirements that all societies have in order to survive.

Here we can see a continuation of Durkheim's positivist approach, with its emphasis on description rather than criticism. Its implication that education contributes towards a meritocratic system (in which pupils' educational achievements are based only on ability and effort) has been severely challenged, as research has repeatedly highlighted the profound effects of social inequalities on educational outcomes. Critics have also argued that education can contribute to both social cohesion and social conflict, and that education does not necessarily serve the needs of either the economy or the individual. There are, moreover, no clear and agreed sets of 'needs' that can be functionally fulfilled. In general, functionalist images of society have been seen as being so unrealistic that they should either be dismissed or be adapted to suit reality.

It would, however, be wrong to assume that functionalist approaches to education are no longer

A closer look

Four functional requirements of society

Adaptation

Education adapts itself and individuals to changes in the cultural, technological and physical environment. It helps to emancipate the child from dependence on the family.

Goal attainment

Education helps individuals to identify and realize their personal and collective needs. Differentiated achievements can contribute to an effective division of labour.

Integration

Education provides some coherence between the relative influences of, for example, family, legal system, church, employment and the wider economic system. It helps individuals to identify themselves within a wider social system.

Latency or pattern maintenance

Educational processes lead to the reproduction of common values and social norms. It teaches us not only how to conform but also how to think.

influential. Some aspects have indeed been adapted or developed more fully in order to incorporate criticisms. For example, theories about social dysfunction (Merton 1938) help to explain how education can not only fail to serve the needs of society but also actually work against the interests of society. It can also reasonably be claimed that it is just as important to observe the role of education in maintaining society as to observe the manifestation of conflict within education.

Structural explanations: conflict and change

Conflict perspectives emphasize inequalities of educational opportunities and the need for social change. These have varied from the revolutionary writings of Marx and Engels to more moderate appeals for reforms within the existing social system. Classical Marxists have emphasized the primary influence of the capitalist economic infrastructure and the secondary role of education in perpetuating the necessary supportive ideology. While others in England were celebrating the arrival of elementary education for all, Marx and Engels were concerned that this would increase opportunities for the state to train docile workers.

Marxist influences continue today but have (like functionalism) been developed and adapted to their changing historical context. They have probed more deeply into the processes by which inequality is perpetuated through education. For example, in *Schooling in Capitalist America*, Bowles and Gintis (1976) analysed the correspondence between children's experiences in school and the inequalities they encountered as adults in the workplace. In this way the school was seen as introducing and reproducing the inequalities of social class perpetuated in a capitalist system, normalizing them in the process so that the working class was hardly aware of them (and therefore in a state of false consciousness).

Case study

Marx and Engels: education and the state

> The communists have not invented the intervention of society in education; they do but seek to alter the character of that intervention, and to rescue education from the influence of the ruling class.
>
> The bourgeois claptrap about the family and education, about the hallowed co-relation of parent and child, becomes all the more disgusting, the more, by the action of modern industry, all family ties among the proletarians are torn asunder and their children transformed into simple articles of commerce and instruments of labour.
>
> (Marx and Engels 1976, Vol. 6: 502)

> Equal elementary education? What idea behind these words? Is it believed that in present-day society (and it is only with this one has to deal) education can be equal for all classes? Or is it demanded that the upper classes also shall be compulsorily reduced to the modicum of education – the elementary school – that alone is compatible with the economic conditions not only of the wage workers but of the peasants as well?
>
> 'Elementary education by the state' is altogether objectionable. Defining by a general law the expenditures on the elementary schools, the qualifications of the teaching staff, the branches of instruction, etc., as is done in the United States, supervising the fulfilment of these legal specifications by state supervisors, is a very different thing from appointing the state as the educator of the people! Government and church should rather be equally excluded from any influence on the school.
>
> (Marx 1969 [1875]: 170–71)

Questions

1. How could education transform children into 'simple articles of commerce and instruments of labour'? Could aspects of your education be interpreted in this way?
2. Compare these views with those of Durkheim. What are the similarities and differences?

> Alienated labor is reflected in the student's lack of control over his or her education, the alienation of the student from the curriculum content, and the motivation of school work through a system of grades and other external rewards rather than the student's integration with either the process (learning) or the outcome (knowledge) of the educational 'production process'. Fragmentation in work is reflected in the institutionalized and often destructive competition among students through continual and ostensibly meritocratic ranking and evaluation. By attuning young people to a set of social relationships similar to those of the workplace, schooling attempts to gear the development of personal needs to its requirements.
>
> (Bowles and Gintis 1976: 131)

Stop and think

- What influences have you had on the content or style of your education (a) at the age of 8; (b) at the age of 12; and (c) now?
- List any aspects of schooling that are essentially (a) cooperative; and (b) competitive.

Yet even in what is often defined as a structural approach, Bowles and Gintis were looking not only at the social structure but also at the way in which small groups and individuals related to each other in schools. This makes it difficult to see where a structural

Case study

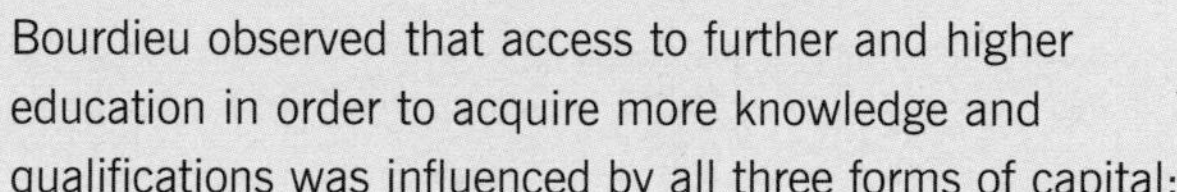

Cultural capital

> . . . capital can present itself in three fundamental guises: as economic capital, which is immediately and directly convertible into money and may be institutionalized in the form of property rights; as cultural capital, which is convertible, on certain conditions, into economic capital and may be institutionalized in the form of educational qualifications; and as social capital, made up of social obligations ('connections'), which is convertible, in certain conditions, into economic capital and may be institutionalized in the form of title of nobility.

Bourdieu criticized economists and functionalists for emphasizing the value of education in terms of national productivity and society as a whole. In doing so they ignored the influence of cultural capital and were 'unaware that ability or talent is itself the product of an investment of time and cultural capital'.

> This typically functionalist definition of the functions of education ignores the contribution which the educational system makes to the reproduction of the social structure by sanctioning the hereditary transmission of cultural capital.

Bourdieu observed that access to further and higher education in order to acquire more knowledge and qualifications was influenced by all three forms of capital:

> Differences in the cultural capital possessed by the family imply differences first in the age at which the work of transmission and accumulation begins . . . and then in the capacity, thus defined, to satisfy the specifically cultural demands of a prolonged process of acquisition. Furthermore, and in correlation with this, the length of time for which a given individual can prolong this acquisition process depends on the length of time for which the family can provide him with the free time, i.e. time free from economic necessity, which is the precondition for the initial accumulation (time which can be evaluated as a handicap to be made up).
>
> (Bourdieu 1983: 183–98)

Questions

1. Discuss what Bourdieu had to say about (a) whose interests are served by education; and (b) connections between educational process, the labour market and national productivity.
2. What are the implications of Bourdieu's arguments now that tuition fees for higher education have been introduced?

approach may end and an interpretative approach may start, and divisions between these approaches become even more spurious when we consider the work of Paul Willis. Willis (1977) analysed the attitudes of a group of working-class 'lads' during their last year at secondary modern school and their first year in the workplace. He highlighted how the 'lads' celebrated their masculine identity and persuaded themselves that the 'earoles' who were school conformists were in some way less masculine. To the 'lads', working-class jobs were masculine and therefore superior to what they regarded as effeminate middle-class jobs. In the process, Willis greatly enhanced our understanding of how the 'correspondence principle' identified by Bowles and Gintis could work in practice.

Pierre Bourdieu provided another explanation of how analysis at a structural level could illuminate our thinking about social inequalities and their effects on our educational experiences. This involved the identification of three types of capital (economic, cultural and social) that could confer advantages on its owners.

The focus of writers working within a Marxist tradition (and critical theorists in particular) has also shifted to an emphasis on hegemony and the role of the ideological superstructure in perpetuating social inequalities. For example, Althusser (1972) saw education as playing a vital role within the ideological state apparatus, perpetuating inequalities by conditioning the masses to accept the status quo. Similarly, feminists have examined the features of education that perpetuate and legitimize gender inequalities (e.g. see Byrne 1978; Deem 1978; Kelly 1981; Stanworth 1983; Arnot 1986; Kenway and Willis 1990; Arnot *et al.* 1999).

One feature that many of these theoretical developments have in common is an emphasis on the use of education as part of a process of liberation. For example, Bryan *et al.* (1987) found that the black girls they studied described their educational experiences as being defined primarily by their blackness in a negative way. The title of their article, 'Learning to resist', suggests that children may not automatically accept this sort of labelling. They (and their teachers) may resist negative influences and not only use education as a source of personal empowerment but also bring about minor or major changes in educational processes. In order to really achieve any depth in our understanding of education, we must therefore look at how individuals relate to structural constraints and at their experiences of small-scale interaction.

Interpretative influences

From the late 1970s onwards the influence of Weber and other action theorists was becoming more noticeable in educational research. More sociologists started to present findings based on classroom observation and interview data; the best known of these in Britain were provided by Ball (1981), Hargreaves (1967), Lacey (1970) and Willis (1977). They were trying to understand the meanings that individuals and groups attached to their behaviour, and to interpret their findings at a theoretical level. However, it would be a simplification to depict these as just interpretative studies, when often they have been motivated by an interest in how structural inequalities are maintained by educational processes. This interest in showing how many 'interpretative' studies of classroom interaction incorporate 'structuralist' issues could be seen as a natural progression from the work of Weber (1964) and part of a general move towards the triangulation of methodological and theoretical perspectives.

Paul Willis's (1977) research has already been mentioned as it relates quite closely to the 'correspondence principle' described by Bowles and Gintis (1976) (notice that his book was published a year after theirs). Willis acknowledged the use of both structuralist and interpretative approaches at the very beginning.

> **The difficult thing to explain about how middle class kids get middle class jobs is why others let them. The difficult thing to explain about how working class kids get working class jobs is why they let themselves.**
>
> (Willis 1977: 1)

He then went on to adhere to one of the essential features of interpretative sociology, as he used the words of 'the lads' themselves and tried to communicate their own sense of reality.

Willis's interests reflect common sociological interests in pro- and anti-school subcultures, the self-fulfilling prophesy and the 'hidden curriculum'. Put simply, teachers' expectations about how well or how badly individuals will behave are likely to influence that behaviour. Pupils are likely to internalize their teachers' expectations and make them their own, eventually matching their behaviour to the predictions made.

Figure 15.1 The classroom jungle or catering for individualism?
Catherine Ledner/Getty Images

Expectations may be derived not only from teachers but also from families, friends and society in general; in this way, social inequalities can be perpetuated by low self-esteem.

Willis, however, added depth to this sort of scenario by illustrating the creative interaction of 'the lads' with social constraints as well as the processes by which they reached a predictable structural location. This creative process has been illustrated more recently by Nayak (2003), who discovered that, over 25 years after Willis's research, 'local lads' in school subcultures still preserved a traditional white working-class masculinity and the grammar of manual labour. This was through a modern 'curriculum of the body', as exemplified through the rituals of football fandom, which provided an illusion of stability in insecure times. (Other well-known studies of the self-fulfilling prophesy include Holt (1969), Rosenthal and Jacobson (1968) and Spender and Sarah (1980).)

Willis's 'lads' may be seen as taking a rather predictable route, but what about the black women interviewed for 'Learning to resist'? Fuller (1980) also found that a group of black girls in comprehensive school created an anti-school subculture, but they still valued academic achievement as a form of resistance. This is something we will consider later when we look at the 'genderquake' in education and also at the achievements of various ethnic groups.

Unity and diversity in the study of education

Developments in sociological theories about education seem to have moved towards a synthesis of structural and interpretative perspectives. For example, critical theory has Marxist origins but emphasizes the ways in which language reproduces or transforms culture. Like classical Marxist approaches, it advocates changes in education to reduce social inequalities, but it also emphasizes individual, rather than social class, empowerment in recognition of the increasingly diverse nature of society and the fragmentation of social classes.

Other approaches also mix theories and techniques. Feminists share a common concern about gender inequalities in society (i.e. a structural emphasis), but the diverse range of sometimes competing feminist theories often seem to share little else. For many years it was assumed that gender disadvantages generally applied to girls, but this assumption has been challenged in many countries, as boys have fallen behind in education. Strategies for tackling boys' underachievements now reflect, in some ways, those advocated by feminists for tackling girls' underachievements in the past. Yet feminists can still identify ways in which females are disadvantaged, including the lack of correspondence between female experiences in education and female experiences in the workplace.

Like feminism, postmodernist ideas challenge even basic assumptions about education:

> **. . . postmodernism does more than wage war on totality, it also calls into question the use of reason in the service of power, the role of intellectuals who speak through authority invested in a science of trust and history, and forms of leadership that demand unification and consensus within centrally administered chains of command.**
>
> (Giroux 1992, quoted in Halsey *et al.* 1997: 118–19)

This calling into question could create some confusion about our ability to theorize in any way. However, Giroux argues that modernism, postmodernism and feminism offer valuable opportunities for rethinking learning processes and relationships between schooling and democracy:

> **To invoke the importance of pedagogy is to raise questions not simply about how students learn but also how educators (in the broad sense of the term) construct the ideological and political positions from which they speak. At issue here is the discourse that both situates human beings within history and makes visible the limits of their ideologies and values. Such a position acknowledges the partiality of all discourses so that the relationship between knowledge and power will always be open to dialogue and critical self-engagement.**
>
> (Giroux 1992, quoted in Halsey *et al.* 1997: 128)

According to Giroux, this partiality of discourse does not exclude an agenda for using education in a transformative and political way. Here he explains how, to him, sociological theories about education are linked inextricably to education policies:

> **A radical pedagogy and transformative democratic politics must go hand in hand in constructing a vision in which liberalism's emphasis on individual freedom, postmodernism's concern with the particularistic, and feminism's concern with the politics of the everyday are coupled with democratic socialism's holistic concern with solidarity and public life.**
>
> (Giroux 1992, quoted in Halsey *et al.* 1997: 128)

To read more about the challenges and dangers in education that have been identified by postmodernists see Hargreaves' (1994) description of seven dimensions of postmodernity (see Activity 1 on pp. 642–643). To Hargreaves, the challenge in reconstructing and redesigning teachers' work is to develop more flexible and responsive structures and processes that also deal effectively and reflectively with the pressures of overload, multiple innovations and accelerated change.

Sociological approaches to education policy

We have seen how educational studies have become more 'political', not only encompassing their traditional interests in educational problems but also increasingly emphasizing debates about how those problems should be tackled. In order to clarify current political debates about educational issues, we shall consider the two main themes of equality/inequality and uniformity/diversity. This is because policymakers' perspectives vary, from those favouring an extremely uniform education system (e.g. in France, where it is assumed that social inclusion is promoted by a uniform school system) to those favouring an extremely diverse system (e.g. in England and Wales, where politicians tend to discount links between schools and wider aspects of social inclusion or exclusion). Similarly, policymakers vary, from those favouring extreme notions of equality (egalitarianism) to those favouring extreme notions of inequality (biological determinism).

The theme of equal (or rather unequal) opportunities is already well-established in educational studies and, although debates about uniformity/diversity are certainly not recent, they have assumed greater prominence, along with increases in migration and religious diversity and the prominence of postmodern ideas about the fragmentation of societies.

Equality or inequality?

There seems to be an almost universal assumption that 'equal opportunities' are a good thing, much in the same way that 'democracy' is regarded as a good thing. Yet, if we try to clarify these concepts, it is likely that individual interpretations of these terms will differ. In educational studies there is a wide range of views as to what 'equal opportunities' means, based on different assumptions about human nature (e.g. that we are basically competitive or basically cooperative) and the purpose of formal education (e.g. to emphasize the needs of the child and/or of the economy). Figure 15.2 reflects a polarity of views about policies, ranging from an emphasis on strong definitions of equality

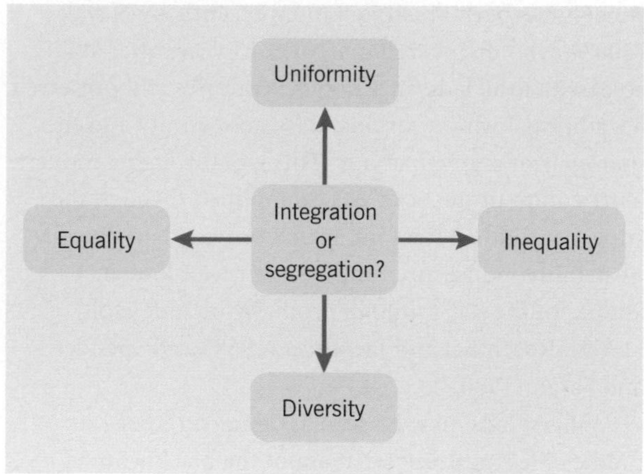

Figure 15.2 Educational policymaking: a model of key themes and polarities

(egalitarian) to an emphasis on strong definitions of inequality (biological determinism).

Egalitarian approaches: equal outcomes

At one end of this range are views often described as 'egalitarian', emphasizing equality of outcomes, in which identifiable social groups are not over- or underrepresented among high or low achievers. This means that the proportion of a social group represented among university graduates (and also among those without qualifications) should correspond with the proportion of that group in the whole population; for example, if 50 per cent of the population is female, then about 50 per cent of all graduates should be female. In the sections on social class, gender and ethnicity, we shall see how far we are from such equal outcomes.

Egalitarian arguments have supported the need for compensatory education. In other words, some children or schools are seen as needing extra resources and extra help in an effort to compensate for wider social inequalities. This can be seen in the use of learning assistants who work alongside children with special educational needs to give them specialized, one-to-one support. Extra help of this sort can allow such children to stay in the classroom alongside other pupils of the same age. However, this is an example of an egalitarian strategy rather than a representation of wider egalitarian assumptions and approaches.

According to egalitarian approaches, social inequalities cannot be tackled by education alone. A new educational power base and other changes in education (such as anti-racism, anti-sexism and anti-heterosexism) are promoted, but egalitarians present these as just part of the necessary shift towards a more equitable and caring society in general. The use of education for personal empowerment fits egalitarian images of enlightenment and emancipation.

> **Education has also been seen as a means to social emancipation. It is through education that socialists and feminists, for instance, have come to know their everyday unhappinesses aren't the fault of personal inadequacies but are common experiences, shared by others, and produced by particular social arrangements.**
>
> (Johnson 1983: 20)

Critical theorists and action researchers have encouraged individuals not only to acknowledge but also to challenge the forces that oppress them, and nowhere can this be seen more forcefully than in the writings of Paulo Freire. Freire worked among poor farmers in northern Brazil during the 1960s. In *Pedagogy of the Oppressed* (1972) he said that they were trapped in a 'culture of silence' by being in an economic and social situation in which critical awareness and responses were virtually impossible. What was needed was teaching as a partnership and dialogue through which people could 'achieve significance as people' (Freire 1972: 61), becoming conscious of the inequalities they had hitherto taken for granted.

> **Conscientization is a permanent critical approach to reality in order to discover it and discover the myths that deceive us and help to maintain the oppressing dehumanizing structures.**
>
> (Freire 1976: 225)

In Britain Freire's approach was adopted by Grant (1989) when she worked with parents and children in a Glasgow slum. Here she explains why her emphasis is on a dialogue between participants:

> **In the context of under-achievement in school, the ultimate goal of such dialogue is an improvement in children's learning. But there are intermediate goals. Parents need to work through hidden fears and feelings which block successful involvement in their children's education. Positive feelings have to be strengthened in two areas; pride in their role as educators of their own children, and interest in widening their own knowledge base and personal scope. The parents are, therefore, the central participants with their own children, with each other and with professional educators.**
>
> (Grant 1989: 132)

At first glance this looks very similar to the British Labour government's emphasis on the need to improve parenting skills, including their skills as educators. Efforts to do this include the introduction of a National Institute for the Family to focus on family and parenting issues, encouraging local self-help groups, a Freephone helpline for parents, and an expanded role for health visitors in advising the parents of children up to ten years old. A Sure Start programme also brings together education, health and child development agencies to promote the welfare of preschool children and their families:

> **Sure Start will work with parents to help them promote the physical, intellectual and social development of their children. The programme will break down the barriers between the different approaches to the family and the child in the crucial early years, and will operate alongside our children and early years' strategies.**
>
> (David Blunkett, then education and employment secretary, quoted in the *Guardian* 24.07.98)

This looks like a remarkably egalitarian approach, but it must be considered alongside claims that New Labour's emphasis on parenting skills and the family in general is focused on an interest in training individuals for responsible citizenship, rather than on tackling the social inequalities emphasized by Freire. In order to evaluate such claims it would be necessary to study Labour policies and draw on the communitarian ideas espoused by Etzioni and others (see Etzioni 1993; Demaine and Entwistle 1996).

Stop and think

➤ How could these debates about the role of parents be interpreted from different theoretical perspectives? (You might consider functionalist, Marxist and feminist perspectives.)

Equal access

A second interpretation of equal opportunities describes a cooperative system in which equal access to a high-quality education, with equal resources, is to be provided for all. The image is of a broad staircase to which all should have access; and it is this sort of definition that supports the provision of comprehensive schools attended by children of all abilities and (in theory) all social backgrounds (see Model 1 in the case study below, which includes international comparisons).

In the past, an equal-access approach was seen as quite radical because of its emphasis on equal treatment for all, irrespective of social origins. Although still popular in many countries, in Britain it is limited in its application to social class inequalities by the existence of a diverse range of schools, and its success is more noticeable in policies relating to gender and racial issues. For example, British efforts to ensure that individuals are not discriminated against on the grounds of gender or ethnicity include the Sex Discrimination Act 1975 and the Race Relations Act 1976. Proposals such as these, couched in terms of equal access, were able to gain more popular and political support than some of the more radical (egalitarian) action promoted by the Equal Opportunities Commission and Commission for Racial Equality.

Case study

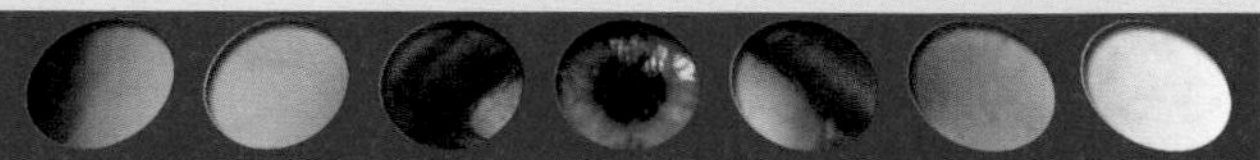

A typology of admission policies

Model 1: zoned comprehensive

In principle, a mixed-ability and mixed-social intake, with delayed specialization into vocational, academic or other tracks, and a broad curriculum. There may be four ways of trying to achieve a mixed ability intake:

- Children are obliged to attend their nearest secondary school or one linked to their feeder primary school. This works when local areas have a relatively mixed social composition.
- Children are 'bussed' into zones in order to achieve a social balance. This has been an unpopular practice in some parts of the USA and has not been government policy in Britain, although there has been some bussing of students to integrated schools in Northern Ireland.
- School catchment areas may be drawn up in ways that include a mixture of social and economic community types.
- Parents may choose from a range of schools, but their applications are judged by schools according to various selection criteria, in order to achieve a socioeconomic balance.

Model 2: open enrolment in comprehensive and partially comprehensive systems

This gives parents more freedom of choice and allows schools to compete with each other for students and, therefore, resources. However, an element of choice suggests diversification in the type of schools provided, and this may contradict the principles of comprehensivization, which is based on the notion of equal entitlement to common learning experiences. In Britain diversification has been encouraged without an emphasis on equality. Since 1997 the Labour government has allowed comprehensive schools to select up to 15 per cent of their pupils on the basis of ability and has retained grant-maintained (now called 'foundation') schools and city technology colleges. This promotes status differentiation between schools.

Model 3: selection by ability

Children are selected according to an assessment of their abilities. This selection may be by examination, by teachers' recommendations or by a mixture of both. Germany has traditionally maintained a selective system for admission to its Gymnasien, Realschulen, Hauptschulen and Gesamtschulen. In Britain this is common in Northern Ireland, less common in England and Wales and quite rare in Scotland. Selection by ability does not allow for real parental choice, although some parents will make a great effort to ensure that their children go to a high-status academic school.

(Adapted from Green *et al.* 1999)

Questions

1. Consider arguments for and against the 'bussing' of students from one area to a school in another area.
2. Green *et al.* (1999) claim that, within the European Union, there has been growing pressure to move towards Model 2. Why might that be the case?
3. Do you favour one of the models? If so, why?

Competitive access

A third approach involves the idea of a competitive system in which only a few children can find a place on the narrow ladder to success (see Model 3 in the case study above). Superior educational provision is seen as being rationed according to ability, the less able being provided with the sort of education that will equip them for relatively undemanding working lives. This sort of approach has supported the provision of scholarships (or the 11+ examination for entry into British grammar schools) and rests on two assumptions – that intelligence can be identified at an early age and that basic aptitudes do not change much over the years.

We have already considered assessment by norm-referencing as a form of selection for places on this narrow ladder and the criticisms of the bipartite system that eventually led to the introduction of comprehensive schools. The next move is to consider the market-led form of competitive access associated with New Right political polices.

Parental choice

Citizens of the European Union are all free to found, organize and run schools (European Communities 2000), which, at least in theory, means that parents in the EU have a considerable amount of power in making decisions about education. A long period of Conservative government in Britain (1979–97, when some other English-speaking countries also had New Right governments) also brought a new emphasis on parental 'choice', and an uncritical approach to inequalities in education. From this perspective more egalitarian approaches to equal opportunities are unrealistic and impractical. They are unrealistic because they do not accommodate our competitive natures, and they are impractical because they demand too much action from the state via the education system.

> **The [Conservative] government views inequality as being helpful to incentives at both ends of the income distribution and does not regard gross inequalities in income and wealth as a problem.**
>
> (Walker and Walker 1987)

Although similar to the third approach (competitive access) because of its emphasis on competition, an emphasis on parental choice no longer sees competition as being only among children, but also among parents, who are expected to act in their children's best interests by sending them to the best-possible schools. The ultimate aim is to provide a free market education system in which only those high-quality schools that attract parents will survive. As schools and families become more self-sufficient, the pressures of education on the state should decrease and consumer-led education should lead to optimum consumer satisfaction.

Stop and think

- In the UK, New Labour has also shifted towards an emphasis on consumer-led education through parental choice. How did this shift take place?
- Has this shift occurred in left-wing parties in other countries? If so, how?

Brown (1989: 42) called this perspective the 'ideology of parentocracy'. However, an emphasis on competitive access does not allow parents complete freedom of choice or eliminate selectivity on the part of the school. Some popular schools have had to adopt stringent criteria for the selection of pupils, and 'parental choice' raises uncertainties about who is really being selected in this sort of competitive system: is it parents or their children? Choice is also limited by practical and economic factors, and many parents cannot afford to pay for private education (see Activity 2 on pp. 643–644).

Inequality: biological determinism

Our earlier extract from Durkheim presented his criticisms of the then orthodox view that educational achievement was based entirely on individual ability, and that this ability was determined at birth. In the early years of the twentieth century, common-sense knowledge suggested that intelligence was innate and could be measured by intelligence tests developed by Binet (1905) in France and Stern (1911; the Intelligence Quotient, IQ) in Germany. Furthermore, it was assumed that once intellectual abilities were measured at (typically) the age of 11 they would remain unchanged. This argument explained why education policies often favoured channelling children into different schools suiting their 'needs', and this policy remains in many countries today. Moreover, where elitist, academic schools exist, affluent parents may argue that their children have a right to places in them because they have inherited their academic abilities. However, assumptions about biological determinism and the measurement of intelligence have been disputed as more children have been found to develop and change their intellectual capabilities later in life.

The influence of more moderate views means that, from the mid-twentieth century onwards, we have seen the prominence of what has often been called the 'nature/nurture debate', its key question being 'To what extent is intelligence determined at birth (innate) and to what extent is it determined by our social experiences?' Sociologists tend to accept that some aspects of educational ability may be biologically determined (for example, the abilities of autistic children) while rejecting absolute biological determinism.

There are, nevertheless, still some academic theories supporting ideas associated with biological determinism. These can be seen in sociobiology, with its emphasis on the importance of genetics (e.g. Dawkins 1976), and in theories about a 'bell curve' and dysgenesis (Murray and Herrnstein 1994). Put simply, a 'bell curve' is the shape of a type of graph representing the way in which intelligence is apparently distributed among the population in the USA. Theories about a 'dysgenesis' have suggested that this bell curve is moving backwards and changing shape, which means that the average intelligence is actually declining. In popular discourse, the claim is that society is 'dumbing down'. Yet what is important to our interest in power, knowledge and education is how power and social position have been presented as being natural outcomes of innate intellectual inequalities.

In *The Bell Curve: Intelligence and Class Structure in American Life*, Murray and Herrnstein (1994) presented the following arguments.

- Intelligence (what some psychometricians call *g*) is quantifiable and can be measured across historical, cultural and environmental differences.
- If we understand this, then we will also understand the social arithmetic that creates the powerful and the powerless, the rich and the poor.
- Innate low intelligence is a major cause of unemployment and poverty and lies behind all sorts of social problems.
- If social hierarchies are determined by innate low intelligence, then public policy is unable to do anything about associated social problems.
- Something could be done to tackle the 'dysgenesis' in America, caused by the higher fertility rates of what they called the 'cognitive underclass'. Changes in immigration law, and welfare and public health reforms, might arrest the genetic degradation of the national stock.

Murray and Herrnstein's theories gained most acceptance in the USA but were also influential in other countries and, in the 1980s and 1990s, were used to support New Right policies in the USA, the UK, Australia and elsewhere. Such policies challenged what was seen as a moral underclass of people with low intelligence, who were trapped in a dependency culture and who must be prevented from living off the state.

There have been many critics of Murray and Herrnstein's theories. Fraser (1995) and others noted the following criticisms of theories about dysgenesis and a moral underclass:

- They ignore the important role of training in the attainment of any kind of intelligence.
- They ignore the past 100 years of biological and psychological research that challenges the notion of a single, uniform and innate human intelligence, or *g*. Gardner (1983, 1993) argued instead for a concept of 'multiple intelligences': those that are typically valued in schools (linguistic, logical-mathematical); those associated with the arts (musical, bodily-kinesthetic, spatial); and 'personal intelligences' (interpersonal, intrapersonal). Goleman (1996) added his theories about the importance of emotional intelligence and showed that it could be developed rather than inherited.
- Murray and Herrnstein's book was published at a time when its explanation justified right-wing politicians' reluctance to commit resources towards the eradication of poverty.
- They did not analyse the criminal behaviour of the white-collar 'cognitive elite'.

The main sociological criticism is that, however we choose to define 'intelligence', any natural abilities cannot be separated from social and cultural influences. Sociologists therefore use the term 'cultural relativism' to acknowledge that it is impossible to distinguish between 'real' knowledge and culturally produced knowledge. We will look at social and cultural influences when we focus on social groups and education.

Stop and think

'He is just naturally very bright.'
'I've always been a bit dim.'
'She went to university because she takes after her mother.'
'The family's artistic ability just seems to be in their genes.'

- Have you ever used similar terms to describe yourself?
- Do you now think that your knowledge is biologically or culturally determined?

Uniformity or diversity?

We have looked at some of the key definitions of equal opportunities, covering the horizontal axis on Figure 15.2. The theme of equal opportunities is well established in the sociology of education, but debates about uniformity and diversity reflect a growing emphasis on policy issues, which is represented in the vertical axis of Figure 15.2. These debates also help us to understand how power is distributed and used, through education systems, in a way that can create a sense of identity or loyalty to the state.

Again, we can see that education systems may vary anywhere along that polarity between extreme uniformity and extreme diversity, and that some systems may include elements of both. The most extreme uniformity may be seen in totalitarian states, where power and conformity are imposed through a rigid education system in which only one ideology or religion can be propagated. However, even in a totalitarian state, there can be elements of diversity; for example, in the separation of the sexes or of various social groups into different schools. This means that it is possible for a society to have a uniform curriculum and a diverse school system or to have a diverse curriculum and a uniform school system. By asking questions about uniformity and diversity in education we can therefore learn more about how power is used to promote or discourage various social divisions within a society.

The French system of education is often cited as an example of a system characterized by centralization and uniformity, and this character dates back to the influence of Napoleon in trying to establish a sense of coherence. France is a secular state and the state education system is used as a way of promoting social integration and national identity by discouraging anything that draws attention to religious differences. Too obvious signs and symbols of a religion (e.g. the hijab, or Muslim headscarf) are discouraged by law, and children may be sent home from school for drawing too much attention to their religious identity. Social integration is also encouraged by a common curriculum. Yet France cannot be defined as having a totally uniform education system because it includes some private schools and some schools founded by religious organizations.

In contrast to France, education in the UK is often cited as an example of a system characterized by diversity, because a history of laissez-faire individualism has allowed a wide range of schools to be established. The UK is not a secular state, and Christianity has been very influential, both in the foundation of many faith schools and in the school curriculum (various government directives having been issued concerning a Christian focus in school assemblies). More, and varied, faith schools have been established in recent years, now including Jewish, Muslim and Sikh (Figure 15.3). In addition, the types of school provided vary between the four countries of the UK. For example, Northern Ireland has traditionally had a particularly diverse system, with children attending different schools according to their gender (single-sex schools), religion (typically on sectarian lines and either Protestant or Roman Catholic), and/or assessment of intelligence at the age of 11 years (grammar schools or secondary modern schools). This has affected social integration and has meant that children have often identified themselves primarily along sectarian lines as either Catholic (and often Republican) or Protestant (and often Unionist). It is therefore interesting to note that in Northern Ireland there has been a forceful movement pressing for the creation of more integrated schools in order to avoid the sectarianism of the past and to create greater social cohesion.

In the UK during the 1980s and 1990s, there were concurrent moves towards both diversification and uniformity in education. The British Labour government elected in 1997 was committed to the decentralization of education in various ways, but in practice it has increased some forms of centralization. For example, a Labour government is inclined to share more powers with (mainly Labour-controlled) local education authorities, and regional assemblies in Scotland, Northern Ireland and Wales have extended

Figure 15.3 Catering for cultural diversity
ALESSANDRO ABBONIZIO/AFP/Getty Images

the distinctions between educational provision in the regions of the UK. For example, central government in Westminster decided to introduce fees for students in higher education in England and Wales, but the Scottish Parliament refused to introduce fees in Scotland. Yet the Labour government has maintained the uniformity of a national curriculum for state schools, despite its reservations when this was introduced by a Conservative government. Indeed, it now seems that opposition to the principle of a national curriculum comes mainly from Liberal Democrats, whose policies have traditionally maintained a strong emphasis on decentralization.

Stop and think

- What sort of assessment should be used in the national curriculum: descriptive or prescriptive, criterion-referencing or norm-referencing? (See A closer look on p. 607)
- Can a national curriculum be politically neutral?

The diversification of educational provision in many countries is in keeping with current postmodern theories about the fragmentation of society in general. In other words, it would bc wrong to associate educational diversity only with government policies without also acknowledging other social trends. One of these trends is the common concern of politicians and academics from many perspectives that ever-increasing demands on the state leave it overburdened or overloaded. Efforts to reduce government responsibilities for education have been in keeping with New Right policies favouring greater self-sufficiency and the 'rolling back of the state'. Yet, writing from a left-wing perspective, Habermas (1971) also observed the problems of an overburdened state and associated them with a legitimation crisis in capitalist societies. All of this might suggest that a shift towards the fragmentation of educational provision is inevitable but, again, it is not as simple as that.

Although some similarities between politically right- and left-wing education policies have been identified, there are certain fundamental distinctions between their perspectives on education, and you should at least start to consider how they relate to wider sociological theories and findings. Left-wing politicians (in both central and local government) are likely to emphasize stronger definitions of equality but are still faced with decisions about uniformity or diversity. An emphasis on egalitarianism and uniformity may lead to the state being overburdened by responsibilities as it tries to reduce social inequalities, but an emphasis on egalitarianism and diversity may have inherent contradictions or, indeed, may just be a utopian dream.

Decisions about the segregation or integration of children within and between various schools also have to be made, and it is often difficult to identify the perspectives on which such decisions are based. For example, arguments about coeducational or single-sex education, schools for separate religious faiths, and the integration (in mainstream schools) or segregation of children with special educational needs are not clearly delineated along political lines. Pressure groups associated with any one of these issues could include members of all political hues and various sociological perspectives. We will now shift from an emphasis on the educational policies that identify different types of pupils and students to focus on inequalities between the groups themselves.

Stop and think

- Consider the arguments for and against the following:
  - (a) single-sex education (either within individual schools or via separate schools);
  - (b) the granting of public finance to Muslim schools;
  - (c) the integration of children with special educational needs within mainstream schools and the various ways in which this can be done.

Social groups and education

If you were asked to explain which social characteristics most influenced your educational experiences and achievements, you would probably be rather baffled. Which was most significant: your parents' economic position, your gender, ethnicity, religion, special educational needs, geographical location or something else? There will probably be no simple answer; it is the same when sociologists study the relationships between social characteristics and education in general. Individual experiences of social inequalities may be very different – so much so that there are even disagreements about what words to use to describe various characteristics. Chapters 4 and 6 considered the problems of defining the concepts of social class, socioeconomic group, race and ethnicity, and those problems are reflected in this chapter. Indeed, the expression 'social exclusion' entered public discourse at the end of the twentieth century with an appreciation that, although concepts were contested, the effects of gross social inequalities could be seen quite clearly. By the end of the twentieth century, sociological studies of education had become more concerned with the cumulative effects of social characteristics than with discrete social groupings. For example, the experiences of working-class black girls may be so different from the experiences of middle-class white girls that it would be totally unrealistic to suggest that 'gender' has had the greatest influence on their educational outcomes.

Social class inequalities in education

The terms 'social class' and 'socioeconomic group' are both used in this chapter, partly as a reflection of the words used in various sources and partly as a reflection of the subjective nature of social class identities. When discussing education, twenty-first-century writers often use the expression 'socioeconomic group' to refer to shared levels of employment and education. Yet many writers still use the expression 'social class' to refer not only refer to levels of employment and education but also to shared identities and conflicts of interest between groups. Irrespective of the terms used, what is important is the finding that relevant inequalities still exist and, in some societies, may even be becoming more pronounced. Sociologists (e.g. Mac an Ghaill 1996) observed the irony of the decentring of class-based analysis at a time when extremes of wealth and poverty were becoming increasingly polarized. It may no longer be appropriate to just label manual workers as 'working class' and non-manual workers as 'middle class', but parents' educational and occupational levels still have a profound effect on their children's opportunities in life.

These inequalities vary between different societies, and class is more influential in some countries than in others. For example, the OECD found that in many countries students were much more likely to be in higher education if their fathers completed higher education. In Austria, France, Germany, Portugal and the UK, students from such a background were more than twice as likely to be in higher education. However, in Spain this ratio dropped to 1.5 and in Ireland to 1.1 (OECD 2007). Similarly, the OECD found that there were significant differences between countries in the proportion of their higher-education students whose fathers were manual workers. In Austria, France, Germany and Portugal, students from such a

A closer look

Scott Lash has suggested that the production of information and communication goods has become 'the new axial principal of capital accumulation' (Beck *et al.* 1994: 129), replacing the production of heavy industry, and that the new middle class work as experts inside expert systems. As information and communication systems have became increasingly important in the workplace, those people with a low level of education and lacking in computer skills have started to be socially excluded.

Lash was impressed by theories about an underclass, arguing that at the start of the twenty-first century we had a 'two-thirds society', consisting of the expanded middle class, who worked in the information and communication sectors, the upgraded working class, who had adapted to the shift from manufacturing to information production, and those who had been downgraded from the classical (Marxist) proletariat to become the new underclass.

Question

Do you agree with the claim that education and skills in information technology have replaced other aspects of production (e.g. work in heavy industry) as the key influence on social class?

background were about one-half as likely to be in higher education, whereas the background of students in Spain and Ireland was more equitable (the UK was not included). In the UK in 2002, there were more than twice as many students in higher education from non-manual worker backgrounds as from manual worker backgrounds (ONS 2004).

It must be emphasized that the influence of socioeconomic inequalities is particularly apparent in the UK and that, in spite of changes in class composition over the years, it is remarkable how consistent some findings are. Many more young people from all socioeconomic groups now have a degree, but inequalities between groups are still extreme. Indeed, these inequalities are more extreme than those found between males and females or between various ethnic groups. Education in the UK has never been based widely on egalitarian ideals, and patterns of inequality remain in spite of the critical research findings produced by sociologists and educationalists over many years.

In the UK, the 1950s and 1960s produced a series of official reports that provided cumulative evidence of the relationship between father's occupation and educational outcomes. Concurrent support for official findings about social class inequalities was provided by sociologists (e.g. Bernstein 1971; Bourdieu and Passeron 1977; Bowles and Gintis 1976; Douglas 1964; Goldthorpe *et al.* 1980; Halsey *et al.* 1961, 1980; Jackson and Marsden 1963; Rutter *et al.* 1979; Willis 1977), and by the end of the 1970s the evidence had became overwhelming. From the 1970s onwards we can see a long list of sociological findings in which the focus is placed more sharply on educational policymaking, with an emphasis on social inequalities (e.g. Flude and Ahier 1974; Institute of Public Policy Research 1993; Karabel and Halsey 1977; Kogan 1975; Lodge and Blackstone 1982; McKenzie 1993; National Commission on Education 1993).

Shortly after the election of the Labour government in 1997, a report called 'Learning works' (the Kennedy Report, published by the Committee On Widening Participation in Further Education) addressed some of these problems and pointed to serious inequities between the funding of further and higher education. It argued that, although they generally came from more affluent backgrounds than other students, students in higher education received more of taxpayers' money and could also achieve a higher income after graduation. This point was later supported by the Report of the National Committee of Inquiry into Higher Education (Dearing 1998) and the government paper 'The learning age: a renaissance for a new Britain' (1998). The Labour government therefore decided to make grants available to students in further education while more restrictions were placed on the maintenance of students in higher education. In 2004–05, 81 per cent of eligible students in the UK took out a loan to support them through higher education, the average being £3390 (ONS, 2005), which could amount to a much larger debt by the time of graduation. Although the government saw its efforts as widening access to further education, its policies could discourage students from less affluent families from entering higher education. Prospective students now face the alternatives of a debt-free start to their adult lives or a foot on the ladder of credential inflation.

Stop and think

- Consider the arguments for and against (a) means-tested fees for students in higher education and (b) grants for students aged 16–18.
- How do these policies relate to the various perspectives about equal opportunities described earlier (egalitarian, equal access, competitive access, parental choice, biological determinism)?

It has long been claimed that children from working-class families are less willing to 'defer gratification' and want to start earning a wage as soon as possible rather than stay longer in education (see Bourdieu's comments on social capital earlier in this chapter). Sociologists have even observed a tendency to split young people into 'sheep and goats', with some being able to take the route to a high-status qualification, and others resigning themselves to low-grade training for low-status jobs or long-term unemployment. We have looked at Willis's (1977) theory about how working-class boys were persuaded (and persuaded themselves) that they wanted working-class jobs. However, outcomes are not simply a matter of choice and McFadden (1996) argues that social advantages can outweigh resistance to education, while social disadvantages can outweigh efforts to study hard and conform.

Socioeconomic inequalities in higher education have now been described, but what about inequalities

Case study

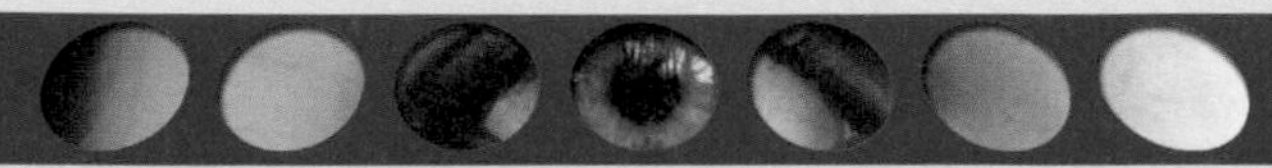

Resistance to schooling

McFadden's analysis of resistance to schooling indicates how social class (and other social inequalities) can be studied in greater depth by linking structural and interpretive approaches:

> The crucial point though – and one that brings questions of class and structure back into the debate – is that the rejection of the offers and advantages of schooling has differential class consequences. Aggleton (1987) found that middle class students who resist schooling are advantaged in the labour market in general terms. The labour market defines class and advantage in the clearest sense (Weiss 1990). At a time of high youth unemployment, all of Aggleton's middle class resisters were in employment six years after his study. They were involved either in service industries or in industries related to symbolic production and the arts. The available evidence suggests that resistance has differential racial, ethnic and gender consequences as well.

While middle-class resisters may still be advantaged, working-class students who comply may still be disadvantaged:

> Willis' counter image to that of the voluntary walk onto the shopfloor, i.e. of 'Armies of kids' who have absorbed 'the rubric of self-development, satisfaction and interest in work', 'equipped with their "self-concepts" . . . fighting to enter the few meaningful jobs available, and masses of employers . . . struggling to press them into meaningless work' . . . is as powerful and applicable an image now as it was then.

McFadden noted that Willis stressed the importance of language as one of the 'underworkings' supporting the continuity of social structures. Bernstein also regarded it as very important:

> Essentially, Bernstein's work shows how power articulates through discursive practices and that schools, through their pedagogic practices – largely but not exclusively rooted in language – can limit the access of certain groups to the language of power and symbolic control.

Yet McFadden was not entirely pessimistic about educational constraints and felt that structuration theory (Giddens 1984) provided the conceptual tools needed to deconstruct such power relationships:

> If, for example, gender/sexual and racial norms of behaviour are said to be reproduced through the actions of individuals, then there exists the possibility of anti-sexist and anti-racist actions, because no matter how narrow the options facing the individual there is always choice.
>
> Taken together with Giddens' formulations about the nature of society and change, Bernstein's work enables us to see the way that students can be positioned within classroom discourse as either producers or passive receptors of knowledge. It also helps to illustrate how the pedagogic device can 'naturalise' a state of affairs, silencing students' voices and allowing no access to the discourse relaying power. Without access to the means of knowledge production no means is available to change or challenge the 'symbolic boundaries regulating classroom practice'.
>
> (McFadden 1996: 297–306)

Questions

1. Research by both Aggleton and Willis was over 20 years ago. Can it still be claimed that middle class resisters are advantaged in the labour market?
2. How can students be 'producers' of knowledge, rather than 'passive receptors'? Again, relate to subjects that you have studied and courses you have followed.

Table 15.2 GCSE attainment:[1] by parents' socioeconomic classification,[2] England and Wales, 2002

	5 or more GCSE grades A*–C %	1–4 GCSE grades A*–C[3] %	5 or more GCSE grades D–G %	1–4 GCSE grades D–G %	None reported %	All %
Higher professional	77	13	6	. . .	3	100
Lower professional	64	21	11	2	2	100
Intermediate	52	25	17	2	4	100
Lower supervisory	35	30	27	4	4	100
Routine	32	32	25	5	6	100
Other	32	29	26	4	9	100

1 For pupils in year 11. Includes equivalent GNVQ qualifications achieved in year 11.
2 See Appendix, Part 1: National Statistics Socio-economic Classification.
3 Consists of those with 1–4 GCSE grades A*–C and any number of other grades.
(Source: *Social Trends 34*, 2004, Table 3.9, p. 42)

among schoolchildren? A diverse range of schools in the UK has obviously meant a diversity of educational experiences. What has remained the same since the 1980s, under both Conservative and Labour governments, has been the shift towards a discourse that accepts socioeconomic inequalities in the form of a 'parentocracy' – in which a child's educational opportunities are more honestly seen to be related to his or her family's social and economic position. Success in a market system has relied more heavily on family background than did even the more moderate forms of competitive access. Under recent British governments some schools have been able to thrive due to their popularity with parents and their position in published league tables. A growing dependence on fundraising by parents for school resources also means that, where a large proportion of pupils come from affluent backgrounds, the school is more likely to prosper. By comparison, some schools in less affluent areas have become what are popularly known as 'sink schools' (i.e. unable to afford proper maintenance and with facilities that are barely adequate), with an intake of children whose parents cannot compete in a market system. Such inequalities are reflected in continuing inequalities in school-leaving qualifications (Table 15.2).

Gender inequalities in education

Research into gender inequalities in education seems to have had a greater influence on education policies than has research into other socioeconomic inequalities, apparently because policymakers were prepared to accept stronger definitions of gender equality than of socioeconomic equality. These definitions can be seen in Weiner's (1985) summary of relevant gender-related strategies and their links to some of the perceptions of equality that we have considered already. What Weiner describes as an 'equal opportunities/girl-friendly' approach is similar to what we have described as an equal-access approach to equal opportunities and reflects a fairly moderate interpretation of equal opportunities. This fits those government policies aiming to discourage gendered subject choice. By comparison, what she describes as an 'anti-sexist/ girl-centred' approach has a stronger egalitarian outlook, which has been influential but has secured less government support in the UK. This egalitarian approach to equal opportunities places more emphasis on equality of outcomes, suggesting that it is important not only to look at access but also to see whether males and females are represented equally at all levels of educational achievement. Applying this sort of definition of equality, there are indications that, in education at least, gender inequalities have been transformed.

Since the 1970s equal access/equal opportunities approaches and anti-sexist/egalitarian approaches have influenced education policies, not only in the UK but also in other European and OECD countries. The effect has been a dramatic turnaround of educational inequalities between the sexes, and a resulting shift from concerns about the underachievement of females (before 1990) to concerns about the underachievement of males (roughly since 1990). Indeed, Wilkinson

(1994) coined the expression 'genderquake' to describe this remarkable shift in the achievements and attitudes of new generations of women.

These findings did not come as a surprise to many educationalists. It had long been claimed that, in general, girls matured at an earlier age than boys and therefore achieved more during their early years at school. This meant that, in Britain, before the equal opportunities legislation of the 1970s, girls often had to get better results than boys to 'pass' a norm-referenced 11+ examination for selection to a grammar school, the assumption being that boys would catch up at a later age. However, the gendered 'catch-up' argument is unconvincing now that girls achieve better results at all stages of education, up to and including degree level.

Shifts towards more equal opportunities were instigated throughout Europe in the 1970s by European Union directives. In Britain, changes were made via the Sex Discrimination Act 1975, which can be clearly associated with an equal-access approach. This Act prohibited sex discrimination in admission to schools, in the appointment of teachers (with some exceptions for single-sex schools) and in careers advice. It also stipulated that neither boys nor girls should be refused access to 'any courses, facilities or other benefits provided solely on the grounds of their sex'. The introduction of a UK national curriculum in 1988 also emphasized equal access by tackling the problem of gendered subject choice – the tendency for girls to favour languages and boys to favour science subjects (except for biology).

The national curriculum has encouraged pupils to make non-gendered subject choices by obliging pupils to take English and another language (not popular among boys), maths and a science (not popular among girls) in their examinations at the age of 16 years. Some educationalists feel that changes in subject choice have still been rather slow; for example, biology is still a particularly popular science with girls and there are gender-based choices in technical subjects. At A level (or Scottish Highers), students have more freedom to choose favoured subjects and gendered patterns continue.

In the UK girls now achieve better results than boys at all ages and levels; for example, in 2007, in England, from Key Stage 1 (age 5–7) to Key Stage 3 (age 11–14) girls' results were higher than those of boys (www.statistics.gov.uk). There was an exception only in mathematics tests at Level 2 of Key Stage 2 (age 7–11), when boys (78 per cent) achieved better results than girls (76 per cent).

Since the mid-1970s more girls than boys have achieved five or more GCSE passes in grades A–C (or their equivalent in SCE, O Level or CSE). In 2005–06, 64 per cent of girls and 54 per cent of boys in the UK achieved five or more grades A*–C in their GCSEs or equivalent, and 44 per cent of girls and 33 per cent of boys gained two or more A Level passes or equivalent (www.statistics.gov.uk). This reflects a pattern that has lasted for over ten years. Also, in 2005–06, females in England, Wales and Northern Ireland performed better than males in virtually all A Level subjects (an exception being the equal proportions of grades A–C in English).

Such national data are reflected in the European Union Labour Force Survey data (http://epp.eurostat.ec.europa.eu) for 2006, which showed that, among 20- to 24-year-olds, more females than males had reached at least upper secondary education attainment level. Across all 27 countries in the European Union, 75 per cent of all males in this age group and 80.8 per cent of all females in this age group had attained that level of education. In the UK, comparable figures were 77.3 per cent of males and 80.3 per cent of females. Of the 27 countries sampled, only in Turkey did more males than females reach that attainment level (51.7 per cent males and 38.9 per cent females).

Stop and think

- Can you think of three possible reasons why the gender differences in achievement in Turkey are so different from those in the European Union?

So, we have seen a tendency for a higher proportion of males to fall behind in their achievements at school-leaving age. What happens after school-leaving age? The EU Labour Force Survey provided data for 2006 showing that, among 18- to 24-year-olds, more females than males were receiving some sort of education or training. Across all 27 countries in the EU, 17.3 per cent of all males in this age group and 13.1 per cent of all females in this age group were *not* receiving some sort of education or training. In the UK comparable figures were 14.6 per cent of males and 11.4 per cent of females. Of the 27 countries sampled, only in Austria

(9.3 per cent of males and 9.8 per cent of females) and Turkey (56.5 per cent of males and 42.2 per cent of females) were more males in education or training.

In 2006 UK females (56 per cent) also outnumbered males (44 per cent) in their achievement of National Vocational Qualifications (NVQ) and Scottish Vocational Qualifications (SVQ). However, some longstanding differences in subject choices remained: for example, 86 per cent of all awards in health, public services and care-related qualifications went to females, and 89 per cent of all awards in construction, planning and the built environment, engineering and manufacturing technologies went to males.

Females and males are collectively achieving more educational qualifications and we have already acknowledged the impact that credential inflation may have on motivation. Between 1970–71 and 1995–96, the number of students enrolling on higher education courses in the UK more than trebled, with one in three young people entering higher education in 1995–96 compared with one in 20 in the early 1960s. In 1970–71 there were twice as many male students as female students in higher education, but by 2001–02 there were more females. The gender distribution of higher education students is therefore changing. We have seen that, in 2006, a higher proportion of females than males aged 18–24 were receiving some sort of education or training, and this was reflected in the same year when 54 per cent of all new entrants to higher education in the UK were female.

The impact of these changes on gender inequalities in society in general is difficult to gauge. It is moderated by access to, and conditions in, the workplace, and sociologists have found that there is no perfect link between educational achievement and advancement in employment and income. The extent of the problem can be illustrated if we look at the influence of gendered subject choice and at occupations in the field of education. Educational achievements are given a social rather than an individual construction: some subjects (maths, science and some technologies) are awarded higher status in employment than others, and these high-status subjects are those favoured by boys. This means that, although females are achieving more qualifications, some of their qualifications are not awarded similar recognition to the fewer qualifications achieved by males. Those technologies that are favoured by females, such as textiles and home economics, tend to be compared unfavourably with 'male' technologies, such as electronics and engineering. For example, keyboard skills assumed greater importance when they were associated with computers rather than secretarial work; yet, as more women gained word-processing skills, that particular application of information technology also lost its relative status.

The findings described above clearly suggest inequalities between the sexes with regard to educational outcomes, although it must be acknowledged that these are structural patterns that conceal variations between individuals. It is now necessary to consider how inequalities between the sexes changed and to acknowledge debates about the apparent underachievement of males.

Structural approaches, illustrating changes in achievement, have to be supplemented by interpretive approaches in order to reach a comprehensive understanding of the nature of gender differentiation in education. Although there is no room for complacency,

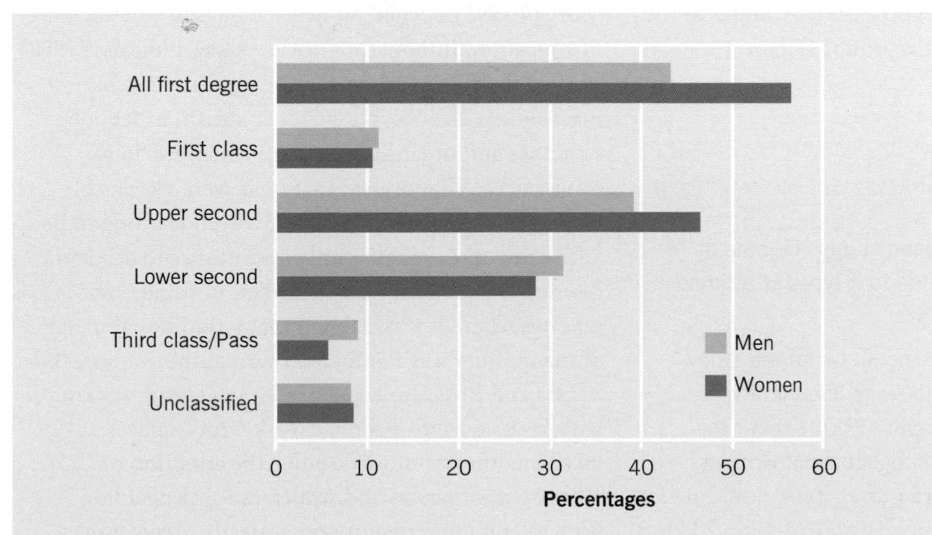

Figure 15.4 Achievement at first degree level, by gender, UK 2005–06
Source: UCAS, www.statistics.gov.uk

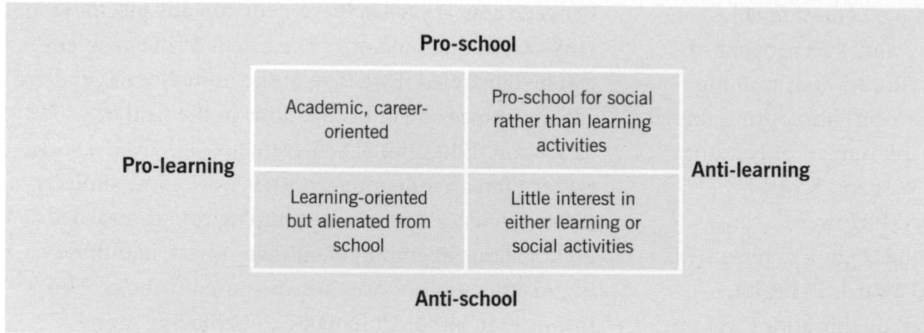

Figure 15.5 Girls' attitudes to schooling
Source: adapted from Lees (1986)

continuous monitoring of resources by sociologists and educationalists has helped to promote more positive images of women in school textbooks and other educational resources (e.g. Nilsen 1975; Statham 1986). This may have affected the way in which young females now perceive themselves.

Feminist studies also raised awareness of sexism in classroom interaction and an understanding of how girls and women perceive themselves in education. For example, Stanworth (1983) and many others observed that boys tended to demand, and get, more of the teacher's attention in class and that girls tended to have unrealistic ideas about their own capabilities. Boys tended to overestimate their own capabilities while girls tended to underestimate their capabilities.

Lees (1986) studied the attitudes of 15- to 16-year-old girls, from various social class and ethnic backgrounds, in three London schools. Her interpretive approach elicited the terms on which the girls described their sexuality and managed their social world and helped to explain how some girls rationalized their lack of achievement. Yet this now rather dated research still offers a possible model for the analysis of girls' and boys' achievements. Lees categorized the attitudes of the girls she studied into four main groups (Figure 15.5).

Stop and think

- What factors could influence pupils (female or male) to adopt each of the four types of attitude described in Figure 15.5?
- How useful would Lees' model be for the study of boys' attitudes to schooling? See the findings by Willis (1977) and Nayak (2003) about the attitudes of anti-school subcultures of working class boys (pp. 613–615).

The growing numbers of mature women students since the 1970s (see Edwards 1993) has also meant that sociologists have become more absorbed in the educational experiences of women as well as girls. Using feminist methods, this research has often been used as a source of empowerment for the subjects, rather than straightforward academic analysis. For example, the Taking Liberties Collective (1989) published accounts of the educational experiences of over 50 women, recording how they had encountered 'oppression in men's education'. One of the themes emerging from this and other studies (e.g. Pascall and Cox 1993) is that mature women have perceived education as playing a dual role: their schools encouraged domesticity and low-status jobs, but further and higher education provided an escape route from traditional roles and into more rewarding jobs.

This emphasis on the empowerment of women through education has tended to dominate feminist research, but what of the gendered experiences of boys and men in education, and why are they falling behind in their educational achievements? Research into the construction of masculinity (e.g. Roper and Tosh 1991; Morgan 1992) opened up new avenues for the sociology of education. In *Boys Don't Cry*, Askew and Ross (1988) studied the role of schools in the construction of masculinity, classroom dynamics, sexism in school structure and organization, and women teachers' experiences. They argued that boys were victims of their own socialization, which involved learning to be aggressive and attaching little importance to academic discourse. Problems were identified in some boys' schools, where it was claimed that a traditional image of masculinity was reinforced by an authoritarian ethos. Askew and Ross also suggested strategies for working with boys and for in-service work with teachers, including the use of workshops, the adoption of anti-sexist initiatives and strategies for persuading boys to talk more openly and honestly. Arnot *et al.*

also addressed these themes during a ten-year (1984–94) study of educational reforms and gender equality in schools:

> **A number of new areas of concern relating to equality issues emerged during the project. One of the most common has pointed to an apparent loss of motivation among working-class and black boys. It was claimed time and time again that as traditional areas of male employment have collapsed or altered, working class (and/or black) male students now tend not to see themselves as benefiting academically or vocationally from schooling. They appear to be less motivated than girls, therefore, and/or alienated from the classroom. Further, while working class boys seem increasingly to stay on into the sixth form, they tend to study for vocational qualifications such as GNVQ (rather than A levels).**
>
> (Arnot *et al.* 1997: 143)

Some remaining problems and policies regarding gender and education centre on the theme of uniformity and diversity. For example, we have already briefly considered the question of whether or not education should be coeducational, but this debate is too large to be probed in depth.

Debates about uniformity and diversity have also encompassed concerns about how attitudes to sexuality are influenced by education. In the UK, Clause 28 of the Local Government Act 1988 forbade local authorities from promoting the 'teaching in any maintained schools on the acceptability of homosexuality as a pretended family relationship'. Critics argued that this could encourage homophobia and the presentation of heterosexuality as a norm from which individuals must not deviate; it was over 14 years before the Clause was withdrawn. Not only does this have implications for the social construction of knowledge, but also interpretative sociologists have generated accounts of the experiences of homosexuals in academic environments. For example, Trenchard and Warren (1984) found individuals who had been expelled or referred to a psychiatrist when they 'came out'. Jones and Mahony (1989) provided an analysis of the historical background to this debate, including criticisms of the sociology of education for the way it ignored the promotion of heterosexuality in the past. In 1998 findings were published from the first survey of homophobia in schools (commissioned by Stonewall and the Terrence Higgins Trust). Clause 28 seemed to have had some impact as, of about 1000 schools taking

A closer look

Yes he can!

More research projects and strategies for tackling boys' achievement have emerged since the 1990s. For example, in July 2003 OfSTED (in the UK) published two reports on boys' achievement: 'Yes he can – Schools where boys write well' (HMI 505) and 'Boys' achievement in secondary schools' (HMI 1659). Another project was undertaken by researchers at Homerton College, Cambridge, who worked with over 60 schools in England for the 'Raising Boys' Achievement Project'. All of these reports acknowledged that improving boys' achievements was a complex matter, including a range of factors. Schools that were successful in raising boys' attainment and writing skills tended to have the following characteristics:

- a positive and stimulating learning culture, with high expectations for all pupils;
- good teaching and learning, with knowledgeable and enthusiastic teachers, effective pastoral systems and extracurricular activities;
- good classroom management, i.e. behaviour was well managed, discipline was fair and praise was used frequently;
- tracking and supporting boys' performance through good use of data and assessment that particularly values their work and always offers them clear advice on how to improve;
- strategies focusing on literacy, which provides intensive support on reading, writing and literacy across the curriculum with careful selection of materials that appeal to boys.

(Adapted from www.standards.dfes.gov.uk/genderandachievement/understanding/faqs)

Table 15.3 Highest qualification held:[1] by sex and ethnic group, Great Britain, 2003[2]

	Degree or equivalent %	Higher education qualification[3] %	GCE A level or equivalent %	GCSE grades A*–C or equivalent %	Other qualification %	No qualification %	All %
Males							
White	18	8	31	18	12	13	100
Mixed	14	7	21	22	17	17	100
Asian or Asian British	20	6	17	11	24	20	100
Black or Black British	19	7	21	16	23	12	100
Chinese	29	4	19	9	28	10	100
Other ethnic group[4]	23	6	11	7	36	18	100
All	18	8	29	17	14	13	100
Females							
White	15	10	18	27	13	16	100
Mixed	21	9	17	21	15	17	100
Asian or Asian British	14	6	13	17	25	24	100
Black or Black British	13	12	16	21	24	13	100
Chinese	26	9	14	10	30	11	100
Other ethnic group[4]	14	9	11	10	34	22	100
All	15	10	18	26	14	16	100

1 Males aged 16–64, females aged 16–59.
2 At spring. These estimates are not seasonally adjusted and have not been adjusted to take account of the Census 2001 results. See Appendix, Part 4: LFS reweighting.
3 Below degree level.
4 Includes those who did not state their ethnic group.
(Source: *Social Trends 34*, 2004, Table 3.17, p. 47)

part in the survey, only a quarter said that their teachers mentioned sexuality when talking about equal opportunities. More than 80 per cent of schools taking part reported that verbal bullying was common, and more than 60 per cent of the respondents felt that schools were an appropriate place for providing information about homosexuality.

The study of gender and education is not only wide-ranging and confusing but also quite fascinating when we look at recent developments in the achievements of males and females (Table 15.3). When the cumulative effects of social inequalities are considered, we get a clearer impression of current debates within the sociology of education.

Ethnicity and education

Chapter 6 has shown that 'ethnicity' and 'race' are confusing concepts. In general, too many studies of education and ethnicity could be accused of gross simplification because they forced individuals into inappropriate, homogeneous categories and thus misrepresented the unique nature of our ethnic backgrounds. Despite the wide range of ethnic backgrounds in Britain, educational research often categorized individuals into three main, and largely incomprehensible, groups – 'West Indian', 'Asian' and 'other'. It is easy to see why this happened. Sociologists study group behaviour and are, by the nature of their subject, obliged to allocate individuals into groups. They are also concerned about inequality in education and make such distinctions in order to identify and measure inequality.

Research into ethnicity and education is therefore fraught with difficulties, first because of the problem of finding suitable ways of labelling groups, second because there is a temptation to generalize from small samples, and third because an emphasis on statistical data often means that qualitative differences in educational experiences are ignored. These reservations help to explain why figures relating to various ethnic groups have been included in official national statistics on education only since 1990–91.

Before the 1990s the existing statistics tended to suggest that 'Afro-Caribbeans' in particular were underachieving when compared with other ethnic groups. This was despite the fact that many of them had English as their first language, while many children of 'Asian' origin and who had learned English as a second language appeared to have thrived in education. What explanations could be found for this? Various writers have claimed that the language problems of 'Asian' children have been recognized more easily, and treated more sympathetically, than the language problems of 'West Indian' children. Children are expected not only to speak English in British schools but also to speak *standard* English or, even more specifically, what Bernstein (1971) called an 'elaborated code' (i.e. complex, analytical and abstract language with explicit meanings). When children learn English as a second language they are taught the 'correct' grammatical constructions; when English is a child's native language, it may be spoken with a wide range of dialects, grammatical constructions and implicit meanings. Labov (1969) maintained that non-standard English was different, rather than inferior, that it could have its own logical structure and could be very effective as a means of communicating complicated arguments. V. Edwards (1976, 1979) argued that the Creole spoken by many West Indian children (and children of West Indian parents) played an important role in their underperformance. Although Creole includes English vocabulary, it has different grammatical constructions and sound systems. These children were therefore at a disadvantage.

Stop and think

- How important is it today to speak standard English or use an elaborated code?

More recent research into achievements in further and higher education has challenged images of the achievements of 'Afro-Caribbeans', suggesting that many have a strong determination to succeed in education. In 1994 the Policy Studies Institute (PSI) published its findings about the different rates of entry of ethnic minorities into higher education in 1992. It considered the percentages of successful applications from various groups and found radical differences in access to universities and polytechnics. When looking only at access to universities, it was found that 'Chinese' and 'black African' applicants were overrepresented compared with their presence in the population as a whole, while 'black Caribbeans' and 'Bangladeshis' were underrepresented. When looking only at access to polytechnics, it was found that 'black Caribbeans' were overrepresented compared with their presence in the population as a whole. However, the PSI (1994) indicated that a simplistic cause–effect interpretation based on ethnic categorization should be avoided; for example, a larger proportion of 'black Caribbeans' applied for access to highly competitive courses, such as medicine and law, and to courses in a relatively small number of universities near their homes. This meant that competition for places was not evenly spread.

Since the 1990s the most significant change has been that, within each ethnic group, a higher proportion of girls than boys have achieved good grades at GCSE/GNVQ level (Figure 15.6). This not only confirms what has already been said in this chapter about gender differences but also challenges various racial stereotypes.

The stereotype of the non-academic 'Asian' female has been challenged by many research findings. For example, Singh-Raud (1997) interviewed nine Asian girls aged 14–18 years (three Muslims, three Sikhs and three Hindus) and reported on their diverse and conflicting views on education. He also surveyed 202 Asian female undergraduates (51 Sikhs, 52 Hindus and 99 Muslims) and found that they were increasingly asserting their rights to have a higher education (Singh-Raud 1998). This was particularly evident among Muslim women. Parker-Jenkins *et al.* (1997) interviewed 100 Muslim women aged 16–25 years in order to chart their career destinations and experiences. The title of their report, 'Trying twice as hard to succeed', reflects some of their findings, but they also found that an apparently common religious identity contained diverse views and wide-ranging multicultural, multiracial and multilingual groupings. Some women said that religious leaders had told their parents not to let them attend university, while one woman reported that her parents had supported her studies because of the emphasis on education in the Koran. Again, we can see the limitations of statistical data in helping us to develop a deeper understanding of educational experiences.

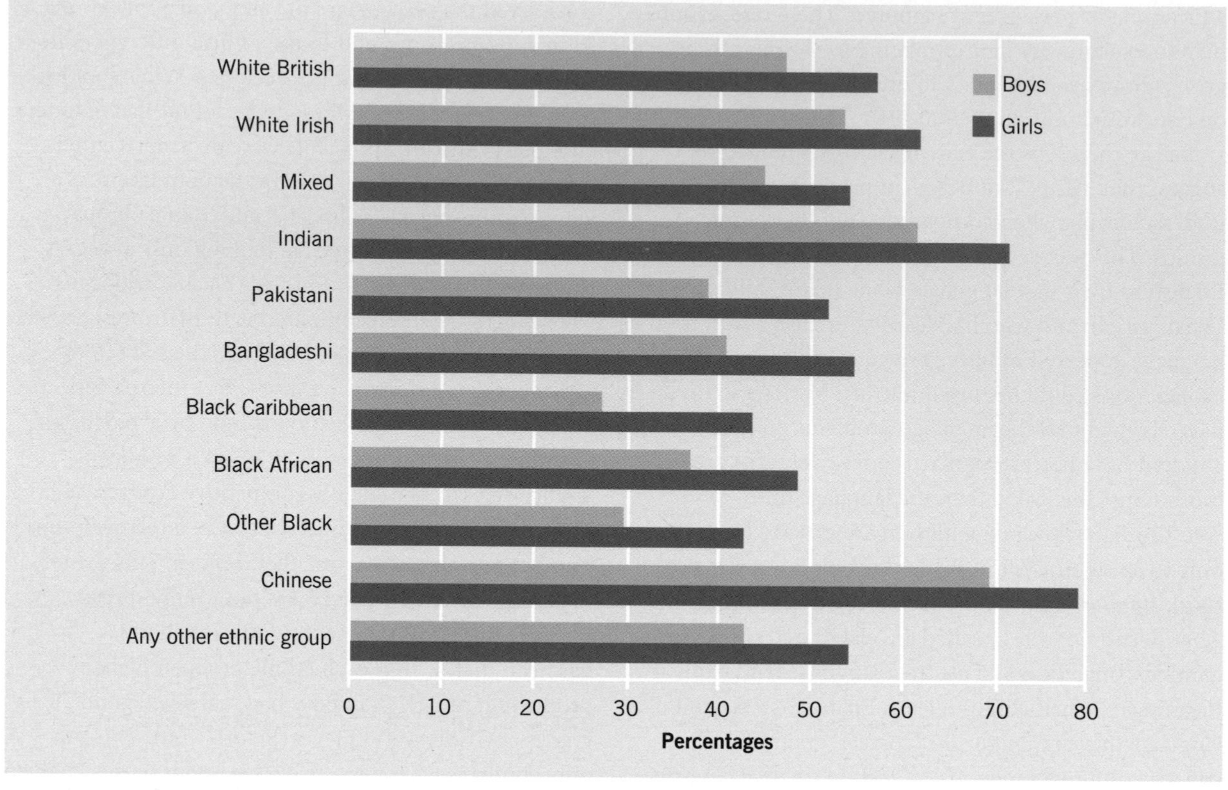

Figure 15.6 Pupils achieving five or more A*–C grades at GCSE/GNVQ, by gender and ethnic group, England 2004
Source: www.statistics.gov.uk

Case study

The secret of Chinese pupils' educational success

A study, conducted by Dr. Becky Francis and Dr. Louise Archer of London Metropolitan University, considered reasons for the academic achievements of children of Chinese origin.

> 'The two-year London study, which surveyed the views of 80 British Chinese boys and girls, 30 Chinese parents and 30 teachers, found that one of the key factors underpinning educational success was the extremely high value placed on education by British Chinese pupils and their parents. This high valuing of education was regarded as a central, defining aspect of British Chinese identity and occurred irrespective of pupils' social class and gender. As one pupil (Amy) put it: "School first, life later". A Chinese parent (HongWah) described education as "a way of life".
>
> Social competition between British Chinese families provided an extra impetus for educational success. ...
>
> But high academic achievement was not won lightly: pupils and their parents described how families often work extremely hard to help their children to do well. Many parents endured long working hours and hard conditions to pay for additional support and to provide their children with more time to study. ...
>
> Many teachers held unintentionally racist and sexist views about British Chinese boys and girls. For example, many teachers described British Chinese pupils as "nice and polite", "hardworking" but also "withdrawn" and "rather quiet". British Chinese girls were described in particularly negative terms, as excessively quiet, overly-diligent and repressed. British Chinese pupils often felt that popular assumptions about their "cleverness" were "a big pressure" and they challenged such narrow definitions, expressing instead a broad range of behaviours and outlooks.'

(London Metropolitan University, extract from News Release, 24 July 2004)

Question

1. Discuss the finding that some teachers were critical of their high-achieving Chinese-British pupils.

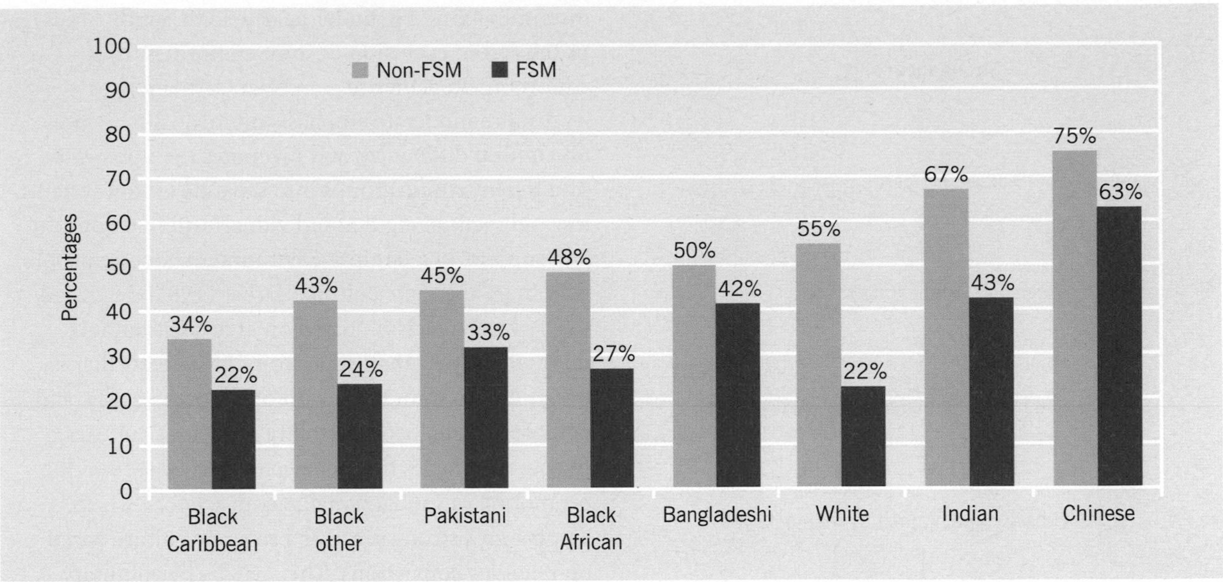

Figure 15.7 Proportion of pupils achieving five or more A*–C grades at GCSE, by free school meals and non-free school meals, 2002
Source: Bhattacharyya, Ison and Blair (2003)

Just as gender and ethnicity may have a combined impact on educational achievement, we could also ask whether ethnicity affects social class and, if so, whether research that intends to study 'ethnicity' is actually studying social class. In 1989 Drew and Gray found that social class explained more variation in examination performance than did either ethnic group or gender. Figure 15.6 shows that in 2004 there was still cause for concern about the achievements of children of black Caribbean, black African and other black origins, although it could be the case that the social class of such children had a greater impact than their ethnicity. To evaluate this further Bhattacharyya *et al.* (2003) analysed pupils by splitting them into eight ethnic categories and considering whether or not they were receiving free school meals (FSM) (Figure 15.7). They noted that

> **These differences may yet be attributable to socio-economic differences: the broad non-FSM category captures a wide range of socio-economic status and income which is not differentiated. Ethnic groups will vary in the extent of this range, with some ethnic groups containing many more people of higher incomes. However, socio-economic factors are not the sole explanation for lower attainment, as not all children from low-income families have low attainment at GCSE. For example, Chinese children eligible for free school meals, whilst a small group, are more likely to achieve five or more GCSEs than all other ethnic groups, except Indian non-FSM pupils.**
>
> (Bhattacharyya *et al.* 2003: 11)

If we look back at Table 15.3 and the working-age population as a whole, we can see that there are marked variations according to ethnic groupings and that only in the 'Mixed' ethnic group were there more female than male graduates. There were the same or higher percentages of women as men with no qualifications, showing that the recent improvements in female attainment had not yet tipped the balance created by lower female attainment in the past. Although Table 15.3 describes the high proportion of working-age women in the Asian or Asian British group in 2003 without any qualifications, it is likely that the proportion will decline as younger generations have more impact over the years.

Researchers today are more sophisticated than they used to be in their attempts to reflect the often complex identity of people from diverse ethnic backgrounds. Yet it is only possible to understand current approaches to issues surrounding ethnicity and education if we also appreciate how perspectives about ethnicity and associated political policies have changed over time. We can begin by acknowledging that political perspectives on ethnicity and racism have tended to encompass all of the approaches we have already encountered in this chapter, ranging from egalitarianism to biological determination and including debates about uniformity,

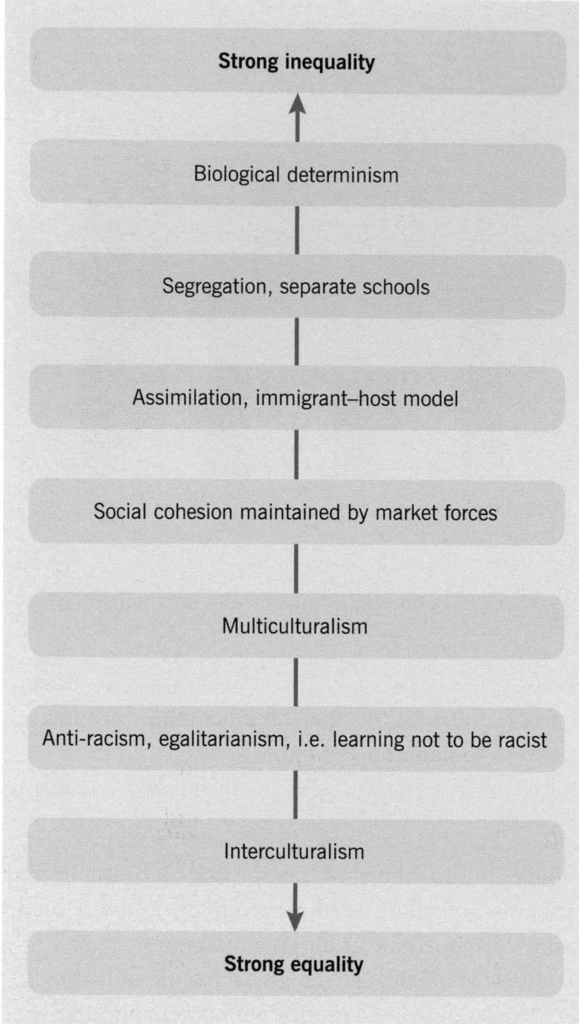

Figure 15.8 Simple polarity of perspectives about ethnicity and education
Source: Adapted from McKenzie 2001: 159

diversity, integration and segregation. Figure 15.8 provides a simplified model of the polarity of perceptions about ethnicity and race, ranging from those with a strong emphasis on apparently natural inequalities being built into the structure of education, to those interpretive approaches with a strong emphasis on combining equality with diversity. You will see that perceptions can overlap and that their actual position on the polarity may be debatable, but the model may still help to highlight ways in which decisions about education can feed into inequalities of power at all levels.

An emphasis on *biological determinism* sees race as linked to innate educational capacities and a natural source of social inequalities. At its most extreme, this approach has been used to justify negative racial discrimination (e.g. under apartheid in South Africa) or the forced exclusion of some minorities from education altogether (e.g. in Nazi Germany).

A more moderate emphasis on inequality focuses on cultural differences and promotes the *segregation* of different ethnic groups into separate school systems, the argument being that individuals will find comfort and support in a familiar environment, among people who share the same culture. Barker (1981) described this as a 'new racism', based on arguments about difference rather than superiority. It suggests that it is 'natural' to want to be with one's 'own people' and emphasizes the incompatibility of various cultures. In some countries this perspective can be seen in the promotion of fundamentalist faith schools, which emphasize a strong sense of a separate culture based on religious convictions. This may be by voluntary arrangements, but at its most extreme it involves segregation by force.

Other right-wing perspectives assume that children from a wide range of backgrounds will be incorporated into the country's existing mainstream 'culture', submerging their own cultural heritage in the process. This *immigrant–host* model sees the 'host' country as a benefactor and the immigrant as being expected to *assimilate* into what is provided by the host. Research in the UK up to and including the 1980s (e.g. the Rampton and Swann Reports) was mainly about unequal educational outcomes, the emphasis being on helping people to fit into British society. This approach is still emphasized in the French model of social integration and was an undercurrent to riots in 2005, when protesters objected to elements of forced cultural uniformity within the education system; for example, Muslim girls were not allowed to wear the hijab in school.

At the centre of Figure 15.8, a New Right emphasis accepts individual diversity but assumes that social cohesion can be maintained and promoted by the sound operation of *market forces*, without government intervention to ameliorate inequalities. In the UK this laissez-faire approach has been associated with Conservative Party policies but has also influenced New Labour policies and has been taken up by local education authorities of various political affiliations. It emphasizes self-sufficiency and the freedom of parents to make decisions about their children's education and has been influential in the creation of a diverse range of schools, the assumption being that each type of school responds to the demands of local consumers.

Centre-ground and left-wing perspectives tend to involve more concern about racism and the negative effects of ethnic inequalities, but they vary in their proposed solutions. For example, a *multicultural* approach tends to assume that, if children can learn about cultures other than their own, then a greater degree of tolerance will be cultivated, not only in the individual but also in society as a whole. This approach has been criticized for being naive in its understanding of the true nature of racism by ignoring the fact that many children who are born to indigenous 'British' families and in the British 'culture' (if that could be defined) suffer from covert or overt racism simply because of the colour of their skin.

Anti-racists argue that it is racism, rather than cultural diversity, that must be confronted. The role of education is to challenge racism in society as a whole by, for example, providing children with positive images of 'blackness' (Bryan *et al.* 1987). As with the anti-sexist approaches described earlier, efforts have been made to make language (spoken and in books) more politically correct. The following quote from one of Bryan and colleagues' (1987) interviewees describes how one black woman responded to the negative images she encountered in her school work:

> **I had always liked reading, and could have really enjoyed literature at school. I suppose I liked the strange and different world I found in books, especially the ones about life as it was supposed to have been in Britain. This couldn't last though, because reading often became a nasty, personal experience. You would be getting deep into a story and suddenly it would hit you – a reference to Black people as savages or something. It was so offensive. And so wounding. Sometimes you would sit in class and wait, all tensed up, for the next derogatory remark to come tripping off the teacher's tongue. Oh yes, it was a 'black' day today, or some kid had 'blackened' the school's reputation. It was there clearly, in black and white, the school's ideology. The curriculum and the culture relies on those racist views.**
>
> (Bryan *et al.* 1987: 93)

In the UK the New Right governments of the 1980s tended to reject anti-racist ideas as too extreme, but

Figure 15.9 Children at school: cultural integration
© Christine Osbourne/CORBIS

anti-racism became more mainstream following the racist murder of an Asian boy in his school playground and the very detailed research that followed (the Macdonald Report of 1990, and associated research). The racist murder of Stephen Lawrence was followed by the McPherson Report of 1999, with an emphasis on institutionalized racism that impacted on schools as well as other institutions.

Another (and there are probably more) approach tries to assimilate multicultural and anti-racist approaches. *Interculturalism* promotes a recognition and acceptance of the uniqueness of the individual and the superficiality of labelling anyone simply by skin colour, 'culture', social class, gender, disability and so on. This approach can be seen in the work of Rassool (1999), who studied the flexible identities of pupils from first- and second-generation immigrant families in an inner London comprehensive school. Rassool found a 'hybridization' of cultures over a period of time, as culture was 'made malleable' in order to support social survival. These pupils were quite comfortable with their multifaceted identities, and Rassool concluded that, rather than assimilation taking place, difference was redefined by individuals and groups in an ongoing process of interaction with their environment and changing circumstances. These findings reinforce well-documented evidence (e.g. Stone 1981; Mirza 1992) about the strong support that many black parents give to their children's education and about their belief in a meritocratic ideal. Immigrant communities throughout the world have tended to regard education as a means of accessing power in a difficult social world, and dissatisfaction among parents about existing education systems has often led them to support some sort of supplementary educational provision.

We have now seen that ethnicity, social class and gender must be recognized as sources of educational inequalities, but their effects and interrelationships should not be distorted by oversimplification. The intercultural approach taken by Bhattacharyya *et al.* (2003: 22) acknowledged a wide range of factors that could influence individual experiences of education, including not only free school meals but also having English as a second language, having special educational needs, being the children of refugees and asylum-seekers, school exclusions, poverty, parental or pupil illness, racial abuse or harassment, lack of role models, unfamiliarity with the workings of the education system, and 'teaching based on unfamiliar cultural norms, histories and points of reference'.

Stop and think

- It is easier to identify and categorize an individual according to sex than according to social class or ethnic group. How has this affected the introduction of education policies that (a) are egalitarian; (b) emphasize equal access; and (c) promote inequality?
- Compare the policies of central government (on social class, gender and ethnicity) with local or independent initiatives that aim to reduce educational inequalities. How effective have local initiatives been, and what challenges have they faced?

Special educational needs

Class, gender and ethnicity are probably the most highly researched influences on educational experiences, but sociologists have now moved towards a greater appreciation of influences that have been relatively ignored in the past. In the UK, the Warnock Report (1978) raised the profile of children with special educational needs (SEN) and was followed by many other research reports, legislation and amendments to practice. Such developments in the UK have been influenced by changes in other countries, and by the late 1970s there were already moves towards integration in North America and much of Europe.

Before 1978 British children with special educational needs were usually educated in 'special' schools and apart from the majority of children in 'mainstream' schools. A movement towards the greater integration of children with special needs into mainstream schools has brought with it a greater appreciation of the diversity of special needs. Some acknowledgement of this can be seen in changes in the discourse about special educational needs, with a shift from an emphasis on 'integration' to an emphasis on a stronger sense of 'inclusion'. This is in keeping with the wider political discourse about social inclusion and social exclusion. However, it is clear that structural changes are not enough and that education can play an important part in generating a more genuine form of social integration. Oliver tries to explain what is needed:

> **All disabled people experience disability as a social restriction whether these restrictions occur as a consequence of inaccessible built environments, questionable notions of intelligence and social competence, the inability of the general public to use sign language, the lack of reading material in Braille or hostile public attitudes to people with non-visible disabilities.**
>
> (Oliver 1990)

There has been an element of consensus about what should be done in order to support children with special educational needs, but there has also been a growing awareness of competing perspectives (see Riddell 1996), including approaches that have been described as essentialist (biological/medical), social constructionist (see the above quote from Oliver), materialist (emphasising poverty and oppression), postmodern (individual experiences), and disability movement (advocating activism in a new social movement).

This short review of special educational needs can be seen as a simple resume of some key features of sociological studies of education. It reiterates that such studies highlight competing perspectives and changing discourse. It also tells us something about how education changes in general.

Multiple disadvantages in education

We have now seen that there are patterns of inequalities in education associated with socioeconomic group, gender, ethnicity and special educational needs and that disadvantages can be cumulative (as shown by Bhattacharyya *et al.* 2003). However, we have also found that our educational outcomes are not simply determined by such structural inequalities, and it is still important to acknowledge the agency of the individual. With this in mind, we must return to the emphasis placed by various governments on parents and children as 'consumers' of education. The important role of parents means that it is possible for them to compensate for their children's social and educational disadvantages or to make them worse, for example by supporting or not supporting their children's access to higher education (see the Case study 'Resistance to schooling'). In extreme cases, when children have no parents or are separated from them, the impact on their education can be dire.

The social exclusion and educational problems of children in the care of local authorities have only started to be appreciated fully (Armstrong *et al.* 1995). Children in care may be fostered or living in children's homes, but in both cases the state has effectively taken the role of the parent. Although it is estimated that at

A closer look

What do changes in special educational needs tell us about change in general?

- New problems are constantly being recognized.
- Although education policies and practices are constantly changing, such changes tend to be evolutionary rather than revolutionary (e.g. the 2001 Code of Practice on special educational needs was explicit in favouring an evolutionary approach).
- Change involves a new rhetoric and evolving discourse. The labels given to various special educational needs have changed over time, and political discourse about such needs has shifted from medical labels to 'integration' and now 'inclusion'.
- Change is often initiated by individual schools and institutions and even individual teachers; for example, a whole-school approach, institutions' codes of practice and providing special equipment.
- Implementation of changes often differs from what has been planned and passed by politicians and other officials; for example, the British government decided to 'cherry pick' from the 2004 Tomlinson Report about changes in assessment.
- Research findings and official changes may not change the way people think.

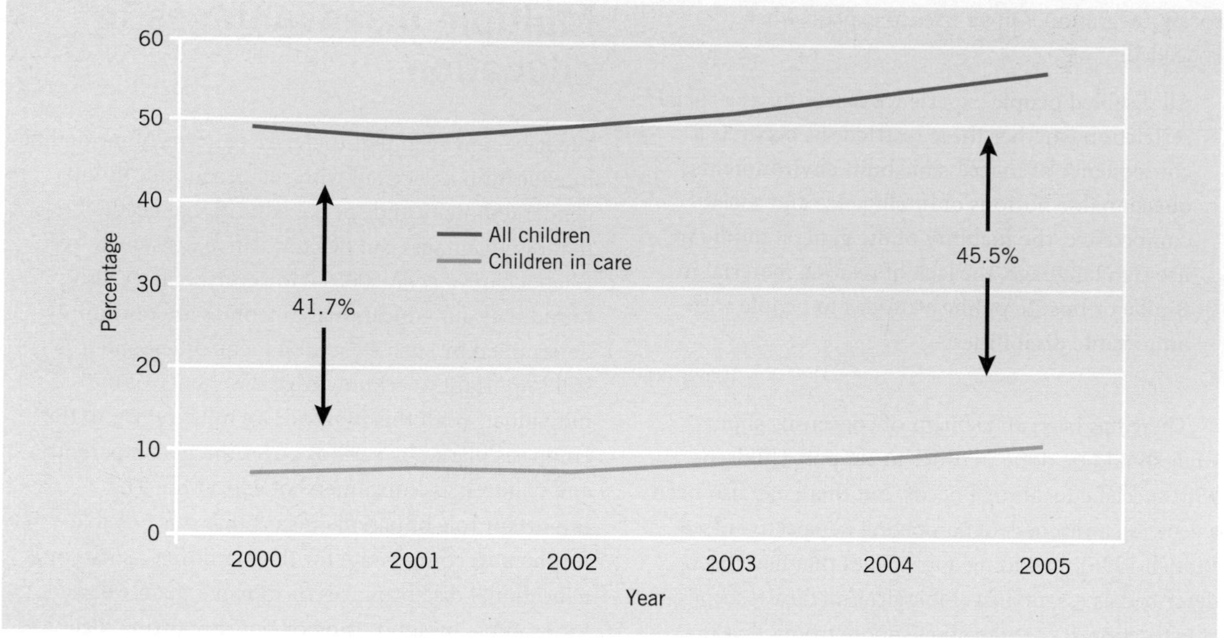

Figure 15.10 Percentage of children in Year 11 who achieved at least five A*–C grades at GCSE/GNVQ
Source: Social Exclusion Task Force (2006)

any one time there are approximately 61,000 children in care in the UK, it has been easy to ignore them in a society promoting the ideals of a parentocracy.

In 1997 Sir William Utting produced a disturbing study of children in local authority care, which led to the setting up of a ministerial task force; in 1998 the Downing Street Social Exclusion Unit (SEU) considered children in community care as part of its wider remit. In 2006 the government's Social Exclusion Task Force published 'Reaching out: an action plan on social exclusion', in which it illustrated the large gap that exists between the educational achievements of children in care and the achievements of other children (Figure 15.10). It noted that

> **. . . the outcomes for the most disadvantaged young people remain unacceptably poor. For example, we typically spend £110,000 each year on a child in residential care, and spending on all children in care has increased by almost 50 per cent in four years. Yet only around 11 per cent of children in care get grades A*–C at GCSE compared with 56 per cent of all children. Such poor outcomes may be a reflection of the trauma and backgrounds experienced by these children, rather than the care itself, but these outcomes contribute to a life of exclusion and need to be improved.**
>
> (Social Exclusion Task Force 2006: 63)

Stop and think

- Compare Figure 15.10 with other statistics about GCSE and the effects of:
  (a) socioeconomic classification (Table 15.2);
  (b) free school meals (Figure 15.7);
  (c) gender (Figure 15.4);
  (d) ethnic group (Figure 15.6).
- How could these findings be interpreted:
  (a) from various sociological perspectives (e.g. structural, interpretive, postmodern);
  (b) using different definitions of equal opportunities?

This chapter ends with an image of educational inequalities in the UK that may cause us to wonder why relatively little was achieved during the twentieth century. Yet we have also encountered disagreements about both the meaning of 'equal opportunities' and the extent to which the state should control the educational experiences of its citizens. Perhaps it may seem that this chapter has provided more questions than answers, but it should now be clear that, although 'education is an eminently social thing' (Durkheim 1956: 114), it is still possible for individuals to become producers rather than passive receptors of knowledge.

Summary

- The sociology of education highlights *power* relationships between children and adults and the important influences of political and cultural perspectives. *Knowledge* is seen as socially constructed and the identification of intelligence as a social and subjective process. Even the use of concepts such as 'intelligence', 'knowledge' and 'ability' is regarded as problematic; for example, qualifications tend to be devalued as more people have them (credential inflation).
- The nature of *schooling* in the UK and many other countries has shifted towards an increasing emphasis on accountability to parents and central or regional government. In the UK, a diverse *school system* has emerged from successive governments' emphasis on parental rights.
- *Sociological explanations and theories* have developed from an early emphasis on the social structure towards a synthesis of structural and interpretative perspectives. Functionalist approaches have emphasized the role of education in maintaining consensus and continuity. Approaches emerging from Marxist influences have emphasized conflict and change within education and inequalities of educational opportunities within a capitalist system. Critical theorists have emphasized the role of education in supporting an ideological superstructure and perpetuating inequalities. Interpretative influences have included descriptions of how working-class boys have interacted creatively with their social constraints to generate self-fulfilling prophesies. Postmodernist ideas challenge even basic assumptions about education.
- Sociologists have identified important themes within *debates about education policy*. These include questions about equality and inequality, and uniformity and diversity. Perceptions of equality include egalitarianism (emphasizing equal outcomes), equal access (to equal resources), competitive access (rationing access to superior education), parental choice (the ideology of parentocracy) and biological determinism (with its emphasis on inequality). There are also debates about how much uniformity or diversity, segregation or integration, there should be in education.
- At a time when class-based analysis has been questioned and partially replaced by an emphasis on *socioeconomic groups*, what is important is the finding that relevant inequalities in education have been remarkably consistent over time and may even be more pronounced. These inequalities can be influenced by the dominant political ideology. Some sociologists have claimed that the acquisition of skills in information technology has become a key influence on social class.
- *Gender inequalities* in education have been transformed since the 1980s as girls have tended to achieve more than boys in education. Improvements in girls' performance have resulted from some policies reflecting an equal-access approach (equal opportunities/girl-friendly) and some reflecting a more egalitarian approach (anti-sexist/girl-centred). In view of such progress for women, sociologists are asking why gender inequalities remain in the workplace (including the teaching hierarchy). They are also focusing on the role of schools in the construction of masculinity and some have argued that boys are victims of their own socialization, learning to be aggressive and attaching little importance to education.
- Research into *ethnicity and education* has been fraught with difficulties. These include forcing individuals into inappropriate categories and questions about whether research that intends to study ethnicity is actually studying social class. However, the role of education in the transmission or amelioration of racism must be considered. Political perspectives on ethnicity and education include the full range, from egalitarianism to biological determinism, and include debates about uniformity, diversity, integration and segregation. Some ethnic groups are over- or underrepresented in access to higher education. However, statistical data are limited in helping us to develop a deeper understanding of educational experiences; for example, the success of children of Chinese origin.
- Sociologists are continually moving towards a greater appreciation of influences on education that have been relatively ignored in the past; these include *special educational needs*. While there has been a growing emphasis on parental choice in education, there has also been a growing appreciation of the *multiple disadvantages* experienced by children who lack parental support and who are in the *care of their local authorities*.

Links

The section on the main sociological approaches to the study of education in society (pp. 609–615) links to the broader theoretical approaches of Durkheim, Marx and other social theorists discussed in Chapter 2.

Issues around inequalities in educational achievement in terms of social class, gender and ethnicity (pp. 624–638) can be related to the general discussion of social class, gender and race in Chapters 4, 5 and 6 respectively.

Further reading

This chapter has shown that educational processes are constantly changing, and you should now appreciate the need to make your reading as up-to-date as possible. You should search out the most recently published books available and remember that by the time of their publication they will already be out of date in some respects. For this reason, it is a good idea to search for up-to-date information in websites, educational journals and magazines.

Educational journals and magazines are useful resources for updating and expanding your existing knowledge of this area. Weeklies in the UK include the *Times Educational Supplement* and *Times Higher Educational Supplement* (see www.tes.co.uk). Academic journals provide your best source of recent research findings, and some of them focus on one aspect of education. Wide-ranging journals include the *British Educational Research Journal* and the *British Journal of Sociology of Education*. Copies of *Sociology of Education Abstracts* are also useful. Many online journals are listed on the Taylor and Francis Group's website www.tandf.co.uk/journals/online.asp.

Websites

www.oecd.org/edu/eag2007

Organisation for Economic Co-operation and Development (OECD)

www.statistics.gov.uk

Office for National Statistics, the UK Statistics Authority

www.statistics.gov.uk/socialtrends

Social Trends, Office for National Statistics

http://epp.eurostat.ec.europa.eu

Statistical Office of the European Communities

www.dfes.gov.uk

UK government's Department for Education and Skills

www.tes.co.uk

Times Educational Supplement

http://portal.unesco.org/education

United Nations Educational Scientific and Cultural Organization (UNESCO)

Activities

Activity 1

Hargreaves' seven dimensions of postmodernity

1. *Flexible economies* (occupational and technological complexity). Teachers need to develop skills and flexibility in their students but also need to address and discuss the uses of technology and patterns of unemployment and underemployment which many young people will face.
2. *The paradox of globalization* creates national doubts and insecurities. There is a danger of resurrecting traditional curricula of an ethnocentric and xenophobic nature, and reinforcing subject-based structures that inhibit organizational learning.

3. *Dead certainties (i.e. moral and scientific uncertainties)* have reduced confidence in the factual contents of what is taught. In response teachers may be involved in developing their own missions and visions or placed at the moral mercy of the market force of parental choice or forced to extol the standards, traditions and basic skills of those who nostalgically reconstruct mythical certainties of ill-remembered pasts.
4. *The moving mosaic (organizational fluidity)* challenges the separation of subjects in secondary schools and addresses the need for more collaboration and shared occupational learning in contexts that are larger and more complex than those provided in small schools.
5. *The boundless self (personal anxieties)* involves a continuous psychological quest in a world without secure moral anchors.
6. *Safe simulation (technological sophistication and complexity) of reality* can be more perfect and plausible than the more untidy and uncontrollable realities themselves. In a world of instantaneous images and artificial appearances, contrived co-operation and contrived collegiality are examples of safe simulations that can deny the collaborative process its vitality and spontaneity.
7. *Compression of time and space* brings real benefits, including increased turnover, quicker travel and communication, speedier decision-making, more responsive services, and reduced waiting-times. It also brings the following costs:
   - Expectations of such rapid responsiveness that decision-making is too swift and leads to error, ineffectiveness etc.
   - Innovation, accelerated pace and so on mean that people experience an intolerable overload and feelings of guilt about their inability to meet goals.
   - People may concentrate on the aesthetic appearance of change or performance rather than on the quality and substance of change or performance itself.
   - Uncertainties can be exacerbated as knowledge is produced, disseminated and overturned at an ever increasing rate.
   - The possible erosion of opportunities for personal reflection and relaxation can lead to increased stress and loss of contact with basic goals and purposes.
   - We can place such a premium on implementing new techniques and complying with new mandates that more complex, less visible, longer-term and less measurable purposes which involve care for others and relationships with others are diminished in importance or sacrificed altogether.

(Adapted from Hargreaves 1994: Chapter 4.)

Questions

1. Consider each of the first six dimensions and:
   (a) whether you agree that it exists;
   (b) what means could be used to tackle it.
2. Can anything be done to tackle the costs listed in dimension 7?
3. Does Hargreaves add anything to your understanding about the pressures of credential inflation and performativity?

Activity 2

Private and 'truly private' schools

The size of the private school sector at the primary stages varies across Europe. In the Netherlands, Ireland and both parts of the Belgium system, it is over 60 per cent; in Denmark, France, Portugal and Spain it is between 10 per cent and 30 per cent; in Austria, England, Germany and Sweden it is less than 10 per cent; whilst in some others it is almost non-existent. The percentages of students attending private schools at the secondary stage tend to be somewhere higher than the figures reported here.

The size of a country's 'private' sector can be somewhat misleading however. Some of our experts reminded us that a more fine-grained distinction is required. In England, for example, there is a group of schools which are almost entirely funded by parental fees. These schools make up around 7 per cent of all secondary schools and are extremely influential in terms of their impact on the whole system, offering a form of 'selective' education which has historically offered advantages in terms of entry to higher education and subsequent life-chances. Ireland also has a group of these 'prestigious' schools which serve the upper/middle classes and charge boarding fees although the bulk of their income comes from the state; however, the numbers involved in this case are limited. Scotland, meanwhile, has a comparable group which makes up around 5 per cent of its school population. Often such schools, by virtue of their missions and intakes, are referred to as 'elitist'. Furthermore, their impact on the entire education system (especially when they attract or select the more able students) can be disproportionate to their size. We refer to such schools as 'truly private' ones to indicate that they are not financed through grant-aid funding from (governmental) authorities but mainly through direct financial contributions by the parents of pupils and, possibly, by donations from industry or by accumulated funds dating back to their foundation. By contrast, in countries such as the Netherlands, Belgium, Spain and Portugal only a very limited number of 'truly private' schools exist at present and they are not widely-perceived to have much influence on the educational systems of which they are a part.

The public/private distinction is an important feature of European educational systems but only part of the overall story. Most systems, we found, had private and public schools. The key difference was in how they chose to fund them. In some countries the state finances both the public and the private sectors equally and implements identical policies across both sectors (the Netherlands, Sweden, Ireland). Furthermore, some countries combine the equal funding and treatment of public and private schools with free parental choice of school (Belgium and the Netherlands). But, whilst the law in many countries permits private schools to be established, it does not necessarily imply that such schools will be publicly-funded. In some countries, the private sector accounts for the majority of schools (Belgium, Ireland, the Netherlands), whilst in others they constitute just a small minority (Austria Germany, Portugal, Sweden). The importance of looking at countries in which education and other services are financed by the government, but operated by private non-profit organizations (often religious by nature) also needs to be taken into account (Ireland and the Netherlands).

(Hofman *et al.* 2008: 97–8)

Questions

1. Do you know of any private schools in your locality? If so, how can you judge whether they are private or 'truly private'?
2. How would you describe the system of private education in the Netherlands? (To help you to do this, look again at Figure 15.2.)
3. What has influenced the mix of private and state schools in your country? (To help you to do this, look again at 'A closer look: Influences on different national education systems' on p. 606.)
4. Is there a difference between parentocracy and elitism?

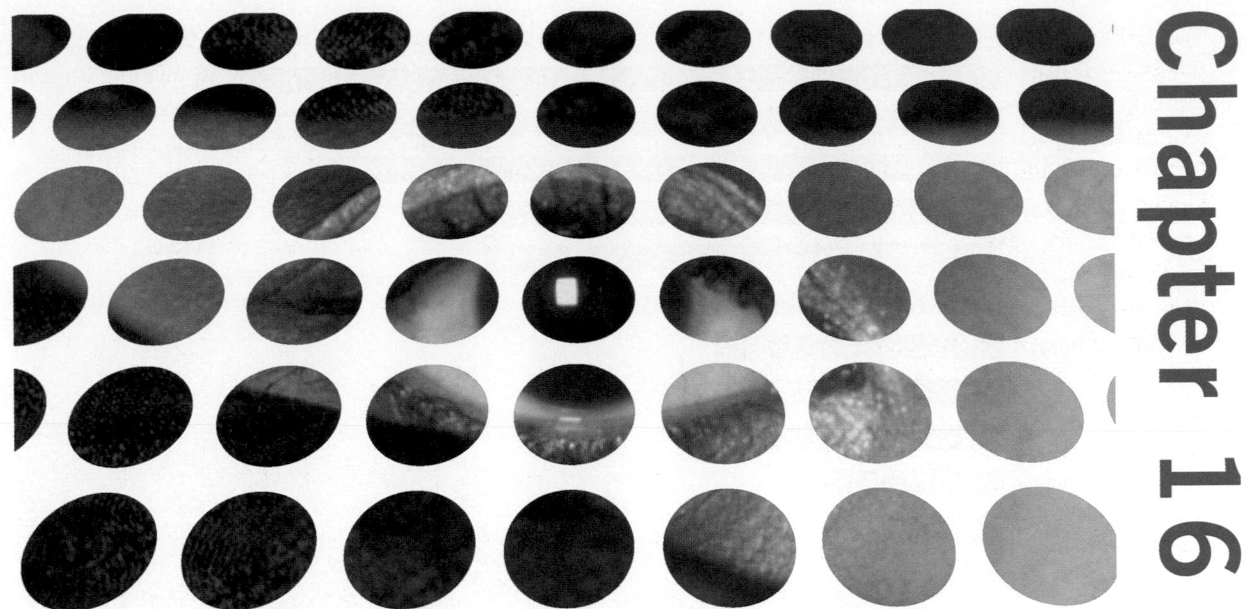

Chapter 16

Religion

Kristin Aune

Texas doomsday prophet faces bigamy charges ABC News, 6 June 2008

Publisher to suspend cartoon sales after Muslims say it insults Islam
Kyodo News Service, Japan, 22 May 2008

Russian expert tags Falun Gong as international cult
Xinhua/China Daily, 13 May 2008

Pagan prisoners allowed twigs in their cells to use as magic wands
Scotland on Sunday, 11 May 2008

Baby with two faces worshipped as reincarnation of Hindu goddess
Straits Times, USA, 8 April 2008

Key issues

- How should religion be defined and measured?
- What explanations have been given for the role of religion in society?
- How does religion affect our daily lives?
- What are the main debates about the decline and future role of religion?

Introduction

In the twenty-first century, religion frequently makes the headlines. Since the attacks of 11 September 2001, questions of religious motivations for acts of terrorism have led some to assume that religion is a cause of conflict rather than integration. Religion is involved in conflicts over territory and political rule, for example between Israelis and Palestinians, and formerly between Catholics and Protestants in Northern Ireland, over human embryo research and over the

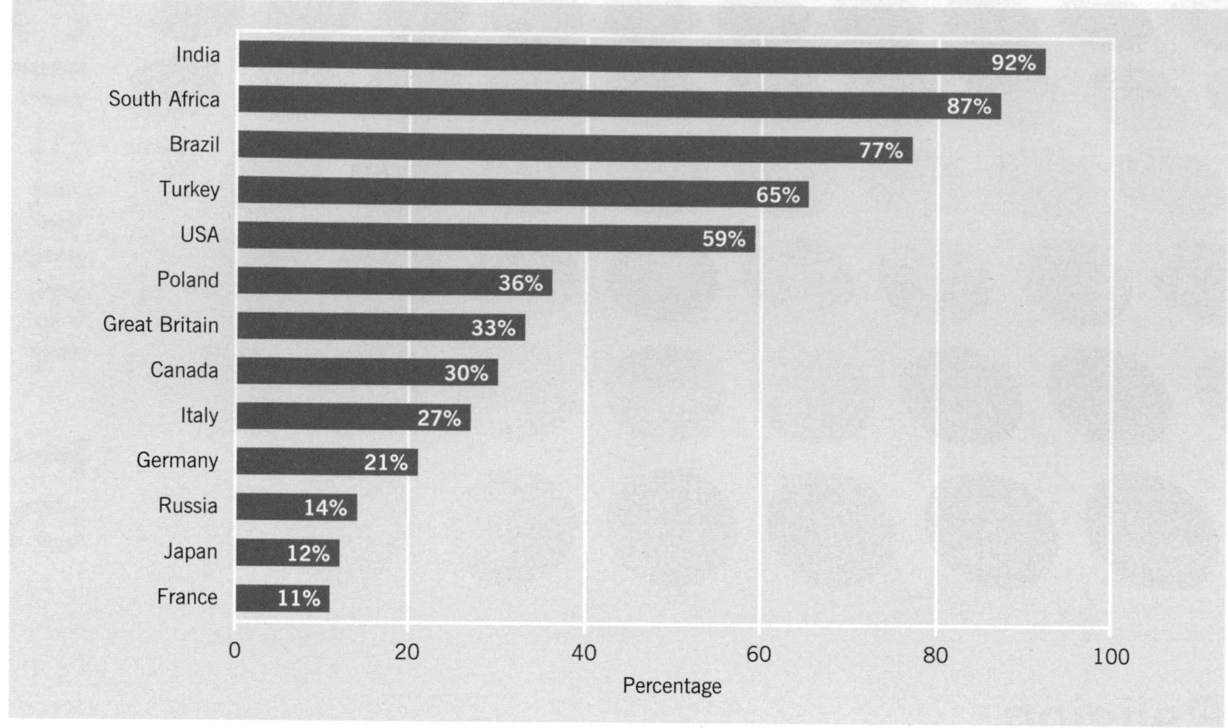

Figure 16.1 Percentage of people for whom religion is important, by country
Source: Pew Research Center 2002. Quoted in the Institute for Public Policy Research (ippr) report *Who are we? Identities in Britain, 2007*

ordination of bishops who are female or homosexual. At the same time, religion unites people. Religious ceremonies and events with religious elements – such as bar mitzvahs, weddings, funerals and singing your national anthem at the Olympics – bring people together. Religion unites people who would not otherwise meet; religion is woven into the fabric of everyday life, in places where we do not expect to find it. Many of us debate what good or harm religion does. Opinion polls about this give conflicting messages: some show that more people think religion does more good, but others see religion as a source of social division (Firth 2008).

Additionally, religion's role in the lives of individuals is important. Most religious people are so because they believe their religion is the only true one. Others may be sceptical of the idea of a single true religion, but the claim is compelling. For religious individuals, faith is therefore an imperative, not a choice. Yet the significance of religion varies by factors such as ethnicity, national identity, age and gender. In different countries, religion takes different forms and attracts different numbers and segments of the population. For example, more than nine out of ten people living in India consider religion important, compared with just over one in ten in France (Figure 16.1).

Sociology of religion is the study of religion in society. As a field within sociology, it is concerned with relations between social structure and human activity, with social order and social conflict, with human interaction, with the relationship between individuals and the collective. As sociology of religion, the fate of religion in modernity and in the shift towards postmodernity has been its chief concern (see the discussion of modernity and postmodernity on pp. 100–105). In this chapter, we will examine the role of religion in societies and the contributions made by key sociologists to advance our understanding. We will look at religion's benefits and problems, at how and why religious organizations form, grow and decline, and at the forms of religion flourishing – and faltering – today.

The development of the sociology of religion

From around the mid-eighteenth century, industrialization transformed Western European and North American societies from feudal agricultural societies to modern capitalist ones. This shift marks the development of modernity and is a chief sociological focus. Before this shift, religion was at the heart of communities and nations. The so-called 'founding fathers' of sociology were fascinated with the role that religion played in societies experiencing this transition, and the impact industrialization had on people's support for religion. They began to tell the story of *secularization* (religious decline), a (contested) story that has become sociology of religion's key concern.

During the twentieth century academic interest in religion waned, and religion became the 'Cinderella' of sociology: dazzling when examined properly, but never invited to the sociologists' ball. Inspired by secular left-wing political and equality movements such as feminism and anti-racism from the 1960s, many scholars neglected religion. But the accelerated decline in churchgoing and the rise of new religious movements from the 1960s also inspired some sociologists. Recently, fundamentalism and New Age spirituality – contrasting kinds of spirituality that have set up home in modern Western societies – have attracted attention too.

Sociology of religion is predominantly, but not exclusively, the study of religion in Western societies. It has connections to anthropology, a discipline that developed alongside sociology during the nineteenth century, when increased travel, the growing British Empire and a (somewhat voyeuristic) fascination with 'other' lands spurred scholars on to study these phenomena. Anthropology contributed a global and empirical (see Chapter 2) dimension to the study of religion. Sociology of religion also overlaps with history, theology, religious studies, psychology, geography and newer disciplines such as cultural, media and gender studies.

Religion today: back on the agenda

In the twenty-first century, religion is returning to centre stage and we – especially those of us studying sociology – can no longer ignore it. Increased migration has brought a diversity of religions to the West. Fewer people are subscribing to Christianity, and more to religions including Islam, Hinduism, Sikhism and Buddhism. The 9/11 terrorist attacks by a group linked to Al-Qaeda and the subsequent American-led invasions of Afghanistan and Iraq brought Islam into the public eye in the West, subjecting it to a new level of political, media and academic scrutiny. It has become clear that a minority of fundamentalist Muslims are reacting against the oppression of Muslims throughout the world through radical action; they also dislike the West's adherence to secular liberal, materialistic values. While the vast majority of Muslims have decried the terrorist attacks, they have nevertheless become victims of the new 'Islamophobia' of many Western non-Muslims. Media portrayals have fuelled the negative portrayal of Muslims; a study found that about two-thirds of all 'hooks' used by journalists for news reports about Islam focused on cultural differences, extremism or terrorism (Bari 2008). Many writers, most publicly the political scientist Samuel Huntingdon (1993), have advanced the idea of a Muslim-versus-Western 'clash of civilisations'; this is unhelpful and inaccurate, but it has fuelled prejudice and forced Muslims to defend themselves, creating a stronger Islamic identity while accentuating social divisions.

In the UK, 'race riots' in the spring and summer of 2001 in several northern towns fed growing government concern about the apparent failure of multiculturalism. People are not interacting with other cultural groups but are segregated in religious or ethnic enclaves, it is claimed, with Muslims in particular concentrated in areas of social deprivation. It is increasingly recognized that issues of 'ethnicity' are at least partially about religion; for example, the lower employment rates of people of Pakistani and Bangladeshi origin compared with people of Indian origin are partly attributable to religion, and Muslims (especially women) have the lowest incomes and employment rates and are most likely to face discrimination (Beckford *et al.* 2006). For the first time since 1851, the 2001 UK Census asked a question about religion. Pressure to develop the religion question came from religious groups who argued that, once people knew how many people belonged to religions other than Christianity, they would take them more seriously and provide for their needs better (Weller 2004). The Census questions were successful in doing this; and, with religious discrimination outlawed in the Employment Equality (Religion or Belief) Regulations in 2003, religion is back on the political agenda, with religious diversity education in schools, universities and workplaces extolled as a way to promote social cohesion.

What is religion?

Stop and think

➤ Without consulting any books or sources, write down your own definition of religion.

The question 'What is religion?' may seem simple to answer. However, to create a definition that serves all forms of religion equally well is not easy. The sociologist Georg Simmel (1858–1918), who, unlike Marx, Weber and Durkheim, was a person of faith, struggled with this. The passage in the box below comes from his essay 'A contribution to the sociology of religion' (1997 [1898]). It raises issues of definition that sociologists

A closer look

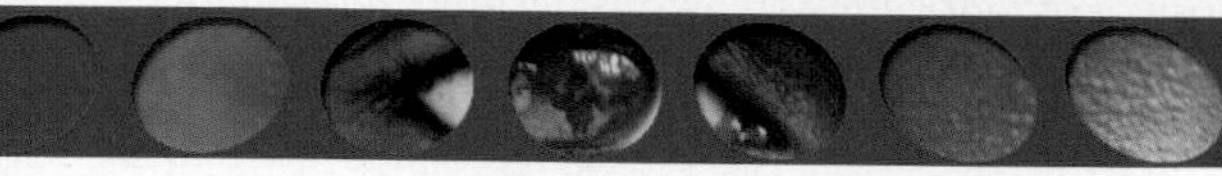

Religion is hard to define We must decide whether and how to distinguish religion from other supernatural beliefs	No light will ever be cast in the sybillic twilight that, for us, surrounds the origin and nature of religion as long as we insist on approaching it as a single problem requiring only a single word for its solution. Thus far no one has been able to offer a definition of religion that is both precise and sufficiently comprehensive. No one has been able to grasp its ultimate essence, shared by the religions of Christians and of South Sea islanders, of Buddha and Vitzliputzi. We have as yet no definition that distinguishes religion clearly from mere metaphysical speculation or from belief in ghosts. As a consequence, not even the purest and highest manifestations of religion can claim exemption from examination for the presence of such contaminations. The multiplicity of psychological motives ascribed to religion corresponds to this ill-defined conception of its nature. It does not matter whether fear or love, ancestor worship or self-deification, the moral instincts or the feeling of dependence are regarded as the root of religion; each one of these theories is entirely erroneous only when it is assumed to be the sole explanation, but is justified when it claims to point out merely one of the sources of religion.	Religion is a complex phenomenon that needs to be explained both precisely and comprehensively, so as to understand its essential characteristics
It is not the sociologist's place to say whether religion is 'true' or real	Hence the solution to the problem will depend on the following preconditions. First, all the impulses, ideas, and conditions operating in this domain must be inventoried. Then it must be determined clearly that the significance of known particular motives may not be expanded arbitrarily into general laws that supposedly govern the essence of anything religious. But this is not the only qualification that must be made in an attempt to clarify the religious significance of the phenomena of social life, which themselves are entirely unrelated to religion. In addition, we must insist that no matter how mundanely and how empirically the origin of ideas about the supramundane and the transcendent is explained, neither the subjective, emotional value of these ideas nor their objective value as matters of fact is at all in question. Both these values lie beyond the limits that our merely causal, psychological inquiry aims to reach.	We must look to see whether there are rules, or forms, that exist wherever religion is at work and that help us to recognize religion
	If we try accordingly to find the beginnings of the fundamentally religious in human relations that in themselves are not yet religion, we merely follow a method that has been accepted for some time. It has long been admitted that scholarship is merely a heightening, a reassembling, a refinement of those means of knowledge which, in lesser and dimmer degree, help us form our judgments and experiences in daily, practical life . . . Thus it may help us to achieve an insight into the origin and nature of religion if we can discover in all kinds of nonreligious relationships and intentions certain religious qualities that, as they become independent and self-sufficient, come to be 'religion.' I do not believe that religious feelings and impulses manifest themselves only in religion; rather, they are to be found in many connections, a contributing factor in various situations.	There are religious aspects, religious-like emotions generated in apparently non-religious elements of everyday life

after him tried to solve. The key points are summarized alongside the passage.

Simmel's contemporary Max Weber, one of the most renowned sociologists of religion, began his book *Sociology of Religion* (1963) with the declaration that we can venture to define religion only *after* studying it, but he never actually produced a definition himself. Instead, he seemed to use a 'common-sense' definition – that religion was what people currently recognize as religion and it may not be necessary to define it precisely in order to study it.

Not all sociologists agreed. The definitions of religion they developed fall into two camps, substantive (what religion is) and functional (what religious does). In her book *Religion: The Social Context*, Meredith McGuire (2002) distinguishes between these definitions using the example of a chair. A substantive definition of chair might be: 'a chair has four legs and a back and is often made of wood or plastic'. A substantive definition is about what the chair is, its essence. A functional definition of chair is instead about what it does: 'a chair is something that one person can sit on, somewhere you can rest, something that can be put at a table so you can work or eat a meal.'

Substantive definitions

Substantive definitions try to capture the substance or essence of religion. Belief is often emphasized. More specifically, substantive definitions often see religion as belief in something non-material, other-worldly or supernatural, often one or more deities who govern or intervene in the world.

Anthropologist Edward Tylor (1873) produced a well-known substantive definition of religion: 'belief in Spiritual Beings'. This could be one god (as in Islam or Judaism), several deities (as in Hinduism), spirits (as in Shintoism and Taoism) or deceased ancestors, revered especially by Chinese and other East Asian cultures. What united all religions, Tylor said, was belief in supernatural forces. As an anthropologist, Tylor was interested in the origin of religion, and so his concern with finding a source or essence is understandable. He believed that early humans attributed supernatural powers to inanimate objects and natural forces such as water and the sun. Gradually, these primitive beliefs evolved into polytheistic systems of many gods and, later, into monotheism (the belief in one god).

Sometimes substantive definitions specify adherence to an orthodox set of beliefs pertaining to one particular religion. Thus, a Muslim is expected to believe in the revelation to the prophet Mohammed, or a Christian to believe in the resurrection of Jesus Christ.

Functional definitions

Functional definitions concern what religion does: what function it has in society. This is about the social activity of believing more than about an essence or belief in a particular thing. For Milton Yinger (1970), religion is something that helps people cope with the ultimate questions of human life. Yinger's is a wide definition that could include systems of thought rarely considered religious. For example, if science helps an atheist to find the meaning of life, then science could be considered a religion, as could capitalism, nationalism or bereavement counselling. The anthropologist Clifford Geertz adds a symbolic element to an otherwise functional definition:

> **. . . a religion is: (1) a system of symbols which acts to (2) establish powerful, pervasive, and long-lasting moods and motivations in men by (3) formulating conceptions of a general order of existence and (4) clothing these conceptions with such an aura of factuality that the moods and motivations seem uniquely realistic.**
>
> (Geertz 1975 [1966]: 90)

Throughout this chapter we will encounter sociologists who take varying approaches to understanding religion, some using a combination of substantive and functional. We will also look at Durkheim's definition, which, although usually considered functional, in fact amalgamates both versions. There are advantages and drawbacks to substantive and functional definitions. We may want to insist that religion is more than simply a quasi-religious event like a football match where people come together to celebrate and find a sense of meaning, and that a supernatural element is involved. Yet to focus purely on subscription to spiritual doctrines without reference to religious practices is also mistaken. In Christianity beliefs tend to be uppermost, but in Judaism social practices, including eating kosher food, taking part in a Passover Seder and lighting Sabbath candles, are paramount. Thus, both functional and substantive approaches contribute welcome insights to the study of religion.

Stop and think

➤ Think back to the definition you gave of religion. Would you consider it to be more of a substantive or functional definition?

Methods for studying religion

When studying religion, sociologists use the sorts of method introduced in Chapter 3. Sometimes only one of these methods is used, but at other times they are combined.

Quantitative methods, including surveys, questionnaires, statistics and large-scale content analysis of religious publications, uncover the macro- or social structural aspects of religion. We might use these methods to investigate how many people attend religious worship or believe in a god, or how religious participation in a nation varies according to ethnicity.

Qualitative methods, including interviews, focus groups, participant observation (also known as ethnography) and small-scale content analysis of religious documents or cultural products, uncover the micro-elements, the detail about individual and group aspects of religion. Qualitative methods would be used to discern how a religious community integrates with its non-believing neighbours or negotiates family life, or how people interact in a religious online forum.

As with social research generally, ethical concerns should be taken into account. The ethics of studying religion can be complicated. For example, approaching a religious group as an outsider might make it hard for you to empathize with the spiritual beliefs of the people you study. Additionally, the religious group might be suspicious and reluctant to let you in, fearing that you might paint a negative picture in your write-up. Conversely, if you share the group's beliefs, you might be tempted to become inappropriately closely involved, and this might jeopardize the quality of your research. So, if you are studying a religious group, you should inform yourself as much as possible about the group before you begin research: Magida (1996) and Weller (2007, 2008) have written helpful guides to visiting places of worship.

Measuring religiosity

Sociologists of religion are preoccupied with discovering the significance of religion in society, especially in individuals' lives. The level of religiousness is called 'religiosity'. This is not directly measurable; it would be impossible to say, for instance, whether 'John' is 50 per cent less religious than 'Rubina'. Nevertheless, it can be useful to break religiosity down into different dimensions; some of these can then be evaluated by means of carefully constructed questions. Here is one example; another is shown in Figure 16.2.

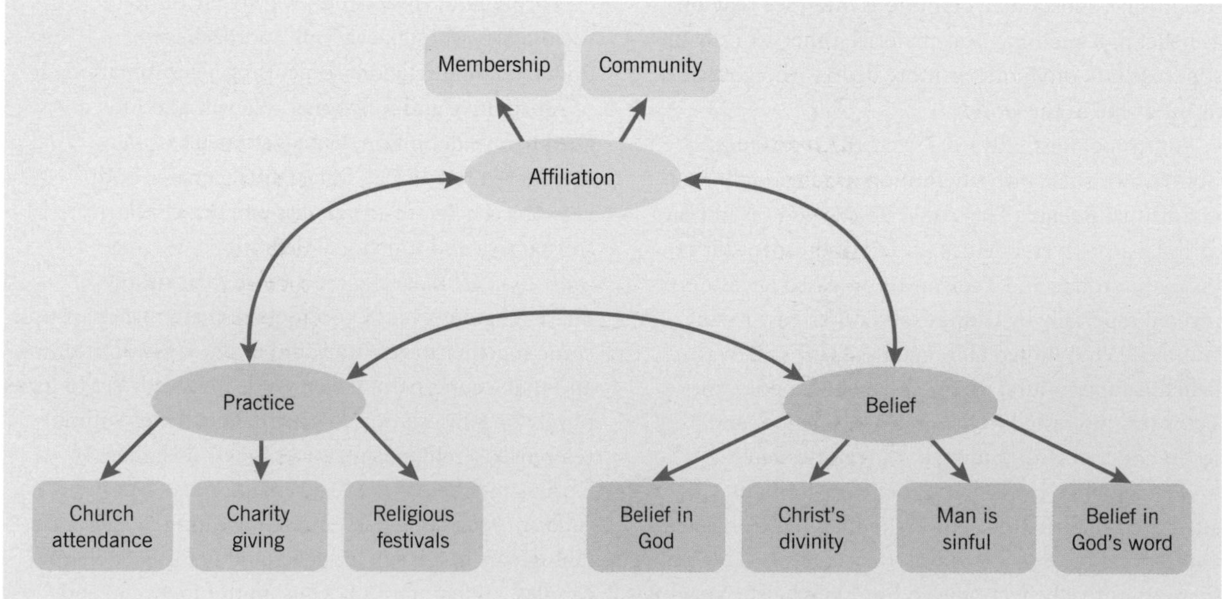

Figure 16.2 Example of measurement model for Christian religiosity dimensions
Source: From Purdam *et al.* 2007: 156

Belief – Adherence to certain doctrines.
Practice – Incorporating ritual (ceremonies and rites of passage) and devotional practices (e.g. private prayer or reading of holy texts).
Experience – Sense of connection with the divine.
Knowledge – Knowledge of religious culture, history.
Consequences – Religious actions in everyday life (e.g. giving to charity, telling the truth) (adapted from Stark and Glock 1968).

Stop and think

Imagine you are a researcher commissioned to undertake a major study of religion in the country where you live.

- Which dimensions of religion would be most important to measure?
- Which would be easiest to measure?
- Design several questions you might use to gauge people's religiosity.

Sociologists studying Islam face the question of how to classify people as Muslim. Should only those who practise the five pillars of Islam – profession of faith, prayer, fasting, pilgrimage and charity – be counted as Muslims? What about those who practise some, but not all, of these? Do you have to go to a mosque regularly in order to be a practising Muslim? If so, how should researchers approach the religiosity of Muslim women, who are often unable to attend prayers at a mosque, either because of family commitments or because not all mosques admit women? Alternatively, should Islam be conceptualized as a cultural identity rather than a currently practised faith? These issues make religion hard to measure.

Stop and think

- How might you adapt Stark and Glock (1968) and Purdam *et al.*'s (2007) models to create questions about religiosity that could be used with a Sikh, Buddhist or Hindu population?

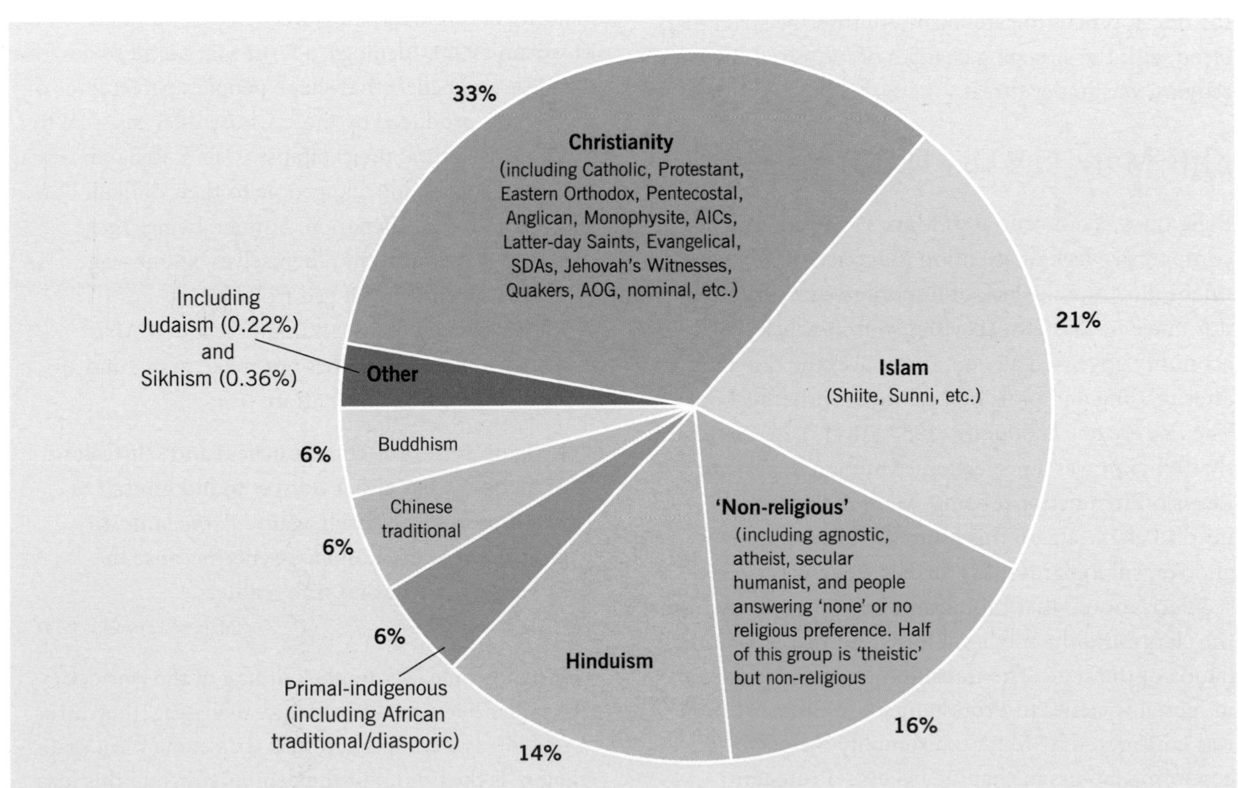

Figure 16.3 Major religions of the world
Note: Total adds up to more than 100% due to rounding and because upper bound estimates were used for each group.
Source: From www.adherents.com

The website www.adherents.com uses a functional definition of religion to produce the chart shown in Figure 16.3. The numbers 'tend towards the high end of reasonable worldwide estimates'.

Religion in classical sociology

The relationship we perceive between religion and society relates to how we understand religion. For example, if we see religion as beliefs in the supernatural that people hold privately as individuals, then religion may seem separate from society and less important. But if we see religion as the various meaningful connections, symbols or rituals around which people gather, then religion will seem to play a more integrative role. These issues emerge in the classical sociologists' theories on religion to which we will now turn. Durkheim was interested in religion's integrative role in society. Marx saw the negative side of this, believing that religion can be used to support a social structure that benefits the rich and harms the poor. For Weber, religion was not simply a servant of the economy but also could and did exert a powerful influence on social change, notably on the development of capitalism. All three believed that, faced with the sweeping changes of industrial societies, religion was under threat.

Karl Marx (1818–1883)

Religion was not central to Marx's analysis. The comparative lack of attention Marx accords religion might illustrate the lack of importance he perceived it to have in capitalist societies, within which the economy governed all else. It was also the case that, after reading and praising Ludwig Feuerbach's book *The Essence of Christianity* (1957 [1841]), his criticism that religion was a projection of human hopes and ideals on to a fictional being, Marx did not see a need to elaborate on this himself. Marx recognized – and we will look into this further when we discuss secularization – that capitalism took power away from the clergy and the medieval lords and placed it in the hands of the state. The transition from Catholicism in feudal societies to Protestantism in capitalist ones was considered by Marx to exemplify the power of economic factors in shaping beliefs – Protestant individualism emerged because it was compatible with the developing individualistic focus of capitalism (Turner 1999).

For Marx, the overarching determinant of what happens in the transition to modern capitalist societies was the economy. Pursuit of profit by business owners drove the separation of production from commerce as the feudal system of the village shifted towards the capitalist urban setting. People were divided into two classes, the owners of the means of production and the (subordinate) workers. In contrast to earlier theorists who had emphasized the importance of ideas and beliefs in determining people's behaviour, Marx believed that the economy was foremost. Religion, along with law and politics, was part of the 'superstructure', the secondary, subordinate level to the productive 'base' of society. Those with economic power could determine the beliefs, thoughts and cultural values that were emphasized and adopted. Those with money could influence the perceptions of others in a way that made their ideas seem like common sense; thus the middle classes lauded 'equality', 'freedom' and individuals' rights to seek material gain as core values, despite the fact that the material conditions of capitalism (the exploitation of the workers' undervalued labour by the owners of the means of production in pursuit of profit) made the majority of population less free (Marx and Engels 1947; Morrison 1995). Ideology, a term Marx used to describe the ideas and beliefs that shape people's perceptions of reality, was produced by those whose interests were to promote as natural the capitalist system. Religion was a form of ideology, inuring people to their difficult lives, and was a kind of alienation. Human beings make society, but they also find themselves, at one stage or another, feeling estranged from it.

Marx saw religion as a human creation ('*Man makes religion*, religion does not make man') and an expression of human alienation:

> **Religion is the self-consciousness and self-feeling of man who has either not yet found himself or has already lost himself again . . . *the fantastic realization* of the human essence because the *human essence* has no true reality.**
>
> (Marx and Engels 1955: 41–2)

When people lack understanding of the world, or when their lives are difficult and alienating, they turn to religion as a compensator. Marx's contention that religion 'is the opium of the people' sums up this idea well. For him, religion dulls people's senses so they cannot see clearly their own oppression. His most famous statement on religion is this:

> ***Religious* distress is at the same time the *expression* of real distress and the *protest* against real distress. Religion is the sigh of the oppressed creature, the heart of a heartless world, just as it is the spirit of a spiritless situation. It is the *opium* of the people.**
>
> **The abolition of religion as the *illusory* happiness of the people is required for their *real* happiness. The demand to give up the illusions about its condition is the *demand to give up a condition which needs illusions.* The criticism of religion is therefore *in embryo the criticism of the vale of woe*, the *halo* of which is religion.**
>
> (Marx and Engels 1955: 41–2)

Marx believed that religion would disappear when people came to understand their true situation. In the passage above, however, there is evidence that religion is not simply a compensator but also a form of protest, both for Marx and even more for later Marxist theorists such as Antonio Gramsci and Louis Althusser, who gave increased credit to the role of non-economic factors (culture, education, the family, politics, religion) in shaping social life. In other words, religion can inoculate us against oppression, but it also carries the seeds of vivification and resistance. Many people in industrial and post-industrial societies are familiar with the idea of religion as the opium of the people. But this latter sense – religion as people's grasping for a better life – has been acquisitioned by Marxist-inspired movements such as the Liberation Theology of the Christian base communities in Latin America (Gutiérrez 1973).

Max Weber (1864–1920)

Weber wrote much on religion and planned to write more; his volumes on Islam and early Christianity, among others, were never completed. Even so, his works advance no single definitive theory of religion, but instead several interlinked themes and arguments surface in different texts. There is not sufficient room to cover even the major ideas here (for an introduction to them, see Whimster (2007), Chapters 3 and 6), so instead we will focus on the relationship between religion and the economy and the evolution of authority in religious organizations. We will consider Weber's work on religious sects later.

We will begin with the relationship between religion, economy and society. Marx argued that the economy governs religion, shaping people's beliefs and values. Weber did not disagree, but he also contended that religion can powerfully influence the economic realm. Evidence for this came from his study of modern capitalism. His famous study *The Protestant Ethic and the Spirit of Modern Capitalism* (1930 [1904–05]) advanced the case that Protestantism was influential (though not the sole factor) in the establishment of capitalism in Western societies. Capitalism, Weber argued, was distinctive in its pursuit of profit through rational means. The capitalist sought profit not for self-advancement or to enable frivolous spending but 'as a calling toward which the individual feels himself to have an ethical obligation' (Weber 1930 [1904–05], cited in Thompson and Tunstall 1971: 410) and as part of an ordered life.

The shift to a modern society incorporated the changeover from Catholicism to Protestantism, setting up a battle between established church and sects that has rumbled on ever since. During the Reformation, the Protestants argued that salvation would be gained not through effort but through faith. Although only faith in the grace of God led to salvation, hard work was also, in Calvinist theology, considered part of the evidence of salvation. Through hard work, the Calvinist can, as Weber puts it, create the conviction of his own salvation. The Protestants dismantled the religious elites of the monasteries, convents and priesthood, saying that all believers were called to a holy life and that earthly work was a vocation too. Luther, the European Calvinists and the later Puritans in North America and Europe considered hard work sacred. Work was not about acquiring money to consume: frivolity was rejected in favour of frugality and investment in enterprises and honest labour. The Protestant entrepreneurs were particularly successful at this, since answering to God made them reliable trading partners. Thus, the concept of 'rational conduct on the basis of the idea of calling' (Weber 1930 [1904–05], cited in Thompson and Tunstall 1971: 413), which percolated through the developing capitalist society, had its origin in Christian asceticism.

Weber's original thesis related especially to Europe, but he later argued, in the essay 'The Protestant sects and the spirit of capitalism' (Weber 1948a [1922–3]) that, based on his observations in the USA, involvement in Protestant sects seemed crucial for a person's success in business. Joining a sect is a voluntary process, whereby congregation members recognize the religious standing of the person before God and his or her moral standing before others. The person's conduct at work provides evidence of his or her religious uprightness.

Acceptance as a member gave the person access to a wide range of business contacts and opportunities; these enabled him or her to achieve, and contribute towards, the advancement of bourgeois individualism. (Here, Weber's focus on the making of successful middle-class individualism contrasts with Marx's concern with the fate of the working classes who were exploited within the same economic system.) What happens in sects is symptomatic of the secularization that Weber believed all religious manifestations experience: that religious impulses are squeezed out by rationalization. Rationalization is a concept that runs through Weber's writings and refers to 'the process by which nature, society and individual action are increasingly mastered by an orientation to planning, technical procedure and rational action' (Morrison 1995: 218). We will return to rationalization, and its role in secularization and contemporary religion, later in this chapter.

Stop and think

- Is the Protestant ethic still visible in today's consumer society?

Weber was not simply interested in Western capitalist societies. He was interested in the world religions, and in why capitalism succeeded in the West where it had not in the East. This, he concluded, was because the approach of Western Protestantism was conducive to capitalism, whereas the Eastern religious outlook was not. India, which Weber discusses in volume 2 of his *Sociology of Religion* (1963 [1920]) and in *The Religion of India* (1958a), provides a contrasting example of the way religion shapes societies and economies. For Weber, just as Protestantism was a powerful influence on the success of capitalism, so the establishment of the Hindu religion in India was a key impediment to capitalism despite evidence of some of the similar conditions out of which capitalism emerged. This is because of the caste system. Established gradually as Hinduism developed in the conducive economic conditions of ancient India, the tribal system was supplanted by the caste system. While this brought changes in some people's social status, it solidified – and sanctified – the existing inequalities in a manner that had (and still has) far-reaching consequences, especially for those at the bottom of the caste system. Here there are echoes of Marx's belief that religion sanctifies social inequality. For example, the lowest-status transient 'guest workers', a Gypsy group who moved from place to place undertaking menial labour, became the 'pariah people' as Hindu ritualism, led by the highest-status Brahmin (priest caste), marked them as 'unclean'. Regulations prohibiting intermarriage between those of different castes (with some exceptions – a man could marry a woman of a lower caste than himself, but a woman could not, and this led to dowry practices that still exist today) kept the caste system in check. The Hindu doctrine of *karma* legitimated the caste system by promising rebirth to a higher position in a future life for those who kept to the sphere of work set by their birth. Weber comments:

> **A ritual law in which every change of occupation, every change in work technique, may result in ritual degradation is certainly not adapted to giving birth to economic and technical revolutions, or even to facilitating the first germination of capitalism in its midst . . .**
>
> **The doctrine of Hindu salvation promises rebirth as a king, noble, and so on (according to his present rank) to the artisan who in his work follows traditional prescriptions and never overcharges or deceives about the quality . . . The neglect of one's caste duties, prompted by high aspirations, unfailingly brings harm in the present or future life.**
>
> **It is difficult to imagine a more traditionalistic conception of professional virtues than those of Hinduism. The castes might face one another with bitter hatred . . . However, so long as the karma doctrine remained unshaken, revolutionary ideas of progressivism were inconceivable, particularly as the lowest castes had most to gain through ritual correctness and were therefore least inclined towards innovation.**
>
> **It was impossible to shatter this traditionalism, based on ritualism and anchored in the karma doctrine, and to rationalise the economy.**
>
> (Weber 1983 [1923]: 107–8)

Weber also examined Confucianism and Judaism, noting that these religions presented obstacles to the adoption of capitalism. Hence, religion is one important force that influences the economic ethic – and thus the economic behaviour – of human populations (Weber 1948b [1922–3]).

Another Weberian concept frequently used to understand the evolution of religious groups and the entrance of rationalization into the social and religious sphere is that of charisma; his typology of the bases of authority is connected to this. Weber identified that, within religion, individuals emerge who stand out as unusually religious, as possessors of the sacred values that are cherished most highly within a religious group; these include monks, shamans, sorcerers and ascetics. Established religious organizations often resent them, since they disrupt the traditions and organizational routines. Their impact on societies varies. As holders of *charismatic authority*, leaders of religious (and other) groups can exert significant influence because 'the governed submit because of their belief in the extraordinary quality of the specific *person*' (Weber 1948b [1922–3]: 295). These extraordinary qualities are revealed and confirmed via miracles, revelations and other kinds of magic. Charismatic authority is unstable, since it has to be reconfirmed through further miraculous instances, and it contrasts with *traditional authority*. Traditional authority is based on tradition, often on patriarchalism (the rule of the fathers). The difference between them, in essence, is that the former requires 'belief in the sanctity or the value of the extraordinary' while the latter requires 'belief in the sanctity of everyday routines' (Weber 1948b [1922–3]: 297). In both cases, once the possessor of the authority dies, authority becomes 'routinized'. A new leader may be chosen, perhaps based on inheritance or on election. By that time, a staff of officials and various bureaucratic systems will often have developed around the leader, which eases a transition towards what Weber calls '*legal* or *bureaucratic authority*'. Here,

> **submission . . . is based upon an *impersonal* bond to the generally defined and functional 'duty of office'. The official duty – like the corresponding right to exercise authority: the 'jurisdictional competency' – is fixed by *rationally established* norms, by enactments, decrees, and regulations.**
>
> (Weber 1948b [1922–3]: 299)

Weber's concept of charismatic authority is still applicable to religious groups today, especially to new religious movements.

Emile Durkheim (1858–1917)

Durkheim was a French sociologist whose approach contrasted with Marx's and Weber's. To understand Durkheim's view of religion, we need to grasp Durkheim's basic sociological principles. Marx saw the economy as the guiding factor in society; Weber seemed to conceive of society as a set of interlinked spheres, all of which were influential. In asserting the importance of the material, Durkheim would have agreed with Marx. Durkheim contended that the 'substratum' (the base of society) provoked changes at the level of 'institutions' and groups (the 'normative sphere'), which in turn influenced 'collective representations' (the 'symbolic sphere', or ideas and beliefs). This approach was broadly structuralist. Where religion was concerned, he emphasized the power of the social structure or collective in shaping religious practices and beliefs. Yet this was not a one-way process, as Durkheim (especially in his later writings) believed that beliefs (including religious ones) could influence wider structural aspects.

Durkheim's key work on religion is *The Elementary Forms of the Religious Life* (1976 [1912]). He was not particularly interested in finding the origin of religion. However, he believed in looking to primitive societies to understand how the elementary ideas at the root of religion function. He believed that, while religion is not a causal factor in producing societies, nevertheless religion has existed in virtually all human societies.

His key argument is that 'religion is an eminently social thing' (Durkheim 1995 [1912]: 9). Durkheim was not a religious believer and did not accept the substantive definitions of religion as belief in the supernatural or a higher power. This does not mean, however, that he thought religion 'false' or rejected it as socially useful. Religions, as systems that incorporate both beliefs and rites, play a vital part in social life because they are 'grounded in and express the real', Durkheim (1995 [1912]: 2) argued. Moreover, religions bind people together.

Durkheim had given an example of the collective usefulness of religion in his 1897 study *Suicide* (1952 [1897]). There, he demonstrated that suicide could not be explained through individual factors such as the reasons recorded on a suicide note or death certificate. For Durkheim, the social environment should be examined in order to explain the variations in suicide rates by things such as nation, location, family situation, occupation and religion. Examining suicide rates in Europe, Durkheim found that suicide rates among Protestants were significantly higher than among Catholics, despite the fact that both religions prohibited suicide. He concluded that the difference was that Protestants exhibited a greater degree of individualism. What kept Catholics from suicide was their strong group ties, their collective life. Extending his investigation to the family and the political life of individuals, Durkheim concluded that suicide is rarer where there is close religious integration, family integration and political integration. In other words, close community ties prevent (though not entirely) suicide. Religion also prevents against suicide by giving people a reason for living and wards off the 'anomie' or alienation that causes suicide in modern societies.

In *The Elementary Forms*, Durkheim notes that religions commonly distinguish between two categories, sacred and profane; this is the key identifying feature of religion. Durkheim explains:

> **. . . the real characteristic of religious phenomena is that they always suppose a bipartite division of the whole universe, known and knowable, into two classes which embrace all that exists, but which radically exclude each other. Sacred things are those which the interdictions protect and isolate; profane things, those to which these interdictions are applied and which must remain at a distance from the first. Religious beliefs are the representations which express the nature of sacred things and the relations which they sustain, either with each other or with profane things. Finally, rites are the rules of conduct which prescribe how a man should comport himself in the presence of these sacred objects.**
>
> (Durkheim [1912] in Thompson 1985: 120)

This division into sacred and profane influenced anthropologists, including Claude Levi-Strauss and Mary Douglas.

Religion is unlike magic because it binds together its adherents into a group who share a faith and life. Thus, if religion's first distinctive characteristic is its sacred/profane division then its second is that it is collective, not individual. Bringing these together into a single definition, Durkheim proposed:

> **A religion is a unified system of beliefs and practices relative to sacred things, that is to say, things set apart and forbidden – beliefs and practices which unite into one single moral community called a Church, all those who adhere to them.**
>
> (Durkheim 1995 [1912]: 44)

Durkheim may have used the term 'church', but he intended his definition to apply beyond Christianity. In fact, the example he uses throughout *The Elementary Forms of the Religious Life* derives not from Christianity but from Australian tribal (Aboriginal) religion.

Helped by the other anthropological studies of Australian tribal life, Durkheim observed the Australian tribal peoples behaving in a particular way in reference to a totem, a representation of a plant or animal that is considered sacred. The totem, he explains, is not significant in its own right, since it is just an object; it is 'before all a symbol, a material expression of something else'. First, it is the outward form of something considered divine or supremely important, 'the totemic principle or god' (cited in Thompson 1985: 121). Second, it is the symbol of the clan or society, their mark of identity. But are not the two connected, he wondered? He went on to reason:

> **So if it is at once the symbol of the god and one of the society, is that not because the god and the society are only one? How could the emblem of the group have been able to become the figure of this quasi-divinity, if the group and the divinity were two distinct realities? The god of the clan, the totemic principle, can therefore be nothing else than the clan itself, personified and represented to the imagination under the visible form of the animal or vegetable which serves as totem.**
>
> (Durkheim, cited in Thompson 1985: 122)

So, the symbols that these tribes use, and that are used today – flags at national parades, for example, or the pentagrams popular with teenagers involved in the heavy-metal subculture – are not intrinsically sacred; they are sacred only because members of their society accord sacredness to them.

A significant question remains: since religion can be argued to be a creation of society, then why does society feel it needs religion? Durkheim reasoned that, by asserting the existence of religion, societies are reacting to the frustration they feel because of social pressures. Living in a community structured by law and regulation, people are used to deferring to authority figures (leaders or monarchs, for instance). It is easy, therefore, to assume that a higher force lies behind these power structures. Being 'acted upon', people 'must invent by themselves the idea of these power with which they feel themselves in connection' (Durkheim, cited in Thompson 1985: 123), and this generates the religious representations that people then and now were familiar with. The sense of spiritual power that comes from acting together with others is socially constructed; but this does not mean it is worthless, and Durkheim recognized that those who come together, believing themselves to be acting out of religious motivations, are capable of great things, as a collective 'effervescence' inspires them to action (Durkheim, cited in Thompson 1985: 123–4, 128). Expressions of religion are also visible in the way that people revere and almost deify selected people (perhaps monarchs, political leaders or, today, actors and respected celebrity figures). Ideas and philosophies are similarly exalted and worshipped. Religion is also an expression of our hopes and ideals, which are realized only imperfectly in the societies we live in. In explaining forces of evil as well as good, religion is also capable of including in its 'mythologies', and explaining, our negative traits.

Overall, for Durkheim, however inspiring and socially useful it is, religion derives only from society's own thoughts and ideals. Yet it is not necessarily desirable to rid ourselves of religion, and this is likely to be impossible, since, as he puts it:

> **there is something eternal in religion which is destined to outlive the succession of particular symbols in which religious thought has clothed itself. There can be no society that does not experience the need at regular intervals to maintain and strengthen the collective feelings and ideas that provide its coherence and its distinct individuality.**
>
> (Durkheim 1995 [1912]: 429)

Whether particular gods, totems or religious representations held at the current time by particular societies change, religion will live on. Religion seems, he writes, 'destined to transform itself rather than disappear' (Durkheim 1995 [1912]: 432).

Stop and think

Durkheim believed that religion is present not only in the traditional or recognized world religions, but also in the veneration of people, ideas or objects in societies. Examples of this might include football teams or political leaders.

➤ What other examples can you think of?

Classical sociology's legacy for the sociology of religion

Much more could be said about these classical sociologists, but, as regards their legacy for the sociology of religion, their writings raise two major issues that have occupied sociology of religion ever since. The first concerns the question of secularization in modern societies. The second concerns religious organizations, both new and old: how they evolve and are structured, why people join them, and the relationship between religious organizations and wider society. In the following sections, we will look at these in turn.

Secularization

Coined by Weber, the term 'secularization' began to be explored in detail by sociologists of religion from the late 1950s. By using the term, Weber was referring to the dual processes of 'rationalization' and 'disenchantment'. We have discussed rationalization briefly already, but, to recap, modernizing societies where capitalism was advancing came to rely increasingly on reason and calculation as the chief source of knowledge and inspiration. In the process, anything irrational or 'other-worldly' was pushed to one side. Mystery, religion and the supernatural were considered conquerable through reason. Relegated to lower status, religion began to lose its influence.

By early 1970s secularization was, as Swatos and Christiano (2000: 1) put it, the 'reigning dogma in the field'. From the mid-1980s, the idea of secularization (at least in its simplest form) has been challenged. For example, in an influential address to the Southern Sociological Society in the USA in 1986, its president Jeffrey Hadden argued that the theory was problematic because it was based on shaky logic, was unsupported by data and ignored the rise of new forms of religion. Accepted 'in faith' by many social scientists, it had become more a doctrine than a theory (Hadden 1987).

For example, if modernization leads inevitably to secularization, then why are Americans, who live in an advanced modern society, so religious? If people are becoming less religious, then how do we account for the growth of new religious movements and the New Age movement in the later twentieth century? And even if fewer people are engaging in traditional religious behaviour such as going to church, then how do we explain the increasing presence of religion in the public realm – in legislation, education, health and welfare services and political debate? Today, many sociologists accept some aspects of the secularization argument: religious institutions, affiliation and, perhaps, beliefs have declined in certain ways. But they believe the situation is complex, that religion and spirituality are here – at least in some form – to stay, and that there are also signs of societies becoming more religious. We will look at a case study of religion in the UK shortly to test out these ideas, but it is important to examine in more detail what sociologists mean by secularization.

Bryan Wilson's definition of secularization is still paramount. Wilson (1966: xiv) defined secularization as 'the process whereby religious thinking, practices and institutions lose social significance'. For Wilson secularization meant the decline of religious *thinking*, religious *practices* and religious *institutions*. Religion has lost its grip on our thinking. We are engaging less in religious practices such as attending places of worship, giving money to religious organizations or praying. Religious organizations have a reduced role in society. In the transition to industrial capitalism, the state took over many of the Church's functions, notably law, education, welfare, housing and health. In different countries, varying degrees of separation between religion and state exist (Table 16.1). In the USA, France and Turkey, Church and state are clearly separate, but even within this there are variations: the US government cannot make alliances with religion or provide religions with financial aid, but it does protect

Table 16.1 Changes in Church–state relations, Europe, 1980–2000

	Religious	Secular	Atheistic
State propagates Christianity	Vatican*		
Massive state subsidies to churches	Monaco, Belgium, Denmark, Finland, Greece, Iceland, Liechtenstein, Luxembourg, Norway, Spain, Switzerland, [Sweden] → *Federal Republic of Germany*	Austria Sweden	
Limited state subsidies to churches	Andorra Portugal, Britain, Italy, Malta, **Armenia** **Poland**	San Marino Netherlands **Russia** **Hungary** **Romania**	
State subsidies only to schools, hospitals, etc.		France	
Complete state non-interference	Ireland, **Macedonia**} **Croatia**} **Slovenia**} **Ukraine, Moldova,** **Georgia**	**Germany**, **Estonia**} **Lithuania**} **Slovakia** **Czech Republic**	
Limited political restrictions		**Latvia**	**Yugoslavia**
Minorities discriminated against	**Bulgaria**	**Albania**	*German Democratic Republic* **[<1991]**
State interference and obstruction	Cyprus, **Belarus** **Bosnia**	Turkey	**Bulgaria,** **Hungary,** **Poland,** **Romania**
State hostility and prohibition	**Azerbaijan**		*Czechoslovakia* *USSR*
State suppression or eradication			**Albania 1967–91**
Totals (2000)	**30**	**17**	**1**

Note: Bold type indicates countries that have changed their classification. Italics indicates states that have ceased to exist since 1980.
(Source: Madeley 2003)

its citizens' religious freedom; France's and Turkey's secularist states also place restrictions on public expression of religion. In contrast, in England and Norway, the monarch acts as governor of the Church and the national Church retains some privileges. Notwithstanding these differences, a considerable degree of separation between Church and state is a mark of the secularization that has impacted on industrial and post-industrial capitalist societies. In the process, religion is relegated to the private realm of society. Even though some people continue to attend church and some consider religion central to their personal and family lives, most view it as a kind of spare-time, leisure activity.

If it is a leisure activity, then religion has become a personal choice. This is what the prominent American sociologist Peter Berger (1973) calls the *individualization* or *privatization* of religion. For us to be able to choose, we need several options, and here religious *pluralism* (different groups following different religions) becomes an issue. As we will explore shortly, religious pluralism is now an important feature of the religious landscape of Western countries.

We might think of secularization as happening on three levels. Chaves (see Roberts 2004) and Dobbelaere (2002) both produced versions of this argument. We can imagine these levels as beginning with the *individual* and moving out towards the *organizational* and then to the *societal* level. At the individual level, secularization means that we make our own decisions free from pressure from religious authority figures, that we practise religion less and believe in it less. At the organizational level, rational principles and bureaucratic structures govern institutions such as schools, universities, hospitals and workplaces, without reference to religious inspiration or sacred texts and traditions. Finally, at a societal level, religion loses its connection to the state, as political debates and decisions make little or no reference to religion. Whether individual or societal aspects of secularization are uppermost is debated.

Secularization does not have to involve the entire disappearance of religion, but it does involve religion's decline and dilution. As Steve Bruce, another important secularization theorist, argues:

> **My explanation of the decline of the popularity and importance of religion in the modern world does not suppose that patently false superstitions will be replaced by patently obvious truth as people become better educated or that modern people will become self-consciously committed to an atheistic and materialistic view of themselves and the universe. We have not all become committed rationalists; rather, in the phrase popularized by Weber, most of us have become religiously 'unmusical'. Like the truly tone-deaf, we know about music, we know that many people feel strongly about it, we might even be persuaded that, in some social sense, it is a good thing, but still it means nothing to us.**
>
> **Belief in the supernatural has not disappeared. Rather the forms in which it is expressed have become so idiosyncratic and so diffuse that there are few specific social consequences. Instead of religiosity expressing itself in new sects with enthusiastic believers, it is expressed through piecemeal and consumerist involvement in elements of a cultic world. To pursue Weber's music metaphor, the orchestras and mass bands with their thunderous symphonies have gone. Handfuls of us will be enthusiastic music-makers but, because we no longer follow one score, we cannot produce the melodies to rouse the masses.**
>
> (Bruce 1996: 234)

Stop and think

Take one of Bruce's concepts from Figure 16.4 overleaf and do some independent research about it. Find out what the term means and how it contributed to secularization. This could be done as a group exercise, with each member of the group tasked with researching one concept.

The UK: losing its religion?

How do these ideas about secularization work in practice? In this section, we will examine the UK as a case study. Britain has a long Christian heritage, but is it becoming less religious? Has there been a growth in non-Christian religious and spiritual beliefs? How relevant is the secularization thesis to the UK, and what other explanations could be given to help us understand its religious climate?

In the past decade, religion has become increasingly evident in public debate in the UK. It has re-emerged in politics: Tony Blair, prime minister from 1997 to 2007, said that religion influenced him and his political decisions, such as his decision to go to war in Iraq. Legislation against discrimination on the grounds of religion has been passed, notably the Employment Equality (Religion or Belief) Regulations 2003 and

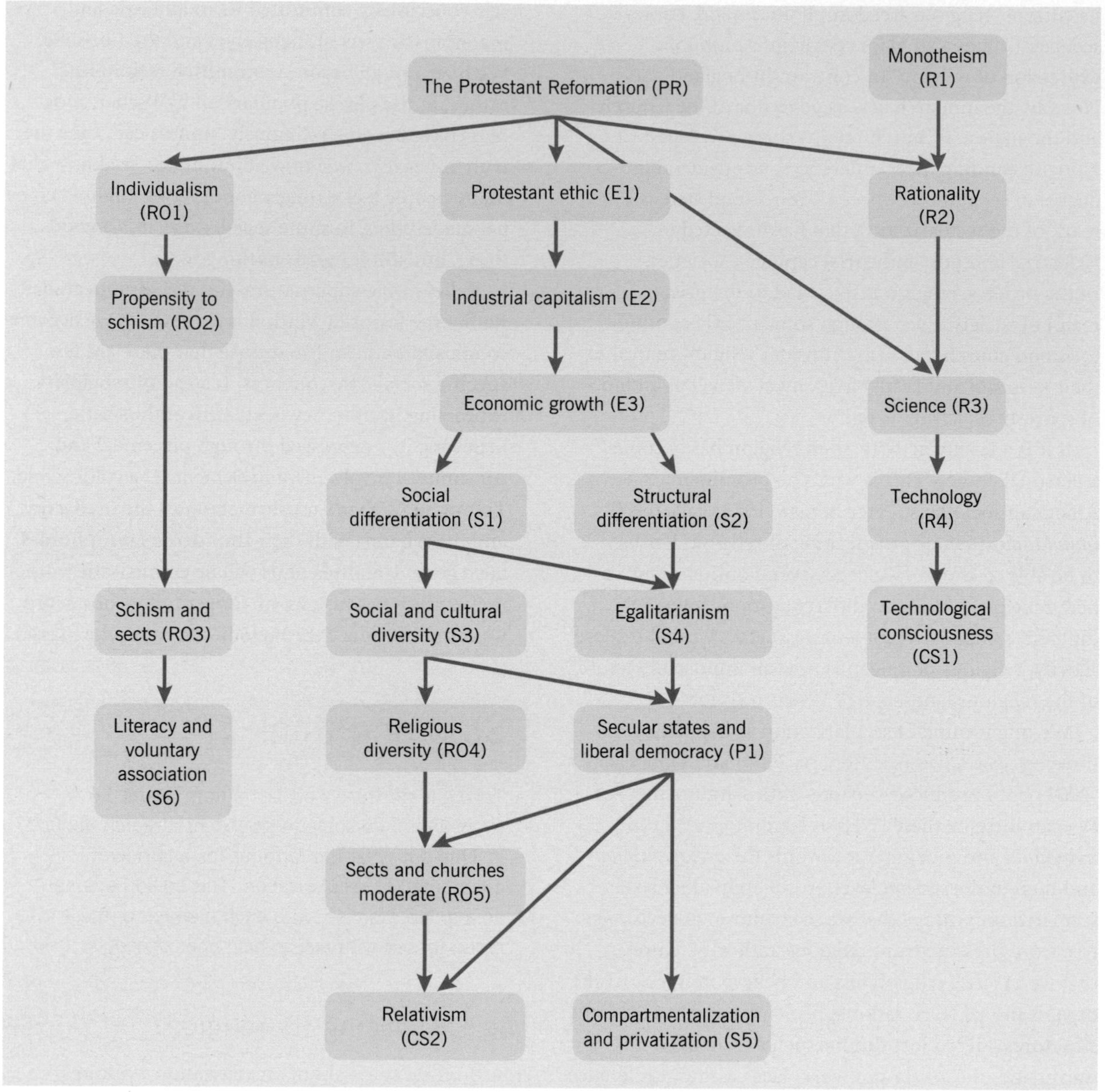

Figure 16.4 The secularization paradigm
CS, cognitive style; E, economy; P, policy; R, rationalization; RO, religious organization; S, society.
Source: Bruce 2002: 4

the Religious and Racial Hatred Act 2006–7, and the government is giving more opportunities to faith-based organizations to provide welfare, social care and education. Religion has re-emerged in the media through debates about the radicalization of young Muslims and the wearing of religious symbols in the workplace. If one aspect of secularization is the removal of religion from the public realm, then its re-emergence in the public realm is a sign of de-secularization (Casanova 1994). In the late 1960s Berger believed that privatization and rationalization were signalling secularization, but by the late 1990s he had changed his mind. Now it seems that these processes are reversing: societies are becoming re-enchanted as religion experiences resurgence. Evangelical Christianity in Latin America and China, and Buddhism in Taiwan, are key examples (Berger 1999). Western Europe has not seen these levels of religious revival, yet nevertheless it is '*differently* religious' (Davie 1999: 65) rather than less religious: religion is more evident in the public sphere and is attracting individuals who, dissatisfied with consumerism, are searching for spiritual meaning (Polak 2006).

As we have discussed, the methods and definitions of religion that we use will affect the answers we get to the question 'How religious is the UK?' We will examine answers produced through quantitative methods and qualitative methods.

Quantitative data

Quantitative data are produced by large-scale surveys and questionnaires, often repeated over time so that trends can be discovered. Key examples of quantitative data on religion include the Census, the European Values Surveys and the English and Scottish Church Censuses.

The 2001 England and Wales Census asked 'What is your religion?', inviting people to tick a box corresponding to the major religions in the UK, 'No religion' and 'Any other religion, *please write in*'. The Scottish and Northern Ireland Censuses phrased the question differently, as 'What religion, religious denomination or body do you belong to?' (Scotland) and 'Do you regard yourself as belonging to any particular religion?' (Northern Ireland), with a follow-up question for those who gave a religion, religious denomination or body. The cumulative UK results in Table 16.2 are not exactly comparable because of the different ways in which the question was formulated, but they do give an indication of general trends (Weller 2004).

On the face of it, the UK looks like a very religious place, with most of its population Christian. If this is true, then it would contradict the secularization thesis. But we should observe also that the way the question ('What is your religion?') was asked assumes that respondents have a religion in the first place and thus directs them to tick one of the given religions. Moreover, enabling people to identify themselves as having a religion, whether or not they attend a place of worship, pray or believe in God, makes it likely that a substantial number will identify themselves as belonging to a religion. Voas and Bruce, two sociologists who argue that secularization is occurring in the UK, were intrigued by why this figure was higher than in other recent surveys, and higher in England and Wales than in Scotland (65%), where a greater proportion of people attend church. They concluded that the figure was high partly because of the way the question was asked and the data collected. But most importantly, it points to a desire among people in England and Wales to assert their national identity at a time when public debates abounded about immigration and the politicization of Islam. As one woman remarked to them, 'I put down C of E because I wanted to say that this is a Christian country' (Voas and Bruce 2004: 26).

There are other surveys that, by asking about religion differently, produce data that suggest lower levels of religiosity. In 1981, 1990 and 1999, the European Values Survey asked people in nine European countries about their views about religion (Table 16.3).

Most countries show a declining commitment to religion. In the UK, belonging to a religious denomination dropped from 85 per cent to 82 per cent and church attendance at least monthly dropped from 25 per cent to 19 per cent. Thirty-three per cent thought

Table 16.2 Responses to religion questions in the UK

Religion	England	Scotland	Wales	Northern Ireland	UK (total)	UK (%)
Buddhist	139,046	6830	5407	533	151,816	0.3%
Christian	35,251,244	3,294,545	2,087,242	1,446,386	42,079,417	71.6%
Hindu	546,982	5564	5439	825	558,810	1.0%
Jewish	257,671	6448	2256	365	266,740	0.5%
Muslim	1,524,887	42,557	21,739	1943	1,591,126	2.7%
Sikh	327,343	6572	2015	219	336,149	0.6%
Other religion	143,811	26,974	6909	1143	178,837	0.3%
Total	**38,190,984**	**3,389,490**	**2,131,007**	**1,451,414**	**45,162,895**	**76.8%**
No religion	7,171,332	1,394,460	537,935	*	9,103,727	15.5%
Not stated	3,776,515	278,061	234,143	*	4,288,719	7.3%
No religion/not stated total	**10,947,847**	**1,672,521**	**772,078**	**233,853**	**13,626,299**	**23.2%**
Grand totals	**49,138,831**	**5,062,011**	**2,903,085**	**1,685,267**	**58,789,194**	**100.00%**

*Separate statistics for those answering 'no religion' and those 'not stated' are not available for Northern Ireland.
(Source: Weller 2004: 4)

Table 16.3 Religious evolution of European countries from 1981 (or 1990) to 1999

	Ireland*		Italy*		Portugal		Spain*		Austria		Belgium*		France*		West Germany*		Netherlands*		Great Britain*		Denmark*		Sweden		Nine countries*	
	81	99	81	99	90	99	81	99	90	99	81	99	81	99	81	99	81	99	81	99	81	99	81	99	81	99
Belong to a religious denomination	98	90	93	82	82	88	91	82	85	87	74	63	73	57	90	82	59	46	85	82	94	88	93	76	85	75
– Catholic	95	87	93	81	70	85	90	81		79	70	55	70	53	40	36	30	24	11	13	1	1	1	2	55	49
– Protestant	2	2	0	0	0	0	0	0		6	2	3	1	2	50	42	25	17	74	51	92	87	90	70	29	22
Church attendance: ≥ once a month	85	67	50	53	41	51	54	36	44	42	36	28	18	12	37	32	39	26	25	19	7	12	13	9	36	30
Religious service/death	96	95	81	86	76	91	73	77	82	83	74	70	70	70	75	75	60	56	84	74	78	79	77	76	74	74
Religion gives comfort and strength	71	80	62	68	62	77	57	49	49	58	43	47	37	32	44	47	39	44	48	33	19	30	27	29	48	45
Confidence in Church (great, quite a lot)	70	52	59	66	56	79	50	41	56	38	55	42	53	44	47	39	36	29	49	33	37	55	37	44	51	43
Church answers spiritual needs	55	57	43	66	49	65	45	48	59	53	37	46	47	51	47	54	32	37	43	47	21	40	37	44	44	52
Church answers moral needs and problems	38	25	39	43	47	42	34	29	29	26	29	29	33	26	36	36	22	24	32	23	9	12	13	14	34	31
Belief: in God	93	93	84	88	81	93	87	81	79	83	74	66	61	56	73	66	62	60	77	61	42	62	51	47	74	68
in a personal god	68	63	51	70	61	77	55	46	41	31	36	29	26	21	25	36	29	23	31	28	15	24	18	16	30	38
in sin	83	79	62	67	63	65	58	44	62	57	43	41	41	37	60	41	46	39	70	57	20	18	34	23	57	47
in a life after death	71	68	48	61	31	37	55	40	50	50	36	40	35	39	38	38	41	46	47	43	23	32	28	39	43	43
in Hell	46	46	31	42	21	31	24	27	36	16	15	18	15	18	15	20	13	13	27	28	7	8	10	9	22	25
in Heaven	86	77	41	50	49	51	50	42	57	38	30	30	26	28	32	31	37	35	57	45	11	16	26	28	39	38
in reincarnation	26	19	20	15	23	24	25	16	26	19	12	17	22	25	19	18	11	20	26		13	15	15	19	21	15

Example of how to read the table: 98% of Irish respondents belonged to a religion in 1981, 90% in 1999.

*Designates the nine countries of the EEC that were surveyed as early as 1981 (the mean is weighted according to the population of each country): Ireland, Italy, Spain, Belgium, France, former West Germany, the Netherlands, Great Britain and Denmark.

(Source: Lambert 2004: 31)

Table 16.4 Results from the English Church Census, 2005

All England	1979	1989	1998	2005	2015*
Usual Sunday attendance	5,441,000	4,742,800	3,714,700	3,166,200	2,474,200
% attending on Sunday	11.7%	9.9%	7.5%	6.3%	4.7%

*predicted figures
(Adapted from Brierley 2006: 12.2, Table 12.2.1)

religion gives comfort and strength in 1999, in contrast to 48 per cent in 1981, and belief in God dropped from 77 per cent to 61 per cent. Like the Census, this survey reveals that most people identify as belonging to a religion. However, it unhelpfully assumes that religion means Christianity, without providing an option to write in the name of another religion. The European Values Survey also reveals that, while most people say they are religious, and quite a few believe in God, sin, life after death and Heaven, only a minority go to church regularly. In other words, there is a difference between religious beliefs (which are quite high) and religious practice (which is much lower). Other Protestant countries, such as Denmark and Sweden, also show religious decline. In the Catholic countries of Italy, Spain and Belgium, religious belonging dropped from 70–93 per cent in 1981 to 55–81 per cent in 1999.

The Church Censuses conducted in England and Scotland focus on Christianity. Rather than asking people whether they go to church, they gather data on actual church attendance, through organizing key people in every church to count numbers of people who go though their doors on a particular Sunday.

Results from the 2005 English Church Census are given in Table 16.4.

These figures teach us several things. First, less than half of the people who say they go to church regularly in the European Values Surveys are actually there on a typical Sunday. Additionally, less than a tenth of those who in the national Census said they were Christian go regularly to church – 71.6 per cent versus 6.3 per cent. This finding poses a clear challenge to the Census figure for Christian adherence. Second, there has been a substantial decline in the number of people going to church – down nearly 2.3 million from 1979 to 2005 in England alone – and a decline in the percentage of the population who go to church regularly. Church attendance has been falling over a long period, since a high point of about 40–60 per cent of adults in 1851 (Bruce 1999). From the 1960s, decline became steeper (Brown 2001): in the period 1998–2005, weekly church attendance reduced from 7.5 per cent to 6.3 per cent – a 15 per cent decrease.

Voas and Crockett examine two other sources of data, the British Household Panel Survey and the British Social Attitudes surveys. These provide challenging evidence for secularization at the level of belief as well as belonging.

Analysing British Household Panel Survey data from people questioned in 1991–92 and then in 1999–2000, Voas and Crockett (2005) examine affiliation (whether people regard themselves as belonging to any particular religion), belief (when people say religion makes a difference to their life) and attendance. Affiliation was highest, attendance lowest and belief in the middle. Over the eight-year period, they found fewer people affiliating, believing and attending, with the decline in each occurring at similar rates. Especially revealing is their finding that it is not so much that individuals become less religious as they get older; rather, the major element of decline is across different age cohorts. Each age cohort is less religious than the last.

British Social Attitudes surveys over a longer period also find relative stability in belief as people age but find that each younger age cohort has lower rates of belief. Age and cohort have the most influence over declining belief. Voas and Crockett argue that this is due to upbringing – secularization relates principally to the relationship between the religiosity of parents and children. Using British Household Panel Survey data from young adults aged 16–29 years, the authors found that, if children have two attending parents, then 46 per cent of them still attend. Brought up with one attending parent, the likelihood of the child attending is 23 per cent; with neither parent attending, the chance is only 3 per cent. They explain:

> **What this suggests is that in Britain institutional religion now has a half-life of one generation, to borrow the terminology of radioactive decay . . . At least in Britain in recent decades, change has**

> **occurred because each generation has entered adulthood less religious than its predecessors.**
>
> (Voas and Crockett 2005: 21, 24)

Combined with low fertility rates among Christians, the 'cohort effect' means that the loss of older people is not replaced by younger people being born into Christian families or choosing to join the church.

Nevertheless, while Voas and Crockett provide evidence for the decline in belief as well as affiliation and attendance, it is important to consider Davie's (1990, 1994) thesis that the hallmark of British religiosity is 'believing without belonging'. Davie argues that Britain may be 'unchurched' but it is not secular. Belief remains high despite falling attendance and affiliation. She examines European Values Surveys and concludes that a high percentage of people believe in God, Heaven, sin and the soul and pray (Davie 1994). Believing without belonging signifies the 'persistence of the sacred in contemporary society' (Davie 1994: 94); she also points out that bare statistics about church decline do not tell us everything we need in order to understand the state of religious belief (Davie 2000). We need to look at the qualitative details of people's experiences and beliefs; when we do, this reveals a complex picture. For example, the death of Princess Diana in 1997 triggered an outpouring of grief and spontaneously constructed shrines in public places, and people turned to the Church for answers.

But what kinds of belief count as legitimate manifestations of religion? This question is important because how we understand belief affects what we are willing to 'count' as religious belief when we do survey research. Here we are back to the issue of what religion is. Voas and Crockett's (2005) data on declining belief come from a definition of belief as 'How much difference would you say religious beliefs make to your life? Would you say they make a little difference, some difference, a great difference, no difference?' This carries the implication that, in order for it to be 'counted' as belief, it has to have an identifiable impact on an individual's life; they also imply that, in order for it to be considered to be persisting, it should be orthodox. For Davie, in contrast, belief in its wider sense is persisting. She believes that it is not secularization that is the most significant issue today; rather, it is the fact that people have religious or spiritual beliefs and yet do not feel they have to go to church to express them. Davie has written about what she calls 'vicarious religion', which is related to believing without belonging (Davie 2007). This is the idea that a smaller group of people perform religion on behalf of a larger group. In other words, because we live in a country where Anglicanism remains the state-supported religion, and because we have access to churches to go to for Christmas, weddings and funerals, we count ourselves as religious even though we leave most of the religious activities to others: to priests, Sunday school leaders and religious broadcasters. It may be that believing without belonging relates to the transition from religious obligation to religious consumption. We used to go to church because it was what most people did and our parents expected us to; today, we have a choice. If we go to a place of worship, we go because *we* want to, not because anyone forces us. This is a general social trend (in the family realm, for instance, people used to marry because of duty and tradition; now they most often marry out of love and personal choice).

Bringing this evidence together, it seems that, in the UK, churchgoing, affiliation and, perhaps, Christian belief, are declining. However, this pattern of decline masks instances of growth for religious organizations and individuals. Notably, growth is occurring in Islam, in pockets of Christianity and in New Age spiritualities.

Muslims are more committed to their faith and more likely than other groups to say that religion is very important to them (Purdam *et al.* 2007). Since Islam is a proselytizing faith, this is significant, since it is likely that conversion to Islam will continue to increase. More than one in ten Muslims in England and Wales, some of whom are converts, identified themselves in the Census as white. As fertility rates account for Christianity's decline, they also explain Islam's rise: compared with other faith communities, Muslims are more likely to have children; when they do have children, they tend to have more of them (Hussain 2008).

Branches of Christianity – notably ethnic minority and Pentecostal churches – are also growing. In 2005, 17 per cent of churchgoers were from non-white ethnic groups, an increase from 12 per cent in 1998. Pentecostal churches (half of which have a predominantly black congregation) have replaced Methodist churches as the third largest Christian denomination and were the only denomination that grew in the period 1998–2005 (Brierley 2006). There has also been some growth in Roman Catholicism. While the Catholic Church lost the greatest number and proportion of members of any denomination from 1998 to 2005, there are reports of revitalization of Catholic communities due to migration from Eastern Europe.

Figure 16.5 Does the Church's future life lie in vicarious religion?
MarioPonta/Alamy Images

New Age and alternative spiritualities are more popular too, and those becoming involved with them might attend yoga classes or practise Wicca. Paul Heelas and Linda Woodhead (2005) conducted a study of Kendal, a town in north-west England, where church attendance was exactly the national average. They tried to document every place of worship or spiritual practice, aiming to test the claim that alternative spirituality is eclipsing Christianity in a kind of 'spiritual revolution'. They found that only 2–3 per cent of Kendal residents were involved in alternative spiritualities, but this had grown by 300 per cent during the 1990s, when church attendance fell from 11 per cent to 7.9 per cent. Heelas and Woodhead conclude that, if change continues at the same rate, then alternative spirituality will eclipse Christianity within the next 30 years; thus, while it would be premature to declare that a spiritual revolution has occurred, there is a good chance that it will do so. And while their numbers are smaller, new religious movements (see below) have retained a significant presence in the UK. Barker (2004) estimates that there are 900–2000 new religions in the UK, mostly with very small numbers of members. While the Census questions did not lend themselves to revealing support for new religious movements, nevertheless some 2500 people in England named their religion as Hare Krishna, Scientology or the Unification Church (Weller 2008).

Qualitative data

We have spent some time looking at quantitative data, for these data are essential in painting the broad brushstrokes of the UK religious landscape. If quantitative data provide information this is countable, then qualitative data provide quality and detail.

A research project by Abby Day investigated what people believe and analysed what people who said they were Christian in the 2001 Census really meant by this. Day talked to 266 people, mostly in schools and colleges, and interviewed 68 at length. One, a 15-year-old student from Yorkshire, told her this:

Abby: What do you believe in?
Jordan: Nowt.
Abby: Sorry?
Jordan: I don't believe in owt. I don't believe in any religions.
Abby: You don't believe in any religions?
Jordan: No. I'm Christian but I don't believe in owt.

(Day 2006: 4)

This example – of someone saying that they are Christian but that they do not believe in any religions – seems contradictory, but it is not unusual. Day explains that only about a quarter of the people who ticked 'Christian' in the Census actually have traditionally Christian beliefs. For most, what is important is not conventional religious belief but what she calls 'believing in belonging'. People have most faith in their relationships with family and friends; for them, religion takes on a more functional than substantive connotation.

There are also signs that belonging is occurring in different contexts than traditional churches, and so conventional measures of religiosity may fail to capture the variety of religious belonging that exists. Jewish Shabbat meals, Islamic study classes and online Pagan communities, for instance, are harder to count than Sunday church attendance. The Internet in particular has enabled new, diverse forms of religious belonging to be brought into being (Dawson and Cowan 2004).

From our examination of religion in the UK, it is clear that there is a good deal of evidence for secularization: the decline in support for institutional religion, and to some extent for traditional religious belief, has been significant. But religion has re-emerged at the societal level, through politics and public debate, and is increasingly active in providing (state-sanctioned) education and welfare services; faith schools (see the case study below) exemplify this. This provides evidence against the secularization thesis. Additionally, some forms of religion are popular, notably Islam, churches attended by immigrant groups and New Age forms of spirituality; we will explore some of these shortly. Some sociologists refer to this re-emergence of religion as 'resacralization' (Woodhead and Heelas 2000). There is thus a mixed picture. Weller (2008) suggests that it may be helpful to see the UK as a three-dimensional society where religion is concerned: Christian, secular and religiously plural. The UK has a

Case study

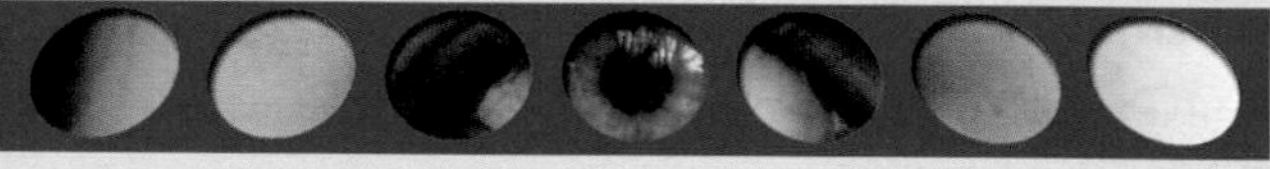

Faith schools

A third of UK schools are faith schools, mostly Church of England and Roman Catholic. Since its election to government in 1997, Labour encouraged the development of faith schools. Faith schools have attracted controversy and media attention. For example:

- A top Jewish school in north-west London was cleared in July 2008 of discrimination after it refused to admit an 11-year-old boy who was not considered 'Jewish enough'. In Judaism, religion is passed down the maternal line, and the boy's mother had converted from Roman Catholicism at a progressive synagogue before her son was born. But progressive synagogues are not recognized as legitimate by the Office of the Chief Rabbi. The barrister supporting the family claimed that other children had been offered places who were 'committed atheists' (Steele 2008).
- The Krishna-Avanti primary school, the first Hindu school in the UK, opened in Edgware in north-west London in 2008. Teaching the national curriculum like any other school, the school's additional aim is to promote 'holistic health through the provision of a safe, caring environment, a balanced vegetarian diet and opportunities to practise yoga, meditation and the arts'. Its head teacher told the press that the school would contribute to 'contemporary British society'. She explained: 'We recognize and take our duty seriously in ensuring that we promote community cohesion, inclusion and value inter-cultural and religious diversity' (adapted from BBC News 2008).
- Emmanuel College, Gateshead, an academy school financed partly by the evangelical Christian businessman Peter Vardy, came under fire for teaching creationism rather than evolution. Creationism (or 'intelligent design') teaches that God made the earth a few thousand years ago. Media commentators and some teachers' groups criticized the government for giving public funding to schools teaching creationism (Branigan 2002).

Questions

1. What do the debates about faith schools teach us about the position of religion in contemporary UK society?
2. Does the presence of faith schools indicate that religion is re-emerging?

Christian heritage, predominantly secular attitudes and organizations, and elements of religious diversity, including significant Muslim, Sikh, Jewish, Buddhist, Hindu and alternative religious populations.

Understanding religious organizations

Churches and sects

To begin our exploration of religious organisations, we return to Weber. Weber distinguished the Church, into which we are born and which offers its grace indiscriminately to all, from the sect, which, by contrast, 'is a voluntary association of only those who . . . are religiously and morally qualified' (Weber 1948a [1922–3]: 306). Sects are tightly bounded communities with limited contact between believers and unbelievers. People earn admittance to the sect by showing the religious community that they possess the requisite religious and moral qualities. Once inside the sect, the member's life is scrutinized, and he or she must '*prove* repeatedly that he was endowed with these qualities' (Weber 1948a [1922–3]: 320). The religious community employs discipline, for example having the power to withhold Holy Communion from those they believe are participating in sin. For this reason, sects are small or organized into small units to keep members' lives visible to others.

Weber's division of church versus sect was developed by Troeltsch (1931 [1912]) and Niebuhr (1929). Niebuhr believed that sects lasted only a generation before succumbing to the bureaucratization that Weber described in his writings on charismatic authority. The second generation, born into the group, are less committed to the idea of voluntary adherence and, in becoming more reconciled to the world, transform from sects to denominations. Wilson's (1970) work was also influential in developing a typology of sects. For them all, sects are religious movements in tension with the wider society. But although they are distinctively different from church-type religion (Table 16.5), they are not wholly different. They tend to be challenging offshoots of the dominant religion of the wider society.

New religious movements

The church–sect categorization was challenged from the 1960s by the arrival of new religious movements (NRMs or 'new religions'). The Unification Church ('the Moonies'), Scientology and the Hare Krishna movement were among the most prominent. Melton provides a helpful definition of new religions:

> **New religions are religious groups that exist socially and culturally on the fringe, differ significantly in belief and practice from the dominant religious institutions of the culture in which they are located, and have minimum ties to and allies within the dominant government, religious and intellectual structures of the society in which they operate.**
>
> (Melton 2007: 33)

Not all sociologists separate sects and NRMs, and some now use the term 'new religious movement' for organizations previously labelled as sects. For the sake of clarity, we might say that the main difference between NRMs and sects is that sects are strict adaptations of the dominant religious tradition in the country in which they are located, whereas NRMs are new, having little or no connection to existing religions in the country where they attract followers.

NRMs gained widespread public attention in the late 1970s, after the mass murder–suicide of 914 members of the People's Temple in Jonestown, Guyana. Since then, NRMs have often been branded as 'cults', with deluded members and power-hungry leaders likely to

Table 16.5 Comparison of Church and sect

	Church	Sect
Membership	Involuntary – by birth	Voluntary – by merit
Type of organization	Traditional impersonal institution	Community of believers
Selection of religious leaders	On basis of educational qualifications	On basis of gift or calling
Relationship with society	Good relations with society	In tension with society
Priority members give to religion	Religion is one of many commitments	Religion is top priority
Religious beliefs	Looser and more open	Stricter and more closed

lead the 'cult' in a harmful direction. In the past few decades, several high-profile groups have ended violently: the 1993 siege at the Branch Davidians' compound in Waco, Texas, led to 80 murder–suicides when government officials stormed the building; the Japanese group Aum Shinrikyō killed 12 and injured thousands by releasing poisonous nerve gas in the Tokyo subway in 1995; and 39 members of Heaven's Gate, an American UFO movement, committed suicide in 1997, believing that they would be taken on board a spaceship to a new life. Apocalyptic motives – that is, factors connected to prophecies about the end of the world – existed in several of these movements. Indeed, apocalyptic themes can inspire religious movements to actions that have wide social impacts; the acts of terrorism or *jihad* perpetrated by Al-Qaeda can be seen as part of a kind of apocalyptic war (Hall 2004). But violence is rare in NRMs, and when it does occur it is prompted by both external (persecution, stigmatization, attempts to intervene) and internal (an apocalyptic outlook in which evil is seen to be so rampant that the group must fight or stockpile weapons to protect themselves, volatile leaders) factors (Robbins and Hall 2007).

The anti-cult movement, populated by aggrieved ex-members, families of people in new religions and 'cult-watching' agencies, has fuelled media criticism of NRMs; an Internet search on a new religion will quickly bring up many sites opposing the religious movement in question. However, as the NRMs have grown older and more established, Western populations have grown more used to them.

Stop and think

➤ What do reactions to new religious movements tell us about our society's attitudes to religion in general?

NRMs are significant on a number of levels. They exemplify social change and have been highlighted as a challenge to secularization. Sociologists have spent much time and energy studying and categorizing NRMs, and we will look at some of their investigations shortly. Today, however, some of the new religions are on the wane. They attracted much media attention but not huge followings. It is difficult to count membership, but estimates suggest that less than 1 per cent of the US and Canadian populations belong to NRMs (Dawson 2006). NRMs that retain popularity tend towards the world-affirming type described by Wallis (Figure 16.6), but they are merging with, or being eclipsed by, alternative New Age spiritualities. We will now turn to the work of Roy Wallis (1984), who classifies new religions into three types.

World-rejecting religious movements tend to be monotheistic. Their god is radically different from, and higher and greater than humans, but is personally concerned with human affairs. From the Indian strand of new religions, the International Society for Krishna Consciousness (ISCKON) exemplifies this, as do fundamentalist Christian-based groups. The Unification Church is a third example; they combine influences from the Judaeo-Christian tradition and from Korea, birthplace of the movement's founder Reverend Sun Myung Moon.

World-rejecting movements reject many features of modern societies, especially affluence and material consumption. They try instead to establish a society that follows God's prescriptions for creation, modelled on patterns outlined in scriptures or revealed via the movement's leader. For instance, the People's Temple originated in Indiana under the leadership of Reverend Jim Jones, and then it moved to California, where it expanded. It moved again to Jonestown, Guyana, establishing a small rural settlement before ending in tragedy in 1978. Life in a world-rejecting movement can be hard work, and members put the good of the community and its leaders first, abandoning secular lives ard surrendering money to the group. Discipline is crucial, and clear boundaries govern personal relationships (in the Unification Church, marriages are often arranged) and restrict contact with non-members. Often apocalyptic or millenarian – that is, believing that the world is in the end times – they believe that their movement will be instrumental in the imminent new world order.

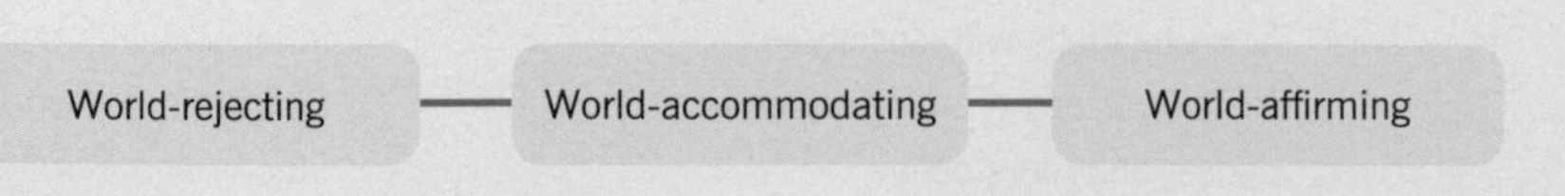

Figure 16.6 Wallis's three types of new religious movement

World-affirming movements take a positive approach to the surrounding world. Rather than changing the world, they try to equip individuals with tools to increase their happiness and self-awareness. Problems are caused primarily by individuals, they believe, and so it is individuals who are responsible for changing their situations. They have few religious structures or doctrines. Absent is the self-denial characteristic of world-rejecting movements; participants may be asked to abstain from drugs or to sit and meditate for periods of time, for instance, but they are not required to make major life changes. Eastern religions and philosophies and modern psychological or scientific ideas are the inspiration for world-affirming movements. Those movements that believe in a divine reality conceptualize divinity as a force pervading the world and the self rather than as an external, all-powerful figure. Achievement of their goals often requires undergoing training or mastering a technique such as meditation or mind control. World-affirming movements are happy using worldly methods – bureaucratic organization, mass production, marketing and even profit – to achieve their ends.

Wallis argues that world-affirming movements prioritize three themes: individual achievement, freeing one's 'real' self from the constraints of conventional social behaviour, and attaining a sense of intimacy to counteract the isolation of modern societies. As Wallis points out, not everyone would recognize these characteristics as religious. Some world-affirming movements prefer the term 'spiritual' to 'religious', and others (see World in focus on pp. 671–672) have fought to be recognized as a religion. Prominent world-affirming movements include Silva Mind Control, Erhard Seminar's Training (est), Transcendental Meditation and Sōka Gakkai (discussed below).

World-accommodating new religions form a mid-point between world-rejecting and world-affirming movements, comprising elements of both, but in diluted form. Their relationship to the world is neither wholly rejecting nor wholly accepting. Like world-affirmers, world-accommodating movements emphasize the individual and their religious experience. They believe that as the individual's religiosity is ignited he or she will be inspired to live in a way that brings some benefit or spiritual challenge to society. Collectivism features more than in the world-accommodating groups but less than in world-rejecting religions. Wallis cites the Charismatic Renewal or Neo-Pentecostal movement of the Protestant and Catholic churches as a key example. Embracing speaking in tongues, healing and other 'gifts of the Holy Spirit', this movement emerged from the established churches as a protest against their perceived spiritual lifelessness. Its constituency was middle-class – people who have achieved relative economic success but still consider religion an important aspect of their lives. Other world-accommodating groups include the Aetherius Society (a movement founded in London in the 1950s that draws on the Theosophical tradition) and the Western versions of Sōka Gakkai.

Why did new religious movements emerge?

We can understand the rise of new religious movements by looking at micro- and macro-explanations. Micro-explanations consider factors within the individual that might lead them to seek out or form new religions. Macro-explanations look at factors within the society as a whole.

Micro-explanations

American sociologists Stark and Bainbridge are interested in why people engage in religion, and especially why they join the religious groups recently popular in the West. Starting from the premise that religion is a human creation, they believe that religion arises because people feel a need for 'compensators', things that make up for the scarcity of rewards available in modern societies. Religions are 'human organizations primarily engaged in providing general compensators based on supernatural assumptions' (Stark and Bainbridge 1985: 8). That is, religions are attractive because they promise future rewards (commonly, in the afterlife) and provide individuals with meaningful lives oriented towards the supernatural in the meantime. Religion will endure because people will always search for compensators.

As for NRMs, Stark and Bainbridge believe that there are three plausible explanations for the creation and successful transmission of new religious ideas. The first is the *psychopathology model.* Cults start with a founder whose ideas or visions originate in mental illness (or occasionally drugs) and provide compensators for his or her own needs. Convinced that their visions are true, the individual can transmit their ideas to others who are vulnerable psychologically or have similar social needs. As followers accept the founder's ideas, a group forms. The founder 'may achieve at least a partial cure of his illness because the self-generated compensators are legitimated by other persons and because the founder now receives true rewards from his followers' (Stark and Bainbridge 1985: 174). The Christian Science founder Mary Baker Eddy seems to conform to this pattern.

The *entrepreneur model* is the second explanation. Put crudely, people start religious movements to make money. More subtly, new religions are businesses that market and sell compensators to people for profit and other rewards, such as power and sexual favours. As in any business, cult entrepreneurs must invent and sell products that appeal to people's desire for compensators. Just as new models of vacuum-cleaner were created once the first was produced and recognized as a desirable product, so it is easier to start new cults that are variations on existing successful ones. Some NRMs have become financially successful; Scientology, which we will examine shortly, is a case in point.

The third explanation is the *subculture-evolution model*. In this model, a kind of 'mutual conversion' (Stark and Bainbridge 1985: 184) occurs as cults form when a group of people with similar needs and backgrounds come together to seek rewards. They fail to achieve the desired rewards, but they develop various compensators that unite them as a group, even enabling growth.

These models are not mutually exclusive; two or three of them may together account for a religious movement's appearance. The People's Temple began as a Christian sect but became esoteric. It evolved from Jim Jones's visions (the psychopathology model), provided him with rewards of power as it expanded (the entrepreneur model) and was strengthened through group interaction as people banded together to support Jones's plans (the subculture-evolution model).

Other micro-explanations seek explanations in the individual characteristics, such as age or social class, of those joining NRMs. Joiners tend to be young, middle-class and people who could be described as 'seekers'; that is, they are on the look-out for some form of spirituality. It is interesting that, in the USA, people from Jewish backgrounds are disproportionately represented in new religions. When sociologists looked at this more closely, they discovered that their families' religion was in fact cultural or secular Judaism. Those who joined NRMs were dissatisfied with the lack of spirituality in their own families and so embraced new religions in search of a more spiritual life (Selengut 1988).

Micro-models concentrate on factors specific to the individuals involved in beginning and joining the religion rather than on the social structural factors that, we might say, fertilize the soil of society so that such religions can grow. We will turn, therefore, to the wider structural factors that account for the rise of NRMs.

Macro-explanations

The classical sociologists suggested that there is a connection between a society and the religions that emerge from within it. Accordingly, the rise of new religions is generally linked to changes that accelerated in the latter part of the twentieth century. Dawson (2006) argues that in North America, where NRMs have proliferated, they are both an *expression of cultural continuity* and *a response to cultural change*; his arguments are expandable to other Western societies. To explain how new religions express cultural continuity, Dawson points out that, unlike in Europe, religion in the USA has never been connected to the state, and so religious movements have developed independently. The USA experienced several Protestant religious movements in the eighteenth and nineteenth centuries. The NRMs that emerged from the 1960s might be seen as a fourth major religious movement. In other words, NRMs are a newer version of an older cultural pattern.

It is more common, however, to see NRMs as a response to cultural change. After the 1950s' baby boom and post-war return to churchgoing and domesticity, the 1960s counter-cultural generation began to shake things up. Challenging the economic, political, social and sexual values, campaigning against war, racism and sexism, the counter-culture was spurred on by the resurgence of Romanticism; it was an 'expressive revolution' (Martin 1981) that sought to dissolve barriers between people and create a new communal ethic. The counter-culture may have rejected traditional religion, but they were open to embracing new kinds of spirituality. This gave NRMs, which even in their stricter sectarian forms often embraced religious expressivism, a fertile soil. Some people connected to the counter-culture joined NRMs that expressed their communitarian or libertarian values. Others, dismayed at the perceived moral laxity of the counter-culture, were attracted to the new Christian-based movements dedicated to recreating a divinely ordered society; some thought it was only a matter of time before the apocalypse arrived. In the aftermath of the counter-culture, NRMs attracted former revolutionaries who were disappointed that their aims had not been achieved or who now questioned those aims.

In experiencing different social changes, different societies have produced different new religions. Japan is an important example. Japan has seen tremendous change, transforming in less than a century from a semi-feudal society to a modern industrialized democratic nation at the epicentre of the electronics, transportation and banking industries. Economic change and new-found religious freedom creates opportunities for religious innovation, and this rapid transition may explain why Japan has seen such a proliferation of sects (Wilson 1970). The sect that has been particularly successful is Sōka Gakkai, founded in 1930 as a variation on Nichiren Buddhism. Sōka Gakkai means 'value creation society'; through the practice of chanting the Lotus Sutra *Nam Myōhō Renge Kyō*, it aims to increase wellbeing, happiness and the ability to contribute to society.

Globalization has aided the spread of new religion. With travel now easier and more frequent, ideas can spread swiftly across nations. In particular, beliefs associated with the East have headed West (Campbell 1999). The mass media is also important, and the Internet is a tool used enthusiastically by new religions. Some new religions have tried to create a new world order, while others have taken advantage of the rapidity with which ideas can spread in a globalized world in order to retain a religious identity that is both global and tied to a specific nation. In trying to forge 'world Hindu' identity, the Indian Rashtriya Swayamsevek Sangh (RSS) movement exemplifies this (Beckford 2004). The movement gave birth to the Bharatiya Janata Party, the Hindu-Right government that headed a national coalition between 1998 and 2004 and endorsed the *Hindutva* ideology of 'one nation, one people, one culture'.

World in focus

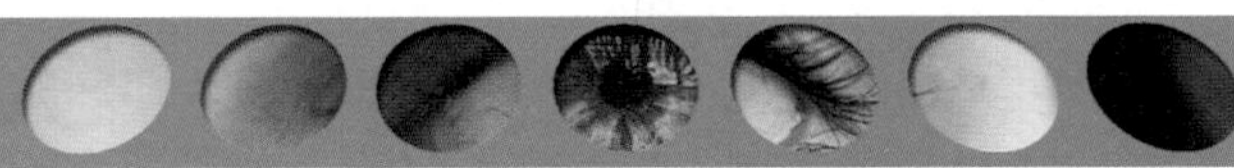

Scientology: a successful new religious movement

Most of us hear about Scientology through stories about high-profile celebrities – Tom Cruise and Katie Holmes, John Travolta or Jason Lee – and the impact of Scientology on their lives (for example, Scientology's criticism of certain medical or psychiatric practices). Scientology was started by L. Ron Hubbard, who can be viewed as a charismatic leader in Weber's sense. Hubbard formulated a system of self-development that he called *Dianetics*; he thought that 'the creation of dianetics is a milestone for Man comparable to his discovery of fire and superior to his inventions of the wheel and arch' (Hubbard 1950, cited in Stark and Bainbridge 1985: 175). Churches of Scientology began to be established from the 1950s, with the international linking association Church of Scientology International founded in 1981. Estimates of membership vary widely: the Church of Scientology often cites its membership as over eight million, but national religion surveys reveal a much lower figure. For instance, the American Religious Identification Survey 2001 reported around 55,000 Scientologists. The website www.adherents.com estimates a worldwide figure of 500,000 (www.adherents.com/Religions_By_Adherents.html#Scientology).

Scientology describes itself as:

> **The only major new religion to emerge in this undeniably turbulent twentieth century, Scientology offers mankind the hope of resolving our most pressing societal problems and of creating a true renaissance of the spirit in the coming century.**
>
> (www.whatisscientology.org/html/Part12/Chp37/index.html)

The International Association of Scientologists' website states:

> **A Scientologist is defined as 'essentially one who betters the condition of himself and the conditions of others by using Scientology technology'.**
>
> (www.iasmembership.org/)

Scientology's aims are ambitious:

World in focus *continued*

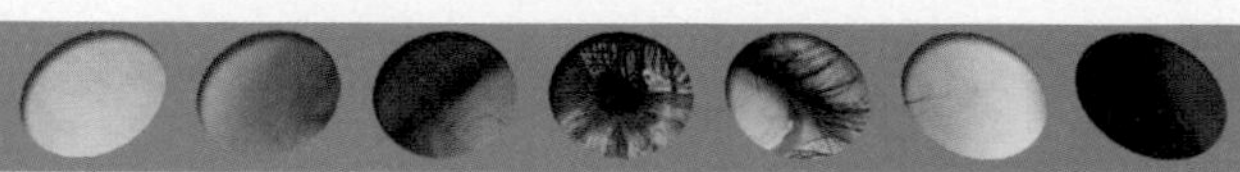

> A civilization without insanity, without criminals and without war, where the able can prosper and honest beings can have rights, and where man is free to rise to greater heights, are the aims of Scientology.
>
> First announced to an enturbulated world in 1950, these aims are well within the grasp of our technology.
>
> Nonpolitical in nature, Scientology welcomes any individual of any creed, race or nation.
>
> We seek no revolution. We only seek evolution to higher states of being for the individual and for society.
>
> We are achieving our aims.
>
> (www.whatisscientology.org/html/Part12/Chp37/pg0684.html)

Controversy has surrounded Scientology. It has fought, with only varying degrees of success, to be seen as a religion. We might think that being officially recognized as a religion is not important. However, being classed as a religion enables groups to have charity status and thus gain tax benefits, something Scientology still lacks in the UK.

What Scientologists believe

Scientologists believe that the 'thetan', the human essence or soul, is immortal and godlike. Having become encumbered with 'Matter, Energy, Space and Time' (MEST) through occupying the human body, the thetan has taken on an emotional 'reactive mind' that stores memories of unpleasant events in the person's life. These act as 'engrams' that impede rational thought. The thetan's aim is to eliminate these memories, thereby attaining a 'clear' and analytical mind. Furnished with an 'e-meter' machine, another person, the 'auditor', aids the 'pre-clear' individual to recall past events and eliminate the engrams. This is done for payment and can take years. Toxins should be avoided in order to speed up the process. Once 'clear', the person may progress through various levels of 'operating thetan'; exactly what this means and how it occurs is a closely guarded secret (Wilson 1990; Chryssides 2004).

Sociological perspectives on Scientology

As we saw, Wallis considered Scientology to be a world-affirming movement. Although it calls itself the 'Church of Scientology', it is not primarily a collective movement. Rather, its activities are techniques embraced by individuals under an auditor's guidance. The aim is to improve the individual's situation rather than to achieve social transformation. Scientology also fits Stark and Bainbridge's entrepreneurial model of cult formation; costs for achieving 'clear' are cited by various unofficial websites as $128,560 (http://en.wikipedia.org/wiki/Scientology_as_a_business#Costs). Later in this chapter, we will look at the implications that postmodernity holds for religion. Because of its individualistic approach, we might argue that Scientology suits the conditions of postmodernity.

In Wilson's interpretation, Scientology can be considered a 'secularized religion' because 'it is a religion that mirrors many of the preoccupations of contemporary society' (Wilson 1990: 288). The various sects and variants of Christianity that have emerged since the Reformation are forerunners of the new religions that exist today. Modern societies have witnessed a shift away from the sacrificial worship of an otherworldly God towards a conception of God as a spirit force that can be manipulated for therapeutic purposes. Scientology represents this shift. Weber described rationalization as an important feature of modernity, and indeed, Scientology's auditing process is a standardized procedure that emphasizes reason over emotion and claims to be scientific. Although it defines itself as a church, the core of Scientology lies in the individual's engagement with the auditing process, and communal gatherings are relatively unimportant.

Table 16.6 A new typology of religious organizations

		Policy towards adherents	
		Relaxed	**Strict**
Policy towards others	*Accommodating*	Liberal	Devout
	Challenging	Activist	Rigorist

(Bruce and Voas 2007: 14)

How religious movements are changing

Theories about churches, sects and NRMs developed in Western environments where Christianity was the most significant major religion. Today, sociologists are questioning the relevance of these frameworks to non-Christian religions. For example, in the Islamic world, there are no Muslim churches, but there are dominant schools of law as well as bodies that could be labelled 'sects' and 'cults' (Sedgwick 2004).

Bruce and Voas (2007) believe that, though useful for describing religion from the Reformation to the late twentieth century, the older typologies for understanding religious organizations are becoming redundant. Using the British example, they argue that Britain has become so secularized that there is no longer a distinction between religious groups that are socially acceptable (church-type groups) and those that are not (sect-type groups). Today, people are more tolerant of religion as a whole (in whatever form it exists) but less tolerant of manifestations of religion that they perceive as extremist (such as high levels of commitment, conservative attitudes to women or creationist beliefs). Extremism is just as likely to be observed in established church-type groups as in sectarian ones. They suggest a new typology of religious organizations, as shown in Table 16.6.

Fundamentalism

If Bruce and Voas are right, then extremism and its close cousin fundamentalism represent the main religious approach in tension with wider society. It is therefore worth exploring what 'fundamentalism' is. Like NRMs and sectarian religion, fundamentalism attracts attention because it is a strict form of religion that contrasts with mainstream social attitudes.

Sectarian religion and fundamentalism overlap: fundamentalism often operates in sect-type organizations, and many sects take a fundamentalist approach to religion. But 'sect' is a name given to a type of religious organization, whereas 'fundamentalism' is a description of a religious approach.

Just as members of new religions deny being in a 'cult', few people call themselves fundamentalist because of its negative connotations. Instead, 'fundamentalists' believe that their religion is the most authentic. They believe they are recreating a past era where religious texts were understood and obeyed literally. As Hunt puts it:

> **Fundamentalism . . . may be broadly understood as a self-conscious attempt to represent or reassert what are perceived to be authentic religious traditions and beliefs, even if they are reconstructed and fall back on myths and subjective interpretations of religious texts.**
>
> (Hunt 2005: 116–17)

Fundamentalists adhere to tightly defined doctrines and believe there is only one true version of religion. For them, 'Truth emerges as an exclusive concept, with no space for error, alternative interpretation or appropriate ambiguity' (Percy 1996: 13).

The concept of fundamentalism originated in the early twentieth-century publication of a series of pamphlets called *The Fundamentals* by a group of Protestant theologians. These theologians sought to defend the inerrancy of the Bible (the view that the Bible is free from error or contradiction) against the threat of modernism. Because of its early association with the Bible, some writers argue that fundamentalism is most at home in 'religions of the book' (Christianity, Islam and Judaism) (Bruce 2000: 5). Indeed, Aldridge points out that, whereas only some forms of Christianity have a fundamentalist biblical approach, in a sense all Islam is fundamentalist:

> **The Qur'an is not simply the Muslims' Bible. Muslims believe that the Qur'an is uncreated and coexistent with God. Qur'an means recitation, and the text is the word of God delivered to the Prophet Muhammad by the Angel Jibreel (Gabriel). Strictly, it is untranslatable from Arabic. In Christian terms, the Qur'an functions less as the Bible than as Christ. It is an object of reverence in ways that the Bible is usually not, even to Christian fundamentalists . . . In the case of the Qur'an, it is not possible to distinguish between liberal and conservative interpretations in the Christian sense of the terms.**
>
> (Aldridge 2007: 136–7)

Yet it is also the case that Islam (like Judaism) places more emphasis than Christians do on religious law; only some of this law is written in the Qur'an, and thus there is an extra-scriptural authoritative tradition to which Muslims look. Additionally, as Bruce points out, it is also the monotheism of Islam, Judaism and Christianity that makes fanaticism more likely. In Buddhism or Hinduism:

> **. . . the variety of Gods (or the varieties of forms that the divine can take) should create a climate of tolerance. After all, if one is used to accepting that people may worship different Gods, it is a little difficult to insist that this particular group deserves to be persecuted and imposed upon.**
>
> (Bruce 2000: 5)

Christian and Islamic fundamentalisms receive most academic attention. Islamic fundamentalism is associated more with the pursuit of political and revolutionary change, with the aim of creating an Islamic state pursuing Sharia law. However, fundamentalism is present in other religions too. There have been Hindu nationalist movements, for instance. In Judaism, the ultra- or neo-orthodox *haredim* Jews aim to strictly observe the *mitzvot*, the

Figure 16.7 Pickets condemning homosexuality, organized by Westboro Baptist Church, a fundamentalist church in Topeka, Kansas, have gained international attention. The church is best known for its 'God hates fags' slogans and for picketing funeral processions of soldiers killed during the war in Iraq
Tim Boyle/Getty Images

613 injunctions in the Torah that prescribe or forbid certain activities (Aldridge 2007).

Like NRMs, fundamentalism is linked to modernity, as its product and as a reaction against it. The strategies and technology that fundamentalists use are often modern: think of the way in which TV evangelists use the mass media to transmit their message or radical Muslims access the sermons of controversial preachers online (Bunt 2003). But fundamentalists also reject modernity, and the liberalization of attitudes to gender and sexuality are aspects of modernity that fundamentalists have especially resisted. Noteworthy examples of Christian fundamentalists in the USA include the 'God hates fags' website (Figure 16.7) and Operation Rescue. Operation Rescue was founded in the late 1980s and has maintained a high-profile campaign of pickets at, and attacks on, abortion clinics. In Europe, Christian fundamentalism is a fringe position that occasionally tries to exert a public presence (protesting against the musical version of the *Jerry Springer Show*, for example) but is diluted by secular culture and exercises little social influence.

Stop and think

- What is your reaction to images like that in Figure 16.7?
- What role do protests such as these play within fundamentalism, and how successful do you think they are?

Alternative New Age spiritualities

'New Age' is an umbrella term for a variety of phenomena that became popular in the 1960s. These have roots in the occult and esoteric movements of the mid- to late nineteenth century (notably spiritualism) and in the 1960s counter-culture. They also overlap with the 'world-affirming' NRMs (Bruce 1996). The term 'New Age' derives from the expectation of the dawning of an 'Age of Aquarius', but these expectations have dulled, and many people now use the terms 'alternative spiritualities' or 'holistic spirituality' instead. Alternative spirituality is more of a 'cultic milieu' (Campbell 1972) than a structured movement. It includes belief in angels, astrology, crystals, feng shui, horoscopes, human potential movements, meditation, Satanism, and Western versions of Taiosm and Zen, to name just a few examples. Neo-Paganism (sometimes just called Paganism) is a strand within the wider New Age movement. Paganism:

> **. . . refers to a number of religions that view nature as sacred, ensouled or alive, which tend to be pantheistic, polytheistic and/or duotheistic rather than monotheistic, including both gods and goddesses in their pantheons, who try to live in balance and harmony, accepting darkness and light, life and death, as part of one sacred whole.**
>
> (Pearson 2002: 20)

The rising fortunes of alternative spirituality relate to the shift from modernity to postmodernity. If modernity championed scientific knowledge, then postmodernity challenges science and bureaucratic hierarchies and prioritizes the individual afresh. In many ways, postmodernity is good news for religion: people are becoming disenchanted with scientific modernity and re-enchanted by spiritual ideas. New Agers often search for lost spiritual mysteries, forgotten kinds of knowledge that were neglected with the rise of science. Goddess religion is a good example: in 1978, Carol Christ's address 'Why women need the Goddess' galvanized the early Goddess religion movement. Carol Christ argued that, in giving women a female symbol of divinity, Goddess religion could do what traditional male-centred religion could not: it could affirm women and relate their everyday experiences to the supernatural realm. Although the Goddess movement dates mainly from the 1970s, it draws on older polytheistic traditions and reclaims a history of powerful female figures that is thousands of years old. They believe that, at this time before patriarchal religion, Europe was occupied by societies that venerated female divinities (Rountree 2004: 4).

New Age religion is often described as 'mix and match'. Indeed, in postmodernity, the idea of there being a single true religion is unpopular, and so it is common to select elements from a variety of sources, including different religious traditions, philosophy and psychology. The New Age is perhaps the closest thing we have to postmodern spirituality. Aupers and Houtman interviewed spiritual trainers at New Age centres in the Netherlands and found this mixture of religious influences, as this quotation shows:

Case study

Muslim women embracing the *hijab*

Islam is the fastest-growing religion in Europe and North America. Although sometimes portrayed as a 'backward' and 'other' civilization on a collision course with the Western Christian tradition, Islam in the West tends to be a Western form of Islam. Muslim women are creating an Islam that comes alive in the contexts where they live. Their decisions about how to dress derive from their own interpretations of the Qur'an and Hadith, interpretations that are made only within their Western environments. In the wake of 9/11, when Muslims in Western countries began to face increased Islamophobic abuse, women began to take up the *hijab* in larger numbers (Figure 16.8). This approach was viewed by some as fundamentalist, as a desire to go back to a literal interpretation of the Qur'an. But women are not covering up as a retreat from modernity. By contrast, they are doing so to create space for themselves in the public sphere (Khan 2007). *If* their Islam is fundamentalist, then it is, like other forms of fundamentalism, modern: that is, women who cover themselves advocate a particular modern interpretation of the Qur'an and use modern tools and structures as part of their Islamic practice. Websites advising women on Islamic clothing are popular; sites such as Hijabs-R-Us and eJilbab.com offer women not only fashionable head coverings but also discussion forums where they can meet as a global *umma* (community of believers). Additionally, feminist values are part of this new Islam. McGinty's interviews reveal how, in Sweden, one of the world's most secular countries, female converts are incorporating feminist values within Islam. Cecilia, a recent convert, explains:

Figure 16.8 Since 11 September 2001, Muslim women in the west have increasingly adopted the *hijab*
© iStockphoto.com/naheed choudhry

> I have rather a feminist view on things. I refuse to see the woman as a second-class citizen. I refuse to see why a woman should be worth less than a man . . . I like Islam's emphasis on the rights and obligations the woman and the man have. This is very, very important. My rights as a woman are very important to me. I would never obliterate myself for a man, never.
>
> (McGinty 2007: 480)

In covering up, she is refusing to allow men to look at her as a sexual object. She says:

> This may sound very . . . complacent, but I have always been slim and I have always had a remarkably good-looking body. And that has been a basis for many people forming a judgment of me. I was only a walking body. And even if you wear jeans and a T-shirt people can tell how you look. With the veil and so-called decent clothes I get judged in a whole different way. Since people can't see my body they can't think 'wow, what a waist, what a sexy butt and what legs!' Instead people have to look into my eyes. Contrary to what most women believe, it is not fun to be so-called 'sexy'. It is not nice when people forget that you actually can have an IQ of 120. Because, in their eyes, if you are sexy you are also stupid.
>
> (McGinty 2007: 480)

> **I feel very connected with the person of Jesus Christ, not with Catholicism. But I also feel touched by the person of Buddha. I am also very much interested in shamanism. So my belief has nothing to do with a particular religious tradition. For me, all religions are manifestations of god, of the divine. If you look beyond the surface, then all religions tell the same story.**
>
> (Aupers and Houtman 2006: 203)

Similarly, some people combine traditional religiosity with New Age alternatives: 'Quagans' are Pagans who are also Quakers (Vincett 2008a) and 'Fusers' fuse Christianity and Paganism (Vincett 2008b). The thirteenth-century-origin Jewish mystical practice of Kabbalah has become increasingly popular in Israel and the USA, and the term 'New Age Judaism' has been coined to describe the Kabbalah revival (Huss 2007).

Alternative spiritualities operate less in collective gatherings than in mainstream religions, and Bruce (1996: 196–7) uses Stark and Bainbridge's concept of 'client cults' and 'audience cults' to describe New Age activities: 'audience cults' are manifestations of spirituality around which people gather as audiences and consumers. This could involve attending a lecture by a New Age practitioner or purchasing books, magazines or DVDs. There is little central organization or group membership. With 'client cults', an individual is a client who obtains (generally for money) a service from a New Age expert or therapist (for example, a tarot card reading).

The individual is at the heart of New Age practices, which aim to bring people in better touch with themselves and the spiritual force within them. As one of Aupers and Houtman's interviewees said:

> **I experience god, the divine, as something within me. I feel it as being present within myself. I connect with it as I focus my attention on my inner self, when I meditate . . . It's all about self-knowledge, being conscious about yourself . . . It has nothing to do with something that's outside you that solves things for you.**
>
> (Aupers and Houtman 2006: 204–5)

Because of this focus on the self, Heelas and Woodhead (2005) describe the New Age as 'subjective-life' spiritualities, and contrast these with traditional 'life-as' religion's prescribed roles (life as a daughter, father, worker, etc.). Several decades earlier, Luckmann (1967: 113–17) identified what he believed was a major trend under way, a turn from church-oriented religion to a privatized religion. At that time, this 'invisible religion' fell outside the scope of sociology of religion; now, it is impossible to ignore. Subjective-life spirituality sees the individual as the source of authority; religion, in contrast, prioritizes external sources of authority (religious texts, rituals or traditions). This attitude is epitomized in the slogan of health-club chain Fitness First: 'Be yourself, only better' (Heelas 2006: 224). Self-spiritualities are symptomatic of a turn in culture that they call 'subjectivization' or the 'spiritual revolution'.

Although some writers criticize alternative spirituality for functioning as a kind of spiritual marketplace that attracts people purely out of self-interest, varying degrees of New Age involvement exist. Heelas (1996: 117–19) identifies three degrees of involvement: the 'fully engaged' may be practitioners with a career as a life coach or Reiki practitioner. There are groups that are tied into larger networks, such as the Universal Federation of Pagans in the USA, to which the fully engaged may belong. Those with mid-range commitment, 'serious part-timers', fit spiritual practices into their daily lives and may, in fact, find this easier to do than those committed to traditional religion, for whom there are set times for worship that may conflict with work or family commitments. The 'casual part-timers' are the least committed; they treat New Age spirituality as a kind of consumer product that can be picked up and put down at leisure.

Alternative spirituality particularly attracts certain sectors of the population, notably women, the middle classes and those in what Bruce (1996: 217–22) calls the 'expressive professions' (writers, artists, counsellors, social workers). Also, different forms are attractive to different groups. While the middle classes may have sufficient money and confidence to invest in self-improvement, the working classes are more likely to view themselves as passive and turn to fortune-telling or horoscopes or spiritualism to contact departed family members (Bruce 1995: 117).

How significant is contemporary New Age spirituality? Some people believe that New Age spiritualities will not endure, because their focus on the self makes them 'existentially vacuous' and the lack of a solid social base renders them 'socially precarious' (Heelas 2006: 227). Bruce argues that alternative spiritualities are too diffuse to be coherent and are insufficiently organized into collective forms. Parents will not socialize children effectively to retain their commitment, he contends, since 'For all its talk of community, the New Age is the embodiment of individualism' (Bruce 1996: 225).

Others counter this, saying that those involved in alternative spiritualities are not selfish and prioritize caring for others; they believe that the improvements wrought within them by New Age practices will make them more effective at work and in relationships (Aupers and Houtman 2006). Also, New Age beliefs may be less rigid than traditional religion, but practitioners share core values, such as belief in some sort of spirit of life force or special healing powers. Moreover, there are strands such as Paganism that are communal and organized, with ritual practices and festivals and where parents bring up children in a spiritual community.

Gender and religion

Gender is an important issue within religion, notably because there are differences between men's and women's religious behaviour. These differences arise from two related factors: the views of religious texts and traditions, and the different experiences of men and women in the societies they inhabit. Three issues stand out where gender is concerned: religious authority, the home and family, and the body and sexuality (Aune 2009).

In some religions, religious authority is given only to men: women cannot be Roman Catholic priests or Muslim imams. Women have campaigned for access to leadership positions and been successful in progressive Judaism and the Anglican Church.

These spatial and role separations bring us to the second key issue, home and family. Many religious groups believe that women's role should be family-centred. We encountered this in the discussion of the difficulties of measuring religiosity; for Muslim and Jewish women, assessing religiosity by attendance at places of worship fails to account for the way women's religious obligations centre around the home and family. Doctrines instructing women to submit to their husbands exist in many religions. For instance, the Hindu Manusmirti scriptures advise women to serve even bad husbands as if they were gods. But submission doctrines can be reinterpreted: Muslim feminists exercise considerable energy refuting the Quranic verse that appears to permit a man to beat his wife. While women care for their homes, their children and the religious community, men take the provider role.

When it comes to the body, religions that adopt a dualistic way of thinking generally associate women with the body and regard their sexuality as unclean or polluting. In Hinduism and Judaism, rules restrict women's movements during menstruation and after childbirth and require them to undergo purification rituals. Concerns that women's bodies are either unclean or unduly arousing to male onlookers provide the rationale for religious restrictions surrounding women's clothing. While most religions endorse sex as an important part of marriage, some, notably Buddhism and Roman Catholicism, keep their most exalted positions of religious authority for celibate men.

In Western societies, women's religious behaviour is changing. For at least two centuries, more women than men have attended church, engaged in private devotional practices and subscribed to religious beliefs. The gender imbalance is most acute in alternative spirituality, where only around a third of those involved are male. But recent research shows a decreasing gender imbalance that is occurring mainly because women's church attendance is experiencing decline. It seems, therefore, that there is a connection between gender and secularization. Brown's (2001) book *The Death of Christian Britain* makes the case that secularization is related to the changing position of women. Until recently, women were the main carriers of religiosity because they spent most of their lives in the private sphere, where the church and home are located and intertwine. Christianity has been a key part of their female identity. But from the 1960s, the feminist movement and sexual revolution challenged traditional views, giving women aspirations that took them away from the housewife role. Even though full gender equality remains elusive, women's opportunities have expanded immeasurably. Women have entered paid employment in much greater numbers, partly out of choice but also because rising living costs have made it difficult to survive on a male partner's wage. Family forms have diversified, with more women remaining single and childless, cohabiting and getting divorced and fewer living in nuclear families. These changes have had a significant impact on their religiosity.

Research on religion in contemporary Western women's lives suggests that women fall into three groups. First are the *home-centred* women, whose priority is their families, even if they engage in part-time work. They tend to be traditionally Christian because Christianity fits around their commitments, affirming their priorities through providing activities such as coffee mornings and mother-and-toddler groups. Next are the *jugglers*, who combine home and work. These women are more likely to be found in alternative or New Age spirituality because alternative spiritualities do most to help women who are negotiating private/public boundaries, affirming their commitments to their families while also endorsing female empowerment and the search for fulfilment outside the home. The last group are *work-centred*. These women are more likely to follow male patterns of religiosity, abandoning church because it does not fit with their demanding work schedules and taking on a more secular outlook (Woodhead 2005; Aune *et al.* 2008).

Where future trends are concerned, home-centred femininity is likely to decline, while numbers of jugglers and career-centred women are rising. This suggests that traditional religion needs to adapt if it wants to retain women whose work schedules cannot easily incorporate weekly church meetings. If this does not happen, then Christianity's likely future lies in 'believing without belonging' or merging with alternative spiritualities.

A closer look

Gender and sexuality in the Anglican Church

Gender and sexuality have been central to debates in the Anglican Church in recent years. The ordination of women and gay men as bishops is so divisive that a split in the Anglican Communion is possible.

In 2008, after intensely emotional debates, the General Synod voted to ordain women as bishops. Some opponents, from the evangelical and Anglo-Catholic wings of the Church, threatened to leave the Communion unless the Church provided alternative structures (known as 'super-bishops') enabling them to avoid taking direction from a female bishop. The Synod rejected the alternative provisions as inappropriate but agreed to devise a code of practice for those who, out of conscience, cannot accept women bishops.

The 2003 ordination of Gene Robinson as Bishop of New Hampshire in America ignited conflicts over gay bishops. Conservative clergy threatened to leave the Anglican Communion if it continued to support homosexuality. Conservatives believe that resolutions of the 1998 Lambeth Conference – which ruled sex outside heterosexual marriage as sinful and rejected the ordination of gay clergy and the blessing of same-sex unions – have been broken. However, liberals argue that there is a theological rationale for same-sex relationships. Although his role as Archbishop of Canterbury has led him to take a more conservative stance in favour of Church unity, before his appointment Rowan Williams contended that faithful homosexual relationships can reflect the love of God just as heterosexual marriage can.

In a move that should have appeased traditionalists and mitigated against future splits, the 2008 Lambeth Conference supported the 1998 regulations and said that the Church should not bless same-sex unions or ordain gay clergy. Yet strength of feeling led over 200 conservative bishops, notably from the global south (mainly Africa), to stay away from the 2008 Lambeth Conference. They held an alternative meeting, the Global Anglican Future Conference, in Jerusalem. This led to the establishment of the Fellowship of Confessing Anglicans, a new network to support bishops who felt they could not submit to the authority of those with liberal views on sexuality. This is not a rival communion, and yet it nevertheless paves the way for more decisive splits in the future.

These debates about sexuality and gender centre on different interpretations of the Bible and Christian tradition. But some observers have argued that these debates are not just theological, and that insecurity and prejudice about identity and gender also explain these fierce divisions.

Question

1. **Why do you think gender and sexuality are so often the focus of religious debates?**

However, the rise of Islam presents a challenge, as Islam is growing in the West (van Nieuwkerk 2006), and Muslim women tend to be home-centred. The future may not be certain, but we need to pay attention to women's lives in order to understand contemporary religion.

Conclusion

In this chapter, we have explored the key issues in the sociology of religion today. We have looked at what religion is and how it is defined and researched. We have considered the structure and formation of religious organizations, especially in relation to sects and new religions. Under the social conditions of late modernity or postmodernity, we have debated whether religion is in decline or whether in fact it is experiencing a resurgence as non-Christian religions and spiritual practices increase in popularity. Sociologists are interested in religion's role in societies and its relationship with social change, and we have explored a range of classical and recent approaches to this. Sociologists of religion have been concerned predominantly with religion in Western societies, and this has been our prime focus. Yet, as globalization continues to reshape the contours of the world and our understandings of it, religion will demand an increasingly global approach. The mass media and new forms of technology are fundamental to the global experience, and the media and popular culture are growing in importance for religion. Additionally, issues of identity – ethnicity, gender, sexuality and age, for instance – are more salient: we are becoming aware that different groups of people experience religion differently and that religion operates alongside other social markers to define who we are. As the twenty-first century progresses, religion will continue, change and adapt to the challenges of the modern – and postmodern – world.

Summary

- Religion is an increasingly important area in the study of contemporary society.
- Religion can be defined by its essence (a substantive definition) or by its role in society (a functional definition). In brief, religions are systems of beliefs and practices that provide meaning or orient individuals and groups to a supernatural realm.
- Classical sociologists, notably Marx, Weber and Durkheim, analysed the role of religion in the transition to modern capitalist societies. They were interested in the relationship between religion and social change.
- Sociologists are interested in discovering how religious people are. This 'religiousness' is called religiosity and can be analysed using quantitative and qualitative research methods.
- Secularization is a hotly debated area in the sociology of religion. Secularization refers to the declining influence of religion in society. Many sociologists believe that Western societies have experienced significant secularization. Others see evidence of a religious resurgence.
- The study of religious organization is another important area. Sociologists have investigated types of religious organization, especially churches, sects and new religious movements.
- New religious movements, alternative spiritualities and fundamentalism are forms of religion that have experienced success since the 1960s.
- Variables such as gender play an important role in religious behaviour. Religion has traditionally been more popular with women than men, but this may be changing.

Links

The theoretical explanations for the role of religion suggested by Marx, Weber and Durkheim (pp. 652–657) can be related to their broader theoretical writings examined in Chapter 2.

The integrative role of religion links to the discussion of cultural identity in Chapter 1.

Further reading

Aldridge, A. (2007) *Religion in the Contemporary World*, 2nd edn, Cambridge: Polity Press.
An accessible and up-to-date sociological introduction to religion in the contemporary world, covering the latest developments and debates about religious diversity in the twenty-first century.

Furseth, I. and Repstad, P. (2006) *An Introduction to the Sociology of Religion*, Aldershot: Ashgate.
A clear and useful introduction to sociological approaches to religion, this book also shows how sociology of religion fits within sociology as a discipline.

Weller, P. (2008) *Religious Diversity in the UK: Contours and Issues*, London: Continuum.
A helpful overview of the variety of religion in the UK, with useful features and activities for students.

Journal of Contemporary Religion
An international academic journal dedicated to contemporary religion, especially in its new and emerging varieties.

Social Compass
An international academic journal publishing articles on the sociology of religion in English and French.

Websites

www.socrel.org.uk

BSA Sociology of Religion Study Group
The website of the British Sociological Association's Sociology of Religion Study Group, with details of activities, membership and resources for postgraduate students.

http://hirr.hartsem.edu/ency

Encyclopedia of Religion and Society
Online version of the *Encyclopedia of Religion and Society*, edited by William H. Swatos and published by AltaMira Press, with entries on many themes and topics in the sociology of religion.

www.intute.ac.uk/artsandhumanities/religion

Intute Religious Studies Resources
Database of religious studies resources for lecturers, students and researchers in UK further and higher education.

www.beliefnet.com

Beliefnet
A non-academic site that includes information and features about religion.

www.adherents.com

Adherents.com
An online index of religious groups and statistics relating to them.

Activities

Activity 1

Exploring horoscopes

Anthony Giddens (1991) argues that a feature of contemporary societies is their preoccupation with 'the reflexive project of the self'. Get hold of a horoscope from a popular magazine. Examine the way it presents the self. What can we learn from the presence of New Age themes in popular culture? How influential do you think horoscopes are?

Activity 2

Religion in your local area

Get hold of a map of your local area and some labels or stick-on notes. Using sources such as local telephone and information directories and the Internet, identify and label places of worship in your local area. These could include Christian churches, Hindu and Sikh temples, mosques, synagogues, Buddhist centres, and centres for alternative spirituality and new religions. You may want to colour-code these according to religion. When you have done this, reflect on what you have learned about religion in your area.

Questions

1. Which religions predominate, and why?
2. How long have these religions existed in your locality, and in what circumstances did they emerge?
3. How might some of the theories about religion introduced in this chapter be applied within your local area?

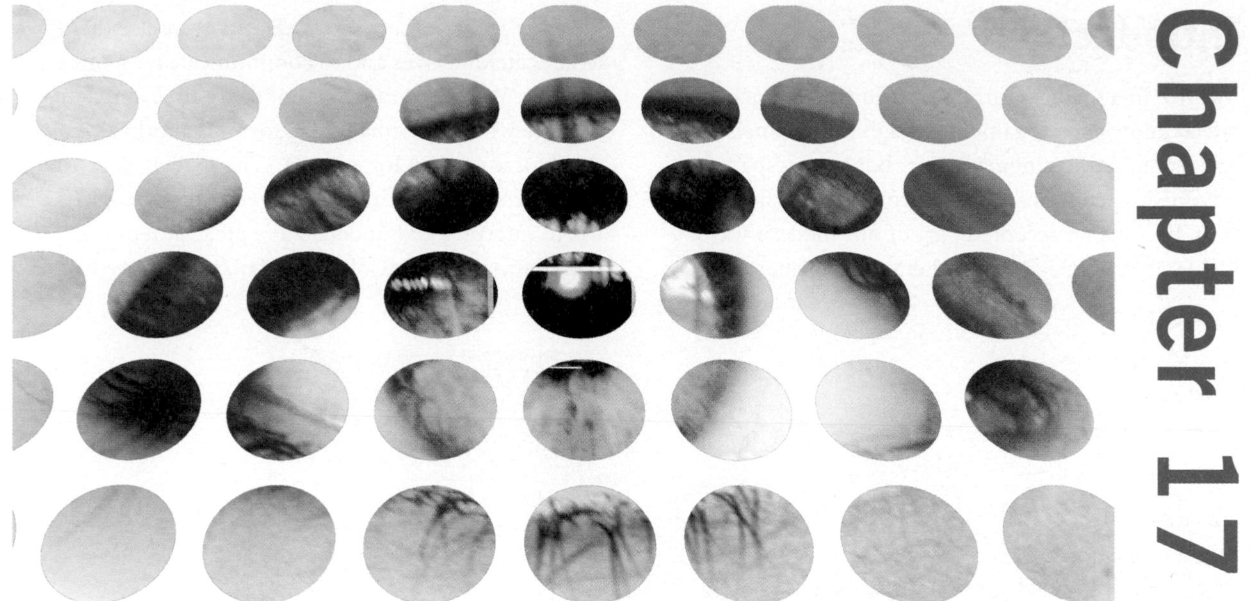

Chapter 17

The mass media

Through [the] networks of direct interpersonal communication we participate in a *situated culture*. We may hear or relay news of recent events in the neighbourhood, likewise rumours, gossip, stories or jokes. We may attend and participate in local events, entertainments, family ceremonies or other rituals. These cultures of situation are primarily oral, by word of mouth relationships and . . . tend to be limited and defined in relation to a particular locale. In certain ways they embody elements of pre-industrial cultures, relatively small-scale forms of social interaction and groupings derived from the immediate, face-to-face environment and its daily experience. Since the mid-nineteenth century, however, we have increasingly learned to live not only in our situated culture, but also in a *culture of mediation*, whereby specialised social agencies – the press, film and cinema, radio and television broadcasting – developed to supply and cultivate larger-scale forms of communication; mediating news and other forms of culture into the situation. 'Our' immediate world co-exists with the mediated 'world out there'. (O'Sullivan *et al*. 1994: 12–13)

Key issues

- How have the mass media developed and extended their influence in modern societies, particularly in Britain?
- What factors determine and constrain the content of the mass media?
- What are the major sociological explanations of the role of the mass media in society?
- How do the mass media influence social and cultural behaviour – in particular, what is the relationship between the portrayal of violence in the media and violent behaviour?

Introduction

We live in a media-saturated world where much of our social knowledge is gained through the channels of television, radio, cinema, video, books, newspapers, advertising, comics and home computers. The media have become an accepted part of our modern way of life: they give us news and entertainment, sell us lifestyles and reinforce social identities; we use them to educate ourselves and to communicate with one another. We spend much of our spare time and a lot of money on the media in one form or another, and much of it is taken for granted. 'The media are central in the provision of ideas and images which people use to interpret and understand a great deal of their everyday existence' (Golding 1974: 78). Twenty-five

Figure 17.1 Freddie Flintoff on the big screen in Liverpool city centre at the start of England's World Cup campaign in 2006 – it ended in a riot! © Mike Keating

years later, Briggs and Cobley (1998: 4) extend this view to assert that 'as we move into the new millennium the media are increasingly a central part of our lives, our cultures and global economies' (Figure 17.2).

Stop and think

- Which of the following media do you use on a regular basis: (a) daily newspapers; (b) magazines; (c) radio; (d) television; (e) video; (f) home computer; and (g) the Internet?
- Which do you use most for news and information?
- Which do you use most for entertainment?
- Keep a diary for a week and record your use of the media.
- What patterns emerge? Are there any surprises? How much of your cultural world is 'situated' and how much is 'mediated'? (See the quote from O'Sullivan *et al*. 1994 on p. 683.) How do you compare with your classmates?

It is clear from market research and social surveys that people in general depend heavily upon the media for information and entertainment. By looking at ownership of media hardware and the purchase of consumer items we can get some idea of the level of media saturation of modern society.

Once regarded as luxury goods and symbols of status, TV sets can be found in 99 per cent of households in Britain, with over 80 per cent owning video recorders and CD players and 80 per cent possessing a DVD player. Mobile phone ownership has increased fourfold in the period 1997–2006, to 80 per cent of households, and there has been a similar rate of increase over the same period in the ownership of home computers (65 per cent) and Internet access (55 per cent). Figure 17.2 only takes us up to 2006, but it shows the rapid growth in the areas of new technology in the UK. However, we should note that globally a 'digital divide' has opened up in terms of access to the Internet, which favours the richer nations (Table 17.1).

Table 17.1 Internet penetration by continent (2007)

Continent	Proportion of population using Internet
North America	71%
Oceania/Australia	57%
Europe	43%
Latin America/Caribbean	22%
Middle East	17%
Africa	5%

(Source: Internet World Stats (2008))

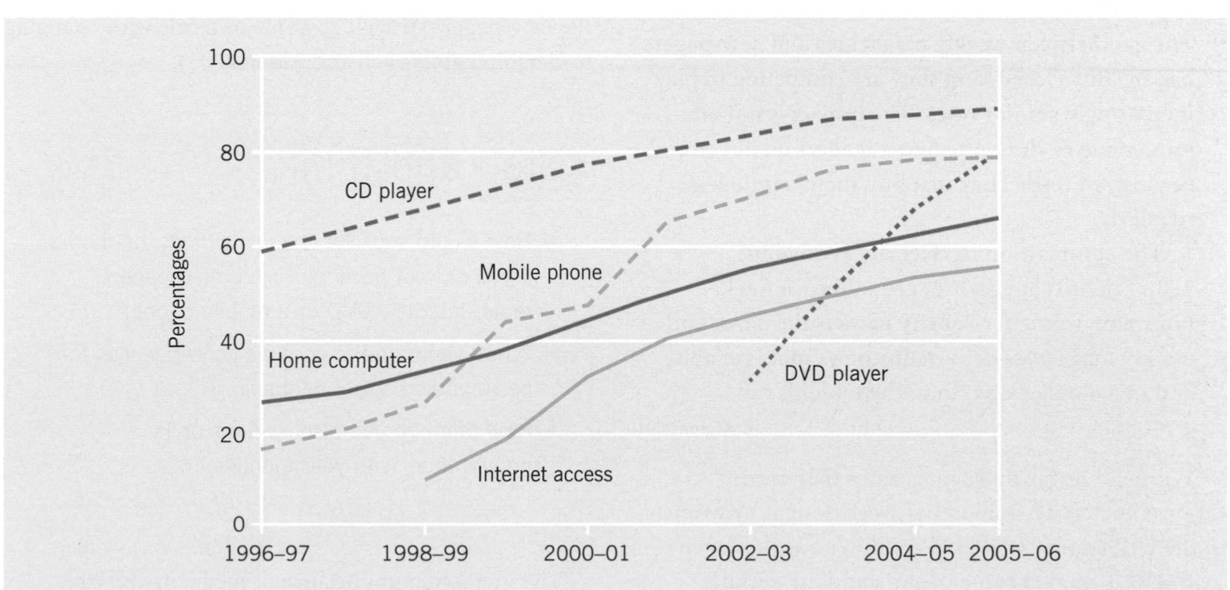

Figure 17.2 New technology in UK households
Source: *Family Expenditure Survey* and *Expenditure and Food Survey*, Office for National Statistics (*Social Trends* 37, 2007)

The computer games market now represents a $25 billion industry, with approximately 70 per cent of UK teenagers gaming online (Macionis and Plummer 2008: 719). In contrast with this drive towards a more privatized leisure culture, the cinema has increased in popularity since the 1980s. According to the British Council's website (www.britfilm.com), there were 167.3 million visits to the cinema in Britain in 2003, with similar growth in the twenty-first century noted in the USA, Europe and Japan. However, by mid-2008, reports in the UK suggested a dramatic reversal of interest, with annual attendances falling by 11 per cent in one year to a low of 151 million. This may be due to the rapid transfer of film to DVD format, but it may also be related to the poor quality of titles turned out in 2008 and the downturn in the economy.

The level of interest in newspapers and magazines has remained high, with 64 per cent of adults in Britain being regular readers of a daily newspaper and 71 per cent reading a Sunday paper. However, there has been an overall drop in readership over the past 50 years of an average two million readers per day, and the 'red-top' tabloids have taken the brunt, with the *Daily Mirror* losing around 7 per cent and the *Sun* 5 per cent per year. In the Sunday market too, the *Sunday Mirror*, the *People* and the *News of the World* are all losing readers. With audiences (especially younger ones) turning to alternative sources (TV, Internet, mobile phones) for their news, newspapers are also losing out to magazines that target the celebrity news once found in the tabloids:

> **The gap between weekly magazines and newspapers has steadily closed, and they are competing to play increasingly similar roles. The impact is not an immediate or dramatic one – readers do not stop buying red tops. They just buy them a little less regularly.**
>
> **The competition in celebrity is obvious: 2.8m celebrity magazines are sold each week. For many women, celebrity news is the news, and weekly magazines deliver this news more reliably, and in a glossier way, than the tabloids can.**
>
> (Ewington 2004)

Women buy far more magazines than men (approximately 17 million per week bought by women in the UK, compared with 4 million bought by men). Within this market some of the standard weeklies (*Woman*, *Woman's Own*, *Woman's Weekly*) are in decline, while those aimed at younger readers (such as *Chat* and *Heat*) are doing well. Women's lifestyle magazines have increased sales overall, with newcomer *Glamour* topping the charts, with sales of over half a million, and older competitors such as *Vogue* just making the top ten, with sales of 200,000. After a dip in fortunes in the mid-term, the *Guardian* reported an upturn in overall sales of 17.3 per cent during 2007.

The other staple diet in a gendered audience, once catered for by the tabloids through soft porn displays on page 3, can now be found in magazines that target 'football-loving, beer-swilling blokes'. Since the 1990s, new magazines such as *Loaded* and *FHM* have emerged with a content that is 'openly juvenile and not ashamed of it' (*Observer* 13.11.1994). More recently, this market has been assaulted by the arrival of men's weeklies *Nuts* and *Zoo*, which if anything are attempting to outdo the competition by taking 'dumbing down' to a new low. After a promising start, all of the above titles dipped and the men's magazine market turned back to its more traditional interest in hobbies such as fitness and motoring. The sales situation has been made been more difficult for the 'lads' mags' with the emergence of titles such as *Sport* and the online *Monkey*, which rely entirely on advertising and are offered free to those who want to read them. (For a useful potted history of men's magazines, see www.magforum.com/mens.htm).

With sales running at £7 billion per year and advertisers spending over £2 billion in this sector (in March 2003, newspaper advertising revenue fell below the £2 billion mark for the first time in 70 years), it is clear that the magazine market remains vibrant while the newspapers struggle to come to terms with changing readership habits (Bell and Alden 2003).

Stop and think

- How would your life change without the media, if you did not have television, newspapers, radio, Internet, DVD or a mobile phone?
- What would be the possible consequences for personal and social interaction?
- How often do you discuss films or TV programmes with your friends?

The increasing importance of media in everyday life led Masterman to argue over 20 years ago that 'Media studies has become as important as reading' and identified the following reasons for its inclusion in the curriculum:

> **high levels of media production, consumption and saturation within contemporary society;**
> **ideological importance of the media and their influence as consciousness industries;**
> **growth in the manufacture and management of information and its dissemination through the media;**
> **increasing penetration of the media into our central democratic processes;**
> **importance of visual communications and data handling in many areas;**
> **increasing cross-media ownerships which concentrate power and influence in fewer hands;**
> **increasing commercialization of the media environment, the privatization of information and the threat to public service obligations.**
>
> (Masterman 1985: 2)

These issues are particularly relevant in a media-saturated world where it is almost impossible to talk objectively about our relationship to them. As Postman has observed, the media are not only taken for granted but also mythologized into part of the natural order; the alphabet and the television set are no longer regarded as human inventions but, like trees and clouds, are seen as elements of natural inheritance (Postman 1987). Fiske and Hartley put their finger on it when they describe our problematic relationship to television:

> **Everybody knows what it is like to watch TV . . . and it is television's familiarity, its centrality to our culture, that makes it so important, so fascinating and so difficult to analyse. It is rather like the language we speak: taken for granted but both complex and vital to an understanding of the way human beings have created their world.**
>
> (Fiske and Hartley 1978: 16)

Our main intention throughout this chapter is to provide a comprehensive grasp of the relationship between the individual, the media and society. Attempts by sociologists to emphasize the social role of the 'mass media' have led to some concern over the use of the term itself, which implies an undifferentiated and passive audience and encourages the simplistic belief that all media operate in more or less the same way with little recognition that individuals may use different media in different ways. We share these misgivings but retain the use of the term 'mass media' to denote the way in which most people rely on the media for much of what passes for cultural activity and information in the modern world.

The rest of this chapter focuses on the historical development of the media, the relationship between the media and society, the power of the media to influence attitudes and behaviour, and the ways in which audiences interpret and respond to media texts.

The development of the mass media in Britain

Over time the mass media have come to play an increasingly important part in the everyday transmission of information and culture. Knowledge based on direct experience and the oral transmission of culture are parts of a fading tradition in which face-to-face communication was crucial. What was once a culture founded in folk tales and contained within clear geographical boundaries has given way to an electronic revolution that respects neither time nor place. The world has been reduced to what Marshall McLuhan (1964) referred to as 'the global village', in which our culture becomes mediated rather than situated (see the quote from O'Sullivan *et al.* 1994 on p. 683).

The rate and scale of these changes are also important aspects of the mediation of culture; as yesterday's technological miracle becomes today's obsolete gizmo, we begin to grasp how rapidly our lives become transformed by media technologies that we take for granted. We focus here on the most widely recognized technologies of the press and broadcasting, as well as the newer technologies of mobile phones, MP3 players and the Internet.

The press

The early development of the British press is often associated with the wider campaigns for individual liberty and workers' rights. In this struggle the newly emerging press was seen as a potential vehicle for political agitation and consequently became a target for government repression. Using a combination of legal sanctions and covert operations, the governments of the late eighteenth and early nineteenth centuries infiltrated, bribed and intimidated newspapers into political obedience. The introduction of a 'stamp tax' on all newpapers simply penalized the mainstream press and created an underground (unstamped) press, which

Case study

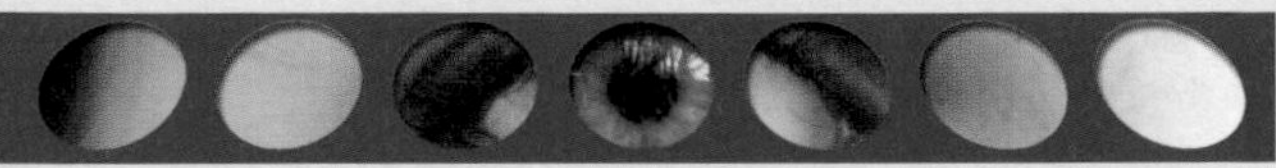

The media in Britain 1945 and 1990

1945 There was no television. About ten million households had a radio set and most were run off the mains, not off a battery. The compulsory licence-fee was ten-shillings [50p]. You had a choice of two BBC stations. One was 'serious'; the other broadcast light music and entertainment. The nine o'clock evening news had an audience of half the population during the war, but this fell quickly in 1945. You could hear music at home on a wind-up gramophone with ten or twelve-inch 78 rpm bakelite records. Most people read one of nine London-edited 'national' morning newspapers. If it was the *Daily Mirror* or *Daily Sketch*, it was tabloid. Local evening papers were smaller, but more numerous. Even more people read a Sunday paper than a daily, often for the sport. The national dailies differed sharply in style between the low-circulation 'qualities' and the mass-circulation 'populars'. All nine were separately owned by press barons, such as Lords Beaverbrook, Kemsley and Rothermere. On the news-stands were several popular illustrated news and feature magazines: *Everybody's*, *Illustrated* and *Picture Post*. There were numerous general magazines and a growing market in women's weeklies and monthlies. You went to the cinema regularly. Thirty million cinema tickets were sold each week. The short weekly 'newsreels', a mix of news and feature stories, gave a foretaste of TV news. Hollywood films predominated. In addition to the main feature, you saw a shorter, low budget 'B' movie.

1990 There was no escape from television. Three homes out of five had two sets and one person in six had three. ITV broadcast round the clock. Viewers had a choice of four channels and between them, BBC1, BBC2, ITV and CH4 provided some 450 hours of programmes a week. The licence fee was £71, all of which went to the BBC. ITV was paid for by advertisements, carefully regulated by the Independent Broadcasting Authority. We spent twenty-six hours a week watching TV: news, soaps, films, the House of Commons, endless studio discussion amongst politicians. Snooker was the most popular televised sport with only one team game [football] in the TV top-ten. We spent eight hours a week listening to the radio, but mainly whilst doing something else. The BBC had four national stations and thirty-two locals. There was a commercial station for most people and any number of overseas stations. Stations mostly broadcast music and 'chat'. BBC Radio 4 was news and talk; Radio 3 for classical music. You could listen almost anytime and anywhere, especially with a Walkman headset. Music of high technical quality was available in the home through CDs, cassettes, LPs and pop-videos. Despite TV, most people still read a daily newspaper. Of eleven main dailies, six were tabloids with 80 per cent of the circulation. Your paper had 30–40 pages or more; a large proportion of features, pages of small ads and, increasingly, colour. The Sunday papers came in sections. Fewer people read an evening paper, primarily to see what was on TV. Half of us bought a local weekly paper, and three-quarters received 'free-weeklies'. The national dailies were bunched into eight ownership groups, headed by Murdoch, Maxwell and Rothermere. They had interests as international multimedia organisations; TV, radio, film, video, music and book publishing. Magazines were very popular, and station news-stands commonly displayed over 700 titles, including music and hi-fi, computing, body-building, sports and so on.

(Seymour-Ure 1992: 1–5)

Question

1. There seems to be a world of a difference, and yet these developments took place in only 45 years. Since 1990 you may have noticed media developments that should be added to an update of this snapshot; what would they be? Which have affected your own life most?

quickly became popular with the new industrial working class for whom they were intended. The government appeared to accept defeat and eventually abolished the stamp tax. This is often hailed as a great achievement in the struggle for democracy but there are two perspectives on what this meant.

The liberal thesis

For some media historians, such as Koss (1973), the end of stamp duty was more than simply a political defeat for the government; it represents a symbolic moment in the emergence of a 'free press' and political democracy. It is associated with a 'golden age' of British journalism that ushered in the transition from official to popular control and took seriously the demands of a newly educated mass audience. Despite the fact that ownership of the new commercial press was concentrated in the hands of a few powerful 'press barons', the liberal thesis suggests that those who own the press are ultimately subservient to the demands of their readers and cannot afford to ignore their interests (sometimes called 'market democracy'). Hence, the twentieth century is characterized by a further 'golden age' in which control shifts from the press baron to the corporate expert and the professional journalist is committed to satisfying their customers and running an efficient business (Koss 1973). There are strong similarities between this liberal historical thesis and the pluralist perspective considered in the section on perspectives on the media (pp. 711–724). See especially Whale (1980) and Veljanovski (1989, 1991).

The 'power without responsibility' thesis

The 'liberalization' of the press perspective is challenged by Curran and Seaton (1991, 1997), who argue that it is a political myth that disguises the real nature of the modern press and its relationship to those who own and control it.

First, they reject the view that the repeal of the stamp tax was a victory for press freedom and identify a range of less obvious purposes for the reform: to destroy the popularity of the radical press, to enhance the power (and profitability) of the 'respectable' press, and to ensure that the newly freed newspapers were owned and controlled by 'men of good moral character, of respectability and of capital' (Curran and Seaton 1991: 29).

Second, they argue that this commercial involvement hardly represents a transition from official to popular control as the ownership of the press rapidly became concentrated in the hands of a few 'press barons'; by 1937, the four major players were Lords Beaverbrook, Rothermere, Camrose and Kemsley, who between them owned 50 per cent of national and local dailies and 30 per cent of the Sunday papers, including most of the popular titles.

Third, this concentration of ownership raised concerns about the extent to which these powerful and politically motivated men used their positions to influence editorial policy and promote their own political interests and careers (see Jenkins 1986: 24–5). Consequently, politicians became concerned about the influence of unaccountable proprietors who enjoyed 'power without responsibility'. After the Second World War, a Royal Commission was set up to investigate 'the growth of the monopolistic tendencies in the control of the press'. Despite its conclusion that concentration of ownership did not represent a threat to freedom of expression as long as the public got what it wanted, the issues of monopoly ownership, editorial freedom and political bias have continued to dominate discussion of the relationship between society and 'its' press and been the subject in Britain of two further Royal Commissions. According to Curran and Seaton, the commercial press did not come into being as a celebration of freedom but as a deliberate attempt at repression and ideological control:

> **The period around the middle of the nineteenth century . . . did not inaugurate a new era of press freedom and liberty: it introduced a new system of press censorship more effective than anything that had gone before. Market forces succeeded where legal repression had failed in conscripting the press to the social order.**
>
> (Curran and Seaton 1991: 9)

Fourth, they argue that 'market democracy' did not enhance or widen political debate. New types of newspaper emerged that were aimed at the literate working and lower middle classes but geared towards entertainment, consensus and patriotism. The *Daily Mail*, *Daily Express*, *Daily Mirror* and *News of the World* all emerged as mass-circulation newspapers for the lower-class reader, with *The Times* and the *Daily Telegraph* providing serious news for the middle and upper classes. In the new commercial environment, advertising revenue enabled the cover prices to fall dramatically and placed the commercial press in a strong position to see off radical competitors that refused to dilute their political seriousness and as a result were unappealing to readers and advertisers alike.

Finally, they point out that the 'second golden age' of press freedom is as illusory as the first, with no serious transfer of control from owners to professional managers and editors taking place. Curran and Seaton argue that some of the old barons clung on to their power well into the 1960s, by which time a new generation of 'interventionist proprietors' had emerged, including Rupert Murdoch (News International), Robert Maxwell (Mirror Group) and Conrad Black (*Daily Telegraph*). Curran and Seaton complain that this is not so much a period of 'market democracy' as one of concentration of ownership and corporate takeover resulting in the 'integration [of the press] into the core sectors of financial and industrial capital':

> **The ownership of newspapers thus became one strategy by which large business organisations sought to influence the environment in which they operated . . . newspapers campaigned more actively for the general interests of big business, under closer proprietorial supervision. This development signified an important, long-term shift: commercial newspapers became increasingly the instruments of large business conglomerates with political interests rather than an extension of the party system.**
>
> (Curran and Seaton 1991: 101)

What is interesting in all of this is the way in which a genuinely radical press has become depoliticized, commercialized and integrated into the economic and political core of society; a medium that began its life as a force for political agitation and social change has become part of the entertainment industry (Pilger 1997: 18).

Broadcasting

Unlike newspapers, whose early evolution appeared in opposition to the state, broadcasting has always been subject to state regulation and control, primarily through the allocation of scarce channel frequencies. In some societies the state has retained strong regulation over the broadcasting media, while in others the airways were quickly opened up to privatization and advertising. According to Negrine (1998), this tension between public service broadcasting and private competition 'reflects different socio-political traditions, economic forces [and] geographic features' to be found in Europe:

> **Unlike the US experience where radio broadcasting developed within a competitive framework with private commercially funded companies running the broadcasting services, European countries mostly favoured some form of state control over broadcasting as a way of avoiding the chaos in the airwaves which was characteristic of an unregulated system and also a way of ensuring that the 'public interest' was not overlooked.**
>
> (Negrine 1998: 225)

In March 2005, the UK government confirmed that the BBC would continue to be funded from a licence fee. This will be reviewed in 2016, when the BBC's Charter comes up for reconsideration. (For a comparative account of the differences in media delivery in Europe, see Kleinsteuber 2009.)

Radio

Radio is often overlooked when we talk about the media, and yet before the advent of television radio was one of the main sources of news and entertainment in the home. Beginning life as a 'wireless' version of the telephone, the radio very quickly emerged as a means of mass communication that, in Britain, came under the regulation of the BBC and its first director John Reith, a strict Calvinist who recognized the importance of the radio to act as 'trustee of the national interest' and to defend middle-class standards of Christian morality. This model of public-service radio broadcasting characterized the BBC for the next 40 years, with a clear mission 'to educate, to inform, and to entertain'.

Since the 1960s the BBC has faced competition from commercial radio stations funded through advertising and appealing to a range of tastes (rolling news, sport, chat shows, etc.). This 'narrowcasting' of 'format radio' is 'the life blood of commercialism' and 'all but unstoppable' (Crisell 1998: 120). Since 1984, when there were only 48 local commercial stations, the independent sector mushroomed to boast 248 by the year 2000, outnumbering the BBC by six to one; the independent sector increased its advertising revenue throughout the 1990s more than threefold to an annual total estimated at £500 million in 2002. According to Robinson (cited in Gibson 2008: 168), the BBC has managed to defend its market share and retains 54 per cent, with Radios 1, 2 and 4 netting regular audiences of ten million or more. Consequently, Crisell argues that commercial radio has done little to increase consumer choice or to challenge the BBC's claim to quality public broadcasting:

> **Commercial radio has enriched output in one or two areas, notably pop and rock music, but not in many others such as documentary, features, drama, comedy and light entertainment, where the BBC's near-monopoly has been left largely unchallenged.**
>
> (Crisell 1998: 115)

Stop and think

How good is radio? Listen for at least an hour to each of the following:

(a) Radio 1

(b) Radio 4

(c) Radio 5 Live

(d) talkSport

(e) Your BBC local radio station

(f) Your Independent local radio station

- To what extent does each fulfil Lord Reith's original mission for public service broadcasting 'to educate, inform and entertain' (see p. 690)?
- Why do you think some media forms are valued more highly than others?

See also Geoff Baldwin's online critique, 'The trouble with modern UK commercial radio', at www.icce.rug.nl/~soundscapes/VOLUME02/Trouble_with_modern_UK_commercial_radio.shtml.

Television

Most people spend some of their daily leisure time watching TV, which is, by far, the most popular form of home-based leisure – the average person watches approximately 27 hours of TV every week. Robert Kubey of Rutgers University has estimated that the average American spends nine years in front of the TV in a lifetime, and figures from Japan and Europe show similar patterns. In a MORI poll conducted for *Radio Times* in the UK, 54 per cent said that they would be lonely without the television, although 67 per cent were prepared to admit that there was 'nothing worth watching'. Viewing figures have had their ups and downs since the 1990s, and both the BBC and ITV have had to face falling audience rates since the start of the twenty-first century, due partly to competition from Sky, cable and digital stations. Whatever the precise picture might be, it is still the case that 'Television remains the number one leisure activity in the UK' (Bell and Alden 2003: 87). This is probably true across Europe and the USA, although new technologies may have some impact over the next couple of decades (see pp. 692–699). All social groups spend roughly a quarter of their viewing time on information and news, and 40 per cent view light entertainment and light drama, though there are differences according to social class and gender: women are more frequent watchers than men, and viewing appears higher among social classes C2, D and E. High-rating soap operas, quiz shows and news programmes tend to be watched by a complete cross-section without any skew towards a particular age group, sex or class.

Development of television broadcasting

Television started life in 1936, and its exciting potential was exploited by commercial broadcasters in the USA after the war, but in Britain it remained under the control of the BBC and developed more slowly. By the end of the 1950s, however, television had supplanted radio as the more popular broadcasting medium. At a time when the disposable income of the 'affluent' working class had increased to the extent that they represented a large consumer market, it was dangerous to ignore their tastes, which were becoming heavily influenced by the popular culture of North America (see Tunstall 1977: 100–101).

A range of reforms and technological developments during the second half of the twentieth century saw great changes in the content and delivery of TV, particularly the introduction of commercial channels. This has led to an ongoing debate on the best way to fund television and the importance of consumer choice. Writers such as Hargreaves have argued that it is unfair for the BBC to be run as a tax-funded monopoly that can afford to ignore the tastes of the public and have demanded an end to the licence fee (Williams 1994: 9). According to Veljanovski, the choices offered to TV audiences represent a triumph for viewer sovereignty and the death knell for publicly funded broadcasting:

> **The viewer will no longer be restricted to a few general entertainment channels, but will be able to create his or her own viewing schedule at times which are convenient to them and not the broadcasters. In the absence of government restrictions on the spread of new technologies and**

programming, viewers will have greater choice, variety and access to more programmes. It follows that British broadcasting should move towards a market system which recognises that viewers and listeners are the best ultimate judges on their own interest, which they can best satisfy if they have the option of purchasing from the broadcasting services from as many alternative sources of supply as possible.

(Veljanovski 1991: 14)

In defence of public service broadcasting it is argued that standards will fall and minority tastes will be axed should the licence fee be dropped in favour of an unregulated commercial system. The Campaign for Press and Broadcasting Freedom has lobbied for the preservation of public-service broadcasting in general and the BBC in particular:

The BBC is a major part of our daily lives. It entertains and informs us across radio, the Internet and TV. It is a testimony to the success of the public funding of broadcasting. It is central to the development of the political and cultural life of the country. We need to build on this success to create a better, more democratic, more creative BBC in the twenty-first century.

(O'Malley 2005: 3)

In a poll conducted in March 2004 by ICM, public opinion was evenly split, with 31 per cent supporting the retention of the licence fee, 31 per cent preferring the BBC to be funded through advertising (like ITV) and 36 per cent opting for subscription (like Sky).

Stop and think

- What assumptions about society lie behind the concept of public service broadcasting? How important is it in a period of rapid commercialization?
- Do you think that the BBC should continue to be funded by a licence fee?

The digital revolution: '57 channels and nothin' on' (Bruce Springsteen)

Since the mid-1990s there have been massive technological changes to the way that TV programmes are broadcast and experienced by viewers. In 1994 Granville Williams predicted that the developments in fibre optics and digitization would create a new interactive multimedia environment in which nothing would be the same again.

Since then, the digital revolution in broadcasting has not only led to improved quality of reception but also dramatically increased the number of channels available and provided the opportunity to interact with TV in a variety of ways. The number of homes receiving digital transmission has increased steadily, so that by 2004 over 50 per cent of households in the UK had digital TV. By the end of the decade, the government intends to turn off analogue transmission altogether.

On the consequences of all this for society, opinion is divided between what Curran and Seaton (1991: Chapter 14) call the 'neophiliacs' on the one hand and the 'cultural pessimists' on the other. In the view of the neophiliacs, we are moving towards a bright new post-industrial future (the information society), where the whole world is at our fingertips thanks to the Internet and the World Wide Web (WWW).

In reply, the cultural pessimists point to the inevitable decline of quality broadcasting and the damage done to cultural standards by the new forms of communication. Concentration of media ownership, the globalization of culture and the distortion of political power represent the unwelcome side of the new, media-saturated order. In the view of Graham Murdock (1990), we run the risk of creating a world where the principle of universal access to information is sacrificed in the interests of diversity of production and consumer choice (see Activity, p. 741).

New media

Apart from the changes in media broadcasting, the technological developments mentioned above have had an impact on our lives in other ways. The invention of the DVD player spells the end of video, while MP3 players make it possible to carry our entire music collections around on a 40-gigabyte iPod (*The Times* on 14 April 2008 reported IBM claiming a breakthrough in digital storage that would enable MP3 players to hold half a million songs). Linked to computer technology, both have transformed the way in which we access, store and distribute information. In social terms, the two most important innovations have probably been the invention of the mobile phone and the emergence of broadband Internet provision. Both have contributed in different ways to the 'network society' predicted by

Figure 17.3 Virtual escapism
Cartoon by Ian Hering

the Spanish sociologist Castells (2000). In his work, the revolution in information technology is as significant to our social experiences today as the Industrial Revolution was to those living in eighteenth-century Europe. The twin forces of digitalization and globalization have created a world in which we become increasingly estranged from fellow human beings and more dependent upon the virtual networks created through cybernetics (see also Flew 2002).

The mobile phone has transformed not only the way we communicate with one another but also our social relationships and the ground rules for social interaction. Hans Geser has attempted a sociological analysis of the impact of the mobile phone on our lives and suggests that, as they provide opportunities to escape the barriers to communication imposed by local and interpersonal settings and to increase our potential range of contacts, they may also alter the way we relate to one another in real time and space – what we referred to as *situated culture* at the start of this chapter. This is particularly apparent in the impact that the 'unpredictable and uneasy intrusions of distant others' may have upon the interpersonal and intimate aspects of social life as well as the disruption caused to everyday interactions by the summons of a ringtone. Apart from turning the thing off, the recipient can respond in three ways:

- *Flight* – The most drastic response is leaving the place of collocal (face-to-face) interaction for a corner or another room, where the phone talk cannot be overheard.
- *Suspension* – While remaining in the same physical location, the recipient suspends current activities or interactions for an undefined time.
- *Persistence* – Keeping current activities ongoing.

Whichever strategy for taking the call is made, the impact on the collocal interaction is inevitably disruptive for those on the receiving end:

> **There can be something comical about the mobile user attempting the difficult task of managing a call whose purpose and emotional registers are at odds with those around them: the conversation with a lover on a train, or with an irate boss in a bar. Certain conversations can induce emotional and**

Figure 17.4 Maria Sharapova keeps Wimbledon waiting while she phones her mother
PA Photos

> **bodily responses, which may be quite incompatible with their perceptions of their physical location. Their participants often look as though they don't quite know what to do with themselves, how to reconfigure the tones of voice and postures which would normally accompany such conversations. The mobile requires its users to manage the intersection of the real present and the conversational present in a manner that is mindful of both.**
>
> (Plant, cited in Geser 2004)

As Goffman has pointed out, rules governing our use of public space and for conducting private communication are taken for granted. The widespread use of mobile phones is beginning to rewrite these rule books. Rob Stones has noted:

> **It is difficult to sustain a mobile phone conversation in a public space without breaking either some of the rules of normal face-to-face interaction or the rules of civil person-to-person phone interactions.**
>
> (Stones 2001)

For a full discussion of these issues, see http://socio.ch/mobile/t_geser1.pdf.

The Internet is the other major development to have transformed our lives. Access to the Internet is not as widespread as mobile phone ownership, but its social impact is far more wide-ranging. Recent developments – particularly through digital technologies and the introduction of broadband transmission – have created an alternative world in which we can shop, play games, download music and create social networks of friends we will never meet (see Longhurst *et al.* 2008: 182–96 for a useful summary of the information society).

After 15 years as the UK media professionals' handbook, the 2008 *Guardian Media Guide* has been divided in two: traditional (offline) media and digital (online) media (Gibson 2008). This reflects the growth of digital platforms into areas such as news coverage, entertainment and advertising; the Internet's market share of advertising revenue, for example, has increased from 0.1 per cent in 1997 to 10.6 per cent in 2006, with Google taking 40 per cent of the £1834 million being spent. Rather than representing a direct challenge, new media technologies may herald an era of potential integration in which the traditional means of communication and the digital means feed off one

Case study

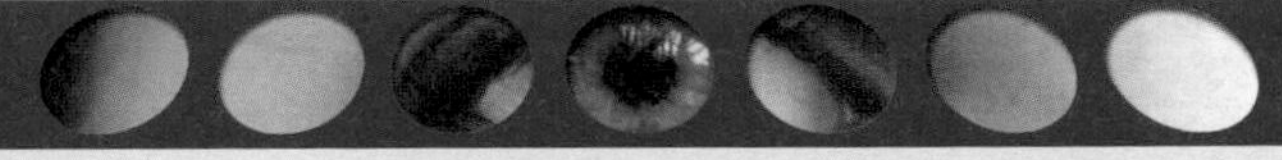

The Internet at its best . . . and worst

Cyberlibrary

As the Internet has expanded it becomes increasingly difficult to find what you want in the ocean of data sloshing around on the World Wide Web, but in 2004 Steven Levy reported on the latest technological breakthrough at Google, which promises to bring together the power of its search engine and the digitization of the printed page. At an average cost of $10 per volume, it would be possible to integrate the world's greatest library collections into its indexes and provide free access to all who need it. The cost of digitizing the 15 million books held in these collections would be covered by pegging adverts to the search results and using the revenue to subsidize the project. As Levy says:

> **Google's goal is to have everything at your fingertips, all the world's information digitized and instantly available to all who have a right to see it.**
>
> (Levy 2004)

The project is well under way, and the Google Library Project plans to harness the entire collections from the libraries of Harvard, Stanford and Oxford universities, as well as the New York Public Library. See http://books.google.com/googlebooks/library.html.

Cyberporn

It has been suggested that 'sex' is the most popular search term on the Internet. Using 'porn' for a search in Google will get you almost ten million hits. Not all of these are linked to porn sites, as some of them involve campaign groups against pornography, but it is clear that the Internet provides an almost unlimited opportunity to access materials that may be seen as offensive and, in some cases, illegal. The images and video downloads offer incest, paedophilia and rape as part of a staple diet that would be banned if offered over the counter. In 2001 several members of the Wonderland Club went to jail following an international police investigation of Internet child pornography across 12 countries. Almost a million images were traded online, and men abused their own children for the entertainment of fellow members using video-conferencing technology. Status within the club was achieved through the nature of abuse on offer. In a disturbing extension of the right to freedom of expression that the Internet provides, sites such as Ogrish.com now serve up videos of murder, torture and the beheading of hostages alongside hard-core porn as part of everyday entertainment. In this sense, the Internet may be seen to undermine general moral standards in ways that were previously unimaginable.

WAP technology

WAP is an attempt to bring together the two developments of mobile phones and the Internet and will enable customers to use their mobile phones to surf the Internet, access news items, interact with their computers, and enjoy the audio and video services already available through the digitization of information. In 2008, the iPhone G3 leapfrogged WAP technology with a mobile phone that links directly to the Internet and incorporates the functions of a digital camera, video player, MP3 player and broadband-connected PC. However, as research suggests, 'mobile entertainment' is not what people want from their phones. As Mike Masnik reports:

> **TV at home works because you turn it on and it works – and the user can sit back and relax while watching it. Radio in the car works, because you turn it on and it starts playing, and the user has nowhere else to go. On a mobile phone, there are other options, and if things cost too much and don't work as easily as consumer electronics, they'll find other things to do.**
>
> **More importantly, people still view their mobile phones as communication devices first. They buy them so they can talk to others or SMS others. Not because it lets them watch TV when they're away from home . . . In fact, study after study after study all seem to show that people want to use their phones to communicate . . .**
>
> **That isn't to say there isn't a market for mobile entertainment. In fact, it's likely to be a huge market – it's just that it has to be built on the foundation of communication and interaction, rather than broadcast. This is in the form of communicating**

Case study *continued*

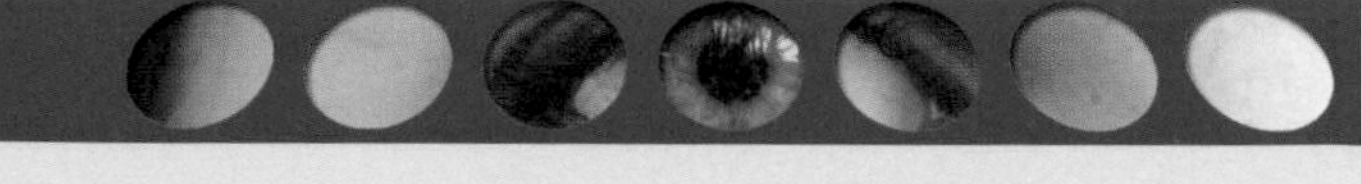

with each other for entertainment purposes, interactive gaming, file sharing and other forms of entertainment that actually take into account that the user is mobile and connected – rather than stationary and isolated. Simply moving entertainment to a mobile device and calling it mobile entertainment is missing the point. If there's no reason for that entertainment to be mobile, there's no reason anyone's going to be willing to pay anything extra to get it.

(www.thefeaturearchives.com 29.1.2005)

Questions

1. What are the likely advantages and disadvantages of the cyber library?
2. Do you think that cyberporn poses a threat to moral standards?
3. Would you welcome the forms of 'mobile entertainment' offered by WAP technology?

Case study

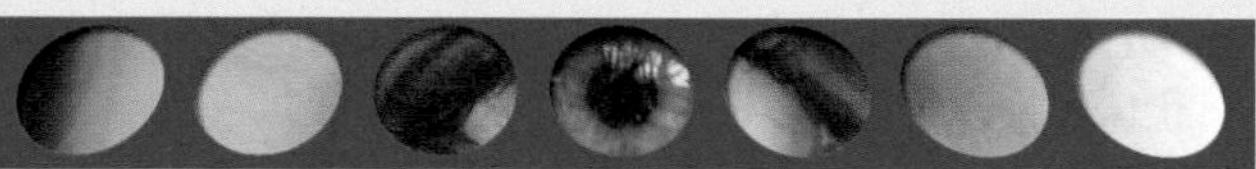

Bloggers of the world unite – virtual community, subversive social network or a global popularity contest sponsored by advertising?

Originally inspired by a handful of enthusiasts, 'blogs' provided links to other websites and enabled bloggers to swap information about sites of shared interest (known as 'blogroll'). In 1998 Jorn Barger first used the term 'weblog' to describe the interaction between these early sites and this became shortened to 'blog'. As the Internet grew and the systems became more user-friendly, the number of 'link-driven sites' mushroomed and within a decade the community of bloggers had increased from 23 (in 1999) to be numbered in millions. One development was for these sites to adopt a journal format on which bloggers could post their personal details and ideas and converse with one another.

Originally it was thought that blogging would create a social network of virtual friends and communities that represented a democratization of communication free from interference by the state and media conglomerates found in the press and broadcasting media. As Rebecca Blood pointed out in 2000, the subversive potential was to be celebrated:

> By highlighting articles that may easily be passed over by the typical web user too busy to do more than scan corporate news sites, by searching out articles from lesser-known sources, and by providing additional facts, alternative views, and thoughtful commentary, weblog editors participate in the dissemination and interpretation of the news that is fed to us every day. Their sarcasm and fearless commentary reminds us to question the vested interests of our sources of information and the expertise of individual reporters as they file news stories about subjects they may not fully understand.
>
> (www.rebeccablood.net/essays/weblog_history.html)

In the early days the Internet did promote serious discussion of culture, politics and social issues, and many serious commentators continue to run their own blogs from where they can invite comment, respond to criticism and engage in debate. However, the popularity of the blog has led to an epidemic that defies comprehension or navigation. In order to impose some sort of order on the chaos of unregulated blogging, social networks ('sites that would seek to wrap and re-centralise communication') emerged that could corral like-minded bloggers by age, taste and interest. By mid-2000, the domain of free-thinking spirits had been colonized by commercially run service providers keen to offer personal space but hungry for advertising revenue. Myspace (owned by News Corporation), Bebo (AOL) and Friends Reunited (ITV) have created a new

Case study *continued*

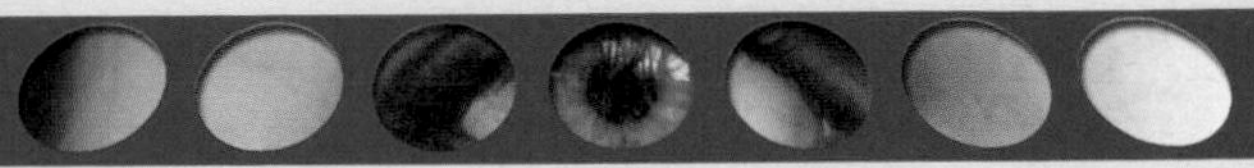

world of online communities where people can chat, download music and video, and sample bands plugging their latest single. By 2007 it was estimated that Myspace had 120 million accounts, with over 50 million regarded as 'active users'. In his critical look at the blogspace phenomenon, Joe Shooman (2007) argues that the power of these social networks may have been exaggerated but that the future has been transformed by the younger 'information aware, technology driven generation' who have grown up within them and seek to use the media in a different way.

These developments incorporate the traditional forms of communication (text, audio and video) into a 'super-medium . . . that brings together a lot of other media as we understand them; things like television or radio can exist in different forms within it' (McNicholas, quoted in Shooman 2007: 112). Consequently, the Internet now poses a threat to established media institutions and practices because it offers the opportunity to pick 'n' mix in a way that leaves the customer in control and spells the end of traditional press and broadcasting media. Digital consultant Sammy Andrews explains:

> A lifestyle site is the future and I'm just waiting for someone to do it properly . . . you can't do it if you force it on people, you have to have grass roots there and that's just how it works on the internet. If the whole internet population is against you, you're out. I honestly think you're going to be able to log on to one page where you've got email, home shopping, a list of friends, music, all in one. Youtube, Skype, all these things added into one. And TV at some point as well; you don't have to pay for any of these individual services, they're all on a computer screen.
>
> (Quoted in Shooman 2007: 162–3)

Not everyone agrees. With regard to music, Conor McNicholas, editor of *NME*, argues that the sheer volume of 'stuff' on the Internet will lead to an increased need to help us work out what is worth spending our time on. In this, the traditional media will take on a new role, filtering out the dross and helping us to make sense of what is left:

> Our role is much more of a filter and an arbitrator now. There's loads of stuff out there . . . so our role is to go 'actually *this* is the thing that you really ought to be looking at, because whether they've got 100,000 friends or not, *this* is the best thing. And also *that* thing that people are going on about, *that's* actually not very good; *this* thing that people are going on about – yes, *this* is the real deal. And we're gonna take it to another level, we're gonna embrace your endorsement, and we're gonna put them on the cover, or give them a feature, or whatever'.
>
> (Quoted in Shooman 2007: 153–4)

Questions

1. How much time do you spend on virtual 'social networks'?
2. Do you agree that social networking represents the end of traditional communication?

another. Roy Greenslade has argued that in the press this has led to the emergence of high-tech newsrooms in which 'the future of news-gathering and news delivery is tied to the screen'. This has allowed editors to merge their Web and print journalists as well as staff on Sunday and daily titles in ways that respond to the demands of audiences familiar with the Internet:

> **(Integration) is really about the creation of a new journalistic culture, a method of working that reflects both the technological possibilities and demands of a wised up, increasingly media – savvy public . . . The challenge is to provide 24/7 news, to offer a minute-by-minute, round the clock news service. This can only be achieved through integration, by journalists responding to the demand of filing for website and newsprint paper, by them bringing into play audio and video material whenever relevant.**
>
> (Greenslade, quoted in Gibson 2008: 26–7)

According to *Guardian* editor Alan Rusbridger, this will create a 'new world order' in which media professionals will have to pay more heed to the people they report on and report to. New networks will evolve in which there will be greater collaboration between the public and journalists 'seeking new ways of disseminating, aggregating and assessing information'

A closer look

An ongoing project called Assignment Zero set itself the following question:

> Can large groups of widely scattered people, working together voluntarily on the net, report on something happening in their world right now, and by dividing the work wisely tell the story more completely, while hitting high standards in truth, accuracy and free expression?

Check out their website and decide for yourself whether it can work: http://zero.newassignment.net.

(quoted in Gibson 2008: 246). In this new order, he argues for the development of 'citizen journalism', where members of the public provide tip-offs, editorial comment and even entire stories. In return, journalists offer 'citizen journalists' professional advice on investigation, writing and editing.

So far we have concentrated on the development of media technologies and institutions. In emphasizing the power and autonomy of media technologies, there is a danger of falling into the trap of 'technological determinism'; as Williams (1974) and Winston (1998) have warned, this diminishes the importance of social, economic and political factors in the development and use of the media. By focusing on the idea that media institutions are driven by technological innovation, we imply that society merely deals with the consequences of change instead of looking at the ways in which media technologies, society and culture shape one another.

In the rest of this chapter, we explore the wider relationship between the media, society, culture and power. The issues raised include media freedom, censorship, social control, public responsibility and the ethics of media production; in particular, four areas will be emphasized. First, *media and control* – the extent to which media communicators and audiences are restricted by social, political, economic and organizational determinants of media production and consumption. Second, *theories of media freedom and control* – an examination of the different theoretical positions that analyse the relationship between the media, the audience and the structure of society. Third, *media power* – a brief review of the debates over the media's influence on culture and social behaviour, focusing on the relationship between media presentations of violence and violent behaviour. Fourth, the '*active audience*' – with a reminder that, far from being an undifferentiated mass of brain-dead cultural dupes, the audience has the potential to discriminate, negotiate and resist media power – an important factor that is often overlooked in the way we talk about 'the mass media' and what it does *to* people.

As we have already noted, the issue of media freedom has been seen as crucial to the development of democratic societies. In opposition to 'authoritarian' and 'soviet' models of deliberate media control, McQuail (1994: 126–31) has noted the emergence of 'public service' and 'libertarian' models, which emphasize the creative freedom of media personnel and the customer's right to choose. These ideas underpin the liberal and pluralist views of media production (see pp. 711–713) that are at the centre of the debate over the relationship between the media and democracy (Keane 1991). In its most idealized form, this view exaggerates the investigative and creative freedom of individual journalists and broadcasters, who, according to Gans (1974), 'fight to express their personal values and tastes . . . and to be free from control by the audience and media executives' (quoted in Lull 1995: 122). However, as Gans recognizes, media personnel are also trained employees of large organizations as well as members of society. Whether producing hard-hitting news, dramatic fiction or alternative comedy, there are institutional restraints placed upon what the media professional can and cannot do. As Brian Whitaker pointed out in his review of the production of 'the news', journalists and editors are not only gatekeepers of news events but also actively involved in the creation of news through the criteria by which they select 'newsworthy' stories:

> **There is no limit to what might be reported. The number of observable events is infinite . . . We often fail to realise what a very, very limited selection of events it is that appears on our table at breakfast time.**
>
> (Whitaker 1981: 23)

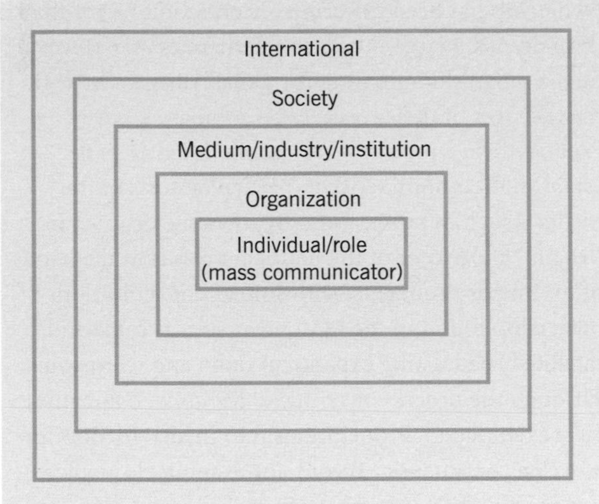

Figure 17.5 The relationship of the individual communicator to the outside world
Source: McQuail 1994: 189

The criteria that govern this selection process involve individuals in making decisions, but they are decisions made in the performance of an organizational role, which in turn has to be placed in the context of wider global and social factors that are economic, political and cultural in nature.

McQuail (1994) identifies a hierarchy of five levels of analysis for understanding the relationship of the individual communicator to the outside world (Figure 17.5).

The range of factors or pressures that journalists have to deal with can be expressed in a different way, which emphasizes the competing interest groups seeking to influence media decisions (Figure 17.6).

The various influences on media content can be referred to as 'determinants'. Some of these determinants operate internally and some are external to the media organization. The external influences include economic, political and legal interventions, while the internal influences relate to the constraints inherent in the structure of media organizations.

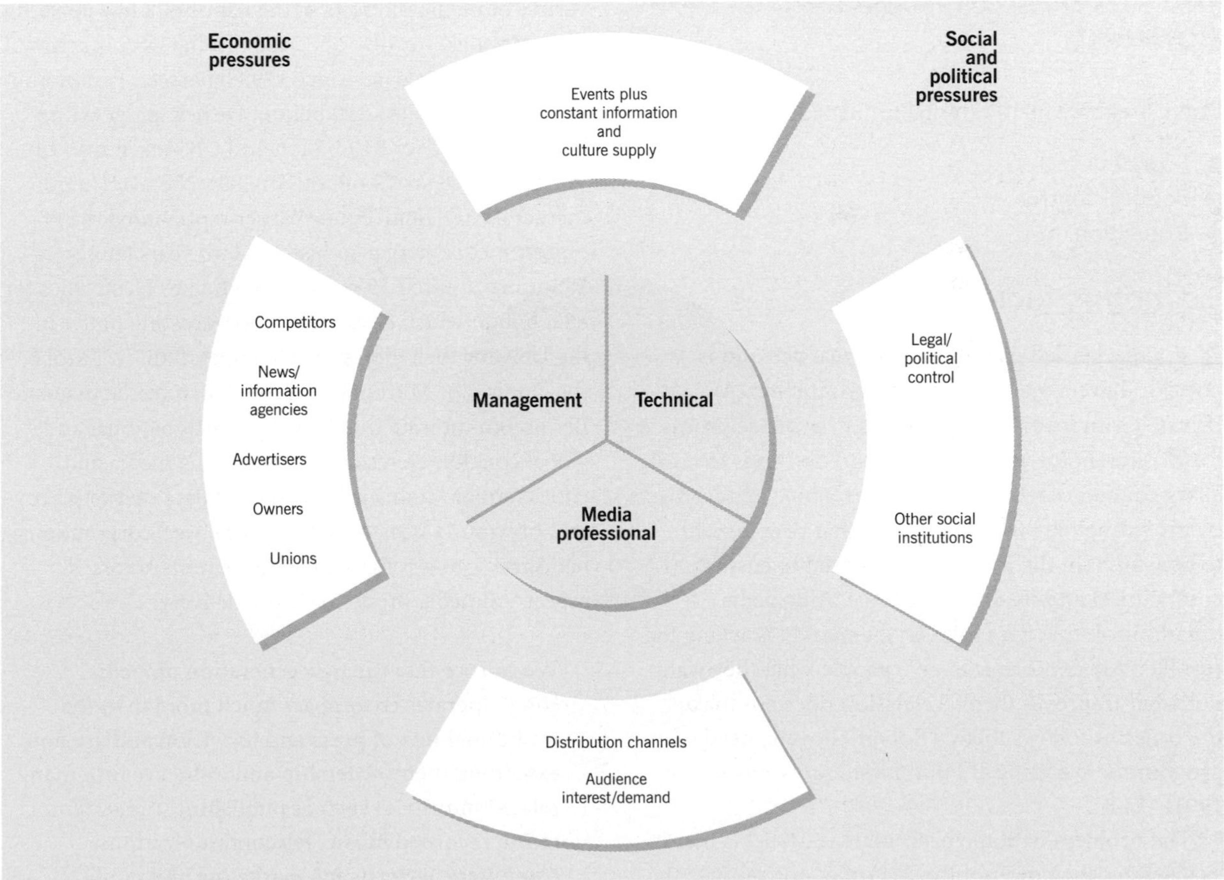

Figure 17.6 Pressures that journalists have to deal with
Source: McQuail 1994: 191

Stop and think

- Provide examples of the ways in which the work of journalists or broadcasters can be analysed at the five levels given by McQuail (Figure 17.5).
- How might the factors identified in the second model (Figure 17.6) influence news production?
- Find some recent examples of media personnel being constrained by these influences.
- When, in 2007, the *News of the World* was caught in a phone-tapping scandal involving members of the royal household, the two journalists responsible were jailed and the newspaper's editor, Andy Coulson, resigned. Using McQuail's models, why do you think Coulson decided to go with the story in the first place, and where do you think the pressures to resign came from?

External influences on media content

There are three main external influences:

- Economic factors
- Political control
- Regulation.

Economic factors

In any market-led operation, audience demand is going to have a major impact on production. A privately run media enterprise has to produce profits for its shareholders. The only way to do this is to create a large audience who in turn are attractive to advertisers by providing the kinds of product that people want to consume. In theory, this is supposed to ensure competition and freedom of choice. Any media organization that tries to buck the market is asking for trouble: 'My concern is to give people what they want, not what improves them. Television does not make the times. It follows them' (Robert Giovalli, head of programme planning at Finninvest, quoted in Keane 1991: 121).

The problem with the basic market model is that it exaggerates the power of the customer and ignores the influence of media owners and advertisers. Since the end of the nineteenth century, the tendency in media ownership has been towards concentration rather than diversity, with large media conglomerates and powerful media moguls dominating the global village. Through the takeover of their rivals, large companies have expanded via a process of *horizontal integration* to establish their dominance in particular areas of the media – such as publication. By the same process, in Britain, 90 per cent of the national press is in the hands of five major producers, with similar concentrations of ownership found in the local press and, as cable and satellite broadcasting expand, in radio and television. Through the process of *vertical integration*, companies have extended their operations into media distribution as well as production. BSkyB, for example, is involved not only in the production of television programmes but also in their transmission, while the Japanese electronics giant Sony has bought out software-production companies, such as Columbia, in order to have greater control over media consumption. This is part of a wider trend towards cross-media ownership on a global scale, which is of great concern to media analysts distrustful of the concentration of a variety of media interests in the hands of a few powerful and extremely wealthy operators. In the USA, a series of mergers and takeovers since 1993 have seen Paramount going to Viacom for $10 billion, Disney merge with CapCities/ABC for $19 billion and CBS taken over by Westinghouse for $5 billion. In 2001, the $165 billion merger of AOL and Time Warner represented the biggest media merger in history. Two years later, Newscorp aquired 19 per cent of Hughes Electronics for $6.6 billion which gave them a broadcasting outlet in the USA for their global satellite operation. In Europe, the empires of Murdoch and the Italian media magnate Berlusconi indicate the extent to which national and global conglomerates can dominate the media and entertainment industries. By the 1990s, a marketplace that previously boasted over 50 'first-tier' corporations had shrunk to less than 20, with interests across all aspects of media production and delivery.

> **We can see that the new generation of media conglomerates encompass much more than the traditional mix of press and television and are now extending their ownership and influence into many related industries such as publishing, radio, film, video, recorded music, telecommunications, computers, advertising, marketing and public relations, cinemas, couriers, hauliers and even postal services . . . We have a highly concentrated**

media in the hands of politically partisan owners who use their power to defend and advance their commercial and political influence. Unrestricted ownership and control will lead to a narrowing of choice and the elimination of diversity in media at a local, regional and national level.

(Williams 1994: 52)

By the end of the 1990s, three new players had emerged (Microsoft, Yahoo! and Google), but the overall trend towards concentration continued so that the global media of the twenty-first century is dominated by eight large conglomerates. The trend towards concentration over the past 25 years is well represented in Figure 17.7. This important work on who owns what in the media is now being updated with a new £50,000 research project by the CPBF into global ownership and convergence. See Granville Williams's first report 'Media ownership in the age of convergence' on the CPBF website at www.cpbf.org.uk/. As the media critic Ben Bagdikian famously observed, 'Trying to be a first-rate reporter on the average American newspaper is like trying to play Bach's St. Matthew Passion on a ukulele: The instrument is too crude for the work, for the audience and for the performer.'

Gillian Doyle has analysed the development of two key processes in the transformation of the media: *globalization* (the erosion of national boundaries to media markets) and *convergence* (the amalgamation of different media technologies through digitization):

The ongoing globalization of media markets and the convergence in technology between media and other industries has caused many media firms to adapt their business and corporate strategies accordingly. As traditional market boundaries and barriers have begun to fade away, the increase in competition among the media has been characterized by a steady increase in the number of perceived distributive outlets or 'windows' available to media firms.

As media markets have been freed up . . . the opportunities to exploit economics of scale and economies of scope have increased. Globalization and convergence have created additional possibilities and incentives to repackage media content for a global audience into as many different

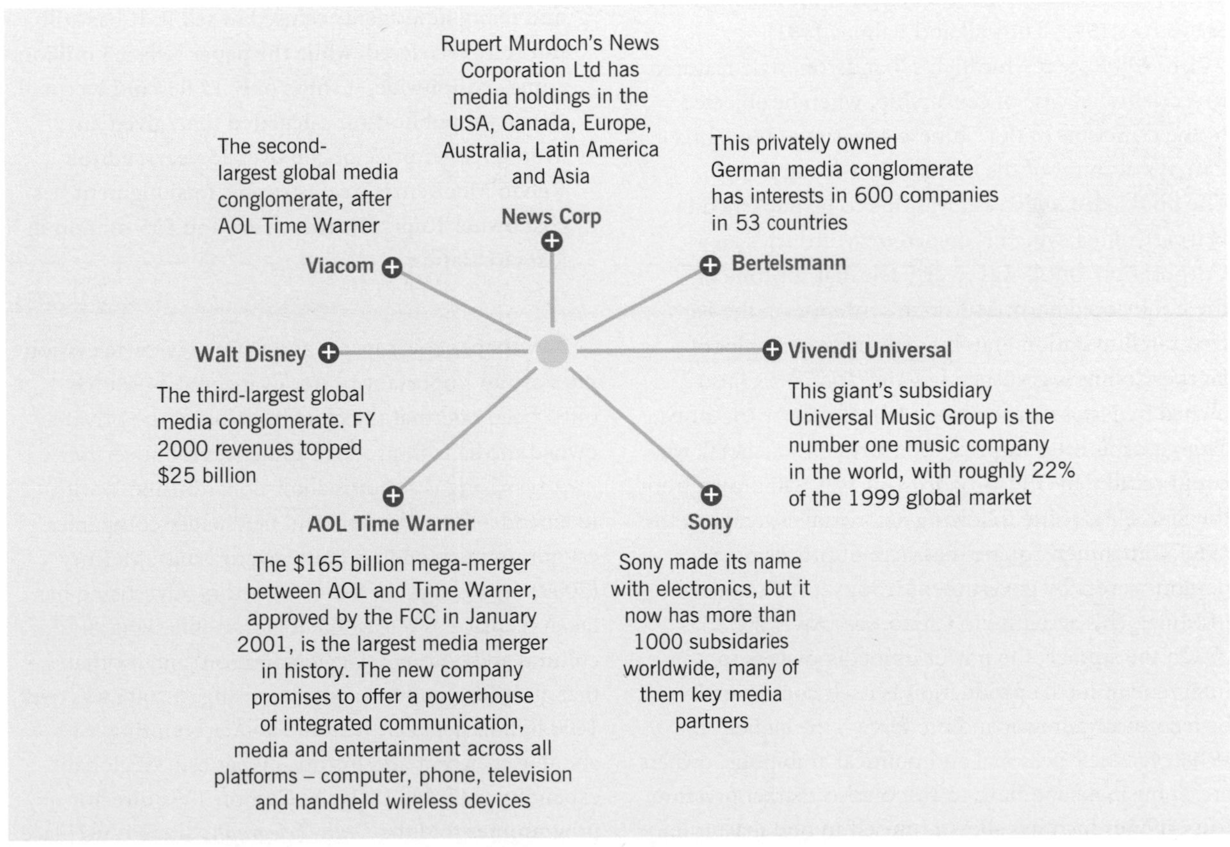

Figure 17.7 Media giants
Source: www.wgbh.org

> **formats as possible (books, magazine serializations, television programme, video) and sell the product through as many distribution channels and to as many paying consumers as possible.**
>
> (Doyle 2004: 3)

Consequently, Doyle argues that the bigger and more convergent organizations are best placed to exploit these opportunities and that this will encourage further mergers by which 'self-interested media corporations' will dominate 'ever-widening spheres of political decision making in the future' (Doyle 2004: 4).

Although writers such as Veljanovski (1989, 1991) have sought to justify unrestricted cross-media ownership on the grounds that it stimulates competition by 'bailing out' ailing newspapers, more critical commentators disagree. While ownership does not automatically imply control, there is much evidence from the history of media institutions and from the biographies of great media moguls such as Beaverbrook that owners have always sought to intervene in media production to further their own commercial and political interests or those of others (e.g. Bower 1995; Clarke and Riddell 1992; Coleridge 1994; Jenkins 1986; Shawcross 1992; Tunstall and Palmer 1991).

In 1998 Rupert Murdoch's 'hands-on' style featured in a celebrated case of censorship, when he objected to the criticisms of the Chinese government in Chris Patten's account of the handover of Hong Kong. The book, *East and West*, was due to be published by HarperCollins, which is owned by Murdoch's News Corporation, but it was clearly felt that the tone of the book could harm Murdoch's interests in the Far East satellite station Star TV. The editor-in-chief of HarperCollins was suspended and *The Times* (also owned by News Corporation) failed to carry the story. This came as little surprise to 'Murdoch watchers', who could recall that BBC broadcasting was withdrawn from the Star TV satellite following its critical coverage of the 1989 Tiananmen Square massacre of pro-democracy demonstrators by government troops. (For a review of Murdoch's activities in China, see Dover 2008.)

On the surface, the power of media owners to intervene in media production is itself constrained by a countervailing economic force – the audience. Whatever their personal and political ambitions, owners are in business and have to respond to market pressure. Rupert Murdoch has shown himself to be a master in the art of giving the punters what they want. When he bought the ailing *Sun* newspaper from the Mirror Group for £800,000 in 1969, he targeted the youthful working-class audience ignored by the *Daily Mirror*:

> **[Murdoch and his editor] felt the *Mirror* had grown old with its wartime generation of readers. They identified the working class, postwar baby-boomers, now in their early 20s as their potential audience. These young people were anti-establishment, sexually experienced and watched a lot of television. Murdoch understood that TV was the new medium (rather than a rival medium) . . . and gave copious coverage to the TV programmes his target readers were watching.**
>
> (Pilger 1997: 7)

The *Sun* quickly became the *Daily Mirror*'s biggest rival and overtook it in terms of sales in 1978. However, audiences can be volatile, and in the late 1980s the *Sun* lost many readers following misjudged and false allegations about Elton John in 1987 and Liverpool fans during the Hillsborough tragedy of 1989. On Merseyside, the *Sun* has not recovered from the decline in sales. Fifteen years later the *Observer* reported:

> **Copies of the *Sun* were burnt in the city's streets and many newsagents refused to sell it. It has still not fully recovered: while the paper sells 3.3 million copies nationwide, it shifts only 12,000 in Liverpool. One rival publication calculated that, given an average cover price of 20p over 15 years, editor Kelvin MacKenzie's catastrophic misjudgment has cost owner Rupert Murdoch around £55 million in lost circulation.**
>
> (*Observer* 11.7.2004)

Newspaper cover prices and pay-per-view television rates are an important source of income, but it has often been said that the chief function of the privately owned media is to produce audiences for advertisers.

Advertising is a multibillion-dollar business, with independent broadcasters and newspaper companies caught up in an endless battle over ratings. McRury (2009) argues that 'In the 21st century advertising has taken its place as one of the major visible signatures of cultural and commercial globalization' and estimates that global expenditure on advertising in 2006 was over $400 billion per year, with the USA accounting for about 40 per cent and Europe 30 per cent of global expenditure (Table 17.2). As Carlton TV's director of programmes told the *Daily Telegraph*, 'there is no place in prime time television for programmes which cannot achieve ratings of six to eight million' (quoted in

Case study

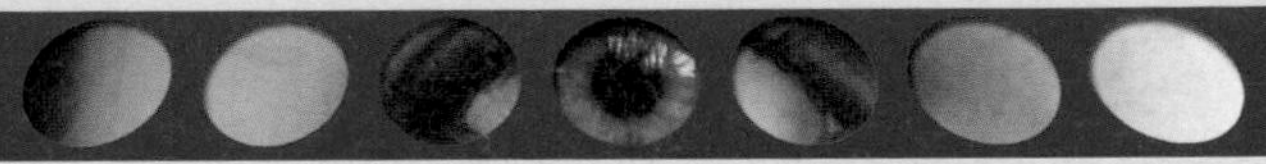

Newspaper owners and journalists

In 2008 a Select Committee of the House of Lords concluded its investigation of concentration of ownership in the UK media. The chairman, Lord Fowler, summarized their findings by saying: 'If you look at the concentration of ownership that there now is in newspapers, TV, radio, there's no question . . . there's a lot of influence and a lot of power in the hands of a small number of owners . . . People are going to become more and more interested and more and more concerned about this. Our new report is not realistically going to be the last word on the issue.' One of the key witnesses was Andrew Neil, who worked for Rupert Murdoch and edited the *Sunday Times* from 1983 until 1994. He told the committee:

> If you want to know what Rupert Murdoch really thinks, read the editorials in the *Sun* and the *New York Post* because he is editor-in-chief of these papers . . . He doesn't regard himself as editor-in-chief of *The Times* and the *Sunday Times* but he does regard himself as someone who should have more influence on these papers than anyone else . . . Although he is not named as the editor-in-chief of the *Sun* and the *News of the World* that is in reality what he is. There is no major geopolitical position that the *Sun* will take whether its attitude to the euro or to the current European treaty or to whom the paper will support in the upcoming general election. None of that can be decided without Rupert Murdoch's major input . . . It would be inconceivable for example at the next election for the *Sun* to say 'vote Cameron' if Mr Murdoch's view was 'vote Brown'.

Questions

1. In what ways and to what ends do owners and shareholders attempt to influence the content of 'their' newspapers or radio and television stations?
2. What kinds of constraints are there on this influence? How effective do you think they are?

Table 17.2 The five largest advertising markets ranked by total expenditure across all media, and including comparison data on ad expenditure as percentage of GDP, per capita expenditure in US$ and expenditure growth 1997–2006

National advertising market placed in rank order of total expenditure	Total spend	% GDP	Per capita expenditure 1997	Per capita expenditure 2006	Growth of ad spend 1997–2006
1. USA	US$163,036	1.23%	US$387.4	US$541.6	21.6%
2. China	US$48,518	1.85%	US$3.0	US$36.7	1,092.3%
3. Japan	US$34,240	0.78%	US$265.0	US$267.1	0.8%
4. UK	US$25,827	1.09%	US$274.5	US$431.4	14.4%
5. Germany	US$21,177	0.75%	US$249.7	US$263.2	–10.1%

Williams 1994: 17). This places advertisers in a strong position to influence programming, production values and even the script: through 'product placement' some shows are thinly disguised commercials. This is less of a problem in the UK, where product placement is strongly controlled by the Advertising Standards Authority.

In the USA, where television has always been a commercial enterprise, even news programmes have to be angled towards dramatic reconstruction of sensational incidents in order to boost audience ratings. K7, the Florida news channel, set a new trend for newscasting in the 1990s when it deliberately shifted towards news as entertainment. 'Tabloid television' is the result, providing a diet of human interest and trivia with a heavy emphasis on violent crime. Special effects, background music and trained presenters work together to turn other people's tragedies into prime-time television; in the pursuit of ratings, sensation, excitement and drama replace the quest for serious news coverage (BBC2 *Late Show*, 25.5.1994).

Case study

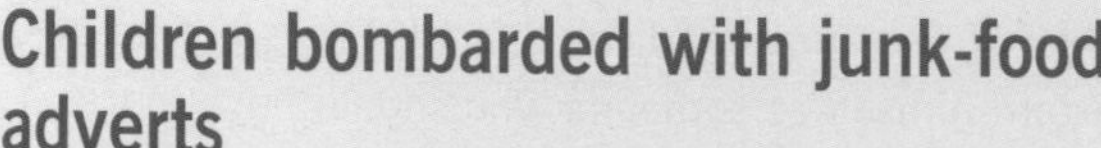

Children bombarded with junk-food adverts

Children are being bombarded with advertising for junk food at the rate of 1,150 television commercials each day, researchers have found. The average child watches 20,000 adverts a year on children's television. Among food commercials, 95 per cent are for products high in fat, sugar and salt. The findings (in a TV documentary called Fat Pushers) come two days after the Government's chief medical officer said obesity in children had shot up by 25 per cent in eight years and now affects one in 10 six-year-olds.

The programme . . . blames Whitehall for failing to crack down on junk food advertising and for allowing it into schools. According to research for the programme, 48 per cent of schools now have vending machines, largely selling sweets and crisps.

Last year, McDonald's spent £32.5 million on television advertisments, while Coca-Cola spent £13 million and Pringles £7 million. The programme suggests that it is money well spent.

While the Government maintains that children are wise consumers who are not manipulated by advertising, when the programme filmed a class of nine-year-olds watching adverts for foods such as Frosties and Dunkers, many of them clearly knew every word and gesture in the commercials.

Nick Barham, of the advertising agency Karmarama, said advertisers try not to talk about the food itself. 'These ads are no longer trying to sell the foods, which are of such poor nutritional value it's hard to say anything good about them,' he added. 'Instead they're promoting a dream; a fun, exciting, seductive lifestyle.'

Although Tessa Jowell, the Culture Secretary, has decided that Britain will not follow other European countries and ban junk food advertising, the Labour MP Angela Eagle told the programme there was 'overwhelming' evidence that advertising was affecting what children eat. 'I would ban advertising of foodstuffs that are unhealthy to children,' she said.

(*Daily Telegraph* 1.5.2004)

Questions

1. What adverts and jingles can you recall from your childhood?
2. Do you think they influenced your diet?
3. Should government regulate advertising aimed at children?
4. Do these findings influence your views on obesity and choice raised in the case study on obesity on p. 527?

In theory, the market-driven media model should guarantee customer choice and satisfy audience needs, but as Keane argues, the outcome ignores the needs and opinions of minority groups. In this relentless pursuit of advertising revenue the media become terrified of controversy and depth and learn to play safe:

> **Advertising works in favour of advertisers and business and against citizens. It privileges corporate speech. Bent on maximising audiences and minimising costs, advertising ensures that material which is of interest to only a small number of citizens will at best be available on a limited scale. Advertising reduces the supply of 'minority interest' programmes, aesthetically and intellectually challenging themes and politically controversial material which fails to achieve top audiences and, hence, does not entice advertisers to open their cheque books.**
>
> (Keane 1991: 83)

Political control

In the twentieth century the potential of the media for political influence and control has been widely recognized (Herman and Chomsky 1988). It is no accident that in times of political upheaval the fiercest battles are often for the control of the radio or television stations as warring factions seek to establish ideological as well as military supremacy (e.g. radio broadcasts whipping up racial hatred played an important role in Rwanda's slide into civil war and genocide in 1994, and in Serbia in 1998 newspapers were closed by the government because they refused to support the Milosovic government line). The bombing in 1999 of the State TV Station in Belgrade, with the loss of 13 lives, was justified by NATO on the grounds that it was broadcasting propaganda. More recently, events in Zimbabwe have seen the imprisonment and torture of journalists critical of the Mugabe regime and the emergence of what Ranger (2005) has termed 'patriotic journalism', which divides the population into 'patriots' and 'traitors' and encourages intimidation of the 'enemy within'. In this world, the job of being a serious political journalist can be a very dangerous one: the Committee to Protect Journalists estimates that, between 1992 and 2008, 693 journalists have been killed. Some have died in combat zones, but over 70 per cent have been murdered (see www.cpj.org).

In periods of political stability, the media also play a major role in establishing and maintaining social order and political control. McQuail describes how the state in totalitarian regimes deliberately suppresses freedom of expression through official censorship, while at the same time seeking to establish ideological hegemony through orchestrated propaganda campaigns. McQuail defines propaganda as 'the deliberate and systematic attempt to shape perceptions, manipulate cognitions, and direct behaviour to achieve a response that furthers the desired intent of the propagandist' (McQuail 2000: 425).

In the 1930s Hitler expressed his opinion on the importance of political propaganda in *Mein Kampf*, identifying two clear objectives in the battle for the hearts and minds of the masses: the silencing of critical intellectuals and the brainwashing of everyone else:

> **All propaganda must be popular and its intellectual level must be adjusted to the most limited intelligence among those it is addressed to. Consequently, the greater the mass it is intended to reach, the lower its purely intellectual level will have to be . . . The art of propaganda lies in understanding the emotional ideas of the great masses and finding . . . the way to the attention and thence to the hearts of the broad masses . . . The receptivity of the great masses is very limited, their intelligence is small, but their power of forgetting is enormous. [Therefore] all effective propaganda must be limited to a very few points and must harp on these slogans until the last member of the public understands what you want him to understand by your slogan.**
>
> ('War propaganda', in Hitler 1969)

In the former Soviet Union, the importance of the press for the purposes of agitation, propaganda (*agitprop*) and organization dates from the victory of Lenin in 1917 and the subsequent domination of Soviet society by the Communist Party.

World in focus

Television in Iran

Parliament in Iran, where clerics want to stop people watching television programmes they see as corrupting, yesterday passed the final parts of a bill which bans the private use of satellite television equipment.

The bill, which prohibits the import, distribution and use of satellite dishes, will become law when the guardian council, a parliamentary watchdog, ratifies it in a fortnight. That is considered all but certain.

The legislation empowers the Ministry of Islamic Guidance and Culture 'to safeguard cultural boundaries of the country and of its families against destructive and indecent satellite programmes'.

Iranians watching programmes with dish antennas have a month to dismantle the equipment or risk its confiscation and fines of 1 million to 3 million riyals (£360–1000).

(*Guardian* 2.1.1995)

Questions

1. Why might satellite broadcasting pose such a threat to regimes such as these?
2. How might the content of satellite programmes be seen as corrupting to Iranian culture?

> **The press is the strongest instrument with which, day by day, hour by hour, the party speaks to the masses in their own essential language. There is no other means so flexible for establishing spiritual links between the party and the working class.**
>
> (Stalin, quoted in Whitaker 1981: 45)

However, such intentions do not always have the desired effect: audiences can react against deliberate attempts at ideological manipulation. Lull points out that many Chinese people ridicule and resist government propaganda:

> **They detest the Communist Party's simple minded self-promotion, its blatantly biased news reports, the laughable TV 'model worker' programmes, the many exaggerated advertising claims about domestic products, and the unavailability of advertised foreign goods.**
>
> (Lull 1995: 62)

In liberal democracies the freedom of the media is a much-valued principle, but in practice there are still many restrictions imposed by the state. Politically sensitive and morally offensive material is often suppressed; the state also uses the media to transmit information (and misinformation) that serves its interests. This is particularly true in times of political crisis or war. During the First World War, for example, press coverage was tightly controlled and manipulated by the British government (Lovelace 1978). Similar criticisms were made of the news coverage of the Falklands War (Glasgow University Media Group 1985; Morrison and Tumber 1988) and the 'Troubles' in Northern Ireland (Curtis 1984).

According to Keane (1991), a characteristic of modern politics is the growth of state power ('the democratic leviathan') at the expense of the citizenry. A key element in this process has been the control of the media, and Keane highlights the four types of political censorship of the media.

First, the British government can exert direct political censorship on the media. It can vet any sensitive material before it is released; the '30-year rule' on Cabinet papers is an example of the automatic 'prior restraint' on information. It can also take legal action against journalists, radio stations and TV companies in order to prevent the dissemination of material already available or in production. This may include banning, shredding, burning or confiscating material.

Second, state officials have involved themselves in surveillance, infiltration and information management, which has 'resulted in a well organised form of permanent political censorship at the heart of state power' (Keane 1991: 99). In 1995 newscaster Jon Snow revealed that, in his first days as a journalist, MI6 (the UK intelligence service) had tried to recruit him as an agent because of his contacts with the radical student movement (Snow 2004: 90–92).

Third, governments may be 'economical with the truth' or deliberately orchestrate a campaign of disinformation. Tactics can include stage-managed briefings, denial of access to official sources and the leaking of misinformation. Those seeking to expose such activities can expect to find their careers destroyed. During the 1980s, civil servants Clive Ponting and Sarah Tisdall both found themselves in court for leaking information that exposed government misinformation strategies. Ponting was aquitted but Tisdall was not so fortunate.

Fourth, governments seek to use the media in order to influence public opinion: 'All governments seek to

A closer look

Film in Tibet

In Tibet the Dalai Lama is seen to be such a subversive figure by the Chinese government that possessing an image of him is treated as a political crime. A recent documentary, *What Remains of Us*, was shown at the Cannes Film Festival under strict security to protect Tibetans who had been filmed watching an illegal recording of their spiritual leader. The movie-makers risked imprisonment themselves by smuggling a video of the Dalai Lama into the country and filming the responses of local people to his first appearance since fleeing the country in 1959. See the website of Students for a Free Tibet at http://studentsfora.tempwebpage.com.

manage the news; to trumpet the good, to suppress the bad and to polish up the image of the Prime Minister' (Cockerell *et al.* 1984: 9). Through 'lobby system' briefings, public information campaigns and the manipulation of links with media organizations, governments and politicians use the media to market political policies and careers. Those who comply may find themselves rewarded; for example, shortly after coming to power, Margaret Thatcher singled out the editors of the *Sun* and the *Sunday Express* for knighthoods, while Victor Mathews, owner of the *Daily Express*, received a peerage (Shawcross 1992: 212). More recently Michael Moore has complained that, by repeating the accusation that a link existed between Saddam Hussein and Osama bin Laden so often, the Bush administration managed to get the American public to believe that the two were allies. By the time war had begun, a poll conducted by Knight-Ridder showed that 50 per cent actually believed that one or more of the hijackers on 9/11 were Iraqis (Moore 2003: 56). In 2008, Scott McClennan (former press secretary at the White House) was branded a traitor for revealing in his memoirs that the US media had been heavily involved in creating a 'culture of deception' aimed at selling the Iraq war to the US public.

As a result of these trends, in what might euphemistically be called 'information management', Keane (1991) suggests that Western democracies have become immune from public evaluation and criticism. Government officials have less interest in consulting the public and little belief in their right to know what is going on. The media have had to become part of a strategy of public deceit or else face the consequences of legally sanctioned intimidation. The Official Secrets Act was extended in 1989 to gag government officials for life and to render it a criminal offence for a journalist to make a 'damaging disclosure'. An example of this official censorship was the dubbing of Sinn Fein members' voices between 1988 and 1994 in an attempt 'to starve [them] of the oxygen of publicity' (Gilbert 1992). In 2007, the editor of *El Jueves* and a cartoonist were fined €3000 each for mocking the Spanish royal family. In a bedroom scene that leaves little to the imagination, Crown Prince Felipe is made to say 'if you get pregnant this will be the closest thing I've done to work in my whole life'. As the issue was also banned by the court, it is necessary to go online (http://forbiddenplanet.co.uk/blog/?p=5721) should you really want to see what all the fuss was about.

Stop and think

The Media Democracy movement involves a variety of groups who campaign for a more representative media. Many of these organizations can be found on the Internet where interactive media technology is being used to challenge the power of the conventional media institutions. One of the pressure groups to check out is www.mediademocracyday.org. A more general political website that also covers the media is www.opendemocracy.net.

- Look these up and see whether you can find evidence to support Keane's argument.
- Do you think such campaigns can bring about change?

Regulation

Most state control of the media is exerted through the law and voluntary codes of conduct entered into by media organizations and journalists and broadcasters. While the USA guarantees freedom of expression in its First Amendment and the European Convention on Human Rights does so in Article 10, British governments are not bound by such rights.

As Robertson and Nicol (1992: 3) observe in a 650-page book devoted to legal restrictions on the media, 'Free speech is what is left of speech after the law has had its say.' We shall touch briefly on these legal constraints and identify the more important regulatory bodies and codes of practice.

Legal restrictions on the media

Under the Official Secrets Act 1911, the leaking of official information by civil servants was forbidden and the use of unauthorized material by journalists became a criminal offence. Since 1989, civil servants were bound by 'a lifelong duty of confidentiality' (Burnet 1992: 54), and journalists could be prosecuted for disclosing information 'damaging the security forces or the interest of the United Kingdom' (Robertson and Nicol 1992: 424). The Obscene Publications Act 1857, which empowered magistrates to confiscate and destroy immoral books, was amended in 1959 to make a distinction between erotic literature of genuine artistic merit and pornography. A number of show trials ensued, the most famous of which in 1961 concerned *Lady Chatterley's Lover* by D.H. Lawrence. It has been used sparingly since, although, in 1991, it was invoked against the misogynist lyrics of rap artists N.W.A. The law has also been used to prosecute for the crime of blasphemy defined as 'any contentious, reviling, scurrilous or ludicrous matter relating to God, Jesus Christ or the Bible'. Again it is rarely used.

Civil law covers private litigation relating to breaches of confidence, copyright, libel and individual rights to privacy. Where libel action is successfully prosecuted, the aggrieved party stands to make a lot of money: in 1987 Elton John was awarded £1 million against the *Sun* for alleged use of 'rent boys'; in 2005 he made out-of-court settlements with two newspapers (for amounts over £100,000) when they had dared to label him 'rude'. We do not know how much Jordan and Peter Andre were awarded, but the *News of the World* was successfully sued in 2008 after printing a story alleging them to be 'bad parents'.

Regulatory bodies and codes of conduct

Through statutory laws and voluntary agreement, regulatory bodies have been set up to establish guidelines on 'public taste' and to maintain decent standards of journalism. Pornography, violence, bias and invasions of privacy tend to be the main concerns of such bodies. However, the codes of conduct they try to enforce are seen by Harris (1992) as a minor part of the regulatory framework as journalists and broadcasters are concerned more with the constraints imposed by proprietors, advertisers, public demand and the law.

The press

Between 1953 and 1989, newspapers were subject to voluntary regulation by the Press Council to ensure 'the highest professional standards' in journalism. Following the highly critical Calcutt Report (1990), the newspaper proprietors rushed to set up their own Press Complaints Commission (PCC). With a clear code of conduct, the PCC deals with complaints from the public and publishes a quarterly bulletin of its judgments. However, the PCC has been criticized for lacking teeth, independence and public confidence.

Broadcasting

The broadcast media have a captive audience and the normal rules that cover the distribution of magazines and newspapers cannot be applied to radio and television programmes, which are beamed into our homes. The power of broadcasters has always been tied closely to government control through the granting of licences and the insistence on clear codes of conduct, particularly in relation to accuracy, impartiality and public taste. In Britain, separate agencies were established in the 1980s to maintain standards and deal with complaints. These were replaced in 2003 by Ofcom, which has a much wider role monitoring sex and violence on television and providing codes of conduct for the portrayal of sensitive and controversial material. According to Bell and Alden (2003: 10),

Case study

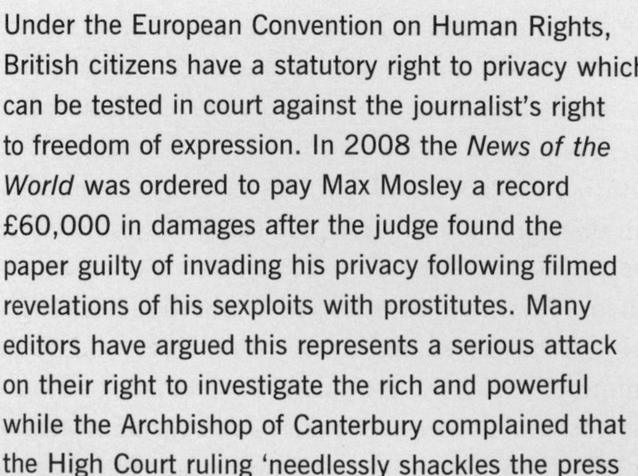

Under the European Convention on Human Rights, British citizens have a statutory right to privacy which can be tested in court against the journalist's right to freedom of expression. In 2008 the *News of the World* was ordered to pay Max Mosley a record £60,000 in damages after the judge found the paper guilty of invading his privacy following filmed revelations of his sexploits with prostitutes. Many editors have argued this represents a serious attack on their right to investigate the rich and powerful while the Archbishop of Canterbury complained that the High Court ruling 'needlessly shackles the press [and] removes the right of the public to make informed moral judgments'.

(Timesonline 29.07.2008)

Look up this case and answer the following questions.

Questions

1. Does the public have a right to know what individuals get up to in their private lives?
2. Do you agree with the judge that 'anyone indulging in sexual activity is entitled to a degree of privacy'?

Figure 17.8 The Press Council fails to curb tabloid trash
Cartoon by Mike Keating

Ofcom has overall responsibility for standards in broadcasting and enjoys 'the power to enforce the public service obligations of broadcasters as well the power to fine them as much as £250,000 for "breaches of taste and decency"'.

Film and video

The licensing and censoring of films, videos and console games has a long history of quasi-statutory regulation. The British Board of Film Classification has become a means of prior classification of films (U, PG, 15, 18, 18R; see www.bbfc.co.uk for definitions) and is the chief censor of films shown in cinemas and broadcast on television. Since 1984, the power of classification was extended to video cassettes in the wake of concern over 'video nasties'. Despite these attempts at prior censorship, it is still possible to bring court action against certified films for obscenity (e.g. *Last Tango in Paris*) or for local authorities to ban any film from cinemas within their jurisdiction (e.g. *The Life of Brian*). In 2003 the original version of the video game *Manhunt* was given an 18 classification, but in 2007 *Manhunt 2* was banned by the British Board of Film Classification for its 'unrelenting focus on stalking and brutal slaying' (see the case study on p. 732).

Advertising

The Advertising Standards Authority has real powers as a self-regulating body to ensure that adverts are 'legal, decent, honest and truthful' because it has the power to hurt advertisers in the pocket by forcing the withdrawal of offensive adverts (Robertson and Nicol 1992: 542–5, 559–61).

Internal influences on media content

There are a number of factors that occur within media organizations and influence media production, including the social construction of 'media reality' by journalists and broadcasters working within media organizations. The 'reality' that journalists produce has to be accounted for in terms of the practices of those who have the power to determine the experiences of others; these practices have to be placed within the context of media personnel working within bureaucratic organizations.

The organizational structure of the media means that media workers are constrained in two main ways. First, they are constrained by the hierarchical and paternalistic nature of media organizations. As with any bureaucracy, the lines of authority are clearly marked and the interaction between journalist and editor and between editor and owner are of crucial importance. Second, the journalist relies on sources and contacts within other organizations. The story of journalism 'is the story of the interaction of reporters and officials' (Schudson 1991: 148).

Journalists are members of a profession governed by its own internal regulations. However, a commitment to professional standards can be a source of conflict with management (Burns 1977). The social backgrounds of media personnel are also important, because their social and educational backgrounds may simply reinforce the taken-for-granted assumptions underlying organizational definitions of 'newsworthiness' and 'professionalism'. According to US critics such as Lichter *et al.* (1986), the liberally educated 'media elite' in the USA are biased towards the Democratic Party. However, the white, male, middle-class profile of most media professionals has led to the criticism that they are too conservative:

> **Journalists, who are better seen as bureaucrats than buccaneers, begin their work with a stock of plausible, well-defined and largely unconscious assumptions. Part of their job is to translate untidy reality into neat stories with beginnings, middles and denouements. The values which inform the selection of news items usually serve to reinforce conventional opinions and established authority.**
>
> (Curran and Seaton 1991: 265)

Case study

Journalists' backgrounds

An investigation by the Sutton Trust in 2006 suggests that top journalists and editors are more likely to come from private schools:

- Over half (54%) of the country's leading news journalists were educated in private schools, which account for 7% of the school population as a whole.
- The proportion of the 'top 100' journalists in news and current affairs who come from independent schools has increased by five percentage points in the past 20 years, from 49 per cent to 54 per cent.
- In 1986 over two-fifths (44%) of national newspaper editors, columnists, and leading broadcast editors and news presenters came from grammar schools; by 2006, however, this had fallen to 33 per cent.
- In 2006 14 per cent of journalists who could be considered to be among the most influential in the country were educated at comprehensive schools, up from 6 per cent in 1986.
- Overall 45 per cent of the leading journalists in 2006 – or 56 per cent of those who went to university – attended Oxbridge. This is slightly lower than in 1986, when the equivalent figures were 52 per cent of the total and 67 per cent of university graduates.
- Just under two-fifths (37%) of the top journalists in 2006 who went to university graduated from one institution – Oxford (40% in 1986).
- Seven in ten (72%) journalists in 2006 who went to university attended one of the country's 13 'Sutton Trust' leading universities – those that have consistently been ranked top when taking the average of major league tables.
- The proportion of women among the top 100 news journalists increased from 10 per cent in 1986 to 18 per cent in 2006.
- A separate survey of leading journalists and editors suggests that the latest new recruits to the national news media are even more likely to come from privileged backgrounds than those from previous generations.

See the full report at www.suttontrust.com/reports/Journalists-backgrounds-final-report.pdf.

Questions

1. Find out whether there are similar differences according to gender, ethnicity or disability.
2. Find out from your local or college career service what the entry requirements are for a future in journalism.

By definition, the experiences and perspectives of those groups who are not part of 'the club' are likely to be undervalued and underrepresented. The formal training of journalists through degree programmes may serve only to reinforce this bias by recruiting into the profession those with formal academic qualifications.

Perspectives on the mass media

In order to understand the relationship between media personnel, media organizations and social structure, it is necessary to examine some of the major theoretical perspectives on the role of the media. The media have to be examined within the context of social interaction and social rules. These rules are formed within the structures of power in society, and within this setup the electronic media have a crucial role to play:

> **The special authority of electronic media, asserting and reinforcing endless streams of ideologically charged information is, without question, an impressive social force . . . Media help shape and maintain rules and the ideological predispositions underlying them because their unique and powerful technical capabilities and appealing content are the most effective means of information diffusion ever invented . . . By articulating ideological syntheses that promote certain perspectives and exclude others . . . the mass media help constitute and regulate social reality by structuring some of their audiences' most common and important experiences . . . Mass media help break down distance between the macro social and the micro social. They bring public themes into private environments where they enter into and are influenced by local conditions, orientations, authorities and practices.**
>
> (Lull 1995: 60–61)

Recognition of this 'special authority' of the media is not a simple acceptance of its social control function; it is the starting point of an exploration of a range of perspectives that ask us to think about the relationship between the media and society in a variety of ways. These perspectives do not fit neatly under the conventional headings for organizing our ideas on social theory (as, for instance, in Chapter 2); McQuail (2005) has shown how difficult it is to talk about media theories as if they exist in a simple and agreed relationship with one another. The comparison of the *dominant paradigm* with *alternative paradigms*, which is the way in which we categorize different media perspectives below, is therefore only one way of presenting media theories. It may be helpful in providing 'the general structure of thinking about the mass media and society' (McQuail 1994: 93), but it can provide only a limited map of the area.

The dominant paradigm

Early theories tended to exaggerate the power of the media to influence behaviour and were associated strongly with fears of 'mass society': in particular, there were fears that developments such as mass education, mass communication and political democracy would cause the collapse of the old order and elite rule, leading to a fragmented society and mob rule. The mass media were seen as part of this 'problem':

> **Rather than being viewed as vehicles for enlightenment, popular education and the press are regarded as reducing intelligence to the level of the lowest common denominator.**
>
> (Bennett 1982: 34).

However, precisely because the new mass media dealt in the artefacts of mass culture, they could also be seen as a popular means by which the masses could be integrated into the social consensus of the new order:

> **The links between popular mass media and social integration were readily open to conceptualisation in terms both negative and individualistic (more loneliness, crime and immorality), but it was also possible to envisage a positive contribution from modern communications to cohesion and community. Mass media were a potential force for a new kind of cohesion, able to connect scattered individuals in a shared national, city and local experience.**
>
> (McQuail 1994: 34)

The dominant paradigm that emerged tended to emphasize a positive view of modern society as liberal, democratic and orderly, within which the media play an important role. These ideas found their early expression through the perspectives of functionalism and pluralism.

Case study

The functions of the mass media

From the early work of Lasswell (1948), Wright (1960) and Mendelsohn (1966), a number of writers have identified the essential functions of the mass media. McQuail (1994) provides a summary of these media functions:

Information

- providing information about events and conditions in society and the world;
- indicating relations of power;
- facilitating innovation, adaptation and progress.

Correlation

- explaining, interpreting and commenting on the meaning of events and information;
- providing support for established authority and norms;
- consensus building;
- setting orders of priority and signalling relative status.

Continuity

- expressing the dominant culture and recognizing subcultures and new cultural developments;
- forging and maintaining common values.

Entertainment

- providing amusement, diversion and means of relaxation;
- reducing social tension.

Mobilization

- campaigning for societal objectives in the sphere of politics, war, economic development, work and sometimes religion.

(Adapted from McQuail 1994: 79)

Question

1. **Give an example of how the television and the national press might fulfil each of the functions listed by McQuail.**

Functionalism

By responding to human needs, social institutions develop that are said to be functional for society as a whole. The mass media can be looked at in this way, with an emphasis on the ways in which they satisfy a range of social needs more effectively than alternative social institutions (e.g. church, family, school). The media according to this model are clearly involved in socialization, integration and the maintenance of social consensus.

> **[We are talking of] the ability of the media to bind together disparate and fragmented audiences into a classless community of individuals who feel others to be their equals, with whom they can share news of events, television characters and fictional narratives.**
>
> (Keane 1991: 120)

Pluralism

Usually associated with theories of power and political participation, the concept of pluralism has been adapted to explain the role played by the media in modern democracies. The pluralist model developed in direct opposition to the negativism of the mass society approach.

In the 1960s and 1970s, the fears endemic to the mass society model were attacked by US writers such as Bramson (1961), Dahl (1961), Gans (1974) and Shils (1959), who argued that such distrust of the masses was elitist and undemocratic. Rather than fearing the totalitarian potential of mass society, these writers celebrated its power to liberate 'the cognitive, appreciative and moral capacities of individuals' and the various 'taste cultures' that make up a heterogeneous popular culture (Billington *et al.* 1991: 17). According to this view, the media play a key role in the democratic process by providing access to information, stimulating open debate, and giving all groups the opportunity to share their beliefs and tastes with others. In exercising political and cultural choices in a democratic society, the freedom of the media is crucial.

Case study

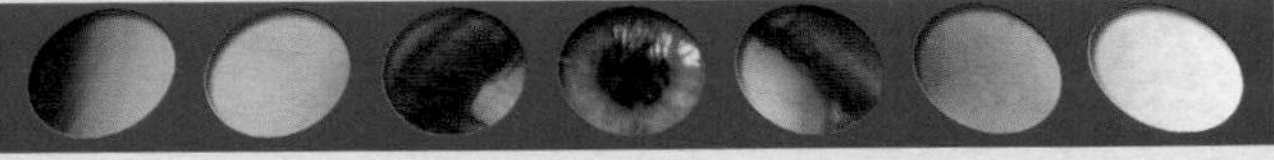

The liberal model of the mass media

O'Donnell suggests that this model has five key elements:

- The freedom to set up media ventures ensures that a range of opinions and interests are represented.
- Editorial freedom and professional standards of journalism underpin an effective media.
- Public access to press and broadcasting allows individuals to express their opinions and criticisms – through, for example, letters to the editor, right to reply or phone-ins.
- A commitment to balance ensures that all groups in society have access to the media and are represented fairly – through programming that reflects minority tastes and interests (for example, Channel 4 was established in part to achieve this).
- Market power enables the audiences to determine in the long run which media prosper and who goes out of business.

(Adapted from O'Donnell 1981: 546)

Whether this represents a normative theory (how things should be) or an actual model of how the media operate is debatable and relates to another key issue: how best to deliver a genuinely pluralist media. On the one hand is the belief that the media (and especially broadcasting) are so important to a free and rational society that they must be controlled for the public good. Hence, regulations are imposed on ownership, offensive content and political balance. Public service broadcasting derives from this 'top-down' approach, with the BBC being an obvious example. On the other hand, such 'nannying' of the public by the state is seen as a threat to liberty. According to the liberal market model, the only means of providing a diverse public with genuine freedom of choice is through a deregulated marketplace. This view was expressed clearly by Rupert Murdoch in his lecture on 'freedom in broadcasting' in 1989, which has been summarized by Keane (1991):

> **Murdoch insists that market competition is the key condition of press and broadcasting freedom, understood as freedom from state interference, as the right of individuals to communicate their opinions without external restrictions. Market led media ensure competition. Competition lets individual consumers decide what they want to try. It keeps prices low and quality high, forces suppliers to take risks and to innovate continually, lest they lose business to rivals offering better, improved products. A privately controlled press and a multi-channel broadcasting system in the hands of a diversity of owners is a bulwark of freedom.**
>
> (Keane 1991: 53)

This confidence in the ability of the market to provide real choice and a genuinely pluralistic media is supported by writers such as Whale (1980) and Veljanovski (1989), but it is rejected by Keane and others, who argue that the marketplace fails to provide genuine competition or free access to all media operations when it is dominated by a handful of global monopolies. Keane also rejects the idea that consumer choice and satisfaction are secured by a liberal market: some consumers are excluded by the purchase costs of media technology, others by their membership of minority groups, who are not attractive to advertisers. The market becomes led by the demands of advertisers and the caprice of private owners and corporate decision-makers. Choice exists within the confines of commercial viability, and this often amounts to broadcasting more of the same in order to satisfy the 'mass audience', which the advertisers demand. In the long run, this will lead to the 'Americanization' of the media and an increase in what Keane (1991: 64) terms 'garbage television' and 'satellite slush'.

Although critical of both the public service and liberal market models, Keane retains a belief in the potential of the modern media to provide

> **a radically new public service model which would facilitate a genuine commonwealth of forms of life, tastes and opinions. Communications media . . . should aim to empower a plurality of citizens who are governed neither by undemocratic states nor by undemocratic market forces. The media should be for the public use and enjoyment of all citizens and not for the private gain or profit of political rulers or businesses.**
>
> (Keane 1991: xi–xii)

Case study

Golden age: myth or reality?

In the 2005 Huw Wheldon Lecture, sponsored by the Royal Television Society, Dawn Airey, managing director of Sky Networks, challenged the idea that TV standards had declined as a result of increasing choice and argued instead that new technologies have liberated the audience from the patronage of the BBC (see the earlier discussion of public service broadcasting and the emergence of digital and satellite TV on pp. 690–700):

> The opportunities for connecting with the audience in ways hitherto unimagined will produce programmes of genius that will exploit the medium's capabilities in ways we haven't even dreamed of. At some point we might be able to choose the ending of a popular drama instantaneously with the click of the red button. Or follow the path of an individual character rather than a linear storyline – much as computer games already do. The one thing that is certain is that in this new era the best television will be saved from oblivion . . . the home entertainment systems of the future will be capable of storing thousands of hours of content, including perhaps every movie ever made, all available on demand at the press of a button in high definition quality.
>
> No longer bound by the tyranny of the schedule, . . . Television will at last be able to emulate one of the great achievements of civilization: the library. Everything will be available for all to see . . . If there is a Golden Age of TV, then I believe that we're only just on the cusp . . . Rather than it being a 'social menace of the first magnitude' as Lord Reith suggested, television has become a powerful means of breaking down mass conformity in order to liberate individual choice . . . Viewers are no longer simply passive observers. Television has broken free from paternalistic rationing by an elite which once decreed what it ought and ought not to do. And, as it does so, the only path for those who work in the industry is to trust the viewers and the infinite choices that they are now capable of making.
>
> There is no alternative because technology has finally set them free.
>
> (www.rts.org.uk)

Questions

1. In what sense do the new technologies set TV viewers free?
2. What criticisms could be made of this argument?

Alternative paradigms

It is difficult to talk about an alternative paradigm as if it comprises a consistent set of ideas and perspectives that constitute a particular school of thought. The challenge to the dominant paradigm includes the work of Marxists, feminists and some strands of postmodernism and cultural theory. There are, then, enough critics who reject the consensus underlying functionalism and the democratic assumptions behind pluralism to talk of an alternative, oppositional paradigm, which McQuail has summarized:

> **Most broadly, an 'alternative paradigm' rests on a different view of society, one which does not accept the prevailing liberal-capitalist order as just or inevitable or the best one can hope for in the fallen state of human kind. Nor does it accept the rational-calculative, utilitarian model of social life as at all adequate or desirable. There is an alternative, idealist and sometimes utopianist ideology, but nowhere a worked out model of an ideal social system. Nevertheless, there is sufficient common basis for rejecting the hidden ideology of pluralism and conservative functionalism.**
>
> (McQuail 1994: 46)

Early radical thinkers seemed to share some of the concerns about the emergence of mass society and the rise of popular culture put forward by conservative thinkers. The first attempts to make sense of the media in modern society from a critical perspective were made by the Frankfurt School (and particularly Horkheimer, Adorno and Marcuse: see pp. 89–92), who argued that the media were a conservative force acting to replace working-class aspirations with a false and one-dimensional consciousness dominated by commercialism, individualism and false needs.

This pessimistic view was endorsed in the USA by C. Wright Mills' (1956) work on the power elite and by Herman and Chomsky's (1988) 'propaganda model', where it was argued that the media were an instrument for manipulation and control that operated in the interests of the powerful. In Europe similar concerns were expressed through the writings of Althusser (1971), Barthes (1972) and the rediscovered works of Gramsci (1971). As a result, Marxists began to develop an interest in the cultural and ideological aspects of social life with an emphasis on the significance of the media and the emergence of popular culture. Not all critics of the dominant paradigm are Marxist, and the following seven elements represent the range of critiques that may be said to form an alternative approach:

- the political economy of the media;
- the media as ideological state apparatus;
- the media and hegemony;
- the Glasgow University Media Group;
- the threat of technology;
- globalization;
- feminism and representations of gender.

The political economy of the media

This approach derives from the classical 'base–superstructure' model in Marxist thought, which focuses on the relationship between the economic base, or infrastructure, and the ideological superstructure. It emphasizes the power of the economy (through, for instance, owners, advertisers and media markets) to determine media content. This power has been enhanced by the moves toward deregulation and the concentration of ownership on a global scale. Such a view is concerned with the power of owners and advertisers to influence public agendas and media content and is sometimes known as the 'manipulative model' (Trowler 1988: 33–7). However, the critical political-economy approach also examines the economic forces that may constrain the extent to which influential individuals can meddle in the media.

> **Government and business elites do have privileged access to the news; large advertisers do operate as a latter-day licensing authority . . . and media proprietors can determine the editorial line and cultural stance of the papers and broadcast stations they own. [However, they] operate within structures which constrain as well as facilitate.**
>
> (Golding and Murdock 1991: 9)

The link between economic power and editorial control, which this model takes for granted, has also been examined by Bagdikian (1997, 2004) and was well summarized by the famous American critic Noam Chomsky in the Massey Lectures delivered in 1988:

> **Media concentration is high, and increasing. Furthermore, those who occupy managerial positions in the media . . . belong to the same privileged elites, and might be expected to share the perceptions, aspirations, and attitudes of their associates, reflecting their own class interests as well. Journalists entering the system are unlikely to make their way unless they conform to these ideological pressures generally by internalizing the values . . . those who fail to conform will be weeded out.**
>
> (Chomsky 1989)

The media as ideological state apparatus

In the writings of structuralists such as Althusser (1969, 1971) and Poulantzas (1973), the state is seen as operating in a mechanical manner to reproduce the social relations of a class society. The involvement of individuals in this operation is irrelevant, as it is the overall function of the apparatus of the state that is important and not the motivations, interests or activities of its agents. In this process, social control is established through physical coercion (repressive state apparatus) or the power to persuade (ideological state apparatus). Along with the school and the Church, the media are clearly regarded as having a key role in establishing ideological domination and false consciousness among those classes whose interests are not served by capitalism. In his attack on humanist Marxism and the Frankfurt School, Althusser established a model that saw all aspects of 'civil society' (family, church, media, for example) as extensions of state power, so that human consciousness and subjectivity are constituted by external forces created by the structures of society. Althusser (1969, 1971) admits that ideas have some 'relative autonomy', but he insists that in the last instance ideology is determined by the economic structure of society and the agencies of the state. It is against this rigid and mechanistic model that Gramsci's (1971) more flexible concept of hegemony has been adopted by European Marxists.

The media and hegemony

Although the concept of hegemony relates to the general discussion within Marxism about the ways in which dominant ideologies encourage a 'false consciousness' among the lower classes in society, it has also been applied to the role of the media in the transmission of popular culture, consumerism and national identity.

In his original use of the term 'hegemony', Gramsci (1971) refers to the 'dual perspective' whereby, as well as using 'levels of force', those in power will seek to establish 'moral and philosophical leadership' over the mass of the population by winning their active consent.

> **The convictions of people are . . . not something manipulated by capitalists or put into the minds of the masses by them, but rather they flow from the exigencies of everyday life under capitalism. The workers, and others, hold the values and political ideas that they do as a consequence both of trying to survive and of attempting to enjoy themselves, within capitalism. These activities require money . . . mediated by ideological means, for people have to come to desire the goods for sale. Such desires . . . are not natural, not inborn . . . These desires to consume various products have to be constructed by ideological apparatus, especially in the mass media.**
>
> (Bocock 1986: 32–3)

As Lull (1995, 2000) has pointed out, such a media-transmitted ideology establishes itself through two processes of mediation – technological and social. *Technological mediation* refers to the power of the media to influence human consciousness on behalf of consumer society. Advertising is a classic example of this:

> **Selection of corporate spokespersons, visual logos, audio jingles, catchy slogans, the style and pace of commercials, special technical effects, editing conventions, product packaging, and the welding of print and electronic media campaigns . . . all combine to generate the desired result, selling capitalism's big and bright products and the political-economic-cultural infrastructure that goes along with them.**
>
> (Lull 1995: 16)

According to this view, media personnel are not coerced or manipulated into deliberately misrepresenting social reality; they have become socialized into accepting the values and techniques of their profession and to a large degree believe in what they are doing and that they are giving the customers what they want.

Social mediation emphasizes the humanism of Gramsci's work by stressing the active involvement of people in the hegemonic process. If we are duped by the system, then we are partly responsible by virtue of our participation in the language and image systems that have been created by the media. In our everyday interaction with one another we give credibility to and reinforce 'media-transmitted ideology' by referring to its content and using its codes and incorporating its messages into our social discourse.

The admission that ordinary people have a part to play in creating and reaffirming their culture raises the possibility that the audience may also reinterpret, resist or reject the preferred messages of those responsible for media production and thus undermine the ideological control of those in power. This 'relative autonomy' in cultural production underpins the work of the Centre for Contemporary Cultural Studies (based at the University of Birmingham; e.g. see Hall and Jefferson 1976). Although they accept the Marxist idea that the media reproduce the relations of class society through the reinforcement of a consensus-based 'common sense', they reject the economic determinism of traditional Marxist models. The meanings of cultural texts are not pre-given but are open to interpretation and negotiation and therefore never ideologically fixed.

This cultural flexibility allows writers such as Hall and Jefferson (1976) and Hebdige (1979) to argue that subcultural groups can express their resistance to dominant ideological forms through their cultural practices (for instance, music, fashion, language):

> **Style in sub-culture . . . challenges the principle of unity and cohesion [and] contradicts the myth of consensus . . . It is this alienation . . . which gives the teds, the mods, the punks a truly subterranean style.**
>
> (Hebdige 1979: 118–19)

In Branston and Stafford (1996: 151–4), Bob Marley's career is used as a case study to demonstrate how ideologies of domination can be opposed by reggae as 'rebel music'. However, they also show how, in order to become successful, Marley had to sign up to Island Records and replace the original Wailers to develop the mainstream sound and star image required by the music business:

Case study

The people's music?

Despite the fact that popular music is produced and marketed by corporations for commercial reasons, it is also possible to regard some elements of popular music as a genuine attempt to wrest creative control and production away from the industry professionals and to produce ideas and music that challenge cultural and political conventions. As MacDonald argues, we may run the risk of romanticizing the rebellious nature of pop music, but some of it certainly set out to change public perceptions and attitudes – especially of the young:

> The first such outburst was the original rock'n'roll outbreak of the mid-fifties. This rebellious spirit reignited in the mid-sixties in the work of Bob Dylan and The Rolling Stones, intensified in the late sixties under the influence of LSD and New Left politics, and turned popular music into a counter-cultural phenomenon expressing itself in gigantic outdoor festivals in the years thereafter. A similar spirit drove the radical politico-theology of reggae Rastafarianism and the anarchistic Punk spasm of the seventies. Hiphop has carried a rebellious torch since the early eighties, while the 'orbital' dance scene of the late eighties in the UK sparked a comparable enthusiasm . . . such eras come and go, being attached to wider social signifiers and deeper cultural upheavals than can be accounted for in purely creative terms. The creativity of rock music rides on a social background and takes much of its cut and colour from what's going on in the wider world. The individual cult figures involved are products of their time . . . popular music is a product of society first, a rebel festivity second (and always in passing).
>
> (MacDonald 2003: vii–viii)

As an illustration of this point it is worth repeating what MacDonald has to say about the Beatles in the latter half of the 1960s. Today their work is part of the nostalgia industry, a trip to Liverpool is not complete without a visit to the Beatles Museum, and Paul McCartney has been knighted for his services to the music industry, but 40 years ago . . .

> Quality of consciousness was the key motif of the counter-culture's revolt against consumer materialism in the sixties, running, for instance, through the Beatles' work from Revolver onwards and reaching a zenith with 'A Day in The Life'. The nub of the countercultural critique was that 'plastic people' of 'straight' society were spiritually dead. New Leftists spoke of 'consciousness-raising' while hippies offered a programme of 'enlightenment' through oriental mysticism supplemented by mind-expanding drugs. In today's pleasure-seeking world, introspection holds no appeal and the sixties focus on innerness is ignored or derided as a cover for nineties-style chemical hedonism. The truth was otherwise in 1965–69.
>
> (MacDonald 2003: 220–21)

See also George McKay's (1996) *Senseless Acts of Beauty: Cultures of Resistance Since the 1960s* for an historical account of the counter-culture and its political manifestation in various movements such as free festivals, anti-road campaigns and New Age travellers. For a critique, see www.geocities.com/aufheben2/aufr5rmckay.html

Questions

1. Do you think pop music has lost its rebellious nature?
2. Which artists in the contemporary pop music scene can be considered rebels?

> **Marley and the new Wailers presented a 'sweeter' and more rock-oriented sound to go with a seemingly less aggressive stance. Where 'roots reggae' set out to exclude whites and to attract an aware audience interested in discovering an African culture and African rhythms, Island was effectively marketing Marley as 'Bob Dylan or Marvin Gaye or both'.**
>
> (Branston and Stafford 1996: 153)

It is also possible within the more liberal Marxist model to recognize the relative freedom of journalists and broadcasters to challenge the ideological consensus. In *Channels of Resistance* (Dowmunt 1994), a variety of media analysts reveal the ways in which television producers around the world have managed to preserve their local identities against the threat of cultural imperialism and global homogenization. Although the contributors are not necessarily Marxist, their conclusions clearly reflect the dialectical notions of domination and resistance found in the concept of hegemony:

> **The fact [of television dominance] does not stop us from imagining, developing and analysing alternatives . . . groups all over the world, in institutional and technological situations not of their own making, have begun to resist this domination in diverse and creative ways . . . Although the economic and political pressures on the global television system are strong, they are not totally determining. We can dare to imagine, and start to create, something different.**
>
> (Dowmunt 1994: 15)

Glasgow University Media Group

Although it does not represent a particular element of Marxist theory of the media, the Glasgow University Media Group has provided much empirical evidence to support the view that the media tend to favour conservative representations of reality. In analysing news coverage of industrial disputes, politics and warfare, it has focused on the ways in which political bias affects the structuring of the news, its content and the language used to report it:

> **The essential thrust of our critique is not against media workers as such . . . Rather, it relates to the picture of society that the media construct with such remarkable consistency. We attribute this artificial and one-dimensional picture to the nature of organisations whose basic assumption is that our industrial, economic and social system operates to the benefit of everyone involved . . . unfortunately [this] involves the mass of the 'public' being misrepresented.**
>
> (Glasgow University Media Group 1982: 144–5)

The Glasgow University Media Group has also become increasingly well known for developing new research methods relating production, content and reception. An example of the group's work is Greg Philo's examination of the 'quantitative imbalance' in the flow of news between the developing world and the developed world, and the negative representations of Africa in particular. By interviewing audience groups, it was confirmed that the coverage had a predictable character and that it was perceived as such:

> **Our own study showed that when the developing world is featured on British news, a high proportion of the coverage is related to war, conflict, terrorism and disasters. This is especially so for the main television channels, with over a third of coverage on BBC and Independent Television News (ITN) devoted to such issues . . . Some people were completely 'turned off' from the developing world (about 25 per cent of the sample), but the reason was in part the constant negative diet of images they were given. As one interviewee put it: 'Well every time you turn on the TV or pick up a paper, there's another [war] starting or there is more poverty or destruction. It's all too much.'**
>
> (Taken from An unseen world: how the media portrays the poor, www.unesco.org/courier/2001_11/uk/medias.htm)

In his critique of the GMG, Shaun Best attacks the group for its positivist methodology (content analysis) and its theoretical approach (Marxist):

> **The Glasgow media group do not pose interesting questions because they have their answers in advance. Greg Philo has no concept of ideology. Ideology is merely news and views that he disagrees with. The whole argument of the Group is wrapped up in a romantic package about what life was like before the new right. One of the reasons why many people have embraced postmodern ideas is because of the total and complete intellectual collapse of Marxism as the basis of an explanatory framework for anything.**
>
> (http://shaunbest.tripod.com/id8.html)

The threat of technology

While Marxist writers tend to blame those who control the mass media for cultural decline and political manipulation, other writers have argued that it is the technology itself that threatens cultural and intellectual life. In the 1960s Marshall McLuhan first warned that the new media technologies were transforming our relationships by promoting lazy and irrational attitudes. Whereas a culture based on reading books demands a level of rational concentration, the television has ushered in a 'couch potato' culture for the masses that makes very little demand on the individual other than turning on the TV set (McLuhan 1964; McLuhan and Fiore 1967).

In the 1980s, Postman (1987) returned to the debate with a blistering attack on television and the threat that it poses to Western culture. He argues not that we are being deliberately misled or brainwashed by those in power but that we are conniving in our own cultural

Figure 17.9 Turn off TV!
www.whitedot.org

and political downfall through our demand for continuous entertainment:

> **Our politics, religion, news, athletics, education and commerce have been transformed into congenial adjuncts of show business, largely without protest or even much popular notice . . . The result is that we are a people on the verge of amusing ourselves to death.**
>
> (Postman 1987: 4)

Television clearly plays a central role in providing this endless stream of amusement, but for Postman the real threat is not in the arena of entertainment (which is after all what television was invented for) but in the belief that television can operate as a serious medium for the transmission of culture and political debate:

> **When a population becomes distracted by trivia, when cultural life is redefined as a perpetual round of entertainment . . . when, in short, a people become an audience and their public business a vaudeville act, then a nation finds itself at risk; culture-death is a clear possibility.**
>
> (Postman 1987: 161)

Postman's argument is compelling, but there are many who reject his 'doom and gloom' scenario, particularly those who feel that television can be a useful educational aid (e.g. Masterman 1985; Cragg 1992; Fiske 1987; Fleming 1993). In his book *Everything Bad is Good for You*, Stephen Johnson (2005) pokes fun at those who automatically assume that popular culture is inferior to literary culture and that TV must be bad for you. Instead, he argues that the plots of TV dramas can be just as demanding as those found in literature and that video games are as intellectually stimulating as playing chess or reading books. In a satirical extract on his website, he turns the tables on those who condemn TV by proposing a world in which interactive technology came first and books have suddenly been discovered.

Case study

Serendipity – dream or nightmare?

In the 1990s Postman broadened the debate by extending his critique to the domination of society by technology and the computer. He described the new technopoly as:

> a state of culture. It is also a state of mind. It consists in the deification of technology, which means that the culture seeks its authorization in technology, finds its satisfactions in technology, and takes its orders from technology.
>
> (Quoted in Longhurst *et al*. 2008: 192)

In 2006 Erich Schmidt, CEO of Google, fulfilled Postman's worst nightmare when he revealed:

> And then there's my dream product – I call it serendipity. It works like this. You have two computers. On one you're typing, on the other comments appear checking the accuracy of what you are saying, suggesting better ways of making the same point. This would be good for journalists and politicians too.
>
> (Quoted in Gibson 2008: 11)

Question

1. What impact would this invention have on (a) journalism; (b) politics; and (c) education?

As this new craze for reading books gains in popularity, he imagines how conservative cultural forces such as teachers and parents might react. He identifies four key areas of potential controversy:

1. Limited cognitive skills
While game playing stimulates a range of mental skills and utilizes the senses, reading books engages children in a very limited set of cognitive skills. This may lead to progressive atrophy and eventual shrinkage of the brain itself.

2. Social isolation
Game playing has a long tradition of promoting pro – social attitudes and behaviour including networking, team work and individual competition. Books, however, are anti-social by nature and reading encourages the reader to participate in a lonely and passive activity.

3. Discrimination
One of the most disturbing consequences of book reading is that it has led to the construction of a new learning disorder called dyslexia which may affect as much as 20 per cent of the population.

4. Mind control
One of the great pleasures of gaming is that the outcome is uncertain and dependent upon the skill of the individual players. Books on the other hand allow the author to dictate what happens in ways the reader is powerless to challenge.

As Johnson concludes, 'Reading is not an active, participatory process; it's a submissive one. The book readers of the younger generation are learning to "follow the plot" instead of learning to lead'.

(Adapted from Johnson 2005)

Cartoon by Mike Keating

The globalization of culture

In 1977, the author of this chapter arrived in Marrakech. The marketplace bustled with the activities of jugglers, musicians and storytellers but, in the shade of a streetside café, Berber tribesmen in traditional dress sipped mint tea and sucked on hookahs as they sat transfixed by the huge monochrome television set that dominated the small bar. As I drank my ice-cold Coke, I realized that I recognized the characters on screen: it was an episode of the TV western series *High Chaparral*, which had been dubbed in French (the colonial language) and subtitled in Arabic (for the hard of hearing). The only thing missing was a Big Mac with fries!

Writers such as Baran and Sweezy (1966) had written about the economic and political domination of global markets and national governments by American multinational companies, and this was also the year that Tunstall (1977) published his warnings about the Americanization of the world's media, but the terms 'globalization' and 'cultural imperialism' were yet to be applied to the impact of Western media on local cultures and identities. Over 30 years later, the terrain has changed (there is now a McDonald's in Marrakech), but the issue remains the same: to what extent can local cultural traditions survive and resist the threat of cultural imperialism that accompanies the rise of the transnational corporation and the monopoly exercised over new media technologies by one or two global powers? (For a more up-to-date exploration of the production and distribution of the media at a global level, see Bakir 2009.)

While the old multinationals that were located within nation-states, such as America or Japan, were subject to government regulation and owed some allegiance to their home base, the emerging transnational corporation has no parents and no obligations other than to itself (see Chapter 9). Using the latest information technologies, it scours the globe in search of expanding markets and cheap labour.

The economic might of transnational production companies is paralleled in the media environment by the emergence of global giants in the shape of Sony, Disney, Time-Warner and Microsoft, and these corporations both convey the commercial ethos of the transnationals and impose their own cultural footprint, through news, information and entertainment, on countries that quite literally cannot afford to produce their own.

There are many who fear that this global influence is eroding local differences and cultural diversity and will lead to a form of cultural imperialism that threatens to engulf us all in a torrent of commercialism dedicated to spreading the gospel of Coca-Cola, McDonald's and Nike Sports Wear. Pessimistic writers such as Schiller (1989, 1993) argue that traditional cultures and national identities may be swept away by the rising tide of (largely) American values, aspirations and popular culture. The world has become a global village, and it is called America.

This grim view of a world in the grip of a homogeneous culture is not shared by many cultural commentators. James Lull (1995, 2000), for example, rejects the simplistic notion of 'cultural imperialism' as an irresistible force for uniformity as it entails the notion of passive audiences and acquiescent cultures. Following the ideas of Smith (1990) and Appadurai (1990), he argues that the idea of a 'global culture' is 'a practical impossibility' because the notion of culture refers to historical differences between peoples in terms of collective beliefs, language and behaviour. As peoples around the world do not share a common past, language or experience, it is a contradiction in terms to refer to a 'global culture'. It is further argued that cultures are dynamic processes, not fixed entities to be confirmed or replaced. In other words, the post-industrial media conglomerates of 'the West' may dominate the transmission of modern culture, but they do not control its reception or the way that it is used. In a process known as 'deterritorialization', cultures become separated from their geographical and social roots and transplanted into other cultural environments. The result is not global hegemony by a dominant Western culture but a transformation of all cultures (including the Western) by the interplay between the local and the global. Big Macs in Marrakech is one side of this coin, Ladysmith Black Mombazo advertising baked beans on British television is the reverse. For a broader discussion of the interrelationship between the global and the local, see Sreberny-Mohammadi (1991), Stevenson (1995) and Back (1997). Not surprisingly, for a computer mogul who has become the world's richest man, Bill Gates's book *The Road Ahead* (1995) is an unashamed tribute to the wonders of globalism.

The idea that there is something inevitable about the globalization of culture has also been challenged by those who point out that the media offers opportunities for initiatives that serve local audiences and celebrate

Figure 17.10 McDonaldization?
Kevin Foy/Alamy

regional, national and ethnic differences. The growth of community radio is a good example, although the form it takes differs from one society to another; in the UK, it is often associated with 'pirate radio' and the musical tastes of different ethnic groups, while in the USA it provides 'micro-broadcasters' with a licensed alternative to commercial radio (Hendy 2000). In Wales and Ireland, the broadcast media challenge the hegemony of English as the dominant language through radio and TV channels in Welsh or Gaelic.

Stop and think

- What examples of globalization have you come across at home or abroad?
- Do you regard them as a threat to national or regional cultures?

Feminism and representations of gender

If the Marxist tradition tends to focus on the ways in which the media reproduce relationships and ways of thinking that are of benefit to capitalism, then feminists concentrate on the ideological work carried out by the media on behalf of men. Van Zoonen (1991) argues that, before the rise of the women's movement, the 'gendered' nature of culture was accepted as natural and consequently the issue of gender was largely ignored by traditional and critical theorists alike. As feminist writers began to examine the personal dimensions of female oppression 'the media became a major focus of feminist research, critique and intervention' (Gill 2007: 9). Attention turned to the ways in which women were represented to 'suit the interests and pleasures of men' through narrow stereotypes that reinforced traditional roles (Marchbank and Letherby 2007: 303). Early research such as Meehan's (1983) study of prime-time television revealed that in North American serials women characters were restricted to a limited number of stereotypical roles. At the same time, Ferguson's (1985) analysis of women's magazines from the 1940s to the 1980s revealed an underlying 'cult of femininity' that defined the ideal woman in terms of getting a good man, keeping him happy and raising his kids. However, Radway's (1984) work on romantic novels and

Winship's (1986) study of women's magazines suggest a more supportive role in what was still a male-dominated culture. Similarly, the work of Geraghty (1991), Hobson (1982) and Kilborn (1992) reveals that strong and positive role models for women exist in soap operas:

> **Many of the British soaps . . . are marked by the presence of women – most of them no longer in the prime of youth – who have remained sturdily independent, in spite of sometimes quite strong social or family pressures to be otherwise. As such their judgement is respected and they often operate as confidantes or advisors to the young, vulnerable or inexperienced. Bet Lynch and Rita Fairclough in *Coronation Street* are good examples of this particular type of strong woman.**
>
> (Kilborn 1992: 47)

Stop and think

- ➤ What strong female characters can you list from British soaps today?
- ➤ Can you identify any who represent the more restricted (traditional) stereotypes?

Changes in the workplace and the family towards the end of the twentieth century, along with the feminist critique of media practices, meant that representations of women became more complex and contradictory. Kath Woodward's (2003) study of motherhood reveals a new image of the ideal mum as one who balances a range of competing demands from family and work alongside the need to look good. As Gill points out:

> **The notion that the media offered a relatively stable template of femininity to which to aspire gave way to a much more plural and fragmented set of signifiers of gender.**
>
> (Gill 2007: 11)

This paradigm shift also involved an increasing fascination with the representation of men, so that Gill's study of gender and the media covers a range of issues, including twenty-first-century representations of both men and women, anorexia, the rise of 'chic lit' and the crisis of identity faced by some men.

David Gauntlett (2002, 2008) suggests that these changes have led to a decline in fixed representations of gender and a more fluid notion of identity:

> **Twenty or thirty years ago, analysis of popular media often told researchers that mainstream culture was a backwards-looking force, resistant to social change and trying to push people back**

Case study

A survey of women's magazines

In 1997 the Social Affairs Unit conducted a survey of women's magazines. Although one or two magazines, for example, Bella and Prima, were found to offer 'useful advice and pleasant entertainment' for the young mothers who form their readership, most magazines targeting the young 'Magazine Woman' of the 1990s were castigated. Magazines such as Marie Claire, Cosmopolitan and, in particular, Company were condemned for ignoring traditional values, child-rearing and family life in an amoral diet of sex, fashion and sensationalism which trivialized the role of women and the issues which they face. They conclude: 'It is a depressing survey . . . the bulk of magazines . . . contain a dominant image of women as selfish, superficial and obsessed with sex'.

(*Guardian* 24.11.1997)

Questions

1. Applying content analysis (see pp. 137–138) to one of the magazines mentioned, examine the report's conclusion that 'Magazine Woman has escaped from the kitchen only to get as far as the bedroom'.
2. What criticisms would you make of the methodology used in the survey? (You will need a copy of the report by the Social Affairs Unit (1997) or the *Guardian* review (24.11.1997).
3. How might the differing feminist approaches respond to the 'Magazine Woman' referred to in the study?

> into traditional categories. Today, it seems more appropriate to emphasise that, *within limits*, the mass media is a force for change. The traditional view of a woman as a housewife or low-status worker has been kick-boxed out of the picture by the feisty, successful 'girl power' icons. Meanwhile the masculine ideals of absolute toughness, stubborn self-reliance and emotional silence have been shaken by a new emphasis on men's emotions, need for advice, and the problems of masculinity. Although gender categories have not been shattered, these alternative ideas and images have at least created space for a greater diversity of identities.
>
> (Gauntlett 2002: 247–8)

Effects of the mass media

The debate over the power of the media to influence attitudes and behaviour goes back to the nineteenth century. It is a controversial area where strength of opinion often outweighs hard evidence; it has therefore become increasingly difficult to talk with any certainty about the power of the media to influence social behaviour. We concentrate on the major areas of concern: the media's economic, political, moral and social influences.

Areas of concern

Economic influence of the media

Apart from their potential for making money, the media are thought to possess the power to influence consumer choice. Billions of pounds are spent on advertising every year by companies seeking to improve their market share, and customers pay over the odds for the privilege. It is estimated that the average American child will have seen 350,000 commercials by the age of 18 (Brierly 1998: 46). The *Guardian* (18.9.1992) estimated that, for every £1.50 spent in Britain on a top brand of coffee, 12 pence goes in profits and wages to the growers but 57 pence is accounted for by the

Case study

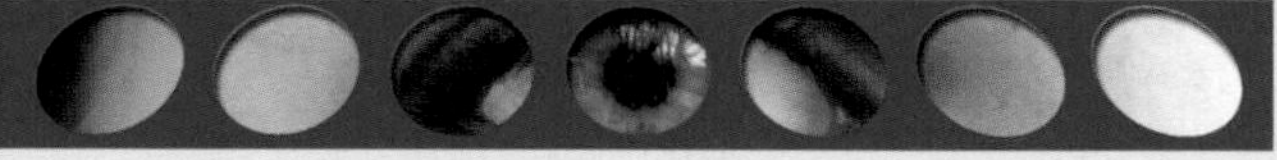

The branding of the media

Advertisers may not be able to directly influence the choices consumers make, but they can have some say over media content as well as ensuring that the line between plot and product become blurred. In her book *No Logo*, Naomi Klein draws on recent history to make the point:

> It is common knowledge that many advertisers rail at controversial content, pull their ads when they are criticized even slightly and perpetually angle for so-called value-addeds – plugs for their wares in shopping guides and fashion spreads. For example, S.C. Johnson & Co. stipulate that their ads in women's magazines 'should not be opposite extremely controversial features or material antithetical to the nature/copy of the advertised product' while De Beers diamonds demand that their ads be far from 'any hard news or anti/love-romance themed editorial'. . . But the advertisers don't always get their way: controversial stories make it to print and air, even ones critical of major advertisers . . . [however] these same media show how deeply distorting the effects of branding can be on our public discourse – particularly since journalism, like every other part of our culture, is under constantly increasing pressure to merge with the brands . . .
>
> The merger between media and catalog reached a new high with the launch of the teen TV drama *Dawson's Creek* in January of 1998. Not only did the characters all wear J. Crew clothes, not only did the windswept, nautical set make them look as if they had stepped off the pages of a J. Crew catalog, and not only did the characters spout dialogue like 'He looks like he stepped out of a J. Crew catalog,' but the cast was also featured on the cover of the January J. Crew catalog. Inside the new 'freestyle magalog', the young actors are pictured in rowboats and on docks – looking as if they just stepped off the set of a *Dawson's Creek* episode.
>
> (Klein 2000: 39–42)

Question

1. What examples of 'branding' can you find in TV series and films?

advertising budget. In 1987, Gold Blend instant coffee launched its successful 'mini-soap' campaign, which saw sales rise by 15 per cent over the first year and by 40 per cent after five years (Cashmore 1994: 76). Despite its success, the series was eventually dropped by Nestlé after 11 years and an increase in overall sales of 70 per cent in order to appeal to a more international market. By the same token, companies are terrified of bad publicity and will resort to the law in order to stifle public complaint. The organizers of the 'What's Wrong with McDonald's?' campaign (see www.mcspotlight.org) ended up in court for spreading anti-Mac propaganda. While it is clearly in the interests of advertising agencies to claim that publicity has a direct influence on consumer choice, there is very little evidence to support this. Brierly (1998) notes research showing that we can barely recall any of the adverts with which we are bombarded every day, while advertising pundit Winston Fletcher argues that, for the amounts they spend advertising their brands, companies get very little in return. As someone who has worked in advertising for most of his life, he comes to the remarkable conclusion that 'at least 96 per cent of all advertising is wasted, but nobody knows which 96 per cent' (Fletcher 1992: 38).

Political influence of the media

Since the advent of public education and mass-circulation newspapers, the role of the media in the coverage of politics has been regarded as important; however, it is with the introduction of broadcasting that the power of the media to influence opinion has been a key issue in political debate. Some of the earliest content analysis of newspapers was concerned with political bias and propaganda (Krippendorf 1980). Original research into media effects concentrated upon the effectiveness of wartime propaganda (Hovland 1949) and the links between election campaigns and voting behaviour (Berelson *et al.* 1954; Katz and Lazarsfeld 1955; Lazarsfeld *et al.* 1944). Despite little evidence that the media can do much more than reinforce existing political attitudes, the media have been heavily involved in election campaigns since the 1950s, with strict controls imposed in some societies on the extent to which political parties may have access to broadcasting at election time.

The first politician to take advice on his election campaign from an advertising agency was Dwight D. Eisenhower, who paid for TV commercials to get his message across in the defeat of Adlai Stevenson in 1952. In 1960, the first real 'election by television' took place, when John F. Kennedy and Richard Nixon debated the issues on both television and radio. It is widely held that, despite a good performance, Nixon came across poorly on television, largely due to his appearance, and that this cost him the election. This success was repeated in the 1964 election, when Lyndon Johnson was advised to use a negative advertising campaign against Barry Goldwater, which highlighted the Republican's desire to use nuclear weapons in Indo-China. In what has become a classic example of the genre, the 'Daisy Girl' commercial shows a young girl plucking the petals from a flower as we hear the countdown to the launch of a nuclear warhead.

By the 1980s, negative campaigns and zappy commercials had replaced the more traditional approaches to electioneering. Political advertising and, to some extent, political discussion became reduced to the wisdom of what works on television. As Kern (1989) has argued, a political broadcast is deemed effective only if it is short, entertaining and capable of provoking a reaction.

These lessons have been learned in Britain, where, despite the restrictions on access to the broadcast media, the major parties engage 'spin doctors' to grab the soundbite and advertising agencies to manage the image (Jones 1995). In his study of the 1987 general election in Britain, William Miller (1991) concludes that, once party identification (partisanship) had been taken into account, the press had some influence in the swing back to the Conservatives, especially among tabloid readers:

> **The influence of the tabloid press was particularly strong on those voters who denied being party 'supporters', even when they had a party preference. They made up half of the electorate. The Conservative lead increased by 50 per cent amongst politically uncommitted *Sun/Star* readers but not at all amongst politically uncommitted *Mirror* readers. Since *Sun/Star* readers as a whole were relatively uncommitted they were relatively easy to influence anyway but, in addition, the tabloids were particularly good at influencing their readers' voting preferences.**
>
> (Miller 1991: 199)

Very few political analysts hold the view that the media can determine what we think or radically alter our political beliefs, but instead they argue that the media play a part in *reinforcing* existing opinions, *setting the agenda* for political discussion and *framing* the way in which the public perceives political events in general. The tabloid press cannot make die-hard Labour

Table 17.3 Election 2005: what the papers said

Newspaper	1997	2001	2005
Sun	Labour	Labour	Labour
Daily Express	Conservative	Labour	Conservative
Daily Mail	Conservative	Conservative	Conservative
Daily Mirror	Labour	Labour	Labour
Daily Star	No party	Labour	Undecided
The Times	No party	Labour	Labour
Daily Telegraph	Conservative	Conservative	Conservative
Financial Times	Labour	Labour	Labour
Guardian	Labour	Labour	Labour
Independent	No party	Labour	Undecided

(*Financial Times* 14.4.2005)

supporters vote against their own party, but by repeatedly placing the 1992 election in the context of Labour's tax plans they may have influenced the less committed voter to vote against a return to power for Neil Kinnock's party. The Labour Party complained that its defeat was a consequence of negative tabloid coverage, while the *Sun* announced the next day that 'It was the Sun wot won it' (Figure 17.11). However, by the election of 1997, many traditional supporters (broadsheet and tabloid) of the Conservative Party had turned against John Major's government and, for the first time since the Second World War, the Labour Party enjoyed a slight advantage in terms of press support, which included a switch by Rupert Murdoch to Tony Blair's side (Figure 17.12). Since coming to power, the Labour Party has continued to get the backing of most of the press, but in the 2005 election support began shifting again (Table 17.3).

In the US elections, some concern was raised over the support for the Bush campaign in 2004 by the boss of Viacom, the parent company of CBS, which is the major news channel in the USA. Sumner Redstone said that, from a 'Viacom standpoint, the election of a Republican administration is a better deal because the Republican administration has stood for many things we believe in, deregulation and so on'. For more on the debate this caused, see www.newsweek.com/id/55035. In the run-up to the 2008 election, John McCain accused the US media of having a 'love affair' with Barack Obama, but this was disputed by analysts, who claim the reverse is true:

> **Over the course of a career, most nationally prominent politicians, particularly those who choose to seek the White House, can expect ups and downs in their treatment by the press . . . But in recent years, there has been one exception to this rule: John McCain . . . McCain and his admirers in the media have cooperated to construct a shimmering image of the senator from Arizona, one that has propelled him to the heights of American politics.**
>
> (Brock and Waldman, quoted in the *Guardian* 28.7.2008)

In Italy the prospect of having someone standing for election when he owns the major independent TV broadcasting group is even greater cause for concern. Berlusconi owns Fininvest, a major shareholder in Mediaset, which controls the three commercial terrestrial channels in opposition to the state-run RAI. This gives Berlusconi around 45 per cent of the audience share in a country that has a low level of newspaper readership and where the majority of people (87 per cent) depend more heavily on TV for their information about political issues than anywhere else in Europe. Fininvest also controls a leading national newspaper and a range of magazines. In 2002 the *Economist* reported:

> **Mr Berlusconi has yet to remove the ubiquitous conflicts between his private and public concerns. Because his companies are embroiled in almost every part of the economy, his failure to do so casts doubts on the motives behind so many of his projects, whatever their merits.**
>
> (From www.ketupa.net/berlusconi.htm)

In their analysis of globalization, Curran and Seaton (1997) touch on a different aspect of political influence; the impact of up-to-the-minute news coverage on the formulation of policy by governments. Particularly in the field of foreign policy, they argue that national governments can be stampeded into hasty responses to world events simply in order to satisfy the media expectation that they 'do something'. The NATO bombing of Kosovo in 1999 by US and British war planes, as well as the invasion of Iraq, can be seen as examples of this.

Moral and social influences of the media

An area that has provoked particular concern has been the effects of media violence and pornography, especially upon children. Historically these fears about juvenile delinquency and the link between mass entertainment and moral degeneration predate the invention of the television set and the 'video nasty' by at least a century. Murdock and McCron (1979) remind us of this when they quote from a concerned observer in 1851, who warns of the corrupting and demoralizing influence of the theatre acting as a 'powerful agent for the depraving of the boyish classes of our towns and cities . . . which are so specially arranged for the attraction and ensnaring of the young' (quoted in Glover 1985: 372). In the 1950s, the comic book became the focus of a moral panic in the USA over educational standards and deviant behaviour, which ultimately led to the official censorship of horror and crime stories (M. Barker 1984). However, it was the issue of violence in the cinema, television and computer games that grabbed the headlines in the 1990s.

Levels of screen violence are notoriously difficult to measure, and comparisons have to be made with care (Gunter 1985). The SDP MP David Alton (now in the House of Lords) claimed in 1994 that by the age of five years the average child will have witnessed 20,000 murders on television. Mary Whitehouse's National Viewers' and Listeners' Association (now renamed Mediawatch) monitored the output of the terrestrial channels in the first half of 1994 and concluded that 'broadcasters are promoting a relentless culture of cruelty and violence' (Denscombe 1994: 43). Studies by less partial bodies such as the Henley Centre (1993), the Broadcasting Standards Council (1994) and the Independent Television Commission (1993) all suggest that, whatever the relative levels of violence on television, sex, violence and bad language remain an issue for many people, with 65 per cent feeling that there is still too much violence on television (Broadcasting Standards Council 1994).

In the run-up to the 2005 general election in the UK, the head of Mediawatch, John Beyer, wrote to each of the party leaders expressing his organization's concern over continued levels of violence and antisocial behaviour on TV. He complained that his researchers had monitored 177 films across the five terrestrial channels during 2004 and had 'identified 900 incidents involving firearms and 680 violent assaults'. Consequently he wanted to know what they intended to do to regulate such coverage:

Parliament legislates on a range of social and moral issues and these have yet to feature very much in the Election campaign. Many people care deeply about standards in entertainment and are concerned about the portrayal of violence, the use of obscene language and the display of nudity and sexual intimacy on television. We believe the quality of our culture matters and that television, in particular, is promoting violence and uncivilised behaviour which validates the social and criminal violence that disfigures our society. The latest statistics on the portrayal of violence on television again show that violence involving firearms is the most common followed by violent assaults – precisely those crimes that are on the increase.

Whether such concerns reflect a real threat or simply represent an imaginary moral panic is difficult to assess, but there is much hearsay evidence that violence on screen is a direct cause of copycat behaviour in society. In 1971, *A Clockwork Orange* was withdrawn from British cinemas by its director because of imitative violence by young gangs. In 1987, the Hungerford massacre was said to have been inspired by Michael Ryan's obsession with *Rambo* films. Three young men were convicted of a murder in Cardiff that followed repeated exposure to the film *Juice*, while the video of *Child's Play 3* was cited in the 1993 murders of James Bulger in Liverpool and Suzanne Capper in Manchester (see Newburn and Hagell 1995). Similar concerns were raised over the film *Natural Born Killers* and apparent 'copycat' killings in the USA and France, leading to much publicized court cases. The murder of London headteacher Philip Lawrence by a teenager has also led to the introduction of guidelines on screen violence being introduced in 1998 by a government convinced that screen violence and street crime are linked.

Since 2000, other films have grabbed the headlines, such as *The Matrix*, which has been related to several 'copycat killings', including the massacre of students at Columbine High School, and *Scream*, which has been associated with many violent murders across Europe and North America: in the USA there have been at least four killings in which *Scream* was cited as a trigger or where a *Scream* mask was worn by the killer; in England and in France there have been three reported cases and one in Belgium where a lorry driver put on a *Scream* costume before killing a 15-year-old girl with two kitchen knives.

(*Observer* 9.7.2002)

On a less serious level, the antics of cartoon characters such as Tom and Jerry, Ren and Stimpy, Beavis and Butthead and the Simpsons have all been

Saturday, April 11, 1992 25p Audited daily sale for March 3,629,449

'THREE DEAD' AS IRA HIT CAPITAL

THREE people were feared killed last night after a massive car bomb blasted the City of London.

Rescue workers said many more were injured and nine ambulances rushed to the scene in St Mary Axe.

A warning call, with a code word used by the IRA, was made to British Rail at Waterloo at about 8.50pm by a man with an Irish accent.

Witness Nick Haycock said: "Dozens of windows have been blown out and there is glass everywhere.

"There are hundreds of police flooding in and people are staggering from the area in each other's arms."

The outrage wa thought to be in retalia tion for the Tory Elec tion triumph.

It posed a fresh chall enge to Premier Joh Major just hours afte his win at the polls.

IT'S THE SUN WOT WON IT

Celebrating . . . roly-poly Page 3 star Pat Priestman at Parliament yesterday

HERE'S HOW PAGE 3 WILL LOOK UNDER KINNOCK!

20mph FRED'S M-WAY CHAOS

Warning . . . Pat as our Page 3 girl

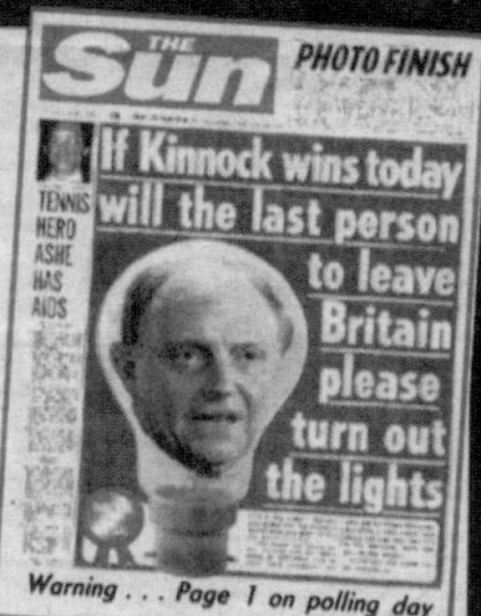

Warning . . . Page 1 on polling day

Big thank-you from MPs

By JOHN KAY and JOHN TROUP

TRIUMPHANT MPs were queueing yesterday to say "Thank You My Sun" for helping John Major back in to Number 10.

They and hundreds of readers hailed our polling day front page — showing Neil Kinnock's head in a light bulb — which alerted people to the dangers of Labour rule.

They smiled at the headline with it: *If Kinnock wins will the last person to leave Britain switch out the lights.*

And they rolled about when we starred roly-poly Pat Priestman, 53, as our Page Three girl —saying she would be the shape of things to come under Labour.

Tory MP Matthew Banks, who won back Southport from the Lib-Dems, could not thank The Sun enough.

He said yesterday: "Wherever I went on polling day everyone was talking about The Sun's front page.

"We even stuck a huge blow-up of it on to the noticeboard in our campaign centre.

"The Sun stuck with the Tories all the way through the campaign and everyone in the party is truly grateful."

SWING

Jubilant Nigel Evans, who won back the Ribble Valley seat snatched from him by the Lib Dems in a recent by-election, joined in praising The Sun.

He said: "The Sun's support for the Conservative cause was vindicated by the

Continued on Page Two

Figure 17.11 Down with Kinnock!
John Frost Newspapers/NI Syndication

THE Sun

An historic announcement from Britain's No 1 newspaper

MAY 1st

Tuesday, March 18, 1997 28p THE PAPER OF THE PEOPLE

THE SUN BACKS BLAIR

Give change a chance

Historic . . Blair reads early copy of today's Sun

THIS is the election for the millennium.

In six weeks' time, Britain will vote for a government to take it into the 21st century.

The people need a leader with vision, purpose and courage who can inspire them and fire their imaginations.

The Sun believes that man is Tony Blair. He is the best man for the job, for our ten million readers and for the country.

It is a momentous decision which we have not taken lightly because we still have reservations about some of New Labour's policies. But for all the Tories' achievements of the past 18 years, they no longer deserve our support.

They are tired, divided and rudderless. They need a rest and so does the country. Blair is the breath of fresh air this great country needs.

On Pages 6 and 7 we explain why we are putting our trust in him.

Election special – Pages 2, 4, 5, 6 and 7

Figure 17.12 Up with Blair!
John Frost Newspapers/NI Syndication

Case study

The history of 'copycat suicides'

Following the publication of Goethe's novel *The Sorrows of Young Werther* in 1774, there were many reports of young men shooting themselves, in what was believed to be copies of the death of the novel's hero. When academic David Phillips studied copycat suicides in the early 1970s, he coined the term 'Werther effect'. Studying suicides in the US between 1947 and 1968, Phillips found that within two months of a front-page suicide, an average of 58 more people than usual killed themselves. And there is also a sharp rise in car crash fatalities and other forms of disguised suicides. Later studies showed that people were more likely to copy the behaviour of others if they felt similar to the person they were copying: it has been argued that social networking sites are a highly effective means of allowing people to communicate with someone they feel similar to.

(Times online 19.2.2008)

Between January 2007 and February 2008, 15 young people in Bridgend committed suicide, leading to claims that media coverage and social networking on Internet sites such as Bebo were to blame for inspiring a 'suicide cult' in the area.

Questions

1. What evidence can you find to support the view that the Bridgend suicides were influenced by the media?
2. What alternative explanations may be offered?

linked to the incitement of violence, vandalism and antisocial behaviour; Mighty Morphin Power Rangers have also been accused of promoting imitative violence in the playground. Professor Provenzo at Miami University has found that, of 47 Nintendo games monitored, only seven were not violent; much of the violence was directed at women, with 'foreigners' most likely to be portrayed as villains (*Guardian* 4.11.1991). Since the early 1990s, computer pornography has been treated as a serious offence as children gain widespread access to acts of buggery, rape and bestiality via the Internet. Butterworth (1993) examined the impact of the new technologies on pornography and the emergence of what she calls 'virtual sex' in wider-ranging and more accessible formats. Catherine Itzin has claimed that such extreme pornography distorts the perceptions that boys have of women and can contribute to sexual violence:

> **Many studies show that if teenage boys are repeatedly exposed to images where women are reduced to their genitals and presented as sexually voracious, passive and servile it desensitises them and increases callous attitudes towards women. Pornography is often a contributing factor in child sexual abuse, sexual harassment and forced sex.**
>
> (Quoted in Bouquet 1994: 2)

In March 1994, Elizabeth Newson, professor of developmental psychology at the University of Nottingham, claimed that the new levels of mindless violence occurring in society could be explained only by the 'easy availability to children of gross images of violence on video' (Newson 1994: 3). From her summary of research findings, she suggested that video violence leads to identification and imitation among the young, but Newson's main concern was with the way in which vicious and cruel behaviour was portrayed as entertainment and amusement, encouraging desensitization. She quotes an American writer to emphasize the point:

> **Not only do these films suggest that brute force is a prerequisite for manliness, that physical intimidation is irresistibly sexy, and that violence offers an effective solution to all human problems; today's movies also advance the additional appalling idea that the most appropriate response to the suffering of others is sadistic laughter.**
>
> (Medved 1992, quoted in Newson 1994: 4)

It is true that many studies, especially those conducted under experimental conditions, support the view that violence on the screen leads to aggressive attitudes and violent behaviour, but whether this is the cause or the trigger of such behaviour is another matter. It should not surprise us that young offenders express an interest in films that sensationalize crime or that sex offenders show an interest in pornography, but this does not demonstrate any original cause; it merely suggests an attraction to the behaviour that has got them into trouble in the first place and accepts that the media play a part in the story. McQuail has summarized this link:

> **The balance of evidence supports the view that media can lead to violent behaviour and probably have done so; these effects occur mainly as a result of 'triggering' of aggressive acts, imitation, identification with aggressive heroes and 'desensitisation', leading to a higher tolerance for real violence.**
>
> (McQuail 1994: 334)

Critics of the violent effects model have argued that there is no clear evidence to prove a link between screen violence and social behaviour. After more than 1000 studies, 'no satisfactory consensus has emerged', with different research techniques tending to produce contradictory results (Newburn and Hagell 1995: 8). The work of Hodge and Tripp (1986) and Gunter and McAleer (1990) has questioned the reliability of studies that show a causal link, while Cumberbatch (1989) has been a persistent critic of those who too readily accept the pessimistic warnings of media-induced violence. Cumberbatch has pointed out the relatively low levels of violence on British screens, especially in comparison with law-abiding societies such as Japan, as well as refuting the evidence that short-term responses to media violence indicate long-term changes in behaviour. The horror stories so often quoted by the press and the largely discredited Newson Report mentioned above have been the subject of detailed examination (e.g. Buckingham 1996; Barker and Petley 1997), where much of the repeated 'evidence' for media-induced rape, murder and violence is denounced as popular myth inspired by tabloid journalists and high-profile moralists. In his summary of the continuing controversy surrounding 'media effects', Cumberbatch (1998) argues that much of the 'evidence' would not be out of place in 'an encyclopaedia of ignorance':

> **The tip of the iceberg of knowledge about media effects is probably akin to a pebble on a mountain: the bit underneath is a colossal mass that geologically might turn out to be reasonably representative of the bit above, but might not bear any relationship to it whatsoever.**
>
> (Cumberbatch 1998: 262)

After reviewing well-known anecdotal cases and the evidence of psychologists, psychiatrists and sociologists who favour the media violence hypothesis, Cumberbatch concludes that, in the face of contradictory data, researchers have been extremely selective in their presentation of findings and overlook suggestions that the audience can handle the material to which it is subjected.

These conclusions are to some extent supported by the work of Gauntlett (1995), who suggests that the link between TV and juvenile crime has been exaggerated by a middle-class moral panic over social order that ignores the more obvious part played by unemployment and poverty. In his revised edition ten years later, Gauntlett (2005) complains that recent studies 'have not only failed to show anything new, but have remained doggedly rubbish'.

Noble (1975) has gone further, by suggesting that some forms of television violence may have the cathartic effect of releasing feelings of aggression. This is a point of view also expressed by Yaffe and Nelson (1982) about the use of pornography in sex education and therapy sessions. However, they also point out that pornography can be used in different ways by different people and will have more than one set of consequences. They conclude that, apart from the harmful effects of violent pornography on children, especially those who are already disturbed, 'pornography might be offensive, distasteful and a nuisance, but it did not appear to pose a threat to society' (Yaffe and Nelson 1982: xii). In his review of the research into the effects of pornography, Goode (1997: 225–30) dismisses the 'catharsis theory' as obsolete and false, but he is equally dismissive of the argument that pornography is by nature a form of violence against women. Following a trawl through a variety of statistical and experimental studies, Goode concludes that 'sexual explicators in pornography, by itself, is not a major determinant of male aggression against women.' However, the case of violent pornography is a different matter, and he agrees with Donnerstein *et al.* (1987) that 'exposure to violent pornography will increase aggression against women . . . it also plays a part in changing the way men think about women.' As Malamuth *et al.* have concluded:

Case study

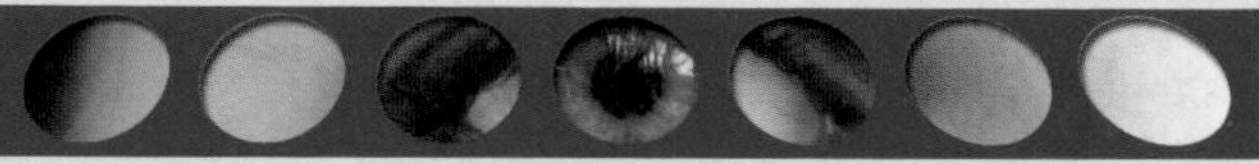

Manhunt

Following the conviction of 17-year-old Warren Leblanc for the murder of 14-year-old Stefan Pakeerah in 2004, many high street stores, including Dixons, have removed the Rockstar game, Manhunt, from their shelves. Leblanc had savagely beaten his victim with a claw hammer and stabbed him several times after luring him into a local park. The defence had suggested that the motive was robbery but Stefan's mother argued that the violence had been linked to Leblanc's obsession with Manhunt, described by reviewer Dave Jenkins as 'perhaps the most violent, amoral video game ever made [in which] you're forced to sneak around a series of maze-like levels killing "hunters" and SWAT-team members as you go, using such unsavoury methods as suffocating them with plastic bags and cutting their throats with shards of glass.' Stefan's father described the game as 'a video instruction on how to murder somebody, it just shows how you kill people and what weapons you use'. Stefan's mother added: 'When one looks at what Warren did to Stefan and looks at the brutality and viciousness of the game one can see links.'

A statement from the game's publishers Rockstar North said: 'We extend our deepest sympathies to those affected by these tragic events . . . Rockstar Games is a leading publisher of interactive entertainment geared towards mature audiences and markets its games responsibly, targeting advertising and marketing only to adult consumers aged 18 and older . . . [We] submit every game for certification to the British Board of Film Certification and clearly mark the game with the BBFC-approved rating.'

A spokesperson for the British Board of Film Classification said the game had been given an 18 certificate. It was also the board's opinion that there were no issues of harm attached to the game and there was no evidence directly linking the playing of games with violent behaviour.

Professor Mark Griffiths of Nottingham Trent University, a psychology expert, said 'Research has shown those aged eight years or below do in the short-term re-enact or copy what they see on the screen. But there's been no longitudinal research following adolescents over a longer period, looking at how gaming violence might affect their behaviour.'

(Adapted from BBC News Online 29.7.2004)

Questions

1. How convincing do you find that statement from Rockstar?
2. Does the research referred to by Professor Griffiths help us to draw any conclusions?

> **if a person has relatively aggressive sexual inclinations resulting from various personal and/or cultural factors, some pornography exposure may activate and reinforce associated coercive tendencies and behaviours . . . [although] high pornography use is not necessarily indicative of high risk for sexual aggression.**
>
> (Malamuth *et al.* 2000: 79–81)

The contradictory evidence and the range of possible responses by different audiences to different stimuli make it difficult to draw firm conclusions. The debate over the effects of the media on children raises important issues about the nature of the society in which we want them to grow up and the kind of people we want them to become, but the evidence, quite simply, fails to resolve these questions. The remarks of Wilbur Schramm in 1961 are still true today:

> **For *some* children under *some* conditions, some television is harmful. For *other* children under the same conditions, or for the same child under *other* conditions, it may be beneficial. For *most* children under *most* conditions, most television is neither particularly harmful nor particularly beneficial.**
>
> (Schramm *et al.* 1961: 1)

Interpreting the evidence

Given the inconclusive nature of the evidence, it is not surprising that several models have developed to explain the relationship between the media and its audience.

While early models emphasized the power of the media, later work has concentrated on the ability of the audience to make its own sense of media texts through the processes of interpretation and negotiation. Similarly, there has been a shift away from short-term effects on the individual towards the long-term impact of media messages within different cultural contexts. The following represent some of the major theoretical positions that characterize the historical development of media effects research.

The hypodermic syringe model

Early ideas tended to be influenced by sociological positivism, behaviourist psychology and popular fears of mass society, all of which created the 'myth of media power'. Although, as McQuail has pointed out:

> **this view was based not on any scientific investigation but on observation of the enormous popularity of the press and of the new media of film and radio that intruded into many aspects of everyday life as well as public affairs.**
>
> (McQuail 2000: 417)

According to this view, the media had the power to change attitudes and behaviour and the potential for prosocial as well as antisocial influence. The panic induced across America by Orson Welles' radio play *War of the Worlds* in 1938 is often quoted as a classic example of the power of the media to influence behaviour (Cantril 1940). Such deterministic ideas still inform modern debates about the use of the media, but, as McQuail (1977) points out, there are at least four methodological issues that prevent an acceptance of such a simplistic model:

- The media are only one of many factors involved in the socialization process. When assessing the possible effects of the media, we must also consider the influence of family, friends and schooling.
- The media themselves consist of many forms that operate in different ways. When discussing 'the media', we have to specify which aspect we are referring to; broadcast media operate differently from the press, tabloid newspapers do not behave like broadsheets, and so on.
- A distinction must be made between effects ('any of the consequences of mass media operation, whether intended or not') and effectiveness ('the capacity to achieve given objectives'). The whole issue of the dichotomy between the intended message and the audience response to it is crucial to the later shift of interest away from the power of media texts towards the reader's interpretation.
- We need to specify the level at which we are measuring media effects; the media may have influences on the individual, the group, the institution or culture in general. Before making general claims for the power of the media to affect behaviour, it is important to be clear about the level at which they are operating.

The 'no effects' model

Empirical research soon revealed the shortcomings of the hypodermic syringe model, and it was recognized that the effectiveness of the media in getting its messages across depended on the personal influences affecting the perceptions of audience members. The direct consequence of this was the development of the 'two-step flow' model by Katz and Lazarsfeld (1955), which recognized that the way we interpret the media usually involves a process of negotiation with other members of the audience; instead of passively absorbing media output, we discuss with family, friends and even perfect strangers the programmes we have seen on TV or the stories we read in the press. In this model, opinion leaders emerge (in families, at work, in the pub) to help interpret the messages we are being sent; the simplicity of the stimulus/response relationship between media and audience was replaced by the complexity of human meaning and personal relationships.

A more extreme variant of audience power that diminished the significance of the media even further was the 'uses and gratification' model, which stresses the ways in which the media respond to the biological, psychological and social needs of the individual members of the audience (Blumler and Katz 1974). In an approach that has similarities with the dominant paradigm mentioned earlier (pp. 711–713), the media are seen as responsive to client needs. McQuail *et al.* (1972) looked at the way in which people use television in particular to satisfy a range of personal requirements; they concluded that, at a general level, four types of gratification were provided for:

- *Diversion* – Media as a form of escapism.
- *Personal relationships* – Media as a means of providing companionship and the opportunity for social interaction.
- *Personal identity* – Media as a device for confirming personal values and concept of self.
- *Surveillance* – Media as a channel for information and ideas.

Stop and think

- Using the two-step flow model, who do you regard as the major opinion leaders who have affected your reading of media events at home? At college? At work? At play?
- Using the uses and gratifications model, provide examples of the four types of gratification identified by McQuail *et al*.

The emphasis of this approach has led to the criticism that it exaggerates the importance and independence of the audience (Elliot 1997), but it has also opened up the possibility of exploring the ways in which media texts may be interpreted (McQuail 1994) and the role of the individual consumer within an 'active audience' (Lull 1995).

Long-term effects

A rejection of both the hypodermic syringe model and the no effects alternative has encouraged the view that the media may influence us in many ways that are hard to measure and have long-term effects on our attitudes, creating new ideas or reinforcing existing ones rather than changing the opinions we already have. When this is combined with the recognition that individuals belong to social groups, a new paradigm emerges that insists on placing media production and audience response within the context of a cultural effects approach that 'seeks to bring together both the way in which meanings are created by the media and the way in which these relate differently to the cultures of particular social groups' (Glover 1985: 380). Another way of interpreting the panic of Martian invasion that gripped Americans in 1938 is to go beyond the polarized debate (which blames the power of the media or the gullibility of individuals) and explore the interplay of various historical, situational and cultural factors, which may lead us to understand the context within which, for some people, the panic took place. Such factors would include the relative newness of the radio as a medium for communication, the dramatic devices employed in the production of the play itself, the point at which individual listeners tuned in, the role of the 'opinion leader' within the family, the fascination with science-fiction film and comics of the time, current speculation over the habitability of the planet Mars, and the serious political situation in Europe as it drifted towards the Second World War.

A further aspect of the long-term view is the role played by the media in reinforcing negative attitudes through the stereotypical portrayal of particular groups by the media. In this, the concept of representation is central because it recognizes the part played by the media in articulating and preserving the values and norms of wider society. Gill Swanson has defined representation as 'the way images and language actively construct meanings according to sets of conventions shared by and familiar to makers and audiences.' However, the construction of these meanings takes place within a system of power, which ensures that some representations enjoy greater legitimacy than others and are dominant; those without legitimate status become marginalized. Branston and Stafford (1996) discuss this power in their examination of the way in which stereotypes categorize and evaluate groups of people in such a way as to explain their social position in terms of the characteristics which form the basis of the stereotype. Briggs and Cobley (1998) argue that the way in which groups of people are represented not only affects the ways that they are seen by others but also influences the way they see themselves. Rather than adopting a Marxist perspective on ideology and 'false consciousness', they are more interested in 'the manner in which ideology underpins and endows with meaning the constituent components of our identities and what these entail.' What it means to be a woman, an Asian, gay, young, British or disabled all entail identities that are constructed partially through the discursive activities of the media.

Moral panics

One aspect of the 'media effects' debate is concerned not so much with its ability to influence behaviour in a direct manner but with the possibility that it can generate widespread feelings of anxiety and concern and exaggerate the risks that the public might face from particular threats or social groups (Goode and Ben-Yehuda 1994). Rather than acting as a cause of individual behaviour in the positivistic sense (see 'The hypodermic syringe model' on p. 733), this approach is more interested in the role of the media in creating a climate of fear in which we become sensitized to certain risks and not others. In general terms, Gerbner (1995) has talked of how the media obsession with violent crime promotes a 'mean world syndrome', which exaggerates the sense of insecurity, anxiety and mistrust that is characteristic of modern life. More specifically, however, the idea of 'moral panic' was originally developed to explain the demonization of young people as a social problem and the scapegoating of certain subcultural groups in particular.

First used by Jock Young to describe the impact upon public anxiety of the creation of 'drug squads' in the 1960s, the concept of *moral panic* was borrowed and extended by Stan Cohen (1972) in his classic study of mods and rockers and their treatment by the media and the police in the early 1960s. Like the Teddy boys before them, the mods and rockers were presented by the media not simply as symbols of youthful style but as an indicator of national decline. This approach reached fever pitch in press coverage of the mod 'invasions' of various seaside resorts in 1964. These events were given front-page prominence by national newspapers, which referred to a 'day of terror' in which whole towns had been overrun by marauding mobs 'hell bent on destruction'.

Such spectacular reportage was generally exaggerated. For instance, in the case of the mod 'invasions', the initial violence and vandalism were minimal. Moreover, it is speculated that press coverage actually engendered and amplified subsequent disturbances. Stanley Cohen defined the moral panic that followed as a situation in which:

> **A condition, episode, person or group of persons emerges to become defined as a threat to societal values and interests; its nature presented in a stylised and stereotypical fashion by the mass media, the moral barricades are manned by editors, bishops, politicians and other right thinking people; socially accredited experts pronounce their diagnoses and solutions; ways of coping are evolved [more often] resorted to, the condition then disappears, submerges or deteriorates and becomes more visible.**
>
> (Cohen 1972: 9)

In such situations distorted media coverage plays a key role in shaping events. Media attention fans the flames of an initially trivial incident and creates a self-perpetuating 'amplification spiral', which generates a phenomenon of much greater significance and magnitude. In his work, Cohen shows how media intervention gave form to these subcultural groups and represented them as threatening 'folk devils'.

In Pearson's (1983) work the idea is used to explore the fears generated by the emergence of urban gangs in the nineteenth century: Girroters, Peaky Blinders, Scuttlers and Hooligans were some of the gangs that gripped public attention at the time, but Pearson concludes:

> **every era has its young gangs that catch the terrified imagination of the respectable. Every era also has its myth about a previous golden age of traditional values, a time when it was safer to walk the streets.**
>
> (Cited in Toynbee 1983)

Hall *et al.* (1979) applied the idea of moral panic to the criminalization of black youth in the 1970s, while Bill Osgerby (1998) points out that Cohen's arguments could easily be applied to media treatment of the various forms of subcultural groups that have emerged since, from the skinheads of the late 1960s and the punks of the 1970s to the New Age travellers and acid house ravers of the late 1980s and early 1990s. These youth subcultures have been subject to a process of stigmatization and stereotyping, which has worked to popularize and lend substance to styles that were initially indistinct and ill-defined. Media intervention, therefore, gives youth subcultures not only national exposure but also a degree of uniformity and definition. As Osgerby points out:

> **Without the intercession of media industries it is unlikely that sub-cultures such as Teddy Boys, Punks or Ravers would have cohered as recognisable cultural formations, instead remaining vaguely defined and locally confined stylistic innovations.**
>
> (Osgerby 1998)

The active audience

Often overlooked in the debate about media effects is the ability of the audience to take control of the media and to respond to its messages in unpredictable ways. Because of its pluralist and individualistic overtones, this view has been unfashionable in sociological circles (Elliot 1977, in Marris and Thornham 1997: Reading 30). However, recent dissatisfaction with the amount of time and funds devoted to inconclusive research and the simplistic thinking about the media it encourages has led to a revisiting of the 'uses and gratifications' model and a more psychological approach to what we do with the media rather than what they do to us. Lull has argued that, despite its mechanistic references to human needs, the uses and gratifications approach, through the research of McQuail *et al.* (1972) and

Figure 17.13 Matt cartoon from the *Sunday Telegraph* 15.5.2005

Blumler and Katz (1974), did show how 'various audiences . . . use media differently and for different reasons' (Lull 1995: 93). By accepting that psychological needs have a cultural dimension, Lull attempts to bring together the social and the psychological strands into a less deterministic approach to the study of communications which recognizes the critical abilities of 'the audience'.

> **In the end it is this tension between the ability of the mass media to influence thought and activity, and the strong tendency of individuals to use media and symbolic resources for their own purposes, that our theory of media, communication, and culture must accommodate.**
>
> (Lull 1995: 105)

This view underpins much of the thinking now to be found in cultural studies and is clearly reflected in the work of Fiske (1989), Ien Ang (1985, 1991), Lewis (1990) and Gauntlett (1997) on the relationship between popular culture and its audiences. Ang's book *Desperately Seeking the Audience* (1991) is a revolt against the models that treat the audience as a homogeneous and passive bunch of 'couch potatoes' in danger of 'amusing themselves to death' or quite literally driving themselves mad. In her attack on this dominant thesis, she argues that the 'viewers' perspective is almost always ignored' in preference to an 'institutional point of view' in which the actual audience is treated as 'an objectified category of others to be controlled' (Ang 1991: 4).

In order to provide an alternative 'microscopic stance', Ang argues that attention should focus on 'actual audiences' that inhabit the real world:

> **The social world of actual audiences . . . [is] a provisional shorthand for the infinite, contradictory, dispersed and dynamic practices and experiences of television audiencehood enacted by people in their everyday lives – practices and experiences that are conventionally conceived as 'watching', 'using', 'receiving', 'consuming', 'decoding', and so on, although these terms too are already abstractions from the complexity and the dynamism of the social, cultural, psychological, political and historical activities that are involved in people's engagements with television. It is these heterogeneous practices and experiences of audiencehood that form the elements to be articulated in discourses of 'television audience'.**
>
> (Ang 1991: 13–14)

This approach requires an 'ethnographic thrust' that is genuinely concerned to produce an alternative body of knowledge 'that is constructed from the point of view of actual audiences'. In an example of patriarchal remote control, Ang borrows the following account from Bausinger's (1984) study, in which a woman talks of her husband's use of the TV: 'Early in the evening we watch very little TV. Only when my husband is in a real rage. He comes home, hardly says anything and switches on the TV.' According to Bausinger, this is not a choice of programme but a well-understood family code for 'I would like to hear and see nothing'.

From this 'microsituational' perspective, the static viewing habits of 'the audience' revealed by empirical research are replaced by a more intimate approach that transforms our understanding of media use by celebrating 'the dynamic complexity of television audiencehood' and recognizing its diversity:

Case study

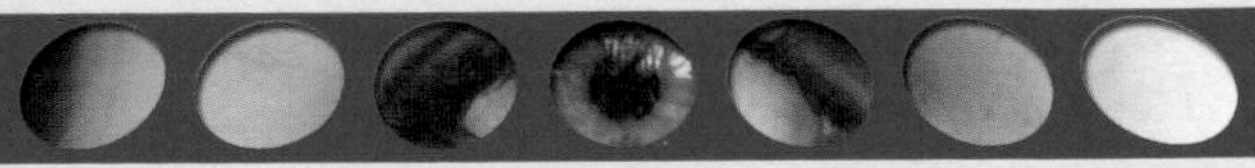

The hoodie: another moral panic?

In May 2005, the Bluewater shopping centre in Kent introduced a dress code for customers which bans youths wearing hoods and baseball caps from their private malls as such young men are seen as intimidating yobs who use the hood to conceal their identities during a day spent shoplifting.

Rachel Harrington, vice-chair of the British Youth Council, says Bluewater's decision demonstrates a growing demonization of young people. 'It's yet another example of a trend – tarring all young people with the same brush and overreacting to any behaviour by young people. You can understand a shopping centre's desire to please their customers, but it doesn't seem to me to be the best response. It's very easy to create the stereotype of the young thug as emblematic of society's problems, rather than seek out the root of the problems.'

Angela McRobbie, professor of communications at Goldsmiths College, says it's the hoodie's promise of anonymity and mystery that both explains its appeal and provokes anxiety. 'The point of origin is obviously black American hip-hop culture, now thoroughly mainstream and a key part of the global economy of music through Eminem and others. Leisure- and sportswear adopted for everyday wear suggests a distance from the world of office [suit] or school [uniform]. Rap culture celebrates defiance, as it narrates the experience of social exclusion. Musically and stylistically, it projects menace and danger as well as anger and rage. [The hooded top] is one in a long line of garments chosen by young people, usually boys, and inscribed with meanings suggesting that they are 'up to no good'. In the past, such appropriation was usually restricted to membership of specific youth cultures – leather jackets, bondage trousers – but nowadays it is the norm among young people to flag up their music and cultural preferences in this way, hence the adoption of the hoodie by boys across the boundaries of age, ethnicity and class.'

However, McRobbie concludes that attempts to ban such clothing will simply make it more desireable: 'Moral panics of this type have only ever made the item, and its cultural environment, all the more attractive to those who prefer to disidentify with establishment figures and assorted "moral guardians" and who enjoy the outlaw status of "folk devil".'

(Gareth McLean, *Guardian* 13.5.2005)

Questions

1. Why would traders at Bluewater want to ban hoodies?
2. In what sense can this be seen as a 'moral panic'?
3. What is the cultural significance (attraction) of the hooded top to young people?

Case study

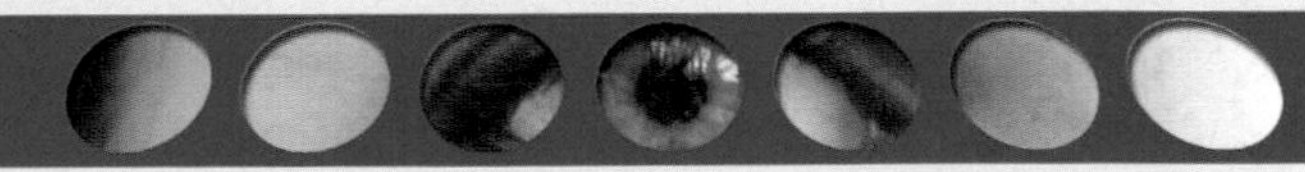

Soap talk: using TV to negotiate identities

In *Television, Globalisation and Cultural Identities*, Chris Barker (1999) discusses the idea that ideologies are not simply imposed upon people by those in positions of power but created in an interactive environment that involves audiences in interpreting texts from popular culture and the 'television talk' which accompanies them. In Barker's view, 'television talk' is an important part of establishing ethical and personal boundaries, particularly through the discussion of soap opera:

> Soap talk is one of the ways in which [people] make intelligible and manageable the moral and ethical dilemmas that face them.
>
> (Barker 1999: 132)

Following writers such as Barthes, Foucault and Gramsci, Barker argues that we make sense of the world around us and our relationship to it within the context of ►

Case study *continued*

power but that audiences have the ability to negotiate and resist ideological control through the imposition of their own 'preferred meanings' upon media texts. Such texts are 'polysemic' and as such can be read in different and oppositional ways. Although the media industry holds most of the cards when it comes to the production of media texts it is powerless to dictate their consumption. In this sense, the power of the audience is important because they bring with them a range of common-sense attitudes by which they interpret the messages they receive and play a major part in judging the relevance of these messages to their own lives. Television, for example, does not tell us how to act but

> forms a resource for the construction of cultural identity just as audiences draw from their own sedimented cultural identities and cultural competencies to decode programmes in their own specific ways.
>
> (Barker 1999: 112)

This means that our reading of texts is tied closely to the major identity elements of our 'self'. Studies of news programmes and soap operas have suggested that our readings of such texts are influenced by cultural background and the identity components of class, gender, ethnicity and locality. In other words, different people 'read' the same text in different ways depending upon the aspects of identity that are of most importance to them.

In Barker's study, he uses qualitative research to examine

> the role of television soap opera as a resource employed by British Asian and Afro-Caribbean teenagers [to show] how a specific group of persons deploy television as a resource for the construction of cultural identities [through] the formative nature of language as a resource in lending shape to ourselves and our world out of the contingent and disorderly flow of everyday talk and practice.
>
> (Barker 1999: 119)

In other words, he records the conversations the sample have about soaps. This 'soap talk' provides the data by which he can examine the process of 'discursive production' through which their 'multiple and gendered hybrid identities' are formed within British culture.

Through their discussion of soaps, the teenagers explore the boundaries of their own identities because, by expressing opinions on the behaviour of others, they are really engaging in the establishment of who they think they are, what issues are important to them and the moral codes by which they establish 'acceptable' behaviour for youngsters like themselves (black/Asian/male/female/working class/middle class/British), even if this is through a discussion of characters who are not like them and in circumstances that they are unlikely to experience.

In this way, the 'self' can reflect upon its relationship to formal morality but also work out its own ethical stance. In Foucault's work this distinction is important, and Barker uses it to focus upon the role of 'ethical reflection' in the social construction of identity:

> Ethics . . . is concerned with the actual practices of subjects in relation to the rules which are recommended to them which they enact with varying degrees of compliance and creativity . . . This more dynamic conception of self suggests a route by which ethics can be seen as the site of a form of self-fashioning activity.
>
> (Barker 1999)

Through the two related but contradictory responses to characters (condemnation and explanation), the audience not only 'slag off' the bad characters for breaking the rules of conventional morality (condemnation) but also come to a more forgiving position that sees behaviour as relative to circumstances as well as some overarching set of absolute rules (explanation). Somewhere between the two, they do some important 'identity work' of their own.

Questions

1. How much time do you spend discussing soaps and reality TV?
2. Which characters and storylines excite the most discussion?
3. Is there a clear moral agenda in these episodes? What is it?
4. Is there much disagreement over such readings?
5. Does the social nature of the audience (class, gender, ethnicity) make a difference to the reading?
6. Does TV play a part in the formation of identity? Who is in control – them or us?

> **Television audiencehood is becoming an ever more multifaceted, fragmented and diversified repertoire of practices and experiences. In short, within the global structural frameworks of television provisions that the institutions are in the business to impose upon us, actual audiences are constantly negotiating to appropriate those provisions in ways amenable to their concrete social worlds and historical situations.**
>
> (Ang 1991: 170)

The active nature of the audience can be seen in many ways, whether it involves swearing back at *Pop Idol* or *I'm a Celebrity: Get Me Out of Here* in the privacy of our own homes or the public demonstrations in Liverpool against the *Sun*'s treatment of Hillsborough. In 1939, a dramatic, if extreme, example of audience power was demonstrated in Ecuador when an attempt to reproduce the *War of the Worlds* hoax backfired; the public took such exception to the joke that they burned the radio station to the ground, killing six members of staff.

The models we have looked at are not supposed to be mutually exclusive but indicate the different perspectives that may be applied to the study of media effects. Depending on circumstances, the effectiveness of a particular message will be affected by the quality of its production, the needs of individual consumers, the social context of its consumption and the cultural circumstances surrounding its transmission. Where the balance between these factors is right, the media have the power to transform people's lives, but when the relationship becomes unbalanced, the magic ceases to work.

In concluding his discussion on the effects of the media, McQuail identifies the ways in which the media demonstrate their power:

> **That we cannot trace very precise causal connections or make reliable predictions about the future does not nullify this conclusion [about media effects]. The question of the power of the mass media is a different one . . . Control over the mass media offers several important possibilities. First, the media can attract and direct attention to problems, solutions or people in ways which can favour those with power and correlatively divert attention from rival individuals or groups. Second, the mass media can confer status and confirm legitimacy. Third, in some circumstances, the media can be a channel for persuasion and mobilisation. Fourth, the mass media can help to bring certain kinds of public into being and maintain them. Fifth, the media are a vehicle for offering psychic rewards and gratifications. They can divert and amuse and they can flatter. In general, mass media are very cost-effective as a means of communication in society; they are also fast, flexible and relatively easy to plan and control.**
>
> (McQuail 1977: 90–91)

Summary

- The mass media play an ever-increasing part in our modern way of life. People depend on the media for information and for their entertainment.
- Technological developments have increased the range and changed the nature of the mass media that are available to people. The diversity of channels and broadcast services available enables consumers virtually to create their own viewing schedules.
- While there have always been attempts by governments to control the mass media, recent developments have led to a greater concern about the power of the media. Restrictions on the media include economic, political and legal controls and regulations.
- There are a number of theoretical perspectives that explore the relationship between the media and society. These perspectives do not fall conveniently under 'conventional' sociological headings. There is a broad distinction between theories that take a generally optimistic view of the media – that emphasize their ability to provide us with more information and a greater choice of material to read, listen to and view – and those that express concern over the negative consequences of the role of the media – highlighting the danger of the media being used as instruments for manipulation and control.

Summary *continued*

- The extent to which the media affect attitudes and behaviour is contentious. While it is clear that people will be influenced by what they read, see and hear, evidence on whether the media directly determine specific forms of behaviour – whether watching violence causes children to behave violently, for instance – is inconclusive.
- There have been various theoretical attempts to explain the relationship between the media and their audience. Early models tended to emphasize the power of the media, and the short-term effects on the individual, while later work has focused on the ability of the audience to interpret the media and has highlighted the longer-term impact of media messages within different cultural contexts.

Links

The media permeates all aspects of modern life, and most of the topics and issues covered throughout this textbook will involve a concern with how they are represented by the media.

Further reading

Briggs, A. and Burke, P. (2005) *A Social History of the Media*, Cambridge: Polity Press.
Provides a clear overview of the communications media and the social and cultural contexts within which they have emerged.

Briggs, A. and Cobley, P. (2002) *The Media: An Introduction*, 2nd edn, Harlow: Longman.

Albertazzi, D. and Cobley, P. (2009) *The Media: An Introduction*, 3rd edn, Harlow: Longman.
This text provides a useful and up-to-date introduction to developments in the media, including some of the less fully researched areas such as comics, advertising, marketing and new technology.

Curran, J. and Seaton, J. (1997) *Power Without Responsibility: The Press and Broadcasting in Britain*, London: Routledge.
A detailed account of the history and development of the media in Britain that also provides an introduction to the main theories of the media.

French, K. (1997) *Screen Violence: An Anthology*, London: Bloomsbury.
A reader that covers a variety of perspectives – personal, professional and political – on this contentious topic.

Gauntlett, D. (1995) *Moving Experiences: Understanding Television's Influences and Effects*, London: John Libbey.
An excellent critical review of 'media effects' research. Updated in 2005 with additional chapters on research techniques and also including his often cited article 'Ten things wrong with the "effects model"'. See website below for links to other texts by Gauntlett.

Gibson, J. (ed.) (2008) *Media 08: The Essential Guide to the Changing Media Landscape*, London: Guardian Books.
Does what it says on the tin – an essential guide for media students and practitioners, with over 13,000 contacts in the worlds of media, politics, sport, culture, etc. An invaluable sourcebook for third-year dissertations. See also *Who's Who in the Media* (2006) also published by Guardian Books, for background information on influential figures in UK media.

Gil, R. (2007) *Gender and the Media*, Cambridge: Polity Press.
Excellent review of the field covering the early research into female representation to the broader concerns with masculinity and postmodernism.

Goldsmith, J. and Wu, T. (2008) *Who Controls the Internet: Illusions of a Borderless World*, Oxford: Oxford University Press.
A critical account of the development of the Internet and its unfulfilled promises of freedom and debate. Will probably date quickly.

Lull, J. (1995, updated 2000) *Media, Communication and Culture*, Cambridge: Polity Press.
A readable discussion of the relationship between social order and the ideological power of the media.

McQuail, D. (2005) *Mass Communications Theory: An Introduction*, 5th edn, London: Sage.
Now in its fifth edition, the standard text on the sociology of the media. Its coverage of theories of the media is particularly extensive.

Williams, G. (1994) *Britain's Media: How They are Related*, London: CPBF.
This brief introduction is packed with information and ideas about media ownership in Britain during the twentieth century. It is available from the Campaign for Press and Broadcasting Freedom (8 Cynthia Street, London N1 9JF). See 'Media ownership in the age of convergence' on the CPBF website at www.cpbf.org.uk for an update on this research.

Websites

www.cpbf.org.uk

A pressure group defending public service broadcasting and the freedom of journalists. Concerned mainly with issues of media ownership and political control.

www.cmpa.com

The site for the US-based Centre for Media and Public Affairs, which conducts research into the news and entertainment media.

www.guardian.co.uk/media

A free-rolling news website with online subscription database access to news stories and also free text search.

www.theory.org.uk/david/index.htm

Professor David Gauntlett maintains his own website, which includes extracts from his books on media. There are also blogs that allow for interactive discussion.

Activities

Activity 1

Neophiliacs and cultural pessimists

In looking at the historical development of the media, some of the range of current technological innovations were introduced and discussed. Such a review is almost bound to be out of date as soon as it is committed to print, as technological innovation shows little sign of slowing up. However, here are differing views of the effects of these developments for society. The positive view that improved media technologies will benefit society through increasing customer choice and providing greater opportunities for education and democratic participation is termed by Curran and Seaton (1991) the *neophiliac approach*. Those adopting a *cultural pessimistic* viewpoint believe that a decline in quality and cultural standards inevitably accompanies new forms of media and communication.

Questions

1. **Look at the following list of positive statements about change in the modern media from the neophiliac approach. Give an example of each one.**
2. **How might a cultural pessimist respond? Again, give an example for each row. The first row has been completed as an illustration. You might find the following chapters useful in completing this task: Curran and Seaton (1991: Chapter 14); O'Sullivan *et al*. (1994: Chapter 8); G. Williams (1994: Chapter 1).**

Neophiliacs	Cultural pessimists
More services offer more choice	More channels = more of the same
End of broadcasting monopoly	
Two-way technology is interactive	
Access to global information/other cultures	
Introduction of new work practices	
End of traditional class divisions	
New educational opportunities	
Political empowerment of individuals	

Activity 2

Life without the media

Have you ever considered what life would be like without the media? Try it out for one day as an experiment – and don't cheat! No newspapers, no radio, no magazines and no television (even if you have to record your favourite programmes for future viewing). Make some notes as to how you feel at different times of the day.

Questions

1. **Which media did you miss most, and for what reasons?**
2. **At the end of the experiment consider the questions asked earlier on p. 686.**
3. **How did your life change?**
4. **What were the effects on social life and interpersonal communication?**

Glossary

A

Active audience A notion used in the study of the media which suggests that the audience has powers of discrimination and uses the media rather than reacts to it. It rejects the simplistic cause–effect model of media influence.

Afterlife A term reflecting belief in life after death in some form. Most religions believe in an afterlife, though the form varies. Examples include heaven and hell in Christianity and Islam and more temporary states such as reincarnation in Hinduism and Buddhism.

Age of majority The age in society at which a child becomes considered an adult in social, legal and/or political terms. The exact age varies across time and culture and the specificities of rights and responsibilities can vary within societies. Some societies have rituals celebrating or marking such 'coming of age'.

Ageing The process of growing old. This is both a physical and a social process, as are the changes associated with old age. **Ageism** refers to prejudice or discrimination on the basis of age.

Alienation The condition in which individuals feel detached or estranged from themselves and others and from specific situations, such as their work situation.

Anglican Communion The fellowship of Churches throughout the world sharing a close relationship with the Church of England, the head of which is the Archbishop of Canterbury.

Anomie A situation where an individual or group no longer supports or follows the norms of society: a condition of normlessness (see Norms).

Anthropocentrism A 'human-centred' perspective that regards humans as the most important and central factor in the universe. Anthropocentrism is believed by some to be the central problematic concept in environmental philosophy, where it is used to draw attention to a systematic bias in traditional Western attitudes towards the non-human world.

Anti-racist education Educational policies aimed at eliminating the practice of labelling people according to the colour of their skin or racial identity.

Anti-sexist education Educational policies aimed at challenging male domination of the education system and society in general.

Articulation of modes of production A term most closely associated with the work of Ernesto Laclau in the 1970s. Laclau uses it as a critique of dependency theory. It refers to the notion that there can be several different modes of production operating at the same time across the globe. The dominant mode of production, for example capitalism, is able to articulate – that is to say direct and control – other modes of production for its own ends.

Artificial insemination A process of unnatural conception involving the injection of semen into the womb by artificial means.

Asceticism A doctrine or practice of self-denial and abstinence in which sensual/physical pleasures are denied in order for spiritual fulfilment to occur.

Assimilation This refers to the process by which 'outsiders' adjust culturally to the host country through a relinquishment of social and cultural characteristics and the adoption of the host culture and identity. Originating in the USA, and having some popularity in political debates in 1960s–1970s Britain, the term has more recently been used by critical writers to refer to a form of social control by the powerful over the powerless.

B

Bahā'īs A religious movement arising out of a Persian Islamic sect in the 1860s. Bahā'īs believe in the oneness of God, the unity of all faiths and the inevitable unification of humankind. Social goals as well as spiritual truth are emphasized.

Bias In sociological research, this refers to the difference between the 'true' value of a characteristic and the value that is found by the research.

Biological determinism The assumption that individual abilities, such as intelligence, are determined at birth by innate, inherited qualities. At its most extreme this perspective ignores social influences.

Biomedicine Western, or cosmopolitan, medicine founded on principles of modern science.

Birth rate The number of births per thousand females of childbearing age per year.

Bourgeoisie In a narrow sense, the term used by Marxists to refer to the owners of property in capitalist society. More loosely, it has been used to describe the middle and upper classes, who are both presumed to support the capitalist system.

Branch Davidians A breakaway from a sect which itself broke away from the Seventh Day Adventists, a millenarian movement. A large number of Branch Davidians following the charismatic authority of David Koresh were killed in a siege and subsequent storming of their compound in Waco, Texas, in 1993.

Buddhism A set of traditions and teachings derived from the Buddha about 2500 years ago. Central teachings include the law of *karma* by which reward or punishment results from good and evil acts. There is much variety within Buddhism and two main historical traditions: Theravada and Mahāyāna.

Bureaucracy A particular form of administration that is characterized by a set of clearly defined rules and a hierarchy and that emphasizes efficiency and impersonality. It is seen as the typical form of largescale organization in modern societies.

C

Calvinism The beliefs and teachings following the theology of sixteenth-century Protestant reformer John Calvin. Key aspects of his theology included the sovereignty of God, the centrality of the Bible, the rule of predestination and justification by faith alone.

Capitalism A form of economic organization in which the means of production are privately owned and controlled.

Capitalist world metropolis A concept derived from André Gunder Frank used to describe those countries at the centre of a chain of exploitation that reaches into some of the poorest societies. The capitalist world metropolis exercises its control over societies at the periphery primarily through economic means.

Carer Someone who provides help or support for a disabled person, usually unpaid.

Case study A piece of research that focuses on a single example or case, rather than a larger sample, and examines it in some depth.

Child abuse Maltreatment of a child. Child abuse may involve physical, verbal and/or sexual abuse and it is important to remember that its effects may not necessarily be visible.

Childhood The state of being a child. In physical terms this usually means the time from birth to puberty. Sociologists are also interested in the social, political and legal meanings of childhood and highlight how the meaning and designation of childhood varies across time and culture.

Children's rights The notion and definition of the just and fair treatment of children. These have been formally outlined and ratified by a number of countries following the United Nations Convention on the Rights of the Child in 1989. In practice, however, children's rights continue to be violated in many ways and throughout the world.

Christianity An inclusive term referring to the world religion founded on the life, teachings and work of Jesus of Nazareth, an Israeli Jew. The term 'Christ', meaning anointed one, refers to the belief that Jesus was the Messiah. There are many branches within Christianity, including Eastern or Orthodox Churches, the Roman Catholic Church and those Protestant Churches arising out of the Reformation.

Citizenship Membership of, and inclusion in, a national community. This usually requires the fulfilment of certain obligations to the state, such as paying taxes, as well as offering entitlements, such as the right to vote in elections.

Civic culture The symbols, norms and attitudes that legitimate a system of political power.

Class A basic type of social stratification. In sociological theorizing, classes have been defined in economic terms, by economic characteristics such as occupation or income. They are used to refer to divisions in society, for instance the dividing of a society into upper, middle and working classes.

Cohabitation The state of living together outside marriage. Cohabitation implies being involved in a sexual relationship. It may apply to both heterosexual and homosexual couples.

Collective conscience The term associated with the work of Durkheim that refers to the moral consensus of society: the beliefs and values that are held by (the majority of) citizens in a particular society.

Colonialism Domination by one country (the colonial power or 'home country') of a territory or culture, often by military force, and exploitation of that territory or culture in order to help the home country's economic development.

Communitarianism A political perspective emphasizing a balance between the rights of individuals and their responsibilities to the community. The aim is to remove severe impediments to community relationships, for example, by providing education for parenthood or devolving considerable government power to a local level.

Complementary medicine Non-biomedical healing traditions such as herbalism, acupucture or aromatherapy founded on principles other than modern science, e.g. humoral balance or energy meridians.

Confucianism Or K'ung Fu-tse. A school of thought following the ideas of the Chinese philosopher Confucius (551–479BC). Confucius emphasized moral values as the basis of the social and political order, including the notion of respect for the family and the state.

Conjugal Of marriage. Traditionally the notion of 'conjugal rights' referred to the right of sexual intercourse with a spouse.

Conscientization A state or process of critical awareness of inequalities that may have previously been taken for granted.

Content analysis A research technique used to quantify media texts according to predetermined and clearly defined categories. By measuring the amount of space or time devoted to stories, images or symbols, it is possible to make comparative assessments of media content.

Core In development theory, these are the most advance industrialized societies. These societies are already developed and in many ways control the process of development for others at the periphery.

Corporatist state A political system in which some large interest groups have become more powerful than others in the political and economic arena. Decision making is generally by compromise between a representative of labour (unions), capital (employers) and the state.

Correspondence principle Similarities between social relationships in schools and the division of labour at work. Associated with the Marxist-based work of Bowles and Gintis.

Credential inflation The tendency for qualifications to be valued less highly as more people have them. In response to the increasing number of candidates with the necessary qualifications, employers will raise the qualifications required for specific jobs.

Crime Behaviour that breaks the criminal law and that can be followed by criminal proceedings and formal punishment.

Criterion referencing Assessing an individual's educational attainment by checking whether items on a list of criteria have been satisfied.

Critical theory A form of social analysis that originally developed in the first half of the twentieth century (particularly the 1930s and 1940s) based around the writing and theorizing of the Frankfurt Institute for Social Research (known as the Frankfurt School). It draws on the work of Marx but criticizes positivism in Marxism and the social sciences in general. It argues that criticism should be self-critical.

Cross-media ownership The diversification of media corporations into several fields of media production and distribution (e.g. News International has interests in book publishing, newspapers and television as a producer and distributor).

Cultural capital This refers to 'ownership' of the dominant culture, including social and linguistic competences and qualities such as style, manners, aspirations and the perception of chances of success. It is associated with Bourdieu, who claimed that the degree of cultural capital individuals possessed the more successful they would be in the educational system.

Cultural deprivation Exclusion from the usual standards of material and social existence experienced by others who live in the particular culture. It is often used by sociologists to refer to educational deprivation.

Cultural diversity The differences in culture between different groups and societies: what is regarded as normal and acceptable by one culture may be quite unacceptable in another.

Cultural relativism Social and cultural forces affect the conditions under which knowledge is produced. Certain knowledge comes to be regarded as superior because people in power define it as such.

Culture The beliefs, values and attitudes shared by a particular group of people or a particular society.

Culture of poverty The phrase originated with the work of US anthropologist Oscar Lewis, who used it to explain how poor people in Latin America reacted to their situation by producing strategies for survival which endured to form a culture, which in turn became an explanation for their continued poverty. These ideas are now strongly associated with the political right in Britain and the USA and in particular with Charles Murray's writings on the underclass.

D

Daoism Chinese philosophy and religion based on the writings of Laozi more than 300 years BC. Key themes include harmony with nature, including balancing the powers of *yin* and *yang*.

Dark figure of crime Crimes that are not included in the official crime statistics. This can include crime not known about by the authorities and also crimes that the police may know about but do not record.

Dealignment Although most voters are still strong identifiers with a particular political party, the notion of dealignment suggests that such 'identifiers' have declined as a proportion of all votes (party dealignment) and that social class is no longer a major influence on voting behaviour (class dealignment).

De-industrialization A term used to describe the decline in the employment in, and scale of, the manufacturing and extractive industries.

Democracy This may be simply defined as 'rule by the people', although this ignores power relationships and fundamental assumptions about human rights. Wider definitions would include some sort of recognition of those who are excluded from influence.

Democratization The process of creating a (usually liberal) democratic system. It is sometimes agreed that, for this to happen, society must already have a civic culture. Giddens argues that in many liberal democracies, democratization occurs through making politicians more accountable to the people.

Dependent variable A variable that changes as a result of changes in something else – another variable. It is sometimes the variable that a particular hypothesis tries to explain.

De-skilling Associated with Braverman, who thought that within the context of capitalist society skilled work becomes increasingly broken down into a series of simple, and hence more easily managed and controlled, tasks.

Development The process by which societies move from agrarian-based economies and social structures to become complex modern industrial societies.

Deviance In sociology and everyday usage, this refers to behaviour that does not conform to conventional standards of behaviour and that is disapproved of. Deviant behaviour may be criminal but can also include behaviour that does not break the criminal law.

Diagnostic assessment A form of assessment which is likely to include a summative assessment but will go further by providing an indication of what the next stage of the learning process should be (by, for example, identifying special educational needs).

Disability (*individual model*) A restriction or lack resulting from an impairment of the ability to perform an activity in the manner considered normal for a human being; or (*social model*) the loss or limitation of opportunities to take part in society on an equal basis with others due to social or environmental barriers.

Disciplinary power In Foucault's writing, the exercise of power over a population through monitoring and surveillance.

Discourse theory Associated with Michel Foucault, this attempts to identify how social institutions, behaviours and identities are historically and culturally constructed by a series of discourses (e.g. legal discourses, medical discourses).

Doctrine The official or orthodox teaching of a religion which is believed to have been divinely inspired. Doctrines may be written (scripture) or passed on orally.

Domestic violence Violence within the home, which may take various forms, including verbal, physical and sexual abuse.

Dysfunctional A word applied to an institution or system that is failing to function effectively, for example a family, school or hospital that is failing to serve a positive purpose.

E

Ecocentrism A holistic view that all organisms have intrinsic value and no single organism is more important than another. This perspective presents a radical challenge to long-standing and deeply rooted anthropocentric (human-centred) attitudes in Western culture.

Ecofeminism Belief that the domination by men both of women and of nature are directly connected. Ecofeminists argue that parallels exist between the subordination of women and the degradation of nature by similarly masculine attitudes and methods. Ecofeminism is a movement that has now expanded to work against what ecofeminists see as the interconnected oppressions of gender, race, class and nature.

Ecological modernization A concept that proposes that economic development and environmental protection can be combined in a progressive manner. For example, new, clean technologies and greater energy efficiency could address energy crises. Ecological modernists identify modern science, technology and the state as key institutions in the dynamics of ecological reform.

Effects model The belief that the media and in particular television can affect the beliefs and behaviour of the audience, usually for the worse.

Egalitarian A word defining principles of equality of opportunities in which identifiable social groups are not over- or underrepresented among high or low achievers.

Elaborated code A complex language code: analytical, abstract and with explicit meanings. It is associated with the work of Bernstein, who contrasted it with a more restricted code which is less analytical and abstract.

Elitism The systematic exclusion of the majority from political influence. The elitist government relies on the deference of the masses, created by their socialization into an acceptance of elite domination.

Embourgeoisment The term used to describe the process by which working-class people come to desire and embrace a middle-class lifestyle and outlook.

Empirical sociology Sociology based on research that involves the collection of real data, for instance, from questionnaires or interviews.

Empty shell marriage A marriage where a husband and wife formally remain together but there is no substance to the relationship in the sense of a conjugal relationship.

Environmental justice Equitable distribution of environmental risks, hazards and benefits, with a lack of discrimination, including access to information and participation in decision making. The central principles incorporate the need to redress unfair and inequitable distributions of *environmental burdens* such as pollution, and access to *environmental goods* such as clean air, water and transport in a variety of situations and social contexts.

Epiphenomenon A secondary symptom of something.

Epistemology The theory of knowledge; in sociology it is used to refer to the procedures by which sociological knowledge is acquired.

Equal opportunities An often unspecified ideal of equal chances in education with definitions varying between weak and strong extremes.

Eschatological Pertaining to 'last things'. Eschatological beliefs often refer to the last days before the end of the world.

Ethics/ethical codes Guidelines relating to correct ways of behaving for individuals or society. All religions develop views about right and wrong, though the nature and degree of prescription varies.

Ethnicity Those cultural values, norms and identities that help to differentiate members of one group of people from those of other groups. A common ethnicity is a sense of shared belonging to a group that has similar cultural traditions, such as language or religion.

Ethnocentrism Viewing one's own community or nation as the model by which all other communities or nations should be judged, implying that, in comparison, they display odd, strange and perhaps inferior behaviours to one's own.

Ethnography The detailed study, based on observation, of a particular group or culture; the description and evaluation of the study.

Ethnomethodology A theoretical branch of sociology that focuses on the ways in which people construct their social world and how they make sense of their everyday lives. It was developed by Harold Garfinkel as a challenge to the conventional sociological view that the social world is ordered and structured and can be taken for granted.

EU 'European Union': the 27 member nations, including the UK, that act as a common trading area within Europe.

Executive Government and civil service.

Experiment A method of research which involves the systematic and controlled analysis of variables. Typically the subjects of the research are assigned to two different groups: an experimental and a control group. The experimental group is then exposed to an independent variable, the control group is not, and the results are observed and analysed.

External locus of control In psychology, a belief that one's destiny is largely controlled by factors outside, and beyond the control of, the individual, such as powerful others or fate.

Externalizing system In the anthropology of health, a set of beliefs which attribute ill health to factors outside the individual, e.g. evil eye, germs.

F

False consciousness A Marxist term used to explain the lack of class consciousness and the failure of revolutionary action. It implies the deliberate use of ideology by those in power to disguise their true interest from the working class.

Fascism Generally described as extremely right-wing views because of the assumption that inequalities are biologically determined, although in some cases fascists have been suspicious of free-market capitalism. Fascism promotes common fears and hatreds, the appeal of superiority and domination over others and strong authoritarian leadership.

Feminism A body of thought that suggests that women are disadvantaged in modern society and that advocates gender equality. There are many different strands within contemporary feminism and it is more appropriate to talk about feminisms, rather than feminism.

Feral children Literally wild children: children brought up without any meaningful contact with other human beings.

Fertility The actual number of live births in a population unit in one year.

Feudalism The social and political structure that characterized medieval Europe, based on a system of mutual obligation and dependence between the nobility and peasants.

First World A now discredited term referring to the more affluent industrialized and developed societies. The USA, UK, France, the Netherlands, Germany and Japan are a few examples of First World countries.

Flexibility An imprecise term that refers to a range of changes in working practices – such as part-time work, casual labour, short-term contracts – which allow for the easier management, deployment and control of labour.

Flexible firm A model developed by Atkinson to highlight purported changes to work organization, particularly the breaking down of the workforce into a core and a peripheral group.

Fordism This term is sometimes seen to be synonymous with mass production, but it is also used to describe a socio-economic system developed in many countries in the postwar period.

Formal health-care system The provision of health care by paid professionals.

Fourth World A term that attempts to make a distinction between Third World societies that have the potential to develop and those that appear destined to remain non-industrial and poverty-stricken (see also **Super-poor**).

Fragmentation The way in which social groups such as classes lose their cohesiveness and feelings of identity and unity because of differentials in pay and status which divide the group against itself.

Functionalism A theoretical perspective that analyses social institutions and phenomena in terms of their function (or contribution) to the maintenance of the particular society: for instance, what function does the family play in the maintenance and running of society.

Fundamentalism A strict approach to, and observance of, religion in the modern world, involving asserting or reasserting that a religious tradition or belief system is the only true religion.

G

G7 A group of leading industrialized economies comprising the USA, Japan, Germany, France, Italy, Canada and the UK. Countries belonging to the G7 are among the most developed societies in the world.

G8 The G7 plus Russia.

Gender The socially produced categories of masculinity and femininity. Refers to the social, cultural and psychological characteristics associated with maleness or femaleness in particular cultures and societies.

Genetic engineering The deliberate modification of hereditary features. The notion that this aspect of reproductive technology may be used for social and political purposes has generated much ethical debate.

Globalization Globalization reflects the growing interdependency of world society. It can take place on any number of levels: economically, culturally, politically and militarily.

Governance In educational terms, processes of coordination and collective decision-making that impact upon education.

Guest worker A system for the employment of non-native workers within an industrial society. The guest-worker system has been widely used in many European societies, such as Germany, France and Switzerland, in the postwar period. Such workers are accorded few, if any, civil rights.

H

Health beliefs model A model which accounts for health behaviour in terms of an individual's assessment of the costs and benefits of that behaviour.

Hegemony A term coined by Gramsci to refer to ideological domination of society by a 'ruling class', whose control depends in part on convincing the mass of society that the *status quo* is inevitable or natural.

Heterogeneity When a group or culture is characterized by differences we refer to it as being heterogeneous.

Heterosexual Sexual desire for members of the opposite sex. How heterosexual desire is formed is much debated.

Hidden curriculum Traits of behaviour or attitudes that are learned at school but which are not included within the formal curriculum (see also **Paracurriculum**).

Hinduism A collective term for a diverse range of religious beliefs and practices developed over thousands of years in India. Hinduism embraces various scriptures, deities and practices, including the notion of reincarnation or rebirth.

Hir A pronoun preferred by some transgendered persons in place of his or her.

Historical materialism Marx's theory of historical development. Different social structures (at different historical periods) are seen as resulting from the ways in which the production of material goods is organized in different societies.

Homogeneity When a group or culture shares similar characteristics we refer to it as being homogeneous.

Horizontal integration The process by which corporations expand to dominate one aspect of media operations within a particular market (e.g. the takeover of one newspaper by another).

Horizontal segregation This describes the way in which women and men tend to be concentrated in different sectors of the labour market, with women being concentrated in a narrower range of sectors.

Human rights The notion and details pertaining to just and fair treatment of all persons on the basis of their humanity. Increasingly such rights are spelt out in written statements or charters.

I

Iatrogenesis Ill health or adverse effects caused by medicine itself, e.g. the side-effects of medications.

Ideal type A general, abstract concept that describes a 'pure' type that does not actually exist. It can be used as a means for comparing and evaluating actual social phenomena.

Identity The distinctive characteristics or elements of a person's or group's character and personality. Both individual and group identities can be marked by factors such as ethnicity, religion and language but also in terms of interests and preoccupations (music, sport, film, etc.).

Ideology In strict terms this is simply the science of ideas. However, as it has been developed in the social sciences it refers to a set of beliefs, values and attitudes that are used to explain and/or justify particular forms of social relationship.

In Marxist thought it denotes thinking which is unscientific and has the function of obscuring the truth. Writers such as Mannheim suggest that all knowledge is ideological.

Illness iceberg The large number of symptoms of ill health for which people do not seek professional help.

Imam A religious leader within Islam. The term means 'model' or 'example'.

IMF The International Monetary Fund, based in Washington, and the organization that attempts to regulate and control, via international agreements, the world monetary system.

Immigrant–host model A perspective built on the assumption that immigrants from a wide range of backgrounds will be incorporated into the host country's existing mainstream culture, submerging their own cultural heritage in the process (see Assimilation).

Impairment An injury, illness or condition that causes a loss or difference in physical, physiological or psychological functioning.

Independence (*individual model*) Being able to meet one's own needs without relying on someone else; or (*social model*) having control over the type and level of support one receives.

Independent variable A variable that is controlled or manipulated by the researcher so as to observe how it affects other variables.

Individual model of disability A model of disability that presumes that disability is caused by an individual's illness or impairment. Also called the medical or personal tragedy model of disability.

Individualization thesis The argument that class is now less important than it used to be in structuring people's lives, since individuals are more likely to determine their own destinies.

Industrialization This refers to the transformation of predominantly agricultural societies into societies where manufacturing and the extractive industries are central to the economy.

Infant mortality rate The number of deaths per 1000 children under one year old in a given year.

Infrastructure A Marxist term meaning the economic base or structure of a society. In some texts it is called the substructure or economic base of society. For Marx, all the non-economic aspects and institutions of a society are seen as being determined by its infrastructure.

Institutionalized racism Used to refer to those instances by which racist attitudes and practices are continuous and integral to the structures of a society; racism, for example, may be institutionalized in the judiciary, the government or the police force. Usually covert in nature, institutionalized racism works to reinforce a society's beliefs about racial characteristics.

Interculturalism A recognition and acceptance of the uniqueness of the individual and the superficiality of labelling anyone simply by skin colour, culture, social class, gender, disability, and so on.

Internal locus of control In psychology, a belief that one's destiny is largely controlled by the self.

Internalizing system In the anthropology of health, a set of beliefs which attribute ill health to factors within the individual.

Interview A method of gathering data by asking people a series of questions.

Interviewer bias This can refer to inaccurate or unrepresentative information given to an interviewer by a respondent, either by consciously misleading the interviewer or unconsciously giving inaccurate information. It can also arise from the actions or background of the interviewer: for example, the status of the interviewer may affect the replies given by the respondent.

Islam A term meaning 'submission'. Followers of Islam (Muslims) see their faith as embracing every aspect of life. They believe God (Allah)'s will was revealed to the Prophet Muhammad and is incorporated in the Holy Book (Qur'an). Most of the 700 million Muslims worldwide belong to the moderate Sunni branch. The largest minority group is Shi'ism.

J

Japanization A broad term which encompasses a range of work and design practices carried out within some Japanese companies, such as the use of teamworking and the just-in-time system.

Jehovah's Witnesses A millenarian movement whose followers emphasize the imminent second coming of Christ and the literal translation of the Bible. Witnessing includes house-to-house preaching, the publication of a newsletter, *The Watchtower* and regular meetings in Kingdom Halls.

Job enrichment This involves an attempt to empower workers by giving them a measure of control, planning and variety within their job in order to counteract the negative consequences of boring and repetitive labour.

Judaism The religion of the Jews, who believe that God delivered their Israelite ancestors out of bondage. There are various branches of Judaism, ranging from the traditional Orthodox strand to more reformed or liberal branches.

Judiciary The legal system.

K

Kinship This refers to blood relations and the social relationships deriving from these. Anthropologists distinguish between ties based on descent and ties based on marriage (or 'affinity').

L

Labelling The process by which individuals and/or types of behaviour are categorized by more powerful groups in society. These labels generally have negative connotations and labelling as a theoretical concept has been applied particularly to the study of crime and deviance.

Labour market This refers to the interactions between the buyers and sellers of labour power.

Labour migration A system found primarily in South Africa under the apartheid system, but also in southern states of the USA. Such workers are often employed in low-wage areas of the economy and are forced to return home when demand for their work decreases.

Labour process This involves purposeful human activity in relation to an object of some kind and the tools with which it is carried out.

Lay health beliefs Concepts used by non-professionals to explain health and illness.

Legislature One or more consultative chambers or assemblies for political debate and the scrutiny and passing of legislation.

Legitimation crisis German sociologist Habermas' theory that capitalism is inherently unstable and the state regularly intervenes in the economy to try to maintain stability. Voters see social problems as political rather than economic and therefore question the legitimacy of the state.

Liberal democracy A form of government in states that have regular and free elections for representative institutions of government and have guarantees of individual rights.

Liberal Democrats The former Liberal Party and its successor the Liberal Democratic Party are associated with *liberal* policies that aim to defend and enhance civil rights, freedom of belief and speech, the protection of minorities and equal opportunities. Liberal Democrats also support radical political change via the decentralization of power and the reform of the electoral system.

Liberalism In general terms this relates to beliefs in personal freedom. There are many forms of liberalism. Classical liberalism emphasized a negative form of freedom, involving freedom from oppression and the economic freedoms promoted by Adam Smith in the eighteenth century. The new liberalism of the early twentieth century emphasized more positive freedoms, including the capacity to make real choice and the redistribution of wealth from the rich in order to help the poor.

Life expectancy The average length of life.

Life history A method of research that consists of autobiographical material that has usually been obtained from a particular individual by an interview or conversation.

Lone/single parent family A family headed by one parent. These tend to be women, though single parents can also be men.

M

Majority world A more recent term for the 'developing world', comprising most of Asia, Africa and Latin America. The term reflects the fact that most of the world's population live in the 'majority world', which also has a greater land mass.

Managerial revolution A theory put forward by US sociologist James Burnham to support the view that the power of a ruling class had been reduced by the emergence of a managerial class who are trained administrators. The control of the economy is transferred away from the vested interests of the owners and into the hands of people who manage according to rational principles on behalf of all parties.

Marginalization The process by which individuals and groups are excluded from the mainstream of social life. Members of such groups often feel they are not receiving the prestige and/or economic rewards they deserve.

Marriage A cultural and legal relationship between partners which confers legitimacy on their offspring. In many societies marriage is based on the principle of romantic love and partners' choice. In other communities marriages may be arranged by parents and may involve consolidating property and forming family alliances.

Mass Observation An organization founded in Britain in 1936 to conduct social surveys on the population. The results of its surveys produced a detailed picture of British life and social change before and during the Second World War.

Mass production The systematic production of large volumes of standardized products for mass consumption.

McDonaldization A term coined by Ritzer, who uses the global fast-food industry as a graphic example of the all-pervasive process of rationalization in contemporary societies.

Mechanical solidarity A form of social integration based on the similarity between individuals who hold the same beliefs and values and feel the same emotions. Durkheim saw this form of solidarity as typical of traditional societies.

Medicalization The process by which aspects of social life (such childbirth, dying, alcoholism) become seen as medical problems.

Medical model of disability See Individual model of disability.

Meritocracy A society in which social rewards are allocated not according to ascribed characteristics, but according to merit: talent and effort.

Methodology The theory and analysis of how research should proceed. It includes the rules and practices that guide the gathering of data and the conclusions drawn from it.

Migration Movement of people, either voluntary or involuntary, from one locality to another, often over large distances and in groups. A recent example is the voluntary movement of Polish people to the UK, driven by economics and the search for higher wages and a better quality of life. Other reasons for migration include war, persecution and poverty.

Millenarianism This refers to the belief within Christianity in the return of Christ based on the Biblical Book of Revelation. Different Christian groups vary in their interpretation of the meaning and significance of this belief. Social scientists use the term more broadly to refer to any religious group stressing the impending end of the world through transformation.

Minority world A more recent term for the 'developed world', comprising mainly Europe, Australia, New Zealand, Japan, the USA and Canada. The term reflects the fact that a minority of the world's population, who generally have more privileged lifestyles, live in the 'minority world', which also has a smaller land mass.

Missionary movements Missionary activity involves active promotion of a faith or cause and attempts to gain new converts. Not all religions engage in active mission; those that do tend to stress a unique or universal truth and emphasize the importance of spreading their message.

Mode of production An abstract analytical model of the relationship between the relations of production (the relationships between people involved in production) and the means or forces of production (factories, machinery and raw materials involved in the production process). Different forms of society have different modes of production, for example, the feudal mode of production. Marx believed that each mode of production contained the seeds of its own destruction. Thus the slave-based mode of production gave way to the feudal mode of production, which in turn gave way to the capitalist mode of production. This in its turn would give way to the socialist, and eventually the communist, mode of production.

Modernization The process by which societies become developed, moving from agrarian to industrial economies. All Western societies can be said to have undergone a process of modernization in the last 200 years. It is associated with the work of Rostow, who defined five stages of modernization.

Monogamy The state of being married to one person at a time. The increase in divorce has resulted in 'serial monogamy', that is, the remarriage of divorcees.

Moral panic Public concern about issues such as drug abuse, teenage violence or football hooliganism are exaggerated or 'amplified' by the media out of all proportion to their real threat to social order. Public reaction often requires 'folk devils' to be identified as scapegoats.

Morbidity Illness and/or disease.

Mortality rate The number of people per thousand who die in a given year.

Multicultural education Teaching pupils and students about a wide range of cultures. The assumption is that this will generate a greater degree of tolerance, not only in the individual but also in society as a whole.

Multiculturalism An approach to public and social policy that acknowledges, accommodates and appreciates the benefits of a variety of different cultural traditions and practices in state and society. It is argued that Britain is a multicultural society.

N

Nation People with a sense of common identity. It may also apply to people who do not share a common territory (for instance, a diasporan nation such as the Kurds or the Jews).

Nationalism A sentiment, an ideology, a social movement or a form of culture that focuses on 'the nation'. Nationalism has often led to conflict both within and beyond multicultural states, but on a day-to-day basis we experience it through flags, national anthems and the 'cultural stuff' of daily life.

Nation-state A form of political authority that comprises various institutions such as the legislature, judiciary, police, armed forces, and central and local administration. Nation-states claim a monopoly of power and legitimacy within a defined territorial area.

Neo-colonialism A new form of economic colonialism that exploits the resources of majority world countries without having direct political or military control over them.

New Age spirituality Spiritual beliefs and practices dating from the 1960s that consider nature and humanity sacred and combine insights from different spiritual and mythical traditions. New Age spirituality rejects external religious hierarchies and values individual empowerment through spirituality.

New Labour The name used to signal the changes that have taken place in the British Labour Party. These changes include the abandonment of Clause 4 of Labour's constitution, which, in theory, had bound the party to a policy of nationalization of industry. New Labour embraces the concepts of enterprise, individual responsibility and the market economy and has been criticized for being a weak version of socialism.

New Religious Movements (NRMs) Relatively new religious organizations, generally dating from the second half of the twentieth century, that operate at the fringes of or outside mainstream religions and contrast significantly from them.

New Right Views within the British Conservative Party which originate in classical liberalism. The state is seen as overloaded by responsibilities as a result of trying to satisfy the ever-increasing demands of various interests. The emphasis is on letting market forces operate naturally.

New social movements Seen (particularly in Europe) as a new style of movement emerging from the protest movements of the 1960s. Critical of established political structures, they are loose, fluid networks with decentralized, open, democratic structures. They emphasize values that are universalistic rather than class-based (e.g. environmentalism, gay rights).

Norm-referencing A form of assessment in which the performance of one individual is ranked in comparison with that of others. Usually the aim of this approach is to ration the number of 'passes' (for example, when selecting pupils at 11+ for a limited number of places in a popular secondary school).

Norms Socially accepted rules or standards of behaviour.

O

OECD The Organisation for Economic Co-operation and Development. This is a Paris-based organization of industrialized economies which attempts to promote trade and economic co-operation between member states. Membership of the OECD extends further than that of the G7 nations to include countries such as Sweden, Finland, Denmark, Switzerland, Australia and New Zealand.

Official statistics Statistical data produced by governments or government agencies. While providing a great deal of useful data, sociologists have to be aware that they are not produced for sociological research and may reflect official (i.e. governmental) priorities.

Oligarchy A political structure in which an individual (oligarch) or small group (oligarchy) control the decision-making process.

One Nation Conservatives Often called Tory 'wets'. These Conservatives have criticized the New Right for disregarding the needs of those unable to thrive in an enterprise culture and thus recreating two nations of rich and poor. They present a benevolent, paternalistic attitude.

OPEC The Organization of Petroleum Exporting Countries. This organization, made up of major oil-exporting countries, attempts to set the worldwide prices for crude oil. It gained prominence in the 1970s when it increased the cost of oil several-fold. Today it is far less powerful than it was.

Organic solidarity A form of social integration or cohesion that Durkheim felt typified modern, advanced societies. In more complex societies, individuals are increasingly interdependent and this interdependence encourages solidarity.

P

Paracurriculum This describes all that is taught in schools alongside the formal curriculum. The term acknowledges a common awareness that this part of the curriculum exists (and is therefore not really a 'hidden curriculum').

Paradigm The ideas, assumptions and rules that form a model for analysing phenomena. The hypothetico-deductive method employed in the natural sciences is a good example.

Paradigm shift A radical change in the theories and concepts used to explain the world.

Parentocracy A market system in education, emphasizing the rights of parents to compete to send their children to what they perceive to be the best possible schools (Brown).

Participant observation A research method in which researchers observe behaviour and situations in which they are participants. Such participation allows the observer to observe either covertly, in other words without the other participants being aware, or overtly.

Part-time work An increasingly common form of work arrangement where people are employed for fewer hours than in a 'normal' full-time job.

Patriarchy The dominance of men over women in a society or a family system. A key concept in feminist theory.

Pauperization A Marxist term that refers to the belief that capitalism could only survive by driving down wages and increasing the exploitation of the workers. This continual impoverishment of the workers would create the conditions necessary for a social revolution.

Pedagogy The science or principles of teaching.

Performativity According to Lyotard, a culture, system or form of regulation in which individual or group performances are monitored to assess their quality, value or productivity. This may incorporate the people being watched so that they continually criticize and monitor themselves.

Periphery Societies which are underdeveloped and connected to the core developed societies by a chain of exploitation (see also **Core**).

Personal tragedy model of disability See Individual model of disability.

Phenomenology A philosophical approach based on the analysis and description of everyday life. Phenomenologists study the ways which people come to understand the world they live in; they emphasize how human beings create social worlds.

Phrenology The now discredited practice of assessing personality traits from head shape.

Pluralism A perspective usually associated with the study of politics or the media which suggests that the institutions of a democratic society are responsive to the diversity of interests in that society. Organizations representing various interests exist because no one interest group is allowed to dominate.

Political economy A Marxist model of the media which emphasizes the influence and power of owners and advertisers in decision making.

Polygamy Having more than one marriage partner at a time. Some religious and cultural communities sanction this type of marriage arrangement. It may involve **polygyny** (one man and two or more wives), **polyandry** (one woman and two or more husbands) or **group marriage** (several husbands and wives).

Positivism A doctrine that science (including the social sciences) can deal only with observable things and that phenomena, in any form, have to be studied in a scientific manner. It does not take account of the individual's interpretation of the situation.

Post-Fordism A conception of socio-economic change which highlights a move away from mass production and mass consumption towards more flexible forms of work and production, often utilizing new technologies, the break-up of mass markets and shifting patterns of consumption.

Post-industrialism A conception of contemporary societies which emphasizes the increasing role of the service industries, the key role of new information technologies and the control, production and manipulation of knowledge.

Postmodernism A theoretical approach or position that emphasizes the uncertain nature of the modern world and the variety of cultural styles and choices in modern societies. It has been applied in a number of disciplines, most notably in literature and the arts. In sociology, postmodernism has been critical of those 'grand' theoretical perspectives that have produced all-encompassing theories based on logical and rational accounts of the development of societies.

Post-structuralism Developed in France in the 1960s and based on the structuralism of linguistics, post-structuralism treats social life in general as 'text' which is open to analysis. It rejects the basic assumption of structuralism that there is a universal principle or structure in the social world.

Prejudice Holding often unwarranted, preconceived ideas about an individual or group. Even in the light of new information, prejudicial attitudes can be stubborn to review and change.

Pressure groups Groups aiming to put pressure on decision-making bodies to support their demands. They are smaller and more formally structured than social movements and, unlike political parties, they seek to influence rather than to govern.

Priesthood A priest is a religious leader, usually ordained, who serves the non-ordained or lay people (laity). Within Christianity the priest may fulfil a range of duties including sacraments. Christian traditions have differing views on the nature and meaning of priesthood based on theological interpretation.

Primary groups Term used by Cooley to describe groups based on close, personal relationships and face-to-face interaction between the members.

Privatization Providing formerly state-owned services through privately owned companies.

Professionalization The process by which an occupational group achieves the status of a profession, through gaining a monopoly over its work.

Proletarianization The term used to describe the process by which some white-collar occupations have become de-skilled and poorly paid.

Proletariat The Marxist term for the working classes: the wage earners and property-less in capitalist societies.

Proportional representation There are several versions of PR, all of which aim to make the proportion of seats held by each party reflect the proportion of the electorate voting for that party.

Protestant ethic The Protestant ethic refers to a particular type of Protestantism that believed in an absolute, all-powerful God who had predestined every individual to salvation or damnation and that advocated a puritanical, austere lifestyle. The Protestant ethic thesis is the title given to Weber's argument that there was a link or 'spiritual affinity' between modern capitalism and this form of Protestantism.

Public service broadcasting The notion that broadcasting is too important to be left to market forces and that regulation is needed to ensure the public gets a balanced diet of education, information and entertainment. As a public corporation financed through the licence fee, the BBC is regarded as the best example of public service broadcasting.

Q

Qualitative research Research which produces data that is not based on precise statistical measurement, and that is often expressed in words. This style of research encourages sociological analysis that aims to understand and interpret experiences and phenomena in ways that do not require detailed statistical comparisons. Typical methods of qualitative research include participant observation and unstructured interviews.

Quantitative research Research which produces data that can be expressed statistically – as numbers, percentages, tables and so on – and that can be subjected to statistical testing. Sociologists adopting this style of research emphasize that the data they collect are less open to bias resulting from the interpretation of the researcher. Typical methods of quantitative research include large-scale social surveys and structured interviews.

Questionnaire A method of collecting information in which the respondents complete a formal and standardized form. The questions may be closed or open-ended or a combination of both. Closed questions are more open to statistical testing and analysis.

R

Race An outdated concept, rejected by most social scientists but persisting to this day, that tends to be associated with an emphasis on supposed biological differences focusing on skin colour.

Race relations A field of study that gained academic and political popularity during the 1970s and continues to have some significance today. It studies a range of phenomena including the development of racial beliefs, the history of 'relations' between racial groups, and the life chances of the black community today.

Racialism This refers to behaviour based on racist beliefs, also known as *racial discrimination.* Whereas *racism* refers to beliefs or ideologies, racialism is confined to the 'acting out' of these beliefs. Examples of racialism include discrimination against individuals by employers on the basis of an individual's membership of a particular group.

Racism A form of prejudice that involves attributing characteristics of superiority or inferiority to a population sharing certain physically inherited characteristics. During Western colonial expansion, for example, 'white' people were usually deemed to be superior while 'black' people were deemed inferior.

Reflexivity In the context of social research this refers to the researchers' examination of their own role and behaviour and their use of this to help make sense of their research. In interpretative sociology it is used more generally to refer to the human ability to reflect on its actions.

Regulation The making of rules and the determination of policies and sanctions; a rule or order.

Reliability The reliability of research is the extent to which repeated measurements that use the same method produce the same results. Data or information that has been collected is said to be 'reliable' if, when the same research method is used again, the same results are produced.

Religion A system of beliefs and practices that provides meaning and/or orients individuals and groups to a supernatural realm.

Religiosity The level of commitment to religion present in and exhibited by individuals, groups or society.

Representation The symbolic construction of meaning through words or images. It is usually used in combination with the concept of stereotyping to understand how the media shapes audience perceptions of other social groups.

Republican This favours a form of government without a monarch. It also means the supporter of a republican party (which in the USA represents right-wing political views).

Rites of passage Public ceremonies to mark and celebrate the transition of an individual or group to a new social, religious or legal status. Rites of passage include marriage, coming-of-age celebrations (e.g. 18th or 21st birthday parties), and funerals.

Roman Catholicism The Roman Catholic Church claims a line of succession from the earliest Christians and the authority of its leader, the Pope, deriving from St Peter (the first 'Bishop of Rome'). During the Protestant ('protesting') Reformation of the sixteenth century denominations broke away from the Church and establishing their own organization, theology and practices.

Ruling class An ambiguous Marxist term which indicates the political power of the dominant economic class. Marx argued that politics can be explained by economic forces and, consequently, the class which controls the economy is the one which runs society.

S

Sacred and **Profane** The sacred refers to that which is set apart, treated with special respect and regarded as holy. It is regarded as distinct from the worldly or profane, which is that belonging to the material world.

Sampling Collecting information from a subgroup of a particular population. Various methods can be used to select a sample, but the aim is essentially the same: to find a sample that will be representative of a wider population or group.

Scientific management This is often associated with the doctrines of F.W. Taylor and involves the systematic breaking down of tasks into simple operations which can be more easily monitored and controlled. Often referred to as 'Taylorism'.

Secondary groups Formal groups or organizations which are less personal and intimate than primary groups – schools, for instance. Such groups will often provide individuals with their first formal contact with society in general and with the generally accepted standards of behaviour in society.

Secularization The declining influence of religion in society.

Self-fulfilling prophecy The theory that pupils and students strive to realize their own self-images and expectations.

Semiotics The process by which meanings can be decoded from media texts. This is sometimes referred to as the 'science of signs'.

Service class Those members of the middle class who are directly responsible for the management of the interests of the capitalist class and most closely associated with it via income, education and lifestyle.

Sex This describes the biological categories of male and female.

Sexual division of labour This describes how the performance of labour, both unpaid domestic labour and paid employment, is shaped by gender. Most commonly it refers to the observation that women have greater responsibility for unpaid domestic labour and child care and that women and men are integrated into the paid labour market on a differential and inequitable basis.

Sexuality This term is used to encompass human sexual desire, pleasure, behaviour and identity.

Shivism Shi'ite Muslims are the largest minority group within Islam, mainly concentrated in Iran, Iraq and the Indian subcontinent. The problem of suffering is a key theme as illustrated in the concept of *Jihad* ('struggle'). One interpretation of this is 'holy war' against those who reject Islam.

Shrine A shrine is a sacred place regarded as having particular power and significance and often associated with key events in a group or society's history and identity.

Sickness A state of being unwell or ill that is assumed to be temporary.

Sick role The set of norms and expectations which pattern a person's behaviour when ill.

Sie A pronoun preferred by some transgendered persons in place of he or she.

Social capital The cultural and social resources held by an individual or community.

Social control The ways by which behaviour is constrained and guided by society, in particular by social institutions. Such control can be exercised informally (through friends and family, for instance) or formally (perhaps through school rules or the law).

Social exclusion A combination of structural and individual factors that prevent people from participating fully in society.

Social mobility The process by which individuals move up or down the social scale. An open society is one characterized by high levels of social mobility.

Social model of disability A model of disability that presumes that disability is caused by the social or environmental barriers experienced by people with illnesses and impairments.

Social movement A collection of individuals who share a common interest (e.g. environmentalism or women's liberation) and the potential for mass mobilization in order to promote their aims.

Socialization The process by which individuals learn the beliefs, values and behaviour that are accepted in and approved by the society in which they are placed.

Socio-biology A field of study that attempts to characterize human and animal kind by reference to biological characteristics (such as genetic and/or chromosomal composition). While not perceived by sociologists as adequately explaining the complexities of human behaviour, recent (albeit controversial) studies from writers such as Charles Murray suggest a revival in approaches to 'race' which posit a biological basis to explain, for example, different levels of educational attainment among social groups.

Special educational needs Although exceptionally gifted children may be seen as having special educational needs, the term is generally used to refer to educational disadvantages caused by physical or mental disabilities.

Stagflation This can best be described as economic recession combined with high inflation levels in the economy. In the developed world, stagflation was evident during the mid-1970s, partly because of the rise in oil prices that took place at that time. Many 'majority world' societies have faced recent periods of stagflation.

Standard English The use of 'correct' grammatical constructions and pronunciation in written and spoken English. Individuals and groups using alternative forms of English language (e.g. dialects) have often been labelled as deficient or incompetent.

Step-family A family resulting from the remarriage of a parent.

Stigma A discrediting attribute or characteristic usually associated with a person, e.g. a disability or HIV.

Structuralism A theoretical approach that in sociology emphasizes the analysis of social structures rather than individuals. It is derived from (and most usually associated with) the study of language, which is seen as the basic structure in society.

Subculture A distinguishable group within a broader culture which has its own beliefs and rules; these differ from those of the broader culture. These beliefs and values are usually exhibited in forms of behaviour that set the subculture apart from mainstream society, for example, in a delinquent subculture.

Summative assessment A form of assessment aiming to describe an individual's current knowledge and/or ability. This may lead to a grading or some other type of summary or label (e.g. GCSE grades, degree classifications).

Super-poor Commonly used to describe societies that are most economically deprived and disadvantaged. As a concept 'super-poor' can be said to unite not just countries sharing common conditions but disparate groups in several societies. Thus many women in 'majority world' societies can be said to be 'super-poor'.

Superstructure A Marxist term used to refer to all aspects of society apart from the economic: so institutions such as the family, the school and the mass media constitute part of the superstructure of a society.

Survey A systematic method of gathering data through asking people a series of questions, either in an interview or in a questionnaire. The data can then be interpreted by statistical analysis.

Sustainable development The need to balance environmental and developmental needs. The influential Brundtland Report described sustainable development as development that 'meets the needs of the present without compromising the ability of future generations to meet their own needs'. Achieving equity and sustainable growth would require technological, social and behavioural changes.

Symbolic interactionism An intrepretative perspective, based on the work of social scientists working at the University of Chicago in the 1920s and 1930s, in particular George Herbert Mead. It suggests that social structures are created and maintained in the course of human interaction. In its focus on human interaction, individuals are seen as learning meanings through their interactions with others; these meanings become the basis around which they organize their lives.

T

Theology The study of the divine or God. Theology is often associated with the study of Christian beliefs and teachings but there are also schools of theology focusing on other religious traditions, such as Islamic or Buddhist theology.

Third way A political perspective that seeks to transcend the traditions of old-style social democracy ('old' Labour policies in Britain) and neoliberalism (the New Right in Britain). It favours a mixed economy and emphasizes citizens' obligations and responsibilities as well as equality and the protection of the vulnerable in society.

Third World A now discredited term used to describe less affluent non-industrialized societies.

Tiger economies A term that refers to the economies of Asian nations that appeared to be undergoing dramatic rises in economic and industrial development during the period from the late 1970s onwards, for example, Malaysia.

TNCs Transnational corporations: globally (transnational) operating companies, very large, very wealthy and very powerful. Examples of TNCs include the Anglo–Dutch oil company Shell Oil and the American-owned telephone corporation AT&T.

Totalitarianism A state in which opposition to the dominant political group and its associated states is not allowed.

Totemism A common religion in tribal societies which involves treating the totem (a symbol of a person or the group) with awe and veneration. Within totemism supernatural powers are attributed to objects and creatures and this is reflected in various rituals involving the totem.

Trade unions Organizations that developed to protect the interests of workers against employers.

Transgender Transgendered persons identify themselves as having a gender that does not match their biology and does not conform to societal norms; this includes people who identify themselves as neither masculine nor feminine but somewhere in between. Transgendered people may or may not change, or wish to change, their biology.

Transnational corporation Often huge companies that can organize production on an international, rather than a national, basis.

Transnational families Families that live apart in different nations for some or most of the time.

Transvestism A term that describes the behaviour of men who identify as male but choose to dress, on occasion, in 'female' clothing.

Triangulation The use of more than one method of research when carrying out a piece of research. This will enable research to benefit from the strengths of (and avoid any problems with) different methods of research. So it is likely to increase the validity of the research.

U

Underclass Used by sociologists to describe those at the very bottom of society with little or no regular connection with the labour market and no stake in society. In general usage, the term has moralistic and negative overtones.

Underdevelopment A condition in which certain societies remain in a permanent condition of poverty, lacking the resources, social structures or political systems to allow them to become developed.

Unemployment The condition of having no paid employment.

Unification Church A religious movement founded by and following Sun Myung Moon (hence followers are known as 'Moonies'). In the past Moonies were accused of 'brainwashing' as a method of recruitment and this phenomenon, as well as practices such as mass weddings, have been studied by sociologists of religion.

Urbanization The growth of city living, although it is often used to refer to the phenomenal expansion of new centres of economic activity and mass living in the nineteenth and twentieth centuries.

Utopia An imaginary, ideal state. The term 'utopian' is often associated with an idealism that can never be achieved.

V

Validity The extent to which a research method measures what it is intended to measure. Although a research method may be reliable, do the data gathered provide a true representation of what the researcher wishes to measure? For instance, is occupation a satisfactory measure for classifying people by social class?

Value-freedom The notion that social research should not be influenced by the researcher's beliefs and ideas. It is particularly associated with the positivist approach in sociology.

Variable A characteristic or behaviour that varies from one individual, group or society to another. For example, age is a variable by which people can be classified according to the number of years they have lived.

Verstehen A German term meaning empathetic or interpretative understanding. It was advocated by Weber as an approach to understanding social behaviour through empathy: through putting ourselves in the position of the individual or group being investigated so as to discover the motives behind our actions.

Vertical integration The process by which a media corporation extends its influence by expanding into areas of operation previously left to other organizations (e.g. the movement of hardware manufacturers into the production of software).

Vertical segregation The way in which within many occupational sectors of the labour market, women are under-represented in the better-paid and more senior positions (i.e. the higher up the occupational ladder, the fewer the women).

Vocationalism Education with the emphasis placed on job-related training.

W

Wage-labour This is often equated with work in general but it involves a monetary payment in exchange for a certain amount of labour.

Welfare Collective responses (on the part of the state, the community and other sectors of society) to meeting the needs of individuals and families.

White-collar crime Crime committed in the context of a legitimate occupational role. It includes crimes committed by employees 'against' their employers, such as fraud or fiddling, and crimes committed by businesses or corporations, such as the breaking of health and safety legislation. This latter form of white-collar crime is more usually considered as 'corporate' crime.

World systems theory A theoretical model developed by Wallerstein which postulates that movement from a condition of underdeveloped to developed is possible. However, such movement can only come about by the express agreement of those societies who are themselves at the pinnacle of development, those at the core.

WTO World Trade Organization: the organization based in Washington DC responsible for the enforcement of free and fair trade agreements at a global level.

X

Xenophobia Fear of strangers. It is generally used to denote negative attitudes towards immigrant groups on account of their cultural differences.

References

A

Abberley, P. (1987) 'The concept of oppression and the development of a social theory of disability', *Disability, Handicap and Society* 2(1): 5–19.

Abbot, D. (2001) 'The death of class?', *Sociology Review*, 11(2): 6–7.

Abbott, P. (1991) 'Feminist perspectives in sociology: the challenge to "mainstream" orthodoxy', in J. Aaron and S. Walby (eds) *Out of the Margins: Women's Studies in the Nineties*, Brighton: Falmer.

Abbott, P. and Wallace, C. (1990) *An Introduction to Sociology: Feminist Perspectives*, London: Routledge.

Abbott, P. and Wallace, C. (1997) *An Introduction to Sociology: Feminist perspectives*, 2nd edn, London: Routledge.

Abbott, P., Wallace, C. and Tyler, M. (2005) *An Introduction to Sociology: Feminist Perspectives*, 3rd edn, London: Routledge.

Abdalla, A. (1988) 'Child labour in Egypt: leather tanning in Cairo', in A. Bequele and J. Boyden (eds) *Combating Child Labour*, Geneva: International Labour Organization.

Abercrombie, N. and Warde, A. (eds) (1992) *Social Change in Contemporary Britain*, Cambridge: Polity Press.

Abercrombie, N. and Warde A. (2000) *Contemporary British Society*, 3rd edn, Cambridge: Polity Press.

Abrams, P. (1968) *The Origins of British Sociology*, Chicago, IL: University of Chicago Press.

Acheson, D. (1998) *Independent Inquiry into Inequalities in Health: Report*, London: HMSO.

Achterhuis, H. (1994) 'The lie of sustainability', in W. Zweers and J.J. Boersema (eds) *Ecology, Technology and Culture: Essays in Environmental Philosophy*, Cambridge: White Horse Press.

Acker, J. (2002) 'The gender regime of Swedish banks', *Scandinavian Journal of Management* 10(2): 117–30.

Adams, J. (2004) 'Demarcating the medical/non-medical border', in P. Tovey, G. Easthope and J. Adams (eds) *The Mainstreaming of Complementary and Alternative Medicine: Studies in Social Context*, London: Routledge.

Adger, W.N., Paavola, J., Huq, S. and Mace, M.J. (eds) (2006) *Fairness in Adaptation to Climate Change*, Cambridge, MA: MIT Press.

Adorno, T.W. (1973) *Dialectic of Enlightenment*, trans. J. Cumming, New York: Continuum.

Afshar, H. (1994), 'Muslim women in West Yorkshire: growing up with real and imaginary values amidst conflicting views of self and society', in H. Afshar and M. Maynard (eds) *The Dynamics of 'Race' and Gender: Some Feminist Interventions*, London: Taylor & Francis.

Aggleton, P. (1987) *Rebels without a Cause? Middle-Class Youth and the Transition from School to Work*, London: Falmer Press.

Agyeman, J. and Evans, B. (2004) '"Just sustainability": the emerging discourse of environmental justice in Britain', *Geographical Journal* 170(2): 155–64.

Ahmed, S. and Dale, A. (2008) 'Pakistani and Bangladeshi women's labour market participation', CCSR working paper 2008–02, Cathie Marsh Centre for Census and Survey Research, University of Manchester, Manchester, www.ccsr.ac.uk/research/ethnic.htm.

Ahmad, W. and Bradby, H. (2007) 'Locating ethnicity and health: exploring concepts and contexts', *Sociology of Health and Illness* 29(6): 795–810.

Albrecht, G. (1976) *The Sociology of Physical Disability and Rehabilitation*, Pittsburgh: University of Pittsburgh Press.

Alcock, P., Glennerster, H., Oakley, A. and Sinfield, A. (2001) *Welfare and Wellbeing: Richard Titmuss's Contribution to Social Policy*, Cambridge: Polity Press.

Aldridge, A. (2007) *Religion in the Contemporary World*, 2nd edn, Cambridge: Polity Press.

Aliaga, C. (2006) *How is the Time of Women and Men Distributed in Europe?*, Luxembourg: Office for Official Publications of the European Communities.

Alinski, S. (1972) *Rules for Radicals*, New York: Random House.

Allan, G. (1996) *Kinship and Friendship in Modern Britain*, Oxford: Oxford University Press.

Allan, G. and Crow, G. (2001) *Families, Households and Society*, Basingstoke: Palgrave Macmillan.

Allen, J. (1995) 'Global worlds', in J. Allen and D. Massey (eds) *Geographical Worlds*, Oxford: Oxford University Press.

Allen, J. and Massey, D. (1988) *The Economy in Question*, London: Sage.

Allen, J., Braham P. and Lewis, P. (eds) (1992) *Political and Economic Forms of Modernity*, Cambridge: Polity Press.

Allen, S. and Walkowitz, C. (1987) *Homeworking Myths and Realities*, London: Macmillan.

Allsop, J. (1995) 'Shifting sphere of opportunity: the professional powers of general practitioners with the

British National Health Service', in T. Johnson, G. Larkin and M. Saks (eds) *Health Professions and the State in Europe*, London: Routledge.

Almond, B. (2006) *The Fragmenting Family*, Oxford: Clarendon Press.

Althusser, L. (1969 [1965]) *For Marx*, London: Allen Lane.

Althusser, L. (1971) *Lenin and Philosophy and Other Essays*, London: New Left Books.

Althusser, L. (1972) 'Ideology and ideological state apparatuses', in B. Cosin (ed.) *Educational Structure and Society*, Harmondsworth: Penguin.

Amnesty International (2004) *Clouds of Injustice: The Bhopal Disaster 20 Years on*, London: Amnesty International Publications.

Amos, V. and Parmar, P. (1984) 'Challenging imperial feminism', *Feminist Review* 17 (July): 3–20.

Anderson, B. (1991) *Imagined Communities: Reflections on the Origins and Spread of Nationalism*, London: Verso.

Anderson, C. (1974) *Towards a New Sociology*, Homewood, IL: Dorsey.

Andreski (1983) *Max Weber on Capitalism, Bureaucracy and Religion*, London: Allen & Unwin.

Ang, I. (1985) *Watching 'Dallas': Soap Opera and the Melodramatic Imagination*, London: Methuen.

Ang, I. (1991) *Desperately Seeking the Audience*, London: Routledge.

Ang, I. (2005) 'Multiculturalism', in *New Keywords*, Oxford: Blackwell.

Ansell, N. (2005) *Children, Youth and Development*, London: Routledge.

Anthias, F. and Yuval-Davis, N. (1993) *Racialized Boundaries: Race, Nation, Gender, Colour, Class and the Anti-Racist Struggle*, London: Routledge.

Appadurai, A. (1990) 'Disjuncture and difference in the global cultural economy', *Theory, Culture and Society* 7: 295–310.

Arber, S. and Evandrou, M. (1993) 'Mapping the territory: ageing, independence and the life course', in S. Arber and M. Evandrou (eds) *Ageing, Independence and the Life Course*, London: Jessica Kingsley.

Arber, S. and Ginn, J. (1991) *Gender and Later Life: A Sociological Analysis of Resources and Constraints*, London: Sage.

Ariès, P. (1962) *Centuries of Childhood*, London: Jonathan Cape.

Ariès, P. (1981) *The Hour of our Death*, London: Allen Lane.

Armen, J.C. (1974) *Gazelle Boy*, London: Bodley Head.

Armstrong, D. (1983) *Political Anatomy of the Body*, Cambridge: Cambridge University Press.

Armstrong, F., Clarke, M. and Murphy, D. (1995) '"... some kind of barmpot": young people in care and their experiences of the education system', in P. Potts, F. Armstrong and M. Masterton (eds) *Equality and Diversity in Education 1: Learning, Teaching and Managing Schools*, London: Open University/Routledge.

Arnold, M. (1963 [1869]) *Culture and Anarchy*, Cambridge: Cambridge University Press.

Arnot, M. (1986) *Race, Gender and Educational Policy Making*, Module 4, E333, Milton Keynes: Open University Press.

Arnot, M., David, M. and Weiner, G. (1997) 'Educational reform, gender equality and school cultures', in B. Cosin and M. Hales (eds) *Families, Education and Social Differences*, London: Open University/Routledge.

Arnot, M., David, M. and Weiner, G. (1999) *Closing the Gender Gap: Postwar Education and Social Change*, Cambridge: Polity Press.

Askew, M. and Ross, S. (1988) *Boys Don't Cry: Boys and Sexism in Education*, Milton Keynes: Open University Press.

Assiter, A. (1996) *Enlightened Women: Modernist Feminism in a Postmodern Age*, London: Routledge.

Atkinson, J. (1984) *Flexibility, Uncertainty and Manpower Management*, Brighton: Falmer and Institute of Manpower Studies.

Audrey, S. (2000) *Multiculturalism in Practice: Irish, Jewish, Italian and Pakistani Migration to Scotland*, Aldershop: Ashgate.

Augoustinos, M. and Reynolds, K.J. (eds) (2001) *Understanding Prejudice, Racism and Social Conflict*, London: Sage.

Aune, K. (2009) 'Religion, gender roles in', in J. O'Brien (ed.) *Encyclopedia of Gender and Society*, Thousand Oaks, CA: Sage.

Aune, K., Sharma. S and Vincett, G. (eds) (2008) *Women and Religion in the West: Challenging Secularization*, Aldershot: Ashgate.

Aupers, S. and Houtman, D. (2006) 'Beyond the spiritual supermarket: the social and public significance of New Age spirituality', *Journal of Contemporary Religion* 21(2): 201–22.

Ayieko, M.A. (2004) 'From single parents to child-headed households: the case of children orphaned by AIDS in Kisumu and Siaya districts', study paper 7, New York: University of Illinois, UNDP HIV and Development Programme, www.undp.org/hiv/publications/study/english/sp7e.htm.

B

Babb, P., Martin, J. and Haezewindt, P. (2004) *Focus on Social Inequalities*. London: The Stationery Office.

Back, L. (1997) 'Globalisation, culture and locality', *Sociology Review* 7(2).

Backett-Milburn, K., Cunningham-Burley, S. and Kemmer, D. (2001) *Caring and Providing: Lone and Partnered Mothers in Scotland*, London: Family Policy Studies Centre.

Bagdikian, B. (1997) *The Media Monopoly*, Boston, MA: Beacon Press.

Bagdikian, B. (2004) *The New Media Model*, Boston, MA: Beacon Press.

Baignent, M., Leigh, R. and Lincoln, H. (1986) *The Messianic Legacy*, London: Corgi.

Baker, S. (2006) *Sustainable Development*, Abingdon: Routledge.

Bakir, V. (2009) 'Global media production', in P. Long, *et al.* (eds) *Doing Media Studies: Texts, Production and Consumption*, Harlow: Pearson Education.

Bakx, K. (1991) 'The "eclipse" of folk medicine in Western society', *Sociology of Health and Illness* 13(1): 20–38.

Baldwin, J. (1955) 'Stranger in the village', in *Notes of a Native Son*, Boston, MA: Beacon Press.

Ball, S. (1981) *Beachside Comprehensive: A Case Study of Secondary Schooling*, Cambridge: Cambridge University Press.

Ball, S. (ed.) (2004) *The RoutledgeFalmer Reader in Sociology of Education*, London: RoutledgeFalmer.

Ballard, C., Guibbay, J. and Middleton, C. (eds) (1997) *The Students Comparison to Sociology*, London: Blackwell.

Banton, M. (1987) *Racial Theories*, Cambridge: Cambridge University Press.

Banton, M. (1998) *Racial Theories*, 2nd edn, Cambridge: Cambridge University Press.

Baran, P. and Sweezy, P. (1966) *Monopoly Capital*, Harmondsworth: Penguin.

Bari, M.A. (2008) 'British Muslims plan a summer vision', *The Times*, 12 July.

Barker, C. (1999) *Television, Globalisation and Cultural Identities*, Milton Keynes: Open University Press.

Barker, E. (1984) *The Making of a Moonie*, Oxford: Blackwell.

Barker, E. (2004) 'General overview of the "cult scene" in Great Britain', in P.C. Lucas and T. Robbins (eds) *New Religious Movements in the Twenty-First Century: Legal, Political and Social Challenges in Global Perspective*, New York and London: Routledge.

Barker, M. (1981) *The New Racism*, London: Junction Books.

Barker, M. (1984) *A Haunt of Fears: The Strange History of the British Horror Crimes Campaign*, London: Pluto.

Barker, M. and Petley, J. (1997) *Ill Effects: The Media/Violence Debate*, London: Routledge.

Barley, N. (1986) *The Innocent Anthropologist*, Harmondsworth: Penguin.

Barnes, A., Elias, R. and Walsh, P. (2000) *Cocky: The Rise and Fall of Curtis Warren, Britain's Biggest Drug Baron*, London: Milo Books.

Barnes, C. and Mercer, G. (2003) *Disability*, Cambridge: Polity Press.

Barnes, C., Mercer, G. and Shakespeare, T. (1999) *Exploring Disability: A Sociological Introduction*, Cambridge: Polity Press.

Barnett, T. and Whiteside, A. (2002) *AIDS in the Twenty-First Century: Disease and Globalisation*, Basingstoke: Palgrave Macmillan.

Baron-Cohen, S. (2003) 'They just can't help it', *Guardian*, 17 April, www.guardian.co.uk/education/2003/apr/17/research.highereducation.

Barrett, M. (1980) *Women's Oppression Today*, London: Verso.

Barrett, M. and McIntosh, M. (1982) *The Anti-Social Family*, London: Verso.

Barron, P. and Sweezy, P. (1968) *Monopoly Capitalism*, Harmondsworth: Penguin.

Barron, R.D. and Norris, G.M. (1976) 'Sexual divisions and the dual labour market', in L.D. Barker and S. Allen (eds) *Dependence and Exploitation in Work and Marriage*, London: Longman.

Barter, C. and Renold, E. (1999) 'The use of vignettes in qualitative research', *Social Research Update* 25.

Barth, F. (ed.) (1969) *Ethnic Groups and Boundaries: The Social Organization of Culture Difference*, London: Verso.

Barthes, R. (1972) *Mythologies*, London: Jonathan Cape.

Bartky, S.L. (1990) *Femininity and Domination*, London: Routledge.

Baubock, R. (1994) *Trans-National Citizenship*, London: Edward Elgar.

Baudrillard, J. (1990) *Cool Memories*, London: Verso.

Bauer, P. (1997) *Class on the Brain: The Cost of a British Obsession*, London: Centre for Policy Studies.

Bauman, Z. (1989) *Modernity and the Holocaust*, Oxford: Polity.

Bauman, Z. (1990) *Thinking Sociologically*, Oxford: Blackwell.

Bauman, Z. (1992) *Mortality, Immortality and other Life Strategies*, Cambridge: Polity Press.

Bauman, Z. (2000) *The Individualized Society*, Cambridge: Polity Press.

Bauman, Z. (2003) *Liquid Love: On the Frailty of Human Bonds*, Cambridge: Polity Press.

Bauman, Z. and May, T. (2001) *Thinking Sociologically*, Oxford: Blackwell.

Baumeister, R. (1986) *Identity: Cultural Change and the Struggle for Self*, Oxford University Press.

Baumgardner, J. and Richards, A. (2000) *ManifestA: Young Women, Feminism, and the Future*, New York: Farrar, Straus and Giroux.

Bausinger, H. (1984) 'Media, technology and daily life', *Media, Culture and Society* 6(4).

Beccaria, C. (1963 [1764]) *On Crime and Punishment*, Indianapolis, IN: Bobbs-Merrill Educational.

Beck, U. (1992) *Risk Society: Towards a New Modernity*, London: Sage.

Beck, U. (1994) *Ecological Enlightenment: Essays in the Politics of the Risk Society*, Atlantic Highlands, NJ: Humanities Press.

Beck, U. (1995) *Ecological Enlightenment: Essays in the Politics of the Risk Society*, Atlantic Highlands, NJ: Humanities Press.

Beck, U. (2006) *The Cosmopolitan Vision*, Cambridge: Polity Press.

Beck, U. and Beck-Gernsheim, E. (1995) *The Normal Chaos of Love*, Cambridge: Polity Press.

Beck, U., Giddens, A. and Lash, S. (1994) *Reflexive Modernization*, Stanford, CA: Stanford University Press.

Becker, G. (1993) *Human Capital*, Chicago, IL: University of Chicago Press.

Becker, H.S. (1963) *Outsiders: Studies in the Sociology of Deviance*, New York: Free Press.

Becker, H.S. (1982) 'Problems of inference and proof in participant observation', in R. McCormick, J. Bynner, P. Clift, M. James and L.M. Brown (eds) *Calling Education to Account*, London: Open University Press/Heinemann.

Beckford, J. (2004) 'New religious movements and globalization', in P.C. Lucas and T. Robbins (eds) *New Religious Movements in the Twenty-First Century: Legal, Political and Social Challenges in Global Perspective*, New York and London: Routledge.

Beckford, J., Gale, R., Owen, D., Peach, C. and Weller, P. (2006) *Review of the Evidence Base on Faith Communities*, London: Office of the Deputy Prime Minister.

Beck-Gernsheim, E. (2002) *Reinventing the Family: In Search of New Lifestyles*, Cambridge: Polity Press.

Beechey, V. (1978) 'Women and production: a critical analysis of some sociological theories of women's work', in A. Kuhn and A.M. Wolpe (eds) *Feminism and Marginalism: Women and Modes of Production*, London: Routledge.

Bell, D. (1973) *The Coming of Post-Industrial Society: A Venture in Social Forecasting*, London: Heinemann.

Bell, D. and Binnie, J. (2000) *The Sexual Citizen: Queer Politics and Beyond*, Cambridge: Polity.

Bell, E. and Alden, C. (eds) (2003) *Media Directory 2004*, London: Guardian Newspapers Ltd.

Bem, S. (1993) *The Lenses of Gender*, New Haven, CT: Yale University Press.

Beneria, L. and Sen, G. (1997) 'Accumulation, reproduction and women's role in economic development: Boserup revisited', in N. Visvanathan, L. Duggan, L. Nisonoff and N. Wiegersma (eds) *The Women, Gender and Development Reader*, London: Zed Books.

Bennett, T. (1982) 'Theories of media, theories of society', in M. Gurevitch, T. Bennett, J. Curran and J. Woollacott (eds) *Culture, Society and the Media*, London: Methuen.

Benton, T. (1993) *Natural Relations: Ecology, Animal Rights and Social Justice*, London: Verso.

Benton, T. (1996) *The Greening of Marxism*, London: Guilford Press.

Benton, T. (2002) 'Social theory and ecological politics: modernity or green socialism?', in R. Dunlap, F.H. Buttel, P. Dickens and A. Gijswijt (eds) *Sociology Theory and the Environment: Classical Foundations, Contemporary Insights*, Oxford: Rowman & Littlefield.

Bequele, A. and Boyden, J. (eds) (1988) *Combating Child Labour*, Geneva: International Labour Organization.

Bequele, A. and Myers, W.E. (1995) *First Things First in Child Labour: Eliminating Work Detrimental to Children*, Geneva: International Labour Organization.

Berelson, B., Lazarsfeld, P. and McPhee, W. (1954) *Voting: A Study of Opinion Formation in a Presidential Campaign*, Chicago, IL: University of Chicago Press.

Berger, A. (1991) *Media Analysis Techniques*, London: Sage.

Berger, P.L. (1967) *Invitation to Sociology: A Humanistic Perspective*, Harmondsworth: Penguin.

Berger, P.L. (1972) *Sociology: A Biographical Approach*, New York: Basic Books.

Berger, P.L. (1973) *The Social Reality of Religion*, Harmondsworth: Penguin.

Berger, P.L. (ed.) (1999) *The Desecularization of the World: Resurgent Religion and World Politics*, Washington, DC: Ethics and Public Policy Center.

Bernardes, J. (1997) *Family Studies: An Introduction*, London: Routledge.

Bernstein, B. (1971) 'On the classification and framing of educational knowledge', in M.F.D. Young (ed.) *Knowledge and Control: New Directions for the Sociology of Education*, London: Collier-Macmillan.

Bernstein, H. (2000) 'Colonialism, capitalism, development,' in T. Allen and A. Thomas (eds) *Poverty and Development into the 21st Century*, Oxford: Oxford University Press.

Bernstein, P. (1998) *Against the Gods: The Remarkable Story of Risk*, New York: John Wiley & Sons.

Best, S. (2005) *Understanding Social Divisions*. London: Sage.

Beveridge, W. (1942) *Social Insurance and Allied Services*, London: HMSO.

Beynon, H. (1975) *Working for Ford*, London: Allen Lane.

Beynon, H. and Nichols, T. (1977) *Living with Capitalism*, London: Routledge.

Beynon, J. (2004) 'The commercialization of masculinities: from the "new man" to the "new lad", in C. Carter and L. Steiner (eds) *Critical Readings: Media and Gender*, Maidenhead: Open University Press.

Bhabha, H.K. (1990) *Nation as Narration*, London: Routledge.

Bhattacharyya, G., Ison, L. and Blair, M. (2003) 'Minority ethnic attainment and participation in education and training: the evidence', Research Topic Paper RTP01-03, London: Department for Education and Skills.

Bhavnani, R. (1993) 'Talking racism and the editing of women's studies', in D. Richardson and V. Robinson (eds) *Introducing Women's Studies*, London: Macmillan.

Biggs, S. (1993) *Understanding Ageing: Images, Attitudes and Professional Practice*, Buckingham: Open University Press.

Billig, M. (1995) *Banal Nationalism*, London: Sage.

Billington, R., Strawbridge, S., Greensides, L. and Fitzsimons, A. (1991) *Culture and Society*, London: Macmillan.

Bilton, T., Bonnett, K., Jones, P., *et al.* (2002) *Introductory Sociology*, 4th edn, Basingstoke: Palgrave Macmillan.

Binet, A. (1905) 'New methods for the diagnosis of the intellectual level of subnormals', *L'Annee Psychologique* 12: 191–244.

BJS (Bureau of Justice Statistics) (2007) *Homicide Trends in the U.S.*, www.ojp.usdoj.gov/bjs/homicide/children.htm.

Blanchet, T. (1996) *Lost Innocence, Stolen Childhoods*, Dhaka: University Press Limited.

Blau, P.M. (1963) *The Dynamics of Bureaucracy*, Chicago, IL: University of Chicago Press.

Blaxter, M. (1997) 'Whose fault is it? People's own conceptions of the reasons for health inequalities', *Social Science and Medicine* 44(6): 747–56.

Bloor, M and Horobin, G. (1975) 'Conflict and conflict resolution in doctor–patient relationships', in C. Cox and A. Mead (eds) *A Sociology of Medical Practice*, London: Collier Macmillan.

Blumler, J.G. and Katz, E. (eds) (1974) *The Uses of Mass Communications*, London: Sage.

BMA (British Medical Association) (1986) *Alternative Therapy: Report of the Board of Science and Education*, London: British Medical Association.

BMA (British Medical Association) (1993) *Complementary Medicine: New Approaches to Good Practice*, London: British Medical Association.

Bocock, R. (1986) *Hegemony*, London: Tavistock.

Bonnet, M. (1993) 'Child labour in Africa', *International Labour Review* 132(3): 371–91.

Bonnett, A. (2000) *Anti-Racism*, London: Routledge.

Booth, C. (1889) *Life and Labour of the People in London*, London: Williams & Norgate.

Bornstein, K. (1994) *Gender Outlaw: On Men, Women and the Rest of Us*, London: Routledge.

Boronski, T. (1987) *Knowledge*, London: Longman.

Boserup, E, (1970) *Women's Role in Economic Development*, London: Allen & Unwin.

Boston Women's Health Book Collective (1973) *Our Bodies, Ourselves*, New York: Simon and Schuster.

Bottomore, T.B. (1963) *Karl Marx: Early Writings*, London: C.A. Watts.

Bottomore, T.B. (1965) *Classes in Modern Society*, London: Allen & Unwin.

Bottomore, T.B. (1983) *A Dictionary of Marxist Thought*, Oxford: Blackwell.

Bouquet, T. (1994) 'Computer porn, a degrading menace', *Reader's Digest*, June.

Bourdieu, P. (1983) 'Okonomisches Kapital, kulturelles Kapital, soziales Kapital', in R. Kreckel (ed.) *Soziale Ungleichheiten, Soziale Welt*. [Extract published as 'The forms of capital' in A.H. Halsey, H. Lauder, P. Brown and A. Stuart Wells (1997) *Education, Culture, Economy, Society*, Oxford: Oxford University Press.]

Bourdieu, P. (1996) 'On the family as a realised category', *Theory, Culture and Society* 13(3): 19–26.

Bourdieu, P. and Passeron, J.C. (1977) *Reproduction in Education, Society and Culture*, Beverly Hills, CA: Sage.

Bowen-Jones, C. (1992) 'Multiple marriage', *Marie Claire* 9 (July).

Bower, T. (1995) *Maxwell the Outsider*, London: Mandarin.

Bowler, I. (1993) ' "They're not the same as us": midwives' stereotypes of South Asian descent maternity patients', *Sociology of Health and Illness* 15: 157–78.

Bowles, S. and Gintis, H. (1976) *Schooling in Capitalist America: Educational Reform and the Contradictions of Economic Life*, London: Routledge & Kegan Paul.

Bowling, B. and Phillips, C. (2002) *Racism, Crime and Justice*, Harlow: Longman.

Box, S. (1983) *Power, Crime and Mystification*, London: Tavistock.

Boyden, J. (1988) 'National policies and programmes for child workers: Peru', in A. Bequele and J. Boyden (eds) *Combating Child Labour*, Geneva: International Labour Organization.

Boyden, J. (1990) 'A comparative perspective on the globalization of childhood', in A. James and A. Prout (eds) *Constructing and Reconstructing Childhood: Contemporary Issues in the Sociological Study of Childhood*, Basingstoke: Falmer Press.

Boyden, J. (1997) 'A comparative perspective on the globalization of childhood', in A. James and A. Prout (eds) *Constructing and Reconstructing Childhood: Contemporary Issues in the Sociological Study of Childhood*, Basingstoke: Falmer Press.

Boyden, J. and Ennew, J. (eds) (1997) *Children in Focus: A Manual for Experiential Learning in Participatory Research with Children*, Stockholm: Rädda Barnen.

Boyden, J., Ling, B. and Myers, W. (1998) *What Works for Working Children*, Stockholm: Rädda Barnen/UNICEF.

Bradley, H. (1996) *Fractured Identities: Changing Patterns of Inequality*, Cambridge: Polity Press.

Bradley, I. (1990) *God is Green*, London: Darton, Longman & Todd.

Bradley, I., Erickson, M., Stephenson, C. and Williams, S. (2000) *Myths at Work*, Cambridge: Polity Press.

Braham, P. and Janes, L. (2002) *Social Differences and Social Divisions*, Oxford: Oxford University Press.

Bramson, L. (1961) *The Political Content of Sociology*, Princeton, NJ: Princeton University Press.

Branca, F., Nikogosian, H. and Lobstein, T. (2007) *The Challenge of Obesity in the WHO European Region and the Strategies for Response*, Copenhagen: World Health Organization.

Branigan, T. (2002) 'Creationist row blamed on support for faith schools', *Guardian*, 19 March.

Brannen, J. (2003) 'The age of beanpole families', *Sociology Review* 13(1): 6–9.
Brannen, J. and Nilsen, A. (2005) 'Individualisation, choice and structure: a discussion of current trends in sociological analysis', *Sociological Review* 53(3): 412–28.
Brannen, J., Heptinstall, E. and Bhopal, K. (2000) *Connecting Children: Care and Family Life in Later Childhood*, London: Routledge Falmer.
Brannon, L. (2005) *Gender: Psychological Perspectives*, Boston, MA: Pearson Education.
Branston, G. and Stafford, R. (1996) *The Media Student's Book*, London: Routledge.
Braverman, H. (1974) *Labour and Monopoly Capital: The Degradation of Work within the Twentieth Century*, New York: Monthly Review.
Bravo, M.J., Royuela, L., Barrio, G., *et al.* (2007) 'More free syringes, fewer drug injectors in the case of Spain', *Social Science and Medicine* 65(8): 1773–8.
Bray, R. (2003) 'Predicting the social consequences of orphanhood in South Africa', *African Journal of AIDS Research* 2: 39–55.
Breen, R. and Goldthorpe, J. (1999) 'Class inequality and meritocracy: a critique of Saunders and an alternative analysis', *British Journal of Sociology* 50: 1–27.
Brierley, P. (2006) *UKCH Religious Trends No. 6 2006/7*, London: Christian Research.
Brierly, S. (1998) 'Advertising and the new media environment', in A. Briggs and P. Cobley (eds) *The Media: An Introduction*, Harlow: Longman.
Briggs, A. (1967) 'The language of "class" in early-nineteenth-century England', in A. Briggs and J. Saville (eds) *Essays in Labour History*, London: Macmillan.
Briggs, A. and Cobley, P. (eds) (1998) *The Media: An Introduction*, Harlow: Longman.
British Association of Aesthetic Plastic Surgeons (2007) *Annual Audit, 2007*, www.consultingroom.com/Statistics/Statistics_List.asp?Category=United%20Kingdom%20Statistics.
British Sociological Association (2001) *Network* 21.
British Sociological Association (2002) Statement of Ethical Practice for the British Sociological Association.www.britsoc.co.uk/equality/Statement+Ethical+Practice.htm
Broadcasting Standards Council (BSC) (1994) *Radio and Audience Attitudes*, London: Broadcasting Standards Council.
Brod, H. and Kaufman, M. (1994) *Theorizing Masculinity*, London: Sage.
Brohman, J. (1996) *Popular Development: Rethinking the Theory and Practice of Development*, Oxford: Blackwell.
Brown, C. (2001) *The Death of Christian Britain*, London: Routledge.
Brown, G., Wilson, C., Brady, G. and Letherby, G. (2008) 'Questioning the inevitability of risk', in N. Johns and A. Barton (eds) *Trusting New Labour: Perceptions Policy and Practice*, Lampeter: Edwin Mellon.
Brown, P. (1989) 'Education', in P. Brown and R. Sparks (eds), *Beyond Thatcherism: Social Policy, Politics and Society*, Milton Keynes: Open University Press.
Brown, R. (1992) *Understanding Industrial Organizations*, London: Routledge.
Brownlie, J. and Howson, A. (2005): ' "Leaps of faith" and MMR: an empirical study of trust', *Sociology* 39(2): 221–39.
Brownmiller, S. (1976) *Against Our Will: Men, Women and Rape*, Harmondsworth: Penguin.
Bruce, S. (1995) *Religion in Modern Britain*, Oxford: Oxford University Press.
Bruce, S. (1996) *Religion in the Modern World: From Cathedrals to Cults*, Oxford: Oxford University Press.
Bruce, S. (1999) *Choice and Religion: A Critique of Rational Choice Theory*, Oxford: Oxford University Press.
Bruce, S. (2000) *Fundamentalism*, Cambridge: Polity Press.
Bruce, S. (2002) *God is Dead: Secularization in the West*, Oxford: Blackwell.
Bruce, S. and Voas, D. (2007) 'Religious toleration and organisational typologies', *Journal of Contemporary Religion* 22(1): 1–17.
Bruges, J. (2000) *The Little Earth Book*, Bristol: Alastair Sawday.
Bryan, B. Dadzie, S. and Scafe, S. (1987) 'Learning to resist: black women and education', in G. Weiner and M. Arnot (eds) *Gender under Scrutiny*, London: Hutchinson.
Bryant, B. (ed.) (1995) *Environmental Justice: Issues, Policies and Solutions*, Washington, DC: Island Press.
Bryceson, D. and Vuorela, U. (2002) *The Transnational Family: New European Frontiers and Global Networks*, New York: Berg.
Bryman, A. (2004) *Social Research Methods*, 2nd edn, Oxford: Oxford University Press.
Bryman, A. (2008) *Social Research Methods*, 3rd edn, Oxford: Oxford University Press.
Bryson, V. (1992) *Feminist Political Theory: An Introduction*, London: Macmillan.
Bryson, V. (2007) *Gender and the Politics of Time, Feminist Theory and Contemporary Debates*, Bristol: Polity Press.
Buckingham, D. (1996) *Moving Images*, Manchester: Manchester University Press.
Bukumhe, R.B. (1992) 'I will definitely go', in D. Driedger and S. Gray (eds) *Imprinting Our Image: An International Anthology by Women with Disabilities*, Ottowa: Gynergy Books.
Bullard, R. (1990) *Dumping in Dixie: Race, Class and Environmental Quality*, Boulder CO: Westview Press.
Bunt, G.R. (2003) *Islam in the Digital Age: E-Jihad, Online Fatwas and Cyber Islamic Environments*, London: Pluto Press.

Burawoy, M. (1985) *The Politics of Production*, London: Verso.

Burchardt, T. (2000) *Enduring Economic Exclusion: Disabled People, Income and Work*, York: Joseph Rowntree Foundation.

Burchielli, R., Buttigieg, D. and Delaney, A. (2008) 'Organising homeworkers: the use of mapping as an organizing tool', *Work, Employment and Society* 22(1): 167–80.

Burke, R.H. (2005) *An Introduction to Criminological Theory*, 2nd edn, Cullompton: Willan.

Burnet, D. (1992) 'Freedom of speech, the media and the law', in A. Belsey and R. Chadwick (eds) *Ethical Issues in Journalism and the Media*, London: Routledge.

Burnham, J. (1945) *The Managerial Revolution*, Harmondsworth: Penguin.

Burningham, K. and Thrush, D. (2001) *Rainforests Are a Long Way from Here: The Environmental Concerns of Disadvantaged Groups*, York: Joseph Rowntree Foundation.

Burns, T. (ed.) (1969) *Industrial Man*, Harmondsworth: Penguin.

Burns, T. (1977) *The BBC: Public Institution and Private World*, London: Macmillan.

Burns, T. (1992) *Erving Goffman*, London: Routledge.

Burrows, R. and Loader, B. (eds) (1994) *Towards a Post-Fordist Welfare State?*, London: Routledge.

Burt, C. (1925) *The Young Delinquent*, London: University of London.

Bury, M. (1982) 'Chronic illness as biographical disruption', *Sociology of Health and Illness* 4: 167–82.

Bury, M. (1997) *Health and Illness in a Changing Society*, London: Routledge.

Butler, J. (1990) *Gender Trouble: Feminism and the Subversion of Identity*, London: Routledge.

Butler, J. (1993) *Bodies That Matter: On the Discursive Limits of Sex*, London: Routledge.

Butler, T. and Savage, M. (eds) *Social Change and the Middle Classes*, London: UCL Press.

Buttel, F.H. (1986) 'Sociology and the environment: the winding road toward human ecology', *International Social Science Journal* 109: 337–56.

Butterworth, D. (1993) 'Wanking in cyberspace: the development of computer porn', *Trouble and Strife* 27.

Byrne, E. (1978) *Women and Education*, London: Tavistock.

C

Calcutt (1990) *Report of the Committee on Privacy*, London: HMSO.

Callicott, J.B. (2001) 'Aldo Leopold', in J. Palmer (ed.) *Fifty Key Thinkers on the Environment*, London: Routledge.

Callinicos, A. (1990) *Against Postmodernism*, London: St Martin's Press.

Callinicos, A. and Harman, C. (1987) *The Changing Working Class*, London: Bookmarks.

Campbell, C. (1972) 'The cult, the cultic milieu and secularization', in M. Hill (ed.) *A Sociological Yearbook of Religion in Britain*, Vol. 5, London: SCM Press.

Campbell, C. (1999) 'The Easternisation of the West', in B. Wilson and J. Cresswell (eds) *New Religious Movements: Challenge and Response*, London: Routledge.

Campion, P. and Langdon, M. (2004) 'Achieving multiple topic shifts in primary care medical consultations: a conversation analysis study in UK general practice', *Sociology of Health and Illness* 26(1): 81–101.

Canton, N., Clark, C. and Pietka, E. (2008) '"The thing is that we haven't come here for holidays": the experiences of new migrant communities from central and Eastern Europe who are living and working in Glasgow', Edinburgh and London: British Council and the Institute for Public Policy Research.

Cantril, H. (1940) *The Invasion from Mars: A Study in the Psychology of Panic*, Princeton, NJ: Princeton University Press.

Carricaburu, D. and Pierret, J. (1995) 'From biographical disruption to biographical reinforcement: the case of HIV-positive men', *Sociology of Health* and Illness 17(1), 65–88.

Carson, R. (1962) *Silent Spring*, Boston, MA: Houghton Mifflin.

Carvel, J. (2004) 'Agencies defy code on poaching foreign nurses', *Guardian* 30.12.2004.

Casanova, J. (1994) *Public Religions in the Modern World*, Chicago and London: University of Chicago Press.

Cashmore, E. (1984) *No Future: Youth and Society*, London: Heinemann.

Cashmore, E. (1994) *. . . And There Was Telev!s!on*, London: Routledge.

Castells, M. (1996) *The Rise of the Network Society*, Oxford: Blackwell.

Castells, M. (2000) *The Rise of the Network Society*, 2nd edn, Oxford: Blackwell.

Castles, S. and Miller, M.J. (1993), *The Age of Migration: International Population Movements in the Modern World*, London: Macmillan.

Catton, W.R. and Dunlap, R.E. (1978) 'Environmental sociology: a new paradigm', *American Sociologist*, 13: 41–9.

Cavadino, M. and Dignan, J. (1993) *The Penal System: An Introduction*, London: Sage.

Cavadino, M. and Dignan, M. (2002) *The Penal System*, 3rd edn, London: Sage.

Chambers, R. (2005) *Ideas of Development*, London: Earthscan.

Chapkis, W. (1986) *Beauty Secrets*, London: Women's Press.

Chapman, T. (2004) *Gender and Domestic Life: Changing Practices in Families and Households*, Basingstoke: Palgrave Macmillan.

Charlesworth, S. (2000) *A Phenomenology of Working Class Experience*, Cambridge: Cambridge University Press.

Charmaz, K. (1983) 'Loss of self: a fundamental form of suffering in the chronically ill', *Sociology of Health and Illness* 5: 168–95.

Charmaz, K. (1995) 'Identity dilemmas of chronically ill men', in D. Sabo and D. Gordon (eds) *Men's Health and Illness: Gender, Power and the Body*, London: Sage.

Chatterton, P. and Style, S. (2001) 'Putting sustainable development into practice: the role of local policy partnership networks', *Local Environment* 6(4): 439–52.

Chawla, L. and Johnson, V. (2004) 'Not for children only: lessons learnt from young people's participation', *Participatory Learning and Action 50*, www.planotes.org/documents/plan_05007.pdf.

Cheal, D. (2002) *Sociology of Family Life*, Basingstoke: Palgrave Macmillan.

Cheney, J. (1989) 'Postmodern environmental ethics: ethics as bioregional narrative', *Environmental Ethics* 11: 117–34.

Chesney, K. (1991) *The Victorian Underworld*, Harmondsworth: Penguin.

Chomsky, N. (1972) 'The fallacy of Richard Herrnstein's IQ', *Social Policy* May–June.

Chomsky, N. (1989) *Necessary Illusions: Thought Control in Democratic Societies*, Pluto Press.

Chryssides, G.D. (2004) 'The Church of Scientology', in C. Partridge (ed.) *Encyclopedia of New Religions: New Religious Movements, Sects and Alternative Spiritualities*, Oxford: Lion.

CIA (Central Intelligence Agency) (2008) *The 2008 World Factbook*, Washington, DC: Potomac Books.

Ciambrone, D. (2001) 'Illness and other assaults on self: the relative impact of HIV/AIDS on women's lives', *Sociology of Health and Illness* 23(4): 517–40.

Cicourel, A.V. (1976) *The Social Organization of Juvenile Justice*, London: Heinemann.

Clark, T.N. and Lipset, S.M. (1996) 'Are social classes dying?', in D. Lee and B.S. Turner (eds) *Conflicts about Class: Debating Inequality in Late Industrialism*, London: Longman.

Clarke, H., Chandler, J. and Barry, J. (eds) (1994) *Organizations and Identities*, London: Chapman & Hall.

Clarke, J., Critcher, C., and Johnson, R. (eds) (1979) *Working Class Culture Studies in Theory and History*, London: Hutchinson.

Clarke, N. and Riddell, E. (1992) *The Sky Barons*, London: Methuen.

Clay, J. (1839) 'Criminal statistics of Preston', *Journal of the Statistical Society of London* 2.

Cloward, R.A. and Ohlin, L.E. (1961) *Delinquency and Opportunity*, New York: Free Press.

Cochrane, A. and Pain, K. (2000) 'A globalizing society?', in D. Held (ed.) *A Globalizing World? Culture, Economics, Politics*, London: Routledge.

Cockburn, C. (1983) *Brothers: Male Dominance and Technological Change*, London: Pluto.

Cockburn, C. (1991) *In the Way of Women: Men's Resistance to Sex Equality in Organizations*, London: Macmillan.

Cockerell, M., Hennessy, P. and Walker, D. (1984) *Sources Close to the Prime Minister*, London: Macmillan.

Coffey, A. and Atkinson, P. (1996) *Making Sense of Qualitative Data: Complementary Research Strategies*, Thousand Oaks, CA: Sage.

Cohen, A.K. (1955) *Delinquent Boys: The Culture of the Gang*, New York: Free Press.

Cohen, R. and Kennedy, P. (2000) *Global Sociology*, Palgrave, Macmillan.

Cohen, R. and Kennedy, P. (2007) *Global Sociology*, 2nd edn, London: Palgrave Macmillan.

Cohen, S. (1972) *Folk Devils and Moral Panics: The Creation of the Mods and Rockers*, London: MacGibbon & Kee.

Coleman, C. and Moynihan, J. (1996) *Understanding Crime Data: Haunted by the Dark Figure*, Buckingham: Open University Press.

Coleman, K., Jansson, K., Kaiza, P. and Reed, E. (2007) *Homicides, Firearms Offences and Intimate Violence 2005/2006: Supplementary Volume 1 to Crime in England and Wales 2005/2006*, London: Home Office.

Coleridge, N. (1994) *Paper Tigers: Latest Greatest Newspaper Tycoons and How They Won the World*, London: Mandarin.

Collard, A., with Contrucci, J. (1988) *Rape of the Wild: Man's Violence against Animals and the Earth*, Bloomington, IN: Indiana University Press.

Collier, R. (1992) 'The new man: fact or fad', *Achilles' Heel* 14: 34–8.

Collins, R. (2002) 'The dirty little secret of credential inflation', *Chronicle of Higher Education* 27 September.

Condry, J.C. and Condry, S. (1976) 'Sex-differences: a study in the eye of the beholder', *Child Development* 47: 812–19.

Connell, R.W. (1987) *Gender and Power*, Cambridge: Polity Press.

Connell, R.W. (2000a) *The Men and the Boys*, Cambridge: Polity Press.

Connell, R.W. (2000b) 'Understanding men: gender sociology and the new international research on masculinities', Clark Lecture, Department of Sociology, University of Kansas, 19 September, http://toolkit.endabuse.org/resources/understandingmen.html.

Connell, R.W. (2002) *Gender*, Cambridge: Polity Press.

Conrad, P. (2006) *Identifying Hyperactive Children*, Aldershot: Ashgate.

Conrad, P. and Gabe, J. (1999) 'Introduction: sociological perspectives on the new genetics – an overview', *Sociology of Health and Illness* 21(5): 506–16.

Conrad, P. and Jacobson, H.T. (2003) 'Enhancing biology: cosmetic surgery and breast augmentation', in S.J. Wiliams, L. Birke and G. Bendelow (eds) *Debating Biology: Sociological Reflections on Health, Medicine and Society*, London: Routledge

Cook, D. (1989) *Rich Law, Poor Law: Different Responses to Tax and Supplementary Benefit Fraud*, Milton Keynes: Open University Press.

Cooke, B. and Kothari, U. (eds) (2001) *Participation: The New Tyranny?*, London: Zed Books.

Cooley, C.H. (1902) *Human Nature and Social Order*, New York: Scribner.

Cooper, D. (1998) 'Regard between strangers: diversity, equality and the recognition of public space', *Critical Social Policy* 18: 465–92.

Coppock, V. (1997) 'Families in crisis', in P. Scraton (ed.) *Childhood in Crisis*, London: UCL Press.

Coppock, V., Haydon, D. and Richter, I. (1995) *Illusions of 'Post-Feminism': New Women, Old Myths*, London: Taylor & Francis.

Corbin, J. and Strauss, A. (1991) 'Comeback: the process of overcoming disability', in G.L. Albrecht and J.A. Levy (eds) *Advances in Medical Sociology*, Vol. 2, Greenwich, CT: JAI Press.

Corby, B. (2000) *Child Abuse: Towards a Knowledge Base*, Buckingham: Open University Press.

Cornwell, J. (1984) *Hard-Earned Lives: Accounts of Health and Illness from East London*, London: Tavistock.

Coser, L.A. and Rosenberg, B. (1969) *Sociological Theory: A Book of Readings*. 3rd edn, London: Macmillan.

Courtenay, R.W. (2000) 'Constructions of masculinity and their influence on men's well-being: a theory of gender and health', *Social Science and Medicine*, 50: 1385–401.

Coward, R. (1989) *The Whole Truth: The Myth of Alternative Medicine*, London: Faber and Faber.

Cowie, J., Cowie, S. and Slater, E. (1968) *Delinquency in Girls*, London: Hutchinson.

Cox, S. and McKellin, W. (1999) '"There's this thing in our family": predictive testing and the construction of risk for Huntington Disease', *Sociology of Health and Illness* 21(5): 622–46.

Cragg, C. (1992) *Media Education in the Primary School*, London: Routledge.

Craib, I. (1992) *Modern Social Theory*, Hemel Hempstead: Harvester Wheatsheaf.

Craig, C. (2005) *The Scots' Crisis of Confidence*, Edinburgh: Big Thinking.

Cranny-Francis, A., Waring, W., Stavropoulos, P. and Kirkby, J. (2003) *Gender Studies Terms and Debates*, Basingstoke: Palgrave Macmillan.

Crawford, R. (2006) 'Health as a meaningful social practice', *Health* 10(4): 401–20.

Crisell, A. (1998) 'Public service, commercialism and the paradox of choice', in A. Briggs and P. Cobley (eds) *The Media: An Introduction*, Harlow: Longman.

Croall, H. (1992) *White-Collar Crime*, Milton Keynes: Open University Press.

Croall, H. (1998) *Crime and Society in Britain*, Harlow: Addison Wesley Longman.

Crompton, R. (1989) 'Class theory and gender', *British Journal of Sociology* 40(4): 565–87.

Crompton, R. (1993) *Class and Stratification*, Cambridge: Polity.

Crompton, R. and Jones, G. (1984) *White-Collar Proletariat: Deskilling and Gender in Clerical Work*, London: Macmillan.

Crook, S., Pakulski, J. and Waters, M. (1992) *Postmodernization: Change in Advanced Societies*, London: Sage.

Crossley, N. (2004) 'Fat is a sociological issue: obesity rates in late modern "body conscious" societies', *Social Theory and Health* (2): 222–53.

Crotty, M. (2003) *The Foundations of Social Research: Meaning and Perspective in the Research Process*, London: Sage.

Cuff, E.C., Sharrock, W.W. and Francis, D.W. (1990) *Perspectives in Sociology*, 3rd edn, London: Unwin Hyman.

Cuff, E.C., Sharrock, W.W. and Francis, D.W. (1998) *Perspectives in Sociology*, 4th edn, London: Routledge.

Cuff, E.C., Sharrock, W.W. and Francis, D.W. (2006) *Perspectives in Sociology*, 5th edn, London: Routledge.

Cumberbatch, G. (1998) 'Media effects: the continuing c4ontroversy', in A. Briggs and P. Cobley (eds) *The Media: An Introduction*, Harlow: Longman.

Cumberbatch, G. and Howitt, D. (1989) *A Measure of Uncertainty: The Effects of the Mass Media*, London: John Libbey.

Cumming, E. and Henry, W. (1961) *Growing Old: The Process of Disengagement*, New York: Basic Books.

Cunningham, J. and Cunningham, S. (2008) *Sociology and Social Work*, Exeter: Learning Matters.

Cunningham, S., Backett-Milburn, K. and Kemmer, D. (2005) 'Balancing work and family life: mothers' views', in L. McKie and S. Cunningham-Burley (eds) *Families in Society: Boundaries and Relationships*, Bristol: Policy Press.

Cunningham-Burley, S. and Kerr, A. (1999) 'Defining the "social": towards an understanding of scientific and medical discourses on the social aspects of the new human genetics', *Sociology of Health and Illness* 21(5): 647–88.

Curran, J., Gurevitch, M. and Woollacott, J. (eds) (1977) *Mass Communication and Society*, London: Edward Arnold/Open University Press.

Curran, J. and Seaton, J. (1991) *Power Without Responsibility: The Press and Broadcasting in Britain*, London: Routledge.

Curran, J. and Seaton, J. (1997) *Power without Responsibility*, London: Routledge.

Curtis, L. (1984) *Ireland: The Propaganda War*, London: Pluto.

D

Dahl, R.A. (1961) *Who Governs?*, New Haven, CT: Yale University Press.

Dahlerup, D. (1986) *The New Women's Movement: Feminism and Political Power in Europe and the USA*, London: Sage.

Dahrendorf, R. (1959) *Class and Class Conflict in an Industrial Society*, London: Routledge & Kegan Paul.

Dahrendorf, R. (1992) 'Footnotes to the discussion', in D. Smith (ed.) *Understanding the Underclass*, London: Policy Studies Institute.

Dale, R. (1997) 'The state and the governance of education: an analysis of the restructuring of the state–education relationship', in A.H. Halsey, H. Lauder, P. Brown and A.S. Wells (1997) *Education, Culture, Economy, Society*, Oxford: Oxford University Press.

Daly, M. (1991) *Beyond God the Father*, London: Women's Press.

Daly, M. and Wilson, M. (1988) *Homicide*, New York: Aldine de Gruyter.

Daniel, P. and Ivatts, J. (1998) *Children and Social Policy*, Basingstoke: Macmillan.

Darwin, C. (1871) *The Descent of Man, and Selection in Relation to Sex*, London: John Murray.

Darwin, C. (1872) *The Expression of the Emotions in Man and Animals*, London: John Murray.

Darwin, C. (1968 [1859]) *On the Origin of Species*, Harmondsworth: Penguin.

Daud, F. (1985) *Minah Karan: The Truth about Malaysian Factory Girls*, Kuala Lumpur: Berita.

Davidson, B. (1984) *Africa in History*, London: Paladin.

Davie, G. (1990) 'Believing without belonging: is this the future of religion in Britain?', *Social Compass* 37(4): 455–69.

Davie, G. (1994) *Religion in Britain since 1945: Believing Without Belonging*, Oxford: Blackwell.

Davie, G. (1999) 'Europe: the exception that proves the rule?', in P.L. Berger (ed.) *The Desecularization of the World: Resurgent Religion and World Politics*, Washington, DC: Ethics and Public Policy Center.

Davie, G. (2000) 'Religion in modern Britain: changing sociological assumptions', *Sociology* 34(1): 113–28.

Davie, G. (2007) *The Sociology of Religion*, London: Sage.

Davis, K. (1949) *Human Society*, London: Macmillan.

Davis, K. (2003) *Dubious Equalities: Cultural Studies on Cosmetic Surgery*, Oxford: Rowman & Littlefield.

Davis, K. and Moore, W.E. (1967) 'Some principles of stratification', in R. Bendix and S.M. Lipset (eds) *Class, Status and Power*, 2nd edn, London: Routledge & Kegan Paul.

Dawkins, R. (1976) *The Selfish Gene*, Oxford: Oxford University Press.

Dawson, L.L. (2006) *Comprehending Cults: The Sociology of New Religious Movements*, 2nd edn, Toronto: Oxford University Press.

Dawson, L.L. and Cowan, D.E. (eds) (2004) *Religion Online: Finding Faith on the Internet*, New York: Routledge.

Day, A. (2006) 'Believing in belonging in contemporary Britain: a case study from Yorkshire', unpublished PhD thesis, Lancaster: Lancaster University.

Dearing (1998) *Report of the National Committee of Inquiry into Higher Education*, London: HMSO.

D'Eaubonne, F. (1974) *Le Feminism ou la Mort*, Paris: Pierre Horay.

De Beauvoir, S. (1974) *The Second Sex*, New York: Vintage.

Deem, R. (1978) *Women and Schooling*, London: Routledge & Kegan Paul.

Delbridge, R. (1998) *Life on the Line: The Workplace Experience of Lean Production and the 'Japanese' Model*, Oxford: Oxford University Press.

Delphy, C. (1984) *Close to Home: A Materialist Analysis of Women's Oppression*, London: Hutchinson.

Demaine, J. and Entwistle, H. (1996) *Beyond Communitarianism: Citizenship, Politics and Education*, Basingstoke: Macmillan.

Denitch, B. (1994) 'Dismembering Yugoslavia: nationalist ideologies and the symbolic revival of genocide', *American Ethnologist* 21(2): 367–90.

Dennis, N., Henriques, F. and Slaughter, C. (1956) *Coal is our Life*, London: Eyre & Spottiswoode.

Denscombe, M. (ed.) (1994) *Sociology Update*, Leicester: Olympus.

Denscombe, M. (ed.) (1998) *Sociology Update*, Leicester: Olympus.

Denscombe, M. (ed.) (2002) *Sociology Update*, Leicester: Olympus.

Department of Health (2003) *Our Inheritance our Future: Realising the Potential of Genetics in the NHS*, London: HMSO.

Dermott, E. (2008) *Intimate Fatherhood: A Sociological Analysis*, London: Routledge.

DES (Department of Education and Science) (1988) *Advancing A Levels*, Higginson Report, London: HMSO.

Desougi, M. (2005) 'It's the end of the world as we know it: meeting sociological ideas for the first time', *Network: Newsletter of the British Sociological Association* Summer (91): 28.

De Vaus, D.A. (1986) *Surveys in Social Research*, London: Allen & Unwin.

Devine, D. (2002) 'Children's citizenship and the structuring of adult-child relations in the primary school', *Childhood* 9(3): 303–20.

Devine, D. (2003) *Children, Power and Schooling: How Childhood is Structured in the Primary School*, Stoke on Trent: Trentham Books.

Devine, F. (1994) '"Affluent Workers" revisited', *Sociology Review* 3(3): 6–9.

Devine, F. (2004) *Class Practices: How Parents Help Their Children Get Good Jobs*, Cambridge: Cambridge University Press.

Dicken, P. (2003) *Global Shift: Reshaping the Global Economic Map in the 21st Century*, 4th edn, London: Sage.

Dickens, P. (1992) *Society and Nature: Towards a Green Social Theory*, London: Harvester.

Dickens, P. (1996) 'Society and nature', *Developments in Sociology* 9: 141–61.

Dickens, R., Gregg, P. and Wadsworth, J. (2004) *The Labour Market Under New Labour: The State of Working Britain*, London: Palgrave Macmillan.

Di Marco, A.D. and Di Marco, H. (2003) 'Investigating cybersociety: a consideration of the ethical and practical issues surrounding online research in chat rooms', in Yvonne Jewkes (ed.) *Dot.cons: Crime, Deviance and Identity on the Internet*, Cullompton: Willan.

Dimmock, B. (2004) 'Young people and family life: apocalypse now or business as usual?', in J. Roche, S. Tucker, R. Thomson and R. Flynn (eds) *Youth in Society*, 2nd edn, London: Sage.

Dingle, C. and Daley, S. (2006) 'Damned by debt relief', www.worldwrite.org.uk/damned/articles.html.

Disability Rights Commission (2002) *Independent Living and the DRC's Vision*, London: DRC.

Dixon, A. (2008) *Regulating Complementary Medical Practitioners: An International Review*, London: Kings Fund.

Dizard, W. (1982) *The Coming Information Age: An Overview of Technology, Economics and Politics*, London: Longman.

Dobash, R.E. and Dobash, R.P. (1992) *Women, Violence and Social Change*, London: Routledge.

Dobbelaere, K. (2002) *Secularization: An Analysis at Three Levels*, Brussels: Peter Lang.

Dobson, A. (1995) *Green Political Thought*, 2nd edn, London: Unwin.

Dollar, D. (2007) *Poverty, inequality, and social disparities during China's economic reform*, Policy, Research Working Paper, No WPS 4253. This is available from the World Bank website as a free download.

Donald, R.R. (1992) 'Masculinity and machismo in Hollywood war films', in S. Craig (ed.) *Men, Masculinities and the Media*, London: Sage.

Donnerstein, E., Linz, D. and Penrod, S. (1987) *The Question of Pornography: Research Findings and Policy Implications*, New York: Free Press.

Doring, N. (2000) 'Feminist views of cybersex: victimization, liberation and empowerment', *Cyber Psychology and Behaviour* 3(5), 863–84.

Dorling, D., Rigby, J., Wheeler, B., *et al.* (2007) *Poverty, Wealth and Place in Britain, 1968 to 2005: Understanding the Transformation of the Prospects of Places*, York: Joseph Rowntree Foundation.

Dostoevsky, F. (1962 [1860]) *The House of the Dead*, London: Dent.

Douglas, J.W.B. (1964) *The Home and the School*, London: MacGibbon & Kee.

Dover, B. (2008) *Rupert's Adventures in China: How Murdoch Lost a Fortune and Found a Wife*, Camberwell, Australia: Mainstream Publishing.

Dowmunt, A. (ed.) (1994) *Channels of Resistance*, London: British Film Institute.

Doyal, L. (1995) *What Makes Women Sick: Gender and the Political Economy of Health*, Basingstoke: Macmillan.

Doyal, L. and Harris, R. (1986) *Empiricism, Explanation and Rationality*, London: Routledge & Kegan Paul.

Doyle, G. (2004) 'Changes in media ownership', *Sociology Review*, 13(3).

Drakakis-Smith, D. (2000) *Third World Cities*, London: Routledge.

Drew, D. and Gray, J. (1989) 'The fifth-year examination achievements of black young people in England and Wales', Sheffield: University of Sheffield Research Centre.

Driedger, D. (1989) *The Last Civil Rights Movement: Disabled People's International*, London: Hurst and Co.

DSS (Department of Social Security) (1994) *Households Below Average Income*, London: HMSO.

Duelli-Klein, R. (1983) 'How to do what we want to do: thoughts about feminist methodology', in G. Bowles and R. Duelli-Klein (eds) *Theories of Women's Studies*, London: Routledge.

Duffy, J. (1987) 'Franklin Roosevelt: ambiguous symbol for disabled Americans', *Midwest Quarterly*, XXIX(1): 113–35.

Duncan, S. and Edwards, R. (1999) *Lone Mothers, Paid Work and Gendered Moral Rationalities*, London: Macmillan.

Dunion, K. (2003) *Troublemakers: The Struggle for Environmental Justice in Scotland*, Edinburgh: Edinburgh University Press.

Dunlap, R.E. (1980) 'Paradigmatic change in social science. from human to an ecological paradigm', *American Behavioral Scientist* 24(1): 5–13.

Dunlap, R.E. (2002) 'Paradigms, theories and environmental sociology', in R.E. Dunlap, F.H. Buttel, P. Dickens and A. Gijswijt (eds) (2002) *Social Theory and the Environment: Classical Foundations, Contemporary Insights*, Oxford: Rowman & Littlefield.

Dunlap, R.E. and Catton, W.R. (1980) 'A new ecological paradigm for a post exuberant sociology', *American Behavioral Science* 24(1): 15–47.

Dunlap, R.E., Buttel, F.H., Dickens, P. and Gijswijt, A. (eds) (2002) *Social Theory and the Environment: Classical Foundations, Contemporary Insights*, Oxford: Rowman & Littlefield.

Dunne, G. (1998) *Living 'Difference': Lesbian Perspectives on Work and Family Life*, New York: Haworth,

Dunne, G. (1999) 'A passion for "sameness": sexuality and gender accountability', in E. Silva and C. Smart (eds) *The New Family?*, London: Sage.

Durkheim, E. (1952 [1897]) *Suicide: A Study in Sociology*, trans. J.A. Spaulding and G. Simpson, London: Routledge & Kegan Paul.

Durkheim, E. (1956 [1903]) *Education and Sociology*, New York: Free Press.

Durkheim, E. (1963 [1897]) *Suicide: A Study in Sociology*, London: Routledge and Kegan Paul.

Durkheim, E. (1960 [1893]) *The Division of Labour in Society*, New York: Free Press.

Durkheim, E. (1964 [1895]) *The Rules of Sociological Method*, New York: The Free Press.

Durkheim, E. (1976 [1912]) *The Elementary Forms of the Religious Life*, trans. J.W. Swain, London: Allen & Unwin.

Durkheim, E. (1995 [1912]) *The Elementary Forms of the Religious Life*, trans. K.E. Fields, New York: The Free Press.

Dworkin, A. (1983) *Pornography: Men Possessing Women*, London: Women's Press.

E

Eckersley, R. (1992) *Environmentalism and Political Theory: Toward an Ecocentric Approach*, London: UCL Press.

Eden, F.M. (1797) *The State of the Poor*, London: Frank Cass.

Edensor, T. (2002) *National Identity, Popular Culture and Everyday Life*, Oxford: Berg.

Edensor, T. (2004) 'Automobility and national identity: representation, geography and driving practice', *Theory, Culture and Society* 21(4–5): 101–20.

Edgell, S. (1993) *Class*, London: Routledge.

Edgell, S. (2006) *The Sociology of Work: Continuity and Change in Paid and Unpaid Work*, London: Sage.

Edgerton, R. (1970) 'Mental retardation in non-Western societies: toward a cross-cultural perspective on incompetence', in H. Hayward (ed.) *Social-Cultural Aspects of Mental Retardation*, New York: Appleton-Century-Crofts.

Edwards, M. (1996) 'New approaches to children and development: introduction and overview', *Journal of International Development* 8(6): 813–27.

Edwards, R. (1979) *Contested Terrain*, London: Heinemann.

Edwards, R. (1993) *Mature Women Students*, London: Taylor & Francis.

Edwards, R., Hadfield, L. and Mauthner, M. (2005) *Children's Understanding of their Sibling Relationships*, London: National Children's Bureau.

Edwards, R., Hadfield, L., Lucey, H. and Mauthner, M. (2006) *Sibling Identity and Relationships: Sisters and Brothers*, London: Routledge.

Edwards, V. (1976) *West Indian Language: Attitudes and the School*, London: National Association for Multiracial Education.

Edwards, V. (1979) *The West Indian Language Issue in British Schools*, London: Routledge & Kegan Paul.

EGRIS (European Group for Integrated Social Research) (2001) 'Misleading trajectories: transition dilemmas of young adults in Europe', *Journal of Youth Studies* 4(1): 101–18.

Eisenstadt, S. (1956) *From Generation to Generation: Age Groups and Social Structure*, New York: Free Press.

Elder, G. (1978) 'Family history and the life course', in T. Hareven (ed.) *Transitions: The Family and the Life Course in Historical Perspective*, London: Academic Press.

Elias, N. (1985) *The Loneliness and Dying*, Oxford: Blackwell.

Elkington, J. and Hailes, J. (1988) *The Green Consumer Guide*. London: Gollancz.

Elkins, S.M. (1976) *Slavery: A Problem in American Institutional and Intellectual Life*, 3rd edn, Chicago, IL: University of Chicago Press.

Elliot, A. (2002) 'Beck's sociology of risk: a critical assessment', *Sociology* 36(2): 293–315.

Elliot, J.A. (1999) *An Introduction to Sustainable Development: The Developing World*, London: Routledge.

Elliot, P. (1997) 'Uses and gratifications research: a critique and sociological alternative', in P. Marris and S. Thornham (eds) *Media Studies: A Reader*, Edinburgh: Edinburgh University Press.

Elliott, A. (1996) *Subject to Ourselves*, Cambridge: Polity.

Elliott, A. (2002) 'Beck's Sociology of Risk: A Critical Assessment', *Sociology* 36(2) 293–315, London: Sage Publications.

Elliott, J. (2006) *An Introduction to Sustainable Development*, 3rd edn, London: Routledge.

Elliott, L. and Atkinson, D. (1999) *The Age of Insecurity*, London: Verso.

Elrich, P.R. (1968) *The Population Bomb*, New York: Ballantine.

Emmer, P.C. (1993) 'Intercontinental migration as a world historical process', *European Review* 1(1): 67–74.

Engels, F. (1958 [1845]) *The Condition of the Working Class in England*, Oxford: Blackwell.

Environics Research Group (2004) *Canadian Attitudes Towards Disability Issues: A Qualitative Study*, Toronto: Environics Research Group.

Erichsen, V. (1995) 'State traditions and medical professionalization in Scandanavia', in T. Johnson, G. Larkin and M. Saks (eds) *Health Professions and the State in Europe*, London: Routledge.

Etzioni, A. (1993) *The Spirit of Community: The Reinvention of American Society*, New York: Simon & Schuster.

European Communities (2000) *Financing and Management of Resources in Compulsory Education*, Vol. 2: Key Topics in Education in Europe, Luxembourg: Office for Official Publications of the European Communities (EUR-OP).

European Opinion Research Group (2004) 'Europeans' attitudes to parental leave', *Eurobarometer 189*, Luxembourg: European Commission.

Eurostat (2007a) 'Gender pay gap in unadjusted form', http://europa.eu.int/estatref/info/sdds/en/earn_gr_gpg_base.htm.

Eurostat (2007b) 'The narrowing education gap between men and women', Statistics in Focus, Population and Social Conditions, 130/2007, Luxembourg: Office for Official Publications of the European Communities.

Eurostat (2007c) 'The flexibility of working time arrangements for women and men', Statistics in Focus, Population and Social Conditions, 93/2007, Luxembourg: Office for Official Publications of the European Communities.

Ewington, T. (2004) 'Red tops need blue-sky thinking', *Financial Times*, 9 March.

F

Fairbrother, H. (1983) 'Who's the brightest of them all?', *Radio Times* 19–25 February: 8–9.

Fairburn, J., Walker, G. and Smith, G. (2005) 'Investigating environmental justice in Scotland: links between measures of environmental quality and social deprivation', Edinburgh: SNIFFER.

Featherstone, M. and Hepworth, M. (1989) 'Ageing and old age: reflections on the postmodern life course', in B. Bytheway, T. Keil, P. Allatt and A. Bryman (eds) *Becoming and Being Old: Sociological Approaches to Later Life*, London: Sage.

Feinberg, L. (1998) *Transliberation, Beyond Pink or Blue*, Boston, MA: Becon Press.

Felstead, A., Jewson, N., Phizacklea, P. and Walters, S. (2000) 'A statistical portrait of working at home in the UK: Evidence from the Labour Force Survey', ESRC Future of Work working paper 4, Leeds: ESRC Future of Work.

Fenton, S. (1999) *Ethnicity: Racism, Class and Culture*, Basingstoke; Palgrave Macmillan.

Ferguson, I. (2008) *Reclaiming Social Work*, London: Sage.

Ferguson, M. (1985) *Forever Feminine: Women's Magazines and the Cult of Femininity*, London: Heinemann.

Ferguson, N. (2004) *Empire*, London: Allen Lane.

Fernando, S., Ndegwa, D. and Wilson, M. (1998) *Forensic Psychiatry, Race and Culture*, London: Routledge.

Festinger, L., Riecken, H.W. and Schachter, S. (1956) *When Prophecy Fails: A Social and Psychological Study of a Modern Group that Predicted the Destruction of the World*, London: Harper & Row.

Feuerbach, L. (1957 [1841]) *The Essence of Christianity*, London and New York: Harper.

Fevre, R. (1992) *The Sociology of Labour Markets*, Hemel Hempstead: Harvester Wheatsheaf.

Field, F. (1989) *Losing Out: The Emergence of Britain's Underclass*, Oxford: Blackwell.

Fielding, T. (1995) 'Migration and middle class formation in England and Wales, 1981–91', in T. Butler and M. Savage (eds) *Social Change and the Middle Classes*, London: UCL Press.

Fiese, B.H. and Skillman, G. (2000) 'Gender differences in family stories: moderating influence of parent gender role and child gender', *Sex Roles* 43(5–6): 267–83.

Finch, J. (1987) 'The vignette technique in survey research', *Sociology*, 21: 105–114.

Finch, J. (2007) 'Displaying families', *Sociology* 41: 65–80.

Finch, J. and Mason, J. (1993) *Negotiating Family Responsibilities*, London: Routledge.

Fincham, R. and Rhodes, P.S. (1994) *The Individual, Work and Organization*, Oxford: Oxford University Press.

Finkelstein, N. (2000) *The Holocaust Industry: Reflections on the Exploitation of Jewish Suffering*, London: Verso.

Finkelstein, V. (1980) *Know your Own Approach: The Handicapped Person in the Community*, Milton Keynes: Open University Press.

Finkelstein, V. (1994) *Getting There: Non-Disabling Transport*, Leeds: Disability Research Centre.

Fiorenza, E.S. and Copeland, M.S. (eds) (1994) *Violence Against Women*, London: SCM Press.

Firth, L. (ed.) (2008) *Religious Beliefs*, Cambridge: Independence Educational Publishers.

Fiske, J. (1987) *Television Culture*, London: Routledge.

Fiske, J. (1989) *Reading the Popular*, London: Unwin Hyman.

Fiske, J. and Hartley, J. (1978) *Reading Television*, London: Methuen.

Fitzpatrick, T. (1998) 'The implications of ecological thought for social welfare', *Critical Social Policy* 18(1): 5–28.

Fivush, R., Brotman, M.A., Buckner, J.P. and Goodman, S.H. (2000) 'Gender differences in parent–child emotion narratives', *Sex Roles* 42(3–4): 233–53.

Flax, J. (1990) *Thinking Fragments: Psychoanalysis, Feminism and Postmodernism in the Contemporary West*, Berkeley, CA: University of California Press.

Fleming, D. (1993) *Media Teaching*, London: Blackwell.

Fletcher, A. (1999) *Gender, Sex and Subordination in England, 1500–1800*, London: Yale University Press.

Fletcher, W. (1992) *A Glittering Haze*, London: NTC.

Flude, M. and Ahier, J. (1974) *Educability, Schools and Ideology*, London: Croom Helm.

Foreman, D. (1989) 'Putting the Earth First' in J.S. Dryzek and D. Schlosberg (eds) *Debating the Earth: The Environmental Politics Reader*, 358–64, Oxford: Oxford University Press.

Foreman, S. and Dallos, R. (1993) 'Domestic violence', in R. Dallos and E. McLaughlin (eds) *Social Problems and the Family*, London: Sage.

Foster, G. (1997) 'Children rearing children: a study of child-headed households', presented at the Socio-Demographic Impact of AIDS in Africa Conference, Durban, South Africa.

Foucault, M. (1967) *Madness and Civilisation: A History of Insanity in the Age of Reason*, London: Tavistock.

Foucault, M. (1976) *The Birth of the Clinic*, London: Tavistock.

Foucault, M. (1977 [1975]) *Discipline and Punish: The Birth of the Prison*, London: Allen Lane.

Foucault, M. (1979) *Discipline and Punish: The Birth of the Prison*, New York: Vintage Books.

Foucault, M. (1984) *The History of Sexuality*, Vol. 1: An Introduction, London: Penguin.

Fox, A. (1974) *Beyond Contract: Work, Power and Trust Relations*, London: Faber & Faber.

Francis, B. (2000) *Boys, Girls and Achievement*, London: Routledge Falmer.

Frank, A.G. (1966) *The Development of Underdevelopment*, Boston, MA: New England Free Press.

Frank, A.G. (1967) *Capitalism and Underdevelopment in Latin America*, New York: Monthly Review.

Frankel, B. (1987) *The Post Industrial Utopians*, Oxford: Polity Press.

Franklin, B. (1986) *The Rights of Children*, Oxford: Basil Blackwell.

Fraser, M. and Greco, M. (eds) (2005) *The Body: A Reader*, London: Routledge.

Fraser, R. (ed.) (1968) *Work: Twenty Personal Accounts*, Harmondsworth: Penguin.

Fraser, S. (1995) *The Bell Curve Wars: Race, Intelligence and the Future of America*, New York: Basic Books.

Fredrickson, G.M. (2002) *Racism: A Short History*, Princeton, NJ: Princeton University Press.

Freeman, T. (2003) 'Loving fathers or deadbeat dads: the crisis of fatherhood in popular culture', in S. Earle and G. Letherby (eds) *Gender, Identity and Reproduction: Social Perspectives*, Basingstoke: Palgrave Macmillan.

Freidson, E. (1970) *Profession of Medicine: A Study of the Sociology of Applied Knowledge*, New York: Dodd Mead.

Freire, P. (1972 [1970]) *Pedagogy of the Oppressed*, Harmondsworth: Penguin.

Freire, P. (1976 [1970]) 'A few notions about the word "conscientization"', in Schooling and Society Course Team, *Schooling and Capitalism: A Sociological Reader*, Milton Keynes: Open University Press.

French, S. (1993) 'Disability, impairment, or something in between?', in J. Swain, V. Finkelstein, S. French and M. Oliver (eds) *Disabling Barriers – Enabling Environments*, London: Sage.

Friedan, B. (1963) *The Feminine Mystique*, London: Norton.

Friedman, A.L. (1979) *Industry and Labour: Class Struggle at Work and Monopoly Capitalism*, London: Macmillan.

Friedman, M. (1962) *Capitalism and Freedom*, Harmondsworth: Penguin.

Friedmann, J. (1995) 'Where we stand: a decade of world city research', in P. Knox and P. Taylor (eds) *World Cities in a World-System*, Cambridge: Cambridge University Press.

Friends of the Earth (2001) *Pollution and Poverty: Breaking the Link*, London: Friends of the Earth.

Friends of the Earth (2002) 'Blair Challenged Over Sustainable Development' (Archived Press Release) Sept 2002, http://www.foe.co.uk/resource/press_releases/0904blar.html.

Frith, K.T. and Mueller, B. (2003) *Advertising and Society: Global Issues*, New York: Peter Lang.

Fritsch, B., Schmidheiny, S. and Seifritz, W. (1994) *Towards an Ecologically Sustainable Growth Society: Physical Foundations, Economic Transitions and Political Constraints*, Berlin, New York: Springer.

Frobel, F., Heinrichs, J. and Dreye, O. (1980) *The New International Division of Labour*, Cambridge: Cambridge University Press.

Fromm, E. (1942) *The Fear of Freedom*, London: Routledge & Kegan Paul.

Fromm, E. (1960) *The Fear of Freedom*, London: Routledge & Kegan Paul.

Fryer, P. (1984) *Staying Power: The History of Black People in Britain*, London: Pluto.

Fukuyama, F. (1989) 'The end of history?', *The National Interest* 16: 3–17.

Fuller, M. (1980) 'Black girls in a London comprehensive school', in R. Deem (ed.) *Schooling for Women's Work*, London: Routledge & Kegan Paul.

Furlong, A. and Cartmel, F. (1997) *Young People and Social Change*, Buckingham: Open University Press.

G

Gabb, J. (2008) *Researching Intimacy in Families*, Basingstoke: Palgrave Macmillan.

Galbraith, J.K. (1967) *The New Industrial State*, Harmondsworth: Penguin.

Gallie, D. (ed.) (1989) *Employment in Britain*, Oxford: Blackwell.

Gallie, D. and Paugam, S. (eds) (2000) *Welfare Regimes and the Experience of Unemployment in Europe*, Oxford: Oxford University Press.

Gallie, D., Marsh, C. and Vogler, V. (1993) *Social Change and the Experience of Unemployment*, Oxford: Oxford University Press.

Gamman, L. and Marshment, M. (1988) *The Female Gaze*, London: Women's Press.

Gans, H. (1974) *Popular Culture and High Culture*, New York: Basic Books.
Gardner, H. (1983) *Frames of Mind: The Theory of Multiple Intelligences*, New York: Basic Books.
Gardner, H. (1993) *Frames of Mind: The Theory of Multiple Intelligences*, 2nd edn, London: Fontana Press.
Garfinkel, H. (1967) *Studies in Ethnomethodology*, Englewood Cliffs, NJ: Prentice-Hall.
Garland, D. (1990) *Punishment and Modern Society*, Oxford: Clarendon.
Garmarnikov, E., Morgan, D., Purvis, J. and Taylorson, D. (eds) (1983) *Gender, Class and Work*, London: Heinemann.
Garner, R. (1996) *Environmental Politics*, London: Prentice Hall and Harvester Wheatsheaf.
Gates, B. (1995) *The Road Ahead*, New York: Viking.
Gauntlett, D. (1995) *Moving Experiences: Understanding Television's Influences and Effects*, London: John Libbey.
Gauntlett, D. (1997) *Video Critical: Children, the Environment and Media Power*, London: John Libbey.
Gauntlett, D. (2005) *Moving Experiences: Understanding Television's Influences and Effects*, 2nd edn, London: John Libbey.
Gauntlett, D. (2002) *Media, Gender and Identity*, London: Routledge.
Gauntlett, D. (2008) *Media, Gender and Identity*, 2nd edn, London: Routledge.
Geertz, C. (1975 [1966]) 'Religion as a cultural system', in C. Geertz, *The Interpretation of Cultures*, London: Hutchinson.
Gelles, R.J. (1997) *Intimate Violence in Families*, London: Sage.
Gellner, E. (1983) *Nations and Nationalism*, Oxford: Basil Blackwell.
Gerbner, G. (1995) 'TV violence and what to do about it', in G. Dines and J. McMahon Humez, *Gender, Race, and Class in Media: A Critical Text Reader*, Thousand Oaks, CA: Sage.
Gershunny, J.I. and Miles, I. (1983) *The New Service Economy: The Transformation of Employment in Industrial Relations*, London: Frances Pinter.
Gerth, H.H. and Mills, C.W. (eds) (1991 [1970]) *From Max Weber: Essays in Sociology*, London: Routlege.
Geser, H. (2004) *Towards a Sociological Theory of the Mobile Phone*, http://socio.ch/mobile/t_geser1.pdf.
Gibson, J. (ed.) (2008) *Media 08: The Essential Guide to the Changing Media Landscape*, London: Guardian Books.
Giddens, A. (1973) *The Class Structure of the Advanced Societies*, London: Hutchinson.
Giddens, A. (1984) *The Constitution of Society*, Berkeley, CA: University of California Press.
Giddens, A. (1986) 'The rich', in M. Williams (ed.) *Society Today*, London: Macmillan.
Giddens, A. (1990) *The Consequences of Modernity*, Cambridge: Polity Press.
Giddens, A. (1991) *Modernity and Self-Identity*, Cambridge: Polity Press.
Giddens, A. (1992a) *The Transformation of Intimacy: Sexualities, Love and Eroticism in Modern Societies*, Stanford, CA: Stanford University Press.
Giddens, A. (ed.) (1992b) *Human Societies: An Introductory Reader in Sociology*, Cambridge: Polity Press.
Giddens, A. (1993) 'Dare to care, conserve and repair', *New Statesman and Society*, 29 October.
Giddens, A. (1997a) *Sociology*, 3rd edn, Cambridge: Polity Press.
Giddens, A. (ed.) (1997b) *Sociology: Introductory Readings*, Cambridge: Polity Press.
Giddens, A. (1998) *The Third Way: The Renewal of Social Democracy*, Cambridge: Polity Press.
Giddens, A. (1999) *Runaway World: How Globalisation is Reshaping our Lives*, London: Profile Books.
Giddens, A. (2001) *Sociology*, 4th edn, Cambridge: Polity Press.
Gide, A. (1952) *The Journals of André Gide 1889–1949*, trans. J. O'Brien, New York: Knopf.
Gilbert, A.G. and Gugler, J. (1992) *Cities, Poverty and Development: Urbanization in the Third World*, 2nd edn, Oxford: Oxford University Press.
Gilbert, P. (1992) 'The oxygen of publicity: terrorism and reporting restrictions', in A. Belsey and R. Chadwick (eds) *Ethical Issues in Journalism and the Media*, London: Routledge.
Gill, R. (2007) *Gender and the Media*, Cambridge: Polity Press.
Gillies, V. (2000) 'Young people and family life: analysing and comparing disciplinary discourses', *Journal of Youth Studies* 3(2): 211–28.
Gillies, V. (2007) *Marginalised Mothers: Exploring Working-class Experiences of Parenting*, London: Routledge.
Gillis, S. (2008) 'Cyberspace, feminism and technology: of cyborgs and women', in D. Richardson and V. Robinson (eds) *Introducing Gender and Women's Studies*, 3rd edn, Houndsmills: Palgrave Macmillan.
Gilroy, P. (2004) *After Empire: Multiculture or Postcolonial Melancholia*, London: Routledge.
Ginn, J. and Arber, S. (1993) 'Ageing and cultural stereotypes of older women', in J. Johnson and R. Slater (eds) *Ageing and Later Life*, London: Sage.
Ginsburg, N. (1992) 'Racism and housing: concepts and reality', in P. Braham (ed.) *Racism and Anti-Racism: Inequalities, Opportunities and Policies*, London: Sage.
Giroux, H. (1992) *Border Crossings: Cultural Workers and the Politics of Education*, London: Routledge.
Gittins, D. (1993) *The Family in Question*, London: Macmillan.
Gittins, D. (1998) *The Child in Question*, Basingstoke and London: Macmillan Press.

Giulianotti, R. and Robertson, R. (2007) 'Forms of glocalization: globalization and the migration strategies of Scottish football fans in North America', *Sociology* 41: 133–43.

Glaser, B.G. and Strauss, A.L. (1965) *Awareness of Dying*, Chicago, IL: Aldine.

Glasgow University Media Group (1982) *Really Bad News*, London: Writers & Readers.

Glass, D. (ed.) (1954) *Social Mobility in Britain*, London: Routledge & Kegan Paul.

Glover, D. (1985) 'The Sociology of Mass Media', in M. Haralambos (ed.) *Sociology, new directions*, Ormskirk: Causeway Press.

Goffman, E. (1968) *Asylums: Essays on the Social Situation of Mental Patients and Other Inmates*, Harmondsworth: Penguin.

Goffman, E. (1969) *The Presentation of Self in Everyday Life*, Harmondsworth: Penguin.

Goffman, E. (1971) *Relations in Public*, Harmondsworth: Penguin.

Goffman, E. (1981) *Forms of Talk*, Philadelphia, PA: University of Pennsylvania Press.

Golding, P. (1974) *The Mass Media*, London: Longman.

Golding, P. and Murdock, G. (1991) 'Culture, communications and political economy', in J. Curran and M. Gurevitch (eds) *Mass Media and Society*, London: Edward Arnold.

Goldman, R. (1992) *Reading Ads Socially*, London: Routledge.

Goldsmith, E., Allen, R., *et al.* (1972) 'A blueprint for survival', *Ecologist* 2: 110–22.

Goldthorpe, J. (1996) 'Class analysis and the re-orientation of class theory: the case of persisting differentials in educational attainment, *British Journal of Sociology* 47: 481–505.

Goldthorpe, J., Lockwood, D., Bechhofer, F. and Platt, J. (1968) *The Affluent Worker: Industrial Attitudes and Behaviour*, Cambridge: Cambridge University Press.

Goldthorpe, J., Lockwood, D., Bechhofer, F. and Platt, J. (1969) *The Affluent Worker in the Class Structure*, Cambridge: Cambridge University Press.

Goldthorpe, J., Llewellyn, C. and Payne, C. (1980) *Social Mobility and Class Structure in Modern Britain*, Oxford: Clarendon Press.

Goleman, D. (1996) *Emotional Intelligence*, London: Bloomsbury.

Goode, E. (1997) *Deviant Behaviour*, New York: Prentice Hall.

Goode, E. and Ben-Yehuda, N. (1994) *Moral Panics: The Social Construction of Deviance*, Blackwell: Oxford.

Goodman, A., Johnson, P. and Webb, S. (1997) *Inequality in the UK*, Oxford: Oxford University Press.

Gordon, C. (1966) *Role Theory and Illness: A Sociological Perspective*, New Haven, CT: Connecticut College and University Press.

Gorz, A. (ed.) (1979) *The Division of Labour*, Brighton: Harvester.

Gorz, A. (1982) *Farewell to the Working Class*, London: Pluto.

Gospel, H. and Wood, S. (eds) (2003) *Representing Workers: Trade Union Recognition and Membership in Britain*, London: Routledge.

Gouldner, A.W. (1954) *Patterns of Industrial Bureaucracy*, New York: Free Press.

Gouldner, A.W. (1971) *The Coming Crisis of Western Sociology*, London: Heinemann.

Gouldner, A.W. (1973) 'Anti-minotaur: the myth of a value free society', in A.W. Gouldner (ed.) *For Sociology: Renewal and Critique in Sociology Today*, Harmondsworth: Penguin.

Gouldner, A.W. (1975) *For Sociology: Renewal and Critique in Sociology Today*, Harmondsworth: Penguin.

Graham, H. (1984b) 'Surveying through stories', in C. Bell and H. Roberts (eds) *Social Researching*, London: Routledge & Kegan Paul.

Graham, H. (1993) 'Women's smoking: government targets and social trends', *Health Visitor* 66(3): 80–82.

Graham, S. (2007) 'Research into child-headed households in Jinga, Uganda', report compiled for Street Child Africa, UK.

Gramsci, A. (1971) *Selections from Prison Notebooks*, London: Lawrence & Wishart.

Grant, D. (1989) *Learning Relations*, London: Routledge.

Gray, E.D. (1981) *Green Paradise Lost*, Wellesley, MA: Roundtable Press.

Green, A., Wolf, A. and Leney, T. (1999) *Convergence and Divergence in European Education and Training Systems*, London: Institute of Education.

Green, D. (1997) *Faces of Latin America*, 2nd edn, London: Latin American Bureau.

Green, D. (2003) *Silent Revolution: The Rise and Crisis of Market Economics in Latin America*, London: Latin America Bureau.

Green, E. and Singleton, C. (2007) 'Risky bodies at leisure', *Sociology* 40(5): 853–71.

Green, E., Hebron, S. and Woodward, D. (1990) *Women's Leisure, What Leisure?*, London: Macmillan.

Grewal, A., *et al.* (2000) *Images of Disability: Evidence presented to the DRC*, London: DRC.

Griffin, S. (1978) *Women and Nature: The Roaring Inside Her*, New York: Harper & Row.

Griffiths, C., Fosgter, G., Ramsay, J., Eldrige, S. and Taylor, S. (2007) 'How effective are expert patient (lay led) education programmes for chronic disease?', *British Medical Journal* 334: 1254–6.

Grint, K. (2005) *The Sociology of Work*, 3rd edn, Cambridge: Polity Press.

Gross, E. (1992) 'What is feminist theory', in H. Crowley and S. Himmelweit (eds) *Knowing Women*, Cambridge: Polity.

Guba, E.G. and Lincoln, Y.S. (1994) 'Competing paradigms in qualitative research', in N.K. Denzin and Y.S. Lincoln (eds) *Handbook of Qualitative Research*, Thousand Oaks, CA: Sage.

Gubrium, J. and Wallace, J. (1990) 'Who theorises age', *Ageing and Society* 10(2): 131–50.

Gubrium, J.F. and Holstein, J.A. (1997) *The New Language of Qualitative Method*, New York: Oxford University Press.

Gunter, B. (1985) *Dimensions of Television Violence*, Aldershot: Gower.

Gunter, B. and McAleer, J. (1990) *Children and Television: The One Eyed Monster*, London: Routledge.

Gutiérrez, G. (1973) *A Theology of Liberation*, Maryknoll, NY: Orbis.

H

Habermas, J. (1971a) *Legitimation Crisis*, London: Heinemann.

Habermas, J. (1971b) *Knowledge and Human Interests*, trans. J. Shapiro, Boston, MA: Beacon Press.

Hadden, J.K. (1987) 'Towards desacralizing secularization theory', *Social Forces* 65: 587–611.

Hafferty, F.W. and McKinlay, J.B. (1993) 'Cross cultural perspectives on the dynamics of medicine as a profession', in F.W. Hafferty and J.B. McKinlay (eds) *The Changing Medical Profession: An International Perspective*, Oxford: Oxford University Press.

Hakim, C. (1979) 'Occupational segregation: a comparative study of the degree and patterns of differentiation between men's and women's work in Britain, the United States and other countries', research paper 9, London: Department of Employment.

Hall, J.R. (2004) 'Apocalypse 9/11', in P.C. Lucas and T. Robbins (eds) *New Religious Movements in the Twenty-First Century: Legal, Political and Social Challenges in Global Perspective*, New York and London: Routledge.

Hall, S. (1977) 'The "political" and the "economic" in Marx's theory of classes', in A. Hunt (ed.) *Class and Class Structure*, London: Lawrence & Wishart.

Hall, S. (1992) 'New ethnicities', in J. Donals and A. Rattansi (eds) *Race, Culture and Difference*, London: Sage/Open University Press.

Hall, S. (1997) (ed.) *Representation: Cultural Representations and Signifying Practices*, London: Sage.

Hall, S. and Jacques, M. (1989) *New Times*, London: Lawrence & Wishart.

Hall, S. and Jefferson, T. (1976) *Resistance through Rituals*, London: Hutchinson.

Hall, S., *et al.* (1979) *Policing the Crisis: Mugging, the State, and Law and Order*, London: Macmillan.

Hall, S., Held, D. and McGrew, T. (eds) (1992) *Modernity and its Futures*, Cambridge: Polity Press.

Halsey, A.H., Floud, J. and Anderson, C.A. (1961) *Education, Economy and Society*, New York: Free Press.

Halsey, A.H., Heath, A.F. and Ridge, J.M. (1980) *Origins and Destinations: Family, Class and Education in Modern Britain*, Oxford: Clarendon.

Halsey, A.H., Lauder, H., Brown, P. and Wells, A.S. (1997) *Education, Culture, Economy, Society*, Oxford: Oxford University Press.

Hammersley, M. (1992) 'Introducing ethnography', *Sociology Review* 2(2): 18–23.

Hamnett, C. (2004) 'In both Britain and United States, wealth inequality has increased since the 1970s', *Independent* 3.8.2004.

Hannigan, J.A. (1995) *Environmental Sociology: A Social Constructionist Perspective*, London: Routledge.

Hansen, E.C., Walters, J. and Wood Baker, R. (2007) 'Explaining chronic obstructive pulmonary disease (COPD): perceptions of the role played by smoking', *Sociology of Health and Illness* 29(5): 730–49.

Harden, J. (2001) '"Mother Russia" at work: gender divisions in the medical profession', *European Journal of Women's Studies* 8(2): 181–99.

Harden, J. (2005) '"Uncharted waters": the experience of parents of young people with mental health problems', *Qualitative Health Research* 15(2): 207–23.

Hardin, G. (1968) 'The tragedy of the commons', *Science* 162: 1243–8.

Harding, S. (1987) *Feminism and Methodology*, Milton Keynes: Open University Press.

Hardman, C. (2001 [1973]) 'Can there be an anthropology of children?' *Childhood* 8(4): 501–17.

Hargreaves, A. (1994) *Changing Teachers, Changing Times: Teachers' Work and Culture in the Postmodern Age*, Toronto: University of Toronto Press.

Hargreaves, D.H. (1967) *Social Relations in a Secondary School*, London: Routledge & Kegan Paul.

Hargreaves, D.H. (1978) 'Power and the paracurriculum', in C. Richards (ed.) *Power and the Curriculum: Issues in Curriculum Studies*, Driffield: Nafferton.

Harraway, D. (1991) *Simians, Cyborgs and Women*, London: Free Association Books.

Harris, N. (1992) 'Codes of conduct for journalists', in A. Belsey and R. Chadwick (eds) *Ethical Issues in Journalism and the Media*, London: Routledge.

Harrison, T. and Madge, C. (1986 [1939]) *Britain by Mass Observation*, London: Hutchinson.

Hart, G. and Carter, S. (2000) 'A sociology of risk behaviour', in S.J. Williams, J. Gabe and M. Calnan (eds) *Health, Medicine and Society: Key Theories, Future Agendas*, London: Routledge.

Hart, J. (1985) 'Why do women commit less crime?', *New Society* 30 August.

Hartmann, H. (1981) 'The unhappy marriage of Marxism and feminism: towards a more progressive union', in

L. Sergent (ed.) *Women and Revolution*, New York: Monthly Review.

Harvey, D. (1990) *The Condition of Postmodernity*, London: Blackwell.

Harvey, D. (1996) *Justice, Nature and the Geography of Difference*, Oxford: Blackwell.

Harvey, J. (1997) 'The technological regulation of death: with reference to the technological regulation of birth', *Sociology* 31(4): 719–36.

Hastings, A. (1997) *The Construction of Nationhood*, Cambridge: Cambridge University Press.

Haug, M. (1973) 'Deprofessionalization: an alternative hypothesis for the future', *Sociological Review Monograph* 2: 195–211.

Hayek, F.A. (1960) *The Constitution of Liberty*, London: Routledge & Kegan Paul.

Hayek, F.A. (1976) *The Constitution of Liberty*, London: Routledge & Kegan Paul.

Hayes, D. and Hudson, A. (2001) *The Mood of the Nation*, Basildon: Demos.

Haymes, S. (1996) 'Race, repression and the politics of crime in the bell curve', in J. Kincheloe, S.R. Steinberg and A.D. Gresson (eds) *Measured Lies: The Bell Curve Examined*, New York: St Martin's Press.

Hearn, G. (1987) *The Gender of Oppression: Men, Masculinity and the Critique of Marxism*, London: Pluto.

Hearn, J. (1996) 'Is masculinity dead? A critique of the concept of masculinity/masculinities', in M. Mac an Ghaill (ed.) *Understanding Masculinities*, Buckingham: Open University Press.

Heath, A. (1992) 'The attitudes of the underclass', in D.J. Smith (ed.) *Understanding the Underclass*, London: Policy Studies Institute.

Hebdige, D. (1979) *Subculture: The Meaning of Style*, London: Methuen.

Hecht, T. (1998) *At Home in the Street: Street Children of Northeast Brazil*, Cambridge: Cambridge University Press.

Heelas, P. (1996) *The New Age Movement*, Oxford: Blackwell.

Heelas, P. (2006) 'The infirmity debate: on the viability of New Age spiritualities of life', *Journal of Contemporary Religion* 21(2): 223–40.

Heelas, P. and Woodhead, L. (2005) *The Spiritual Revolution: Why religion Is Giving Way to Spirituality*, Oxford: Blackwell.

Heery, E. and Salmon, J. (eds) (2000) *The Insecure Workforce*, London: Routledge.

Hegewisch, A. and Pilinger, J. (2006) *Out of Time: Why Britain Needs a New Approach to Working-Time Flexibility*, Manchester, Trades Union Congress.

Heidensohn, F. (1989) *Crime and Society*, London: Macmillan.

Heidensohn, F. (2002) 'Gender and crime', in M. Maguire, R. Morgan and R. Reiner (eds) *The Oxford Handbook of Criminology*, 3rd edn, Oxford: Oxford University Press.

Held, D. (ed.) (1991) *Political Theory Today*, Cambridge: Polity Press.

Held, D. (1995) *Democracy and the Global Order*, Cambridge: Polity Press.

Held, D. (2000) *A Globalizing World? Culture, Economics and Politics*, London: Routledge.

Hendy, N. (2000) *Radio in the Global Age*, Cambridge: Polity Press.

Henley Centre (1993) *Media Futures*, London: Henley Centre.

Henry, C. and Hiltel, M. (1977) *Children of the SS*, London: Corgi.

Henwood, F., Wyatt, S., Hart, A. and Smith, J. (2003) 'Ignorance is bliss sometimes: constraints on the emergence of the informed patient in the changing landscapes of health information', *Sociology of Health and Illness* 25(6): 589–607.

Herman, E. and Chomsky, N. (1988) *Manufacturing Consent: The Political Economy of the Mass Media*, New York: Pantheon Books.

Hermes, J. (1995) *Reading Women's Magazines*, London: Routledge.

Herrnstein, R. and Murray, C. (1994) *The Bell Curve: Intelligence and the Class Structure*, New York: Free Press.

Hettne, B. (1995) *Development Theory and the Three Worlds*, London: Longman.

Heywood, C. (2001) *A History of Childhood: Children and Childhood in the West from Medieval to Modern Times*, Cambridge: Polity Press.

Hibbert, A. and Meager, N. (2003) 'Key indicators of women's position in Britain', *Labour Market Trends* 111(10).

Hibbett, A. (2002) *Ethnic Minority Women in the UK*, London: Women and Equality Unit.

Hiestand, Katherine R. and Levitt, Heidi M. (2005), 'Butch Identity Development: The Formation of an Authentic Gender', *Feminism and Psychology*, 15(1), 61–85.

Hill-Collins, P. (1990) *Black Feminist Thought: Knowledge, Consciousness, and the Politics of Empowerment*, London: Unwin Hyman.

Hilton, R.H. (1969) *The Decline of Serfdom in Medieval England*, London: Macmillan.

Hirst, J. (2004) 'Sexuality', in G. Taylor and S. Spencer (eds) *Social Identities: Multidisciplinary Approaches*, London: Routledge.

Hirst, P. and Thompson, G. (eds) (1996) *Globalization in Question: The International Economy and the Possibilities of Governance*, Cambridge: Polity Press.

Hitler, A. (1969 [1925]) *Mein Kampf*, trans. R. Manheim, London: Hutchinson.

Hobsbawm, E. (1998) 'Markets, meltdown and Marx', *Guardian*, 20 October.

Hobsbawm, E. and Ranger, T. (1983) *The Invention of Tradition*, Cambridge: Cambridge University Press.

Hockey, J. (1997) 'Women and health', in D. Richarson and V. Robinson (eds) *Introducing Women's Studies*, 2nd edn, London: Macmillan.

Hockey, J. and James, A. (1993) *Growing Up and Growing Old*, London: Sage.

Hockey, J. and James, A. (2003) *Social Identities across the Life Course*, Basingstoke: Palgrave Macmillan.

Hodge, B. and Tripp, D. (1986) *Children's Television*, Cambridge: Polity Press.

Hofman, R.H., Hofman, W.H.A. and Gray, J.M. (2008) 'Comparing key dimensions of schooling: towards a typology of European school systems', *Comparative Education* 44(1): 97.

Hollway, W. (1994) 'Women's power in heterosexual sex', *Women's Studies International Forum* 7: 66–8.

Holland, J. (2005) www.thinkingpeace.com/pages/arts2/arts352.html 22/1/05

Holliday, R. (2008) 'Media and popular culture', in D. Richardson and V. Robinson (eds) *Introducing Gender and Women's Studies*, Houndsmills: Palgrave Macmillan.

Holmes, E.R. and Holmes, L.D. (1995) *Other Cultures, Elder Years*, London: Sage.

Holt, J. (1969) *How Children Fail*, Harmondsworth: Penguin.

Home Office (1992) *Criminal Statistics*, London: HMSO.

Home Office (2002) *Annual Abstract of Statistics*, London: HMSO.

Home Office (2008) *Home Office Department Report*, London: HMSO.

Hood-Williams, J. (1990) 'Patriarchy for children: on the stability of power relations in children's lives', in L. Chisholm *et al.* (eds) *Childhood, Youth and Social Change: A Comparative Perspective*, London: Falmer Press.

hooks, b. (1984) *Feminist Theory: From Margin to Center*, Boston, MA: South End Press.

Horkheimer, M. and Adorno, T. (1973 [1944]) *Dialetic of the Enlightenment*, Harmondsworth: Allen Lane.

Horowitz, I. (2001) 'Cultural practices of masculinity in post-apartheid South Africa', in B. Pease and K. Pringle (eds) *A Man's World? Changing Men's Practices in a Globalized World*, London: Zed Books.

House of Lords Select Committee on Science and Technology (2000) *Sixth Report on Complementary and Alternative Medicine*, London: HMSO.

Houtt, M., Brooks, C. and Manza, J. (1996) 'The persistence of classes in post-industrial societies', in D. Lee and B.S. Turner (eds) *Conflicts about Class: Debating Inequality in Late Industrialism*, London: Longman.

Howson, A. (1999) 'Cervical screening, compliance and moral obligation', *Sociology of Health and Illness* 21(4): 401–25.

Howson, A. (2004) *The Body in Society: An Introduction*, Cambridge: Polity Press.

Hoyles, M. (ed.) (1979) *Changing Childhood*, London: Writer and Reader Publishing Cooperative.

Hubbard, L.R. (1950) *Dianetics: The Modern Science of Mental Health*, New York: Paperback Library.

Hughes, J. (1984) 'The concept of class', in R. Anderson and W. Sharrock (eds) *Teaching Papers in Sociology*, London: Longman.

Hughes, K. (2004) 'Health as individual responsibility: possibilities and personal struggle', in P. Tovey, G. Easthope, and J. Adams (eds) *The Mainstreaming of Complementary and Alternative Medicine: Studies in Social Context*, London: Routledge.

Human Development Report (1992) Global Dimensions of Human Development (UNDP). Published for the United Nations Development Programme, New York: Oxford University Press. http://hdr.undp.org.en/reports/global/hdr/1992/chapters/

Humm, M. (ed.) (1992) *Feminisms: A Reader*, Hemel Hempstead: Harvester Wheatsheaf.

Hunt, S. (2005a) *The Life Course: A Sociological Introduction*, Basingstoke: Palgrave Macmillan.

Hunt, S. (2005b) *Religion and Everyday Life*, Abingdon: Routledge.

Huntingdon, S. (1993) 'The clash of civilizations?', *Foreign Affairs* 72(3): 22–49.

Huss, B. (2007) 'The New Age of Kabbalah: contemporary Kabbalah, the New Age and postmodern spirituality', *Journal of Modern Jewish Studies* 6(2): 107–25.

Hussain, S. (2008) 'Counting women with faith: what quantitative data can reveal about Muslim women in "secular" Britain', in K. Aune, S. Sharma and G. Vincett (eds) *Women and Religion in the West: Challenging Secularization*, Aldershot: Ashgate.

Huxley, J.S. and Haddon, H.C. (1935) *We Europeans*, London: Jonathan Cape.

I

Ignatieff, M. (1994) *Blood and Belonging: Journeys into the New Nationalism*, London: Vintage.

Illich, I. (1976) *Limits to Medicine*, London: Boyers.

Independent Television Commission (ITC) (1993) *Television: The Public's View*, London: Independent Television Commission and John Libbey.

Institute of Public Policy Research (IPPR) (1993) *Education: A Different Vision*, London: Institute of Public Policy Research.

IPCC (1990) *IPCC First Assessment Report: Climate Change 1990*, http://www.ipcc.ch/ipccreports/assessments-reports.htm

IPCC (1995) *IPCC Second Assessment Report: Climate Change 1995*, http://www.ipcc.ch/ipccreports/assessments-reports.htm

IPCC (2001) *IPCC Third Assessment Report: Climate Change 2001*, http://www.ipcc.ch/ipccreports/assessments-reports.htm

IPCC (2007) *IPCC Fourth Assessment Report: Climate Change 2007*, http://www.ipcc.ch/ipccreports/assessments-reports.htm

Itzin, C. (1990) 'Age and sexual divisions: a study of opportunity and identity in women', PhD thesis, Canterbury: University of Kent.

Itzin, C. (1994) 'A harm-based equality approach to legislating against pornography without censorship', paper presented at Sexualities in Social Context Conference, University of Central Lancashire, Preston, 28–31 March.

J

Jackson, B. and Marsden, D. (1963) *Education and the Working Class*, London: Routledge & Kegan Paul.

Jackson, D. (1990) *Unmasking Masculinity: A Critical Autobiography*, London: Routledge.

Jackson, P. (1968) *Life in Classrooms*, New York: Holt, Rinehart & Winston.

Jackson, S. and Scott, S. (eds) (1996) *Feminism and Sexuality: A Reader*, Edinburgh: Edinburgh University Press.

Jackson, S. and Scott, A. (2000) 'Childhood' in G. Payne (ed.) *Social Divisions*, London: Macmillan.

Jacobs, M. (1999) 'Sustainable development as a contested concept', in A. Dobson (ed.) *Fairness and Futurity Essays on Environmental Sustainability and Social Justice*, Oxford: Oxford University Press.

Jacobs, S., Jacobson, R. and Marchbank, J. (eds) (2000) *States of Conflict: Gender, Violence and Resistance*, London: Zed Books.

Jagger, G. and Wright, C. (1999) 'Introduction', in G. Jagger and C. Wright (eds) *Changing Family Values*, London: Routledge.

James, A. and Prout, A. (1990) *Constructing and Reconstructing Childhood: Contemporary Issues in the Sociological Study of Childhood*, London: Falmer Press.

James, A., Jenks, C. and Prout, A. (1998) *Theorizing Childhood*, Cambridge: Polity Press.

James, W. (1890) *Principles of Psychology*, London: Henry Holt.

Jamieson, L. (1998) *Intimacy: Personal Relationships in Modern Societies*, Cambridge: Polity Press.

Jamieson, L. (2005) 'Boundaries of intimacy', in L. McKie and S. Cunningham-Burley (eds) *Families in Society: Boundaries and Relationships*, Bristol: Policy Press.

Jamrozik, A. and Nocella, L. (1998) *The Sociology of Social Problems*, Cambridge: Cambridge University Press.

Jasanoff, S. (2007) 'Bhopal's trials of knowledge and ignorance', *Isis* 98: 344–50.

Jayaratne, T.E. (1993) 'The value of quantitative methodology for feminist research', in M. Hammersley (ed.) *Social Research Philosophy, Politics and Practice*, London: Sage.

Jeffrey, B. and Woods, P. (1998) *Testing Teachers: The Effect of School Inspections on Primary Teachers*, London: Falmer Press.

Jeffrey, C. and McDowell, L. (2004) 'Youth in a comparative perspective: global change, local lives', *Youth and Society*, 36(2): 131–42.

Jeffreys, S. (1990) *Anticlimax: A Feminist Perspective on the Sexual Revolution*, London: Women's Press.

Jeffreys, S. (1994) *The Lesbian Heresy: A Feminist Perspective on the Lesbian Sexual Revolution*, London: Women's Press.

Jencks, C. (1993) *Culture*, London: Routledge.

Jenkins, P. (1987) *Mrs Thatcher's Revolution*, London: Jonathan Cape.

Jenkins, R. (2008) *Social Identity*, 3rd edn, London: Routledge.

Jenkins, S. (1986) *Market for Glory*, London: Faber & Faber.

Jenks, C. (1996) *Childhood*, London: Routledge.

Jensen, A. and McKee, L. (2003) 'Theorising Childhood and Family Change', in A. Jensen and L. McKee (eds) *Children and the Changing Family: Between Transformation and Negotiation*, London: RoutledgeFalmer.

Jensen, A.R. (1973) *Educational Differences*, London: Methuen.

Jermier, J.M., Knights, D. and Nord, R.W. (eds) (1994) *Resistance and Power in Organisations*, London: Routledge.

Jess, P. (1995) *A Place in the World?: Places, Cultures, and Globalization*, Oxford: Oxford University Press.

Jewson, N.D. (1976) 'The disappearance of the sick man from medical cosmology', *Sociology* 10(2): 225–44.

Johnson, J. and Bytheway, B. (1993) 'Ageism: concept and definition,' in J. Johnson and R. Slater (eds) *Ageing and Later Life*, London: Sage.

Johnson, R. (1983) 'Educational politics: the old and the new', in A.M. Wolpe and J. Donald (eds) *Is There Anyone Here from Education?*, London: Pluto.

Johnson, S. (2005) *Everything Bad is Good for You*, London: Allen Lane.

Johnson, V., Hill, J. and Ivan-Smith, E. (1995) *Listening to Smaller Voices: Children in an Environment of Change*, Chard: ACTIONAID.

Jones, C. and Mahony, P. (1989) *Learning our Lines*, London: Women's Press.

Jones, N. (1995) *Soundbites and Spindoctors*, London: Cassell.

Jones, P. (2003) *Introducing Social Theory*, Cambridge: Polity Press.

Jordon, B. (1984) *Invitation to Social Work*, Oxford: Blackwell.

Jupp, V. and Norris, C. (1993) 'Traditions in documentary analysis', in M. Hammersley (ed.) *Social Research: Philosophy, Politics and Practice*, London: Sage.

K

Kabeer, N. (1994) *Reversed Realities: Gender Hierarchies in Development Thought*, London: Verso.

Kabeer, N. (2001) 'Conflicts over credit: re-evaluating the empowerment potential of loans to women in rural Bangladesh', *World Development*, 29(1): 63–84.

Kamin, L. (1977) 'Heredity, intelligence, politics and psychology', in N. Block and G. Dworkin (eds) *The IQ Controversy*, London: Quartet.

Kaplinsky, R. (2005) *Globalization, Poverty and Inequality*, Cambridge: Polity Press.

Karabel, J. and Halsey, A.H. (1977) *Power and Ideology in Education*, Oxford: Oxford University Press.

Karlsen, S. and Nazroo, J.Y. (2002) 'Agency and structure: the impact of ethnic identity and racism on the health of ethnic minority people', *Sociology of Health and Illness* 24(1): 1–20.

Kassebaum, G. and Baumann, B. (1965) 'Dimensions of the sick role in chronic illness', *Journal of Health and Social Behaviour* 6: 16–25.

Kastenbaum, R.J. (2004) *Death, Society, and Human Experience*, Boston, MA: Pearson Education.

Katz, E. and Lazarsfeld, P. (1955) *Personal Influence*, London: Free Press.

Kaul, H. (1991), 'Who cares? Gender inequality and care leave in the Nordic countries', *Acta Sociologica* 34: 115–25.

Keane, J. (1991) *The Media and Democracy*, Cambridge: Polity.

Kefyalew, F. (1996) 'The reality of child participation in research: experience from a capacity-building programme', *Childhood* 3(2): 203–13.

Kellehear, A. (1990) *Dying of Cancer: The Final Year of Life*, London: Harwood Academic Publishers.

Kellner, D. (1995) *Media Culture*, London: Routledge.

Kelly, A. (ed.) (1981) *The Missing Half: Girls and Science Education*, Manchester: Manchester University Press.

Kelly, E. (1988) *Surviving Sexual Violence*, Cambridge: Polity.

Kelly, E., Regan, L. and Burton, S. (1992) 'Defending the indefensible: quantitative methods and feminist research', in H. Hinds, A. Phoenix and J. Stacey (eds) *Working Out New Directions for Women's Studies*, Brighton: Falmer.

Kempe, H. (1962) 'The battered-child syndrome', *Journal of the American Medical Association* 181: 17–24.

Kemshall, H. (2003) *Understanding Risk in Criminal Justice*, Buckingham: Open University Press.

Kennedy, P. (1993) *Preparing for the 21st Century*, London: Random House.

Kent, J. (2000) *Social Perspectives on Pregnancy and Childbirth for Midwives, Nurses and the Caring Professions*, Buckingham: Open University.

Kent, R. (1981) *A History of British Empirical Sociology*, Aldershot: Gower.

Kenway, J. and Willis, S. (1990) *Hearts and Minds: Self-Esteem and the Schooling of Girls*, Darwin, Australia: Darwin University Press.

Kern, M. (1989) *30 Second Politics: Political Advertising in the Eighties*, New York: Praeger.

Kerr, C., Dunlop, J.T., Harbison, F.H. and Mayers, C.A. (1962) *Industrialism and Industrial Man*, London: Heinemann.

Khan, S. (2007) 'Creating new gender identity and space in the public sphere', in C. Beckett, O. Heathcote and M. Macey (eds) *Negotiating Boundaries? Identities, Sexualities, Diversities*, Newcastle: Cambridge Scholars Publishing.

Kiely, R. (1998) 'Introduction: globalisation, (post) modernity and the third world', in R. Kiely and P. Marfleet (eds) *Globalisation and the Third World*, London: Routledge.

Kiernan, K. (1992) 'The impact of family disruption in childhood on transitions in young adult life', *Population Studies* 46(3): 51–82.

Kilborn, R. (1992) *Television Soaps*, London: Batsford.

King, A. (1993) 'Mystery and imagination: the case of pornography effects studies', in A. Assiter and C. Avendon (eds) *Bad Girls and Dirty Pictures*, London: Pluto.

Kingdom, J. (1991) *Government and Politics in Britain*, Cambridge: Polity.

Klein, N. (2000) *No Logo*, Flamingo: London.

Kleinman, A. (1980) *Patients and Healers in the Context of Culture: An Exploration of the Borderland Between Anthropology, Medicine, and Psychiatry*, Berkeley, CA: University of California Press.

Kleinsteuber, H. (2009) 'The media in Europe', in D. Albertazzi and P. Cobley (eds) *The Media: An Introduction*, Harlow: Pearson.

Kodz, J., Harper, H. and Dench, S. (2002) *Work–life Balance: Beyond the Rhetoric*, Brighton: Institute for Employment Studies.

Kogan, M. (1975) *Educational Policy Making*, London: Allen & Unwin.

Kohn, M. (1996) *The Race Gallery*, London: Vintage.

Koss, S. (1973) *Fleet Street Radical: A G Gardiner and the Daily News*, London: Allen Lane.

Krippendorf, K. (1980) *Content Analysis: An Introduction to its Methodology*, London: Sage.

Kritzman, L. (1988) *Michel Foucault: Politics, Philosophy and Culture: Interviews and Other Writings 1977–1984*, New York: Routledge.

Kumar, K. (1978) *Prophecy and Progress: The Sociology of Industrial and Post-Industrial Society*, Harmondsworth: Penguin.

Kumar, K. (1995) *From Post-Industrial to Post-Modern Society*, Oxford: Blackwell.

Kurz, R. (1981) 'The Sociological Approach to Mental Retardation' in A. Brechin, P. Liddiard and J. Swain (eds) *Handicap in a Social World*, London: Open University Press.

Kvale, S. (1996) *Interviews: An Introduction to Qualitative Research Interviewing*, London: Sage.

L

Labov, W. (1969) 'The logic of non-standard English', in Giglioli, P.P. (ed.) *Language and Social Context*, Harmondsworth: Penguin.

Lacan, J. (1968) *The Language of the Self: The Function of Language in Psychoanalysis*, Baltimore, MD: Johns Hopkins University Press.

Lacey, C. (1970) *Hightown Grammar: The School as a Social System*, Manchester: Manchester University Press.

Lacquer, T. (1990) *Making Sex: Body and Gender from the Greeks to Freud*, Cambridge MA: Harvard University Press.

Lambert, Y. (2004) 'A Turning Point in Religious Evolution', *Journal of Contemporary Religion*, 19(1): 29–45.

Lash, S. and Urry, J. (1994) *Economies of Signs and Space*, London: Sage.

Lasswell, H. (1948) 'The structure and function of communications in society', in L. Bryson (ed.) *The Communication of Ideas*, London: Harper.

Lather, P. (1988) 'Feminist perspectives on empowering research methodology', *Women's Studies International Forum* 11(9): 569–81.

Laungani, P. (2005) 'Changing patterns of family life in India', in J. Roopnarine and U. Gielen (eds) *Families in Global Perspective*, London: Pearson Education.

Lavalette, M. and Cunningham, S. (2002) 'The sociology of childhood', in B. Goldson, M. Lavalette and J. McKechnie (eds) *Children, Welfare and the State*, London: Sage.

Lawson, T. (1986) 'In the shadow of science', *Social Studies Review* 2(2): 36–41.

Lawton, J. (1998) 'Contemporary hospice care: the sequestration of the unbounded body and "dirty dying"', *Sociology of Health and Illness* 20(2): 121–43.

Lazarsfeld, P., Berelson, B. and Gauder, H. (1944) *The People's Choice*, New York: Duell, Sloan & Pearce.

Lea, J. and Young, J. (1984) *What's to be Done About Law and Order?*, Harmondsworth: Penguin.

Lee, C.H. (1995) *Scotland and the UK*, Manchester: Manchester University Press.

Lee, D. and Newby, H. (1983) *The Problem of Sociology*, London: Hutchinson.

Lee, D. and Turner, B.S. (1996) *Conflicts about Class: Debating Inequality in Late Industrialism*, London: Longman.

Lees, S. (1986) *Losing Out: Sexuality and Adolescent Girls*, London: Hutchinson.

Lees, S. (1993) *Sugar and Spice: Sexuality and Adolescent Girls*, Harmondsworth: Penguin.

Lee-Treweek, G. (1994) 'Bedroom abuse: the hidden work in a nursing home', *Generations Review* 4(1): 2–4.

Lemert, C. (1997) *Social Things*, Oxford: Rowman & Littlefield.

Leonard, D. (1990) 'Persons in their own right: children and sociology in the UK', in L. Chisholm (ed.) *Childhood, Youth and Social Change: A Comparative Perspective*, London: Falmer Press.

Leopold, A. (1949) *A Sand Country Almanac and Sketches Here and There*, New York: Oxford University Press.

Lepkowska, D. (2004) 'Unsung success of Chinese pupils', *Times Educational Supplement*, 27 August.

Letherby, G. and Marchbank, J. (2003) 'Cyber-chattels: buying brides and babies on the net' in Y. Jewkes (ed.) *Dot.cons: Crime, Deviance and Identity on the Internet*, Collumpton: Willan.

Letherby, G., Williams, K., Birch, P. and Cain, M. (eds) (2008) *Sex as Crime?*, Cullompton: Willan.

Levin, I. (2004) 'Living apart together: a new family form,' *Current Sociology 52*(2): 223–40.

Levin, J. (1993) *Sociological Snapshots*, Newbury Park, CA: Pine Forge Press.

Levi-Strauss, C. (1994) 'Anthropology, race and politics: a conversation with Didier Eribon', in R. Borofsky (ed.) *Assessing Anthropology*, New York: McGraw-Hill.

Levy, S. (2004) 'Google's Two Revolutions', *Newsweek*, 27 December.

Lewis, G. (1986) 'Concepts of health and illness in a Sepik society', in C. Currer and M. Stacey (eds) *Concepts of Health, Illness and Disease: A Comparative Perspective*, Leamington Spa: Berg.

Lewis, J. (2001) *The End of Marriage*, Cheltenham: Edward Elgar.

Lewis, J. and Ritchie, J. (2003) 'Generalising from qualitative research', in J. Ritchie and J. Lewis (eds) *Qualitative Research Practice*, London: Sage.

Lewis, L. (1990) *The Adoring Audience*, London: Unwin Hyman.

Lewis, O. (1961) *The Children of Sanchez*, New York: Random House.

Lichter, S., Rotham, S. and Lichter, L. (1986) *The Media Elite: America's New Powerbrokers*, Bethesda, MD: Adler & Adler.

Light, D. (1995) 'Counterveilling powers: a framework for professions in transition', in T. Johnson, G. Larkin and M. Saks (eds) *Health Professions and the State in Europe*, London: Routledge.

Lijphart, A. (1977) *Democracy in Plural Societies: A Comparative Exploration*, New Haven, CT: Yale University Press.

Linzey, A. and Barsam, A. (2001) 'St Francis of Assisi', in J. Palmer (ed.) *Fifty Key Thinkers on the Environment*, London: Routledge.

Littler, C.R. (1982) *The Development of the Labour Process in Capitalist Societies*, London: Heinemann.

Llobera, J.R. (1994) *The God of Modernity: The Development of Nationalism in Western Europe*, Oxford: Berg.

Lock, M. (2002) *Twice Dead: Organ Transplants and the Reinvention of Death*, Berkeley, CA: University of California Press.

Lockwood, D. (1989 [1958]) *The Blackcoated Worker*, 2nd edn, Oxford: Oxford University Press.

Lodge, P. and Blackstone, T. (1982) *Educational Policy and Educational Inequality*, Oxford: Martin Robertson.

Lomborg, B., with Action Aid (2002) Special report: earth – health check for a planet under pressure, *Guardian*, 21 August.

Lombroso, C. (1876) *L'Uomo Delinquente [The Criminal Man]*, Turin: Fratelli Bocca.

Longhurst, B., Smith, G., Bagnall, G., Crawford, G., Ogborn, M., Baldwin, E. and McCracken, S. (2008) *Introducing Cultural Studies*, Harlow: Pearson Education.

Lovelace, C. (1978) 'British press censorship during the First World War', in G. Boyce (ed.) *Newspaper History: From the Seventeenth Century to the Present Day*, London: Constable.

Lovelock, J. (1979) *Gaia: A New Look at Life on Earth*, Oxford: Oxford University Press.

Low, J. and Murray, K.B. (2006) 'Lay acquiescence to medical dominance: reflections on the active citizenship thesis', *Social Theory and Health* 4: 109–27.

Luckmann, T. (1967) *The Invisible Religion: The Problem of Religion in Modern Society*, New York: Macmillan.

Lull, J. (1995) *Media, Communication and Culture*, Cambridge: Polity Press.

Lull, J. (2000) *Media Communication Culture: A Global Approach*, 2nd edn, Cambridge: Polity Press.

Lupton, D. (1994) *Medicine as Culture*, London: Sage.

Lupton, D. (1997) 'Consumerism, reflexivity and the medical encounter', *Social Science and Medicine* 45(3): 373–81.

Lupton, D. (2003) *Medicine as Culture: Illness, Disease and the Body in Western Culture*, London: Sage.

Lupton, D. and Barclay, L. (1997) *Constructing Fatherhood: Discourses and Experiences*, London: Sage.

Lyndon, N. (1992) *No More Sex War: The Failures of Feminism*, London: Sinclair-Stevenson.

Lyotard, J. (1985) *The Postmodern Condition*, Minneapolis, MN: University of Minneapolis Press.

M

Mac an Ghaill, M. (1996) 'Sociology of education, state schooling and social class: beyond critiques of the New Right hegemony', *British Journal of Sociology of Education* 17(2): 163–76.

Mac an Ghaill, M. (1999) *Contemporary Racisms and Ethnicities*, Buckingham: Open University Press.

Mac an Ghaill, M. and Haywood, C. (2007) *Gender, Culture and Society: Contemporary Femininities and Masculinities*, Houndsmills: Palgrave Macmillan.

MacDonald, I. (2003) *The People's Music*, Pimlico.

Macionis, J. and Plummer, K. (1998) *Sociology: A Global Introduction*, London: Prentice Hall.

Macionis, J. and Plummer, K. (2002) *Sociology: A Global Introduction*, 2nd edn, Harlow: Pearson Education.

Macionis, J. and Plummer, K. (2008) *Sociology: A Global Introduction*, 4th edn, Harlow: Pearson Education.

Mackay, H. (2000) 'The globalization of culture?', in D. Held (ed.) *A Globalizing World? Culture, Economics, Politics*, London: Routledge.

Mackenbach, J. (2006) *Health Inequalities: Europe in Profile*, London: Department of Health.

MacKinnon, C. (1982) 'Feminism, Marxism, method and the state: an agenda for theory', *Signs* 7(3): 515–44.

MacKinnon, C. (1987) *Feminism Unmodified: Discourses on Life and Law*, Cambridge, MA: Harvard University Press.

MacLean, C. (1977) *The Wolf Children*, London: Allen Lane.

Macpherson, W. (1999) *The Stephen Lawrence Inquiry*, London: The Stationary Office.

MacRury, I. (2009) 'Advertising and the New Media Environment' in D. Albertazzi and P. Cobley (eds) *The Media: An Introduction*, 3nd edition, Harlow: Longman (forthcoming).

Madeley, J.T.S. (2003) 'European Liberal Democracy' in J.T.S. Madeley and Z. Engedi (eds) *Church and State in Contemporary Europe*, London: Frank Cass.

Magida, A.J. (ed.) (1996) *How to Be a Perfect Stranger: A Guide to Etiquette in Other People's Religious Ceremonies*, Woodstock, VT: Jewish Lights Publishing.

Maguire, M. (2002) 'Crime Statistics: the "data explosion" and its implications', in R. Morgan and R. Reiner (eds) *The Oxford Handbook of Criminology*, 3rd edn, Oxford: Oxford University Press.

Malamuth, N., Addison, A. and Koss, M. (2000) 'Pornography and sexual aggression: are there reliable effects and can we understand them?', *Annual Review of Sex Research* 11: 26–91.

Malson, L. and Itard, J. (1972) *Wolf Children*, London: New Left Books.

Mannheim, K. (1952) *Essays in the Sociology of Knowledge*, London: Routledge.

Manning, P. (1992) *Erving Goffman and Modern Sociology*, Cambridge: Polity.

Mao Zedong (1966) *Quotations from Chairman Mao Tse-Tung*, Beijing: Foreign Languages Press.

Marchbank, J. (2000) *Women, Power and Policy: Comparative Studies of Childcare*, London: Routledge.

Marchbank, J. (2008) 'War and sex crime', in G. Letherby, K. Williams, P. Birch and M. Cain (eds) *Sex as Crime?*, Cullompton: Willan.

Marchbank, J. and Letherby, G. (2007) *Introduction to Gender: Social Science Perspectives*, Harlow: Pearson Education.

Marcuse, H. (1964) *One Dimensional Man: Studies in the Ideology of Advanced Industrial Society*, Boston, MA: Beacon.

Marris, P. and Thornham, S. (1997) *Media Studies: A Reader*, Edinburgh: Edinburgh University Press.

Mars, G. (1982) *Cheats at Work: An Anthology of Workplace Crime*, London: Allen & Unwin.

Marsh, I., Campbell, R. and Keating, M. (eds) (1998) *Classic and Contemporary Readings in Sociology*, Harlow: Addison Wesley Longman.

Marshall, G. and Swift, A. (1993) 'Social classes and social justice', *British Journal of Sociology*, 44: 206.

Marshall, G., Newby, H., Rose, D. and Vogler, C. (1988) *Social Class in Modern Britain*, London: Hutchinson.

Marshall, T.H. (1950) *Citizenship and Social Class*, Cambridge: Cambridge University Press.

Martin, J. and Roberts, C. (1984) *Women and Employment: A Lifetime Perspective*, London: HMSO.

Martin, K.A. (2002) '"I couldn't ever picture myself having sex . . .": gender differences in sex and sexual subjectivity', in C.L. Williams and A. Stein (eds) *Sexuality and Gender*, Oxford: Blackwell.

Marx, K. (1959 [1844]) *Economic and Philosophic Manuscripts of 1844*, Moscow: Progress Publishers.

Marx, K. (1967 [1867]) *Das Kapital*, Vol. 1, London: Lawrence & Wishart.

Marx, K. (1969 [1875]) 'Critique of the Gotha Programme', in L.S. Feuer (ed.) *Marx and Engels: Basic Writings on Politics and Philosophy*, London: Fontana.

Marx, K. (1970 [1845]) *The German Ideology: Students' Edition*, London: Lawrence & Wishart.

Marx, K. and Engels, F. (1947 [1846]) *The German Ideology*, New York: International Publishers.

Marx, K. and Engels, F. (1952 [1848]) *The Manifesto of the Communist Party*, Moscow: Progress.

Marx, K. and Engels, F. (1955) *On Religion*, Moscow: Foreign Languages Publishing House.

Marx, K. and Engels, F. (1976) *Collected Works*, 10 vols, London: Lawrence & Wishart.

Mason, J. (2002) *Qualitative Researching*, 2nd edn, London: Sage.

Massey, D. (1994) *Space, Place and Gender*, Oxford: Polity Press.

Massey, D. and Allen, J. (1988) *Uneven Re-Development: Cities and Regions in Transition*, London: Hodder & Stoughton.

Masterman, L. (1985) *Teaching About Television*, London: Macmillan.

Masterman, L. (ed.) (1986) *Television Mythologies*, London: Comedia.

Matthews, B. (2000) 'The body beautiful: adolescent girls and images of beauty', in L.G. Beauman (ed.) *New Perspectives on Deviance: The Construction of Deviance in Everyday Life*, Scarborough, ON: Prentice Hall.

Matza, D. (1969) *Becoming Deviant*, London: Prentice-Hall.

Mauthner, M. (2000) 'Snippets and silences: ethics and reflexivity in narratives of sistering', *International Journal of Social Research Methodology*.

Mauthner, M. (2002) *Sistering: Power and Change in Female Relationships*, Basingstoke: Palgrave Macmillan.

Mauthner, M. (2005) 'Distant lives, still voices: sistering in family sociology', *Sociology* 39(4): 623–42.

Mauthner, N., McKee, L. and Strell, M. (2001) *Work and Family Life in Rural Communities*, Bristol: Policy Press and Joseph Rowntree Foundation.

Mayall, B. (2002) *Towards a Sociology for Childhood*, Buckingham: Open University Press.

Mayerfield-Bell, M. (1998) *An Invitation to Environmental Sociology*, Thousand Oaks, CA: Pine Forge Press.

Mayhew, H. (1949) 'Mayhew's London', in P. Quennell (ed.) *Mayhew's London*, London: Pilot.

Maynard, M. (1990) 'The reshaping of sociology? Trends in the study of gender', *Sociology* 24(2): 269–90.

Mays, J.B. (1954) *Growing up in the City*, Liverpool: University of Liverpool Press.

McCormick, J. (1995) *The Global Environmental Movement*, 2nd edn, London: Belhaven.

McCrone, D. (1998) *The Sociology of Nationalism*, London: Routledge.

McCulloch, J.R. (1825) *Principles of Political Economy: With a Sketch of the Rise and Progress of Science*, London.

McDowell, E. and Chalmers, D. (1999) 'Sustainable development in Scotland: responses from the grassroots', in E. McDowell, E. and J. McCormick (eds) *Environment Scotland: Prospects for Sustainability*, Aldershot: Ashgate.

McDowell, L. (1999) *Gender, Identity and Place: Understanding Feminist Geographies*, Cambridge: Polity Press.

McFadden, M.G. (1996) 'Resistance to schooling and educational outcomes: questions of structure and agency', *British Journal of Sociology of Education* 16(3): 293–308.

McGee, R. (2002) 'Participating in development', in U. Kothari and M. Minogue (eds) *Development Theory and Practice: Critical Perspectives*, Basingstoke: Palgrave.

McGhee, D. (2005) *Intolerant Britain: Hate, Citizenship and Difference*, Maidenhead: Open University Press.

McGinty, A.M. (2007) 'Formation of alternative femininities through Islam: feminist approaches among Muslim converts in Sweden', *Women's Studies International Forum* 30: 474–85.

McGrew, A. (2000) 'Sustainable globalization? The global politics of development and exclusion in the new world order', in T. Allen and A. Thomas (eds) *Poverty and Development into the 21st Century*, Oxford: Oxford University Press.

McGuire, M. (2002) *Religion: The Social Context*, 5th edn, Belmont, CA: Wadsworth.

McIlroy, J. (1995) *Trade Unions in Britain Today*, 2nd edn, Manchester: Manchester University Press.

McIntosh, I. (1991) 'Ford at Trafford Park', unpublished PhD thesis, Manchester: University of Manchester.

McIntosh, I. (1995) 'It was worse than Alcatraz: working for Ford at Trafford Park', *Manchester Regional History Review* May: 9.

McIntosh, I. and Broderick, J. (1996) 'Neither one thing nor the other: competitive compulsory tendering and Southburch Cleansing Services', *Work, Employment and Society* 10: 2.

McIntosh, I. and Punch, S. (2005) *Get Set for Sociology*, Edinburgh: Edinburgh University Press.

McIntosh, I. and Punch, S. (2009) '"Barter", "deals", "bribes" and "threats": exploring sibling interactions', *Childhood* 16(1): 49–65.

McIntyre, L.J. (2005) *Need to Know: Social Science Research Methods*, New York: McGraw-Hill.

McKay, G. (1996) *Senseless Acts of Beauty: Cultures of Resistance Since the 1960s*, London: Verso.

McKenzie, J. (1993) *Education as a Political Issue*, Aldershot: Avebury.

McKenzie, J. (2001) *Changing Education: A Sociology of Education Since 1944*, Harlow: Prentice Hall.

McKie, L., Cunningham-Burley, S. and McKendrick, J. (2005) 'Families and relationships: boundaries and bridges', in L. McKie and S. Cunningham-Burley (eds) *Families in Society: Boundaries and Relationships*, Bristol: Policy Press.

McKinlay, J. and Stoekle, J. (1988) 'Corporatization and the social transformation of doctoring', *International Journal of Health Services* 18: 191–205.

McLaughlin, J. (1997) 'Feminist relations with postmodernism: reflections on the positive aspects of involvement', *Journal of Gender Studies* 6: 1, 5–15.

McLuhan, M. (1964) *Understanding Media*, London: Routledge & Kegan Paul.

McLuhan, M. and Fiore, Q. (1967) *The Medium is the Message*, Harmondsworth: Penguin.

McMichael, P. (2000) *Development and Social Change: A Global Perspective*, 2nd edn, London: Pine Forge Press.

McNeill, P. (1990) *Research Methods*, 2nd edn, London: Routledge.

McQuaide, M. (2005) 'The rise of alternative health care: a sociological account', *Social Theory and Health* 3: 286–301.

McQuail, D. (ed.) (1972) *Sociology of Mass Communications*, Harmondsworth: Penguin.

McQuail, D. (1977) 'The influences and effects of mass media', in J. Curran, M. Gurevitch and J. Woollacott (eds) *Mass Communication and Society*, London: Edward Arnold/Open University Press.

McQuail, D. (1994) *Mass Communications Theory: An Introduction*, London: Sage.

McQuail, D. (2000) *McQuail's Mass Communication Theory*, London: Sage.

McQuail, D. (2005) *Mass Communications Theory: An Introduction*, 5th edn, London: Sage.

McQuail, D., Blumler, J.G. and Brown, J. (1972) 'The television audience: a revised perspective', in D. McQuail (ed.) *Sociology of Mass Communications*, Harmondsworth: Penguin.

McRobbie, A. (1982) 'Jackie: an ideology of adolescent femininity', in B. Waites (ed.) *Popular Culture: Past and Present*, Milton Keynes: Open University Press.

McRobbie, A. (1991) 'The politics of feminist research', in A. McRobbie (ed.) *Feminism and Youth Culture*, London: Macmillan.

Mead, G.H. (1934) *Mind, Self, and Society*, Chicago, IL: University of Chicago Press.

Mead, M. (1935) *Sex and Temperament in Three Primitive Societies*, London: Routledge & Kegan Paul.

Meadows, D.H., Meadows, D., Randers, J., *et al.* (1972) *The Limits to Growth*, New York: Universe Books.

Meadows, D.H., Meadows, D, Randers, J. (2002) *Limits to Growth: The 30-Year Update*, White River Junction, VT: Chelsea Green Publishing Company.

Medved, M. (1992) *Hollywood vs America*, New York: HarperCollins.

Meehan, D. (1983) *Ladies of the Evening: Women Characters on Prime Time TV*, Metuchen, NJ: Scarecrow.

Meighan, R., Shelton, I. and Marks, T. (eds) (1979) *Perspectives on Society*, Sunbury on Thames: Thomas Nelson.

Mellor, M. (1997) 'Gender and the environment', in M. Redclift and G. Woodgate (eds) *The International Handbook of Sociology*, Cheltenham: Edward Elgar.

Melton, J.G. (2007) 'Introducing and defining the concept of a new religion', in D.G. Bromley (ed.) *Teaching New Religious Movements*, New York: Oxford University Press.

Mendelsohn, H. (1966) *Mass Entertainment*, New Haven, CT: College and University Press.

Merchant, C. (1989) *The Death of Nature: Women, Ecology and the Scientific Revolution*, San Francisco, CA: Harper & Row.

Merchant, C. (1992) *Breaking the Boundaries: Towards a Feminist Green Socialism*, London: Virago.

Merton, R.K. (1938) 'Social structure and anomie', *American Sociological Review* 3: 672–82.

Merton, R.K. (1952) 'Bureaucratic structure and personality', in R.K. Merton, *A Reader in Bureaucracy*, New York: Free Press.

Meyer, S. (1981) *The Five Dollar Day*, New York: Albany.

Mies, M. (1986) *Patriarchy and Accumulation on a World Scale*, London: Zed.

Miles, R. (1982) *Racism and Migrant Labour: A Critical Text*, London: Routledge & Kegan Paul.

Miles, R. (1987) 'Recent Marxist theories of nationalism and the issue of racism', *British Journal of Sociology* 38(1): 24–43.

Miles, R. (1989) *Racism*, London: Routledge.
Miles, R and Brown, M. (2003) *Racism*, 2nd edn, London: Routledge.
Miles, S. (1997) 'How to present your sociological education to the labour market', in Ballard, C. *et al. The Student's Companion to Sociology*, London: Blackwell.
Milgram, S. (1974) *Obedience to Authority*, London: Harper & Row.
Miliband, R. (1969) *The State in Capitalist Society*, London: Weidenfeld & Nicolson.
Miller, H. (1970 [1945]) *The Air-Conditioned Nightmare*, New York: New Directions.
Miller, W. (1991) *Media and Voters*, Oxford: Clarendon.
Miller, W.B. (1958) 'Lower-class culture as a generating milieu of gang delinquency', *Journal of Sociological Issues* 14: 5–19.
Millett, K. (1970) *Sexual Politics*, London: Abacus.
Mills, C.W. (1970) *The Sociological Imagination*, Harmondsworth: Penguin.
Mirza, H. (1992) *Young, Female and Black*, London: Routledge.
Mishler, E. (1981) 'Viewpoint: critical perspectives on the biomedical model', in E. Mishler (ed.) *Social Contexts of Health, Illness and Patient Care*, Cambridge: Cambridge University Press.
Mitchell, G.D. (1968) *A Hundred Years of Sociology*, London: Duckworth.
Modood, T., Berthoud, R., Lakey, J., *et al.* (1997) *Ethnic Minorities in Britain: Diversity and Disadvantage*, London: Policy Studies Institute.
Mohanty, C., Russo, A. and Lourdes, T. (eds) (1991) *Third World Women and the Politics of 'Feminism'*, Bloomington, IN: Indiana University Press.
Moir, A. and Jessel, D. (1989) *Brain Sex: The Real Difference Between the Sexes*, London: Mandarin.
Mol, A.P.J. (1997) 'Ecological modernization: industrial transformations and environmental reform', in M. Redclift and G. Woodgate (eds) *The International Handbook of Sociology*, Cheltenham: Edward Elgar.
Monbiot, G. (2006) *Heat: How to Stop the Planet Burning*, London: Allen Lane.
Monbiot, G. (2007) 'Ethical shopping is just another way of showing how rich you are', *The Guardian*, 24 July, 27.
Moore, M. (2003) *Dude Where's My Country?*, London: Penguin.
Moore, S. (1988) *Investigating Deviance*, London: Unwin Hyman.
Moran-Ellis, J. Alexander, V.D., Cronin, A., Dickinson, M., Fielding, J., Sleney, J. and Thomas, H. (2006) 'Triangulation and integration: processes, claims and implications', *Qualitative Research* 6(1), 45–59.
Morgan, D. (1981) 'Men, masculinity and the process of sociological enquiry', in H. Roberts (ed.) *Doing Feminist Research*, London: Routledge & Kegan Paul.
Morgan, D. (1991) *Discovering Men*, London: Routledge.
Morgan, D. (1992) 'Sociology, society and the family', in T. Lawson, J. Scott, H. Westergaard and J. Williams (eds) *Sociology Reviewed*, London: Collins.
Morgan, D. (1996) *Family Connections: An Introduction to Family Studies*, Cambridge: Polity Press.
Morris, J. (1991) *Pride Against Prejudice: Transforming Attitudes to Disability*, London: The Women's Press.
Morris, J. (2004) 'Independent living and community care: a disempowering framework', *Disability and Society* 19(5): 427–42.
Morrison, D. and Tumber, H. (1988) *Journalists at War: The Dynamics of News Reporting During the Falklands Conflict*, London: Sage.
Morrison, K. (1995) *Marx, Durkheim, Weber: Formations of Social Thought*, London: Sage.
Morrow, V. (1994) 'Responsible children?: aspects of children's work and employment outside school in contemporary UK', in B. Mayall (ed.) *Children's Childhoods: Observed and Experienced*, London: Falmer Press.
Moser, C. (1993) *Gender Planning and Development*, London: Routledge.
Moxnes, K. (2003) 'Children coping with parental divorce: what helps, what hurts?', in A. Jensen and L. McKee (eds) *Children and the Changing Family: Between Transformation and Negotiation*, London: RoutledgeFalmer.
Muggeridge, M. (1978) *Things Past*, London: Collins.
Murdock, G. (1949) *Social Structure*, New York: Macmillan.
Murdock, G. (1990) 'Redrawing the map of the communications industries', in M. Ferguson (ed.) *Public Communication*, London: Sage.
Murdock, G. and McCron, R. (1979) 'The broadcasting and delinquency debate', *Screen Education* 30: 51.
Murphy, L. and Livingstone, J. (1985) 'Racism and the limits of radical feminism', *Race and Class* 4 (spring): 61–70.
Murphy, R. (2002) 'Ecological materialism and the sociology of Max Weber', in R. Dunlap, F.H. Buttel, P. Dickens and A. Gijswijt (eds) *Social Theory and the Environment: Classical Foundations, Contemporary Insights*, Oxford: Rowman & Littlefield.
Murray, C. (ed.) (1990) *The Emerging British Underclass*, London: IEA Health & Welfare Unit.
Murray, C. and Herrnstein, R. (1994) *The Bell Curve: Intelligence and the Class Structure in American Life*, New York: Free Press.
Murray, W. (2006) *Geographies of Globalization*, Abingdon: Routledge.
Myrdal, G. (1968) *Asian Drama*, New York: Pantheon.

N

Naess, A. (1973) 'The shallow and the deep, long-range ecological movement', *Inquiry* 16: 95–100.

Nakane, C. (1973) *Japanese Society*, Harmondsworth: Penguin.

National Commission on Education (1993) *Learning to Succeed*, London: HMSO.

Navarro, V. (1978) *Class, Struggle, the State and Medicine*, London: Martin Robertson.

Nayak, A. (2003) '"Boyz to men": masculinities, schooling and labour transitions in de-industrial times', *Educational Review*, 55: 2.

Negrine, R. (1998) 'Media institutions in Europe', in A. Briggs and P. Cobley (eds). *The Media: An Introduction*, Harlow: Longman.

Neihardt, J.G. (1932) *Black Elk Speaks, Being the Life Story of a Holy Man of the Oglala Sioux*, New York: Marrow.

Nelson, T.D. (2005) *The Psychology of Prejudice*, Harlow: Allyn and Bacon.

Nettle, D. (2003) 'Intelligence and class mobility in the British population', *British Journal of Psychology* 94: 551–61.

Nettleton, S. (2006) The *Sociology of Health and Illness*, 2nd edn, Cambridge: Polity Press.

Nettleton, S. and Watson, J. (eds) (1998) *The Body in Everyday Life*, London: Routledge.

Newburn, T. and Hagell, A. (1995) 'Violence on screen: just child's play', *Sociology Review* February: 7–10.

Newburn, T. and Stanko, E. (eds) (1994a) *Just Boys Doing Business: Men, Masculinities and Crime*, London: Routledge.

Newby, H. (1997) 'One world two cultures: sociology and the environment', in L.T. Owen and T. Unwin, (eds) *Environmental Management: Readings and Case Studies*, Oxford: Blackwell.

Newson, E. (1994) 'Video violence and the protection of children', Nottingham: Child Development Research Unit, University of Nottingham.

Newton, M. (2002) *Savage Girls and Wild Boys: A History of Feral Children*, London: Faber and Faber.

Nichols, T. (1979) 'Social class: official, sociological and Marxist', in J. Irvine, I. Miles and J. Evans (eds) *Demystifying Social Statistics*, London: Pluto.

Nichols, T. (1999) 'Death and injury at work: a sociological approach', in N. Daykin and L. Doyal (eds) *Health and Work: Critical Perspectives*, London: Macmillan.

Nicholson, L. (ed.) (1990) *Feminism/Postmodernism*, London: Routledge.

Nicholson, L. and Fraser, N. (1990) 'Social criticism without philosophy', in L. Nicholson (ed.) *Feminism/Postmodernism*, London: Routledge.

Niebuhr, H.R. (1929) *The Social Sources of Denominationalism*, New York: Holt.

Nilsen, A. (1975) *Women in Children's Literature*, Englewood Cliffs, NJ: Prentice-Hall.

Niro, B. (2001) *Race*, Basingstoke: Palgrave Macmillan.

Nisbet, R.A. (1970) *The Sociological Tradition*, London: Heinemann.

Noble, G. (1975) *Children in Front of the Small Screen*, London: Constable.

Noon, M. and Blyton, P. (2007) *The Realities of Work: Experiencing Work and Employment in Contemporary Society*, 3rd edn, Houndmills: Palgrave Macmillan.

Nozik, R. (1974) *Anarchy, State and Utopia*, Oxford: Blackwell.

O

Oakley, A. (1972) *Sex, Gender and Society*, London: Temple Smith.

Oakley, A. (1974a) *Housewife*, London: Allen Lane.

Oakley, A. (1974b) *The Sociology of Housework*, Oxford: Martin Robertson.

Oakley, A. (1981) 'Interviewing women: a contradiction in terms', in H. Roberts (ed.) *Doing Feminist Research*, London: Routledge & Kegan Paul.

Oakley, A. (1984) *The Captured Womb: A History of Medical Care of Pregnant Women*, Oxford: Blackwell.

Oakley, A. and Oakley, R. (1981) 'Sexism in official statistics', in J. Irvine, I. Miles and J. Evans (eds) *Demystifying Social Statistics*, London: Pluto.

O'Brien, M. (1981) *The Politics of Reproduction*, London: Routledge & Kegan Paul.

O'Brien, M., Peyton, V., Mistry, R., *et al.* (2000) 'Gender-role cognition in three-year-old boys and girls', *Sex Roles* 42(11–12): 1007–25.

O'Connell Davidson, J. and Layder, D. (1994) *Methods, Sex and Madness*, London: Routledge.

O'Connor, J. (1996) 'The second contradiction of capitalism', in T. Benton (ed.) *The Greening of Marxism*, New York: Guilford Press.

O'Connor, J. (1998) *Essay's in Ecological Marxism*, London: Guilford Press.

O'Donnell, K. (1999) 'Lesbian and gay families: legal perspectives', in G. Jagger and C. Wright (eds) *Changing Family Values*, London: Routledge.

O'Donnell, M. (1981) *A New Introduction to Sociology*, London: Harrap.

OECD (Organisation for Economic Co-operation and Development) (2007) *Education at a Glance*, Paris: Organisation for Economic Co-operation and Development.

O'Faolain, J. and Martinez, L. (1979) *Not in God's Image*, London: Virago.

Office of Climate Change (2006) *Stern Review on the Economics of Climate Change*, London: HM Treasury/Cabinet Office.

Okun, L. (1986) *Woman Abuse: Facts Replacing Myths*, New York: State University of New York Press.

Oliver, M. (1989) 'Conductive education: if it wasn't so sad it would be funny', *Disability, Handicap and Society* 4(2): 127–200.

Oliver, M. (1990) *The Politics of Disablement*, Basingstoke: Macmillan.

Oliver, M. (1996) *Understanding Disability*, London: Macmillan.

O'Malley, T. (2005) *Keeping Broadcasting Public: The BBC and the 2006 Charter Review*, 2nd revised printing, London: CPBF.

Onion, A. (2005) 'Scientists find sex differences in brain', http://abcnews.go.com/Technology/Health/story?id=424260&page=1.

ONS (Office for National Statistics) (2001a) *Labour Force Survey*, London: HMSO.

ONS (Office for National Statistics) (2001b) *Living in Britain 2001*, London: HMSO.

ONS (Office for National Statistics) (2002) *Living in Britain: Results from the 2002 General Household Survey*, London: HMSO.

ONS (Office for National Statistics) (2003a) *Labour Force Survey*, London: HMSO.

ONS (Office for National Statistics) (2003b) *Census 2001*, London: HMSO.

ONS (Office for National Statistics) (2003c) *Social Trends*, London: HMSO.

ONS (Office for National Statistics) (2004) *Social Trends 34*, London: HMSO.

ONS (Office for National Statistics) (2005) *National Statistics*, London: HMSO.

ONS (Office for National Statistics) (2006) *Labour Market Trends*, London: HMSO.

ONS (Office for National Statistics) (2007a) *Labour Force Survey*, London: HMSO.

ONS (Office for National Statistics) (2007b) *Social Trends*, London: HMSO.

ONS (Office for National Statistics) (2008) *Society*, London: HMSO.

Osgerby, B. (1997) *Youth Culture in Post-War Britain*, Oxford: xxxxx.

Osgerby, B. (1998) ' "The Good, The Bad and the Ugly": Media Representations of Youth Since 1945', in A. Briggs and P. Cobley (eds), *Introduction to the Media*, London: Longman.

Osheron, S.D. and Amara Singham, L.R. (1981) 'The machine metaphor in medicine', in E.G. Mishler (ed.) *Social Contexts of Health, Illness and Patient Care*, Cambridge: Cambridge University Press.

Osler, A. and Starkey, H. (2005) *Changing Citizenship: Democracy and Inclusion in Education*, Maidenhead: Open University Press.

O'Sullivan, T., Dutton, B. and Raynor, P. (1994) *Studying the Media: An Introduction*, London: Edward Arnold.

Osuwu, J.A. (1992) 'Struggle of disabled women in Ghana', in D. Driedger and S. Gray (eds) *Imprinting Our Image: An International Anthology by Women with Disabilities*, Ottowa: Gynergy Books.

Oxford, C. (2005) 'Protectors and victims in the gender regime of asylum', *National Women's Studies Association (NWSA)* 17(3): 18–38.

P

Pachman, J. (1981) *The Children's Generation*, Oxford: Blackwell.

Pahl, J. (1989) *Money and Marriage*, London: Macmillan.

Pahl, R.E. (1984) *Divisions of Labour*, Oxford: Blackwell.

Pahl, R.E. (ed.) (1988) *On Work*, Oxford: Blackwell.

Pahl, R.E. and Wallace, C. (1988) 'Neither angels in marble nor rebels in red: privatization and working-class consciousness', in D. Rose (ed.) *Social Stratification and Economic Change*, London: Hutchinson.

Pakulski, J. and Waters, M. (1996) *The Death of Class*, London: Sage.

Palmer, J. (ed.) (2001) *Fifty Key Thinkers on the Environment*, London: Routledge.

Panelli, R., Punch, S. and Robson, E. (eds) (2007) *Global Perspectives on Rural Childhood and Youth: Young Rural Lives*, London: Routledge.

Parekh, B. (2008) *A New Politics of Identity: Political Principles for an Interdependent World*, Basingstoke: Palgrave Macmillan.

Parfitt, T. (2002) *The End of Development: Modernity, Post-Modernity and Development*, London: Pluto Press.

Park, C.C. (1976) *History of the Conservation Movement in Britain*, Conservation Trust.

Park, R.E., Burgess, E. and Mackenzie, R. (1923) *The City*, Chicago, IL: University of Chicago Press.

Parker-Jenkins, M., Haw, K. and Khan, S. (1997) 'Trying twice as hard to succeed: perceptions of Muslim women in Britain', *Times Educational Supplement*, 24 October.

Parkin, F. (1972) *Class, Inequality and Political Order*, London: Paladin.

Parpart, J. (1995) 'Deconstructing the development expert', in M. Marchand and J. Parpart (eds) *Feminism, Postmodernism and Development*, London: Routledge.

Parrott, L. (1999) *Social Work and Social Care*, London: Routledge.

Parsons, H.L. (1977) (ed.) *Marx and Engels on Ecology*, Westport, CT: Greenwood Press.

Parsons, T. (1951) *The Social System*, London: Routledge & Kegan Paul.

Parsons, T. (1959) 'The school class as a social system: some of its functions in American society', *Harvard Educational Review* 29. Also in A.H. Halsey, J. Floud and C.A. Anderson (eds) (1961) *Education, Economy and Society*, New York: Free Press.

Parsons, T. (1966) *Societies: Evolutionary and Comparative Perspectives*, London: Prentice-Hall.

Parsons, T. and Bales, R.F. (1955) *Family, Socialization and Interaction Process*, New York: Free Press.

Parton, N. (1985) *The Politics of Child Abuse*, London: Macmillan.

Pascall, G. (1995) 'Women on top? Women's careers in the 1990s', *Sociology Review* February: 2–6.

Pascall, G. and Cox, P. (1993) 'Education and domesticity', *Gender and Education* 5(1).

Paton, D. (2004) No Bond but the Law: Punishment, Race and Gender in Jamaican State Formation, Durham, CT: Duke University Press.

Pawson, R. (1989) 'Methodology', in M. Haralambos (ed.) *Developments in Sociology*, vol. 5, Ormskirk: Causeway.

Payne, G. (2000) *Social Divisions*, New York: St Martin's Press.

Payne, G. (2006) 'An introduction to social divisions', in G. Payne (ed.), *Social Divisions*, 2nd edn, London: Macmillan.

Payne, R. (2007) 'Child-headed households and their experiences of support in Zambia: a continuing role for the family', presented at Extended and Extending Families, Edinburgh University, Edinburgh.

Payne, R. (2008) '"Emerging adulthood"? Growing up in child-headed households in Zambia', workshop presentation, London: British Academy.

Pearson, G. (1983) *Hooligan: A History of Respectable Fears*, London: Macmillan.

Pearson, J. (1972) *The Profession of Violence: The Rise and Fall of the Kray Twins*, London: Weidenfeld & Nicolson.

Pearson, J. (2002) 'The history and development of Wicca and paganism', in J. Pearson (ed.) *Belief Beyond Boundaries: Wicca, Celtic Spirituality and the New Age*, Buckingham: Open University Press.

Pearson, R. (2000) 'Rethinking gender matters in development' in T. Allen and A. Thomas (eds) *Poverty and Development into the 21st Century*, Oxford: Oxford University Press.

Pearson, R. and Jackson, C. (1998) 'Introduction: interrograting development: feminism, gender and policy', in C. Jackson and R. Pearson (eds) *Feminist Visions of Development: Gender Analysis and Policy*, London: Routledge.

Pease, B. (2001) 'Moving beyond mateship: reconstructing Australian men's practices', in B. Pease and K. Pringle (eds) *A Man's World? Changing Men's Practices in a Globalized World*, London: Zed Books.

Pease, B. and Pringle, K. (2001) 'Introduction: studying men's practices and gender relations in a global context', in B. Pease and K. Pringle (eds) *A Man's World? Changing Men's Practices in a Globalized World*, London: Zed Books.

Pepper, D. (1996) *Modern Environmentalism: An Introduction*, London: Routledge.

Percy, M. (1996) *Words, Wonders and Power: Understanding Contemporary Christian Fundamentalism and Revivalism*, London: SPCK.

Persell, C.H. (1990) *Understanding Society: An Introduction to Sociology*, 3rd edn, New York: Harper & Row.

Petchesky, R. (1985) *Abortion and Woman's Choice*, New York: Northeastern University Press.

Peters, T.J. and Austin, N. (1985) *A Passion for Excellence*, New York: Random House.

Peters, T.J. and Waterman, R.H. (1982) *In Search of Excellence: Lessons from America's Best Run Companies*, New York: Harper & Row.

Peterson, A. (2005) 'Securing our genetic health: engendering trust in UK Biobank', *Sociology of Health and Illness* 27(2): 271–92.

Phillips, A. (1987) *Divided Loyalties: Dilemmas of Sex and Class*, London: Virago.

Phillips, A. (1999) *Which Equalities Matter?*, Cambridge: Polity Press.

Phillipson, C. (1998) *Reconstructing Old Age: New Agendas in Social Theory and Practice*, London: Sage.

Philo, G. (ed.) (1996) *Media and Mental Distress*, Harlow: Addison Wesley Longman.

Phizacklea, A. (1994) 'A single or segregated market? gendered and racialised divisions', in H. Afshar and M. Maynard (eds) *The Dynamics of 'Race' and Gender*, London: Taylor & Francis.

Phoenix, A. (1991) 'Mothers under twenty: outsider and insider views', in A. Phoenix, A. Woollett and E. Lloyd (eds) *Motherhood: Meanings, Practices and Ideologies*, London: Sage.

Pilcher, J. (1995) *Age and Generation in Modern Britain*, Oxford: Oxford University Press.

Pilcher, J., Williams, J. and Pole, C. (2003) 'Rethinking adulthood: families, transitions and social change', *Sociological Research Online* 8(4).

Pilger, J. (1997) *Breaking the Mirror*, Central Television.

Pilkington, A. (2003) *Racial Disadvantage and Ethnic Diversity in Britain*, Basingstoke: Palgrave Macmillan.

Pill, R. and Stott, N. (1982) 'Concepts of illness causation and responsibility', *Social Science and Medicine* 16: 43–52.

Pines, M. (1981) 'The civilising of Genie', *Psychology Today* 15.

Piore, M. and Sabel, C. (1984) *The Second Industrial Divide*, New York: Basic Books.

Plant, S. (1996) 'On the Matrix: cyberfeminist simulations', in G. Kirkup, L. Janes, K. Woodward and F. Hovenden (eds) *The Gendered Cyborg: A Reader*, London: Routledge.

Platt, L. (2007) *Poverty and Ethnicity in the UK*, Bristol: Policy Press.

Plint, T. (1851) *Crime in England: Its Relation, Character and Extent, as Developed from 1801 to 1848*, London: Charles Gilpin.

Plummer, K. (1975) *Sexual Stigma: An Interactionist Account*, London: Kegan Paul.

Plummer, K. (1995) *Telling Sexual Stories: Power, Change and Social Worlds*, London: Routledge.

Plumwood, V. (1988) 'Women, humanity and nature', *Radical Philosophy* 48(spring): 6–24.

Plumwood, V. (1991) 'Nature, self and gender: feminism environmental philosophy, and the critique of rationalism', *Hypatia* 6(1): 3–27.

Plumwood, V. (1993) *Feminism and the Mastery of Nature*, London: Routledge.

Pointing, C. (1991) *A Green History of the World*, London: Sinclair-Stevenson Ltd.

Polak, R. (2006) 'Re-emergence of religion?', in V. Mortensen (ed.) *Religion and Society: Crossdisciplinary European Perspectives*, occasional paper no. 9, Højbjerg, Denmark: University of Aarhus, Centre for Multireligious Studies.

Policy Studies Institute (PSI) (1983) *The Police and People in London*, London: Policy Studies Institute.

Policy Studies Institute (PSI) (1994) *Ethnic Minorities and Higher Education: Why are There Different Rates of Entry?*, London: Policy Studies Institute.

Pollard, C. (1998) 'Keeping the Queen's peace', *Criminal Justice Matters* 31: 14–16.

Pollard, N., Latorre, M. and Sriskadarajah, D. (2008) *Floodgates or Turnstiles? Post-EU Enlargement Migration Flows to (and from) the UK*, London: Institute for Public Policy Research.

Pollert, A. (1981) *Girls, Wives, Factory Lives*, London: Macmillan.

Pollert, A. (1988a) 'The flexible firm: fact or fiction?', *Work, Employment and Society* 2(3): 281–316.

Pollert, A. (1988b) 'Dismantling flexibility', *Capital and Class* 34: 42–75.

Pollock, L. (1983) *Forgotten Children: Parent–Child Relations 1500–1900*, Cambridge: Cambridge University Press.

Popay, J., Bennet, S., Thomas, C., *et al.* (2003) 'Beyond "beer, fags, eggs, and chips"? Exploring lay understanding of social inequalities in health', *Sociology of Health and Illness* 25(1): 1–23.

Porritt, J. (1984) *Seeing Green*, Oxford: Basil Blackwell.

Porritt, J. (2005) *Capitalism: As If the Earth Matters*, London: Earthscan Books.

Porter, D. (2001) *The Enlightenment*, Basingstoke: Palgrave.

Postman, N. (1987) *Amusing Ourselves to Death*, London: Methuen.

Potter, G. (2000) *Deeper than Debt: Economic Globalisation and the Poor*, London: Latin American Bureau.

Potter, R. (2002) 'Global convergence, divergence and development', in V. Desai and R. Potter (eds) *The Companion to Development Studies*, London: Arnold.

Potter, R. and Lloyd-Evans, A. (1998) *The City in the Developing World*, Harlow: Pearson Education.

Potter, R., Binns, T., Elliot, J. and Smith, D. (2008) *Geographies of Development*, 3rd edn, Harlow: Pearson Education.

Poulantzas, N. (1973) 'The problems of the capitalist state', in J. Urry and J. Wakeford (eds) *Power in Britain*, London: Heinemann.

Poulantzas, N. (1979) *Class in Contemporary Capitalism*, London: New Left Books.

Pressman, S. (2002) 'Explaining the gender poverty gap in developed and transitional economies', *Journal of Economic Issues* 36(1): 17–40.

Primary Review (2007) *Community Soundings: The Primary Review Regional Witness Sessions*, Cambridge: University of Cambridge Faculty of Education.

Pugh, A. (1990) 'My statistics and feminism: a true story', in L. Stanley (ed.) *Feminist Praxis*, London: Routledge.

Punch, S. (2001a) 'Negotiating autonomy: childhoods in rural Bolivia', in L. Alanen and B. Mayall (eds) *Conceptualising Child–Adult Relations*, London: Routledge Falmer.

Punch, S. (2001b) 'Household division of labour: generation, gender, age, birth order and sibling composition', *Work, Employment & Society* 15(4): 803–23.

Punch, S. (2002a) 'Youth transitions and interdependent adult–child relations in rural Bolivia', *Journal of Rural Studies* 18(2): 123–33.

Punch, S. (2002b) 'Research with children: the same or different from research with adults?', *Childhood* 9(3): 321–41.

Punch, S. (2003) 'Childhoods in the majority world: miniature adults or tribal children?', *Sociology* 37(2): 277–95.

Punch, S. (2004) 'The impact of primary education on school-to-work transitions for young people in rural Bolivia', *Youth and Society* 36(2): 163–82.

Punch, S. (2005) 'The generationing of power: a comparison of child–parent and sibling relations in Scotland', *Sociological Studies of Children and Youth* 10: 169–88.

Punch, S. (2008a) ' "You can do nasty things to your brothers and sisters without a reason": siblings' backstage behaviour', *Children and Society* 22: 333–44.

Punch, S. (2008b) 'Negotiating the birth order: children's experiences', in M. Klett-Davies (ed.) *Putting Sibling Relationships on the Map: A Multi-disciplinary Perspective*, London: Family and Parenting Institute.

Purdam, K., Afkhami, R., Crockett, A. and Olsen, W. (2007) 'Religion in the UK: an overview of equality statistics and evidence gaps', *Journal of Contemporary Religion* 22(2): 147–68.

Q

Qvortrup, J. (1994) 'Introduction', in J. Qvortrup, M. Bardy, G. Sgritta and H. Wintersberger (eds) *Childhood Matters: Social Theory, Practice and Politics*, Aldershot: Avebury.

R

Radcliffe-Brown, A.R. (1952) *Structure and Function in Primitive Society*, London: Cohen & West.

Radford, G., Hester, R. and Kelly, L. (eds) (1995) *Women, Violence and Male Power: Feminist Activism, Research and Practice*, Milton Keynes: Open University Press.

Radway, J. (1984) *Reading the Romance: Women, Patriarchy and Popular Literature*, Chapel Hill, NC: University of North Carolina Press.

Ramazanoglu, C. (1991) 'Feminist epistemology and research', in J. Gubbay (ed.) *Teaching Methods of Social Research*, report of a City conference, City University, London, November 1991.

Ramazanoglu, C. (1993) *Up Against Foucault: Explorations of Some Tensions Between Foucault and Feminism*, London: Routledge.

Ramesh, R. (2005) 'This UK patient avoided the NHS list and flew to India for a heart bypass: is health tourism the future?', *Guardian* 1 February.

Ranger, T. (2005) The rise of patriotic journalism in Zimbabwe and its possible implications [Special issue: Media and Zimbabwe]. *Westminster Papers in Communication and Culture*, November, 8–17.

Rappley, T. (2008) 'Distributed decision making: the anatomy of decisions-in-action', *Sociology of Health and Illness* 30(3): 429–44.

Rassool, N. (1999) 'Flexible identities: exploring race and gender issues amongst a group of immigrant pupils in an inner-city comprehensive school', *British Journal of Sociology and Education* 20(1): 23–36.

Rattansi, A. and Westwood, S. (1995) *Racism, Modernity and Identity: On the Western Front*, Oxford: Blackwell.

Redclift, M. (1997) 'Sustainable development: needs, values, rights', in I. Owen and T. Unwin (eds) *Environmental Management: Readings and Case Studies*, London: Blackwell.

Reed, J. (2004) 'Review: *Class Practices: How Parents Help Their Children Get Good Jobs*', *Sociological Research Online* 9(4).

Regan, C. (2002a) 'Aid and development', in C. Regan (ed.) *80:20: Development in an Unequal World*, Wicklow, Ireland: 80:20 Educating and Acting for a Better World.

Regan, C. (2002b) 'HIV/AIDS and Development', in C. Regan (ed.) *80:20: Development in an Unequal World*, Wicklow, Ireland: 80:20 Educating and Acting for a Better World.

Regan, C. and Ruth, D. (2002) 'Development: describing and debating the idea', in C. Regan (ed.) *80:20: Development in an Unequal World*, Wicklow, Ireland: 80:20 Educating and Acting for a Better World.

Reicher, S. and Hopkins, N. (2001) *Self and Nation*, London: Sage.

Reid, I. (1989) *Social Class Differences in Britain*, 3rd edn, London: Fontana.

Reid, I. (1998) *Class in Britain*, Cambridge: Polity Press.

Reiner, R. (1992) *The Politics of the Police*, 2nd edn, London: Harvester Wheatsheaf.

Reinharz, S. (1993) 'The principles of feminist research: a matter of debate', in C. Kramarae and D. Spender (eds) *The Knowledge Explosion: Generations of Feminist Scholarship*, Hemel Hempstead: Harvester Wheatsheaf.

Renan, E. (1990 [1890]) 'What is the nation?', in H. Bhabha (ed.), *Nation as Narration*, London: Routledge.

Rex, J. and Tomlinson, S. (1979) *Colonial Immigrants in a British City: A Class Analysis*, London: Routledge & Kegan Paul.

Reynolds, J. (2008) Factories shut as crisis hits China. BBC News website, 19 November 2008.

Reynolds, P. (1991) *Dance Civet Cat: Child Labour in the Zambezi Valley*, Athens, CH: Ohio University Press.

Reynolds, T. (2002) 'Re-analysing the black family', in A. Carling, S. Duncan and R. Edwards (eds) *Analysing Families*, London: Routledge.

Ribbens McCarthy, J., Edwards, R. and Gillies, V. (2003) *Making Families: Moral Tales of Parenting and Step-Parenting*, Durham: Sociology Press.

Rich, A. (1977) *Of Woman Born: Motherhood as Experience and Institution*, London: Virago.

Rich, A. (1980) 'Compulsory heterosexuality and lesbian existence', *Signs*, 5, 631–60.

Riddell, S. (1996) 'Theorising special educational needs in a changing political climate', in L. Barton (ed.) (1996) *Disability and Society: Emerging Issues and Insights*, London: Longman.

Ridge, D., Ziebland,, S. Anderson, J., Williams, I. and Elford, J. (2007) 'Positive prevention: contemporary issues facing HIV positive people negotiating sex in the UK', *Social Science and Medicine* 65(4): 755–70.

Riessman, F. (1962) *The Culturally Deprived Child*, New York: Harper & Row.

Ritchie, J., Spencer, L. and O'Connor, W. (2003) 'Carrying out qualitative analysis', in J. Ritchie and J. Lewis (eds) *Qualitative Research Practice*, London: Sage.

Ritzer, G. (1992) *Sociological Theory*, 3rd edn, New York: McGraw-Hill.

Ritzer, G. (1993) The McDonaldization of Society, London: Sage.

Ritzer, G. (2004) *The McDonaldization of Society*, 3rd edn, Thousand Oaks, CA: Pine Forge Press.

Robbins, T. and Hall, J.R. (2007) 'New religious movements and violence', in D.G. Bromley (ed.) *Teaching New Religious Movements*, New York: Oxford University Press.

Roberts, H. (1990), *Doing Feminist Research*, London: Routledge and Kegan Paul.

Roberts, K. (2001) *Class in Modern Britain*, London: Palgrave Macmillan.

Roberts, K., Cook, F.G., Clark, S.C. and Sememeoff, E. (1977) *The Fragmentary Class Structure*, London: Heinemann.

Roberts, K.A. (2004) *Religion in Sociological Perspective*, 4th edn, Belmont, CA: Thomson/Wadsworth.

Robertson, G. and Nicol, A. (1992) *Media Law: The Rights of Journalists*, Harmondsworth: Penguin.

Robertson, S. (2006) '"I've been like a coiled spring this last week": embodied masculinity and health', *Sociology of Health and Illness* 28(4): 433–56.

Robins, K. and Webster, F. (1986) 'Today's television and tomorrow's world', in L. Masterman (ed.) *Television Mythologies*, London: Comedia.

Robinson, M., Butler, I., Scanlan, L., Douglas, G. and Murch, M. (2003) 'Children's experience of their parents' divorce', in A. Jensen and L. McKee (eds) *Children and the Changing Family: Between Transformation and Negotiation*, London: RoutledgeFalmer.

Roper, H.T. (1983) 'The invention of tradition: the Highland tradition of Scotland', in E. Hobsbawm and T. Ranger (eds) *The Invention of Tradition*, Cambridge: Cambridge University Press.

Roper, M. and Tosh, J. (1991) *Manful Assertions*, London: Routledge.

Rose, D. (ed.) (1988) *Social Stratification and Economic Change*, London: Hutchinson.

Rose, D. and Gershuny, J. (1995) 'Social surveys and social change', *Sociology Review* 4(4): 11–14.

Rose, D. and O'Reilly, K. (eds) (1997) *Constructing Classes*, Swindon: ESRC/ONS.

Roseneil, S. (2005) 'Living and loving beyond the boundaries of the heteronorm: personal relationships in the 21st century', in L. McKie and S. Cunningham-Burley (eds) *Families in Society: Boundaries and Relationships*, Bristol: Policy Press.

Roseneil, S. and Budgeon, S. (2004) 'Beyond the conventional family: intimacy, care and community in the 21st century', *Current Sociology* 52(2): 135–59.

Rosenthal, R. and Jacobson, L. (1968) *Pygmalion in the Classroom*, New York: Holt, Rinehart & Winston.

Ross, N., Hill, M., Sweeting, H. and Cunningham-Burley, S. (2005) *Relationships Between Grandparents and Teenage Grandchildren*, CRFR research briefing 23, Edinburgh: Centre for Research on Families and Relationships.

Rostow, W.W. (1960) *The Stages of Economic Growth: A Non-Communist Manifesto*, Cambridge: Cambridge University Press.

Rountree, K. (2004) *Embracing the Witch and the Goddess: Feminist Ritual-Makers in New Zealand*, London: Routledge.

Rowbotham, S. (1982) 'The trouble with patriarchy', in M. Evans (ed.) *The Women Question*, London: Fontana.

Rowntree Foundation (1995) *Income and Wealth*, York: Rowntree Foundation.

Roy, D. (1954) 'Efficiency and the fix', *American Journal of Sociology* 60: 255–66.

Rubin, G. (1993) 'Misguided, dangerous and wrong: an analysis of anti-pornography of politics', in A. Assiter and C. Avendon (eds) *Bad Girls and Dirty Pictures*, London: Pluto.

Rummery, K. (2002) *Disability, Citizenship and Community Care: A Case for Welfare Rights?*, Aldershot: Ashgate.

Rummery, K. (2006) 'Disabled Citizens and Social Exclusion: the role of direct payments', *Policy and Politics*, 34(4): 633–50.

Runciman, W.G. (1990) 'How many classes are there in contemporary society?', *Sociology* 24: 377–96.

Rusche, G. (1980 [1933]) 'Labour market and penal sanctions: thoughts on the sociology of punishment', in T. Platt and P. Takagi (eds) *Punishment and Penal Discipline*, Berkeley, CA: University of California Press.

Rusche, G. and Kirchheimer, O. (1968 [1939]) *Punishment and Social Structure*, New York: Russell & Russell.

Rutter, M., Maughan, B., Mortimore, P. and Ouston, J. (1979) *Fifteen Hundred Hours: Secondary Schools and their Effects on Children*, Shepton Mallet: Open Books.

S

Sabel, C. (1982) *Work and Politics*, Cambridge: Cambridge University Press.

Safilios-Rothschild, C. (1981) 'Disabled persons' self-definitions and their implications for rehabilitation', in A. Brechin, P. Liddiard and J. Swain (eds) *Handicap in a Social World*, Sevenoaks: Open University Press.

Saks, M. (ed.) (1992) *Alternative Medicine in Britain: Professions and Self-Interest*, Oxford: Clarendon Press.

Sandbach, F. (1980) *Environment, Ideology and Policy*, Oxford: Basil Blackwell.

Sanders, C., Donovan, J. and Dieppe, P. (2002) 'The significance and consequences of having painful and disabled joints in older age: co-existing accounts of normal and disrupted biographies', *Sociology of Health and Illness* 24(2): 227–53.

Sangar, T. (2008) 'Transgovernmentality: the production and regulation of gendered subjectivities', *Journal of Gender Studies* 17(1): 41–53.

Saporiti, A. (1994) 'A methodology for making children count', in J. Qvortrup, M. Bardy, G. Sgritta and H. Wintersberger (eds) *Childhood Matters: Social Theory, Practice and Politics*, Aldershot: Avebury.

Saraga, E. (1993) 'The abuse of children', in R. Dallos and E. McLaughlin (eds) *Social Problems and the Family*, London: Sage.

Sarantakos, S. (2004) *Social Research*, 3rd edn, Basingstoke: Palgrave.

Satterthwaite, D., UNICEF, *et al.* (1996) *The Environment for Children*, New York: UNICEF/Earthscan.

Saunders, P. (1987) *Social Theory and the Urban Question*, London: Unwin Hyman.

Saunders, P. (1996) *Unequal but Fair? A Study of Class Barriers in Britain*, London: IEA.

Saunders, P. (1997) 'Social mobility in Britain: an empirical evaluation of two competing explanations', *Sociology* 31: 261–88.

Saunders, P. (2002) 'Reflections on the meritocracy debate in Britain: a response to Richard Breen and John Goldthorpe', *British Journal of Sociology* 53, 559–74.

Savage, M. and Egerton, M. (1997) 'Social mobility, individual ability and the inheritance of class inequality', *Sociology* 31: 645–72.

Savage, M., Barlow, J., Dickens, A. and Fielding, T. (1992) *Property, Bureaucracy and Culture: Middle Class Formation in Contemporary Britain*, London: Routledge.

Sayer, A. and Walker, R. (1992) *The New Social Economy*, Oxford: Blackwell.

Scambler, A., Scambler, B. and Craig, D. (1981) 'Kinship and friendship networks and women's demands for primary care', *Journal of Royal College of General Practitioners* 26: 746–50.

Scase, R. (1992) *Class*, Milton Keynes: Open University Press.

Schiller, H. (1989) *Culture, Inc.: The Corporate Takeover of Public Expression*, Oxford: Oxford University Press.

Schiller, H. (1993) *Mass Communication and the American Empire*, Boulder, CO: Westview Press.

Schlosser, E. (2002) *Fast Food Nation*, London: Penguin Books.

Schnaiberg, A. (1980) *The Environment: From Surplus to Scarcity*, New York: Oxford University Press.

Scholes, R.J. (1999) 'The "mail-order bride" industry and its impact on US immigration', Appendix Q, Washington, DC: Immigration and Naturalization Service.

Schramm, W., Lyle, V. and Parker, E. (1961) *Television in the Lives of our Children*, Stanford, CA: Stanford University Press.

Schudson, M. (1991) 'The sociology of news revisited', in J. Curran and M. Gurevitch (eds) *Mass Media and Society*, London: Edward Arnold.

Schuman, H., Steel, C. and Bobo, L. (1985) *Racial Attitudes in America: Trends and Interpretation*, Cambridge, MA: Harvard University Press.

Scott, J. (1991) *Who Rules Britain?*, Cambridge: Polity Press.

Scott, J. (1994) *Poverty and Wealth: Citizenship, Deprivation and Privilege*, London: Longman.

Scott, J. (1997) *Corporate Business and Capitalist Classes*, Oxford: Oxford University Press.

Scott, J.F. (2002) 'The nature of social research and social knowledge', in I. Marsh (ed.) *Theory and Practice in Sociology*, Harlow: Pearson.

Scott, P. (1999) 'Black people's health: ethnic status and research issues', in S. Hood, B. Mayall and S. Oliver (eds) *Critical Issues in Social Research: Power and Prejudice*, Oxford: Oxford University Press.

Scottish Government (2007) *Statistics on Health Inequalities: An Overview*, www.scotland.gov.uk/Topics/Health/inequalitiestaskforce/overviewofstatistics

Scully, D. (1990) *Understanding Sexual Violence: A Study of Convicted Rapists*, London: Unwin/Hyman.

Seager, A. (2004) 'Women close the pay gap', *Guardian* 29.10.04.

Seager, J. (1993) *Earth Follies: Feminism, Politics and the Environment*, London: Earthscan Books.

Sedgwick, M. (2004) 'Establishments and sects in the Islamic world', in P.C. Lucas and T. Robbins (eds) *New Religious Movements in the Twenty-First Century: Legal, Political and Social Challenges in Global Perspective*, New York and London: Routledge.

Segal, L. (1994) *Straight Sex: The Politics of Pleasure*, London: Virago.

Seidler, V. (1989) *Rediscovering Masculinity*, London: Routledge.

Seidler, V. (ed.) (1991) *Men, Sex and Relationships*, London: Routledge.

Selman, P. (1996) *Local Sustainability: Managing and Planning Ecologically Sound Places*, London: Paul Chapman.

Sennet, R. (1998) *The Corrosion of Character*, New York: Norton.

Seymour, J. (2005) 'Entertaining guests or entertaining the guests: children's emotional labour in hotels, pubs and boarding houses', in J. Goddard, S. McNamee, A. James and A. James (eds) *The Politics of Childhood: International Perspectives, Contemporary Developments*, Basingstoke: Palgrave Macmillan.

Seymour, J. (2007) 'Treating the hotel like a home: the contribution of studying the single location home/workplace', *Sociology* 41(6): 1097–114.

Seymour-Ure, C. (1992) *The British Press and Broadcasting since 1945*, Oxford: Blackwell.

Shalleh, A.K. (1992) 'Deeper than deep ecology: the ecofeminist connection', *Environmental Ethics* 6(1): 339–45.

Sharpe, S. (1994a [1976]) *Just Like a Girl*, 2nd edn, Harmondsworth: Penguin.

Shaw, M. (1995) *The Global State and the Politics of Intervention*, London: Centre for Study of Global Governance.

Shaw, M., Galobardes, B., Davey Smith, G., *et al.* (2007) *The Handbook of Inequality and Socioeconomic Position*, Bristol: Policy Press.

Shawcross, W. (1992) *Murdoch by Shawcross*, London: Chatto & Windus.

Shepherd, A. (1998) *Sustainable Rural Development*, Basingstoke: Palgrave.

Shilling, C. (1993) *The Body and Social Theory*, London: Sage.

Shils, E. (1959) 'Mass society and its culture', in N. Jacobs (ed.) *Culture for the Millions? Mass Media in Modern Society*, London: Van Nostrand.

Shiva, V. (1994) 'Development, ecology and women', in C. Merchant (ed.) *Ecology Key Concepts in Critical Theory*, Atlantic Highlands, NJ: Humanities Press.

Shiva, V. (1989) *Staying Alive*, London: Zed Press.

Shooman, J. (2007) *Whose Space is it Anyway?*, Church Stretton: Independent Music Press.

Shrader-Frechette, K. (1999) 'Chernobyl, global environmental injustice and mutagenic threats', in N. Low (ed.) *Global Ethics and the Environment*, London: Routledge.

Sillence, E., Briggs, P., Harris, P.R. and Fishwick, L. (2007) 'How do patients evaluate and make use of online health information?', *Social Science and Medicine* 64: 1853–62.

Silva, E. and Smart, C. (eds) (1999) *The New Family?*, London: Sage.

Simmel, G. (1997 [1898]) 'A contribution to the sociology of religion', in G. Simmel (ed.) *Essays on Religion*, trans. H. Jürgen Helle in collaboration with Ludwig Nieder, New Haven, CT: Yale University Press.

Sinclair, J. (1974 [1791–99]) *Statistical Account of Scotland drawn up from the Communications of Ministers of the different Parishes*, 21 vols, Edinburgh: William Creech/Witherington & Grant, E.P. Publishing.

Singh-Raud, H. (1997) 'Educating Sita: the education of British Asian girls', *Times Educational Supplement*, 24 October.

Singh-Raud, H. (1998) 'Asian women undergranduates in British universities and the dangers of creedism', *Times Educational Supplement*, 30 October.

Skeggs, B. (1997) *Formations of Class and Gender*, London: Sage.

Skeggs, B. (2003) *Class, Self and Culture*, London: Routledge.

Sklair, L. (1991) *Sociology and the Global Process*, Hemel Hempstead: Harvester Wheatsheaf.

Skuse, D. (1984) 'Extreme deprivation in early childhood', *Journal of Child Psychology and Psychiatry* 25(4).

Smart, C. (2007) *Personal Life*, Cambridge: Polity Press.

Smart, C., Neale, B., and Wade, A. (2001) *The Changing Experience of Childhood: Families and Divorce*, Cambridge: Polity Press.

Smith, A.D. (1986) *The Ethnic Origin of Nations*, London: Blackwell.

Smith, A.D. (1998) *Nationalism and Modernism: A Critical Survey of Recent Theories of Nations and Nationalism*, London: Routledge.

Smith, A.D. (2001) *Nationalism: Theory, Ideology, History*, Cambridge: Polity Press.

Smith, D. (1990) 'Towards a global culture' in M. Featherstone (ed.) *Global Culture: Nationalism, Globalisation and Modernity*, London: Sage.

Smith, D. (ed.) (1992) *Understanding the Underclass*, London: Policy Studies Institute.

Smith, D.J. and Gray, J. (1983) *Police and People in London IV: The Police in Action*, London: Policy Studies Institute.

Snow, J. (2004) *Shooting History*, London: Harper Collins.

Sobotka, E. (2003) 'Romani migration in the 1990s: perspectives on dynamic, interpretation and policy', *Romani Studies* 13(2): 79–121.

Social Affairs Unit (1997) 'The British woman today: a qualitative survey of images in women's magazines', London: Social Affairs Unit.

Social Exclusion Task Force (2006) *Reaching Out: An Action Plan on Social Exclusion*, www.cabinetoffice.gov.uk.

Sokolovsky, J. (ed.) (1990) *The Cultural Context of Aging: Worldwide Perspectives*, New York: Bergin and Garvey.

Solomon, Y., Warin, J., Lewis, C. and Langford, W. (2002) 'Intimate talk between parents and their teenage children: democratic openness or covert control?', *Sociology* 30: 965–83.

Sontag, S. (1972) 'The double standard of aging', *Saturday Review of the Society* 23 September.

Southern, R.W. (1988) *The Middle Ages*, Harmondsworth: Penguin.

Soysal, Y. (1994) *Limits of Citizenship*, Chicago, IL: Chicago University Press.

Spaargaren, G. and Mol, A.P.J. (1992) 'Sociology, environment and modernity: ecological modernization as a theory of social change', *Society and Natural Resources* 5: 323–44.

Spencer, C. (1986) *Colin Spencer's Fish Cookbook*, London: Pan.

Spender, D. (1981) *Men's Studies Modified: The Impact of Feminism on the Academic Disciplines*, Oxford: Pergamon.

Spender, D. and Sarah, E. (1980) *Learning to Lose: Sexism and Education*, London: Women's Press.

Sreberny-Mohammadi (1991) 'The global and the local in international eommunications', in J. Curran and M. Gurevitch (eds) *Mass Media and Society*, London: Edward Arnold.

Stacey, J. (1988) 'Can there be a feminist ethnography?', *Women's Studies International Forum* 11(1): 21–7.

Stacey, J. (1993) 'Untangling feminist theory', in D. Richardson and V. Robinson (eds) *Introducing Women's Studies*, London: Macmillan.

Stacey, J. (1994) *Star Gazing: Hollywood Cinema and Female Spectatorship*, London: Routledge.

Stafford, C. (1995) *The Roads of Chinese Childhood: Learning and Identification in Angang*, Cambridge: Cambridge University Press.

Stanley, L. (ed.) (1990) *Feminist Praxis: Research, Theory and Epistemology in Feminist Sociology*, London: Routledge.

Stanley, L. and Wise, S. (1983) *Breaking Out: Feminist Consciousness and Feminist Research*, London: Routledge & Kegan Paul.

Stanley, L. and Wise, S. (1993) *Breaking Out Again: Feminist Ontology and Epistemology*, London: Routledge.

Stanworth, M. (1983) *Gender and Schooling: A Study of Sexual Division in the Classroom*, London: Women's Research and Resources Centre.

Stanworth, M. (1984) 'Women and class analysis: a reply to John Goldthorpe', *Sociology* 18(2): 159–70.

Stark, R. and Bainbridge, W.S. (1985) *The Future of Religion: Secularization, Revival, and Cult Formation*, Berkeley, CA: University of California Press.

Stark, R. and Glock, C.Y. (1968) *American Piety*, Berkeley, CA: University of California Press.

Starkey, P. (2007) *The Essentials of Community Care*, Basingstoke: Palgrave.

Statham, J. (1986) *Daughters and Sons: Experiences of Non-Sexist Childraising*, Oxford: Blackwell.

Steele, J. (2008) 'School was right to ban "non-Jew"', *Metro*, 4 July.

Stern, W. (1911) *Differential Psychology in its Methodological Principles*, Grundlagen: Jena Fischer.

Stevens, P. and Willis, C. (1979) *Race, Crime and Arrests*, London: HMSO.

Stevenson, N. (1995) *Understanding media cultures: Social theory and mass communications*, London: Sage.

Stewart, A., Prandy, K. and Blackburn, R.M. (1980) *Social Stratification and Occupations*, London: Macmillan.

Stewart, J. and Stoker, G. (eds) (1989) *The Future of Local Government*, London: Macmillan.

Stone, M. (1981) *The Education of the Black Child in Britain: The Myth of Multiracial Eduction*, London: Fontana.

Stones, R. (2001) 'Mobile phones and the transformation of public space', *Sociology Review* 11(2).

Strangleman, T. and Warren, T. (2008) *Work and Society: Sociological Approaches, Themes and Methods*, London: Routledge.

Strate, L. (2004) 'Beer commercials: a manual on masculinity', in M.S. Kimmell and M.A. Messner (eds) *Men's Lives*, 6th edn, Boston, MA: Pearson Education.

Strinati, D. (1992) 'Postmodernism and popular culture', *Sociology Review* 1(4): 2–7.

Strong, P.M. (1979a) 'Sociological imperialism and the profession of medicine: a critical examination of the thesis of medical imperialism', *Social Science and Medicine* 13A: 199–215.

Strong, P.M. (1979b) *The Ceremonial Order of the Clinic: Parents, Doctors and Medical Bureaucracies*, London: Routledge & Kegan Paul.

Sullivan, O. (2004) 'Changing gender practices within the household: a theoretical perspective', *Gender and Society* 18(3): 207–22.

Summit, R.C. (1984) 'Beyond belief: the reluctant discovery of incest', *American Journal of Orthopsychiatry* 56: 167–81.

Sumner, A. and Tribe, M. (2008) *International Development Studies: Theories and Methods in Research and Practice*, London: Sage.

Sumner, C. (1979) *Reading Ideologies*, London: Academic Press.

Sutton, P.W. (2004) *Nature, Environment and Society*, London: Palgrave Macmillan.

Swatos, W.H. and Christiano, K.J. 'Secularization theory: the course of a concept', In W.H. Swatos and D.V.A. Olson (eds) (2000) *The Secularization Debate*, Lanham, MA: Rowman & Littlefield.

Swimme, J. (1990) 'How to cure a frontal lobotomy', in I. Diamond and G.F. Orenstein (eds) *Reweaving the World: The Emergence of Ecofeminism*, San Francisco, CA: Sierra Club Books.

Swingewood, A. (1991) *A Short History of Sociological Thought*, London: Macmillan.

Sydie, R. (1987) *Natural Women, Cultured Men*, Milton Keynes: Open University Press.

T

Taking Liberties Collective (1989) *Learning the Hard Way: Women's Oppression in Men's Education*, London: Macmillan.

Tasker, F. and Golombok, S. (1991) 'Children raised by lesbian mothers: the empirical evidence', *Family Law* 184–7.

Taylor, F.W. (1967 [1911]) *The Principles of Scientific Management*, New York: W.W. Norton.

Taylor, I., Walton, P. and Young, J. (eds) (1975) *Critical Criminology*, London: Routledge & Kegan Paul.

Taylor, M. (2008) 'Disabled in images and language', in J. Swain and S. French (eds) *Disability on Equal Terms*, London: Sage.

Third Wave Foundation (TWF) (2006) 'About us', www.thirdwavefoundation.org/about/growth, accessed August 2008.

Thomas, K. (1983) *Man and the Natural World: Changing Attitudes in England 1500–1800*, Harmondsworth: Penguin.

Thomas, W.I. and Znanieki, F. (1918) *The Polish Peasant in Europe and America*, Chicago, IL: University of Chicago Press.

Thompson, E.P. (1968) *The Making of the English Working Class*, Harmondsworth: Penguin.

Thompson, H.S. (1967) *Hell's Angels*, Harmondsworth: Penguin.

Thompson, I. (1986) *Religion*, London: Longman.

Thompson, K. (ed.) (1985) *Readings from Emile Durkheim*, London & New York: Routledge.

Thompson, K. and Tunstall, J. (eds) (1971) *Sociological Perspectives*, Harmondsworth: Penguin.

Thompson, P. (1989) *The Nature of Work*, 2nd edn, Basingstoke: Macmillan.

Thompson, P. and McHugh, D. (2003) *Work Organisations*, 3rd edn, London: Palgrave Macmillan.

Tierney, J. (1996) *Criminology: Theory and Context*, Harlow: Longman.

Toffler, A. (1970) *Future Shock*, New York: Random House.

Toffler, A. (1980) *The Third Wave*, London: Collins.

Tomlinson, J. (1999) *Globalization and Culture*, Cambridge: Polity Press.

Torpey, J. (1999) *The Invention of the Passport*, Cambridge: Cambridge University Press.

Touraine, A. (1971) *The Post-Industrial Society*, New York: Wildwood House.

Townsend, P. (1981) 'The structured dependency of the elderly: creation of social policy in the twentieth century', *Ageing and Society* 1: 5–28.

Toynbee, P. (1983) 'The crime rate', *Guardian* 10 October.

Toynbee, P. and Walker, D. (2008) *Unjust Rewards: Exposing Greed and Inequality in Britain Today*, Cambridge: Granta Books.

Trenchard, L. and Warren, H. (1984) *Something To Tell You*, London: Gay Teenage Group.

Trigg, R. (1985) *Understanding Social Science*, Oxford: Blackwell.

Troeltsch, E. (1931) *The Social Teaching of the Christian Churches*, London: Allen & Unwin.

Trowler, P. (1988) *Investigating the Media*, London: Collins.

Tumin, M.M. (1967) 'Some principles of stratification: a critical analysis', in R. Bendix and S.M. Lipset (eds) *Class, Status and Power*, 2nd edn, London: Routledge & Kegan Paul.

Tunstall, J. (1962) *The Fishermen*, London: MacGibbon & Kee.

Tunstall, J. (1977) *The Media are American*, London: Constable.

Tunstall, J. and Palmer, M. (eds) (1991) *Media Moguls*, London: Routledge.

Turmunsani, M. (2003) *Disabled People and Economic Needs in the Developing World: A Political Perspective from Jordan*, Aldershot: Ashgate.

Turner, B. (1987) *Medical Power and Social Knowledge*, London: Sage.

Turner, B.S. (1994) *Orientalism, Postmodernism and Globalism*, London, New York: Routledge.

Turner, B.S. (1997) *The Blackwell Companion to Social Theory*, London: Blackwell.

Turner, B.S. (1999) *Classical Sociology*, London: Sage.

Turner, E. (1965) *The Young Man's Companion*, London: Hugh Evelyn.

Turner, R. (1961) 'Modes of social ascent through education', in A.H. Halsey, J. Floud and C.A. Anderson (eds) *Education, Economy and Society*, New York: Free Press.

Tutt, N. (1974) *Care or Custody: Community Homes and the Treatment of Delinquency*, London: Dartford Longman & Todd.

Twomey, B. (2002) 'Women in the labour market: results for the spring 2001 LFS', *Labour Market Trends* 110(3).

Tylor, E. (1873) *Primitive Culture*, Vol. II, London: John Murray.

U

Udall, A.T. and Sinclair, S. (1982) 'The luxury unemployment thesis: a review of recent evidence', *World Development* 10: 49–62.

UNCED (United Nations Conference on Environment and Development) (1992) *Agenda 21: Action Plan for the Next Century*, Rio de Janeiro: United Nations Conference on Environment and Development.

UNDP (United Nations Development Programme) (2002) *The Human Consequences of the Chernobyl Nuclear Accident: A Strategy for Recovery*, New York: United Nations Development Programme.

UNDP (United Nations Development Programme) (2006) *Human Development Report 2006*, New York: United Nations Development Programme.

UNFCCC (United Nations Framework Convention on Climate Change) (1990) 'United Nations Framework Convention on Climate Change', Bonn: United Nations Framework Convention on Climate Change.

UNICEF (1997) *The State of the World's Children*, Oxford: Oxford University Press.

UNICEF (2006) *The State of the World's Children*, Oxford: Oxford University Press.

UNICEF (2008) *Our Climate, Our Children, Our Responsibility: The Implications of Climate Change for the World's Children*, London: UK Committee for UNICEF.

Union of the Physically Impaired Against Segregation (UPIAS) (1976) *Fundamental Principles of Disability*, London: Union of the Physically Impaired Against Segregation.

United Nations (1989) *United Nations Convention on the Rights of the Child*, Geneva: United Nations.

Ussher, J.M. (1997) *Fantasies of Femininity: Reframing the Boundaries of Sex*, London: Penguin.

Ussher, J.M. (2000) *Women's Health: Contemporary International Perspectives*, Leicester: The British Psychological Society.

Ussher, J.M. (2006) *Managing the Monstrous Feminine*, London: Routledge.

V

Vance, C. (1992) *Pleasure and Danger: Exploring Female Sexuality*, London: Routledge.

VanEvery, J. (1999) 'From modern nuclear family households to postmodern diversity? The sociological construction of "families"', in G. Jagger and C. Wright (eds) *Changing Family Values*, London: Routledge.

Van Nieuwkerk, K. (ed.) (2006) *Women Embracing Islam: Gender and Conversion in the West*, Austin, TX: University of Texas Press.

Van Zoonen, L. (1991) 'Feminist perspectives on the media', in J. Curran and M. Gurevitch (eds) *Mass Media and Society*, London: Edward Arnold.

Veljanovski, C. (1989) *Freedom in Broadcasting*, London: Institute of Economic Affairs.

Veljanovski, C. (1991) *The Media in Britain Today*, London: News International.

Victor, C. (1994) *Old Age in Modern Society: A Textbook of Social Gerontology*, 2nd edn, London: Chapman & Hall.

Vincent, J. (2000) 'Age and old age', in G. Payne (ed.) *Social Divisions*, London: Macmillan.

Vincent, J. (2003) *Old Age*, London: Routledge.

Vincett, Giselle (2008a) 'Quagans: fusing Quakerism with contemporary Paganism', in B.P. Dandelion and P. Collins (eds) *The Quaker Condition: The Sociology of a Liberal Religion*, Cambridge: Cambridge Scholars Press.

Vincett, G. (2008b) 'The Fusers: new forms of spiritualized Christianity', in K. Aune, S. Sharma and G. Vincett (eds) *Women and Religion in the West: Challenging Secularization*, Aldershot: Ashgate.

Visvanathan, N. (1997a) 'General introduction,' in N. Visvanathan, L. Duggan, L. Nisonoff and N. Wiegersma (eds) *The Women, Gender and Development Reader*, London: Zed Books.

Visvanathan, N. (1997b) 'Introduction to Part 1', in N. Visvanathan, L. Duggan, L. Nisonoff and N. Wiegersma (eds) *The Women, Gender and Development Reader*, London: Zed Books.

Voas, D. and Bruce, S. (2004) 'Research note: The 2001 Census and Christian identification in Britain', *Journal of Contemporary Religion* 19(1): 23–8.

Voas, D. and Crockett, A. (2005) 'Religion in Britain: neither believing nor belonging', *Sociology* 39(1): 11–28.

W

Waddington, D. (1992) *Contemporary Issues in Public Disorder*, London and New York: Routledge.

Waddington, P.A.J. (1993) *Calling the Police: The Interpretation of, and Response to, Calls for Assistance from the Public*, Aldershot: Avebury.

Wade, R. (2004) 'Is globalization reducing poverty and inequality?', *World Development*, 32(4): 567–89.

Waitzkin, H. (1991) *The Politics of Medical Encounters*, New Haven, CT: Yale University Press.

Waksler, F. (1996) *The Little Trials of Childhood and Children's Strategies for Dealing with Them*, London: Falmer Press.

Walby, S. (1986) *Patriarchy at Work*, Cambridge: Polity.

Walby, S. (1990) *Theorizing Patriarchy*, Oxford: Blackwell.

Walby, S. (2004a) 'The European Union and gender equality; emergent varieties of gender regime', *Social Politics: International Studies in Gender, State and Society* 11(1): 4–29.

Walby, S. (2004b) *Globalization and Difference: Theorizing Complex Modernities*, London: Sage.

Waldby, C. (1996) *Aids and the Body Politic*, London: Routledge.

Walker, A. (1983) *In Search of Our Mothers' Gardens: Womanist Prose*, San Diego, CA: Harcourt Brace Jovanich.

Walker, A. (1990) 'Blaming the victim', in C. Murray (ed.) *The Emerging British Underclass*, London: IEA Health & Welfare Unit.

Walker, A. and Walker, C.A. (1987) *The Growing Divide: A Social Audit 1979–87*, London: Child Poverty Action Group.

Walker, L. (2002) '"We will bury ourselves": a study of child-headed households on commercial farms in Zimbabwe', Harare, Zimbabwe: Farm Orphan Support Trust of Zimbabwe (FOST), www.sarpn.org.za/documents/d0000070/index.php.

Walker, N. (1991) *Why Punish?*, Oxford: Oxford University Press.

Walker, R. (1992) 'Becoming the Third Wave', *Ms* January/February: 39–41.

Wallis, R. (1976) *The Road to Total Freedom: A Sociological Analysis of Scientology*, London: Heinemann.

Walters, R. (2003) *Deviout Knowledge: Criminology, Politics and Policy*, Cullompton: Willan Publishing.

Wanless, D. (2004) *Securing Health for the Whole Population*, London: HM Treasury.

Ward, C. (1972) *Work*, Harmondsworth: Penguin.

Warnock, M. (1978) *Special Education Needs: Report of the Committee of Enquiry into the Education of Handicapped Children and Young People*, London: HMSO.

Warren, K. (1994) *Ecological Ecofemism*, London: Routledge.

Warren, K (1998) 'Ecofeminism', in M.E. Zimmerman, J.B. Callicott, G. Sessions, *et al.* (eds) *Environmental Philosophy: From Animal Rights to Radical Ecology*, Upper Saddle River, NJ: Prentice Hall.

Wasoff, F. and Jamieson, L., with Smith, A. (2005) 'Solo living, individual and family boundaries: findings from secondary analysis', in L. McKie and S. Cunningham-Burley (eds) *Families in Society: Boundaries and Relationships*, Bristol: Policy Press.

Waters, M. (2001) *Globalization*, London: Routledge.

Watson, J. (2000) *Male Bodies: Health, Culture and Identity*, Buckingham: Open University Press.

Weaver, J. (2002) 'Court-ordered caesarean sections', in A. Bainham, S. Day Schlater and M. Richards (eds) *Body Lore and Laws*, Oxford and Portland, OR: Hart Publishing.

Weber, M. (1930 [1904–05]) *The Protestant Ethic and the Spirit of Capitalism*, trans. Talcott Parsons, London: Allen & Unwin.

Weber, M. (1948a [1922–3]) 'Die Protestantischen Sekten und der Geist des Kapitalismus', *Gesammelte Aufsaetze zur Religionssoziologie*, Vol. 1, reprinted as 'Protestant sects and the spirit of capitalism' in H.H. Gerth and C. Wright Mills (eds, trans.) *From Max Weber: Essays in Sociology*, New York: Routledge.

Weber, M. (1948b [1922–3]) 'Die Wirtschaftsethik der Weltreligionen', *Gesammelte Aufsaetze zur Religionssoziologie*, Vol. 1, reprinted as 'The social psychology of the world religions' in H.H. Gerth and C. Wright Mills (eds, trans.) *From Max Weber: Essays in Sociology*, New York: Routledge.

Weber, M. (1949) *The Methodology of the Social Sciences*, New York: Free Press.

Weber, M. (1958) *The Religion of India: The Sociology of Hinduism and Buddhism*, trans. H.H. Gerth, New York: Free Press.

Weber, M. (1963 [1920]) *The Sociology of Religion*, Boston, MA: Beacon.

Weber, M. (1964 [1922]) *The Theory of Social and Economic Organization*, Oxford: Oxford University Press.

Weber, M. (1974 [1904–05]) *The Protestant Ethic and the Spirit of Capitalism*, London: Unwin.

Weber, M. (1983 [1923]) *Gesammelte Aufsaetze zur Religionssoziologie*, Vol. 2, in S. Andreski (ed., trans.) *Max Weber on Capitalism, Bureaucracy and Religion*, London: Allen & Unwin.

Webster, A. (1990) *Introduction to the Sociology of Development*, London: Macmillan.

Webster, F. (2002) *Theories of the Information Society*, 2nd edn, London: Routledge.

Weeks, J. (1986) *Sexuality*, London: Tavistock.

Weeks, J. (1990) *Coming Out*, Aylesbury: Hazell.

Weeks, J. (1991) *Against Nature: Essays on History, Sexuality and Identity*, London: Rivers Oram.

Weeks, J. (2000) *Making Sexual History*, Cambridge: Polity Press.

Weeks, J., Donovan, C. and Heaphy, B. (1999) 'Everyday experiments: narratives of non-heterosexual relationships', in E. Silva and C. Smart (eds) *The New Family?*, London: Sage.

Weeks, J., Heapy, B. and Donovan, C. (2001) *Same Sex Intimacies*, London: Routledge.

Weiner, G. (1985) *Just a Bunch of Girls*, Milton Keynes: Open University Press.

Weiskel, T.C. (1989) 'The ecological lessons of the past: an anthropology of environmental decline', *Ecologist* 19(3): 98–103.

Weiss, L. (1990) *Working Class Without Work: High School Students in a De-industrializing Economy*, New York: Routledge.

Weller, P. (2004) 'Identity, politics, and the future(s) of religion in the UK: the case of the religion questions in the 2001 decennial Census', *Journal of Contemporary Religion* 19(1): 3–21.

Weller, P. (ed.) (2007) *Religions in the UK Directory 2007–2010*, Derby: Multi-Faith Centre and University of Derby.

Weller, P. (2008) *Religious Diversity in the UK: Contours and Issues*, London: Continuum.

Wellman, D. (1977) *Portraits of White Racism*, Cambridge: Cambridge University Press.

West, P.C. (1984) 'Max Weber's human ecology of historical societies', in V. Murvar (ed.) *Theory of Liberty, Legitimacy and Power*, Boston, MA: Routledge and Kegan Paul.

Westergaard, J. (1970) 'The rediscovery of the cash nexus', in R. Miliband and J. Saville (eds) *The Socialist Register*, London: Merlin.

Westergaard, J. (1995) *Who Gets What? The Hardening of Class Inequality in the Late Twentieth Century*, Cambridge: Polity Press.

Westergaard, J. and Resler, H. (1976) *Class in a Capitalist Society*, Harmondsworth: Penguin.

Westwood, S. (1983) *All Day and Every Day: Factory and Family in the Making of Women's Lives*, London: Pluto.

Whale, J. (1980) *The Politics of the Media*, London: Fontana.

Wheen, F. (1982) 'Having a smashing time', *New Statesman*, 22 October.

Whelehan, I. (1995) *Modern Feminist Thought: From the Second Wave to 'Post-Feminism'*, Edinburgh: Edinburgh University Press.

Whimster, S. (2007) *Understanding Weber*, New York: Routledge.

Whitaker, B. (1981) *News Ltd*, London: Minority.

White, B. (1996) 'Globalization and the child labour problem', *Journal of International Development* 8(6): 829–39.

White, L., Jr (1967) 'The historical roots of our ecological crisis', *Science* 155: 1203–7.

Whitehead, S.M. and Barrett, F.J. (eds) (2001) *The Masculinities Reader*, Cambridge: Polity.

Whiteside, N. (1991) *Bad Times*, London: Faber & Faber.

WHO (World Health Organization) (1980) *International Classification of Impairments, Disabilities and Handicaps*, Geneva: World Health Organization.

WHO (World Health Organization) (2008) *World Health Statistics Report*, Geneva: World Health Organization.

Whol, A.S. (1983) *Endangered Lives: Public Health in Victorian Britain*, London: Dent & Sons.

Wiegersma, N. (1997) 'Introduction to Part 5', in N. Visvanathan, L. Duggan, L. Nisonoff and N. Wiegersma (eds) *The Women, Gender and Development Reader*, London: Zed Books.

Wilkinson, H. (1994) *No Turning Back: Generations and the Genderquake*, London: Demos.

Williams, F. (2004) *Rethinking Families*, London: Calouste Gulbenkian Foundation.

Williams, G. (1984) 'The genesis of chronic illness: narrative reconstruction', *Sociology of Health and Illness* 6(2): 175–200.

Williams, G. (1994) *Britain's Media: How They are Related*, London: Campaign for Press and Broadcasting Freedom.

Williams, G. (1996) 'Representing disability: some questions of phenomology and politics', in C. Barnes and G. Mercer (eds) *Exploring the Divide: Illness and Disability*, Leeds: Disability Press.

Williams, K., Cutler, T., Williams, J. and Haslam, C. (1987) 'The end of mass production?', *Economy and Society* 16(3): 405–39.

Williams, M. (1986) *Society Today*, London: Macmillan.

Williams, R. (1974) *Television, Technology and Cultural Form*, London: Fontana.

Williams, S.J. (2000) 'Chronic illness as biographical disruption or biographical disruption as chronic illness? Reflections on a core concept', *Sociology of Health and Illness* 22(1): 40–67.

Williams, S.J. (2003) *Medicine and the Body*, London: Sage.

Williamson, J. (1978) *Decoding Advertisements*, London: Marion Boyars.

Willis, K. (2005) *Theories and Practices of Development*, London: Routledge.

Willis, P. (1977) *Learning to Labour: Why Working-Class Kids Get Working-Class Jobs*, Farnborough: Saxon House.

Wills, W., Backett-Milburn, K., Gregory, S. and Lawton, J. (2006) 'Young teenagers' perceptions of their own and others' bodies: a qualitative study of obese, overweight and "normal" weight young people in Scotland', *Social Science and Medicine* 62(2): 396–406.

Wilson, B. (1966) *Religion in Secular Society*, Harmondsworth: Penguin.

Wilson, B. (1970) *Religious Sects: A Sociological Study*, London: Weidenfeld & Nicolson.

Wilson, B. (1990) 'Scientology: a secularized religion', in B. Wilson (ed.) *The Social Dimensions of Sectarianism: Sects and New Religious Movements in Contemporary Society*, Oxford: Oxford University Press.

Wilson, C., Letherby, G., Brown, G. and Bailey, N. (2002) 'The baby brigade: teenage mothers and sexuality', *Journal of the Association of Research on Mothering* 4: 1.

Wilson, E. and Rodgerson, G. (1991) *Pornography and Feminism*, London: Lawrence & Wishart.

Wilson, G. (2000) *Understanding Old Age: Critical and Global Perspectives*, London: Sage.

Wilson, M. (1967) 'Nyakyusa age villages', in R. Cohen and J. Middleton (eds) *Comparative Political Systems*, Garden City, KS: Natural History Press.

Wilson, S. (2007) '"When you have children, you're obliged to live": motherhood, chronic illness and biographical disruption', *Sociology of Health and Illness* 29(4): 610–26.

Winship, J. (1986) *Inside Women's Magazines*, London: Pandora.

Winston, B. (1998) *Media, Technology and Society: A History – From Printing Press to the Superhighway*, London: Routledge.

Witz, A. (1992) *Professions and Patriarchy*, Routledge, London.

Wolf, M. (2004) *Why Globalization Works*, New Haven, CT: Yale University Press.

Wolf, N. (1991) *The Beauty Myth*, London: Vintage.

Wollstonecraft, M. (1982 [1792]) *A Vindication of the Rights of Woman*, Harmondsworth: Penguin.

Wood, S. (ed.) (1982) *The Degradation of Work?*, London: Hutchinson.

Woodhead, L. (2005) 'Gendering secularisation theory', *Køn og Forskning* [*Women, Gender and Research*] 1–2: 24–35.

Woodhead, M. (1998) *Children's Perspectives on their Working Lives: A Participatory Study in Bangladesh, Ethiopia, The Philippines, Guatemala, El Salvador and Nicaragua*, Stockholm: Rädda Barnen.

Woodhead, M. (1999) 'Combating child labour: listen to what the children say', *Childhood* 6(1): 27–49.

Woodhead, L. and Heelas, P. (eds) (2000) *Religion in Modern Times: An Interpretive Anthology*, Oxford: Blackwell.

Woodward, K. (2003) 'Representations of motherhood' in S. Earle and G. Letherby (eds) *Gender, Identity and Reproduction: Social Perspectives*, Basingstoke: Palgrave Macmillan.

Woodward, K. (ed.) (2004) *Questioning Identity: Gender, Class, Ethnicity*, 2nd edn, London: Routledge.

Woodward, K. (2008) 'Gendered bodies, gendered lives', in D. Richardson and V. Robinson (eds) *Introducing Gender and Women's Studies*, 3rd edn, Houndsmills: Palgrave Macmillan.

Woolley, B. (2004) *The Herbalist: Nicholas Culpepper and the Fight for Medical Freedom*, London: Harper.

World Commission on Environment and Development (1987) *Our Common Future (The Brundtland Report)*, Oxford: Oxford University Press.

Wrench, J. and Modood, T. (2000) *The Effectiveness of Employment Equality Policies in Relation to Immigrants and Ethnic Minorities in the UK*, ILO Report, www.ilo.org.

Wright, B. (1995) 'Environmental equity justice centres: a response to inequity', in B. Bryant (ed.) (1995)

Environmental Justice: Issues, Policies and Solutions, Washington, DC: Island Press.

Wright, C.R. (1960) 'Functional analysis and mass communication revisited', *Public Opinion Quarterly* 24: 606–20.

Wright, E.O. (1997) *Class Counts*, Cambridge: Cambridge University Press.

Wright, P. & Treacher, A. (eds) (1982) 'Introduction', in P. Wright and A. Treacher (eds) *The Problem of Medical Knowledge: Examining the Social Construction of Medicine*, Edinburgh: Edinburgh University Press.

Wright Mills, C. (1956) *The Power Elite*, Oxford: Oxford University Press.

Wright Mills, C. (1970 [1959]) *The Sociological Imagination*, London: Oxford University Press.

Wyn, J. and Dwyer, P. (1999) 'New directions in research on youth in transition', *Journal of Youth Studies* 2(1): 5–21.

Wyness, M. (1997) 'Parental responsibilities, social policy and the maintenance of boundaries', *Sociological Review* 45(2): 304–24.

Wynne, D. (1990) 'Leisure, lifestyle and the construction of social position', *Leisure Studies* 9: 21–34.

Y

Yaffe, M. and Nelson, E. (1982) *The Influence of Pornography on Behaviour*, London: Academic.

Yearley, S. (1991) *The Green Case: Sociology of Environmental Issues, Arguments and Politics*, London: Harper Collins.

Yearley, S. (1997) 'Science and the environment', in M. Redclift and G. Woodgate (eds) *The International Handbook of Sociology*, Cheltenham: Edward Elgar.

Yinger, J.M. (1970) *The Scientific Study of Religion*, New York: Macmillan.

Young, J. (1992) 'The rising demand for law and order and our Maginot lines of defence against crime', in N. Abercrombie and A. Warde (eds) *Social Change in Contemporary Britain*, Cambridge: Polity Press.

Young, J. and Mathews, R. (eds) (1992) *Rethinking Criminology: The Realist Debate*, London: Sage.

Young, K. (1997a) 'Gender and development', in N. Visvanathan, L. Duggan, L. Nisonoff and N. Wiegersma (eds) *The Women, Gender and Development Reader*, London: Zed Books.

Young, K. (1997b) 'Planning from a gender perspective', in N. Visvanathan, L. Duggan, L. Nisonoff and N. Wiegersma (eds) *The Women, Gender and Development Reader*, London: Zed Books.

Young, L. and Ansell, N. (2003) 'Fluid households, complex families: the impacts of children's migration as a response to HIV/AIDS in southern Africa', *Professional Geographer* 55(4): 464–7.

Young, M. and Willmott, P. (1962 [1957]) *Family and Kinship in East London*, Harmondsworth: Penguin.

Young, M.F.D. (ed.) (1971) *Knowledge and Control: New Directions in the Sociology of Education*, London: Collier-Macmillan.

Yuval-Davies, N. (1997) *Gender and Nation*, London: Sage.

Z

Zeitlin, M. (1989) *The Large Corporation and Contemporary Classes*, Cambridge: Polity Press.

Zola, I. (1972) 'Medicine as an instrument of social control', *Sociological Review* 20: 487–504.

Index

Note: page numbers in **bold** indicate chapter extents; those in *italics* are glossary definitions

A

B

C

D

E

H

I

K

M

N

O

P

Q

R

T

U

V

W

Y

Z